THE MORAVIAN MISSION DIARIES OF DAVID ZEISBERGER

The Moravian Mission Diaries

of David Zeisberger

is published as part of the

Max Kade German-American

Research Institute Series.

This series provides an outlet for

books that reflect the mission of the

Penn State Kade Institute:

to integrate the history and culture of

German-speakers in the Americas

with the major themes of early

modern scholarship from the

sixteenth to the

early nineteenth century.

IN MEMORIAM

Carola Wessel

The

Moravian Mission Diaries

of

DAVID ZEISBERGER

1772–1781

Edited by

HERMAN WELLENREUTHER
CAROLA WESSEL

Translated by

JULIE TOMBERLIN WEBER

THE PENNSYLVANIA STATE UNIVERSITY PRESS
UNIVERSITY PARK, PENNSYLVANIA

This English translation
was made possible through the kind support of
Goethe Institut Inter Nationes

Library of Congress Cataloging-in-Publication Data

Zeisberger, David, 1721–1808.
[Herrnhuter Indianermission in der Amerikanischen Revolution. English]
The Moravian mission diaries of David Zeisberger, 1772–1781 /
edited by Hermann Wellenreuther, Carola Wessel ; translated by Julie Weber.
p. cm.— (Max Kade German-American Research Institute series)
Translation of: Herrnhuter Indianermission in der Amerikanischen Revolution.
Includes bibliographical references and index.
ISBN 978-271-05813-9 (alk. paper)
1. Zeisberger, David, 1721–1808.
2. Zeisberger, David, 1721–1808—Diaries.
3. Indians of North America—Missions—Ohio—History.
4. Indians of North America—History—Revolution, 1775–1783.
5. Moravian Church—Missions—Ohio—History.
I. Wellenreuther, Hermann.
II. Wessel, Carola.
III. Title.
IV. Series.

E98.M6Z3713 2005
305.897′345′009033—dc22
2004017540

First published in Germany in 1995 by Akademie Verlag
as *Herrnhuter Indianermission in der
Amerikanischen Revolution:
Die Tagebücher von David Zeisberger,
1772 bis 1781*

CONTENTS

PREFACE AND ACKNOWLEDGMENTS

When Carola Wessel and I worked on the German edition of the diaries of David Zeisberger, many helpful American souls confided to us with sadness in their voices that they would never be able to read this source. The implication of this confession was that we should publish the diaries immediately in a language that all people interested in North American ethno-history, church and mission history, and the history of the American Revolution would be able to read. It is indeed one of the tragedies of early modern American history that so many of the historians working in this field are unfamiliar with quaint European languages like Latin, French, Dutch, and German. These days, German politicians bemoan the fact that immigrants into Germany do not speak the country's language; they demand that the acquisition of citizenship be tied to proof that the prospective German citizens speak German. Had it been adopted in the seventeenth century, such a measure would have produced uniformity in early modern American historical sources and saved a considerable number of friends and institutions the trouble of having to come up with ways and means to publish an English-language edition of Zeisberger's diaries.

With one important exception I will not repeat the acknowledgments with which we have prefaced the German edition. What we said then is still true today. Without the generous assistance of major libraries this whole project would not have been possible. That there is an English edition is due to the energetic support of many colleagues and friends. But our first thanks must go to the Elders of the Moravian Archives at Bethlehem, who through the Rev. Vernon Nelson generously and most kindly granted us immediate permission to publish an English edition. As before, this friendly support of the Moravian Church and of Vernon Nelson and his staff, notably Lothar Madeheim, was absolutely vital to the project. Second, the material means for producing an English edition were provided by the German Federal agency *Inter Nationes* and the *Deutsche Forschungsgemeinschaft*. At a crucial moment, when we realized that these funds would not cover all the costs, a close friend, A. Gregg Roeber from Penn State, stepped forth and offered help. He not only brought us together with Peter Potter, a most patient and understanding editor, of The Pennsylvania State University Press, but on behalf of the Max-Kade Foundation pledged to close the gap between what we had and what we needed. Without their unfailing help and encouragement this project would have failed.

The German text had to be turned into readable English. We were particularly glad to find in Julie Weber a translator who was willing to get involved with the intricacies of the Moravian terminology and who coped with patience and forbearance with our numerous and time-consuming suggestions and criticisms. Julie translated the diaries themselves; the introduction was partially translated and partially written anew by me. My two student assistants, Julia Braun and Lasse Hoyer, went over the translation with a fine-tooth comb and caught more errors than I care to admit; they checked and rechecked the notes, the introduction, the numerous appendices, and the bibliography. Their thoroughness and dedication has saved us from many embarrassing mistakes. Frauke Geyken, who is currently editing the letters of David Zeisberger, was always willing to leave her own work and help us out whenever we needed her; and my secretary, Ms. Steneberg, not only coordinated the flow of e-mail communication related to the project but made sure that everything ran smoothly so that we could focus on "Brother David." I am very grateful to the staff of Penn State Press for their kind and generous assistance—particularly for turning my introduction into something close to readable English prose.

Carola Wessel would have written this introduction somewhat differently. Her style would have had fewer flourishes, been more factual, more straightforward—she would have written in plain style, the seventeenth-century term for it. We worked together on the English translation until early summer 2003, when Carola suddenly fell ill. By autumn she seemed to have made a fine recovery and began to look again at translated texts; e-mail once again flew back and forth. In October she had a severe relapse and never recovered. She died on February 14, 2004. I am still at a loss to describe how much this work owes to her expertise, knowledge, and fine scholarship. It was a great honor and pleasure to work with her. I cannot think of a more friendly, patient, honest, and forthright editor than she was. We spent weeks in Chicago and Göttingen mulling over details of text, ethnological terminology, and other intricacies. Never once did she lose her patience; often she had the better argument.

Carola Wessel was a quiet person; she did not shout her expertise to the world, she did not push herself into the foreground. She was modest to a fault, and yet all who knew her were deeply impressed by her scholarship. She was an excellent historian, a wonderful editor, and a first-rate bibliographer. David Zeisberger's diaries simply could not have been published without her. I dedicate this book to her.

Hermann Wellenreuther
Göttingen/Indianapolis

LIST OF ABBREVIATIONS

AA, 4th series	Peter Force, ed., *American Archives: Consisting of a Collection of Authentick Records, State Papers, Debates, and Letters and Other Notices of Publick Affairs,* 4th series. 6 vols. Washington, D.C., 1837–44.
AA, 5th series	Peter Force, ed., *American Archives: Consisting of a Collection of Authentick Records, State Papers, Debates, and Letters and Other Notices of Publick Affairs,* 5th series. 3 vols. Washington, D.C., 1848–53.
CLP	Carnegie Library, Pittsburgh, Pa.
DHDW	Reuben G. Thwaites and Louise P. Kellogg, eds., *Documentary History of Dunmore's War, 1774.* Madison, Wis., 1905.
FAO	Louise P. Kellogg, ed., *Frontier Advance on the Upper Ohio, 1778–1779.* Publications of the State Historical Society of Wisconsin, Collections 23, Draper Series 4. Madison, Wis., 1916.
FDO	Reuben G. Thwaites and Louise P. Kellogg, eds., *Frontier Defense on the Upper Ohio, 1777–1778.* Publications of the State Historical Society of Wisconsin, Collections, Draper Series 3. Madison, Wis., 1912.
FRO	Louise P. Kellogg, ed., *Frontier Retreat on the Upper Ohio, 1779–1781.* Publications of the State Historical Society of Wisconsin, Collections 24, Draper Series 5. Madison, Wis., 1917.
GD	Tagebuch von Gnadenhütten II, MAB, B 144
H2	Copy of MS Diary at Moravian Archives, Bethlehem, Pa.
H3	Copy of MS Diary at Moravian Archives, Herrnhut
HP	"The Haldimand Papers." *Michigan Pioneer and Historical Collections* 9 (1886): 343–658.
JP	James Sullivan et al., eds., *The Papers of Sir William Johnson.* 14 vols. Albany, N.Y., 1921–65.
LOC	Library of Congress, Washington D.C.
MAB	Moravian Archives, Bethlehem, Pa.

NYCD   E. B. O'Callaghan, ed., *Documents Relative to the Colonial History of the State of New York; Procured in Holland, England and France.* 15 vols. Albany, N.Y., 1853–87.

PA   *Pennsylvania Archives,* 1st–9th series. Philadelphia and Harrisburg, Pa., 1852–1935.

PCR   Samuel Hazard, ed., *Colonial Records. Minutes of the Provincial Council of Pennsylvania from the Organization to the Termination of Proprietary Government.* 16 vols. Harrisburg, Pa., 1852–53.

RUO   Reuben G. Thwaites and Louise P. Kellogg, eds., *Revolution on the Upper Ohio, 1775–1777.* Draper Series 2. Madison, Wis., 1908.

WHC   Lyman C. Draper and Reuben G. Thwaites, eds., *Collections of the State Historical Society of Wisconsin.* Madison, Wis., 1855–1911.

ZE   *Nikolaus Ludwig von Zinzendorf. Ergänzungsbände zu den Hauptschriften.* 14 vols. Ed. Erich Beyreuther and Gerhard Meyer. Hildesheim, 1966–85.

ZH   *Nikolaus Ludwig von Zinzendorf. Hauptschriften.* 6 vols. Ed Erich Beyreuther and Gerhard Meyer. Hildesheim, 1962–63.

INTRODUCTION

Prologue

On 9 November 1781 the commanding officer of British forces, Major S. De Peyster, and his interpreter met with some Delaware chiefs and Shawnee warriors in the council chamber of Fort Detroit for the interrogation of six missionaries of the Moravian Church. This interrogation indirectly praised the accomplishments of David Zeisberger's work, which had begun in 1768 in the Ohio region. After a slow and difficult start, the successful mission congregations, to their dismay, found themselves gradually involved in the War for Independence between Great Britain and her colonies. The missionaries and their Christian Indian Helpers tried to work for peace and remain neutral in the conflict. They failed; the combatants perceived their neutrality as sympathy for the opposite camp. Thus the Native American allies of Great Britain, especially the Shawnee and factions of the Delaware, repeatedly lodged complaints with the governor of Fort Detroit, stating "that the Moravian Teachers had always apprised the Enemy of our Manoeuvres by which means they were always frustrated."[1]

The missionaries had repeatedly been asked to remain strictly neutral, but these warnings had been ignored. Finally a group of Indian warriors under the command of British officers was dispatched to conduct, if necessary with force, the missionaries with their congregations to Upper Sandusky. They left on 11 September 1781. A few weeks later the missionaries were brought to Fort Detroit for an interrogation.

After introductory remarks by Delaware Captain Pipe, Major De Peyster addressed the missionaries directly. The protocol records the following dialogue between De Peyster and Zeisberger:

Q. How many are there of your mission?
A. Six

1. The full text of the proceedings of the interrogation is printed as Document No. 5 in the appendix. We are quoting from the introductory remarks of De Peyster, the commanding officer.

Q. Where are you from?

A. Bethlehem in Pennsylvania and two sent to each Town—

Q. By what authority do you act?

A. By that of our Bishops at Bethlehem.

Q. How long have you been in the Indian Country?

A. I have been on the Muskingum River since 1768 and many followed me.[2]

Q. By what did you pass?

A. By permission of Congress.

Q. I suppose you must have rec'd instructions from the Congress.

A. Not any of us—

Q. What correspondence could you have carried on with the Enemy, which I have been informed by my Interpreters that you have practised from time to time.

A. Being obliged to draw near to the Kooshaking Indians we were often importuned by them to write to Fort Pitt and after two years residence with them we found they were rather troublesome which obliged us to quit their Towns and retreat to our former villages as we had long declined writing for them, we drew their resentment upon us, since when we have never wrote any.

Q. How many Indians are there who belong to your Mission?

A. Including Men, Women and Children 350.

Q. Have they ever joined in the War?

A. Not any.

Zeisberger's responses summarized the factual history of the Moravian mission in the Ohio region. After early unsuccessful trials between 1768 and 1771 northeast of Fort Pitt, the missionaries founded mission congregations in the upper Muskingum River valley region. The beginnings, the rise, the life, and the problems of these mission congregations are detailed in these diaries, published here in English for the first time.

The diaries, most of which were written by David Zeisberger, transport the reader into a strange world. This world was unknown to Europeans, including the Moravian Missionaries when they first came to the Muskingum valley. The region seemed just as alien to the British soldiers who were sent there some years after the Moravians arrived. The soldiers of the Continental army were no more familiar with the territory; probably only Indian traders and the Native Americans residing in the area were familiar with the region.

Were Zeisberger to visit the region today, he would scarcely recognize it. Creeks have disappeared, rivers have been tamed, and extensive works to control floods have changed much of the surface, topography, and vegetation of

2. This answer identifies Zeisberger as the speaker for the missionaries, as he was the only one who had been in the region since 1768.

the region around what today is New Philadelphia. What sounds strange to our ears today, what seems incomprehensible to us now, was normal and familiar to the Mingo, the Delaware, and the Shawnee. David Zeisberger and the other missionaries shared in that knowledge after 1772.

Their ignorance of the Ohio region did not mean that European settlers were not interested in it. On the contrary, the region had become the subject of intense dispute between English and French colonists as well as their mother countries long before the features of the country had been fully explored. Indeed, France and England both claimed exclusive right of possession to this region. It is the purpose of this introductory essay to make the reader of these diaries familiar with this strange world. We begin with a sketch of the general historical background and then turn to a description of what was known to the people in the early 1770s about the Ohio region. A brief description follows of the Native American tribes in the region and of how their settlements moved west over time. Finally, we turn to a narrative of Lord Dunmore's war as the last war between Native Americans and white settlers over land before the beginning of the War for Independence.

This, of course, is the Euro-American perspective. In the Native American perspective that I attempt to recover in the next section of this introduction I pay special attention to Lord Dunmore's war. For it was this conflict that ushered in an era of warfare that led to the eventual dislocation of all native settlements in the area and the loss of large parts of native hunting grounds. For the indigenous tribes, this greatest crisis in memory ended with a series of peace treaties in 1782 and 1783; but the final curtain in the drama fell only with the Treaty of Greenville a decade later.

The third part of this essay focuses on the Moravians, their missionaries, and their theology. Here I sketch the mission congregations in the Ohio region and offer biographical details about David Zeisberger, the author of these diaries.

The final part of the introduction describes the diaries themselves, their physical features, how they have survived over time, and their value as sources for the history of mission, for the life and history of Native Americans, and for the war in the Ohio region. The introduction concludes with a discussion of the problem of translation as a process of transferring a text from one culture to another. The appendix to the diaries reproduces some key documents. We have also included indexes of the geographical terms and a complete list of names, together with the vital data that we could locate, including variations in the spelling of contemporary Native American and European names.

1. Historical Contexts, 1750–1782: The Seven Years' War and Its Consequences

For North America, the Peace of Paris of 1763 changed the conditions that had dictated the relations between the British colonies, their mother country, and the Native American tribes. For England, the peace not only ended the rivalry with France in North America but secured huge territorial gains—in addition to Canada, the whole region between the Alleghenies and the Mississippi. Only a small part of this region was peopled by European settlers; the largest section was settled by its original inhabitants, Native Americans, only some of whom had earlier acknowledged English supremacy.

Leaving aside the problems Native American tribes associated with the term "supremacy," this huge increase in its territory presented massive administrative problems for Britain. It quickly transpired that the English government was totally unprepared to meet this challenge. Two problems required urgent attention. First was the necessity to establish some kind of administrative structures for the new region—this need was addressed in the early 1770s with the passage of the Quebec Act. Second, and for British ministers and military even more urgent, was the need to secure the region from threats of violence, both external and internal. After what colonists and Europeans called "Pontiac's Rebellion," colonists agreed with British politicians that only the British army had the means to secure this new conquest. While most of the army was demobilized, some regiments were stationed in forts in the Ohio region; in addition to covering the region militarily, they were assigned responsibility for supervising trading relations between Native Americans and colonists and relations between tribes and colonies. Since these were services provided by the mother country for the benefit of the colonists alone, the British government decided that the costs should be borne by the colonies themselves. From a British perspective, taxation of the American colonies for these purposes made sense; the colonists, not surprisingly, disagreed. The resulting bitter controversy between colonies and mother country ended with the signing of the peace treaty at Paris in 1783.

The peace treaty of 1763 freed the colonies from the ever-present French threat. The colonists feared more than France's supposedly unlimited thirst for territorial expansion. Of equal importance was the widespread conviction, shared by colonists and Englishmen alike, that France was determined to establish a Catholic "monarchie universelle" and thus in one stroke destroy the constitutional achievements of both Protestant England and British colonial North America. The vast concessions the colonists were prepared to offer in 1754 in Albany, New York, in order to achieve a "union" of the colonies are telling proof of how seriously colonial politicians took the French threat.

The Peace of Paris had other consequences for the relationship between the colonies and England. One was the decision of the British government to suspend, for the duration of the war, the reforms of imperial relations governing the colonies that had begun in 1748–49. These reforms had been designed to increase the crown's influence on inner-colonial decisions and to strengthen Britain's influence on colonial politics. Implementation of these reforms was hampered by the presence of France in North America. The colonial assemblies were always able to claim that the French presence precluded the financial reforms demanded by the ministry, and that reforming commercial relations with Native American tribes would push the tribes into the French camp. Both arguments induced the Board of Trade and Plantations to lower its expectations.[3] With the British conquest of Canada, this argument lost its plausibility. The story after 1763 is well known. Relations between the colonies and the crown moved from misunderstandings to constitutional disputes that became increasingly bitter; in the end colonial writers argued for the colonies' internal sovereignty as a means of freeing them from the British Parliament's supposed tyranny.

The successes of British and colonial arms raised another fundamental question that was debated in 1760–61: which of the conquered territories should Britain retain? This issue, in turn, raised questions about England's expectations of the colonies—were they to be producers of vital products like sugar, or markets for English manufactured goods? Those who believed that the colonies should continue to supply England with much-needed raw materials pleaded for retaining the French sugar islands, especially Guadeloupe. This camp argued that it was in England's best interest to return Canada to France, for this would make the colonies dependent on the British navy for protection from French tyranny, thus curbing their tendency toward independence. The advocates for retaining Canada (among them Benjamin Franklin) did not deny the colonies' importance as producers of raw material. But they stressed the vast quantity of manufactured goods the colonies consumed yearly. This market function, Franklin and others argued, came at a price: colonies would refrain from manufacturing their own goods only so long as they had enough land to cultivate. Retaining Canada, Franklin argued, would satisfy the British colonists' land hunger for a long time, provide English manufactures with a growing market for their products, and strengthen the bonds between mother country and colonies.[4]

In Virginia, expansionists eager to secure new land had founded the Ohio Company in the early 1740s. In the following decade their efforts to survey land beyond the Alleghenies had met with fierce resistance from Native Americans, but this did not deter the Virginians. In negotiations with the French and British regarding the Native Americans' allegiance in the forthcoming war, the security of Delaware and Shawnee lands emerged as the paramount issue. When, after the defeat of the French, European settlers began flooding into the Ohio region in search of land, the Delaware and Shawnee fought for their land, joining what historians have called "Pontiac's Rebellion." The British

3. As a rule, all references will be cited in shortened form; full titles are given in the bibliography. On the Board of Trade's attitude toward colonial–Native American trade relations in the context of French-English rivalries in North America, see Greiert, "Board of Trade and Defense of the Ohio Valley"; Cutcliffe, "Colonial Indian Policy."

4. [Franklin], *Interest of Great Britain Considered.*

crown responded by closing the land beyond the Alleghenies to European settlers and ordering the British army to crush the Native American uprising. With peace reestablished, settlers resumed their migration into the fertile Ohio region despite the royal proclamation banning settlement. The blood and treasure spent in the long war, they believed, justified their taking the land they needed. In this belief they were only implementing the theory advanced by Benjamin Franklin in his pamphlet *The Interest of Great Britain Considered.*

If the colonists profited from the outcome of the war, the Native Americans were the losers. The Native Americans had been losing land in conflicts with the Euro-Americans from the beginning. But with the stipulation in article 15 of the Treaty of Utrecht of 1713, this had achieved a new meaning. That article proclaimed that because the Five Indian Nations had acknowledged the sovereignty of Great Britain over their land, France had to do so, too. The British interpreted this article to mean that by acknowledging British sovereignty, the Five Indian Nations had transferred legal title to their territory to the British crown. France, on the other hand, claimed that the Five Indian Nations meant only to establish a special relationship with Great Britain.[5]

Article 15 served as a model for the peace treaty of 1763, but times had changed. Before the war, the bargaining position of Native Americans had been determined by their ability to choose sides.[6] With the French gone, they faced a difficult future. Native Americans bitterly resented the implication that the peace treaty of 1763 gave European powers the right to transfer ownership of *their* land without consulting them. They had never, so they informed English representatives, transferred their right of ownership to the French—neither had they transferred land wholesale to the English. True, they had sold land, but selling land meant something different to them than it did to Europeans, as a Delaware warrior angrily explained to the Presbyterian missionary David McClure in 1772:

> Some of the warriors had expressed to me their extreme resentment at the encroachments of the white people, on their hunting ground, and extending their settlements to the Ohio. I asked one of them, "Have not the white people bought the land and paid you?" "Yes." "Well, then they have a right to use it." "No; not so," he replied, "for when you white men buy a farm, you buy only the land. You don't buy the

5. On the international implications and for a discussion of the importance of article 15 of the Treaty of Utrecht, see Savelle, *Origins of American Diplomacy*, 150, 250–52.

6. As late as 1768 the English government assumed that an imaginary French presence shaped Native American behavior toward the British colonies. Cf. the report of the Board of Trade and Plantations, dated 7 March 1768, to the king, and Earl of Hillsborough to Sir William Johnson, dated 15 April 1768. In this letter Hillsborough justified the transfer of responsibility for the Indian trade from the superintendents for Indian Affairs to the colonial governments, with the results of the Seven Years' War. O'Callaghan, *Documents Relative to the History of the State of New-York*, 8:19–31, 57–58.

horses and cows & sheep. The Elks are our horses, the Buffaloes are our cows, the deer are our sheep, & the whites shan't have them."[7]

In the Ohio region the cruel truth dawned on the Native American tribes that they must either accede to English policies, retreat to the interior of the continent and rediscover their old Indian ways, or fight. The last option, for the time being, at least, was ruled out with the defeats between 1763 and 1765—with the exception of the Shawnee and Mingo, as we shall see. The second option was advocated by the Delaware prophet Neolin. But most Native Americans realized that retreat was unrealistic, because Native American ways of life had been too deeply affected by European goods. Thanks to long use of European goods such as pots, pans, cloth, and blankets—not to mention the guns and the ammunition vital for hunting—the tribes no longer knew how to produce these things themselves. Neolin's words fell on deaf ears.[8]

From the Native American perspective, 1763 represented a watershed. Their options for preserving their territory intact were diminished dramatically, despite the British ban on settlement west of the proclamation line of 1763 and, indeed, despite the transfer, in 1756, of responsibility for supervising Indian trade, purchasing Indian lands, and enforcing observance of the proclamation line from the colonies to the army and to superintendents for Indian Affairs. Sir William Johnson, responsible for the northern and middle districts, an area stretching from Maine to Pennsylvania, and John Stuart, superintendent for Indian Affairs for the southern colonies, tried hard to assert their authority against colonies and army officers commanding posts in Indian country. Caught between colonial demands for more land and royal insistence that the proclamation of 1763, forbidding colonists' expansion beyond the Alleghenies, be respected, the superintendents pursued a middle course that, at least as far as Sir William Johnson was concerned, lined their own pockets rather nicely.

The new regulations transferring responsibility for Indian trade back to the individual colonies did not make the superintendents' role easier. This became evident in the negotiations at Fort Stanwix, where the 1763 proclamation line was to be modified in order to meet at least some of the colonial needs. Contrary to royal instructions, Sir William Johnson accepted the arguments of Virginia and Pennsylvania for a dividing line on colonial settlement further to

7. Dexter, *Diary of David McClure*, 85. Cf. Heckewelder, *History, Manners, and Customs of the Indian Nations*, 102. According to Heckewelder, the Board of Trade in the 1760s seems to have assumed that the Native American tribes had good and extensive property titles to their lands. See the report to the king dated 7 March 1768 in O'Callaghan, *Documents Relative to the Colonial History of the State of New-York*, 8:19–31. For a discussion of the different concepts of land ownership and their effects on different perceptions of the peace treaty of 1763, see Wellenreuther, "Der Vertrag zu Paris (1763)."

8. On prophets such as Neolin and their teachings, see Dowd, *A Spirited Resistance*.

the west. The treaty of 5 November 1768 pushed the border from the mouth of the Kanawha River at the Ohio to that of the Tennessee River into the Ohio. According to Johnson, the Six Indian Nations had insisted on the sale of the land up to that new borderline. Rejecting the demand of the Six Indian Nations would have meant insulting the most important Native American ally of England and risking a new war in the western lands. David Zeisberger, the Moravian missionary, probably assessed the effects of this purchase on the Native American tribes more realistically in a diary entry of 25 August 1768.

> We found that Mr. Crawford and Andrew Montour and some twenty odd Shawanose had arrived on their way to Sir William Johnson, who had invited them to a Treaty with the Six Nations. . . . I learned from him [Crawford] that the present treaty contemplated a purchase of extensive territory. . . . The Indians are generally of the opinion that if this land-sale, on the part of the Six Nations, should be consummated, a war will be inevitable. For even if the Seneca Chief consents to sell the land that Johnson has wished to have for several years he would do so unwillingly. They say, further, that should the land be sold, the entire Seneca Nation and those of the Six Nations that are not favorable to the whites would move away far to the west, after which the war with the whites should begin. One may not credit all that one hears among the Indians, but it is said to be certain that this is the project of the Six Nations and, particularly, of the Senecas."[9]

Since John Stuart, representing the crown and the southern tribes, had signed a treaty at Hard Labor, according to the royal instructions that treaty—and of course not the one for the northern border line—had to be renegotiated. The new treaty, signed at Lochaber (18–22 October 1770), failed, however, to meet the border line as established at Fort Stanwix. Yet Virginia's governor Lord Dunmore's manipulative interpretation of older Virginian laws finally extended the southern borderline to the mouth of the Tennessee into the Ohio, and in 1773 this new and fairly extensive region was opened to white settlers.[10]

The revision of the proclamation line of 1763 had three consequences. First, it granted what would later become Kentucky to Virginia and awarded a sizeable region west of the Alleghenies to Pennsylvania; second, it seriously reduced the hunting grounds of the Shawnee; and third, it represented the final expression of a policy that subordinated the interests of the tribes in the Ohio region (including the Cherokee) to those of the Six Indian nations.[11]

9. [Sensemann and Zeisberger], "Continuation of the Diary of the Brethren in Goschgoschuenk," 71–72.

10. For the treaties, see Robinson, *Virginia Treaties, 1723–1775*, 326–30, 370–76; cf. Alden, *John Stuart and the Southern Colonial Frontier*, 215–93.

11. McConnell, *A Country Between*, 242–54; Alden, *John Stuart and the Southern Colonial Frontier*, 269–82.

The beginning of this policy can be traced back to the early eighteenth century. It substituted the complex system of relations between colonies and tribes in the middle Atlantic region with the straightforward relation with one partner, the Five, then Six, Indian Nations. This powerful confederation had historically claimed overlordship over all the smaller tribes in these regions, which from the middle of the century onward had moved back into the Ohio area. The policy simplified matters immensely for the colonies, dramatically increased the Six Indian Nations' influence, and proved very profitable to that confederation at the expense of the smaller tribes. These smaller, less powerful tribes had been excluded from the negotiations and from the profits of land sales since the early 1730s—including those held at Fort Stanwix. Finally, the results of the negotiations at Fort Stanwix, Hard Labor, and Lochaber increased the alienation between the tribes of the Ohio region and the Six Indian Nations and weakened the latter's control over the region, while furthering contact between the region's tribes and those of the Great Lakes area. These regional realignments determined the battle lines of the coming conflicts, Lord Dunmore's war and the Revolutionary War.

2. The Ohio Region

THE CONTOURS OF THE LAND

Most readers of Zeisberger's diaries will be familiar with the present-day geographical location of the state of Ohio. In the eighteenth century, however, the Ohio region encompassed large parts of what is today the state of Illinois. Indeed, the border regions of the eighteenth-century Ohio region reached into Indiana to the west, West Virginia and Kentucky to the south, and of course to New York and Pennsylvania to the east. The region is dominated by the Ohio River, "la belle rivière," as the French called it, and the many creeks and smaller rivers that flow into it.

In order to capture something of what eighteenth-century people knew about the region, we have used contemporary maps as guides. The first significant factor of eighteenth-century cartography is the prominence of the mountains as a natural border between the British colonies and the Ohio region. In his memoirs, which describe his first trip to the Ohio region, John Lacey called them "monstrous Mountains."[12] Equally significant is that many of the mountains and passages through them remained mysterious to European travelers; without European names they retained their original Native American identity. Thomas Pownall included on his 1776 map the "Ouasioto Mountains, a Vein of Mountains about 30 or 40 Miles right across thro' which there is not yet any

12. [Lacey], "Memoirs of Brigadier-General John Lacey," 6.

occupied Path in these Parts."[13] Pownall was referring to the frontier region between Virginia and the Ohio region in the early 1760s; thereafter a flood of settlers from Virginia entered the Ohio region through the Great Kanawha River Valley.

From Pennsylvania, too, valleys offered the easiest access to the Ohio region. Most travelers and soldiers used the route constructed in 1758 for the British army of General John Forbes. It linked "Ray's Town," now Bedford, Pennsylvania, with the French Fort Duquesne, later Fort Pitt and then Pittsburgh. This route offered two distinct advantages over others: it ran a pretty straight line and included a number of river passages that facilitated the transportation of heavy goods. Goods were shipped up the Susquehanna and Juanita Rivers to Fort Bedford and were then carried over land to Fort Ligonier. From that fort the goods were shipped down the Loyalhanna Creek to the Allegheny River and thence down to Fort Pitt.[14]

Another route began at the Moravian town of Bethlehem and in a pretty direct line reached Venango on the Allegheny River. Again travelers could transport their goods part of the way on the west branch of the Susquehanna River. Travelers from Virginia followed the Monongahela River. Christopher Gist, the surveyor, and George Washington used this route—the latter in 1754 in his failed attempt to prevent a French army from building Fort Duquesne.[15]

Most travelers stopped in the region of Fort Pitt; only Indian traders, soldiers on their way to military outposts further west, and missionaries ventured further into the wilderness. They usually stopped at one of three centers of Native American settlements—the Shawnee villages on the Scioto River were the farthest to the west; about fifty miles to the east of them on the upper Muskingum River lay Delaware villages. Finally, north of Fort Pitt on the Beaver Creek and northeast from Venango on the Allegheny River, travelers found a group of Seneca and Mingo villages. In other words, the settlement patterns followed the structures inscribed on the land by the river systems.

Travelers such as the Baptist missionary Charles Beatty, who toured the region in 1766, were dependent on information provided by Indian traders like Levi Hicks, John McClure, John Petty, John Gibson, George Croghan, John Freeman, and James Forbs.[16] This information was, at least from our perspec-

---

13. *A General Map of the Middle British Colonies in America . . . from Governor Pownall's Late Map 1776* (London: Sayer & Bennett, 1776). We have consulted the reprint in Nebenzahl, *Atlas of the American Revolution*, 14–15.

14. Our guide for this description is Jakle, *Images of the Ohio Valley*, 167–70.

15. Gist's travel diaries are printed in Mulkearn, *George Mercer Papers*, 7–40; Washington's diaries are in [Washington], *Diaries of George Washington*, 1:118–210.

16. Beatty met these Indian traders on his trip. [Beatty], *Journals of Charles Beatty*, 46, 55, 56. According to John Lacey, John Gibson was married to a woman from Gekelemukpechünk (Newcomer's Town). In 1773 he accompanied two Quakers on their trip from Pittsburgh to Gekelemukpechünk; at this village Lacey met the two Indian traders "John Freeman & James Forbs," who had brought to the settlement "a store of goods." [Lacey], "Memoirs of Lacey," 6, 8.

tive, not particularly precise, yet it offers a glimpse into how geographical information was conveyed and what terms were used. Thus on 21 August 1766 Beatty noted the information he received in the valley of the Tuscarora, a creek that flowed into the Juanita River:

> Here we met with Levi Hicks—who had been captive with the Indians, and informs us that at the Big Beaver Creek about 25 Miles from Fort Pitt there used to be a small Town but now only a tavern is kept by an Indian called white Eyes—that at Tuskalawas is an Indian Town—that about 17 miles from that is another Indian Town called Standing Pond *Kighalampegha* of about 40 houses & another about 10 miles thence called worm Town (*Moghwheston*) of about 20 houses— about 17 miles thence another called Oghkitawmikaw or white corn Town the largest Town in these Parts, a Shawana Town; about 20 miles from this another called *Sughchaung* the Salt Lick of about 20 houses where the first Indian preacher lives—from thence about 40 or 50 miles To Mighchetaghpie[or: pu]stagh, the Big Lick of about 10 Houses—at Kighalampegha lives Netatwhelman the King or Headman of the Delaware Nation—between all these Towns is a pritty good riding Road—between Pittsburgh & Tuskarawas is in some part hilly, but beyond that a level Country.[17]

Beatty's entry illustrates how difficult it was to find reliable information about a region subject to rapid changes thanks to heavy in-migration. At least some of his remarks can be explained: the little village on the Big Beaver Creek twenty-five miles north of Fort Pitt, where in 1766 an Indian by the name of "white Eyes" was operating a little "tavern," probably meant Kuskuski (today New Castle in Lawrence County, Pennsylvania), the chief village of the Delaware until the end of the 1750s. A decade later Munsees resettled that place after White Eyes and the inhabitants of the village had moved to a new location near Gekelemukpechünk. John Lacey recalls in his memoirs that in 1773 White Eyes "resided a few miles below New Comer's Town on the Muskingum River called White Eyes Town."[18] "Tuskarawas," in Beatty's diary, referred to Tuscarawas, a Delaware village located on the river of the same name, one of the two source rivers of the Muskingum River. This was where Chief Beaver lived; the little town still exists today.[19] The settlement Kighalampegha, which the Presbyterian missionary David McClure called Kekalemahpehoong[20] and

---

17. [Beatty], *Journals of Beatty,* 46.
18. McConnell, *A Country Between,* 126–27, 208, 226–28; [Lacey], "Memoirs of Lacey," 6. On Crèvecoeur's map, southwest of the "Village de Newcomers" the "village de White Eyes" is marked on the same river.
19. For a biographical note on Chief Beaver, see Mulkearn, *George Mercer Papers,* 512–18.
20. Dexter, *Diary of David McClure,* 61.

the Moravian missionaries referred to as Gekelemukpechünk (the name we will use in this text), is identical with what the two Quaker missionaries and David Jones called "Newcomer's Town," the chief settlement of the Delaware in the upper Muskingum valley, where the head chief of the Delaware, Netawatwees, or Newcomer, as the English called him, resided. Again, the little town survived the troubles of the times.[21] The village Beatty called "worm Town (*Moghwheston*) of about 20 houses" is probably the same as the "Village de Moughwerssing" at the confluence of the Tuscarawas and the Walhanding Rivers on Crèvecoeur's map. This is probably the settlement that English maps call "Little Shawnee Womans." The "Oghkitawmikaw or white corn Town the largest Town in these Parts, a Shawana Town" refers, we believe, to Woaketameki (today Dresden) on the Muskingum. John Heckewelder mentions the place in his travel diary, which narrated events on his trip from Langundoutenünk (Friedensstadt on the Beaver Creek) to Schönbrunn.[22] We think that what Beatty describes as "*Sughchaung* the Salt Lick of about 20 houses where the first Indian preacher lives" is identical with the settlement Beatty later styles "Sukahunig." Heckewelder, in his 1773 travel diary, mentions without further comment a place called "Sikhewünk."[23] We assume that the three names refer to the same village. Heckewelder again offers a clue to the identity of the village Beatty calls "Mighchetaghpie[or: pu]stagh, the Big Lick of about 10 Houses." Immediately after mentioning "Sikhewünk," Heckewelder wrote: "Together with some of our Brethren I went about ten miles up this creek to see the famous salt spring, which is embedded in a sand creek." The editor of Heckewelder's journal identifies this place as today's Salt Creek Township.[24]

Analysis of the geographical information Beatty received from Levi Hicks proves two points. First, knowledge of the topography of the Ohio region was still very sketchy in the 1760s. Second, it was largely dependent on the reliable memory of the few who had lived or traveled in the region, either as prisoners, like Levi Hicks or James Smith,[25] or as Indian traders. A comparison of George

21. McConnell, *A Country Between*, 208–9; Heston and Parrish, "Journal of a Mission to the Indians in Ohio," 104 (for 19 July 1773). A less polished version of this diary is published as [Parrish], "Extract from the Journal of John Parrish." The second Quaker missionary was Zebulon Heston; the two Quakers had been accompanied by Heston's nephew, John Lacey, who narrates the events of this trip in his memoirs, "Memoirs of Lacey," 2–8. Jones, *Journal of Two Visits*, 23. The map by Hector St. John de Crèvecoeur in *Letters from an American Farmer* notes the place as "village de Newcomers" (see map 6 in the appendix).

22. [Heckewelder], "Canoe Journey from the Big Beaver to the Tuscarawas," 296. Heckewelder notes that the Shawnee were in the process of giving up their settlement: "most of them had already moved away" (296). Upstream Heckewelder passed another Shawnee settlement whose name he does not give; we assume on the basis of other sources that this was Moghwheston, alias Little Shawnee Womans.

23. [Beatty], *Journals of Beatty*, 67; [Heckewelder], "Canoe Journey from the Big Beaver to the Tuscarawas," 295.

24. [Heckewelder], "Canoe Journey from the Big Beaver to the Tuscarawas," 295–96.

25. Darlington, *Scoouwa: James Smith's Indian Captivity Narrative*.

Mercer's and Lewis Evans's pre-1755 maps with the map of Thomas Hutchins and the one reproduced in Crèvecoeur's *Lettres d'un cultivateur Américain* shows the progress in knowledge achieved between 1755 and 1787.[26] The 1750s maps indicate that the topographical structure of the Ohio region was largely unknown; by the late 1780s, thanks to the many travel reports and the wealth of other information available, this gap had been filled. This was largely due to the large number of settlers that had poured into the region, settlers John Heckewelder met not only in the Pittsburgh area but even in the lower Muskingum valley. No wonder, then, that the Native American tribes were deeply concerned about the integrity of their territories.

THE NATIVE AMERICAN TRIBES IN THE OHIO REGION

Migration, Settlement Patterns, and Imperial Rivalries, 1720–1782

After the wars of the seventeenth century, the Ohio region became one of the important areas into which Native American tribes retreated. This was particularly true of parts of the Six Indian Nations, especially the Mohawk, the Delaware, and the Shawnee. These three tribes were linked by a complex system of cultural and geographical ties; until the end of the Seven Years' War their relations were further complicated by the rivalry between the colonies of the two European colonial powers.[27]

Since the 1720s the Seneca, whose settlement area as "guardians of the West" reached up to the northern parts of the Ohio region, and especially the Mohawk and Oneida, had moved into the Ohio region. This migration increased in the following decades, with two results. First, the representative of the Six Indian Nations in Shamokin, the Oneida chief Shikellemi, gradually lost control over those Iroquois who were now usually called by their Delaware name, "Mingo."[28] Second, in the late 1740s these Iroquois migrants, led by the Seneca Tanaghrisson and the Oneida Scarouady, intensified their efforts to unite the various settlements and tribes of the region. Their likely aim was to keep the region free of the over-mighty influence of either the English or the French. Pennsylvania in the early 1750s acknowledged Logstown officially as a separate council fire for the Ohio region as distinct from Onondaga, the official council fire of the Six Indian Nations.[29]

At the same time, the Six Nations intensified their efforts to gain and retain their control over the whole region. In the 1720s the confederation had

26. See maps 2–6 in the appendix.

27. This part of the introduction is much indebted to volume 15 of *Handbook of North American Indians;* to Jennings, *Ambiguous Iroquois Empire* and *Empire of Fortune;* to McConnell, *A Country Between;* to White, *Middle Ground,* 366–412; to Dowd, *A Spirited Resistance,* 65–89; to Merrell, *Into the American Woods;* and to Merritt, *At the Crossroads.*

28. Heckewelder, *History, Manners, and Customs,* xxiv.

29. McConnell, *A Country Between,* chaps. 4–5; Merritt, *At the Crossroads,* 78–80.

already successfully subjected the Shawnee to their overlordship; during the negotiations at Lancaster in 1744 they succeeded in subjecting the Delaware as well. Yet already in 1727 the confederation had tried, albeit unsuccessfully, to degrade the Delaware to the status of "women who had lost the ability to declare war or conclude peace."[30] In 1742 the Six Indian Nations, with the energetic support of Pennsylvania, successfully disputed the competence of the Delaware to sell land to the colonies. From then on, Pennsylvania paid the Six Indian Nations for land belonging to Shawnee or Delaware. Those Delaware and Shawnee,[31] however, who lived beyond the mountains in the Ohio region, were outside the control of the Six Indian Nations.

For Shawnee and Delaware living *east* of the Alleghenies, the process of becoming dependent clients of the Six Indian Nations had been concluded at the treaty of Lancaster in 1744. Again the English colonies, this time in the form of Virginia, played an important role in this process. After Virginia had acknowledged at Lancaster the claim of the Six Indian Nations to ownership of the land down to the Shenandoah River Valley, their chiefs and the governor of Virginia signed a purchase treaty under which the Six Indian Nations sold all the lands within the Charter of Virginia—which, theoretically, stretched to the Pacific!—to the colony. Virginia thus acquired the right to settle all the land east and west of the Alleghenies within its charter boundaries. It was this treaty on which the colony based its opposition to the proclamation line of 1763 and to the line agreed by John Stuart at Hard Labor and at Lochaber. It is at least possible that the efforts of the Mingo, Shawnee, and Delaware settling west of the Alleghenies to unite in an alliance independent of the Six Indian Nations represented a reaction to these treaties at Lancaster.

Analysis of the spatial distribution of the tribes in the Ohio region from 1750 to 1790 reveals the relative strengths of the tribes, as well as the direction of migrations and the whereabouts of the many tribes. Such an analysis reveals that the three tribal groups, the Iroquois, the Delaware, and the Shawnee, each preferred specific settlement regions.[32] Until Lord Dunmore's war, most of the settlements of the Iroquois migrants (the Mingo) were in the area of the Beaver Creek and the Allegheny River in the eastern section of the Ohio region. Their most important settlements were Venango (on the Allegheny River, Seneca), Logstown (fairly close to Pittsburgh), and Logan's Town (further down the river toward the Ohio). This was the settlement of the Oneida John Logan, until his death in 1780 one of the most influential chiefs of the Mingo.[33] After the Seven

30. See note 66 below for a discussion of this contentious issue.
31. By the end of the 1740s almost all the Shawnee had left their settlements in Pennsylvania.
32. This section is based on an analysis of the settlement data found in the map "Indian Villages: Ohio, Pennsylvania, New York," in Cappon et al., *Atlas of Early American History,* 21. Since the data for this map are derived from diaries like Beatty's, data on migration may not always reflect the actual process of migration.
33. Mayer, *Tah-Gah-Jute.*

Years' War the Iroquois relocated some of their settlements farther west; after 1760 they founded Salt Licks on the Scioto River and Kekionga on the Maumee River. Within the next decade Darbys, on the Sandusky, and Pluggys Town, on the Scioto River, were settled. Probably toward the end of the 1770s or in early 1780 Mingo started the settlement called Zane's on the Miami River and Little Turtles on the Maumee River close to Lake Erie. Both villages were close to newly founded Shawnee villages.

The Delaware, too, migrated west. Since the 1730s part of the Delaware tribe had gradually settled the villages of Kuskuski, Salt Licks, Shenange, and Mahoning on the Beaver Creek. But some of the Delaware moved even farther west to the Muskingum valley. By the end of the Seven Years' War this tribe had founded thirteen settlements in that valley; it clearly formed the new center of the tribe. In the 1770s its head village was the seat of Chief Netawatwees (in English, Newcomer), Gekelemukpechünk (Newcomer's Town). When the War of Independence reached the region, white settlers poured into the valley, and disagreements erupted in the tribe between 1776 and 1780. A significant number of Delaware moved farther west, to the Miami and Sandusky. In the 1790s some Delaware settled on the Maumee River.

The Shawnee kept the greatest distance from sprawling white settlements. Earlier than the other tribes, they responded to the influx of white settlers by moving west. Until the 1770s the settlements of the Shawnee were concentrated in two river systems: the Muskingum (Shawnee Womans, Snakes, Woaketameki), and the western part of the Scioto, where Shawnee settled in nine villages until the war broke out. Around 1774, the year of Lord Dunmore's war, the Shawnee began to transfer the center of their settlements to the headwater region of the Scioto and Maumee Rivers. From the middle of the 1770s through the 1780s the Shawnee founded ten villages. In the 1780s some Shawnee moved even farther west, to the Maumee River region, where between 1783 and 1794 they founded five settlements. In migrating farther west, both the Delaware and the Shawnee moved closer to some of the larger tribes of the Great Lakes region, notably the Wyandot and the Ottawa, but closer, too, to the British Fort Detroit. The settlement known as Snipes I was not only close to the Mingo village Darbys but also to the Delaware settlement Hell I, on a side branch of the Mohican. Within a day it was possible to reach the center of the Shawnee settlements. At Zane's, originally founded by Mingo, Wyandot settled, too. Yet the bulk of that nation lived closer to Lake Erie, especially on the Sandusky River.

Of all these tribes the Shawnee were the first to cross the border between present-day Ohio and Indiana, in the late 1780s. Within half a century they had retreated from settlements east of the Alleghenies to the valley of the Mississippi in response to white encroachment. Their enforced retreat, like that of the Delaware, who followed them, documents the process of involuntary migration and illustrates one of the fundamental problems of the region.

Initially, all of the tribes had shared the hope that they could establish a safe haven from white settlers once they had moved beyond the Alleghenies. Their efforts to establish effective control over the Ohio region reflected that hope. At the same time, the experience of retreat before unending waves of white settlers produced not only a new religiosity within these tribes but visions about a new Native American way of life from which they hoped to gain strength for a new beginning. There were two possible ways to accomplish this. The tribes could renounce everything European and return to their roots; or they could adapt even more thoroughly to European religion, culture, and ways of life. Both the Shawnee and the Delaware were deeply divided over these diametrically opposed options. After fierce and prolonged infighting, the Delaware finally opted for the second path, one propagated by Moravian missionaries, and they pursued this course for a number of years. The Shawnee, by contrast, attempted to recapture their old forms of living, believing, happiness, life, and death. Both stories are told in the diaries of David Zeisberger.

The Ethnography of the Native American Tribes in the Ohio Region

The Delaware, who play a central role in Zeisberger's diaries, belonged to the northeastern woodland tribes and to the east Algonquian language family.[34] When the Europeans arrived they settled in small groups in what are today New Jersey, southeast New York, southeast Pennsylvania, and Delaware.[35] The Munsee in the south spoke a different dialect from the Unami, who lived further north. The Unami were the first to migrate to the Ohio region and settle in Gekelemukpechünk; the Munsee arrived in the region only in the 1770s.[36]

34. Accounts of the Delaware in the seventeenth century include Lindeström, *Geographica Americae* and [Penn], *William Penn's own Account of the Lenni Lenape*. In the eighteenth century the Moravian missionaries Zeisberger and Heckewelder acquired the most extensive knowledge about this tribe. See Zeisberger, "History of the Northern American Indians," written about 1780–81, and entries in the diaries below; Heckewelder, *History, Manners, and Customs*. We have used shorter accounts of visitors to the Ohio region, among them [Beatty], *Journals of Charles Beatty;* Thornely, *Journal of Nicholas Cresswell;* Jones, *Journal of Two Visits;* [Lacey], "Memoirs of Brigadier-General John Lacey"; Dexter, *Diary of David McClure*.

35. See Kraft, *Lenape;* Newcomb, *Culture and Acculturation of the Delaware;* Wallace, *Indians in Pennsylvania;* Weslager, *Delaware Indians;* Merritt, *At the Crossroads*.

36. Occasionally the Unami are further distinguished into the Unami and the Unalachtigo. Scholars are divided about whether the Monsy or Munsee belonged to the Delaware and were only distinguished by their dialect, or whether they were, to use Zeisberger's terminology, a distinct nation. Zeisberger was familiar with the Munsee; they lived for example in Goschgoschünk, where Zeisberger began his missionary work in 1768; the following year this congregation moved to Lawunnakhannek. See [Sensemann and Zeisberger], "Diary of Zeisberger and Zenseman." The Munsee represented a significant portion of the congregation at Schönbrunn. We assume that Zeisberger considered the Munsee a distinct nation. In the entry for 6 June 1778 he himself speaks of the "Monsy Nation." And in the entry for 21 March 1777 he indicates that in light of the differences between the two it may have been wrong to unite both in one mission congregation and would have been better to let them have separate congregations. On the other hand, that the Munsee were invited to participate in a Head Council meeting in 1771 to which all settlements sent representatives speaks against their being

It was in this region that the tribe reconsolidated and gained military and political influence. The population of the Delaware, estimated at some 11,000 people in 1600, had fallen by 1779 to about 3,200 owing to war, disease, and abuse of alcohol.[37]

The tribe consisted of three phratries[38] named after animals: Turtle, Wolf, and Turkey.[39] The Turtle tribe was the most highly respected. Each phratrie had its own chief. The chiefs' role as partners in negotiations with Europeans strengthened their position, yet chiefs in general did not command much power. They led hunting expeditions and performed religious functions, but in the political sphere they could carry a point only by convincing their councils. Decisions were made by the council, which was composed of advisors and, when important concerns were debated, of all men of the tribe. In times of war the direction of affairs was transferred to the war chiefs, whose authority was defined by their exploits in the war.[40]

Gekelemukpechünk, the central village, was settled mostly by members of the Turtle tribe under chief Netawatwees. The war captain was White Eyes. Yet the leaders of the other phratries also played an important role. The chief of the Wolf tribe was Pachanke (Custaloga) and from 1773 on Captain Pipe. Their central village was first Venango and afterward Kuskuski. In 1769 Welapachtschiechen (Captain Johnny) became chief of the Turkey tribe, whose central village was at first Kuskuski and later Tuscarawas.[41]

Owing to the closeness of Schönbrunn to Gekelemukpechünk, David Zeisberger was often invited to council meetings, which followed a particular ceremony. After being invited by special messengers to attend a council meeting, representatives of other tribes were invited to the house of the chief, where they stayed as guests. The council meetings were opened with formulaic rituals

---

a distinct nation. Cf. Zeisberger, Friedensstadt [i.e., Langundoutenünk] Diarium, entries for 4–9 Oct. 1771, MAB 137, 1770–72. Becker, in "Boundary Between the Lenape and Munsee," has suggested that the Munsee should be considered distinct from the Delaware; the opposite view is advanced by Goddard in "Delaware," 225. Cf. entry for 17 Oct. 1772, note 94, below.

37. Goddard, "Delaware," 214.

38. A "phratrie" was an association of groups within one ethnic union that traced their kinship to one mythical ancestor. In the context of this definition, the groups are defined as "lineages." See note 42 below.

39. For defining these phratries as representatives of land (Wolf), air (Turkey), and water (Turtle) on the basis of a cultural and semantic analysis, see Miller, "Delaware Clan Names"; Goddard, "Further Note on Delaware Clan Names"; Miller, "Cultural View of Delaware Clan Names"; and Dean, "Reply to 'A Further Note,'" 63–65. On animal and plant terminology of the Delaware as employed by Zeisberger, see Mahr, "Delaware Terms for Plants and Animals." When Zeisberger speaks of a phratrie, he uses the German word "Stamm," but once he uses the English word "tribe" (entry for 13 Aug. 1775). On other definitions, see note 42 below.

40. Zeisberger, "History of the Northern American Indians," 92–102.

41. The name first given was used by the Moravians and was usually identical with that used by the Indians, while the name in brackets was that used by the English. There were of course other names and variations of names. Gekelemukpechünk was situated on the Tuscarawas River in what is today Tuscarawas County, Ohio. Venango (today Franklin, Pennsylvania) and Kuskuski (today New Castle, Pennsylvania) were east of Gekelemukpechünk.

that cleansed and opened the senses. One of the members of the council functioned as its speaker. He related the concern of the council in a speech that was accompanied by the presentation of a string or belt of wampum whose colors and patterns symbolized the message. Accepting them implied acceptance of the message; the string or belt was retained as a confirmation and remembrance of the transaction. If the wampum was refused, it meant that the negotiations had failed.

For subgroups of the Delaware nation, Zeisberger uses the terms "tribe" ("Stamm") and "friendship" ("Freundschaft"). As he understood it, the Unami and the Munsee were "nations"; phratries he calls "Stamm" or "tribe." He calls larger kinship groups "friendships" or "lineages," which means, too, that "friend" is his term for a "relative."[42] These groups of families were related matrilinearly; together they formed the phratrie. They fulfilled ceremonial functions and were exogamous. Marriages were not formed for life; separation of partners was simple and occurred frequently, and was facilitated by the partners' not possessing common property.

Men and women had separate spheres of work. Men were responsible for hunting, fishing, trade, and the production of tools and instruments, while women ran the house, worked the gardens, cooked the meals, mended and made dresses and cloth, and educated the children. The traditional crops of the Delaware were a variety of corn, beans, and squash. These crops were supplemented by plants collected in the forest, berries, and nuts. The most important hunting season was in late autumn, when deer were well fed. Deer were the preferred prey, supplemented by bear later in the winter. The meat of smaller animals enriched the diet.

The Delaware had learned from Europeans to keep cattle and cultivate other plants. Pigs, cows, and chicken, which they had either bartered from white farmers or acquired in the war, were a familiar sight in Native American settlements and necessitated the fencing of fields.[43] These animals contributed meat, milk, and eggs to the diet. Delaware women usually prepared two meals per day. Corn and meat were staples and were prepared in different ways and

42. Zeisberger calls a lineage within a tribe a "friendship." For an extensive definition, see his diary entry for 14 Jan. 1773. The larger category, superior to "friendship," is the "Stamm" ("tribe" in English). See the protocol of peace treaty negotiations in 1764, in *PCR*, 9:214–33, esp. 226; Weslager, *Delaware Indians,* 250–51. Elsewhere Zeisberger himself calls the social units "lineage, tribe [and] nation" (see entry for 7 April 1775). The terms "friendship" or "matrilinear lineage" include in their meaning the religious and ritual elements that are not comprised in the term "tribe." Cf. Goddard, "Delaware," 222, 225, and Hodge, *American Indians North of Mexico,* part 1, 385–87. See, in general, Hedican, "Algonquin Kinship Terminology." The "friendships" were the next-lowest social and ritual forms of organization within what Zeisberger calls a "tribe."

43. The fencing of fields had only recently been introduced in the Delaware villages. On arriving at Goschgoschünk, Zeisberger noted on 11 June 1768 in his diary: "they have no fences, so that their corn is liable to be damaged by cattle." [Sensemann and Zeisberger], "Diary of Zeisberger and Gottlob Zenseman," 50.

seasoned with different herbs, sugar from maple trees, or berries. Salt was seldom used.[44]

Meals were prepared in metal kettles and in other dishes acquired through barter from European traders; by the middle of the eighteenth century these goods had become vital parts of Native American life. Guns were substituted for bows and arrows, metal utensils supplanted tools and pots made from bones, wood, or clay. To pay for these goods, hunters had to bring back as many furs as possible; the meat of these animals, however, was often not used. The necessary extension of the hunting territories not only created conflicts with other tribes but meant that men had to stay out hunting longer, which affected the gender balance within the village community.

Another negative effect of trade with Euro-Americans was the abuse of alcohol in Native American communities. The Delaware were well aware of the baneful effects of alcohol on communal life, but attempts to prevent drinking usually failed, with consequences for tribal relations with mission congregations.

The dress of the Delaware changed little over the years, although Europeans introduced new materials. The Delaware wore shirts, leggings, and moccasins, as well as coats and capes in cold weather. The deer skins of earlier times were supplanted by cloth that could be cleaned more easily but was of course not as durable. Men plucked the hair from their faces and heads, leaving just the scalp lock, while women wore their hair long and uncurled. For decoration women used paint and wore wampum.

Some Delaware copied the European way of building block houses—sometimes even building two stories and a chimney. More often they lived in traditional wigwams, the frames of which were constructed from branches linked together and covered with bark. Smaller houses were preferred, but some longhouses offered room for more than one family. When the Moravians arrived in the Muskingum valley, about one hundred families lived in Gekelemukpechünk in as many houses. The layout of the houses followed no regular plan, and even in those built in the European blockhouse style traditional internal arrangements were retained. Along the walls were benches, covered with furs and mats, on which one could sit as well as sleep at night. Other mats, decorated with various patterns, were hung on the walls, both as decoration and as protection against cold weather. Available spaces in the houses were used for storing food.[45]

All villages boasted sweating huts that were used for cleaning the body

---

44. On the Delaware diet and food, see Zeisberger, "History of the Northern American Indians," 44–48, 57–75, and passim; Newcomb, *Culture and Acculturation of the Delaware*, 13–24; Kraft, *Lenape*, 138–58.

45. See Zeisberger, "History of the Northern American Indians," 17–18, 86; Newcomb, *Culture and Acculturation of the Delaware*, 24–30; Kraft, *Lenape*, 122–27. On Gekelemukpechünk in the 1770s, see Hamilton, "Ettwein and the Moravian Church," 3–4, 342–57, esp. 348.

and treating illnesses. In addition, Delaware medicine men used herbs and different methods of treating illnesses; these were adopted also by the missionaries. Healing ceremonies were frequent because the Delaware were convinced that many illnesses were caused by magic, spells, and evil spirits.[46] In other ceremonies people sang, danced, made sacrifices, or narrated visions. On these occasions the priestly functions were performed by wise old men. Magic was important; for love and hunting magic, the Delaware often used a "medicine" called "beson" that consisted of different herbs.[47]

Religion played a central part in Delaware culture. The tribe believed in one all-powerful god or spirit, who through Manitus (little spirits) could be met indirectly and offered sacrifices. These little spirits were everywhere; they resided in animals, plants, and the elements. It was possible to communicate with them through visions; one's personal Manitu acted as a "guardian angel."[48] The soul of a dead person lived on. It remained for about a year in the vicinity of the dead person's body and had to be appeased through sacrifices to prevent it from inflicting illness on the tribe. Thereafter the soul, depending on the lifestyle of the deceased, either migrated to a land of plenty or wandered aimlessly about in the vicinity forever.[49]

Interaction with Euro-Americans affected Native American religious beliefs. From mid-century onward, Native American preachers increasingly tried to preserve traditional Indian ways of life, inveighing against loose morals, abuse of alcohol, and many other negative consequences of contact with Euro-Americans, as they saw it. In order to survive, the Delaware would have to return to their traditional way of life, these prophets maintained. Only then would God return to them and help them drive the whites away. Although these teachings were directed against the Euro-Americans, they were unwittingly influenced by Christian beliefs and concepts such as God in heaven, his son, the devil, and hell. The mixture of Christian and Native American beliefs had significant political implications.[50]

The other Native American tribes mentioned in the Zeisberger's diaries belonged to the Woodland Indians, too; their lifestyles were not dramatically different from that of the Delaware. The Mahican, the second-largest group among the converted native members of the mission congregation, had been the northern neighbors of the Delaware in the seventeenth century, in what is today the state of New York; as part of the mission congregation they migrated with the other converted Indians to the Upper Ohio region.[51]

Important unconverted tribes were the Shawnee and the Iroquois. The

46. Zeisberger, "History of the Northern American Indians," 23–27, 55–57.
47. Ibid., 125–39, 148–50; see also note 117 to entry for 25 Dec. 1772 below.
48. Newcomb, *Culture and Acculturation of the Delaware*, 59–76.
49. Zeisberger, "History of the Northern American Indians," 88–89, 129–30.
50. See p. 123 below.
51. See Brasser, "Mahican."

Shawnee (Zeisberger refers to them in the German text as "Schawanosen") lived southwest of the Delaware.[52] The north was dominated by the Six Indian Nations;[53] Kayahsota, the Seneca chief and resident watchdog of the confederation, did his best to maintain oversight of the region, with mixed results. Relations between the mission congregations and the Mingo in the Ohio region were often fraught with tension and misunderstanding.

Alliances and other relations between the Delaware and other tribes were expressed in kinship terms. The Delaware were usually addressed as "grandfather," which implied an especially honored position. "Grandchildren" of the Delaware were the Mahican, the Shawnee, the Cherokee, and the Chippewa. The Wyandot were addressed as "uncles" or "cousins" of the Delaware.[54] The members of the Six Indian Nations were "cousins," on the same terminological kinship level as the Delaware.

FROM LORD DUNMORE'S WAR TO THE PEACE OF PARIS IN 1783

The culture, kinship-based relations, and land of the Native American tribes were endangered by the treaties of Fort Stanwix, Hard Labor, and Lochaber. With the opening of territory for settlement, settlers from Virginia flooded into the region south of the Ohio in the early 1770s. Clashes between settlers and Shawnee multiplied. The Shawnee argued that these settlers were moving into their territory, while settlers perceived these clashes as further proof of Indian malice and deviousness.

The Shawnee looked in vain for allies; not only did the Delaware decline to help them, but White Eyes even went so far as to accompany Virginia's soldiers in their march to the Shawnee settlements. The Wyandot and the Cherokee, the latter after some soul searching, also failed to come to the aid of the Shawnee tribe. The exception were the Mingo, especially those from Logan's Town, who had suffered badly from white settlers' attacks and stood by the Shawnee despite the Seneca's attempts to hold them to the official line of the Six Indian Nations. In response to what Virginia considered unjustified attacks, the colony's governor, Lord Dunmore, moved with two armies into the Ohio region determined to "chastise" the Shawnee. After the battle at Point Pleasant, the Shawnee were forced to sign a peace treaty on 10 October 1774 that declared the Ohio River the border between Virginia's settlers and Shawnee hunting ground. In the following years the Shawnee moved westward.[55]

Neither the Shawnee nor the Mingo accepted the outcome of Lord Dun-

52. See Callender, "Shawnee."
53. See Tooker, "League of the Iroquois," and Fenton, *Great Law and the Longhouse.*
54. See entry for 8 Aug. 1777 below.
55. On Lord Dunmore's war, see *DHDW*, 1–8, 22–25, 30–35, 47–49, 66–67, 72–73, 308–10, 341–44, 368–95. According to Dunmore's official report to the English government, the Virginians lost forty-six militiamen and the Shawnee thirty warriors in the battle.

more's war; they continued to maintain that the territory south of the Ohio between the Kentucky and the Tennessee Rivers was their hunting ground. Siding with the British army after 1775, the Shawnee concentrated their attacks on the settlers in this disputed territory.[56]

The Delaware pursued a different course. At least since 1773 White Eyes had adopted a persistent and energetic policy of acculturation to European forms of life. It clearly was no coincidence that on 12 October 1775, at the congress at Fort Pitt, White Eyes confessed:

> "I for my part will be Strong and Prevent my young Men from hunting thereon [i.e., on land ceded to Virginia] for I had rather they wou'd employ themselves in planting Corn in their Own feilds than that any Mischeif shou'd happen by their hunting." And a little later he confessed: "I wou'd wish to Comply with the dictates of the Christian Relegion and Commands of our Saviour whose hands were Nailed to the Cross and sides Peirced for our Sins as far as I am Capable in my Dark Present State."[57]

In the following years the Delaware stuck to this course; in the winter of 1775–76 White Eyes even went to Philadelphia to argue his policy of acculturation, albeit with few tangible results. The Continental Congress sent him home with sweet words and encouragement but little real help.[58]

In 1774–75 two centers of power emerged in the Ohio region: Fort Detroit and Fort Pitt. Both England, at Detroit, and the colonists (as revolutionaries), at Fort Pitt, enlarged their military posts into strategic military headquarters for the region; they were command centers as well as places where all negotiations with the Native American tribes as prospective allies took place. At Detroit between 1775 and 1776 the commanding officer was Richard B. Lernoult, followed by Henry Hamilton and Arent S. De Peyster; at Fort Pitt the military command until 1777 lay in the hands of Edward Hand, followed by Lachland McIntosh, who in the following year was succeeded by Daniel Brodhead.[59]

While indian affairs at Detroit were more and more controlled by the commanding officer of the fort, who from 1778 on enjoyed the advice of Alex-

56. On the other hand, Chief Cornstalk, at that time probably the most influential of the Shawnee chiefs, pursued until his death a pro-American policy; tragically, he was murdered by an American soldier while imprisoned in an American fort (see note 75 below); after his death the nativist party among the Shawnee gained control of the tribe. See Dowd, *Spirited Resistance*, 66–68.

57. *RUO*, 109, 110. On Moravian figurativeness as mission method, see pp. 51–58 below.

58. See the resolve of the Continental Congress dated 10 April 1776 about White Eyes' proposition in *AA*, 4th series, 5:1664; on the same day the Congress appointed George Morgan Indian agent of the Middle Department, which included the Ohio region.

59. Orrill, "General Edward Hand"; Stevens, "Indian Diplomacy of Lernoult"; Orrill, "'Placing Proper Persons at their Head.'"

ander McKee, Andrew Montour, Matthew Elliot and Simon Girty,[60] the Continental Congress on 12 July 1775 separated Indian Affairs from the administration of the fort. The responsibility for Indian Affairs was transferred to a newly created Middle Department; its commissioners were Benjamin Franklin, Patrick Henry, and James Wilson. Richard Butler was appointed the first Indian agent; he was, as already mentioned, succeeded by George Morgan, who remained in that office until May 1779.[61]

Both Fort Pitt and Fort Detroit were more than just military strongholds and trading centers. Native Americans viewed them as "Brothers the English" and "Big Knife," which is how Native American speakers addressed the representatives of England, the united colonies, and the Continental Congress; the Euro-American representatives accepted these titles and used them in their own speeches. Until 1775 "Big Knife" had been the natives' name for Virginia; the transfer of this term, immediately after Lord Dunmore's war, to the united colonies and the Congress was more, from a native perspective, than semantic: it conflated Virginia's aggressive land policies, which had triggered Lord Dunmore's war, with those of the colonies and the fledgling United States.[62]

Fort Detroit and Fort Pitt were at the extreme margins of the Ohio region, for which both were militarily responsible. Their marginality and distance from each other meant that their communication networks did not intersect. Fort Pitt received its supplies overland, as the few attempts to supply the fort by ships up the Mississippi and Ohio were less than satisfactory. Supplying Detroit was simpler as long as the British controlled the Great Lakes and the connection to the St. Lawrence River, which they did until 1782. Keeping Fort Pitt supplied proved difficult and dangerous and the problem was aggravated by the financial constraints of the Continental Congress and the British sea blockade, both of which prevented stockpiling a large enough assortment of goods to satisfy Native American demands.[63] Fort Detroit, by contrast, was always well supplied with goods its Indian allies needed and expected to receive for their services.

From a Native American perspective, old problems were compounded by new ones in 1775–76. The old questions of whether, or how deeply, to acculturate themselves to European ways, like the old problems associated with land, persisted. But now whites talked with two tongues, and the tribes found

60. Horsman, *Matthew Elliott*, 23–43; Hoberg, "Tory in the Northeast"; Lewin, "Andrew Montour."

61. On Fort Pitt, see Williams, "Note on Fort Pitt" and *Fort Pitt and the Revolution;* on Richard Butler, see Williams, "Journal of Richard Butler." On George Morgan, see Savelle, *George Morgan,* 130–82; and on Detroit, see Kellogg, *British Régime in Wisconsin,* 130–79.

62. Heckewelder reports the speech of Pachgantschihilas [Buckaghihitas] (who was, according to Heckewelder, "head war chief of the Delaware") to the Christian Indians in March 1781, in *Narrative of the Mission,* 217–19, and the speech of Half King, chief of the Wyandot, to the same group in August 1781 in Salem (ibid., 236–37, 240).

63. Savelle, *George Morgan,* 167–82.

that they suddenly had to deal with "Brothers the English" and "Big Knife" as enemies. In 1775 and 1776 both British and American representatives toured the Native American tribes and tried to win their sympathies and support, each side offering its particular version of the conflict between the colonies and England as the true one.

Both the British and the Americans won some Native American tribes to their side while still claiming to maintain peace in the region. In the name of "the father," George III, the commanding officer of Fort Detroit liberally distributed gifts to the tribes of the Great Lakes region while cautioning the natives against attending conferences at Fort Pitt, for these were organized by rebels who were out to grab their land and cheat them of their inheritance.[64] Thanks to Richard Butler, the British efforts failed. Between 7 and 19 October 1775 all the important tribes of the region, including representatives of the Six Indian Nations, attended the congress at Fort Pitt. All of them, including the Wyandot, assured the commissioners of the Continental Congress that they would remain neutral in the fight between the "Brothers the English" and "Big Knife."[65]

In the ensuing conflicts between 1775 and 1779, the Delaware played a key role in determining the attitudes of other tribes of the region. There was a natural reason for this: the Delaware settlements on the Muskingum River were halfway between Fort Pitt and Fort Detroit. In addition, in the complex communication networks between the Native American tribes of the region, the Delaware played a special role as "peacekeepers," particularly in times of conflict and strife.[66] This at least had been the function the Delaware tried to perform in 1774 in the conflict between the "Big Knife" and the Shawnee.

Efforts to mediate that conflict were seriously hampered by the representa-

64. Stevens, "Indian Diplomacy of Lernoult," 75–77. Cf. the speech of the lieutenant-governor of Detroit in August 1776 to the assembled tribes, in *AA*, 5th series, 2:516–17.

65. The protocol of the Congress is printed in *RUO*, 70–125. See also *AA*, 5th series, 1:36–37.

66. According to Heckewelder, *History, Manners, and Customs*, xxvii–xxxix, 56–65, the Delaware were invested by representatives of the Five Indian Nations at a conference attended by the Dutch with this function as "peacekeepers" in the 1640s. The function implied too, that the Delaware were seen as "women." Later that view became particularly controversial. In general, "women" among the natives of the woodland region were considered responsible for keeping and maintaining peace; this was uncontroversial. But the term "women" usually also implied those unable to determine their own fate. This was undoubtedly understood both by Pennsylvania and by the Six Indian Nations, since the treaty negotiations at Philadelphia in 1742 specifically invested the term "women" with the latter meaning, thus essentially robbing the Delaware of their ability to determine their own fate. See speech of Canassatego on 12 July 1742, in *PCR*, 4:578–80; the relevant passage reads: "We conquer'd You, we made Women of you, you know you are Women, and can no more sell Land than Women" (579). As a consequence the Six Indian Nations insisted that henceforth the Delaware not be invited to treaty negotiations or other conferences. See the remarks accompanying "A list of all the Indians names present at the treaty held in Lancaster in June, 1744," in *PA*, 1st ser., 1:656–57: "the Delawares wer forbid to Come to the treaty by the Chiefes of the Six Nations." White Eyes clearly was familiar with this meaning of the term, as we shall see. Only in light of this aspect of the strained relationship between the Delaware and the Six Indian Nations do the efforts of White Eyes to disassociate the Delaware from the Six Indian Nations at the conferences at Fort Pitt make any sense.

tives of Pennsylvania, Virginia, and the Continental Congress, who embraced the concept that the Delaware were still under the overlordship of the Six Indian Nations. This is what the Continental Congress told White Eyes when he asked the Congress's help in securing legal title to the land the Delaware were living on.[67] It is this background that gives White Eyes' speeches in October 1775 and at later congresses at Fort Pitt their significance.

In October 1775 the Delaware captain made two speeches. After warning the other participating tribes not to meddle in the conflict between England and the colonies, White Eyes informed the Congress on 9 October 1775:

> I now also Acquaint you that my Uncles the Wiandots have bound themselves the Shawanese Tawaas and Delawares together and have made us as one People and have also given me that Tract of Country Beginning at the Mouth of Big Beaver Creek and running up the same to where it interlocks with the Branches of Guyahoga Creek and down the said Creek to the Mouth thereof where it empties into the Lake along the Side of the Lake to the Mouth of Sanduskey Creek and up the same to the head untill it interlocks with Muskingum down the same to the Mouth where it Empties into the Ohio and up the said River to the Place of Beginning. I also now Acquaint my Uncles the Six Nations that my Uncles the Wiandots have given me that Tract of Country as we have now Acquainted you what Lands belongs to us I desire you will not Permit any of your foolish People to sit down upon it that I cannot suffer it least other Nations shou'd be Uneasy.[68]

White Eyes' meaning becomes clearer when contrasted with the statement of the speaker of the Six Indian Nations in Philadelphia on 12 July 1742: "We . . . Assign you two Places to go—either to Wyomin or Shamokin. You may go to either of these Places, and then we shall have you more under our Eye, and shall see how You behave. Don't deliberate, but remove away and take this Belt of Wampum. . . . This String of Wampum serves to forbid You, Your Children and Grand Children, to the latest Posterity, for ever medling in Land Affairs."[69]

White Eyes' speech contained two bombshells: first, his news that the Delaware had concluded an alliance with the Wyandot, the Shawnee, and the Tawas. This implied that the Delaware considered themselves entitled to act as

---

67. Resolve of 10 April 1776 on White Eyes' demand to grant a legally secure title to land the Wyandot had granted the Delaware, AA, 4th ser., 5:1664. According to Heckewelder, *Narrative of the Mission*, 240, the Wyandot chief Half King threatened on 25 August 1781 "that the Six Nations would not suffer us to stay!" yet added that other nations, too, were objecting to the presence of the Moravian mission congregation in the Muskingum valley.

68. *RUO*, 86–87

69. *PCR*, 4:580.

an independent Native American nation that concluded its treaties with whom it pleased. The second bombshell was White Eyes' announcement that the Delaware were living on land granted to them not by the Six Indian Nations but by the Wyandot. This second announcement had a further implication. By insisting that the land the Delaware lived on had been granted to them by the Wyandot, White Eyes disputed the Six Indian Nations' claim of having conquered the Ohio region in the seventeenth century[70]—a conquest from which they claimed the right of exclusively disposing of and selling the land to others. According to White Eyes, the Wyandot, not the Six Indian Nations, were the rightful owners of the Ohio region.

As far as the problem of ownership was concerned, White Eyes failed in the months following to wrest a land title from the Continental Congress. The Commissioners of the Congress, and especially the Congress's Indian agent, George Morgan, whom the Natives called Tamenend ("the affable one"), did accept the Delaware's important role as mediators between the conflicting parties in the Ohio region. Given the special relationship between the Delaware, the Shawnee, and the Wyandot, this made sense, and through this recognition of their peacekeeping role the Delaware temporarily joined the Mingo as one of the most influential tribes in the region. The following year, however, the Wyandot refused to attend the congress at Fort Pitt; the Six Indian Nations, the Delaware, Shawnee, and Mingo met in congress without them.

The tribes close to the two military strongholds of the contending parties were subjected to strong pressures. The Wyandot had to decide between their loyalty to the neighboring British at Fort Detroit and their alliances to other Native American tribes, while the Delaware and Shawnee had to make the same decision with respect to their native allies and the Americans at Fort Pitt. With their native allies they wanted to maintain sovereignty over the Ohio region. According to a report submitted in September by William Wilson, the Wyandot were already divided on this issue in August 1776. About half of the tribe wanted to side with England, while the other half opted for the rebels' cause.[71]

The Wyandot were not alone. Divisions were visible among the Mingo, Shawnee, and Delaware as well. The fundamental issue continued to be whether the tribes should adapt to European ways of life or try to retain their old ways. Within the Delaware this issue became personalized in the figures of Captain Pipe and the Wolf tribe on the one hand, and Captain White Eyes and the Turtle and Turkey tribes on the other. Not surprisingly, the latter sided with the Moravian mission congregations. According to John Heckewelder,

---

70. It was undisputed that the Five Indian Nations had fought wars with the Wyandot in the middle of the seventeenth century and had been victorious in those wars. It is equally true that the Iroquois had destroyed the tribal territory, Huronia, of the Wyandot. Yet this territory was far to the north and not between Lake Erie and the Ohio. See Trigger, *The Huron.*

71. Report of William Wilson dated 26 Sept. 1776 in *AA,* 5th series, 2:514–18, esp. 518.

this conflict reached a crisis point after White Eyes' October 1775 speech dissociating the Delaware from the Six Indian Nations at Fort Pitt.[72] Pipe, who enjoyed only minority support within the Delaware, now began actively to recruit allies among the Wyandot, the traditional allies of the Delaware, and the British at Detroit; the events of 1781 were to reveal his success.

The situation changed in 1777. In June Governor Henry Hamilton received orders from London actively to recruit allies among the Native American tribes of the region. The resulting British initiatives prompted the Shawnee, Mingo, and Delaware, who were determined to maintain Native American sovereignty and control over the Ohio region, to cement their bonds and join the British. The Shawnee especially had not yet given up the fight for their hunting grounds south of the Ohio. Their decision to ally themselves with the British also reflected their desire to gain access to badly needed European goods. At a conference in June–July 1777, Hamilton formally enlisted the support of the Wyandot for the British side.[73]

A number of incidents in the following months favored the British cause, among them American attacks on Indian delegations on their way to a planned congress at Fort Pitt in July 1777 (the congress had to be canceled owing to poor attendance).[74] More serious was the murder of the most influential chief of the Shawnee, Cornstalk, by America militiamen.[75]

As a consequence, the Shawnee accepted the war belt from Hamilton in March 1778 and entered the war on the British side. Some time earlier the Six Indian Nations had already joined the British; by winter 1777–78 the Delaware alone remained neutral, and their neutrality isolated them.[76]

The strategy of the American states that had declared their independence on 4 July 1776 hung on a number of factors. For one thing, the theater of the Revolutionary War was largely confined to the older settled regions; it was a fight between the British and Continental armies. For another, between 1775 and 1781 the states were not exactly spoiled by military success. Moreover, the Ohio region was outside the key area and thus enjoyed only marginal funds

72. Heckewelder, *Narrative of the Mission,* 141–43. One indication that this was much more than a power struggle between the two captains was the presence and energetic support Captain Pipe received from Wangomen, the preacher and prophet. Ibid., 136.

73. See Hamilton's report in *FDO,* 7–13. The Wyandot were appointed "guardians of the Hatchet" at that conference.

74. *FDO,* 85–87; Heckewelder, *Narrative of the Mission,* 159.

75. *FDO,* 157–63.

76. See William Wilson's report dated September 1776, according to which White Eyes had been determined "that as soon as they [i.e., the Delaware] find they [i.e., western tribes] were determined for war, he would collect all his people together, and would apply to his *American* brothers to send men to him, and erect a strong fort; that then he should not regard them, for the western tribes were but very indifferent warriors." On 27 March 1777 the governor of Virginia instructed the commanding officers of the Virginia militia companies in the frontier counties to provide the Delaware with military protection should they so wish. *RUO,* 203–4, 244–45; *FDO,* 93–95; *AA,* 5th series, 2:518.

and attention. The military at Fort Pitt had to make do with the meager resources at their disposal. This meant, among other things, that George Morgan, the Indian agent, had to resort to words, rhetoric, promises, and symbolic gestures. He and the military simply did not have the means to offer protection to their Indian allies; they had to leave military protection to the individual state militia units, which of course held the same negative ideas of the "savages" that other Euro-American settlers did.[77]

The militiamen considered it their first and most important duty to protect their families and farms. They were convinced that they had a clear and legal title to their land; God's commandment and the treaties of Lancaster of 1744 and Fort Stanwix of 1768 were on their side. As they saw it, their property was endangered less by the British than by the Native Americans, about whom they heard daily rumors and from whom they expected savage atrocities and surprise attacks. The Indian was the devil personified, and the settlers and militiamen did not feel they could differentiate between tribes allied with the Americans and those allied with the British. On 24 December 1774, in a letter to Lord Dartmouth, the last royal governor of Virginia, Lord Dunmore summarized the problem:

> In this Colony Proclamations have been published from time to time to restrain them [settlers]: But impressed from their earliest infancy with Sentiments and habits, very different from those acquired by persons of a Similar condition in England, they do not conceive that government has any right to forbid their taking possession of a Vast tract of Country, either uninhabited, or which serves only as a shelter to a few Scattered Tribes of Indians. Nor can they be easily brought to entertain any belief of the permanent obligation of Treaties made with those People, whom they consider, as but little removed from the brute Creation.[78]

What this meant for the Delaware was that by 1777 they were threatened not only by the Native American allies of Britain but also by those who perceived them as Britain's allies. Soon the pressure on the Delaware emanating from Fort Detroit became almost unbearable. In August 1777, during a visit of the Wyandot chief Half King with a large band of warriors, the Moravian missionaries were able to conclude a treaty for the protection of the "Moravian Indians"; but it was unclear whether Half King would be able to get the endorsement of his council and the British for this agreement.[79] The danger emanating from the American side was vividly demonstrated by the murder of

---

77. Report of the Indian Commissioners to the Continental Congress, March 1778, *FDO*, 238–40.

78. *DHDW*, 371.

79. See entries for 7 and 8 Aug. 1777 below; Heckewelder, *Narrative of the Mission*, 160–62.

Cornstalk by soldiers from Fort Randolph. Cornstalk, the Americans' only staunch ally among the Shawnee, and his son had paid the fort a friendly visit. There both were arrested and taken hostage in retaliation for Shawnee attacks on white settlements in Kentucky. According to David Zeisberger, the Delaware were so much troubled by this incident that Zeisberger advised General Hand at Fort Pitt that if White Eyes were to stay longer than a few days at the fort, Hand should "let the people here know of it that they may not be uneasy about him, for some apprehend because Cornstalk is taken fast at the Kanhawa, White Eyes may be served so too."[80] When a few weeks later the news of Cornstalk's murder arrived in the Delaware villages, confidence in the reliability of the Americans was shaken even more deeply.

The next year witnessed increased attacks on settlers by Mingo, Seneca, and Wyandot; and now the Shawnee, bent on avenging the injustice done to them, joined in the attacks on white settlements. Worse was to come. After the failure of the "Squaw Campaign" against the settlements on the Cuyahoga and Sandusky Rivers in the winter of 1777–78, in which a son of Captain Pipe was killed and his mother badly wounded, everyone expected that Pipe and his followers would actively enter the war effort on the British side.[81]

On 11 March 1778 the Delaware accepted the declaration of war; in June of the same year, at a congress in Detroit, they were nevertheless sharply criticized by other tribes for their ambivalent and reluctant attitude toward the war. Chaminitawaa, whom the Ottawa, Chippewa, and Potowatomi had appointed their speaker, concluded his pointed critique with a veiled threat: "this is the last time we intend speaking to you." Indeed, by now the pressures on those Delaware who were leaning to the British side to pack up and move to the Detroit region became almost unbearable. The Delaware speaker at the congress must have sensed this. His answer illustrates the dilemma these Delaware warriors faced. Captain James, as he is called in the protocol, assured his listeners: "I am well pleased with what you & your children have said this day, you have cleansed my heart, and the hearts of those who live at my village, there are sixty of us for whom I will be answerable, tho' I cannot say anything for the rest of the nation. To convince you of my sincerety, I desire to sing the War Song, on that Belt you gave me."[82]

At the same time Captain James admitted that only two villages, his own and that of Captain Pipe, had openly joined the British side; the larger part of the Delaware still stuck to the neutral course outlined and pursued by White Eyes. How dangerous that course was, however, the resolutions and speeches at the Detroit congress made perfectly clear. The news of these speeches and resolutions traveled fast to the villages in the Muskingum valley.

80. Zeisberger to General Hand, 16 Nov. 1777, *FDO*, 167.
81. General Hand's report dated 7 March 1778 and report of Samuel Murphy, both in *FDO*, 215–20.
82. Lieutenant Governor Henry Hamilton to Governor Guy Carleton, 25 April 1778, in *HP*, 434; for the protocol of the congress from 14 to 29 June at Detroit, see ibid., 442–58.

One of the immediate consequences of the congress at Detroit was that the Wyandot rather rudely rejected White Eyes' efforts to dissociate them from the British. In communicating the resolutions of the Detroit congress to George Morgan on 19 July, the captain added: "the Nations have agreed to fall upon the Delawares, & the Wiandots are to make the beginning. . . . I believe it to be true." After David Zeisberger, on 9 June 1778, had conveyed the soothing news to Fort Pitt that "among the Delawares all is quiet and peaceable, they are now in a fair way again,"[83] the Delaware were suddenly faced with their most serious crisis. White Eyes knew this: "Brother," he wrote Morgan, "I have always told you that I shall hold fast to our friendship so long as the Sun shall shine & the Rivers run, & so my heart is yet. I still hold fast to our friendship, but you know that I am weak & am in need of your assistance. If you do not assist me now as soon as possible then I shall be ruin'd & destroy'd, but if you will assist me now at this dangerous time then nobody will be able to break our friendship."[84] Thus it comes as no surprise that White Eyes proposed to the congress at Fort Pitt on 19 September 1778 that the American army should "build some place for our old men, Women & Children to remain in safety, whilst our Warriors go with you."[85]

During this congress the Delaware signed a remarkable treaty containing three provisions. First, they gave up their neutrality and joined the war on the American side; American troops were allowed to march through Delaware territory. Second, the treaty guaranteed the Delaware the land they lived on

83. Zeisberger to George Morgan, 9 June 1778, FAO, 82–83.
84. White Eyes to Morgan, 19 July 1778, FAO, 117–18.
85. It is not clear who first proposed in 1778 to build a fort on the Muskingum for the protection of the Delaware. During the second half of 1777 the isolation of the Delaware in the Ohio region increased. FDO, 93–95. Nevertheless, White Eyes on 22 September 1777 demanded from the Continental Congress that an army against Detroit should not march through Delaware territory but "above and below the towns" (ibid., 97). In the following weeks the danger to the Delaware increased; Mingo and Wyandot in particular who came through Delaware villages insulted them as "Virginians" who would soon be given the same treatment as the white settlers (ibid., 100). The first unequivocal proposal to build a fort in the Delaware settlements in these dire times seems to have been made by General Hand in his letter dated 1 Oct. 1777. Hand wrote that he would march his expeditionary army, as desired, around the Delaware settlements, and continued, "if you think it necessary I will build a fort & Garrison it either at your Town or at any other Place near to it that you think proper and when Peace shall be restored the fort shall be burned & our People shall all come out of your Country" (ibid., 113). Shortly thereafter the tensions eased, which accounts for Zeisberger's letter cited above. In a letter accompanying White Eyes' message of 19 July 1778, Zeisberger explained White Eyes' plea for help thus: "he wisheth an army might come out now—the sooner the better, for its high time. All thoughts of bringing about a peace with the Nations, especially with the Wyandotts, are in vain, & time only is lost; therefore White Eyes thinks, that the only help you can afford him, is to send an army against the Wyandotts &c, except you should know another remedy" (FAO, 119). The first real proof that the Delaware wanted a fort built within their settlements is White Eyes' letter of 19 Sept. 1778 (FAO, 43); a second plea for a fort is contained in a letter copied into Robert McCready's regimental diary about the march of the expeditionary army from Fort McIntosh to the Delaware settlements. The last entry, dated 20 Nov. 1778, reads: "they [the Delaware] likewise Insisted much on the Generals going down to their Town to Build A fort for their Defence and Safety" (Williams, "Revolutionary Journal and Orderly Book," 17).

forever. Third, the treaty promised that the Delaware and their land were at a later time to be admitted to the United States as a separate state; in this context the treaty promised further assistance to the Delaware in their efforts to adopt more features of Euro-American culture, civilization, and agricultural practices.[86]

The treaty of 19 September 1778 was signed for the Delaware by White Eyes, Captain Pipe, and Captain Killbuck. It marked a turning point in the relations between the Delaware and the United States in more than one sense. First, the treaty seemed to indicate that the Delaware, faced with grave dangers, had, under White Eyes' leadership, given up their policy of neutrality and without any reservations joined the American side. This at least was the understanding of the Commissioners of the Continental Congress; the Delaware, however, disputed this reading of the treaty. Among many of them the feeling quickly spread that they had been betrayed during the treaty negotiations. Captain Pipe, for example, when he saw the text of the treaty, insisted that it was a forgery; the chiefs, he maintained, had never signed such a text. In particular he disputed the stipulation that the Delaware had joined the war on the American side.[87]

The circumstances that caused such denials are difficult to unravel because the one person who could have explained the stipulations of the treaty was by then unable to do so. For in October 1778, White Eyes, en route from the expedition army that was to conquer Fort Detroit, was murdered by American settlers or militiamen.[88] With this murder the American side lost its most energetic supporter among the Delaware. His ability to mediate and to explain complex and contradictory behavior to his tribe and to the other councilors was sorely missed during the events of November 1778, when General Hand, commanding officer of the American expedition force, during the building of Fort Laurens[89] near Coshocton (Goschgashünk) mightily irritated the Delaware through his haughty behavior. If the record of White Eyes' last words at the Congress is accurate, then we must assume that White Eyes shared the Continental Congress Commissioners' and General Lachlan McIntosh's understanding of the treaty.[90]

The contradiction was too obvious: the treaty's promise of help, goods, and

86. Peters, *Public Statutes at Large*, 7:13–15; cf. Abel, "Proposals for an Indian State," 89. Different versions of the conference protocol are printed in Bushnell Jr., "Virginia Frontier in History," and in *FAO*, 138–45.

87. White, *Middle Ground*, 382–83.

88. *FAO*, 20–21; see entry for 20 Nov. 1778 below.

89. Gramly, *Fort Laurens;* Pieper and Gidney, *Fort Laurens;* Williams, "Revolutionary Journal and Orderly Book."

90. In his last words White Eyes demanded the building of a fort close to the Delaware settlements "whilst our warriors go with you." If only White Eyes and a few warriors were to accompany the American army, as had been the case with Lord Dunmore's expedition, the fort would have been unnecessary, for enough warriors would have been left at home to protect the elderly and children.

support could never have been fulfilled by the miserable army, which scarcely had enough food for itself and which had brought no goods at all to the Delaware villages but in fact begged the Indians for provisions. During the winter of 1778–79 relations between army and Delaware gradually collapsed. An open break was only a matter of time.

The break came later than one would expect. In the meantime, in a surprise attack, George Rogers Clark and a few militiamen from Virginia conquered the former French settlements on the Illinois, first Kaskaskia, then Vincennes, and thus brought the French people of that region—whose knowledge of the recently concluded French-American treaty of Amity helped them switch their allegiance—into the American camp. In April 1779 the Wyandot, too, joined the American side. Even the Shawnee distanced themselves from Detroit, but for different reasons: they had learned that the Virginia militia was planning a new expedition against Shawnee settlements.[91] A third factor contributed to easing tensions: in July 1779 the new commanding officer of Fort Laurens, Frederick Vernon, who had relieved the former commander, John Gibson, abandoned the fort with the approval of McIntosh's successor, Daniel Brodhead.[92] At the same time, the army gave up the idea of conquering Detroit or gaining military control over the Ohio region. The few soldiers available were to be spared for smaller military expeditions—against the Seneca on the Allegheny River in July and August 1779, for example.[93] From now on, the local militias were to be responsible for securing the settlements of Virginia and Pennsylvania.

During the fifth congress at Fort Pitt, in September 1779, everything pointed to quieter times. With the exception of the Mingo and the Seneca, all of the larger tribes in the Great Lakes region and Ohio area were impressed by the impending and much-discussed American expedition against the Seneca and by the French-American treaty of amity. They indicated their willingness to live in peace with the United States henceforth.[94]

The relative quiet prompted the commander of the American army at Fort Pitt to revive the idea of organizing an expedition against Fort Detroit, which still represented a threat to the white settlements and the villages of the allied Native American tribes.[95] George Washington approved of the plan but was unable to send Brodhead soldiers. Even Virginia and Pennsylvania denied the commander, who had only 722 soldiers at his disposal, reinforcements, arguing that the militia was needed for the protection of the settlements. Finally, in January 1780, Washington ordered that preparations for the expedition be cut

91. On Clark's expedition, see James, *Clark Papers*, 40–207.
92. FAO, 389.
93. FAO, 388–405; FRO, 55–66, 235.
94. FRO, 66–67; The American expedition army destroyed the settlements of the Seneca but the warriors had retreated and avoided meeting the soldiers in battle.
95. FRO, 98.

short, reasoning that "we cannot at present furnish either the men or supplies necessary for it."[96] At the same time it became clear that General Sullivan's army had been unable to conquer Fort Niagara, which would have cut off the stream of goods flowing to Detroit.

The idea had been to diminish the attraction of Fort Detroit as a source of European goods. This was considered important because the Americans had neither the means nor the opportunity to compete with the rich assortment of goods stored at Detroit. The American army was simply unable to protect the supply lines to Fort Pitt; this enabled Simon Girty and about 130 Indians to hijack a large train of goods en route from New Orleans on 4 October 1779.[97] At roughly the same time, Brodhead's relations with the commanding officers of the militia regiments of the surrounding counties of Virginia and Pennsylvania worsened. The general's attempts to requisition Pennsylvania militia units for the service of the army met with resistance from Archibald Lochry, as the Seneca had resumed their attacks on white settlements in the spring of 1780.[98] The attacks were to continue until 1782.

In 1780 the desperate situation of the Continental army in the east made it impossible to send reinforcements to Fort Pitt; plans to "chastise" (as contemporaries put it) the Shawnee and Wyandot—in the winter of 1779–80 both had again switched sides—had to be shelved.[99] In autumn the shortage in army provisions was so desperate that Brodhead was forced to requisition food from the settlers of the region,[100] but fierce resistance forced him to end that practice and instead send his soldiers out to hunt for food.

At the same time, relations with the Delaware steadily deteriorated. In the summer of 1779 Brodhead had been unable to re-man Fort Laurens. In the autumn a flood of white settlers poured into the area and settled close to the Delaware villages; again the commander could only look on helplessly, for he had no means to stop the tide or disperse the squatters. Meanwhile, the threats not only from Detroit but also from the Shawnee, Mingo, and Wyandot against the Delaware multiplied. On 23 April 1780 the Council of the Delaware wrote Brodhead: "I am so much mocked at by the Enemy Indians for speaking so long to them for You. Now they laugh at me, and ask me where that great Army of my Brothers, that was to come out against them so long ago, and so

96. *FRO*, 123–24.

97. *FRO*, 79–94, 103–6; Killbuck and John Heckewelder informed Brodhead on 23 October about the successful attack on the transport. Ibid., 105–6.

98. *FRO*, 150–51, 154–55, 160, 163–64, 170–71, 179–81, 183–87, 192–95; on the differences with the militia, ibid., 125–26, and on the links between these disputes and the border controversy between Virginia and Pennsylvania, see ibid., 127–28, and passim.

99. Report on the congress at Detroit with Native American tribes, early July 1780, in the handwriting of David Zeisberger, dated 19 July 1780, in *FRO*, 217–20. This was not a proper congress because, as the British governor pointed out, most warriors were out on the warpath. De Peyster (at Detroit) to Sinclair, 15 June 1780, in HP, 585; De Peyster to Alexander McKee (at Detroit), 22 June 1780, in HP, 404.

100. *FRO*, 273.

often, stays so long. . . . They further desire me to tell You now to make haste and come soon, the sooner, and the greater Number the better."[101]

A number of factors helped tip the scales in the council, among them the isolation of the Delaware, the constant reproaches of the pro-British tribes, and the attacks from the American side, provoked by the Delaware's continued profession of neutrality. These factors widened the rift between the followers of Captain Pipe and the other leading chiefs in the council at Goschachgünk. With the death of White Eyes, the advocates of a pro-British course had slowly gained ground, especially among the younger warriors. Even before the Continental Congress finally resolved, in March 1781, not to grant new funds for remanning Fort Laurens, the war party in the council at Goschachgünk finally gained the upper hand. When Brodhead read John Heckewelder's letter informing him of the council's turnabout, he decided on a preventive strike against the tribe.[102] When he arrived in April 1781 at Goschachgünk, the settlement had been deserted. He destroyed its buildings as well as those of the nearby Moravian town of Lichtenau, which the Moravian congregation had left in April 1779; since then non-Christian natives had lived there.[103] The expedition produced two results. First, the pro-American party within the Delaware was reduced to the followers of Gelelemind (Captain Killbuck); they followed Brodhead back to Fort Pitt.[104] Second, the Moravian missionaries realized that with the departure of Gelelemind and his followers they were without any protection, for it would have been foolish to expect protection from Fort Pitt.

For the Americans at Fort Pitt, the situation was further complicated by the dispute between George Rogers Clark and Brodhead about the resolve of the Continental Congress that Fort Pitt lend two hundred of its soldiers to Clark for his expedition against Fort Detroit. Brodhead refused to honor that resolve, which in turn increased already existing tensions between Virginia and Pennsylvania. Nevertheless, Clark succeeded in collecting four hundred soldiers for his expedition. The enterprise failed thanks to Mohawk chief Joseph Brant's carefully planned ambush.[105]

Two weeks earlier, the event David Zeisberger had been dreading had finally occurred: on 9 August 1781 Captain Pipe, Matthew Elliott, and the Wyandot chief Half King, together with 140 warriors, arrived at Salem and demanded that the Moravian congregations relocate their settlements to the Sandusky. After long negotiations and the imprisonment of the missionaries, the congregations finally gave in. On 9 September the Christian Indians buried their possessions and winter provisions and left the settlements of Schönau, Gnadenhütten, and Salem.[106]

101. FRO, 172; cf. Downes, Council Fires, 264.

102. FRO, 334–40, 342–43.

103. FRO, 376–81, reprints the official report of Brodhead.

104. See memorandum of the commander of Fort Detroit dated 26 April 1781, in HP, 476.

105. See the report of General Haldimand to Lord St. Germain, Quebec, 23 Oct. 1781, in HP 530–31.

106. Heckewelder, Narrative of the Mission, 232–77.

Shortly after the deported congregations had arrived at the region where Captain Pipe and his followers had their village, the commander of Fort Detroit called the missionaries and speakers of the Christian Indians to attend a conference. The Delaware and Shawnee, but not the Wyandot, obeyed the summons. At the center of the talks was the question whether the Moravian missionaries had been truly neutral or had been collaborating with the American side and had thus hindered the war effort of the British.

The protocol of this conference[107] offers insights not only into the decision-making process at Fort Detroit but into the nature of the relationships between the Native American tribes and the British, the extent of factionalism within the Delaware, attitudes toward the Moravian mission, and, finally, into the way David Zeisberger, as spokesman for the missionaries, justified Moravian behavior during the war years. The protocol reveals three different attitudes toward the Moravian mission. First was the attitude of the "Kooshacking Indians," to use the terminology of the protocol, which meant the inhabitants of the settlement Goschachgünk with their chief, Netawatwees, until 1776 and, thereafter, the chief's successor, Gelelemind or Killbuck. Until 1780 these Delaware had consistently maintained friendly relations with the Moravian congregations and their missionaries. Second was the attitude of Captain Pipe and his followers, who between 1774 and 1776 had separated from the tribes at Goschachgünk and later moved to Sandusky, where they settled close to the Wyandot. The size of this group is not quite clear; it differed from the Goschachgünk group in two respects—a certain shyness toward the Christian congregations and, more important, a totally different attitude toward the "Big Knife," the Americans. Since 1775 a series of controversies between White Eyes and Captain Pipe had focused on their different perceptions of the Americans. Third was the attitude of the followers of chief Pachgantschihilas; the protocol gives their number as "240 Delaware warriors, 70 women, and 90 children"; this group's attitude was decidedly pro-British—something one cannot really say of Captain Pipe if one takes his speech of 9 December 1801 into account.[108] Chief Pachgantschihilas obviously rejected Christianity in general and the Moravian mission in particular even more energetically than Captain Pipe did. He did not want the Moravians to settle either in the Muskingum valley or in the Sandusky region, and he demanded that the missionaries be imprisoned by the commander of Fort Detroit and then removed from Indian territory, and that the Christian Indians return to their native beliefs. These demands confronted De Peyster with a set of difficult choices. He could not afford to brusquely reject these demands and alienate such a large group, so he temporized, promising to call a second meeting that would examine Pachgantschihilas's charges and,

---

107. Printed as Document No. 5 in the appendix.

108. See speech of Pipe dated 9 Dec. 1801, in Heckewelder, *History, Manners, and Customs*, 134–36, which is characterized by skepticism about the British.

should they be substantiated, act according to his wishes. Such a meeting, however, apparently never took place, and the missionaries remained with their congregations.[109]

Since 1775 Netawatwees, his successor Gelelemind, and White Eyes had worked for the reestablishment of Delaware unity; they believed that the Delaware as a nation should adopt European ways of life, agricultural practices, and religious beliefs, and that they should sometime join the American confederation as a separate state. For these chiefs the Christian mission congregations were important in helping the Delaware to achieve these goals. Sadly, viewed from the perspective of 1781, the exact reverse happened. The events of November and December 1781 revealed that the Delaware nation was split into four blocks: a pro-American block somewhat larger than that headed by Pachgantschihilas, which had retreated to Fort Pitt; a second group, headed by Gelelemind, that was probably as large as the first; a third group, of unknown size, headed by Captain Pipe; and, finally, the group led by Pachgantschihilas. The tensions caused by the American Revolution and the challenges posed by the Moravian mission had split the nation asunder.

While the Moravian congregations tried to adjust to the new situation in Sandusky, events in Fort Pitt had not improved. Brodhead had been unable to come to the assistance of the Moravians; he was now planning a new expedition against the Wyandot, who together with Delaware had been carrying out a series of attacks on frontier settlements. Just when Brodhead intended to leave with his soldiers, in September 1781, a letter from David Zeisberger informed him that Delaware under Pachgantschihilas and Wyandot under Half King intended to attack Wheeling in Pennsylvania. Seeking revenge for these Native American attacks, which had resulted in severe damages but fortunately cost almost no lives, a militia unit under David Williamson marched from Washington County to Gekelemukpechünk. This unit found the village deserted; its inhabitants had fled to Fort Pitt.

In March 1782 Williamson repeated the exercise. This time he stumbled over ninety Christian Indians who had returned to Gnadenhütten to fetch the provisions they had left behind. None of the Christian Indians survived the militia's assault; again, the Delaware warriors had eluded the militia soldiers.[110]

Frustrated, four hundred militiamen marched to the Delaware settlements on the Sandusky in May 1782; once and for all they wanted to extirpate the source of the attacks on their villages. On 4 June 1782 the American militiamen were severely defeated. William Crawford, the commanding officer, and many of his soldiers were made prisoners, but Williamson, who had led the expedition in March 1782, and the bulk of the soldiers got away. Crawford was

109. At least Heckewelder does not mention such a meeting in *History, Manners, and Customs*.
110. Much has been written on the Gnadenhütten massacre; I am following here the account of Heckewelder, *Narrative of the Mission*, 313–27.

killed in the cruelest way the Delaware could devise; he was slowly burned to death.[111] While the preliminaries of the peace treaty were signed in Paris by the representatives of Great Britain and the United States, war in the Ohio region continued.

General William Irvine, Brodhead's successor as commander of Fort Pitt from winter 1781–82, planned a new punitive expedition against the Delaware; its date of departure had to be postponed several times because the regular troops did not arrive. The last date Irvine had set was 20 October 1782, but on 19 October news of the signing of the peace preliminaries arrived. On 7 November Irvine wrote George Rogers Clark: "This news gained universal belief in the country and I fear would have mutilated my plan [even] if the report had proved premature."[112]

The War of Independence had come to an end. In the Ohio region the Native American tribes faced the same dismal conditions and circumstances that they had in 1763. Once again they lost the option of siding with a power that might support them in their efforts to preserve their independence, their way of life, and, most important, the integrity of their lands, while at the same time maintaining access to much-needed European goods. Until the conclusion of the Treaty of Greenville in 1794, the events of the 1760s in many respects repeated themselves. The Treaty of Greenville accomplished what Virginia, with the Treaty of Lancaster, and what Sir William Johnson and the colonies of Pennsylvania and Virginia, with the Treaty of Fort Stanwix, had hoped to accomplish in 1768: a clear and undisputed title to the Ohio region as a land open to white settlers.

3. The Ohio Region as Mission Country

MISSIONARY ACTIVITIES IN THE OHIO REGION BEFORE 1772 AND CONCEPTS OF CHRISTIAN MISSION

The Moravians were not the first missionaries to settle in the Ohio region. From the seventeenth until the early eighteenth century, Jesuits had been preaching the gospel among the Seneca; they stayed among the Wyandot until the end of the Seven Years' War. Since then the Catholic Church had maintained clergy only in the French settlements. In the 1770s only a few priests were active in the Ohio region, for example, in Detroit. Yet the Native Americans in the region were under the impression that Christian teachings had been preached there since time out of mind. David Zeisberger's diary reports a furi-

111. Brown, "Battle of Sandusky," and "Fate of Crawford Volunteers," 65.
112. Cited in Downes, Council Fires, 275.

ous dialogue between a Mingo and a Christian Delaware, in which the Mingo maintained that Christianity was a long-established tradition in the region.[113]

On the Protestant side there had been few mission attempts. By and large these efforts were restricted to short visits; no one attempted to establish a long-term mission program in the region. This is the more remarkable because the importance of Protestant mission for drawing the tribes to the English side had played a large role in the political discussion about relations with Native Americans in the Ohio region. Since the 1720s English reports had persistently claimed that tribal sympathies for the French were usually due to the influence of Catholic missionaries.[114] The French colony, the argument went (and not without justice), would use mission as a political weapon in the fight for the Native Americans' allegiance. Catholic missionaries were no more than political agents and helpers in the efforts to establish political tyranny in North America. This belief was so widespread that it is surprising that the colonial governments did not try harder to counteract the influence of Catholic missionaries with Protestant mission efforts.

There were some early efforts to introduce Protestantism among Native Americans. In 1649 the Society for the Propagation of the Gospel in New England had been founded to spread the gospel among the Native American tribes of Massachusetts and Connecticut; John Eliot was one of the more important of the society's missionaries.[115] At least in theory, the scope of the Society for the Propagation of the Gospel in Foreign Parts, founded in 1701, was wider, though in reality that society focused its efforts on non-Anglican Protestant congregations and on Anglican parishes in the southern colonies, in New York, and in New England that were without a pastor.[116] Overall, the Anglican Church provided very few missionary impulses in the colonial period.[117]

A shortage of clerics hindered other Christian confessions, too, from getting involved in missionary work. The Dutch Reformed Church suffered from too few pastors because the Amsterdam classis provided too few new clerics for the parishes. There were additional reasons for the lack of clergy in North America. Among the larger churches, the Presbyterians in the middle Atlantic colonies were preoccupied with fighting among themselves. They had been deeply divided since the theological disputes of the Great Awakening; only after 1760 did they reestablish harmony and unity among themselves. This accomplishment freed Presbyterian energies for other activities, mission work

---

113. See entry for 20 Sept. 1773 below.

114. Contemporaries were firmly convinced that the behavior of the Abenaki in Nova Scotia and Maine was largely influenced and shaped by the Catholic missionary Sébastian Rasle; this belief figured heavily during the negotiations at the Albany Congress of Union in 1754.

115. Simmons, "Conversion from Indian to Puritan"; Cogley, "John Eliot."

116. Bonomi, *Under the Cope of Heaven*, 49–54, 121.

117. Axtell, *Invasion Within*, 259–63; Hawkins, *Historical Notices of the Missions of the Church of England*; Goodwin, "Christianity, Civilization, and the Savage."

among them. At the behest of the Presbyterian Synod, the first Presbyterians to visit the Ohio region were Charles Beatty and George Duffield; according to David McClure they reported in 1772 favorable prospects for "Christianizing" the Native American inhabitants of the Ohio region. In the same year the Scottish Society for Propagating Christian Knowledge commissioned McClure and Levi Frisbie to again tour the Ohio region.[118] Neither initiative was of consequence, since both the Shawnee and the Delaware rejected the missionaries' offer to stay on.[119]

From the middle of the century the Baptists had expanded so widely that they had barely enough migrant preachers to minister to their own congregations. Yet at least one, David Jones, visited the Ohio region in the early 1770s.[120] He too was rebuffed by the tribes.[121] The Methodists made similar attempts and met with similar responses.[122] The failure of the Society of Friends, the Quakers, to gain a foothold was due to different causes. The Quakers believed that everyone had the principle of God, the "Inner Light," within himself, and their avowed mission was to proclaim the existence of this "Inner Light" within each person. The nonbeliever could thus accept the existence of the "Inner Light" and experience conversion or reject his own "Inner Light." The nature of the Quaker mission encouraged individual short excursions into the Ohio region but discouraged the foundation of permanent mission settlements.[123] The "Friendly Association," a group of Quakers influenced by the "social concerns" of the Quaker revival of mid-century, worked hard to protect the Native American tribes in the Ohio region against the aggressions of white settlers and the problematic land policies of the proprietor of Pennsylvania.[124]

The experience of long exposure to Catholic missionary efforts was matched on the Protestant side by only one Native American tribe: the Delaware. A number of Delaware had lived in Moravian missionary congregations before the Seven Years' War. Before the war many Delaware returned to their villages, where they contributed to the emergence of new religious concepts

---

118. Dexter, *Diary of David McClure*, 26–27; on McClure, see entries for 13, 16, and 26 September and 7 October 1772 below. See also [Beatty], *Journals of Charles Beatty;* Ramsay, "Francis Borland"; Conrad, "Cherokee Mission of Virginia Presbyterians," 58; Smylie, "United Presbyterian Church in Mission," 57.

119. On the reasons for this, see pp. 40–41 below.

120. Jones, *Journal of Two Visits;* see entry for 13 Feb. 1773 below; Sacks, *Philadelphia Baptist Tradition.*

121. On the reasons for this, see pp. 40–41 below.

122. Barclay, *History of Methodist Missions,* dates the first missionary efforts to the 1790s.

123. Wellenreuther, *Glaube und Politik in Pennsylvania,* 2–3; Tolles, "Nonviolent Contact"; Daiutolo, "Early Quaker Perception of the Indian." An example of this kind of declaratory mission sermon and work is the visit of John Parrish, his friend Zebulon Heston, and their youthful companion John Lacey toward the end of July 1773 in the Delaware settlements on the Muskingum. See entry for 30 July 1773 below.

124. Wellenreuther, *Glaube und Politik in Pennsylvania,* 285–86, and passim.

that fused Native American and Christian thought.[125] Some of these Delaware later returned to Moravian congregations.[126]

Other reasons for the relatively meager efforts of Protestant missionaries in the Ohio region before the Seven Years' War were the distance between that region and the white settled areas, and the proximity of small Native American villages to white settlements east of the mountains that offered missionaries enough opportunities to preach the gospel. No Protestant missionary before 1760 had subscribed to the idea that successful missionary work depended largely on minimizing white influence on Native American society. For these influences too often had seriously disruptive effects on Native American life. Other reasons were connected to the imperial rivalries in the region. Competing French and English activities for dominance contributed to the increasing political and social instability in the region. And, finally, both before and during the Seven Years' War, frequent military clashes between the French and English would have endangered the lives of missionaries.

Yet these reasons, important as they are, do not explain the almost total failure of the visits of Beatty, Jones, McClure, and Parrish *after* 1763. Their failure was largely the result of changing conditions and of three factors in particular. First, conflicts with colonies and settlers had increased Native American awareness of the importance of the land issue. This was particularly true for those tribes that had gradually retreated from the East Coast to the Ohio region. Their mistrust of the intentions of white settlers had increased sharply, and settlers, more than the colonial governments, were increasingly identified as the Native Americans' worst enemies. This general mistrust greeted missionaries, too. The Baptist missionary David Jones reported to David Zeisberger that during his visit to Shawnee villages, the Shawnee, in Zeisberger's words, "had not allowed him to speak privately with Indians, much less to preach a single time. He finally fled in secrecy to save his life. They actually set out after him, but fortunately he escaped their hands."[127] The second factor was the result of increased immigration from Europe after 1763, which increased demand for new land everywhere, but especially in the Ohio region. Settlers saw land in this region as "underused" and "uncultivated," and their fascination with the land in the Ohio region infected many missionaries, whose diaries sometimes read like the advertisements of land agents. During their visits in Native American villages missionaries made no effort to hide their disdain for "wasteful" Native American attitudes toward the valuable agricultural potential of land. David McClure's diary is a telling example of this attitude. An entry in Zeisberger's diary of 7 October 1772 reports the remarks of McClure's interpreter, the Christian Joseph Peepi, at the end of McClure's visit:

125. The most important example is chief Teedyuskung. See Wallace, *King of the Delaware*.
126. See entry for 25 Dec. 1772 below, note 114 (for Stockbridge Indians), and note 116 for earlier members of the Indian congregation of David Brainerd in New Jersey.
127. See entry for 13 Feb. 1773 below.

As we heard personally from *Joseph Peepi,* he [McClure] talked very carelessly. For example, he supposedly said often that the Indians had so much beautiful and good land, but it was lying in waste and they did not use it because they were lazy people who did not want to work and resented the White people using it. In a few years all the land would be taken away from them. The White people would establish cities and towns there and drive the Indians away or even destroy them. He also said other such things, so it is no wonder that they sent him away.[128]

Finally, skepticism and hostility toward white settlers was supplemented by increasing nativism among the tribes, particularly among the Delaware and Shawnee. Although it is not quite clear how important a role nativism played among the Shawnee and Delaware during the so-called "Pontiac's Rebellion" of 1763–64, travel diaries from the 1760s and 1770s make it quite clear that the rediscovery of values and beliefs associated with the Native American past played an increasingly important role.[129] Missionary activity had to take these changing conditions into account and develop strategies for coping with them if they were to have a hope of success. Of all the Christian missionaries who attempted this, only one seems to have enjoyed a measure of success in the eighteenth century: the Moravian Unity.

MORAVIAN MISSION ACTIVITY IN NORTH AMERICA BEFORE 1772

The mission work of the Moravian Church in North America has been often described, yet we still lack a satisfactory ethno-historical analysis that sets that mission in the context of the encounter of European with Native American cultures. Apart from the 1956 doctoral dissertation of Ilse Loges,[130] existing scholarship has with few exceptions—the work of Merritt and Wessel among them—usually used traditional methodological and historiographical concepts.[131] Among the older works, David Cranz's, George Heinrich Loskiel's, and John Heckewelder's are of particular value. All three men were members of the Moravian Church; while Cranz and Loskiel had unrestricted access to the Moravian archives, Heckewelder, a missionary himself, wrote his *Narrative* as an extremely well informed participant and witness.[132] Cranz's work is charac-

128. See entry for 7 Oct. 1772 below.
129. Dowd, *Spirited Resistance.* Zeisberger's diaries contain numerous additional references that testify to the importance of the nativist revival.
130. Loges, "Irokesen und Delawaren."
131. Merritt, *At the Crossroads;* Wessel, "Missionsvorstellung und Missionswirklichkeit" and *Delaware-Indianer und Herrnhuter Missionare;* Kaiser, "Delaware und die Herrnhuter Brüdergemeine"; Hertrampf, *Herrnhuter Missionare bei den Indianern Pennsylvanias.*
132. Cranz, *Alte und Neue Brüder-Historie;* Hegner, *Fortsetzung;* Loskiel, *Geschichte der Mission.* These three authors wrote their histories at the behest of the Unity's Elders' Conference, the directorate of the Moravian Church. Heckewelder wrote his history, *Narrative of the Mission,* as a participant and close ethnographic observer. Of the older histories of the mission, Schweinitz's *Zeisberger* is by far the

terized by his perception of the Moravian mission as part of a worldwide effort
to Christianize all "heathens" of North and South America, Greenland, Europe,
Asia, and Africa. Like David Zeisberger, Moravian missionaries not only wrote
diaries but circulated them via either Herrnhut, the center of the Moravian
Church in Germany, or Bethlehem, the center of Moravianism in North
America, to all the other congregations.[133] Missionaries and authors knew that
they were part of an international Christian community.

The origins of the first Renewed Moravian congregation go back to the
1720s and are linked to the life and deeds of Nikolaus Ludwig Imperial Count
of Zinzendorf and Pottendorf—thus his full title. Until his death on 9 May
1760, Zinzendorf shaped, guided, and directed the thinking, activities, and
work of the Moravians, who as persecuted members of the old Moravian
Church had fled to Saxony, where they joined Lutherans and Calvinists to form
the constituent parts of the Moravian Church. In the rise, growth, and consoli-
dation of the Moravians' mission work in North America, its first bishop, August Gottlieb Spangenberg, played a leading role.[134] After Zinzendorf's death,
Spangenberg was recalled to Germany and quickly became one of the leading
members of the Unity's Elders' Conference. He wrote not only the first comprehensive biography of Zinzendorf but the first comprehensive treatise of Moravian theology in the post-Zinzendorf era.[135]

In the early 1730s the Moravians' focus on mission began to crystallize. At
Halle more than twenty years earlier, August Hermann Francke and his pietistic followers had taken the biblical command (Matt. 28:19) seriously. In
1707 that center of pietism, in cooperation with the Danish court and the
Society for the Propagation of Christian Knowledge, started mission work
among the Hindu population at Tranquebar in Southern India.[136] Halle, where
Zinzendorf himself had been educated, was the example. The precarious position of the Moravian Unity as a radical and persecuted pietistic sect within the
German territories became an additional incentive to branch out into the wider
world.[137] Under constant attack from the Lutheran Church as well as from
the competing pietistic movements in Halle and Württemberg, the Moravian
Church started to search for countries whose governments were willing to tolerate this radical pietistic sect. Because of its pacifism and its rejection of the

best informed. For concise summaries of the Moravian mission work, see Hutton, *History of Moravian Missions,* and Beck, *Brüder in vielen Völkern.*

133. Gollin, *Moravians in Two Worlds,* and esp. Wessel, "Connecting Congregations."

134. Bechler, *Spangenberg.*

135. Spangenberg, *Zinzendorf* and *Idea fidei fratrum.*

136. The latest comprehensive accounts of pietism in the eighteenth century are the contributions to Brecht, *Geschichte des Pietismus,* vol. 2; Brunner, *Halle Pietists in England,* chap. 4. Of particular
importance were the translation activities of these early Halle missionaries; see Victor, "Tamil Translation of the Bible"; Sandgren, *Ziegenbalg;* Jeyaraj, *Inkulturation in Tranquebar;* and for a comparison of
the Halle mission and the Moravian mission, Wellenreuther, "Deux modèles de mission piétiste."

137. The most recent accounts of the Moravian Church in eighteenth-century Europe and North
America are Meyer, "Zinzendorf und Herrnhut," and Roeber, "Pietismus in Nordamerika."

oath, authorities viewed the Moravians with suspicion.[138] According to
Spangenberg, only his visit to the Danish court at Copenhagen induced Zinzendorf to combine the search for a safe haven with defining mission as an
overriding concern of the Moravian Unity.[139]

After Zinzendorf's death the administrative structure of the Unity was
overhauled. The Unity's Elders' Conference became the administrative directorate; first located in Herrnhut it was later moved for a while to Barby, close to
Magdeburg. The church's North American center was at Bethlehem in Pennsylvania, founded in 1740–41.[140] The direction of the church activities was
entrusted to committees, where decisions were made collectively. The Unity's
Elders' Conference for the whole church had its equivalent in the Provincial
Elders' Conference responsible for affairs in North America. Leading members
of this committee, responsible for directing the mission activities between 1761
and 1801, were Nathanael Seidel and Johann Ettwein.[141] Other important
persons to whom the missionaries directed their correspondence were Matthäus
Hehl and Bernhard Adam Grube.[142] All the committees and institutions were
subordinated to the General Synod, the meeting of delegates from all parts of
the church, and to the Provincial Synod, in which representatives of the particular provinces assembled.

In the 1730s, news of the foundation of the colony of Georgia induced
Moravians to consider for the first time the possibility of extending their activities to the New World. A few years later the settlement in Pennsylvania—
Bethlehem—was founded. The Moravians preferred Pennsylvania because it
permitted the affirmation instead of the oath, granted liberty of conscience,
and did not require military service of the men.[143] How wise the selection of
Pennsylvania was became obvious when Moravian missionaries in Checomeco,
the first mission station in the middle colonies, encountered problems with the
government; Checomeco was in the colony of New York.

The problems the first missionaries encountered are spelled out in the report of a justice of the peace on his visit to Checomeco in March 1744. The

---

138. For the Moravians' justification of these tenets, see "Aufsatz wegen der Eydes-Verweiger-
ung einiger Mährischer Brüder," in *ZE*, 1:401–3.

139. Spangenberg, *Zinzendorf*, 3rd part, 690–91.

140. Neisser, *Beginnings of Moravian Work in America*; Levering, *History of Bethlehem*; Erbe, *Bethlehem, Pa.*

141. Hamilton, "Ettwein." Nathanael Seidel (1718–82) was bishop of the Unitas Fratrum since
1758; in 1762 he had been entrusted with the leadership of the Moravian Church in North America.
John Ettwein (1721–1802) became his successor and chairman of the Provincial Helpers' Conference;
in 1784 he was consecrated bishop.

142. Matthäus Hehl (1704–87) grew up in Württemberg, had read theology at Tübingen, and
came to Bethlehem as assistant to A. G. Spangenberg. He became pastor of the Moravian congregra-
tion at Lititz in Pennsylvania. Bernhard Adam Grube (1715–1808) was born in Erfurt, was missionary
at Wechquetank, and accompanied Christian Indians to Philadelphia and stayed with them until the
end of their internment in the City of Brotherly Love. In 1780 he visited the mission congregations
in the Ohio region.

143. Wellenreuther, *Glaube und Politik in Pennsylvania*, chap. 1; Schwartz, *"A Mixed Multitude."*

justice asked whether the missionaries would absolve from sin Indians who had killed a human being; were the Moravians "Roman Catholicks"? He also wanted to know whether the missionaries accompanied the Indians in their assaults on white settlements and in the killing of white settlers.[144] The Moravians refused to answer any of these questions. Nevertheless, on 9 June 1744 the missionaries were ordered to appear at the muster of the militia; at the same time rumors and unrest increased "in the country because we were papists," as the diary reports.[145] The missionaries refused to appear at the muster. On 4 July 1744 this refusal caused them to be called before the governor and his council.[146] Attempts to diffuse the situation failed, and on 21 September 1744 the assembly of the colony passed a law that stipulated

> that no Vagrant Preacher Moravian or Disguised Papist shall preach or teach either in publick or private without first taking the Oaths appointed by this Act, and Obtaining a Licence from the Governor or Commander in Chief for the Time being . . . [and that] . . . no person or persons whatsoever shall take upon them to reside among the Indians under the pretence of bringing them over to the Christian Faith, but such as shall be duly Authorized . . . and every Vagrant Preacher Moravian or Disguised Papist or any other person presuming to reside among and teach the Indians without such Licence aforesaid, shall be taken up and treated as a person taking upon him to seduce the Indians from his Majesties Interest.[147]

All churches located in the colony were exempted from this law. On 15 December 1744 the act was handed to the missionaries together with the governor's order to desist immediately from further activities. The missionaries entrusted the direction of the mission congregation to baptized Indians and left the colony.

These difficulties illustrate that from the perspective of colonial governments mission activities were politically important; at the same time, they show why the Moravians missionaries' insistence on preaching the gospel in politically neutral territory was always defeated by political exigencies.

The experiences at Checomeco prompted Zinzendorf to seek the advice of John Carteret, second Earl of Granville, who advised Zinzendorf to petition Parliament. On 8 May 1749 the English Parliament approved a law that exempted the Unitas Fratrum within the British Empire from military service

144. "A Journal of Shekomeko. From Feb. 23 to March 15," n.s., 1744, MAB, B 112, F 1, no.2.

145. Ibid., no. 3.

146. Printed in Hastings, *Ecclesiastical Records, State of New York*, 4:2847–48.

147. Copy of the act in MAB, B 112, F 7, no. 9, "Shecomeco New York, Miscellaneous Documents. 1744."

and from swearing the oath.[148] In 1746 the mission congregation at Checomeco was dissolved.[149] Its baptized members, mostly Mahican, accompanied their missionaries to Pennsylvania, where they started a new settlement where the Mahony Creek joined the Lehigh River. This settlement the Moravians named Gnadenhütten. Delaware and Munsee settled in this region. The mission was extended to these two tribes and a growing number of them joined the mission congregation. Toward the end of July 1746 the protocol of the "Pennsylvania Religious Conference," which had sat at Philadelphia between 31 July and 3 August, reported that "not only the Delaware had in a friendly way established a new contact with our Indian brethren in order to renew their old kinship but that divers Indians that lived in Wayomik, had cordially invited them to preach to them the good word."[150]

The movement of the mission into this region implied, first, that henceforth the Moravians' activities would be focused particularly on these two tribes and, second, that the Moravians had to cope with the Six Indian Nations' claim as overlords of these tribes, as Spangenberg was aware. Since the mid-1740s, at the behest of Conrad Weiser, who was familiar with Native American affairs and had recently been appointed Indian agent for Pennsylvania,[151] the Moravian church had attempted to establish closer relations with the confederation. As a result, the confederation requested in 1746 that the Moravians provide a missionary and a smith for Shamokin. The missionary was to preach the gospel and the smith was to repair the guns of Iroquois warriors en route to battles against the Catawba and other tribes to the south.[152] At Shamokin, at the confluence of the two rivers that form the Susquehanna, Shikellemi resided as representative of the Six Indian Nations. By September 1746 at the latest, Spangenberg was aware of the political and military implications of the confederation's request. By this time he had received a letter from Charles Brockden dated 7 September 1746: "Yesterday our honourable Governour . . . said unto me . . . viz. The five Nations of Indians have taken up the Hatchet against our Enemies. Therefore you may write to Mr. Spangenberg That we may send People among the Indians when he will."[153]

148. Stock et al., *Proceedings and Debates of the British Parliaments,* 4:301–4, 362–63.
149. The mission congregation Pachgatgoch among the Wampanoag had been founded in Connecticut in 1742 and was continued until 1770. Pachgatgoch is identical today with the village Scaticook, close to Kent.
150. "Verlaß der General Synode in Philadelphia vom 25.-27. März 1746," MAB, uncatalogued. "Verlaß der pennsylvanischen Religions Conferenz gehalten zu Philadelphia, Julii 31 seqq. 1746," fol. 2a-3 (citation), ibid. "Wayomik" is identical with the central village of the Delaware at that time, Wyoming, on the east branch of the Susquehanna River, about ninety kilometers northeast of Shamokin.
151. Wallace, *Conrad Weiser;* on the claims to overlordship of the Six Indian Nations over the Shawnee and Delaware, see pp. 13–14 above.
152. "Heyden Sachen. Bruder Martin Macks Diarium von seiner Reise und Aufenthalt in Shomoko. Sept.-Okt.-Nov. 1745," entry for 6 Nov. 1745, MAB, B 121, F 2; Conrad Weiser to A. G. Spangenberg, Tulpehokin, 5 May 1746, ibid., F 8, no.1.
153. MAB, B 121, F 8, no. 5.

The Moravians faced a problem. They knew that the continuation of their missions among the tribes depended on the good will of the Six Indian Nations. Every missionary activity among the Delaware or Shawnee, including the mission work at Gnadenhütten, depended on the permission of the confederacy. If they denied the chief at Shamokin the smith he had requested, he might put an abrupt end to all of their missionary activities. Spangenberg tried in the spring of 1747 to avoid complete dependence on Shikellemi by requesting that the Delaware participate in the negotiations about the future status of the Moravians at Shamokin. In this context Martin Mack had been asked, on 14 April 1747, to open negotiations with "Shikellemi and Alomosbey, King of the Delawares, and the Council in Shomoco." A few days later, however, the Delaware chief was described as "old and deaf," and the discussions with Shikellemi took place without him.[154]

In the negotiations Shikellemi demanded that the guns of the warriors be repaired free of charge; all other services would be paid. Faced with the dilemma of either violating their pacifistic convictions or endangering their missionary activities, the Provincial Helpers' Conference opted for a remarkable compromise. Bishop Cammerhoff handed missionaries Joseph Powell and John Hagen the following message to be delivered to Shikellemi: "Shikellemy! You asked us to mend the warrior's guns, who go against the Flatheads gratis. As they have no money to pay or use what little they have. We love peace rather than war, but as the warriors use their guns to shoot deer, we will repair them gratis. Shikellemy! We ask that you have all Indians pay for their work, and the warriors too, on their return home."[155]

According to the Shamokin diary, the Iroquois chief accepted the decision and from then on supported the mission effort at that place.[156] In November 1749 he even visited Bethlehem. Conard Weiser claimed to have been told that Shikellemi had been converted by the Moravians.[157] The mission flourished under the confederation's protection and thanks to the cooperation of the Delaware in Gnadenhütten, too, while in Shamokin success was barely visible.[158]

The concentration of missionary activities in the middle colonies had changed the basic character of the Moravians' work. The widely dispersed mission fields, which included activities among the Cherokee (in the 1730s these

154. Spangenberg to Alomosbey, 14 April 1747; negotiating power for Mack, dated the same day, and memorandum for the Delaware chief in MAB, B 121, F 9, nos. 1–2.

155. Copy of letter in "Bishop Cammerhoff's Letters to Zinzendorf, 1747–1749," transcripts by J. W. Jordan, Historical Society of Pennsylvania, Philadelphia.

156. MAB, B 121, F 4, no. 1.

157. Conrad Weiser to Richard Peters, Heidelberg, Pa., 21 Nov. 1749, Peters Manuscripts, vol. 2, fol. 112, Historical Society of Pennsylvania. The rumor was without substance.

158. "With respect to Shamokin the question was raised how to continue there; more than once one had thought of giving it up but Christ had not granted permission for this. It was necessary to keep a careful eye on it and especially keep a smith there because without one disorderly circumstances would immediately cause trouble for the brothers there." Conferenz über die Heyden-Sache, den 8ten Sept. 1755," MAB B 315, F 2, no. 2.

had been started in Georgia), the Wampanoag, and the Mahican in Connecticut and New York, had been exchanged for a much narrower focus on the Delaware as the most important mission concern of the Moravians. Even before the Seven Years' War, then, the Moravian mission became part of the wider conflict between the Delaware and the Six Indian Nations. When the Shawnee and the Delaware sided with the French at the outset of the war, the Moravian missionaries were perceived as partners of the enemy. Immediately after the defeat of General Braddock's English army, settlers in the vicinity of Shamokin on 24 November 1755 advised the Moravian missionaries to run for their lives. The missionaries refused.[159] On 24 November Delaware and Shawnee warriors surprised Gnadenhütten and killed ten missionaries; the village was burned down. The rest of the congregation, more than one hundred persons, escaped to Bethlehem.

THE MORAVIAN MISSION TO THE DELAWARE BEFORE 1772

The Christian Indians who had fled from Gnadenhütten and Shamokin settled at Nain, a village not far from Bethlehem. In the winter of 1759, when the war was almost over, the Moravian Unity bought land for a new mission settlement, called Wechquetank, between today's towns of Stroudsburg and Weissport in western Pennsylvania.[160] The new settlement was only five miles from Meniolagomeka, where Moravian missionaries had preached for five years in the 1750s. In April 1760 most of the inhabitants of Nain moved to this place. They were accompanied by missionary Heinrich Joachim Sensemann and his assistant, John Joseph Bull.[161] From this new settlement contacts with the Delaware were reestablished and intensified. Friedrich Post, who since the 1750s had gradually drifted away from the Moravian Church and who had played an important role in reopening talks between the Delaware and Shawnee in 1758 and 1759, lived at that time in Tuscaroratown, a Delaware village

159. "Diarium von Schomoko," entry for 26 July 1755, MAB, B 121, F 7, no. 2.
160. Leibert, "Wechquetank." Members of the Moravian congregation in Philadelphia had originally purchased the land, but most of them had died during the war. The land, about fourteen hundred acres, was bought from the administrators of the original owners' estates.
161. Heinrich Joachim Sensemann (d. 1774), by occupation a baker, had grown up in Hessen-Kassel, arrived in Bethlehem in 1742 with his wife, Anna Katharina, and began missionary work the following year. He worked as a missionary both in Checomeco and in Gnadenhütten, where his wife was killed in 1755 in the massacre. Together with his second wife, Christina, he left North America for a mission congregation in Jamaica in the West Indies, where he died in 1774. Gottlob Sensemann (1745–1800) was his son by his first wife. Neisser, *Beginnings of Moravian Work in America*, 173. In 1768 he had accompanied Zeisberger on his trip to Goschgoschink; like Heckewelder, he later served as Zeisberger's adjunct in Schönbrunn, until 20 August 1781. John Joseph Bull (1721–88) was the son of a Quaker family in Skippack, Pennsylvania; he joined the Moravian Church in 1742, married Christiana, a Mahican, and remained adjunct until his death. Zeisberger usually called him by his Indian name, Schebosh ("running water"). Schweinitz, *Zeisberger*, 120, 131, 134.

on the Tuscarawas River.[162] In the summer of 1760 Post returned from his new home and for a few months took over the mission at Wechquetank, where Sensemann had fallen ill; in October of that year he was replaced by Bernhard Adam Grube.

It was during this time that contacts were established with the influential Delaware preacher Papunhank; in 1763 he invited the Moravian missionaries to his village, Machiwihilusing. The Provincial Helpers' Conference sent David Zeisberger, who was, if possible, to found a new mission congregation there. In the same year, on 26 June, Papunhank was baptized Johannes. These early successes were rudely interrupted by the so-called Pontiac's Rebellion. Zeisberger returned to Bethlehem. A bit later the mission congregation at Wechquetank had to flee as well, to Nazareth. The risk of being held responsible for Indian attacks on white settlements had become too great. On 6 November 1763, in response to the threats of white settlers, the governor of Pennsylvania ordered the Christian Indians to Philadelphia to be interned in barracks. A few days later Papunhank, baptized Johannes, followed with another twenty-one of his followers from Machiwihilusing. They remained there until 27 February 1765, when they were allowed to return to Papunhank's village, which was now renamed Friedenshütten. For the time being, it became the central mission congregation of the Moravians.

Three events characterized the development of the Moravian mission: the politics of the Six Indian Nations, the increasing hostility of the Indian preachers toward the Moravian mission, and the fact that the missionaries themselves became increasingly convinced that successful mission work was possible in the long term only in mission congregations far removed from the corrupting influences of white settlements. The relationship to the Six Indian Nations became ever more difficult. The Moravians' first message to the regional council of the Six Nations for the region at Cayuga resulted in permission for them to preach among the Delaware, but they were informed at the same time that they could not remain at Friedenshütten. Only the direct intervention of David

---

162. Loskiel, *Geschichte der Mission*, 458. Christian Friedrich Post (1710–85) was one of the most remarkable missionaries of his time. Born and raised in Conitz in Prussia, he came to Bethlehem in 1742; beginning in 1743 he worked in the mission stations Checomeco and Pachgatgoch. In 1751 he visited Europe and was co-founder of a mission station among the Eskimo. After the failure of this mission he returned to Bethlehem, whence he was sent to Wyoming in 1754. While serving as a messenger between the colonies, the Shawnee, and the Delaware he became estranged from the Moravians; in 1761–62 he worked as an independent missionary at Tuscarawas. The new war forced him to give up this mission and move to Mosquito Coast, Nicaragua, where he preached the gospel between 1762 and 1784. He died in April 1785 in Germantown, Pennsylvania. Post was the only Moravian missionary besides John Joseph Bull to marry a Native American—in his case, in fact, two of them. On 4 September 1743 at Checomeco he married Rachel, a Wampanoag. She died in Bethlehem on 26 December 1747. His second wife was Agnes, a Delaware. The marriage was celebrated on 24 September 1748; Agnes was baptized only after the marriage, in March 1749. She died on 8 July 1751. Post took a third wife, Margaret Miller, on 25 August 1767. Neisser, *Beginnings of Moravian Work in America*, 180–82.

Zeisberger with the central council at Onondaga, in mid-October 1766, reversed this decision. Shortly thereafter the news reached the mission congregation that the Six Indian Nations had sold to the English colonies the land on which Friedenshütten was built.

In October 1767 this news prompted Zeisberger to travel with Johannes Papunhank to the three Delaware settlements comprised by Goschgoschünk on the Allegheny River near the mouth of Tionesta Creek. At the invitation of the old, blind chief Allemewi and his council, Zeisberger founded a new mission congregation there. The Delaware preacher Wangomen, who also lived there, remained silent, but the mission activities soon led to serious internal disputes among the Delaware. One group, hostile to the mission, was led by Wangomen, the other, friendly to the Moravians, was led by Allemewi, the chief.[163] By relocating the mission congregations to a new village called Lawunnakhannek, about three miles distant, the missionaries attempted to stay out of this controversy, but this effort failed—as did efforts to alleviate the pressures brought to bear by Wangomen's followers on those Delaware who wanted to attend the religious services of the mission congregations. The small mission congregation forming in Schechschiquanünk, where missionary Johann Roth[164] had been sent in early February 1769, was likewise dragged into the factional disputes at Goschgoschünk. After war between Seneca and Cherokee had broken out again in 1770, on top of all these difficulties, the missionaries decided to accept the invitation of the Delaware council at Kuskuski and move the mission congregation from Lawunnakhanneck to that center of the Delaware tribe; the new place was christened Langundoutenünk or "Friedensstadt." One of the prime movers behind this decision was the Delaware war captain of the Wolf tribe, Glikhican, who some months later joined the mission congregation. Yet the events of Goschgoschünk repeated themselves in the new surroundings: the surrounding villages were soon divided between enemies and supporters of the mission. Packanke himself, the chief of the Wolf tribe, led the hostile faction.

In the spring of 1771 the plot thickened. A new message from the Head Council of the Delaware at Gekelemukpechünk repeated an earlier, somewhat mysteriously worded invitation to transfer the mission congregations to the

163. Allemewi was baptized Salomo on 25 December 1769; on Wangomen, see Dowd, *Spirited Resistance*, 32–38.

164. Johann Roth (1726–91), born at Saarmund in the Mark Brandenburg, Germany, by occupation a locksmith, had joined the Moravian Church at Neusalz in Prussia and came to Bethlehem in 1756. He had gained some experience as a missionary in other mission congregations before marrying Maria Agnes (1735–1805) on 16 August 1770. Their first child was born in August 1771 in Schechschiquanünk; they were stationed at Langundoutenünk and from April 1773 onward at Gnadenhütten II in the Muskingum valley, where their son John Lewis was born. After the arrival of the missionary couple Schmick in August 1773, the Roths transferred to Schönbrunn, whence they returned to Bethlehem in May 1774. Johann Roth died on 22 July 1791 in Yorktown, Pennsylvania, and Anna Maria Roth on 25 February 1805 in Nazareth. Diary of Anna Maria Roth in MAB, Memoirs B 6, 1805; Diary of Johann Roth in MAB, Memoirs Gemeinnachrichten 1793, Beilage 2.

Muskingum valley. At the same time, the number of settlers who had come into the region of Kuskuski following the purchase of this region at Fort Stanwix increased markedly. Meanwhile the opposition of Wangomen and his followers, and of the Seneca in general, to the Moravian mission continued unabated and did not bode well for the peaceful development of the mission congregation.[165] These developments, combined with the prospect of soon being surrounded by Euro-American settlements, induced the Provincial Helpers' Conference at Bethlehem, in the presence of two members of the Unity's Elders' Conference, Christian Gregor and Johann Loretz,[166] and on the advice of Zeisberger, to accept this invitation. As a first step it was decided to transfer the mission congregations from Friedenshütten and Schechschiquanünk to Friedensstadt. From there the Christian Indians were to be moved step by step to the new mission settlements in the Muskingum valley.[167]

The resolution of the Provincial Helpers' Conference was motivated by a number of developments. From the beginning of the mission, the work of the Moravians had suffered from the proximity of white settlers. In times of peace, the trade and consumption of rum had been a disturbing feature. In times of war, the hostility of white settlers had exposed the Christian Indians to many dangers. There seemed only one solution to these problems: to locate the mission settlements as far as possible from Euro-American settlements in order to protect the Christian Indians from the corrupting influences of the white settlers.[168] The missionaries were convinced that in the long run only such a move would enable them to preach the gospel with success. And preaching the gospel meant more than converting the Native Americans to "the cross."[169] Mission implied, too, teaching the Indians a Christian way of life as embodied in the rules for the mission congregations that had been agreed upon in the 1740s.[170]

The decision of the Provincial Helpers' Conference was also motivated by disillusionment with the attitude of the Six Indian Nations. Since 1744 the Moravians had tried hard to establish good relations with the confederation. For every new initiative the church had always asked the permission of the confederation, but these efforts had failed to secure the quiet, steady development of the mission congregations. The conference's decision reflected a learning process: over the years white settlers had sooner or later caught up to the mission congregations. The frontier expanded ever more rapidly after the Seven Years' War; not even the mountains provided a secure barrier. The distance

165. On the nativism of these tribes, see Dowd, *Spirited Resistance.*
166. In May 1771 both visited Friedenshütten as inspectors.
167. Loskiel, *Geschichte der Mission,* 580–81.
168. In the early nineteenth century the American government reached a similar conclusion under President Jefferson; it was used as a justification for relocating the tribes from the East Coast to reservations in the future state of Oklahoma. See Sheehan, *Seeds of Extinction.*
169. On the meaning of the term in Moravian theology, see pp. 52–55 below.
170. On the statutes of mission congregations, cf. pp. 60–68 below and appendix, Document No. 3.

between Friedenshütten and Friedensstadt and white farms narrowed by the month. So fast did the settlement line move that in 1773 John Heckewelder met white settlers at the mouth of the Muskingum River.[171] Finally, the mission congregations' removal represented a reaction to the growing nativism of the Delaware settlements of the eastern Ohio region. The missionaries and the Provincial Helpers' Conference probably hoped that mission congregations under the direct protection of the Delaware Head Council would be spared nativistic hostility. This expectation was disappointed. As David Zeisberger was to learn between 1772 and 1775, the Head Council's invitation had itself been motivated by nativistic considerations; the council hoped that by luring the mission congregations to the Muskingum Valley it would succeed not only in reuniting its Native American members with the tribe but in recovering old Indian ways and beliefs. Once this had been accomplished, the white missionaries would be sent back to where they had come from.

MORAVIAN METHOD AND THEORY OF MISSION

Within three decades the Moravian missionaries had converted a respectable number of Native Americans—Mahican, Wampanoag, some Nanticoke,[172] and Delaware—to Christianity. For the times this was a surprising achievement. It illustrates the importance of Zinzendorf's theory of mission and of the Moravian mission method.[173] Zinzendorf had begun rather early to discuss problems related to mission. His early letters to missionaries and his trip to St. Thomas and North America in the early 1740s demonstrate his interest and concern. Reading the mission diaries prompted him in 1740 to insist on formulating principles of a mission method that reflected Moravian theology. He complained to the synod at Gotha that no mission method existed and that the success of the mission depended on the personality of the individual missionary. In December of that year, at the synod at Marienborn, Zinzendorf elaborated: "There exist two wrong methods to propagate the Gospel among the heathen: 1) That one tells them too much about God and too little about the lamb and its redemption, and that most often comes from the heart. 2) That in propagating the gospel one first tells them of the Father and then of the Son. Done this way they have to believe in the trinity before one propagates to them the word about the wounds of the lamb."[174] With these remarks Zinzendorf criticized Moravian missionaries who still followed the methods of their brethren at

171. [Heckewelder], "Canoe Journey from the Big Beaver to the Tuscarawas."
172. Until the early 1750s the Nanticoke had lived in the Wyoming valley; Moravians had enjoyed good relations with this settlement and repeatedly contemplated establishing a mission there. In 1753 the Six Indian Nations ordered the Nanticoke to settle in the territory on which the Tuscarora had formerly lived. Schweinitz, *Zeisberger*, 206; Feest, "Nanticoke and Neighboring Tribes," 246.
173. See [Zinzendorf], *Texte zur Mission;* Wessel, "Missionsvorstellung und Missionswirklichkeit."
174. Cited in [Zinzendorf], *Texte zur Mission,* 63.

Halle, for whom the sermon came first and was followed by catechizing those interested in Christianity and teaching them the Bible in the mission school.[175]

An analysis of Zinzendorf's critique reveals the theological concepts from which he deduced his ideas about a new mission method. Zinzendorf based his ideas on the notion that all human beings, and not just Christians, had an idea about a god. Speculating about God was pointless. Even the cleverest were unable to argue away the existence of God; nor could they dispute his nature as the highest being. Everyone knew "that there is a God" since God had "revealed" this to all mankind.[176] Even non-Christians knew that a God existed.[177] "That a God exists, has been revealed to them," Zinzendorf added to the instructions for the missionaries who went to the Samoyeds in Russia in 1735.[178] Therefore it was unnecessary to preach to people something they knew already. The missionaries ought to focus instead on the one thing that was fundamental to Christianity: "the lamb and its redemption." They must talk about "the wounds of the lamb." And, in his speech at Herrnhag of 11 June 1741, Zinzendorf added that the lamb "was their Special God . . . their Particular God."[179] What was true for God, i.e., that it was unnecessary to prove his existence, applied even more to the fundamental message of the missionaries: "for the absurd doctrine of the cross."[180] Since that doctrine was "absurd," irrational, and thus not rationally intelligible,[181] and since this "absurd and ridiculous thing" contained the "gem of religion," it was impossible to explain, discuss, or preach this absurdity with the language of reason to rational minds. Elsewhere Zinzendorf called this the "secret truth"[182] that the mind was unable to comprehend. At Bethlehem, on 11 November 1742, Zinzendorf defined truth as "what is revealed to us within us as true and proven incorrigible in the sense that food and drink prove themselves as real to our palates and stomachs or as illness and health, heat and cold are real to our bodies. Everything must prove itself as real to our inner being which is to be true; truth generally is distinguished between sad and blessed truth, between the gospel truth and the

175. In the 1730s both the Halle and the Moravian missionaries based their methods and procedures on J. A. Freylinghausen, *Grundlegung der Theologie*. See Brunner, *Halle Pietists in England*, 102–3, and for a comparison of the mission methods of Halle missionaries and Moravian missionaries, see Wellenreuther, "Deux modèles de mission piétiste."

176. Zinzendorf, *Berlinische Reden* (23 Feb. 1738), in *ZH*, 1:10. Zinzendorf considered proofs of the existence of God a waste of time.

177. Zinzendorf, *Sieben Letzte Reden* (Herrnhag, 11 June 1741), ed. 1743, in *ZH*, 2:4. Zinzendorf cited Rom. 1:19 as proof.

178. [Zinzendorf], *Texte zur Mission*, 40. These instructions were similar to his general instruction to missionaries in 1738. Ibid., 55.

179. Zinzendorf, *Sieben letzte Reden* (Herrnhag, 11 June 1741), ed. 1743, in *ZH*, 2:11–12.

180. For Zinzendorf's remark at the synod of Gotha, see [Zinzendorf], *Texte zur Mission*, 62.

181. Zinzendorf , *Sieben Letzte Reden*, ed. 1746, in *ZH*, 2:91–95; *Berlinische Reden*, ed. 1758, in *ZH*, 1:172–74.

182. In his sermon in the Lutheran church at Philadelphia on 11 March 1742, he said: "Our doctrine is the secret truth." Zinzendorf, *Sammlung Öffentlicher Reden*, part 1, 2d ed. 1746, in *ZH*, 2:108.

law."[183] Zeisberger echoed this concept of truth in his diary: "We ourselves have now heard what is preached here and believe it is the truth";[184] "surely you speak the truth";[185] "this had touched their hearts. Therefore they believed that what we told them was certainly true."[186] Moravians did not use the term "truth" in the sense of a rational statement but as their emotional consent to what had been preached to them.

Zinzendorf's definition of "truth" and his emphasis on the importance of emotion for recognizing the Christian message had direct consequences for his concept of the Moravian mission method. Faith was a matter not of the head but of the heart, as expressed in phrases such as "to paint the doctrine of the cross for eyes to see,"[187] to bring "the word to the heart," "only with few words but with the strength of God and with such a Mother-Heart,"[188] to talk "truthfully to the Heart."[189] Zinzendorf believed that both conversion and conversation should be approached as intimate matters of the heart, not of the understanding. In this he differed markedly from conventional views of the function, form, and importance of the sermon.

Within both the larger Moravian and the narrower mission congregations, "Speakings," the Moravian term for the intimate religious conversation that can be understood as "honest and thorough talk," played a most important role. There were also so-called "Gelegenheiten" (translated as "devotional services"), religious meetings in which members of the congregation met. At these services the missionaries not only preached but sang.[190] The purpose of word, song, and sermon was always to touch the "heart."

The heart played a decisive role in Zinzendorf's theology for the process of conversion as well as for the "new life" after the "new birth." The desire for conversion had to come, Zinzendorf insisted as early as 1725, "from an *urging Heart*."[191] The "urging" in this case was the work of the Holy Spirit, the pioneer for all mission activities. Already in 1732 Zinzendorf had written: "Do not work with a heathen who does not display a happy disposition to become a

183. Zinzendorf, *Sammlung Öffentlicher Reden*, part 2, 2d ed. 1746, in *ZH*, 2:168.

184. See entry for 29 July 1772 below.

185. See entry for 10 Oct. 1772 (diary of journey to the Shawnee) below.

186. See entry for 3 March 1773 below.

187. Zinzendorf, *Berlinische Reden*, 1758, in *ZH*, 1:13.

188. Andreas Grasmann, Amsterdam, 29 Feb. 1741, to the missionaries in Greenland, in *ZE*, 8:411–12.

189. [Zinzendorf], *Texte zur Mission*, 63.

190. Thus special singing services were introduced in which verses of songs fit a particular theme. The general synod of 1775 addressed the importance of sermons in services: "It would be a pity if the thought that has been uttered here and there that in the meetings of the congregation the public sermon should play the most important role, and that this would be considered satisfactory. If a congregation loses its taste for liturgies, homilies, etc., then this is proof that their hearts do not live in Jesus as they should." MAB, "General-Synode 1775" in Barby, in the hand of John Ettwein, fol. 12.

191. Zinzendorf, *Der Teutsche Socrates*, 1732, in *ZH*, 1:241.

true and honest person."[192] Citing Acts he stressed the preparatory role of the Holy Spirit: "First the savages' heart has to be prepared, something from the Lord had to come down to them, so that they confess with Cornelius: We are here. This preparation is alone Christ's work."[193]

Once the heathen's heart had been prepared by the Holy Spirit, the missionary's most important task was to structure his message in such a way "that Christ gains the features of a real person in the heart."[194] "[A]s soon as their mind is so enlightened that they understand the necessity of these things, the urgent demand and praying for the forgiving of sins and for rebirth . . . as soon as their craving, trust and vision gets mixed with the godly truth that reaches their hearts through God's spirit, and if these then catch thirst and hunger, then the seed will open the heart, the fire will raise the love of God; this then is called the new birth."[195]

It followed that the missionaries had to preach forgiveness and salvation, what Zinzendorf had called the "doctrine of the cross." "Whenever they talk with people, they preach to them the crucified Christ into their hearts and paint Him before their eyes how he really had died for them and was dead."[196] The message to turn to Christ was not directed to the mind but "is brought before the Heart." If the soul "with a true and honest heart considers itself condemned," the soul is already saved. For only in such a state could one achieve the "pleasure of redemption."[197] Conversion was therefore defined as "the piercing strength of the blood of Christ, which streams through the human heart and soaks it so intensely that all hardness is melted away as if it were in a glow so that even the most renitent and opposing hearts experience the mighty hand."

Only then could the person know that "the heart is no more dead, that they are miserable, that they are condemned."[198] The precondition for conversion was the knowledge that one is condemned, that one "has a genuine feeling of death." This feeling emerges in the "moment of conversion." Only "if someone has experienced in his heart the strength of death" could he experience the gift of conversion.[199] According to Zinzendorf, in the process of conversion the individual relived the death of Christ on the cross: "To what do we have to pay particular attention when we experience Christ's death struggle and sweat of blood? Only this: We have to be so long afflicted in our hearts . . . until we

---

192. ZE, 9:810.
193. Cited in Uttendörfer, *Missionsinstruktionen*, 45–46.
194. Zinzendorf, *Der Teutsche Socrates*, 1732, in ZH, 1:167.
195. Zinzendorf, "Antwort auf die solide Anfrage in den Franckfurter Gelehrten Zeitungen," 1737, in ZE, 7:330–32.
196. Zinzendorf, *Berlinische Reden*, ed. 1758, in ZH, 1:62.
197. Ibid., 1:95.
198. Ibid., 1:93–94.
199. Zinzendorf, *Sonderbare Gespräche*, ed. 1739, in ZH, 1:83.

know that we profit from his bloody sweat, the struggle, from the fight for redemption of Jesus Christ."[200]

Zinzendorf emphasized that conversion had nothing to do with the mind: "one has to admit: that *Jesus lost his life on the cross* is not a thing for the human mind."[201] In Philadelphia Zinzendorf coined a phrase that sums up the difference between his theology and that of orthodox Lutheranism: "On the side of Christ is his word, on our side sentiment and feeling."[202]

Zinzendorf's theology is extraordinarily Christ-centered.[203] The description of the suffering, crucifixion, death, and resurrection of Jesus forms the centerpiece not only of conversion but of all Moravian religious services. In the "sifting period"—a period in the 1740s of radical theological sentimentality—the focus on Christ's suffering reached its rhetorical peak. The contemplation focused on two phenomena: Christ's wounds, which the soldiers had inflicted on him on the cross, especially the hole in his side ("Seitenhölgen") and the wounds in his hands and feet, and Christ's blood, "the strength of the blood in the covenant," through which man could attain absolution for his sins and "exclaim: He is butchered, and he has purchased me with his blood."[204] This meditation on and visualization of the sufferings on the cross as an act of salvation Zinzendorf defined as the distinctiveness of Moravian theology. "To become part of the man Jesus Christ as he hung on the cross and gently bled to death and become as a fruit of his bloody merit blessed, this is the secret of the congregation."[205]

In countless songs, sermons, and conversations, the missionaries contemplated with the Christian Indians these sufferings in a language that today is difficult to understand. The emphasis on sentiment and feeling influenced the diaries of mission congregations of the 1740s more so than those written later by David Zeisberger. The following chart summarizes these linguistic and semantic peculiarities; the data are taken from the German version but we have added the English meaning of the words in italics.[206]

200. Zinzendorf, *Sieben Letzte Reden*, ed. 1743, in *ZH*, 2:120–21.

201. Ibid., 2:91, 1:77 (sermon dated 30 July 1741).

202. Zinzendorf, *Sammlung Öffentlicher Reden*, part 2, 2d ed. 1746, in *ZH*, 2:111, 114.

203. Beyreuther, "Christozentrismus"; Meyer, *Christozentrismus des späten Zinzendorfs*.

204. Zinzendorf, *Berlinische Reden*, ed. 1758, in *ZH*, 1:99.

205. Zinzendorf, *Sieben Letzte Reden*, sermon at Herrnhag dated 11 June 1741, ed. 1743, in *ZH*, 2:3. We have translated "Gemeine" as "congregation" but Zinzendorf means the whole Moravian Church.

206. The data were gained from a complete word analysis (performed by the Concord program) of three texts of roughly equal length. The first is the mission diary of Checomeco for the period 9 April through 8 August 1743, which in its published form is signed "B. M. S. P." but was probably composed by Gottlob Büttner (1716–45). We have used the printed edition in *Büdingische Sammlung*, vol. 3, in *ZE*, 9:252–82. The second is the mission diary of Schönbrunn for 19 Oct. 1772 to 22 March 1773, MAB, B 141, F 3a The third text is the mission diary of Lichtenau for the period 12 April through 1 July 1776, MAB, B 147, F 1; the latter two diaries were composed by David Zeisberger. Not all variations were included in the columns, but we have counted all variations of a word stem highlighted by the program.

Terms with their variations	C	S	L
Abendmahl—*holy supper*	9	8	1
Blut/Blute/Bluts—*blood*	16	7	9
Fühlbar/fühlen, gefühlt, etc.—*feel, feeling*	18	1	2
Heiland—*savior*	34	31	27
Herz/Hertz/Hertzen—*heart*	32	10	16
Lamm/Lamme, etc.—*lamb*	26	0	2
Marter—*martyr*	1	1	0
Wunden—*wounds*	5	1	1
Thränen—*tears*	0	4	0
weinen/weinte/weinete—*to weep, wept*	3	0	0
Gnade—*grace*	15	5	2
Innig—*fond, intimate*	6	0	0

C = Checomeco; S = Schönbrunn; L = Lichtenau

The focus on Christ's sufferings, together with the derationalization of religious belief, prepared the genesis of a particular mission method that was incompatible with rational discourse. Mission method focused instead on presenting the fundamentals of Christian doctrine in images and pictures that were full of poetic beauty, sensuality, and metaphor. This language was designed to speak only to the senses of those to be converted. Zinzendorf himself has given us a telling example of this method:

> It surely expresses a godly assurance that a person who believes that Christ has died, yea that he who has envisioned Him in his bloody body hanging on the cross, could not remain without feelings if he otherwise has a rational soul that has not been turned by lusts into insanity. When he appears in the imagination how he gently bled to death on the cross and if one considers this is not a fantasy and therefore refuses to have others convince him to the contrary, one attains a permanent remembrance of this vision, which one will never forget as long as one lives. One either does nor really love it, gets anxious and desolate, or, one becomes blessed, nay more than blessed if from thence on one is able to deeply contemplate death and its causes.

From these insights Zinzendorf deduced what he considered the task of preachers and missionaries: "This is the work of those who testify for Christ whenever they talk with people, to preach to them the crucified Jesus into their hearts and paint him before their eyes how he died really for them and was then dead, although he now liveth from eternity to eternity and holds the key to hell and death in his hands."[207]

"To paint for the eyes" was the essence of the mission method. The purpose was to describe the suffering, the torture, and the wounds so vividly that the

207. Zinzendorf, *Berlinische Reden*, speech dated 9 March 1738, ed. 1758, in *ZH*, 1:62.

hearer "would be enraptured."[208] The listener began to identify with the suffering. In this respect the mission method was similar to the way Native American preachers acquired religious insights through visions and thus was not unfamiliar to the tribes.[209] In his imagination the potential convert appropriates the sufferings and the causes of these sufferings and thus understands these as *real sufferings;* they become true. Zeisberger's diary often describes this process metaphorically. One example may suffice:

> Seth's wife, who had no feeling or life in her heart until now, told us with many tears how the Savior had entered her heart last night. All of a sudden she felt she could believe he had received the wounds in his hands and feet and in his side for the sake of her sins. She could imagine how the crown of thorns had torn and wounded his head, so that her heart was completely filled. Now, however, she really wanted to be cleansed of her sins with his blood.[210]

Zinzendorf describes the process of conversion with remarkable clarity:

> A person that becomes converted with all his heart has to confess with this experience . . . I am a damned and lost person; death sits on my tongue. . . . In the sadness in which the soul believes to be lost, Christ appears to her as a completely crucified person; While she feels she is condemned, Christ at the Cross with his wounds in his death is so present to this soul, as if he had been crucified before her eyes . . . thus she loses her burden, everything falls from her that had oppressed her; she is full of joy: and it says within her, I have become before his eyes the person that has found peace. . . .
>
> A soul that attains absolution experiences a moment it will never experience again. The memory will last forever; even if one gets doubts, one always remembers the sight. One thinks: I have seen Him; he has kissed, blessed, and received me; he will never leave me.[211]

Getting lost in the sufferings and wounds of Christ not only caused the conversion; the wounds remained in the memory of the converted as the visible sign of his or her salvation. In his sermon on the second Advent, in 1742 at Philadelphia, Zinzendorf discussed the eschatological meaning of his insight: "He will appear marked. The sermon on wounds—what good does that bring us? The Sermon will last until eternity. . . . If we want to talk about something in this life that would edify us, something permanent: something that would

---

208. See entry for 13 Oct 1772 below.
209. On the term "vision," see Wellenreuther, "Bekehrung und Bekehrte."
210. See entry for 23 Dec. 1774 below.
211. Zinzendorf, *Sammlung Öffentlicher Reden,* part 2, 2d ed. 1746, in *ZH,* 2:154, 156, 157.

lead us to talk about eternity, about something that satisfies our heart, then we must talk about his wounds and death. . . . Why? These are the signs, the marks, on which we will recognize him on his day. Mark this sign."[212] Both the Moravians and the Native Americans experienced religious salvation through visions and ecstatic meditation in which they appropriated what they saw. This affinity is probably the most fundamental reason for the success of the Moravian missionaries—a success the more remarkable because there is no indication that Zinzendorf and the missionaries tailored this approach to the needs and predispositions of the tribes. The Moravians' Christological concepts and theology of conversion long predate their focus on mission, and only slowly were the implications of that theology applied by missionaries in the field. Zinzendorf's critique of the methods of missionaries focused essentially on the fact that missionaries only reluctantly began to put the doctrine of the cross into the center of their mission efforts, as his remarks at the synod of Marienborn, cited earlier, make clear.

At the end of December 1740 the synod at Marienborn approved as a guide for missionaries a catechism that put the theological fundamentals into simple question-and-answer form that could be easily understood by the unconverted.[213] This was especially evident in the concluding section, a model conversation between missionary and potential convert in which the latter asks what will happen after "Jesus had poured his love into his Heart." He will then, the answer reads, be baptized in the name of the Father, the Son, and the Holy Spirit.

Q. "Who are these?
A. First the Father of Lord Jesus.
Q. Who is that?
A. This is impossible to describe to you, he is so high that I cannot reach him and it needs time for you to get to know him.
Q. How do I learn to know him?
A. Well, the Lord Jesus will tell that to you himself when his father will be your father too.
Q. Who is the Holy Ghost?
A. He is our Lord's Father's assistant and he is the mother of the baptized, who teaches him to pray.
Q. Why do I have to be baptized with water?
A. The blood that the Lord Jesus in his death has shed for you is invisibly added to it and washes all your sins and punishments from your heart.
Q. Please, tell me more.
A. After you are baptized, we will from time to time."[214]

---

212. Ibid., part 1, 2d ed. 1746, in *ZH*, 2:208–9.
213. The catechism is printed in [Zinzendorf], *Texte zur Mission*, 64–69.
214. Ibid., 68.

The final answer indicates an important part of the daily life in a mission congregation: in the "Speakings," the intimate and intense personal conversation between the missionary or the head of the choirs and the baptized, the biblical teachings as the Moravians understood them were explained to the newly converted. Other occasions for explaining the biblical texts and Watchwords were the religious services and "occasions," as they were called. Yet all these teachings and explanations retained their close links to Christology. The diaries of David Zeisberger offer many examples of this reality of congregational life.

THE MISSION CONGREGATIONS[215]

The decision to accept the invitation from Gekelemukpechünk marks the end of the older type of mission and the beginning of the mission activities on the Muskingum. In April 1772 Zeisberger brought the first group of converted Indians to the new region; with him he brought well-prepared plans and concepts for both the internal structure and the external relations of the new mission settlements. Mission congregations were to be founded only where the missionaries had received explicit invitations. From the beginning the Moravians had observed the principle that both missionaries and Native American converts would not oppose the secular authorities but would seek their protection. Earlier and later mission activities were characterized by continuous efforts to establish harmony and good relations with the regional and transregional Native American councils and tribes. Requests to found mission congregations, however, always included the condition that neither members of the mission congregation nor missionaries should be asked to concern themselves with political matters or warlike efforts; missionaries always insisted that they retain complete freedom in shaping their own lives, rules, and daily routines in their mission congregations.[216]

Four mission congregations were founded in the Muskingum valley. First was Schönbrunn, whose settlement began with the arrival of the first group led by Zeisberger in early May 1772. With the arrival of the Mahican on 18 September 1772, the second congregation was founded; it was baptized Gnadenhütten. Schönbrunn and Gnadenhütten were about ten miles apart. At the urgent request of Netawatwees and the General Council at Gekelemukpechünk in the spring of 1776, the third settlement was founded near the new head village of the Delaware, Goschachgünk; on 9 April 1776 the place was named Lichtenau. In the spring of 1777, when the Native American tribes allied with

---

215. This section is largely based on Wessel, *Delaware-Indianer und Herrnhuter Missionare.*

216. See "Des C. L. Schreiben wegen einiger Verfolgung," dated Marienborn, 6 May 1739, in ZE, 8:515–17. The line was drawn there when authorities requested from Moravian congregations things that conflicted with biblical commands. The missionaries answered these requests with the principle that "we cannot accept that, we have to obey God more than men." Ibid., 516.

the British threatened the very existence of the Delaware as well as of the mission congregations, most of the inhabitants of Gnadenhütten moved to Lichtenau, where they lived under the protection of the Delaware warriors from nearby Goschachgünk. After the crisis had passed, the Mahican moved back to their old village, Gnadenhütten. Schönbrunn, which had been given up after the foundation of Lichtenau, was refounded in April 1779. Lichtenau was given up and in 1780 Salem was begun as a new mission congregation. On 11 September 1781 the members of the congregations together with their missionaries were deported by the Wyandot to the Upper Sandusky region controlled by the British and beyond the influence of the American side. The diary ends half a year earlier, on 25 March 1781, with Zeisberger's departure for Bethlehem.

The missionaries had received statutes for the mission congregations early on.[217] These statutes contained rules for admission to the congregation and rules that regulated living together and the sharing of responsibilities. The institutional structure of the congregations, though never spelled out in detail in the statutes, included a congregation council that was responsible for settling the worldly affairs. Religious life and questions related to it were dealt with and shaped by the various religious institutions and meetings; by and large they were the same as those that had been developed in the European Moravian congregations. These fell into two groups—those to be attended by all inhabitants of the settlement and those open only to the baptized members of the congregation.

Among the inhabitants of the mission congregations, four groups can be distinguished. The first group consisted of all those who had received permission to live in the settlement. Such permission was granted once the applicant expressed a serious desire to join the mission congregation in conversation with one of the Indian Helpers or one of the missionaries. If there was any doubt, only a temporary permission was granted. The second group was composed of all those who had been baptized, or, if an applicant had been baptized elsewhere, by the laying on of hands. The relative size of the two groups changed continuously, as the following table shows:

Proportion of Baptized to Unbaptized in Schönbrunn, 1774–81[218]

| Year | Schönbrunn | | |
	All	B	UB
1774	184	106	78
1775	220	123	97
1776	263	185	78
1777	—	—	—
1778	—	—	—

217. These statutes are printed in the appendix, Document No. 3.
218. The figures are based on the statistics in the diary compiled at the end of the year by Zeisberger.

1779	—	—	—
1780	—	—	—
1781	143	116	27

All = all inhabitants of settlement; B = baptized inhabitants; UB = unbaptized inhabitants

Everyone who had received permission to live in the mission settlement was admitted to the congregation council. All inhabitants and their guests, whether baptized or not, were welcome to attend every type of religious gathering. These gatherings took place both in the morning and in the evening. Sermons were preached only on Sundays; in the quarter-hour meetings only the Watchwords and the daily texts were explained.

Some religious meetings were open only to the baptized. If someone desired to be baptized, missionaries and Indian Helpers reviewed his life and assessed his religious development;[219] if they agreed that the candidate's desire was serious, a missionary questioned the candidate "about his heart's feelings" in a long and intimate conversation. After receiving absolution, the candidate was then "baptized with Jesus' blood."[220] The baptism itself was often part of the Sunday service but could also be performed in the quarter-hour meetings or in the meetings of the choirs. Especially important days for baptisms were the first day of the year and 6 January, Epiphany, the "festival of the Heathens," Easter Sunday, Pentecost, and Christmas day. The number of baptisms confirms that the missionaries baptized only after careful consideration:

Baptisms in Schönbrunn and Lichtenau, 1772–81[221]

	Schönbrunn			Lichtenau		
Year	All	AB	CB	All	AB	CB
1772	92	2	3	—	—	—
1773	184	9	9	—	—	—
1774	220	21	7	—	—	—
1775	263	22	15	—	—	—
1776	—	—	—	59	3	3
1777	—	—	—	232	8	3
1778	—	—	—	328	23	12

219. Early on the Moravians tried to define criteria for baptism. See "Eine Hayden-Boten Instruction nach Orient," c. 1740, in ZE, 8:632–36. This instruction named four criteria: "1) A simple understanding of God who became man . . . and after a long and difficult life a sacrifice for the sins of the whole world . . . , 2) an understanding of the evil spirit as someone who as great power over all who do not know Jesus . . . , 3) an understanding of the good spirits that are invisible . . . , 4) An idea that the baptism is mixed with Christ's blood, and that according to God's command it washes the nature of all from their sins and makes them into newborn children." But it was not necessary that the candidate be already familiar with the "secrets of the holy supper and all other secrets." On the contrary, these should not be revealed to him or her "until they grow as ours do in wisdom and understanding." Ibid., 635–36.

220. Wessel, *Delaware-Indianer und Herrnhuter Missionare*, 121–23.

221. The figures are based on the statistics compiled by the missionaries at the end of each year.

| 1779 | 100 | 1 | 4 | — | — | — |
| 1780 | 143 | 3 | 5 | — | — | — |

All = total number of inhabitants; AB = baptisms of adult persons; CB = baptisms of children

By and large, missionaries refused to baptize the children of unbaptized parents. They made an exception if the child was terminally ill; the wish of gravely ill adults to be baptized was likewise usually honored. Moravian congregations were divided into choirs that were organized by sex, age, and marital status; each baptized person belonged to one of these choirs. There was a choir for young boys and one for older boys, for young and older girls, for single men and single women, for married couples, for widows, and for widowers.[222] Baptisms were often performed in the meetings of the choir to which the candidate belonged. If someone who had been baptized earlier desired admission to the congregation, she usually was admitted by the laying on of hands in the respective choir's meeting. In a similar fashion, marriages were celebrated in the meetings of the choir for married couples. The statutes of the congregation decreed monogamy as the rule and not, as was practiced among the Delaware and neighboring tribes, polygamy. Permission to marry was granted by the missionaries.[223]

The choirs held regular quarter-hour meetings and occasionally assembled for "lovefeasts." At the yearly choir festival held in all Moravian congregations, each choir celebrated on the same predetermined day a love feast consisting of a simple dinner, singing, and praying. On these occasions the respective choirs at Bethlehem often sent little presents to the choir at Schönbrunn, and occasionally, too, the so-called Festival Ode.[224] These love feasts, which mixed sociability with religious activities, were celebrated at other holidays as well, usually remembrance days that recalled special events within the history of the Moravian Church. Thus on 13 August the congregations recalled what had happened in 1727, when the Moravian refugees at Herrnhut decided to form a congregation. On 16 September 1741 the lot, through which Christ as "Elder of the Church" communicated his decisions, had decided that henceforth Jesus himself would accept its leadership. On 13 November this important decision was communicated to all congregations and both days were devoted to the

222. On this system, see Smaby, *Transformation of Moravian Bethlehem*, 10–11.

223. See article 16 of the statutes for Schönbrunn, printed in the appendix, Document No. 3. The Moravians considered marriage not a compact concluded between two persons out of affection and love but a union predetermined by God. Thus the English Provincial Conference resolved at their meeting between 17 and 19 May 1752 that "Those brothers and sisters who for themselves consider marrying each other we consider absurd. They are not only sinning but behave extravagantly and are a bit out of their mind if they do not want or if they want out of their own will to marry. Yet it is good to keep the exception in mind as well as the difference between genders." Minutes of the Provincial Conference at Ingatestone Hall, 17–19 May 1752, fol. 13, John Rylands Library, MSS R 92072, Ryl. Engl. MS 1054, No. 9.

224. MAB, B "Odes," no. 4.

remembrance of this decision. Over and above these holidays, "epiphany" had a special meaning as the "Festival of the Heathen," an occasion, as mentioned above, for baptizing the newly converted.

The third and innermost group of the congregation consisted of those who participated in the holy supper. Candidates for baptism were allowed to witness but not to partake of the Lord's Supper and again they were required to converse with missionaries beforehand. Afterward, the Moravians tried to determine the effects on the candidate. If they believed that she was worthy to participate in this honor, she was admitted to the Lord's Supper for the first time as a participant and thus belonged, as the annual reports stated, to the group of communicants. From this group alone the Indian Helpers were recruited, as we shall see. If, during an intimate conversation, a missionary decided that a participant at Holy Communion had slackened in his religious fervor or, worse, that he had violated an article of the statutes of the congregation, he lost his status and rejoined those who were not allowed to partake of the Lord's Supper.

We have meaningful data on the number of participants in Holy Communion only for the years 1772 to 1775, from the annual reports for the mission congregation in the Muskingum valley. These data underline how sparingly permission to participate in the Holy Communion was granted and give us a sense of how frequently the Lord's Supper was celebrated.

The Communicant Congregation at Schönbrunn, 1772–75[225]

Year	Frequency	Admissions	Communicants	Total
1772	5	4	?	92
1773	7	5	50	184
1774	8	4	51	220
1775	9	18	68	263

Frequency = number of times the holy supper was celebrated; Admissions = number of baptized who were admitted as participants to the holy supper; Communicants = number of members of the communion congregation; Total = all inhabitants in the mission congregation

If these figures are representative of the other years, the innermost group of the mission congregations made up about one-fourth of the total population. The communicant congregation was the core group of the congregation. The celebration of Holy Communion approximately every six weeks represented *the* highlight of Moravian religious life. On these occasions the communicants merged with Jesus, the Elder of the Church, into one mystical body.

At the head of the mission congregations were the missionaries themselves.

225. The data are based on the year-end reports in the diaries printed below. According to Wessel, *Delaware-Indianer und Herrnhuter Missionare*, 200–202, the relationship between baptized and communicants was as follows: Schönbrunn, 1773, 56:50; 1774, 72:51; 1775, 117:68; Gnadenhütten, 1773, 53:31; 1774, 62:38; 1775, 73:43; 1776, 65:52; 1779, 52:34; 1780, 50:33; Lichtenau, 1779, 55:42; Salem, 1780, 51:27.

The direction of one or more mission congregations was usually entrusted to one missionary. Zeisberger was responsible for the mission congregations in the Muskingum valley. The Provincial Helpers' Conference, however, frequently had to remind Zeisberger and the other missionaries to get together regularly in conference to coordinate common concerns. These reminders were necessary because relationships between the missionaries did not always reflect the highest standards of loving charity.[226]

The missionaries were assisted by their wives. Since Zeisberger was not married, Anne Margarethe Jungmann had to shoulder the burden of working with the female members of the congregation. She had been involved in mission work almost from the beginning of the Moravian mission in North America; she had been at Checomeco as well as at other mission congregations, spoke Mahican as well as Delaware, and was very experienced. Until August 1773 she and her husband conducted the intimate conversations at Gnadenhütten as well as at Schönbrunn on occasion. On 29 January 1775 she was entrusted with the special care of the girls while John Heckewelder was entrusted with the special care of the boys.

Aside from these assignments, the wives of the missionaries were responsible for all problems related to the female members of the mission congregation as well as for providing their own families with food, although the diaries are silent on these points.[227] The missionaries had their meals together. Moravians considered marriage a union designed to optimize the efficiency of both sexes in the mission congregation. The autobiographies tell us that the affection of the converted female Indians compensated the wives of missionaries for their hardships and privations.

Apart from the numerous reports of women conducting intimate conversations with members of the congregation, the diaries reveal little about the other religious tasks and activities the women performed. Since they were ordained as acolytes or deacons, they would have been qualified to perform liturgical functions. We know that at least one wife of a missionary, Anna Margarethe Jungmann, absolved a member of the congregation by the laying on of hands.[228]

Mission statutes defined the authority of the missionaries; in the end, they

226. See note 549 to entry for 12 Nov. 1774.

227. Even the autobiographies of these women to not reveal the range of their activities in the mission congregations, see the autobiography of Sarah Heckewelder, née Ohneberg (1747–1815), which John Heckewelder wrote after her death, MAB, Memoirs B 7, F 1815, 15; the autobiography of Anna Margaretha Jungmann, née Bechtel (1721–93), MAB, Memoirs Diary Bethlehem, vol. 37, fol. 474–87; Maria Agnes Roth, née Pfingstag (1735–1805), MAB, Memoirs, B 6, 1805, 113; biography of Johanna Schmick (1721–95), MAB, Memoirs Diary Bethlehem, vol. 38, fol. 152–55; autobiography of Anna Maria Sensemann, née Brucker (1747–1815), MAB, Memoirs, B 7, 1815, 112; autobiography of Susanna Zeisberger, née Lecron (1744–1824), MAB Memoirs B 8, 1824, I 13. For more biographical details, see Register of Persons below.

228. The sin in question was an unknown misdemeanor. See entry for 7 Jan. 1776.

alone decided what happened in the mission congregation. They were, as the converted Indians always stressed, the "teachers," and as such they demanded recognition of their authority. But the diaries reveal too that in secular affairs the missionaries rarely made decisions without consulting the Indian Helpers. The Indian Helpers likewise regarded the missionaries as their speakers vis-à-vis the colonial authorities. Even in Checomeco the Indians had made this very clear.[229] In the Delaware Council, by contrast, the Indian Helpers functioned as speakers of the mission congregation.

The Indian Helpers were usually selected from the small group of reliable Indian communicants. They were responsible for caring for visitors ("servants of strangers"), for orderly behavior in religious assemblies ("servants at meetings"), and had other duties, such as organizing communal work—for example, the construction of buildings for communal use or fences around cleared fields. The diaries report that Indian Helpers preached the "doctrine of the cross" to unconverted visitors as well as to those they met on their travels. In the absence of a missionary, the Indian Helper led the religious meetings.

Although the missionaries had the final say in all religious and secular affairs, they were also, in a very direct and practical sense, members of the mission congregations, and in this they differed from all missions of other confessions.[230] They were distinguished from the other congregants only by their authority as religious teachers. They participated in the building of houses as well as in tilling the soil and planting and harvesting the fields. They were responsible for earning their own livelihood and producing the things they needed themselves. Only cloth, writing utensils, tea, coffee, medicine, herbs, spices, and a few other amenities of European civilization were sent to them from Bethlehem.

In these practical activities the missionaries profited from the fact that most of them were not theologians who had studied at a university, but had usually been apprenticed to particular crafts. Johann Roth had been apprenticed to a locksmith, Johann Jakob Schmick learned the trade of a joiner,[231] while Johann Georg Jungmann was a miller. Only Zeisberger had not learned a particular trade. Instead, he and Schebosch, originally the son of Quakers, belonged to the few who, after their arrival at Bethlehem, had visited a school founded at the instigation of Spangenberg, where between 1744 and 1746

229. "Heyden Conferenz den 29. Jan. o. s. 1745/46," MAB, B 315, F 1, no. 6.

230. See the diary of William Richardson, a Presbyterian, who between 1757 and 1759 worked as a missionary among the Cherokee. According to Richardson a missionary needed "a hundred and twenty pounds sterling yearly, at least, let him be as frugal as he will . . . he must keep three or four horses a Servant or Negro Man, two would not be amiss, to guard him from Town to Town." Williams, "Presbyterian Mission to the Cherokees," 136.

231. Before Schmick joined the Moravian Church in 1748, he had been a pastor in a Lutheran congregation; as a university-educated theologian among the missionaries he was the exception to the rule. It is telling for the Moravians' scale of values that Schmick learned joinery after joining the Moravian Church.

Johann Christian Pyrlaeus prepared prospective candidates for work as mission-aries.[232]

In many respects the missionaries lived the same life as the Indian members of the congregation. They carved their dishes from wood or made their own pottery.[233] The missionaries used other metal utensils for their housework—probably more than could be found in the average Native American household. The 1780 inventory for Schönbrunn lists the following items: "Kitchen utensils: 3 tin pots, 4 tin plates, 2 iron kettles, 2 coffee pots, 1 large brass kettle holding 4 to 5 buckets, two small ones, 1 small iron carder [?], 1 funnel, one pan, one grater, one iron skimmer, two candlesticks, and one snuffer."

A coffee mill and a tea kettle were also common household items of the missionaries.[234] The household items were supplemented by an order for wick for the production of candles, of hard soap for cleaning, and of pipe bowls for pleasure. Zeisberger owned a pocket watch.[235] On the missionaries' crude bookshelves were exegetical, liturgical, and history books.[236]

In furnishings, the missionaries' houses differed from those of the converted Indians. The missionaries owned tables and chairs, stored their belongings in trunks, and probably even slept in feather beds.[237] Their houses were heated by either fireplaces or stoves.[238] In addition, the missionaries built a baking oven, while the converted Indians baked their bread in hot ashes.[239]

Their sharing in almost all aspects the lifestyle of the Indian members of the congregation was one reason why the Moravians succeeded as missionaries. Living together, contact between Native Americans and missionaries was not restricted to religious meetings, as it was in non-Moravian mission congregations. Moravians and Indian converts shared the same concerns of daily life and worked side by side in the fields. Yet there were limits. The missionaries, probably for lack of numbers, did not go out hunting with their converted Indian

232. Schweinitz, *Zeisberger,* 120; MAB, Bethlehem Gemeinediarium, vol. 2, 45. On Johann Christoph Pyrlaeus (1713–85), see Neisser, *Beginnings of Moravian Work in America,* 149–50.

233. Schmick carved his dishes from pine wood (GD, 28 June 1773). Johann Jungmann built his own potter's wheel (GD, 16 July 1774) with which he produced milk pots and tiles (GD, 22 July 1774).

234. Besides the inventory for Schönbrunn, see the one for Salem (n.d.) and the list of items which "Schmick has left back on the Muskingum and has sold to the Mission Deaconry," all in MAB, B 311, F 5.

235. Cf. the inventories in MAB, B 311, F 5; Zeisberger to Seidel, 20 May 1773, B 229, F 4, 17b.

236. "Von Jungmanns am Muskingum zurückgelassene Sachen," MAB, B 311, F 5.

237. In 1780 the Jungmanns left behind on the Muskingum one "feather bed and one eider-down with four cushions" (3 May 1780, MAB, B 311, F 5), while the Schmicks owned strawsacks ("Von Schwester Schmickin am Muskingum zurückgelassen," MAB, B 311, F 5). When the Indians chased the missionaries away in 1781, they, among other things, cut up their eiderdowns ("Diario der pilgernden Indianergemeine," entry for 3 Sept. 1781, fol. 2037a, MAB, B 148, and curriculum vitae of Susanna Zeisberger, MAB, Memoirs B 8, 1824, I 13). The couple Roth owned featherbeds in Langundoutenünk in 1772. See Dexter, *Diary of David McClure,* entry for 5 Sept. 1772.

238. GD, 20 Aug. 1773, 13 Dec. 1774.

239. GD, 18 June 1774.

brothers and only rarely accompanied them to the sugar huts, where the Indians made sugar from maple sap. Nevertheless, the kind of social hierarchy that prevailed in the mission congregations of other confessions was notably absent from the Moravian congregations.

Being the authority of last resort in all cases was limited by the will of the Chief Elder of the Unity, Jesus Christ. This should be taken literally. When an important question was put to the lot, it was understood that the lot drawn represented the will of the Chief Elder. Among the important concerns addressed to the lot were the worthiness of a candidate requesting baptism, whether two people should be united in matrimony, or whether a new mission settlement should be started. The reasoning behind this procedure was simple: what looked like an arbitrary decision-making process could be determined by an all-powerful Christ. At the same time, the missionaries were warned not to misuse the lot; it was not to be used if human insight could sensibly decide the case.[240]

The statutes contained little about the structure of the congregation or its institutions; what little was said there was said indirectly. The statutes dealt mostly with the basic rules of communal life, as shown by the "Statutes & Rules" in Document no. 3 in the appendix. The basic tendency of the statutes was clear; their purpose was to introduce certain European Christian values and moral concepts as general behavioral rules to be obeyed by all. These rules included the command to obey one's parents, not to kill another human being, to live in modesty, to be married to one wife, to behave peacefully and honestly, and to work hard. Everyone admitted to the congregation had these statutes read to her or him. All new members were told that violations would automatically result in expulsion from the congregation. The statutes left no doubt that this was a Christian congregation in which the practice of Indian religious or ritual customs was forbidden.

Perhaps surprisingly, however, the statutes did not mandate that converted Indians had to give up their former way of life. The Indians were allowed to maintain their huts in the usual way. The division of labor reflected the Native American economic order; women were responsible for agriculture, men for hunting. The diaries do tell us, however, that the strict division along gender lines gradually weakened. Indeed, the missionaries themselves set an example by participating in tilling the fields. They practiced the principle expressed in "Methods with the Heathens," a circular written in 1742, which read: "Your heavenly walk in life should be such that the Heathen would be provoked to ask: Who are these people?"[241]

The values inherent in the statutes made a sharp contrast between Euro-

240. On the usage of the lot, see Beyreuther, "Lostheorie und Lospraxis."

241. "Brief an die damals in allen Religionen und Secten durch America verstreute prediger des Evangelii geschrieben." Philadelphia, 17/25 May 1742, in Zinzendorf, *Naturelle Reflexiones*, in ZE, 4:37–40.

pean Christian moral concepts and Native American values; conversion to Christianity and admission to the congregation required a total restructuring and civilizing process that unconverted Indians considered a threat to their own lifestyle and that they therefore repeatedly rejected. These Native Americans contrasted the Christian-European way of life with a native path to redemption in harmony with other features of the Indian way of life.[242]

Zeisberger's diary shows beyond any doubt that this contrast was not "discovered" by twentieth-century scholars. Indians who asked for admission to the mission congregation knew what they were getting into and what they were expected to give up.[243] Present-day critics who argue that Christian missions were mechanisms of oppression and social control underestimate the intelligence and awareness of the tribes. At the same time it is important to recognize that the Moravian religious system was similar to the Native American in at least one important respect: both achieved religious insight through "visions."[244] And, as we have seen, Zinzendorf stressed repeatedly that Christian teachings must be "painted into the heart," an approach consistent with Native American understandings of spirituality.

The mission congregations were part of the Delaware Nation in both a political and an economic sense. After the Great Council of the Delaware in February 1775 assigned the mission congregations official status as Native American settlements, with all the rights and duties that went with that status, the mission congregations formed an integral part of the Delaware Nation. In return, the Council expected the mission congregation to contribute its share to the costs of the diplomatic and other activities of the Delaware.

Before Lord Dunmore's war, the opinion of converted chiefs had carried considerable weight in the Great Council; after the decision of February 1775 it gained even greater weight. At the same time, David Zeisberger and John Heckewelder were gradually adopted as communication links between the Great Council and the American Continental army at Fort Pitt. White Eyes, at least, tried to exploit the mission for political purposes. It is remarkable that in this whole process the converted chiefs and the missionaries did not lose sight of their own interests. They certainly contributed to the efforts to marginalize Captain Pipe and his followers, who still looked at the mission warily if not with outright hostility; Captain Pipe and his people finally left the area. This was the doing not only of the Great Council but of the Moravians. They

---

242. See the reasons the Shawnee gave for their skepticism and rejection of the Moravian mission, entry for 25 Dec. 1772; and see the teachings of the Delaware preacher Scattameck, entry for 1 Jan. 1773.

243. The diary repeatedly and explicitly states that Indians were read the statutes after they received permission to join the mission congregation. See, e.g., entry for 28 June 1772.

244. For a modern analysis of the meaning of vision among Shawnee at the turn of the century, see Dowd, *Spirited Resistance*, 123–31; Native American visions are mentioned in entries for 7 May 1772, 1 Jan. 1773, and 13 April 1774 (Scattameck), and entry for 11 June 1775 (Wangomen); see pp. xx–xx above.

felt that the loss of Pipe and his faction was justified by the positive effects they imagined it would have on the position of the mission congregation within the Delaware Nation. Undeniably, the presence of the mission congregations had changed the political landscape; for one thing, it increased, at least for a while, the political weight of the Delaware within the Native American Nations of the Ohio region.

The Moravian missions had their effects, too, on the Native American economic structures and conditions of life in the region. The Native American economy was based on agriculture. The mission congregation's agricultural pursuits, however, were more intense and produced more per head than the Native American settlements. The Indians planned primarily for immediate needs, while the missionaries based their planting on longer-term needs and tried to account for unforeseen developments. Indian agriculture remained the concern of women, but the mere fact that male missionaries participated in working the fields heightened female expectations of their husbands. Zeisberger disapproved of these female expectations.[245] Raising cattle was more important in the mission congregation than in the Native American villages. The missionaries owned animals—cows, hogs, horses, and chickens—jointly; the individual native families in Schönbrunn worked plots allotted to them for their own use; they probably owned their own cattle, too.

More important, because they stocked provisions, the mission congregations developed into an important regional economic center. Word spread quickly that between February and May, when in native villages food became scarce and famine was not unknown, provisions could be bought from the mission congregations at pre-crisis prices.[246] As Indian families flocked to the mission congregations in search of food, many of them heard for the first time of the missionary purpose. Widows and single pregnant women, who had to make do without the support of a family and who suffered especially in times of need, were particularly attracted to the missions, and the percentage of widows among converted Native Americans was always fairly high.[247]

The missions were part not only of the Delaware Nation but also, of course, of a worldwide network of Moravian mission congregations. Bethlehem was the link between the congregations of Ohio and those of the wider world. Ideally, all mission diaries were dispatched every third month to Bethlehem, where they were read, copied, and sent to other congregations. Excerpts and summaries of diaries from other mission stations were sent in turn to the congregations of the Ohio region, along with letters in which Nathanael Seidel and John Ettwein discussed problems common to missions and answered queries from missionaries in the Muskingum Valley. The missionaries occasion-

---

245. See Wessel, *Delaware-Indianer und Herrnhuter Missionare*, chap. 2.

246. See entry for 7 June 1772 and entries for the months of March, April, and May 1775.

247. The 1775 annual report for Schönbrunn lists 22 widows and 2 widowers; in Lichtenau, according to the same source for 1778, there were 31 widows and 9 widowers.

ally read these reports and diaries to each other; Zeisberger's diary occasionally reports that particular accidents were shared with the whole congregation. Thus all learned about the hard times that had befallen the Moravian congregations in Greenland and Russia, and were made to feel part of a transcontinental Christian community.[248]

The process of converting the Indians began the transformation of a tribal community into something new. In the words of the Provincial Conference held at London in 1749, this community defined itself as a "pure Pilgrim society" to which "all in the whole world belong who bore witness to Jesus."[249] Zeisberger emphasized this repeatedly, commenting proudly on how many tribes were represented in the Ohio mission congregations.

Less in the German but certainly in the English congregations, the idea of a transnational community of Christ was greeted with little enthusiasm. These different attitudes about the nature of the church as a national or transnational body reflect contrasting understandings of the term "nation" in Germany and England.[250] In Germany "nation" was defined as a cultural entity, whereas in England it was understood in both its political and its cultural meanings. Zeisberger seems to have used the term in the sense of a cultural unity.[251] In 1754, at the Provincial Synod in London, Zinzendorf himself discussed the conflicting concepts of the term:

> . . . there are two different kinds of principles and modes of thinking among us: Some people merge their identity totally with Christ when they become converted. And from that moment on their mode of thinking is ruled by the *reglement* of Christ and the congregation. There is another group of people that, when being converted to Christ and to the church, yet they want for the rest of their life to retain their fatherly and national way of life. . . . For those to whom the church is not so important that he wants to think only in the way the church does, but juxtaposes his national, his regional etc ways of thought to those of Christ in such a way that the concerns of Christ have to give way to those national and regional ones—these persons I will remember when they have passed away. That person who prefers an English

---

248. See entries for 19 Jan. 1774, 6 Jan. 1775, 30 May 1775.

249. Minutes of the Provincial Conference at Northampton House, Bloomsbury Square, London, 16–20 Jan. 1749, fol. 29, in Minutes, etc., of Provincial Conferences and Synods of the Moravian Brethren in England, 1743–55. Copied from the records in the Provincial Archives of the Moravian Church at 22 Fetter Lane, London, vol. 1, in John Rylands Library, Manchester, R 92072, Ryl. Engl. Ms. 1054.

250. On the English definition of the term "nation," cf. Wellenreuther, "England und Europa," 104–23, and "Volk, Nation, Nationalismus, Masse," in Brunner et al., *Geschichtliche Grundbegriffe,* 7:302–9.

251. See entry for 5 June 1772.

hat to a Moravian or another dress does not belong to the Moravian cemetery.[252]

The next day Zinzendorf returned to the subject: "Yet the Germans know what they want. They do not care whether a thing is English, Bohemian or Swedish—if it is the Lord's thing they will contribute to it with their utmost abilities. We Germans have not been converted to a nation and therefore do not want to be turned from any nation. If God elects a nation and even if it is that of Ethiopia, we have to serve it even if in doing so we are being deprived; this means thinking German."[253]

Within the English Moravian Church the subject continued to be controversial. The problem of the transnational character of the Moravian Church was discussed on at least two occasions. After the synod in May 1765 had reiterated the concept of a transnational "Pilgrim Society" in its fullest meaning, the synod the following year finally agreed on a compromise formula, stating: "National distinctions should cease entirely amongst us, and it was wished that the name of nations might never be thought of. In the House of God we are all but one nation. We have but one saviour, one Blood of Atonement, one faith, one Bible etc. A different way of thinking in immaterial points, which does not clash with our fundamental principles, may, however, be born with."[254]

Surprisingly, similar problems existed in the mission congregations. These discussions shed new light on the concept of "nation" and "tribe" among Native Americans. For example, the Mahican insisted on settling together in a separate settlement; Gnadenhütten, which Zeisberger initially had opposed, was their foundation. The Munsee, too, had demanded a separate settlement, but Zeisberger had refused the request. Zeisberger, who was unfamiliar with the political dimension of the term "nation," recognized his mistake too late.[255] By then he could not prevent a substantial number of Munsee from leaving the mission congregations; soon they joined the ranks of inveterate enemies of the Moravians. In order to not endanger the mission, the missionaries by and large tried to steer a restrictive but generally not inflexible middle course.

---

252. Minutes of the Provincial Synod at Lindsey House, London, 13–20 May 1754, fols. 45–46, in Minutes, etc., of Provincial Conferences and Synods of the Moravian Brethren in England, 1743–55. Copied from the records in the Provincial Archives of the Moravian Church at 22 Fetter Lane, London, vol. 1, in John Rylands Library, Manchester, R 92072, Ryl. Eng. MS. 1054.

253. Ibid., fols. 75–76.

254. Ibid., vol. 3, fol. 5 (Synod at Lindsey House 12–22 May 1765), fol. 167 (Synod of 3–14 Aug. 1766). From the early 1760s English synod protocols are written not in German but in English. In North America the percentage of non-German members was so small that a similar controversy about the national or transnational character of the church could not arise.

255. See entry for 2 March 1777 below.

DAVID ZEISBERGER, THE AUTHOR OF THE DIARIES

The diaries were written almost exclusively by one person—David Zeisberger. They narrate the stories of Schönbrunn and Lichtenau between 1772 and 1781; they describe these events from a missionary's perspective, shaped by a specific biography and by cultural notions filtered through long experience and wide knowledge of Indian modes of thought and ways of life. In order more precisely to understand the biases and perspective of the diaries, we must look more closely at David Zeisberger's world.

David Zeisberger was born on 11 April 1721 in Zauchenthal, a village in the Carpathians.[256] Five years later his parents, David and Rosina Zeisberger, fled persecution and came with their children to Herrnhut.[257] In 1736 the parents emigrated, with other members of the congregation, to Georgia, the British colony in North America. Their son, David, who had learned Latin, among other things, at Herrnhut,[258] remained in the Moravian congregation at Herrendyk, Netherlands, where he worked as an errand boy and learned Dutch. Dissatisfied with the conditions there, the young boy ran away, traveling on his own initiative to England, whence, with the assistance of James Oglethorpe, he finally reached Georgia, where he rejoined his parents. Like most other members of the Moravian Unity, the Zeisbergers remained in Georgia until the beginning of the War of Jenkin's Ear. In April 1740 they migrated to Pennsylvania, where they helped build the new settlement of Bethlehem.

David Zeisberger was one of the first students of Johann Christian Pyrlaeus, whose task was to educate young members of the congregation as potential missionaries.[259] In the spring of 1745 Zeisberger and Friedrich Post traveled to Onondaga, where they were to perfect their knowledge of Iroquois. In Albany, New York, they were arrested as potential spies and spent a couple of weeks in the local prison. After their release, they accompanied Spangenberg to Onondaga. It was on this trip that Shikellemi adopted Spangenberg and Zeisberger into the Oneida tribe. Spangenberg was given the name Tgirhitontie, Zeisberger Ganousseracheri.

During his visit Zeisberger was introduced to the mysteries of Iroquois

---

256. The best account of Zeisberger's life is Schweinitz, *Zeisberger*. Zauchenthal or Zauchtl is situated south of Troppau, southwest of Ostrau, and east of Ölmütz. See Scobel, *Andrees Allgemeiner Handatlas*, 61–62, square M 4.

257. David Zeisberger (1696–1744) and his wife Rosina (d. 1746) had three children, David, Anna, and George. Anna (1725–63) married George Jäschke (1718–62); both went as missionaries to Tranquebar in India, where they died. George (before 1726–42) went as a missionary to Surinam, where he died. Neisser, *Beginnings of Moravian Work in America*, 76–77.

258. Schweinitz, *Zeisberger*, 17.

259. Little is known about this school. Pyrlaeus ran it and he seems to have taught Native American languages, especially Mohawk, and to have given lessons on how Native Americans lived. John Joseph Bull, alias Schebosch, Michael Schnall, Joseph Möller, Abraham Büninger, and Johann Hagen were Pyrlaeus's other original students. Ibid., 120.

diplomacy, and began his long, close relationship to Onondaga and the Six Indian Nations. He visited Onondaga five times before 1769 and got to know all the important members of the Chief Council of the Six Indian Nations as well as Sir William Johnson, the superintendent for Indian Affairs. During a long visit in 1753–54, he picked up a solid knowledge of Mohawk, and, though he was less fluent in it, of Onondaga. During the Seven Years' War Zeisberger's extensive familiarity with Native American languages prompted the colonial authorities to employ him as translator in the treaty negotiations at Easton, Pennsylvania. He played the same role in conferences at Fort Pitt during the American Revolution.[260]

Zeisberger had a unique opportunity to familiarize himself with the whole spectrum of Native American life and customs, power relationships between tribes, languages and rituals,[261] and religious beliefs. At the same time, he became familiar with the problems of mission congregations. Over the years, he stayed at all of the important North American Moravian mission congregations—before 1755 at Checomeco, Gnadenhütten, and Shamokin, after 1763 at Machiwihilusing, Friedenshütten, and Friedensstadt. He worked with Mahican, Mohawk, Onondaga, and Delaware. On numerous trips he accompanied the leading theological thinkers of the Moravian Unity, which extended his knowledge. He profited from Petrus Böhler, one of the most educated members of the Moravian congregation in Georgia, from August Gottlieb Spangenberg, next to Zinzendorf probably the leading theologian of the Moravian Unity, from Johann Christoff Friedrich Cammerhoff, the radical exponent of the theology of the sifting period, and from Johann von Watteville, Zinzendorf's son-in-law. But Zeisberger's primary interests were the practical concerns and needs of the mission. He was interested in Native American languages and ways of life, and in pursuing these interests he made good use of his extensive knowledge of languages. He was fluent in German, Dutch, English, Mohawk, and Delaware, and understood Onondaga and Shawnee.

Unlike most missionaries, Zeisberger remained unmarried for a long time. It was only during his visit to Bethlehem in 1781 that he finally gave in to the repeated wishes of the Provincial Helpers' Conference and agreed to a marriage with Susanna Lecron.

Lecron was born on 17 February 1744 at Lancaster to German immigrants. The whole family joined the Moravian Unity in 1764. In 1781 Johann Friedrich Reichel, a member of the Unity's Elders' Conference and bishop of the church who visited the Moravian congregations in North America, wrote to

260. On Spangenberg's and Zeisberger's Indian names, see ibid., 133–34; on Zeisberger's visits to Onondaga, 156–75, 187–90, 205–12, 215–19, 318–20; on his knowledge of tribal languages, 212; and on his role as translator, 242–51, 253 (and see below numerous entries documenting his activities as a translator and interpreter).

261. In 1754 Zeisberger functioned for some time as the official keeper of the archive of the Six Indian Nations. Ibid., 217.

Susanna requesting that she marry Zeisberger. She recalled in her autobiography receiving the request to "join the single brother David Zeisberger, already aged 60, in matrimony and work with him in the mission congregation."

> . . . this request was almost too much for me. I thought the strength of my love and my soul would be too weak for this service; yet the obligation to be obedient to Jesus despite my weaknesses did not permit me to deny the request. And since the above named brother had been called back from his mission congregation we were joined in matrimony at Lititz on 4 July 1781. On 10 June I was consecrated a deaconess and soon after we began our journey into the Indian country.

Almost immediately after their arrival in the mission congregation, they were deported, along with the rest of the congregation, to the Upper Sandusky region, where they endured many difficulties and privations. While all the contemporary reports of this period emphasize its hardships, Zeisberger's wife seems to have experienced it as a particular ordeal to which she almost succumbed. She wrote vividly in her autobiography of the "horrible Indians" who carried everything away. After Zeisberger's death, on 8 January 1808, she returned to Lititz; on 8 September 1824 she died at Bethlehem.[262]

Zeisberger left behind a large body of material that remains a rich source of information on the history and language of the Delaware; only part of his papers have been published. Together with John Heckewelder's work on the Delaware, Zeisberger's *History of the Northern American Indians*, which was finally printed in 1910, has largely shaped our understanding of the Delaware in the eighteenth century.[263]

4. The Diary

PHYSICAL SHAPE, PROVENANCE, AND TRADITION

Whenever the opportunity arose, David Zeisberger sent his diaries from Schönbrunn and Lichtenau to Bethlehem; this happened at irregular intervals and depended on when opportunities arose to entrust the diaries to people traveling to Pittsburgh. In Bethlehem the diaries were first read and then copied; the originals were stored in the archives, while copies were sent to the Unity's

---

262. Autobiography of Susanna Zeisberger, MAB, Memoirs B 8, 1824, I 13. The excerpt illustrates the Moravian concept of marriage as a mutual service contract. It was not the first time that a woman married a much older man in order to become his "helper."

263. A list of the published writings of Zeisberger can be found in Schweinitz, *Zeisberger*, 686–92.

Elders' Conference in Europe.[264] The Moravian Archives at Bethlehem own the originals and in many cases one or more copies; another copy of the diary can be found in the central Moravian Archives at Herrnhut, Germany.[265] Wherever we found variations between original and contemporary copies, we have marked and annotated them in the notes. Carl John Fliegel later sorted Zeisberger's individual diaries into the following folders, which are preserved in the Archives at Bethlehem in boxes 141 and 147. Material enclosed in brackets has been added by the original editors at Bethlehem. Material enclosed in {braces} was crossed out in the original.

Diary part 1: "Bruder David Zeisbergers Diarium von seiner Reise und Ankunft mit 5 Familien Indianer Geschwister in der Gegend von Gekelemukpeckünk," Box 141, F 1, fols. 1–8a, covering the period 14 April–2 September 1772 inclusive. The pagination is that of the archivist, Carl John Fliegel. The cover of the individual diary received only one page number without the additional "a" or "b"; the following pages were in addition to the single page number identified as "a" (left-hand page) and "b" (right-hand page).

Diary part 2: "Diarium des Indianer Gemeinleins in Welhik-Thuppeck an der Mushkingum vom Monat September bis 18ten October 1772," Box 141, F 2, fols. 9–16b, covering the period 3 September–18 October 1772.

Diary part 3: "Diarium von Welhik Thuppeck und Gnadenhütten an der Mushkkingum vom 19ten October [1772 bis 22. März 1773]," Box 141, F 3, I 1, fols 17–30b, covering the period 19 October 1772–22 March 1773.

Diary part 4: "Diarium des Indianer Gemeinleins in Welhik Thuppek und Gnadenhütten an der Mushkingum vom 24ten Martius {–} [bis 8ten] Juni 1773," Box 141, F 3, I 2, fols. 31–37b, covering the period 24 March–8 June 1773.

Diary part 5: "[Diarium der Gemeine in Sch]önbrunn an der Ohio vom Monat [Juni bis zum] October 1773," Box 141, F 4, I 1, fols. 38–52a, covering the period 10 June–18 October 1773.

Diary part 6: "Diarium des Indianer Gemeinleins in Schoenbrunn am Mushkingum vom October 1773 bis im Februar 1774," Box 141, F 4, I 2, fols. 53–58b, covering the period 22 October 1773–13 February 1774.

Diary part 7: "Diarium der Indianer Gemeine in Schoenbrunn an der Muschkingum vom Februar bis 21ten May 1774," Box 141, F 5, I 1, fols. 59–66b, covering the period 19 February–21 May 1774.

Diary part 8: "Diarium von Schoenbrunn am Mushkingum vom 22ten May–12ten September 1774." Box 141, F 5, I 2, fols. 67–84b, covering the period 22 May–12 September 1774.

264. It is not possible to say who copied which diary; but the names of Immanuel Nitschmann and Henry Lindenmeyer are often mentioned. In one case Ewald Gustav Schaukirch received five shillings "for copying the journal of Lichtenau." MAB, Diaconate of Bethlehem, Ledger A, 5 Nov. 1778.

265. Unitäts-Archiv, Herrnhut, R 15, H 1, b 14–17.

Diary part 9: "Diarium von Schoenbrunn am Mushkingum vom 13ten September 1774 bis zu Ende Februarij 1775," Box 141, F 6, I 1, fols. 85–103a, covering the period 13 September 1774–28 February 1775.

Diary part 10: "Diarium von Schönbrunn am Mushkingum vom Monat Martius April und May 1775," Box 141, F 6, I 2, fols. 104–112a, covering the period 1 March–30 May 1775.

Diary part 11: "Diarium von Schoenbrunn am Muskingum vom {Monat Juni Juli und August} [1.Juni bis 7.September] 1775," Box 141, F 7, I 1, fols. 113–120a, covering the period 1 June–7 September 1775.

Diary part 12: "Diarium von Schoenbrunn am Muskingum von September 1775 bis 23ten Februar 1776," Box 141, F 7, I 3, fols. 121–133b, covering the period 9 September 1775–23 February 1776.

Diary part 13: "Diarium von Schönbrunn vom 28ten Februar bis 10ten April 1776," Box 141, F 7, I 4, unpaginated, covering the period 28 February–10 April 1776. The archivist erroneously continued the pagination for this diary on the copy of part 13 of the diaries. The page numbers 134 to 203 were used for the pagination of other documents that pertained to this mission or for copies of the original.

Diary part 14: "Diarium vom Anbau und Fortgang in Lichtenau am Mushkingum vom 12ten April bis Juli 1776," Box 147, F 1, fols. 204–216a, covering the period 12 April–1 July 1776.

Diary part 15: "Diarium von Lichtenau am Muskingum vom Juli 1776 bis 21ten Juni 1777," Box 147, F 2, I 1, fols. 216–249b, covering the period 7 July 1776–21 June 1777.

Diary part 16: "Diarium der Indianer-Gemeine in Lichtenau am Muskingum vom 22ten Juni bis 5ten August 1777," Box 147, F 3, I 1, fols. 250–259b, covering the period 22 June–5 August 1777. The page numbers from 251b to 255a are missing in the pagination.

Diary part 17: "Diarium von Lichtenau vom 6ten August bis 23ten September 1777," Box 147, F 4, I 1, fols. 393–403, covering the period 6 August–23 September 1777. The page numbers 260 to 278 were used for the copy of the original.

Diary part 18: "Diarium von Lichtenau am Muskingum vom 24ten September 1777 bis 10ten Martius 1778," Box 147, F 5, I 1, fols. 278–295b, covering the period 24 September 1777–10 March 1778.

Diary part 19: "Diarium von Lichtenau am Muskingum vom 15ten Martius bis 6ten Julij 1778," Box 147, F 6, I 1, fols. 296–306a, covering the period 15 March–6 July 1778.

Diary part 20: "Diarium von Lichtenau am Muskingum vom 10ten Julij bis 17ten August 1778," Box 147, F 7, fols. 306b–312a, covering the period 10 July–17 August 1778.

Diary part 21: "Diarium von Lichtenau am Muskingum vom 19ten August bis Ende des Jahres 1778," Box 147, F 8, I 1, fols. 312b–326a, covering the period 19 August–31 December 1778.

Diary part 22: "Diarium von Lichtenau am Muskingum vom Januario bis April [und von der Wieder Besezung von Schönbrunn und dessen Fortgang bis November 1779]," Box 147, F 9, fols. 326b–332a (i.e., 342a), covering the period 1 January–14 November 1779. Page 335a was erroneously numbered 325a. This error was continued until the end of this part. Another hand then added the correct pagination to the original.

Diary part 23: "Diarium von Schönbrunn und Gnadenhütten am Muskingum vom November 1779 bis in August 1780," Box 141, F 10, fols. 540–555b, covering the period 18 November 1779–9 August 1780.

Diary part 24: "Diarium von Schönbrunn vom 13ten August 1780 bis 25ten Martius 1781," Box 141, F 11, pages 556–570a, covering the period 13 August 1780–25 March 1781.

Copies of the diary are preserved in the Ohio State Historical Society at Cincinnati, Ohio, and in the Archives of the Moravian Unity at Herrnhut. Although some attempts have been made to publish the diaries, none was realized. The archives at Bethlehem preserve in boxes 141 and 147 manuscript translations of the diary by the archivist Rev. William N. Schwarze. The archives of the Ohio Historical Society at Columbus, Ohio, preserve extensive notes and comments by August C. Mahr. Mahr was professor of German Philology and Literature at the Ohio State University at Columbus. Between 1948 and 1955 he transcribed the diaries for Schönbrunn and Gnadenhütten for the years 1772 to 1777 as well as a number of shorter travel diaries. In addition, he translated parts of the diaries and composed annotations to that for Schönbrunn. In connection with his preparations for a critical edition of the diaries, he wrote a series of scholarly articles that we have used with great profit in our edition.[266] In recent years the American theologian George Wolfgang Forell has been particularly interested in the diaries.[267]

American and German historians and ethno-historians have long been aware of the existence of these diaries. In 1951 Paul A. W. Wallace called attention to the valuable ethnographic material contained in the Moravian Archives at Bethlehem.[268] Aside from the studies by Ilse Loges, Siegrun Kaiser,

266. August Mahr, "Delaware Terms for Plants and Animals"; and "Early Ohio Natural History"; "Indian River and Place Names in Ohio"; "Health Conditions in the Moravian Indian Missions"; and "How to Locate Indian Place Names." In addition, Mahr has translated and edited the valuable editions of John Heckewelder's diary, "A Canoe Journey from the Big Beaver to the Tuscarawas."

267. Forell, "Moravian Mission Among the Delawares." Forrell's transcriptions of some parts of the diaries and of Zeisberger's letters from 1775 to 1781 remained unpublished. These are preserved in the Moravian Archives at Bethlehem and in the Moravian Theological Seminary as manuscripts under the title George Wolfgang Forell, "Revolution at the Frontier. Reports from Moravian Missionaries Among the Indians, 1775–1781."

268. Wallace, "They Knew the Indian."

Carola Wessel, and Jane Merritt, and the analytically not very satisfactory but biographically valuable work by Earl P. Olmstead, ethno-historians have thus far made only superficial use of these diaries. This is true, too, of the work of James Axtell, Richard White, Michael N. McConnell, Gregory Evans Dowd, James Merrell, and Eric Hinderaker.[269]

Zeisberger's diary is not an isolated find but one of a number of diaries. Only as an ensemble do these diaries reveal the wealth of information Moravian missionaries noted about the life, customs, culture, economy, and politics of the Indians in the Ohio region. This is true not only of the diaries for Friedenshütten and Friedensstadt[270] but also of that for Gnadenhütten, which was written at the same time as the diary published here and which we have occasionally used for identifying persons.[271] How intimately Gnadenhütten and Schönbrunn, and later Lichtenau, were linked to each other is revealed by these diaries. It is this close relationship that prompted us to draw on all the diaries of the Ohio mission congregations when we compiled the extensive register of persons printed at the end of this volume.

THE DIARY AS A SOURCE

Since the sixteenth century much has been written on the source value of written documents, on the need for rigid rules for their interpretation, on the problem of discovering the true meaning of texts, on the difficulties of disentangling various influences that shaped the texts, and on discovering the forces that shaped their structure. Some have maintained that linguistic and related concepts have offered important insights. We will not repeat their arguments or those of their opponents. In this section we offer some clues to the material conditions that shaped the diaries published here, and to the limitations of their value as sources.

In a very practical sense, the material conditions for writing a diary mean the availability of feather, ink, and paper.[272] Ink and paper had to be brought

269. Axtell, *Invasion Within;* White, *Middle Ground;* McConnell, *A Country Between;* Dowd, *Spirited Resistance;* Merrell, *Into the American Woods;* Hinderaker, *Elusive Empires.*

270. The diary for the period from 20 Nov. 1767 to 9 Jan. 1769, which describes the mission activities at Friedenshütten on the Allegheny River, is published in Hulbert and Schwarze, "The Diaries of Zeisberger." These diaries contain the "Diary of David Zeisberger's Journey to the Ohio called in Delaware the Allegene, From Sept. 20th to Nov. 16, 1767" (8–32); "Report of the Journey of John Ettwein, David Zeisberger, and Gottlob Sensemann to Friedenshütten and Their Stay There, 1768" (32–42); "Diary of David Zeisberger and Gottlob Senseman. Journey to Goschgoschink on the Ohio and Their Arrival There, 1768" (42–69); "Continuation of the Diary of the Brethren in Goschgoschuenk on the Ohio, August 1768" (69–104).

271. "Diarium der Indianer-Gemeine in Gnadenhütten am Muskingum, 1. Mai 1773–30. Juli 1777," MAB, B 144.

272. In order to finish the last entries of part 5 of the diary on p. 47a and not begin a new page, Zeisberger reduced the size of his handwriting for the entries from 16 to 18 October 1773; at Gnadenhütten Schmick had to cope with similar problems. He had to deny the request of White Eyes to compose a message for the Delaware because he had only half a sheet left. GD, 16 July 1774, F 3, I 2.

or sent from Bethlehem. Their arrival depended on how fast requests traveled to Bethlehem and how quickly orders were filled and dispatched to Ohio.[273] Transport was often slow, and in addition orders had to be brought from Bethlehem to Schönbrunn, which in wartime was always hazardous.[274]

Writing the diaries required time and opportunity, and both were usually in short supply. It would be very convenient if we knew that Zeisberger had made daily entries, but the diary tells us otherwise. It contains indications that Zeisberger noted daily events only in rough notes that he usually expanded into diary entries on a weekly basis; occasionally the time between entries was even longer. When he wrote the diary entries, he relied on rough notes as well as on his and his companions' memories. For his biographical notices he could draw on special registers for baptism, marriage, and death, and for the religious meetings he could consult the register of Watchwords and Texts for each day of the year to refresh his memory. His accounts of these religious occasions are characterized by a certain repetition.

Zeisberger's diaries belonged to a tradition that stretched back to the early 1740s and influenced his decisions on what to include and how, what to stress and what to gloss over. In 1741 Zinzendorf had sent out a circular that asked all congregations to note daily events in their diaries. "Not only the big, but the small and little things as well as the quaint affair" should be reported, he wrote.[275] Secular and religious events, the dates of festivals and the holy supper, the start and completion dates of new building construction, and many other things were noted in these diaries. An early copy of the diary of Checomeco is printed in the *Büdingische Nachrichten*.[276]

The purpose of the diaries was to note the religious development in order to allow the readers in congregations to take part in the life of the congregation. They diaries were not the private record of the author. On the contrary, the diaries were written for the benefit of the other congregations and were usually read in public assemblies.

This explains their style and their content: Zeisberger referred to himself in the third person as "Brother David," and in describing events he always selected particular ones. This made it difficult to strike the right balance between a description of the political events and the narration of the religious progress of the mission, and Zeisberger was conscious of this problem. In the

273. In compiling at Lichtenau in July 1777 the list of things he needed for the following year, Zeisberger requested "three books of paper" and then added: "I have to request that the last ones should not be dealt with the same way as last year," when the orders had been filled incompletely and Zeisberger had received not three but only one book with empty pages, MAB, B 311, F 5.

274. Since communication between Fort Pitt and Schönbrunn in wartime was rather infrequent, occasionally the missionaries had to ask Christian Indians to go to the fort and fetch the goods that had arrived from Bethlehem. See entry for 7 April 1778. Occasionally even letters addressed to the missionaries remained at the fort for longer periods. See entries for 21 July and 17 Dec. 1774.

275. Unitäts-Archiv, Herrnhut, R 3, A 8, 2a.

276. See note 206 above.

spring of 1778 he wrote to Matthäus Hehl that he was not sure whether he had not discussed the events of the war in too great detail and suggested that the members of the Provincial Helpers' Conference decide "whether everything could be read in public."[277] Especially in this eighteenth part of the diary, members of the Provincial Helpers' Conference bracketed many sections that were to be omitted in the copies and not read in public.[278]

Zeisberger was aware that his diaries were read carefully in Bethlehem—not only because the readers wanted to share the difficulties and hardships of the missionaries but to make sure that the diaries met the expectations of the Provincial Helpers' Conference. Thus, after reading the eighteenth and nineteenth parts of the diary, John Ettwein concluded that Zeisberger had gotten too deeply involved with the military and political events of the Ohio region. In the spring of 1779 he communicated his critique to the missionaries: "we cannot conceal from you our concerns, that the news we have received from you has caused. It seems to us that you got yourself too much involved in the troubles of this world and thus are losing the character of a friend of all the world."[279]

Ettwein's letter may be the reason why political events after 1779 move into the background and why thereafter the diary focuses more on the daily religious events of the mission congregation. Another cause may be related to the move, in early 1779, from Lichtenau to Schönbrunn, which was farther away from the Delaware's main settlement, with the result that Zeisberger was asked less often to participate in the political affairs of the Delaware.[280]

Two other questions are important in evaluating the reliability of these diaries. First, how reliable are Zeisberger's accounts of conversations with Native Americans, and what do we make of his reports on Native American thoughts and beliefs. Second, how does one evaluate Zeisberger's observations about Native American behavior? In general we have tried to compare Zeisberger's reports about particular events with other sources; our copious annotations indicate that in general Zeisberger's reports were accurate.

Next to the narration of political and military events in the Ohio region, descriptions of the life and behavior of Native Americans, both converted and unconverted, make up the bulk of the diary. The authorities in Bethlehem made no objections to the diary passages on Native Americans (unlike the entries on political and military affairs). We have found no indication that the Provincial Helpers' Conference bracketed passages relating Native American

---

277. Zeisberger to Hehl, 14 March 1778, MAB, Lititz Records: Indian Mission. See entry for 1 Nov. 1774 below.

278. Parts bracketed and thus not included in the copies we have marked and annotated in this edition.

279. MAB, E. P., B 965, F 42, no. 1047. The letter is undated; its content places it at the time we suggest.

280. Zeisberger to Seidel, 17 Nov. 1779, MAB, Lititz Records: Indian Mission.

criticism of white settlers or Native American lifestyle or cults. On the contrary, John Ettwein specifically requested that the missionaries report these things in their diaries and reports.[281]

Zeisberger's *History* and Heckewelder's *History, Manners, and Customs* are supplemented by the ethnographic reports and observations in Zeisberger's diaries. In many cases we had to omit supplementary information or annotations because Zeisberger and Heckewelder were the only ones to report particular events. This raises a significant number of new issues about which we previously knew very little. Scholars, for example, have hitherto assumed that the Native Americans' method of selecting new chiefs—it would not be strictly accurate to speak of "election"—was heavily influenced by colonial authorities by the second half of the eighteenth century. It has been assumed that in certain cases these authorities forced their own decisions on particular tribes.

Zeisberger's account of how Netawatwees' successor was chosen suggests that this view needs revision. According to Zeisberger, the choice of successor was predetermined by the kinship of the potential candidate. Yet this was only one precondition, for the new chief needed the consent not only of the other chiefs and war captains but the approval of the nation as a whole. This process took rather a long time, as the selection of Gelelemind as Netawatwees' successor indicates.[282]

This is not to suggest that Zeisberger's ethnographic observations are always reliable. Despite his obvious interest in Native American customs and religious beliefs, Zeisberger's observations were clearly colored by Moravian religious doctrines. Zeisberger was no more free of European prejudices about "heathens" than were other missionaries of the era. His interpretations of Native American ways must always be taken with a grain of salt.[283]

Zeisberger distinguishes consistently between "friends" and "enemies" of the mission. In addition to the Mingo and the Munsee, he initially ranked as enemies the members of the Wolf tribe and parts of the Turtle tribe. Once the Head Council had in principle decided to grant the mission congregation equal status with the other Delaware settlements, Zeisberger considered only the Wolf tribe hostile to the mission. The reader learns little about the reasons for Zeisberger's impressions and must form his or her own opinion, relying primarily on Zeisberger's occasional remarks about Native American prophets and his reports of the statements of Scattameck and Gischenatsi. Zeisberger apparently saw tribal opposition in terms of Satan's unending desire for the mission's destruction, and he always perceived Native American support or opposition through this eschatological lens.

281. John Ettwein wrote to the Christian Indians at Gnadenhütten in 1774 requesting that they relate their stories, ideas, and traditions to the missionaries. These narratives were then to be compared with similar reports from mission congregations in other countries. MAB, E. P., No. 964.

282. See the annotation to the entries for 21 April 1776, 8 May 1777, 21 April 1778, and 27 Nov. 1778.

283. See entries for 12 Feb. and 1 June 1773.

This interpretative framework also guided Zeisberger in his observations of unconverted Native American settlements. The Native American as "other" was for Zeisberger always a potential convert to Christ. Given this view, he understandably tended to see the tribes' "heathenish" customs as obstacles in the path to Christ, and he naturally sought to learn as much as possible about them so as to wean the Indians away from them. The diary does not tell us clearly whether the missionaries also sought to find common religious ground with the natives, the better to convert them. What little it does say on this issue suggests that this is unlikely.

In Zeisberger's account of Native American confessions of their own feelings and states of mind, his reliance on Moravian terminology comes through clearly. Indians are "touched in their hearts," they confess that they have become "restless," they admit that something is "true," they shed "tears." The same kind of language is common to other Moravian diaries. The careful scholar should probably distinguish between Zeisberger's stereotypical terms for emotion and the actual emotion that the diary describes.

One must ask where Zeisberger got his knowledge of the feelings of Native Americans. Most probably came from the "Banden," the personal and intimate conversations between missionaries and would-be Indian converts. As we have seen, the Moravians considered these conversations a much more important tool of conversion than sermons. The Banden played crucial roles in all stages of the religious development of prospective and actual Indian members of the mission congregation. They were decisive in assessing the prospects of a person who wanted to be admitted to the settlement, who requested baptism, and who wanted to partake in the holy supper. Even when Zeisberger does not always mention a personal conversation with a given individual, we can assume that his remarks are often based on such personal conversations.

Again one must keep in mind that Zeisberger's perceptions were rooted in his eschatological framework, and that he interpreted the Indians' statements as steps in a conversion process that, to his mind, had definite and foreordained stages. According to his scheme, the process of adopting the "doctrine of the cross" had to be preceded by the unruly heart—that the process might work the other way around apparently did not occur to Zeisberger; in any case, it was not part of the schedule and the diary nowhere acknowledges this possibility. There are occasional reports of converted Indians who doubted their redemption—often as the result of conversations with non-Christian friends or of human weaknesses.

Normally, Zeisberger interpreted the increase of the mission congregation as an expression of inner unrest and of longing for Christian redemption. Only occasionally does he mention other motives—for example, that members of a particular lineage might follow their chief and convert in order to avoid being without spiritual guidance. Less dramatically, families often followed one of their members on the path of conversion to eliminate the strained relations that tended to result when only one family member converted. The conversion of Glikhican and Welapachtschiechen triggered such a response in their families. In addition, there were economic motives for conversion, especially in times of economic crisis and famine. As we have seen, Native Americans knew that even in the worst of times the Moravians would always provide food to the needy, and this was no small incentive for many natives.

Finally we must raise the question, how reliable are Zeisberger's reports of conversations between Native Americans? It is necessary to keep in mind that all such reports formed part of the general discourse about mission, except in times of severe crisis such as Lord Dunmore's war or the War for Independence. The missionaries' reports had to meet the expectations to which all Moravian mission diaries were held. With a report of conversion, the mission transcended the activity of the missionary and became the affair of the whole congregation; after their conversion, members automatically became propagators and preachers of the redemption they had found. We can draw two conclusions here. On the one hand, we can assume that such reports usually were based on personal knowledge of such conversations. And yet, in the majority of cases, the report follows a stereotypical pattern in which the newly converted confesses that he has been told "the truth." A few reported conversations end differently and thus deviate from the usual pattern. That they do not conform to the pattern suggests that these reports, too, are based on actual conversations. Since Zeisberger and the other missionaries participated in daily chores, they had many opportunities to talk to members of the congregations and witness discussions between them.

Zeisberger's reports of the conversations of others about Native Americans suffer from a second limitation in that they are usually limited to the small circle of Native American converts who had previously been chiefs, preachers, or war captains. Zeisberger's account of the conversion of Welapachtschiechen or Gelelemind is much more extensive than that of an ordinary Indian. Former chiefs such as Isaac, Israel, Augustinus, and Johannes belonged to the small circle who accompanied Zeisberger on his travels and whose words and deeds are reported in some detail. The emotions, thoughts, and adventures of others are given much less space in the diary. In other words, Zeisberger's description of Christian and non-Christian Native American society represents to a considerable degree the perspective of the chiefs and leading families of that society. Clues about the life, emotions, and worldview of ordinary Indians must be sought in occasional hints and observations. The diary offers many such clues, which is part of its extraordinary value.

THE TRANSLATION

When the German edition of the diaries was published, many American friends asked us why we had gone to the trouble of producing an edition of obvious use to American ethno-historians and historians of mission in a language we knew they would be unable to read. Our response was always that we thought it vitally important to produce a scholarly edition of the original before undertaking an English translation.

A translation can never measure up to the original, a truism that we trust finds wide acceptance. Yet the consequences of this truism have been elaborated only within recent decades by scholars who specialize in analyzing translations.[284] Closer to these diaries is the relatively recent discussion of the problem of translation in eighteenth-century treaty negotiations between colonial authorities and Native American tribes.[285] Zeisberger's diary is a document already one step removed from the original, in that Zeisberger communicated with the Delaware in their own language but wrote his diary in German. He transferred the cultural meanings associated with the language of the Delaware into the cultural meanings of German; in the process he not only lost indigenous cultural meanings but added new cultural meanings to his German words.

We are familiar with this phenomenon in reverse: the British assigned English names to Native American offices, positions, activities, and customs. Thus they called speakers of Indian settlements "kings" and Indian governing bodies "councils." These terms stuck, and by the eighteenth century, whites, both laypeople and scholars, were using them without giving the matter much thought. Zeisberger uses some of these English terms, notably "chief" and "war captain"; he combines these with other German words. Thus, for example, he calls the matters with which chiefs dealt "chief affairen";[286] in eighteenth-century German an "affair," a word taken from the French, means an individual event. Zeisberger's words, then, suggest less the range of competences associated with the office but an ensemble of individual events and matters, although he was of course familiar with the idea that a ruler or officeholder was defined by a range of duties, functions, tasks, and rights that defined his authority. In order to remain as close as possible to Zeisberger's terminology, we have translated "chief affairen" as "chief affairs." In general, Zeisberger's English terminology—"town," "Nation," and so on—have been retained. Since Zeisberger wrote these words in Latin, we have set them in italics. And we have retained Zeisberger's use of uppercase with certain English and Latin terms. All underlining in this translation is Zeisberger's.

284. I am drawing here on Kittel and Frank, *Interculturality and the Historical Study of Literary Translations*, and on Frank et al., *Übersetzen, verstehen, Brückenbauen*.

285. See Fausz, "Middlemen in Peace and War." In general, see Szasz, *Between Indian and White Worlds*, a collection of important essays; especially valuable is Hagedorn, "'Faithful, Knowing, and Prudent': Andrew Montour as Interpreter" (44–60), and Szasz, "Samson Occom" (61–78). See also Hagedorn, "'A Friend to Go Between Them'"; Galloway, "Talking with Indians"; Richter, "Cultural Brokers and Intercultural Politics"; Merrell, "Shikellemi, 'A Person of Consequence'"; McConnell, "Pisquetomen and Tamaqua"; and Merrell, *Into the American Woods*. A list of participants in treaty negotiations between the Six Indian Nations and colonial authorities is published in Jennings and Fenton, *History and Culture of Iroquois Diplomacy*, 229–55.

286. See, e.g., entry for 24 Aug. 1774 below.

Other terms pose more serious problems. For example, Zeisberger calls a kinship group within a clan a "Freundschaft." Today this German word means what binds two friends together: affection, but in the eighteenth century it also meant a kinship tie. What the German word does not mean and has never meant is something equally important within Delaware and other tribal cultures: a kinship group bound together in a particular cult. Zeisberger says that the eldest member of the "friendship" had to "perform the annual sacrifices," but "friendship" is not really an adequate translation here.[287] In the case of Welapachtschiechen's "friendship," Zeisberger offers more details: in the middle of the house of the "friendship," he writes, was "ein Pfosten, woran ein ausgeschnitztes Gesicht . . . und welches ihr Haus Göze ist." We have translated this as: "a post . . . where there was a face carved out and which is their house idol."[288] Clearly, Zeisberger knew of the religious aspect of a "friendship." The Delaware of course automatically associated the religious component with their word, whereas Zeisberger associated that meaning with "Freundschaft" whenever he used it in this particular sense (he does use it, too, in the modern sense of "friendship"); nevertheless, in the process of translation from Delaware to German to English, the religious and cultic meaning is lost for twenty-first-century readers.

The translation sometimes adds fuzzy meanings to terms, or puts them in different contexts in which their original meaning is altered significantly. Zeisberger undoubtedly used German terms that he thought best captured the spirit of the Delaware, but we can only try to recapture these associations. In the case of "Freundschaft" this is not so difficult; in other cases it is not so easy.

Another semantic aspect of the diary poses equally serious problems for the translator. The Moravians' religious language was influenced by their theological views; they invented their own language to describe the intensity of their religious emotions. Had we tried to translate this kind of language into English word for word, the result would have been incomprehensible to English speakers. In making the fundamental decision to produce a readable text, we have consciously decided to accept the loss in intensity of religious feelings embodied in Moravian pietistic language.

For example, on 14 April 1775 Zeisberger wrote:

> Den 14ten Frühe nach der AbendMahls *Liturgie* wurde der Anfang gemacht mit Verlesung der Marter Geschichte, welche mit weichen und zerflossenen Herzen angehört wurde und Nachmittags hatten die Getauften Geschwister eine *Liturgie* zur Eröfnung der Seite.[289] Es waren so viele fremde Indianer hier als noch nie gewesen, so daß unser

287. See entry for 14 Jan. 1773.
288. See entry for 10 Feb. 1777.
289. On the meaning of "Piercing of the Side," see p. 55 above.

Saal der doch gut 300 Menschen fassen kann, zu klein wurde und manche wurden kräftig gerührt und angefaßt.

We have translated this entry as:

THE 14TH.   Early in the day after the *Liturgy* for Holy Communion, we began reading the Passion story. People listened with tender and melting hearts, and in the afternoon the baptized Brothers and Sisters had a *Liturgy* commemorating the Piercing of the Side.[290] There were more Indian strangers here than there had ever been, and our Meeting Hall, which can easily hold 300 people, was too small. Many were powerfully moved and touched.

Here we have translated "Marter Geschichte" into "Passion story"—knowing full well that "Marter" means "torture" in English. Had we translated "we began reading the torture story," this would not have made any sense to the reader. Yet "torture," of course, is more direct and explicit, and it evokes the pictures of horror that, in Moravian theology, Christ suffered for our sins. His sacrifice is greater when described as "torture" than when simply called "passion."

"Weichen and zerflossenen Herzen" we rendered as "tender and melting hearts." Again, we tried to stay as close as possible to the original, but transferring it into another linguistic culture has again meant a loss of meaning, for "weich," literally translated, means "soft"—but a "soft heart" does not convey the correct meaning to the modern reader. "Weich" in Moravian parlance indeed comes close to "tender"; but in this case the Moravians used the word "weich" in the sense of "easily to be shaped"—in contrast to "hart" (English "hard"), that which resists impressions, refuses to be shaped or influenced by affections. "Zerflossenen" we have rendered as "melting." "Zerflossen," however, in this specific context means something closer to "melted in tears" "dissolved under the weight of emotional impressions," while "melting" may suggest to today's reader something more like the melting of ice cream. Again, a bit of the emotional and religious intensity is lost in translation. Finally, we have translated "Eröffnung der Seite" as "Piercing of the Side"—in this case we have added a note explaining the image involved. Yet again the translation has created new meanings: "Eröffnung" means "opening," a fairly neutral term; the word "piercing," by contrast, suggests the action of the Roman soldier who pushed his spear into the side of Jesus on the cross—the image depicted in the paintings with which we are familiar. The English emphasizes the horror; the German stresses the creation of a place where the soul of the con-

290. Cf. notes 204–5 above.

verted can rest and become one with the dying Jesus—a particularly important concept in the Moravian liturgy of the "sifting period."

Translations are transfer processes from one culture into another; they lose meanings and create new meanings, however faithfully the translator tries to stay close to the original. The reader who wants to make sure that he has understood Zeisberger's meanings must therefore consult not only the English translation but the German original as well. And this is why we first published a scholarly edition of the original text.

A final remark. The original edition reproduces the idiosyncrasies of the manuscript, with its erasures, additions, omissions, marginalia, and so on. Zeisberger used many abbreviations, all of which we have spelled out and rendered in English in this translation. To reproduce these idiosyncrasies in the English translation in a way that was faithful to the letter of the original would have again produced an unreadable text. We refer readers to the German original if they are in any doubt as to the accuracy or faithfulness of the English translation. The German edition, like this one, includes the page references of the original. Words or sentences crossed out by Zeisberger appear enclosed in {braces}. Words or sentences bracketed by others are annotated. Spelling variations in the diaries have not been corrected.

The
Moravian Mission Diaries
of

DAVID
ZEISBERGER

1772–1781

Brother David Zeisberger's Diary of his trip and stay with Five Families of Indian Brothers and Sisters in the Area of Gekelemukpechünk.[1]

APRIL 14TH   We began our journey with the Watchword, *And I will make an everlasting covenant with them, that I will not turn away from them, to do them good; but I will put my fear in their hearts, that they shall not depart from me. Grant that we remain with you and join us to your body. . . .*[2] The following Indian Brothers and Sisters went with us: *Jeremias* and *Anna Caritas, Lucas* and *Pauline, Isaac* and *Agnes, Nicolaus* and *Amalia, Levi* and *Salome,* and the single Brother *Jacob.*[3] In the evening we arrived at *Sakunk*[4] and the following day we crossed the *Fall* with all of our belongings. One *Canow* almost had an accident when they tried to ride down with it loaded. They would certainly have lost everything if they had not gotten it back onto land, which was really difficult. Originally we had intended for some people to go with the cattle directly by land from here, but at this point we decided to stay together, or at least that we should all meet in the night camp each evening.

THE 16TH   We had to stay where we were because of strong winds. In our devotional service we reflected on the Savior's bloody sweat on the Mount of Olives.[5]

THE 17TH   We continued on and in the evening we arrived at the little *Beaver Creek,* where we all spent the night together. In the evening devotion we described the Savior in his complete suffering, from head to foot, to the Brothers and Sisters. There was a very blessed feeling during this.

THE 18TH   We continued on. However, those who were going with the cattle on land had to take a bad road. Actually there is not a road at all, and they just cut through the bush. Some cattle lagged behind because of the steep mountains and we left them some miles behind. Late in the evening we all reached the night camp. Here the *Ohio* runs directly east for a while, but then it turns back toward the south. Across from us we also passed a couple of fields where White people have settled.

THE 19TH   Early in the day we had a service celebrating our Lord's

---

1. MAB, B 141, F 1, fol. 1. Zeisberger and the converted Indians had set out from Langundoutenünk. Gekelemukpechünk was the center of the Delaware settlements on the Muskingum and seat of the Council and chief of the Delaware; see notes 6 and 15 below.

2. Jer. 32:40. "Gib daß wir an dir bleiben und uns dir einverleiben," etc. *Das kleine Brüder-Gesang-Buch,* hymn no. 338.

3. For short biographical notes on persons mentioned in the text, see the Register of Persons. An important reason for choosing these particular Christian Indians was that they had been members of the congregation for long periods and had proved themselves trustworthy. Another reason was their familiarity with both the Ohio region and the Delaware who settled there.

4. For short descriptions of the villages and towns mentioned in the text, see the Index of Place and River Names.

5. Luke 22:44. In their religious meditations the Moravians focused on the sufferings of Christ on the cross. See Introduction, 52–55.

resurrection. Then some of us went and fetched the cattle. We stayed here and rested today because it was raining and the cattle were sickly.

THE 20TH   We sent a *Canow* and two messengers ahead with a message to the *Chiefs* in *Gekelemukpechünk*[6] to find out if they could meet us at the river with horses. In the meantime, we continued on slowly until the afternoon of THE 21ST, when we reached a *Mingo Town*.[7] Below this a *Creek*[8] runs into the *Ohio* and the road turns off to *Gekelemukpechünk*. We camped here and waited for our messengers. These *Mingo,* who are *Senecas,*[9] told us that when they heard we were moving away from *Langundouteniünk*[10] they had already decided to take possession of our *Town*. However, they later heard that only some of us were moving away, so then some of them went down the *Ohio* and some went upstream. The few who are still here all want to move away in a few days. Their leaders and *Chiefs* ordered them to leave because many complaints had been made against them, since they are a very slovenly people who do nothing but rob, steal and murder among the White people.[11]

THE 22ND AND 23RD   Many of them visited us, as did the *Delaware* who were staying in this area. We proclaimed the Savior to many of them. Our people also bought a couple of horses here.

THE 24TH   Our messengers returned from *Gekelemukpechünk* with the news that almost no Indians were at home there. They had all scattered into the bush to hunt because of a shortage of food, and so they did not see how

6. In 1771 Zeisberger described the settlement thus: "Gekelemukpechünk on the Muskingum River is a pretty large Indian town which, as I am told, consists of about 100 houses, which agrees with my own personal observation. Most of them are block houses. The house of the chief is built of squared wood with a wood floor and stairs made of wooden boards and masoned chimney; it is certainly the most spacious in the town covered with shingles, as are some others. The region is pleasant, it is a big flat countryside, the soil is very good on both sides of the river which is here as wide as the Delaware at Eastown. Yet six miles further down it is joined by another river which is as large. Tuscarawi, a settlement that is now deserted, was situated at a branch of this river about 40 miles north from here; many travel from Pittsburgh to this place on the river." Friedensstadt [i.e., Langundoutenünk] Diary, entry for 23 March 1771, report of Zeisberger about his travel to Gekelemukpechünk, MAB, B 137, 1770–72.

7. Probably Logan's Town. The town had been named after Chief Logan, a son of the Oneida Shikellemi (see note 432) below for entry of 26 June 1774).

8. Ohio Cross Creek.

9. In calling these Indians "Mingo" (occasionally "Minque"), Zeisberger uses the Delaware's summary designation for Iroquois who had migrated into the Ohio region. On the migration of Iroquois, especially Seneca, into the Ohio region and their role there between 1772 and 1782, see Introduction, 13–16. The Seneca were one of the Six Indian Nations.

10. The German name of this settlement was Friedensstadt; this Moravian mission town on the Beaver River in the neighborhood of Kaskaskunk had been founded in 1770.

11. With these remarks Zeisberger echoes Delaware antipathy toward the Six Indian Nations in general and toward the Mingo in the Ohio region in particular. For background, see Introduction, 13–14. Since the Seven Years' War, the Council of the Six Indian Nations had tried in vain to induce the Mingo to leave the Ohio region and return to their original tribal areas (McConnell, *A Country Between,* 136–37, 246–47); between 1772 and 1782 they continued these efforts. See entries for 26 Aug., 12 Sept., and 3 Dec. 1774.

they could help us. The *Chief*[12] was indeed very concerned and wanted to help us. He promised to do what he could. He advised us to have a couple of *Canows* brought around with the heavy *Baggage,* which we managed to do on THE 25TH. We had originally intended to go by water this far, and to travel together from this point on over land as far as the *Gekelemukpechünk Creek.*[13] Brother *Levi* and Sister *Salome's* baby daughter, who was just a few weeks old, died yesterday evening and she was buried here this evening. Then those of us who were going by land set out early on THE 26TH. Some of our people suggested it might be better to spend the summer here and to plant, and then perhaps to move on in the fall or next spring since it is already pretty late in the spring and we had an empty *Town* and a large area of clear land, the *Mingo's* fields, ahead of us. We did not decide on this for various reasons, however.

THE 28TH   We arrived at the source of the *Gekelemukpechünk.* The road leading there is very mountainous and although the mountains are not high, they are still very steep. There is plentiful limestone in this area, which is otherwise scarce in this part of the country.

THE 29TH   We were just getting ready to leave in the morning when *Echpalawehund,* one of the *Chiefs* in *Gekelemukpechünk,*[14] and a couple other Indians met us with some horses they had rounded up hastily. So today we got as far down the *Creek* as it is navigable. We spent the night here.

THE 30TH   We constructed a large *Canow* out of reeds for our children and heavy *Baggage,* because from here we had to *march* straight through the bush without any paths. I spoke a great deal with the *Chief.* He told me that since he had heard about the Savior during my visit in *Gekelemukpechünk*[15] and had begun to realize that he was a wretched human, he had already reflected a great deal upon himself. I extolled to him the Savior as the redeemer of our sins; he saves sinners.

[May]

MAY 1ST   We continued on, some by water and the rest on land. The *Chief* returned home with his people after they had instructed our people which route we should take to get through the bush as easily as possible.

12. Netawatwees (Newcomer, in English), chief of the Turtle clan and at the same time chief of the Delaware (see Introduction, 17); he died on 31 October 1776.

13. There existed two routes to the Muskingum region. The shorter and more difficult one was overland; the Zeisberger party used this road. The longer route used the Beaver, Ohio, Muskingum, and Tuscarawas Rivers and Gekelemukpechünk Creek (today Stillwater Creek). The group led by Heckewelder used this route in 1773; see entry for 3 May 1773.

14. On 6 February 1774 Echpalawehund was baptized "Petrus" in Gnadenhütten.

15. Zeisberger had visited Gekelemukpechünk in March 1771. On that occasion he had agreed with the Council on the establishment of a mission town. See Introduction, 49–50.

THE 2ND   Our boat of reeds did not return to us until this morning. We were already on the *Mushkingum*,[16] and we continued upstream on it. In our night camp we received many visits from Indians who were hunting around here, including some acquaintances. They expressed their joy that we had come so far and told us they would visit us often.

MAY 3RD   We were overjoyed to arrive at our site on the big *Spring* toward noon, on exactly the same date on which we arrived in *Langundouteniink* 3 years ago.[17] Our hearts were happy and grateful that the Savior had assisted us so mercifully on this difficult journey. We camped here and erected huts today and looked around the area again for the best site to establish the *Town*. However, we did not find one more suitable or better than the one we had previously designated for this. The Watchword was noteworthy and comforting to us, *Their children also shall be as aforetime, and their congregation shall be established before me.*[18]

THE 4th   We laid out the fields and everyone began clearing land right away. We continued with this until we were finished.

THE 7TH   One of our Indian Brothers came and brought us news that they had made it as far as *Gekelemukpechünk* with the *Canows*. They were quite worn out, so four Brothers went there today to relieve them and bring the *Canows* all the way here. They arrived with them on THE 9TH. After they had left us, they traveled 3 more days down the high waters of the *Ohio* and then 12 days up this river. This is indeed a very big detour, but the *Mushkingum* is quite navigable and does not have any falls. They passed various Indian *Towns* as well as a *Shawnee Town*.[19] There is great famine everywhere, for which the Indian preacher *Scattameck*[20] is responsible. A year ago he deceived them by saying that if they just believed in him, enough Indian corn would grow even if they only planted a little. *Chief Netawatwees* therefore called all his people together and warned them not to believe these lies any more. They should plant as much as possible so that they could share with their friends they were expecting from *Fridenshütten* this summer. In the meantime, the young people should hunt diligently and provide meat for those who are working there. Many of those there who are unfavorably inclined, who are opposed to the preaching of the Gospel, left and moved far away when they heard that we were approaching. Just recently the *Chief* told his people in a public *Councel* that they should be happy the Brothers were coming into this area to preach the Gospel to them, and he advised them to accept it. He also told them that

16. "Mushkingum," more often spelled in this diary "Muskingum," a branch of the Ohio River, where most of the settlements of the Delaware were situated. Farther north the Muskingum divides into the Walhanding and the Tuscarawas.

17. See Introduction, p. 49.

18. Jer. 30:20.

19. The reference is to Woaketameki on the Muskingum, the main settlement of the Shawnee in this region; it was deserted around 1774. See entry for 17 Oct. 1772.

20. On preachers in Native American societies, see Introduction, p. 20.

anyone who wanted to listen to us or to live with us would not be prevented from doing so. Then a head man from a small *Town*[21] above *Gekelemukpechünk* stood up and said he would never agree to this; even if they all wanted to live as we do, he would not. Therefore he left the area with all of his people and left his *Town* and fields lying abandoned.

THE 10TH   We had blessed Sunday services, and although there are now only a few of us, the Savior very graciously allowed himself to be felt among us.[22]

THE 11TH   *Michael* and two other Indians who had helped us this far returned to *Langundoutenünk.*

THE 13TH   Some Indians from *Gekelemukpechünk* who were visiting us spent the night here. Because they wanted to listen, we explained our God and Savior on the cross to them. They were very attentive during this.

THE 18TH   Once again an Indian, a very reasonable man, came from there for a visit. He found me completely alone in the field,[23] greeted me cordially, and said that he came to visit us because he had heard that there would be preaching here and he really wanted to hear this. I told him that what he had heard was indeed true, sat down with him, and explained to him the way to salvation, that there is no other way to be saved except through faith in Jesus Christ who bought us with his precious blood and freed us from Satan and eternal damnation. He was very attentive and said he had already heard all the Indian preachers in this whole area, but found nothing in their preaching which blessed him. Therefore he doubted whether they were preaching the truth. I replied that I could assure him he would not find anything for his heart anywhere except in the word of Jesus' death and sufferings. If he could sincerely believe that God, the creator of heaven and earth, became human and shed his blood for him, then he would feel blessed from that hour on. The Indians had lived in ignorance and blindness for so many years and did not know anything about God. Now, however, He had also remembered them in grace and was having his word proclaimed to them. Whoever accepted this now and believed it would be saved. He spent the night with us and also

21. On 17 October 1772 Zeisberger passed this settlement on his way to the Shawnee settlements farther south. According to his report there were three Delaware settlements between Gekelemukpechünk and the first small Shawnee settlement. One of the three was White Eyes' Town; the southernmost of the three and the one closest to the Shawnee towns was the settlement where there lived those "who fled from us last spring when they heard that we would settle in the region of Gekelemukpechünk, because they do not want to listen to the gospel." See Zeisberger's report inserted for 17 Oct. 1772 below.

22. In a letter to Johann Georg Jungmann dated 10 May (MAB, B 229, F 4, I 2), Zeisberger reported on the arduous trip and the heavy physical labor in building the settlement. He had his own hut but shared a fireplace with Jeremia. Zeisberger does not use the term "religious service" but speaks of religious "occasions," a term that encompasses all kinds of religious assemblies. We have translated his terms as "service" or "devotion." In these services he spoke Delaware, although occasionally he lacked the right words. En route, the Holy Communion cup and the baptismal font broke.

23. On the missionaries' participation in tilling fields, see Introduction, p. 65–66.

attended our services. Afterward he told our Indian Brothers, who also spoke a great deal more with him, that he was surprised he could understand me so well, since he could not understand anything from the Indians' sermons or make any sense out of them. He could even understand some when we sang, although not all of it, and he was happy to hear that we sing in his language.[24]

THE 19TH   He returned home and was very grateful for what he had heard. Today we began to clear a piece of land together for our Indians from *Fridenshütten* and to plant as much as we will be able to manage.

THE 23RD   There was a powerful storm with rain and hail. Because of the many trees around us, we had to flee from our huts during the worst weather. We fled together to an open site where there were few trees and watched as the storm blew down trees like people mow grass. None of our huts was actually damaged after all, but part of our town square and especially some of our fields were badly damaged.

THE 28TH   It was Ascension Day and we had a blessed Service of Adoration in the morning, during which we prayed for the Savior's precious presence forever. Through an Indian who was recently in *Langundoutenünk*, I received a letter from Brother *Jungmann* which had already been opened.[25] Because of all the rainy weather lately, the water was very rough.

THE 30TH   I was delighted that *Isaac* and *Jacob*, who returned from *Langundoutenünk*, brought me letters from Bethlehem and *Litiz* as well as Watchwords and Texts for this year from *Philadelphia*.[26]

[June]

JUNE 5TH   Recently many guests have come to visit us. Some of them really wanted to listen, and our Indian Brothers are always prepared and willing on such occasions to proclaim the Savior and his death to them. The Indians said that their *Chief, Netawatwees,* always told them they should give up their

24. From the beginning of his missionary work, Zeisberger translated biblical texts and Christian songs into Delaware; he discussed his translations with experienced Delaware members of the congregation. See entry for 31 Jan. 1773. The first printed collection of hymns was published in Philadelphia in 1803 under the title *A Collection of Hymns for the Use of the Christian Indians, of the Missions of the United Brethren in North America*. Other missionaries, too, had translated hymns, e.g., Bernhard Adam Grube, who in 1763 in Friedensthal published a collection under the title *Dellawaerisches Gesang-Büchlein. Wenn ich des Morgens früh aufsteh etc. Translat. 1. Enda wopanachinaane*.

25. In September, Johann Georg Jungmann (1720–1808) came from Friedensstadt to Schönbrunn. See entry for 29 Sept. 1772 below.

26. The Watchwords were drawn by lots in Herrnhut and thence sent to North America. Until 1776 Henry Miller, the Philadelphia printer, printed the required number of copies, for this year under the title *Die täglichen Loosungen der Brüder-Gemeine für das Jahr 1772*. See Arndt and Eck, *First Century of German Language Printing*, 1:180. By "Texts" Zeisberger means the Lehrtexte, which suggested particular Bible verses for daily meditation. Published by Henry Miller in Philadelphia under the title *Die Lehr-Texte der Brüder-Gemeine für das Jahr 1772*, they were usually bound together with the Watchwords.

slovenly and bad life, and instead should work diligently and attend services here. He sent all the Indians from this area and from *Kaskaskunk*[27] out to hunt, and each hunter was supposed to bring back 3 buckskins which would be used for the peace negotiations with other *Nations*[28] such as the *Wyandot, Chippewa,* and *Shawnee,* as well as for messages to the *Mohicans* in *Stockbridge* and that area, who have been called to this area.[29] He did not request anything like this from us.

It seems that the Indian preachers, two of whom had come to *Gekelemuk-pechünk* recently, have already lost heart and are no longer preaching. Instead they now said they wanted to come to our place and hear if they could perhaps also become believers.

JUNE 7TH   We asked our dear Mother[30] for merciful *Absolution* for all the ways we so often cause her sorrow and for not listening to her voice adequately. We commended ourselves anew to her faithful care and promised her faithfulness and obedience. We also had visitors from elsewhere. Most of them came here just to find food though, because there is great need everywhere. Most of the Indians are now living only from hunting, wild potatoes, and other edible plants.[31]

THE 9TH   I moved into my house, which we had built some days ago

27. Main Delaware settlement on the Beaver River.

28. The term "Nation" designates for Zeisberger a specific ethnic unity characterized by a governing council, common history, culture, and belief system, as well as a common language whose dialects may have differed significantly. For Zeisberger, the Deleware "Nation" is divided into the three tribes of Turtle, Turkey, and Wolf. A clan was composed of so-called "lineages," which Zeisberger calls "Freundschaften" ("friendships"). See Introduction, p. 18, note 42, and p. 17, notes 38 and 39.

29. Since February 1772 both John Stuart and Sir William Johnson (on Johnson, see note 120 for entry under 26 Dec. 1772) knew of efforts to organize conferences whose purpose was to mediate the conflicts between the southern, western, and northern Indian nations. The first such conference, at which no whites participated, seems to have met in the spring of 1772 at the Scioto River in the main settlement area of the Shawnee. The second conference, which had been convened at the Scioto River in September or October 1772, was not very successful, according to reports by Thomas Gage and Sir William Johnson. A number of western tribes do not seem to have participated. Davies, *Documents of the American Revolution,* 5:34–35, 58–61, 203, 211–14. French sources usually refer to Wyandot as "Huron," yet Zeisberger and Heckewelder prefer their Delaware name, *Delamattenos* or *Delamattenoos,* which means "people who live in the hills." In this translation, we always use the term "Wyandot." For information on this tribe, see Tooker, "Wyandot"; on the Shawnee, see Callender, "Shawnee"; on the Mahican, who had migrated from Stockbridge to the eastern region of the Ohio, see Brasser, "Mahican." The Moravian missionary Johann Jacob Schmick wrote a dictionary of their language; see [Schmick], *Schmick's Mahican Dictionary,* 197, and note 114 for entry under 25 Dec. 1772. On the Chippewa, who were called Ojibway in Canada, see Rogers, "Southeastern Ojibwa."

30. The reference to the Holy Spirit as "Mother" was part of Moravian religious terminology. Zinzendorf called the Holy Spirit "beloved Mother," because the Holy Spirit cared for Christians in a motherly fashion. Together with God the Father and Jesus Christ the Son, this trinity was perceived as a family. See Reichel, *Dichtungstheorie und Sprache bei Zinzendorf,* 61; Bettermann, *Theologie und Sprache bei Zinzendorf,* 61. In the diaries these terms are used in connection with Pentecost or in the concluding formulas at the end of the year; sometimes "beloved Mother" is crossed out by another hand and replaced by "Holy Spirit." In 1772, 7 June was Pentecost Sunday.

31. On the importance of the mission settlements as supply centers for the region, see Introduction, p. 69.

after we were completely finished planting. For the time being, we will also hold our devotions in it. Thus far we have been holding them under the open sky.

THE 12TH   Brothers *Jeremias* and *Nicolaus* returned from *Gekelemukpechünk* where they had gone on business the day before yesterday. A letter had come there from *Virginia* for the *Chief* and his *Councel*. In this they are asked to accept a preacher or *Minister* from the White people, but, it seems they do not approve of this.[32] The *Chief* says, We already have preachers, the Brothers. Anyone who wants to hear can go there. We do not need any more preachers.

THE 14TH   Via *Langundouteniünk*, I received letters from *Litiz* and from Brother *Ettwein* in Bethlehem.[33]

THE 15TH   Another family came here for a visit. They said they also hoped to live with us and to become believers. We hear similar things from many Indians in the area. If only we were somewhat settled in; currently we are not yet set up for many visitors because we have neither rooms nor food.

THE 20TH   *Echpalawehund*, the *Chief* who met us with horses on our journey here, passed through here on his return journey from *Kaskaskunk*. He was happy to see us here. He said that since he did not have much time to spend with us, we should preach to him a little bit quickly. He has not heard anything more since he left us. We did so and acquainted him with the Savior who accepts sinners and gladly saves them, until he said a cordial farewell and continued his journey. He is a forthright and honest man, loves us, and wishes us well.

THE 25TH   A family of ten from *Gekelemukpechünk* arrived here to live with us. We would have preferred that they wait, but they refused to be turned away. They said they had considered this well and were completely resolved to belong to the Savior.

THE 27TH   After we had spoken with the Brothers and Sisters, we celebrated the first Holy Communion here. The Savior very graciously revealed himself to us. *Agnes*, *Isaac*'s wife, observed for the first time and *Nicolaus* and *Amalia* for the second time.[34]

THE 28TH   We held our usual Sunday services. We talked with the family who moved in with us, asked about their circumstances, acquainted them with our rules,[35] and accepted them provisionally. The woman is our

32. This was probably not an official request of the governor and council of Virginia, for no such thing is mentioned in the official protocol of the council. McIlwaine et al., *Executive Journals of the Council of Colonial Virginia*, 6: passim.

33. The Moravian congregation at Lititz, Pennsylvania, was served by Mattheus Hehl (1704–87); see Schweitzer, "Significance of a Newly Discovered Volume." Ettwein refers to Johann [John] Ettwein (1721–1802).

34. Participation in the Holy Communion depended on one's spiritual status, which on the same or the previous day was assessed by the missionaries in an intimate conversation with the member of the congregation. See Introduction, p. 63.

35. The rules of statutes for Schönbrunn are published in the appendix.

Lucas's sister.[36] They are very poor people materially, and also sickly. This is generally how the Indians are when they come to us. They hardly have enough to cover their bodies and no food at all, until they have stayed with us a while and learned to live properly.

THE 30TH   The woman spoke with her brother *Lucas* and told him she had been so sick for a long time that she could not walk another step. She had always wanted to postpone moving here until she was better. Finally she felt that she would not become well until she came to our place, so she asked her husband to bring her here and he did so. She had to be carried to a *Canow*. In the first night's camp she had begun to walk again for the first time and by the time she arrived here she was so strong that she could have come to us herself from the *Canow*; now she felt completely well. Therefore she fully believed that it was the Savior's will for her to live with us and to believe in Him, and she really desires this.

[July]

JULY 4TH   *Gertraut's* brother *Zeno* came here for a visit. He is another of those who committed the massacre on the *Mahony*.[37] Because he expressed a desire to hear the Gospel, we extolled to him the Savior as the redeemer of all the world's sins and explained that we all had to be saved through faith in Him. However, we soon saw that he was not yet concerned about his salvation and about the Savior, but just wanted to hear something new and unusual.

THE 7TH AND 8TH   More visitors came and our services were well attended. Some of our people went to *Langundouteniünk*.

THE 13TH   *Jacob* returned from there. I was delighted that he brought along letters from Brother *Matthao* in *Litiz* and from Brother *Ettwein* in *Great Island*[38] and also a message to the *Chiefs* in *Gekelemukpechünk* from our Indians in *Fridenshütten*.[39]

36. A high percentage of those Indians who joined the mission congregations between 1772 and 1781 were relatives of converted Indians. Lucas is a good example; after his sister and her large family had joined the settlement, Lucas's brother followed suit. He was baptized Jonas on 1 January 1774. Among the strangers who visited Schönbrunn on 24 April 1775, during the famine, were "Lucas['s] friends from Goschgoschünk." On 4 May 1775 that family received permission to move to Schönbrunn.

37. On 24 November 1755 a group of Indians who were French allies joined French soldiers in an assault on the Moravian mission settlement Gnadenhütten I on the Mahony and killed nine missionaries. See Schweinitz, *Zeisberger*, 220–40; Heckewelder, *History, Manners, and Customs*, 44–46; for a contemporary report, see [Franklin], *Papers of Benjamin Franklin*, 6:340–42, 348–51.

38. "Brother Matthao" refers to Mattheus Hehl, "Brother Ettwein" to Johann Ettwein. "Great Island" is today named Lock Haven on the right bank of the west branch of the Susquehanna River in Clinton County, Pa. See map in the appendix.

39. The members of this mission place on the Susquehanna were on their way to their new abodes in the Ohio valley. On the mission in Friedenshütten, see Introduction, p. 48.

THE 14TH   We sent this on. It brought much joy there and they were very excited when they heard they are actually on their way here.

THE 20TH   A couple of Indians who are staying not far from here while hunting came here for a visit and they wanted to listen. One said he had been trying to find the right way to salvation for many years. Therefore when he met Indians whom he believed knew more than he did, he gave them gifts and many *Belts of Wampum*[40] in the hope that they would tell him something. However, no one yet has been able to teach him how to be saved. Those to whom he had given gifts just greeted him cordially when he went to see them. The Brothers then told him that if that was what he was seeking, he had now found it here. He did not need to look any further or give any gifts. They would gladly tell him at no cost. He should believe in the Savior who became human for us and shed his blood for us. In this way he would attain forgiveness for his sins and eternal life and salvation.

THE 25TH   An old woman had been here visiting for a number of days and had not missed any services. She returned home. She had liked it so well that she said she would move here to our place in the fall, along with her children who are already grown and of the same mind she is. They moved over here from *Kaskaskunk* last spring and settled on this river.

THE 29TH   Some people came from *Gekelemukpechünk* in order to pick up their friends, the family who moved here to live with us, because evil Indians had threatened them by saying things would not go well for them and that they would be burned alive if they stayed here. They said this to frighten them and scare them away. However, they could not be persuaded to move away from here. The woman particularly said she could not live with the savages[41] again; she wanted to turn to the Savior with her whole heart. Those who wanted to take them away also changed their minds after they had been here for several days and had attended our services regularly. They said, far be it from us to oppose our friends. We ourselves have now heard what is preached here and believe it is the truth, and we hope to become believers yet.

[August]

AUGUST 2ND   The sermon was about the words: Go ye therefore, and teach all nations.[42] During this the baby girl born to Brother *Lucas* and Sister

---

40. Wampum were beads made of shells polished and strung together in belts. They were not only used as currency but also had ceremonial significance. In formal negotiations they symbolized the contents of a speech and served as reminders. If a belt was accepted, the message conveyed in the speech was accepted, too. Wampum belts are described in Duke, "Iroquois Treaties," 88–90. On their function, see also Foster, "Another Look at the Function of Wampum."

41. I.e., non-Christian Indians.

42. Matt. 28:19.

Pauline on the 30th of last month was baptized with the name *Anna*. They were the first ones baptized in *Lawunakhannek* and their child is now also the first here. Some of the guests present, including our *Abraham*'s sister, were very moved and touched.

THE 5TH   An elderly Indian spent the night with us. He is well known for having been a great sorcerer[43] who could travel a long distance through the air and return in one night. He is now in such miserable circumstances that he can hardly get around on horse and would starve if others did not share with him, yet he continues to deceive the Indians, saying he could still do exactly the same thing if he wanted. *Jeremias*, in whose house he was, preached to him a little and told him that all Indians lived in blindness and would be lost if they did not come to know the Savior. No feeling or life could be seen in him, however.

THE 7TH   *Echpalawehund*, the often-mentioned *Chief*, came here on his return journey from *Langundoutenünk* and brought me a letter from Brother *Ettwein*. From this I was delighted to learn of his safe arrival there.[44] The *Chief* spent the night with us and stayed in my house with me until midnight. He discussed various matters and shared his heart with me. He was now trying to free himself of the *Affairs* of *Chief* and to come to our place, where he believed he would have a blessed life. The office of *Chief* was nothing after all, and all his efforts and work were in vain. He asked me what I thought about this. I answered him that he should not be too hasty, but should consider well what he was doing. As long as he could stay in *Gekelemukpechünk*, he should not leave. In the meantime he could visit us occasionally and hear about the Savior as often as he wanted to, and he should love us as we loved him in return. Yes, he said, but the Indians who are not your friends are already saying I am one of you now. This will not cease, but will continue so that in the end I will not be able to stay there. I told him we were not very eager for the *Chiefs* to come live with us. We would be very happy with them if they just remained our friends and loved the faithful Indians, and we would thank the Savior for this. However, if a person could no longer endure it among the savages and then came to us, we would not send him away.

He is *Netawatwees*' best and most reliable man in carrying out *Affairs* in the *Council*, and we feared that if he came to our place all our good friends in the *Council* would follow him and *Netawatwees* would eventually get weary of this and lay down his office as *Chief* and come to our place. Then there would be no one to keep control over the savages who oppose us.[45]

43. On the function of sorcerers and their relation to Indian preachers in Native American societies, see entry for 11 Sept. 1773 and note 264 thereto.

44. On 1 and 5 August, respectively, Johann Ettwein and Johannes Roth (1726–91) arrived in Langundoutenünk from Friedenshütten and Schechschiquanünk together with 204 Indians. See [Ettwein,] "John Ettwein's Notes of Travel."

45. On the difficult relationship between Christian mission and politics, see Introduction, pp. 44–51.

THE 8TH   We had Holy Communion after having Speakings with the Brothers and Sisters. *Nicolaus* and *Amalia,* after they had first been confirmed, participated for the first time.

THE 9TH   At noon I left for *Langundoutenünk* with the Indian Brother *Jeremias.*

THE 12TH   I arrived there and to my heart's delight I ran into Brother *Ettwein* and Brother and Sister *Roth* and was able to welcome them. I was there until THE 19TH, but I was sick most of the time. Then after we had discussed everything, I left for *Welhik Thuppeck* in the company of Brothers *Ettwein, John Heckewelder* and some Indian Brothers and Sisters from *Fridenshütten.*[46]

THE 23RD   We found the Indian Brothers and Sisters there happy and well, and they were delighted when we arrived there at noon. The Watchword was, And whatsoever ye do in word or deed, do all in the name of the Lord Jesus, giving thanks to God and the Father by him.[47]

THE 24TH   We went a few miles up the river and took a look at the area. Brother *Ettwein* led the devotions about the text, I would have you wise unto that which is good, and simple concerning evil.[48]

THE 25TH   We marked out the *Town* again and added another street as well as a congregation house or meeting house.[49]

THE 26TH   We put up the bell. Brother *Ettwein* went to *Gekelemukpech-ünk* with some Indian Brothers to greet the *Chief* and his *Councel* and to deliver the message[50] agreed upon in *Langundoutenünk* about our Indian Brothers and Sisters who had come.

THE 28TH   They returned from there. They had been well treated there and were received with much joy. Many who had previously opposed the preaching of the Gospel have completely changed their minds and now support the Brothers.

THE 29TH   We looked for a site for God's Acre. We spoke with the Brothers about various points that everyone who wants to live here must observe, and we agreed on these. We also announced *Johannes* and *Nathanael-Davis* as Elders.[51] We two single Brothers were with our Choir[52] in heart and spirit[53] today and prayed for his blessing in fellowship with them. We also

46. See Conferenz-Protocoll Langundo-Utenünk, 12–19 Aug. 1772, MAB, B 315, F 2, I 4, reprinted in the appendix. John Heckewelder (1743–1823) became Zeisberger's assistant; Welhik Thuppeck is the Delaware name for Schönbrunn (lovely spring).

47. Col. 3:17.

48. Rom. 16:19.

49. See Heckewelder's map of Schönbrunn, reprinted in the appendix.

50. See paragraph 3 of the protocol of the Conference of 19 August 1772, reprinted in the appendix.

51. On the offices in the congregation, see Introduction, pp. 63–65. The conference protocol for 17 Aug. 1772 in paragraph 10 contained decisions concerning the two elders of the congregation.

52. On the system of choirs in the Moravian congregations, see Introduction, p. 62.

53. End of page, diary continued on the margin of page.

experienced the special joy of receiving letters from Brother *Nathanael*[54] and *Matthaus* in *Litiz* along with our celebration ode.

THE 31ST   The Brothers went to make some more hay for the winter. In the meantime Brothers *Ettwein* and *David* discussed all the necessary aspects of the entire work here.

[September]

SEPTEMBER 2ND   In the evening devotion Brother *Ettwein* said farewell. He reminded the Brothers and Sisters of the grace they had received and admonished them to remain in this so that they might bring light among the other Indians. He also added other necessary and useful admonitions and reminders. It is our sincere desire that the Savior might prepare himself a people from among them who follow his rules and customs.

Diary of the little Indian Congregation in Welhik-Thuppeck *on the* Mushkingum *from the Month of* September *until* October 18, 1772.[55]

SEPTEMBER 3RD   After a tender and touching farewell, Brother *Ettwein* left for *Langundouteniink* with *Schebosch*[56] and some Indian Brothers. He parted with the Watchword for today, Watch ye, stand fast in the faith, quit you like men, be strong. This is the hand, Lord help us act. . . .[57] Some Indians from *Gekelemukpechiink* came here for a visit.

THE 4TH   Our people began to clear their lots, fell wood, and make preparations for building.[58]

THE 6TH   In the morning was the sermon about the Epistle of the great blindness in which humans live by nature, how they are not even able to think good thoughts, and how nothing but the blood of Christ can transform us and make us new people.[59] We had a discussion with the Brothers about

---

54. Nathanael Seidel (1718–82).

55. MAB, B 141, F 2, fol. 9.

56. John Joseph Bull, alias Schebosch, son of Quaker parents, was baptized in Skippack, Pa., in 1721; he was again baptized in the Moravian congregation at Lancaster in 1742; in 1746 he married Christiana, a Mahican from Esopus. His wife died on 7 September 1787; he followed her on 4 September 1788. He was not ordained. Zeisberger usually refers to him by his Indian name, Schebosch. See Olmstead, *Blackcoats Among the Delaware*, 78–79.

57. 1 Cor. 16:13; this represented, however, the text for 3 Sept. 1772. "Da ist die Hand, Herr helfs uns thun," etc. *Das kleine Brüder-Gesang-Buch*, no. 1600, verse 2.

58. At first the Indian members of the congregation lived in simple huts made of bark, so-called wigwams. After the fields had been cleared, they used their free time to build proper houses from the trees they had cut down.

59. Rom. 11:25–27.

considering an *Interim* meeting house until we can find time to build the permanent one.

THE 7TH   In the morning devotions we commended our married Brothers and Sisters here and in *Langundouteniünk,* as well as all of our native congregations, to the Savior for blessing according to the Watchword for today. In the afternoon they had a service about today's text.[60]

THE 8TH   An Indian came here from *Gekelemukpechünk* for a visit. Through him we learned that a party of *Chippewa* had returned from the *Cherokees* with many *Scalps.* The *Delaware* are afraid the latter suspect them in this and might want to take revenge on them. Therefore the *Chief* sent 5 men with a message to the *Chippewa Nation* and reproached them and told them not to do anything like this again. He will also send a delegation to the *Cherokees* to clear himself from suspicion.[61]

THE 11TH   The Brothers began a Meeting House. They started serious treatment of Brother *Heckewelder,* who had already been suffering with *Rheumatism* for several days and could not go out.[62]

THE 13TH   Brothers *Isaac* and *Nathanael Davis* returned from *Gekelemukpechünk* where they had gone yesterday. They brought us news from the *Chief* that the site 10 miles down the river from us, where the old *Town*[63] stands, was now ours to settle. They arranged this in their *Councel.* Another letter from two *Ministers* also arrived there. They are supposed to be in *Pittsburgh* currently and are expected in *Gekelemukpechünk* very soon. They have offered to preach to the Indians there.[64]

THE 16TH   Some of our Indian Brothers and Sisters from *Langundoutenünk* came here to stay. *Echpalawehund* also came with them from *Gekelemukpechünk.* Our *Isaac* spoke with him a great deal again, especially about the two *Ministers* they were expecting. He said they should not think they were teaching the same thing as the Brothers were, and they should consider well what they were doing before they gave an answer.

THE 18TH   *Josua* arrived at our place from *Langundoutenünk* with a party of our people. He brought me a letter from Brother *Ettwein* there.

60. The appointed text was Eph. 5:25, 22, 24. On September 7 the married Brothers and Sisters celebrated their choir festival. See Introduction, pp. 62–63.

61. Neither John Stuart nor Sir William Johnson seems to have known of this incident, for neither mentioned it in his report. Yet both mention for 1772 and 1773 conflicts between the Wabash and the Cherokee. See Davies, *Documents of the American Revolution,* 4:33, 375. On the Cherokee, see Woodward, *The Cherokees,* and on the southern Indian tribes during the American Revolution, see O'Donnell, *Southern Indians in the American Revolution.*

62. Heckewelder reports that the sweating in a hot hut cured his rheumatism. *History, Manners, and Customs,* 226, 229.

63. Formerly this old town had been settled by King Beaver and Delaware of the Turkey clan; later the site became Gnadenhütten (see entry for 17 Oct. 1772 below). On chief Beaver King, who died in 1771, see Mulkearn, *George Mercer Papers,* 512–18; entry for 15 Dec. 1772 below.

64. The two missionaries were David McClure and Levi Frisbie of the Society in Scotland for Propagating Christian Knowledge. See Dexter, *Diary of David McClure,* and entry for 26 Sept. 1772.

THE 19TH   We finished our Meeting House and had our first service in it this evening. *Josua senior* went out with some of his people to take a look at the area and to select a suitable site.[65]

THE 20TH   The sermon was about the Gospel lesson for today,[66] how gracious and merciful the Savior is toward all poor sinners who call upon Him for help, but that some people easily forget what He has done for them and are ungrateful. While discussing the [page 10b][67] Watchword in the Congregational Service in the evening, we noted that when the Savior wants to bring light into a region which was previously dark, he sends his servants and messengers to prepare the way so that his people can then live and grow in peace. We have a clear example and proof of this in the area here.

THE 23RD   The Indian Brothers helped us[68] frame in our house. *Josua* went out with others to look at a site up the river, and he really liked it. It is 3–4 miles from us on the west side of the river.

THE 24TH   He went there with all of his people after we had given them some of the food which had been planted for them here, because they had none at all.

THE 26TH   We heard from *Gekelemukpechünk* that the English *Minister* had arrived there some days ago with *Joseph Peepi,* had addressed the Indians, and was now waiting for an answer.[69]

THE 27TH   After the sermon, which some strangers also attended, Brother *David* went to the *Town* being laid out and held a service for them there. Then he looked around the area and site of the town to see how it could be most suitably laid out. He returned home in the evening.

THE 28TH   Some Indians passed through here on their way from *Gekelemukpechünk* to the upper *Town* to visit their friends. Brother *Heckewelder,* who has been ill for almost 3 weeks, has now recovered enough that he can go out

65. Before his conversion, Josua had been a chief of the Mahican and had served as the speaker of the Christian Indians. Since Mahican and Delaware did not get along too well, they settled in places of their own. On 24 September 1772 the Mahican moved to the "upper town" and on 9 October to the settlement of King Beaver, later to be named Gnadenhütten II.

66. We cannot be certain which gospel lesson Zeisberger is referring to here. As a rule, we assume that the missionaries followed the regular canon of texts for the ecclesiastical year. But, since within certain limits this canon is flexible, we have decided to err on the side of caution in cases like this and not provide the text. In cases where Zeisberger offers additional information—e.g., "today's Gospel about the Canaanite woman" for the sermon on 15 March 1778 (similar entries for 4 April 1779 and 30 Jan. 1780)—we give the biblical text, in this case Matt. 15:21–28. We assume that whenever the text for the sermon is stated without the addition "today's Gospel," the text differs from the canons. For the Moravians, the sermon was less important than it was in other denominations. See Introduction, p. 53, note 190.

67. Isa. 58:12. The page number in brackets refers to the page of the original manuscript.

68. I.e., Zeisberger and Heckewelder. Both had probably felled trees for building their houses.

69. David McClure carried with him a message from George Croghan that recommended him to the Delaware. Dexter, *Diary of McClure,* 46. Frisbie fell ill and was therefore unable to come along.

again.[70] Many of our people had attacks of fever, which is very common in this area at this time of year.[71]

THE 29TH   Brother and Sister *Jungmann*[72] arrived here with some Indian Brothers and Sisters. In the evening the former led the service about the protection and guidance our heavenly Father provides through the service of the dear angels, and afterward extended greetings to the Brothers and Sisters once again from Brother *Ettwein* and the Brothers and Sisters in *Langundoutenünk*.

THE 30TH   The Brothers and Sisters returned here from the upper site for a service, during which they were told about Holy Communion next Saturday and they were invited as poor sinners. We concluded this month with reflection upon the Watchword for today The Lord bless thee, and keep thee etc.[73] which was meaningful and comforting to us.

October

THE 1ST   Brother and Sister *Jungmann* went to the upper *Town*, held a service for them there, and had Speakings with the Brothers and Sisters for Holy Communion. They found them all contrite and humble. Once again, some people came from *Langundoutenünk* to live here.

THE 2ND   We had Speakings in *Welhik Thuppeck*. *Killbuck* and 3 other White people[74] from *Pittsburgh* passed through here on their way to the upper *Town*, the latter to see if there was anything to be done about the arrangements here. The former brought a message to the *Mohicans* from the *Chiefs* saying: My grandchildren[75] (this is what they call the *Mohicans*) 36 days ago I learned that you have arrived here. We had designated and prepared a site for you, the old *Town* below *Gekelemukpechünk Creek,* to settle you there. However, now we see that you wanted to settle and build somewhere else. This is not your rightful place and you should move away from there. We really want our grandchildren to live close to us.[76]

THE 3RD   Therefore *Josua* came to our place early in the morning to learn what they would reply to him. We sent word that we would consider the *Chief's* words together and would send him an answer as soon as possible. The

70. See entry for 11 Sept. 1772.

71. Schönbrunn was located in a mosquito-infested swamp, and many of its inhabitants were infected with malaria, especially in the fall. Whenever Zeisberger mentions a three-day fever, he is talking about malaria. Duffy, *Epidemics in Colonial America,* 204–6.

72. Johann Georg Jungmann was married to Anna Margaretha Jungmann (1722–93).

73. Num. 6:24–26.

74. Unidentifiable.

75. On the usage of kinship terms, see Introduction, p. 21.

76. See entries for 13 and 19 Sept. 1772, with notes. The location was considerably closer to Gekelemukpechünk than to Schönbrunn.

reason they had settled there was that they still did not have a teacher with them and therefore wanted to live close to us.[77] In the afternoon we had Holy *Communion,* for which the Brothers and Sisters from the upper *Town* had come. In all there were 36 Indian Brothers and Sisters. *Andreas* and *Anna Justine* were *readmitted.*[78] Then the Brothers and Sisters went home.

THE 4TH   Those from the upper *Town* also came for the sermon, which Brother *Jungmann* preached. Afterward we joined the Helpers in considering the *Chief's* message to the *Mohicans.* We noted that we must make it clear to these *Chiefs* that we are not two people but one, so that they do not think we are to be distinguished, and they must know that none of us does anything without the previous knowledge of the others.[79]

THE 5TH   *Josua senior* and some others went down to look at the site. They liked it and decided to move there. We could not do much in this matter or advise them against it. It is just a little difficult because it is somewhat too far and they do not have a Brother with them. During winter or spring the waters often cannot be crossed and it is possible that no one will be able to reach them for long periods of time. The *Chiefs* had agreed on this same site for the Indian believers a number of years ago. However, last year when we were in *Gekelemukpechünk* they explicitly named only the area from the *Gekelemukpech-ünk Creek* to *Tuscarawi*[80] for us to look for a site and thus we chose *Welhik Thuppeck,* until Brother *Ettwein* went there with the Indian Brothers and spoke with them. Then they mentioned this site for the first time and said they would extend our *District* and move the border to there. However, before that they had always said that the site was reserved for the *Munsee* in *Goschgosching.*[81]

OCTOBER 7TH   Brother *Jungmann* went to the upper site and held a service for them there, because Brother *David* was not well.

Joseph Peepi arrived here from *Gekelemukpechünk* where he had been the *Inter-preter* for the English *Minister*[82] who had been staying there for a while and had

---

77. The location chosen by the Council was ten miles from Schönbrunn. See entry for 9 Oct. 1772.

78. See entry for 27 June 1772 and note 34.

79. Despite tensions between Christian Mahican and Christian Delaware, Zeisberger's reasoning was surely sound insofar as neither made a move without informing the missionaries or receiving their assent. Josua and Zeisberger agreed that the various ethnic groups represented one Christian community. Within this Christian community, however, Josua insisted on the independence of his ethnic group. He demonstrated this by moving without coordinating the move with the missionaries; similarly he sent a message to Gekelemukpechünk without informing the missionaries. See [Ettwein,] "John Ettwein's Notes of Travel," 211.

80. According to Zeisberger (see entry for 20 April 1772, note 6), Tuscarawi was deserted in 1771. By the winter of 1772 (see entry for 31 Dec. 1772), Tuscarawi was inhabited again.

81. On the relationship between the Monsy (modern spelling Munsee) and the Delaware, see Introduction, pp. 16–18.

82. Joseph Peepi had been baptized by Presbyterians before 1748; his independent behavior brought him into conflict with Zeisberger more than once. Between 1777 and 1780 Peepi lived outside the Moravian congregation. Interpreters played a vital role in the communication between white people and Native Americans. Members of the Moravian congregation were preferred translators

preached a number of times. However, he was called to the *Councel* then and told that they were pleased he had come to them and preached during his time there. There had been enough preaching now, however, and he should stop. It would be good for him to return home. He was very upset about this and told them that they would have no more good fortune if they did not accept the Gospel. God would send judgment upon this city and eradicate them from the face of the earth.

As we heard personally from *Joseph Peepi,* he talked very carelessly. For example, he supposedly said often that the Indians had so much beautiful and good land, but it was lying in waste and they did not use it because they were lazy people who did not want to work and resented the White people using it. In a few years all the land would be taken away from them. The White people would establish cities and towns there and drive the Indians away or even destroy them. He also said other such things, so it is no wonder that they sent him away.[83]

THE 9TH   The *Mohicans* and those living with them moved down to their designated site. It lies half way between *Gekelemukpechünk* and us, a good ten miles from us on the east side of the river. It sits on a good-sized hill on the river and the land there is nice and level. The fields, however, are across the river from them.

THE 10TH   Brother *David* also went there with a couple of Indian Brothers. From there they continued on to *Gekelemukpechünk* with *Josua* and his people.

THE 11TH   Brother *Jungmann* preached the sermon about the Savior's love for all who are poor and sick, who just approach Him faithfully and call upon Him for help. An Indian and his wife came here from *Gekelemukpechünk* to visit their friends here. He offered them a *Canow* load of Indian corn if they wanted it. They gratefully accepted this.

THE 12TH   *Willhelm* also returned from there. He brought along a letter for Brother *David* informing us[84] that he would make a further journey to the *Shawnee* with the 2 Indian Brothers *Isaac* and *Joseph Peepi.*

THE 15TH   A baby boy was born to Brother *Anton* and Sister *Juliana.* The Brothers were busy building houses, as they usually are these days.

THE 17TH   Late in the evening Brother *David* returned from his visit among the *Shawnee.* He reports the following from his journey:

On THE 10TH of this month we arrived in *Gekelemukpechünk,* where we

because their knowledge of the language was good and both sides trusted them. See Hagedorn, "'A Friend to Go Between Them.'"

83. See McClure's report in Dexter, *Diary of David McClure,* 26–27, which corroborates Zeisberger.

84. The diary is in Zeisberger's handwriting. Jungmann and Heckewelder probably jotted down the major events in a book which later served Zeisberger as a basis for the diary. On the genesis and authorship of the diary, see Introduction, pp. 72–80.

were cordially received. Because there was a pretty large number of us, we were lodged in a house where we were alone. On THE 11TH I held a service in the morning and various people from the *Town* were present for this. In the afternoon we were called to the *Councel* so they could learn what our people had to say to them. *Josua senior* addressed the *Chief* and thanked him for directing them to the proper place for them to live. He said that when they had arrived, they had not known where to go and therefore had looked for a little place. They had just been preparing to build houses when they received his message. They had then immediately decided to move there. Now they were indeed there at that place, and he should take care of his grandchildren (the *Mohicans*) who were living close to them now. The road to them should be open, so that anyone who would like to hear the Gospel would be free to come. In brief, that was the message of his talk. After this he presented 2 *Strings of Wampum.* They approved and agreed with everything, but no formal answer followed. They had put together a quantity of Indian corn out of gratitude that our people had accepted and followed their message. They dedicated this and gave it to them.

Although I learned there that the men were already out hunting, I felt I should still undertake this journey and see if I found any of them at home or not. Therefore I asked the *Chief* if he had ever reported anything to his grandchildren, the *Shawnee,* about us and that we had come into this region and were living here now. He replied that this had indeed been done long ago. I informed him that I wanted to visit them. He approved and said, yes, that would be very good and he would like that. Therefore in the morning on THE 12TH I left with the 2 Brothers *Isaac* and *Joseph Peepi.* We passed by two *Delaware Towns* to our right and 2 large flat stretches of land where there is nothing but grass for a number of miles. At one of these we also saw the site where *Colonel Bouquet* camped[85] with his army and then turned back. Toward evening we entered another *Delaware Town* where we stopped in for a little while. Those who had fled last spring, when they heard we were coming into the region of *Gekelemuk-pechünk,* live here because they do not want to hear anything about the Gospel. Despite this, *Isaac* joyfully preached to the Indian at the place where we stopped. Finally he replied, Surely you speak the truth. Then we went a little further, and in the evening we came to the first *Shawnee Town* where there are just 3 huts and we spent the night there. Here we were delighted to learn that the *Shawnee* in the *Town* where we wanted to go had been out hunting for 3

85. In the second half of October 1764 Colonel Henry Bouquet (1719–65) established camp for his army "near Tuscarrowas," while he negotiated with the Delaware the release of white prisoners and a new armistice; he then moved on to Woaketameki, where he concluded similar agreements with the Shawnee. On 28 November 1764 he returned with this army to Fort Pitt. Stevens and Kent, *Papers of Henry Bouquet,* 15:233–52; *JP,* 6:570–71, 585–86, 606–7; [Smith], *Expedition Against the Ohio Indians.* Thomas Hutchins's map of Bouquet's march, the first really reliable map of the Muskingum region, is reprinted in the appendix.

weeks but had all returned home a couple of days ago. It turned out that without knowing it we had stopped in at *Paxenoos's* son's house. He knew me right away,[86] welcomed me cordially, and was happy to see me. All three of us preached the Savior to him half the night and he seemed to receive this well. After he had listened to us for a while he said he surely believed that our teaching was the right one and that we preached the correct way to salvation. They had tried for a long time to find the way to eternal life. Now, however, they saw that everything they had tried and all their efforts and attempts were in vain. They had almost given up because they knew nothing else good they could do. He offered to go with us on the morning of THE 13TH and hear more. We were happy about this because he understands and speaks *Delaware* well. We passed through a couple more small *Shawnee Towns*, each of which has only 4–5 huts. As we passed through we informed them that anyone who would like to listen should follow us, because we had precious words to tell them. They did so, and those who were home came. Toward noon we arrived in the *Town* where we wanted to go.[87] It is the main town and their *Chief* lives there. We stopped in at the preacher's, as *Paxenoos's* son had advised, because his word counts the most and governs everything, so to speak. The *Chief,* on the contrary, only takes care of *Chief Affairs.*[88] We were cordially received, and when we informed them that we had come to visit them and had something to tell them, the preacher asked what kind of things we had to tell them. When we told him we had the words of eternal life to tell them, he answered, We are happy about this and we would like to hear it. They immediately made preparations to clear a house and get it ready for this purpose. However, because many people, and especially the women, were busy in the fields harvesting their corn,[89] it got too late for a public service today. In the meantime, we did not wait that long but preached in the house where we were staying to the Indians who came to us, one after the other. Since our house was always full and they listened very attentively, we continued until after midnight, when the roosters were already crowing and we lay down to rest a little. However, as soon as day broke we began again. The preacher had not replied at all until then, but just listened very attentively. Now, however, he began to speak and told us he had not been able to sleep all night; he had just kept thinking and *meditating* about what he had heard. Now he wanted to share his heart with us. He believed everything we preached was the truth. For a year it has been clear to him and he has realized that they were all poor, sinful humans despite all their deeds. However, they did not know what else they could decide and do

86. Paxenoos was a Shawnee chief. Zeisberger and Christian Seidel had visited him and his family in Wyoming in 1755. Schweinitz, *Zeisberger,* 225–26; Heckewelder, *Narrative of the Mission,* 49.

87. I.e., Woaketameki.

88. On the functions of chiefs, preachers, and captains, see Introduction.

89. On the role of women in Native American societies, see Introduction, p. 18.

in order to be saved. He always consoled his people that someone would certainly come and tell them the right way to salvation, because they were not on the right path. Just the day before we arrived he had told them they should have just a little more patience; someone would surely come soon. Now that we had come, he believed God had sent us to them to proclaim his word to them.

For some years the *Shawnee* had often practiced vomiting in order to free themselves of sins and to cleanse themselves.[90] They ceased this practice a year ago because they had seen that sin still prevailed among them. Then, however, they began to lead a good and pious life, in their own way, for which their preacher had given them instructions as well as he understood. For example, they should not become drunk, dance, fornicate, steal, lie and deceive, and so on. He said they would continue doing this until God had something different and better proclaimed to them in one way or another. He is the same kind of preacher our *Isaac* was;[91] he sticks to his conviction only until he discovers and agrees with something better. *Isaac* told him from his personal experience how things had been for him and what he had felt the first time he had heard the Brothers, and how the word of Jesus' death and suffering had tugged at his heart so that he immediately affirmed publicly that this is the truth. This morning they all gathered in the house that had been prepared for this. My heart was open and the Savior granted me grace to extol his death and bloody merit as the source of our salvation. At the beginning I told them they did not need to respond during the sermon. They should not ask questions as they had done previously in the house where we had spoken with them. Instead they should just listen until the sermon was over. Then they could ask as much as they wanted to. They did this and things proceeded very quietly and orderly. The *Chief* and *Captain* were also present. The former is already pretty old and seems to be a nice man. Afterward the Indian Brothers spoke with them and further explained my sermon to them. Then they asked various questions, all of which we answered to their *Satisfaction*. In the afternoon we learned that they wanted to hold a *Councel* among themselves, so we left them alone. In the

90. "They [i.e., teachers] declared to the Indians that God had commanded their cleansing from sin and to this end they gave them twelve different kinds of Beson to drink, supposed to cause vomiting to free them from sinful taint. Some Indians followed these injunctions, vomited so often that their lives were endangered by it. They were, further, ordered to fast, and to take nothing but Beson. Few persevered in this absurd practice the required length of time." Zeisberger, "History of the Northern American Indians," 133–34. This cleansing ritual is first described for Shawnee and Delaware by Dowd, *Spirited Resistance*, 33–34. For other rituals research usually relies on the 1824 report of C. C. Trowbridge, who does not mention such rituals and declares categorically that Shawnee had no preachers (in ethnological literature usually referred to as "prophets"). Kinietz and Voegelin, *Shawnee Traditions*, 40–43; Edmunds, *Shawnee Prophet*, 23–26; Howard, *Shawnee!* 196–212. Gilbert, *God Gave Us This Country*, 216, believes that each Shawnee settlement had its own preacher.

91. According to Zeisberger, on 12 August 1773 another Indian characterized Isaac thus: "he had previously been the second to the Chiefs and their advisor. He had been a Captain, Doctor and also a preacher. Now, however, he had become a believer."

evening, however, they sent for *Isaac* and *Joseph Peepi,* and informed them first of what they had arranged and decided among themselves. They also wanted to hear their thoughts about this, and when they showed their joy and pleasure at this, they asked what else they should do to reach their goal. The Brothers answered them that they should tell me what they thought. I would answer and advise them. However, because it was already too late this evening, we did this the next morning when they gathered in our house. The preacher, who was their speaker, addressed me and said, Brother, we are very happy that you have come to visit us and have brought us God's word, which we are happy to hear. Now we want to let you know what we decided unanimously in our *Councel* yesterday. It is true the women were not present, because they are very busy harvesting their fields now. This is not important, however, because they are in agreement with what we men decide. We agreed that from this day on we want to accept God's word and also live according to it. We say this not only with our mouths, but also from our hearts. Our hope and wish is that not only Indian believers, but also White Brothers, will come to us, live with us, and instruct us in how we can be saved. We are planning to go on our fall hunt as soon as possible now. Then when we return home, in a little over 2 months, we would be very happy if someone came to our place then and stayed with us. We present our request to you. We are poor, bad people, but do not scorn us because we are so bad and do not deny our request. This *Shawnee* talk touched my heart so that I had to promise to help in one way or another, although I saw in advance that it would be very difficult for us because there are so few of us. Therefore I told him I was very glad to hear that they not only want to accept God's word but also to live accordingly; we Brothers were always happy to hear about Indians, regardless of which Nation they are from, who desire the Savior and his word, and we would be happy to serve them. However, at present there were too few of us White Brothers and Sisters and one site was still not occupied. Therefore I could not promise them that some-one would come to them as soon as they asked and desired. I would promise them, however, that we would help them as soon as possible and from now on would not neglect them any more. When I got home I would not only speak with my Brothers about this but also would write to my Brothers in Bethlehem about sending us more helpers. In the meantime, perhaps there would be an opportunity this winter for us to communicate with each other. Perhaps some-one from our place would also visit them this winter. They should just remain steadfast in what they had agreed upon together and not allow themselves to lose faith. From now on they should surely believe that the Brothers remember them well. However, I also had to tell them now how things would have to be in their *Town* if we lived with them and how they would have to behave: there could be no sign of dances, pipes, drunkenness, gaming, commotion, and so on, as is common in other Indian *Towns.* Otherwise we could not live with them. Everything had to be quiet and orderly. They answered that they had already managed this on their own for a long time; we would not be bothered by such bad things because they themselves did not like them. They really wanted to have Brothers to tell them always what they had to do, because they really wanted to live as believers should. He said furthermore that they had also already deliberated and discussed leaving this place and looking around for a better one, because they did not live in a place suitable for many Indians to gather. Then other members of their Nation who wanted to live in this way, but who are scattered around, could move in with them. Therefore when they returned home from hunting, the first thing they would do would be to look for a suitable site for such a *Town,* where only believers and those who at least intended to become believers would live. I was even happier to hear this. However, it would be good and necessary for us to be there from the beginning of such a *Settlement,* so that nothing would be overlooked or ruined that afterward could not be corrected. This would also be good because then we would always be free to act as we wanted and should. This *Town* is commonly referred to among the Indians by the name of the Vomit-*Town;*[92] this is another reason it would be good to begin a new one. Thus we have reached the *Shawnee* border now, because their *District* begins here. However, it is still probably another 100 miles from here to their primary seat.[93] There are many other *Towns,* all *Shawnee,* in between, though, and this continues westward from *Gekelemukpech-ünk.* This *Town* consists of 17 houses and is the largest in this area. In addition 4 small *Towns,* 3–4 miles at the furthest and each consisting of only a few huts, belong to it. Most of them understand *Delaware* and some also speak it well, so that language issues will be relatively easy for us. This will provide a good beginning among this *Nation.* It is indeed very good and necessary for the Savior to enter this *Nation* with his Gospel, for the sake of His work among the Indians. If a beginning is made among them then we can count on peace prevailing, because this *Nation* is always ready for war if one breaks out, and I was told here that the *Lower Shawnee* definitely have a large supply of *Ammunition* on hand at all times. Moreover each hunter here and in other *Towns* has a supply keg of gunpowder and lead in *proportion.*

After I had agreed on everything with them, we said farewell and admonished them not to forget what they had heard. Then toward noon we left with *Paxenoos's* son. On the way we took a look at a stretch of beautiful land, suitable for a *Settlement* on the river. Since our Indian Brothers and Sisters from *Fridens-hütten* arrived, I have always wished we might perhaps have another *Settlement* here in this area. This would do more for the Savior's work than if they all lived together, and now this is working out by itself and the Savior is providing ways and means. Today we went about 10 miles and spent the night with a *Shawnee*

92. On vomiting as a cleansing ritual, see entry for 12 Oct. 1772 and note 90 above.
93. Zeisberger is thinking of the settlements on the Scioto River, where at this time most of the Shawnee lived, See Introduction, pp. 15–16.

who received us very well and provided us with the best hospitality. *Isaac,* who can speak *Shawnee* pretty well, joyfully preached the Savior to him. In the evening on THE 16TH we arrived back in *Gekelemukpechünk* and spent the night with *Netawatwees,* who was glad to hear good news about his grandchildren. The *Delaware* call the *Shawnee* their grandchildren. They in turn call them their grandfathers. The *Munsee* call the *Shawnee* their youngest brothers and these in turn call them their elder brothers.[94] We found many of our Sisters here. They were helping to harvest the Indian corn, for payment.[95] We arrived at the homes of our *Mohicans* toward noon on THE 17TH, where I held the first service for them and also announced that this place would be called *Gnadenhütten.*[96] They were all very happy about this. During that time they had already framed some houses and were busily building. In the evening we arrived in *Welhik Thuppeck,* happy and grateful that the Savior had been with us and had blessed our journey. That is all the news of this trip.

OCTOBER 18TH   In the morning was the sermon. After the Congregational Service in the evening, Brother *David* told the Brothers and Sisters about his journey to the *Shawnee* and commended this people to their remembrance before the Savior. This brought them great joy, and you could sense a special affection and love for them among our people.

Diary *of* Welhik Thuppeck *and* Gnadenhütten *on the* Mushkingum *from* October *19th 1772 until* March 22, 1773[97]

OCTOBER 19TH   Brother *David* left for *Langundouteniink* with Brothers *Heckewelder* and *Schebosch.*

THE 21ST   Brother and Sister *Jungmann* went down to *Gnadenhütten* for a visit. They found everyone there well and busy building, and they returned on THE 22ND.

THE 25TH   After the sermon about the Gospel, the baby boy born to Brother *Anton* and Sister *Juliana* on the 15th of this month was baptized with the name *Joseph. Josua* senior and *Joseph Peepi* came from *Gnadenhütten* for a visit here.

---

94. This entry indicates that Zeisberger considered the Munsee a separate nation. See note 81 to entry for 5 Oct. 1772.

95. The women worked in order to be able to buy corn for the winter, for they had been unable to plant enough corn for the year owing to their late arrival. Non-Christian Indians worked for Christian Indian women on other occasions. See entry for 24 June 1775.

96. Officially the name had been chosen by throwing the lot. Yet the name, meaning "huts of Grace," symbolized the continuity of Moravian missions in North America. Gnadenhütten on the Mahony Creek had been founded in 1746; it was destroyed on 24 November 1755. In Moravian martyrology this day loomed large.

97. MAB, B 141, F 3, I 1, fol. 17; although Zeisberger was not, as the following entry indicates, at Schönbrunn, he is the author of the diary. See note 84 to entry for 12 Oct. 1772. Entries between 19 Oct. and 8 Nov. 1772 are understandably short.

THE 28TH   Old *Hanna* from *Langundouteniink* came here to stay. Her friends in *Gekelemukpechünk* had picked her up there with horses and brought her here.

November

THE 8TH   Brothers *David* and *Heckewelder* returned from *Langundoute-niink*. Some Indian Brothers and Sisters also came with them to stay here. The former led the evening service and greeted the Brothers and Sisters.

THE 9TH   During the devotion in preparation for Holy Communion[98] we announced the upcoming Holy Communion to the Brothers and Sisters and invited them to attend as poor and needy people. We also spoke with the Brothers and gave them good advice about their building activities.

THE 10TH   2 more families from *Langundouteniink* arrived to live here. Brother *David* went to *Gnadenhütten,* held services for them there, and had a Speaking with the Brothers and Sisters in preparation for Holy Communion. Brother and Sister *Jungmann* did the same here. In both places we found hearts hungry and thirsty for Jesus' Body and Blood.

THE 13TH   In response to the Watchword[99] we discussed our Lord's office as Chief Elder.[100] We also dealt with this subject during the Holy Communion service the next day. The Brothers and Sisters from *Gnadenhütten* had come for this. During this service we knelt and prayed for His merciful *Absolution* for all our insufficiencies, and we promised Him new obedience and faithfulness. He looked upon us lovingly, and then we shared blissfully in his Body and Blood in the Holy *Sacrament*. One person was readmitted after receiving *Absolution*. Two Brothers and Sisters observed for the first time, and two for the second time.

THE 15TH   The sermon about the Gospel addressed how we all are and remain the Savior's debtors, and if He treated us justly we could not stand before Him. We had a Conference with the Brothers who are Helpers about various matters.[101]

THE 16TH   *Traders* from *Pittsburgh* arrived here. They sold a good portion of their wares to our Indians.[102] Otherwise our people were busy building their houses.

98. This service should not be confused with the religious conversations in preparation for the Holy Communion, which were conducted on 10 November 1772. See note 34 for entry 27 June 1772.

99. The Watchword was Exod. 34:10.

100. See Introduction, p. 62, on the importance of commemorating Christ's acceptance of the office of Chief Elder on 13 November 1741.

101. The missionaries appointed trusted Christians as National Helpers; they assisted in the missionary work and were members of the Helpers' Conference. See Introduction, p. 65.

102. Traders were the most important link between the mission settlements and the colonies; at the same time they tried to ensure that Native Americans got those European goods they most

THE 18TH   Brother and Sister *Jungmann* went to *Gnadenhütten* for a visit, held services for them, spoke with some Brothers and Sisters, and returned here on

THE 19TH   In the presence of the Helpers' Conference, we spoke with an Indian who is not baptized and with his wife. They came here from *Schechschiquanünk*[103] and asked to live here. They received provisional permission for this.

Most of our Indian Brothers went out for the fall hunt. We advised them to stay close to the Savior while they are alone in the bush. Brother *David* had practical and blessed conversations with *Isaac* about our Savior's work among the Indians. Not until this occasion did I learn that the reason our Indians were called here from *Fridenshütten* was actually not so virtuous at first. *Isaac,* who had been present in the *Councel* in *Gekelemukpechünk*[104] when the matter was set into motion, said that some people had suggested they should have the Indian Believers called here. They should allow them to bring their teachers along, because they would certainly not want to come here without them. After they had built here and gotten settled in, then they should send their teachers back home. In this way the entire work would be destroyed and the Indians would be returned to the old ways they had abandoned.[105] At that time some not only thought like this but even talked this way. However, all indications now are that they were deceived in their thoughts and have already lost the courage to disrupt the Savior's work, especially now that they see what a large number of Indian believers there is. It is certainly possible that in this area the smallest number of people to convert will be from the *Delaware Nation,* although we came to this country because of them. This will not deter us, however. He will know how to gather in the reward for his sufferings from various *Nations,* because what the Savior has done so far is just the beginning.

---

urgently needed (see Introduction, pp. 19–21). The most important traders for Gekelemukpechünk and Schönbrunn were probably John Gibson and John Anderson. John Gibson (1740–1822), prominent Indian trader and later commanding officer of Fort Laurens, was married to a Shawnee who had lived in Gekelemukpechünk and who was killed in the massacre in late April 1774. She had intimate relations both with Shawnee and Delaware. Gibson represented an important link between the missionaries and Bethlehem. DHDW, 11, 15, 17; Butterfield, *Washington-Crawford Letters,* 69; Jones, *Journal of Two Visits,* 63; Gibson, "General John Gibson," 298, 310. John Anderson, according to Heckewelder dubbed "the honest Quaker trader" by his Indian customers, was in 1774 actively involved in efforts to prevent the outbreak of a war. From 1775–76 on the Continental Congress trusted him with numerous important tasks. Heckewelder, *History, Manners, and Customs,* 241; DHDW, 137.

103. Schechschiquanünk was founded in 1769; this mission settlement served as a link between Friedenshütten and Schönbrunn. See Index of Place and River Names.

104. Isaac, whose Indian name was Glikhican, was Packanke's most trusted adviser, according to Heckewelder. Packanke was chief of the Wolf clan. Heckewelder, *Narrative of the Mission,* 186–91; Weslager, *Delaware Indians,* 284–85. In his function as trusted counselor, Glikhican attended all meetings of the Delaware's central Council in Gekelemukpechünk. He ceased to do so after his conversion. See Introduction, pp. 16–17.

105. See entries for 23 Feb. 1773, 23 June 1774, and 1 Nov. 1774.

THE 22ND   We were delighted to receive letters from our dear Brother *Matthao* in *Litiz* and some of the Watchwords for next year. They came by way of *Langundouteniünk*.[106]

THE 29TH   On the First of Advent, the sermon was about the text, He came unto his own, and his own received him not,[107] which deals with the Savior's incarnation. Some Sisters returned from *Gekelemukpechünk* where they had gone some days ago to buy Indian corn. They had a very difficult journey because of the high waters. For this same reason we also could not reach *Gnadenhütten* for some time.

Brother *Jungmann* led the Congregational Service about the promise given to the pagans in ancient times that many more would be converted to the Lord. In the evenings, we congregational Brothers and Sisters are now reading either the congregational newsletters or the *Historie of the Brothers*[108] to bless our hearts.

December

THE 4TH   A woman who had been with us often in *Langundouteniünk* and had attended many of our services came here for a visit.

THE 8TH   Some of our Brothers and Sisters who were in *Gekelemukpechünk* spoke with some Indians there about the salvation we have in the Savior and how this can be attained, since a number of people showed a willingness and desire to hear this.

THE 15TH   Brother *David* went to *Gnadenhütten* for a visit. In the meantime, we were delighted to receive letters and news from Bethlehem that a *Trader* brought us via *Pittsburgh*. The former returned from there on THE 17TH. He had found everyone well. They have started building a house there for a couple of Brothers and Sisters, and they will also hold their services in this *ad interim*. It is noteworthy that the former *King Beaver* lies buried there. During his life he worked hard to establish such a *Town* with a church where the Gospel would be preached, but he never accomplished this. After his death this was accomplished after all, and the Gospel is now being preached in his *Town*.

This evening *Samuel's* child was baptized with the name *Catharina*. She was on the verge of death.

THE 18TH   Brother *David* spoke with *Killbuck*,[109] who had come here

106. The Watchwords were published under the title *Die täglichen Loosungen der Brüder-Gemeine für das Jahr 1773*.

107. John 1:11.

108. On the communication system within the Unity, see Introduction, p. 42, and Cranz, *Alte und Neue Brüder-Historie*.

109. Killbuck, Indian name Bemineo, son of Netawatwees and chief of the Wolf clan, was one of the most adamant enemies of the Mission congregation until the spring of 1775; on 19 May 1775 he participated for the first time in one of the religious services of the missionaries. See also Mulkearn, *George Mercer Papers*, 514–15. He is not to be confused with his son, Killbuck Jr., whose Indian name was Gelelemind, grandson of Netawatwees and from 1776 on influential member of the Council at

3 days ago and declared himself to him because we had already heard all sorts of things about *Joseph Peepi's* negotiations in *Philadelphia*.[110] He was happy about this.

THE 21ST   There was a congregational council[111] since there were various reminders to be made. The Brothers and Sisters received everything well and said they wanted to bring joy and honor to the Savior.

THE 22ND   Brother and Sister *Jungmann* went to *Gnadenhütten* for a visit. The Brothers and Sisters here cut a quantity of firewood for them. *Traders* arrived here from *Pittsburgh*. When people like this come here they behave orderly and quietly as long as they are here, even if they are still very crude. Today the Brothers began building a schoolhouse.[112] It is important to all the Brothers and Sisters that their children be instructed. We announced the upcoming Holy Communion for next Saturday in a separate service. This delighted the Brothers and Sisters.

THE 24TH   We had Speakings with the Brothers and Sisters both yesterday and today. We sensed the blessed work of the dear Mother in most of them. We celebrated Christmas Eve with a Lovefeast, during which we read the story of our Savior's birth and then discussed the Watchword and daily text.[113] Afterward we knelt and worshipped the baby child in the manger and thanked Him with many tears for his holy incarnation. We concluded with the church benediction.

THE 25TH   In the morning was the sermon and in the afternoon the Children's Service. Brother and Sister *Jungmann* returned from *Gnadenhütten* where they had spoken with the Brothers and Sisters and held services for them. During the sermon this morning they received one Sister, *Mary* from *Stockbridge*,[114] into the congregation. Some Brothers and Sisters also came here

---

Gekelemukpechünk; for a short biographical note on him, see *Pennsylvania Magazine of History and Biography* 10 (1886): 116–17.

110. See entry for 26 Dec. 1772.

111. All baptized members were admitted to and participated in the community council. According to Zeisberger's diary it was convened on 26 Jan., 17 May, and 13 Sept. 1773, on 7 May 1774, 13 May 1775, and 15 Jan. 1776; thereafter the community council met at Lichtenau on 30 Oct. 1778 and 14 Feb. 1779. While the worldly affairs of the mission congregation were dealt with in the community council, the daily meetings of the congregation were reserved for religious problems like the confirmation of new members and conversations about the day's Watchword.

112. It was completed on 29 July 1773; affairs of the school are discussed in entries for 3 Feb. and 29 July 1773, for 11 Jan. and 2 Sept. 1774, for 22 Nov. and 4 Dec. 1775, for 14 Jan., 13 Feb., and 4 Nov. 1777, and for 12 Jan. 1778. Delaware as a language of instruction is mentioned for the first time in 1775.

113. The Watchword for the day was Ps. 98:3, the text for the day was Gal. 4:4–5.

114. Indians from the Housatonic tribe had lived in Stockbridge since the early eighteenth century; from 1735 to 1749 they were under the care of the congregational minister John Sergeant, from 1751 to 1758 the charge of the congregational minister and theologian Jonathan Edwards. During and after the Seven Years' War, the congregation slowly disintegrated; in the 1770s a significant number moved west, where, in the 1780s, they founded New Stockbridge in western New York. This settlement was only a few miles from the mission settlement of Brotherton, headed by the Mahican missionary Samson Occom. The Moravians enjoyed close contact with the Stockbridge Mahi-

with them for a visit. In the Congregational Service two individuals were baptized into Jesus' death after a meditation on the Watchword.[115] *Pommachgutte*, who is blind, received the name *Ephraim*, and *Aaron's* wife received the name *Henriette*. *Mary*, *Samuel's* sister from the *Jerseys*,[116] was also received into the congregation. This was a blessed proceeding, which *Echpalawehund* attended along with other Indians who had come here from *Gekelemukpechünk* for a visit. We heard some news about the *Shawnee* we had visited in the fall. It was completely contrary to what we had agreed upon at that time. Supposedly they told the Indian who brought us this news that they had not considered the matter adequately; they had many things to consider about this and they could not accept the Gospel for three reasons. First, at one time their entire *Nation* had been completely destroyed except for a few survivors. Then God had given them a certain *Beson*[117] or medicine, and since they had this they had taken courage again and multiplied so that they were now strong again. Second, God had given them bread from heaven in the following manner: Two Indians had gone where the sun sets, brought it back from there, and now they had bread to eat. Therefore they held a festival and dance annually, during which they thanked God for giving them bread. Third was the festival of death or the dance of death, which they held so that their friends who die would go to

---

cans dating from 1742. See Kellaway, *New England Company*, and, especially, Frazier, *Mohicans of Stockbridge*.

115. Ps. 31:9.

116. As a rule, when Zeisberger refers to "the Jerseys" he means Delaware who belonged to the mission congregation founded in 1745 by David Brainerd, which remained the charge of Brainerd's brother, John, until his death in 1777. Thus Mary, Samuel's sister, had been baptized. She was now formally admitted to the congregation. "Samuel" is Samuel Moor, the grandson of Papunhank; see Register of Persons. On Christian mission in New Jersey, see Edwards, *Life of David Brainerd*; Brainerd, *Life of John Brainerd*. On John Brainerd, see also the entry for 16 June 1780 below.

117. "Beson," according to Zeisberger's *Delaware Indian and English Spelling Book*, 10, meant "physic"; even today the Delaware use the term "Be-soon" for "medicine"; see Hale, *Turtle Tales*, 200. On 1 Jan. 1773 Zeisberger described Beson as "Medical herbs and roots." Beson also meant "Wapachsigan (a poison warriors use; this is the Beson they received from God, as has already been reported above)," entry for 19 Jan. 1773; this Beson was boiled; see entry for 12 Oct. 1774. Heckewelder reports the sermon of a prophet from Cayahaga in 1762 who called the white people's rum "beson" and told his listeners that "above all, you must abstain from drinking their deadly beson, which they have forced upon us, for the sake of increasing their gains and diminishing our numbers." Heckewelder, *History, Manners, and Customs*, 293–294, where it is reported as part of the sermon of Wangomen. See note 90 for entry for 17 Oct. 1772. Elsewhere Zeisberger defines Beson as medicine: "If they [Indians with knowledge of the virtues of roots and herbs] give a dose, which, as, indeed, all roots and herbs used for medicinal purposes, they call *Beson*, i.e., medicine, and which consists commonly of quite a kettle full—for with them quantity signifies much and the decoction usually being weak is rarely an overdose—none can see or know of what roots and herbs it has been prepared, for they are pounded very fine. . . . For the bite of every variety of snake they have a special Beson" ("History of the Northern American Indians," 24–25). Tantaquidgeon's *Folk Medicine of the Delaware* is based on the published writings of Zeisberger and Heckewelder. Herrick consulted many more sources for the Six Indian Nations in "Iroquois Medical Botany"; see esp. chap. 3 and 195–99 for a study of the plants that could cause or prevent magic. For a brief survey of white settlers' knowledge of Native American medical and pharmaceutical expertise, see Vogel, *American Indian Medicine*, 36–93.

God.[118] They could not abandon these three practices and especially not the first one, because they would all perish as had almost happened in olden days. We will investigate this matter further when we have time and opportunity. Satan will spare no means to prevent the Savior's work and to destroy it wherever possible.

THE 26TH   Toward noon the communicant Brothers and Sisters from *Gnadenhütten* gathered here and we joined in partaking blissfully in his Body and Blood in the Holy *Sacrament*. There were 49 of us. Two Brothers and Sisters enjoyed this great gift for the first time, and 3 observed for the 2nd time.

Today *Joseph Peepi* also returned here from his business with the *Gouverneur* in *Philadelphia* and brought us welcome letters from Bethlehem and *Litiz* along with Watchwords and texts for next year, as far as they have been printed.[119] He took the message from the *Chief* in *Gekelemukpechünk* upon himself and as we had heard, involved himself in this. We were concerned that he might be hurt or even separated from us. However, the Savior prepared us the joy of having him return to us a true, poor sinner, and he repented of his misdeeds with many tears. Regarding his business in *Philadelphia*, the *Chiefs* had instructed him to negotiate with the *Gouverneur* for transportation to England for some Indians, at their expense. Second, the *Quakers* should provide them with a preacher and schoolmaster. They asked for this a year ago and had not yet received anything. The *Gouverneur* answered that this *Affair*, transporting Indians to England, was not his concern, but *Sir William Johnson's*.[120] They should ask him about this. To the 2nd point he replied that he could not understand why they were requesting another preacher and schoolmaster. After all, they already had preachers, the Brothers, and so many Indian Brothers were living with them already. Why would they want to have others? He thought they should be satisfied with this; they should just do what the Brothers told them. The *Quakers* also sent word that they did not see how anyone could live with them to instruct them and their children unless they led an orderly life. The elders would have to begin, and then the children would follow.[121]

THE 28TH   The Savior took young *Catharina, Samuel's* baby daughter,

118. On the meaning of these dances, see Voegelin, *Shawnee Female Deity*, 12–16, and Kinietz and Voegelin, *Shawnee Traditions*, 49–51. The authors of these works are unaware of the dances' origins and therefore assign different meanings to them. In general, see Fenton and Kurath, "Feast of the Dead," and Kurath, "Native Choreographic Areas."

119. The words "as far as they have been printed" suggest that Peepi brought only the first batch from the printers; the second batch, pp. 57–128, arrived on 14 March 1773. See also note 106 for entry for 22 Nov. 1772.

120. On behalf of the English government, Sir William Johnson and John Stuart as superintendents of Indian Affairs were responsible for all dealings with the Native American tribes; Johnson for those in the middle and northern districts and Stuart for those in the southern. See also entry for 8 Sept. 1773, note 261.

121. See message of Netawatwees, which Peepi delivered to Governor John Penn on 26 Nov. 1772, *PCR*, 10:61–64. The message of the year before and the answer given at the conference in Philadelphia 7–13 May 1771 are printed in *PCR*, 9:735–42.

to her eternal rest.[122] She was a quiet and dear child, very patient in her illness. At the very beginning of her illness she asked her grandmother to take her to the Brothers. They could wash away her sins with the Savior's blood and then she would gladly go to Him. After she had experienced this grace, she went to Him, blessed beyond her 3 years and 11 months. This evening Brother *Heckewelder* led the Singing Service.

THE 29TH   Brother *Jungmann* held the early devotion about the Watchword, Then the Lord will sprinkle clean water upon you, and ye shall be clean.[123] Then the little earthly dwelling was taken to its resting place, and we dedicated our *God's Acre* with a sincere prayer.

THE 31ST   A very old woman from *Tuscarawi* came here for a visit. She has been here a number of times already and wants to belong to the Savior. Brother *David* went to *Gnadenhütten* and held the New Year's Watchnight Service, as Brother *Jungmann* did here. With grateful hearts we remembered all the grace and good deeds the Savior granted us during this year, being with us and blessing us, and comforting us with his dear presence and allowing us to experience richly the dear Father's protection and the Holy Spirit's care and guidance. After a reflection upon the Watchword,[124] we knelt and thanked Him for this and commended ourselves further to his faithful guidance and care.

At the conclusion of this year the following should be noted:

After the Savior revealed his will and pleasure last spring[125] to see a new *Settlement* begun for the Indian Believers in this area, Brother *David* and 3 Indian Brothers traveled here from *Langundoutenünk,* looked at the town and the area, and arranged the matter with the *Chiefs* in *Gekelemukpechünk.* After their return, he moved away from *Langundoutenünk* with 5 families of Indian Brothers and Sisters. After a journey lasting 20 days, they arrived here on *May* 3rd and began this new town in the name of the Lord. It was then called *Welhik Thuppek.*

Then in *August* we were delighted by the arrival of our Indian Brothers and Sisters from *Fridenshütten,* accompanied by Brother *Ettwein,* especially since the latter soon arrived here with some of them. Since that time the little gathering here has gradually increased. In the following *September Josua* also arrived here with a number of Brothers and Sisters. Following the advice of the *Chiefs* they established a 2nd *Town* in this area, which was named *Gnadenhütten.* For the time being they do not actually have any Brothers or Sisters with them,

122. Catharina had been baptized on 17 Dec. 1772. She was the daughter of Samuel Moor; her mother had probably died, which explains why the child was under the care of the grandmother. On 13 June 1773 Samuel Moor married the widow Helena. See Register of Persons.

123. Ezek. 36:25.

124. Ps. 52:11.

125. Zeisberger used this formula to indicate that the question had been decided by submitting it to the lot and that the lot had determined the foundation of a new settlement; on decisions by lot, see Introduction, p. 67.

but Brother *David* and Brother and Sister *Jungmann* visit them as often as possible. The latter arrived here from *Langundouteniünk* on 20 *September,* as Brother *Heckewelder* already had in *August.*

We especially thank the Savior for bringing all of our Brothers and Sisters safely here; during the move no one suffered spiritual harm or erred into the world. Even when it seemed that someone had suffered harm, the Savior and the dear Mother made everything right.

The heavenly Father also mercifully helped the Brothers and Sisters manage despite great shortages and satisfied the desire of every living thing.[126] He also inclined the hearts of the savages to share with our Brothers and Sisters, which we gratefully acknowledge.

With gratitude we also acknowledge the *Communication* of the Congregational Newsletters as a special act of kindness. They are very beneficial for our hearts and souls.

Two adults and 3 children have been baptized here.

Two Sisters have been received into the congregation, one here and one in *Gnadenhütten.* We have had Holy Communion five times at this new site, and each time the Brothers and Sisters from *Gnadenhütten* came here for this.

Four Brothers and Sisters partook in this for the first time.

Three children were born.

Two children died. One died on the journey here in the spring and was buried on the *Ohio,* and one died here. Our God's Acre was dedicated on this occasion.

Currently 92 people, children and adults, live in *Welhick Thuppeek* and 94 in *Gnadenhütten.*

Total 186.

January 1773

THE 1ST   In the morning was the sermon. Toward evening Brother *David* returned from *Gnadenhütten. Echpalawehund* and his wife also came with him. They had gone there from *Gekelemukpechünk* and attended the services this morning. Brother *David* spoke with him several times the next day. Since his desire to live with us and for the Savior has been stirred up anew, we shared good advice with him. When people like this want to come to our place we must exercise great caution. Through him we also received more news about the *Shawnee* and the reason they have changed their minds again. Soon after our visit there, some Indians went there and worried them and scared them and told them that they had not considered well what they had done; they could not do such things without the consent of their *Chiefs.* Then they sent a

126. Ps. 145:16.

message to the *Chief* of the *Lower Shawnee*,[127] who gave them this same answer and added that their grandfather (the *Delaware Chief*) had not informed them about this. Without this they could not do anything like this. A main article in the *Alliance* the *Shawnee* and *Delaware* concluded with each other is that they would not do anything without informing each other about it. The former must especially have their grandfather's consent first.[128] The matter stands as follows: After our first visit to *Gekelemukpechünk*[129] in the year 1771, the well-known Indian preacher *Scattameek* went there and changed everyone's mind again, including the *Chief*, when he pretended he had been in heaven and had had a conversation with the Son of God. He had told him that just as the Indians have different skin and coloring[130] from the White people (because it pleased him to make them like this) he also wanted them to come to him through a different way than the White people. He had also revealed to him that the Indians should drink *Beson*[131] (medicinal herbs and roots) and cleanse themselves from sins. If they did this diligently they would come to him, and if they believed him they would be able to walk on water as on land; even if they only planted a little they would still have enough to live, and many more things like this. Everyone immediately approved of this teaching, which was supported by two other preachers, and soon afterward *Netawatwees* sent a message to the *Shawnee* and shared the news about all this with them, saying that 3 of their preachers had received a new revelation from God and indeed had personally spoken with him.

The *Shawnee* accepted this joyfully and sent the message on to the *Wyandot*,[132] and they sent *deputies* from their midst to *Gekelemukpechünk* to learn about the heart of this matter. They also approved of it, although soon afterward they had seen enough to realize that they had been deceived, to their great detriment, because as a result they experienced the worst famine. Last summer I heard from the *Chief* himself that it was their own fault they ended up in such misery because had believed the lies. Despite this, things remain the same and have not been rescinded, nor repealed through a contrary message. Until this happens, nothing will change.

While we were there, the *Shawnee* had decided together to accept God's

127. Zeisberger refers to the settlements on the Scioto River.

128. According to Zeisberger, "History of the Northern American Indians," 108–9, both tribes concluded this treaty some time before the Seven Years' War; as a result of the treaty the Delaware henceforth called the Shawnee "Grandchildren" and the Shawnee addressed the Delaware as "Grandfathers." Heckewelder, *History, Manners, and Customs,* 86–89, mentions two agreements, an older one that probably dates from the first part of the eighteenth century (86–87), and an agreement in 1768 at the time of the Treaty of Fort Stanwix and the peace treaty with the Cherokee. Weslager, *Delaware Indians,* does not mention such an agreement.

129. This visit occurred in March 1771.

130. Here, for the first time in the diary, skin color is used to distinguish Europeans and Native Americans.

131. See entry for 25 Dec. 1772, with note 117.

132. On the Delaware name for the Wyandots, see entry for 5 June 1772, with note 29.

word and asked the Brothers to send someone at Christmas to live with them and preach the Gospel to them. I had objected then and asked them if they could do this of their own accord without the prior consent of their superiors. I was told that they had been separated from their *Nation* for more than 2 years because they intended to lead a pious life. Therefore they were not dependent on anyone. No one was concerned about them and no one would take any notice of them. This is indeed partially true, because no one objected as long as they remained in their self-made and self-invented worship (as they call it), but remained blindly within this. They remained peaceful and no one checked on them. However, as soon as the Savior allowed himself to be seen with his Gospel, it immediately seemed like Satan was busy with his whole army trying to prevent the work and destroy it. Should Satan always conquer and the Savior and his work be defeated? Should His joys always be curtailed and His reward, which He earned so bitterly with blood, be limited and withheld? Oh, if the Father of our Lord Jesus Christ would soon make things right and save his dear Son's honor!

THE 3RD   The sermon was about the bliss we enjoy when we are made worthy of participating in Jesus' shame and suffering for his's sake. In the afternoon was the Children's Service and in the evening the Congregational Service about the Watchword, Seek the Lord etc.[133] The Brothers were busy with *Echpalawehund* and diligently presented to him the Savior in his suffering and death, during which he was very touched and shed many tears. He had even spoken with an Indian in *Gekelemukpechünk* just recently and asked him why he kept his wife, who wants to become a believer, away from the Brothers. He should try to save his own soul and get advice from the Brothers. They would certainly advise him well. He told him what the Savior has done out of love for us, and how His hands and feet were pierced with nails for the sake of our sins. He said he had hardly been able to speak these words, because he himself was choked by tears. *Traders* from *Pittsburgh* arrived at our place[134] and we also had visitors from *Gekelemukpechünk* again.

THE 4TH   Brother *Jungmann* held the early devotions about the Watchword, But they that wait upon the Lord shall renew their strength etc.[135] He said we are all received through the Savior's hand and are maintained daily in grace through the fluid from his wounds. 3 White people were also present.

THE 6TH   In the morning service we prayed for His precious presence today and committed ourselves and all of our native congregations to him for blessings.[136] In the second service there was a talk about the text, I will also give thee for a light to the Gentiles, etc.,[137] and then two people, *Ignatius* and

133. 1 Chron. 16:11.
134. Not identified.
135. Isa. 40:31.
136. On the meaning of 6 January, see Introduction, xx–xx.
137. Isa. 49:6.

Catharina, were baptized into Jesus' death. This was a very blessed event, which *Echpalawehund* and others from *Gekelemukpechünk* also attended. They were very touched. In the afternoon there was a Lovefeast. During this we remembered that on this day one year ago some of us were in *Fridenshütten,* some in *Schech-schiquanünk,* and some in *Langundoutenünk,* and now the Savior has brought us together here. We had a blessed Service of Adoration with all those who have been baptized. Brother *Jungmann* led the Congregational Service about the Watchword for today,[138] which told how the Savior wants to confirm his promises and what He has done for us on this day, so that we retain an eternal impression of this.

THE 7TH   *Echpalawehund* returned home early in the day. He was powerfully touched during his visit this time and shed countless tears. The Savior will surely be too powerful for him. He went to Brother *David* very early this morning, shared his heart with him once again, and told him then that he has decided to move here to our place now. However, he will surely find a good bit more work before he frees himself, because he is the *Chief's* right hand in the *Council.* Because he realizes all this lies ahead of him, he asked Brother *David* for good advice about how to behave in various situations. He then shared this with him to his *Satisfaction.*[139]

Brother and Sister *Jungmann* went to *Gnadenhütten* to make up the celebration from yesterday. They had not been able to get there earlier because of the high waters.

THE 9TH   They returned from there after leading holiday services and a Lovefeast for them. There were also various matters to clear up there.

THE 10TH   Brother *David* left for there and held the Sunday services and *Conference* with the Helpers there, as Brother *Jungmann* did here. During this he especially impressed on their hearts that they should maintain order among themselves since they are now somewhat settled in. We read them the rules we agreed on during Brother *Ettwein's* stay here, in both *Welhik Thuppeek* and in *Langundoutenünk.* Everyone who wants to live with us has to observe these. They were also told that we congregational Brothers and Sisters do not rule over them, but just want to help them with good advice if they want to become the Savior's people. They would have to try to do what we advised them as well as they could. They received everything well and agreed to all the points, and we then communicated this to all the residents of *Gnadenhütten* the next day. We told them that we will follow these rules from now on and we would expel anyone who opposed them and did not behave according to them. In a service for the married Brothers and Sisters, *Gabriel* and *Lydia,* who were

138. 2 Sam. 7:25.
139. On the problems connected with the conversion of chiefs, see note 243 to entry for 17 August 1773. Echpalawehund was baptized in Gnadenhütten on 6 February 1774.

engaged on the 8th of this month, were married.[140] The 3 Brothers *Isaac, Joseph Peepi,* and *Marcus* traveled to visit the *Shawnee* to find out from them personally how things stand. A *Shawnee,* who lives not far from them and came to *Gnadenhütten* the day before yesterday for a visit, gave us the news that they would hold a *Councel* precisely for this reason and would consider one more time what they had originally proposed.

THE 12TH   Brother *David* returned from *Gnadenhütten.* Some Brothers and Sisters went from here to *Gekelemukpechünk* to fetch Indian corn. Brother *Heckewelder* led the Singing Service in the evening.

THE 13TH   In the Bible reading, held instead of the Singing Service, we read from the Acts of the Apostles about Paul's conversion.[141]

THE 14TH   Through some of our Indian Brothers who returned from *Gekelemukpechünk,* we received news about our 3 Brothers who were continuing their journey to the *Shawnee* from there. When they informed the *Chief* about it, he replied that it was still too early; he wanted to send a message to them on our behalf, but he could not do this yet because his *Councel* was not gathered. However, they could still continue their journey and visit them, which I was glad to hear. A man like *Netawatwees* could be very helpful to the Savior's work among the Indians if he had enough insight and were willing to do this. However, he lacks both.

They had also visited *Echpalawehund* and discussed many things with him. He no longer feels peaceful there, but he has not yet revealed his intention to come to us to *Netawatwees.* This is his only hesitation and what he fears. Without a doubt, it will not be easy and the *Chief* will be upset. Time will tell. However, we feel no joy in our hearts about advising *Echpalawehund* to stay away from us. It is customary among the Indians for the eldest in the friendship[142] to perform the annual sacrifice[143] to keep illnesses away and so things will go well for them. Three or four or more deer or bears are required for this. If this is not observed, but is neglected, and one of them becomes ill, then it is surely because the sacrifice was not made. *Echpalawehund* is the eldest in the family and has performed the sacrifice each time. His friends now see that he is abandoning his old customs and traditions and wants to become a believer. Therefore they have already said that they would have to follow him if he did this. Otherwise things would not go well for them.

---

140. On the Delaware concepts of marriage, personality, childhood, and adulthood, see Miller, "Delaware Personhood," which is based on the published writings of Zeisberger and Heckewelder. There was no place for the solemn vow or for the idea of duration expressed in "till death do us part" in the Delaware concept of marriage. Zeisberger, "History of the Northern American Indians," 78–79.

141. Acts 9:1–9.

142. For Zeisberger's meaning of "friendship," see Introduction, p. 18, and note 42. For a more extensive description of the religious meaning and function of "friendship," see entry for 10 Feb. 1777.

143. On the importance of the sacrifice for the Delaware, see entry for 23 Jan. 1774 and note 330; the importance of sacrifice is downplayed in the answers to Lewis Cass's questions. Weslager, *Delaware Indian Westward Migration,* 114, answer no. 12.

THE 17TH   The sermon was about Moses' words, The Lord thy God will raise up unto thee a Prophet from the midst of thee, unto him ye shall hearken etc.[144] The Savior himself came and revealed God's counsel and will to us and His plans of peace for us. It is now up to us to accept this and to believe with our hearts what He has done for us. Brother *Jungmann* led the Congregational Service and talked about how He approaches the wretched and needy, gladly becomes involved with them, and grants his grace.

THE 19TH   *Isaac* returned from a visit with the *Shawnee*. Yesterday he went to *Gnadenhütten* with *Joseph Peepi* and *Marcus* and they really enjoyed their visit. The preacher was especially happy to see them again. Although they were not all at home, those who were there were just as eager to hear the Gospel as we had found them and left them last fall. They asked the Brothers to hold services for them and also to sing verses, and they gladly did so. The preacher also gave them the news about everything we had heard about them since our first visit. All of it is partially true, because many of them did allow themselves to be turned away, and they told the preacher they could not live as we did. They still liked to make sacrifices and dance, and they did not want to abandon the warrior *Wapachsigan* (a poison warriors use; this is the *Beson* they received from God, as has already been reported above).[145] A rift has developed among them, but their preacher said that he and some others were still of the same mind and were sticking to what they previously told us, and they had not changed. He had once said that he wanted to become a believer, and he still did. If his people did not agree with him, then he and those who agreed with him would leave the rest of them and live with us alone somewhere. The last understanding they had had with each other was that the preacher would visit us before spring and bring us more news. The 3 Brothers also visited a *Delaware Town*[146] where they preached the Savior to them and indeed found ears to hear.

THE 20TH   In the evening there was a Bible reading instead of the Singing Service. The Brothers and Sisters always find this blessed and enjoyable.

THE 24TH   In the morning was the sermon. In the afternoon we read the Brothers and Sisters a talk by a Brother from Greenland, as well as some letters from the Brothers and Sisters there. This delighted them.[147] We had a

---

144. Deut. 18:15.

145. Wapachsigan was produced from herbs; see entry for 25 Dec. 1772, and note 117.

146. See note 21 above. The manuscript map "A Sketch of Muskingum River and Big Beaver Creek" (1775?) (Bibliothèque National de la Service Hydrographique, C.4044, no. 92, photocopy in Library of Congress, Map Division) lists the following settlements on the Muskingum between Woaketameki and Gekelemukpechünk: Mouhweissing, Cushaughking, and White Eyes Town. Thus, according to this map, Mouhweissing would be identical with Mochwesüng, the settlement of the Munsee (cf. note 252 to entry of 2 Sept. 1773), and Cushaughking would be the settlement of those who left Gekelemukpechünk in 1771 in protest.

147. On the Moravian mission in Greenland in the eighteenth century, see Cranz, *Historie von Grönland;* Hegner, *Fortsetzung,* 125–39.

Conference with the Helpers about various concerns, especially about using our time well this winter so that not all of the work lies waiting for us until spring.

THE 26TH   A *Trader* came here, and because he was going to *Pittsburgh* I wrote letters to Bethlehem.[148] In the evening we had a congregational council, during which there were reminders about various things and our congregational rules were read and renewed.

THE 31ST   Brother *David* preached the sermon about Isaiah 42, Behold my servant etc.[149] Brother *Heckewelder* held the Children's Service and Brother *Jungmann* the Congregational Service. With the help of the Brothers, we revised some of the hymns which have been translated into the Indian language.[150]

February

THE 2ND   During the early devotion we committed our widowers and widows to the Savior and all the Brothers and Sisters for blessings. Then they had a separate devotion and Service of Adoration.[151] The Savior revealed himself graciously to them, comforted them, and blessed them. In a separate service we also announced Holy Communion for next Saturday.

Today the Brothers began making rails to fence in about 40 acres of land, which is laid out in fields. This does not include what had already been cleared last year. We also began school for our youth today and will continue this daily.[152]

THE 3RD   Brothers *Josua* and *Johann Martin* came from *Gnadenhütten,* and *Echpalawehund* came from *Gekelemukpechünk.* Both of the former were on business and the latter came here for a visit. The high water has prevented us from being able to get to *Gnadenhütten* for a while now.

THE 5TH   We had Speakings with the Brothers and Sisters. Today the Brothers finished making rails to fence in their land.

THE 6TH   A couple of Brothers from *Langundouteniink* came here for a visit and brought us letters from Brother and Sister *Roth,* along with many sincere greetings. We had not heard anything from them in a long time, so we were even happier about it. After all the services, we 34 Brothers and Sisters partook of the *Sacrament* of the Body and Blood of our Lord, during which He

148. Zeisberger to Seidel, read in Bethlehem on 5 March 1773, MAB, B 229, F 4, I 5. As in later letters, Zeisberger recounted briefly what he described in greater detail in this diary.

149. Isa. 42:1.

150. See entry for 18 May 1772, and note 24.

151. This was the day of the widows' and widowers' choir festival.

152. In 1776 Zeisberger published a *Delaware Indian and English Spelling Book* for the mission schools. On teaching in these schools, see entry for 4 Dec. 1775, and on schools in general, entry for 22 Dec. 1772, with note 112.

revealed himself to us in an exceptional manner. Two Brothers and Sisters participated for the first time, and one observed for the first time.

THE 7TH   Brother and Sister *Jungmann* traveled downriver to *Gnaden-hütten* to hold Holy *Communion* there. We cannot travel there by land since everything in the *Lowland* is covered with ice.

In the meantime Brother *David* held a Conference with the Helpers to consider matters regarding our Brothers and Sisters in *Langundouteniink* who need our help since they want to move here in the spring. They also discussed *Echpalawehund*, who has now decided to move here. He was then called and the Brothers heard his explanation first-hand. Today was an especially blessed day for our Brothers and Sisters. You could tell from their faces that they had eaten Jesus' Body and drunk his Blood.

THE 10TH   The 2 messengers returned to *Langundouteniink.* Some Brothers and Sisters from here also went there with them to pick up all their belongings. Brother and Sister *Jungmann* returned from *Gnadenhütten,* where they had spoken with the Brothers and Sisters and then had a blessed Holy Communion.

There was a Conference with the Helpers there, and some individuals from here also went for this. During this they discussed how they should exercise caution regarding the *Chiefs* so that they do not bring all kinds of burdens and difficulties upon themselves, which they would regret later. In short, they should not undertake anything without our previous knowledge.[153] The Conference advised two people who were not baptized to seek their fortune elsewhere, since they do not fit in here with their improper lifestyle.

THE 12TH   Various Brothers and Sisters returned from *Gekelemukpech-iink.* They had bought Indian corn there and they found the Indians there involved in sacrifices and celebrations. One of them told some of our people that they should not hold out any hope that he would give up that way of life and accept our way of life. He wanted to retain his brown skin and not become white. When they carry out their heathen ways and celebrate festivals, the enmity against the Gospel expresses itself anew.

THE 13TH   Brother *David* went to *Gnadenhütten* and held the Sunday services for them on THE 14TH and spoke with some of the Brothers and Sisters. An English *Baptist Minister*[154] who had already sent letters to *Gekelemuk-pechiink* a number of times and had offered to preach to them, had heard about us and went there for a visit. He told us he had spent this winter among the *Shawnee* with the *Intention* of preaching the Gospel to them. However, he did

153. Since Gnadenhütten was considerably closer to Gekelemukpechünk, it was tempting for Netawatwees to involve Christian Indians like Josua (who had been a chief before his conversion) in Council affairs in times of crisis. See entry for 10 June 1774. Zeisberger was the more worried about this because there was still no missionary permanently stationed in Gnadenhütten. See Introduction, pp. 59–60.

154. This was David Jones (1736–1820), a Baptist minister. See Jones, *Journal of Two Visits.*

not find one person who was inquiring about God, indeed not even one in whom he had observed signs of wondering if there was a God in heaven. He had been in 5 of their *Towns,* but they had not allowed him to speak privately with Indians, much less to preach a single time. He finally fled in secrecy to save his life. They actually set out after him, but fortunately he escaped their hands. He said he would certainly never go into that area again because that is not how he had imagined things would be. Now he wanted to see if they would give him a *favorable* answer in *Gekelemukpechünk,* where he also made a request. If that happened, he would stay there for a while. However, soon afterward we heard that they did not accept his offer and they also did not allow him to preach a sermon.[155] Therefore he praised and lauded the work of the Brothers among the Indians and said we had done more than they would manage in their whole lives. From his *Certificate* from the *Baptist Society* in *Philadelphia,*[156] we saw that he was an ordained preacher. He had also shown this to the Indians everywhere he went, but it did not help him accomplish his goal. He seemed to be a nice man and he also said he had preached in *Brother Gambold's*[157] church. He gave a nice talk admonishing our Indians, at his own request and with Brother *David's* permission. He told them they were fortunate and blessed and commended them to God's protection, which they needed because they lived in the midst of the enemies of Christ's kingdom. He also wanted to go to *Welhik Thuppeck* with Brother *David* and have a look at the town. The ice had blocked the river and the waters were swollen though, so he gave up his plans and returned to *Gekelemukpechünk.* He told us that on his journey here in *November* last year, he had received a *Paquet* of letters from Brother *Bill Henry*[158] in *Lancaster* to send us. Because he took a different route than he had originally planned, he had given them to a White man below *Pittsburgh* on the *Ohio* to send on. We have not received them yet, however. Brother *David* asked him to send them to *Pittsburgh* if he could get them back on his return journey.

THE 16TH   Brother *David* returned from *Gnadenhütten* and led the Singing Service in the evening. Our Indian Brothers and Sisters made preparations for boiling sugar,[159] which they do close to here. The Brothers began framing a house for *Echpalawehund.*

155. Ibid., 92–105. Remarks like these indicate how Zeisberger composed his diary. Obviously, every week or two Zeisberger wrote out the diary on the basis of short notes.

156. On Baptists in Philadelphia, see Sacks, *Philadelphia Baptist Tradition.*

157. Hector Ernest Gambold (1719–88) was one of five Moravian preachers who had been born in England and who at first had worked as itinerant Moravian preachers in Pennsylvania, New Jersey, and New York before they were assigned districts. Between 1764 and 1784 Gambold was minister of the Moravian congregation at Staten Island. Leibert, "History of the Congregation on Staten Island," 61–62; Glatfelter, *Pastors and People,* 2:82–83.

158. William Henry (1729–86), merchant and member of the Moravian congregation at Lancaster, Pa., was often involved in transporting mail and goods for the Moravian mission settlements, thanks to his excellent connections to other places. Jordan, *William Henry of Lancaster.*

159. The boiling of maple sap for sugar was an important part of securing provisions and food for Native Americans. See in general Keller, "America's Native Sweet," 119–21, and, for the Delaware, Zeisberger, "History of the Northern American Indians," 48–51.

THE 19TH   In the evening was the Bible Reading from the Old Testament about how God led his people out of *Egypt* with a mighty hand.[160]

THE 23RD   *Isaac* returned from *Gekelemukpechünk,* where he had to listen to much being said against us. He had an answer for everything, however. Things there are very disorganized and there is great *Confusion* among them. They do not know how they should handle the matter, and it is all just because they see that *Echpalawehund* wants to leave them and come to us. They also foresee that if he comes to us, others will follow. Now they do not want this to happen (because the people can come to listen, but they should not convert), so they are considering ways to control the situation and stop it. People have different ideas about it, and each one thinks he is the cleverest. The *Chief* surely does not want to see his people go to us, but he is watching the matter and has remained neutral toward us thus far. Those who are antagonistically inclined, however, are trying the old *Project* again and are talking a lot publicly about getting us White Brothers and Sisters out of the country. They are saying that some of our Indians have already been instructed in the word and in the teaching daily for 20–30 years. They could certainly instruct others, and then they would not need teachers anymore. As long as the Indians have existed, it has been unheard of for them to have White preachers among them or for them to need instruction. This was surely the case among the White people across the sea, but not among the Indians. They were not at all happy that we were here. They could not live as peacefully as before, because now they always have to hear how various things they did were not right and were sinful, and that their sacrifices and everything they did to please God was useless. Some of our Indian Brothers thought we should submit a *Declaration* to the *Chief* stating that if their teachers were not allowed to stay with them, they would all go with them wherever they went. After all, they had not come here because of the land; there was other land. They had come to be a blessing and help to their *Nation.* However, we thought it would be better to remain quiet and bide our time in this matter.

THE 24TH   In the early devotions, the Watchword for today seemed very noteworthy and fitting, But Israel shall be saved in the Lord with an everlasting salvation etc.[161] In the evening we had the Bible reading. Brother *Jungmann* returned from *Gnadenhütten* where he had visited and held services.

THE 25TH   Some Brothers and Sisters from *Gnadenhütten* came here for a visit and some returned from *Langundoutenünk* with Indian corn and their belongings.

THE 28TH   Brother *Jungmann* preached the sermon and Brother *David* held the Children's Service and Congregational Service. We learned from *Gekelemukpechünk* that they have now finally agreed upon some measures to prevent

160. Exod. 12:31–15:27.
161. Isa. 45:17.

their people from coming to us. The *Chief* submitted these to his *Councel* to consider what would be best for them. Then they deliberated for three days in a row and after they had all reached an agreement, they gathered again before the *Chief* and informed him that they had decided they would lead a better life from now on, that they would admonish and punish the young people for their disorderly and bad life. From now on they would completely forbid and put an end to drinking, dancing, gaming, and such vices, and if anyone brought *Rum* there, whether it was an Indian or White person, they would destroy the kegs and pour the *Rum* out onto the floor.[162] They had designated six men to do this and they could also get more helpers if needed. They also said, Why should we also not be able to live as the Indian believers, without having teachers here. If we just want to do this, it will work. Then they called *Echpalawehund* and asked him why he wanted to leave them and what it was that he did not like among them. If he just told them, they would change and stop it. He replied, You have decided to rid yourselves of the four matters of drinking, dancing, cards, and dice games. Is that all? I could name many more things you should get rid of. However, I know in advance that nothing will come of this. He had to listen to many lies and vicious remarks about us, especially concerning baptism, and he was really not in a position to answer everything. However, he told them in conclusion that even if he did not go to us yet, they should know that he would not watch them and wait for them much longer, because it was his absolute intention to become a believer. They had also decided not to tolerate any *Traders* among them, because they continue bringing more sinful things among the Indians. Now they also wanted to begin leading a pious life, but they will not get far with this. It may work for a little while, but then it will become even more difficult. Because they are now making a new beginning and want to lead a good life and have good conduct, they had also decided in their *Councel* to establish a new site and town. It could hardly work at the old site because evil had become too strongly entrenched. The *Chief,* however, did not approve of the suggestion and asked them if they did not have more considerations and if there was no one among them who had the ability to understand the matter better. They had built nice houses where they lived, which had cost a lot. They had cleared land and fenced it in, and now they wanted to turn their backs on all this? Most importantly they needed to consider that their friends from the *Susquehanna* lived close to them. They had called them there and now they had established 2 *Towns*. What would they say to this if they went away now and left them alone? It is true that many of them preferred to

162. For both the missionaries and most Native American chiefs, the introduction of rum and other alcohol was one of Europe's worst influences on the Native American tribes. See Vachon, "History of Brandy in Canada"; Salone, "Sauvages du Canada"; Jacobs, *Wilderness Politics and Indian Gifts,* 52–55; White, *Middle Ground,* 334–36, 497–99; and Mancall, *Deadly Medicine.* On the effort to realize the resolve in Gekelemukpechünk, see entry for 14 March 1773; on the importance of rum for the Shawnee, see speech of Gischenatsi, entry for 17 Sept. 1773.

avoid us so they could continue undisturbed in their heathen life, but where would they flee so that we would not get in their way? The Indians are very uneasy; Satan is putting up a fight and is seeking to claim his place. In the end, however, he will have to give up the fight. Today a messenger also brought us word from *Gekelemukpechünk* that the *Shawnee* were on the way to visit us.

March

THE 3RD   *Lucas* returned from *Gekelemukpechünk,* where he had gone on business yesterday. He had spoken quite emotionally to some Indians there about the Savior's great love for poor sinners and all that He had suffered and endured for our sake. A couple of them replied that this had touched their hearts. Therefore they believed that what we told them was certainly true. Through him we also received the news that the *Shawnee* preacher and someone else had gone to *Gnadenhütten* for a visit yesterday and had spoken with the Indian Brothers there. Because he had heard them himself, he gave us the following news about this. They said that when some of our Brothers had visited them this winter, they had been very happy and listened gladly to what they had discussed with them.[163] Then after all their people had come home, they had held a *Councel* again, in which they decided among themselves for a second time to accept the word of God and also to live accordingly. All the people in their *Town,* men and women, young and old, were in agreement about this. Soon, when they got home, they would move away from there and a good day's journey further on, where no one would disturb them.[164] Their *Chief* had sent them here to inform us of this and they were glad to have seen us and spoken with us. *Josua* and the Brothers who had gathered then told them they could not give them an answer to this and advised them to go to *Welhick Thuppeek,* where they would receive a reliable answer. However, they replied that they were out of time and it was already past the time they had promised they would be back home.

We later heard that when they left home they had all been in a good frame of mind to discuss everything with us and to work things out. Unfortunately they arrived at *Gekelemukpechünk* at a time when everything was very confused[165] and they were making up all the lies about us they could come up with. They did not miss any chance to turn them away. Therefore they did not convey their message completely, but just half way. We see nothing more we can do in this matter for now. We will wait until we get another opportunity and there is a *Prospect* to reach them again.

163. See entries for 1 and 19 Jan. 1773.
164. See entry for 28 Feb. 1773 as a parallel to the Council's resolves in Gekelemukpechünk to justify the foundation of a new settlement with the need for fundamental reforms.
165. On the reasons for this confusion, see entry for 28 Feb. 1773.

THE 8TH   Brother *David* returned from *Gnadenhütten* where he had gone on a visit the day before yesterday. He was accompanied by *Isaac,* who had been on business in *Goshahossink*[166] some 20 miles below *Gekelemukpechünk,* where he had proclaimed the Savior in a service for many Indians. Everyone was very attentive during this. 2 days ago in *Gekelemukpechünk,* they carried out the first *Execution* of the *Acta* they had made, destroying 10 kegs of *Rum* a *Trader* brought and pouring it out onto the ground before he even reached the *Town.*[167]

THE 14TH   We were delighted to receive letters by way of *Pittsburgh,* along with the *Continuation* of the Watchwords for this year.[168]

THE 21ST   Brother *Jungmann* held the services here and after the sermon he baptized the baby daughter born to Brother *Levi* and Sister *Salome* on the 18th of this month with the name *Rebecca.* In the evening Brother *David* returned from *Gnadenhütten.* He had gone there yesterday, held services for them, and had Speakings with some of the Brothers and Sisters.

THE 22ND   The Helpers gathered, spoke with a woman who has been staying here for a long time, and advised her to go somewhere else since things were not working out with her. However, *Gertraut's* daughter, another person who has wanted to come to us a number of times and has often visited but always allowed herself be turned away, received permission to stay for a trial, in reply to her persistent requests.

Schebosch and his wife drove a couple of days journey down the river to visit their friends and get Indian corn.

Diary of the little Indian Congregation in Welhik Thuppek *and* Gnadenhütten *on the* Mushkingum *from March 24th until the 8th of* June 1773[169]

MARCH 24TH   Brother *Heckewelder* and some Indian Brothers left for *Langundoutenünk* to assist the Brothers and Sisters there with their move here. We also sent letters for Bethlehem with them.

THE 25TH   In our services we reflected on how the Savior dressed himself in our poor flesh and blood, and this nourished our hearts.[170] A certain Indian *Doctor,*[171] who had often visited our services in *Goshgoshüng* but later left

166. See note 146. Goschahossink is identical with Cushaughking.

167. See entry for 28 Feb. 1773.

168. The first installments for 1773 had arrived on 22 Nov. and 26 Dec. 1772.

169. MAB, B 141, F 3, I 2, fol. 31.

170. The Moravian Festival Calendar marked this day as "The Festival of the incarnation of Christ."

171. Zeisberger, "History of the Northern American Indians," 25–27, uses the terms "Doctor" and "medicine man" interchangeably and considers them "nothing other than charlatans" (25, 148), although he expresses appreciation for Indian knowledge of medicinal herbs (24–25), an expertise belonging only to "Doctors": "They [i.e., doctors] prescribe some sort of Beson prepared from herbs and roots, of which they know the properties very well" (148). Heckewelder, *History, Manners, and*

there, came here yesterday for a visit. Since then he has been wandering from one place to another. He was very moved by the word about Jesus' incarnation, sufferings, and death. Both he and his wife expressed their desire to belong to the Savior and to live with us. The man told us about his circumstances and asked for our advice, which we gave him.

THE 28TH   Brother *David* went to *Gnadenhütten* and held the Sunday services there, as Brother *Jungmann* did here.

THE 29TH   Some more Brothers and Sisters left to assist in *Langundoutenünk*. The high waters had delayed them for several days.

April

THE 5TH   Brother *David* returned from *Gnadenhütten,* where he had Speakings with the Brothers and Sisters in preparation for Holy Communion. *Echpalawehund* had gone on his way to *Welhik Thuppeck*. However, since he found Brother *David* there, he spoke with him and asked him for advice about various things. He had spoken with the *Chief* once again about moving to our place. He objected and asked who would assist him in his affairs if he moved to our place and whether *Echpalawehund* would come to his *Councel* when he sent for him if he were living with us. Then he wanted an answer from Brother *David*. He replied that he could not promise such things, because if he wanted to live with us he must not commit to anything else, so that he could always act in accordance with his heart. Even if he thought that he could do this now, and even if we advised him to go to the *Councel* now and then, he did not know how he would feel when he was living with us and he might not be able to keep his promise then. Brother *David* advised him to stay in *Gekelemukpechünk* until his circumstances were cleared up better, because he is still very obligated by the *Chief's* business and by his family, and he cannot yet free himself completely. He should remember us lovingly, as we would also remember him, and come to visit us now and then when things there became too difficult for him. He was very satisfied with this, said a cordial farewell, and returned home. Now we also learned that the latest commotion and *Confusion* in *Gekelemukpechünk* was caused by none other than *Killbuck*. He had secretly incited the people against us, deliberated with them, and made up all sorts of evil accusations against us. He always pretended he had orders from the *Chief* to do this, until

---

Customs, 225–38, emphasizes that many "Doctors" used medical knowledge *and* religious rituals to treat disease (see also [Sensemann and Zeisberger], "Diary of Zeisberger and Zenseman," 57, 66), yet stresses that he knew of "practitioners among them . . . who are free from these prejudices, or at least do not introduce them into their practice of the medical art" (224). Heckewelder stresses the close relationship between magic, cult, and medicine in the description of Isaac as "Captain, Doctor and Preacher" (entry for 10 Aug. 1773) and of Queelpachano as "formerly a great Doctor," who had been bothered by hallucinations (entry for 29 Dec. 1773). See note 117 for entry for 25 Dec. 1772.

the truth was finally discovered. When the *Chief* found out, he publicly shamed him, after which he left the *Town* for a time. Thus all of their attacks came to nothing.[172]

THE 6TH   The early devotion was about the promise the Savior gave us that we will receive whatever we ask from the Father in his name, if we just believe.[173] Brother and Sister *Jungmann* had Speakings with the Brothers and Sisters in preparation for Holy Communion. In the evening we read the Bible text for the day.[174]

THE 8TH   In the morning the communicant Brothers and Sisters from *Gnadenhütten* gathered here, and we celebrated the *Pedilavium*[175] and the Holy *Sacrament* of the Body and Blood of our Lord with 32 Brothers and Sisters. *Anton* from *Schechschequanünk* joined us in this for the first time. Most of our Brothers were not home this time, but in *Langundoutenünk*.

In the afternoon Brother and Sister *Jungmann* traveled to *Gnadenhütten* to take care of the services there. In the evening we read the story of the Savior's anguish on the Mount of Olives and his arrest. Our tender hearts melted.

THE 9TH   We read the Bible story for the day. Our hearts melted during this. To commemorate the piercing of Jesus' side,[176] we had a blessed *Liturgy* and Service of Adoration, and in this way we accompanied Him through all his *Scenes* of suffering until the grave.

THE 10TH   At noon was the Lovefeast and in the evening a talk about the Watchword,[177] which told of the comfort we have in the Savior because he lay in the grave for us.

THE 11TH   Early in the morning the congregation was greeted with the words, The Lord is risen. They replied: He is risen indeed! Then we prayed the Easter *Litany* on God's Acre and prayed for eternal fellowship with those Brothers and Sisters who died during this year. In a service afterward, we read the story of our Savior's resurrection and then there was the sermon. The Congregational Service was about the Watchword and the text.[178] During this we wished that the Holy Spirit might illuminate what we have felt and enjoyed in our hearts in these days, and that when He helped us in judgment He would confirm that God was in Christ.

---

172. The reference is to John Killbuck Sr. (Bemineo). On his role and function, see entries for 7 Sept. 1773, 19 Dec. 1774, and 12 Aug. 1775.

173. John 14:13.

174. In fact the text for the day is not what they read—for 6 April 1773 it was Luke 23:11, the story of Herod and his court's mockery of Jesus—but in general the stories reported are for the high days of the Christian church calendar. For Holy Week these of course were accounts of the Passion. Daily readings were divided into sequences; thus on Good Friday the story of the crucifixion was read (see entries for 1 April 1774 and 14 April 1775); see Smaby, *Transformation of Moravian Bethlehem*, 18–19.

175. Foot washing.

176. On the importance of the piercing of Jesus' side in Moravian theology, see Introduction, pp. 55–56.

177. Ps. 23:4.

178. Isa. 27:8; text, 2 Timothy 2:8.

THE 12TH   Brother and Sister *Jungmann* returned from *Gnadenhütten,* where they had many visitors from *Gekelemukpechünk* during the holidays.

THE 17TH   We received letters from *Langundoutenünk,* in which Brother *Roth*[179] announced their departure from there.

THE 18TH   It was the festival day of those baptized during this year, and all those who have been baptized had a service to remember the covenant they made with the Savior in their baptism. We especially committed to Him the five who were baptized here this year and one who was received into the congregation. We admonished them to strengthen their profession and election and to hold fast to this until their end. This was a blessed service. An Indian stranger named *Leonhard* came here and attended our services. He was baptized in *Meniolagameka,*[180] knew Brothers *David* and *Jungmann* well, and now lives 60 miles from here. The Indian Brothers and we spoke with him a great deal and admonished him to seek the Savior on the cross again, whom he had lost, and to approach him as a sinner.

THE 19TH   Brother *Jungmann* baptized the baby girl born on the 9th of this month, who was on the verge of death, at the persistent request of the parents who were not yet baptized. She received the name *Salome,* and then she did die on the following day and was buried in our God's Acre on THE 21ST.[181]

THE 24TH   *Johann Martin* and *Marcus* came here from *Gnadenhütten.* Brother *David* went there with them. In the afternoon Brother and Sister *Roth*[182] arrived here on land with the Indian Brothers and Sisters.

THE 25TH   Brother *Jungmann* preached a sermon about the Good Shepherd. The Brothers and Sisters who became communicants this year had a service. There were 11 of them. He laid on their hearts the absolute necessity of remaining in Him, the Vine,[183] and of continuing to grow. Brother *Roth* led the Congregational Service. Brother *David* returned from *Gnadenhütten* where he had held the services and baptized the baby boy born to Brother *Daniel* and Sister *Johanna* on the 22nd of this month with the name *Benjamin.* A number of Indian strangers came here to visit, including 3 *Mohicans* from *Walhanding,* a day's journey away from here.[184] They brought a message and a *String of Wampum* for our *Mohicans* from the *Shawnee.* The message was:

We were happy and pleased to learn of your arrival on the *Mushkingum* in the summer of last year. However, we are sorry to hear now that you are

---

179. Johannes Roth accompanied the group of Christian Indians who traveled by land from Langundoutenünk to Schönbrunn, while John Heckewelder accompanied the group that traveled by water.

180. Meniologomeka was situated on the Aquanshicola in eastern Pennsylvania. Between 1749 and 1754 it had been an outstation of Gnadenhütten I. Müller, *200 Jahre Brüdermission,* 219–23.

181. Under normal circumstances, children of unbaptized parents were not baptized.

182. Johannes Roth was married to Maria Agnes, born Pfingstag (1735–1805).

183. John 15:5.

184. It is not possible to identify this settlement clearly.

turning your faces back where you came from. Turn your eyes here toward us and do not worry about where you should settle. If you really do not like where you are now and you cannot be at peace there, then come to us. We will find you a place where no one will disturb you or offend you.

As far as we know, the confused and worrisome events which had recently taken place in *Gekelemukpechünk* are what prompted this message. At that time some of the *Shawnee* had come up to visit us since they had seen and heard that the Indians were very prejudiced against us and were saying a lot of bad things about us. They took this news and how they had found things in this area to the *Lower Shawnee* and told them everything there.[185] Whenever Satan rages, he hurts himself and loses. We gave the messenger the answer that we could not give any definite response to this now. We had just recently come here and had not even all gathered. We would keep their words and not forget them. However, they had not been correctly informed when they heard we were turning our faces away again. We were, rather, remaining completely quiet. We also heard that the *Wyandot*[186] were not very satisfied that the *Chief* in *Gekelemukpechünk* had not reported the arrival of our Indians here to them in good time, so that they could have sought and designated a place for the Indian Believers to live comfortably and peacefully. They surely knew how things were with them, and that they would have to live alone so they would not be disturbed and bothered by the savages.

THE 26TH   Everyone who was there went out to clear land. This had been substantially slowed down by those moving here from *Langundoutenünk*. We congregational Brothers and Sisters had a *Conference* about getting settled in, as well as about *Gnadenhütten* receiving either a Brother or a couple. Brother and Sister *Roth* were willing to go there.

THE 27TH   We spoke with some Brothers and Sisters whom we thought could move to *Gnadenhütten*. There are only a very few of them, however, and *Welhik Thuppeek* will therefore be almost too large. For now we cannot help this.

THE 28TH   Some more of our Brothers and Sisters arrived here by way

185. See entry for 8 March 1773.
186. The Wyandot (Delamatteno) had given permission to the Delaware to settle on their territory and therefore demanded a say in the decisions respecting land use. See Introduction, pp. 25–26. For 9 Aug. 1768 Zeisberger noted in his Goschgoschünk diary that during a negotiation there in the presence of the Indian preacher, the following proposal had been advanced: "They would send a message to the two Delaware Chiefs at Kaskaskank on the Beaver Creek, which empties into the Ohio below Pittsburg, acquainting them with their desire to live differently in the future and to hear the gospel which was being preached to them by the brethren whom they had with them. They did not doubt that they would gladly receive them and, in case they received their consent, would move thither this fall. These two chiefs [Packanke and Glikhican, the latter baptized in 1770 as Isaac] are said to be peaceable, to avoid entanglement in wars, to listen to no Indian preachers and to be desirous of leading a good life. *The land in question*, which is said to be excellent, *was given by the Delamattenos to the Delawares to live upon and it lies three days journey from here to the west-south-west*." [Sensemann and Zeisberger], "Diary of Zeisberger and Zenseman," 69–70, emphasis added.

of *Tuscarawi.* They made reed *Canows* and then traveled the rest of the way down by water. A couple of families moved from here to *Gnadenhütten* today.

THE 29TH   Brother *Roth* held the early devotions about praising and thanking the Lord for all the good things He has done for us. Afterward we spoke with some Indians who were not our members but who had followed along on the move from *Langundouteniink.* Some received permission to live with us; some were turned away.

May

THE 1ST   After the early devotions, Brother and Sister *Roth* left by water for *Gnadenhütten,* where they will stay for now. Today the first heralds of those who had traveled from *Langundouteniink* by water arrived at our place. They had left the rest of them on this river 6 days ago.[187]

THE 3RD   All the Brothers and Sisters got to work making fences. Some of the Brothers from here and *Gnadenhütten* went out to meet those who were traveling up by water in order to help them. On the 5th they all arrived here safely, for which we thanked the Savior in a childlike way, in accordance with our Watchword for today.[188] In the evening we welcomed the Brothers and Sisters in the Singing Service. The report from their journey can be seen enclosed here.[189]

THE 6TH AND 7TH   We tried to lodge all of our Brothers and Sisters as well as we could, divided up the fields and building sites,[190] and each person immediately began working to prepare for planting.

THE 9TH   In addition to the usual Sunday services, there was a *Conference* with the Helpers. We also spoke again with some of those who had come here about their living here, and they received provisional permission.

THE 10TH   We built an addition to our Meeting Hall, which was too small. There were Indians from *Shenenge*[191] here for a visit. They are moving down this river. A family of Indians from there had settled not far from us on *Sugar Creek* and are planting there. We are afraid that this might become another Indian *Town,* which would be disadvantageous and harmful especially to

187. See note 182 above.

188. 1 Chron. 16:34. The enumeration of chapters differs in the 1745 Bible edition of the Halle Orphanage from the standard Bible edition; in the Halle edition the correct reference is 1 Chron. 17:34.

189. The enclosure is published by [Heckewelder], "Canoe Journey from the Big Beaver to the Tuscarawas."

190. See entry for 24 Aug. 1772, and map in appendix.

191. Shenenge, more often spelled Shenango, was a Delaware settlement on the Shenango, one of the headstreams of the Beaver River north of Kaskaskunk. The chief of this settlement, Lawelooch-walend, visited Schönbrunn on 20 September 1773; nine days later he received permission to move with his family to Schönbrunn. He was baptized Simon on 2 April 1774; see entry for 6 July 1778.

our young people. Therefore we sent Brothers *Isaac* and *Wilhelm* to *Gekelemuk-pechünk* to inform the *Chief* about this.

THE 12TH   *Schebosch* and his wife returned from visiting their friends 20 miles below *Gekelemukpechünk*. They had received them well there and given them Indian corn as a gift. Through them we received letters from *October* last year, via *Gekelemukpechünk*. We had already assumed that those were lost. The *Lower Shawnee,* about whom we heard bad news a while ago, came up here with some white *Scalps* which they had killed down the *Ohio*.[192] They were turned away with a serious rebuke, however, before they reached *Gekelemukpechünk*.

THE 15TH   The Brothers finished making fences and more than 80 acres[193] have been fenced in now on three different sites. All of it will be planted this year.

THE 16TH   The sermon about today's Gospel lesson discussed how the Savior, who proceeded from the Father and came into the world, accomplished the entire work of our redemption through his sufferings and death.

THE 17TH   There was a congregational council. During this people were reminded of various matters, especially that parents should be more concerned about raising our children for the Savior.

THE 18TH   We were delighted to receive letters from Bethlehem and *Litiz* by way of *Pittsburgh*. These brought us news of our many Brothers and Sisters who have gone home, which really touched us.[194]

THE 20TH   Early in the day we read the Bible story for Ascension Day[195] and then we knelt and worshipped Him and prayed for his precious presence and his further walk among us. Then there was the sermon, which many strangers also attended. In the Congregational Service in the evening there was a talk about the Watchword,[196] and then *Lazara's* husband was baptized into Jesus' death with the name *Esra*. This was a blessed event for our Brothers and Sisters as well as for the strangers.

192. Alexander McKee's report to Sir William Johnson, dated 3 July 1773 from Pittsburgh, mentions incidents; unfortunately the crucial parts are mutilated and offer no further details, *JP*, 8:842–43; see Sir William Johnson to Earl of Dartmouth, 22 Sept. 1773, *JP*, 8:888–91. According to Rice, *Allegheny Frontier*, 80, in April 1773 Indians killed trappers George Yeader and Adam Strader. It is likely that these incidents are the same mentioned in the court protocol of the *Camp Cat Fish Court Record* as "Upper Battle of Tingooqua Creek" from 8 May 1773; see entry for 22 May 1773 and note 197.

193. Although Zeisberger used the German terms for weights and measures, he seems to have given the German terms English meanings—thus the "acre" in the text conforms to an English acre, etc.

194. In February 1773 American correspondents reported to Franklin in London about extremely cold weather in Pennsylvania; see [Franklin], *Papers of Benjamin Franklin,* 20:194 note 9. Zeisberger's remark more specifically refers to the death of David Nitschmann, the first bishop of the Unity, on 8 October 1772, and to that of Timothy Horsefield on 9 March 1773 and his wife on 14 March 1773. MAB, Memoirs, B 3, 1771–85, F 1773.

195. The text for the day was Acts 1:1–14.

196. Song of Sol. 7:30.

THE 22ND   Indians from *Gekelemukpechünk, Goshahossünk,* and other towns came here to visit. Some time ago it seemed that a war with the *Shawnee* and *Virginians* who live far down the *Ohio* was almost unavoidable, because the former had already killed and *scalped* many White people.[197] Now we received the happy news that everything has been put aside and peace will prevail. The *Wawiachtanos* and *Kickapoo,* 2 *Nations* who are their neighbors,[198] held a council with them and offered to keep peace. The *Chief* in *Gekelemukpechünk* also did this and told them that if they did not keep peace they could expect complete ruin because no one would support them.

THE 23RD   In the morning the sermon was about all those who will be lost because of their unbelief. Afterward there was a service for the married Brothers and Sisters and a *Conference* with the Helpers.

THE 24TH   The strangers who were here visiting returned home, some of them with blessings for their hearts. Brother *David* went to *Gnadenhütten,* discussed various matters with the Brothers and Sisters, and returned from there on the 25TH.

THE 30TH   In addition to the usual Sunday services, all the baptized residents had a blessed Service of Adoration, thanked our dear Mother for all the faithful care and guidance she has shown us, and asked her for merciful *Absolution.*[199] *Echpalawehund* and some others came here from *Gekelemukpechünk* for a visit.

THE 31ST   A certain Indian who was returning from *Gekelemukpechünk* and passing through here called some of our Brothers together. He gave them a *String of Wampum* and told them that they should consider among themselves whether they could tell him anything about *Machtapassican* (about the poison

197. The date of the incident is 8 May 1773, when (according to the protocol of the *Camp Cat Fish Court Record,* 45) Cherokee assaulted four white families. Between March 1772 and May 1773 in this region alone more than thirty people, among them twenty-two Indians, were killed (Horn, *Horn Papers* 1:100–101). McConnell, *A Country Between,* 258–60, emphasizes that in the region claimed by Virginia relations between Shawnee, white hunters, and traders were tense and led to numerous incidents.

198. For the context and background of these conflicts, see Introduction, pp. 21–24. According to Zeisberger, Wawiachtano (Wah-w(-ah'-tung-ong; see Dunn, *True Indian Stories,* 315; also spelled Wewischtano, see entry for 15 July 1777, a synonym for the Wea) around this time settled in the region between the river systems of the Scioto and Wabash, while the Kickapus (Kickapoo) lived on both sides of the Wabash; both tribes were allies of the Delaware. The language of the Wawiachtano was linguistically related to that of the Shawnee; that of the Kickapus on the other hand differed in many respects from that of the Delaware, although the relationship between Delaware and Kickapus was close, "for many live along the Wabash river where the Kickapus have given them hunting grounds. Every year Delaware hunters go thither for the chase and return" (Zeisberger, "History of the Northern American Indians," 108–10, 142). See Callender, Pope, and Pope, "Kickapoo." After 1763 the Kickapus were willing to listen to Spanish agents, as Sir William Johnson, the English agent responsible for relations to these tribes, learned. These alliances between Delaware, Shawnee, and the western tribes were not in Britain's interest, and with the support of the Six Indian Nations Johnson tried to destroy this wide network of alliances. White, *Middle Ground,* 354–57.

199. Whitsunday was on 30 May 1773.

that is supposed to exist among the Indians).[200] He did this here recently for the second time. The first time they returned his *Belt* to him, but he forced this *String* upon our Indian Brothers and left. He is the one who alarmed everyone in this area and *Kaskaskunk* last year. He has now spent more than a year trying to discover the poison among the Indians and has not yet been able to find the smallest amount. Now he wants to begin again and would like to entangle our people in this.[201]

June

JUNE 1ST   In the early devotion about the Watchword[202] we talked about how nothing but the word of Jesus' death and blood can melt and make tender the hard and dead hearts that people have by nature.

Echpalawehund returned home and promised to visit us again soon. His visit was a blessing to him once again.

Some of our Indian Brothers had considered it good and necessary for us to submit[203] another *Declaration* to the *Chief* in *Gekelemukpechünk*, because he has not yet replied to any of our words. We have waited until now for a good opportunity. Since people are trying to bother us with such things now, we thought the time had come to explain ourselves to them directly again. Brothers *Johannes, Isaac, Wilhelm, Nathanael,* and *Joseph* were appointed to do this and some others from *Gnadenhütten* were supposed to join them. The next day, the 2ND, they passed through *Gnadenhütten* and went to *Gekelemukpechünk* and returned here in the evening on the 3RD. They gave the following talk to the *Chief* and his *Councel* in the presence of a great crowd of listeners: My friends! It has already been 3 years, and indeed it was just 2 days after our arrival in *Kaskaskunk*, when all the residents of *Kaskaskunk, Shenenge* and the whole area had gathered, that we told *Packanke* and his *Councel* about our teaching, life, and walk, and that we have abandoned all heathen ways and all sinful Indian customs and traditions and do not want to have anything to do with them. We want, instead, to live in the world in a manner pleasing to God.[204] We explained this same thing to you in a *Councel* a year ago, when our friends and

200. On the poison Wapachsigan, see entry for 19 Jan. 1773, note 145 and for 25 Dec. 1772, note 117. The term (or its variant, Mattapassigan) does not appear in Zeisberger's *Delaware Indian and English Spelling Book* or in his more comprehensive *Lenapé-English Dictionary*. On Machtapassican, see entries for 3, 6, and 25 June and for 11 Sept. 1773 and 5 Nov. 1774.

201. The name of this Indian was Gulpikamen or Ludwig, a son of Glikhican, alias Isaac. See entry for 25 June 1773 and Register of Persons under Ludwig (baptized before 1749).

202. Ezek. 11:19.

203. See entry for 23 Feb. 1773.

204. On the background for this message to Packanke in Kaskaskunk, see entry for 9 Aug. 1768 in [Senseman and Zeisberger], "Diary of Zeisberger and Zenseman," 69; also see Introduction, pp. 48–51.

Brothers whom you had called from the *Susquehanna* [page 36a][205] arrived here. You will remember this all well. However, you have not yet given us an answer, although it will soon have been a year. Instead you have caused us trouble with your bad affairs. We have nothing to do with them and we have done away with all of them. Therefore, we think the time has come and we expect to hear your thoughts about this soon. Then *Isaac,* whom the Brothers had previously chosen as speaker while they were here and had told them that they all agreed to what he said, gave them a *String of Wampum.* He continued and said: My friends! We are informing you once again that we have accepted the sweet and saving word of God, not only with our mouths but also with our whole hearts. We have brought the word God sent us here with us. We hold firmly to this as to a great treasure we have found, and we will hold firmly to this until our end. Now anyone among the Indians who would like to hear this and accept it should come to us. We will consider it a pleasure to teach him about this. Then he gave a *Belt of Wampum* and added: Send this *Belt* with our words to your grandchildren the *Shawnee* and to your uncles the *Wyandot.*[206] Both the first *String* and this *Belt* were passed around in the *Councel* and when they were finished with this, *Isaac* continued: My friends! You have heard enough about what kind of people we are now. One of you forced a *String of Wampum* upon us with angry words and asked us to consider matters which are against our hearts.[207] It is not our business to deliberate about the *Machtapassican* and this does not belong before us but before you. We have cast all this aside. We do not want to consider this nor to have anything at all to do with it. Then he threw the *String* on the floor in the middle of the *Councel.* None of them picked it up until a woman who was sweeping took it and hung it up. It was still hanging there when they left the next day. After a short pause he also said, My friends! Your grandchildren the *Mohicans,* who live close to you here, have had to go without a teacher for a long time because they left them behind when they moved here from the *Susquehanna.* The one who came recently was just lent to them since we had compassion because they had to live alone like this. We want to inform you now that they will pick up their teacher[208] as soon as possible and bring him here. Then they separated until the next morning when they gathered again, and the *Chief* gave them the following answer through his speaker *Echpalawehund,* I am glad that I have heard your words. Indeed I have not forgotten what you told us a year ago, and I have indeed often reminded my *Councel* that it is time to give you an answer. However, we have not yet

205. See entries for 14 July, 26 Aug., and 5 Oct. 1772.

206. On kinship terminology between tribes, see Introduction, p. 21. Between the Shawnee and the Delaware relations were especially close; see entry for 1 Jan. 1773, note 128. This explains the proposal to officially inform the Shawnee of Moravian mission activities. As proprietors of the land, the Delamattenoos had to consent to the settlement and activities of the Moravians.

207. See entry for 31 May 1773.

208. For Johann Jacob Schmick and his wife, see note 212 below. The missionary on loan is Johannes Roth, who was supposed to be stationed at Schönbrunn.

been able to reach a conclusion. I will answer you soon now. I will send this *Belt* of yours to the *Shawnee* and the *Wyandot* as soon as I can. Then you will hear what they have to say to you. I think it is unnecessary for my grandchildren the *Mohicans* to fetch their teacher. They have enough teachers and if they bring more here then they will preach the same thing to them and nothing different from what they are preaching. *Isaac* replied, We just wanted to inform you about this; we do not know if your grandchildren will be satisfied with your answer. They can speak for themselves. They were not present, so this is how things remained since *Josua* had refused to go with them. The *Chiefs* had deliberated together before they gathered and were unsure of what they should answer. However, *Echpalawehund* said to them, What is there to consider? You hear well enough that they want to live like this and not otherwise.

THE 4TH   Both yesterday and today we had Speakings with the Brothers and Sisters in preparation for Holy Communion. We found them hungry and thirsty for Jesus' Body and Blood, which we enjoyed most blessedly with 54 Brothers and Sisters in the Holy *Sacrament* on THE 5TH. One person observed for the first time.

THE 6TH   In the morning was the *Liturgy for Communion* and the sermon.[209] In the afternoon Brothers *David* and *Isaac* went to *Gnadenhütten*.

THE 7TH   They returned from there. We heard from *Gekelemukpechünk* that our words and the talk we had presented to them had led them to much reflection and consideration. As long as our Brothers were there, they were very friendly and accommodating toward them. However, after they had left, they began to really consider and their opinions were then divided again. We also learned that the *String of Wampum* that had been forced upon us did not actually come from the *Chief*. Still, he may not have been completely ignorant of it. Some of them were unhappy that *Isaac* had spoken too directly and sharply and interpreted it as if he had thrust all evil things, and especially the *Machtapassican* (poison) upon their heads when he had thrown the *String* to the floor. Now they had to bear everything alone and be the scapegoat, because we no longer wanted to have any part in this or to help them eradicate it. Generally they were surprised that he spoke with such courage and audacity to such a gathering of Indians in the presence of the *Chiefs*. Some said mockingly that he was so brave and courageous because he was baptized with the brain and heart of a white *Minister*. This statement requires further explanation. Just recently a certain Indian invented a lie which he proclaimed as the truth: a certain pious *Minister*[210] had lived among the White people some years ago. He was a very reasonable and wise man and had led such a pious life and flawless walk that he had no equal. Now when he died, his followers and believers tried to get

209. According to the Festivity Calendar of the Unity this day was the "Festival of the Holy Trinity."
210. Not identified.

another *Minister* like him but could not find anyone else like him anywhere. Then they took his brain and heart from his body, dried it, and pulverized it. They had saved this to try an experiment with it, to see if this powder would not perhaps have a good effect on others. Then it happened that someone went mad and was in such a rage that no one could control him, although many *Ministers* and others had tried everything with him. Finally it occurred to them to attempt the first trial with this powder. They put just a little of this in a vessel with water and baptized him with it. After this he immediately came to himself and became as reasonable, wise, and pious as the *Minister* had been. They say now that we baptize all the Indians who come to us with this powder.[211]

THE 8TH   *Isaac* returned from *Gekelemukpechünk.* He had gone there yesterday with *Josua* and some other Brothers from *Gnadenhütten* to speak with the *Chief* once again about bringing Brother and Sister *Schmick*[212] here. They responded to all his objections and answered everything he said, and then he agreed they could do this.

Herewith we greet the entire Unity very sincerely and we commend all who are gathered here and ourselves to their faithful remembrance before the Savior.

Diary of Schönbrunn *on the* Ohio *from the Month of* June–*the 18th of* October *1773*[213]

JUNE 10TH   Brothers *Johannes, Willhelm,* and *Nicolaus* left for Bethlehem. We sent letters and our diary along with them. Others went to *Kaskaskunk* to pick up their Indian corn and cattle, which they had left there in the spring.

THE 11TH   In a service for the married and older Brothers and Sisters, we talked at length about marriage of our young single people, especially children of our Brothers and Sisters. We told them about our rules and this satisfied all the Brothers and Sisters, because many Brothers and Sisters, and especially new ones who came to us several years ago, were under the illusion that their

211. According to Francis Jennings (interview conducted on 9 Sept. 1993), the custom of eating the hearts and brains of prisoners as a means of acquiring their bravery and wisdom was common among tribes of the Six Indian Nations and others. After the conquest of Pickawillany in 1752, Chief La Demoisselle was killed and his heart and brain devoured. See McConnell, *A Country Between,* 98–100.

212. Johann Jacob Schmick (1714–78) hailed from Königsberg and was a trained Lutheran clergyman who joined the Unity in 1748, arrived in North America in 1751, and in the same year married Johanna Heid (1721–95). They both were active missionaries from 1757 until 1777; from 1774 to 1777 they directed the Moravian mission at Gnadenhütten II.

213. MAB, B 141, F 4, I 1, fol. 38; two lines at top of left-hand page are missing and the page on the whole is very spotty. The title was completed by consulting the copy in MAB, B 1411, F 3.

children could not marry among us. We announced the engagement of Brother *Samuel Moor* to *Helena* to the Brothers and Sisters and commended them in a prayer before the Savior.

THE 13TH   Brother *Jungmann* joined them in holy matrimony during the service for married Brothers and Sisters. Indians from *Gekelemukpechünk* were here visiting. They attended our services regularly and listened attentively.

THE 17TH   Some of the Sisters returned from the other side of *Gekelem-ukpechünk*, where they had gone some days ago to buy Indian corn. We acknowledge it as the special providence of our dear heavenly Father that our Brothers and Sisters do not have to suffer shortages when there has been such great famine among all the Indians in the entire area for a year. He provided for them in advance. Now our Brothers and Sisters are able to get enough Indian corn this year and at a very low price.

THE 19TH   The Brothers also returned from *Kaskaskunk* with their Indian corn and cattle. Several Indians from there also came to visit us. Some Indians from that area have taken possession of *Langundouteniünk* and are living there. It is now a real drinking nest.

THE 20TH   A messenger came from *Gekelemukpechünk* with a *String of Wampum*. Through this the *Chief* there invited our *Salomo* to a *Councel*. At the same time we received the news that the *Cherokees* had declared war against the *Wawiachtano Nation* and had already destroyed an entire *Town*. They killed all the Indians there, not even sparing the children.

They did not take any prisoners, but killed them all.[214] Because of this, the *Chief* in *Gekelemukpechünk* wants to send a delegation of 12 men to the *Cherokees* with suggestions for peace.

THE 21ST   Brothers *Abraham, Samuel,* and *Jacob Gendaskund* accompa-

---

214. According to Alexander McKee, the Cherokee gave as a reason for this war that "their [i.e., tribes on the Wabash River] bad Conduct toward the Reconciliation talk'd of between all Nations." McKee to Sir William Johnson, Pittsburgh, 3 July 1773, in *JP*, 8:842–43, and John Stuart (reporting more comprehensively from the perspective of the Cherokee) to Earl of Dartmouth, 21 June 1773, in Davies, *Documents of the American Revolution*, 6:158–59. The relations were complex: for reasons not clear the Cherokee had waged war against the two tribes in the region of the Wabash River for a number of years. For Sir William Johnson and the other agents of Indian Affairs, this war was of interest only because it provided an opportunity to prevent the union of the western tribes with the tribes of the Ohio region, and because it prevented an increase in the influence of French and Spanish Indian traders, who were still roaming the Mississippi River Valley. The English viewed Shawnee and Delaware attempts in 1772–73 to end this war as a potential threat to their interests in the region; see entry for 5 June 1772, note 29. Obviously neither Johnson nor Alexander McKee were aware of the larger context. While McKee, on 3 July 1773, reported new war expeditions of Cherokee against the "Oabaches," Sir William Johnson wrote the Earl of Dartmouth on 22 Sept. 1773: "The Indians in April last at S[c]ioto returned my deputy [Alexander McKee] for answer to the information," that the crown was seriously considering founding a new colony in the Ohio region, and "that they were very thankful for the notice they had thereof. . . . After this they proposed to hold conferences with the Ouabache Indians and Cherokees etc. in July and then if the season would admit of it purposed to come to a congress with me." *JP*, 8:889–90.

nied *Salomo*[215] to the council, and we had a *Conference* with the Helpers about affairs[216] regarding our town.

THE 24TH The early devotion was about the joy we have in the Lord[217] once we have found Him and become acquainted with Him.[218] Some strangers also came here for a visit. We had heart-to-heart talks with them about the importance of their spiritual salvation.

THE 25TH The above-mentioned Brothers from *Gekelemukpechünk* returned. The reason they had called our *Salomo* there was because he is already an old *Chief*,[219] and they wanted to learn what he had heard about *Machtapassigan* (the poison) in olden times and who among the Indians had anything like this. He told them as much information about this as he knew, but said that he had only heard this and had never seen it with his own eyes. A certain Indian named *Gulpikamen*, who was baptized by the Brothers and is called *Ludwig*, has tried to find this substance for several years, acting very important. Presumably he has done this only in an attempt to become a great man among the Indians.[220] They were well satisfied with *Salomo's* information and answer, put together *100 Strings* of Indian corn for his family and him, and gave him gifts so that his journey would be well rewarded. The *Chief* was very friendly toward him. Our Brothers also gave him an additional 12 Klafters[221] of *Wampum* from here and *Gnadenhütten* for the *Expedition* to the *Cherokees*.[222] This was very well received by the entire *Councel*. 4 men from the *Lower Shawnee* had arrived there with news they were taking to *Pittsburgh* as well: the *Mingo* had given the White people a *District* of land below the *Canhawa* in addition to the last *Purchase*.[223] This was supposed to be compensation for the cattle stolen in the White people's *Settlements* some years ago. Many White people had already arrived there to establish a *Settlement*.[224] This really alarmed the *Shawnee* and it

215. Original torn, supplemented by copy in MAB, B 1411, F 3. The original probably read "Jacob Gendaskund and Salomo."

216. Original torn, supplemented by copy in MAB, B 1411, F 3.

217. Original torn, supplemented by copy in MAB, B 1411, F 3.

218. According to the Festivity Calendar, this day was devoted to the memory of John the Baptist.

219. Salomo, Indian name Allemewi, had been chief of the Munsee.

220. See entries for 31 May, 1 June, and 6 June 1773.

221. One German "Klafter" measures between 1.7 and 1.83 meters. See Witthöft, *Umrisse einer historischen Metrologie*, 1:430.

222. Zeisberger refers to a delegation whose job was to mediate in the newly erupted conflict between the Cherokee and the tribes on the Wabash. See note 214 to the entry for 20 June 1773.

223. I.e., the land purchase connected with the Treaty of Fort Stanwix. See Introduction, pp. 7–8.

224. On 28 June 1773 six Shawnee complained in a speech to Alexander McKee at Fort Pitt that shortly before Michael Cresap had come to their settlements on the Scioto River and told them of a new land purchase by the Six Indian Nations and the Cherokee; he told them that he would soon come to survey these lands. The Shawnee warned the agent of the dire consequences of such a step. Alexander McKee to Sir William Johnson, 28 June 1773, in *JP*, 8:834–35. On 31 August 1773 this information was related by General Frederick Haldimand to the Earl of Dartmouth. Davies, *Documents of the American Revolution*, 6:166–67.

is generally believed that this will lead to a war because that land belongs to so many of the *Nations* who live around there; therefore the *Mingo* cannot give it away, and they were doing this just to entangle the Indians in a war which would eventually wipe them out.

THE 27TH   The Savior took young *Abigail,* the 16-month-old baby daughter of Brother *Willhelm* and Sister *Martha,* home to himself in blessing. Her little earthly dwelling was then buried on THE 28TH.

THE 30TH   Brother *Isaac's* two-and-a-half-year-old baby boy, who was ill, was baptized into Jesus' death with the name *Jonathan.*

July[225]

THE 2ND   A youth was buried into Jesus' death with the waters of Holy Baptism and named *Benjamin.* He has already been ill with consumption for a year and has longed for this.

THE 4TH   Brother *Jungmann* preached the sermon and Brother *Hecke-welder* led the Children's Service. In the Congregational Service in the evening the talk was about the Watchword, Then was I in his eyes as one that found favour.[226] The First Fruit[227] of the *Cherokees* was then baptized with the name *Noah,* and at the same time his wife was baptized with the name *Wilhelmina.* We sensed the Savior's presence during this. He had been captured in a war about 20 years ago and brought to this area.[228] Last winter he and his family came to us in *Langundoutenünk.* They then came along here. He speaks his native language better than the *Delaware* language; his wife is *Unami.*[229] When peace was concluded between the 6 Indian *Nations* and the rest of the *Nations* in this area and the *Cherokees* a number of years ago,[230] he was free to return to his fatherland or to remain here. He chose the latter, however, and now acknowledges it as providence of the Savior's grace, who wanted him to become saved.

THE 5TH   Brother *David,* Brother and Sister *Jungmann,* and some In-

---

225. Added by another hand: "1773."

226. Song of Sol. 8:10.

227. The Moravians considered it their mission to visit and convert people who had heard nothing about Christianity and make first conversions ("First Fruits").

228. Warriors frequently captured members of hostile tribes or white settlers and adopted them into their own tribe. These captives often replaced warriors who had been killed; they enjoyed all the rights and privileges of a regular member of the tribe. If no family was interested in adopting a prisoner, he was often killed. There is a description of the adoption ritual in Darlington, *Scoouwa: James Smith's Indian Captivity Narrative,* 29–31.

229. Unami represent one of the three linguistic groups within the Delaware Nation. See entry for 5 Oct. 1772, note 36.

230. Peace had been concluded during the treaty negotiations between 4 and 11 March 1768 in Sir William Johnson's residence. *NYCD,* 8:38–53; Alden, *John Stuart and the Southern Colonial Frontier,* 222–24.

dian Brothers and Sisters went to *Gnadenhütten* for the baptism of the baby boy born to Brother and Sister *Roth* yesterday.[231] The former returned home in the evening.

THE 6TH   Brother and Sister *Jungmann* returned home from there, but Sister *Jungmann*[232] was ill. In the evening we talked about the Watchword[233] for today, which says that the Savior finds ways and means in our time and clears the obstacles out of the way so that the Gospel will be preached to all *Nations*. News arrived from *Gekelemukpechünk* that 6 *Shawnee* are supposed to have been killed by enemy Indians. However, they could not find out to which *Nation* the perpetrators belonged.[234]

THE 9TH   We received letters by way of *Pittsburgh* from Brother *Mattheus* and Brother *Grube* in *Litiz*.[235] Today the Brothers went fishing and got some very large fish, 4 to 5 feet long. This evening the Savior took *Tobias*, the little son born to *Nicolai* and *Amalia* in *Langundouteniink*, home to himself in blessing. He was in his second year. On the following day, the same thing happened to *Benjamin* who was baptized on the 2nd of this month. He came here from *Friedenshütten* with his mother one and a half years ago, and he was always a quiet boy. His illness was protracted and lasted almost a year. After his baptism he became very clear and seemed to revive, but then 9 days later things changed suddenly and he went in blessing to the one who purchased him preciously with his blood. He was 14 years old.

THE 16TH   *Michael* and *Charlotte's* baby girl, young *Sabina*, died. She was one and a half years old. Then on the 17th Brother *Levi* and Sister *Salome's* baby girl *Rebecca*, who was 4 months old, died. A bad cough has been raging in this entire area. Since spring it has taken more than 50 children in *Gekelemukpechünk* alone, and now it has also appeared among our children here. Very few have been spared.

THE 19TH   The Brothers had another successful fishing trip and got 2 *Canow* loads of all kinds of fish, some of the exceptional size of 6 to 7 feet long. *Philippus junior* from *Gnadenhütten*, who had been hunting up the *Creek*, returned from there. He reached the end of that *Creek* with the *Canow* and entered the *Lake* from which it originates. He traveled as far as a few miles from the *Cayahaga*. It is supposed to be another day's journey from there to *Lake Erie*.[236]

231. Johannes Ludwig Roth (1773–1841).

232. Anna Margaretha Jungmann.

233. Isa. 57:14.

234. These Shawnee had probably settled between the Cherokee and the Indian tribes on the Wabash River. See entry for 20 June 1773, note 214.

235. Before joining the Unity, Bernhard Adam Grube (1715–1808) had been a Lutheran pastor in Erfurt. He worked as missionary at Wechquetank, accompanied and took care of the spiritual needs of the Christian Indians in Philadelphia between 1763 and 1765, and in 1780 inspected the mission congregations on the Muskingum.

236. Philippus Jr. (baptized 1749) had canoed up the Tuscarawas. The lake from which the Tuscarawas originated was mentioned along with the Cayahaga in Thomas Hutchins, "Map of Colonel Bouquet's Indian Campaigns" (1764), reproduced in appendix, map no. 4.

THE 20TH   A woman from *Tuscarawi, Michael's* mother, came here to stay. She has been asking to live with us for a year. Various Indians from *Gekelemukpechünk* and that area came here for a visit. We extolled to them the Savior as the one who saves us.

THE 24TH   We celebrated the Lord's Supper in the Holy *Sacrament* with 50 Brothers and Sisters. *Michael* watched for the 2nd time during this. Brother *Jungmann,* who has been ill with a fever for some time already, received it in his sickbed.

THE 25TH   After the *Liturgy* for Holy Communion we had the sermon and in the afternoon the Children's Service. A woman named *Hanna,* who was baptized in *Gnadenhütten* on the *Mahony* and had come here for a visit, was very touched during the services.

THE 26TH   Brother *Nathanael* and his wife traveled 2 days' journey from here to visit a woman who is sick. She is friends with them and had asked for them, and she also wanted to hear about the Savior again before she dies.

THE 27TH   The *Chief* in *Gekelemukpechünk* had sent a letter to Brother *Samuel Moor* inviting him to come there for a few days and serve as *Interpreter* in *Affairs* with White people, so he left for there today. *Mr. Anderson*[237] arrived here from *Kaskaskunk* on a journey to *Gekelemukpechünk*. The strangers who had been here visiting for several days returned home after receiving blessings for their hearts.

THE 29TH   Our schoolhouse was completely furnished so that Brother and Sister *Roth* can live in it for a while when Brother and Sister *Schmick* come to *Gnadenhütten*. We also began building a house for Brother and Sister *Jungmann*.

THE 30TH   Brother *Samuel* returned from *Gekelemukpechünk,* where he had interpreted for the Quakers who had come there from *Philadelphia*. They had given a talk to the Indians and reminded them of the friendship they had maintained with the Indians since they came into this country.[238] The *Chiefs* then addressed them and told them they would like it if they not only sent them preachers, but also taught the Indians various kinds of work and trades so that they would become an orderly people. They also asked them for assistance transporting some of their people to England to talk with the King.[239] As far as we heard, however, the Quakers would not agree to these suggestions and made excuses that this was not their concern and it was not fitting for them to do so. The Indians, however, were not satisfied with this. They forced them, so to speak, at least to promise them the last article concerning a journey to England. The Indians are not as concerned with hearing the Gospel as with

237. John Anderson. See entry for 16 Nov. 1772, note 102.

238. Three reports describe the visit of the Quaker missionary John Parrish, his friend Zebulon Heston, and their youthful companion John Lacey. See Introduction, p. 39 and note 21.

239. At least since the beginning of the 1770s, it had been the Council's policy to introduce the basics of European education and culture and to secure the land they were settling on. See entry for 26 Dec. 1772.

acquiring gifts through this and profiting materially, under the guise of good intentions.

August

THE 1ST   The sermon was about the assurance of the salvation we attain through Jesus' blood. Afterward the baptized Brothers and Sisters had a blessed service. Many of them examined their hearts during this and found they were lagging behind in grace. They resolved again to belong completely to the Savior.

THE 3RD   After the early devotion, the Board of Supervisors spoke with some of those who have not been baptized and admonished them about various concerns. This had the desired *Effect*. Strangers came up the river for a visit, and toward evening the 3 Quakers who have been visiting in *Gekelemuk-pechünk* also came here. One of them is a preacher. They looked around the site and they liked it. In the evening service they were also pleased with our Indian Brothers and Sisters, whose reverence and order they praised. The next day they traveled back to *Pittsburgh*.

THE 10TH   We baptized a sick child with the name *Anna,* and then she died in blessing several hours later. She is the daughter of an Indian woman who had brought her here for a visit some time ago, and who asked for this insistently. The mother is *Salomo's* grandchild.

THE 11TH   We had Indian visitors from both *Gekelemukpechünk* and from the *Mahony* on *Beaver Creek*. A respected Indian from the latter town was also here. He had previously visited in *Langundouteniünk*. He enjoyed hearing about the Savior and is convinced of the truth, but is very rich.[240]

THE 12TH   Because we had gotten some news about our horses which had been lost since spring, Brother *Heckewelder* went to *Beaver Creek* with *Scheb-osch* and a couple of Indian Brothers in the hope of getting them back.

Isaac, who had gone to *Gekelemukpechünk* on business, returned from there and said that he was very well received there by the *Chief* and the Indians and that they had followed him from one house to another to hear him. One of them particularly engaged him in discussions and told him among other things that he had already thought about this a lot and considered becoming a believer too. He was just afraid of the Indians and especially the *Chiefs*. He had often thought to himself that *Isaac* knew everything about the Indians and nothing was hidden from him; he had previously been the second to the *Chiefs* and their advisor. He had been a *Captain, Doctor* and also a preacher. Now, however, he

---

240. The reference is to Laweloochwalend. See entry for 20 Sept. 1773. Zeisberger's words recall the story of the rich young man whose wealth prevented him from following Christ (Matt. 19:16–26).

had become a believer. Therefore what we Brothers were teaching must really be the truth, because he was a reasonable man after all, who could judge whether something was right or not, whether it was the truth or not the truth. *Isaac* answered him: You have considered correctly. There is nothing about the Indians that I do not know. I know all of their affairs well because I was among the head men everywhere and have tried to go deeply into everything. However, I found nothing to satisfy my heart and bless it. I can bear witness to you that the Brothers' teaching is the truth, because I have felt it and experienced it in my heart as the truth. The Indian, who is also one of the head people, then asked what he thought about all the suggestions they had made to the Quakers. *Isaac* answered him that he believed they would not complete their *Projects* in many years, and perhaps nothing would come of it in the end. The Gospel would be preached here indeed, and whoever wanted to hear it could come and hear it. Why would they want to look any further? This was nothing more than obstacles laid in the path so that the Indians could not and would not hear it. The Indian said, I think this too. It is remarkable that we want to send to the King first. It may be a long time before we carry this matter out, and during this time we could all die. Then what have we gained?[241] I would rather come to you now so that I can hear the Gospel before I die. *Isaac* told him and all those who were there, Even if you get more preachers and teachers, I tell you that you will not be any better off, because no one will preach God's word and the way to salvation as clearly and meaningfully as the Brothers. *I* tell you this, and not the Brothers, so that one or the other of you does not go there and say that the white Brothers, their teachers, said this. No, I have said it myself. No one told me to do this, and I know that it is so.

THE 14TH   This morning we received the happy news that Brother and Sister *Schmick* had arrived in *Pittsburgh*. Therefore this very day we sent some Brothers with horses to meet them. An Indian and his family from *Tuscarawi* came here to visit. He really wanted to hear about the Savior.

THE 15TH   *Echpalawehund* came here with a couple of Indians from *Gekelemukpechünk* for a visit. They attended our Sunday services, and the Indian Brothers spoke a great deal with them about the salvation in Jesus' meritorious sufferings.

THE 16TH   At noon we were delighted when Brother *Johann Jungmann*[242] arrived at our place from *Bethlehem*. Brother and Sister *Schmick* had taken a different route from them, directly to *Gnadenhütten*.

241. It is at least questionable whether this really represents the opinion of the non-Christian Indians. One should probably interpret Isaac's arguments as an instance of the missionaries' objections against the program of the Delaware. The missionaries would not have understood the concern about securing a secure title to the land because their eyes were so firmly fixed on the aspect of saving souls through their missionary activities that they lost sight of the civilizing aspects of their mission; the reverse may have been true of the Delaware. Another reason for the missionaries' opposition may have been their determination to prevent competition from other Christian denominations.

242. John Jungmann (1749–1843) was the son of Johann Georg and Anna Margaretha Jungmann, who lived at Schönbrunn. Until September 1775 John lived in Gnadenhütten in order to learn

THE 17TH   We received delightful letters from Bethlehem and *Litiz* by way of *Gnadenhütten*. We enjoyed them today.[243]

THE 18TH   We were overjoyed that Brother and Sister *Schmick* also arrived at our place from *Gnadenhütten,* and we welcomed them very sincerely as did all the Indian Brothers and Sisters. At the same time, Brother and Sister *Roth* also arrived here by water to stay. They had had heavy thunderstorms with rain on the way and were completely soaked. In the evening the former led the Singing Service and extended many sincere greetings from the Unity to the Brothers and Sisters.

THE 19TH   We congregational Brothers and Sisters held a *Conference,* partly about a letter from the Provincial Helpers' Conference from *Bethlehem* and partly about our plan in this area. We discussed various points and agreed to carry out the work of the Lord among the Indians with one mind, in harmony and love. We then covenanted together through the Cup of Covenant to do this and promised Him we would be his faithful servants.[244]

Brother *Schmick* held the early devotions this morning about the peace we have in Him, which He accomplished for us with God through his sufferings and death.[245] He and his wife also delighted the Brothers and Sisters by visiting them in their huts and houses, and Brother *Roth* led the Singing Service.

THE 20TH   Brother *Schmick* held the early devotion about praising and thanking the Lord for all the good things He has done for us, especially for winning all good things for us through his death and blood. We should not forget to be grateful to Him for this.[246] He and his wife then traveled back to *Gnadenhütten* by water, after they had been provided with the necessary supplies from here. Brother *Johann Jungmann,* however, stayed here until he gets a place to live there.

This afternoon old *Cornelia, Isaac*'s mother, went home very suddenly and unexpectedly. She came to the Brothers in *Goshgoshing* in the year 1768, en-

---

Mahican. MAB, Bethlehem Diary, 24 Feb. 1773, fol. 216. On his travels, see "Reise-Diarium des Br. Joh. Jungmann von Bethlehem nach Schönbrunn, 20. Juli bis 16. August 1773," MAB, B 217, F 6.

243. Especially important was John Ettwein's letter to the missionaries of both congregations dated 20 July 1773, MAB, Ettwein Papers [hereafter E.P.], B 965, F 42, no. 1041. Ettwein informed the missionaries of the resolves of the Mission Conference concerning their individual fields: the Schmicks were to superintend Gnadenhütten, the couple Roth was to return to Schönbrunn, John Jungmann, who came along, was to go to Gnadenhütten and if possible run a school there, and Heckewelder was to do the same in Schönbrunn. Toward the end of the letter Ettwein turned to the anticipated conversion of Echpalawehund and in this context discussed the complex issue of "concerns of chiefs": "the principle: No chief is allowed to convert to Christianity! And if he nevertheless insists he is then first to give up his office as chief! is unreasonable for us to maintain. As long as the Indians are willing to admit a chief who is pondering conversion to their council, it is not for the Brethren to object to this so long as his own concerns and conscience will allow it . . . such a man is to be considered in the same light as a member of a white magistracy who wants to convert." See note 139 for entry of 7 Jan. 1773.

244. The protocol of this conference (MAB, B 229, F 4, I 9) is printed in the appendix.

245. The text discussed is Matt. 5:9.

246. The Watchword discussed in the early morning meeting was Ps. 107:30–32.

joyed hearing about the Savior, and was concerned about her salvation. She often spoke very sincerely with them about this, so that we had high hopes for her. However, when the Brothers moved to *Lawunahannek* the following year, she remained behind. Later she went to *Kaskaskunk* to be with her son, now known as *Isaac.* When the Brothers came to *Kaskaskunk* in 1770, she was very happy to see them again and immediately asked if she could come to our place again and live with us. She received permission to do this and was very happy and grateful. In 1771 she was baptized on Epiphany[247] and then led a blessed life. She could not thank the Savior enough for what He had done for her and we all rejoiced over her. She also became a *Candidate* for Holy Communion. However, last year something very peculiar happened to her. Her advanced age contributed a lot to this, because she became completely childlike. Her mind got very weak and she could not remember things or make sense of them. However, whenever we spoke with her and directed her to the Savior, she came back to herself. A year ago she came here from *Langundouteniink* and spent her time here in quiet. She attended the services, which were always very important to her, as often as she could. This was always a big undertaking for her though, because walking was very difficult. For a number of days we had noticed that she was not as well, which had happened before, and today she suddenly lost her speech and died gently. No one knew her age, but she was well over 100. Her earthly dwelling was then laid to rest the next day on THE 21ST. We congregational Brothers and Sisters had a *Conference* about our external business.

THE 22ND   Brother *Roth* preached the sermon about the text, Look unto me, and be ye saved, all the ends of the earth,[248] and in the Children's Service this morning he baptized the baby boy born to Brother *Samuel* and Sister *Sara Nantikok* with the name *Heinrich.* Then there was a *Conference* with the Helpers.

THE 25TH   The Savior took *Beata,* the previously mentioned baby daughter of Brother and Sister *Nantikoks,* home to be with Him. She was born on *August* 28, 1771 in *Schechschiquanünk* and was baptized at the same time as her mother on the 27th of *January,* 1772, in *Friedenshütten.* She came along here last year.

THE 27TH   In the morning young *Beata* was buried. Many Brothers and Sisters are starting to become ill with fever and our Brother *Anton Senior* also became ill with a high fever today.

THE 29TH   The sermon was in the morning and in the afternoon the devotions for married Brothers and Sisters. The single Brothers celebrated their festival and today joined their Choir with heart and mind. We had a sweet

247. On 6 Jan.
248. Isa. 45:22.

Lovefeast together and reflected on the ode sent to us and dedicated ourselves anew to the youth Jesus, to be his faithful Choir Brothers.[249]

THE 31ST   Our dear Sister and colleague of many years, *Lucia,* went to her eternal rest. She came to Bethlehem with her husband *Lucas* in 1756 on the occasion of a treaty in Easton. He had strayed from the Unity during the first Indian war.[250] Her husband was ill there for a long time but also found his heart again during that time. She served him with much care and faithfulness, so that she legitimated herself with the Brothers and Sisters. Before his end, her blessed husband admonished her to remain with the Unity and to come to love the Savior. She promised him this and then faithfully did so. As soon as he closed his eyes, she turned to the congregation, asked for permission to stay there, and received it. That was in 1757. The word of Jesus' sufferings quickly made a deep *Impression* on her heart. She soon longed to see herself cleansed of her sins with Jesus' blood. She attained this grace on *April* 10th of the same year in the *Sacrament* of Holy Baptism, and in 1758 she attained Holy Communion with the congregation. She loved the Savior and His people and was loved by everyone. Her walk among us was contrite and solid and for many years she was a faithful co-worker among her fellow women. She was especially happy when anyone from her *Nation* expressed a desire for the Savior. Her heart was strongly attached to the Savior and the Unity. She endured many trials when people tried to lead her away from the congregation, especially in her last marriage. If she had thought like her husband, whom she married in *Wequetank,*[251] she could easily have been separated from the Unity. As it was, however, she kept him close to the Unity until his blessed end. After that she spent her 10 remaining years as a blessed widow, although her earthly dwelling was already sick. For 2 years she had not been able to do anything, but this did not prevent her from undertaking the long journey with the Indian congregation from the *Susquehanna* to here. When she came to *Langundoutenünk* she asked the Brothers for permission to be one of the first here in *Schönbrunn,* because she wanted to rest again soon. Therefore in *September* of last year she arrived here, weak and sickly. From that time on her strength continued to fail and she waited with much patience, surrendered to the Savior's will, for him to take her home. Three days before her end she sent for the white Brothers and Sisters and asked them to send her greetings to all the Brothers and Sisters here, in *Gnadenhütten,* and Bethlehem once more, and to say she loves everyone and is happy that she will soon go to the Savior now. She was granted this joy today,

249. Each year special festive hymns were usually printed for the festivals of the individual choirs; for most years, but not for 1773, these are preserved in MAB, B "Odes," no. 4.

250. The negotiations in Easton, Pennsylvania, lasted from 24 to 31 July 1756, from 8 to 17 Nov. 1756, from 7 to 26 Oct. 1758, and from 3 to 12 Aug. 1761; Delaware and representatives of the Six Indian Nations participated. *PCR,* 7:204–20, 313–38, 8:174–223, 630–54.

251. Wechquetank or Wequitank was a Moravian mission town, where the Christian Indians from Gnadenhütten I, accompanied by the missionary Gottlob Sensemann, settled in 1760. Threatened by the hostile actions of the "Paxton Boys," they left the settlement on 11 October 1763.

when she fell into a blessed sleep with the blessing of the congregation. We keep her memory among us in blessing.

September

THE 1ST   Her earthly dwelling was accompanied to its rest. We announced the upcoming Holy Communion in a service and the Brothers and Sisters, as poor and needy individuals, were invited to it. Brother *Jungmann* has now pretty well recovered from his fever. His wife, however, has also been ill with the fever since yesterday.

THE 2ND   Brother *Isaac* returned from *Mochwesüng*[252] where he had gone to take care of *Affairs* for some Brothers and Sisters in *Gnadenhütten.* On his way there he attended a *Councel* in *Gekelemukpechünk* to which he was invited. 2 *Shawnee* from the *Lower Towns* had also come to this. They were given the following message for their *Chiefs:* 3 of the *Quakers* had visited in *Gekelemukpechünk* and admonished them to accept God's word. They told them that they would do this on the condition that they assist them in sending a delegation to the King in England, which they had also promised to do.[253] After the messengers had returned, this message to the King would indicate where things stood. The King would then decide which party or religion they would join, because the French claimed they had the right teaching, and now there were 2 *Towns* of Indian believers in their neighborhood who also said they had the right teaching, as did the Quakers and the English Church. Now they wanted the King to instruct them in this.[254] They, the *Shawnee,* should consider the matter and also inform the *Wyandot* about it, and within 10 days (this means in a period of 10 months) both should prepare to set out from there and begin their journey. They should collect hides and use the profit to cover the expenses[255] of those making the journey.

Isaac, who continued his journey with these 2 *Shawnee,* took advantage of the opportunity to discuss various things with them on the way. Among other things he asked if *Chief Netawatwees* had ever sent them a message from us, because twice already we had given him a message to send on to the *Shawnee* and *Wyandot,* and he had promised to do this.[256] They asked what the message had been, and when *Isaac* told them, they replied that those were indeed very good words. They were glad they had now heard this, but they had never heard a word about it before.

---

252. Mochwesüng, a Munsee settlement, was only a few miles from Woaketameki. See note 455 for entry for 7 July 1774.

253. See entry for 30 July 1773.

254. See entry for 12 Aug. 1773.

255. See entry for 6 Nov. 1773.

256. See entry for 1 June 1773.

THE 4TH   With 52 Indian Brothers and Sisters, we blissfully partook of the Body and Blood of our Lord in Holy Communion. One Brother participated for the first time and one Sister observed for the 2nd time.

THE 5TH   In the morning, it pleased our dear Lord to take our dear Brother *Anton,* faithful colleague of many years, into the joy of his Lord. He came to the Unity in Bethlehem in *January* 1750. He was baptized there in *February* of the same year by blessed Brother *Cammerhoff*[257] and joined us in Holy Communion the next fall. We loved this Brother from the very beginning because we quickly realized how attached his heart was to the Savior and to the Unity. This blessed Brother served as interpreter among his *Nation* after the Indian congregation had left *Gnadenhütten* and retreated to Bethlehem, and then established another site behind the Blue Mountains in *Wequitank* with some Indians in 1759.[258] The Savior granted him special grace and a special gift for this, and he had no equal in it. He carried out this office with much faithfulness and it was a blessing for his own heart. The Savior had given him the gift of expression and wisdom, and a special insight into the Gospel and the Unity. Therefore afflictions, persecution and danger did not disturb his spiritual life in the least, but brought him ever closer to the Savior and the Unity.

In 1763, when the Indian congregation moved to the *Susquehanna* and established the well-known site of *Fridenshütten,* he faithfully helped to oversee the Lord's work there. He called many through his preaching of the Gospel, especially during the first year. Almost all of them prospered. The poor, touched Indians asked him to repeat in his house what had been taught in the services, and he did this day and night with special grace and untiring faithfulness. He was thus a blessing for many, until he received a call from the Unity to move to *Goschgosching* with Brother *David Zeisberger* in 1768. He joyfully accepted this call and was a proven helper and servant of God in his measure there as well. The Savior had made him worthy to tolerate pain, persecution, even danger to his life for his name's sake, with the rest of the servants of his church. He joyfully proclaimed the Savior and his death there and the next year in *Lawunakhannek,* where they had to retreat from the savages. He did not allow himself to be deterred by persecution or scorn, until he left *Lawunakhannek* in 1770 with the rest of the residents there and came to *Kaskaskung,* where they established a 3rd town, *Langundouteniünk.* He stayed there until this was

257. During his time in Bethlehem, Bishop Johann Christoff Friedrich Cammerhoff (1721–51) was the most prominent representative of the sifting period; on this period, see Introduction, pp. 55–58.

258. Anton (baptized Feb. 1750) was a Delaware; it is not possible to assign him to one of the linguistic groups. See Carl John Fliegel, "Catalog of Indians," MAB, no. 249. Fliegel, *Index to the Records of the Moravian Mission,* offers a number of entries that report Anton's translating activities, among them one that relates to the Delaware language (Diary of Friedenshütten, 27 July 1765, MAB, B 131, F 2). Between 1761 and 1763 Anton assisted Bernhard Adam Grube in the translation of hymns that were published in 1763 (see note 24 above). Newollike, chief of the Munsee, baptized on 12 May 1774, was Anton's brother.

abandoned once again this spring, and he made the journey with the company by water. This journey was difficult for him though. Upon his arrival in *Schoenbrunn* he expressed his sincere joy and hope that he would now be able to rest, because he believed that this town would last at least several years. However, he soon became ill, and people attributed this illness to his journey. He actually recovered from this pretty quickly, but after a while he got the cold fever and this turned into yellow fever, which he had for 11 days. During this time he often expressed his longing to go to the Savior, but he surrendered himself to the Savior's will in this. Four days before his end, he told a company of Brothers who visited him, I am going to the Savior and so I ask you not to renounce the faith, not to tear down what the Savior has built among you, but to guard it. Obey your teachers and do what they tell you. Do not make things difficult for them and do not let anyone mislead you. Also do not think that the Savior's work will suffer when I am no longer with you. He will continue his work as he has done until now and He will also prepare the Brothers He needs for this. He gave them other nice admonitions. During this, the hearts of those present became tender and their eyes overflowed. We did not really think his end was so close and we hoped for his recovery, especially because we would like to have kept him here longer. However, yesterday was Holy Communion day, and when we wanted to serve him Holy Communion for the ill, he was no longer able to receive it. He told those watching over him that they should not sleep, but should watch him well. In the morning between 3 and 4 o'clock he died with the blessing of the congregation, at least 76 years old. His death is painful for us, but we are happy for him to receive his rest and the great joy of being at home with his Lord. His earthly dwelling was buried on THE 6TH, accompanied by a large procession.

THE 7TH   In our morning devotion we prayed for a special blessing from the Savior for our Married Choir on their festival day today. Afterward they had a festive talk about the text for today,[259] followed by a Lovefeast, and in conclusion a blessed Service of Adoration. He revealed Himself very mercifully to them and blessed them.

THE 8TH   We had a *Conference* with the Indian Brothers about the construction of our Meeting House and we decided to begin right away. *Isaac,* who returned from *Gekelemukpechünk,* had heard a lot there again. An Indian (named *Killbuck*)[260] addressed him and said, You know that your teachers here do not have anything of their own and do not possess any land. Should they continue living there and teaching the Indians like this? That could not possibly work out, he said. He was now going to see *Johnson.*[261] When he returned we would see that this would not be allowed, and the white Brothers should leave.

259. Eph. 1:10.
260. John Killbuck Sr.
261. As superintendent of Indian Affairs Sir William Johnson was also responsible for problems related to whites settling on tribal land.

Isaac replied, You are right that they have nothing of their own and no land here. They are very well aware of this. Nor do they desire to own any land. The land is not my land or yours and yet we live on it; in the same way they also live there. I tell you that as long as there are Indians, the Gospel will be preached unceasingly since God has decided it should be preached to all *Nations,* because he wants all humans to be saved, including you. Therefore no one can prevent it or stop it. The Indian had no reply to this, but remained silent and left.

THE 9TH   Brothers *Nathanael* and *Anton* left for *Great Island* to pick up the things that had been left behind a year ago, some of which we now need to build our Congregation House.[262]

An Indian named *Leonhard* came here from *Gekelemukpechünk* for a visit. Both Brother *David* and the Indian Brothers spoke with him a great deal. They reminded him of his baptism and admonished him to seek again what he had lost. He often feels very restless in his heart, as he himself told us.

THE 11TH   The Brothers of the Board of Supervisors spoke with the woman who recently moved to our place from *Tuscarawi* in the presence of two Indian strangers from *Gekelemukpechünk.* They were present as witnesses. She is accused of having *Machtapassigan* (poison).[263] She is supposed to be taken to *Gekelemukpechünk* and examined there. If she is found guilty, she is to be burned.[264] However, she explained herself well here to everyone's *Satisfaction* and revealed her innocence. We were thus spared many unpleasantries.

THE 12TH   In addition to the usual Sunday services, a service and talk about the doctrinal texts for yesterday and the day before yesterday were held for the children.[265] Some Sisters from *Gnadenhütten* came here to visit.

THE 13TH   In the evening there was a congregational council instead of the Singing Service. We reminded people of various matters, and we especially commended to the Brothers and Sisters the construction of our Congregation House. They began preparing wood for this on THE 14TH.

THE 16TH   The early devotion was about the Savior's office as Chief Elder in his Unity, which he had chosen from the world and which he wants to

262. At first huts were made of bark and simple houses were constructed from trees. For the permanent houses, logs that had been sawed and planed into square beams were used.

263. See entry for 25 Dec. 1772 and note 117, and entries for 31 May, 1 June, and 25 June 1773.

264. We have no proof that Native Americans were burned at the stake for knowledge or possession of poison. Yet see the case of Josua Jr., a Mahican (baptized before 1747 in Bethlehem; see Register of Persons). On 17 March 1806, in a witch hunt similar in scope to that of Salem, Massachusetts, Josua was accused of sorcery in Wah-pi-kah-me-kunk on the White River and burned. White River was a Delaware settlement and at that time the residence of the Shawnee prophet. Dunn, *True Indian Stories,* 48–71; for the witch hunts started by Wangomen, for example, in 1771 and 1775, see also Dowd, *Spirited Resistance,* 37–40. See entry for 16 May 1775.

265. This was the day of the children's choir festival. The text for 10 Sept. was Eph. 6:1 and the text for 11 Sept. was Luke 2:40.

form and prepare according to his heart so that He will experience joy and honor from them.[266]

THE 17TH   In the early devotion the Watchword[267] provided an occasion to talk about how we can venture everything on the Savior's *Credit,* and no one should doubt that he will indeed carry out what he has decided among the Indians. Then Brother *David* and Brothers *Isaac* and *Wilhelm* began a journey to visit the *Shawnee.*[268]

THE 18TH   In the afternoon was the burial of our blessed Sister *Rebecca,* our *Salomo's* eldest daughter. She went home yesterday. She came to *Fridenshütten* with her husband when the Indian congregation moved from the *Barraks* in *Philadelphia* to the *Susquehanna.*[269] She was baptized on *June* 7th, 1767, and she became a communicant in the Unity in *June* 1769. From then on she lived a blessed life. After the death of her husband, she was a blessed widow for a long time. However, when she came to *Langundoutenünk* with her 3 sons in 1770, her friends treated her well and made much of her, and she also began to please herself. People then became aware of all sorts of unpleasant traits in her. She lost her sensitivity, did not bring honor to the Savior, and forfeited Holy Communion. In this condition, she was overcome by a serious illness, and she became completely lame and the *Object* of true pity to all Brothers and Sisters. On this occasion, however, she found her heart again, was ashamed, asked for forgiveness, and was readmitted to Holy Communion. She cried a lot about her unfaithfulness and expressed a great longing to be redeemed, especially at her last Speaking for Holy Communion. Two days before her end she had an attack of gout and did not come back to her senses until it pleased the Good Shepherd, for whom nothing is too bad, to transport her to the kingdom of health in her 60th year.

THE 20TH   In the presence of the *Conference* of Brothers and Sisters, we spoke with an Indian from *Packanke's* friendship[270] who had lived in *Kaskaskunk* before and had often visited in *Langundoutenünk.* He had come here on the 18th of this month and asked for permission to live with us. He was overjoyed to be allowed to stay here.

This afternoon we laid the foundation for our congregational Meeting Hall, dedicated this site to the Lord, and commended the workers to his merciful watch. *Laweloochwalend,*[271] the *Chief* of *Shenenge,* arrived here from *Beaver Creek.* He soon spoke with some of our Indian Brothers and told them that he did not come just to visit as previously; his intention now was to become a believer in

266. See entry for 13 Nov. 1772, note 100.

267. Isa. 46:9–10.

268. They returned from this trip on 23 September. A report on their trip is entered in the diary entry for 23 Sept. 1773.

269. See Introduction, xx–xx.

270. On Zeisberger's meaning of the term "friendship," see Introduction, p. 18, and note 42.

271. He was baptized on 2 April 1774; his new name was Simon.

the Savior. He had now considered everything adequately and was completely ready. Therefore he had hurried to our place to inform us of this and to tell us his heart and his mind. He wanted to stay with us for a short time, until his wife, who is of one mind with him, had harvested her fields. Then he would fetch her with his whole family and bring them here as well. It had seemed too long for him to wait until his wife was finished with the fields, so he had come on ahead.

THE 22ND   Brother *Roth* held the early devotion about the Watchword, The works of the Lord are great etc.[272] He told of the great work of our redemption which cost him more than creating a world. The Indian mentioned on the 20th of this month sent us his idol[273] through Brother *Abraham*. This consisted of a face carved from wood. An Indian had given it to him and told him that if he sacrificed bear meat to the image, he would never become ill and would always have good luck hunting. If he did not do this, however, he would die. He gave it to us now to burn or do with as we wished. He was afraid to get rid of it himself, but he still wanted to be free of it.

THE 23RD   Brother *Jungmann* held the early devotion, and toward evening Brother *David* and his traveling companions returned from the *Shawnee*. A brief report from this journey follows.[274]

THE 24TH   The Brothers all went out to hunt and collected meat for the construction of the Congregational House. In the evening Brother *Isaac* reported the events of our journey and the talk we had with the *Shawnee Chief Gischenatsi* to the Brothers of the Helpers' *Conference*.[275]

THE 25TH   In the evening we refreshed ourselves by reading some news from the Unity.

THE 26TH   Some Indians from *Gekelemukpechünk* were also present for the sermon. It was about how the heathen have also been included in the promise and inheritance of eternal salvation since the Savior's incarnation, sufferings, death, and resurrection. Otherwise, today was a day of preaching. Brothers *Johannes, Abraham,* and *Isaac* were busy serving the strangers visiting here with the word of Jesus' death and sufferings. Brother *Jungmann* held the Congregational Service and we congregational Brothers and Sisters had a house *Conference*.

272. Ps. 111:2.

273. Zeisberger, "History of the Northern American Indians," 141, suggests the following explanation: "The only idol which the Indians have, and which may properly be called an idol, is their Wsinkhoalican, that is, image. It is an image cut in wood, representing a human head, in miniature, which they always carry about them either on a string around their neck or in a bag. They often bring offerings to it. In their houses of sacrifice they have a head of this idol as large as life put upon a pole in the middle of the room." See, too, entries for 9 Feb. 1777 and 23 Oct. 1781; Krusche, "Origin of the Mask Concept"; and Miller, "Delaware Masking."

274. See pp. 164–73 (fols. 47b–52a) below.

275. See pp. 169–70 below. Gischenatsi ("Hard Man") was one of the influential Shawnee chiefs.

THE 27TH   *Isaac* went to *Gnadenhütten* to travel with another Indian Brother from there to visit three Indian preachers who have asked to hear and speak with one of our Brothers.

THE 29TH   Along with the Brothers from the Helpers' *Conference*, we spoke with the *Chief* from *Shenenge*, mentioned on the 20th of this month. He had said he wanted to come here with his family and live with us, and he is waiting for an answer from us. He visited here occasionally this summer and we could see that he had considered the matter a great deal. However, he had not revealed his thoughts to anyone before now. He is the one who spent a whole night with Brother *Isaac* on his first visit in *Langundouteniünk* and talked with him and asked about all kinds of things. Since then he had not been able to forget this.[276] He expressed himself again very nicely and directly and told us about all of his circumstances. We also told him our thoughts. After we had read him our town *Statutes* and explained them, we granted him permission to move here with his family. He expressed his joy over this. In the evening there was a talk about the text for today, about the service which the Savior provides us through the dear angels, and we also sang Him our prayer of thanksgiving for this.

October

THE 1ST   In the early devotion the Watchword read, For he said, Surely they are my people, children that will not lie etc.[277] This provided an opportunity to admonish listeners sincerely to remember that the Savior does not dwell on our shortcomings and mistakes, but sees a faithful, honest heart, and various aspects of this point.

THE 2ND   Brother *Isaac* returned from visiting the 3 Indian preachers who live 2 days' journey from here and who had asked to hear Brothers. He and another Brother from *Gnadenhütten* preached to them about the crucified Savior as the redeemer of our sins and clearly explained the basis of our salvation. They listened to this with great *Attention*. They were well received and no one raised objections. In conclusion they replied that they were happy they had seen and heard the Brothers, but they could not reply at that time. They wanted to consider it first and then let us know their thoughts. Brother *Roth* preached the sermon in the morning, Brother *Jungmann* led the devotions for married couples, and Brother *David* the Congregational Service.

THE 4TH   Indian strangers passed through here again. Some of them spent the night, and the Brothers were busy building the Congregation House.

276. Another hand wrote the following addition at the bottom of the page: "and who met the Indian congregations who came from the Susquehanna, over one hundred miles before their destination."

277. Isa. 63:8.

A sad and painful event took place today when we had to inform *Abigail, Peter's* wife, our *Abraham's* daughter,[278] that she could no longer stay here because of her bad behavior. She had to leave today, which she did. May the Savior allow this to serve her best interests and salvation.

THE 9TH   The *Chief* from *Shenenge*, who has enjoyed his time here, traveled back home to get his family. Brothers *Nathanael* and *Anton* returned safe and sound with the things from *Great Island*,[279] and Indians from *Kaskaskunk* also arrived here.

THE 13TH   The Watchword[280] for today was sent to us by the Unity Elders' Conference for *Schönbrunn*, and upon reading it we encouraged the Brothers and Sisters to be faithful to the word of Jesus' death and sufferings, which He revealed to them, and to feed their hearts daily with this. Then they would remain protected from all the evil enemy's temptations.

THE 14TH AND 15TH   We had Speakings with the Brothers and Sisters for Holy Communion. Brother and Sister *Jungmann* spoke with the married Brothers and Sisters and widows and Brother *Roth* with the widowers and single Brothers. Then on THE 16TH we, 56 Brothers and Sisters, participated most blessedly in His Body and Blood in the Holy *Sacrament*. One Sister joined us in partaking for the first time.

Today we also received the news that all the *Traders* in the *Lower Towns* had fled and returned to the *Fort* because some of their lives had been threatened.[281]

THE 17TH   The first heavy frost of this fall fell. It turned out well for our Brothers and Sisters, some of whom had planted very late and some not until the end of June and beginning of July. They did not lose anything since everything was done in time.

278. What the "bad behavior" had been is not mentioned. Already on 7 Sept. 1774 Abigail had been denied the right to settle with her family in Gnadenhütten. On 13 Nov. 1796 she was readmitted into the congregation. She died in 1804; her husband, Petrus, remained a member of the congregation; he died in the Gnadenhütten II massacre on 8 March 1782. Fliegel, *Catalog of Indians*, MAB 556 and 564. Father Abraham refers to Abraham alias Sakima (baptized 25 Dec. 1765).

279. See entry for 9 Sept. 1773.

280. The Watchword was Jer. 32:19. Each year the Unity's Elders' Conference chose by lot special days for a congregation whose Watchword had a special significance for that congregation. The dates were forwarded to the Provincial Helpers' Conference in America. See, e.g., Unity's Elders' Conference to Provincial Helpers' Conference, Barby, 6 Jan. 1773: "As an addendum, beloved Brethren, you will find all those Watchwords, which we have chosen for all those congregations and posts under your special care. We command you to forward these Watchwords immediately to the specific congregation." MAB, Letters Received by the Provincial Helpers' Conference in General, from the Unity's Elders' Conference, 1770–93. The Watchword here mentioned thus related to all congregations but had a special significance for the inhabitants of Schönbrunn.

281. On 25 September 1773, Cornstalk, chief of the Shawnee, informed Richard Butler, an Indian trader, that the Shawnee advised the Indian traders to return to their white settlements because the Shawnee had to go out hunting and thus were unable to keep an eye on the Mingo in their region and could not guarantee the safety of the Indian traders. Should the Mingo do any damage to the Indian traders, the Shawnee would be considered responsible, and Cornstalk wanted to avoid this. On 6 October Butler delivered this message at Pittsburgh. "Journal of Alexander McKee," in *JP*, 12:1032–33. On Cornstalk, see [Cornstalk], "Sketch of Cornstalk."

THE 18TH   Indians from *Walhanding Creek*, 2 days' journey from here, came here for a visit and to hear the word of God.[282] They spent two days here and the Indian Brothers presented the crucified Savior to them and invited them to join in the salvation He won for us through his blood.

Brief Report on Brother David Zeisberger's *Journey to the* Shawnee *with the Indian Brothers* Isaac *and* Willhelm.[283]

We left from *Schoenbrunn* on the 17TH OF SEPTEMBER, spent the night in *Gnadenhütten,* and arrived in *Gekelemukpechünk* at noon on THE 18TH where we visited the *Chief* and met a party of *Wyandot* and *Tawas*[284] on their journey to *Pittsburgh.* We greeted them cordially and welcomed them. I spoke with them as much as time allowed and let them know who I was. They were all very friendly and orderly. One of them could speak English pretty well. He was my interpreter. They soon gathered for a *Councel,* during which they gathered the bones from the dead on both sides, mixed them together, buried them, cleaned and decorated the graves, and protected them from rain and storms. This is the usual *Ceremony* when the *Chiefs* of such *Nations* come together. In brief, this means they removed the mourning from them and comforted them over their deceased. Their language is most similar to the *Mingo* language and I could understand a word here and there, but it was also quite different. Right at the beginning we had informed the *Chief* of our intention to travel to the *Lower Shawnee Towns.* However, he told us that they were expecting the *Chief* from there and our journey would therefore be in vain. We stayed until almost evening and then we traveled with an Indian named *White Eye* to his *Town* 6 miles further on, where we spent the night.[285] He is a *Chief* and his word carries the most weight here. There I resolved to continue my journey either until we met the *Shawnee Chief* or arrived at our intended destination. Both *Isaac* and I discussed many things with *White Eye,* and among other things we also had an opportunity to discuss the Savior with him. He is a *Captain* and *Chief* and a reasonable man. *Isaac,* who used to be his best friend and who knows him very well, believes that if he were ever convinced of the truth it would be difficult for anyone to change his mind again or mislead him. I also used the opportunity to tell him about the Brothers' work among the Indians, and I explained that we seek only the eternal well-being and salvation of the Indians. We also told

282. See entry for 25 May 1773.
283. In the right margin another hand added "1773."
284. This is the Delaware name for the Ottawa, on whom see Feest and Feest, "Ottawa."
285. This is the first time that White Eyes, possibly the most influential member of the Delaware Chief Council at this time and later probably the most important ally of the Moravian missionaries in Gekelemukpechünk, is mentioned. Yet White Eyes was not a chief, but a captain, who could act as chief only in wartime.

him that we had heard much about how we white Brothers were supposed to be driven away, but that the 6 *Nations* had not put any obstacles in our way the entire time our Indians lived on the *Susquehanna*. They had been sad when they moved away from there and had told them they would be sorry about it and would remember their words. What did he think our Indians would say, therefore, when they heard now that their teachers were supposed to leave the country? Would they not have to believe that what the 6 *Nations* told them is the truth? He replied that we should not worry much about such talk. The Indians sometimes spoke very foolishly and without much consideration, as did the White people, who were supposed to be more reasonable than the Indians. However, if we heard anything from their *Councel* and if they sent us anything, we should take this as the truth. I told him this is what we had done previously and we had not been very concerned when we heard such things.

THE 19TH   We traveled further on. When we left, he told us that if we met the *Shawnee Chief* on the way we should follow his advice about continuing our journey or turning back. In the evening we arrived at *Woaketammeki*, a *Shawnee Town* 2 miles from where I had been a year ago. When we were still a number of miles away from there, we heard that *Gischenatsi*, the *Shawnee Chief*, had arrived there yesterday. We went directly into the house where he was and he welcomed us very cordially in the manner of the *Chiefs* with great formality. While shaking hands with each of us, he said among other things, God allowed this day to come. He is the one who decided we would see each other face to face and speak with each other today. After a short time we shared with him our plans and the purpose of our journey, and we told him that we had learned while we were on our way that he was expected in *Gekelemukpechünk*. Because we knew you could not always believe such news, we had decided to continue our journey until we met him, either on the road or at home. In the next *Town* we learned that he was here, and we immediately spoke with an Indian and asked him to go with us and be our interpreter so that we could understand each other well. The Indian could not get away today, however, so he promised us he would come here tomorrow. Therefore we would wait for him first and then speak with him. Finally, we told him that he could show us where we should spend the night, because we saw that the house was very full. He immediately gave orders and we were lodged with our *Timothy junior's* mother, who is a *Shawnee* and lives here.

In the evening, actually it was already night, he came to our lodgings with another *Shawnee* and a *Mingo Indian*. He talked with *Isaac*, who understands *Shawnee* pretty well and can also speak it a little, and asked him about *Gekelemukpechünk* and what things are like there and about the affairs of the *Wyandot* there. *Isaac* told him all the news he had heard about this. Then he told him what things were like in the *Lower Towns* from where he came, and that there was much drunkenness. This was causing great harm. He warned his young people urgently, but they no longer wanted to obey him and he could hardly keep them from robbing the *Traders* any more. They were beating each other to death; a great many had died recently and he did not know what would come of this. He pointed to me and said, Presumably he is coming here to tell us good things. You all may go wherever you want. Perhaps you will manage to do more than I have. Perhaps they will listen to you and obey. The White people have done this as long as I have known them. They always tell us they possess great understanding and wisdom from above. They just deceive us in this, however, in any way they want to, because they consider us fools. They say the Indians do not know anything or understand anything and are poor people. Indeed this is partly true. Now because the White people realize the Indians' weaknesses and inability, they always have a certain power over us. Therefore it is very easy for them to deceive the Indians and trick them into thinking that they only mean well for the Indians, although they are deceiving them. They come and bring *Rum* into our *Towns,* offer it to the Indians and say, here, drink, which they do until they become foolish and act like crazy people. Meanwhile the White people stand there, point their fingers at them, laugh at them, and say to each other, There, you see what great fools the *Shawnee* are. But who makes them so foolish, and whose fault is it? He pointed at me and said, He and those like him are responsible for this, and in the meantime they keep telling us nice words. See, they say, God has taught us thus and so. He has given us reason, so that we far surpass the Indians in knowledge and insight. This is the wisdom they possess: to deceive the Indians, to take their land and possessions. He continued, Some years ago when the White people came into their land with an army, and their leader or *General* asked for the prisoners, their flesh and blood, [page 49a]²⁸⁶ they did not want to give them up. However, because they were promised so many good things, they allowed themselves to be persuaded and gave them many of them, although not all.²⁸⁷ After this they moved on and invited the Indians to a *Treaty* in *Pittsburgh*. They had also allowed themselves to be talked into this because they believed there was nothing to fear; he himself had even gone there. When they got there, they had gathered in a large house. They were told that the house was built for the Indians; all *Nations* could gather there and peace would be concluded and maintained. One time when he wanted to go in to speak with the *Gouver-*

286. A notice at the end of the page in another hand reads: "Note, that when Brother David Zeisberger recalls in his report of his conversation with the Chief of the Shawnee a hymn that describes the Shawnee's character rather well, he is referring to the hymn in the Addition to the 11th added Part, no. 1853, especially verse 13, 'The King loves us rather well, Conf. Verse 12.'"

287. This is a reference to the expedition of Henry Bouquet. See entry for 17 Oct. 1772, note 85. The prisoners were released at a conference at Fort Pitt on 10 May 1765. Gischenatsi probably recalls the words that Lawoughgua used in his speech during the ceremony for the release of the prisoners: "Father, Here is your Flesh and Blood, except—, a few that was out with some of our hunting parties. . . . They have been all tied to us by adoption, and altho' we now deliver them to you, we will always look upon them as our relations whenever the great Spirit is pleased that we may visit them." *PCR,* 9:259. On the adoption of prisoners, see entry for 4 July 1773, note 228.

neur,[288] however, they did not want to let him in. When he insisted on going in, because he thought it was his house after all, he was almost stabbed and it was lucky that the *Bajonet* only went through his clothing. When he later complained about this, the *Gouverneur* had said such nice things to him that he was satisfied once again and believed what he told him. This had always been his experience: the White people said nice things, when in their hearts they thought evil and bad things about the Indians and had already decided upon it.[289] This is the gist of the most important things he said, but not nearly half of it. We had already told him that we wanted to speak with him tomorrow and since it was now midnight, we made no other reply to his words. It seemed, however, as if he wanted to scare us off through this and to quiet our mouths so that we would not talk with him anymore, but might go back without accomplishing what we came for. *Isaac* also believed this.

THE 20TH   When our interpreter did not come as he had promised, we invited him[290] to come to us. It also turned out there were two interpreters in the house where we were who could speak *Delaware* well. When he came, *Isaac* began with the following words, Grandchildren, a year ago we visited here twice. We told our grandchildren who live here in this area about the great, saving word of God, which God himself revealed to us and through which we have been saved. We were glad to hear that some people here wanted to accept this. Then in the spring we received a message[291] from you, which was probably actually sent to the *Mohicans*. This also concerns us after all, because we are not two people, but one, made up of 4 *Nations: Unamis, Unalachtigo, Munsee,* and *Mohicans*. There are also Indians from other *Nations* with us, the *Nanticokes, Shawnee, Canais, Mingo,* and *Cherokees*.[292] All of them live in 2 *Towns* on the *Mushkingum,* above *Gekelemukpechünk*. Therefore we undertook this journey to visit you and your people in your *Towns*, to bring you the great word of life and to see if some would like to hear it and accept it. Since we have met you here now, we are glad that we can speak with each other.

Then I said to him, Brother, I know that you are little or not at all acquainted with us, who call ourselves the *Brothers*, and I see that you do not

288. Governor John Pitt was present at Fort Pitt during the negotiations but did not participate officially in that conference. See Sir William Johnson to Lords of Trade, 24 May 1765, *NYCD*, 7:711–18. The negotiations were chaired by George Croghan as lieutenant of Sir William Johnson. McConnell, *A Country Between*, 204.

289. Peace between the crown, the colonies, the Shawnee, and the Delaware was proclaimed at the conference at Fort Pitt between 8 and 11 May 1765; it had been concluded at the end of negotiations at Johnson Hall, New York, between 8 and 11 May 1765. *NYCD*, 7:718–41. The incident Gischenatsi refers to is not mentioned in the protocol of the conference. *PCR*, 9:256–64.

290. Refers to Gischenatsi.

291. See entry for 25 April 1773.

292. On these tribes and the subdivision of the Delaware, see Introduction, p. 16; on the meaning of the term "nation" see note 28 to entry of 5 June 1772, and Introduction, pp. 70–71. Usually Zeisberger calls Unami and Unalachtigo simply Delaware and does not designate them as separate "nations."

distinguish between us and other White people. I do not hold this against you because you do not know us, because if you knew us better you would think completely differently about us. Therefore I want to tell you now what kind of a people we are. We Brothers have already been among the Indians[293] for over 30 years and no one can say that we have misled the Indians in the least or ever deceived them or cheated them. We seek only to acquaint them with our God and show them the right way to eternal life. This is our only purpose, because we know well that they are completely ignorant of this. We do not seek their land, or hides, or money or wealth, but only what serves their best interest and eternal well-being. All those who know us know this. I must also tell you, however, that there are two kinds of people on earth, because perhaps you only know of one kind and have never seen the other kind. There are good and evil people, children of God and children of Satan and of ruin, faithful ones who believe in God and are already blessed here in this world and then non-believers who live on the earth without God. They do not know him, and take their pleasure only in doing evil. Whoever remains in his unbelief will be eternally lost. Therefore you must not think that I and my Brothers are *Schwonnaks*[294] as you generally see here. Many White people know the Scriptures, can read them, and therefore also know well what God's will is and what He wants us to observe and do. However, not all of them act and live accordingly. The Indians, on the other hand, know nothing of God or His word, because they have never heard it and also cannot read. Therefore the White people who know the Scriptures and do not live according to them are not better, but even worse, than the Indians who know nothing. We Brothers, however, are not like this. We seek to follow what God requires of us, to love Him with all our hearts and strength, because He first loved us and showed His love for us and also for all Indians when He gave up His life for us and shed His blood for our sins and those of the entire world, and thus also for the Indians. Now whoever believes this will be saved. However, whoever does not believe it will be eternally lost and condemned.[295] These are the Savior's own explicit words, and He commanded us to preach the word of His sufferings and death to all Nations[296] because He is full of grace and mercy and does not want anyone to be lost. It will indeed be preached as long as the world exists, because God decided that

293. Zeisberger is recalling the beginning of the mission among the Mahican in Checomeco in 1742. See Introduction, pp. 43–45.

294. "Schwonnaks" or "Schwannack . . . signifies *salt beings,* or *bitter beings;* for in their language the word *Schwan,* is in general applied to things that have a salt, sharp, bitter, or sour taste. The object of this name, as well as of that which the Mohicans gave to the eastern people, was to express contempt as well as hatred or dislike, and to hold out the white inhabitants of the country as hateful and despicable beings." Heckewelder, *History, Manners, and Customs,* 142–43. Zeisberger, *Delaware Indian and English Spelling Book,* 11, translates it only as "Europeans, White People." The word's relationship to salt becomes clear in similar words such as "Schwennak," which means salted meat.

295. John 3:16–18.

296. Mark 16:15; Matt. 28:29.

all humans should hear it. The way to salvation should be made known to them so that whoever wants to be saved should also hear how he can attain this. Whoever accepts our words will experience this as the truth. We do not want to force ourselves on anyone though. We leave alone anyone who does not want to listen and does not want to accept our testimony. Each person makes his own decision to be saved or to be lost. However, we consider ourselves responsible and obligated to preach the Gospel because God commanded us to do so; if people in one place do not want to hear us, then we go to another one. We therefore hope you elders and *Chiefs* do not prevent this, but rather might be supportive since it concerns your eternal well-being and that of your people. If you assist in this, God will reward you for this. If not, however, God's word will still be preached and you will receive no thanks for this. Even if you do not believe my words right away, the time will come some day when you and I and all of us will appear before God. Then everything will be revealed and made known. It will also be revealed that I was speaking the truth now, and you yourself will acknowledge this.

Then he gave a talk and said, Many years ago the *Guhnawage* Indians (baptized by the French in *Canada*)[297] sent word to us here saying, We want to let you know that we have changed our way of life. We have left our old way of life and accepted a new one. There are people with white skin who have come across the great salt sea to us. They have brought scriptures with them and told us, Behold! This is God's word that we are bringing you here. Consider it well and accept it, and things will go well for you, because it is something precious and will give you great knowledge and wisdom from above. The time will come when the earth will be destroyed and everything around you will become bloody. Fear and horror will overcome you and you will try to hide but not find any place to do so. The baptized *Mohicans* (presumably those in *Stokbridge* and around *Albany*)[298] spoke like this afterward and said the same words. Some years ago we saw the White people move into our land with an army, threatening our destruction, and the rest of the Indians persecuted the baptized *Mohawks, Oneidas,* and *Mohicans,* killed many, killed or took away their cattle and burned down their cities.[299] I thought then about the words we had received at that time. Yes, I thought, it is now going to be fulfilled. The *Gendowe* (the Sunday Indians),[300] who have attained such great understanding from

---

297. With the word "Guhnawage" Zeisberger repeats the phonetic structure of the Shawnee term "kànawaꞏki," meaning Mohawk. Gischenatsi is referring here to the Mohawk who had been Christianized by Catholic missionaries and who settled in Canada in Caughnawaga. See Bonvillain, *The Mohawk,* 48:73–75, and Fenton and Tooker, "Mohawk," 467–69.

298. See entry for 5 June 1772, note 29, and for 25 Dec. 1772, note 114. Albany, New York, was the center of the fur trade with the Six Indian Nations and the most important center for treaty negotiations between the English colonies and the tribes of the middle Atlantic and northern colonies.

299. On the conflict in the 1750s between the Christian Mohawk (Caughnawaga) and Delaware, see McConnell, *A Country Between,* 103; White, *Middle Ground,* 291.

300. "Gendowe" is the word for Sunday or holiday in Unami. Zeisberger, *Delaware Indian and English Spelling Book,* 17. These Native Americans celebrated the Sunday.

above through the White people, did this. Last year the *Mohicans* from the *Susquehanna* came here to *Allegheny* (those from *Friedenshütten*). Now when they crossed over the mountains, they looked all around and said among themselves, Where will we end up? We are completely blind here. We cannot see anything and do not know where we should go. With much effort they finally found their way to the area of *Gekelemukpechünk* and then they sent us word saying, We are poor and blind; we cannot see where we should stop or settle. Those were *Josua's* words to the *Chief* in *Gekelemukpechünk* a year ago, when he acted on his own and did not follow what had been agreed in the *Conference* with the Indian Brothers.[301] All the Indians know that a great fire had been lit among the *Shawnee* many years ago, from which the smoke rises toward heaven and makes everything clear and bright. All the surrounding *Nations* will come to this fire and warm themselves at it and through this peace will be maintained.[302] Now why is it that this person is blind, taps around, does not know where he should turn and cannot see the great fire from which the smoke rises to heaven? Why is it that he is so poor? Who made him so poor and who is responsible for all his misery? Once again he pointed at me and said, It is his fault. He made him so poor and blinded his eyes so that he cannot see, and it was not even enough that he was there. They had to bring another like him here. Whose fault is it that we are in such miserable circumstances, that the young people no longer want to be obedient to the older ones, that they no longer listen to their leaders and *Chiefs*, do nothing but drink, rob, steal and beat each other to death? You all are the cause of all the unhappiness and harm which has come to the Indians for a number of years, because things were not like this before. He turned to me and said, You can certainly go to our *Towns*. I will not forbid it, and to the 2 Indian Brothers, You may take him there, but you must expect them to knock out his brains.

I answered him, Brother, you completely misunderstood the *Mohican's* words. He did not mean them as you interpreted them here, and if you yourself would speak with him, he would explain it to you very differently. He meant that they had come into a strange, unfamiliar country where they have never been before. It is like this for everyone who comes to an unknown area. Everything is unfamiliar to him, both the area and the residents, until he has been there a while and become familiar. Then he feels at home again. Concerning the other point, that I and those like me are responsible for your miserable circumstances, I already told you at the beginning of my talk that there are two kinds of people on the earth, evil and good. Therefore I cannot do anything about it if other White people cause trouble and unhappiness among the Indians. It is not within my power to keep them away. My concern and intention

301. This sentence was added in the margin.

302. On the importance of the Shawnee's chief settlement in the Scioto region as the primary site for negotiating the union of the western and the Ohio tribes, see entry for 5 June 1772, note 29.

is to tell the Indians what is good or evil, what they should do and not do, in order to be saved. When someone says something nice and brings you something good, accept it. If someone brings you something evil, you should not accept it. Therefore when someone brings *Rum* into your *Town,* as you say, so that so much misfortune occurs, then do as we do in our *Town.* We do not accept them, but send them away with it. Or if they want to stay overnight, we take it into our custody until they want to go on. Then we return to them what is theirs and let them go in peace. Why should your *Chiefs* not have as much authority in your *Towns* as we do? Concerning the rest of your talk, my Brothers who are here with me can witness to what we teach the Indians and to my walk and that of my Brothers. I do not like to testify about myself, but prefer to leave this up to others. They know and can tell you how they were taught. Then he was completely silent and could not reply. In a while Brother *Isaac* spoke to him saying, Listen to me once again. You have surely seen and heard that the Indians baptized by the French and English go to war, drink, steal, rob, kill, and continue to live in all kinds of sin. Thus they have not become any better than they were before; you are also correct that the latter persecuted our *Nation* in the last war, killed many of our people, and burned their cities. It does not follow, however, that we are also like these people. Those of our people who have become believers no longer do such things. We do not go to war and do not kill people; we do not drink, steal, and lie. We find all such things repulsive and our teachers instruct us how to behave. They teach us daily (because we have services every morning and evening) only how we can be saved and how we can lead a life pleasing to God, and they live as they teach us. We have never seen them do anything bad as we have seen other White people do, since many of them are no better than the Indians. Therefore you must not think that we are the same kind of people as Indians baptized by other *Ministers.* Recently some Indians in *Gekelemukpechünk* wanted to have other preachers come. I told them that this would not improve them, because I know this and have seen that the Indians baptized by those besides the Brothers are not better, and indeed become worse, than others.

Finally I also told him that when I left home, I had departed with the *Intention* of visiting him and his people, and if I had not met him here I would certainly have gone on to their home. However, because I had seen him here now and had spoken to him and had also heard that they were going hunting, and those whom we especially wanted to see were not at home, I wanted to tell him now that I would not go on any further. I was glad I had seen him and just hoped he might take my words to heart and think about them. He had now completely emptied himself and poured out his heart and pulled himself together. It was already midnight. Therefore he said a cordial farewell, shook hands with each of us, and went to his lodgings.

THE 21ST   We stayed there because our horses had gotten lost. Since we were there, we also had the chance during that time to talk with various

Shawnee who visited us about the salvation in Jesus' blood. Among them were also some of those we had visited a year ago. However, they seemed fearful and shy, not so much of us as of the others and perhaps only of the *Chief.* They listened very attentively, and when they were leaving some of them said they were happy they had heard a little bit again. The *Shawnee* we were with last year have scattered; some have gone to the *Lower Towns* and the rest have spread out around here. As happy as I was at that time to see such a beautiful *Prospect,* it now hurts me to see that all has come to nothing and been destroyed. I am no longer very surprised as I really see now that it could not have turned out any other way, because this is the border and Satan is resisting and watching to see that we do not come further into his territory. Now we will hope where there is nothing to see and to hope, and will believe steadfastly what was in the Watchword we read upon leaving home, For I am God, and there is none else; I am God, and there is none like me. Declaring the end from the beginning, and from ancient times the things that are not yet done, saying, my counsel shall stand, and I will do all my pleasure,[303] and the closing hymn, Er hat noch niemals was versehen in seinem Regiment. Nein, was Er thut und läst geschehen, das nimmt ein gutes End.[304] {He has never neglected anything in his order. No, whatever He does or leaves undone always turns out well.} No less the Watchword with which we arrived here and met the *Chief,* which was fitting for the day he first addressed us, which strengthened me and provided me with much comfort. It said, The Lord is on my side; I will not fear: what can man do unto me? Unverzagt und ohne Grauen soll ein Christ, wo er ist, stets sich sehen lassen schauen. {Wherever he is, a Christian should always show himself undaunted and without fear.}[305]

THE 22ND   After discussing various matters with the *Chief,* we said farewell to him and others, and also invited him to visit us in both of our *Towns* when he travels to *Pittsburgh.* He promised to do so, and once again said a *solemn* and very friendly farewell. We then began our return journey and in the evening arrived in *White Eye's Town* where they were preparing for a festival and sacrifice, for which some Indians from the area had gathered. It was supposed to take place the next day, and they made preparations for it and already started celebrating this evening. When they asked him to join in with them, because he used to be a master in such events, Isaac used the opportunity to preach a sermon. He witnessed to them that there is no salvation to seek or to find in anything except in Jesus' blood, which he had found and experienced.

303. Isa. 46:9–10.
304. The "closing hymn" was sung at the end of the service by pastor and congregation together; the Watchwords suggested for each day the verse of a particular hymn; for 17 Sept. 1773 this was hymn no. 190, verse 5, in *Das kleine Brüder-Gesang-Buch.*
305. Ps. 118:6. The hymn cited in addition to the Watchword was in *Altes und Neues Brüdergesangbuch, Theil I* (London, 1753) [hereafter *Londoner Altes und Neues Brüdergesangbuch,* pt. I or pt. II], no. 736, verse 5.

They received this well. Then on THE 23RD we passed through *Gekelemukpech-ünk* and *Gnadenhütten* and arrived in *Schoenbrunn* again, happy and grateful for all the good things the Savior had done for us on the journey.

Diary of the little Indian Congregation in Schoenbrunn *on the* Mushkingum *from* October, 1773 *until* February 1774[306]

THE 22ND   We sent letters and our diary to Bethlehem via *Pittsburgh* with *Traders* who were passing by here.

THE 24TH   In the morning we knelt and dedicated our Meeting House with a sincere prayer[307] and commended this site to the Savior's grace, so that many more Indians might be brought to Him yet through the word of redemption. Then there was the sermon and in the afternoon a Lovefeast.

THE 25TH   *Theodore's* little grandchild, who went home the day before yesterday, was buried. At the request of the parents (who are not baptized), he had first been baptized with the name *Samuel.*

THE 26TH   *Laweloochwalend,* the *Chief* of *Shenenge,* arrived here with his family to stay, and some Indians from *Gekelemukpechünk* came here to visit.

THE 27TH   The Brothers completely finished Brother and Sister *Roth's* new house. They are now living temporarily in our schoolhouse. Brother *Jungmann junior* came here from *Gnadenhütten* for a visit.

THE 31ST   Brother *Roth* preached the sermon in the morning. In the afternoon we shared some news from the *Caribbean Islands*[308] with the Brothers and Sisters, which really delighted and interested them.

November.

THE 1ST   The earthly dwelling of our dear old Brother *Simon,* who died in blessing yesterday, was accompanied to its rest. He became acquainted with the Brothers in 1768 in *Goschgoschünk,* showed his love for them right at the beginning of their presence there, regularly attended their services there and also later in *Lawunakhannek,* and his entire family, which was quite large, often came on Sundays to the latter place. When the Brothers later moved from there to *Kaskaskunk* in 1770, he could not bear to stay there and he followed

---

306. MAB, B 141, F 4, I 2, fol. 53.

307. Construction began on 14 September. The meeting house measured 40 x 36 feet. Heckewelder, *Narrative of the Mission,* 244.

308. Moravian missionaries worked on the islands of St. Thomas, St. John, St. Croix, Jamaica, Antigua, St. Kitts, Barbados, and Tobago. On the history of these missions in the years 1771–73, see Hegner, *Fortsetzung,* 101–9, where the beginning of a great awakening in the wake of a disastrous hurricane in Antigua in August 1772 is reported. The missionaries on these West Indian islands wrote diaries, too, which were circulated to the other congregations. See Oldendorp, *Geschichte der Mission.*

us after several months. On *January* 1, 1772, he was baptized, and in *February* 1773 he joined us in the celebration of Holy Communion. Since his baptism he has also followed a blessed walk and never allowed himself to be disturbed by anything, even in the often-difficult circumstances of his friendship, but proved himself to be in the Father. During his illness, which was a high fever, he proved that he believed, and before his end he also urged his wife to tell all of his friends who are still wandering around in confusion that they should follow him if they wanted to be saved. He was a little more than 80 years old and he leaves behind a widow and two daughters who are communicant Sisters.

THE 3RD The baby daughter born to Brother *Jacob* and Sister *Johanette* yesterday was baptized with the name *Maria Magdalena*. We received the news from *Gekelemukpechünk* that 4 *Shawnee*[309] are supposed to have been killed at 2 different sites on the *Ohio* where they had stolen horses. Our people began going out for the fall hunt, and the Brothers and Sisters were reminded to remember the poor people who could not earn anything and told that they should share meat with them.

THE 6TH *Marcus* came from *Gnadenhütten* with a message to our Indians in both *Towns* from *Chief Netawatwees* in *Gekelemukpechünk*. In this he informed us that things looked pretty serious for both the *Shawnee* and the *Mingo*,[310] and that he did not know where else to turn except to the King across the great water. He still had hope that through him they could become a calm and peaceful people. For this reason, he asked both of our *Towns* to provide assistance, so that this undertaking could be carried out for the general good. Therefore he asked us to collect hides for this *Expedition* when our people came home from hunting, to cover the expenses of those who were prepared to go there. This was supposed to take place in 5 months. The *Shawnee* and *Wyandot* had already been encouraged to do the same.[311]

THE 10TH After the early devotion there was the burial of the one-and-a-half-month-old baby boy *Heinrich,* son of Brother *Samuel Nantikok* and Sister *Sarah Nantikok*. He had died yesterday.

THE 13TH OF NOVEMBER Early in the morning we knelt and paid homage to our Chief Elder and High Priest, prayed for his merciful *Absolution,*

309. The diary entry for Gnadenhütten for 3 Nov. mentions only three Indians. MAB, B 144, F 2, I 2. It is not possible to identify them further.

310. Irrespective of the fact that Shawnee and Mingo, and especially those Seneca who lived close to or even in the settlements of the Shawnee on the Scioto, were divided in their attitudes toward white settlers who poured into the region from Virginia, relations between Mingo and Shawnee had deteriorated in the previous year. See the message of the Shawnee that arrived on 6 Oct. 1773 at Fort Pitt, entry for 14 Oct. 1773, note 281.

311. On the intention of Netawatwees and the Delaware to confront the English king in person with their concerns and request a guarantee for their lands, see entries for 18 Dec. and 26 Dec. 1772 and for 30 July 1773. See Jones, *Journal of Two Visits,* 99. Netawatwees expected that the settlements of Schönbrunn and Gnadenhütten would contribute to meeting the general expenses. His request thus indicates in general how such costs were financed in Native American societies. See entry for 2 Sept. 1773.

promised Him anew obedience and faithfulness, and commended ourselves and those who were absent to his further *Direction*.[312] He looked upon us kindly and comforted us. *Laweloochwalend* returned from *Mahony* on *Beaver Creek,* where he had gone some days ago to get his belongings and food for the winter.

THE 17TH   We white Brothers and Sisters joined in reading the *Memorabilia* of the *Unity Elders' Conference* from the year 1770 and took special interest in what was written about the messengers to the heathen. We let this serve as a lesson and admonition for us.[313]

THE 27TH   Many of our Brothers and Sisters returned home from hunting and on the 28TH we had blessed *Advent* services celebrating our Savior's arrival in flesh.

December

THE 1ST   We received delightful letters from our dear Brothers and Sisters *Nathanael, Mattheus,* etc. from *Litiz,* which we enjoyed today. Some Sisters from here went to the hunting huts to fetch meat.

THE 2ND   A child who was born here on *November* 20th was baptized into Jesus' death and named *Ludwig,* and on THE 3RD *Jannetje's* baby boy, who was born in *Langundouteniünk,* was baptized with the name *Johanan*. Both were *Margaretha's* grandchildren.

THE 18TH   Today as in recent days all the Brothers have returned home from hunting, and Indians from *Moochweshüng* came here to visit. The Board of Supervisors gathered to arbitrate a matter and straighten it out.

THE 19TH   Brother *Roth* preached the sermon in the morning. In a separate service, Holy Communion was announced for next Saturday and the Brothers and Sisters were invited to this as hungry and thirsty people. In the congregational service about the Watchword,[314] we discussed how each person

---

312. On the importance of the day commemorating Christ's acceptance of the position of Elder in the Unity on 13 November 1741, see Introduction, p. 62.

313. In 1764 the directory of the Unitas Fratrum resolved to distribute weekly or biweekly a "really short relation" of her work to all congregations. These were soon called "Weekly News of the Conference of the Unity's Elders' Conference." As soon as these arrived in Bethlehem, they were copied and sent to the missionaries along with the addenda that were of special interest to the missionaries. For the years covered by the diary, the "Weekly News of the Conference of the Unity's Elders' Conference" are collected in the volumes 1764–73, 1774–80, and 1781–85, MAB. The "Memorabilia of the Unity's Elders' Conference" were separate, unbound addenda to the "Weekly News of the Conference of the Unity's Elders' Conference," which were usually incorporated into the "Congregational News" for the fifty-second week of the congregation of Bethlehem as addenda. Thus the "Memorabilia of the Unity's Elders' Conference for the Year 1770" were an addition to the fifty-second week of the "Congregation News." Corresponding to the "Weekly News" of the Unity, "Weekly News" bulletins were composed for Bethlehem as well. These contained not so much reports on the affairs of Bethlehem but excerpts from reports that had come to Bethlehem from other missionaries.

314. 2 Chron. 19:11.

in the congregation must show faithfulness in his calling, in small and large matters; the Savior really pays attention to who is faithful in small matters so that he can then be entrusted with greater things.

THE 21ST   We began having Speakings with the Brothers and Sisters. The Brothers collected hides for the congregational *Expenses*.[315] In remembrance of this day,[316] there was a talk about the Watchword[317] in the evening. This dealt with how we, like *Thomas*, recognize our Lord and God by his five sacred wounds and as soon as we catch a glimpse of our election by grace through this, we must call out and say, My Lord and my God!

THE 24TH   The congregation gathered for the Christmas Eve service, which began with a Lovefeast. During this we read the story of our Savior's birth. We reflected upon the little baby in the stall and in the manger and celebrated Him in song and worshipped Him on our knees. He comforted and delighted our hearts so that they melted and tears flowed from our eyes. In conclusion we passed out written verses and candles to the children, who also joined in singing their childlike *Gratias* to Him and who really rejoiced over baby Jesus in the manger.

THE 25TH   Brother *Roth* preached a sermon about Isaiah 9, For unto us a child is born, unto us a son is given etc.[318] There was a blessed feeling during the Children's Service, which Brother *Jungmann* led. The children sang very sweetly of the Savior's birth and incarnation, so that the older people shed many tears during this. In the evening in the congregational service old *Sarah Nantikok* was baptized into Jesus' death with the name *Rebecca*. The Savior blessed this event. Then we 54 Brothers and Sisters experienced the most blessed enjoyment of His Body and Blood in the Holy *Sacrament*.

THE 26TH   In the morning was the *Liturgy* for Holy Communion, which Brother *Roth* led, and then the sermon, which Brother *Jungmann* preached about the great love our dear Father in heaven has for us lost humans. At the appointed time, He sent His only son, born of a woman, to release us from Satan's power. We felt the powerful work of the Holy Spirit among the hearts of our people and especially among those who have not been baptized; no one remained untouched. In the evening we concluded this blessed holiday in the congregational service with the Church Benediction,[319] during which we also shared the kiss of peace.

---

315. The method of funding expenses was through voluntary contributions and thus was the same in Schönbrunn as in the Indian settlements. See entry for 6 Nov. 1773 and note 311.

316. The 21st of December was St. Thomas Day. The Bethlehem diary entry read: "With Thomas we gazed with believing eyes at the wounds of our Lord and Master. In the evening in the meeting of the congregation we celebrated with an affected heart with hymns our eternal happiness." Bethlehem Congregational Diary, entry for 21 Dec. 1773, MAB.

317. The Watchword for this day was Deut. 32:4; the relation about Thomas is in John 20:24–29. The relationship with the wounds of Jesus was likewise suggested by the hymn for the day's Watchword: "Ich leg die Hand in Seine Seite und sage mein Herr und mein Gott!" (I put my hand into your open wound and proclaim my Lord and my God). *Das kleine Brüder-Gesang-Buch*, no. 1851.

318. Isa. 9:5.

319. See 24 Dec. 1772.

THE 29TH   *Queelpacheno,* who was formerly a great doctor among the Indians and who has been living with us for more than 2 years, came to us and complained about his miserable condition. He has been hearing about the Savior for so long, but has always remained dead in his heart. He told us about his circumstances and what has held him back until now. Ever since he had been living with us a little man had been with him constantly and he had been around him wherever he went. He had also accompanied him into the services, where he had either been behind him or beside him; he had always prevented him from engaging in thoughts about changing. When he sometimes wanted to listen reverently to what was said in the services, he had kicked him in the head so that he almost fell off the bench. However, since he came here last spring, he had left him and he had not seen him for some time. Now he hopes and desires to be cleansed from his sins with the Savior's blood.

THE 30TH   We were delighted to receive letters from Bethlehem and *Litiz* through Mr. *Anderson* via *Pittsburgh,* along with Watchwords and texts for next year.[320]

THE 31ST   At half past ten in the evening we gathered to conclude the old year and begin the new one. First we read the *Memorabilia*[321] and after a talk about the Watchword and text,[322] we fell on our knees before our dear Lord and thanked him for all the kindness and faithfulness He has shown us, His poor Indian people, this year despite our innumerable shortcomings and failures, for all of His forgiveness, for living and walking among us, and for the heavenly Father's protection of His dear Son's people and the Holy Spirit's care and instruction of hearts. In conclusion the Lord's blessing was laid upon the congregation, during which we shared the kiss of peace for the New Year.

This year the following items of note took place in the Indian congregation here:

1) The change in *Langundouteniünk,* the town we completely vacated in *April* and *May.* The little congregation there moved, some here and some to *Gnadenhütten.* Brother and Sister *Roth,* who came here with them, then served the little congregation in *Gnadenhütten* temporarily until Brother and Sister *Schmick* arrived there from Bethlehem on *August* 16th, after which the former came here as assistants.

2) *Isaac* and another Brother from *Gnadenhütten* made two visits, one to the *Shawnee* and one to another area. Brother *David* also visited the *Shawnee* last fall with *Isaac* and *Willhelm.*

3) We thank our dear, heavenly Father that He also provided for the material needs of our Brothers and Sisters, mercifully assisted them, and richly blessed them so that they have now survived the most difficult part.

---

320. *Die täglichen Loosungen der Brüder-Gemeine für das Jahr* 1774; *Die Lehrtexte der Brüder-Gemeine für das Jahr* 1774.

321. The "Memorabilia" contained the summary of the most important events of the year; at the year's end they were incorporated into the diary.

322. Deut. 7:9. The text was 1 John 2:28.

4) The holidays were especially blessed days for us all, accompanied by the Savior's presence, which we still remember vividly.

5) Along with many other buildings, we finished our Meeting House in *October,* and on the 24th we dedicated it in His presence.

6) We celebrated Holy *Communion* 7 times this year, during which the Savior graciously showed Himself among us each time, and revealed Himself to us in a special manner.

7) Although there were fewer visits from Indian guests than before, because *Gnadenhütten* is closer for them, we still had many visits from both this area and others, and some heard the word of redemption and received blessings for their hearts.

8) We also acknowledge the *Communication* of the congregational newsletters as a special act of kindness. We receive this with sincere gratitude, and ask our dear Lord to provide us more in the future.

This year 2 families and 3 single people joined the congregation, in all 9 people. 9 adults and 9 children were baptized. 5 Brothers and Sisters were *admitted* to Holy Communion. One couple was married. 7 adult Brothers and Sisters and 9 children died.

At the conclusion of this year 81 baptized adults live here, including 50 communicant Brothers and Sisters, 2 older boys, 11 younger boys, 1 older girl and 11 younger girls.

Unbaptized: 15 adults, 4 older boys, 3 older girls, 23 younger boys and 33 younger girls. Total: 184 people.

January 1774

THE 1ST   In the morning Brother *Roth* preached the sermon and in the afternoon there was a service for those who have been baptized, during which we could feel the presence of the dear Savior. We commended ourselves to Him anew for grace, and promised Him our willing obedience and faithfulness. In the Congregational Service in the evening 4 people were baptized: *Jonas, Lucas's* brother who came to us in the beginning in *Goschgoschünk, Stephanus, Silas,* and *Debora* from *Tuscarawi.* During this the Savior's presence could be felt powerfully, so that many tears were shed during this.

THE 3RD   The early devotion dealt with Christ and His blood as the foundation upon which His congregation is built. It will stand unmovable, even if heaven and earth are destroyed. Today we had Speakings with various Brothers and Sisters. Some who have lagged behind for a while examined their hearts and found their own fault themselves, so that we were able to thank the

Savior for this. Today the Brothers took up a collection for the *Chief* to be used for *Public Affairs.*[323]

THE 6TH   Early in the morning devotion we commended the entire little congregation and ourselves to the Savior for blessing today, and we prayed for His dear presence. In the second service, after a talk about today's text, And in his name shall the Gentiles trust. Willkommen theure Heiden—am blutgen Wunden Loch, {Welcome precious heathen—at the bloody wound}.[324] 3 people were buried into Jesus' death through baptism, *Queelpacheno* with the name *Jephta, Ignatius's* wife with the name *Christina,* and *Jacob Gendaskund's* daughter with the name *Sophia.* God's sacred peace prevailed during this, so that even the strangers who were present were powerfully touched. During the Lovefeast in the afternoon we remembered all of our native congregations and also expressed desire that the Savior might soon gather His reward for suffering from among the heathen here and in all places. In the evening was the Congregational Service, and to conclude this blessed day there was a holy Service of Adoration with all those who have been baptized.

THE 8TH   We talked to a widow with 2 children who had come here before the holidays for a visit and has now decided and requested to live with us.[325] We granted her permission to do this.

THE 9TH   Brother *Jungmann* led the Children's Service. On this anniversary day,[326] he mentioned when Jesus was twelve years old, and in the Congregational Service in the evening *Noah's* boy, more than 14 years old, was baptized into Jesus' death with the name *Heinrich.* During this the Brothers and Sisters were urged to remember our children and youth diligently before the Savior, so that they might grow up in the love and knowledge of Jesus Christ. We also cannot thank the Savior enough for this and it awakened our hearts to praise that He revealed Himself especially graciously among our children in the recent holidays and allowed Himself to be felt among them.

THE 11TH   We began school again with the children. They showed a great desire for this, and they were up stomping their Indian corn and taking care of their work a number of hours before daylight so that they would not miss school.[327] Some Sisters from *Gnadenhütten* came here for a visit.

THE 16TH   In a service for married Brothers and Sisters, our Brother *Abraham* was promised to Sister *Anna* in marriage and married by Brother *Roth.*

---

323. See entry for 6 Nov. 1773.

324. The text was Matt. 12:21, and the hymn in *Londoner Altes und Neues Brüdergesangbuch,* pt. I, 2065, verse 11; 6 Jan. was the day for commemorating the heathens.

325. Economic considerations made the congregation attractive for widows because they could always count on provisions and security there. See Introduction, p. 69.

326. In the Unity the big boys celebrated their choir festival between 7 and 12 January. Since only a few big boys lived in Schönbrunn, this festival was usually not observed. See entry for 12 Jan. 1777. Nevertheless Zeisberger refers to this festival. The history of the twelve-year-old Jesus in the temple is in Luke 2:41–52.

327. In the previous year school had started on 2 Feb. 1773.

THE 17TH   The Board of Supervisors gathered to take care of an inheritance matter from the *Susquehanna*. This morning our Sister *Phoebe* entered the kingdom of health.[328]

THE 18TH   Her earthly dwelling was buried in the morning. She came to the Unity in *Fridenshütten* in 1765, was baptized on *January* 8, 1767, and was admitted to Holy Communion with the Unity in 1768. Since her baptism her heart has remained firmly attached to the Savior and to the Unity. Her earthly body was very sickly the entire time she was with us, but for a year her strength had been declining significantly and her illness worsened so that she had to lie down almost constantly. She spent her time happily in fellowship with the Savior. She often longed for her release, and she experienced this great grace and died gently and happily with the blessing of the congregation.

Today we spoke with *Gutgigamen, Isaac's* son, from *Mochwesüng*. Before Christmas he had come here from *Tuscarawi* where he had been hunting, and he has been staying here since then. During this time he has often been powerfully moved and convinced of the truth. Now he has also decided to stay here with his wife and children, and he received permission to do so.

THE 19TH   The Brothers and Sisters collected some Indian corn for the 2 families who arrived recently, so that they will have something to eat until the hard winter is past and they can go fetch their own. In the evening service we remembered the first *mission* to the natives 41 years ago in Greenland, and with grateful hearts we remembered what the Savior has done among the heathen in all places since that time, including here.[329] 8 Indians came from their hunting huts in the bush above *Tuscarawi* for a visit. They attended our services and our Indian Brothers preached to them almost the entire night and the following day, because this is what they had come for. They returned on

THE 21ST   Some of them were very touched, and with emotional hearts and tears in their eyes they said that they could now believe that what they had heard here was the truth. They wanted to think about it some more. Brother *Jungmann junior* came here from *Gnadenhütten* to visit and the next day Brother *Heckewelder* went there from here.

THE 23RD   The previously mentioned Indians returned here and said they had not forgotten what they had heard here; they had thought about it day and night, and they felt no peace until they decided to come here again. Therefore they wanted to hear more about the Savior. They stayed here until THE 27TH and could not hear enough. One of them said that he had pre-

---

328. This formula expresses, as does the term "hut" for "body" and "pass away" for "dying," the Moravian conception of life and death. Life on this earth and the body are preliminary and fragile; the real home of a Christian is heaven, and death is the gateway to a better, "healthy" life in a "healthy empire." See entry for 18 Sept 1773.

329. The calendar of the Moravian festivals notes for this day: "19 January 1733: Mission under the Heathens in Greenland." For the beginning of the mission in Greenland and for Zinzendorf's relations with the royal court at Copenhagen, which are related to this event, see Cranz, *Alte und Neue Brüder-Historie*, 186–88, and entry for 24 Jan. 1773.

viously made sacrifices so things might go well for his children in this world and the next. However, now he had heard that nothing could be attained through sacrifices, neither temporally nor eternally. He believed this is really the truth, and from now on he did not want to sacrifice any more but would rather move here with his children, where they could hear good things and learn.[330]

Some Sisters came here from *Gnadenhütten* for a visit, as did *Nathanael's* son and whole family from *Gekelemukpechünk*.

THE 28TH   Brother *David* went to *Gnadenhütten* and returned on the 29TH.

THE 30TH   Brother *Roth* preached the sermon, and then the communicant Brothers and Sisters had a blessed service, and those who have been baptized did so afterward. We announced to the former that there will be Holy Communion next Saturday.

February

THE 2ND   In the early devotion we blessed our widowers and widows and prayed for the Savior's close presence for them on their joyful festival day.[331] In the morning they had a service about the doctrinal text[332] and in the afternoon a sweet Lovefeast, for which the widows in Bethlehem had sent them tea. During this we remembered with gratitude to our dear Lord what He has done for us during this year, in which 3 widowers and 2 widows were baptized. 1 widow was admitted to Holy Communion. 2 couples were married and 4 joined the congregation on high. Currently there are 4 widowers and 17 widows[333] here, including 14 communicant Brothers and Sisters and one who is not yet baptized. At the conclusion of their blessed day they had a joyful Service of Adoration.

THE 3RD   We were extremely delighted to receive letters from *November* of last year from Brother *Matthao* from Litiz.

---

330. The diaries of the Moravian missionaries offer a number of interesting entries on the function and importance of sacrifices among Indians. The entry for 27 July 1768 reads in part: "the Indians of the neighborhood had a spirits- or ghost-feast, on which occasion a hog was sacrificed. Such sacrifices are occasionally arranged by the Indian doctors, who allege that the spirits are dissatisfied and must be appeased by the sacrifice of a hog, a deer or a bear. The feast takes place at night in a house that is entirely dark. In course of the feast, the doctor converses with the spirits, gives them of the flesh and, afterwards, declares that the spirits have been reconciled, whereupon the Indians disperse." [Sensemann and Zeisberger], "Diary of Zeisberger and Zenseman," 66. See entry for 22 Sept. 1773. The Indian concept of sacrifice was replaced by the missionaries with the Christian concept of sacrifice as Christ's sacrifice for all men. See entries for 14 Jan. 1773 (and note 143), 2 April 1775, 8 Oct. 1775, and 24 Dec. 1775.

331. This refers to the choir festival of the widows and widowers.

332. Matt. 11:28–30.

333. The relation of these figures underscores impressively the importance of the mission congregation as a providing and protecting community for single women.

THE 4TH   Yesterday and today were the Speakings with the Brothers and Sisters. We found them contrite, hungry and thirsty for the Body and Blood of our Lord.

THE 5TH   They partook of this most blissfully in the Holy *Sacrament. Jacob Gendaskand* was readmitted, and one Sister observed for the first time.

THE 6TH   In the morning was the *Liturgy* for Holy Communion and then the sermon. We sensed a blessed awareness of the aftertaste of what the Brothers and Sisters had enjoyed yesterday in the Body and Blood in Holy Communion among them.

THE 7TH   A number of Brothers and Sisters from *Gnadenhütten* came here for a visit. The Brothers made rails here to fence in our *Town* as soon as the weather permits. Since Christmas it has been continuously cold without any change and the winter this year is much colder and more relentless than last winter.

THE 11TH   Various Indians came here to visit, including one who lives close to the *Wyandot.* He asked to hear much about the Savior and listened with great *Attention.* Today *Esther* also moved from here to *Gnadenhütten.* We accompanied her with our blessings.[334]

THE 13TH   In the Congregational Service another individual was added to the congregation through Holy Baptism and named *Adolph.*

Diary of the Indian Congregation in Schoenbrunn on the Muschkingum from February *until* May 21, 1774.[335]

FEBRUARY 19TH   A widow from *Kaskaskunk* and her son received permission to live with us. She is from *Packanke's* friendship,[336] had often visited in *Langundouteniünk,* and has actually set out to follow us twice since the Indian congregation moved away from there, but Indians had always prevented her from reaching her goal until last Christmas. She has been staying here since then and has received blessings for her heart.

THE 25TH   Most of the Brothers and Sisters went out to look for sites for boiling sugar[337] and to make preparations for this. Some strange Indians from *Tuscarawi,* who had been here visiting for a number of days, returned home today. They had heard the Gospel with *Attention,* which was the main reason they had come here.

THE 27TH   Yesterday and throughout the night there was one thunderstorm after another with heavy rains. The snow disappeared quickly and the

334. In this and in other cases the reason for moving was usually marriage to a member of another mission congregation. See entries for 22 and 26 April 1774.
335. MAB, B 141, F 5, I 1, fol. 59.
336. On Zeisberger's meaning of the term "friendship," see Introduction, p. 18, and note 42.
337. See entry for 16 Feb. 1773, note 159.

water rose very rapidly. *Traders* arrived here from *Pittsburgh,* and Indians from *Kaskaskunk* came to visit their friends here.

March.

MARCH 2ND   After the early devotion, a child named *Ludwig,* who went home yesterday, was buried in the 8th month of his life. Indians had come here from *Pittsburgh* and were transporting *Rum* so that they could trade it among the Indians, so we talked with them about this and told them if they were carrying such goods they should not pass through here, but should take another way. We want to let all *Traders* who come here or pass through here know this too.[338]

THE 3RD   Our God's Acre was fenced in. 2 Sisters, *Pauline* and *Anna Salome,* joined the Helpers' Conference again.

THE 6TH   All of our Brothers and Sisters came home from the bush where they were boiling sugar. They had to flee because of the extremely high water. All the *Low Land,* not only here on the river but also on all the *Creeks* in the bush, was also under water. In the Children's Service, the baby daughter born to Brother *Jacob* and Sister *Rosine* on the 1st of this month was baptized with the name *Philippina.*

THE 7TH   Through an *Express* messenger from the *Chief* in *Gekelemuk-pechünk,* we received news and the reply to their message they had received from the *Cherokees,* which was very *favorable.* They accepted the suggestions for peace, opened the road here[339] and will begin next summer, when a party of them will come to *Gekelemukpechünk* where the peace will be concluded finally. Those *Towns* which have accepted the message are supposed to include 3,900 men, not counting women and children. However, this is still not the entire *Nation.* They call the *Delaware Nation* their grandfather and these call them their grandchildren.[340] On this occasion the *Chief* of a certain *Nation* even further to the south informed *Netawatwees* that he was his brother.

338. This represents one of the few proofs that not only colonists but Indians, too, carried rum to Indian settlements. See, for further evidence, entries for 6 April, 16 July, and 11 Nov. 1775 below, and [Sensemann and Zeisberger], "Diary of Zeisberger and Zenseman," 73, 91, where Zeisberger noted: "Every spring and fall Goschgoschuenk was the rum market for the Senecas, especially those of Garochiati. They secured the rum in Niagara and brought it thither for sale. Now this is forbidden them." During treaty negotiations with colonists, both Indian speakers and European reports represented the trade in rum as a European monopoly (see too Gischenatsi's speech on p. 166). On the alcohol issue in general, see entry for 28 Feb. 1773, note 132.

339. Here Zeisberger is using Indian diplomatic rhetoric, according to which it was a precondition for opening negotiations that "the road to the place of negotiation be cleared from dirt and rubble." On this usage, see the entries for 20 and 25 June 1773.

340. On kinship between tribes, see Introduction, p. 21. Heckewelder explains the relationship between the Delaware and the Cherokee as that of grandfather to grandson, according to the Delaware belief that all tribes descended from two primary tribes. Heckewelder, *History, Manners, and Customs,* 95–96. Zeisberger, "History of the Northern American Indians," 33–34, suggests that the Cherokee acknowledged the Delaware as their grandfathers in the peace of 1768.

THE 11TH   *Newollike* and his family came here to stay after a journey of almost two years, and with him another family from the *Susquehanna*.[341]

THE 19TH   A number of Indians from *Kaskaskunk* came here to visit and many of our Indian Brothers came home from bear hunting, where they had been very successful.

THE 25TH   We read the Bible story of this remarkable day and when the Watchword was read[342] we talked about how the Savior perfected His plan of mercy for the human race through the Savior's holy incarnation and death.

THE 27TH   Brother *Roth* preached the sermon. In the service for married couples, Brother *Jungmann* married *David* from *Gnadenhütten,* who had come here several days ago to stay, to *Salome,* daughter of *Timothy* and *Martha.*

THE 28TH   *Newollike* and his wife explained to the entire Helpers' Conference why they had come here to our place and what had moved them to do this. They had already been considering this 3 years ago and had felt the desire in their hearts to come to us and become believers in the Savior. Now they were happy they had arrived at our place with good hope that the Brothers would receive them. They sought nothing in this world except to be saved. He said this with tears in his eyes. They were overjoyed when we answered that we would gladly receive them and hoped they might soon become participants in the salvation in Jesus' blood and would bear fruit for Him.

THE 30TH   We spoke with 3 more people who came here to stay. After they had heard and agreed to our *Statutes,* they also received permission to live here. We heard from *Gekelemukpechünk* that they were indeed starting to send away disobedient and unruly people. In time they will learn even more from us.

Two *Cherokees* who came here yesterday for a visit, and with whom our *Noah* spoke a great deal,[343] traveled on today. They were planning to go to *Pittsburgh.* At their request Brother *David* gave them a letter for Mr. *Croghan,*[344] because they do not understand any English or the Indian language from this area. Otherwise, we had Speakings with the Brothers and Sisters yesterday and today for Holy Communion, and in the evening the reading of the Bible story.

THE 31ST   Toward evening we read the story of our Savior's anguish

341. The arrival of Newollike further increased the number of former influential chiefs in Schönbrunn. See entry for 10 April 1774, note 348.

342. The story for the memorial of Jesus becoming human is reported in Luke 1:26–38; the Watchword was Ps. 72:11.

343. Noah was the first Cherokee to be baptized by the missionaries. See entry for 4 July 1773.

344. George Croghan (d. 1782), Indian trader, land speculator, and until 1771 representative of Sir William Johnson in the Ohio region, was surely the most knowledgeable colonist in the region around Fort Pitt, although his support of Virginia's claims to this region made him one of the most controversial as well. See Wainwright, *George Croghan.* After 1771 Croghan had no official function; his successor as representative of Sir William Johnson was Alexander McKee. From the Indians' perspective, however, Croghan was still the most important and trustworthy of the colonists. At least informally, Croghan accepted this role. His economic interests as a trader and land speculator depended on friendly relations with the Six Indian Nations as well as with the Delaware.

on the Mount of Olives and of His arrest, with emotional hearts.[345] Then 54 Brothers and Sisters celebrated the *Pedilavium* and afterward Holy *Communion*. One person was readmitted and one person observed for the 2nd time.

April

THE 1ST   After the *Liturgy* for Holy Communion in the morning, we began reading the Passion Story, and we continued with this throughout the day. Our hearts melted during this. When we came to the piercing of Jesus' side, we read the *Liturgy* on our knees, during which the Meeting Hall was covered with countless tears, and young and old cried tears of love at His pierced feet over His bitter atonement.

THE 2ND   For Great Sabbath we had a Lovefeast, and early on THE 3RD the congregation was greeted with the words, The Lord is arisen! to which they replied, He is risen indeed. Then we went to our God's Acre, prayed the Easter *Liturgy* in the Indian language[346] for the first time, and prayed for eternal fellowship with our 17 Brothers and Sisters who have died since last Easter. Afterward was the sermon, and in the afternoon a reading service about our Lord's Resurrection. During the Congregational Service in the evening, the following three people were buried into Jesus' death through Holy Baptism: *Laweloochwalend* with the name *Simon*, *Newollike's* wife with the name *Regina*, and a widow with the name *Magdalena*. This took place in the close presence of the Holy Trinity, and very few eyes remained dry.

THE 7TH   Once again a family who had arrived from the *Susquehana* received permission to live with us.

THE 9TH   Our Brothers and Sisters finished boiling sugar for this year. We did not have a very good spring for this work this year, because the high waters prevented it and then the warm weather began too soon. Still most people made more than 100 pounds.

Indians from both *Kaskaskunk* and *Gekelemukpechünk* came here for a visit, including a widow with 4 children from the *Susquehannah*, our *Margreth's* daughter, who came to stay.

THE 10TH   This was the festival day for all those who have been baptized in the past year,[347] and all the baptized Brothers and Sisters had a service in which we could sense the Savior's presence. We commended to His grace anew the 16 Brothers and Sisters who have joined in this grace during this year.

---

345. Luke 22:39–53.

346. Meaning in the Delaware language. The text is included in Zeisberger, *Collection of Hymns for the Use of the Christian Indians*, 13–19.

347. This festival had been omitted in 1773 (in that year it had been set for 18 April), probably because too few congregants had been baptized.

An Indian from the Council in *Gekelemukpechünk* tried to find out from *Newollike* where he was planning to stay and what his thoughts were.[348] *Newollike* answered him, If you would like to know, I will tell you straight out. I want to live here and I want to live and die with these people, and nowhere else, because here I have found what I have sought for many years: the salvation of my soul, earthly and eternal well-being. Now you know my thoughts. You should also know that I will not change my mind about this.

THE 11TH   With the Helpers' Conference we discussed the physical work of getting our fields in order, and because our town has grown this spring, we must be sure that everyone is helped according to his need. The Brothers and Sisters also collected Indian corn, which was distributed among those who have recently arrived.

THE 13TH   Brothers and Sisters from *Gnadenhütten* came here for a visit, and others who had been to *Gekelemukpechünk* on business returned from there. We hear that a new preacher has come forward there who had dreams and saw apparitions and is greatly deceiving the Indians again. He is warning them against us and says they should not believe the White people who were trying to mislead them, although they have seen that he was not of sound mind but foolish. However, he explains this as if he were in a rapture and had seen visions and had a revelation from God.[349] Many follow him and say that there has never been a preacher like him, who is certainly speaking the truth.

THE 15TH   Brothers *Jungmann* and *Schebosch* traveled to *Pittsburgh* on business. Our people here went out to make *fences*. The high waters had destroyed them all and swept some of them away.

Brother *David* baptized a sick child with the name *Joseph*. He did so at the persistent request of the parents, who have not been baptized. He then died early on the 16TH and was buried in the evening.

THE 18TH   We had a *Conference* with the Helper Brothers and Sisters about various concerns. The woman from the *Susquehanna* with 4 children, who was mentioned on the 9th of this month, received permission to stay here.

THE 19TH   Brother *David* went to *Gnadenhütten* along with Brothers *Abraham, Isaac,* and *Jacob,* to accompany *Newollike* to *Gekelemukpechünk* and to assist him in his *Affairs* with the *Chief* there.

Brothers *Jungmann* and *Schebosch* had taken the same road to *Pittsburgh.* Their horses ran away there, so they returned here today, took other horses and began their journey anew on THE 20TH, and Brother *David* returned from *Gnadenhütten.*

348. Until his admission to Schönbrunn, Newollike had been chief of the Munsee and thus a member of the High Council.

349. On the importance of preachers in Native American societies, see Introduction, pp. 48–49. Messages of Indian preachers were legitimized by visions; see the message of the preacher Scattameck in entries for 7 May 1772 and 1 Jan. 1773. On women preachers among the Delaware, see note 611. and on preachers among the Shawnee, see entry for 17 Oct. 1772, note 90.

THE 22ND   The Brothers *fenced* in our *Town* after they had finished *fencing* in the fields. *Salome* came here from *Gnadenhütten* to stay. The above-mentioned Brothers returned from *Gekelemukpechünk*. They had given the *Chief* the hides they had collected for him,[350] and at the same time they had given a reply to the *Belt* they had received from the *Cherokees*.[351] They said we were happy about the good news from them and hoped that the peace with them might be completely carried out. Afterward *Newollike* addressed the *Chief* and in conclusion explained his thoughts[352] and said he had already considered and sought his spiritual well-being on his own for a number of years. However, he had never found anything among the Indians that could calm his heart. There was certainly nothing like this to be found among them except in both of the Brothers' *Towns*. There he had found it. Therefore he wanted to let him know that he would live with them there and spend the rest of his life with them. The *Chief* could hardly keep from crying at his words, presumably from sorrow because he was again losing a man for whom he had waited so long and in whom he hoped to have a faithful helper. However, he answered him that he was glad to hear this and was happy, and since he lives close now, they will often have the opportunity to communicate. Among other things, *Newollike* also still had in his hands the *Belt of Wampum* from *Netawatwees,* which he had received from him on the *Susquehanna,* through which he had called him and our Indians to come here. However, when he repeated the message as he had received it, and came to the statement that he called us, *Netawatwees* inter-rupted him and said, I did not say that. I did not call their teachers here. This message must have been sent there from *Goschgoschüng*.[353] *Newollike,* however,

350. On 6 November 1773, in a message to the inhabitants of Schönbrunn and Gnadenhütten, Netawatwees had requested that they contribute to the financing of the delegation that was to visit the king of England.

351. See entry for 7 March 1774.

352. With this declaration Newollike responded to the query reported in entry for 10 April 1774.

353. See entries for 14 Sept. and 21 Oct. 1771 in the Friedensstadt [i.e., Langundoutenünk] Diary, MAB, B 137, F 3. According to that diary Netawatwees suggested that the mission congrega-tion ask that he assign them a better place than Langundoutenünk. Such a message would then be discussed in council, "and then they would assign a large and nice piece of land to the Christian Indians, where they could live . . . without disturbances." In mid-October Netawatwees confirmed this message to Abraham and Jeremias in Gekelemukpechünk in response to their query—but with a difference. Netawatwees confirmed that his message had been correctly reported, "and he intended to repeat to him, namely, that if the brothers with some or all of the Christian Indians would come to them and live with them they would be very welcome; there would be a very nice place only half a day's journey above Gekelemukpechünk large enough for many Indians to live there and it would not be too close to other towns." Ibid., entry for 21 Oct. 1771. See ibid., entry for 27 Dec. 1771, and summary report for the year, where Zeisberger under paragraph 1 noted: "The visit of Gekelemuk-pechünk in the spring from where we received good tidings and an invitation to settle in that region." On 12 January the following official message reached the mission congregation from Gekelemukpech-ünk via Kaskaskunk: "This is to let you know, that I have designated a straight route from here to the Suesquehanna and cleared it, which route you can securely and without any danger take. The land in Kaskaskung and on the Beaver Creek is not really owned by the Delaware, but the Mingoe still

did not allow himself to be interrupted, but repeated the message to the end and gave the *Belt* back to him. *Abraham* then witnessed to him that we had received precisely this *Belt* in *Langundouteniünk* with exactly the same message, and even named the person who delivered it. He had not come there from *Goschgoschüng,* but from *Gekelemukpechünk.* However, he maintained that it had not come from him.

The Indians' eyes are now being opened. They are beginning to realize a little bit what they have done. They would like to have us, at least the white Brothers, out of their way. They do not see how this is possible, however, because they realize that if they send us white Brothers away, then the Indians will follow us. The *Chief* is worried for his life because he is accused, and rightfully, of having called us; he fears that all guilt will be placed on his head and things will not turn out well for him in the end. Therefore he is now trying to save himself and squirm his way out of this matter by saying he did not do it.[354]

THE 23RD   We learned through Indians who came here from *Pittsburgh* that the 3 *Cherokees* who had been here recently had killed two White people. They were traveling down the *Ohio* from *Pittsburgh* with *Traders,* and the *Traders,* of whom there were only 3, made the mistake of letting them see that they had many silver utensils with them to trade, which led them to commit this murder.[355]

THE 26TH   A sad event took place here. *Jacob Gendaskund's* daughter, a 10-year-old girl, was in a field planting when she was struck and killed

---

have a certain claim to it. The Delaware have their land on the Muskingum River from its mouth up to Cayahaga. You settled at Kaskaskung because you knew then of no other place to settle. Send this belt with its message to Newollike at the West Branch so that he can hand it on to Fridenshütten, Schechschiquanünk and to all other Indian settlements at the Susquehanna and inform those Indians in Fridenshütten and Schechschiquanünk that they should not go to Kaskaskunk but continue their journey directly to Gekelemukpechünk, where they will surely be well received. There they should have a separate settlement where they would be secure and live unmolested from savages and drunk Indians. This piece of land the Delamattenoos gave us for our property." Zeisberger conducted the final negotiations with his companions in Gekelemukpechünk on 20–21 March 1772; in these negotiations, according to Zeisberger, Netawatwees confirmed emphatically the invitation of the mission congregation *and* the missionaries.

354. Obviously Zeisberger was unaware that decisions in the Council had to be unanimous; on the question whether the Moravian missionaries were allowed to stay and continue with their work the Council was divided, with the Munsee, Captain Pipe, and John Killbuck Sr. opposed. On how things developed, see entry for 28 Feb. 1775.

355. According to the diary of Alexander McKee Pitt, on 1 May 1774 there arrived at the fort "one Stephens, who had proceeded in a Trader's Canoe which was attacked on the 16th by the Cherokees in order to have carried her to the Scioto." *JP,* 12:1095. According to the letter of Devereux Smith to Dr. Smith, on 15 April 1774 the Indian trader William Butler sent "a canoe loaded with goods for the Shawanese Towns, and on the 16th it was attacked about forty miles from here [Pittsburgh] by three Cherokee Indians. . . . They killed one white man, and wounded another, and a third made his escape. They plundered the canoe of the most valuable part of the cargo and made off." *AA,* 4th series, 1:468.

suddenly by a tree which was burning[356] and suddenly snapped off. Because she was completely alone, no one realized it right away. For some time we had noticed she had a special desire and love for the Savior and the Brothers and Sisters. On THE 27TH she was buried and commended to the Savior's grace in a prayer by Brother *David*. With this we began a God's Acre for those who have not been baptized.[357] In a service for the married Brothers and Sisters, *Stephanus* was married to *Salome* by Brother *Roth* [page 63a].[358]

THE 30TH   Brothers *Jungmann* and *Schebosch* returned from *Pittsburgh*. Through them we received the news that a change had taken place in the *Gouvernment* there and that it now belongs to *Virginia*.[359] Also things looked bad for the *Shawnee*, and people presumed they would attack the new *Settlement* of White people down the *Ohio* across from them, because this is a thorn in their eye. However, a message from *Johnson* has been sent to the rest of the *Nations* warning them not to unite with them.[360]

May

THE 2ND   Guests came here to visit. One of them asked one of our people who had not been baptized why he had moved here to our place, and many Indians had intended to speak sharply to him about leaving there when he went back to *Gekelemukpechünk* some day. He answered, All Indians know how godlessly I lived. There was none like me in *Gekelemukpechünk* any more, and my grandfather *Netawatwees* and all my friends bore me ill will because of my godless life. They often told me I should leave and not let them see me any more. Then last winter I came here. The Believers took mercy on me and took me in. I am happy and grateful for this. I am planning to stay with them and to become a believer in the Savior, because I long for this. However, now that my friends and the Indians see that I am here and want to become a believer, this annoys them much more than my previous godless life did.

THE 4TH   It snowed this morning and last night and was very cold.

356. In order to clear the land of trees and prepare it for cultivation, fires were lit under the trees, which after a while fell and could be carried away.

357. It is not clear whether this cemetery was separate from or part of the consecrated cemetery.

358. From here to the end of entry for 20 May 1774 the diary is in parts printed in English. *PA*, 1st ser., 4:495–97.

359. Dr. John Connolly (c. 1743–1813), in accordance with his position as captain of the militia of Augusta County, Virginia, claimed with the Virginia's governor's support control over Fort Pitt, which had been given up by the British army in August 1771; on the whole affair, see Williams, *Fort Pitt and the Revolution*, 18–28, and [Connolly], "Narrative of the Transactions," both parts.

360. On 3 May 1774 Alexander McKee assembled the influential Seneca chief Kayashota and other chiefs of the Six Indian Nations who lived in and around Fort Pitt and discussed with them the dangerous situation, especially the murder of members of Chief John Logan's family on 30 April 1774; the chiefs assured McKee that the Six Indian Nations would work for peace. *JP*, 12:1098.

This is very unusual here for this time of year. Some time ago the weather was already very warm. The trees were blooming and had almost all of their leaves, but they are all frozen now.

THE 6TH   Indians from *Mochwesüng* came here for a visit. We also received news that a *Shawnee Chief* was apparently killed by the White people on the *Ohio* some days ago and another one was wounded.[361] It looks like an Indian war might break out. We hear that the *Virginians* on the *Ohio* are threatening to attack the *Shawnee* in their *Settlements* and destroy their *Towns*.[362]

THE 7TH   After the early service we had a *Conference* with the Helpers and there was a congregational council in the evening. We heard much about war from strangers who were visiting here. Among other things one of them asked our Indians what they would do if their teachers could no longer be here. They answered him, Then we go with them wherever they go. Then he asked, Are your teachers your gods then? No, they answered, but they have acquainted us with the one and only true God and his word. If they had not done this we would still be as blind as all the Indians who know nothing about God. Therefore we love them and will not leave them.

THE 8TH   In the morning there was a sermon, in the afternoon a service for the communicant Brothers and Sisters, and afterward one for those who have been baptized. Toward evening an *express* messenger arrived here from *Gekelemukpechünk* with the unpleasant news that the White people on the *Ohio* had killed 9 *Mingo* and wounded 2. This news alarmed everyone.[363] The

361. This incident was connected with the Cherokee ambush of William Butler's transport. See entry for 23 April 1774, note 355. Devereux Smith's letter of 10 June 1774 says: "As Mr. Butler was under the Necessity of sending people to assist in bringing his peltry from the Shawanese Towns, he sent off another canoe on the 24th of April in care of two Indians, who were well known to be good men, and two white men. On the 27th, about ninety miles from here, they were fired upon from shore, and both the Indians were killed, by Michael Cresap, and a party he had with him; they also scalped the Indians. Mr. Cresap then immediately followed the above mentioned Shawanese Chiefs some small distance lower down, where they were encamped, and fired upon them, killed one and wounded two more. The Indians fled to the Delaware Towns." *AA*, 4th series, 1:468. See also Doddridge, *Notes on the Settlements and Indian Wars*, 230. After the Shawnee's message to George Croghan on 20 May 1774, the Shawnee chief Othawakeesquo was killed. "Speech of the Shawanese to Alex. McKee, May 20th, 1774," *PA*, 1st ser., 4:497–98. On incidents before 26 April 1774, see John Floyd to Colonel William Preston, 26 April 1774, *DHDW*, 7–8.

362. The rumor was correct; before 1 May 1774 Michael Cresap (1742–75) and other colonists from the region of Wheeling had been prepared to go to war for Virginia; on 25 April 1774 a proclamation by the governor of Virginia had been published asking the militia to protect settlers from Indian attacks. Dr. John Connolly, commanding officer of Fort Pitt, published a similar proclamation. *AA*, 4th series, 1:283, 468. On 8 May 1774 William Crawford wrote to George Washington: "I am now setting out for Fort Pitt at the head of one hundred men." Butterfield, *Washington-Crawford Letters*, 49.

363. On 30 April 1774, close to where the Yellow Creek enters the Ohio (about forty miles above Wheeling and about fifty-five miles from Fort Pitt), settlers from Virginia led by Daniel Greathouse murdered ten Mingo, among them the mother, brothers, and sister of the influential chief John Logan. See William Crawford to George Washington, 8 May 1774, Butterfield, *Washington-Crawford Letters*, 46–50; *DHDW*, 9–19.

messenger arrived here with a horrible cry, as is customary among the Indians in times of war.[364] He also brought a message from the *Shawnee,* which the *Chief* in *Gekelemukpechünk* sent on to us to inform us about this. It said, Our grandfather, the *Delaware Nation,* should not be worried. They should remain completely quiet and calm. They should also allow the *Traders* to trade among them and not put any obstacles in their way or in that of other White people who are there. The women should not let themselves be prevented from planting until they see what is going to happen. From this it really seems that they will keep the road to *Pittsburgh* open and not harm them or the *Pennsylvanians,* but are concerned only with the *Virginians.* However, it is very likely that this resolution will not be kept.[365]

THE 9TH   Both the message we received yesterday and the messenger himself gave us reason to meet with the Brothers of the *Conference* and consider what we could do to keep our White Brothers and Sisters safe, here and in *Gnadenhütten.* We decided to send some Indian Brothers with a message to the *Chief.* However, the *Chiefs* cannot protect us; they have no power or force. We must expect our help and protection from the Lord alone. He will not abandon us, but will assist us with good counsel because He knows that we are in great need of this.

In the evening Mr. *Anderson,* another White man,[366] and the Indian *Chief White Eye* arrived here from *Pittsburgh* on their way to the *Shawnee* on business.[367] We were delighted that they brought us letters from *Litiz* dated *April* 16 of this year. These messengers had almost fallen into the hands of the *Mingo* who had fled here across the *Ohio* and were camping on the road to *Gekelemukpechünk,* but Indians who were going from here to *Kaskaskung* warned them about those. Then they immediately went back and took a detour and thus arrived here safely. They were sent to make another attempt at bringing the *Shawnee* to peace and preventing further hostilities from taking place.

We now hear that there is supposed to be a gang of White people on the *Ohio* who committed the murders against these Indians, as happened in the

364. Heckewelder describes the shout as an "alarm-whoop," used only in times of greatest danger. In quick succession and in a high-pitched voice, "aw" and "oh" sounds would be shouted. Heckewelder, *History, Manners, and Customs,* 217.

365. This message indicates that the Shawnee were still determined to consider the incidents as a limited conflict. It is possible that the news of the declaration of the Six Indian Nations and of Killbuck Sr. and White Eyes for the Delaware, at a conference convened between 3 and 5 May 1774 by Alexander McKee, that in case of war the Shawnee could count on the support of neither the Six Nations nor the Delaware, played a role in this decision. *JP,* 12:1100; *NYCD,* 8:465.

366. The diary for Gnadenhütten II gives the name of the person as "Dunker," MAB, B 144, F 3, I 1, for 10 May 1774. They were John Duncan and John Anderson, both Indian traders. *DHDW,* 28–30.

367. White Eyes, John Duncan, and John Anderson had been commissioned by the conference at Fort Pitt on May 3 to explore the willingness of the Shawnee to maintain peace (see note 360 to entry for 30 April 1774).

previous war in *Pennsylvania*.[368] People in *Pittsburgh* do not believe that they have orders from the *Gouverneur* in *Virginia* to carry out hostilities against the Indians. They have also killed *Traders* because they provide the Indians with goods and ammunition.[369] We have also heard that all the *Traders* who traded among the *Shawnee* throughout the winter are still there and therefore they would all be killed if there should be a war. Apparently many White people around Pittsburgh and down the Ohio have already fled back to the *Settlements*.[370]

THE 10TH   A couple of Brothers went from here to *Gekelemukpechünk* on horse to announce the messengers[371] so they can prepare to receive them, and they went there soon afterward. First however, *Isaac* spoke privately with *Captain White Eye,* who used to be his most trusted comrade.[372] He now has the most say among the *Delaware.* He told him among other things, You will surely remember our old friendship and the covenant we made to remain faithful to each other and to love each other as long as we live. We laid our *Schewondionn* (that is a *Pouch*) between us so that each of us could make use of it, one like the other. We also promised each other that if one of us should receive special knowledge or insight about eternal life while still in this world, and find the way to salvation, then he should reveal this to the other and make it known to him. Both should have a share in this. Now I can testify to you with truth and certainty that I have found it, I have heard the saving word of God which is preached here, and I have accepted it. I have found what leads to salvation and to eternal life. Therefore I would now like for you to share in this as well, and you will have it if you just accept it. During this tears flowed down *White Eye's* cheeks and he said, Yes, what you say is the truth. I believe that the true and only way to salvation is preached here. I have already thought about it a lot and have not yet forgotten what I heard the first time in *Langundoutenünk*. I am still thinking about becoming a believer. *Isaac* also informed him that we were planning to send a message to the *Chief* in *Gekelemukpechünk* about us White Brothers and Sisters here and in *Gnadenhütten,* saying we would like to be recognized and respected among the Indians, not like other White people and *Traders,* but as people who are concerned with the best interests and well being of the Indians. One message just like this was already sent to *Packanke*

368. This refers to the Paxton Boys, who in 1763 had threatened the Christian Indians in Pennsylvania and forced them to seek protection in the barracks at Philadelphia. Heckewelder, *Narrative of the Mission,* 68–92; Loskiel, *Geschichte der Mission,* 472–92; Hindle, "March of the Paxton Boys"; Vaughan, "Frontier Banditti and the Indians." On the social causes, see Franz, *Paxton.*

369. A reference to the attack on the convoy of goods owned by William Butler. See entry for 6 May 1774.

370. William Crawford confirmed this in his letter to George Washington of 8 May 1774, cited in note 362; see also *DHDW,* 19–20.

371. That is, White Eyes, John Anderson, and John Duncan; see entry for 9 May 1774.

372. Zeisberger, "History of the Northern American Indians," 119, describes the friendship between White Eyes and Isaac (Glikhican) as a kind of a model friendship among the Delaware.

in *Kaskaskunk,* but it remained there.[373] He approved of this completely and expressed his pleasure about it, but said it made him sad because he knew the Indians would not understand it or realize what it meant. He understood it well and therefore wished that he could be present when we presented our concern, and he would speak then. He is our good friend and almost of the same mind as some of our Brothers were in the beginning, like *Isaac, Jacob,* etc., who almost wore themselves out trying to get the Brothers' work with the Gospel recognized and accepted everywhere among the Indians. This has not yet been accomplished, however.

THE 11TH   Brothers *Roth* and *Jungmann* married *Tobias Melimius* to *Rebecca* and *Petrus* to *Jannetje.*

THE 12TH   Those who have been baptized had a blessed service on Ascension Day. We knelt and worshipped our dear Lord and prayed to Him for his priceless presence forever. Then there was the sermon, and during the Congregational Service in the evening 2 were added to the congregation through Holy Baptism: *Newollike,* who received the name *Augustinus* in baptism, and *Simon's* wife *Judith.* God's blessed peace prevailed during this.

THE 13TH   Both yesterday and today we had Speakings with the Brothers and Sisters in preparation for Holy Communion. We received the unpleasant news from *Gekelemukpechünk* that the *Shawnee* had not received *Captain White Eye* and his message, much less heard it,[374] and that they had shot at him and a White man who was with him when they were returning to *Gekelemukpechünk.*[375] The *Chief*[376] himself now wants to go there with a pretty large party to see if they can get the *Shawnee* to listen.

THE 14TH   We partook most blessedly in Holy Communion. One Sister was admitted to this for the first time and 2 Brothers and a Sister watched for the first time.

THE 15TH   Early in the morning a messenger came from *Gnadenhütten* and called some of our Indians hastily to a *Councel* in *Gekelemukpechünk.* Brothers *Johannes, Isaac, Jacob, Augustinus, Wilhelm,* and *Joseph* soon left for there.[377] Toward evening the former returned from *Gnadenhütten* with the news that things looked pretty bad, that the *Shawnee* and *Mingo,* who have at least marched out of *Gekelemukpechünk,* were very angry and were threatening to kill

373. The problem of officially acknowledging both mission congregations had last been mentioned in council by Newollike; see entry for 22 April 1774.

374. See entry for 9 May 1774.

375. "One of the Traders who went with White Eyes was detained at New Comerstown; they, it seems, thought it imprudent that more than one should go, very soon the others left it, they were met by a Shawanese Man, who fired at Duncan within a very small distance but fortunately missed him. White Eyes immediately called to him to make back to the Town, and he himself got betwixt the Indian and him, and came up with him when he had stopped to load his gun, and disarmed him." Arthur St. Clair to Governor John Penn, 29 May 1774, *PA,* 1st ser., 4:502.

376. Netawatwees.

377. All these Christian Indians had been chiefs before their conversion.

all the White people they met. These *Mingo,* of whom there were about 20, all fled here from the last massacre on the *Ohio,*[378] when 9 of them were killed and 2 wounded at one time, and 4 more had been killed at other times. Now they are inciting the *Shawnee,* who have not suffered much yet although a few of their people have been killed.[379] They would like to start a war with the White people. The *Delaware,* however, will do their best to prevent this and to advise them to peace. May the Savior rule and guide their hearts, destroy all of their evil attacks, and not allow Satan to succeed against us. It is indeed his plan to get us out of the way and to destroy the Savior's work among the Indians. They have taken all the White people in *Gekelemukpechünk* into safekeeping where they are guarded at night so that the *Mingo* who are roaming around will not kill them.[380] The Brothers here gathered and agreed that no one should go into the bush alone or go far from the *Town,* because of the *Mingo.* There is a party of them in this area who are very angry at the *Delaware* because they are protecting the White people. They arranged for some Brothers to keep watch in the *Town* at night until we see how things develop.

THE 16TH   The Indian Brother *Joseph* returned from *Gekelemukpechünk.* He had accompanied the Brothers as far as *Gekelemukpechünk,* and this morning they left with the *Chief* and a number of Indians to go on from there to the *Shawnee.*[381] He brought the news that it is not safe yet and that a party of *Mingo* is still roaming around in this area. They are lying in wait for White people, but they do not let themselves be seen in the *Town.* We were also overjoyed to receive the packet of letters from the month of *March* along with congregational newsletters. We had already assumed they were lost because we had heard some days ago that Mr. *Jones,*[382] whose father lives close to Bethlehem and who had taken them along to send on from *Pittsburgh,* had been killed. He was traveling by water, but when he got close to the *Shawnee Towns* someone warned him to flee for his life. In his haste he had grabbed the letters and news reports, abandoned everything else, and hurried away with his people. One of them fell into the hands of the *Mingo* close to *Gekelemukpechünk* and was killed.

THE 17TH   During the early service, the Watchword[383] was a great

378. See entry for 8 May 1774.

379. See entry for 6 May 1774.

380. "They [Duncan and Anderson] got safely back to the Town [Gekelemukpechünk], and were immediately shut up in a strong house and a guard kept on them day & Night to preserve them from any attempt that might be made by the Shawanese or Mingoes." St. Clair to Governor John Penn, 29 May 1774, cited in note 375 to entry for 13 May 1774.

381. The delegation went to Woaketameki, the first substantial Shawnee settlement on the Muskingum.

382. John Jones (1714–81) had bought land close to Bethlehem in the early 1750s. By profession a smith, he had been a member of the Unity for a number of years; thereafter he belonged to a Lutheran congregation. Toward the end of his life he rejoined the Moravian Church. We have been unable to identify his son at Pittsburgh. See Dubbs, "Jones Family of Bethlehem Township."

383. Ps. 139:16.

comfort and encouragement to us with its words that all the rest of our days are written in his book and that He knows everything in advance and sees what we are supposed to become, to be called, and to have.[384]

THE 18TH   Since we presumed that they would be gathered in *Councel* with the *Shawnee* today, we uttered countless sighs to the Savior's heart for ourselves and for all of his work here, prayed that he would rule over the hearts of the *Chiefs* and leaders and guide them to do the best. Toward evening *Jacob senior* returned from the Brothers who had gone to the *Councel*. He brought news that was not yet definite but still offered hope that things would turn out well. Yesterday the *Chief* had addressed the *Shawnee* and presented his concerns. They listened to him and asked for time to consider it until today.[385]

THE 19TH   When we read the Watchword, Speak to my soul: I am your help,[386] we were able to look to our dear Lord confidently and to trust Him as children to be our help and our salvation. From Pittsburgh, a messenger from Mr. *Croghan* arrived here with a message to the *Delaware, Mingo,* and *Shawnee* that they should remain calm and not have thoughts of war; they should go about their lives and not offend the *Traders*. In *Pittsburgh* they were trying to find and capture all the White people who had committed the murders, and they had caught one already.[387] Everything in *Pittsburgh* was calm and the Indians came and went undisturbed. We were glad to hear that there was no more danger from the White people.

THE 20TH   In the afternoon our Brothers returned from the *Shawnee* and brought us the good news that they had accepted the suggestions offered to them and the good admonitions given them, and that we have reason to hope peace will be restored.[388] They also made an agreement with them and warned them not to harm the *Traders* among them, but to assist them in

---

384. The text of the hymn added to the Watchword was: "Was ich in dieser Zeit soll werden, heissen, haben, das alles liegt schon heut in Deinem Sinn begraben" (What in due time shall become of us, shall be called and shall own, is today already inscribed in your mind). We were unable to locate this hymn.

385. See letter of "The Cosh (alias John Bull)" (evidently an incorrect reading of Schebosch, alias John Joseph Bull; see Register of Persons) dated 24 May 1774, and the report about the negotiations at Woaketameki: "The Chief addressed the Shawanes & Mingues present in a fatherly manner, showing unto them the blessings of Peace and the Folly of War, and pressed it very much upon their Reason, what misery they would bring upon themselves and others by their madness, & told them positively that they had not to expect any Help or Assistance from the Delawares, and enjoyned them very earnestly not to stop the Road to Philadelphia, but to let it be free & open. The Shawnese gave him in answer: They did believe his Words to be good, and they would take notice of them, and desired him to give also a fatherly Admonition to their Wives, to plant Corn for them, which he did, but they seemed more inclined to move off than to plant." *PA*, 1st ser., 4:499–500.

386. Ps. 35:3.

387. The complete text of Croghan's message of 6 May 1774 could not be located. It is summarized and printed in part in Smith, *St. Clair Papers*, 1:297n1, and in the letter of Devereux Smith to Dr. Smith dated 10 June 1774, *AA*, 4th series, 1:468.

388. See the response of the Shawnee on 25 May 1774 to the message of George Croghan and Alexander McKee, which was unrelenting in its language against Virginia (*AA*, 4th series, 1:480). Arthur St. Clair characterized this message as "insolent." Smith, *St. Clair Papers*, 1:297.

returning safely to their people. There were about 50 *Delaware* and *Munsee* present. The first day they arrived from *Gekelemukpechünk* in *Mochwesüng*, where mostly *Munsee* live, they saw that they were doing the *War* Dance there because they believed there was already full-scale war since the *Mingo* had arrived with a White *Scalp*. Our Brothers *Jacob, Isaac,* and *Augustinus,* who are *Munsee,* spoke sharply with their *Chiefs* and told them they should consider what they were doing, abandon their plan, and join the rest of their *Nation* and the *Delaware* who were bringing peace and wanted to admonish everyone to this. Then they ceased immediately and the next day attended the *Councel* of the *Shawnee* with them and added their consent to this.

Upon their return to *Gekelemukpechünk,* Chief *Netawatwees* and the Indians expressed their pleasure and satisfaction over the service and assistance our Brothers had provided during this matter. Concerning the matter noted on the 10th of this month, which we wanted to submit to the *Chief,* Captain *White Eye* advised us to save this for a more opportune time, when he could also be present. The way things stand now, we hope that there will not be an open war. In the meantime, however, the *Shawnee* and *Mingo* could still take revenge on the White people and many innocent people would suffer from this. May the Savior soon grant us peace and calm and spread his wings over us so that the evil enemy does not carry out his tricks on us or trouble us in body or in spirit. Herewith we commend ourselves and the entire Indian congregation to the remembrance of all the congregations before the Savior.

Diary *of* Schoenbrunn *on the* Mushkingum *from May* 22–September 12, 1774.[389]

MAY 22ND   The *Traders* who had arrived here yesterday left for Pittsburgh as part of a *Convoy* of a party of Indians from *Gekelemukpechünk.* We took advantage of this opportunity to send letters to Bethlehem.[390]

Brother *Roth* preached the sermon about the work of the Holy Spirit, who convicts humans to believe in the name of God's Son so that they will not be lost because of their unfaith. In the afternoon there was a Service of Adoration with those who have been baptized. We thanked our dear Mother[391] for all the efforts and faithfulness exerted on our behalf and promised her obedience anew. Late this evening a messenger came from *Gnadenhütten* with the unpleasant news that, although the *Shawnee* had promised to listen to their grandfather

389. MAB, B 141, F 5, I 2, fol. 67.

390. Zeisberger to Nathanael [Seidel], MAB, B 229, F 4, I 14. White Eyes, who returned with the traders from the Shawnee settlements, brought with him the message from the Shawnee that they were committed to protecting the traders from the Mingo who had threatened to kill them, *PA,* 1st ser., 4:497–98.

391. On the term, see note 30 above.

Netawatwees and to abandon their evil plan at the last *Councel* in *Woaketammeki,* they are still preparing for war and a party had already gone out to attack the *Settlements* of the White people.[392] The messenger from *Gnadenhütten* and another one from here left immediately this evening to catch up with *Killbuck* and the White people[393] and to deliver this news to them in a letter, and to take them along to the *Fort.* They found them still in their night camp.

THE 23RD   In the early service today's Watchword, When I am afraid, I put my trust in you,[394] comforted us richly. In keeping with today's text we were able to call out with childlike, simple hearts, Abba, dear Father,[395] remember your dear Son's people and protect us against Satan's army.

We White Brothers and Sisters considered the circumstances of Brother and Sister *Roth* and their children. We cannot know what else might happen to us and whether we might not all have to flee, so we decided that our Indian Brothers should take them to *Pittsburgh,* and the sooner the better. They can continue their journey on to Bethlehem from there, since the road there is still open now. We immediately informed the Brothers and Sisters of the *Conference,* and they approved and were willing to escort them to the *Fort.*

THE 24TH   In the early service Brother *Jungmann* said, in keeping with the Watchword,[396] that we should always keep in mind what the Lord had done for us and how he has guided us. This awakened our hearts to praise and thanks. Some Brothers and Sisters went to *Gnadenhütten* and some came back from there. Again, we heard horrible stories about war, among others that the second group of *Shawnee* has gone to war.

THE 26TH   Brother *Roth* led the early service about the grace and release from our sins we attain through Christ's Blood.[397] We received news through Indians from *Tuscarawi* that everything is calm and peaceful in that area. *Traders* from the *Wyandot* passed through there traveling to *Pittsburgh.* We also heard that the *Lower Shawnee* were still well disposed and had taken the *Traders* among them into their protection after the *Mingo* had gone out to kill them. Thus only those in *Woaketameki* are causing all this trouble, about which we heard much bad news and many threats again today.[398]

392. See David Zeisberger's letters of 27 and 28 May 1774, excerpts of which are printed in *PA,* 1st ser., 4:498–99. According to a letter from Schebosch (cited in note 385 for entry of 18 May 1774), the Shawnee explicitly excluded Virginia from their assurances to keep the peace. Netawatwees had likewise not mentioned Virginia in his earlier message. If Schebosch's report is correct, then it is obvious that the Shawnee pursued a consistent course, while Zeisberger and others, in their joy about the supposedly peaceful intentions, overlooked this reservation.

393. Killbuck Sr. escorted the traders White Eyes had brought back from the Shawnee settlements to Fort Pitt.

394. Ps. 56:4.

395. Rom. 8:15.

396. Ps. 66:16.

397. 2 Cor. 3:17.

398. John Gibson was among these traders. GD, 26 May 1774, F 3, I 2. According to Zeisberger, this information corresponded to that reported in "Indian Intelligence," dated 5 June 1774

THE 27TH   After a warm farewell, Brother and Sister *Roth* left for *Bethlehem* via *Pittsburgh*. During the Singing Service the previous evening we had blessed them for their journey, and a party of Indian Brothers and one Sister escorted them as far as the *Fort*.[399] We commended them to the protection and guidance of the dear angels to keep all evil and danger mercifully from them, especially since we heard today that 6 *Mingo* had been in *Tuscarawi* yesterday and they would surely run across them if they took their road to *Pittsburgh*. However, no one could say where they have gone.[400]

THE 29TH   In the morning the sermon was about spiritual rebirth and about the fellowship we enjoy with the Father, Son, and Holy Spirit through this. In the devotions for Married Couples, Brother *Jungmann* married *Adolph* to *Susanna* from *Gnadenhütten*. Two *Mingo*, our *Agnes's* friends, came here from *Woaketammeki* for a visit. Such visits are not very pleasant for us just now, because we cannot know what such people are up to or if they might be spies. We cannot prevent them, however. Therefore we found it all the more necessary to be careful and to keep good watch.

THE 30TH   A messenger from *Gekelemukpechünk* passed through *Gnadenhütten* and came here with a *String of Wampum* and some tobacco from the *Cherokees*. He brought the news that they were on the way to *Gekelemukpechünk* with these words, Their grandfather should raise his eyes and look in that direction; then he would see his *Grand Children* coming and smoke tobacco. That would do him good. We sent this message on to *Packanke*[401] in *Kaskaskung* with a couple of Indian strangers. We also heard that news had arrived that 10 White people had apparently been killed at the mouth of the *Muskingum*.[402] In the evening there were strong winds and a storm. It was more like a hurricane

(*PA*, 1st ser., 4:508–9). It originated with Richard Conner, who later was to move to Schönbrunn (see entries for 4 and 9 May and 27 Sept. 1775, 6 April 1776).

399. They took with them Zeisberger's letters to Nathanael Seidel and Matthäus Hehl, MAB, B 229, F 4, I 15 and 16. In a letter to Governor John Penn dated 7 June 1774, Arthur St. Clair interpreted the return of the Roth family as an alarming sign: "The most alarming One however is the retreat of the Moravian Minister." Smith, *St. Clair Papers*, 1:304. On the tensions between Roth, Schmick, and Zeisberger, see note 549 for entry of 12 Nov. 1774.

400. It is possible that these Mingo were also responsible for the death of a "Mr. Campbell," who was killed close to Gekelemukpechünk, which Devereux Smith reported on 10 June 1774. *PA*, 1st ser., 4:511–13.

401. Packanke was chief of the Wolf clan (see entry for 19 Nov. 1772 and note 104) and member of the Great Council.

402. Probably a reference to the incident on "Dunkard's creek about ten miles from the mouth of Cheam River on the west side of Monongahela," in which "at least six persons [were] killed . . . and there are three missing. On Sunday, a man who left a party is supposed to be killed, as he went off to hunt some horses, and five guns were heard go off. The horse he rode away returned to the house where the party was." William Crawford to George Washington, 8 June 1774, Butterfield, *Washington-Crawford Letters*, 50. Devereux Smith reports this incident in his letter of 10 June 1774; he assigns the responsibility for it to Chief Logan yet gives the location as Muddy Creek (*PA*, 1st ser., 4:513). Arthur St. Clair also mentions the incident on the same day in his letter to Governor John Penn. Smith, *St. Clair Papers*, 1:306.

and damaged many houses and blew down trees, and the air was full of fire. We have had such wind and storms here every year.

THE 31ST   The early service was about praise and gratitude to the Lord for everything good he has done for us and continues to do each day, especially for allowing us to find peace with God and humans.[403] 4 *Munsee* head people came here from *Mochwesüng* on their way to the Fort. They asked us for assistance for their journey, and we heard from them how the war is actually going now. Two *Shawnee* who had been sent out to spy where the *Mingo* had been killed had returned with a White *Scalp* and the news that the White people on the *Ohio* had all fled. Ten *Shawnee* and *Mingo* had gone out to attack the *Settlements* of the White people. A large party of warriors had also been prepared to go out, but would still wait and watch a little. The *Lower Shawnee,* however, had not yet declared war but were quiet, so that there is hope everything can be settled again. Still, we fear the 10 warriors who went out will do much harm and get the White people very agitated.

June

THE 2ND   The Indians from *Mochwesüng* left here, two of them going to *Pittsburgh* and the other two back home. After they had left today, we heard the news that they are being deceitful and had sent a *War Belt* to the *Shawnee* just before they came here. Thus they are secretly on their side, but they speak nicely in front of the White people and look innocent. *Netawatwees* called them liars and did not listen to them.

THE 3RD   *Killbuck* returned from the *Fort*. The *Traders* had been escorted there under his command, and all of them arrived there safely. We were even happier to hear this because we had sent letters and our diary to Bethlehem[404] with Mr. *Anderson,* who was also among them. We had recommended these especially to him in case they should be attacked. We were very delighted and grateful to our dear Lord to learn that Brother and Sister *Roth* and their company had arrived safely as far as *Sakunk,* one day's journey from *Pittsburgh.* They were already out of danger there. *Killbuck* also brought good news for the *Delaware Nation,* saying that the White people would always be their good friends. They should just remain firm, not get entangled in war, and call back all their people who might be among the *Shawnee.* They also should refrain from hunting among the White people so that they would not be harmed innocently, because they could not distinguish between the *Delaware* and the *Shawnee.* They would also be glad if this road to *Pittsburgh* remained open for the sake of *Communication.* Furthermore, they thanked *Netawatwees* for his ef-

403. Ps. 71:23.
404. See entry for 22 May 1774.

forts to move the *Shawnee* to peace and also for the protection the *Traders* enjoyed from him and for taking them safely to the *Fort.* He should continue to advise the *Shawnee* to peace and explain to them what would happen if they began a war. They should realize that they would cease being one people and one *Nation;* now they were just waiting and watching to see what they would do, and if they caused further harm and committed more murders among the White people, they would experience the bad consequences of this. Their soldiers were ready and just wanted to hear from the *Shawnee* whether they wanted war or peace. This message was sent in writing and signed by *Captain Connely,* commanding officer of the *Virginia* troops in *Pittsburgh,* along with a *Belt* and 2 *Strings of Wampum.* This was also communicated to our Indian Brothers.[405] Thus war and peace still hang in the balance. If the *Shawnee* who have gone out commit many murders and do much harm, there might be war after all. The Savior, however, is sitting on the throne. He has never failed at anything and whatever He does or allows must have a blessed end. We comfort ourselves with this.

THE 4TH   In the early service we read the Watchword[406] and remembered that wherever the Savior has put us, we should seek what is best for the country with body and soul, and we should be a blessing to them. A messenger came from *Gnadenhütten* with a *String of Wampum* for *Packanke* in *Kaskaskung.* He has been summoned to appear at a large council[407] in *Gekelemukpechünk* within 8 days. We immediately sent this message on. We also got good news from there that the *Lower Shawnee* had received *Netawatwees'* message and admonition to peace very well and they have promised to be obedient to their grandfather. This news was also confirmed from other places and they added that they had already mobilized their warriors and they were on the verge of war. Then they received *Netawatwees'* message and ordered a truce as a result. Now there only remain the *Shawnee* who are closest to us, with whom the *Mingo* in the area have united. They will not accept any warnings. However, they will not push things far enough to agitate the White people, who would then attack the Indians.

THE 5TH   The Indian Brothers returned from the *Fort* where they had arrived safely with Brother and Sister *Roth* on the 1st of this month, and the latter were planning to continue their journey on the 3rd of this month. On this occasion we were also very happy to receive a packet of congregational newsletters and letters from Bethlehem and *Litiz,* dated the 9th and 10th of *April.*

THE 6TH   Our *Noah* returned from *Gekelemukpechünk,* where he had seen and spoken with the 5 *Cherokees* who had been sent to the great council in

405. The message is printed in the entry for 26 May 1774 in the diary of Alexander McKee. *AA,* 4th series, 1:480–81.

406. Ps. 85:12.

407. See entry for 30 May 1774. On the council meeting, see entry for 23 June 1774.

Gekelemukpechünk as *deputies* of their *Nation*. They were very glad to see him and almost did not want to let him go even though he did not know any of them, since he had left his fatherland at a very young age. He heard that two of them are related to him.[408] When they had traveled through *Woaketemmeki* they admonished the *Shawnee* to keep peace and not to act like the drunkards. The parrots[409] have come here in droves recently, although we had not seen any in this area before.

THE 7TH   Once again we heard bad news; another party of *Shawnee* had gone out to kill again. Several Indians from *Kaskaskunk* and *Goschgosching* arrived here on their move down the river. An Indian woman was found dead in the bush between here and *Kaskaskunk* and people are guessing that the *Mingo* did this to trick the *Delaware* into thinking White people had done it and would then incite the *Delaware* against the White people.[410]

THE 9TH   *Captain White Eye* came from the *Fort,* on his way to the *Shawnee* on business again. He stayed here for a couple of hours and talked with our Indian Brothers about being prepared to go to *Woaketammeki* with him as soon as he sent them a message from *Gekelemukpechünk.*[411] Two messengers who had come with him as far as *Tuscarawi* left here today to go to the *Wyandot* with a message from *Sir William Johnson* and the *Nations*. The message

408. The German original for "related to him" is *befreundet*. On Zeisberger's meaning of "Freundschaft," see Introduction, pp. 17–18, and note 42, and p. 97 note 28.

409. On the parrots (*Conuropsis carolinensis ludovicianus*), see Mahr, "Early Ohio Natural History," 50.

410. Toward the end of May, rumors grew of intended or supposed activities of various groups of warriors. See Arthur St. Clair to Governor Penn, 12 June 1774, Smith, *St. Clair Papers,* 1:306–8, and *DHDW,* 36–37. In fact only two groups of warriors seem to have been out: a group led by John Logan, and possibly a group of Shawnee from Woaketameki. The interpretation of the murder on the path to Kaskaskunk is an indication of how important the Delaware's attitude in this conflict was both for the Shawnee and the Mingo and how afraid the missionaries were that the Delaware would be drawn into this war.

411. According to Alexander McKee's diary, two messengers from Gekelemukpechünk arrived in Pittsburgh on 5 June 1774. They brought the information from Richard Conner mentioned above (entry for 26 May 1774, note 398) about the attitude of the Shawnee and about the imminent arrival of the Cherokee (see entry for 30 May 1774). These messengers "then produced some belts of wampum, which had been delivered to them by Sir William Johnson, several years ago, desiring them to collect themselves together, and sit in the center between their brethren the white people, Six Nations, and Western Indians, where they were required to hold fast by the middle of the chain of friendship, and that they were thereby empowered to speak strongly to any Nation who might attempt to disturb it." After consulting Croghan, McKee handed the messengers a new message in which he applauded the Delaware for their intention to preserve and further the peace. The message continued: "Be strong brethren in doing what you have been desired; you have now an opportunity of exerting your good intentions that way, by speaking to those foolish people, who have not listened to the accomodation [*sic*] our wise people were endeavouring." This message was obviously addressed to the Delaware, who understood it as a forceful encouragement to continue their role as mediator in the conflict. The last part of the message was obviously addressed to the Shawnee, who were asked "to follow the advice that has been sent to you by Captain White Eyes, which was to abstract yourselves from bad people who may be obstinate in pursuing their own destruction." In addition, the messengers received the response of the governor of Virginia to the message of the Delaware dated 7 May 1774, both printed in *AA,* 4th series, 1:480–83.

said, We are covering one of your ears so that you do not hear how the boys (the *Shawnee*) are fighting. They are like unreasonable boys. Do not give in to them. Incline your second ear this way to those who preserve peace (namely the *Delaware*, 6 *Nations* and the English) and stand firmly by us.[412] Many Indians who had come here recently from *Kaskaskunk* and *Goschgoschink* moved further down the river, and others arrived. There is great unrest among the Indians everywhere. Some are moving downriver, while others are moving up this way, as if they themselves did not know where they should go. Other messengers from the *Munsee* in *Mochwesüng* also returned from *Pittsburgh* with news *favorable* to the Indians, which they had in writing.[413] From all the news and messages it seems that the *Virginians* will not begin a war if they are not forced into one and the *Shawnee* can be talked into peace. *Sir William Johnson, Mr. Croghan,* and the *Virginians* are telling the *Delaware* that they are the ones who can restore and maintain peace, because from olden times they have been entrusted with keeping and preserving it since the peace *Belt,* the chain of the friendship, is under their care. They tell them it will therefore be a great embarrassment to them if they do not remain firm in this.[414] *Mr. Croghan* also especially commended our Indians and sent us word in writing that our people should work for peace and should support the *Chiefs,* so that the *Shawnee* might consider their words. We will certainly do this to the extent we are able, and we have already done so.

THE 10TH   The Brothers of the Helpers' *Conference* gathered and prepared a speech they will deliver to the *Shawnee* when they are called to the *Council.* This happened on THE 11TH when a messenger came from *Gnadenhütten* and informed us that they wanted 3 Brothers from the *Munsee Nation* to go there. Today Brothers *Isaac, Cornelius,* and *Jacob* went as far as *Gnadenhütten* so that they could go on to *Gekelemukpechünk* tomorrow with some Brothers, and from there to a *Council* with the *Shawnee* in *Woaketammeki.* They asked for

412. According to Alexander McKee's diary, between 1 and 7 May no new message from Sir William John was forwarded to the Delaware. Zeisberger therefore must be referring to the message McKee had sent to the Delaware. See previous note.

413. McKee's diary suggests that this can only refer to a message similar to that sent to the Delaware.

414. This can only mean that Zeisberger had now accepted without reservation the Delaware's reasoning for their role as mediators. A letter from Sir William Johnson to Thomas Gage dated 4 July 1774 indicates that Johnson continued to accept the overlordship of the Six Indian Nations over the Ohio region. He wrote Gage that he "had . . . once more dispatched Kayashota the noted [Seneca] Ohio Chief on an Embassy in which he was Joyned by some principal Sachims, to bring the troublesome Tribes about the Ohio, the Ouabache [Wabash] etc, to make amends for their past irregularities." According to the protocol of the conference with the Six Indian Nations, Johnson (after a futile effort to justify the behavior of Michael Cresap; see entry for 8 May 1774, note 363 and note 361) demanded from the Six Indian Nations on 9 July "that they should exert more authority over their allies, and keep them in better order" (*NYCD*, 8:477). The letter also proves that on 4 July Johnson was informed about events only up to 25 May 1774. *JP*, 12:1113–16. He was unaware of the Delaware's assumption of the role of mediators. Johnson died in the night of 11–12 July 1774. *JP*, 12:1121–24.

Munsee Brothers because there are no head people from that *Nation*[415] whom they can rely on, and because they are well aware that the *Munsee* down in *Mochwesüng* are no better than the *Shawnee,* and side with them. Therefore they want to have Brothers they know will speak for peace. The same is also true for our *Mohicans* in *Gnadenhütten* because there are plenty of others in *Gekelemukpechünk* from the *Delaware Nation.*

THE 13TH   In the early service the Watchword declared that we are the work of His hands and were purchased preciously with the Blood of Christ, and we should always remember this.[416] *Michael,* who had accompanied a messenger from *Pittsburgh* to *Gekelemukpechünk* yesterday, returned from there with the news that our Brothers had left there yesterday with a good number of Indians to go to *Woaketammeki,* where some of the *Lower Shawnee* had already arrived. *Netawatwees* also sent word to our people here and in *Gnadenhütten* that they should not be so worried and afraid that they abandoned their fields or neglected them. If they failed to plant, they would have to suffer want whether there was war or peace. Despite all the unrest, we have not allowed ourselves to be kept from planting, and indeed we have diligently admonished our people to do this and have encouraged them. They have actually all planted a good bit more than last year. It is true, the Sisters have often been chased away from the fields several times a day when there was a rumor that *Mingo* or *Shawnee* had been seen, and even though it was just talk most of the time, it still caused many disturbances and the Sisters were afraid of going outside of the *Town.* Anytime there was such a commotion, however, the first thing the Indian Brothers and Sisters did was to look for us if we were out in the fields or somewhere else,[417] and to take us home.

THE 14TH   *Netawatwees* sent us word through a messenger that a great council would be held soon in *Gekelemukpechünk* with the *Shawnee, Wyandot* and *Cherokees.*[418] Because many people would be gathering now and they were short of food supplies, he asked both of our *Towns* to make a contribution.

THE 15TH   Through an *express* messenger we received news that a party of *Shawnee* has returned from the war with 10 *Scalp*s and 3 prisoners,[419] and also that the *Virginians* were on the march to the *Shawnee* and had been tracked just one day's journey from there. This last claim was unfounded, as we heard a couple of days later.

415. On the relationship between the Munsee and the Delaware, see Introduction pp. 16–17, and note 36.

416. Ps. 138:8.

417. This is one of the few clear hints that the missionaries participated in cultivating the fields.

418. Originally this conference had been called for different reasons that had nothing to do with the differences between the Shawnee and Virginia; for details, see entries for 20 and 25 June 1773 and 7 March 1774.

419. The captain of this group of warriors was John Logan. See GD, 15 June 1774, F 3, I 2. The group consisted not only of Shawnee but also of Mingo. See White, *Middle Ground,* 361.

JUNE 16TH   A couple of Brothers took a *Canow* loaded with Indian corn and meat down to *Gekelemukpechünk* for the council meeting.

THE 17TH   A messenger from *Gnadenhütten* arrived very early to inform us that a couple more Brothers were asked to come to the *Councel* in *Gekelemukpechünk*. Therefore we immediately sent Brothers *Willhelm* and *Augustinus*. The former returned from there with *Cornelius* on THE 18TH and brought us news about the state of things, that the *Lower Shawnee* and some from *Woaketammeki* had arrived there, as well as the *Wyandot*. The latter had already declared that their *Chiefs* sent them for the sole purpose of negotiating peace, and therefore they did not want to hear anything about war. However, at the *Councel* in *Woaketammeki*[420] the *Shawnee* did not respond well to *Netawatwees'* words and the message from *Pittsburgh*. *Captain White Eye* threw the *Belt* down before the *Shawnee Chief Gischenatsi* every time he addressed him, because he was not willing to accept it. This essentially means, You can accept it or not, but you will at least listen to it.[421] A party of *Traders* with 120 loaded horses arrived there from the *Lower Shawnee Towns* on their way to the *Fort*. They had *Delaware* Indians as escorts. Before they reached the *Town*, the *Shawnee*[422] went out with spears and weapons to meet them. None of them would have escaped if they had not been fortunate enough that the *Delaware* from *Gekelemukpechünk* came along, as if they had been called, and rescued them. *Captain White Eye* immediately placed himself between the *Traders* and the *Shawnee* and ordered the latter not to dare lay a hand on them. They helped them make it safely to *Gekelemukpechünk* and from there on to the *Fort*.

THE 19TH   Brother *Jungmann* preached the sermon about how we are tested through sufferings and are firmly grounded in the Savior. Afterward there was a service for the communicant Brothers and Sisters. We announced to them that there would be Holy Communion next Saturday and admonished them to examine their hearts and their relationship with the Savior, so that they would not approach the Body and Blood of the Lamb unworthily.

THE 23RD   All of our Brothers and Sisters returned from *Gekelemukpechünk* and brought us the good news that the *Nations* had decided unanimously to maintain the peace. The Watchword for today was, His work is honourable and glorious: and his righteousness endureth for ever.[423] Therefore I let him take charge. At this council there were *deputies* from the *Shawnee*, *Wyandot*, *Cherokees*, and from the *Gachnawage* Indians[424] from *Canada*, along with the *Delaware*. The *Shawnee Chief* had not come, but two of their *Captains*

420. The date of the council was 12–13 June 1774; see entry for 13 June 1774.

421. In his report of 29 June 1774 about the negotiations at Fort Pitt, White Eyes neglected to mention that the Shawnee chiefs had refused to accept the message. *AA*, 4th series, 1:545.

422. See note 419 above for 15 June 1774. The traders had been protected by Shawnee from the "Lower Towns." See Arthur St. Clair to Governor John Penn, 22 June 1774, Smith, *St. Clair Papers*, 1:314–16.

423. Ps. 111:3; *Das kleine Brüder-Gesang-Buch*, hymn no. 890.

424. On the "Gachnawage" Indians, see note 297 for entry of 20 Oct. 1773.

and many from the *Lower Towns* and *Woaketammeki* were present. They gave no answer until the end when they realized they stood completely alone and the other *Nations* insisted they declare themselves, so they answered that those who were present acknowledged what the great council had decided. They could not give a final *Resolution*, however, because their *Chief* was not present. They would inform their *Chief* and their *Nation* that peace had been concluded and they had no doubt that they would also agree to this. The council appointed the *Wyandot* and the *Cherokees* to admonish the *Nations* bordering them to peace, the former to the north and west and the latter the *Nations* that were on their border to the south. They (the Cherokees) had also brought a *Belt of Wampum* from the *Catawbas*, who also wanted to join the peace. They were told that if they wanted to take part in this alliance and peace treaty they should move away from the White people among whom they were living and come to live with the *Cherokees*.[425]

After they were completely finished with their *Affairs* in the great council, there was a council gathering of the *Delaware Nation* from this entire area. Our Indian Brothers once again offered a *Belt of Wampum* in the name of both of our *Towns*, because as long as we have been here we still do not know how things stand between them and us. No *Chief* wants to acknowledge that he called us White Brothers here, and we have thus not yet been recognized or accepted in Indian country for the reason we are actually here. Presumably we have only been tolerated because they think if they drive us away our Indians will not remain either. Sooner or later they will find a suitable occasion to drive us away, which many people would like to see. *Isaac* recently spoke with *Captain White Eye* about this here and revealed to him our intention and our plan. He not only approved, but he considered it an important matter that really pleased him, and he encouraged our Indian Brothers to carry out their plan. He promised to do what he could and to help us so that it would be accepted,[426] because his voice carries the most weight in the council and the *Chief* does not do anything without him. The point is to try to achieve what we were aiming for

425. It is unclear whether this refers to the Shawnee Chief Gischenatsi or to Cornstalk. The "Catabes" or Catawba were the neighbors of the Cherokee to the east; they lived in the southwestern part of South Carolina and in the northern section of Georgia on the river of the same name. Hudson, *Catawba Nation.* See the description from the year 1775 by the Indian trader James Adair, in Williams, *Adair's History of the American Indians,* 233–36. The participation of this tribe in the negotiations can only be explained in light of the original intention to put relations between Delaware, Shawnee, and Cherokee on a firmer basis. As far as it relates to the Shawnee, Zeisberger adds a more positive twist to the results of the negotiations than is warranted by the conference protocol itself, dated 21 June 1774. White Eyes reported this protocol at Fort Pitt on 29 June 1774, saying only: "We cannot inform you any more of our grandchildren the Shawanese, than that they are gone home, and intend soon going to Fort Pitt, to hear of the disturbances which have happened between your foolish people and theirs, when you will then hear from their own mouths what they have to say. . . . The head men of the Shawnese are gone to Wagetomica [Woaketameki], and intend to send their King up to Fort Pitt, that he may himself hear what his brothers the English have to say." *AA,* 4th series, 1:545.

426. See entry for 10 May 1774.

4 years ago with the *Goschgosching Affair,* with which they personally assisted us and which later went to *Packanke,* where it then remained.

Isaac, who was the speaker, therefore addressed the council with the following words: My friends, we, the Indian believers in both *Towns* below and above the *Gekelemukpechünk Creek,* in *Schönbrunn* and *Gnadenhütten,* first extend our sincere gratitude that we have now lived for 2 years in peace and calm where we have settled. We hope this will continue. On this occasion we must also report to you what the leaders in *Philadelphia* told us when they let us go in peace, after they had protected us for about one and a half years, showed us much love, and provided us with food and clothing. After peace had been restored[427] they said to us, Now go in peace to your friends and to your *Nation.* We will watch where you go and we wish you good luck on your journey. We know that you have accepted God's word, which you enjoy hearing, and that you might not want to leave without your teachers. If you are concerned about his, you should know that your teachers are free to go with you. However, you should consider them your own flesh and blood. Whatever you have, they should also have. If things are going well for you, then they will also go well for them. If you suffer hunger, they will suffer hunger with you and endure everything. But love them, because we give them to you as a sign of our love to you. They will not neglect to preach the Gospel to you wherever you go.

Then he took the *Belt* and said, My friends, you called us here with our teachers, so treat these Brothers of ours, *David* in *Schönbrunn* and *Schmick* in *Gnadenhütten,* as we have done. Accept them as we do. Look upon them as upon us because we are one body, and what you do to them you also do to us.

Then he gave the *Belt* to *Netawatwees* who gave it to *Captain White Eye.* He returned it, however, saying it was customary for such a *Belt* to be passed around in the *Councel,* which was then done. During this time, however, *White Eye* called to the *Counsellors* that they should consider this. Finally it was given back to *White Eye.* Everyone was quiet and no one made a sound. After a while he began to talk and said, Now I am happy because this is a good thing. He was quiet again for a while. Since no one wanted to say anything, he finally said, My friends, this is a great word and worth considering. I do not consider myself worthy of this, because I know I am a poor human. Surely none of us is worthy of having such a word from God arrive in our *Councel.* God has never before honored us by sending us his word. Therefore consider it well. He could barely say this much before tears welled up in his eyes and he had to stop. Those present accompanied and affirmed each word with a *Shout.* The *Belt* was then given to the *Chief* to keep and the matter was submitted to the *Councellors* for further consideration until another suitable time, because *Captain White Eye* had to hurry to *Pittsburgh* now to deliver the good news of the peace that had been concluded there. Our *Noah,* who was in *Gekelemukpechünk* for several days

427. See note 368 to entry for 9 May 1774 above.

during this council, spoke with the *Cherokees* a great deal as well. They were planning to visit us, and we would have enjoyed this. However, their time and their *Affairs* did not permit this.

So that is what happened at the great council. I do not think it would be unpleasant if I included a talk about us that two *Captains* from the *Lower Shawnee* had with *Captain White Eye* during the breaks at the council. One of the former asked *White Eye* what he thought about the Indian believers, whether what they were doing was really right and if it would be good for him to become a believer also and to live as they live. *White Eye* answered him that what they were doing was certainly right and well founded, and it would be good if all Indians became believers. You see that they lead an orderly and quiet life. They do not harm anyone and are happy to live in peace with everyone. Therefore if all Indians lived like this, we would be a peaceful and happy people and not have to be in constant fear of war. You hear nothing among them of robbery, lying, and deception, much less of drunkenness, murder and such. All of these things, however, and many more things, are common among the other Indians. Therefore no one can truthfully say that what they are doing is not right. It is right and will remain right. Many are opposed to it now, but just wait 20 years and then we will see what a large number of Indian believers there will be, and in 50 years there will probably be very few left in this area who are not believers. Then the *Shawnee Captain* said, I too have often thought about this and sometimes prayed to God that he would reveal to me what He would like me to do so that I might be saved. But I always think I am too bad and have sinned too much, and therefore perhaps cannot become a believer. *White Eye* told him, If you talked like this to the believers, they would answer, You are on the right path and are close to becoming a believer. The *Shawnee* continued questioning. He knew that there were many among them who liked hearing God's word and who also wanted to live like the Indian believers. Their *Chiefs* and *Captains*, however, had not yet granted them the freedom to do this. *White Eye* answered him that it would be good if a couple of them went to our place, observed, and listened. Then they would become convinced of the truth and they could then convince their people from their own personal experience. Perhaps that would help more than if the *Delaware* preached to them, because they would not believe them. He told them further that they had an example in our *Isaac,* so that they could not doubt that the *Captains* could also convert. He was a completely different man now than he had been before. He had actually only been with us for a short time, but if they spoke with him and listened to him they would not be able to argue, but would have to admit that everything he says is the truth. This is how all the Indian believers were when they began to talk; even the most reasonable Indians could not argue against them.

THE 24TH   Yesterday and today we had Speakings with the Brothers and Sisters in preparation for Holy Communion. Otherwise many guests came to visit today.

THE 25TH   3 *Shawnee* arrived here from *Pittsburgh.* They had escorted some *Traders* from the *Lower Shawnee Towns* by water to the *Fort.* On the return journey they had been attacked on *Beaver Creek* in *Sakunk* by White people who were presumably watching them. They had shot after them and wounded one of them.[428] We were not happy to hear this because we fear this situation might agitate the *Shawnee,* who have not declared themselves completely for the peace anyway, and they might go out to commit murders. Therefore this evening we sent a messenger after an Indian who was traveling through here to *Pittsburgh* with a letter for Mr. Croghan, to report this to him and to prevent the road from being closed and even more harm perhaps being done.[429] A *Mohawk* Indian messenger from *Pittsburgh,* who had traveled through *Kaskaskung,* had a message to all the Indians from *Captain Sinclair,*[430] *deputy* of the *Gouverneur* in *Philadelphia.* This written message reminded them of their old friendship and admonished them to remain firm in this. He also informed them that he has a considerable *Present* prepared for them, which he would deliver to them as soon as he gets a chance.[431]

In the evening there was a Congregational Service first, and after receiving *Absolution,* the *Communicants* partook most blessedly in the enjoyment of the Body and Blood of the Lord in the Holy *Sacrament.* Two Brothers and two Sisters watched for the first time.

428. After being informed that these traders had been escorted secretly to the residence of George Croghan, the commanding officer ordered forty militia soldiers to pursue the Indians and traders, and on 18 June 1774 issued a proclamation that forbade all contact with Shawnee. Arthur St. Clair, among others, interpreted this as a sign of Virginia's determination to prevent a peaceful settlement of the colony's conflict with the Shawnee. *AA,* 4th series, 1:475; *DHDW,* 66; Smith, *St. Clair Papers,* 1:314–16. On 26 June St. Clair reported to Governor John Penn: "Mr. Connolly sent two parties down the river in pursuit of the Shawanese who escorted the traders, who intercepted them at Beaver Creek, fired on them, and wounded one, and then ran off in the most dastardly manner." Smith, *St. Clair Papers,* 1:318–19.

429. We have not found Zeisberger's letter to Croghan.

430. At that time Arthur St. Clair (1736–1818) was one of the justices of the peace for Westmoreland County, Pennsylvania; the land on which Fort Pitt stood, which was claimed at that time by both Virginia and Pennsylvania, was part of Westmoreland County. St. Clair was Pennsylvania's leading opponent of Dr. John Connolly, Virginia's representative. In view of the dramatic increase in tensions, St. Clair, George Croghan, and some other leading Indian traders formed an association that advanced money for the enlistment of one hundred soldiers. From mid-May at the latest St. Clair acted as mouthpiece of the governor of Pennsylvania, with whom he was in regular correspondence. Smith, *St. Clair Papers,* 1:10–11, 274–91, 302–3.

431. The text of the message is not preserved; neither is it reported in the letters of St. Clair to Governor John Penn dated 22, 26, and 28 June 1774. Ibid., 1:314–21. St. Clair's letter of 22 June, however, reports the following: "I mentioned something of a condolence [ceremony] in my last, and as the Shawanese were up, I suffered myself to be persuaded by Mr. Croghan to collect a small present of goods for that purpose, . . . the Indians . . . were brought down to Mr. Croghan's, and were shown the condolence, and acquainted that it was ordered for them by you, and that when their chiefs arrived they would be spoken to, and the present delivered, and a messenger was sent after the Shawanese to acquaint them likewise."

THE 26TH   We sang our childlike *Gratias* to the dear Lord for the
merciful protection we have enjoyed from Him until now, with faith and confidence that He will soon restore peace for us completely. In the morning there
was a sermon about Isaiah 26: 1–5. Afterward was the burial of Brother *Nicodemus* who died in blessing yesterday. He came to the Brothers in the *Barracks* in
Philadelphia at the end of the year 1763, was baptized there on *June* 10, 1764,
and became a communicant on *October* 11, 1766. After his baptism he lived a
blessed life and his heart was firmly attached to the Savior and the Unity. In
the fall of 1771 he arrived in *Langundoutenünk* with some Brothers and Sisters
from *Fridenshütten,* and in the spring of 1773 he went from there to *Schönbrunn*
with the rest of the Brothers and Sisters. However, he was already very weak
because of his advanced age and last winter he spent almost all his time ill. For
the last month he had become increasingly weak, although he was not really
sick. He often longed to be home with the Savior, and this happiness was
granted him yesterday on the Communion Day of the congregation, and he
died with the blessing of the congregation.

There was a lovefeast in the afternoon, during which the Brothers and
Sisters were reminded how much the Savior had guided them during the last
war and had brought them through so many dangers, and how He had also
kept all harm and danger from us until now. We therefore have sufficient cause
to worship and adore Him for this and to praise Him. We also remembered
the Watchwords our Savior had given us on those days when things looked
the worst. Then we knelt and thanked Him for his merciful protection and
commended his little Indian congregation to Him for further grace. Among
the strangers who were here visiting was also one of the former *Shikellemis'*[432]
sons, who also attended our services. The 3 *Shawnee* who came here from the
Fort yesterday continued their journey today. They were attentive in our services, and also attended the burial today. They talked a lot with our Indian
Brothers about our life and way of living, and asked them many questions.
Among other things they said that the *Lower Shawnee* had decided in their
council to call the Indian believers from the *Susquehanna* first, even before the
Delaware in *Gekelemukpechünk* had thought about it. They had also designated
a site where they could live, which was not far from their *Towns,* so that those
of their people who wanted to hear the Gospel could go there. However, when
those in *Gekelemukpechünk* had received news of their plans, they had gotten
ahead of them, held a *Councel,* and sent a message to our Indians calling them
there. When they saw this and knew that our Indians had actually come, they
had done nothing more in the matter; they thought it would be good to have
Indian believers so near. Surely someday they could work it out to have some

432. Shikellemi, a chief of the Oneida, was to represent in the Ohio region the interests of the
Six Indian Nations vis-à-vis Pennsylvania; according to Loskiel he died in 1748 in Shamokin, in the
presence of David Zeisberger. Loskiel, *Geschichte der Mission,* 351–53. One of his sons was John Logan.

come to their place. They knew that this had been agreed in their *Councel* because they themselves had been present. They still hoped this would happen, because many of them really wanted to hear the Gospel. However, many were also against it. Last winter they had heard that a White Brother and a couple of Indians had been on the way to visit them, but that their *Chief* had stopped him. They were not happy when they heard this.[433]

THE 27TH   Sister *Schmick* and some Indian Sisters came here from *Gnadenhütten* for a visit, and she returned there on THE 28TH. Otherwise, bad news arrived here from the *Shawnee;* they had killed some White people again.[434] Because of this the Indians once again feared that the White people might attack them. The Watchword for today was very comforting to us, The Lord is my light and my salvation; whom shall I fear? the Lord is the strength of my life; of whom shall I be afraid?[435]

THE 29TH   Indians arrived here who wanted to go to *Pittsburgh* with the *Traders* who had come from the *Shawnee* several days ago. However, they had turned around at little *Beaver Creek* out of fear of the White people, because the *Traders* had told them something that made it seem like things did not look very good regarding the White people. Therefore they turned around in silence, without learning the real truth of the matter. They brought along the news that a large party of *Virginians* was waiting in *Sakunk* on the large *Beaver Creek* and were keeping guard there. They presumed that the *Traders* and the Indians all would have been captured.[436]

THE 30TH   Another party of Indians returned here. Some of them had been in the *Fort;* some of them had turned around before they got there. They brought along the news that the *Virginians* were there in great numbers and more were arriving every day. Therefore it was very unsafe for the Indians there, because the White people were very stirred up against them.[437] This is surely no surprise because the *Shawnee* have not stopped murdering. We heard again today that a party of 20 of their men had gone out again to murder.[438] We did not know what things were like among the White people in *Pittsburgh* and we have not received anything certain and also no news *favorable* for us, so

433. See Zeisberger's report about this visit in entry for 19 Sept. 1773. The chief had been Gischenatsi.

434. In the second half of June rumors about incidents circulated, most of which proved wrong. *DHDW*, 38–56.

435. Ps. 27:1.

436. See note 428 for entry for 25 June 1774.

437. Arthur St. Clair reported to Governor John Penn on 4 July 1774: "I can not suppress my fears that it [i.e., peaceable aspect] will soon be interrupted, as a large body of Virginians are certainly in motion. Colonel Henry Lewis is ordered to the mouth of Kenhawa to build a fort there; and Major McDonald with about five hundred, is to march up Braddocks road and down to Wheeling to build another there; and Cresap, with three others, are appointed to raise ranging companies." Smith, *St. Clair Papers,* 1:322.

438. Probably a reference to Chief John Logan, who according to the editor of the *St. Clair Papers* was on the warpath at this time. Smith, *St. Clair Papers,* 1:316n2.

we were mostly worried that gangs[439] of White people might possibly be formed to go out against the Indians. This would be the most dangerous thing for us because people like this are not under anyone's command, and we have nothing to fear now from the Indians, who are most likely to seek protection from us and believe they are safe with us. Our *Town* is therefore constantly filled with strangers who come and go daily. There is also a party of *Virginians* like this in *Sakunk* on *Beaver Creek*.[440] They rob and plunder in the fields where people have fled, and they make the road here unsafe. We also heard afterward that the commanding *Officier* in the *Fort* sent people out after them to look for them, but could not find them.[441] Under such circumstances we commend ourselves and our entire people to the Savior for grace, and we pour out our worry and concern to his faithful heart, according to our Watchword for today, Redeem Israel, O God, out of all his troubles and protect us from all sin and all earthly turmoil.[442]

July

THE 1ST   Early in the day we strengthened our hearts with today's Watchword, but we will remember the name of the Lord our God. Do you know who it is? It is Jesus Christ, the Lord Sabbaoth,[443] and we poured out our need and distress to Him, in accordance with our text for today, Ask, and it shall be given you.[444] We call upon him for help and salvation, as children to their dear father.

We learned from the Indians who returned from the *Fort* yesterday that they had tracked the party of *Virginians* who are camping on the *Beaver Creek* and are patrolling up and down as far as halfway here, and also that they have seen White people from *Wisancksican*,[445] where the *Mingo* were killed,[446] as close as 20 miles from here on the road, where they turned around again. We could only conclude that they were trying to become familiar with the roads and the area and that they were planning something against our *Towns*, because the

---

439. For Zeisberger this term covers all white settlers who had organized themselves in volunteer vigilante groups and were not part of the regular militia structure. In regions not yet organized into counties—and this meant most of the Ohio region—this represented the only possibility for settlers to associate themselves in larger military units. Michael Cresap, for Virginia, and Arthur St. Clair, for Pennsylvania, organized such vigilante groups as "gangs" ("Frey Parthien"). *DHDW*, 11–12; Smith, *St. Clair Papers*, 1:299–301.

440. These were three hundred men. GD, for 30 June 1774, F 3, I 2.

441. See note 428 to for entry for 25 June 1774 above.

442. Ps. 25:22; *Das kleine Brüder-Gesang-Buch*, hymn no. 2390, verse 4.

443. Ps. 20:8; *Das kleine Brüder-Gesang-Buch*, hymn no. 47.

444. Matt. 7:7.

445. Not identified.

446. On 30 April 1774 Mingo, among them relatives of John Logan, had been murdered on the Yellow Creek; see entry for 8 May 1774.

Indians have warned us to be on our guard. Therefore we sent 4 Brothers to the place where our road meets the other one, a day's journey from here, to stay in the area there for a number of days and watch the bush and roads there until we receive more detailed and more certain news form *Pittsburgh*. Brother *Johann Jungmann* and some Indian Brothers and Sisters came here from *Gnadenhütten* for a visit.

THE 2ND   All sorts of bad news arrived, including word that the *Virginians* are already supposed to have arrived in the area of *Gekelemukpechünk Creek* and would attack *Gnadenhütten* tonight. We did not pay too much attention to this, because many lies are circulating which mostly frighten the Indians. Still, *Netawatwees* sent word to us here and in *Gnadenhütten* to be on our guard and to send people out daily to keep watch on the roads and the area around us. They would do the same close to them and station guards on the road to the *Ohio* so that we would have adequate warning if the White people attempt anything against the Indians.

THE 3RD   We heard from Indian strangers who came here frequently that 8 parties of *Shawnee* and *Mingo*, 100 warriors in all, had already gone out to murder and that the women and children from *Woaketammeki* had fled to the *Lower Towns*.[447] We even heard that the Indians in *Gekelemukpechünk* were already wavering and no longer standing firm. The young people were very agitated and wanted to join the *Shawnee* because they believed they would get the upper hand; if they did not join with them then they would not only have the *Shawnee* against them but also the White people.[448] Therefore they are beginning to say it is our fault the *Delaware* are retreating, because we did not want to have war. It would be twice as dangerous for us because we would not only have the *Shawnee* at our throats but also the *Delaware*. This was thus a very dangerous *Prospect* and we certainly had cause to call to the Savior for help, as it says in our Watchword for today, Arise, o Lord, let not man prevail. *Help us, Lord God, in this distress, so that those who do not consider, who despise your word and teach others to do so, might also convert.*[449] Because we have heard so much bad news, we sent our *Isaac* to the *Chief* in *Gekelemukpechünk* this morning to find out what was going on and how things looked. Josua from *Gnadenhütten* also went with him. They learned that what we had heard was correct. A crowd of Indians immediately gathered around them in the *Chief's* house, where they talked with them a lot, encouraged them, and calmed the people again somewhat, because they had already exhausted the *Chief*. He had already ordered his people to prepare to flee to *Walhanding*.[450] One of the main reasons the

447. While the news that eight groups of Mingo and Shawnee were on the warpath represents a considerable exaggeration and indicates the extent of the anxieties, the news that women and children had left Woaketameki was probably accurate, because at this time the Shawnee were probably expecting a counteroffensive by Virginia. See entry for 14 July 1774, note 464.

448. This fear proved unfounded.

449. Ps. 9:20; *Londoner Altes und Neues Brüdergesangbuch*, pt. I, 435, verse 5.

450. See the reproduction of Thomas Hutchins's map of 1778 in the appendix. The settlements on the Walhanding Creek offered greater security because they were at some distance from the paths

people got so upset was because *Captain White Eye* and most of the Head people had gone to the *Fort*. They had already been gone too long, and they had not been able to find out if they had arrived there safely or not and so they think they were either all killed or taken prisoner. All of this and the evil rumors about the *Shawnee* frightened and horrified the Indians, who are runnung from one *Town* to another carrying countless lies with them. On such occasions you can really feel the power of Satan and of darkness that rules among the Indians. Despite this, the Savior does not fail to reveal himself and to profit from this. Our *Simon's* Brother, a respected Indian and preacher among them,[451] who used to be a big enemy, did not want to hear anything about God's word, and therefore was always careful not to come into our *Town* in *Langundouteniünk*. He came here for a visit about 8 days ago, heard the Gospel for the first time, was powerfully convicted and touched, and now is asking for permission to move here with his family. He received this and expressed his heart as solidly as a Brother who has already lived with us for a number of years. This spring he moved from *Kaskaskunk* to *Gekelemukpechünk*. On his journey there, however, he happened to be in *Minque Town*[452] when it was attacked by White people and they had to flee.

THE 6TH   In the morning the Indians who had gone to the *Fort* with *Captain White Eye* and were now returning from there brought us the happy news that there was nothing to fear from the White people and that they were sending the *Delaware* Indians many assurances of their good intentions toward them. Also, no White people were supposed to come across the *Ohio* onto their land. However, they could not say or promise this about the *Shawnee,* because they had not yet declared if they wanted war or peace.[453] We were especially happy to hear this for the sake of the Indians in *Gekelemukpechünk,* who are encouraged through this. This will give them new courage to stand firm. If they did not remain firm, then we could not make it. Three *Shawnee* and 2 *Mingo* from *Woaketammeki* passed through here on their journey to the 6 Nations, whom they will ask for help against the *Virginians.*[454] They had 3 White

---

that led to the Shawnee settlements. Indians from those settlements had visited the mission congregations on 25 May 1774; on 11 July 1774 Netawatwees demanded that the mission congregations prepare themselves to move at a moment's notice to the settlements on the Walhanding Creek. In February 1775 most inhabitants of Gekelemukpechünk moved to the confluence of the Tuscarawas and the Walhanding Creek and founded there the new town of Goschachgünk, which Zeisberger describes in the entry for 8 Feb. 1775.

451. Simon, Indian name Laweloochwalend, had been baptized on 2 April 1774. Netawastond was his brother; see entry for 17 July 1774.

452. Logan's Town.

453. This report summarizes the results of the negotiations at Fort Pitt on 29 June 1774; see note 425 for entry for 23 June 1774.

454. After it became evident during the negotiations at Woaketameki and Gekelemukpechünk that the Delaware and Cherokee were not prepared to start a war with Virginia despite the murder of Chief John Logan's family members and despite the land problem, the Shawnee intensified their search for other allies. The message to the Six Indian Nations and that to the Wyandot were part of these efforts. Officially, at least, the Shawnee were still unaware that the Six Indian Nations had already determined to side with the peace party. Given that many Mingo were as angry as they were about

*Scalp*s with them. A couple of Brothers led them through the middle of our *Town* and escorted them on up the road beyond our borders.

THE 7TH This storm had hardly died down when another arose which was even more dangerous for us and was not just noise. We had already noticed that the strangers who had been filling our *Town* for some time are not doing any good work, and they are frightening our people and their lies are causing harm. They are working on their friends to see if they can get them away from here. Even though we had seen that they were trying to misguide our people, we could not get rid of them. In addition, 3 *Munsee* from *Mochwesüng*[455] brought a message which arrived here today. The message, which they said was from the *Shawnee,* said, The Indians should all come join their women and children in their *Lower Towns,* where their women, their children, and they themselves would be safe. Finally the *Delaware* were also told in a mocking way that they should watch their fields well, so that their warriors would find something to eat when they returned from the war. We did not accept this message, however, although they asked us to send it on. They also said that the *Wyandot, Twichtwees,*[456] *Cherokees,* and other *Nations* also had already joined the *Shawnee* to help them against the White people. This is not true however; they are making up lies in order to scare the *Delaware* and win them to their side. They had also sent to the French on the *Illinois* and asked them for help. However, they replied that they could not help them in any way unless they brought them skins. Then they would receive what they wanted in return.[457] Tonight there was a false alarm. Some shots were heard not far away in the bush, and many people thought that the White people must be advancing. Some Indian Brothers were sent out to scout, but found nothing. Without a doubt some Indians had shot at deer at the *Salt Licks* not far from here. In the meantime, some Brothers and Sisters prepared to flee. All of these circumstances, as well as the threats we have to listen to constantly from the *Shawnee,* and the Indians who are trying to talk their friends here into leaving because we would be the first ones attacked by the White people, caused *Salomo* to leave here with his family on THE 9TH. He wanted to go to the *Shawnee* with another family. It really hurt us to have to watch how intentionally they threw themselves into misery and physical and spiritual ruin. At the same time, however, this will free us of much trouble and distress we have had with them for some time now because

the white settlements, the Shawnee had good reason to think that they could garner the support of the Six Indian Nations. On the negotiations to form alliances, see entries for 7 July, 14 July, and 6 Aug. 1774.

455. See note 146 to entry for 19 Jan. 1773 and note 252 to entry for 2 Sept. 1773. On the location and attitudes of the two settlements, Mochwesüng and Woaketameki, see entries for 31 May, 2 June, and 13 June 1774.

456. See entry for 6 Aug. 1774, note 488.

457. Like the Delaware, the Shawnee maintained close relations with the tribes on the river Wabash, among whom French fur traders wielded considerable influence; see entry for 22 May 1773 and note 198.

of their bad friends.[458] It would also not be good for us to try to persuade and keep people like this, because we could turn the Indians into enemies by keeping their friends, and that would be very dangerous for us White Brothers and Sisters. They stayed on the river a couple more days, then traveled to *Gnadenhütten*. From there, one family turned around and came back here, but *Salomo* went on to *Gekelemukpechünk*.

THE 10TH   A messenger came from *Gnadenhütten* very early and brought us news from *Netawatwees* that the message attributed to the *Shawnee* was not genuine; it actually came from the *Munsee* in *Mochwesüng*, who were trying to separate their friends from us on this occasion. They have worked very hard on some of their friends, especially on the *Munsee*, while they were here. However, they realized and admitted themselves that they could not achieve their goal[459] and so they left today. Then we were able to sense a blessed quiet and the peace of God among us, so that the Watchword for today was really fulfilled, Thou hast caused men to ride over our heads; we went through fire and through water: but thou broughtest us out into a wealthy place.[460] We have surely experienced this inwardly and outwardly.

Captain White Eye arrived here from *Pittsburgh* with a message for the *Delaware* and *Shawnee*. The latter were informed that there could be no more thoughts of peace unless those guilty on both sides were delivered and punished. They were also informed that a large number of *Virginians* have marched to the big *Canhawa*.[461]

THE 11TH   After the early service, Brother *David* went to *Gnadenhütten* with Brothers *Johannes* and *Nathanael*, where he talked for a number of hours with Brother and Sister *Schmick* and then returned home in the evening. We received a message from *Netawatwees*, who sent word that we should prepare *Canows* so that we would be ready if we needed to flee. They, the Indians

458. Salomo (alias Allemewi before his conversion) had been one of the chiefs of the Munsee; "bad friends" must therefore refer to Munsee, whose behavior in this conflict Zeisberger strongly disapproved of.

459. Except that Salomo was determined to move away from the congregation.

460. Ps. 66:12.

461. In his letter of 8 July 1774, Aeneas Mackay wrote from Pittsburgh to Joseph Shippen: "We have no room to doubt that Doctor Conally, by Order Lord Dunmore, sent a Speech to the Shauneaze [Shawnee], Importing that Logan & his party be immediately deliver'd up, with the three prisoners that he had taken, & some Other Shauneaze that are supposed to have committed a murder last Winter. That on Refusal, they (the Virginians) are determined to proceed against them with Vigour & will shew them no Mercy." PA, 1st ser., 4:541. According to Mackay, this message contained no offer to exchange the culprits; this part of Zeisberger's diary entry could—as far as it relates to the implied intention to punish the perpetrators—originate with the Virginia governor's message of 7 May 1774 to the Delaware and Six Indian Nations, which according to the diary of Alexander McKee arrived at Fort Pitt on 9 June. The message read: "And to that end [i.e., life in peace, amity, and good correspondence], if you can point out the offenders against our peace, we will on our parts omit nothing in our power to overtake the transgressors on our side with the punishment due to such crimes." AA, 4th series, 1:482. Lord Dunmore had approved the latter's intention "of marching into the Shawanese Towns, if you think you have a sufficient force" as early as 20 June 1774, in a letter to Captain John Connolly (AA, 4th series, 1:473).

in *Gekelemukpechünk,* would send their women and children and supplies ahead up the *Walhanding Creek,* where they would be out of danger[462] and we should also do this and take our women, children, and elderly there to join theirs. Young and strong people, however, could stay here until they saw imminent danger. Because this suggestion did not suit us, however, we did not consider it.

THE 12TH   The early service was about the comfort and certain assurance we have in the Savior when we have met Him in his suffering and have tasted his wounds. Many Indians from *Kaskaskunk, Walhanding,* and other places came here to visit. *Netawastond,* who had permission to move here with his family, arrived here today from *Gekelemukpechünk.*[463] Toward evening a message came from *Gekelemukpechünk* that Brothers *Isaac, Johannes, Augustinus,* and *Willhelm* should go there tomorrow, and some of them went as far as *Gnadenhütten* this evening.

THE 14TH   They returned from there. They had been called to confer with them about what to do under these circumstances, and whether they should flee or remain since 8 parties of *Shawnee* had gone out to murder.[464] Some were in favor of taking the women, children, and elderly away and building them a *Fort* where they could be safe. When they wanted to hear the Brothers' thoughts and opinions about this, they went aside with Brother *Schmick,* who was with them, deliberated, and decided to stay together as long as we could until we see that there was really danger. We would keep the peace recently concluded with the *Nations.* If we fled now, it would look like we were not standing firmly. When they called *Captain White Eye* and told him their opinion, he was very happy about this. He had really tried to persuade the Indians and the *Chief* there to stay. They all agreed to this as well then.

An Indian who had been far out west and had traveled through many *Nations* brought news that all the *Nations* were peacefully inclined and there was no talk of turmoil or war. The *Wyandot* had asked the *Shawnee* why they were going to war against the White people when all the *Nations* were at peace. However, the *Shawnee* had denied this and refused to admit it.[465] It is now only too true and clear, however, and it is presumed they are planning to move far away. The *Shawnee Chief* even implied this when he said they would leave because their grandfather wanted to leave them. First they would turn around and defeat those who were closest to them, because this was the *Shawnee* way.[466]

462. See entry for 3 July 1774, note 450.

463. Permission had been granted on 3 July 1774.

464. The previous day at Dunkard Creek, six settlers had been killed and three injured (see note 402 above); two were still missing. The Shawnee were blamed. On 19 July the commanding officer of Fort Pitt used the occasion to accuse those representing Pennsylvania of a share in the blame, since their talk "of the Indians, has unluckily lulled the inhabitants into suppineness and neglect." Smith, *St. Clair Papers,* 1:327–30.

465. See entry for 6 July 1774, note 454.

466. On the rumor that the Shawnee intended to give up the settlement of Woaketameki and move further west, see entry for 3 July 1774 and note 447. Zeisberger would be proved right. The dangerous part of this message was the conviction of the Shawnee that they had been left in the lurch by the Delaware. According to White Eyes' speech of 23 July 1774 (see note 468 below), the threat

The *Delaware* are also afraid of them, therefore, because they are always threatening them. Further, *Captain White Eye* had also addressed a great gathering of people in the *Councel* about the Brothers and Indian believers, and said that they should act peacefully and cordially toward us and not speak badly of us, because we were their friends and belonged to them. The *Delaware Nation* was already known for having accepted God's word and although it was not yet true of everyone, there was already a large group of Indian believers. It would be better if they lived in peace with them and did not speak badly of their own *Nation,* because some day they would all call upon God's name, especially when they got into trouble and distress, or if they saw that they were going to die and did not see any other assistance ahead of them. Then it would occur to them that there was a God in heaven who created all things, and they would turn to him in their distress. Therefore they should not be hostile toward us, but love us so that some day when they were in need of help and comfort they would not have to despair. They also could surely believe that if they hurt us, they did the same to God.[467] Surely the Savior had awakened the man for our sake in this unrest of war, so that he can speak so confidently to the people for us. If the Indians were against us in the current circumstances as they had been previously, things would be all the more dangerous for us White Brothers and Sisters. Our lives would not be secure.

THE 16TH   *White Eye* came here from *Gnadenhütten* with *Petrus* and a couple other Indians from *Gekelemukpechünk* to talk with our wisest Indian Brothers and consider what was best for the *Delaware Nation* and both of our *Towns,* and also what they still had to say to the *Virginians* about the *Shawnee,* because they could not quite figure it out in *Gekelemukpechünk.* This was done early in the morning on THE 17TH. In the message, which was put in writing, the three *Towns, Gekelemukpechünk, Gnadenhütten,* and *Schoenbrunn,* were especially commended to them and they were told not to come into this area if they were planning anything against the *Shawnee.*[468] The rest of the *Delaware* Indians, who live here and there in small *Towns* close to the *Shawnee,* had already been told a while ago to leave and go to *Gekelemukpechünk,* which they have done. Thus we can only expect that the *Virginians* will move into *action* after this message and pay them a *Visite.* When they first began acting with hostility

against the Delaware was part of the message of the Shawnee captain "Keesnateta," who is identical with the chief whose name Zeisberger spelled "Gischenatsi." Smith, *St. Clair Papers,* 1:332.

467. According to the protocol that guided the Delaware's negotiations, the speech of White Eyes became possible after the status of the mission congregations was mentioned in Isaac's speech to the Great Council on 22 June 1774; see entry for 23 June 1774.

468. White Eyes' message, which he delivered in Pittsburgh on 23 July 1774, is printed in Smith, *St. Clair Papers,* 1:331–33. In this message White Eyes argued that the Shawnee had given up their settlements on the Muskingum and that therefore no troops should come near the Delaware settlements. At the same time he officially demanded that Virginia inform the Delaware formally of the outcome of the conflict with the Shawnee, "that we may acquaint all other Nations of it" (ibid., 332).

toward the White people, they had surely not imagined things would be like this, but had believed they would be able to get the *Delaware* on their side. This might well have happened if it were not for both of our *Towns*, because fear would have moved them to join them. We recently had evidence enough of this when *Captain White Eye* was gone for so long. He also realizes that we are a good support for him; if it were not for the Brothers he could not reach his goal of keeping the *Delaware* at peace. From the beginning of this trouble, he always tried to arrange things with the *Virginians* so that if they took action against the *Shawnee*, they would march down the *Ohio* rather than through this area. He told them that if they marched through their country it would be considered a breach of peace.

In the Congregational Service in the evening there was a talk about the text for today, For ye are bought with a price: therefore glorify God in your body, and in your spirit, which are God's.[469] *Netawastond*, who moved here for good on the 12th of this month, was buried into Jesus' death through baptism and received the name *Seth* in Holy Baptism.

THE 18TH   The widow *Magdalena* returned safely from *Kaskaskunk* with her 2 children. She had gone there several days ago to pick them up, because she had left them there when she came to us in the spring.

THE 19TH   Many people went out hunting for several days because it was relatively quiet now. No one had been able to go out before because of the unrest.

THE 20TH   We received news that another party of *Shawnee* had returned with 8 *Scalp*s and 2 prisoners, and that one *Shawnee* had been killed.[470]

THE 21ST   *Traders* from *Pittsburgh* arrived here via *Kaskaskunk*. On this occasion we were very delighted to receive letters from Bethlehem and *Litiz* from *April* 28th and the beginning of *May*. They had already been lying around in the *Fort* for a while because there was no transportation. At the same time we learned that *Captain Crysop*[471] and 500 men were on the march to *Woaketammeki*, but the commanding *Officier* in the *Fort* had sent an *express* messenger after them with orders to wait until *Captain White Eye* returned from here with more news.[472] We hear they are not planning to harm the *Delaware*. However,

469. 1 Cor. 6:20.

470. This is a reference to the incident on the Dunkard Creek of 13 July 1774; see entry for 14 July 1774, note 464. In his letter of 24 July 1774 to Colonel Andrew Lewis, Lord Dunmore used this incident to justify his expedition against the Shawnee (*DHDW*, 97–98). In autumn 1774 Colonel Andrew Lewis (1720–81) commanded the second militia army of Virginia against the Shawnee. For a short biographical memoir and many documents on Lewis's role during Lord Dunmore's war, see *DHDW*, 426–28 and passim.

471. In June 1774 the governor of Virginia appointed Michael Cresap captain in the expedition against the Shawnee (*DAB* 4:538). Zeisberger's information was based on an error. Colonel Angus McDonald (1727–79) was in command of the army against the Shawnee settlement of Woaketameki; under McDonald's command Cresap was in charge of one of the regiments. *DHDW*, 151–56.

472. The expedition could not have been delayed for long, for on 26 July four hundred militia soldiers left Wheeling under the command of McDonald. They reached the largely deserted Shawnee

it is possible that when they see what is happening to the *Shawnee* they will all flee. Then we would not be able to keep our people and to comfort them. If we fled, even for a little while, we would fear that angry Indians from the *Delaware* would come and destroy our *Towns* and fields.

THE 22ND   Brother *Schmick* came here from *Gnadenhütten* for a visit. We strengthened ourselves by reading the letters and news we had received yesterday[473] and we discussed our current circumstances, which are still very serious. On the 23RD he led the early service about the Watchword, All my bones shall say, LORD, who is like unto thee?[474] Anyone who has experienced him as his redeemer in his heart must say, Who is a more faithful friend than you? Then he returned to *Gnadenhütten* with his company. We heard from *Gekelemukpechünk* that they are beginning to flee there, because they have heard that the *Virginians* are approaching.

THE 26TH   There was a Helpers' *Conference.* Among other things the Brothers and Sisters were advised to remain orderly among the strangers who come here, not to allow things that conflicted with our congregational rules, and to make sure that they do not come to the services in a disrespectful manner. We also spoke with some strangers who had been here for a while already, and asked them what their intention and desire here is.

THE 27TH   Early in the day an Indian arrived here as an *express* messenger from the commanding *Officier* in *Pittsburgh.* He brought news to all the Indians that the *Virginians* were marching to the *Shawnee* and requested that some *Delaware* join them at the mouth of the *Muskingum.* This message was immediately sent on to *Gekelemukpechünk.*[475] In the evening service the baby daughter born yesterday evening to Brother *Samuel* and Sister *Helena* was baptized with the name *Louisa.*

---

settlements in August 1774 and after a short battle plundered and burned them together with the adjoining fields. *DHDW,* 151–56; Butterfield, *Washington-Crawford Letters,* 95–97.

473. The Indian trader William (?) Thompson brought letters from Lititz from Matthäus Hehl and Bernhard Adam Grube, from Bethlehem from Nathanael Seidel, and from Barby, Germany, from Petrus Böhler, all addressed to Zeisberger. In addition, he had a letter from Bethlehem addressed to the sisters and brothers of the conference (GD, 22, July 1774, F 3, I 2). The identity of William Thompson is not certain; in all the published correspondence for this period we find only one William Thompson, who had bought some buildings within Fort Pitt in 1772, after the fort had been given up by the British army. On 12 July 1774 the settlers of Cumberland County elected this man to the Committee of Correspondence of the county. From 1775 he had the position of a general in the Continental army. See *DAB,* for Thompson, William, and *RUO,* 143. In early April 1774 there lived in Pittsburgh one Edward Thompson, who, according to a report dated 8 April 1774, had been arrested a few days earlier by supporters of Dr. John Connolly. See Butterfield, *Washington-Crawford Letters,* 46. It is not impossible that Edward, not William, Thompson was the bearer of these letters.

474. Ps. 35:10.

475. In his response to White Eyes' speech of 23 July 1774, George Croghan had said: "brothers, I would have you consider well whether you would not in the present circumstance think it prudent for some of your people to accompany ours when they go to chastise the Shawanese, in order to enable them to make a proper distinction between our friends and our enemies." White Eyes refused to answer but promised to send Croghan's query to Gekelemukpechünk, "and as soon as I have their sentiments and advice will speak to you, which I expect in two days." Smith, *St. Clair Papers,* 1:333.

THE 28TH   In the early service, we considered the text for today,[476] discussing how we should examine our hearts every day and check our relationship with the Savior to see if our love for Him might have cooled somewhat. Then we would not be in danger of falling away from the first love, as we often see among the Brothers and Sisters. A messenger from *Gekelemukpechünk* informed us that one or a few Brothers from here and from *Gnadenhütten* were asked to meet the *Virginians* at the mouth of the *Muskingum* and to assist them in their *Affairs* with the *Shawnee*.[477] They want to send another message to the *Lower Shawnee* and demand a final answer from them.

THE 29TH   A messenger from the *Lower Shawnee* arrived very early with a *String of Wampum*. They are asking their grandfather, the *Chief* in *Gekelemukpechünk,* for help and want him to send a couple of wise men and *Captains* to *Assünnünk*.[478] Those who come to them should advise them about how to escape their dangerous situation and what they should do to set right their misdeeds, which were great. *Isaac* went to *Gnadenhütten* in order to join those from *Gekelemukpechünk* who were continuing on to meet the *Virginians*.[479]

THE 31ST   Brother *Jungmann* preached the sermon about the righteousness in Jesus' Blood as the only thing necessary for us to stand before God. In the preparatory devotion for Holy Communion, we announced Holy Communion for next Saturday. *Mr. Gibson* and another White man[480] arrived here from *Pittsburgh*. We were delighted to receive a letter they brought from Brother *Grube,* dated *June* 20th. Both of them came here primarily to stay in *Gekelemukpechünk* and to be on hand long enough that the Indians here would not be so frightened if the *Virginians* should attack *Woaketammeki,* and to stop them if they came into this area. *Mr. Gibson,* who was there when the troops were read the rules they had to observe when they marched out of *Pittsburgh,* told us they had been given very strict orders, especially about *Gnadenhütten* and *Schoenbrunn.* They were not to hurt a single one of our Indians if they should meet them in the bush, and they were not supposed to come into this area so the Indians would not be alarmed. We heard from the *Shawnee* that 60 more warriors had gone out to murder and that the *Lower Shawnee* had burned 3 prisoners alive.

August

THE 1ST   Mr. *Gibson* continued his journey to *Gekelemukpechünk,* although in his opinion there was no need to fear the *Virginians* since nothing

476. Rev. 2:4.

477. Isaac went from Schönbrunn to the Virginia army; see entry for the following day.

478. "*Assünnünk* is a tough 3 day journey from here on the *Hokhokung* Creek, a short day's journey from the *Shawnee Towns,*" according to Zeisberger's entry for 30 Jan. 1776.

479. See entry for 10 Aug. 1774.

480. The GD for 1 Aug. 1774 gives his name as "Wilson" (GD, F 3, I 2). Probably it was George Wilson, who in the following year was involved in the arrest of Dr. John Connolly. Butterfield, *Washington-Crawford Letters,* 102. On John Gibson, see note 102 above.

had been heard of them yet and they might perhaps have changed their plans to go to *Woaketammeki*. In the evening service the baby boy born yesterday to *Esra* and *Lazarus* was baptized and named *Thomas*.

THE 2ND   We received news from *Gekelemukpechünk* that White people had been seen in the bush near the *Ohio*. Because of this, some Indians fled here with all their possessions. *White Eye's* wife also came here from *Gekelemuk-pechünk* with her children. Our Indian Brothers and Sisters here had a very plentiful fishing trip, so that the whole *Town* had enough to carry home.

THE 3RD   During the early service there was a talk about the Watchword for the day, *For he spake, and it was done; he commanded, and it stood fast.*[481] Then a messenger came here from *Gnadenhütten* with the news that more than 500 *Virginians* had moved into *Woaketammeki* yesterday, where they had fought for a good while with the *Shawnee* and *Mingo* who were there. Then the latter fled and the former took *Possession* of the *Towns* and camped there overnight. In the afternoon another messenger came to inform us that they had moved into the upper *Shawnee Towns,* where they also had a skirmish in which some Indians were killed.[482] *Mr. Gibson* had gone down with some Indians from *Gekelemuk-pechünk* to tell them that they should not advance further up toward the *Delaware Towns,* but he had not found them. We just sit in amazement and watch what the Savior does and how He arranges everything so wisely and well, so that his Indian congregations are diligently protected like the little children here on earth.

THE 4TH   In the early service the Watchword was discussed. We are here to make his name known to humanity, to praise him and to proclaim his countless wonders.[483] We received more news of the *Virginians* in *Woaketam-meki;* they had had 3 skirmishes with the *Shawnee,* all of whom, however, had fled after some were killed and several wounded, and the *Virginians* kept the site. Some of them were wounded, but none killed, as we later also learned from *Pittsburgh*. And after they had burned down all 4 or 5 of the *Towns* in that area, cut down the Indian corn fields, and destroyed everything, they marched back again yesterday and captured a *Minque* Indian and took him with them.[484] A *Delaware* Indian came to them and paced back and forth the whole time they were there. They sent him out to call more Indians to speak with them. Some *Delaware* came then, and they told them they would not harm their people nor would they come close to their *Towns*. But they should tell them

---

481. Ps. 33:9.

482. On 2 August 1774 a Virginia army commanded by Major Angus McDonald consisting of between four and five hundred soldiers burned five Shawnee settlements, among them Woaketameki. As a result, the Shawnee did not negotiate in Pittsburgh. Tanner, *Indians of Ohio and Indiana*, 35, 79. The second battle took place at Snakes, where one Indian warrior and one militia soldier were wounded. *DHDW*, 151–54.

483. Ps. 71:15.

484. See "Extract of a Letter from a Gentleman at Redstone, Received at Williamsburg, 18 August 1774," *AA*, 4th series, 1:/22–24.

where the *Shawnee* and *Mingo* were. They had come here because of them, because they wanted to have this war. They sent some Indians from *Gekelemuk-pechünk* to observe the White people and to keep them posted on how far they had advanced. They always followed them on their return *Marches* and watched them to see what road they took, because the Indians always feared they might come up into this area.

THE 5TH   Today and yesterday there were Speakings with the Brothers and Sisters in preparation for Holy Communion. An Indian from *Gekelemukpech-ünk* requested permission to move here with his family and he received it. His wife was baptized as an older girl in *Nain*[485] near Bethlehem, and her name is *Helena*.

THE 6TH   Some of the head people in *Gekelemukpechünk* came here on their journey to *Pittsburgh*.[486] They brought another message from the *Shawnee*, urgently asking the *Delaware* to speak to the *Virginians* and put in a good word for them, so that they will make a truce and enter into peace negotiations with them. They will leave it up to their grandfather, the *Chief* in *Gekelemukpechünk*, to decide what he will arrange with the *Virginians*. They will agree if they just reach peace. They have dismissed their *Chief Gischenatsi* and chosen another in his place,[487] and they have asked him to see that peace is restored before the *Virginians* go any further in their plan against them. They, the *Shawnee*, had sent to the *Twichtees*[488] and the *Wyandot*, given them the hatchet, and asked for their help and support. Both, however, replied, You alone want war. We do not. All the *Nations* have united for peace and you alone arise with the hatchet in your hand and act against the decision of the great council. So be brave and prove yourself as men. You will certainly need to, because there are only a few of you. You will surely receive what you have sought and earned as a reward. We will remain quiet and watch you. We will not meddle in your actions or help you.[489] This answer, and the fact that the *Virginians* destroyed *Woaketam-*

485. Nain was founded as a mission settlement in 1757 close to Bethlehem, in order to protect the Christian Indians during the French and Indian War.

486. Among these were Killbuck Sr. and John Gibson; see entry for 8 Aug. 1774. On 3 August 1774 George Croghan and Alexander McKee informed the chiefs of the Delaware of the arrival of a message from the Six Indian Nations. They requested that Delaware chiefs come to Pittsburgh to receive the message, which is printed in Wainwright, "Turmoil at Pittsburgh," 158.

487. The statement is based on a misunderstanding. Gischenatsi, chief in times of peace, had handed over his function as a chief during the war to the war captains, of whom Cornstalk was probably the most influential. Schaaf, *Wampum Belts and Peace Trees*, 95, 152; see entry for 17 June 1774.

488. The Iroquois and the Delaware call the Miami Twightees; in the eighteenth century this tribe lived in the region of what is today the state of Indiana. Callender, "Miami." In the entry for 7 July 1774, Zeisberger meant the same tribe when he spoke of the "Twichtees."

489. On 8 August 1774 Arthur St. Clair reported to Governor Penn: "I am just returned from Pittsburgh, where the Pipe, Guyasutha, and the White Mingo are arrived, and bring favorable accounts from the Indian Nations about the lakes. They say they are all disposed to continue in friend-ship with the English; but the Wyandotts, the Hurons, and the Tawas have been waivering. The Shawanese had applied to them, and it was so long that they heard nothing from our people, that they were inclined to assist them, but these chiefs have persuaded them to sit still, and to send to the

meki, frightens them, and now they are asking the *Delaware* to help them gain peace again. In the meantime, they had threatened them before they received this answer and had deceived them with lies claiming they already had the *Wyandot, Twichtees,* and *Cherokees* on their side, hoping thus to scare them and force them to join them.

After the Congregational Service in the evening, the Communicants celebrated Holy *Communion.* During this a Brother and a Sister watched for the second time.

THE 7TH   Early in the day was the *Liturgy* for Holy Communion and then the sermon, which many guests attended. A number of Brothers and Sisters from *Gnadenhütten* came here for a visit, as did *Johann Martin, Marcus,* and our Brothers and Indians from *Gekelemukpechünk* to consider what they could do to help the *Shawnee,* who are in great trouble and distress.

THE 8TH   Mr. *Gibson* and *Killbuck* left with some Indians for the *Fort.* With the former we sent a letter to our Brothers and Sisters in Bethlehem, sharing news that we are doing well.

THE 10TH   In the morning our Brother *Isaac* returned from the mouth of the *Muskingum,* where he and 2 other Brothers from *Gnadenhütten* and some Indians from *Gekelemukpechünk* had gone to join the *Virginians.* They had not found anyone, however, and so their journey was in vain.[490] We thanked the Savior for bringing our Brothers back to us safe and sound. There had been a rumor that they were killed by the *Virginians,* because the Indians thought they had seen their horses with them in *Woaketammeki.* This was not true, however.

THE 12TH   Brother *Nathanael* and Sister *Anna Salome* took their daughter *Catharina* down to *Gnadenhütten* to be married there. There was a *Conference* with the Helper Brothers about a matter concerning *Augustinus* and Chief *Netawatwees.*

THE 15TH   After the early service, which Brother *Jungmann* led, Brother *Schmick* came here from *Gnadenhütten* for a visit. We discussed various things together, and then he returned home in the evening. *Joseph Peepi* returned from *Pittsburgh* with a message to the *Delaware* and *Shawnee.* The latter, who had asked for peace now, were told that it was very difficult to believe them. If they were serious, they should prove it and turn over the murderers. Then they would believe they were really serious about having peace.[491]

Wabash Indians to be quiet likewise; so that it is probable they arrived amongst them in a favorable time." Smith, *St. Clair Papers,* 1:338.

490. See entries for 27, 28, and 29 July 1774.

491. The identity of the author of the message Joseph Peepi received is unclear, because Alexander McKee's Indian journal for the month of August is lost. There is no doubt that the message bears no relation to the two letters Governor Penn wrote on 6 August 1774 to the chiefs and warriors of the Shawnee and Delaware. In his letter to the Shawnee, Penn expressed his pleasure about their support of the traders but added that he was concerned about their conflicts with Virginia. To the Delaware he wrote that, despite the murder of Joseph Wipey, they were holding fast to the treaty of amity. He assured them that he was working for peace and justice and asked the Delaware to continue

THE 17TH   Very early, Marcus came here from *Gnadenhütten* as messenger. He brought *Captain White Eye* the news that another party of *Shawnee* had come from the war with 8 *Scalp*s. He arrived here yesterday evening on his way to *Pittsburgh* and was going to continue his journey from here today.

White Eye had come to *Gekelemukpechünk* from the *Fort* some days ago, when they were just getting ready to have a council about us and very bad plans were in the works to chase us White Brothers and Sisters away. In brief, the reason is this: they see that they cannot do whatever they want to with our Indians, and we are not willing to participate in certain *Affairs*. We refuse, for example, when they want us to send some of our Indians with them to the *Fort*, and other things of this nature that we cannot do. They also had many other objections against us. They have finally decided, therefore, that we White Brothers and Sisters, their teachers, are responsible for this and they have concluded that if they just got them out of the way they could soon be done with the Indians. We had heard much about this in recent days. We expected to learn the outcome of this matter any day and thought we would receive a message from the *Chief* about this. However, *White Eye* ruined their plan and all their attacks and told them he would not support them at all in this or give his *Consent* to this. They were not acting at all like reasonable people; if they heard anything bad about us they believed it right away and made no effort to find out if it were true. And if they heard anything good about us they did not even make an effort to consider it. He proved this to them by reminding them that a *Belt of Wampum* we had recently submitted[492] had still not been answered. They did not indicate that they were very willing to consider the matter.

THE 18TH   Once again an Indian, with his wife and child, requested and received permission to live here, after our *Town Statutes* had been read to them.

THE 22ND   In the morning there was a *Conference* with the Helpers. Among other things we spoke with them about bad people who have no mind for the Savior but who stay here when they really do not belong. Our Brothers and Sisters must free themselves of such people, who are their friends, if they want to be otherwise happy in the congregation. We have sufficient examples that Brothers and Sisters who hang around their bad friends do not amount to anything in the congregation, and indeed are finally separated from the congregation. The same is true when people like this have been here for a while and have no desire to convert, but just want to be here on account of their friends. In the end they become enemies of the Savior and the congregation. Therefore it is better for them to leave before they sin against the congregation.

THE 24TH   Brother *David* went to *Gnadenhütten* with Brothers *Corne-*

---

their mediation (PCR, 10:203–5). These letters seem to have arrived at Pittsburgh around 20 August; see Arthur St. Clair to Governor Penn, 25 Aug. 1774, Smith, *St. Clair Papers*, 1:341.

    492. See entry for 23 June 1774.

lius, Isaac, Jacob, and *Augustinus,* and returned home in the evening after a *Conference* with the Brothers there about *Chief Affairs* concerning other places. We have been overwhelmed with these since spring, because the Indians and *Chiefs* in *Gekelemukpechünk* no longer want to do or undertake hardly anything without our Indian Brothers. They claim they are too weak and there are too few of them, and they do not have enough wise men.[493] At this time we cannot really make a decision about this. We are in Indian country now and have a lot to learn, but we must keep one eye focused on being sure we do not surrender anything or give up our freedom. We must not become so involved with the *Chiefs* that they later gain power over us and can order us to do things opposed to our congregational rules.

THE 26TH   A *Wyandot* Indian, a *Chief* among his *Nation,* came here from Cayahaga[494] with his son. The old man was a nice, upstanding, and friendly man. He was very happy to see such a large *Town* of Indian believers, and he had not expected this here. In the evening he attended the service and afterward said this was a different kind of worship service from what they had in *Detroit.* They also had a church and a priest as a preacher,[495] but he was often drunk when he was supposed to preach and then people said he was sick and could not preach. Our Indian Brothers spoke with him a lot the next day about what kind of people we are, about the life and walk of the Indian believers. They also told him there was another Indian *Town* like this not far from here. He was glad to hear all of this. He said that when he got home, he would tell his *Nation,* because they had never heard that such people lived here. He understood the *Minque* language and our *Noah,* who can speak the *Wyandot* language pretty well, was the Brothers' interpreter. They gave him gifts of Indian corn and Brother *David* had to make him an Indian *Calendar* so he would know when it was Sunday. He was baptized by a French priest in *Detroit,* and he said his name is *Tschano.* When he left he said he would visit us again.

Indians came from *Pittsburgh* with a message from the *Gouverneur* in *Philadelphia* to the Indians. He admonishes the *Delaware* Indians to do their best to talk the *Shawnee* into peace.[496] He also informed them that the *Pennsylvanians* wanted to establish another *Trading* site in *Attike,* a distance above *Pittsburgh,* because the *Virginians* in the *Fort* had stopped all *Trade.* Work would begin on this immediately.[497] At the same time another message went from the 6 *Nations*

493. The discussions in the Council had focused on the dangerous situation caused by the Shawnee resolution to defend their lands; see entry for 17 Aug. 1774. This is one of the few entries in which Zeisberger discusses the problem of getting involved in "worldly affairs."

494. On Cayahaga, see entry for 19 July 1773, note 236.

495. From 1754 to 1784 Simplicius Bocquet, member of the Recollet, had been parish priest of the congregation Ste. Anne in Detroit; in English documents he is usually referred to as either Father or Père Simple. Thwaites, "British Regime in Wisconsin," 235, 310–11.

496. A reference to the message mentioned in note 491 to entry for 15 Aug. 1774 above.

497. Under the pretense of stopping trade with hostile Shawnee, the commanding officer of Fort Pitt had forbidden all trade between Pennsylvania traders and Indians, including trade with those Indians not involved in the war between the Shawnee and Virginia—this on the basis of numerous complaints by Indian traders Arthur St. Clair reported to Governor Penn. Penn responded by pro-

to the *Mingo* among the *Shawnee,* that they should leave there and go to their *Nation.*[498]

THE 28TH   Brother *Jungmann* preached the sermon in the morning. In the Children's Service the baby daughter born to Brother *Nathanael* and Sister *Anna Salome* on the 21st of this month was baptized with the name *Eleonora.* We were delighted that Indians brought us letters via *Pittsburgh* from Brother *Mattheus,* dated *July 27.* Brothers *Isaac, Augustinus,* and *Jacob* went to *Gekelemuk-pechünk* where they had been called to a *Councel.*

THE 29TH   The single Brothers dedicated themselves anew to the Prince of their Choir, to bring Him joy and honor with body and soul. Brother *Jungmann junior* had already arrived here yesterday from *Gnadenhütten.* They listened to a choir talk by the blessed disciple[499] and enjoyed themselves very much during a lovefeast with their ode.[500]

THE 31ST   Brother *Jungmann* held the early service about the comfort we receive daily from the Savior's death. Brothers *Jacob* and *Augustinus,* who returned yesterday from *Gekelemukpechünk* where they had been at a *Councel* concerning the *Shawnee,* left for there again today. From there they will go to the *Lower Shawnee Towns* to hold a council with them and see if they will not incline their ears to peace.[501]

September

THE 1ST   The Brothers of the Helpers' *Conference* spoke with some strangers who have been staying here for a while and told them what rules they needed to observe even if they are not residents here. Today and in recent days many strangers from *Kaskaskunk* and the surrounding area came to visit. There were some among them who were glad to hear about the Savior and responded with emotional hearts.

---

claiming Attike the new trade center between Pennsylvania traders and Indian tribes; see Smith, *St. Clair Papers,* 1:314–41. Attike, formerly a settlement of the Delaware, was situated at the confluence of the Cowanshannock Creek and the Allegheny River.

498. Around 3 August 1774 delegates from the Council of the Six Indian Nations had arrived at Pittsburgh; see entry for 6 Aug. 1774, note 486. According to Arthur St. Clair they brought news of the death of Sir William Johnson but also reiterated their intention "to adhere firmly to the treaties subsisting betwixt the English and them, and to endeavor to retain the other Nations in peace." St. Clair does not report that these delegates admonished the Mingo again to return to the original lands of the Six Indian Nations. Smith, *St. Clair Papers,* 1:338–39.

499. Nikolaus Ludwig Graf von Zinzendorf.

500. This was the day the single brothers celebrated their choir festival.

501. So far as we have been able to establish, this is the first mention anywhere in the literature and documents of the era of this new effort at mediation by the Delaware. The effort demonstrates the Delaware's particular interest in preserving political stability in the Ohio region, while at the same time it documents the conviction, expressed more than once by White Eyes, that the Indians could only lose in any conflict with the colonists—even if all tribes were united. On the result of the negotiations, see entry for 12 Sept. 1774.

THE 2ND   We began singing instruction with the children to teach them some new verses.[502] During a service of the Brothers and Sisters, a sick woman who came to us in the spring was baptized into Jesus' death with the name *Anna Regina.* She had earnestly requested this.

THE 5TH   In the early service we talked about how it is not sufficient to be baptized and cleansed of your sins; it is also necessary to become obedient to God's word, to learn all that goes with this, and to live according to and honor his teaching. The Savior said, Baptize them and teach them to observe all things whatever I have commanded you.[503] A number of Brothers and Sisters came here from *Gnadenhütten* for a visit and we had a *Conference* with the Helpers.

THE 11TH   The married Brothers and Sisters celebrated their choir festival.[504] The blessing and presence of the Savior could be felt during this. He revealed himself very graciously to them. We had postponed this until today because some of the Brothers from here and *Gnadenhütten* had gone to see the *Shawnee.* Early in the day was the morning devotion. Then they had a choir service about their doctrinal texts for recent days.[505] In the afternoon after the sermon was a Lovefeast, and during the Congregational Service in the evening a couple were buried into His death through baptism with the names *Thomas* and *Sabina.* We felt the close presence of the Holy Trinity.

SEPTEMBER 12TH   Our Indian Brothers *Jacob* and *Augustinus* returned from the council with the *Lower Shawnee.* They brought us the happy news from there that they wanted to keep the peace. They have heard the whole story from the *Shawnee* now, what the circumstances are, that the *Mingo* or 6 *Nations* are responsible for the whole war, they had stirred up the *Mingo* among them and those in turn the *Shawnee.* They would also be glad to be free of the *Mingo* who were living with them because they were misleading their people, but they were afraid to order them to leave.[506]

502. Up till now the singing hour had been only in the evenings; the singing school was a new institution.

503. Matt. 28:19–20.

504. Festival of the choir of the married couples.

505. The texts from 9 to 11 Sept. 1774 were 1 Tim. 2:8 (9 Sept.); Eph. 6:4 (10 Sept.); Mark 10:14 (11 Sept.).

506. Zeisberger's report is confirmed in its essential points by the diary of Prevost: "18th September. Captain Pipe sent to the Shawnese with a speech returned to Colo. Croghan's The Shawanese are willing to make restitution as soon as they are permitted to go out ahunting" (Wainwright, "Turmoil at Pittsburgh," 140). To interpret this result of the negotiations is difficult: on the one hand it is supported by the widespread conviction that the Mingo were the single most important destabilizing factor in the region. This conviction had often prompted the Six Indian Nations—and the last time had been only days away (see entry for 28 Aug. 1774)—to ask the Mingo to return to the tribal regions of the Six Indian Nations. The Shawnee had repeated this request. The results of the negotiations are, at least according to Zeisberger's diary but also according to other sources (see *DHDW,* 102–88), substantiated by the fact that since the end of July the war activities of the Shawnee had declined drastically. After the destruction of the upper Shawnee settlements on 2 August, Zeisberger himself reported, with one exception, no new incidents. Yet beginning in the second half of September

The Lord has helped us this far and will continue to help us, because He alone is our hope. Otherwise we have none. We join all our people in greeting all the congregations very sincerely and we commend ourselves to their remembrance before the Savior.

Diary of Schoenbrunn on the Mushkingum From September 13, 1774 until the end of February 1775[507]

SEPTEMBER 13TH   An Indian from *Kaskaskunk* passed through here as a messenger to *Gekelemukpechünk*. He brought us the news that the *Virginians* in *Pittsburgh* had killed two more *Delaware* Indians. The Indians in *Kaskaskunk* were apparently very upset and wanted to take revenge, but the matter was later worked out with the Indians and resolved.[508]

---

reports of Shawnee attacks again increased. In light of these developments the question asked by representatives of Pennsylvania—why Lord Dunmore planned, and in October–November executed, a large-scale expedition against the Shawnee—is understandable (see Smith, *St. Clair Papers*, 1:341–42). It is possible that the answer is contained in a circular of Colonel William Preston dated 20 July 1774 and addressed to potential volunteers for an expedition against the Shawnee: "it appears reasonable, we should turn out cheerfully On the present Occasion in Defence of our Lives and Properties, which have been so long exposed to the Savages; in which they have had too great Success in taking away [sic]. We may Perhaps never have so fair an Opportunity of reducing our old Inveterate Enemies to Reason, if this should by any means be neglected . . . it will be the only Method of Settling a lasting Peace with all the Indians Tribes Around us. . . . This useless People may now a[t] last be Oblidged to abandon their Count[r]ly Theire Towns may be plundered & Burned, Their Cornfields Distroyed; & they Distressed in such a manner as will prevent them from giving us any future Trouble" (*DHDW*, 91–93). Prevost confirmed that this was the conviction of leading Virginia politicians. In his diary, immediately after the arrival of Dunmore in Pittsburgh, he noted: "This instant the Deputy Agent of Indian Affairs & Mr. Ross are come from the Fort. They seem to think that Conolly has so far succeeded with his Lordship as to lead him to adopt his measures & ways of thinking with respect to the Shawanese, that that nation had a long time since maltreated the Virginians, that the latter had never scourged them for it, & that now he was come with the troops of that Province to chastise them" (Wainwright, "Turmoil at Pittsburgh," 131). This opinion was shared by neither the Delaware nor the Six Indian Nations. This is confirmed by the mediation of the Delaware and by the remark Prevost added to his former entry: "The Deputy Agent acquainted him that there were deputys from the Delawarres, Mingos, & Six Nations come *to intercede in behalf of the Shawnese*" (Wainwright, "Turmoil at Pittsburgh," 131, emphasis added). Prevost's remarks clearly prove that Dunmore himself pursued a middle course between the extreme policies of Connolly and the policy of pacification followed by Pennsylvania, the Delaware, and the Six Indian Nations (Wainwright, "Turmoil at Pittsburgh," 142–43).

507. MAB, B 141, F 6, I 1, fol. 85.

508. On 4 September 1774 Aeneas Mackay reported to Arthur St. Clair from Pittsburgh: "On my return to this place, last Friday evening, I received the disagreeable information of two friendly Delaware Indians being massacred on their way from this place to Mr. Croghan's, in cool blood, by notorious villains that premeditated the matter before hand, and stationed themselves behind brush near the roadside upon the occasion. It is impossible to discover the murderers at this time, and much more so to bring them to condign punishment, because they have all the force and power the place can afford in their favor." Clearly Mackay was convinced that the perpetrators were to be found among the supporters of Virginia. Smith, *St. Clair Papers*, 1:343–44; for a similar opinion, see entry for 3 Sept. 1774 in the diary of Augustine Prevost, in Wainwright, "Turmoil at Pittsburgh," 127.

THE 14TH   Brothers *Hekewalder* [*sic*] and *Johannes*[509] and a couple other Indians left from *Gnadenhütten* for Bethlehem via *Great Island*. We accompanied them with our prayers and blessings and commended them to the Savior's protection and to his dear angels. The two *Captains Pipe* and *Winginund,* who had gone to the *Shawnee* on business and held a council with them, left for *Pittsburgh* via *Kaskaskunk*.[510] The wife of the former had stayed here during his journey to the *Shawnee*. She really liked it here, and when she left she said she hoped she could come again soon. She enjoys hearing about the Savior.

THE 17TH   We partook most blessedly in the Lord's Body and Blood in Holy Communion. *Noah* and *Henriette* joined us in partaking for the first time. 3 Brothers and Sisters watched for the first time and one for the second time.

THE 18TH   In the morning, after the *Liturgy* for Holy Communion, we had the sermon. During the Children's Service the baby boy born to Brother *Thomas* and Sister *Sabina* on April 23 this year was baptized with the name *Johannes*. The parents had been baptized 8 days ago.

THE 19TH   A poor widow with 3 children received permission to stay here for a probationary period, after persistent requests. However, *Levi,* who had done much harm here, was told to stay away from our town in the future.

THE 24TH   Some Sisters went to *Gnadenhütten*, and Brother *Johann Jungmann* came from there for a visit. We heard that another party of *Shawnee* had returned with *Scalps* and some prisoners, and that they were not yet planning to make peace.[511]

THE 26TH   *Traders* from *Attike*[512] arrived here with some goods to trade. This was good for our Indian Brothers and Sisters because they were not well supplied and they needed some things. The *Traders* did not go any further than here because they did not dare to at this time. They also brought along the news that the *Shawnee* had been murdering again, and also that *Gouverneur Don Moore* from *Virginia* had arrived in *Pittsburgh*.[513]

509. I.e., Johannes Papunhank

510. This can only refer to the Council meeting in which both Jacob and Augustinus participated for the mission congregations, the resolutions of which were reported under the date 12 Sept. 1774. Captain Pipe (d. after 1823), Indian name Kogeshquanohel, led as successor of Packanke, who nevertheless participated as chief in the conference at Pittsburgh in early September (see entry for 26 Sept. 1774, note 513). The Wolf clan's captain, Winginund (d. 1791), lived in the settlement Kinhanschican on the Scioto, close to the settlements of the Shawnee. Although friendlier in his attitude to the mission congregations, he nevertheless stuck to the policies of Captain Pipe.

511. Reports of Indian attacks are contained in letters from Arthur Campbell to Colonel William Preston dated 9 and 17 Sept. 1774, *DHDW*, 192–94, 202–5.

512. See entry for 26 Aug. 1774, note 497.

513. John Murray (1732–1809), fourth earl of Dunmore, and Lord Dunmore, governor, had arrived at Pittsburgh on the evening of 10 September 1774 (Wainwright, "Turmoil at Pittsburgh," 131); on 12 September he met the representatives of the Delaware, White Eye and Packanke, as well as those of the Six Indian Nations. On this occasion White Eyes shared his assessment of the nature of the conflict between the Shawnee and Virginia with the governor; on 17 September Dunmore responded to the chiefs' speeches (ibid., 134–35, 138–39, and *AA*, 4th series, 1:872–74). On the same day Dunmore published a proclamation in which he claimed the region around Pittsburgh for

THE 28TH   The *Shawnee* and *Mingo* who had passed through here with *Scalp*s this summer[514] returned from *Onondago*. However, they had not received what they expected, because they had hoped to get assistance from the 6 *Nations* against the *Virginians*. The council in *Onondago* had told them they should remain quiet and abandon their warlike thoughts. Next spring they would come to them and discuss this further with them. Presumably the 6 *Nations* will tell them that the land on the *Canahawa* has been sold and the *Virginians* therefore have the right to settle it. The Indians also believe this.[515]

THE 29TH   In the evening devotions we discussed the service the dear angels provide for us and for all those who will inherit salvation. We have indeed experienced this in rich measure in these dangerous times. We sang our childlike *Gratias* to the Savior for this.

October

THE 1ST   During the early service we warmly reminded the Brothers and Sisters the fact that a relationship with the Savior is the only necessary thing. Through this we become closer to Him in many ways and our inner person grows and deepens.

Jacob Gendaskund went to *Gekelemukpechünk* so he could join some Indians there who are going on to *Hochhocküng*[516] to talk with the *Shawnee* again. He asked to be excused, however, so he returned on THE 3RD with the news that the *Shawnee* were very angry. They did not want to listen to any more explanations or suggestions for peace. They also did not want to allow the *Delaware* in *Assününk*, and those who live close to them and want to come here, to leave them. They are threatening to kill them if they run away. They also wanted to attack those in *Gekelemukpechünk* and both of our *Towns* and kill everyone be-

---

the jurisdiction of Virginia (*AA*, 4th series, 1:790–91). At a new conference between the representatives of the Delaware and the Six Indian Nations after the arrival of Captain Pipe and Winginund in Pittsburgh, Pipe and Winginund reported the results of their talks with the Shawnee. See entry for 12 Sept. 1774, note 506, and *AA*, 4th series, 1:874–76.

514. See entry for 7 July 1774.

515. Under the treaty of Fort Stanwix of 1768, the Six Indian Nations had ceded the region of Kentucky to the colonies. The Delaware had accepted the treaty, but the Shawnee refused to acknowledge it. On the general issue involved, see Introduction, pp. 8–9.

516. This is a settlement on the Hocking River close to Assünnünk that had originally been inhabited by Delaware but was now peopled by Shawnee. Christopher Gist had visited it on 19 January 1751; he described it as "a small town with only four or five Delaware Families" (Mulkearn, *George Mercer Papers*, 105, 495). The place is not mentioned in the map of Cappon et al., *Atlas of Early American History*, 80; the settlement spelled "Hockhocking" is mentioned as the central meeting place for the militia of Virginia. See Arthur St. Clair to Governor Penn, 2 Nov. 1774, Smith, *St. Clair Papers*, 1:345.

cause we were on the side of the *Virginians*.[517] The *Chiefs* and all the Indians are very frightened about this and are calling all their people together. The *Chief* and *Captain White Eye* also sent us word not to let our people go out hunting and to call those who were out to come home quickly. They should stay together until we really know that there is peace.

Captain White Eye once again spoke very confidently and frankly to the Indians in a public council meeting, which our *Jacob* also attended. He told them he did not see how they could become a happy and peaceful people. No matter where he turned among the Indians, he could not find anything good or anything that could bring spiritual happiness. This could be found among the Brothers, however. If they resolved to accept God's word, they would enjoy only good things from this. This talk once again was referring to our *Belt*,[518] which votes had not yet accepted. *Jacob* said that all the people accompanied his talk with a general *Shout* and *Kehella*[519] as had never happened before. *Nathanael Davis* returned from *Pittsburgh* where he had been on business. Near *Sakunk* he had met the *Gouverneur* of *Virginia* with 2,500 men and 150 *Battows* on their *march* to the *Shawnee*.[520] The *Gouverneur* was very happy to see one of our Indians, as *Mr. Gibson* who was with him told him, and he greeted *Nathanael* very cordially.

We also learned from *Gekelemukpechünk* that another party of *Shawnee* and *Mingo* have returned with *Scalps* and prisoners.[521]

THE 4TH   We sent messengers to various places in the bush to call our people home, and some arrived early on the following day. Others, however, whom we did not know how to find, became so restless that they could no longer stay away and therefore hurried home. Later they thanked the dear Savior that they had followed their intuition.

THE 6TH   We received 2 messages from the *Shawnee* via *Gekelemukpechünk* and *Gnadenhütten* to send on to *Kaskaskunk*. The first, which came with a *String of Wampum* from the *Shawnee Chief*, indicated that they would keep the

517. The Shawnee's change of mind is surprising, for as late as 18 September 1774 Captain Pipe had reported that the Shawnee were willing to keep the peace (see entry for 12 Sept. 1774, note 506). The new attitude can be explained by the fact that in the meantime the Shawnee had heard that Virginia was massing troops in the region and that Lord Dunmore had refused any concessions in his speech of 17 September 1774.

518. See entry for 23 June 1774.

519. "Kehella" means "yes" and was generally used as a shout signifying consent. Zeisberger, *Delaware Indian and English Spelling Book,* 18.

520. On Sakunk, see entry for 14 April 1772, note 4. The numbers basically agree with those Lord Dunmore stated in his official report to the English government. Dunmore to Earl of Dartmouth, 24 Dec. 1774, Davies, *Documents of the American Revolution,* 8:261. "Battows" is a perversion of the French *bateaux,* i.e., riverboats with a flat keel.

521. According to reports from commanding officers of the Virginia militia, Shawnee attacks on white settlements in areas settled from Virginia increased significantly in mid-September. *DHDW,* 205–12, 226–36.

peace which their grandfather had made with the *Pennsylvanians* in olden days and advised their grandfather to remain in this and stand firm. A second *String* from the *Shawnee Captains* indicated that because the *Virginians* were gathering in great numbers at the big *Canhawa*, they were prepared to meet them with all their warriors and would engage in a battle wherever they met them. This was *Colonel Lewis*,[522] who was coming down the *Canhawa* with 1,200 men to join *Gouverneur Don Moore*. We hoped and prayed that *Captain White Eye* might still prevent the *Shawnee* from carrying out their plan, since he is traveling to see them and had met these messengers on the way.[523]

THE 9TH　Brother *Jungmann* preached the sermon and in the afternoon those who have been baptized had a blessed service. We heard from *Kaskaskunk* as well as from this area that things seemed very uneasy among the Indians, because many of them can hardly watch and just be observers while the *Shawnee* are left alone.

THE 10TH　The comforting Watchword, which the Unity Elders' *Conference* had drawn for us,[524] was the object of our reflection in the early service. With praise and gratitude to our dear Lord, we acknowledged what He has done for us in this area and everywhere, and with faithful hearts we look ahead to the complete fulfillment of this.

THE 11TH　Brother *David* went to *Gnadenhütten* and returned in the evening. Once again we received news that 600 *Shawnee* had gone to meet the *Virginians* to engage them in a battle. The *Delaware* and the *Wyandot* had sent messengers after them to stop them. They had actually caught up with them and found them just as they were getting ready to cook *Beson* (their warrior *Beson*, which they use when they go into war so that they will have good fortune).[525] However, they would not be stopped. They talked big and said they did not care. If they all died and were wiped off the face of the earth, this would be better than having the *Virginians* live so close to them. As critical

---

522. Colonel Andrew Lewis.

523. At the conference at Fort Pitt between 18 and 23 September 1774 (see note 513), White Eyes, Pipe, and Winginund promised that they would join the Virginia militia at the Shawnee settlements (*AA*, 4th series, 1:872–76). The reasons for this commitment are given only indirectly in White Eyes' speech: "When the Delawares, the Six Nations, the Shawanese, and you, our elder brother, meet together, you will then see who are sincere in their friendship. In a short time it will be seen; for those who are determined on good, will not fail to meet you. I shall speak to the Shawanese, and, if their intentions are equal to their professions, they will see you." The meaning of this passage is clearer in the version of the speech reported by Prevost in his diary: "Brother, we thought you was inclined to peace. Now, if we are to act as mediators, name a place where we may depend to meet you, as the generals & great men before you was used to do, & then we will be answerable to bring you the Shawnese to treat, & subscribe to the terms you limitt, otherwise we have nothing to say." Wainwright, "Turmoil at Pittsburgh," 143.

524. Ps. 66:4; see note 280 to entry for 13 Oct. 1773. For the year 1774 the Unity's Elders' Conference in Barby had chosen the Watchword for October 10 as the special Watchword for Schönbrunn. Letter of the Unity's Elders' Conference dated 14 Jan. 1774, MAB, "Letters Received by the Provincial Helpers' Conference in General, from the Unity's Elders' Conference, 1770–1793."

525. On Beson, see notes 90 and 117.

and serious as things look once again, we still hope in our dear Lord; he alone is our comfort and does not lack means and ways to arrange everything so that we will praise and honor Him for this.

THE 12TH   We sent *Isaac* to *Gekelemukpechünk* to return a *String of Wampum* we had received yesterday from *Netawatwees* along with the request that some of our people should go on horse to help pick up the Indians from *Assünnunk*. They do not live far from the *Shawnee,* who have threatened to attack and kill them if they made any motions to leave there. However, we refused this request politely and the *Chief* took this well.

THE 16TH   Brother and Sister *Jungmann* visited *Salomo,* who had come here with his family a couple of days ago and was camping on the river.[526] He was happy about their visit and you could see that he still loves the Brothers.

In the evening *Johann Martin* came here from *Gnadenhütten* as an *express* messenger. He brought news an Indian had delivered to *Gekelemukpechünk* this morning that the *Shawnee* had skirmished with the *Virginians* at the mouth of the *Canhawa* 6 days ago. The former had to flee, however, after 50 of their men had died on the site. We later heard it was only 25, but that many men were wounded. At the same time we also heard that they were recruiting again and wanted to attack the *Virginians* once more.[527]

THE 18TH   The Watchwords today and in recent days were very encouraging and strengthening and provided us with new courage and comfort.[528] We were thus able to trust in a childlike manner that the Savior will still carry out everything gloriously and to the honor of His name so that the heathen will not mock us and say, as we have already heard and had to listen to, their God in whom they hope and in whom they trust could not help them after all. He could not save them and he was not able to accomplish the work begun in Indian country. Therefore we sighed countless pleas to the Savior to change the circumstances to the advantage of his Indian congregation, which has been denied all external help. If the Lord were not our comfort and help, then we would have to die.

THE 20TH   A baby daughter was born to Brother *Willhelm* and Sister *Martha.* She received the name *Elisabeth* in Holy Baptism.

THE 21ST   One of the Indians who was here for a visit discussed various things with *Jacob Gendaskund.* We learned from him that our *Belt,* which

526. On 9 July 1774 Salomo and his family had left the mission congregation.

527. The only battle of Lord Dunmore's war between the Virginia militia and the Shawnee was fought at Point Pleasant, above the confluence of the Ohio and Kanawha Rivers, on 10 October 1774. Reports on the number of warriors and militia soldiers who participated, and the number killed, vary. According to the official report Dunmore sent to the Earl of Dartmouth, the Virginians lost forty-nine soldiers and the Shawnee thirty warriors. Eighty Virginians were wounded, but according to Dunmore only "some" of the Shawnee. Davies, *Documents of the American Revolution,* 8:261–62; DHDW, 253–77.

528. The Watchwords for 15 to 18 October 1774 were Ps. 79:13 (15 Oct.); Ps. 92:6 (16 Oct.); Ps. 31:8 (17 Oct.); Ps. 30:12 (18 Oct.).

we submitted to the *Councel* in *Gekelemukpechünk* last summer,[529] was causing much discussion among the Indians and that many have joined *White Eye's* party. They were not satisfied with the *Chief's* behavior since he hesitated so much and did not give us an answer when after all so many were in favor of accepting the Brothers in Indian country and letting them enjoy all freedoms, as people who are seeking the best interests of the Indians. Now we will joyfully watch what the Savior will do.

THE 24TH   Brother *Schmick* came here from *Gnadenhütten* for a visit. We agreed on the necessary matters in a couple of hours and then he returned toward evening.

THE 25TH   *Maria Elisabeth, Salomon's* daughter who had left here with her parents last summer,[530] received permission to return here again. She had urgently requested and desired this.

THE 27TH   Brother *David* returned from *Gnadenhütten,* where he had gone yesterday with the Indian Brothers *Isaac, Jacob,* and *Augustinus,* whom the *Chief* in *Gekelemukpechünk* had called. In the meantime Brother and Sister *Jungmann* had had Speakings with the Brothers and Sisters in preparation for Holy Communion.

THE 29TH   Brother *David* visited old *Salomo,* who had expressed a desire to return to us. We promised to assist him in this, if he would just free himself of his bad friends who had caused us much anguish. In the evening the *Communicants* partook most blessedly of the Lord's Body and Blood in Holy Communion.

THE 30TH   In the evening we received the news that the *Gouverneur* of *Virginia* had set up his camp with his army on the *Plaine* near the *Lower Shawnee Towns,* that the *Shawnee* are engaging in negotiations with him, and that they had already agreed to carry out the main articles he had presented to them.[531] However, late in the night *Marcus* came from *Gnadenhütten* with more news. The *Virginians* had captured 60 prisoners and either captured or killed a whole *Town* of men, women and children.[532] The person who had sent this news to *Gekelemukpechünk* added finally: the *Delaware* should now come and see what has happened. The *Chief* asked some of our Indian Brothers to confer with him about this, so some of them went there during the night. However, we advised

529. See entry for 3 June 1773.

530. The exact date was 4 July 1774.

531. In the peace treaty of Camp Charlotte, the Shawnee ceded the land south of the Ohio, which permitted the settlement of Kentucky and for the next three years secured peace in this area. In addition, the Shawnee were to deliver all prisoners, horses, guns, and furs taken from traders and had to accept new trading regulations. They had to deliver hostages until all conditions of the treaty had been met. DHDW, 304–5; Dunmore's summary in his letter of 24 Dec. 1774, in Davies, *Documents of the American Revolution,* 9:262. The official text of the treaty seems to be lost. See also GD entry for 8 Nov. 1774, F 4, I 1.

532. Dunmore ordered the attack on the Mingo settlement Salt Lick Town; five Indians were killed in this attack and fourteen made prisoners. Tanner, *Indians of Ohio and Indiana,* 79–81; DHDW, 303–4.

them against going to the *Shawnee Towns* and suggested they recommend to the *Chief* that it would be better to send a messenger there and find out more about this, which they did.

November

THE 1ST   The Brothers returned from *Gekelemukpechünk*. We heard from them that the Indians there and everywhere are very agitated and most were very angry at the *Virginians* because people said all the *Shawnee* had either been captured or killed, including *White Eye*, who is with the *Gouverneur*,[533] and that the *Virginians* had already gone as far as *Assünnunk* on their *march* to the *Delaware Towns*. They would destroy them after they had finished with the *Shawnee*. Our Indian Brothers said that things would be more dangerous for us than ever if better news did not come soon; the *Chief* would not be able to control his young people any longer, especially since they all presumed that *Captain White Eye* was dead, because they had not heard from him since his departure. Another circumstance also added to our problems: the *Shawnee* and *Munsee* had always mockingly called us and those in *Gekelemukpechünk Virginians* and *Schwonnaks*.[534] The *Chief* had already sent them a message saying they should not do this any longer; after all they were all like one *Nation* and were united in an alliance. However, they were still forced to listen to this constantly, and the Indians in *Gekelemukpechünk* believed that now they not only had to endure this shame on our account but also feared the *Shawnee* might attack them and begin a war against them, as they have always threatened. Therefore they sent them a message once again and said they did not want to be called *Virginians* or *Schwonnaks*. If they were called this because the Indian believers and their teachers lived close to them in 2 *Towns*, they should know that they personally had not called them to come here; one of their unreasonable and foolish people must have done this. They should also know that they had not joined us and they would never accept God's word, much less live as we did.

The combination of all this indeed presented us with a bad *Prospect*. However, our Watchword today was, *This is the day which the LORD hath made; we*

---

533. White Eyes had joined the Virginia army as mediator between Virginia and the Shawnee, as he had announced at Pittsburgh (see note 523 above), yet he had failed in his efforts to prevent the battle at Mount Pleasant. Little more is known about White Eyes' role in the negotiations about the peace treaty than what Zeisberger reports in the entry for 5 Nov. 1774. In his report dated 24 Dec. 1774 to the Earl of Dartmouth, Dunmore remarked about White Eyes (see note 531): "The Delawares, notwithstanding, remained steady in their attachment, and their chief named Captain White Eyes offered me the assistance of himself and whole tribe; but apprehending evil effects from the jealousy of and natural dislike in our people to all Indians, I accepted only of him and two or three, and I received great service from the faithfulness, the firmness and remarkable good understanding of White Eyes." Davies, *Documents of the American Revolution*, 9:261. This description indicates that Dunmore and White Eyes differed in their understanding of White Eyes' role as mediator.

534. See note 294 to entry for 20 Oct. 1773.

will rejoice and be glad in it.[535] We believed this and therefore we were not so afraid or worried about it.

In the meantime, we saw the consequences of the *Chief's* statement about us in the message very soon, because the Indians entered our *Town* with great arrogance, made noise and shrieked with delight, which they had never done before. They told our people that very soon they would see dancing here in our *Town* and it would be no different than in their *Towns*. We had nothing here of our own, did not live on our own land, and should just clear out and go back where we had come from, along with other such things. This continued until THE 4TH when a messenger hurried here from *Gnadenhütten* with the happy news that *White Eye* had arrived in *Gekelemukpechünk* and some Indian Brothers should go there immediately for a *Councel*. This was done. Then all the strange and slovenly riff-raff hurried there to hear something new, hoping the war would now begin. We got some rest as a result, because when they returned they were very quiet and orderly.

THE 5TH   Late in the evening Brothers *Willhelm* and *Augustinus* re-turned from *Gekelemukpechünk* and brought us the happy and reliable news we had earnestly hoped for for so long, and which *Captain White Eye* had brought: there is now peace, and although it is not yet completely concluded, we can be sure there is nothing else to fear. The *Shawnee* had to surrender and were forced to agree to all the *Conditions* Lord *Don Moore* set forth. The army marched back there 7 days ago now and the *Gouverneur* took 4 *Shawnee* and 10 *Mingo* as hostages.

I will only touch upon the most remarkable aspects of this *expedition* we heard about from *White Eye*, who was present from the beginning to the end. When the *Gouverneur* set out to march with his troups from the *Ohio* to the *Shawnee Towns,* he wanted to have them march through the bush in parties at first. However, *White Eye* advised him against this and objected that if he did this, it would not look like he came to the *Shawnee* to negotiate peace with them; everywhere his people met Indians, they would immediately engage in a skirmish with each other and then it would not be possible to make peace. He was there to assist them in their peace negotiations with the *Shawnee.* However, if they wanted to march in parties, he would leave them.[536] The *Gouverneur* accepted his suggestion and they marched to the *Towns* with no obstacles except one time when they met some *Shawnee. White Eye* called to them, spoke with them, and sent them to their *Towns* to announce them and prepare for a talk with the *Gouverneur.* When they arrived there, they set up their camp on a great flat area where there are no trees, and the *Shawnee Chief*[537] soon paid the *Gouverneur* a visit and asked him what had brought him there. He replied that

---

535. Ps. 118:24.
536. See note 523 to entry for 6 Oct. 1774.
537. I.e., Cornstalk (*DHDW*, 433).

he came to see if they wanted peace or war, and he was prepared for whatever they decided. The *Chief* answered that this was not the place to negotiate peace; *Pittsburgh* was the place. He should turn around immediately. The *Gouverneur* told him he had come to get his flesh and blood, the prisoners. They should also return the stolen horses and everything they had taken from the *Traders*. The *Chief* said he was sorry he could not do this because the things he demanded were no longer all available, and he said once again he should turn around. Then the *Gouverneur* replied that he should hand over 6 of his men first. He would keep them until they made arrangements to do what he asked of them. Then he would turn around. The *Chief* then went home to confer with his people and returned with even more men the next day. Then they began to speak very nicely and tried to apologize politely. They said they were not the ones who had begun the war; the White people had. They promised that as long as the sun shone and the world lasted, they would never harm the White people again. They were told that since *General Bouquet* concluded peace with the Indians in *Tuscarawi* in the previous war, they had never intended to follow it. Since that time they had continued robbing, stealing, and murdering. Then he listed all of their misdeeds in great detail, including the times and places they had committed these. Furthermore they had not surrendered the prisoners at *Bouquet*'s peace treaty, as the *Delaware* had done. Then he told them they should know now that he would not leave there until they had done everything he demanded of them, even if he had to stay there 7 months.[538] When the *Shawnee* heard this tone of talk, they went home, brought the prisoners, the stolen horses, and what they could collect of the rest of the things, and returned everything. They also promised that they would bring what they could not get now as soon as possible. The *Gouverneur* had asked the *Chief* a number of times where the *Mingo* were and why none of them had reported to him. He had always told him that he did not know where they where. However, now the *Gouverneur* insisted that he wanted to know and asked him why they dealt in lies, when they lived with them. When he then learned that they lived together not far away in one *Town*, he immediately sent several hundred men there, without the *Shawnee* knowing it, because they were in the middle of the camp and the 400 men were not missed. They surrounded the *Town*, captured men, women and children and brought them to the camp. Three *Mingo* were killed, however, because they tried to defend themselves at first.[539] The leader of the *Mingo* was soon humbled when the *Gouverneur* addressed him, and knew of no way to excuse himself for carrying out the hostilities other than saying that an

538. At the end of Pontiac's War, General Henry Bouquet conducted peace negotiations with the Indian tribes of the Ohio region during the second half of October 1764. On that occasion the Delaware and Mingo delivered their prisoners, but the Shawnee did not (see note 85 to entry for 17 Oct. 1772 and note 287 to entry for 18 Oct. 1773). The agreement between Bouquet and the tribes is printed in Stevens Kent, and Waddell, *Papers of Colonel Henry Bouquet*, 25:251.

539. See Crawford's report in Butterfield, *Washington-Crawford Letters*, 54–56.

evil spirit had made him do this, Satan was the cause of all evil. Both the *Shawnee* and the *Mingo* promised that from now on they would refrain from their evil deeds. As long as the world existed they would not do this any more, and they called upon God as their witness that they were speaking the truth.[540] The *Gouverneur* answered the *Minque Chief:* because such an evil spirit lives in you, who as you say tempted you to do evil, I will arrest you. You will not escape my hands. The men had to be arrested therefore, but the women and children were released at the repeated request of *Captain White Eye.*

In his talk to the *Shawnee* the *Gouverneur* praised the *Delaware* and told them that He and the *Delaware* were joined in one body. Whoever offended them, offended him, and if he should hear that one of the *Nations* harmed them, then he would seek revenge. The *Shawnee* should thank their grandfather that they had not been destroyed already this summer, because he did not want to stain his Brother's land with blood and he would not treat them so harshly because they were his *Grand Children.* Therefore they should show their gratitude to their grandfather, live peacefully with him, and follow his example. The *Delaware* in *Gekelemukpechünk* had surely not earned this praise, because as long as the negotiations had lasted terrible lies had been spread among the Indians about how the *Virginians* were liars, that they pretended they came to make peace, but would destroy and wipe out the Indians. The *Chief* in *Gekelemukpechünk* himself had spoken against *White Eye* and said he was on the *Virginia*ns' side and would bring them all bad luck. This and similar things reached the ears of the *Shawnee.* During his stay there, they confronted *White Eye* with all that his *Nation* accused him of and at the same time told him if they had him alone, he would soon be a dead man.[541]

He had related all the events and his negotiations during his absence, and the *Chief* and all the Indians were very pleased with this and expressed their satisfaction and pleasure with his *expedition.* He had certainly earned honor and was worthy of this, because he had been busy with this all summer and had endured much. He had traveled constantly between here and *Pittsburgh* and the *Shawnee* and had not been deterred by any trouble. Now in the presence of the entire people he replied to everything he had heard about himself during his absence, both while he was with the *Shawnee* and among the *Delaware* on his return journey, and how only bad things were said about him. He expressed his displeasure over one thing in particular, however, the message the *Chief* had sent to the *Shawnee* some days ago[542] which had reached his hands on the road and which he brought back with him before it reached its destination. In this

540. Others report that on this occasion Chief John Logan made a speech in which he declared that the attack of 30 April 1774 had been the motive for his behavior during the war. *DHDW*, 305–6; *AA*, 4th series, 1:1020.

541. See entries for 1 Oct. and 1 Nov. 1774 for the accusations and reproaches the Shawnee leveled against the Delaware and for the meaning of the term "Schwonnack."

542. See entry for 1 Nov. 1774.

there were 2 points, the first of which was dangerous for the *Delaware Nation* in general and the 2nd for us. 1) The *Chief* asks why he was called a *Schwonnak* or *Virginian,* since he himself had put 20 hatchets in peoples' heads (that means that so many Indians had been killed by White people since the last peace treaty; therefore it is easy to guess the interpretation of this. How can it be possible that we are in such perfect agreement and alliance with the White people?)

2) If they were called *Schwonnaks* or *Virginians* because the Indian believers had set up their night camp with their people on the *Gekelemukpechünk Creek* (that means: they are not staying here permanently, do not belong there, and also will not stay there long) then they should know that they do not listen to us and would never accept God's word. In reference to the first point, *White Eye* said that this was not the *Chief's* business. He had overstepped the line, because as *Captain,* this was *White Eye's* business and no one had the power or authority to send such a message except for him, because the hatchet (that is war) was associated with this.[543] Furthermore he had already acted very foolishly, because surely he knew that they were currently involved in peace negotiations with the *Shawnee.* However, regarding the 2nd point, he had been more than a little shocked, indeed very distressed that the *Chief* said they would never accept God's word. He continued, I have worked this whole summer so that peace might be restored. I invested my physical powers and health, my mind and understanding in this and I did all that was within my power to bring this about so that our people, men, women and children could sit peacefully beside their fire and would not always need to spend their time in fear and mortal danger, as we experienced to some extent this summer. During this my attention was primarily focused on this: if calm and peace were restored externally, we would then concern ourselves with the one necessity, which is so necessary for all of us, that we might also enjoy God's peace in our hearts. My intention was that we would make better use of the precious word of God, which He had sent to us, than we had previously done. We would admonish our young people and lead them by good example for their own good, because I do not see how we can be a happy and peaceful people and how our hearts can be well, until we accept God's word.

This was what I was working for the entire summer, and because I was already looking forward to this, I did not mind any efforts and paid no atten-

543. The differences between the functions and duties of both offices were clear: in peacetime Netawatwees was the highest chief, while White Eyes, Pipe, and Winginund were captains and chiefs only in wartime. In matters that concerned the war only they could speak for the tribe and send out messages. For a parallel case, see the two messages of the Shawnee in entry for 6 Oct. 1774. On 5 January 1774, during a conference with the Six Indian Nations at Johnson Hall close to Albany, New York, George Croghan had announced the deposition of Packanke (Custaloga) and declared Captain Pipe his successor; similarly he had announced the deposition of Netawatwees and declared Captain White Eyes (Grey Eyes) his successor (*JP,* 12:1047–48). Neither Zeisberger nor (as this passage demonstrates) White Eyes had any doubts that Netawatwees was still the chief of the Delaware.

tion to difficulties. I did everything joyfully in the good hope of reaching my goal. We just received hope that peace will be restored, although it is not yet completed. However, before I could return here I had already received the news that you never want to accept God's word. This causes me the most sorrow because I realize that all of the efforts and work are in vain, and with this he broke down in tears in front of the whole assembly and had to step back, because he could not say another word for crying. Some of our Indian Brothers, *Isaac, Jacob*, etc. accompanied his tears with theirs. After a while, when he had collected himself again, he laid the *Belt* with the above message at the *Chief's* feet and said that since they had done this, he wanted to remove himself from everything and have nothing more to do with the *Chief's Affairs*. With this he left the meeting. He later sent Brothers *Isaac* and *Petrus* to the *Chief* with a *Belt of Wampum* and sent word that he should now look for another man to assist him in his place. Herewith he freed himself from him completely, because he saw that all of his work was in vain. The *Chief* and all the Indians were very upset about this. Because they did not think they were able to reconcile these 2 great leaders and did not even know how they should go about this, they asked our Brothers to mediate, to advise them, and do their best to make things right again. They did as much as they could for now and encouraged negotiations between them by carrying messages back and forth. The following day the *Chief* sent a *String of Wampum* to *White Eye* through the Brothers and sent word that he should not take what he had done so hard and seriously. He had not meant it badly and also did not mean to affront or offend him. He would be very sorry if they were at odds with each other. He should forgive him for everything and forget it. They would be and remain good friends. *White Eye* told the Brothers that what the *Chief* said was well enough, but he wanted to make him think about the real matter and reflect. He wanted to teach him something. If he were reasonable, he would figure out what he meant. If not, then he was not capable of being *Chief*. He then sent the *String of Wampum* back along with the reply that he was glad to hear his words. He was pleased with them for the most part, and he himself would gladly forgive and even forget what concerned him, for example that an attack had been made on his office, all sorts of bad things said, and that he had been slandered by both the *Shawnee* and his *Nation*. However, this was not his main concern. His greatest distress, rather, was that the *Chief* had declared in the message that they despised God's word and would not accept it in eternity (they used this expression). He was inconsolable over this; it had so wounded his heart that it was *incurable* until they convinced him of something better. He also gave Brothers *Isaac* and *Petrus* instructions to provide the *Chief* further interpretations and explanations about his desire and request. God had sent the Gospel to them through the Brothers, and they had considered it something great that they had been so honored, so his desire and wish was that the Brothers and their Indians who have accepted God's word and become believers should have freedom of conscience in Indian country. They should be their own people and live separately. Anyone who wanted to accept God's word and become a believer should have the freedom to do so. The nonbelievers should also live separately, but not hinder the believers in any way, and see them as their friends who share a bond as one *Nation*. However, when the Brothers brought these words to *Netawatwees* and explained to him what *Captain White Eye* meant by this, he made harsh accusations against our Indians. One of the main points in this was that we had the *Mattapassican* (the poison)[544] among us, that we took in such bad people and sorcerers, protected them, and when they lived with us they were considered believers and were respected. He was right that such Indians had come to us.[545] However, he lacked the understanding and knowledge that people like this could also convert if they renounced Satan, with all of his essence and black magic. In conclusion the *Chief* told the Brothers that he would have to straighten out the matter of the land with the *Wyandot* before their proposal regarding the Indian believers could be carried out. Many *Belts of Wampum* were required as a sign of gratitude and acknowledgement of the land they had given the *Delaware*. They could not do this earlier because there were too few of them. This was why they had called the Indians, and particularly the *Chiefs* from *Susquehanna,* to come here and it was also one reason they had invited our Indians here. All the Indians, not just we, should agree to this so that when it gets to that point we will be ready. This will surely work itself out now and be handed to us, since we really do contribute to this, and then we can insist that the Chief designate a particular *District* of land for our *Settlements* and where our Indians could hunt. This would be for the Indian believers alone, so that other people who would only bother us could not settle all around us as had always been the case before. The point of the whole matter is the same as we had already requested from *Packanke* in 1770 in *Kaskaskunk,* which we brought up again this summer, as was mentioned on *June* 23rd. The only difference now is that it will be done much more completely, because at that time we did not dare to ask for what is going to be done now. Our request would have been completely rejected at that time. We had realized before that all of our efforts and explanations were in vain, and in our earlier relationship with him we could not survive with our Indian congregation in Indian country. I often remembered and comforted myself with the knowledge that the Savior's kingdom is a kingdom of the cross and his work continues under oppression and opposition, but even so, it cannot continue like this in the long term because we will always increase. We sit like the bird on the branch, with no certain or lasting home, and the longer we are constantly restless and fleeting, the more difficult it becomes. When his time comes, the Savior will indeed

544. On Mattapassican or "Machtapassican," see entries for 31 May, 1, 3, and 25 June, and 11 Sept. 1773.
545. Zeisberger was thinking of Salomo (see entry for 25 June 1773) or of the old woman from Tuscarawi (see entry for 11 Sept. 1773).

grant this and provide the Unity of the Brothers peace and freedom among the Indians. He himself will awaken people from among them for this purpose, just as *White Eye* has already made a good beginning. We pray for the Savior's protection and support for him in this.

It becomes increasingly clear how the *Chiefs* were claiming false pretexts and being deceptive when they decided to call our Indians here from the *Susquehanna*. *Netawatwees* told *Petrus* from *Gnadenhütten* to his face in a public council meeting that he and *Jacob Gendaskund*[546] were there in person, that they had voted to call the Indian believers here and said that after they were here with their teachers and had settled in, they would chase their teachers away. If they would not go, they would kill them. Then they would be able to subdue the Indian believers. Neither *Petrus* nor *Jacob* denied this, but admitted it was true. However, at that time they had not understood things any better, they had been blind. But now, said the *Chief,* you yourselves have joined them and you have not yet told me, It is now time to chase their teachers away, and I have been waiting for this. They set a trap for us and they themselves fell into it. They wanted to deceive us and catch us with tricks, but they themselves were caught. They would like to have chased us White Brothers and Sisters away a long time ago, but they realized they would not be better off if they did this, because they feared that our Indians would also leave then. This would cause more than a little commotion among other *Nations* as well. Indeed, they would be shamed when they saw that other *Nations* received us. We have no reason to doubt that if we turned to the *Wyandot,* who live closest to us, they would gladly clear a *District* of land for us. We even have indications of this, because the *Wyandot* were not pleased that the *Chief* here had not informed them first that the Indian believers were moving here. They said they knew well what they were like; they must live alone and not among the savages. Therefore they would have sought a better and more suitable area for them. That is probably enough about that now. I have gone on about this matter at some length, and I will try to make up for this with brevity in other places.

THE 6TH   In the morning was the sermon which Brother *Jungmann* preached. In the afternoon the Brother who had returned from *Gekelemukpech-ünk* informed our people of the happy news of peace, and they expressed their sincere joy and interest.

In the Congregational Service about today's text, God is faithful, who will not suffer you to be tempted above that ye are able; but will with the temptation also make a way to escape, that ye may be able to bear it. The burden that is laid upon us poor little worms is measured. That what would be too much will not dare to come too close to us, He knows what we can bear.[547] We

---

546. Petrus, before his baptism Echpalawehund, as well as Jacob, Indian name Gendaskund, had been captains before their baptisms on 24 December 1770 and as such had been members of the central Council of the Delaware.

547. I Cor. 10:13; *Das kleine Brüder-Gesang-Buch,* hymn no. 847.

remembered with tender and melted hearts the faithfulness and merciful protection of our dear Lord, which has hovered above us during all need and danger. With shame and humility we must acknowledge and praise Him: He has not allowed trouble and temptation beyond our capabilities to overcome us. He surely knew what we could bear. And indeed we have reached the peak now, because we saw clearly that if this *expedition* to the *Shawnee* did not turn out well, things would have looked bad for us. Then we would have experienced and felt the power of Satan, of which we had already received a number of tokens and previews. Then He, who does as He pleases in heaven and on earth, commanded Satan, You should go this far, and no further. That is enough now! And with that the air was cleared and the heavy, oppressive feeling we had experienced despite all confidence and childlike trust in the Savior, disappeared. How could we praise Him and thank Him adequately for this? Our tongues are too few and even if every beat of our heart were an expression of gratitude and every breath a song of praise, it would not suffice.

THE 8TH   *Isaac* returned from *Gekelemukpechünk*. He and *Petrus Echpalawehund* had done as much as possible in the matter between *White Eye* and the *Chief*. However, things remained unresolved because *White Eye* will not give in until the *Chief* accepts his suggestions.

THE 12TH   We were very joyful and grateful when Brothers *Johann Heckewalder* and *Johannes* returned from Bethlehem.[548] More than 8 days ago we had heard from Indians that they were returning via *Goshgoschünk*. However, they came by way of *Great Island*. We were powerfully strengthened and refreshed through letters and news, from which we saw and felt the compassionate and motherly heart of the dear Unity toward us as her members.[549]

THE 13TH   We worshipped our dear Lord and Chief Elder in the dust with our baptized Brothers and Sisters, asked for his merciful *Absolution* for all of our mistakes and faults, thanked Him for his special guidance and protection, and dedicated ourselves to Him anew to be his property with body and soul. During this He let us feel his peace in a very blessed manner. We extended greetings from Bethlehem and other congregations to the Brothers and Sisters, assured them of their sincere love and participation in our joy and suffering. We also read a letter from Brother *Ettwein* to the Indian congregation here and

548. They had left Schönbrunn on 14 September 1774.
549. They brought a letter dated 14 May 1774 from John Ettwein to the missionaries. In this letter Ettwein addressed the tensions between Roth and Zeisberger on the one hand and Roth and Schmick on the other: "David has now broken with him completely and Schmick's breach with Roth happened a long time ago. They bitterly complain about how he is dominating the Indians and about his rigor in his behavior. Brother David wrote: 'The Indian brothers and sisters cannot stand him and have no heart for him; with his behavior he has lost all credit with them.' Roth would accept no resolves except those he had taken. As a solution, the Mission Conference has therefore decided to reallocate Roth; one possibility would be the beginning of a new mission settlement on Lake Erie which would be assigned to Roth. Beyond that Ettwein discussed and approved the proposals to intensify contacts with the northwestern tribes and the Cherokee." MAB, E.P., B 965, F 42, no. 1043. The Roths had started their journey to Bethlehem on 27 May 1774.

in *Gnadenhütten,* which really delighted them.[550] Yesterday *White Eye* and other Indians also came here from *Gekelemukpechünk* for a visit.

THE 14TH   An *Onandaga* Indian, Brother David's uncle,[551] the natural brother of the man who died several years ago in Bethlehem, came here a couple of days ago, visited us with his wife today, and asked urgently for permission to live with us. They came to *Goshgoschünk* 5 years ago, where they had also attended our services a number of times. Even then they had wanted to move to our place, but they had hesitations because of their children, who would not want to or be able to live as we did. Then when we went to *Kaskaskunk,*[552] they followed us with the *Intention* of coming to us. However, when they got to *Pittsburgh,* the *Shawnee Chief* persuaded them to go with him. Then they lived among the *Shawnee* for 2 years. During that time they always planned to come to us, but they did not see how they could work this out because people there did not want to let them go. Then recently, during the unrest among the *Shawnee,* fear and terror drove them away and they left there in the dead of the night, leaving all their food behind. Because they were afraid people might set out after them, they did not stay on the road but fled through the bush until they came to the *Delaware Towns,* where everyone offered to let them stay with them. They refused this, however, and never said where they wanted to go until they got here. They told us this and were happy that they had arrived here, and hoped we would not turn them away. We told them about our situation and that no one could live here who was not concerned about the Savior and his salvation. They answered that they already knew this. This was precisely why they had come, because they had spent the 5 years since they were here on the *Ohio* in great uneasiness about their hearts. Therefore on THE 15TH we considered their situation with our Helpers. *White Eye* was here, so we called him into our *Conference* and heard his thoughts about this as well and asked him primarily if we might have difficulties with their *Nation* or the *Mingo* in this area on their account. We found no hesitations, so some Brothers went to them and had a thorough talk with them. They told them about our rules and that anyone who did not want to submit to these must not be annoyed if we sent them away. They did not let this deter them, however, but continued asking even more insistently for us to take them in.

We had a good opportunity, now, so we had a thorough talk with *White Eye* for once and shared information about our congregational rules with him. We read these out loud to him and adequately explained the reason for everything, because he had heard much said against us among the Indians, for

550. Possibly the same as the undated letter "An die lieben Indianer-Brüder in Gnadenhütten," MAB, E.P., no. 964.

551. During a mission journey to the Iroquois in May and June 1745, Zeisberger, Spangenberg, and Schebosch had been adopted by the Indians, and Zeisberger had been accepted into the Onondaga tribe.

552. In 1770 the mission settlement Langundoutenünk had been founded close to Kaskaskunk.

example that we often sent people away. This happened when they did not behave according to our rules. He understood everything and received it very well. We especially testified to him that the Brother's work among the Indians was not the work of humans, but was God's work; if it were the work of humans it could not last. However, if it were from God, it would not only last but would increase with time. It would also spread among other *Nations,* because what we now saw with our eyes was just the beginning. This really pleased him and he was quite happy about it, because it is very important to him that the Gospel be extended among the Indians everywhere. He was going to the *Fort,* so he told our Indian Brothers that they should not be worried or fearful in his absence. They should not pay attention if they heard all sorts of bad things. On THE 16TH he visited Brother *David* alone, and he clearly explained his *Affairs* to him and what his intentions were among the Indians. He did not want to do this yesterday in the presence of our Indians. His *Intention* was to arrange for the *Delaware Nation* to declare that they wanted to accept God's word, live in peace and friendship with the Indian believers and their teachers, and be given complete freedom. At this, Brother *David* told him that if they wanted to accept God's word, they should not think that they all had to become faithful and live as we do, because this could hardly happen. However, they should let the Indian believers and their teachers enjoy the same rights and privileges as they, and all the Indians should know we were privileged so that they would not put obstacles in our way. He said he already saw that many Indians were against us and said the Indian believers had no right to be here. This was because the *Chief* had said they would not accept God's word. Therefore he told him that he was separating himself from him and he would stand by this until the *Chief* agreed to what he asked. He would require this of him, and still hoped that he would agree to this. However, if he did not want to agree to this, against his expectations, then he would resign completely and leave him. He would help us, however, and support us. In this way the *Chief* would essentially be deposed.[553] His further plan was that once the primary issue was put right, then he wanted to try to see that the Indian believers received their own *District* of land, along with the other Indians. He was planning for all the Indians around us to move further away so that they would not overrun us or disturb us. He had not yet revealed his *Project* to any Indians and did not yet dare to tell them everything because they would not understand and grasp it all at once. Therefore he had to go to work quietly and just take one step at a time so that he could accomplish his goal for them without being noticed.

Finally he got around to himself, talked about his heart, and said he be-

553. Since Netawatwees as chief needed the consent of the whole Council, the abdication of White Eyes would have deprived him of the consent of White Eyes and his supporters. Such a development would have destroyed his basis for acting as chief.

lieved and was convinced in his heart that the word of the Savior we preached was the truth. He loved to hear it and he confesses that he has accepted it. He also hopes that God will provide him the grace to live according to it (at this tears stood in his eyes). Therefore he was really planning to come and live with us. However, Brother *David* advised him not to hurry, to wait patiently, and for now to remain among his people and in his affairs for the good of the people. Once he was living with us, they would no longer listen to him. After everything he was planning had been done, the Savior would also prepare the road to us for him. In the meantime he should keep us in his heart, and be assured of our love for him. Here, however, he objected that if the *Chief* stood firmly in this matter, he could not and would not stay with them but would come to our place. He told us that he believed he could do more with the Indian believers than with the nonbelievers, who had very little understanding. He regretted that he had not been at home when we first came here and said things would have been very different for us. At that time he had been making a journey down the *Ohio* and *Mississipi* and returned home by sea via *New York* and *Philadelphia*. Brother *David* visited him for the first time last year on his journey to the *Shawnee*, and sat down with him on a small hill that lies in the middle of his *Town* and discussed the Brothers' work among the Indians with him in great detail and explained it to him.[554] Since that time he had tried to get to know us better. In the evening a *Trader* who had been in the army came here from the *Shawnee*. After their retreat he had stayed with them for a while and said the *Shawnee* were now the best people. It was now much safer to be among them than ever before. They had shown him all love and kindness and proved themselves very willing to replace everything the *Traders* had lost as soon as they returned home from the fall hunt. He said they had approved of *Lord Don Moore's* treatment of them and praised it. They said they had not imagined he would be such a kind and friendly gentleman. They gave him a horse to ride and a quantity of skin for shoes for his soldiers because they thought their shoes must be pretty torn up since they had had to *march* such a long way through the bush.

THE 17TH   We granted the *Onondaga* and his family, which consists of 6 adult people, permission to move here. They responded with much joy and gratitude. The entire family was baptized on the *Mohawk River*. His name is *Thomas*, his wife *Maria*, the two sons *Nicolaus* and *Joseph* and the two daughters *Christine* and *Polly*. Because we were short on space, we cleared out our school-house for them until they can build themselves a place. More than once in the past Brother *David* had stayed in his house above *Zeninge*,[555] where they had lived on an arm of the *Susquehanna*.

554. See entry for 18 Oct. 1773.
555. Zenenge, i.e., "Shenenge"; see entry for 10 May 1773, note 191, and Tanner, *Atlas*, 75, c6.

THE 23RD   During the early service we discussed the text[556] which said that if our hearts really lived on the subject of Jesus' death and sufferings and found nourishment in this, we would be prepared in all situations to bear witness to his bloody redemption and what the blood of the wounds does for sinners.

Today and in recent days, our people went out for the fall hunt. Praise be to God they can now do this peacefully and without worrying, since many are in dire need and are absolutely in tatters because they have not been able to earn anything the entire summer. We have now received a nice supply of congregational newsletters from Bethlehem, for which we are sincerely grateful, so we are spending part of the evenings reading these for ourselves. This brings many blessings to our hearts.

THE 26TH   Brother *David* spoke with his uncle and his wife, and extolled to them the crucified Savior, who saves sinners. They listened very attentively, as did their children. We still sense little life and feeling in their hearts, but they do not miss any services and are happy to be there. He understands *Delaware* but cannot speak it. I speak *Delaware* with him because I am completely out of practice with the *Mingo* language and he speaks *Onondaga*. Still, I am gradually getting it back. All of their children are more quiet and orderly than you ever find among the Indians.

THE 27TH   It was the first of Advent and our Savior's arrival in flesh and his holy incarnation was the subject of all of the services. During this we could sense a blessed feeling of his presence.

THE 29TH   A message to the *Delaware Nation* from *Onondago* arrived here via *Pittsburgh*. It said they should keep the peace firmly and unwaveringly, and not be concerned about the *Shawnee* threats. If they should ever attack them or harm them in any way, they should just let them know. They would come and support the *Delaware*.[557] The 6 *Nations* had received news that the *Shawnee* wanted to fight the *Delaware*, whom they had always threatened. This is what led to this message. We can therefore presume the 6 *Nations* did not have a hand in the war, but the *Sennecas* probably did.[558]

556. 1 Pet. 3:15–16.

557. In early November a Great Council of the Six Indian Nations at Onondaga resolved to send a message to the Shawnee asking them to maintain peace; the protocol of this council does not mention any message to the Delaware, however (*NYCD*, 8:524–27). In his cover letter to the Earl of Dartmouth, the successor of Sir William Johnson as superintendent for Indian Affairs, Guy Johnson (1740–88), also discussed the apprehension with which the Six Indian Nations observed the worsening relations between the colonies and England (*NYCD*, 8:516–17).

558. Zeisberger's suspicion is based on the fact that the Mingo, whose settlement Salt Licks I had been attacked and destroy by the militia of Virginia (see note 532 above), as well as the hostages from that settlement, were mostly Seneca. This again prompted the Shawnee to ask the Six Indian Nations to intervene with Virginia on their and the Mingo's behalf. At the same time the Shawnee invited the Six Indian Nations to a congress to be convened in the Ohio region the following spring. The Six Indian Nations rejected both the invitation (as presumptuous on the part of a dependent tribe) and the complaint against the Mingo. The Seneca had not participated in the discussions from 20 to 28 Jan. 1775 (*NYCD*, 8:534–42).

THE 30TH   The Watchword at the beginning of this month and the one for its conclusion today were especially noteworthy to us.[559] The Savior has redeemed us from many troubles and has filled our hearts with comfort and joy. He has not disappointed our trust in Him, we can see with our eyes what we believed. Can anything like this be found on earth or in heaven? We say: No.

December

THE 1ST   Upon reading the text for today, we encouraged the Brothers and Sisters to remain faithful to the Savior until the end and to hold firmly to Him in faith even when they experienced their misery and in all external difficulties.[560] An Indian woman who was a stranger came here a few days ago to give birth. This took place successfully today. We have already had many cases like this, when Indians in this same situation, in illness, or in danger of their lives, have fled to the Brothers. They say very openly that even if they die while they are with us, they still have hope of being saved before their end. Just recently we had a case when Indians became ill on a journey. They hurried to come here and after they were here said that even if they should die, they still would have the opportunity to hear about the Savior first and to turn to Him in their distress. It may be that not much comes of this, because when people are in trouble they gladly make many promises but few keep them when it is over. Even so, we do have examples that people can be won for the Savior in such a manner and can also prosper. It is like *Captain White Eye* said to the Indians in *Gekelemukpechünk,* it will get to the point that they all call upon God's name when they are in need and will put their hope in Him.

THE 3RD   A couple of *Sennecas* who came here from *Pittsburgh* yesterday continued their journey on to the *Shawnee.* They have a message to send them. They also had a message from the 6 *Nations* to the *Mingo* living among the *Shawnee* that they should leave there and go to *Onenga,* and the sooner they do this the better.[561] The 4 *Shawnee* whom the *Gouverneur* was holding as hostages were taken to *Williamsburg* in *Virginia.* The 11 *Mingo,* however, will be kept in *Pittsburgh.* These two messengers were from them.

THE 11TH   The sermon was about the words, The poor have the gospel preached to them.[562] Most people had returned home from their hunting in the bush, along with various strangers. Brother *Heckewalder* led the Children's Service and Brother *Jungmann* the Congregational Service.

---

559. The Watchword for 30 Nov. 1774 was Ps. 116:10, and for 1 Nov. Ps. 118:24.

560. Rev. 2:10.

561. This was the message agreed on in the Council in Onondaga in early November; see note 558 to entry for 29 Nov. 1774.

562. Matt. 11:5.

THE 16TH   Yesterday and today we had Speakings with the Brothers and Sisters in preparation for the upcoming Holy Communion. During this we found many reasons to thank the Savior that his grace is not in vain in their hearts. The 8 *candidates* for Holy Communion had a separate service, accompanied by his sweet presence.

THE 17TH   *White Eye* arrived here from *Pittsburgh* with *John Montour*.[563] We were delighted to receive letters through him from Brother *Matthao* in *Litiz*. They had been lying in the *Fort* for a long time already because there was no opportunity to send them.

We heard that *Colonel Lewis* is accused of having sent only 300 men against 600 *Shawnee* in the battle in *Canhawa*. We had already heard this.[564] Some of them had to go back and get *Ammunition* because most of them had used up all their rounds. Their victory and all that resulted from it therefore cannot be attributed to their caution and skill, but to the Savior alone.[565] The entire matter with the *Shawnee* remains *status quo* until next spring or summer, when a *Treaty* is supposed to be held in *Pittsburgh*.[566] In the evening we celebrated the *Sacrament* of the Body and Blood of our Lord. One Brother participated in this high grace for the first time. One Brother and one Sister observed for the 2nd time, and 3 Brothers and 3 Sisters for the first time.

THE 19TH   Early in the day *White Eye* and *Montour* visited Brother *David*. Once again the former talked with him a lot about us and about our Indians. He told him among other things that because *Netawatwees* cannot understand the Brothers' work and thus was not planning in the best interests of the Indians, he could not be *Chief*. He has already sent a message to the 6 *Nations* about this. In favor of *Netawatwees*, Brother *David* said that he did not believe he was as responsible for this as *Killbuck* and his followers, who might make him very opposed to us and our teaching. He said further that as soon as the Indians were home, a big council would be held in *Gekelemukpechünk* primar-

563. John Montour (1744–after 1789), son of Andrew Montour and the daughter of a Delaware chief, attended an English school in Philadelphia, where he was enrolled in April 1756. Until 1775 he lived at Fort Pitt; in early October 1774 he had gone with White Eyes, whose friend he probably was, to the army of Lord Dunmore at the Great Kanawha; see notice in *Pennsylvania Magazine of History and Biography* 7 (1883): 494; Hanna, *Wilderness Trail*, 1:246, 2:80; DHDW, 302n15.

564. The rumor was true. According to the report of Colonel William Fleming, who had been wounded in the battle, after receiving a report that Indian warriors had been spotted Colonel Lewis detached "150 from Augusta line and as many from the Botetourt" under Fleming's command. These troops bore the brunt of the fighting; a skillful strategy secured them further detachments in time (DHDW, 253–54).

565. Whether it was justified to speak about a victory of the Virginia militia contemporaries considered doubtful. One of these was Guy Johnson; see his letter to the Earl of Dartmouth dated 14 Dec. 1774 (NYCD, 8:517). Considerable evidence suggests that the Shawnee simply retired in the late afternoon and did not consider themselves beaten. According to Lord Dunmore's report (see note 527 to entry for 16 Oct. 1774), the losses of the Virginia forces exceeded those of the Shawnee considerably.

566. The negotiations took place at Fort Pitt on 10 and 11 October 1775 and were parallel to but separate from the general congress (RUO, 94–105).

ily concerning us, and some of our Brothers would be called to this. Therefore we should consider this in the meantime and tell him our suggestions. Furthermore, when everything was in order and things regarding us looked like they were on the right track, he was planning to travel to England with *John Montour* and straighten out the matter of the *Delaware's* land with the King, so that no one would ever stain their land with blood and the White people would never drive them out. *Gouverneur Don Moore* had promised to assist in this plan with the King and also at the *Treaty* which would be held with the *Wyandot* soon.[567] Finally Brother *David* told him that during his previous absence, our opponents among the Indians had caused us trouble and difficulties. He would have to be absent for a pretty long time again now, so he might consider how to prevent this in the future. He promised to do this and said he would get everything on a sure footing before his departure so that no one would lay any obstacles before us. He would also put other people at the rudder.

THE 20TH   In the early service about the Watchword, His foundation is in the holy mountains,[568] Brother *Jungmann* talked about how His Unity was gathered through the work of his blood and death, founded in this, and maintained through this. Afterward *White Eye* continued his journey to *Gekelemukpechünk*. While he was here he had not missed any services and enjoyed hearing about the Savior, and upon leaving he told some of our Indian Brothers that they should remember him. He had brought along some goods, especially powder and lead, because no *Traders* were allowed out here[569] and our Indians were really in short supply. Many had had no gunpowder for a long time. He let our people here and in *Gnadenhütten* have all of it, so that they would be supplied again.

THE 21ST   Brother *David* went to *Gnadenhütten* with *John Jungmann*, who had come here a couple of days ago. He returned on THE 22ND, but his journey had been difficult because the waters were high and the *Low* country was very flooded.

THE 23RD   After the early service the children had a happy service, during which there was a blessed feeling. There were also many adults and strangers present who could not keep from crying when they heard the children singing alone so sweetly. Some of them came and told us of their spiritual

567. White Eyes pursued a double plan: on the one hand he wanted to receive a legally binding grant of territory for the Delaware similar to the "colonial grants." This would have had the advantage of security from colonial attacks—at least that is what White Eyes hoped. On the other hand, he intended to use the land grant from the Wyandot to sever the dependence on the Six Indian Nations. See White Eyes' speech to the Congress at Fort Pitt in September 1775. It seems likely that White Eyes had discussed these problems with Lord Dunmore during his stay in the camp of the Virginia army at the Great Kanawha in early October and that Dunmore had promised him assistance in bringing these two strategies to fruition.

568. Ps. 87:1.

569. The conflict between Pennsylvania and Virginia over who had jurisdiction over the Pittsburgh region reached a crisis point in December 1774. *PA,* 1st ser., 4:589.

concerns and their desire for the bath of Holy Baptism. Life and feeling is growing within the *Onondaga* family, so that they themselves do not know what is happening to them. They said they had never felt anything like that in their hearts, although they were baptized.

Seth's[570] wife, who had no feeling or life in her heart until now, told us with many tears how the Savior had entered her heart last night. All of a sudden she felt she could believe he had received the wounds in his hands and feet and in his side for the sake of her sins. She could imagine how the crown of thorns had torn and wounded his head, so that her heart was completely filled. Now, however, she really wanted to be cleansed of her sins with his blood.[571]

THE 24TH   During the Christmas Eve service, which we began with a Lovefeast, there were one hundred and fifty people present, including the guests. The story was read,[572] and we celebrated the birth and incarnation of our Savior with sweet singing and a talk about it. Then we worshipped and adored the baby in the stall and in the manger and commended ourselves to His further grace. During this He let us sense his presence in a blessed manner and he graciously revealed himself to us. In conclusion, we distributed written verses and candles to the children, and then they went home happily.

THE 25TH   In the morning Brother *Jungmann* preached the sermon about the Gospel lesson for today. In the afternoon the children had a blessed service, during which they were encouraged to give their hearts to the Savior as a gift and to surrender completely and become his own. During the Congregational Service there was a talk about the Watchword, Behold, how good and how pleasant it is for brethren to dwell together in unity etc.! How could his heart not be with us when we rejoice over his incarnation.[573]

After this 3 were joined to the congregation through Holy Communion and one was received into the congregation. One of them was the above-mentioned *Seth's* wife, who received the name *Verone* in Holy Baptism; her daughter received the name *Justina* and her husband the name *Gottfried*. The one received was *Susanna, Margreth's* daughter. This was a blessed event.

THE 26TH   In the morning was the sermon about the text, And the Word was made flesh, and dwelt among us etc.[574] In the afternoon most of the strangers who had come here to visit returned home. Some of them had been very moved and touched, as their tears testified. A little seed that will sprout in its time is indeed planted here and there. Honor and glory be to the Savior, who has shown himself anew so mercifully and powerfully among his

---

570. On 17 July 1774 Netawastond was baptized Seth; his wife was yet unbaptized.

571. This was one of the most favored images of the Moravians. At the same time this image illustrates the importance of images and metaphors in Moravian mission theology that speak to the senses; see Introduction, pp. 56–59.

572. Luke 2:1–20.

573. Ps. 133:1; hymn in *Des Evangelischen Lieder-Buches unter dem Titel Brüder-Gesang von den Tagen Henochs bisher Zweyter Band* (London, 1754), hymn no. 72, verse 33.

574. John 1:14.

Indian people after so many trials and who has revealed himself to them. May his holy name be praised!

THE 28TH   *Thomas,* the *Onondaga,* had an honest and thorough talk[575] with us and shared his whole heart with us. He has already spent a number of years in great spiritual turmoil. During this time he had reflected and searched a great deal to see where his heart would be happy, but he had never found it until he came here now and heard about the Savior's incarnation, sufferings, and death. He said, Now I believe that he shed his blood for me, a sinner, as well. I want to become His property completely. There is not a hair on my head which will not be his. He said this with tears in his eyes.

THE 31ST   During a service for the Communicant Brothers and Sisters, one Sister was absolved through the laying on of hands, during which the Savior graciously revealed himself. In our Watchnight Service, which began with a Lovefeast, we contritely and happily concluded the old year, prayed at his feet for the forgiveness of our mistakes, shortcomings, and all our misdeeds. We thanked the Savior for the many good deeds, powerful protection, and support we experienced so clearly and in such rich measure during this year. We commended ourselves anew to his faithful hands and blessed guidance, to the protection of the heavenly Father, and the care of the dear Mother. Our hearts were surrounded by God's blessed peace, which accompanied us into the New Year.

Besides the events which have already been mentioned adequately, we have the following to report about this year: more strangers visited us than ever before, not only from this area but also from distant areas, from the *Shawnee, Cherokees, Wyandot,* and *Mingo.* The Indians came here in especially large numbers on holidays such as Easter, Pentecost, and Christmas. These were days of special blessing, and many people heard the word of redemption through Jesus' blood and were blessed.

Brother and Sister *Roth* and their children left here for Bethlehem in *May.* Brother *Heckewalder* also visited there in the fall.

We partook of Holy Communion 8 times most blessedly. 4 Brothers and Sisters became participants in Holy Communion this year.

21 adults and 7 children were baptized, and one Sister was received into the congregation.

5 couples were married.

46 people, adults and their children, came to the congregation.

2 came here from *Gnadenhütten* and 3 from here went there.

6 children were born. 4 who had been baptized died.

We sent 6 people away and *Salomo* and his wife and 2 young children left on their own.

---

575. These were individual and intense discussions about the person's relation to and attitude toward Christ; see Introduction, pp. 61–63.

At the conclusion of the year the number of residents in *Schönbrunn* consists of 123 who have been baptized, including 51 communicant Brothers and Sisters, and 97 who have not been baptized, including children.

Total: 220 souls, which is 36 more than last year.

January 1775

THE 1ST   Brother *Jungmann* preached the sermon in the morning. In the afternoon first the children and then the baptized Brothers and Sisters had a service accompanied by the close presence of the Savior. We surrendered ourselves to him anew, renewed our covenant with Him to remain his property, and promised Him faithfulness and obedience. In the Congregational Service we reflected on the Watchword and text[576] for today, and then *Thomas* the *Onondaga* and his son *Nicolaus* were received into the congregation amidst many tears. Then the congregation fell down and Brother *David* prayed to the Savior of the heathen for grace for the whole little gathering, especially the two who had been received, and for God's entire work among the heathen here. He asked that the light of the wounds might break through the darkness soon and bring warmth and life to cold and dead hearts, so that many more might become rewards for his pain.

THE 2ND   Brother *Jungmann* led the early service about the Watchword, For ye shall go out with joy, and be led forth with peace etc.[577] The Savior very much wants to fulfill his promises in us, if we just remain willing to surrender ourselves to his hands. For a number of days, a widow from *Gekelemukpechünk,* our *Gertraud's* sister, had been asking us constantly to take her in and to allow her to live here. We finally told her we would let her try it for a brief time. During this time she could consider it better.

THE 3RD   *Salomo* also sent us a message saying he was tired of being away from the congregation any longer. Therefore he asked the Brothers to have mercy on him and take him in again.[578] He came here in the fall, and even at that time showed a desire to live with us again. However, because we would not allow him to bring along his bad children and friends, who had caused us much anguish, they set up their winter quarters on the other side of the river. Now he is in miserable physical circumstances as well, because his friends, who promised him so many good things and took him away from the congregation, have left him and he is completely helpless. We considered his

---

576. Isa. 44:22; John 8:12. It is likely that on 17 December White Eyes brought with him, together with other letters, the Collection of Watchwords and Texts for the year 1775, *Die täglichen Loosungen der Brüder-Gemeine für das Jahr 1775; Die Lehrtexte der Brüder-Gemeine für das Jahr 1775.* The second installment arrived on 11 January 1775.

577. Isa. 55:12.

578. See entries for 9 July and 29 Nov. 1774.

situation with the Helpers. We felt compassion for him and decided to take him in again. Therefore on THE 5TH some Indian Brothers went to him and talked to him. He then returned to us, happy and thankful that the Brothers had accepted him.

THE 6TH   In the morning devotions we prayed for a sense of the Savior's presence and blessing for today. He let his peace descend on us very blessedly. Afterward Brother *Jungmann* preached the sermon, during which he read and discussed the story. In the afternoon during the Lovefeast, we reminded the Brothers and Sisters of God's work among the heathen in South and North America and on the West Indian Islands. For 42 years the Savior has blessed these through the Brothers' service, and there are now thousands who have been brought to faith in Him through the word of his death. He will also gather his elect from various *Nations* in this country.[579] During the Congregational Service, *Nathanael Davis's* son and his wife were baptized into Jesus' death, the former with the name *Leonhard* and the latter *Rahel*. The Savior's presence could be felt powerfully during this. All the Brothers and Sisters rejoiced over these two who were baptized, because the former has been with the Brothers for many years already. Although his heart was always dead and without feeling for the Savior, still he could not stay away from them. His wife is from *Gekelemukpechünk*.

White Eye and *Montour,* who had come here a couple of days ago, attended this service and the rest of them. The former told some Indian Brothers that when he hears about the Savior, his heart becomes tender and he gets worried and concerned about himself. His intention is to become a believer and live with us. However, he now has so much business he wants to take care of first, and he also wants travel to England. He often asks himself, Who knows if I will live long enough to get all this done and if I might not miss out on my salvation because of this? We hope that the Savior might grant him success in his plan and then also allow him to participate with his believers in the salvation in his blood in this time of blessing.

THE 7TH   He returned to *Gekelemukpechünk* and *John Montour* traveled to *Pittsburgh*. We sent letters to Bethlehem with him.[580]

THE 8TH   In the Children's Service we read them the story about when Jesus was 12 years old and commented on how He submitted to his parents and minded them. He thus left an example so that we could follow in his footsteps. If they would try to follow this, then they would grow in wisdom, in stature, and in grace like the boy Jesus.[581]

---

579. On the meaning of 6 January, see Introduction, pp. 62–63. Zeisberger and the other missionaries could read either from the letters or from the diaries written by missionaries working in the West Indies, in so far as these had been incorporated into the "Weekly News" of the Bethlehem congregation.

580. On 6 January 1775 Zeisberger wrote to Matthäus Hehl, MAB, Litiz Records: Indian Mission, and on 6 and 7 January to Nathanael Seidel, MAB, B 229, F 4, I 21 and 22.

581. Luke 2:41–52, esp. verse 51.

THE 9TH   We read the beautiful Watchword, Behold, thou shalt call a nation that thou knowest not etc.[582] If our hearts just lived rightly in Jesus' bloody merit and burned with love for Him, we would invite many more unknown heathen and *Nations* to salvation in his blood. They would gladly accept the sweet Gospel. Each person should make sure that they do not lag behind in grace, so that others do not exceed us and shame us.

THE 11TH   *Traders* arrived here from *Pittsburgh*[583] and brought us letters from *Litiz* dated *December* 5th and 6th along with a Daily Text Book for this year[584] from Brother *Matthao*.

THE 16TH   2 children were baptized in the Children's Service, during which most of the adults were also present. Brother *Leonhard* and Sister *Rahel's* baby daughter received the name *Lucia,* and *Gottfried* and *Justina's* baby daughter received the name *Lydia.* A blessed feeling of God's presence prevailed.

We spoke with some Indians who are not from here. Some of them had informed us of their desire to live with us, but some of them were advised to look around elsewhere for a way to manage.

THE 17TH   We spoke once again with a family who really want to live with us. The woman is *Salomo's* grandchild, who has already been with us a number of times but always had to be sent away from us. We gathered with the Helpers to listen to them and to give them an answer. However, the woman did not want to explain herself and also did not show remorse for her previous behavior, and we let the man know that we had nothing to say to them in this manner. The man then began sharing his heart with us. He had already been uneasy about his situation for a long time and he did not know anywhere to turn for his heart to be happy except to the Brothers. That was indeed the reason he had come, hoping the Brothers would have mercy on him. However, now he realized he was at the point of being turned away. He saw himself standing on the brink of ruin and all that was left was for him to be pushed in. Then he cried bitterly. We expressed our sincere compassion and advised him that he and his wife should be of one mind about this first. While we were still talking with him his wife's heart became tender, she asked for forgiveness for her previous deeds, and with tears she promised to use her time better now. Then we informed them that we would take them in, and they were comforted and joyful. One of their children had been baptized here previously and was buried on our God's Acre.

582. Isa. 55:5.

583. These are the first Indian traders from Pittsburgh that Zeisberger mentions since 21 July 1774. On 26 September 1774 Indian traders from Attike had arrived at Schönbrunn but had not dared to continue their journey. On 20 December White Eyes had brought some goods from Pittsburgh to Schönbrunn. Despite these visits from traders, on 20 December Zeisberger had already commented that the goods brought by White Eyes were especially welcome because they were badly needed; this need was probably much greater in the Delaware settlements because the traders from Attike had not dared visit them.

584. See note 576 to entry for 1 Jan. 1775.

THE 20TH   Today and yesterday we had Speakings with the Brothers and Sisters in preparation for Holy Communion. We found most of them in a contrite, blessed relationship with the Savior and we were able to rejoice over them. This indescribably blessed enjoyment of the Body and Blood of our Lord then took place on THE 21ST in his close presence. Two Brothers and Sisters were readmitted after receiving *Absolution*. One Brother and one Sister joined us in partaking for the first time; one Sister watched for the 2nd time and one Brother for the first time.

THE 22ND   After the *Liturgy* for Holy Communion Brother *Jungmann* preached the sermon about the text, We love him, because he first loved us.[585] The love that drove Him to death stirs our hearts to love him in return. In the afternoon the baptized Brothers and Sisters had a blessed service. The Congregational Service was about the text, A little one shall become a thousand, and a small one a strong nation.[586] During this service an older boy and an older girl shared in the waters of Holy Baptism and received the names *George* and *Sybilla*. A powerful feeling of grace was felt especially among the children, who shed many tears.

THE 25TH   A couple of messengers who came here yesterday on their way to *Kaskaskunk* continued their journey. We provided them with food for the journey. Their job there is to call *Captain Pipe* to a large Council in *Gekelemukpechünk*.[587] Sister *Jungmann* had gone to *Gnadenhütten* with some Indian Sisters the day before yesterday, and she returned from her visit there. Some Brothers and Sisters from there also came along for a visit.

THE 27TH   There was a Helpers' *Conference*. Among others we spoke with some Indians strangers who had been camping here and there on the river for a while already and who are causing disturbances. Some Indian Brothers went to see them, spoke with them, and warned them to look for quarters further away. They promised to do this.

The Brothers recently talked with a family who had already been here for a long time and told them that if they did not know why they were there, it would be better for them to go. This made them reflect and although the woman had always disagreed with her husband, they agreed with each other now and urgently asked us to take them in. We called them, talked with them, and listened to them. Among other things, the man said he would consider himself fortunate if we just allowed him to listen to the services from the door. It brought them all the more joy when we informed them that we would take them in for a trial. *Traders* came from *Pittsburgh,* and we heard many things from them about the difficult circumstances in the *Colonies* of this land. We fervently remembered our congregations before the Savior with compassionate

---

585. 1 John 4:19.
586. Isa. 60:22.
587. For this meeting of the Council, see entry for 28 Feb. 1775.

hearts and uttered many sighs to His heart, praying that the Watchword for today, The year of my redeemed is come etc.[588] might soon be fulfilled.

THE 29TH   In the morning the sermon was about the text, Seek ye the Lord while he may be found, call ye upon him while he is near.[589] In the Children's Service Brother *Heckewalder* introduced himself to the boys. He will be caring for them especially, as Sister *Jungmann* looks after the girls.[590]

February

THE 1ST   We had a *Conference* with some Indian Brothers concerning some *Affairs* in other places and considered in advance what kind of measures we would take if the land *Affaire* comes up at the *Councel* in *Gekelemukpechünk*[591] and they ask for our help, so that we are in agreement with each other and know what we have to do.

THE 2ND   *John Montour* brought us a letter and a Daily Text Book via *Pittsburgh* from Brother *Krogstrup* in *Lancaster*.[592] At the same time, *Mr. Gibson* informed Brother *David* in a letter that he was getting ready to travel to *Gouverneur Don Moore* in *Virginia*. He was expecting to meet *White Eye* there very soon, because a *Deed* for the *Delaware* Indians' land is supposed to be made there and they would take this with them to England.[593] Therefore he asks for *White Eye* to set out from here as soon as possible. All the Brothers and Sisters

---

588. The Watchword was Isa. 63:4. The controversies between England and the colonies had become more bitter by this time. England answered the Boston Tea Party of 1773 with the passage of the so-called Coercive Acts between 31 March and 20 May 1774; the Continental Congress (5 Sept.–26 Oct. 1774) responded to these acts with resolves that declared them illegal and against the British constitution. At their behest the colony of Massachusetts received permission to form an independent government, while the Congress encouraged all colonies to form and muster their militias and to boycott English goods. On 18 October 1774 the Continental Congress finally formed the so-called Continental Association, whose aim was the total stoppage of all trade with England and the other parts of the British Empire.

589. Isa. 55:6.

590. With this assignment the mission congregation had completed its internal administrative structure. David Zeisberger had the overall charge; the sermons were preached either by Zeisberger or by Johann Georg Jungmann. The male youth were the special concern of John Heckewelder and the female youth and women that of Anna Margaretha Jungmann. This implies, too, that all offices related to teaching and spiritual concerns were filled by missionaries. All other offices that were concerned with concrete administrative matters were administered by Indian members of the congregation. See Introduction, pp. 64–65, and protocol of conference from 17 Aug. 1772, appendix.

591. With this remark Zeisberger recalls Netawatwees' demand that the consent of the Wyandot to the settlement of the Brethren required their material contribution; see entry for 5 Nov. 1774.

592. Otto Christian Krogstrup was born on the Danish island of Fünen on 18 August 1714. After studying theology he arrived in America in 1753, where he served as pastor to the Moravian congregations at Lititz, Graceham, York, and Lancaster; he died in Bethlehem on 10 October 1785. We are grateful to Professor A. Gregg Roeber, The Pennsylvania State University, University Park, for this information.

593. See entry for 20 Dec. 1774.

went out to boil sugar because we keep having such nice spring weather. This is extremely early in the year for this, but we have had almost no winter.

THE 5TH *Willhelm* returned from *Gekelemukpechünk*. We had sent him there the day before yesterday with a *String of Wampum* in all of our names for the *Chief*, asking that he call away the Indians who have settled close to us since last fall and some even several years ago. They cause us all sorts of problems. We had actually already sent a message about this to the *Chief*[594] but it had no *Effect*. It is still continuing and more and more are joining them under the pretense that they would have the opportunity to hear God's word. Nothing more comes of this, however, except that it causes us trouble and hardship. Therefore we tried again and the *Chief* received it well and promised to present the matter in his next *Councel*. In addition to the usual Sunday services, the widowers and widows made up their day of study from THE 2ND of this month, because they had not all been at home. Brother *Jungmann* led them in a blessed service for this.

THE 6TH *Captain Pipe* returned here from *Kaskaskunk* yesterday and continued his journey to *Gekelemukpechünk,* where an *express* messenger had called him to a council, along with some other Indians who went with him.[595]

THE 9TH An Indian family from *Mechedachpisink*[596] came here for a visit. They expressed a desire and an inclination to hear God's word, so we proclaimed the Savior on the cross and his death to them. The man finally said he was not a nonbeliever; he believed our teaching was the truth. However, he asked what kind of things he must put aside and renounce if he wanted to become a believer. Then he said that just two things stood in his way: hunting and drinking. If it were not for these, he would become a believer.

THE 12TH Brother *Jungmann* preached the sermon. In the afternoon we read some letters from the Brothers and Sisters in Greenland.[597] This delighted and interested everyone, and in the Congregational Service we received one Sister, *Maria,* wife of *Thomas* the *Onondaga,* into the congregation.

THE 13TH During a congregational council we gave the Brothers and Sisters some necessary and practical reminders and admonitions, especially regarding their friends who are nonbelievers, and about being honest in their daily interactions with each other and with the *Traders.* They should especially treat the latter courteously, because they are known among the White people as a Christian people and are respected for this.

THE 18TH *Captain Pipe* arrived here with his people on their return journey from the council in *Gekelemukpechünk* to *Kaskaskunk.* He told us we would be informed about what had happened and what they had arranged. Therefore he did not want to say anything about this.

---

594. The diary does not mention an earlier message.
595. See entry for 25 Jan. 1775.
596. Not identified.
597. On the Moravian mission in Greenland, see entry for 24 Jan. 1773, note 147, and for 19 Jan. 1774, note 329.

THE 24TH   Many Indians came here today, as they have done recently, some to visit, and some to buy Indian corn. The food situation among the Indians will be bad again this year because they planted little last year due to the unrest, and some of them planted nothing at all. Praise be to God, our Indian Brothers and Sisters have plenty and now will be able to help others who are in need. A White man and his wife came from *Pittsburgh*. She had been captured by the *Shawnee* and was released in the fall. They were traveling back there to get their child whom she had had to leave there.[598]

THE 25TH   In the evening a messenger came from *Gnadenhütten*. He told us that some of our Indian Brothers should go there. *Chief Netawatwees, Captain White Eye*, and other *Counsellors* had already arrived there and they had something to tell us.

THE 26TH   5 Brothers therefore went there. The sermon was about our Savior's journey to his sufferings. In the Children's Service the baby boy born to Brother *Anton* and Sister *Juliana* yesterday evening was baptized into Jesus' death with the name *Marcus*, and after the Congregational Service in the evening there was the devotional service in preparation for Holy Communion.

THE 28TH   Our Brothers returned here from *Gnadenhütten* and soon afterward *White Eye* also came here with a couple of other Brothers from there. We received the happy and welcome news that the *Chief*, in the presence of his *Councellors*, had told our Indians he was in favor of the Brothers and their work; from now on they would also support this; they would accept God's word;[599] the Indian believers and their teachers should enjoy complete freedom in Indian country and enjoy equal rights and privileges. The country was now open to us and the Indian believers would have as much right and participation in the country as the nonbelievers. Any Indians who wanted to turn to the Brothers and become believers would be free to do so and would not be stopped. No Indians should *settle* close to us and those who are there now have already been informed that they should move down to where they live.[600] The *Chief* also announced that they would leave *Gekelemukpechünk* and move further away in a couple of days.[601] We should not think badly of this or conclude that they wanted to leave us. We were their friends and they were very happy and grate-

598. The couple referred to were Richard and Peggy Conner, who on 8 May 1775 had been provisionally accepted as the first white members of the congregation.

599. The entry reports the resolve of the Council from 23 June 1774. It is unlikely that the Council agreed at that time that all Delaware should become Christians; this had certainly not been the intention of Isaac, who had introduced the propositions on behalf of the mission congregation. Rather, it is to be understood that Zeisberger used "God's word" in the same sense as "those who propagate God's word." Then the sentence would read: we have accepted "those who propagate God's word," i.e., the missionaries. This corresponds exactly to what Isaac had introduced as a proposition in his speech on 23 June 1774.

600. See entry for 5 Feb. 1775.

601. As a result of this resolve, Gekelemukpechünk was given up, and Goschachgünk ("Coshocton," "Newcomerstown II") was founded as a new settlement some distance away. See the description of this settlement in entry for 7 April 1775.

ful that we had come to them. At this he repeatedly expressed his gratitude in a very solemn manner. They were moving away because they were too close to us; they wanted to give us room so that we could live with plenty of space for our cattle and they would not have to suffer. There was already a large number of us and we would surely have to establish another *Town*,[602] so we should look around to see where we liked it best. He said this is what he wanted to tell us. He was already an old man and did not know how much longer he would live here on earth. Therefore he was happy that he was still able to carry out this work, so that their children and heirs could enjoy it. Now he could die when it pleased God. The *Chief* and *White Eye* and their *Council* thus testify in the name of the entire *Nation* that they want to accept the Christian faith.[603] Although many Indians are still opposed to this, indeed are enemies, this will close their mouths. They are no longer allowed to attack us so publicly. *Netawatwees* also sent word to *Packanke*[604] in *Kaskaskunk* saying, You and I, we are both old already and do not know how much longer we will live, so let us do one more good act before we die and leave our children and heirs the knowledge that we have accepted God's word. Let this be our last will and *Testament*.

With this we close our diary for now with praise and thanks to our dear Lord for his many proofs of grace and the miracles He has performed for us. These are the pure fruits of the prayers of the congregations for us. He has heard them and they will surely bring Him praise, honor, and gratitude. We join our whole little gathering in greeting all the congregations very warmy, and we commend ourselves to their remembrance and blessing.

Diary of Schönbrunn *on the* Muskingum *from the Months of* March, April, *and* May 1775.[605]

MARCH 1ST   In the early service we talked about how our creator is also our redeemer and the source of our salvation.

Captain White Eye had a *Conference* with some of our Indian Brothers and prepared the message he is planning to take along to England. They want to ask the King to let the *Delaware Nation* remain in possession of its land and never be driven off of it.[606] On this occasion he gave our Brothers a good, encouraging talk, told them to be courageous, firm, and steadfast, not to be deterred by anything but to remain with God's word which would be preached to them, and not to weaken or give in. He said, If you do not remain firm, you will be shamed before all Indians. But I trust in you and depend on you. When

602. This part of the resolve caused the foundation of Lichtenau; see entry for 9 April 1776.
603. See note 599.
604. Packanke was chief of the Wolf clan; its war captain was Pipe.
605. MAB, B 141, F 6, I 2, fol. 104.
606. See entry for 19 Dec. 1774 and note 567.

you are strong, then I am also strong. Then he left for *Pittsburgh* early on THE 3RD, after he had discussed various aspects of his journey with Brother *David* and asked him for advice. We sent letters and our diary to Bethlehem with him. Yesterday and today we had Speakings with the Brothers and Sisters in preparation for Holy Communion. We then partook of the blessed Body and Blood of our Lord on THE 4TH. One Sister participated in this for the first time and two watched for the 2nd time.

THE 5TH   After the *Liturgy* for Holy Communion Brother *Jungmann* preached the sermon about the text, I am not come to call the righteous, but sinners to repentance.[607] The Brothers and Sisters had much work to do boiling sugar since the trees were running heavily, so we let them get to their work early in the afternoon.

THE 7TH   Indians from *Gekelemukpechünk* came to hear God's word. One said he had come to us a year ago and wanted to convert, and he had also informed *Netawatwees* and other *Chiefs* of his intention. However, they had advised him against it. Afterward he thought about the fact that when he had wanted to drink or do something else bad, he had not asked the *Chiefs* first if he should do this or not, and they had not forbidden him from doing such things. Why then did he ask the *Chiefs* first now that he was seeking something good?

THE 9TH   *Willhelm* returned from *Gekelemukpechünk,* where he had been on business. He had proclaimed the Savior and his death to a respected Indian there who used to be a big enemy of ours and was opposed to the preaching of the Gospel. Now, however, he has completely turned around and is our good friend. If the Brothers visit him, he does not know how he can show them enough kindness. A well-known Indian preacher[608] was there with him, but *Willhelm* did not know that he was a preacher. When he witnessed against sacrificing, vomiting, and purging to get rid of sins, the Indian clapped his hands and said to the preacher, This is certainly the truth! What do you say to this? The preacher did not say a word.

THE 10TH   A whole party of Indians came here from *Beaver Creek* and a couple of White people on their way from the *Shawnee* to *Pittsburgh*. The *Mingo* who live among the *Shawnee* still do not want to obey. Now they have been called home by their Nation.[609] They are not going, but want to *settle* 50 miles further toward the *Lakes*.

THE 13TH   A woman who was ill had asked urgently to be baptised, and early in the day she was baptized with the name *Marie Magdalene*. She had already come and gone here for a number of years and felt a yearning in her heart to give herself to the Savior. She had always wanted to but could not commit to doing this, and her circumstances did not allow her to stay with us.

607. Matt. 9:13.
608. On the function and importance of preachers in Native American societies, see entry for 13 April 1774 and note 349.
609. See entry for 3 Dec. 1774 and note 561.

Therefore we had sent her away a number of times. She could never stay away from us for long without coming back though. This winter she returned, but she was sickly. Instead of improving she got worse. A couple of days ago she gave birth to a baby girl and then yesterday evening she suddenly got worse. She told her uncle, *Isaac,* right away that she would probably not live much longer. Then she became very worried about herself, sought forgiveness for her sins, and throughout the night she asked to be cleansed from her sins with the Savior's blood. She prayed to the Savior to let her live until this morning, when she hoped she would experience this. She prayed repeatedly, Dear Savior, have mercy on me! Come and wash me of my sins with your blood. Then I will go to you gladly and joyfully. Do this while I am still in my right mind though, because soon I will not be lucid. She died early on THE 14TH and left behind a sweeter look than she had ever had in her life. Her earthly dwelling was then laid to rest in the evening.

THE 17TH   Many Indians arrived again from *Kaskaskunk* and *Goschgosching.* We heard that after he had returned home from the council in *Gekelemukpechünk, Captain Pipe* had called the Indians in *Kaskaskunk* and the entire area together and told them what they had agreed upon about us in the council.[610] Anyone who wanted to go to the Brothers to hear God's word and to become a believer was free to do so. This is more evidence that not only the *Chiefs* know this among themselves, but all the Indians know. We can now enjoy this and see the fruits of it daily, because we are not aware that they are acting improperly toward us at all; they are all friendly and very courteous.

THE 19TH   Brother *Jungmann* preached the sermon. In the Children's Service, which all of the adults and strangers also attended, the baby boy born to Brother *Lucas* and Sister *Pauline* this morning was baptized with the name *Paulus,* and toward evening the previously mentioned *Marie Magdalene's* baby girl, who received the name *Gertraud* in Holy Baptism yesterday and then died this morning, was buried. Some of the strangers were very emotional and were touched. One of them who heard about the Savior for the first time said that although he really could not understand what was preached, much less remember it, he believed it was all the truth and now he sees that everything he had heard among the Indians was nothing but lies and deception. Nothing good could be found among them. His wife had always said that what was preached here was all lies. She knew better because she had been to the place of the spirits, where there was an abundance of strawberries and blueberries as big as apples, and she was also planning to go there. She did not want to go where we were going, and therefore she did not attend any services.[611] She came to

610. See entry for 28 Feb. 1775.

611. There were women preachers in other settlements, too; see entry for 4 July 1768: "An old woman of the town [Goschgoschünk], who is very hostile toward us, preaches industriously against us, persuading her people that whoever will go to our meetings will be tempted by the devil and greatly troubled," in [Sensemann and Zeisberger], "Diary of David Zeisberger and Gottlob Zenseman," 57–58, 99–100. Scattameck was a preacher whose influence in 1771–72 was at its height; see entry for 1 Jan. 1773.

the Children's Service today, however, presumably because she had heard there would be a baptism. She also received her share, because she could not stop crying, and afterward she said that from now on she would not say we were preaching lies anymore. She was now convinced otherwise and actually wanted to become a believer.

THE 20TH   The baby girl born yesterday to Brother *Ignatius* and Sister *Christina* was baptized and received the name *Beata*. We received news from the *Fort* that *White Eye* was dangerously ill there and the *Doctors* doubted he would recover. This was not good news for us, because we would be very sad to lose him now.

THE 23RD   Our Brothers and Sisters all returned home from their sugar huts and had finished boiling sugar for now. It was a good spring for this and it was very plentiful.

THE 24TH   We had a *Conference* with the Helper Brothers. They were given some matters to settle and straighten out and were asked to speak with some people who have not been baptized. Also to consider if and what we might reply to the *Chief's* statement about us and what else needed to be done about this matter.

THE 25TH   In the early service we remembered the significance of today, that the eternal Good had dressed himself in our poor flesh and blood.[612] Then the children had a service during which they were also told about this same subject, and we knelt and thanked the Savior for his holy incarnation and death and especially commended our children to His grace. There was a Service of Adoration with the baptized Brothers and Sisters. He revealed himself graciously to us in all of our services and blessed us with his holy incarnation.

THE 27TH   All the residents were home now, and after the early service we informed them what the council in *Gekelemukpechünk* had agreed upon about us and decided. We had not been able to do this before because the Brothers and Sisters were all scattered about boiling sugar and in other places. All the Brothers and Sisters responded with much praise and gratitude toward our dear Lord for this. Brother *Heckewelder* returned from *Gekelemukpechünk,* where he had been visiting for a couple of days.

The wolves have done much damage recently and have already destroyed many head of cattle, and we realize we cannot raise our young cattle if we do not get rid of them. Therefore we set a price on their heads, one *Dollar*. We counted this against the common *Expences* and are paying it from that.[613] This had a good and desirable *Effect,* because within 8 days probably 10 of them were killed, and in a short time they were all wiped out.

THE 29TH   During the Children's Service, the baby daughter born to Brother *Samuel* and Sister *Sarah Nantikok* yesterday was baptized with the name *Anna Helena*.

612. The 25th of March was the commemoration day for Christ's incarnation.
613. On handling congregational expenses, see entry for 21 Dec. 1773 and note 315.

THE 30TH   The Helpers spoke with some strangers who have been here for a long time already and would really like to live here. All of them said they would become the Savior's property and submit to and obey the Brothers.

April

THE 1ST   Many Indians arrived here from *Goschgosching, Kaskaskunk* and the area near *Beaver Creek.* News arrived that some *Delaware* Indians in the area of *Sioto,*[614] where they were hunting, were apparently killed. No one knows which *Nation* committed the murders, but people guess that the *Shawnee* caused it. Last year they sent a message to all the surrounding *Nations,* asked them to help against the *Virginians,* and shouted at the *Delaware* for being on the side of the *Virginians.*[615] Two people, a man and his wife, received permission to live here.

THE 2ND   In the morning we had a sermon about the sacrifice of Jesus, who sacrificed himself for our sins and thus attained eternal redemption. In the Children's Service they were reminded that we are now in the blessed season of Lent, when our Savior so willingly endured his sufferings. They should consider this well and reflect upon what He has done for us.

THE 3RD   4 Brothers, *Willhelm, Isaac, Abraham,* and *Nathanael,* went to *Gnadenhütten* to have a talk with them. The first two then went on with some others from there to see the *Chief* in *Goschachgünk.* The latter two, however, returned the following day. Brother *John Jungmann* had come here a couple of days ago for a visit and he returned there.

THE 6TH   During the early service Brother *Jungmann* talked about how the Savior is a master at helping when we are in the greatest trouble and distress.

Drunken Indians came here from the *Fort* with several horseloads of *Rum.* They bothered us for a little while, then we took their *Rum* for safekeeping and it got quiet. We do this with all Indians and White people who enter our *Town* or area with such goods, regardless of who they are. They are not masters of it as long as they are here, and when they leave we accompany them beyond our borders.[616]

THE 7TH   Brothers *Isaac* and *Willhelm* returned from *Goschachkünk,* the new *Town* the people from *Gekelemukpechünk* are now establishing.[617] In a public

614. I.e., "Scioto."

615. The incident is not reported in other sources; the main settlements of the Shawnee were in the Scioto River system; see Introduction, p. 15. On the Shawnee accusing the Delaware of siding with Virginia, see entry for 1 Nov. 1774.

616. See entry for 2 March 1774 and Zeisberger's response to Gischenatsi in his report on his trip to the Shawnee, in entry for 20 Sept. 1773.

617. The Delaware had argued that their move was necessary because the Christian Indians needed more space; see entry for 28 Feb. 1775. On other reasons for founding new Indian settlements, see entry for 3 March 1773 and note 164.

council meeting there, they thanked the *Chief* on behalf of both our *Towns* for the *Declaration* he made about the Indian believers and their teachers. Before this *Isaac,* who was the speaker, had first repeated the talk the *Chief* had given us, and he confessed before all the people not only that he had called us but also everything that had been said. After his talk was repeated, a *String of Wampum* was presented[618] and one *Belt* in gratitude and 2 more *Belts,* one from here and the other from *Gnadenhütten,* in gratitude for the land given to the *Wyandot.* Each *Belt* was ¹/₂ *Klafter*[619] long and proportionately wide. As *White Eye* himself had indicated to us, the *Belts* were not made in the traditional Indian manner but were plain, with no figures. Down the middle of the length was a street and above this was a cross. This had the following significance: these *Belts* are being sent to the *Wyandot, Tawas, Twichtwees,* and *Wawiachtanos.* Because they are different from others, the *Nations* can immediately see that they mean something different, and that they come from the Indian believers. They can thus tell right away that the Indian believers have now been accepted and are recognized and respected as their friends. Finally, the *Chief* told the people that they had all heard what the *Chiefs* had unanimously decided now. This is how things would stay and if anyone had not heard this before, they had heard it now. He gave the Brothers a *Belt* as a sign of his pleasure over the matter.

Their new *Town* is planned and staked out with cross streets and lies on the *Muskingum.* They copied this from us because otherwise the Indians never build in a regular pattern, but each person builds his house wherever it suits him. Each race, *Tribe,* or *Nation*[620] is supposed to have its own street. There is also a street designated for those Indians whom we send away or who leave us of their own accord. They have much work to do and there are also many people there. They are only in each other's way, though, because they do not know how to divide their work. There is also no one to organize the people. At their request, therefore, the Brothers advised them and told them how we did things among ourselves. This pleased them and they said they would follow our example. They will profit from us materially after all and learn to become more orderly. *White Eye* also returned from the *Fort* to *Gekelemukpechünk.* We were happy to hear that he has recovered pretty well.[621] However, once again nothing came of his trip to England. *Gouverneur Don Moore* sent him word that

618. Isaac and the other Christian Indians followed the traditional ceremony. The speaker of the group repeated the message, which a string or belt of wampum was used to confirm. The pattern on the belt signified the cause and content of the transaction, which was to be documented for future reference. Missionaries knew that they had to follow Indian customs and therefore had asked White Eyes for advice. See entry for 20 July 1772, note 40.

619. On the size of a "Klafter," see note 221. The belts were almost eighty-six cm. long.

620. On the meaning of lineage, see Introduction, pp. 17–18, and notes 32–42. See, too, the formula "A message with a *String of Wampum* came to *Israel* from his tribe and friends in *Goschachgünk*" in entry for 20 Jan. 1779.

621. See entry for 23 March 1775.

they could not make the journey now until after everything had been worked out with the *Shawnee* and the rest of the *Nations,* and the peace had been completely concluded.[622] An Indian had come to us recently with his wife and received permission to live here. His uncle in *Gekelemukpechünk,* who had really worked to turn him against us, had called him for the 2nd time now. He returned from there and had explained why he lived with us so well that his friends had no more objections to this. Instead, they said they were glad they had learned what he thought. A whole party of Indians from *Cayahaga* arrived here, including the *Wyandot* and his wife who had been here a year ago.[623]

THE 11TH   Once again a family received permission to live here. They had already been with us for a while in *Kaskaskunk,* but when we moved away from there they had stayed behind. In the evening we continued reading the story as we had done in recent days. Everyone was very, very attentive and interested during this. The Savior especially blessed people's hearts with this.

THE 12TH   We had Speakings in preparation for Holy Communion. We found much cause to praise and glorify the Savior for his many proofs of grace in our Brothers' and Sisters' hearts.

THE 13TH   The *Wyandot* returned to *Cayahaga* with his wife. He had spoken a lot more with the Brothers and especially with *Thomas* the *Onondaga* and learned a lot about our teachings and life. He said that when he came here a year ago he had been happy to see such a large *Town* of Indian believers. At that time he had also realized that their worship must not have been right, because no change or improvement was seen in those who had been baptized. He had even discussed this with various people from his *Nation* and told them what things were like here and what he thought about this. They had answered him that they would come live with us if some of us came to *Cayahaga* to live. He also said that he was supposed to go to a council across the *Lake* this spring. Since he knew us better now, he will tell his *Nation* about us, and especially the *Chiefs,* and tell them what he has seen and heard. Both of them really like it here and when we persuaded them the slightest bit they stayed with us.

In the evening the communicant Brothers and Sisters had a blessed *Pedilavium*[624] and the most holy *Sacrament* of His Body and Blood. One Sister participated in this for the first time, another was readmitted, 3 Brothers and Sisters watched for the second time, and 3 for the first time. We were sincerely delighted to received letters via *Pittsburgh* from Bethlehem and *Litiz,* dated *January.*

THE 14TH   Early in the day after the *Liturgy* for Holy Communion, we began reading the passion story. People listened with tender and melting

---

622. At least White Eyes had intended to travel to England with Lord Dunmore. The real reason for Dunmore's deferral of the trip was the mounting crisis between the defenders of British policy and its opponents in Virginia. See Scribner et al., *Revolutionary Virginia,* 2:251–388.

623. See entry for 26 Aug. 1774. On Cayahaga, see entry for 19 July 1773 and note 236.

624. Foot washing.

hearts, and in the afternoon the baptized Brothers and Sisters had a *Liturgy* commemorating the Piercing of the Side.[625] There were more Indian strangers here than there had ever been, and our Meeting Hall, which can easily hold 300 people, was too small. Many were powerfully moved and touched.

THE 15TH   It was Great Sabbath. At noon first the children and then the adult residents had a Lovefeast, sang songs, and reflected upon Jesus' body in the grave.

THE 16TH   Early in the day we prayed the Easter *Litany* on our God's Acre, joyfully aware of his close presence.[626] We remembered the 4 Brothers and Sisters who have died since last Easter and asked for eternal fellowship with them. Both strangers and residents took their places in a more orderly manner around God's Acre than they had ever done before. Afterward the story of the resurrection was read. Then there was the sermon, which Brother *Jungmann* preached. During the Congregational Service in the evening 4 people were baptized: *Ludwig,* who was mentioned in the entry for *January* 17 in the previous diary and who had seen himself on the brink of ruin, *Debora,* a widow, and two older girls *Anna Elisabeth* and *Phoebe.* The close presence of the Holy Trinity prevailed during this.

THE 17TH   Some Indian Brothers went to the *camps* of Indians who had been staying in our area recently. We learned that they were after our cattle, because they have nothing to eat and are trying to feed themselves by stealing. They made them pay for the cattle they had killed and told them either to stay in our *Town* while they were here or to leave our area. They then left.

THE 19TH   In our Helpers' Conference we discussed some people who have already been here for a long time but who do not belong here, and we spoke with them. One widow who had asked to live here received permission for this. However, *Margreth* and her daughter left us today. Her second daughter had already left some time ago.[627] The mother and both of her daughters had been received into the congregation. They had also set out on the road to leave a year ago, but had turned back in *Gnadenhütten.* Since then, however, they have not been able to shape up and all the efforts we made were in vain. Therefore we did not oppose their plan, but actually supported it.

THE 22ND   There was a Helpers' *Conference* today, as there had been throughout the week. At various times we talked about our congregational rules, taught the Brothers and Sisters common principles, and admonished

625. See note 176 above.

626. One and a half lines are crossed out but should probably read, "everyone, strangers and inhabitants had placed themselves so nice on God's acre [cemetery] as had never happened before."

627. The diary notes for 10 April 1774 that a widow with four children had arrived from the Susquehanna River and desired to live in the congregation. This widow is described as "our Margreth's daughter." On 25 December 1775 Susanna, "daughter of Margreth" was admitted to the congregation. According to these entries it is not clear which of the daughters came earlier and which arrived with Margreth.

them to follow these. We sincerely commended our children to them and admonished them to provide them more guidance and care. Recently we spoke with some people who have not been baptized and who have already been living with us for a year. We told them to move to *Goschachgünk* because we did not see why they were living here. We confronted them about their behavior during the war last year, when they had acted badly. One of them had recently brought his mother, his brother, and his wife here from *Goschgosching*. They received permission to live here, but we informed him that they could no longer stay here like this. When they heard that we would send them away, they became very worried, and came and asked us to keep them and to give them one more chance. A young, single Indian whom we had sent away last year also came and asked us to have mercy on him and take him in again. He said he could not remain among the Indian savages any longer. Therefore he had thought to himself that he should turn back, go to the Brothers, and ask them to forgive him and take him in again. They were all asking us to have mercy on them again, so we had no choice but to take them in with hope.

THE 23RD   4 *Mingo* who had come here yesterday on their way from the *Shawnee* to the *Fort* continued their journey. We later heard that they kept two of them in the *Fort* in the place of two others they had sent out as messengers this winter but who had not come back.[628]

Today was the festival day for those Brothers and Sisters who have been baptized this year, 18 of them, and 3 who were received into the congregation. During a service attended by all the Brothers and Sisters, we reminded them of the covenant they had made with the Savior. They were admonished to renew this daily and to grow in grace every day. The most important thing, however, is to realize their deep wretchedness and go to the doctor of their souls each day and seek forgiveness through his blood. In conclusion, we knelt and commended these 21 Brothers and Sisters especially, as well as ourselves, to His further grace, to the Father's protection, and to the Holy Spirit's care. During this we could sense a blessed feeling of his dear presence and of God's peace.

THE 24TH   A whole crowd of Indians, including *Lucas's* friends from *Goschgosching*, came from *Kaskaskunk*, and they were all starving. *Lucas* reminded them that the Gospel had come to them first and had been preached in their house during Brother *David's* first visit. It was their own fault that they were still wandering around in confusion, living a miserable life and without even a permanent home, and almost dying of starvation. He told them how good things could be for them if they would surrender to the Savior.

THE 27TH   Yesterday and today large parties of Indians came once again. There is famine everywhere among the Indians, because last year they

628. Lord Dunmore had taken hostages from the Mingo because they had refused to sign a preliminary treaty with him; see entry for 30 Oct. 1774.

were always busy thinking more about fleeing than planting. It is good for them that they can still purchase here and indeed at a low price, 6 shillings for a bushel as we have agreed among ourselves. They are very satisfied with this. There were some Indians among them who had never heard anything about the Savior. They were quite attentive during the service and asked the Brothers many questions. Today the Brothers finished repairing the fences and enlarging the fields, so that the people who have come to us recently will all receive fields.[629]

In the Singing Service in the evening, which only the residents from here attended, we reminded the parents to be more concerned about what was best for their children, to encourage them to work more, especially the boys, and also that they should appear very orderly in the services, clean themselves, comb their hair, and bathe.

THE 29TH   The often-mentioned *Wyandot* came with other Indians from *Kaskaskunk* and *Cayahaga*. He brought along his rosary and prayed this aloud in his language. It is accurate not only to call this an unwise form of worship, but also idolatry and paganism.

THE 30TH   Brother *Jungmann* preached the sermon. The 8 Brothers and Sisters who have joined in partaking of Holy Communion this year had a service on the text for their festival day today, I am come that they might have life, and that they might have it more abundantly.[630] During this the Savior revealed himself in a blessed way.

May

THE 3RD   The Helpers spoke with a woman, our *Molly's* daughter, who had come here from *Goschachgünk* with her 4 children several days ago and requested permission to live here. We advised her to stay away from us because it might not suit her to live with us, and we also told her why. However, she would not be refused at all and had an answer to all our objections. Therefore we had to allow her to stay here, but only on the *condition* that she behave according to our rules. We have done the same with many young widows who did not receive full permission to live with us until they had been baptized and received their inheritance and privileges with God's house and people.

THE 4TH   The early service was about the growth of faith, love, and knowledge of Jesus Christ, and how we increase in these when we remain in Him, the vine.[631]

In the Helpers' *Conference* afterward we considered two families who had

---

629. The formulation implies that families were assigned individual pieces of land for planting, for which they were responsible.

630. John 10:10.

631. The text was John 15:4.

asked to stay here, and we spoke with them. Both received permission to do so. One of them was one of *Lucas's* friends. Our *Town* had just barely emptied out a little from Indian visitors yesterday, and by early today another group had already arrived from *Beaver Creek*.

Some time ago *Mr. Richard Conner* had come here from the *Fort*[632] and gone to the *Shawnee Towns* to see if he could retrieve his child, who is still there. In the meantime he left his wife here. She had been their prisoner and had grown up among the Indians. Today he returned from there without accomplishing his goal. However, the *Chiefs* promised him that he would get his child back. He told us he could not remember ever wanting his actual father as much as he now longed to be back with us. His wife has gotten very used to us while she has been here, and is so obliging toward the Sisters, especially Sister *Jungmann*, that we could see it would be difficult for her to leave here. In the fall when she was set free she was taken to *Pittsburgh*, where she spent the winter with her husband. However, she did not like it at all there. She cannot fit in with White people, especially people like those in the *Fort,* and she also does not want to live among the savage Indians any more.[633] Therefore her husband spoke with us today and said he wanted to ask us for a big favor; he asked if he and his wife could stay with us. He was tired of his previous life and his wife had already asked him numerous times to go with her to our place, several years ago when they still lived among the *Shawnee*. However, at that time he could not do this, because he was not master of his wife while he lived among the *Shawnee.* Brother *David* had spent the night with them on his journey to the *Shawnee* and at that time had a conversation with the man half a night about being saved and what is required for this.[634]

THE 5TH   After the early service was the burial of *Anna Helena,* the

632. That is, 24 Feb. 1775.

633. On the fundamental issue, see Axtell, "White Indians." In the same sense that whites were attracted to Native American societies, Indians seem to have been attracted to the lifestyle of the mission congregation; they repeated Conner's argument that they could not, after having lived in a mission congregation, live again among the "savages." See entries for 27 July 1772, 22 April, and 28 Oct. 1775.

634. Zeisberger's report of his trip does not mention that he stayed overnight at Richard Conner's place. Generally whites were not accepted in mission congregations; Conner was asking for special permission. His wife had been released as a prisoner in consequence of the treaty of Camp Charlotte; see entry for 30 Oct. 1774. On 11 February 1773 Jones traveled through the settlement in which the Conners lived at that time (Jones, *Journal of Two Visits,* 88–89). According to Jones, Conner and "the chief Indian of this town . . . [were] married to two sisters. These women were captives, and it is likely from childhood, for they have the very actions of the Indians, and speak broken English." In the settlement in which Shawnee and Delaware lived, Conner ran "a sort of a tavern, and has moderate accommodations." Probably Conner was unable to act the commanding husband to his wife because she had been assigned, as a prisoner, to a Shawnee family who had adopted her and who claimed prior possession and the right to determine her whereabouts. These rights expired with the treaty of Camp Charlotte. On Conner, see entries for 26 May 1774, note 398, and for 24 Feb. 1775.

baby girl born to Brother *Samuel* and Sister *Sarah Nantikok* on *March* 29th this year. She died yesterday.

THE 6TH   Once again a family received permission to live here. Actually more new people are coming to us than we desire or like. We cannot turn them away though. When they ask so urgently and we have no reason to send them away, we have no choice but to take them in. Still, we have refused some people when we had concerns.

THE 8TH   In our Helpers' *Conference* we especially admonished the Brothers and Sisters to receive the new people well, so that they are not only satisfied to live here, but might also flourish. *Mr. Conner's* situation also came under consideration, as it has many times. He requests that we allow him to stay here. We have explained everything to him and made enough objections, but he refuses to be deterred by this. He promised to submit to our rules just as the Indians who come to us must do, and not to undertake anything without our knowledge or consent. We have examined the matter from all sides with the Indian Brothers and Sisters, primarily considering if and to what extent it might be disadvantageous or harmful to us if we take them in. We found nothing significant, particularly at this time. We really would have had more concerns earlier. Therefore we decided to make a trial with both of these people, but first to discuss it with *White Eye,* whom we expect here soon. He is not ignorant about the situation either, because the man had already talked to him about it before he came to us and had shared his thoughts with him. He was born in *Maryland.* His brothers and friends live there, actually in *Fridricks-town,*[635] and he said they are acquainted with the Brothers.

THE 9TH   The Brothers fenced in another new piece of land for those who have arrived recently. A couple of *Traders* came here from the *Wyandot* on their way to *Pittsburgh,* and they said they had come specifically to see our *Town,* although it is far out of their way; our *Town* was well known among White people and Indians everywhere, and they had heard so much about us in *Detroit* and about what good people and truly Christian Indians lived here. They said the *Wyandot* were also called Christian Indians, but there was no sign of this in them. We also heard now that if the *Tawas*[636] had agreed to this a year ago, the *Wyandot* would have united with the *Shawnee* against the *Virginians.* If that had happened, there would have been a general Indian war and all the *Nations* would have been entangled in it.

Willhelm came from *Gekelemukpechünk* where he had been on business. An Indian from the *Councel* had spoken with him and told him that the *Chiefs* were thinking about getting Brothers who would preach the Gospel to them there.

635. Frederickstown, Maryland, which later became Frederick County. See Scharf, *History of Western Maryland;* Williams, *History of Frederick County, Maryland.*
636. On the Tawas, see note 284 to entry for 18 Oct. 1773.

Another Indian who came here confirmed this and also said that they had talked about building a meeting house where there would be preaching in the middle of their *Towns*. Some who were opposed wanted to leave then and move somewhere else. The *Chief* had told them that they should not balk like this; they would surely have to join in because in 6–7 years there would be very few Indians left who were not believers. Therefore they should just start now and get used to it. The *Chiefs* are working hard to become at least an orderly people, but they will not get far because they cannot get the Indians to be obedient. They have agreed that they should all move to *Goschachgünk* so that they all lived together. Instead of this, however, they are now scattering out more than ever and settling all over the place. Those who lived close to us have all moved away, though, which we are happy about. The Indians are really working through things and are getting agitated. The Savior always profits from this, though. They move around from one place to another and finally run into His hands.

THE 12TH   In the early service it was said that we should surrender to the Savior like clay in the hands of a potter[637] so that he can form and shape something according to his heart. Afterward there was a Helpers' *Conference*. A family who was often with us in *Langundouteniünk* had come here some time ago and asked to be taken in. They received permission to stay here.

THE 14TH   In the morning was the sermon, which many strangers attended. Brother *Heckewelder* led the Children's Service. Various Brothers and Sisters came from *Gnadenhütten* to visit our Brother *Johannes,* who was ill. On THE 15TH the Savior took him to his eternal rest.

THE 16TH   His earthly dwelling was buried, accompanied by a large procession including many Brothers and Sisters who had come from *Gnadenhütten.* He was baptized on *June* 26, 1762, during Brother *David Zeisberger's* 2nd visit in *Wyalusing,* where he had preached for a short time.[638] An Indian war broke out at that time, though, and Brother *David* returned to Bethlehem, but he stayed there. During that time he made arrangements with the 6 *Nations* to allow Brothers to live with them and preach the Gospel to them as he had been assigned to do. Soon afterward he came to Bethlehem and brought the Brothers this news and told them they were now free to come to them and to live there. He left it up to them to do as they saw fit, however. This was not possible because of the Indian war, however, so that same winter he went to *Philadelphia* since our Indians were there. The Quakers there knew him and made much of him, and they kept him with them and took care of him and his people. However, he just did not feel satisfied until he was with the Brothers, although things could have been much better for him, and indeed had been better, than

637. Jer. 18:6.
638. This refers to Wyalusing. On the mission in this place, see Introduction, pp. 48–49.

they would be with us.[639] Then in May 1765 he went to *Wyalusing* on the *Susquehanna,* which was later named *Friedenshütten,* with the Indian congregation, and he participated in the first Holy Communion there. He served the congregation and the Brothers faithfully according to his abilities, went with them to *Langundouteniink* on the *Ohio* in *August,* 1772, and soon afterward came here. He said a number of times during the journey that if he reached the destination and the Indian congregation was well established again, he would gladly lay his bones down to rest, and the Brothers and Sisters remembered this now. The Savior allowed him to witness this and even more. In the beginning he did not like it here very much. Things here were a bit too lively for him and he was not used to hearing the savages utter so many lies, blasphemies, and words of abuse about us. However, after he returned from Bethlehem last fall, he came to like it here better than all the other places and he was content. He was already sickly on that journey, and he had never really recovered since then. He was glad that he had seen Bethlehem once again, though. His heart was firmly attached to the Savior and the Unity, and he endured sufficient tests of this. But he had many enemies among the Indians who accused him of various bad things. They particularly accused him of having the poison about which the Indians have made so much, and this caused him many difficult hours.[640] He held all the more firmly to the Savior and did not let himself be bothered, much less deterred, and we were often more worried about him than he himself was. Even this had also calmed down for some time, though, and we did not hear anything else about it. Recently he had been especially blessed and happy, did his work with great cheerfulness and faithfulness, because he had the care of the external affairs.[641] About 12 days ago he got pains in his side and began coughing, which really bothered him. During his illness he only talked about how he wanted to die and he did not want to get well again. He asked us to send his greetings to all the Brothers and Sisters in Bethlehem, and he said he loved everyone and did not hold anything against anyone. He then died with the blessing of the congregation, at about 70 years old.

THE 20TH   Brother *David* went to *Gnadenhütten* with Brother *Schebosch* and returned home in the evening.

THE 22ND   In the Helpers' *Conference* the Brothers and Sisters were reminded about filling blessed Brother *Johannnes's* place, as well as Brother *David's* trip to Bethlehem with Brother *Schebosch* and a couple of Indian Brothers. We spoke with some Brothers and Sisters about their friends who were not believers. We cannot lead the Indians enough in the verse, He that loveth

---

639. On these times in which the Christian Indians had to be protected against attacks by white settlers and live in barracks in Philadelphia, see note 368 and entry for 9 May 1774.

640. See the reproach of Netawatwees reported by Zeisberger in entry for 5 Nov. 1774. In 1771 Johannes had been suspected of possessing poison that had threatened his life. Loskiel, *Geschichte der Mission,* 581–83.

641. On the offices within the congregation, see Introduction, pp. 64–65.

father or mother more than me is not worthy of me: and he that loveth son or daughter more than me is not worthy of me.[642] When you think you are finally finished, then you must begin again, especially since there are always more people coming to us. There are also other matters just like this that we never finish.

THE 25TH   We joined our baptized Brothers and Sisters in worshipping our dear Lord in the dust, and prayed we would sense his presence among us and walk constantly with Him, our unseen friend. Brother *Jungmann* preached the sermon. In the Congregational Service 2 Brothers and Sisters, *Joseph* and *Polly*, the children of the *Onandaga* family, were received into the congregation. Then we knelt and commended this Brother and Sister and all God's work among the heathen here and everywhere to the Savior's faithful heart in prayer.

THE 26TH   During the Speakings with the Brothers and Sisters in preparation for Holy Communion, we found much reason to praise Him and worship Him for the Holy Spirit's motherly care,[643] which is never in vain in hearts. This blessed enjoyment of his Body and Blood in the holy *Sacrament* then took place on THE 27TH. 4 Brothers and Sisters participated for the first time and 3 watched for the 2nd time during this.

THE 28TH   Two people received the waters of Holy Baptism, a woman named *Johanna Sophia* and a widow named *Cornelia*. We especially rejoiced about the good fortune of the former, because she is from the family we wanted to send away recently, but who asked so urgently for us to give them another chance,[644] and the latter because she never really had permission to live here.

THE 30TH   In the Helpers' *Conference*, Brothers *Abraham* and *Nathanael* were assigned the care of external affairs[645] and we announced this to the Brothers and Sisters during the Singing Service. *Johann Jungmann*, who had been here visiting for several days, returned to *Gnadenhütten*. *Mr. Gibson*, who invited the *Delaware*, *Shawnee*, *Wyandot*, *Mingo* etc. to a *Treaty* in *Pittsburgh*[646] passed through here on his return journey. We received letters from *Litiz* dated *April* 13–28, with the touching news about *Sarepta* and *Nain* in Labrador.[647]

642. Matt. 10:37–38.

643. On the terminology, see note 30 above.

644. See entry for 22 April 1775.

645. With the death of Johannes on 15 May 1775 the office had become vacant. On 22 May the Helpers' Conference had been reminded that the office needed to be filled again.

646. On 20 and 21 May 1775 Dr. John Connolly, commanding officer of Fort Pitt, and Alexander McKee, deputy superintendent for Indian Affairs, invited the Mingo, Shawnee, and Delaware to a "meeting" at the Fort. See Scribner et al., *Revolutionary Virginia*, 3:152–53, 155–56; Arthur St. Clair to Governor Penn, 25 May 1775, Smith, *St. Clair Papers*, 1:355; and [Connolly], "Narrative of the Transactions," 12 (1888): 315–16. The Six Indian Nations were also invited; their chiefs arrived at Fort Pitt on 19 June 1775 (Scribner et al., *Revolutionary Virginia*, 3:208).

647. In early September 1774 a large part of the Moravian congregation at Sarepta (Russia) fled to Astrakan because they feared the rebels led by Pugachev. Sixty-five of the brethren who had stayed behind left Sarepta only after the plundering had already begun (Hegner, *Fortsetzung*, 148–57). After an exploratory trip to the Labrador to investigate the possibility of erecting two new mission stations,

Diary of Schoenbrunn *on the* Muskingum *from* June *I through* September 7, 1775[648]

JUNE IST   After Brother *David* had said farewell in the early service, he and Brother *Schebosch* and 2 Indian Brothers began their journey to Bethlehem.[649]

THE 4TH   We knelt and asked God, the worthy Holy Spirit, for merciful *Absolution* for all of our mistakes and for things in which we have fallen behind, and promised him new obedience and faithfulness.[650]

THE 5TH   Brother *Heckewelder* went to *Gnadenhütten* on business. *White Eye,* who had come here with his family for a visit on the 3rd of this month, informed our Indian Brothers of the contents of the message and the *expedition* to the *Wyandot,* from where the messengers have returned. *Chief Netawatwees* had renewed his *Alliance* and covenant of friendship with them and the rest of the *Nations* to the north and west, and expressed gratitude to the *Wyandot* for the land they had given them some years ago. A lot of *Belts* and *Strings of Wampum* were required for this.

THE IITH   *Wangomen,*[651] the Indian preacher from *Goschgosching* who had arrived here from *Onenge*[652] yesterday, was also present during the sermon about the Gospel, and he had a conversation with the Indian Brothers. At first he wanted to join with the Brothers immediately and said that his teaching was pretty much the same as ours. There were just a few things in ours that he did not support, for example the fact that so many people lived together and that people who had never seen God learned to talk about God. Not a single one of them had ever been to heaven. He, however, had already been there very often and he sent his soul there, where it got its nourishment, as often as he thought it necessary. Therefore he only had to take care of his body.[653] *Isaac* told him, Oh, how blind you are, and possessed by Satan! Do not think we believe a word of what you say. We used to believe you because we did not

the ship that had carried four missionaries on 14 September 1774 capsized on its return journey to Nain; two of the missionaries drowned and the others saved themselves (ibid., 135–37).

648. MAB, B 141, F 7, I 1, fol. 113. The same folder contains a copy of this diary in another hand in which all texts that have been bracketed in the original are omitted.

649. Zeisberger arrived at Bethlehem on 21 June 1775. See John Ettwein to the missionaries, c. first half of July 1775, MAB, E.P., B 965, F 42, no. 1044.

650. On 4 June 1775 the feast of Pentecost was celebrated.

651. Wangomen had been the great adversary of the Moravian missionaries in Goschgoschünk and the decisive cause of the congregation's relocation to the Muskingum. On the conflict in Goschgoschünk, see Introduction, p. 49.

652. Onenge is a settlement on the Allegheny River. Tanner, *Atlas,* 75, d2.

653. The formula "and he sent his soul there, where it got its nourishment, as often as he thought it necessary" clearly indicates that Wangomen is referring to visions. The more far-reaching formula "that whatever he said to him he said to God" indicates, if Zeisberger translated Wangomen's words correctly, that the preacher considered himself God's deputy on earth. See note 349 to entry for 13 April 1774.

understand any better. Now we know in whom we believe and that our teaching of the crucified Savior will last eternally. You, however, will be ruined with your teaching. *Wangomen* then answered him and said he should not talk so much, but should consider that whatever he said to him he said to God. He wanted to preach more to the Brothers, but they told him it would be better if he sought instruction from our children. They could tell him what he needed for his salvation.

Another well-known Indian from *Goschgosching* who had come with him listened as the Brothers extolled the Savior to him and urged him, a poor sinner, to seek his redemption at the cross. He cried a lot, stood up, and shook hands with all the Brothers who were present.

THE 14TH   *Chief Netawatwees* and *White Eye* stopped in here with some other Indians on their way to the *Fort.*[654] After a long drought, we had a pleasant rain this afternoon. We were all grateful to our dear Lord for this. It was delightful that just when an Indian who is not well disposed toward us and who mocks us expressed his *sentiments* that it was indeed amazing that it did not rain where the believers were, while they had enough rain where he lived among the unbelievers, the heavy rain came and he was ashamed.

THE 16TH   The *Chief, White Eye,* and other strangers went with the Brothers and Sisters to cut Indian corn today, and our Brothers and Sisters praised them for working diligently with them.

THE 17TH   The *Chief* and his people continued their journey to the *Fort.* Brother *John Jungmann* from *Gnadenhütten* came here for a visit.

THE 19TH   *White Eye* also left for the *Fort.* Immediately upon his arrival he had chosen *Wangomen,* who was already prepared to go home, as his traveling companion as far as *Kaskaskunk* and he kept him there that long. He certainly would not have done this without a reason, because his conversations with him in recent days clearly showed that he would like to lead him away from his heathen superstitions and make him a friend of the Brothers. Once when many Brothers had gathered around, he told them among other things, My Brothers, if I learned that our whole *Nation* was prepared to believe in the true God and was organized in congregations like the one you have here, then I would be happy and thank the Savior. I would be happiest if I could live with you right away and hear about the Savior every day. However, I do not yet see a real chance for this, because I fear the Brothers' enemies might tear down again what has been built up. I am not yet giving up hope, though, of either moving to your place or having you move to mine. He told *Isaac* he realized

654. Connolly and McKee had invited the Mingo, Shawnee, Delaware, and Six Indian Nations to Fort Pitt; see note 646 to entry for 30 May 1775. When the Six Indian Nations arrived at Fort Pitt on 19 June 1775, Connolly welcomed them; yet the following day, when the negotiations began, Connolly was arrested and they had to be content with being treated to some polite speeches by representatives from Pittsburgh, among them George Croghan. Scribner et al., *Revolutionary Virginia,* 3:214–15. Official negotiations began on 29 June 1775; ibid., 238–40, 246–49, 257–61, 262–68.

there were already enough Indians here. Therefore he had thought of giving us his *Town* including all the houses standing there. He hoped we would accept this offer because he believes many Indians would come there if there were Brothers there.

THE 20TH   Many of the Sisters went out to pick berries, which are very plentiful this year. They are a kind of wild cherries and are very sweet.[655] Many Indians are living on them during the current serious famine.

THE 21ST   Many strangers came from *Walhandünk* and *Sikhewünk*[656] again, some to visit and some to buy Indian corn. Most of them were so starved and emaciated that you would think they had just gotten up after a long illness if you did not know their circumstances.

THE 24TH   Several days ago an Indian had asked for permission to live with us and we accepted him on probation. He had planted in *Goschachgünk,* so the Brothers advised him to wait until his Indian corn was harvested, and in the meantime to consider the matter well. Today he came with his family and said that he had considered it well and his fields should not prevent him; he would let that go immediately. He would earn what he needed to support himself through the work of his hands. Different strangers had come here in recent days to work for our Brothers and Sisters in order to earn food, although they are so weak from hunger that they can only work a little. The famine continues to worsen and there is no more Indian corn to be found among the Indians except in both our *Towns*.

July

JULY 4th   A messenger came here from *Gnadenhütten* yesterday to call some of our Indian Brothers there because the *Shawnee Chief* and his people, who had arrived there on their journey to the *Fort,* have something to say to them. Therefore Brothers *Isaac* and *Cornelius* set out to go there today and returned here on the 5TH. The *Shawnee Chief* told them the following: We admit we acted badly last summer and were disobedient to our grandfather, despite the fact that you warned us several times not to continue with our evil plan, first in *Woaketameki* and finally at the *Great Plaine,*[657] but to join our grandfather in holding firmly to the chain of friendship. We did not do this, but followed our own will. Now some of your people have been killed through

---

655. Probably *Prunus serotina*. Mahr, "Delaware Terms for Plants and Animals," 11.

656. Walhandünk, usually called Walhanding, was a settlement on the river with the same name. It was about seventeen miles upstream from Goschachgünk. Sikhewünk, occasionally called Salt Licks, at the confluence of Salt Creek and the Muskingum, was a day's journey from Lichtenau. See entry for 5 Sept. 1778.

657. See entry for 17 June 1774; and for White Eyes' role in October 1774, see entries for 1 to 5 Nov. 1774. The chief of the Shawnee was Cornstalk; see next note.

our disobedience, so we want to express our remorse and wipe the tears from your eyes. We hope this might be buried and forgotten, and we promise to be obedient to our grandfather in the future. The Brothers expressed their satisfaction and pleasure at this statement, but directed them to the *Chief* of the *Delaware Nation,* whom they would surely find in the *Fort.*

THE 7TH   A white man, the *Shawnee Chief,* his wife, and 5 others came here for a visit and after staying for several hours they returned to *Gnadenhütten* so they can leave for the *Fort* early tomorrow. The former had been sent out by the *Committee* in *Pittsburgh*[658] to find out what things looked like for them among all the *Nations* and to bring them reliable news about this, and also to take the *Shawnee* to the *Fort.* He had also learned from there that the *Commandant* in *Detroit* had sent *Belts* and messages to the *Nations* through the French, encouraging them to raise the hatchet against the *Colonies.*[659] Therefore the *Committee* in *Pittsburgh* had taken measures as hastily as possible to prevent this from happening, and this seems to have had a good *Effect.* The misfortune this could have caused has been subdued and buried.[660]

Our Brothers could not tell one of the *Shawnee* who was here visiting enough about the Savior. He said, I believe everything I hear from you is the truth, and I really like to hear it. I will be happy if you visit us in our *Towns* some day, and then I will listen to you even more. I know there are also many more of our people who would like to hear this. Another *Shawnee* who could speak *Delaware* well and was interpreter, said, If you come down to visit us I will interpret for you, because I like listening to you. However, a third said, These people can speak well; this is true. But where did they learn this? They learned it from the White people; otherwise they would not know any more than we do.

THE 8TH   54 Brothers and Sisters partook of the Lord's Supper through the Holy *Sacrament.* One Brother and 2 Sisters participated in this for the first time.

---

658. On 24 June the Virginia House of Burgesses had asked a committee consisting of George Washington, Thomas Walker, James Wood, Andrew Lewis, John Walker, and Adam Stephen "to meet the Chiefs or head Men of the said *Ohio Indians,* as soon as that same can be done, at such place, as they shall find most proper, to ratify and confirm the said Treaty [of Camp Charlotte], on the part of this Colony, and to demand and receive of the said *Indians* the ratification and full performance of the said Treaty on their parts." McIlwaine et al., *Journals of the House of Burgesses of Virginia,* 282. The chief of the Shawnee mentioned is Cornstalk, GD for 3 July 1775, F 5, I 2. We are unable to identify the white companion of Cornstalk.

659. James Wood reported similar French activities in his letter to the Commissioners of Virginia, 9 July 1775, *RUO,* 35–38.

660. From "He had also learned," the text is bracketed by another hand. As yet the committee had not yet taken any measures to curb these activities. James Wood, however, informed the commissioners that he intended to visit not only the settlements of the Shawnee but those of the Wyandot and the other western tribes in order to represent the cause of the colonies, "and to Counteract any diabolical Schemes formed by the Enemies of this Country to remove any bad Impressions which may have been made on the Minds of these Savages" (*RUO,* 36).

THE 9TH   Early in the day was the *Liturgy* for *Communion,* then the sermon, and in the afternoon a service for those who have been baptized.

THE IITH   The *Wyandot* we know came from *Cayahaga* with his daughter and others for a visit. *Chief Netawatwees* and some of his people also arrived at our place from the *Fort.* He was very satisfied with the *Speeches* given by *Colonel Connely* in the name of the *Virginians* and by *Colonel Croghan* in the name of the *Pennsylvanians.* He told the Brothers a few things about this, but said they should wait until *White Eye* would bring the entire negotiations in writing.[661] He felt very much at home with us and we provided him hospitality. On the I2TH he continued his journey home. A woman whom we do not know brought her dead child here from *Sugar Creek* and asked our Brothers and Sisters to bury the child because she herself was very ill, and they did so.

THE I3TH   A number of Brothers went to *Sikhewünk,* some by water and some on land, to boil salt there and to hunt.

THE I6TH   There were 7 *Mingo* among those who attended our services. They had been imprisoned in the *Fort* since last fall.[662] About 20 Indian strangers came here who were moving to the *Shawnee.* They had 6 kegs of *Rum* with them.[663]

THE 2IST   *Isaac* and some other Brothers returned from *Cayahaga* where they had gone a number of days ago to buy some things from the *Traders* there.[664] The *Wyandot* who lives there had received them very cordially and offered them hospitality.

THE 27TH   *White Eye,* who came here from the *Fort* yesterday, continued on to *Goschachgünk. Isaac* escorted him as far as *Gnadenhütten.*[665]

661. The protocols of the negotiations from 29 June to 6 July 1775 at Fort Pitt are printed in Scribner et al., *Revolutionary Virginia,* 3:238–40, 246–49, 257–61, 262–68.

662. The hostages had been freed during the negotiations at Fort Pitt; see note 661.

663. On the function of Indians as traders in rum, see entry for 2 March 1774, note 338.

664. Within the previous year trade relations between Cayahaga and the Delaware had improved considerably, as may be seen not only in the repeated visits of Wyandot but also in the fact that Christian Indians went to Cayahaga to purchase goods brought over from Detroit. This indicates changes in trading patterns: the Delaware had not accepted Attike, the place Pennsylvania had designated as the new trade center (see entry for 26 Aug. 1774, note 497), nor had they bowed to Virginia's attempts to corner all Indian trade at Pittsburgh; see entry for 25 Aug. 1775.

665. At the conference at Pittsburgh White Eyes pursued his plan to achieve a secure legal title for the land the Delaware were settling on. After Dr. John Connolly, who had been released from prison for the duration of the conference, had in a dramatic gesture handed the Delaware "A Large Belt representing The Chain of Friendship" and had empowered them to keep the peace in the Ohio region—an empowerment confirmed by the Six Indian Nations the following day—White Eyes combined this empowerment symbolized in the large belt with his own concerns: "[He desired] the Big Knife to put one End of this Belt into the Hands of King George our mutual Father and acquaint him we are setled at Quisoching [i.e., Coshocton or Goschachgünk] where we hold fast by the other End being the Centre of a tract of Country given to us by our Uncles the Wyandots." Scribner et al., *Revolutionary Virginia,* 3:259, 263–64, 265. The speaker of the Six Indian Nations ignored White Eyes' statement that the Delaware were settling on a piece of land transferred to them by the Wyandot and the elevation of the main Delaware settlement as the center of negotiation for the Ohio region. John Connolly, by contrast, interpreted White Eyes' linking of the land problem with the attitude

THE 28TH   We learned that a *Belt* and a *String of Wampum* had actually been presented to the *Delaware* in *Goschachgünk* with the words, Be prepared, my children and brothers, because in 20 days the *Virginians* will attack you and kill you all. However, we, your father and your brothers, will support you and help you. The expression father and brother shows clearly enough that the message comes from the French and English in *Canada*.[666] However, the *Chief* gave the *Belt* to a *Virginian Captain* who had just arrived there from the *Fort* to take it along and answer it.[667]

THE 31ST   *Abraham, Willhelm,* and some other Brothers went to *Gnadenhütten* to visit Brother *Josua,* who is ill there. The Brothers who were mentioned on the 13th of this month returned from boiling salt. They had made enough salt to make it worth their while. *Thomas* from *Gekelemukpechünk*[668] was with them and had various opportunities to witness for the Savior both in *Goschachgünk* and *Sikhewünk.* Many hearts came who really wanted to hear and they kept him there for several days. He had been a notorious, evil Indian among the savages before he came to us. Although he told them he was one of the least of his fellow Brothers, since he was still a newcomer and had not been with us for long and also had not yet experienced as much in his heart as some among us, they still insisted he tell them what he believes and what he has experienced during his time with us. He agreed to do this. All the Indians in

toward George III as a victory of loyalism over rebellious colonial ideas. He intended at the same time, as he confided to Arthur St. Clair, to use White Eyes' intentions to Virginia's advantage. According to St. Clair he said: "He is immediately to go England [sic] with White Eyes and some other Delaware chiefs, to solicit for them a confirmation of the country which they now live in, great part of which is within the bounds of this Province, and Lord Dunmore is to back it with all his interest. They are to represent to the King's ministers that they have received the Christian religion, have got notions of property, and in a great measure changed their way of life, and can not change their place of abode as they have heretofore done, and which they must again do if Pennsylvania is allowed to extend beyond the Ohio." St. Clair considered these ideas "ridiculous." Smith, *St. Clair Papers,* 1:358.

    666. From the words "The expression" bracketed by another hand. On the supposedly French activities—in reality pro-English activities against the rebellious colonies—see entry for 7 July 1775, and Wood, "Journal," entry for 20 July 1775, Scribner et al., *Revolutionary Virginia,* 3:326, and sworn deposition of Garret Pendergast Jr., ibid., 3:327. According to this deposition the Delaware had been at Detroit themselves and had participated in a conference held under the leadership of Duperon Baby, an influential French trader and experienced advisor of the commanding officer of Fort Detroit. According to Pendergast, Baby asked the Indians "immediately to strike the white people, that the Wiandots and all other tribes would join, that he would furnish them and at the same time Offered them Ammunition for that purpose. He also told them, the White People were now quite Round them and Intended soon to fall on the Indians."

    667. James Wood and Simon Girty had left Fort Pitt on 18 July in order to invite Delaware, Shawnee, Wyandot, Mingo, and Seneca to peace negotiations at Fort Pitt and to explain the conflict between the colonies and England to the Indian representatives. They visited Gnadenhütten on 21 July and on the following day arrived at Goschachgünk, where they obviously received the French belt. Wood's diary is printed with modern annotation in Scribner et al., *Revolutionary Virginia,* 3:271–74, 316–17, 334, 337, 343–44, 352–53, 362–63, 377, 383–84, 388–90, and as one complete text in *RUO,* 34–67.

    668. Thomas was a grandson of Netawatwees and thus belonged to one of the most influential families; see entry for 24 Jan. 1776.

the *Town* and in that area were then called together and he proclaimed the Savior to them with tears in his eyes, so that many of those present also cried. When he wanted to go, they asked him to stay longer because they had already called the Indians for another meeting in the evening. He then did so and spoke with them about the Savior until late in the night. One of his listeners, who is a *Chief* and his uncle, asked him to visit again and said he would go with him then to *Schoenbrunn*. Another who had cried a lot said, You will see me there soon as well.

August

THE 2ND   Many Brothers and Sisters went to *Gnadenhütten* to attend the burial of Brother *Josua senior* who died yesterday, and they returned home in the evening.

THE 6TH   At the request of the parents, a sick child was baptized into Jesus' death with the name *Sulamith*.

THE 10TH   We were happy to see our dear Brother *David* and his company among us again after his visit in Bethlehem.[669] During the evening service he extended greetings to the Brothers and Sisters from the Brothers and Sisters in Bethlehem and *Nazareth*. This brought everyone much joy.

THE 12TH   Brother *Schmick* came back here from *Gnadenhütten* for a *Conference,* to which the Savior added his blessing. *White Eye* also came here for a visit. He told us that they had held a *Councel* in *Goschachgünk* a few days ago, when *Chief Netawatwees* had declared openly to the people that he was concerned about his *Nation's* welfare and wanted them to be a peaceful and happy people. The only way he knew they could achieve this was to accept God's word, and this was the best advice he could give them. They could see from the Indian believers that this is the truth. They could become a people like this as well since they had sufficient examples before them, if they followed these. Finally he closed with the words, Now I have told you my thoughts; consider this. If you accept my advice and follow it, you will see that I have spoken the truth and that things will go well for you. However, if you do not accept it you should know that I will not advise you any more and will turn away from you. Then two of the leaders replied that they were happy about the talk *Chief* had just given. They had waited a long time for such a statement from him. As soon as they saw how they could carry this out, they were prepared to join with their people in doing this and they really hoped it might happen soon. *White Eye* continued by saying that there was a special stirring among the Indians;

---

669. Zeisberger probably carried with him the letter John Ettwein had written to the missionaries in July, MAB, E.P., B 965, F 42, no. 1044; the most important concern of this letter had been to encourage better cooperation and coordination of activities between Gnadenhütten and Schönbrunn by monthly or quarterly meetings of the missionaries of both places.

people everywhere were talking about the Brothers and they hoped that they might come to them and preach the Gospel. They realized it would not work for them to come to us because our *Town* was already so heavily populated. Therefore they preferred for Brothers to come to them. He said that when he came to our place now, many Indian men and women had followed him a long way and asked him to look out for their best interests, because they believed he would talk with the Brothers about this. Therefore we can expect to receive an *Invitation* soon to go to them. However, *Killbuck* and his followers, the *Wolf's Tribe*,[670] are still opposed to this although *White Eye* has already worked hard to persuade the former.

THE 13TH   The sermon was about the redemption for all humans achieved through Christ's blood. In the Children's Service Brother *David* extended sincere greetings to them from the children in Bethlehem, which delighted everyone. Then there was the devotion in preparation for Holy Communion, which was announced for next Saturday.

THE 14TH   *White Eye,* who had a happy visit here and said he had completely regained his strength, returned home and promised to return again in 3 weeks.

THE 19TH   We had the most blessed enjoyment of the Body and Blood in Holy Communion. 3 Brothers and Sisters watched for the first time and 3 for the 2nd time. Two *Onondagas* and 2 *Senecas* arrived here from *Onondago* on their journey to the *Shawnee.* The first two are friends of our *Thomas* and had a message from *Onondago* to all of their people among the *Shawnee,* saying they should all come home by next spring and not stay there any longer.[671] They also wanted to take our *Thomas* with them down to the *Shawnee* to hear everything, but he refused, telling them he did not want to leave. He was happy that he was finally here where he could hear about the Savior every day. Otherwise they brought good news from the 6 *Nations* that things there were peaceful. They continued their journey very early on THE 20TH. After the *Liturgy* for Holy Communion, Brother *Jungmann* preached the sermon. During the Congregational Service, which *Killbuck* and some other strangers attended, two participated in the waters of Holy Baptism; their names are *Christoph* and *Priscilla.* Two Sisters were received into the congregation, *Christina* from the *Onondaga* family and *Sara.* Both had been baptized on the *Mohawk River.* In conclusion, we knelt in prayer and commended these 4 Brothers and Sisters and God's entire work among the Indians to His grace.

THE 21ST   Sister *Schmick*[672] and a group of Sisters came from *Gnadenhütten* for a visit, and they returned there toward evening.

---

670. Killbuck was Netawatwees' son but was a member of the Wolf clan on matrilineal grounds; see Introduction, pp. 17–19. Captain Pipe, also a member of the Wolf clan, also opposed Christianization.

671. By this time there was a history of efforts to persuade the Mingo to return to the homelands of the Six Indian Nations. See entry for 12 Sept. 1774 and note 506.

672. Johanna Schmick.

THE 23RD   After the early service was a Helpers' *Conference*. We had learned that a French *Trader* from *Detroit*[673] wanted to come to our *Town* also now to trade, but we had good reasons[674] not to approve of this. Therefore we sent *Isaac* to *Cayahaga* with a message forbidding the *Traders* from coming into our *Town* or into our area, because we might have difficulties under the current serious circumstances. We received news through White people who came from *Detroit* that 300 *Volunteers* had arrived there for the security of the *Town,* as people say, because they are afraid that the *Virginians* might make themselves masters of the *Fort*.[675]

THE 25TH   The Savior took a little boy named *Johannes* home to himself. He was one year and 4 months old. He was a sweet child who loved the Savior and was especially happy when songs were sung to him. His earthly dwelling was laid to rest on the 26TH.

THE 27TH   At the request of the parents, Brother *David* baptized the baby boy born to *Mr. Conner*s on the 19th of this month with the name *John*. We received a packet of congregational newsletters and letters from *Pittsburgh*. They had been in *Lancaster* since spring waiting for transportation.[676]

THE 29TH   After the single Brothers had contritely concluded their Choir year, asked the Prince of their Choir for merciful *Absolution* for all their mistakes and shortcomings and promised anew to become his property with body and soul, they celebrated their festival today in his sweet presence. They reflected in blessing on their ode, read a Choir talk, and in conclusion had a blessed Choir communion.

THE 31ST   During the early service we commended our widowers and widows to the Savior for blessing on their festival day today. Afterward they had a Choir service, which Brother *Jungmann* led. In the afternoon they had a Lovefeast. During this they remembered that since their last festival 4 widows have been baptized, one attained Holy Communion, one died, and one, that is *Anna Johanna,* has joined the Choir. In all, there were 18 widows and 2 widowers. In conclusion they had a blessed Service of Adoration. The Savior revealed himself graciously to them during all the services and laid his peace upon them.

September

THE IST   Early in the day Brother *David* went to *Gnadenhütten* and returned home in the evening. Brother *Schmick* then came from there for a visit

---

673. "French" and "from Detroit" bracketed by another hand.
674. See entries for 21 and 28 July 1775.
675. We found no evidence to confirm this rumor.
676. On 27 August Nicholas Cresswell visited Schönbrunn and noted his friendly impressions in his diary. Thornely, *Journal of Nicholas Cresswell,* 106–7.

ON THE 2ND. *Isaac* returned from *Cayahaga*. He had taken the message that the French[677] *Trader* should not come to our *Towns* to trade, as he had planned. At first he had not paid much attention to this, but said he would come anyway. However, when *Isaac* emphatically and earnestly forbade him from doing this, he finally promised to refrain.[678]

THE 5TH *White Eye,* who had come for a visit yesterday, spoke with Brother *David* today and told him how far they have gotten in their undertakings and also where they were having trouble. They had held another *Councel* in *Goschachgünk* with all of their people, and the *Chief* reminded them of his recent address to them. He asked them again to accept the Gospel and told them the best advice he had was for them to choose the Brothers as their teachers; they had the right teaching. He would like to see this done soon, and every day seemed long to him until it happened. Then they discussed the matter together a great deal and the people wanted the *Chief* and *White Eye* to give them suggestions. However, they quickly said that they could not do this before they had spoken with the Brothers about it, because they did not want to do or undertake anything without their knowledge and *consent*. Therefore, *White Eye* came here this time just to tell us of this in advance and to talk with us. He said that when the *Chief* went to the *Fort* he would come through here and also speak with us, so that we could give him an answer to take home when he returned. Brother *David* asked him if they wanted to have Brothers in *Goschachgünk* or if they were planning to establish a separate *Town* for those who wanted to accept God's word. He replied that they had not wanted to decide anything, and therefore they had not even asked much until they had spoken with us. They had discussed the fact that when we originally came here we were planning to establish 3 *Towns* for the Indian believers. Two were there already and were pretty well occupied. Therefore it would be good if the 3rd were established now. If they did this it would be better for them to cancel their fall hunting and work on the *Town* instead. Brother *David* replied that it would certainly be better if a *Town* were established for the Indian believers and for those who wanted to become believers, so that we would have a free hand and could arrange and do everything as we wanted, and all those who wanted to live there would have to agree to our rules. It was also not really best for a large crowd of them to come right in the beginning, but preferably gradually so that things did not get disorderly. They had surely already done a lot of work and building in *Goschachgünk*. He said they had never really had much desire to do much work there, though, because they always believed they were working in vain and would not stay there long. Brother *David* told him further that he should not keep the Indians from their fall hunt because of that, because even if it does happen they cannot do anything before spring. *Schön-*

677. "French" bracketed by another hand.
678. See entry for 23 Aug. 1775.

brunn and *Gnadenhütten* were not well enough supplied with workers anyway that we could spare anyone. However, after *Netawatwees* has spoken with us we would consider it and give them a decision. In the meantime, he should be considering a place where such a *Town* could be laid out, because he is better acquainted with the land in this country than any of us. If he had more than one place to suggest, then we could take a look at it ourselves later and choose the one of them which suits us best. He was very satisfied with everything and happy that he had learned what we thought thus far, and then he returned home.

THE 7TH   The married Brothers and Sisters celebrated their festival with much grace and many blessings. After the morning devotions they had a Choir Service, a Lovefeast in the afternoon, and then a Service of Adoration with those who have been baptized. During the Congregational Service, the baby boy born to *Timothei junior* and *Sarah* this morning was baptized with the name *Nathan*. Circumstances did not allow Brother and Sister *Jungmann* to go to *Gnadenhütten* this morning, so they had a blessed Choir Communion together.

Diary of Schoenbrunn *on the* Muskingum *From* September *1775* until February *23,* 1776[679]

SEPTEMBER 9th   We sent letters through *Pittsburgh* to *Litiz* and Bethlehem with some White people[680] who were passing through here.

THE 14TH   Brother *Schmick* came here from *Gnadenhütten* and after we had consulted with each other about various things, he returned toward evening.

THE 16TH   Brother *Schebosch* left for *Litiz* with *John Jungmann*.[681] The latter's father accompanied us as far as the first night's lodging and then returned.

THE 17TH   Brother *David* preached the sermon and Brother *Heckewelder* led the Children's Service. *Mr. Gibson* and another White man[682] and a

---

679. MAB, B 141, F 7, I 3, fol. 121.

680. The white people were Nicholas Cresswell and John Anderson; see Thornely, *Journal of Nicholas Cresswell,* 113.

681. For John Jungmann, see note 242 to entry for 16 Aug. 1773. Zeisberger indicates in his letters that Jungmann posed considerable problems; it is likely that he was psychologically disturbed. The diaries offer no specific information, however; in his letters Zeisberger describes Jungmann's problems as frenzy, caused by haughtiness. He adds that John never talked with the brethren about these problems. The decision to send him back to Bethlehem was confirmed by the lot. Zeisberger to Seidel, 5 and 15 Sept. 1775, MAB, B 229, F 4, I 25 and 26.

682. On 12 September 1775 the Commissioners of the Virginia Convention had asked John Gibson to go with Allaniwisica (probably one of the sons of the Shawnee chief Cornstalk) to meet the delegations of the western tribes and bring them to the planned conference in Fort Pitt as fast as possible (Scribner et al., *Revolutionary Virginia,* 4:98). Gibson had returned to Fort Pitt by 24 September 1775, where he and "James Rogers an Adopted Shawnese" provided information about hostile activities; Rogers reported events that had their origins at Fort Detroit, while Gibson told of a letter

Mingo Chief returned from the *Shawnee* on their way to the *Fort*. They had picked them up to go to a *Treaty* and left them in *Gekelemukpechünk*. The former told us that the gentlemen in the *Fort* who had been authorized by *Congress*[683] to hold the *Treaty* with the Indians were glad to see that some of our Indians were there, too. However, we told him that we would prefer for our Indians to be spared this because we knew they suffered harm on such occasions and would not be treated well by the Indian savages. Furthermore our Indians had never had anything to do with the *Treaties* and had never even been called to these before.

THE 19TH   A couple of *Shawnee* came here on their journey to the *Fort* and stayed with us for a couple of days.

THE 21ST   During the Helpers' *Conference* Brothers *Abraham* and *Nathanael* were given the job of the care of external affairs in general. Our blessed *Johannes* had served in this office. On the Sisters' side 2 Sisters, *Anna Salome* and *Anna Caritas,* were appointed to this and we announced it to the congregation today.[684] We also spoke with an Indian and his wife who had come here and requested to live with us. We told them they had permission to be here as long as they followed our rules.

THE 24TH   Through an *express* messenger we received a letter from the gentlemen in *Pittsburgh* authorized by *Congress* to hold the current *Treaty* with the Indians. In this Brother *David* was cordially invited to attend this with some of our Indians.[685]

THE 25TH   The twins born to Brother *Nicolaus* and Sister *Amalia* yesterday were baptized with the names *Lea* and *Amalia*.

THE 26TH   *White Eye* came here to spend a few days with us until the rest of the Indians gather here. Then he will leave with them for the *Fort*.

THE 28TH   We buried the earthly dwelling left behind by our Brother *Salomo,* who entered his eternal peace yesterday. He became acquainted with the Brothers during their first visit to *Goschgosching* in 1767, when he heard the Gospel for the first time, acquired a taste for it, and believed the Brothers' witness about the redemption in Jesus' blood. Then when the Mission on the *Ohio* was begun in 1768, he came to the Brothers right away. Because he was a *Chief* of the *Munsee Nation,* he helped them much in their dangerous situation, when they were experiencing much opposition among the Indians there as well as from the *Seneca Chief* in whose country they were. When the latter sent a

---

from Dr. John Connolly to White Eyes. All of this indicates that the "white man" Zeisberger mentions must be James Rogers. Ibid., 4:140–41.

683. On 13 July 1775 the Continental Congress appointed Benjamin Franklin, Patrick Henry, and James Wilson "Commissioners for Indian Affairs of the Middle Department"; on 14 September the Congress approved the proposal that Lewis Morris, who at that time was in Pittsburgh, replace Benjamin Franklin as commissioner, and the next day Thomas Walker replaced Patrick Henry. Ford, *Journals of the Continental Congress,* 2:183, 251.

684. See entry for 30 May 1775.

685. See entry for 17 Sept. 1775.

message to all Indians on the *Ohio* saying not to tolerate or listen to the Brothers, he openly declared to them in a message that he had accepted God's word and would never abandon it. Then the Brothers actually received permission to stay there because they were already there. Although the Indians were forbidden to listen to them, this was enough for the Brothers at that time.[686] On *December* 25, 1769 he was baptized in *Lawunakhannek*. On *March* 28, 1771, he became a communicant. After his baptism he lived a blessed life, so that we could only rejoice over him. He had life and feeling from the Savior in his heart. You could sense this in him each time you spoke with him. He also had ears to hear and he was able to grasp and remember what he heard in the services. He was always as happy as a child when Indians were baptized, and his heart was always revived anew when he saw the Savior's work being done among them. When the war with the *Shawnee* began last year, however, he left the congregation, partly for the sake of his children and friends, who misled him to do this, but primarily due to disbelief; he thought our work would come to an end and we would be bothered or maybe even destroyed by the *Shawnee* and Indian savages or by the White people.[687] However, he could not live among the savage Indians either. Therefore he always stayed alone, but he had no peace in his heart. In the fall he moved closer to us and when he heard that more had been baptized and saw that the Savior's work was continuing after all, he could no longer stay away from us. Therefore he asked the Brothers to take him in again.[688] Then on *January* 5th of this year he returned to us, grateful and happy that he could be in the congregation again. He said now he would never leave it again as long as he lived. During his illness he often prayed to the Savior, Dear Savior, come and take me to you, until he died with the blessing of the congregation, accompanied by the beautiful Watchword, I, even I, am he that blotteth out thy transgressions for mine own sake, and will not remember thy sins.[689]

SEPTEMBER 29TH   Yesterday and today *Delaware* head people and Indians gathered here to go to the *Fort* for the *Treaty*. Chief *Netawatwees* had let us know some time ago that he would pass through here on his journey to the *Fort* since he had something to tell us then, but he was not able to come because of illness. Therefore he instructed his *Councellors* to tell the Brothers and Indian believers the following: Brothers and Friends! It has now been 3 years since you came to us in this area. All of us including myself are happy and grateful to you for this. Immediately upon your arrival here you informed us that you were planning to establish 2 or 3 *Towns* for the Indian believers in this area. There are two now, and we see that they are already pretty densely occupied. We have agreed and decided unanimously to accept God's word,

---

686. See Introduction, pp. 47–49.
687. See entry for 9 July 1774.
688. See entry for 3 Jan. 1775.
689. Isa. 43:25. This was the Watchword for 27 Sept. 1775.

after long and thorough consideration, so we think it is now time to establish the 3rd *Town* so that our people can see that they have a place for as many of them as want to become believers. We ask you to do this as soon as possible. You should begin to lay the foundation, plant God's word there, and begin the initial institutions there that you understand best. These institutions should not just be for the elderly and adults, but primarily for our youth and children, because our plan and desire is that this should become something that lasts eternally, as long as there are Indians. Therefore we hope and desire that our children will be instructed in reading the Holy Scriptures, so that it will never be forgotten. To this end, we are asking the Brothers and Indian believers to help us with this and we hope that you will have mercy on our people, old, young, and children, and that you will serve them gladly and willingly with the word of God. We look to you, because we are not able to do this. *White Eye* said these were the *Chief's* words to us and he would like to see this done as soon as possible. He would like to see the beginning of this at least before he dies, because he will not live much longer.

During *White Eye's* absence the *Chief* had instructed one of his *Councellors* to present these words to us. However, he had appointed the latter to do this and sat next to him during the talk. We replied that their words pleased us and were good to hear. We wanted to consider this further, and because we could see from the talk that the *Chief* and the others would like to have a *Resolution* from us soon, we hoped to give them an answer when they returned from the *Fort*.

Some Indian Brothers have to go to the *Fort* tomorrow,[690] so we had Holy Communion today. 3 Brothers and Sisters participated for the first time, 3 watched for the 2nd time, and 1 for the first time.

THE 31ST   *White Eye* left with a large entourage of Indians to go to the *Fort* for the *Treaty*. During their stay here they were extremely quiet, orderly and friendly. Immediately upon their arrival they had informed us that they wanted to hear the Gospel, so there was a sermon in the morning and in the evening as long as they were here. They listened very attentively during these and some were also very touched. There are many nice people among them, among the leaders as well, who enjoy hearing about the Savior.

Brother *Jungmann* has had a fever for a while now, which worsened, and he had to lie down today. Therefore Brother *David* wrote to the *Commissioners* in the *Fort* and informed them why he could not come to the *Treaty*.[691]

October

THE 6TH   Some Brothers spoke with an Indian stranger who comes here often, and who is half *Mingo*, about a White boy who was a prisoner of

690. See entry for 24 Sept. 1775. The mission congregations were represented at the congress by Willhelm, Nathanael, and Isaac. See entry for 29 Oct. 1775.

691. Letter not found.

theirs. He told him he should deliver him to the *Fort*. If he did not do this, he should never let himself be seen in our *Town* again. He promised to hand the boy over as soon as he was asked to.[692]

THE 8TH   The sermon was about Jesus' sacrifice for our sins, which is good through eternity. Then there was a service for the baptized Brothers and Sisters, during which the Savior revealed himself quite graciously, and in the evening there was a Congregational Service.

THE 10TH   Brother *Schmick* came here from *Gnadenhütten* for a *Conference*. During this we discussed the *Chiefs'* suggestion that we establish a 3rd *Town* and considered what answer we should give them about this. We all agreed that we should accept their suggestion, but that we would first look for a suitable site for this and discuss it with them again. Then toward evening Brother *Schmick* returned.

Otherwise the Brothers and Sisters were very busy throughout the week harvesting their fields, and some houses were built.

THE 22ND   After the sermon Brother *David* baptized the baby boy born to Brother *Gottfried* and Sister *Justine* on the 19th of this month. He received the name *Martin*. Sister *Jungmann*, who had already had the three-day fever for a long time, became very ill today with pains in her side. She improved the following days after she was bled and given some medicine. The fever left her and she recovered completely. We were very happy and grateful to the Savior for this.

THE 27TH   We were delighted by our Brother *Schebosch's* safe return from *Litiz*.[693] He brought us many warm greetings and letters from there. During the evening service, he extended sincere greetings from there to the congregation, which delighted everyone.

THE 29TH   Brothers *Willhelm, Nathanael,* and *Isaac* returned from the *Treaty* at the *Fort* and 6 *Wyandots*, including one *Chief*, came with them. They stayed here for a couple of days and attended the services regularly. Indians from 6 different *Nations* were present at this *Treaty* and people believe they will remain quiet and act peacefully toward the *Colonies*, which is the main thing they were admonished to do.[694] On this occasion *White Eye* had addressed both the *Nations* and the *Commissioners* on behalf of his *Nation* and informed them

692. The Virginia Commissioners' rebuke to the Shawnee (the Mingo were not officially represented at the conference) that they had not yet given up all their prisoners was not unjustified. Scribner et al., *Revolutionary Virginia*, 4:198.

693. See entry for 16 Sept. 1775.

694. Between 10 and 19 October 1775 the Commissioners of the Continental Congress, Lewis Morris and James Wilson, as well as the Virginia delegates Thomas Walker, Andrew Lewis, John Walker, Adam Stephen, and James Wood, met the chiefs and captains of the Delaware, Shawnee, Wyandot, Mingo, Six Indian Nations, and Ottawa. The representatives of the Continental Congress explained the conflict between the colonies and England and asked the tribes to remain neutral. In separate negotiations between the Virginia delegates and the representatives of the western tribes, the results of the negotiations at Camp Charlotte (see entry for 30 Oct. 1774 and note 531) were confirmed and sealed. *RUO*, 79–127.

that they wanted to accept God's word.[695] He repeated this frequently during his talks at the *Treaty.* He then traveled on to *Philadelphia,* so many people think he went there to get either an English or Quaker preacher. However, no one knows the purpose of his journey. Because of this, the leaders from *Goschachgünk* did not come through here on their return journey from the *Fort,* but went straight home. We thus did not have to give them an answer as we had promised, and this will wait until he himself comes or we hear more about how the matter turns out.

[November]

NOVEMBER 1ST   During the evening service there was a talk about the text, which dealt with our fellowship with the congregation triumphant; we are prepared and made ready here to go before Him one day and face to face to see Him in whom we believe and for whom we have so often longed.[696]

THE 8TH   Brother *David* went to *Gnadenhütten* to talk to Brother *Schmick* about various things, and he returned home in the evening. Many Indians returned from the *Fort.* We had to tell some of them to go on because they had *Rum* with them.

THE 11TH   After we had Speakings with the Brothers and Sisters yesterday and the day before yesterday, 62 Brothers and Sisters partook of his Body and Blood with hungry and thirsty souls in the holy *Sacrament.* 4 Brothers and Sisters participated in this high grace for the first time and 3 watched for the first time.

Mr. Gibson, the current *Agent of Indian Affairs,* arrived here from *Pittsburgh* with 3 other white people and some *Mingo.* They were on a journey to the *Shawnee* to receive the prisoners and what they had promised them in the *Treaty.*[697] Another man named *Dodge,* however, came with a couple of *Mingo* to go to the *Wyandot* and western *Nations* with the large *Congress Belt,* 6 feet long and over half a foot wide, to inform them of the conclusion of the *Treaty.*[698]

695. White Eyes spoke three times during this conference; the first time on 12 October, the second time on 16 October, and the third time on 17 October 1775.

696. Luke 20:35–36.

697. On 19 October 1775 John Gibson, "with one other white Man," were appointed by Virginia's delegates to receive the "Prisoners Negroes and Horses which remain among the Indians" (Scribner et al., *Revolutionary Virginia,* 4:241). At the same time the Commissioners of the Continental Congress seem to have assigned him specific tasks. On 24 April 1776 the Congress approved the sum of £141.14.00 for "John Gibson, agent appointed by the commissioners for Indian affairs, for sundry services in the middle department." Ford, *Journals of the Continental Congress,* 4:304.

698. John Dodge (1749–94), an Indian trader from Connecticut who lived in the Wyandot settlement Sandusky, had met James Wood during his trip to the western tribes and supported Wood in his efforts to win the tribes' confidence and trust. He accompanied the Wyandot delegation to Fort Pitt. In January 1776 the commanding officer of Fort Detroit had Dodge arrested for his pro-American attitude and had him brought to Quebec, whence Dodge was able to flee to Boston in 1778. *RUO,* 55, 143; [Dodge], "Narrative of the Capture and Treatment of John Dodge."

THE 12TH   In the morning was the sermon about today's Gospel and during the Congregational Service 4 people received the waters of Holy Baptism. Their names are *Renatus, Moses, Nehemia,* and the latter's wife *Johanna Maria.* During this event we could sense the close presence of the Savior. *Mr. Gibson* and his company attended this event and showed much *Respect.* They themselves confessed and said that even if they never heard more in their life, they had clearly heard enough today about what was important for being saved and had had some conversations among themselves.One of them, the one who is a Baptist[699] but has not yet been baptized, said that sometimes he had thought he should convert, but he had always put it out of his mind. He had never considered it as much as today. He saw he was on the way to being lost and therefore would pay more attention to his salvation in the future.

THE 13TH   We prostrated ourselves and worshipped our Lord and Chief Elder for his blessed rule among us, surrendered ourselves anew to Him, prayed that He would remain among us, and promised Him faithfulness and obedience.[700]

THE 14TH   There was a Helpers *Conference* and then some Brothers from here went to *Gnadenhütten* to discuss various matters with the Brothers there. They returned the next day.

THE 16TH   In the early service the baby boy of *Jeremia* and *Catherine* from *Gnadenhütten* was baptized with the name *Johanan.* She had delivered him yesterday just after their arrival from there.

THE 19TH   We sent letters to *Litiz* with some white people who were passing through here going to the *Fort.* We learned from others who came from *Sandusky* that the *Wyondats* were not very happy when they came home from the *Treaty* in *Pittsburgh* and would not be easy to talk to. They were taking sides with the *Commandant* in *Detroit.*[701] The Indian *Captain Pipe* and his family arrived here from *Kaskaskunk.* He stayed with us a number of days and then went back. His wife likes to hear about the Savior and he is not peaceful either. He feels tugs in his heart and is convinced that the Brothers are preaching the only way to salvation, but he cannot make up his mind to follow his urgings and surrender to the Savior. However, when he hears Indians say that they want to come to our place and hear the Gospel, he always advises them to do so and not to allow anyone to prevent them.

THE 22ND   Brother *Jungmann* led the early service about how, out of love for the Savior, we should not neglect to witness to what He has done for our souls and what the blood of the wounds does for sinners. We began holding

699. On Baptists in the middle and southern colonies, see Boyd, *History of Baptists in America,* 179–81, 189.

700. On the importance of commemorating Christ's acceptance of the office of the Elder on 13 Nov. 1741, see Introduction, pp. 55–56, 62.

701. It is likely that this entry reflects information derived from John Dodge's reports. *RUO,* 92n15; [Dodge], "Narrative of the Capture and Treatment of John Dodge," 73–74.

singing lessons for the children, who learned some new verses that have been translated.[702]

THE 26TH   Brother *David* preached the sermon about the growth and increase in the knowledge of Jesus Christ, through whose blood we receive redemption. Brother *Heckewelder* held the Children's Service and Brother *Jungmann* held the Congregational Service. Some Indians who had come here recently to visit expressed a desire to hear about the Savior and they informed us of this.

When they make such requests, it is always understood that listening during the services is not enough; the Indian Brothers should also preach to them wherever they are staying and explain everything well and interpret it for them. Our Brothers do this very gladly and joyfully. They left on THE 28TH and said they were happy about what they had heard. They would return soon and listen to more.

[December]

DECEMBER 3RD   During our blessed Advent services we remembered how the eternally good one had dressed himself in our poor flesh and blood. We also spoke with the children separately about this subject and celebrated the Savior's incarnation with sweet singing.

THE 4TH   We began holding school with the children again and they were happy about this.[703] Brothers *David* and *Heckewelder* agreed to do this together and to teach in the Indian language. We do not have any books yet, so for now we have to copy some for them. This is very tedious since there are almost 100 children. Still, it is worth the effort if they learn something.[704]

THE 7TH   A sick Indian fervently requested baptism, and he was baptized into Jesus' death with the name *Nicodemus*. When he came to us in the spring of this year he already had consumption. For a long time he could not bring himself to ask for baptism because of a certain superstitious fear which many Indians have.[705] Finally he became so worried about his soul that all this dissolved and he surrendered himself to the Savior and asked him to have mercy on him. After his baptism he was content; he spent his time very blessedly and happily. He testified to everyone who visited him how happy he was now. He died on THE 10TH and his earthly dwelling was then laid to rest the following day.

THE 23RD   The Brothers and Sisters came home from the fall hunt in the past few days and we had Speakings with them yesterday and the day

---

702. The last singing school had started on 2 Sept. 1774; see entry for that date.
703. In the preceding year school had started only on 11 Jan. 1774; see entry for that date.
704. The result of these efforts was Zeisberger's *Delaware Indian and English Spelling Book.*
705. For examples, see entries for 22 Sept. 1773, 23 Jan. 1774, and 23 Oct. 1781.

before yesterday. Then 65 Brothers and Sisters enjoyed the Body and Blood of the Lord most blessedly in Holy Communion. During this 3 Brothers watched for the first time and one Sister for the second time.

THE 24TH   After the *Liturgy* for *Communion,* Brother *Jungmann* preached the sermon about the text, Rejoice in the Lord always,[706] and the joy believers experience through the incarnation and birth of the Savior. We spent Christmas Eve in praise and gratitude, beginning with a Lovefeast. During this the children celebrated our Savior's birth with very sweet singing, which brought much joy and encouragement to all the Brothers and Sisters. We knelt and with gentle tears brought our sacrifice of thanksgiving to the baby in the manger. We then concluded by giving the children Christmas verses we copied recently and candles. Then everyone went happily home. Some of the children were so excited, however, that they slept very little during the night.

THE 25TH   The sermon was about the words, Behold, I bring you good tidings of great joy, which shall be to all people. For unto you is born this day in the city of David a Saviour, which is Christ the Lord.[707] During the Congregational Service in the evening there was a talk about the Watchword, I, even I, am he that comforteth you: who art thou, that thou shouldest be afraid of a man that shall die, and of the son of man which shall be made as grass,[708] and then 4 people were buried into His death through Holy Baptism and added to the congregation: a man named *Sem* and 3 older girls, *Bibiane,* *Cathrine* and *Jael.* During this we could feel the powerful presence of the Holy Spirit and many tears were shed. Some were tears of joy over the Savior's proofs of grace and others came from a desire and longing to participate in this grace as well.

THE 31ST   In the New Year's Watchnight service we concluded this year contritely and happily, prayed to Him for continued release from all our debts, *Absolution* for all of our mistakes and shortcomings, our dear Lord's precious presence, our dear Mother's care, and the dear heavenly Father's protection and guidance. We commended ourselves anew to His grace and then entered the New Year with comforted hearts. In conclusion, the Lord's blessing was laid upon the congregation while we shared the kiss of peace. To the glory of the Savior, we must note at the conclusion of this year that He has done great things to further His work in Indian country. The Brothers are now recognized and accepted by the leaders of the *Delaware Nation* and they have granted them privileges. In addition to granting the Brothers freedom to preach and carry out the Savior's work without obstacles, they also have all decided to accept God's word. This means that the *Chiefs* have unanimously

706. Phil. 4:4.
707. Luke 2:10–11.
708. Isa. 51:12.

agreed they would like to see the whole *Nation* turn to the Brothers, accept the Gospel, and become believers, and they have requested this. They cannot actually force anyone to do this, but they are doing what they can to admonish and encourage them to do so. This is indeed sufficient on their part and all they can do. The Savior must do the primary work and grant the Indians hearts for it. He will certainly do this.

We also acknowledge his act of great kindness in giving us external peace. When people tried to inflame the *Nations* against this country, our dear heavenly Father graciously kept all misfortune away.

The congregational newsreports always provided a sweet and pleasant pasture for our hearts; we enjoyed them with appreciative and grateful hearts.

In *June* Brother *David* paid a visit to the Unity, and he returned from there in *August*.

In keeping with the Watchword the Unity Elders' Conference drew for *Schoenbrunn*, the dear Savior also brought us much joy through the Indian people. Through his blood He blessed them, washed away their sins, and clothed them in the garb of righteousness. This year 22 adults, 15 children, and 7 individuals who had been baptized in other places were received into the congregation.

We celebrated Holy Communion 9 times; the Savior revealed himself to us very graciously each time and blessed us inexpressibly. 18 Brothers and Sisters participated in this for the first time.

2 people from here went to *Gnadenhütten* to stay and one from there came here.

4 adult Brothers and Sisters and 3 children were released to the Congregation Triumphant.

The residents of *Schoenbrunn* include:

98 married Brothers and Sisters
17 single Brothers and older boys
20 single Sisters and older girls
2 widowers
22 widows
104 children

Total: 263; which is 43 more than a year ago. Of these, 68 are *Communicants* and 78 are unbaptized.

[January 1776]

1776. JANUARY 1ST   Brother *Jungmann* preached the sermon about the text, For ye are all the children of God by faith in Christ Jesus. For as many of you as have been baptized into Christ have put on Christ.[709] In the Children's

709. Gal. 3:26–27.

Service which followed, we encouraged them to give themselves to the Savior during the New Year and to become completely his. He revealed himself to the children during these days. We can sense the blessed work of grace among them and feel their emotion, and we are sincerely grateful to Him for this. 6 people received the waters of Holy Baptism during the Congregational Service. Their names are *Joel, Adam, Joachim, Loide, Anna Sybilla*, and *Dorothea*. This was a happy event, and in conclusion we celebrated a blessed Service of Adoration with those who have been baptized.

THE 2ND   Some Brothers and Sisters went to *Gnadenhütten* and some from there came here for a visit. We met with the Brothers who are Helpers and decided to divert water from the *Muskingum* into the little *Lake* by our *Spring*, so that we will have a flowing stream standing here near the *Town* in the summer, rather than foul, stagnant water. We hope this will not only be healthier for the *Town*, but might also bring many other comforts with it. We can do this without great effort or work if we make a ditch of about 30 Ruthen.[710] The Brothers began this immediately on the 4TH and in a couple of days had done as much as they can do for now because of the water. We have to leave the rest until the weather is warm.

THE 5TH   The baby boy born yesterday to Brother *Jacob* and Sister *Johanette* was baptized and named *Michael*.

THE 7TH   We had postponed the celebration of Epiphany until today,[711] and we celebrated it with grace and blessing. During the morning devotions we commended ourselves and all the congregations among the heathen to the Savior of the gentiles and prayed for his continued walk among us. Then there was a sermon about Isaiah 60. This concerned the promise given to the gentiles in the old covenant, which we have seen being fulfilled in so many *Nations*, tongues and languages.[712] In the afternoon we had a Lovefeast with all of our residents, and in the Congregational Service 5 people were baptized into His death through baptism and joined to the body of the Unity. Their names are: *Laban, Andreas, Benjamin, Maria Juliane* and *Johanna Christina*. One Sister was *absolved* at the same time as those being baptized, and Sister *Jungmann* laid hands on her. At the conclusion of this blessed day we worshipped our dear Lord for all the grace and blessings we have enjoyed during recent days and especially today, and we asked him to maintain this in each heart so that it might become something lasting.

THE 11TH   *Jonathan* talked with us. He was baptized by the Brothers in *Meniolagameka* but has been wandering around lost for many years now. Since we have been here he has come and gone at our place a great deal. He shared his heart and mind with us and said he was tired of living among the

---

710. In the eighteenth century in the various German territories the "Ruthe" was of different length. In Saxonia, for example, in the context of road construction it measured 4.53 meters.

711. Epiphany should have been celebrated on 6 January.

712. Isa. 60:3.

wild Indians. He wanted to give himself to the Savior anew and he asked that he and his wife, who is a Black woman, be allowed to live with us.[713] We granted this request and they were very happy. They will move here in the spring. Today we received news that the *Minque* had committed murders again in *Virginia* and had gone to the *Shawnee Town*s with some *Scalps* and prisoners.[714]

THE 14TH   The boys held their make-up services to celebrate their choir festival,[715] which could not be held 8 days ago. A sweet feeling could be sensed among them.

THE 15TH   There was a congregational council in the evening instead of the Singing Service. During this we reviewed our rules once again because there are always new people coming to us who have not heard them yet. Among other things we talked about clothing and said that we really like to see the Brothers and Sisters walking around dressed very properly and clean, at least on Sundays and holidays. However, they should not adorn themselves with silver and many ribbons on their coats in the manner of the savages; this was inappropriate for Brothers and Sisters.

THE 16TH   We were very happy to receive congregational newsletters and letters from Bethlehem and *Litiz,* along with the Watchwords and Daily Texts for this year and some of the weekly newsreports from the *General Synod.*[716] We enjoyed these today and in the following days.

THE 19TH   We remembered the *Mission* among[717] the heathen in *Greenland* and with praise and gratitude to our dear Lord considered what He has done among so many heathen *Nations* in these 43 years, and especially that He has sounded the hour of visitation among the Indians here as well and allowed the word of redemption to be proclaimed to them. This has already brought many to eternal life.

THE 21ST   Indians from *Cayahaga* attended our Sunday services. They were very attentive and paid attention to everything they saw. Brother *Heckewelder* held the Children's Service and Brother *Jungmann* the Congregational Service.

713. It is likely that the wife of Jonathan (baptized 18 April 1749) had been captured as a slave during the war and that Jonathan had adopted her and chosen her as his companion.

714. Neither the protocols of the Virginia Committee of Safety nor the newspapers of this colony report any Indian attacks.

715. See note 326 to entry for 9 Jan. 1774.

716. *Die Täglichen Loosungen der Brüder-Gemeine für das Jahr 1776; Die Lehrtexte der Brüder-Gemeine für das Jahr 1776. Enthaltend lauter Worte unsers lieben Herrn und Heilandes.* A complete protocol of the general synod of 1775 held at Barby together with a register and the most important resolves of the earlier general synods in the handwriting of John Ettwein is preserved in the Bethlehem Archives (without a call number). Zeisberger's reference is to the reports on the synod, which, according to the "Wöchentlichen Nachrichten der Unitäts-Ältesten-Conferenz" dated 30 June, started under the title "Wöchentliche Nachrichten aus dem Synodo der Brüder Unitaet zu Barby vom 1.ten Jul. 1775." These reports were continued in fourteen separate issues until 9 Oct. 1775. A handwritten copy is in MAB.

717. The 19th of January was the day commemorating the beginning of the Moravian mission in Greenland in 1733.

THE 24TH   Indians from *Goschgosching* came here for a visit. Among them was our *Thomas'* brother, *Netawatwees'* grandchild. He feels a longing in his heart to give himself to the Savior and to join the congregation, but his friends, with whom he has talked about this, always advise him not to. He said they had no reply when he asked them if they knew about anything better or about a way to salvation besides the Brothers. He told them that they surely knew that many preachers had already arisen among the Indians but had not done anything, and not a single person had ever become a believer through their preaching. The Brothers, however, had only been here a short time and you could already see 2 large *Towns* of Indian Believers, the likes of which you could not find anywhere you went. He concluded that the teaching of the Brothers must therefore be the truth, while that of the Indians was lies. No one could argue with this.

THE 29TH   A message came from the *Cherokees* reporting that a party of them had arrived at the *Shawnee* on their way to *Goschgosching.* When they were in *Gekelemukpechünk* 2 years ago, they had promised to be here again around this time.[718] It seems they consider it important to have good relationship and friendship with the *Delaware Nation,* and perhaps the Gospel might one day reach the *Cherokees* through the latter. They could at least provide an opportunity for this, especially since *they* now accept the Gospel.

THE 30TH   A headman[719] among the Indians and another man from *Sikhewünk* on this river came here to visit, to talk with the Brothers, and to hear about the Savior. He did not miss any services and was very attentive, and the Indian Brothers did not fail to proclaim the Savior and his death to this Indian, who is a wise man and loves and seeks what is good. They talked sincerely with him. The next day he told the Brothers his thoughts and plans. First, however, he reported that *Netawatwees* had given him a *Belt* of *Wampum* last year[720] and testified to him that the entire *Nation* should and would accept the Gospel; he had advised and encouraged him in particular to do this because he was one of the head people in his tribe. He had been very happy about this, especially since he had already thought about this matter for a long time and had considered becoming a believer. He had been very pleased and happy to hear this from the *Chief.* Now, however, it looked as if they wanted to call other preachers here (they believe that *White Eye* went to *Philadelphia* for this reason).[721] He was not happy about this because he had moved from *Assünnünk* to where he is now in the hope that a 3rd *Town* would be established for the Indian Believers. Now he saw that nothing would come of this, so he wanted

718. On the visit of the Cherokee and the grand meeting of the Great Council, see entries for 30 May and 6, 14, and 23 June 1774.

719. This refers to Welapachtschiechen; see entry for 22 April 1776.

720. See entry for 25 Feb. 1775. Netawatwees informed Packanke as well as all the other chiefs and captains about the resolve of the Council.

721. See entry for 29 Oct. 1775.

to inform us that he was planning to move back to his old place in *Assünnünk* in the spring. He would set out on the road where the word of God was sure to come and then it would also come to him. He was certainly too lowly and there were too few of them to call us to go there. If we did, though, we should know that he would be very happy and would really welcome us. *Assünnünk* is a difficult 3-day journey from here on the *Hokhokung* Creek, a short day's journey from the *Shawnee Towns*. This Indian stayed here 3 days and then traveled back home via *Gnadenhütten*.

[February]

FEBRUARY 2ND   A baby boy belonging to Brother *Ludwig* and Sister *Maria Juliane* was baptized with the name *Christian*. During the Speaking we sincerely rejoiced over the spiritual state of our Brothers and Sisters and thanked our dear Mother for her faithful care and work. We found them hungry and thirsty for Jesus' Body and Blood, and on the 4th He joined us into one body by giving us the bread to eat and into one spirit by giving us the cup to drink. One Sister participated in this high grace for the first time. A Brother and Sister were readmitted. 4 Brothers and Sisters watched for the 2nd time, and 6 Brothers and Sisters, 3 Brothers and 3 Sisters, for the first time.

THE 4TH   After the *Liturgy* for *Communion* and Holy Communion for the Sick, Brother *Jungmann* preached the sermon and then Brother *Heckewelder* led the Children's Service. Brothers *Willhelm*, *Cornelius,* and *Nathanael* went to *Gnadenhütten* this morning. Some Brothers from here had been summoned to listen to a message from *Chief Netawatwees*.

In the Congregational Service there was a talk about the Watchword, I, even I, am the LORD; and beside me there is no saviour,[722] and then the following 7 people were buried into His death and added to the congregation: *Maria Theresia, Lucia, Maria Susanna, Ruth, Anna Cathrine, Jacobina, and Johannes*. At the same time *Helena* was *absolved* and reaccepted. She is an older girl in *Gnadenhütten* who was baptized on the *Mahony* but was misguided into leaving the congregation. During this proceeding the Holy Trinity revealed itself mightily and powerfully.

THE 5TH   We buried the earthly dwelling of Brother *Jephta,* who died in blessing the day before yesterday. In 1771 he came from *Goschgosching* to *Kaskaskunk*, where his daughter, our Sister *Lazara* was the reason he came to the congregation in *Langundouteniünk* soon afterwards. She is still alive and in the Savior performed an obvious miracle in her. She had been so sick and emaciated for a long time that no one believed she could live. On several occasions she was unconscious for a long time so that they thought she was

722. Isa. 43:11.

dead, but she always recovered. She asked her father very fervently to take her to the Brothers so that she could hear about the Savior again before her end. After he had requested and received permission, he and his family came to our place. One time when his daughter was so weak that we did not think she could live until the next morning, she was baptized into Jesus' death at her urgent request. From that moment on she improved so much that within a short time she was healthier than she had ever been in her life. This led the blessed Brother and other heathen Indians to much reflection. He was baptized on *January* 6, 1774 in *Schönbrunn*, and on *July* 8, 1775 attained the enjoyment of Holy Communion. After his baptism he led a blessed life, was very loving towards all the Brothers and Sisters, and was loved in return. Although he was deaf and could not understand what was being said in the services, he never missed any of them as long as he could still walk around, which he was still doing 3 days ago. Early on the day of his death he said he was going to the Savior and he was really looking forward to this. A few minutes before his death he told the Brothers and Sisters who were with him (because he was always alert) that he felt quite well now; he was not sick but completely healthy, and he died gently and happily during the congregation's Holy Communion.

THE 7TH   Both yesterday and today we had a Helpers' *Conference*. Among other things, we discussed and considered a couple of people who want to live in the congregation. Before we give them final permission, we want to observe them a little and see if it their serious intention to live for the Savior.

THE 8TH   In the early service the baby boy born to Brother *Andreas* and Sister *Maria Theresia* was baptized with the name *Philippus*. We had received a message from *Chief Netawatwees* once again on the 4th of this month asking the Brothers to establish a 3rd *Settlement* for Indian Brothers soon, as soon as possible. It also informed us that all the heads of this *Nation* had agreed to accept the Gospel,[723] and that we should come and look for a site. They had already suggested 2 sites we might look over. Therefore Brother *David* left for *Goschgosching* with Brother *Schebosch* and 5 other Indians this afternoon. He reports the following about this:

We spent the night in *Gnadenhütten*. 3 more Indian Brothers from there went with us, and on the 9TH we arrived, via *Gekelemukpechünk*, at *White Eye's Town* while it was raining heavily and was very windy. We spent the night there and were well received. On THE 10TH we looked over the first site and the entire area, which was not half bad, and then made a big detour down

---

723. Future events proved that this report was not correct. The Wolf clan stuck to its rejection of the Moravian mission. The conflict continued for a number of years; it was often mixed with other issues such as the conflict between England and the colonies (see entry for 1 March 1775) and White Eyes' plans for a program of acculturation for the Delaware. Finally, in October 1779, the captains Pipe and Winginund reallocated the settlements of the clan from the Walhanding creek to the region of the Wyandot, closer to Fort Detroit. See entry for 28 Oct. 1779.

along the *Muskingum*. We looked at all the land and thought it was really very good, but we did not find a suitable site to establish a *Town*. Where there was good land for fields, there was no site close by to build and likewise where there was a site for building there was neither land for fields, nor wood, nor water. Towards evening we came to *Goschgosching* and they were not expecting our arrival at all, because the messengers had not received a definite answer in *Gnadenhütten* about if or when we would come. The *Chief* and his *Councellors* and all the Indians were therefore even happier. We were very well received and a separate fire was cleared for us in the *Chief*'s house, which is the largest, where we could sleep. The Indians soon began coming frequently and welcomed us very cordially. Their *Town* lies on the east side of the *Muskingum* directly across from where the *Walhanding*, which is just as big, flows into it.[724] It is pretty large but built in a rambling manner and consists mostly of huts. Although it is laid out and the streets have been staked out, I could still not see a single street built at all regularly. Instead, each person had built according to his *Phantasie*, along the length, the width, diagonally, or even right in the middle of the road. In the evening a large number of Indians gathered in the *Chief*'s house and I preached about the text, I am come that they might have life, and that they might have it more abundantly.[725] This deals with the miserable circumstances in which people exist by nature and what the Savior has achieved for us through his incarnation, death and sufferings, so that we can have eternal life through faith in Him. During this, everyone listened very attentively and the Indian Brothers then continued and confirmed my testimony about Jesus' merits.

THE 11TH   Early in the day we talked with the *Chief* and informed him that we had come at his request, to look for a place for a *Settlement* for Indian Brothers. We had examined the area from top to bottom this far along the river, but we had not yet found a place we liked except for *White Eye*'s *Town*. This site, however, was not appropriate for us because Indians already lived there. Therefore we were planning to go further down the river today as far as *Mochwesüng*. We would probably not be able to go any further this time because of the high water and the ice, which was just breaking up. We would look over the area that far to see if we could find a suitable place and then let him know more about what we thought. After the *Chief* had listened to us, he went to talk with his *Councellors* for a while. Our horses had run far away and it was late before we found them, and we decided to stay here today because it had also snowed and was very cold. It would be better to set out early tomorrow. Soon afterwards the *Chief* came, and his speaker told us the following in

---

724. Zeisberger considered the Walhanding a branch of the Muskingum, which suggests that he called Muskingum what today is the Tuscarawas. While, according to modern geography, Schönbrunn and Gnadenhüten were situated on the Tuscarawas, according to Zeisberger they were located on the Muskingtum.

725. John 10:10.

his name. He was really very happy to see us working on this planned undertaking. He had longed for this so much throughout this winter that sometimes he had dreamed he saw us working on it in his house, which pleased him and he told his *Counsellors* about it. However, when he called us he had not intended for us to live so far away from them. If we established this new *Town* so far away from them it would not help them or serve them at all. He wanted to have God's word preached here, and therefore he would have preferred to call the Brothers directly to *Goschgosching*. However, he always had many dealings with other *Nations* and many *Chief Affairs* to take care of, and he knew well enough this was not our kind of business and we would like to be spared it. Therefore he thought we should live separately, but not too from them so that he and his people could visit us and hear the Gospel. At this point we objected that we had learned from experience in *Goschgosching, Kaskaskunk, Schönbrunn,* and *Gnadenhütten,* that we could not live so close to other *Towns* for various reasons, which we then named for him. He told us things would not be the same among the Indians any more; times had changed. The Indians had all agreed to accept the Gospel. They supported the Brothers and everyone accepted and acknowledged them as their friends. Therefore we no longer needed to fear things like we did before this happened, and if anything should come up, he and his *Counsellors* were close at hand to help us and support us. He made this statement: If the Brothers are close to me, I will be strong. They will make me strong against the disobedient. My *Counsellors* and I, he continued, therefore thought you should establish a *Town* below us on this river. We have reserved this place for you and you can take a look at it. If you do not like it, you should build at *White Eye*'s place. I understood the *Chief* very well and did not want to raise any more objections. At the same time it occurred to me that perhaps it should just be a preaching site and not a settlement congregation. From his talk we realized that we did not need to make a further journey. Therefore we decided to look at the site today since it was not far, and then we would be finished with this *expedition.* We went there together on foot and some of the head people went with us. We soon entered an extremely beautiful area and went about 3 miles through a *Bottom,* the likes of which cannot be found near *Schönbrunn* or *Gnadenhütten,* or along this whole river, and then we came to a hill. This was the site they wanted to show us and had designated for us. It is truly a beautiful place, and it seemed to smile at us. We all felt so happy about this place and our hearts were so filled with joy that we could hardly hide it, although we did not yet know the Lord's will and pleasure about this.

    We went on a little further to another hill, which lies somewhat higher. It is not as well situated in relationship to the water though, because the *Bottom* is between the hill and the river. The site lies on the east side of the *Muskingum* very close to the river, which is twice as broad here as near *Schönbrunn,* and about three miles wide. It is a beautiful flat area, just as the entire area between

Goschgosching and here is flat, and it might be about three miles. You could establish fields either above or below the building site, as you wanted. It is a better site than *Goschgosching* in every respect and it is amazing that they did not build here, except that there is no *Spring* close by. It is not easy to find one close to the river in this area. On the hill where the building site would have to be there is no wood except for black walnut, wild cherries, ash, hickory and such,[726] but not far from there river there is plenty of wood for construction. We looked at this on the return trip, when we went through the upper land. We also found a nice spring, but it is a little bit too far away. When we returned home I immediately looked to see what today's Watchword was. It was so delightfully hopeful and appropriate that you could not have picked a better one: *Arise, shine; for thy light is come, and the glory of the LORD is risen upon thee.*[727] Then I immediately preached about this to a crowd of Indians that was so large the house could not hold them and many had to stand around outside the house. The time and hour had come for the Savior to fulfill the plan of peace He had in his heart for the Indians. Until now they have lived in blindness and had not heard or known anything about their Creator and Redeemer, and He would reveal himself to them in his suffering and with all the wounds He received for them, and let them recognize him, because they had been preciously purchased with his blood. He would now invite them to the salvation he had won with his blood through the Gospel He had sent to them, and on account of which they also had a right to share in the promise of eternal life. He would give the power to become God's children to all who would now accept it, and who believe in his name.[728] Everyone was very quiet and attentive and I felt really happy during the service. The *Chief* himself sat among us Brothers both yesterday and today. He is a dear, old, honorable man who is very concerned about the welfare of his people and who puts much hope and trust in the Brothers to make the Indians a happy people. May the Savior grant this and let him experience joy yet. During this visit we also sensed a different atmosphere. A completely different spirit reigns among the Indians than previously. We have seen some who used to be our bitter enemies and did not want to hear or know anything of God's word who were now very kind and trusting towards us and did not want to be out of our company the whole time we were there. Much has changed in the span of one year.

THE 12TH   Early in the day we spoke with the *Chief* and his *Counsellors* and let them know that we really liked the site we had seen yesterday and had no objections to it. We were glad we had seen it now and we would return home and consider further with our Brothers if and when we would come to them. It was still very cold anyway and the river was not yet open, so nothing

726. Zeisberger's botanical terminology is analyzed in Mahr, "Delaware Terms for Plants and Animals," 3–10. Zeisberger's "Hikri" is "hickory."

727. Isa. 60:1; *Das kleine Brüder-Gesang-Buch*, hymn no. 749.

728. John 1:12.

at all could be done. However, we hoped to give them a final decision as soon as we had a chance. Also, *Schönbrunn* and *Gnadenhütten* were not adequately supplied with workers to spare anyone without hurting ourselves. However, at the first opportunity we would write Bethlehem and ask them to send us help. They did not seem very satisfied with this, because they wanted to hear that we would come as soon as possible. It seemed to them that we still had doubts, although I personally had no doubts. One of them told us that the time would seem long to him. He could hardly wait; he no longer had peace or a permanent home. If he only knew that we would come there for sure, he would begin working at the site right away and fell wood for a house. He believed things would go pretty well for him, but as it was he did not know where he stood. That was *Killbuck*'s son; in *Pittsburgh* he had been designated the next *Chief* after *Netawatwees*.[729] He decided to come to *Gnadenhütten* tomorrow or the day after tomorrow because it was very important to him to have certainty in this the matter soon. So we said farewell to them for now, started back, and arrived in *Gekelemukpechünk* in the evening. On the way back we chased the horses through the *Muskingum*, which was very high. A horse that could no longer swim almost drowned while we were swimming them through. We hurried with a *Canow* to help him and got him to land while there was still a little life in him. He recovered in a while.

In *Gekelemukpechünk* we met an Indian preacher with whom our Indian Brothers discussed various things. There are 3 of these preachers[730] who used to preach a lot and had many followers. They are now very quiet and have given this up, but they make very good excuses to the Indians for themselves and why nothing came of their work. They say they were seeking something good and thought they had found it. However, it had not been the right thing. Now the Brothers had come, and they had brought them what they had been seeking for a long time: the right teaching. The Brothers preached the truth. At noon on THE 13TH we arrived at *Gnadenhütten*, where we stayed. Brother and Sister *Schmick* and I had a little *Conference* together. Now for various reasons we found it necessary to learn our dear Lord's mind about the *Town* to be laid out soon, so we could get ready for this in time since spring is approaching. Therefore we allowed ourselves to be instructed in this by Him.[731] Oh, what joy and praise it awakened in us when He revealed His approval and pleasure that not only a preaching site but a congregational settlement for Indian Brothers would be established below *Goschgosching*, on the site we had looked at today

---

729. This refers to Gelelemind (John Killbuck Jr., later baptized William Henry), Olmstead, *Blackcoats Among the Delaware*, 220–23. On his supposed designation as successor of Netawatwees during the Fort Pitt conference in October 1773 (and not, as Zeisberger thought, in 1775), see entry for 21 April 1776 and note 765.

730. See entries for 27 Sept. and 3 Oct. 1773.

731. This formula means "drawing of the lot," through which God revealed his intention; see Introduction, p. 67.

and where we had felt his peace so blessedly. We see clearly that the Indians' time is approaching with great strides, when the Savior will visit them and gather from among them his reward for suffering. Therefore we want to take note and be aware of his glance and to fulfill his will and please Him. He will grant us his grace for this. We arrived in *Schönbrunn* in the evening, grateful and happy that He was with us and been merciful to us on our journey.

THE 14TH   The diary from *Schönbrunn* continues: The early service was about the childlike trust and confidence we have in the Savior, so that we can turn to Him confidently with all of our external and internal concerns and take our refuge in Him. We then informed the Helpers about the journey we made and told them how we had found things. They were all very pleased about this, especially that a new *Town* should be started this spring. We also decided to work together to make some *Canows* for this purpose, which we will then sell there and use to get the things necessary for a *Congregational Meeting Hall*. Everyone was very willing to help with the new settlement congregation and some said that even if they could not move there, they would consider it a joy if they could help the Brothers and Sisters who are moving there with their work there.

THE 18TH   In the Children's Service *Helena*'s six-month-old baby boy was baptized into Jesus' death with the name *Sigmund*.

THE 21ST   During the early service we talked about the work of the Holy Spirit, how he often reminds us to send our hearts to the Savior so that he can write upon our hearts what and how we should pray to Him, like dear children to their kind father, that He also justifies our prayer before God so that it is pleasing to Him. Therefore we should listen to his voice and obey Him.

Most of the Brothers and Sisters went out to their sugar huts because the weather was so nice.[732]

THE 23RD   One Sister said: The services are extremely important to me and I do not like to miss any, but Holy Communion is more important to me than anything else. That is my greatest and highest good. A Brother said, I have thought about the Indians and considered their situation, how they are bound and imprisoned by Satan. Some of them who have already heard about the Savior hope for redemption and think about how they might escape their miserable state and sigh about this. Others however, who did not yet know or had not yet heard anything about the Savior, were without a care and thought it should be like this and not otherwise. He had been moved to great pity for both and prayed to the Savior to let the hour of their redemption approach soon and to transport them into heavenly freedom.

732. In a different hand.

Diary of Schönbrunn *from* February *28th until* April *10th* 1776[733]

FEBRUARY 28TH   We sent letters and our diary to *Bethlehem* via *Pittsburgh*. A *Trader* came from *Sandusky* and brought us news that through Indians the *Commandant* in *Detroit* had captured *Mr. Dodge* and put him in chains.[734] The *Commissioners* from the last *Treaty* had sent him as an envoy to the western *Nations* and he traveled through here in the fall. We also heard that *Netawatwees* had not received any good news from the *Wyandot* and therefore he sent *Deputies* to warn them to remain peaceful.

{March}

MARCH 8TH   During the Speakings in preparation for Holy Communion with Brothers and Sisters we were able to rejoice over most of the hearts and to thank our dear Mother in a childlike manner for her[735] faithful care. The Brothers and Sisters had already been scattered about in the bush for more than 14 days boiling sugar, and during a strong storm a couple of days ago some of them experienced special protection; so many trees were knocked down that it is a miracle no one was harmed. We are now hearing about many proofs of the protection of the dear angels.

THE 9TH   We had a blessed Holy Communion. 3 Brothers and 1 Sister participated in this for the first time. Two of the Brothers and one Sister watched for the 2nd time and one Sister for the first time.

THE 10TH   Early in the day was the *Liturgy* for *Communion*. First, however, there was a blessed talk about the words, The cup of blessing which we bless, is it not the communion of the blood of Christ? The bread which we break, is it not the communion of the body of Christ?[736] The sermon followed. All the Brothers and Sisters were home now, so in a separate service we told them about what had taken place between the *Chiefs* and us and that they are asking the Brothers to establish a 3rd *Town* close to them so they would have a better opportunity to hear the Gospel. We really should not postpone this any longer; it would be best to do it right away. Since we had already chosen a site for this, we informed them that about 8 families would move there this spring. We already knew 4 families for this and we are just waiting to see who else will volunteer. Therefore we suggested the Brothers remember we would need to make as many *Canows* for this as are needed and they should begin this

---

733. MAB, B 141, F 7, I 4. In the right margin another person, possibly Fliegel, noted: "Version A: Schönbrunn only B-Version adds Lichtenau." There is no pagination.

734. See [Dodge], "Narrative of the Capture and Treatment of John Dodge," 73–75.

735. In copy substituted with "the Holy Spirit."

736. 1 Cor. 10:16.

week, so that everything would be ready before the Easter holidays and we could set out from here right after that. We saw that all the Brothers and Sisters were willing and interested. On THE 12TH the Indian Brothers set about making *Canows* in 2 *Parties*. Some of our Brothers were asked to go to *Goschgosching* to attend a council with the *Cherokee* who have arrived there.[737] We had to decline, however, because our people were out working and were not at home. We left it up to Brother *Schmick* to send someone there from *Gnadenhütten*.

THE 15TH   Indians from *Walhanding* came here for a visit and stayed for several days. Some of them enjoyed hearing about the Savior and were looking for opportunities to hear this.

THE 18TH   *Mr. Conner* returned from the *Shawnee*. He had followed *Mr. Gibson* there some time ago[738] to retrieve his child from them. With great effort, he finally got him after paying another 40 *bucks* or dollars[739] for him. The boy is 4 years old and cannot speak anything but *Shawnee*.

THE 21ST   A couple of White people passed through here on their way to see the *Wyandot* in *Sandusky*. We always hear that they are very restless and have not agreed among themselves whether they want to remain quiet or not.[740]

THE 25TH   We prostrated ourselves and worshipped our Lord and God who came in the flesh, and we thanked Him for His blessed incarnation, sufferings, and death.

THE 27TH   Many Indians from *Goschgosching* came here yesterday and today for a visit, and we heard from them that the Indians in that area who are not inclined to hear the Gospel are considering going far away, because they know the time is approaching for us to go there.[741] We sent news to the *Chief* that we would set out from here in 14 days now, so that the time would not seem so long to him.[742]

THE 29TH   *Mr. Gibson* came here from the *Shawnee* with a party of warriors and about 20 white prisoners. He had spent the winter there and had much work and trouble and had endured many dangers until he got a party of warriors on his side. They took the prisoners away by force and said if they

737. See entry for 29 Jan. 1776.
738. See entry for 12 Nov. 1775.
739. "A large buckskin is valued at a Spanish dollar; two doeskins are regarded as equal in value to one buckskin." Zeisberger, "History of the Northern American Indians," 57.
740. James Wood's reports of pro-British leanings had been troubling; these concerns were heightened by the news of John Dodge's arrest (see entry for 28 Feb. 1776). From the Wyandot's perspective the question was not whether to side with the colonies or England but how to secure an adequate supply of European goods; and these were only available at the cost of supporting England in the conflict.
741. See entry for 8 Feb. 1776.
742. On 26 March Netawatwees informed Schmick that he would welcome Unami-speaking Christian Delaware in the new settlement because this was his own dialect. GD, F 6, I 2.

could not take them to the *Fort* alive, they would take their *Scalps* there.[743] We were delighted to receive letters and news from Bethlehem and Litiz via *Pittsburgh*, including a letter dated *December* 3rd last year from the *Provincial Helpers' Conference* in Bethlehem. This provided us new encouragement and comfort, and new energy.[744]

THE 31ST Many of the *Shawnee* and prisoners attended the sermon for the beginning of Passion Week. The older girls then had a blessed service, because many of them could not come home on the 25th of this month.[745] There was a blessed feeling during this.

[April]

APRIL 2ND *Mr. Gibson* continued his journey to the *Fort*. They were all very grateful and appreciative of the good hospitality they had enjoyed here. Today our Brothers and Sisters finished collecting sugar for this year, and there was a plentiful yield this time.

Among the strangers who were here visiting was a well-known Indian preacher who attended our services and had the Brothers tell him about the Savior.

THE 4TH In the evening we read the story of the day as we had done in previous days. Then 74 *Communicants* celebrated the *Pedilavium* and *Holy Communion*. 3 Brothers and Sisters participated in this for the first time, 3 watched for the 2nd time, and 2 for the first time.

THE 5TH We spent the day reflecting on the many and great sufferings and torments our Savior endured for us.[746] The story of this great day was heard with melted hearts, and the Brothers and Sisters would have been glad to listen even longer. Many tears were sent to Him during the *Liturgy* and Service of Adoration for the Piercing of the Side. We prayed that He would grant us a lasting impression of His entire passion, and that we might always keep in our hearts and minds what it cost Him to redeem us. Many strangers who were here visiting listened very attentively, and some said they had never seen or heard anything like this in their life.

THE 6TH In the afternoon we had a Lovefeast and on THE 7TH we prayed the Easter *Litany* on God's Acre and asked for asked for eternal fellowship with the 6 Brothers and Sisters who have died in the past year. Afterwards

743. See entry for 12 Nov. 1775. On the Native American perspective of adopted white prisoners, see the speech of Gischenatsi as reported by Zeisberger in his account of this visit of the Shawnee on 19 Oct. 1773.

744. Zeisberger's reference is to John Ettwein's letter to all missionaries, 3 Dec. 1775, MAB, E.P., B 965, F 36, no. 866a, in which Ettwein, among other things, asks for the missionaries' views on sending Roth to the Ohio region again.

745. The 25th of March was the choir festival for the big girls.

746. 5 April was Good Friday.

we read the story of the resurrection. Then there was the sermon about the text, I am he that liveth, and was dead; and, behold, I am alive for evermore, Amen; and have the keys of hell and of death.[747] In the afternoon the baptized children had a service. In the evening during the Congregational Service there was a talk about the Watchword and text[748] and then the blood and water of Jesus' side flowed over 4 people.[749] The names of these individuals who were received in Holy Baptism are *Fridrich, Abel, Bethseba, and Anna Helena.*

Brother and Sister *Conners* received their inheritance and privilege with God's house and race through reception into the congregation. During this entire proceeding a powerful sense of grace prevailed and many tears were shed.

THE 8TH   In the *Helpers' Conference* we filled the places of the Brothers and Sisters going to *Goschgosching* who had served in congregational offices. In *Abraham*'s place, Brother *Cornelius* was given the Care of External Affairs. *Jacob senior* was named as Servant for Visitors and the married Brother and Sister *Esra* and *Lazara* were named Congregational Servants. All accepted their positions willingly and joyfully.

2 Brothers, *Tobias* and *Timotheus*, and 2 Sisters, *Martha* and *Anna*, were added to the *Helpers' Conference*. We talked a great deal about the responsibility of the *Helpers*, what they should pay attention to, and how they should behave towards the Brothers and Sisters. In the evening we announced these changes to the entire congregation.

THE 9TH   The Brothers and Sisters who are moving to the new *Settlement* prepared for their departure and we loaded the *Canows*. We also agreed in the presence of our dear Lord that the *Town* being established should be called *Lichtenau*, and we announced this to the Brothers and Sisters today.

APRIL 10TH   In the early service Brother *David* baptized the baby daughter born to Brother *Leonhard* and Sister *Rahel* yesterday evening into Jesus' death with the name *Hanna.* He then set out for *Lichtenau* with Brother *Heckewelder* and 7 families of Indian Brothers and Sisters.[750]

Diary of the Construction and Progress in Lichtenau *on the* Muskingum *from* April *12th until* July *1776*[751]

For a year we had already been planning to establish a third *Settlement* on the *Muskingum* for Indian Brothers, and the Brothers were just waiting for a good and suitable opportunity. Things were then set into motion last fall when *Chief*

---

747. Rev. 1:18.

748. The Watchword for 7 April, eastern, had been Isa. 42:1; text for the day was John 11:25–26.

749. This is the Moravian formula for "baptizing."

750. MAB, B 141, F 8; pp. 134–136b are copies of the preceding diary and pp. 136b–151 are the first parts of the Lichtenau Diary and are identical with those beginning with p. 204; these are in Zeisberger's handwriting.

751. MAB, B 147, F 1, fol. 204.

Netawatwees sent the Brothers in *Schönbrunn* and *Gnadenhütten* a message in *November* informing them that the time had come and he would like the Brothers to establish a 3rd *Town* soon. Then those Indians who want to hear and accept God's word could live with us, because *Schönbrunn* and *Gnadenhütten* were already so densely occupied that they could not all live comfortably and have food in our two *Towns*. At that time the Indians were going to a *Treaty* in *Pittsburgh*, and the Brothers promised to give them an answer when they returned from there. This did not happen, however, because they did not come through *Schönbrunn* on their return journey, and because *White Eye* had asked the gentlemen at the *Treaty* for a preacher and schoolmaster.[752] Although he did not name the Brothers or any other denomination or sect, it seemed as if the matter had come to a *Stop*. Therefore we all remained quiet and just waited. Then in *February* of this year the *Chief* sent us two of his *Counsellors*, reminded us once again about the message he had sent us that we had not yet answered, and asked us to come and select a site as soon as possible. A number of days later Brother *David* traveled to *Goschgosching* with Brother *Schebosch* and some Indian Brothers and listened to the *Chief*'s suggestions. He hoped and wished we would settle close to them so that they would have the opportunity to hear the Gospel often. They suggested a site not far from their *Town* for this. We looked it over on *February* 11th and read the beautifully comforting *Watchword*, *Arise, shine; for thy light is come, and the glory of the LORD is risen upon thee.*[753]

After learning our dear Lord's pleasure and will concerning this, we soon began preparations to carry this out in the spring, and we soon reported this to the *Chief*, to reassure him.

APRIL 10TH   Brother *David*, Brother *Heckewelder*, and 7 families of Indian Brothers and Sisters left *Schönbrunn*, accompanied by the beautiful *Watchword*, *Ye are my witnesses, saith the LORD, and my servant whom I have chosen: that ye may know and believe me, and understand that I am he: before me there was no God formed, neither shall there be after me.* We, and the Lamb's Congregation of Blood, we want to be eternal witnesses, so that grace and freedom from all sins are found in Jesus' sacrifice alone, for all the world.[754] The following Brothers moved with their families: *Abraham, Willhelm, Isaac, Jeremias, Thoma, Ignatius,* and *Joel.* One party went by land with the cattle, the others by water with the baggage, and some more Brothers went along to help and escort them. Towards evening we all met in *Gnadenhütten*, where we spent the night. *Christian* and his family also went with us from there. Our company thus consisted of 8 married couples, 1 single Brother, 1 single sister, 2 widows, 10 girls, and 5 boys, a total of 35 Indian souls who are Brothers and Sisters.

752. See entry for 29 Oct. 1775, where it is reported as a rumor only.
753. Isa. 60:1; *Das kleine Brüder-Gesang-Buch*, hymn no. 749.
754. Isa. 43:10; *Das kleine Brüder-Gesang-Buch*, hymn no. 2284.

THE 11TH   We continued our journey after reflecting on our Watchword for today in the early service, Therefore thy gates shall be open continually; they shall not be shut day nor night; that men may bring unto thee the forces of the Gentiles, and that their kings may be brought.[755] We went past *Gekelemukpechünk*, had many snow flurries throughout the day, and it was very cold. Towards evening we met those who were going by land, helped them swim the cattle through the *Muskingum*, and camped together.

THE 12TH   We arrived in *Goschgosching* in the afternoon, after we had passed *White Eye's Town* and a bad place in the river where we first had to clear out trees that were lying in the water. We put in and greeted the *Chief*, who welcomed us very cordially and later had one of his *Counsellors* tell us how happy they were about our arrival and that we were very welcome among them. They told us much bad news they had heard recently about the *Wyandot* and other *Nations*; they had attacked *Settlements* of White people and also wanted to attack the *Delaware* because they were on their side. Many of the *Munsees* in this area had fled because of this. Actually they were fleeing from us because we were getting too close to them and because they are enemies of the Gospel; they made up lies so they would have a reason to leave and not have to say they were leaving because of us.[756]

Towards evening we arrived at our designated little spot in *Lichtenau*, and everyone was happy and thankful. We had agreed on the name for this place in *Schönbrunn*, before our departure. Those who went by land arrived several hours earlier and had already set up camp and looked around the area for the spot where we held the first service in this new little town, and everyone really liked it. We were encouraged by our beautiful Watchword for today, Thou shalt no more be termed Forsaken; neither shall thy land any more be termed Desolate: but thou shalt be called Hephzi-bah, and thy land Beulah: for the LORD delighteth in thee, and thy land shall be married. *Oh great, and good, and kindly nature, you have chosen to desire something bad, and the text which said, And as they thus spake, Jesus himself stood in the midst of them, and saith unto them, Peace be unto you.*[757] *Oh, Lamb of God, who bears the sins of the world, give to us your peace!*[758] The Savior revealed himself to us and allowed us to blissfully sense his peace and his presence among us.

THE 13TH   After the early service, our first work was to stake out the *Town* and show each family their lot so that they could set up and get settled in as well as possible for now. Then each person went to work diligently and cut down wood on the building site in every direction. Five Brothers had accompanied us here from *Schönbrunn* and helped us. They offered to frame in a

755. Isa. 60:11; *Das kleine Brüder-Gesang-Buch*, hymn no. 1034.

756. On similar negative remarks by Zeisberger about the Munsee, especially at Mochwesüng, see entries for 20 May and 11 June 1774.

757. Isa. 62:4; *Das kleine Brüder-Gesang-Buch*, hymn no. 245.

758. Luke 24:36.

house for Brothers *David* and *Heckewelder* and get it under roof before they returned home, and they immediately got to work on this.

We had many Indian visitors from *Goschgosching* today. They wanted to hear about the Savior, and the Indian Brothers were immediately prepared to serve them in this way. Then they looked around the place where the *Town* is being built and how it is laid out, and they returned home towards evening. Currently we have only 1 road staked out with 2 rows of houses, running from north directly south following the lay of the land along the river, and we have designated the site for the Congregational and Meeting House.

THE 14TH   *Chief Netawatwees* traveled here by water and many of his people by land for the sermon, which was preached under the open sky. It was about the text for today, Ought not Christ to have suffered these things, and to enter into his glory?[759] Some *Cherokees* who live in *Goschgosching* also came with them. Everyone was very attentive during this and afterwards the Indian Brothers continued talking about this subject in companies where they had gathered by the fires, and they discussed many aspects of this with them. Then they returned home in the evening.

THE 15TH   We continued cutting down wood and preparing to build. Our building site looked like a wasteland and there was so much destruction so that you could hardly figure how to get through it. There are sometimes very strong storms here, so it necessary to cut down the nearby trees nearby to be safe. *Munsee* and *Minque* Indians visited us. The latter were *Agnes'* friends. They spent the night with us and *Isaac* proclaimed the Savior to them. However, the *Minque* had no ears to hear; he painted himself the next morning and went away, leaving behind his wife who wanted to stay here longer.

THE 16TH   *John Killbuck*,[760] *Netawatwees'* grandchild (he is like the superintendent of *Goschgosching*)[761] arrived with a pretty large number of Indians and offered to help us with our work. We gratefully accepted this and we put them to work framing in houses. They also helped us on the 17TH and yesterday and today the 4 *Cherokee* joined in the work diligently. Our *Noah*, who had come with us in order to see them, had an opportunity to talk to them a good deal about the salvation the Savior won for us through his blood.

THE 20TH   We moved from the river, where we had been camping until now, to the site of our *Town*, and each person went to his lot. One family from *Goschgosching* asked for permission to live with us and we agree to this. They are the first to come to us and there are 6 of them altogether. The man

759. Ibid.
760. Gelelemind.
761. Zeisberger's description of Gelelemind's position as "elder" ("Vorsteher")—a term whose equivalent in the contemporary terminology would be "chief," which reflects the terminology associated with the hierarchical structure of the mission congregation (see entry for 29 Aug. 1772, note 51)—suggests a distinct gradation for the term "chief." The term could mean "head" of a settlement, "head of a clan" (e.g., Packanke), or "head of the Great Council of a Nation" (e.g., Netawatwees).

is *Netawatwees'* grandchild, our *Thomas'* brother,[762] and the wife was baptized in the *Congregational Meeting Hall* in Bethlehem by Brother *Joseph*[763] when she was 13 years old. She was given the name *Hanna*. Her mother had also been baptized and received the name *Magdalena,* and then died some years ago in *Gekelemukpechünk*, but she had led her away from the congregation. She came here with her belongings in a *Canow* early the next morning and moved in with us for good.

THE 21ST   Before the sermon, which was the first service we had on the site of our *Town*, we dedicated this little place with prayer and supplication. We prayed that the Savior would enter with us and remain with us, that He would gather a congregation from the Indians in this area for himself, to honor and glorify His name, through the word of his cross that will be preached here, and that thousands more might seek and find their salvation in his wounds. Our Watchword for today also provided the most beautiful assurances of this. It said, In righteousness shalt thou be established: thou shalt be far from oppression; for thou shalt not fear: and from terror; for it shall not come near thee. Guard your house and your herd, which are so dear and worthy to their shepherd. Guard them from outside and from inside, and may the entire beginning of the residents be well founded.[764]

Netawatwees was present with a great number of his people, both men and women. The Brothers spoke separately with the former for a long time about the foundation of our salvation in Jesus' blood, that he shed for our sins. He listened attentively during this and you could see that he was seriously thinking about it.

There was another man named *Gelelemend*, or *John Killbuck*, who was designated to be *Chief* after *Netawatwees*.[765] Among other things he asked Brother

---

762. This refers to Johannes Netanewand, a blood relative of Thomas. See entry for 28 July 1776.

763. August Gottlieb Spangenberg (1704–92) had read law and theology at the University of Jena, had been closely associated with Zinzendorf in Herrnhut since 1733, and had been in charge of the North American Moravian settlements from 1735 to 1739, from 1744 to 1749, and from 1751 to 1762. After 1762 he was the presiding member of the directorate of the Unity, in which position he was responsible for all the mission activities.

764. Isa. 54:14; *Das kleine Brüder-Gesang-Buch*, hymn no. 1278.

765. Scholarship is confused about the succession of Netawatwees. Zeisberger's words suggest that within the Delaware Nation there existed clear rules concerning the designation of a successor to the office of chief of the whole nation. On the basis of a report by George Croghan dated winter 1774, however, Weslager, *Delaware Indians*, 297, suggests "that the Delawares at Newcomer's Town had chosen White Eyes as their chief in place of Netawatwees." White, *Middle Ground*, 382, implicitly accepts this theory when he suggests that in 1778 "Quequedegatha (or George White Eyes) had abdicated his chieftainship to become first captain of the Turtle phratry; Captain Pipe, chief of the Wolf phratry, had similarly given up his office to act as war captain." Both suggestions can be traced back to George Croghan's report to the conference at Johnson Hall close to Albany on 5 Jan. 1774 about the congress of October 1773 at Fort Pitt: "Then Mr. Croghan in conjunction with the Seneces [*sic*] added that he was to acquaint, and propose to the Nations then present that the Delaware Chief Custalogo was superannuated, and unfit to preside over that Nation, that they had with the old Man's Consent, and Approbation made Choice of his Nephew Capt. Pipe, a sober sensible Indian to take upon him the Charge of the Delaware Nation, and that he was henceforth to be looked upon as their

David to what extent a believer or person who wants to become a believer could be involved with *Chief Affairs*. Brother *David* answered him: to the extent that a person could be spared heathen matters, *Ceremonies* and traditions. Then his office of *Chief* would not get in the way, and a *Chief* could become a believer as well as someone else who was not a *Chief*. However, he must renounce pagan ways once and for all.[766] He then said that since the fall he had felt a desire in his heart to move to our place. He had also told his uncle the *Chief*[67] some time before he had come here that he had wanted to move to *Gnadenhütten*. At that time he had not really objected to this. However, later he had told him he should not hurry but wait a little, because he hoped the Brothers would come here. Since this was now happening and we were there, he thought he would talk to him again and see if he could move in with us now. Brother *David* answered him should just do it, but if he met any hesitation it would be better to wait before moving here. He had already chosen himself a site and lot where

---

Chief. In like manner the Delawares of Newcommer's Town below Tuscarawas had appointed Captain Grey Eyes al. Sir William [i.e., White Eyes], to be their Chief in the place of their former Chief Newcommer who they thought unfit for the charge, & desire that all the neighbouring Nations will take notice of these Appointments accordingly" (*JP*, 12:1047–48). This report is directly contradicted by what is reported in Zeisberger's diary; in November 1774, according to Zeisberger, White Eyes acted, without any doubt, first as speaker of the great Council and second as captain of his clan (see entry for 5 Nov. 1774). According to Zeisberger, Pipe was still Captain at that time. The report about Croghan's communication may suggest that some Delaware were thinking about Netawatwees' succession. In April 1776 this internal discussion process may have reached the point where Gelelemind was determined upon as successor *designatus*. The reasons for his designation are as yet unclear. Gelelemind was the son of John Killbuck Sr., the eldest son of Netawatwees. This suggests the designation of a direct descendant of Netawatwees. However, this is contradicted by Zeisberger's unequivocal statement in "History of the Northern American Indians," 98–99: "In the matter of choice of a chief various things are to be observed. The Principal captain may choose a chief and inaugurate him, and it is also in his power to take him out of office if the chief proves a poor regent, acts contrary to customs, does according to his own wishes and refuses to accept councel. . . . The chief must always be a member of that tribe in which he presides. The sons of a chief cannot inherit their father's dignity, for the reason that they are not and cannot be, according to established usages, members of the tribe, inasmuch as children do not inherit tribal rights from the father but from the mother . . . as his sons cannot . . . succed [*sic*] him, a great grandchild, or nephew may become chief, that is, either his daughter's daughter's son or his sister's son, so that the privilege of becoming Chief cannot be confined to too intimate relationships." When Zeisberger wrote these words in 1779–80, he had lived for seven years in close proximity and daily contact with the Delaware; his careful wording suggests that he had labored hard to gain a clear understanding of this important issue. At the same time, his statement that only a "great grandchild, or nephew" could inherit the office of a chief was false; a grandson could belong to the same clan as his grandfather—which was true for Gelelemind. More probably the reason for the considerations about the succession of Netawatwees lay elsewhere. From a later perspective, Heckewelder noted: "The Person on whom, *by lineal descent*, the station of head chief of the Nation devolved, being yet young in years, the surviving chiefs . . . officiated in his stead" (*Narrative of the Mission*, 193). The lengthy discussions about Netawatwees' successor may therefore have been due to the youth and inexperience of Gelelemind.

766. See entry for 5 April 1773; if one compares both entries it becomes evident that Zeisberger's views had changed over the course of three years.

767. Gelelemind occasionally calls Netawatwees uncle and sometimes grandfather. Both names are used more in the sense of honorary titles than as reflections of kinship relations. See entries for 16 April 1776 and for 30 May and 17 June 1775.

he would plant and live, and he asked that we keep this place for him. We promised we would do so. It is no wonder that until now *Netawatwees* has not wanted his best and most useful people to leave him and go to us. You cannot think badly of him for this, because he would be an afflicted man if his *Counsellors* left him. Now that we live here, though, he will not be opposed to this.

THE 22ND   *Welapachtschiechen*, the *Chief* of *Assünnünk* arrived here yesterday and had also visited in *Schönbrunn* last winter, as was reported in the diary.[768] He spoke with us once again and said, We should know and believe that in his heart he is still inclined as he told us last winter. He had left home with the intention of visiting in *Schönbrunn* because he had not heard God's word for a long time. He was even happier, however, to meet us here where he could talk with us. He wanted to tell us was he and the Indians who lived with him, currently about 10 families although he knew more who wanted to move there, wanted to accept God's word. He had talked with them about this and learned their intention before he came to us. Therefore he wanted to ask the Brothers to come to see them and preach the Gospel, for which they longed. However, first they should find the most suitable place to establish such a *Town*, because he could see that the Brothers understood this best. They had just recently moved back there from *Sikhewunk*, into the old huts where they had lived before, and they did not want to begin anything new until the Brothers came to them. When they came to them then they would move their place. He would be very happy if a Brother lived with them and preached the Gospel to them. We replied that we were always happy and pleased to hear that Indians wanted to hear God's word, and we would gladly serve everyone in this way. However, it was not possible for us to give them a Brother now because our 3 *Towns* were not sufficiently staffed. For now we could not even promise when they would get someone. However, we would not forget them. We had heard that he had called a White man, a smith currently living in *White Eye's Town*, to move to *Assünnünk*, so we told him if he wanted to have Brothers living in his *Town* he should not become involved with White people and take them in. They usually had other reasons for living among the Indians than we did and therefore they did not fit in well with us. We wanted to have freedom to act and live in our *Towns* as it pleases God and according to his word. He answered he was very glad we spoke with him so directly, because he had not understood this. It was true that he had called the White man. However, he would go now and tell him not to come, because he did not want to do anything that would keep the Brothers from granting his request. On THE 23RD he traveled on and promised to stop in at our place in a number of days on his return journey.

THE 25TH   The Brothers who escorted us here from *Schönbrunn* and

768. Welapachtschiechen, or Captain Johnny, was baptized Israel on 25 December 1777. He had been at Schönbrunn on 30 January 1776.

helped put our house under roof returned home. During this time *Noah* had frequent opportunities to speak with his countrymen the *Cherokee* and to proclaim the Savior and his death to them.

Today we staked out our fields to see how much land we have to fence in. *John Killbuck* and his wife and others came here from *Goschgosching* for a visit. The former spent the night here. We talked with a woman about the Savior and said she was completely astonished. She had already heard some about the Savior but had never thought about it. She thought about it a lot, however, since we had come here. In her heart she always sensed it must be the truth after all and it had to be so.

THE 26TH   *John Heckewelder* and I moved into our house. We will also have our services there for now, so we made it quite spacious.

THE 27TH   There was much preaching because there were many visitors. *Anna*, who went to *Goschgosching* on business, had talked a lot with the Indians there from her tribe the Savior and among others she had a heart to heart talk with a woman whose husband had died recently. She had been baptized by the Brothers, and she admonished her to turn to the Savior again and not to throw away her eternal salvation since she had such a good opportunity now.

THE 30TH   The Indian who had moved to our place with his family and is very restless about his miserable condition came on his own and brought Brother *David* his hunting *Beson*.[769] He said he did not want to have anything more to do with this, because he had once promised to live for the Savior. It is very common among the Indians to use *Beson* on the hunt, and it is either a certain seed from herbs or there are certain roots. Not just anyone can make it, however, because Indian sorcery has to be used. They sell it among themselves for a very high price, and if they have it they believe they are especially lucky while hunting. However, it does not help anyone who is not a good hunter without it or who is already so old that he can no longer hunt well, even if he has it. It is thus nothing but superstition.

[May]

MAY 1ST   We began fencing in our fields. An Indian had come here to *Goschgosching* from *Wobash,* 1000 miles from here and not far from the *Illinois.*[770] A couple of days ago he came to Brother *David* and asked if he were the preacher there. When told Yes, he said, Do you think what you preach is the truth and is good? Brother *David* answered him, I preach God's word and this is the truth and will remain the truth into all eternity. He answered, But I still

769. On Beson, see entry for 25 Dec. 1772 and notes 90 and 117.
770. On the "Illinois," see Callender, "Illinois."

cannot believe it is the truth. Brother *David* told him, That is easy for me to believe, because you do not know anything about God or his word, and perhaps you have never before heard about it. Therefore you can neither say it is the truth or is not the truth. Once you have heard it, however, and receive life and feeling in your heart, you will no longer say that it is not true. It will become life and truth in your heart. He said, I know nothing about what you know. I only know about Indian *Affairs*. However, I would really like to hear what your teaching actually is. Brother *David* replied, If you would like to hear it, then go and visit the Brothers, your countrymen. They will tell you everything and explain what you want to know. However, he said he did not want to go there where there were so many people, because then he would not have a chance to speak. He would prefer to speak with just one person. Brother *David* then told him, Our teaching in brief is this: we believe that we are saved through faith in Jesus Christ, who purchased us with his blood and redeemed us from eternal death and from the power of Satan, under which all humans live by nature. He finally said, if you taught the Indians to make powder, *Blankets*, *Strowds*, linen and such, that would be worth the effort. However preaching does not do us any good. Brother *David* replied, If I tell the Indians how they can come to know their God and Creator and be saved here on earth and in eternity, is that not worth more and much more precious than powder and clothing? If you have everything that you desire in the world and are lost eternally because you do not know your Savior and Redeemer, what good does this do you? Therefore all those who are not concerned about their spiritual salvation here and now are fools. It is the only necessary thing. Afterwards, he often came here to visit and attended services. However, it still always remained a mystery to him and he could not understand what was said to him.

THE 2ND   After the early service Brothers *Isaac* and *Willhelm* went to *Goschgosching* to see the *Chief* about external matters, but they also had a good spiritual talk with him. The *Chief* said he was very happy that the Brothers lived there now and that he saw that his plan was being carried out. However, it was not yet enough sufficient for him personally. He would like to experience more in his heart soon. *Isaac* told him what it had been like for him when he was convince of the word of redemption through Jesus' Blood, and how he had always meditated about this and could not hear enough. Yes, said the *Chief*, it is like that with me. I would just like to be free of my office as *Chief* and I think a lot about how and in what manner I can become free of this, but for now I see no good escape.

THE 3RD   He came with a whole crowd of Indians, men and women, to help us make fences. They worked very hard on them the whole day. The women chopped the wood for this and the men carried it. Everything was done very quietly and orderly and we got a lot of work finished. Before he and his people returned home, a letter for the *Chief* arrived from *Captain White Eye* in

Philadelphia from the month of *March*. In this he informs him that he is planning to leave there soon to come home and that *Congress* promised him to give him a *Minister* and schoolmaster, and had also promised to provide him with other kinds of assistance.[771] Therefore they should build a church and schoolhouse in *Goschgosching*. He said nothing more about what kind of preacher he would bring, so it occurred to us he might be bringing Brothers and Sisters from the Unity. The *Chief* was very quiet at the news and said nothing for or against it.

THE 4TH   A family was here visiting. The wife spoke a lot with the Sisters and lamented the restlessness in her heart. She was worried that she was throwing away her salvation, and therefore she really wanted to live with us, if only her husband would agree to do this. He had also already promised her this, but he had told her she should have a little more patience.

THE 7TH   *John Killbuck* came here for a visit. Brother *David* asked him what they thought about *White Eye*, and if they thought he was bringing Brothers or another preacher with him. He answered they did not know at all what they should think or what he was planning. They would really like it if he brought Brothers with him. Everyone is now waiting to see what he has done, and we are anxious to find out soon. If he brings another *Minister*, we will oppose his settling in *Goschgosching*.

THE 8TH   We finished making fences. We have fenced in 17 acres, all of which should be planted this year. One of those visiting here today was an Indian who was baptized in old *Gnadenhütten* as a child with the name *Fridrich*. Brother *David* spoke with him and asked him if he did not sometimes think about giving his heart to the Savior since he was, after all, baptized. He answered that he often thought about it and it was still his intention to live in the world for the Savior. There were many strangers visiting, so the Savior and his death were proclaimed in most of our homes, just as they are for now. It sounded quite pleasant and sweet. Praise to the Lord, who allows his word to live richly among us. This gives us hope that it will also bear beautiful fruit in his time.

THE 10TH   *Netawatwees* visited us. He said that his thoughts and longing were always with us. He would like to come every day if he were not

---

771. On 16 December 1775 the Continental Congress, in response to White Eyes' petition, promised to fund a "minister and a schoolteacher" for the Delaware (Ford, *Journals of the Continental Congress,* 3:433). On 10 April 1776 this promise was elevated to a formal resolve (ibid., 4:301). See note 773 to entry for 11 May 1776 below, and John Ettwein on ? January 1776 to the missionaries, MAB, E.P., B 965, F 42, no. 1046. Ettwein reported that he met both White Eyes and George Morgan in Philadelphia and that he discussed his plans with White Eyes at some length. White Eyes intended to attract European settlers to a newly founded settlement as part of his efforts to make the Delaware more familiar with European civilization. Morgan had asked Ettwein to support these efforts, and Ettwein in turn had invited Morgan to come to Bethlehem. In Philadelphia White Eyes had been looked after by Quakers and was a houseguest of Israel Pemberton, head of the "Friendly Association" that was founded in 1756 for the improvement of Pennsylvania's relations with Native American Nations. Thayer, "Friendly Association."

prevented so much. First *Willhelm* spoke with him about the Savior for a long time, then he went to *Isaac*, who talked with him until almost evening, when he returned home.

THE 11TH   We were delighted to receive letters from Bethlehem and *Litiz* via *Schönbrunn*. *White Eye*, who arrived there yesterday evening, had brought them along. He came completely alone, however, without anyone else. *Isaac Still*, who was his traveling companion and interpreter, died of smallpox on the way between *Middle Town* and *Harrison's Ferry*.[772] We heard preliminarily from *Mr. Anderson*, who brought us these letters, that *Congress* had finally agreed that he should confer with his *Nation* and agree with them about what kind of preacher they wanted. When that had been done and everyone had agreed, then he should let them know.[773] We had actually hoped to learn from the letters that we could expect Brothers and Sisters from the Unity soon, or that they were already on the way. Unfortunately our hopes were misplaced.

THE 12TH   In the sermon the baby daughter born to Brother *Thomas* and Sister *Sabina* on the 7th of this month was baptized with the name *Johanna*. *Netawatwees* and his wife, grandparents of *Thomas*, were very attentive and took careful note of everything during this.

THE 13TH   We talked a lot with *Welapachtschiachen*, who came here from *Assünnünk* yesterday evening for a visit. This man has been awakened and his heart is restless. He said, When I am with you and hear about the Savior, my heart is very happy. But when I get home again and have been there for a little while, time goes so slowly that I cannot stand it and I set out to come

772. According to Ford, *Journals of the Continental Congress*, 4:271, and Ettwein (see preceding note), White Eyes' interpreter had been Isaac Stillé. This person is probably identical with the Delaware Isaac Still, who in 1758 accompanied Friedrich Post on his second journey as ambassador of the governor of Pennsylvania to the Indian tribes in the Ohio region who were allied with the Nouvelle France. Reuben G. Thwaites calls him "a Moravian Christian Indian, frequently employed as a messenger and interpreter" (*Early Western Travels*, 1:235n67).

773. On 16 March 1776 the Continental Congress read White Eyes' petition and asked a committee consisting of Lewis Morris, James Wilson, and Richard Henry Lee to report on it (Ford, *Journals of the Continental Congress*, 4:208). On 10 April the committee recommended in its report that the promises made to White Eyes on 16 December 1775 be supplemented by granting the Delaware funds for a smith and for a congress in Pittsburgh to which all tribes of the Ohio region were to be invited in 1776 (ibid., 266–67; see note 771 to entry for 3 May 1776). At that congress the tribes were to be informed of American efforts to increase the provision of European goods to the tribe and to do everything possible to quiet the general unrest among the tribes in that region. With regard to White Eyes, the committee recommended that the differences between him and the company Bernard Gratz and Michael Gratz be settled by a commission consisting of George Morgan and Aeneas Mackay, the two Indian agents, and John Neville, the commanding officer at Fort Pitt. Finally, the Congress approved a present of $300 and asked George Morgan, whose appointment as "Indian Agent of the Middle Department" was recommended, to purchase at the public's expense two horses, including saddles and gear, for White Eyes. All recommendations were approved. In the speech drafted by the committee, White Eyes was to be informed of these resolves; at the same time he was assured that the Congress would try to find "a sober man to instruct you in agriculture." In return, White Eyes was asked to assure the western tribes of the Congress's good will. As for the secure legal title to the land given the Delaware by the Wyandot, Congress suggested that the Six Indian Nations' express consent be sought. Ford, *Journals of the Continental Congress*, 4:208, 266–70.

here to your again. When Brother *David* asked him if he could understand what was discussed in the services, he replied that he understood some of it but not everything. Brother *David* told him he could attain the forgiveness of his sins and be saved through this if he could just understand and believe one thing: the Savior died and shed his blood for his sins. Then everything would come to him through faith in Jesus Christ, who is the source of all knowledge and wisdom. He would receive understanding of the Gospel and all of this would be given to him for nothing.

THE 15TH   *Zacharia* came here from *Gnadenhütten* to stay.[774] *John Killbuck* (he is old *Killbuck*'s son)[775] who came here for a visit said he was amazed how the *Chief* had changed since his last two visits here. He had said if *White Eye* brought a preacher who was not one of the Brothers,[776] he did not want to have anything to do with it and would have no part in it. He had called the Brothers and explicitly named them, and he was very happy that they were now there. He would remain faithful to them. He had said further, Do we not already see 2 *Town*s of Indian believers before our eyes and the 3rd one that has been started? Where else can we find such a *Town* among the Indians? Or has anyone ever seen anything like now? Do we then have reason to doubt this matter, that it is right and the truth? I am completely convinced that the Brothers have the right teaching and preach the truth. At the same time *John Killbuck* informed us that *White Eye* had arrived in *Goschgosching* just a little while ago and that a council would be held tomorrow. We were also invited to this and he would like to know when it would be convenient for us to come. We replied that we would be ready by the time they could gather and send us word.

THE 16TH   We prayed to our dear Lord, who ascended into heaven for us, and asked for his invisible but powerful presence, and for a constant relationship with him. Very early, a messenger came to us from *Goschgosching* to call Brother *David* to the *Council* there with as many Indian Brothers as wanted to come. He went with 5 Brothers and the Indians soon gathered in the *Chief*'s house. In a little while *White Eye* came as well and greeted us cordially. We returned the greeting and told him how happy we were to see him here again. Much food had been brought and *White Eye* talked a lot about his trip and the negotiations in *Philadelphia* and what he had seen and heard there, including *Conversations* he had had with people of many opinions and with the Brothers. Everyone had received him very well. Finally he got to the reason we had come together and said they would not separate until they had reached a conclusion and formulated a *Resolution*. First Brother *David* was given *White Eye*'s letter, which he had written to the *Chief* from *Philadelphia*. He read it aloud again.

774. See entry for 8 Aug. 1776.
775. Gelelemind; see note 765 to entry for 21 April 1776.
776. See entry for 11 May 1776.

This reported that the *Congress* had promised him a preacher and schoolmaster, as well as further assistance, and also that the *Chief* should tell us Brothers here that we had nothing to fear if we received an English *Minister* as a result, nor would we have any difficulties because of this. The second thing was an address from the *Congress* to the *Chief* and his *Council* which he had in writing and which Brother *David* also read aloud to them.[777] I will only mention what concerns *us* in this, however. In the name of the *Chief* and his *Nation*, *White Eye* had asked *Congress* for a preacher and schoolmaster. He also asked that arts and science might be introduced among the Indians, but nothing like this could happen unless White people from whom they could learn lived and settled among the Indians. However, this required the entire *Nation* to agree on this. Only then would they assist them as far as they were able. Everyone present listened with great *Attention*. No one said anything, however, and afterwards other matters were discussed, until one person after another left the *Council* House and we were left alone with the *Chief* and the head people. We saw that they were all leaving and nothing else would be done, so Brother *David* finally told the *Chief* that we were also going home. However, first we wanted to tell him that we did not want to have any part in this matter currently in progress about which we had heard so much, nor did we consent to it. If they wanted good advice, we would gladly share it with them if they asked for it. They had good reason to be concerned and to consider well before they made any decisions. We wanted to tell him this because He had called us Brothers here and we hoped we were not just there out of boredom or to be observers; we wanted to be useful to our friends, since we now lived right among them, and to advise them for the best. Then we said farewell. Brother *David* also told *John Killbuck*, whom we met in the road as we were leaving, what the *Chief* had said. He added that if something happened or was supposed to happen, of if they wanted to know something further from us or needed some explanation, they should just let us know. We would then provide them with this as far as we were able. He promised to do this. We heard the next day, after the council had gathered again, that the *Chief* had made sharp inquiries among his *Councellors* about which of them had made an agreement with *White Eye* behind his back to ask *Congress* for a *Minister* who was not one of the Brothers; this had not been his intention at all. He had explicitly named the Brothers. Nor could this have been the result of a misunderstanding, because all the Indians had heard him talk about this matter very clearly not just once, but often. When no one answered him, he asked *Welapachtschiechen* from *Assünnünk*, who was the head *Chief* from *White Eye's Tribe*[778] if he knew anything about this matter. However, he replied that he was completely ignorant and innocent in this.[779] The matter

777. See note 773 to entry for 11 May 1776.
778. White Eyes was a member of the Turkey clan, Netawatwees a member of the Turtle clan.
779. See entry for 30 Jan. 1776.

was not touched upon at all the rest of the day. They took up other matters instead; and hopefully it will indeed be buried. *White Eye* cannot carry out his business without the *Chief's Consent*. All he can do is to quit serving to him. This is how he forced the *Chief* to accept the Brothers last year, but he will not succeed in this. Previously, he won because he was for the Brothers. Now it is the *Chief's* turn; he has taken his place.

We had come here at just the right time, and we have had much contact with the *Chief* while we have been here and before *White Eye* arrived with his *Project*, since he visited us often as we did him. We have had the opportunity to discuss many things with him, and this is an important reason why he supports the Brothers so strongly now. May the Savior maintain him as our friend among us for the furthering of his Kingdom.

THE 18TH   *Welapachtschiechen*, who had spent a happy 6-day visit with us and heard much encouragement, returned to *Assünnünk* and promised to visit us again soon. Today we 16 Brothers and Sisters had our first Holy Communion here and our dear Lord blessed us unspeakably with his Body and Blood in the Holy *Sacrament*. One Brother, *Thomas*, participated in this for the first time.

THE 19TH   *Netawatwees, White Eye,* and the entire *Councel* from *Goschgosching* came here for the sermon with a whole crowd of Indians. Therefore we postponed the *Liturgy* for Holy Communion until evening. The Savior granted me the grace to testify that all poor sinners and those who have a humble heart can find forgiveness for our sins, eternal life, and salvation only in Jesus' sacrifice, which is good for all eternity, and that no further sacrifice is necessary. However, this is not for the great, the proud, and those who want to become rich. *White Eye* was very friendly and also obliging towards us, but he looked dejected and restless. He stayed here for several hours, went into the bush alone with Brothers *Willhelm* and *Isaac,* and talked and discussed with them. From all his talking and questioning, however, you could see that he has gotten very distracted from the main concern; his thoughts were gloomy and focused on secondary issues and *Projects* of great undertakings he is still planning to accomplish with the Indians in order to turn them into a respected and rich people. He hopes in vain that the great people in the country will help him do this. In contrast, the Brothers and their work seem too lowly to him, to speak plainly, and he does not like poverty and baseness. However, Brothers *Willhelm* and *Isaac* kept trying to convince him of the right way and confronted him with the Savior's words, But seek ye first the kingdom of God, and his righteousness; and all these things shall be added unto you.[780] They offered readings perfectly fitting for him and told him things that I could hardly have dared to tell him. He complained that he had had to suffer much since his return home; everyone was against him and he had to listen to almost more than he could bear. This did not happen by chance, however.

780. Matt. 6:33.

THE 22ND   He came to Brother *David* with some others from the council and asked him to write down a message to *Wobash*, not far from *Fort Charter*[781] on the *Missisippi* [sic!] for them. He did this and the 2 messengers immediately left for there.[782]

THE 24TH   Brother *David* traveled to *Schönbrunn* and returned from there on the 28th. In the meantime Brother *Heckewelder* held the services here. Despite the rain on THE 26TH, the *Chief* and *White Eye* came with a whole crowd of their people for the sermon. Afterwards, the Indian Brothers continued proclaiming the Gospel to them until almost evening, when they returned home. We talked a lot in private with *White Eye,* and *John Killbuck*'s heart was very touched.

A couple of days ago the *Chief* received a message from the *Wyandot* saying that they had learned that their *Cousins* the *Delaware* have accepted God's word, which would make them and their children a happy people. They were very happy to hear this about their *Cousins.*[783] They should remain with this. They, the *Wyandot* would also follow them and were especially concerned that their children might also attain this. People usually call them the *Wyandot*, and they live on both the near and far sides of *Lake* Erie around *Detroit.*

THE 27TH   The *Chief* learned that we were planting, so he had an ox slaughtered without our knowledge and told his people to come here with him and help us plant our fields. For this they would feast on the ox when they were finished. Then a crowd of Indians, as well as *White Eye* and all the head people, came with him and planted all our fields in one day. He himself was always present and encouraged the people to work, and they were very diligent. When they returned home in the evening the *Chief* also sent us a quarter of the ox.

THE 30TH   *Michael* and his wife and Magdalena, a widow, came here from *Schönbrunn* and *John Killbuck* and his wife from *Goschgosching* for a visit. They spent the night here. He shared his heart with us and said that he was tired of living among the nonbelievers and he was very weary of dealing with *Chief Affairs*. His desire to live with us was growing greater and greater. He had spoken with his uncle *Netawatwees* about this just a couple of days ago. However, he always objected saying, What will happen to the *Chief* affairs and the worldly government and who will take care of this if you leave me? This is really true and we also need to make sure that everything does not land on *Netawatwee's* shoulders, because if he gets tired of it and perhaps even lays down

781. Zeisberger is referring to Fort Chartres. See the description of George Rogers Clark in his letter to Patrick Henry (?) dated 1777, in James, *Clark Papers,* 30–32, and on the insignificant role of the fort during the American Revolution, see Alvord, *Mississippi Valley in British Politics.*

782. See entry for 1 May 1776, in which Zeisberger reports the visit of an Illinois from that region. The message is certainly related to that visit.

783. See entry for 29 Oct. 1775. The term "Wyandot" in the following sentence is unusual; usually Zeisberger calls the Wyandot Delamattenos.

his office, as he has mentioned to us before, it could be disadvantageous for us if there was either no ruler, or a bad one, among the Indians. Therefore we will have to try to find a middle road so that they are helped on both sides.

The *Chiefs* are always working to see that the Indians follow what they have decided among themselves and since we are now living here they would also like to demonstrate this. However sometimes they lose heart when they see that so many have no inclination to this or are even against it. *White Eye* is supposed to have told *Netawatwees* recently (and he has even said this here at our place) that he sometimes doubted that they would accomplish what they were intending, because so many lacked ears to hear the Gospel and many were even against it. Therefore he believed that many would leave. *Netawatwees* replied, If they want to go, they may do so, because they have no mind for what is good. Let them go. Even if they do go, they will return, and where do they want to go that they will find things any better? Fear and horror will drive them back here.

[June]

JUNE 1ST   *Michael* returned to *Schönbrunn*. 4 *Wyandot* came here from *Goschgosching* for a visit. They had gone there from *Sandusky* some days ago.[784] We heard from them that the *Nations* were all quiet and peaceful.

THE 2ND   Two *Wyandot* were among those who came here for the sermon today. We spoke with *Netawatwees* and told him that because he and others had already expressed to us their desire to learn our thoughts and advice with respect to *Chief* affairs, we would talk to them about this when *White Eye* and *John Killbuck* were at home and would hear their thoughts as well as telling them ours.

THE 5TH   An *express*[785] messenger from *Pittsburgh* passed through here going to the *Shawnee*. We learned from him that *Mr. Morgan* would follow in a few days. He brought us a *Proclamation* from him. One point in this was that the *Traders* or White people should not bring any *Rum* or strong drinks into our *Towns* or into our area. We were happy about this because it has happened before that those who had *Rum* did not actually bring it to our *Towns*, but hid

---

784. See entry for 26 May 1776.
785. The messenger was William Wilson, George Morgan's interpreter. See GD for 3 June 1776, F 7, I 1, and "Report of William Wilson to the Commissioners for Indian Affairs," dated 20 Sept. 1776, *AA*, 5th series, 2:514. He had been accompanied by Joseph Nicholson. Their message asked the Delaware and the Shawnee not to join the British side but to await the arrival of George Morgan before making a decision. See Schaaf, *Wampum Belts and Peace Trees*, 87–88; Savelle, *George Morgan*, 136–38. On 10 April 1776 the Continental Congress appointed George Morgan (1742–1810), an Indian trader and land speculator, "Indian Agent of the Middle Department," an office he held until May 1779.

it in the bush some miles away. A lot of wild Indians became drunk afterwards from this and we experienced many difficulties as a result.

THE 6TH   Some of our Indian Brothers went down to *Sikhewunk* to hunt for 14 days.

THE 10TH   *Welapachtschiechen* came here from *Assününk* for another visit. He is always happy to make the trip to our place. The Savior who won salvation for us through his death was proclaimed to him until late in the night.

THE 11TH   Some of our Indian Brothers were asked to come to the *Council* in *Goschgosching* because *Mr. Morgan* had arrived there, and then *Willhelm* and another Brother went there. The main issue they were informed of was that a *Treaty* would be held with them in *Pittsburgh* as soon as the *Nations* could be gathered. *Mr. Morgan* asked the headmen of the *Delaware Nation* for help sending out messengers to all the *Nations* as far down as *Wobash* to invite them. They promised to do this. Finally he reminded them that they had asked for a preacher and *Congress* was willing to help them. They should think about this and consider the matter well.[786]

THE 13TH   He[787] came here, stayed for a few hours, and then continued his journey on to the *Shawnee*.

THE 14TH   *White Eye*, old *Killbuck,* and his son[788] came here with *Willhelm*. He had told them a few words yesterday about the issue of a preacher, which *Mr. Morgan* had mentioned to them. They had come to consider this and discuss it further. *White Eye* said we should not believe that they knew everything and were as experienced as we were. We surely knew and understood better than they did what was best for them. Therefore we should advise them what to do in this matter. *Willhelm* told them, I am glad to hear you seek our advice. I will tell you my thoughts and opinions as far as I understand the matter. However, what I do not understand and cannot clarify for you, we can ask our teachers who are there and they will always advise us well. You will do well to accept their advice, because this has been my experience as long as I have been with the Brothers. You have heard from *Mr. Morgan*s' address to you that you should consider well what you ask. What do you have to consider now? I will tell you this: consider what you have ahead of you and already in your hands. You have declared you would accept God's word. You have desired to have this preached among you, and you have this now. Stick with this. Why are you looking for something else? You have made a mistake; you have left the right road and have forgotten what you were seeking in the beginning. Turn back and remain faithful to what you have. Then things will go well and the mistake you have made will be rectified. As soon as you give up your plan to calling another *Minister* and remain with the Brothers, things will work out

786. See note 773 to entry for 11 May 1776. Morgan's notes about this meeting in his diary are printed in Schaaf, *Wampum Belts and Peace Trees,* 120–26. The preacher is not mentioned.
787. George Morgan.
788. White Eyes, John Killbuck Sr., and John Killbuck Jr., alias Gelelemind.

and you will reach your goal. However if you continue with this plan, you will run into more *Confusion.* They were all very pleased with what he told them and *White Eye* seemed to have found his way out of the *Labyrinth.* He himself now realizes that he brought the hate of the Indians upon himself and that this went so far that some said although his tribe was the smallest among the *Nation* he wanted to be its sovereign, command them, and force them to do something they had no interest in doing. They would rather do him in. What had agitated the Indians against him so much though was that they realized he was not only planning to call another *Minister* into the country, but also many other White people like *farmers* and tradesmen.[789]

THE 16TH   Once again, many strangers including a *Wyandot* had come for the sermon about how the Savior, through his servants, invites people to the salvation He won for us through his Blood. He sends them the message, Come; for all things are now ready![790] Examples of the kinds of excuses the Indians use for not being able to come were then offered. Old *Killbuck*'s wife[791] spoke with our Sisters and said she really wants to live in the congregation. She also wanted to live for the Savior, and in her heart she always felt she should come to us. She had also spoken with her husband more than once about arranging for them to move there. He replied that she should have a little patience; it could still happen. He has changed a lot since we have been here. He attends the services very regularly and is very obliging to us. This is even more surprising because it has not been very long at all since he told some of our Indians that only when all the Indians had converted and he was left alone would he consider what he would do.[792] It is doubtful now whether he will be able to wait that long, and he may yet become one of the first, which would bring us much joy. However, it is really good that people do rush to us right in the beginning, before we have built ourselves up a little, and if *White Eye*'s *Affaire* served no other purpose, it was useful to us because it held people back a little. They will come soon enough.

THE 17TH   *John Killbuck*[793] spoke with us and complained about his circumstances and his request. He was still so tied up and did not yet see how he could get free from his external *Affairs,* and he still wanted to live with us. From the beginning he had always thought that as soon as the process of the Brothers moving was under way, as soon as they came, he would also move to our place immediately, but now he had still not gotten any further. He was often very upset about this. We encouraged him to bide his time patiently and comforted him that the Savior will certainly help and prepare the way for him.

---

789. See note 773 to entry for 11 May 1776 and entry for 16 May.

790. Luke 14:17.

791. Wife of John Killbuck Sr. and mother of Gelelemind.

792. The diary does not repeat his earlier remarks; on Killbuck's opposition, see entry for 13 Aug. 1775.

793. Gelelemind.

He said his uncle *Netawatwees* had advised him to build a house in *Goschgosching* if he moved to our place. From this we can conclude that he will not let him go completely, but will always want to use him in his service.

THE 23RD   The sermon was about the Gospel lesson of the lost sheep; the Savior came to seek and save the lost,[794] and the *Chief* and many others had come. The Indian Brothers then repeated this sermon and tried to make it quite clear to them.

THE 24TH   A family from *White Eye's Town* came here for a visit and to hear about the Savior. The man and the woman are no longer at peace in their circumstances and would like to come to the congregation.

THE 27TH   Brother *Heckewelder* returned from *Schönbrunn* and on THE 28TH *Willhelm* returned. They had gone there on the 24th. Brothers *Boas*, *Abel*, and *Nehemia* came here with them.

THE 29TH   Our dear Lord blessed us inexpressibly with his Body and Blood in the Holy *Sacrament*.

[July]

JULY 1ST   Most of the Brothers and some Sisters went to *Schönbrunn* to pick up all the rest of their things and the cattle they had left there. Some went on land and some by water. After a pretty long drought, we received a pleasant and welcome rain today. *Willhelm* came immediately thereafter, and those from *Goschgosching* later told him that they had caused the rain, because this morning they had all collected tobacco for an Indian who was supposed to make it rain, and this had now happened. There are Indians who say it is very easy for them to make rain, and the others believe it.

That is all for our diary at this time. We commend our little gathering in *Lichtenau* and ourselves to the prayer and remembrance of the congregations before our dear Lord.

Diary of Lichtenau *on the* Muskingum *from* July *1776 to* June *21 1777.*[795]

THE 7TH   *Chief Netawatwees* came with a whole crowd of Indians from *Goschgosching* and *White Eye's Town* for the sermon. He walked around in the *Town* right away this morning, admonished his people to go with him into the services, and told them that anyone who did not want to go should not work that day, much less play games. They should celebrate Sunday.

794. Luke 15:1–7.
795. MAB, B 147, F 2, fol. 216.

THE 10TH   A couple of *Wyandot* who had come from *Sandusky* with their families came here and stayed until almost evening. They understood *Minque* pretty well, so Brother *David* spoke with them a lot about how we accomplish the forgiveness of sins in Jesus' blood alone and will be saved through this, and our Indian Brothers also did so through an interpreter.

THE 11TH   Various Indians from *Goschgosching* came for the early service with women and children. The news arrived from *Niagara*, where a *Treaty* was held with the Indians,[796] that many from the 6 *Nations* and *Tawa*[797] had gone to war against the residents of this country,[798] and we heard from *Pittsburgh* that a White man had been killed there and people believed the *Minque* had done it.[799] This news made the Indians fearful, because they could only presume that the 6 *Nations* had taken up the hatchet against the *Colonies*. This made them pick up their people who still live in *Gekelemukpechünk* and take them quickly to *Goschgosching*. We lent them *Canows* for this.[800]

THE 13TH   *Mr. Morgan* came here on his return journey from the *Shawnes* and they spent the night with us. He brought along 2 boys who had been captured. A party of *Minque* had brought them in during his stay there and he had gotten them out again.[801] Things do not look *favorable* enough among the *Nations* that we can hope for quiet and peaceful times, because something is going on among them. We cannot yet figure out what it is. It is commonly believed, however, that if an Indian war breaks out it will be the most violent one there has ever been. *Mr. Morgan* also believes this and agrees. Because times seemed very serious, Brother *David* suggested talking urgently with the *Delaware** about the *Communication* from *Pittsburgh* so that the spirit of lies will be thwarted and the Indians will always know where they stand. He

---

796. During the congress at Niagara, which lasted from 29 May to 5 (?) June 1776, Colonel John Butler tried to win the Indians for the British side. The majority refused and argued for peace. Schaaf, *Wampum Belts and Peace Trees*, 100–110; Graymont, *Iroquois in the American Revolution*, 97–100.

797. See entry for 18 Oct. 1773, with note 284.

798. This was incorrect information purposely circulated by the British side (see previous note); only the Mohawk and some Seneca proved receptive to British enticements. In mid-May, according to Patrick Lockhart, this rumor had already been circulated by Colonel John Gibson in Williamsburg; this is particularly strange because on 6 July the Seneca chief Kayahsota had reported the resolves of the Niagara conference to the participants in the conference at Fort Pitt. At the same time he had communicated to the tribes assembled at Fort Pitt the message that the Six Indian Nations recommended neutrality and had resolved to deny both American and British soldiers the right of passage through the confederation's territory. *AA*, 5th series, 1:36–37, 867–68; *RUO*, 155.

799. This news could be linked with a number of incidents that George Morgan reported on 15 Aug. 1776. *AA*, 5th series, 1:137–38.

800. The reaction of the Delaware is difficult to understand, for in the meantime Captain Pipe, who had participated at the conference at Fort Pitt and listened to Kayahsota's report, could have been back in Goschachgünk or could have forwarded a report about the conference. The reaction suggests the possibility that the rumor originated with a nascent pro-British fraction among the Delaware.

801. The children were Adam and William McConnell, who on 23 June 1776 had been made prisoners by Pluggy's warriors and were liberated on 9 July 1776 by Morgan. Schaaf, *Wampum Belts and Peace Trees*, 158–60; *AA*, 5th series, 1:137–38.

agreed to this and on the following day proposed to the *Councel* in *Goschgosching* that they send an *express* messenger to the *Fort* every 14 days, or as often as they thought good. This was accepted and resolved and begun immediately, and it will be continued as long as necessary. At the same time he asked Brother *David* to put it in writing if the *Chiefs* have anything to report to him at the *Fort*, which he promised to do.[802]

THE 16TH   We began framing in a house where we will hold our services *ad interim* until we can build the actual Meeting House. It will be the schoolhouse in the future. We finished it this week and the first sermon was held in it ON THE 21ST. The *Chief* and some of his people came for this. We had not yet been able to arrange getting *Netawatwees* and his *Counsellors* together to speak with him, and they have already asked a number of times to learn our opinions about the *Chief* issue, as well as what would happen if someone from the *Councel* wanted to move to our place and become a believer. Therefore we did this today and told him our intention about this alone, and he was completely satisfied. Since this matter has already come up and been mentioned numerous times, it will not be repeated here. Brother *David* once again received an *Invitation* from *Welapachtschiechen* in *Achsünnünk* [sic!] to go there for a visit and look around the area to establish a *Town* for Indian believers.[803] The reason he would like this to happen soon now, he reported, was because in one month he would be traveling and then nothing would come of it.

THE 23RD   A couple of White people arrived here. *Mr. Morgan* had sent them to the *Wyandot* with a party of *Shawnee* as messengers. However, when they got to *Minque Town*[804] on the way and were stopped there, they thought the safest thing to do would be to sneak away in the middle of the night if they did not want to be taken prisoners, delivered to *Detroit*, or even killed.

THE 25TH   We received the news that a party of *Minque* and *Shawnee* who had brought the *Cherokees* the *War Belt* in the spring asking them to raise the hatchet against the White people returned from there with the news that the *Cherokees* were already engaged in a war with the White people and as a token they had brought along 2 *Scalps* from there to the *Wyandot*.[805] We also

802. This agreement formed the basis for the numerous reports and letters Zeisberger and Heckewelder sent to the commanding officer of Fort Pitt and to the representatives of the Continental Congress.

803. See entry for 22 April 1776.

804. It is evident from Zeisberger's description that this settlement was situated north of Gekelemukpechünk on the road to the Sandusky River. We know of only one Mingo settlement—Hell 1—on this route. See Cappon et al., *Atlas of Early American History*, 80. We believe that Hell 1 is identical with the settlement Kinhanschican, which Zeisberger mentions on 24 Feb. and 14 March 1777 and on 13 Feb. 1781.

805. The Cherokee attacks had commenced at the end of June 1776. For a lengthy report on the negotiations of this delegation with the Cherokee and the Creek, see Henry Stuart to John Stuart, Pensacola, 25 Aug. 1776, in Davies, *Documents of the American Revolution*, 12:191–208, esp. 198–203; John Stuart correctly reported in his letter to Lord Germain, dated 23 Aug. 1776, that this delegation

heard then that the *Shawnee* or some of them were preparing for war at this news. All of this presented us with horrible *Prospects*.

THE 27TH   *Samuel Moor* came from *Schönbrunn* and really delighted us by bringing letters from Brother *Matthao* as well as the weekly reports from the *General Synod* numbers 13-18. At the same time we received the official news that it has pleased our dear Lord to call home his faithful servant, our dear Brother *Thrane*.[806]

JULY 28TH   The first baptism here was carried out and the blood and water from Jesus' side was poured upon *Netanewand, Netawatwee*'s *Grandson*, who received the name *Johannes* in Holy Baptism.[807] At the same time his wife *Hanna*, who was baptized as an older girl in Bethlehem by Brother *Joseph*[808] but was then led away from the congregation, was *absolved* and received again. During this the presence of the Holy Trinity could be felt powerfully and many tears were shed.

THE 29TH   A *Council* was held in *Goschgosching*, because in recent days horrifying news has arrived that the *Nations* seem to be planning evil attacks and that 6 *Nations* had united for war against the White people. The *Chief*, however, cannot remember such things taking place secretly[809] and the *Delaware* should not be told anything about this. A *Council* was held about this in *Goschgosching* and our Indian Brothers were also called to this. They decided right away to send messengers to the *Wyandot* to find out more about the matter. Some *Delaware* Indians who returned from the *Shawnee* had been told that the *Delaware* Indians would not receive news of this until things had gone so far that the war could no longer be stopped, because they knew that they would not consent to this.

[August]

AUGUST 2ND   We responded to *Welapachtschiechen's Invitation* to come to *Assünnünk*[810] by sending word that we would wait and see how things went

---

contributed decisively to the Cherokee's determination to repel the American settlers (ibid., 188–91, esp. 189). The American side interpreted the Cherokee's decision as support for the British. O'Donnell, *Southern Indians in the American Revolution*, 40–43. George Sackville Germain, 1st Viscount of Sackville (1716–85) was the British government's "Secretary of State for the American Colonies" from 1775 to 1782. He is usually called "Lord Germain."

806. Paul Thrane had died at Bethlehem on 19 April 1776. He had been the pastor of the congregation there (Hegner, *Fortsetzung,* 243). Amadaeus Paul Thrane (1718–76), hailed from Aalberg, Jüttland, whence he had arrived at Bethlehem in 1761 (Hamilton, "Ettwein," 236).

807. With the baptism of Netanewand, two grandsons of Netawatwees lived at Schönbrunn, Thomas alias Gutkigamen (baptized 11 Sept. 1774, entry for 14 Aug. 1776) and Johannes, alias Netanewand. A third grandson, Gelelemind, was closely attached to the mission congregation.

808. August Gottlieb Spangenberg; see entry for 21 April 1776.

809. It was possible that messages concerning military alliances were addressed only to captains and not to chiefs; in any case they had to be dealt with in the Council in private session, where chiefs were also present.

810. See entry for 21 July 1776.

because currently we are hearing only bad news and there would be no purpose in going there now. He should be patient until circumstances have cleared up more and settled down.

THE 4TH   Many strangers from the neighborhood were present for the sermon, as was the *Chief*, who told the Indian Brothers that he had made a notched stick[811] and had already marked 13 Sundays on it when he had come to the services. He said that sometimes when he thought about how long he had been hearing about the Savior or if he just looked at his notched stick, his heart became so tender that he had to cry. He did this in private, however, as much as possible.

Referring to the news we heard recently about something dangerous going on, he said he did not doubt that the *Nations* were planning war. However, he believed nothing would come of this because there would be discord among them and thus their plans would come to nothing. This is how things actually turned out.[812]

THE 7TH   The *Chief* sent one of his *Counsellors* to share a message he had received from the *Minque*. It was similar to the *Seneca Chief's* message to the Indians in *Goschgosching* in 1768.[813] The *Delaware* should not believe the preaching of the White people, who were only trying to mislead them. The *Virginians* wanted to deceive them, which was why they sent *Ministers* to them, and they should protect themselves from them. However, the Indians did not consider this and did not accept it. The *Shawnee* also received this same message from a different source.

THE 8TH   The single Brother *Zacharias* was married to the single Sister *Anna Elisabeth* during the devotions for married couples.

THE 10TH   7 White people passed through here going to the *Shawnee*; they said they were going to visit their friends there.[814] Five of them had been prisoners among them previously. The communicant Brothers and Sisters strengthened themselves on the Body and Blood of the Lord in the *Holy Sacrament*. One Sister observed for the first time during this. *Johannes*, who was in

---

811. The Delaware and all other tribes of the region were unfamiliar with letters but used pictograms. See Bray, "Indian Method of Picture-Writing." More difficult is their attitude toward figures. Zeisberger describes one way in which they used figures; see Heckewelder, *History, Manners, and Customs*, 128–31. Zeisberger described their method of counting: "They count up to ten, make a mark, proceed to the next ten and so on to the end of the account" ("History of the Northern American Indians," 144). This is not to say that the Delaware knew only figures up to ten; Zeisberger's dictionary makes it clear that they were familiar with larger figures; see *Zeisberger's Indian Dictionary*, passim.

812. See entry for 11 Aug. 1776.

813. On 1 August 1768 the following message from the Seneca chiefs at Venango arrived at Goschgoschünk: "Cousins, who dwell in Goschgoschuenk and along the Ohio and you Shawanose! I have arisen and looked about me, to find out what is going on in the land. I have seen that somebody in a black coat has arrived, beware of the black coat. Believe not what he tells you, for he will pervert and alienate your hearts." [Sensemann and Zeisberger], "Diary of Zeisberger and Zenseman," 67.

814. See entry for 4 May 1775.

Goschgosching on business today, had the opportunity to witness for Him and the Savior granted him grace to do so with sincere emotion.

THE 11TH   A relatively large number of strangers and the *Chief* came for the sermon, so that our place seemed too small. Today after the messenger had returned from the *Wyandot*,[815] we received the news that neither this nor the other *Nations* had agreed among themselves to begin a war against the residents of this country. A number of *Minque* had persuaded many of the *Shawnee* to go with them and to commit murders in *Virginia* or perhaps to attack the *Fort* on the *Canhawa*.[816] The 6 *Nations* called back all of their people who had gone to the army in *Canada*. They wanted to remain neutral and also will not allow an army to march through their country.[817]

THE 13TH   During our services we remembered the important anniversary today of what our dear Lord did for his house and people 49 years ago.[818] We thanked Him that through grace we are also members of his Unity, which is founded in his Blood and Death, and which the gates of hell cannot overcome.

A family, *White Eye*'s brother and his wife, who is our *Isaac*'s sister,[819] came here with their sick child, a 9-year-old girl. She had continued asking her parents to bring her here to us until they did so and she said, Perhaps I will die, and I want to die with the Brothers. Perhaps I can be baptized first and then I will go to the Savior. They visited very often this summer, and this made an impression on the child. This evening she asked her mother to carry her to the Meeting Hall, because she really wanted to hear about the Savior. This was done, and then she rested and slept better than she has in a long time, and in a short time she became completely well. This was a great miracle for her parents and they thought about this a lot.

We received news that this past spring a *Treaty* had been held with the *Cherokees* in the name of the King at the mouth of the *Cherokee River*. They were given many *Presents* there and much *Ammunition*, along with a *War Belt*. They accepted this, and it is the 2nd one they have accepted.[820]

815. See entry for 29 July 1776.

816. This message seems to indicate that the Wyandot were as yet unfamiliar with the alliance between the Shawnee, Mingo, and Cherokee; see entry for 25 July 1776, note XXX. The "Fort on the *Canhawa*" refers to Fort Randolph, which had been built as a substitute for Fort Blair, which the Shawnee burned down in 1775; the commanding officer of Fort Randolph was Matthew Arbuckle. See Jefferds, *Captain Matthew Arbuckle*.

817. See entry for 11 July 1776 and note 796.

818. On this memorial day, see Introduction, pp. 62–63.

819. Isaac and White Eyes had been close friends before Isaac's conversion (see entry for 9 May 1774); the marriage between Isaac's sister and White Eyes' brother suggests that this friendship should be interpreted within the context of a close alliance between the two families.

820. See note 805 to entry for 25 July 1776. On 24 April 1776 Henry Stuart had brought ammunition and presents to the Cherokee; after talking to the chiefs he reported to his brother, on 7 May, that the Cherokee had pledged their allegiance to George III. Davies, *Documents of the American Revolution*, 10:361–62; O'Donnell, *Southern Indians in the American Revolution*, 36–38. Zeisberger's interpretation of the Cherokee's behavior suggests that not only the revolutionary colonists but the Delaware, too, now viewed the Cherokee as pro-British.

THE 14TH　　Brother *Schebosch* came from *Schönbrunn* and delighted us with letters from Bethlehem and *Litiz*. Brother *David* left with him on the 16th to go there and returned from there on the 21st. In the meantime Brother *Heckewelder* had taken care of the services here. The *Councel* forbade a man from *Detroit* from taking cattle from here to there, because that *Colony* was not at peace with this one.[821] He had come to *Schönbrunn* and *Gnadenhütten* as well as *Goschgosching* to buy cattle. *Netawatwee's* son and his family, 9 people altogether, moved here after he had discussed it with his father first. He was not only very satisfied with this, but even quite happy about it.[822] He also has 2 other grandchildren here, *Johannes* and *Thomas*. The latter is a great amazement to him, because he was one of the worst kinds of Indians. He had chased him away and told him never to show up again; he was too bad a person. Now, however, he is happy every time he sees him. It is clear what has happened to him, because he has changed from a bear to a lamb.

THE 23RD　　Brother *David* was called to *Goschgosching* where he had to read aloud a letter from the *Commissioners* in the *Fort* to the *Councel*.[823]

A White man passed through here on his way from the *Shawnee Towns* to the *Fort*. He brought news that 60 *Minque* warriors were lying there waiting for reinforcements to attack the *Fort* on the *Canhawa*. He said that it looked as if a general Indian war was unavoidable, and that the *Nations* already had an agreement with each other. They should not let the *Delaware* know about this until everything was ready, however, so they could not intervene in it. He had been told this in confidence.[824]

THE 25TH　　*Netawatwees* and others came here for the sermon. We

821. From "a man from . . ." not in H3. In GD, entry for 24 Aug. 1776, the name of this trader is given as "Forsiht." The denial was justified on the grounds that the cattle were needed at Pittsburgh (GD F 7, I 1). The trader was William Forsyth. Born in Ireland, Forsyth had emigrated to North America in 1750; during the Revolution he played an important role at Fort Detroit. George Morgan objected violently to Forsyth's purchasing provisions for Detroit in the Indian settlements of the region and demanded that Forsyth be given up to Fort Pitt. George Morgan to William Wilson, 11 Aug. 1776, George Morgan Letterbook, vol. 2, fol. 6, CLP. On 20 September 1776 the trader John Anderson, for example, bought "10 pieces of cattle for the Treaty" at Gnadenhütten (MAB, B 144, F 7, I 1).

822. This refers to Saktelaeuche, who, on 16 Dec. 1776, considered "getting saved" and who was baptized Gideon on 25 Dec. 1776. In addition to Saktelaeuche and Killbuck Sr., Netawatwees had at least one daughter; see entry for 3 Oct. 1776.

823. Bracketed in a different hand. The letter was dated 17 Aug. 1776 and had been brought by the Delaware George Willson. Commissioners Thomas Walker, John Harvie, John Montgomerie, and Jasper Yeates encouraged the Delaware to remain faithful to the American cause, informed them that at their expense they had sent the trader John Anderson to Goschachgünk, warned them about evil rumormongers, and expressed the hope that White Eyes or another chief would visit them soon. George Morgan Letterbook, vol. 2, fols. 8–9, CLP.

824. The Commissioners for Indian Affairs describe the same informant in a circular dated 31 Aug. 1776 as "a Gentleman from the lower Shawanese Towns"; he was supposed to have reported a "General Confederacy of the Western Tribes . . . in order to Strike our Frontier Settlements" after the harvest. "[T]heir plan of Operation is that the Chippewas and Ottawas two numerous Tribes should attack this place [Fort Pitt], and the Shawanese the Settlements on this side the Ohio" (*RUO*, 190–91). The addition that the Delaware were to be left uninformed of the alliance until the alliance had

heard from him that a couple of *Wyandot* had come to *Goschgosching* with the message for the *Delaware* that they should keep their shoes ready and remain prepared, because bad times were coming. Also the *Wyandot Chief*[825] sent word to *Netawatwees* that he should keep his people together and if a war begins they should move together to the *Heads* of the *Walhanding*, where they would tell them where they could live then.[826] *Netawatwees* replied that they should remember that all the *Nations* had united in peace last year and remain with this. They should remain very still and not become mixed up in war with the White people. They still remembered what had happened to them when the French and English were at war; the Indians had allowed themselves to become entangled in this and had lost many people.[827]

THE 27TH   Mr. *Anderson* came here. The *Commissioners*[828] had assigned him to stay in *Goschgosching* for a while to take care of *Affairs* for the good of the country and to assist the *Chief*s in sending messages to other *Nations* when necessary.

THE 29TH   Yesterday we 2 single Brothers made a contrite conclusion to our choir year and asked the Prince of our Choir to grant us merciful *Absolution* from all of our failures and faults and to heal our souls and bodies through his blood. We then celebrated our festival very blessedly in his dear presence and dedicated ourselves anew to his service, to do as He pleases with us, and to remove from us what saddens him. In conclusion we had a blessed choir communion.

THE 30TH   *Welapachtschiechen*, who had come here yesterday from *Assünnünk* for a visit, had to hurry back home today because a messenger from the *Shawnee* arrived with the news that 10 *Minque* had gone out to commit murders in the *Settlement*s of the White people and they had passed through *Assünnünk*. He said as soon as he saw that the warriors had passed through his *Town*, he would come to our place here and stay wherever the Brothers stayed.

[September]

SEPTEMBER 1ST   Many strangers from *Goschgosching* and the *Munsee Town* visited us here.[829] They had come for the Sunday services. We extolled

---

been concluded had been circulated earlier. On 29 July 1776 such a rumor had originated with the Wyandot.

825. Probably Half King, Indian name Pomoacan, who wielded the largest influence over the Wyandot in the Sandusky region. His village was on the Upper Sandusky.

826. This announcement should be viewed in the context of the Wyandot's having granted land to the Delaware on the Muskingum for the latter's settlement; see entries for 1 June 1773 and 5 Nov. 1775. Already during Lord Dunmore's war the headwater region of the Walhanding had been considered a retreat area; see entries for 3 and 11 July 1774.

827. This refers to the Seven Years' War, which lasted in North America from 1754 to 1760.

828. See note 823 to entry for 23 Aug. 1776.

829. Probably Memehusing; see entries for 7 March 1777 and 29 April 1778.

the Savior's love for poor sinners to them and invited them to accept the grace he has offered them.

THE 3RD   Early in the day 3 *Minque* came here, claiming they wanted to see how things looked among the *Delaware*, and whether they were still or on the move. They said you could hear nothing but talk about war at their place and that 2 parties of *Wyandot* and *Minque* had already gone out to wage war against the White people. We could not trust them, and more importantly we concluded from what they said that they were after some *Traders* who went from the *Shawnee* to the *Fort*; they were asking where they had gone. We took them to *Goschgosching*, where they asked and inquired more and kept a good watch on them until they left.

THE 6TH   An Indian from *Goschgosching*, our *Johannes'* brother, was visiting here and he asked about many things. Among other things, he told *Johannes*, If it were God's will for the Indians to live differently and for them to be preached to, why did he not let them know this before now? Why did he not make it known to their forefathers, because knew nothing about this and had never been told that they had to change. *Johannes* answered him, And if God had let this be proclaimed to them, they would probably not have accepted it, because even now there are many Indians who neither accept it nor want to hear anything about it. Should we not accept his word that He is having proclaimed to us just because our forefathers did not hear it or know anything about it? Should we not rather be happy and grateful to Him for letting us know about it? Anyone who accepts this now and believes in Him will be saved. However, anyone who does not believe will be lost.[830] We who believe in Him know that this is the truth and if you try to discover if it is the truth, you will soon be convinced, as I was convinced in my heart. The Indian answered he was not actually an unbeliever in this matter; he almost believed all that he heard was the truth. He just wanted to tell him and his brother *Thomas* that they should not talk to the Indian savages about what they knew and felt in their hearts. They should keep it to themselves, because they could lose their lives over it. *Johannes* answered him, Then I will speak all the more confidently. Do you think we still fear Indian sorcery and therefore will keep our mouths closed and not speak about what the Savior has done and suffered for us and for all people, even for the Indians, and that he shed his blood for everyone? Far from it! We want to tell all the Indians how they can come to the Savior and be saved and not to be silent about it as long as we live, because that is God's will.

SEPTEMBER 7TH   The married Brothers and Sisters enjoyed a day of true blessing on their festival day. The Savior graciously revealed himself to them and granted them new grace. During the Lovefeast we noted that this choir has increased by 4 couples since we came here. We hoped they might prosper in the congregation and come to belong to the Savior completely.

830. John 3:18.

THE 8TH   Among other Indians, *Netawatwees* and his wife came for the sermon. It was about the ten lepers.[831] We told them that the Savior is merciful and compassionate to all people who turn to Him in their trouble and need and who call upon Him for help. Unfortunately some of them do not apply this well afterward. After they have received peace in their hearts they leave it at that, forget the trouble that had oppressed them, and even return to the world. Therefore we had to ask the Savior to keep us from this through his grace. We could feel among our new people a sense of life, an awareness of their misery, and a desire to be cleansed of their sins through Christ's blood.

THE 10TH   Many Indian visitors from the neighborhood were here. We extolled the Savior's incarnation, sufferings, and death to them as the only cause and source of our salvation. Their blindness is great, however, and their understanding is surrounded by darkness so that they cannot understand or grasp this even when it is explained very clearly to them. A bad typhus has been raging among the Indians everywhere since spring and many have already died from this. Most of them die on the third day after they become ill. This has also reached our people and most of them had it very badly, as did Brother *Heckewelder*. Everyone is improving now.[832]

THE 14TH   *White Eye* returned from *Detroit*. Everyone had been waiting anxiously for him for a while now to learn what is going on with the *Wyandot* and other *Nations*. He traveled there with a White man who had been sent from *Pittsburgh*. Both of them delivered their messages to the *Wyandot*. However, they were only able to do this in the presence of the *Gouverneur*[833] there. He cut up their *Belts* and stepped on them and gave them no reply except that they had better leave within the hour and not let themselves be seen after that. He told *White Eye* he was a *Virginian*;[834] he would attack him and he would have fought against them with the *Shawnee*. If he did not want to lose his head he should leave the *Fort* hastily, which they then did.[835] From this it was clear enough to us that things did not look good. The *Gouverneur*

---

831. Luke 17:11–19.

832. This probably refers to the three-day fever, that is, malaria. See note 71 to entry for 28 Sept. 1772.

833. Lieutenant Governor Henry Hamilton (c. 1734–96), hailed from Ireland and came to North America with the British army during the Seven Years' War. He was appointed civil governor of the Detroit region; his efforts to block George Rogers Clark's attempts to occupy the formerly French settlements in the Mississippi Valley ended in his capitulation at Vincennes on 25 February 1779. For the next eighteen months Hamilton was an American prisoner. From 1781 to 1785 he served as lieutenant governor of Quebec and thereafter acted as governor of various English colonies in the West Indies.

834. Remarkably, the governor appropriated the Shawnee's rebuke of the Delaware during Lord Dunmore's war, which turned Lord Dunmore's original argument on its head. See entry for 1 Nov. 1774.

835. White Eyes and William Wilson, and not Killbuck Sr., who was ill, had gone to Detroit. See William Wilson's long report dated 26 Sept. 1776, in *AA*, 5th series, 2:514–18, and Lieutenant Governor Henry Hamilton to Earl of Dartmouth, 29 Aug. 1776, with postscript dated 2 Sept. 1776, in *Michigan Pioneer and Historical Society Collections* 10 (1888): 264–70.

has the *Wyandot* in his power; he does whatever he wants to with them and they cannot do anything without him. Everyone now believes that there will be a general Indian war. People say the *Senecas* have taken up the hatchet, so it looks like it will break out on all sides. *Mr. Gibson,* who came from the *Fort* yesterday, had orders from the *Commissioners* to sound out the headmen from the *Delaware* to see if they would be willing to take refuge among the White people, where they would be taken for protection and kept if a *general* Indian war should break out. However none of the *Chiefs* have the heart or courage for anything like what they were proposing. They realize that this would not be well received, and also that they would have to expect the Indians to become rebellious and then most of them could join the hostile parties. This would just intensify the problem and promote the Indian war.[836]

THE 15TH   Among others attending the sermon were 5 *Shawnee,* a *Wyandot,* and a *Welapachtschiechen* who came from *Assünnünk* yesterday. He brought the news that the *Shawnee* were still quiet, but that the *Minque* were trying to get them to join in the war with them.

THE 17TH   *Mr. Anderson* came here and in the name of the *Commissioners* in the *Fort* asked one of our Indians to serve as *Interpreter* at the next *Treaty.* He really wanted our *Willhelm* for this. We had to decline however, because times are bad and the Indians are pretty restless, and also because the *Chiefs* in *Goschgosching* are all going to the *Fort.* There is thus no one there to take care of things if something should happen,[837] and he himself understood this. We directed him to see Brothers *Schmick* and *Jungmann.*

THE 20TH   *Netawatwees* came here for a visit, walked around, and looked at our *Town.* He is always very happy when he sees that another house has been built or something has been done, and he wishes *Jerusalem*[838] good fortune.

THE 21ST   We received the news that 19 *Wyandot* had passed through *Assünnünk* going to war in the *Settlements.*[839] *Welapachtschiechen* came to us, therefore, and asked that we send a messenger there to call his family here so that they would be out of danger. We promised to do this, because he himself

836. According to William Wilson, White Eyes' plan for the Delaware in case of a general war was different: "[He said] that, as soon as they found they [meaning the western tribes, especially the Wyandot] were determined for war, he would collect all his people together, and would apply to his *American* brothers to send men to him, and erect a strong fort; that then he should not regard them, for the western tribes were but very indifferent warriors, and if they struck he would soon return the blows." Report of William Wilson, dated 26 Sept. 1776, *AA,* 5th series, 2:518.

837. This argument implied that the leading Christian Indians would take over the functions of chiefs as long as the non-Christian chiefs and other Council members were at Fort Pitt and thus absent from Goschachgünk. It is equally possible to interpret this as a necessity for the Christian Indians to take over the functions of the non-Christian chiefs in order to protect the mission congregations.

838. The term "Jerusalem" denotes a "city of God"; see Ps. 122:6.

839. John Cook's report, dated 2 Oct. 1776, mentions four groups of warriors, among them at least one Mingo (*RUO,* 205–6).

could not go there since he had to go to the *Treaty*. He immediately told us it was still his intention to live for the Savior, as he had told us many times before.

The communicant Brothers and Sisters had the most blessed enjoyment of his Body and Blood in the Holy *Sacrament*, during which one Brother watched for the first time.

THE 22ND   We had the *Liturgy* for *Holy Communion* and then the sermon, for which many Indians from *Goschgoschink* had come.

THE 24TH   Our Indian Brothers had been called to the *Councel*, so Brothers *Willhelm* and *Isaac* went there. The *Chiefs* addressed their people there and warned them not to get involved in the current war at all. They should stay out of it even if all the other *Nations* began a war, as it appeared was happening. Therefore none of their young people should let themselves be tempted into joining in the war.

Finally *White Eye* informed the *Councel* that his *Chief Welapachtschiechen* and his family would move here to *Lichtenau*, and he expressed his pleasure at this.

THE 25TH   We received news that a party of *Minque* and *Wyandot* had caught a *Trader* in *Assünnünk*, taken everything away from him, and taken him to *Detroit*.[840] Mr. *Anderson*, who came here, gave us little hope that we will be able stay here this winter because almost everyone believes there will be an Indian war. He told us that the best and safest thing for us would be to retreat among the White people and put ourselves under their *Protection*. The *Commissioners* in the *Fort* had written to *Congress* about this and were waiting until they had received an answer from there. Then they would propose this to the *Delaware* in general and also to our Indians. This would presumably take place at the *Treaty*.[841] If we had our choice, we would prefer to stay here in Indian country despite all the wars, because we can see in advance that some harm will be done if we go to the *Settlements* of the White people. Therefore we will watch and believe that the Savior knows how to arrange things so that his will is done.

THE 26TH   Brother *David* and *Isaac* left for *Gnadenhütten* and *Schönbrunn*.

THE 30TH   6 *Wyandot* warriors who had crossed the river from the *Settlements* came here. They had no *Scalps* and had not killed anyone. They

840. The GD entry for 26 Sept. 1776 gives the name of this trader as "Macarmick" (GD, F 7, I 1), meaning Alexander McCormick (d. 1803), who had been taken prisoner by the Wyandot in November 1776. At the request of the Delaware, McCormick had been adopted by the family of the wife of Half King, who granted him his freedom. Thereafter McCormick settled as a trader in the village of Half King on the Upper Sandusky; originally he had belonged to the group of traders based at Pittsburgh. FAO, 246; David Zeisberger to George Morgan, 21 Nov. 1776, George Morgan Letterbook, vol. 1, fol. 19, CLP.

841. The Commissioners for Indian Affairs, in their letter dated 25 Sept. 1776, did not make the proposal indicated by Anderson but reported, on the contrary, that tensions had eased and that they had disbanded the larger part of the militia. AA, 5th series, 2:511–13.

went from here to *Goschgosching* and returned from there towards evening the following day. They looked around here one more time and then left. No one knew where they had gone, though. Therefore we were worried that they might be hiding in the bush around here, because they had seen Brother *Hecke-welder*.[842] We were expecting Brother *David* from *Schönbrunn*, so we sent an Indian Brother to meet him. He met up with him and arrived here safely in the evening.[843]

[October]

OCTOBER 3RD   *Stephanus* had come from *Schönbrunn* the day before yesterday, and he returned there. A hut was built for *Welapachtschiechen* and his family. *Gelelemind* asked us to let his wife and children stay with us until he returned from the *Treaty*,[844] and we agreed to this. *Netawatwees* also talked with our Brothers about his daughter, who has been sick for more than a year now and has gone completely blind. He wished she could be with the Brothers and hear about the Savior, and he said he would be happy if she then died in blessing. Because he was going to the *Fort* now, he asked the Brothers to visit her sometimes and to tell her about the Savior. A couple of Sisters therefore went to see her and extolled to her the Savior who died and shed his blood for the sins of the whole world, and they told her that she can be saved through faith in Him alone. She thanked them for their visit, but said she could not think or consider much in her current miserable condition. We visited her often after that, but we could sense no true desire for the Savior in her.

THE 8TH   We heard that another *Company* of *Wyandot* had gone to the war, and also that the Indians from *Assünnünk* were on their way here. *Johannes* went by *Canow* to meet them to assist them on their journey. We got roofs on some houses in recent days.

THE 11TH   *Gelelemind's* wife spoke with one Sister and said she had long desired and hoped to become part of the congregation. However, she was often sad and worried that her husband had no real desire for this yet. Each time she hoped this would change the next time, but nothing ever came of it. Her children often said to her, Let's go see the Brothers, where we can hear

---

842. In a different hand.

843. See, with similar and further information, "Report Mr. [John] Anderson" dated 12 Oct. 1776, George Morgan Letterbook, vol. 2, fols. 61–62, CLP.

844. The congress took place from 15 Oct. to 6 Nov. 1776; some 644 Indians from the Six Indian Nations, Delaware, Shawnee, Munsee, and Mahican participated; they pledged to remain neutral in the conflict between the colonies and England. In his speeches White Eyes stressed the independence of the Delaware from the Six Indian Nations and called the Confederation a liar. See memorandum on conference for the Seneca, *Notes and Queries*, 3rd ser., 3 (1896): 347–49; *RUO*, 185–220; Schaaf, *Wampum Belts and Peace Trees*, 161–96; *AA*, 5th series, 3:599–600; Savelle, *George Morgan*, 140–41.

about the Savior, because we really want to live like the believers. It hurt her when she heard her children talking like this. She was advised to be patient with her husband and wait for the time when he shared her way of thinking.

THE 16TH   Yesterday and today a crowd of *Shawnee* passed through here on their way to the *Treaty. Johannes* returned from the *Falls* where he had met the Indians from *Assününk* and he brought along a *Canow* loaded with their things. A couple of messengers going from *Sandusky* to *Goschgosching* came here with the news that over 100 *Wyandot, Tawa,* and others had gathered in *Detroit* and they would march to *Virginia* on an *expedition*[845] any day now.

THE 19TH   Brothers *Johann Heckewelder* and *Willhelm* went to *Schönbrunn. Martha,* wife of the latter, gave birth to a baby boy today. He was baptized this evening with the name *Jacob.*

THE 20TH   The Indians from *Assününk* arrived here, and it was a great procession. There was a White man with them whom the *Wyandot* had captured and the Indians had paid ransom for him.[846] They brought along a lot of cattle, but they had abandoned their fields and Indian corn.

THE 21ST   After the early service, *Rahel, Welapachtschiechen's* wife who is a White woman, told the Sisters, Oh, how happy I am to be here at last and to have heard God's word for the first time in 19 years (because it had been that long since she was captured by the Indians and taken from *Virginia*). I have often longed to come to your place and live with you, and now God has granted my desire. I woke up happier this morning than I can ever remember being. She has 3 children with her husband and she is bringing them along. The *Commissioners* of *Indian Affairs* are very familiar with her circumstances and they do not want to separate her from her husband, but they have always advised her and her husband to go to the Brothers. When *Welapachtschiechen's* Brother learned that his brother wanted to go to the Brothers, he traveled there to dissuade his brother. He told him he would be taken across the ocean and sold as a slave if he did this. *Welapachtschiechen* replied, I am glad that you are telling me this and warning me in advance. If what you say happens to me, then you are certainly not responsible; I myself am. I will not change my mind because of this though.

This evening *Willhelm* returned from *Schönbrunn* and brought along his wife's sister, who recently had come from the *Susquehanna.* On THE 23RD Brother *Heckewelder* also returned from there. Many *Wyandot* and *Minque* are crossing the *Ohio* here where they are doing much harm. We heard that on one field they killed 11 people at one time.[847]

THE 24TH   *Abraham* and his family returned from *Schönbrunn,* where

845. *RUO,* 185, 190, 199; Zeisberger to George Morgan, 21 Nov. 1776, George Morgan Letterbook, vol. 1, fol. 19, CLP. See entry for 23 Dec. 1776.

846. For Alexander McCormick, see note 840 above.

847. There are many reports of attacks. On 9 October eleven settlers were killed in an attack at Fish Creek. Schaaf, *Wampum Belts and Peace Trees,* 169; *RUO,* 212–14.

he had been visiting for 14 days and had been a blessing to many who were weak and ill.

THE 27TH   Various visitors from the neighborhood attended our Sunday services. The Brothers and Sisters diligently visited with those who had come to us from *Assünnünk* and admonished and encouraged them to faith in Jesus Christ.

THE 28TH   Our Sisters helped the 2 families who had moved here from *Goschgoschink* to harvest and bring in their Indian corn there. Meanwhile, the Brothers helped each other finish their houses. A *Trader* with goods came here from *Pittsburgh* on his way to the *Shawnee*. He said they had not only promised to escort him there when they returned from the *Treaty* but also to protect him against the hostile Indians in their *Towns*. We joined the other Indians in advising him not to go there and explained to him the danger that lay ahead of him, but nothing helped. We really do not like to see *Traders* staying here during these dangerous times, and we encouraged him to leave our place as soon as possible so that the warriors would not come here and cause us trouble when they heard about him. Therefore he decided to ride quickly to the *Shawnee Towns* and get help to escort him there. He promised to return here in a few days, so we had to agree to this. He did not keep his promise, but stayed much longer, which was his own misfortune.

THE 31ST   A *Company* of warriors passed close by *Goschgoschink* and went to the *Settlements*. *Isaac*, who had been down the river a way, returned and brought news that a party of *Wyandot* had returned with 3 *Scalps*.

[November]

NOVEMBER 1ST   Last night hostile Indians were seen in *Goschgoschink* and people also observed things like this here. They sneak around in the *Towns* during the night to see if they can perhaps see and track down White people. Because they made such a good catch in *Assünnünk*,[848] they hope to get some here as well. Therefore we commended ourselves every day and night to the protection of the dear heavenly Father and to the dear angels. The Watchwords in recent days were especially relevant and comforting to us. We made them our own and applied them to our circumstances.[849]

THE 5TH   We were extremely delighted to receive letters via *Schön*-

848. On 11 October seven men were attacked at the mouth of the Hocking River on their return trip from Kentucky. Since Assünnünk was at the mouth of that river, it is likely that this is the incident mentioned. Two settlers died and three were wounded, and the Indians plundered the camp (*RUO*, 213).

849. The Watchwords were Isa. 26:1 (26 Oct.); Isa. 26:9 (27 Oct.); Isa. 38:15 (28 Oct.); Isa. 60:20 (29 Oct.); Isa. 44:8 (30 Oct.); Isa. 59:1 (31 Oct.), and Isa. 50:7 (1 Nov.). Zeisberger probably considered the Watchwords for 26, 27, 29, 31 Oct. and 1 Nov. especially appropriate.

brunn from Bethlehem and *Litiz*, as well as the wonderful news of our dear Brother *Edward's*[850] arrival in *Schönbrunn*. We also received news that our friend Chief *Netawatwees* had died in the *Fort*, and we reported this to *Goschgosching* this evening.[851] The day before he left he had visited us once again, looked around a *Town* a good bit, and said he wanted to see us once more; this was perhaps the last time. He also had an emotional farewell with his son and grandchildren who live here, admonished them to stick with the congregation and left word his daughter in *Goschgosching* should go to the congregation, because that was the only and best advice he could give them. He was a true friend of the Brothers. May the Savior remember him and grant him his share in our eternal dwellings.

THE 6TH   A couple of Indian Brothers who had gone out for a little hunting ran into a *Company* of warriors in the bush not far from here. They are traveling back and forth a lot, so it is very unsafe for our White Brothers to go outside of the *Town*. Nonetheless on THE 7TH Brother *David* went to *Gnadenhütten* and *Schönbrunn* for a *Conference* with Brothers and Sisters *Schmick* and *Jungmann,* and the Indian Brother *Thomas* accompanied him. He returned from there on THE 11TH to a very unpleasant event, just as if he had been called.

THE 12TH   When Brother *Heckewelder* got up at daybreak and opened the doors, 6 *Minque* warriors were standing directly across from our house. It was a while before one of the Indian Brothers went to them, because everyone was still sleeping. When asked what they wanted here, they replied, We are looking for White people so we can beat in their heads. At first the Indian Brothers told them there were no White people here. Why were they looking for White people in the *Delaware Towns*? They replied, We know some are here and we want to see them. The Brothers told them there were none here except for their teachers, and they were their friends. They would not allow anyone to harm them. The warriors answered, We know they are there (and pointed to our house) and if we had wanted to kill them, we would have done so before you knew anything about it. We do not want to do anything to them; we are looking for *Traders* we heard came through here. We told them they were no longer here, because the *Shawnee* had picked them up yesterday. The Brothers did not want to reveal this to them, however. They ran around in the *Town*, looked and searched until they found out where they had gone, either from the Sisters or the unbaptized women. They may have told them this just to get them out of the *Town*, because they were worried about us White Brothers. As

850. William Edwards (1724–1801), born in England, had joined the Moravian Church in 1749; he was sent to replace Zeisberger, who had transferred from Schönbrunn to Lichtenau. Edwards carried with him the letter of John Ettwein to the missionaries of the three villages dated [?] Sept. 1776, MAB, E.P., B 965, F 42, no. 1045. Ettwein expressed regret over the continuing tensions between the missionaries and then discussed the future tasks of Edwards.

851. Netawatwees had died on 31 October. Schaaf, *Wampum Belts and Peace Trees,* 193, and GD, 4 Nov. 1776, F 8, I 1.

soon as they found out, 3 of them set out after them. However, the other 3 stayed here until about noon.[852] This caused a little disturbance for about an hour. We did not let them bother us, and after things were pretty much over we held our early service about today's Watchword, When the Lord shall have washed away the filth of the daughters of Zion, and shall have purged the blood of Jerusalem from the midst thereof by the spirit of judgment, and by the spirit of burning. Oh Father! Bless and protect the Son's territory, etc.[853] In the meantime, *Isaac* had taken them into his house, and he told them that they did not come as warriors, but as thieves at daybreak to steal and rob in their *Cousins' Towns*. If they were men and had *Courage*, they would not act like this but would go into the White people's *Settlements* where they lived rather than looking for them in the Indian *Towns*. They would also let people know what they were planning. They had not even informed the *Delaware* that they were at war. They said the reason they did not inform the *Delaware* of this was because they betrayed all the Indians' plans to the White people. Any day now they would be hearing from *Niagara* that the 6 *Nations* and those in the west had united to wage war against the White people.[854] *Isaac* told them, If you want to wage war, then stay out of our *Towns*. Take another road and do not stain our land, that the *Wyandot* gave us, with blood. They replied, The *Wyandot* gave the land to the *Delaware*; this is true. They did not give it to the White people, though. Therefore we want to round them all up. You allowed yourselves to be seduced by the *Virginians* and now they have sent you *Ministers* who deceive you and turn you against us, and we have heard that if someone wanted to hurt them you would become very angry. *Isaac* answered them, Did the *Minque, Wyandot* and others not accept *Ministers* many years before we did, and do they not have them among them even today?[855] Are we the first who have done this, and do we not have just as much freedom to do so? Or are we someone's servants or slaves, so that we cannot do what we want to? I tell you, we are as free a people and as much our own masters as you and the other *Nations* are. Then they followed after their *Company*. However, in the evening we heard through Indian visitors that they had stolen some horses from around here when they were leaving. Some of our people therefore set out after them

852. From "They ran around . . ." bracketed by another hand.
853. Isa. 4:5; *Das kleine Brüder-Gesang-Buch*, hymn no. 1055.
854. On 25 November 1775 Guy Johnson reported to Lord Germain his efforts to win the Six Indian Nations for the British side (*NYCD*, 8:687–88). In the end, in the winter of 1776, Joseph Brant, chief of the Mohawk, succeeded in drawing the Six Indian Nations, with the exception of the Oneida, to the British side (Graymont, *Iroquois in the American Revolution*, 108–15; Kelsay, *Joseph Brant*, 186–88). The Oneida's attitude was largely influenced by Samuel Kirkland, a missionary among that tribe; see [Kirkland], *Journals of Samuel Kirkland*, 91–114.
855. Until 1763 Jesuits had worked as missionaries among the Wyandot (Palm, *Jesuit Missions of the Illinois Country*); unceasing opposition induced the Jesuits to end their missionary work at the beginning of the eighteenth century (Abler and Tooker, "Seneca," 507, 509). But see entry for 26 Aug. 1774; toward the end of the century Methodist missionaries resumed mission work among the Seneca (Marsh, *Moccasin Trails to the Cross*). On the Oneida, see preceding note.

during the night, caught up with them the next day, and brought back a horse they had stolen. They had already caught the *Traders* the first three had set out after and taken everything away from them, even though they had a couple of *Shawnee* escorting them.[856]

THE 13TH   We worshipped our Chief Elder and High Priest in the dust, commended ourselves and all his Indian people to His grace, and prayed He would continue to dwell among us and to protect us against all the deceitful attacks of the evil enemy.[857] *Netawatwees*'s widowed wife, who has diligently attended our services, moved in with us permanently today. She is already quite old and is planning to spend the rest of her life here.

NOVEMBER 16TH   *Samuel* came here from *Schönbrunn* for a visit and *Welapachtschiechen* came from the *Treaty* at the *Fort*. The gentlemen there had acted and spoken very favorably toward the *Delaware* and *Shawnee* there and showed them much respect and kindness. In contrast, they had told the *Minque* very directly and gravely that if they did not stop robbing and murdering immediately, they would come and visit them in their *Towns*. However, they would give them 2 months to consider.[858] Brother *David* received a friendly letter from an Indian *Minister* from Long Island, near New York, named *John Fowler*. He was ordained in England[859] and has preached in *Pittsburgh*, but he cannot speak an Indian language. We later heard that he halfway promised *White Eye* he would come here and serve his *Nation*.

THE 17TH   The baby boy born to Brother *Johannes* and Sister *Hanna* on the 12th of this month was baptized into Jesus' death with the name *Joseph*.

THE 18TH   *Gelelemind* sent a messenger in advance from *Pittsburgh* informing all the Indians and us that that no one should go out hunting. We learned the reason for this when he himself arrived here on THE 19TH. They had kept him back after the *Treaty* was over until the Indians were gone and then explained to him that because the *Minque* and *Wyandot* had done so much harm in the *Settlements* and had murdered their people, innocent women and children, they could no longer hold back their *Captains* and warriors who were ready to go after their enemies.[860] Therefore the *Delaware* should not be afraid or frightened if they saw an army marching through their land. It would not do them any harm or damage, and they would not steal anything at all. If their

---

856. From "they had caught" bracketed by a different hand. The traders were probably employees of Matthew Elliott. David Zeisberger to George Morgan, 21 Nov. 1776, George Morgan Letterbook, vol. 1, fol. 19, CLP.

857. On the importance of commemorating 13 November 1741 as the day when Christ accepted the office of Elder, see Introduction, pp. 62–63.

858. On the congress, see note 844 to entry for 3 Oct. 1776.

859. This is probably the preacher from Newark who twice preached to the Mohawk in English in the 1790s. Wallace, *Travels of John Heckewelder*, 362–63.

860. Interestingly enough, the justification is adapted to the mode of argument used by Native Americans; they always stressed that under certain circumstances they were unable to prevent their young warriors from attacking or assaulting whites.

troops should need anything, they would pay for it. The Indians were quite upset and frightened by this news. *Gelelemind* was mostly concerned that if they did not come with a sufficient army (because he had heard of only 1000 men) and were defeated, the hostile Indians would then come after them, attack the *Delaware Towns*, and kill the White Brothers.[861] We can do nothing but remain quiet and hope in the Lord who is our help and protection.

THE 20TH   Early in the day a messenger came from *Goschgosching* with the news that messengers from the *Wyandot* had arrived. *Gelelemind* and some of our Brothers went there to hear what they have to say. The *Wyandot Chief* from *Sandusky*[862] was there himself, and he informed the *Delaware* that the *Nations* had forced them to go to war against the *Colonies*. They really did not want to do but had been forced to do so. 1000 Indians from various *Nations* had gathered near *Detroit*; they were going on an *expedition* against the White people. The 6 *Nations* and all the western *Nations* had united as one man and wanted the *Delaware* to tell them which side they would join. They replied that they would remain quiet and not join any side. They would be at peace with everyone because they hoped to manage best in this way. They told the *Wyandot Chief* that the gentlemen in *Pittsburgh* had also advised them to do this and had not asked the Indians for any help at all. They reported to him what had been negotiated at the last *Treaty* and that the White people wanted to shake hands with all *Nations* who would accept peace. Finally they advised him to forbid their warriors from entering or going close to the *Delaware Towns*.

THE 21ST   At the request of the *Chief* in *Goschgosching*, Brother *David* wrote to *Mr. Morgan* in *Pittsburgh* and informed him about the situation among the *Nations* in Indian country and what bad *Prospects* we have. They dispatched this with an *express* messenger.[863] Almost every day we hear of warriors passing close by here, because they do not stay on any road but go through the bush. Therefore the Indians really cannot go out to hunt; the *Wyandot* had also ordered them not to stay away longer than one day.[864]

THE 23RD   Before daybreak, a couple of our people who had gone out yesterday to hunt a little came home. They had met warriors not far from here and spoken with them, and then this morning they came here. There were 6 of them and they were carrying 2 *Scalps* on a pole. They had killed these people close to a *Fort* on the *Ohio*.[865]

861. This message stands in strange contrast to other messages. According to a letter from Colonel Dorsey Pentecost to Captain William Harrod on 12 Nov. 1776, Americans were concerned about the activities of the Shawnee, Mingo, and Wyandot, but up till then no one had been talking about military countermeasures (*RUO*, 218–20). On 12 March 1777, however, Virginia decided to send a military expedition against the Mingo settlement Pluggy's Town. Such an expedition would have had to march through Delaware territory (Savelle, *George Morgan*, 143–44). It is therefore possible that the motive for the conversation with Gelelemind was to prepare him for this expedition.
862. I.e., Half King. See note 825 to entry for 25 Aug. 1776.
863. Zeisberger to George Morgan, 21 Nov. 1776, George Morgan Letterbook, vol. 1, fols. 18–20, CLP; Wheeler-Voegelin, "Ethnohistory of Indian Use and Occupancy," 2:412.
864. Whole paragraph bracketed by another hand.
865. Not identified.

THE 24TH   Although we do not really know yet how many of them will live here, we read our *Statutes*[866] to the Indians who came to our place from *Assünnünk*[867] so they will know how they need to act. We added the 3 following points: 1) Anyone who doctors or is doctored in the heathen manner may not live here, 2) nor could anyone who would consider going to war or even participating in the warriors' stealing and robbing. 3) Anyone who wants to live here should not paint himself or adorn himself with *Wampum*, silver, or various other items. Anyone who does this will not be tolerated here.[868] A *Wyandot* Indian who lived in *Goschgosching* for many years returned to his *Nation* because he was frightened by the news the *Wyandot Chief* brought here. His wife, who is a *Delaware*, told him, If you go to war, then kill the *Ministers* first, the White Brothers here. They have misguided all my friends so that they have abandoned me and left me all alone.

THE 26TH   Brother *David* had a long talk with *Gelelemind* about moving to the congregation, which he has been considering for a year already. He said the Brothers had always advised him to wait until circumstances allowed him to be free of his *Affairs* among the Indians, but this had not yet been possible. Now that his uncle[869] was dead we should tell him what we thought. We told him he would be needed in *Goschgosching* more than ever during this time of war, because neither *White Eye* nor any of the *Chiefs* was there. For the sake of the people, we could not advise him to move to our place since we feared the Indians could still become entangled in the war if there was no ruler among them. We encouraged him to continue his responsibilities here among the Indians, as well as with the other *Nations*. He agreed to do this and said he would stay in *Goschgosching* until he could free himself from this completely. Still, he asked earnestly that we keep the doors to the congregation open for him, and we promised him we would.[870]

[December]

DECEMBER 3RD   Brothers *Marcus* and *Samuel* came from *Gnadenhütten* and *Nathanael* from *Schönbrunn* to present an answer to the *Chiefs* who had recently sent them a message. We considered this together, and then they delivered the answer to the *Councel* in *Goschgosching* on the 4th. You can also see what the message was from the answer, My friends, we learned some days ago in a *Message* from you that we are living in dangerous times and therefore it is

866. Printed in the appendix.
867. See entry for 20 Oct. 1776.
868. On the last sentence, see entry for 15 Jan. 1776.
869. Netawatwees.
870. On the position of Gelelemind as designated successor of Netawatwees, see entry for 21 April 1776 and note.

not good for us to be gone long for hunting.[871] We are always glad when you send us news about danger you see at hand, so that we can act accordingly. We will now put hunting aside and only hunt a little when we are in great need.

We also learned from you that you want us to assist you by supporting you in your *Councels* and advising you, since the *Chief* has now died. We are prepared and willing to do this, as long as you seek to fulfill the *Chief*'s last will and *Testament*. He accepted God's word, often encouraged and admonished you to accept it as well, and he was faithful to this until his end. Therefore let us all hold to this and not waver. You can count on us being loyal to it, and you should join us in doing so.[872]

One *String* was presented at the first point and one *Belt* of *Wampum* for the 2nd. This answer was extremely agreeable to *Gelelemind* and pleased him because it provided an opportunity to remind people of the *Chief*'s advice about the Brothers and to set this in motion. *Isaac*, the speaker, then explained this to them further and told them if they had anything to consider in their *Councel* or in any other matters and wanted our advice and help, we would always be willing to provide this. However, they should not expect us to carry messages to the *Fort* or to *Detroit*, or to other *Nations*. This was not appropriate work for us. They answered that this is not what they meant and they would not expect this of us.

THE 5TH   *Gelelemind* came here for a visit and spent the night. When news arrived that the *Wyandot* had been committing murder in the *Settlements* again, he used this opportunity to talk with the Indian Brothers a lot about the White Brothers and what should be done if things got even more dangerous because of the warriors. They had already come here to *Lichtenau* several times. He said, It is possible that the *Delaware Nation* might get involved in bargains or even in a war with other *Nations*, if large parties of warriors should come here to harm the White Brothers and the Indians fend them off. He suggested that it might be possible to protect them if our Indians from *Schönbrunn* and *Gnadenhütten* all moved here to *Goschgosching* and took the White Brothers among them. The Brothers from *Gnadenhütten* thought that if times got even worse and there was full-scale war, the best thing to do would be to take their teachers to the *Fort*. Brother *David*, who came during the talk, replied, If their teachers were no longer with them, our entire Indian congregation would be finished. They would all be scattered and perish. Finally he said he would take a chance on them killing him and on dying with them. *Isaac*, however, said he could not allow this to happen; if he saw that their teachers were being harmed, he would say to them, Before you kill our teachers, you should kill me. As long as I am alive, you will not do anything to them. On this occasion he told them that he had recently been wounded in the side by a

871. See entries for 18 and 21 Nov. 1776.
872. See entry for 30 May 1776.

fall, and he had lain there a long time and could hardly move. However, when he had heard that there were warriors in the *Town* looking for White people,[873] he had gotten up immediately and gone all around the *Town*. He had not thought once about being sick and had not felt any pain either.

THE 6TH   Early in the day the Brothers returned home from *Schön-brunn* and *Gnadenhütten*. *Gelelemind* and his wife were present in the early service. Afterwards, *Isaac* talked very emotionally with him in our house. He told him about how he was led to join the congregation, and they cried together.

THE 7TH   Brother *David* and some Indian Brothers were called to *Goschgosching* where he had to read a message aloud to the *Councel*. It was from Mr. *Morgan* in *Pittsburgh* and he proposed that they build a *Fort* for their safety anywhere they wanted to, if they thought this necessary. He also promised to defend them if other *Nations* should attack them or force them to wage war against the White people.[874]

THE 9TH   In the early service we read the text for today, And ye shall hear of wars and rumours of wars: see that ye be not troubled: for all these things must come to pass, but the end is not yet,[875] and we reminded the Brothers and Sisters that we put our trust in the Savior, especially in such times. We do not become afraid or feel discouraged. We should rejoice that we have a Lord who is our help and protection. *Gelelemind* came from *Goschgosching* and asked Brother *David* to write a reply to the message he had received from the *Fort* yesterday, which he did.[876]

A certain Indian in *Goschgosching* is calling attention to himself by reintroducing paganism, sacrificial offerings, and preaching among the Indians. He says he really regrets that the Indians had gotten completely away from this for a while. He did not see anyone else doing anything about this, so he would do it himself. Therefore he was planning to establish a separate *Town* and anyone who thought the same way he did should go there with him. They would start anew in earnest and would continue there, because the Brothers are in his way here. He preaches freely and publicly that the Brothers' teaching is not for the Indians, but for the White people. God had designated a different way for the Indians to be saved and he wanted to show them this now. The Brothers should leave, because he would not rest until they all left the country.

873. See entry for 12 Nov. 1776.

874. George Morgan to Captain John Killbuck, 30 Nov. 1776, George Morgan Letterbook, vol. 1, fols. 21–22, CLP. Morgan assured Killbuck that the expedition forces would be strong enough and would not march through Delaware territory; they would only be sent if Pluggy refused the peace offer. He asked Killbuck to inform Pluggy of this condition. At the same time Morgan requested that a Delaware be sent as a spy to Detroit and that Caleb be dispatched for translating services to Philadelphia. He assured Killbuck that he was prepared to erect a fort close to Goschachgünk for the protection of women and children but asked for Killbuck's views on this matter. In a cover letter of the same day, Morgan asked Zeisberger to explain to Killbuck carefully the passage about the fort.

875. Matt. 24:6.

876. From "From Goschachgünk . . ." bracketed in a different hand.

In order to achieve his goal more easily, he is determined to get another family line in the office of *Chief* and to install someone who is an enemy of the Brothers. He is encouraging the Indians to vote for this person.[877]

THE 11TH   In the morning Brother *Edwards* and a couple of Indian Brothers from *Schönbrunn* came here to stay with Brother *David*. Brother *Heckewelder* then went there on the 13TH to stay with Brother and Sister *Jungmann* and to hold school there.

THE 15TH   The sermon was about the light that came into the world and illuminates all humans. There was a blessed feeling during this and many tears were shed.[878] Then we had the Children's Service and we presented the Savior in his incarnation, sufferings, and death to them. Then Brother *Edwards* led the Congregational Service about the beauty of our suffering Savior, as He so kindly shed his blood for us on the cross.[879]

THE 16TH   The Brothers who had been out hunting for 10 days returned home. We were glad to hear that they had not heard anything about warriors during that time or seen any traces of them. *Saktelaeuche*, *Netawatwe's* son, who is generally considered one of the best hunters among the Indians, did not shoot a deer. However, he remained very contented and explained that although he had shot plenty of deer in his life and had never missed one, this had not saved him. While walking around in the bush he had not been able to concentrate on hunting because he was busy thinking about himself and his lost condition. He had not thought about the deer until he had seen them jumping away. This is what happens to most of those who find themselves in this state; they cannot hunt anything because their hearts are not in it.

THE 19TH   We heard that 14 warriors had passed by here hardly a mile below us on their way to the *Settlement*s of the White people.

THE 21ST   With hungry and thirsty hearts, the Communicants enjoyed His holy Body and His precious Blood in the Holy Sacrament. One Brother and one Sister experienced the grace of watching for the 2nd time.

THE 22ND   Early in the day was the *Liturgy* for *Communion*. It was clear that the Brothers and Sisters had been close to Jesus' body. Many people had come from *Goschgoschung* for the sermon, which was about the text, Behold the Lamb of God, which taketh away the sin of the world. Behold, the lamb of

---

877. In contrast to this entry, Dowd assumes that the Delaware unanimously supported the neutral course (*Spirited Resistance*, 68–72). Dowd is not aware that the opposition to the Moravian missionaries continued and that it acquired nativistic traits and was linked to the succession issue. Moreover, this entry poses important questions about the succession to the old chief. Even if we assume that it would be inappropriate to speak of regular voting on this issue, it seems clear that a designated successor did not automatically enter the new office after the death of the incumbent. See entry for 21 April 1776.

878. The sermon was probably on John 3:19.

879. Meditation on the crucified Jesus in the week before Christmas demonstrates once more how strongly Moravian mission theology was based on the sensual imagination of Christ's torture. The subject of the Watchword (Isa. 33:17) had been the King in all his beauty. For the Moravians, "the beauty" of Christ the King was most fully recognized in his wounds.

God who bears the sins of the world.[880] You could sense and see from the tears running down people's cheeks that the word of the Savior's redemption had entered into many. Brother *Edwards* led the Children's Service.

THE 23RD   He also led the early service. Messengers who had been sent out from *Goschgosching* 14 days ago and were returning brought us good and happy news from the *Wyandot*. They and the *Tawa*[881] received the *Delaware*'s message and statement[882] that they do not want to get mixed up in the war very well and also declared their support for this. They also informed them that when the *Chief* from *Sandusky* brought them peaceful news from the *Delaware*, the Indians from many *Nations* who had gathered in *Detroit*[883] all went back home and had given up their plan to wage war against the White people. They had spoken pretty sharply with the *Governeur* in *Detroit* and told him he was always inciting them to go to war against the White people, while he sat quietly and did not do anything. He just wanted the Indians to be worn down. They would continue to watch until tomorrow, which means until spring. If they saw that he did not do anything, they would trample all of his *Speeches* under their feet, come to *Goschgosching*, renew their friendship with the *Delaware*, and then go with them to *Pittsburgh* and declare friendship with the *Colonies*.[884]

THE 24TH   A crowd of Indians, including *Gelelemind*, came from *Goschgosching* for the Christmas Eve service. What can you say about such a Christmas Eve celebration? I have never seen one like it. From beginning to end it was nothing but a service of very loud crying, and many thousands of tears were shed. At the beginning Brother *David* wanted to control this but there was nothing he could do. The tears had to flow freely, because they broke out

---

880. John 1:29.

881. See entry for 18 Oct. 1773 on the report of Zeisberger's visit to the Shawnee, and note 284.

882. In his letter dated 21 Nov. 1776, Zeisberger reported Half King's visit to Goschachgünk. The chief took back with him the Delaware's message that they were determined to maintain peace. The entry here refers to this message; see entry for 20 Nov. 1776.

883. Half King and Cornstalk for the Shawnee had participated in this conference (*RUO*, 185).

884. From "They had spoken pretty sharply . . ." bracketed by another hand. The message poses a number of problems. According to Paul Stevens, three letters of Hamilton survived: the letter from Hamilton to the Earl of Dartmouth, already cited (see note 835 to entry for 14 Sept. 1776), a letter to Guy Carleton dated 4 Sept. 1774, and a letter to Simon Earl Harcourt, his political patron, dated 6 Oct. 1776, the last printed in Harcourt, *Harcourt Papers*, 8:195–202 (Stevens, "'Placing Proper Persons at their Head,'" n. 3). In none of the three letters does Hamilton mention a larger congress with the western tribes in November 1776. The congress mentioned in this entry could only have been a minor gathering of a few Indians. On the basis of these letters, researchers have thus far assumed that the Wyandot attacks on settlements in Pennsylvania and Virginia occurred without the encouragement or approval of the commanding officer of Fort Detroit. See esp. Sosin, "Use of Indians in the War of the American Revolution," 119–20, and Stevens, "'Placing Proper Persons at their Head,'" 284. According to Zeisberger's diary, however, since the summer of 1776 the Wyandot felt urged by Governor Hamilton to go to war. Of this White Eyes too was convinced. According to Sosin (119), the commanding officer of Detroit considered White Eyes an *agent provocateur* of the rebels.

like a flood. All who were there, young and old, with children in their arms, were transported and a stream of tears was shed for Baby Jesus in his manger. It did not look like a very typical service for the Unity, because there was a very large crowd of unbaptized people and friends, and the spirit of the Unity was very subdued. The Savior will be satisfied with this, because they do not understand any better yet.

THE 25TH   The sermon was about the words, Behold, I bring you good tidings of great joy, which shall be to all people,[885] and many gentle tears flowed during this. Brother *Edwards* led an emotional service for the children. During the Congregational Service in the evening, Brother *David* baptized *Netawatwe's* son[886] into Jesus' death with the name *Nathanael*. During this we were powerfully aware of the Holy Trinity's close presence.

The *Wyandot Chief's*[887] wife came here from *Sandusky* with two of her sons. They brought a White man who had been captured some time ago in *Assünnünk*[888] and given to this woman in the place of her brother, who had been killed. She had released him, but because he had lived with *Welapachtschiechen* for some years and feels at home there, he came back here to him. This woman attended our services the next day and paid attention to all she saw and heard here and asked the Sisters many questions. She is baptized and could speak a little *Delaware*. She was sorry they had not attended the baptism yesterday but she thought that we did things here the same way they did; when someone was baptized there only a few of the Indians, those considered the best, are present.

THE 28TH   We spoke with *Welapachtschiechen* and told him that we could not allow any White people to live here. We advised him to free himself of the man who had come here from the *Wyandot*. Another man who had come here with them from *Assünnünk* had already left here of his own accord, as some of the Indian had separated themselves and moved to *Goschgosching*. Thus only *Welapachtschiech's* friendship and one other family from there remain here. This makes about 20 people.

THE 29TH   Many Indians from *Goschgosching* and that neighborhood came back for the Sunday services. We heard many pleasing testimonies about the blessed effect of the holidays on the hearts of many friends and residents. *Netawatwe's* widow also expressed her desire to participate in the grace of Jesus' blood, which we hope for her with all our hearts. *Welapachtschiechen* said that twice he had felt something in the services that made him shed many tears, but he could not name it. He hoped he would experience this feeling again. It was the same for *Gelelemind* and his wife and for others in *Goschgosching*.

THE 30TH   The *Wyandot Chief's* wife returned home. She had seen and

---

885. Luke 2:10.
886. This was Saktelaeuche; see entry for 16 Dec. 1776.
887. Half King.
888. I.e., Alexander McCormick; see note 840 to entry for 25 Sept. 1776.

heard much here and acknowledged that our Indians lead a very different life from the *Wyandot*. They also think they are Christians since they are baptized, but otherwise they are blind heathens. They believe if they just keep their rosary with them it will help them get into heaven, even if they cannot pray.

THE 31ST   We concluded this year contritely and blessedly, and prayed for the *Absolution* from all of our mistakes and shortcomings and brought him our childlike thanksgiving for all the kindness he has shown us during this year, for peace and protection, and all the good things he has allowed us to receive and enjoy. The Savior mercifully revealed himself to us and laid his peace upon us, and then we entered blissfully into the New Year. The most noteworthy items to report about this year, to the glory of the Savior, are as follows:

Chief Netawatwes and his *Councel* repeatedly informed the Brothers of their desire to have a congregational *Settlement* of Brothers established close to *Gosch-gosching*. Brother *David* and some Indian Brothers looked over the site they had suggested to us, and we received the Savior's approval for this. Right after the Easter holidays, he and Brother *Heckewelder* and some families of Indian Brothers and Sisters, 35 people all together, set out on the road, arrived here on APRIL 12TH and began the new *Settlement* for Indian Brothers in the name of the Lord. May the Savior, who knows best why he wanted to have this little *Town* established, carry out his purposes for it to the glory of his name and make it his joy. Since we have been here we have not only enjoyed great friendship but also assistance from them. This has continued since the death of our friend *Netawatwes*, as it was during his life. The *Councellors* value living in harmony and good relationship with us. They have even wanted our Indian Brothers to assist them in their *Councels* more than previously and to provide them with good advice. This is something I had long desired for the good of the *Delaware Nation* in general, as well as for our Indian congregations. Our Indian Brothers who go to the *Councel*, most of whom are Helpers, are legitimated among them[889] and they believe that our Indians are much more prudent than they. We cannot adequately thank the Savior for the peace we have enjoyed here among this otherwise savage people. In the beginning everyone predicted things would be difficult for us and we would experience much trouble from them, but we have experienced the opposite. In fact, the Indians will leave their savage and bad life; in the short time since we have been here there have already been remarkable changes among them. Wherever the Gospel is preached, the people there become meek.

In the fall it seemed like a general Indian war was going to break out. We received news that the *Nations* in the north, south, and west had all united for this. They had in fact begun to do so, and everyone believed things had gone far enough that they could no longer be stopped. However, the one who reigns

---

889. Meaning that before their conversion they had been either chiefs or captains.

destroyed their evil plans and fulfilled the Watchword we had just when things looked so dangerous, Take counsel together, and it shall come to nought; speak the word, and it shall not stand: for God is with us.[890] Warriors came into our *Town* several times but did not want to harm us.

Welapachtschiechen came here with his family and we hope and pray that they might receive a rich blessing here at our place.

In the last month of this year, Brother *Edward* came here to help and Brother *Heckewelder* went to *Schönbrunn*.

3 people have been baptized: *Johannes, Gideon,* and *Nathanael.* 3 children were born and baptized—*Johanna, Jacob, Joseph.*

1 couple was married: the single Brother *Zacharias* and the single Sister *Anna Elisabeth.*

The current residents of *Lichtenau* are:

12 married couples

1 single Brother

3 older boys

3 widows

3 older girls

14 little boys

11 little girls

Total: 59 people including 37 baptized and 22 who are unbaptized, not including the 20 from *Assünnünk*.

January 1777

THE 1ST   In the morning we had the sermon. We presented our baptized Brothers and Sisters and ourselves to our dear Lord, and we surrendered ourselves anew to Him so that we might become completely His and He can do with us whatever he pleases and remove from us whatever saddens Him. We prayed for his continued walk among us, for the care of the dear Mother[891] and the protection and preservation of the heavenly Father throughout the entire year. We had not received Daily Texts for this year, so we decided to use the one from 1775 until we receive one. Brother *Edward* led the Congregational Service about the Watchword, Return unto me; for I have redeemed thee. Turn to me, because I will redeem you.[892]

THE 3RD   A party of *Shawnee* returning from the war was seen a couple

---

890. Isa. 8:10. This was the Watchword for 28 Sept. 1776.

891. On the term and its theological meaning, see note 30 above.

892. Isa. 44:22. For 1777 neither the Texts nor the Watchwords could be printed in North America, probably because of the widespread disruption of communication between Europe and America in 1776. Following Zeisberger's instructions, we have therefore cited the Texts and Watchwords for 1777 according to the collections of 1775.

of miles from here. They had 3 *Scalps* and a White prisoner with them and were going to the *Wyandot*.

THE 4TH   A messenger came early in the day and called our Brothers to the *Councel*. *Gelelemind* had already announced this yesterday. People are starting to get *Rum* from the *Fort* again and some Indians feel free to do this because no *Chief* has been elected yet.[893] Once again this was seriously forbidden, and they asked for our Brothers' help and voices in this matter. They did not fail to speak against this matter and to explain to the people the kind of harm this causes.[894] An Indian from *Gekelemukpechünk* stated, among other things, that he wants to reject getting *Rum* and drinking alcohol, and indeed the entire Indian way of life. He wants to move to *Gnadenhütten* and he had already received permission to do so. The *Counsellors* approved and praised his plan and said, You have chosen the best and surest way. We can believe you will not drink any more if you move to *Gnadenhütten*, because we know the Believers do not drink. Finally *Gelelemind* admonished the people to live in friendship with the Indian Believers and not to speak ill of them, because they were their friends and the *Chiefs* had called them here so they would have the opportunity to hear God's word.

THE 6TH   We enjoyed a day of true blessing with our little gathering. During the morning devotion the Savior revealed himself to us in a blessed way and gave us his peace. Brother *Edward* then preached the sermon, and during the Lovefeast in the afternoon we read the story[895] and remembered our other congregations among the heathen in the north and south and in the West Indian Islands.[896] During the service which followed, Brother *David* baptized *Gideon*'s wife into Jesus' blood with the name *Sara,* and Brother *Edward* baptized *Isaac*'s sister with the name *Helena*. Those being baptized and those watching shed countless tears. To conclude the day, we celebrated a Service of Adoration with those who have been baptized and thanked the dear Savior for the blessings He has granted us from the richness of his blood.

THE 7TH   *White Eye* had returned from *Philadelphia* a few days ago and he visited us. He told us a little about the confused circumstances in the country down there.[897]

893. Netawatwees had died on 31 October 1776; see note 851 to entry for 5 November 1776. That three months after his death the new chief had not yet been chosen is a further indication that the succession of chiefs was a highly complex affair.

894. On the Moravians' and mission congregations' attitudes toward alcohol, see entry for 5 June 1776.

895. Matt. 2:1–12.

896. On 6 January, see Introduction, pp. 62–63.

897. After the negotiations at Fort Pitt, twelve chiefs and captains, among them White Eyes, traveled to Philadelphia at the invitation of the Commissioners for Indian Affairs, where they visited the Continental Congress on 7 December 1776 to receive messages and presents (*RUO*, 216–17; Ford, *Journals of the Continental Congress*, 6:1010–11). The chiefs responded to the messages of the Congress on 9 December 1776; their speeches were not included in the protocol, however, they "having said nothing relative to matters between them and the United States" (Ford, *Journals of the*

Here, the *Wyandot* and the *Minque* continue crossing the *Ohio* and going into the *Settlements* to cause harm. We received news again today that a large party of them was *Marching* there.[898]

THE 8TH   The baby boy born to *Gideon* and *Sara* was baptized into Jesus' death with the name *Johannes*. This was a blessed service, during which most of our children and adults shed many tears. The two recently baptized sisters came and could not adequately describe how blessed, happy, and grateful they are for what the Savior has done for them. *Sara* said, Oh, how long I tortured myself in vain, when I did not need to; now the Savior has given me everything at no cost. He has forgiven my sins and cleansed me with his blood.

THE 9TH   Brothers *Jacob junior* and *Michael* came here from *Schönbrunn* for a visit. They brought us letters and news of how our Brothers and Sisters are doing.

THE 10TH   *Welapachtschiechen* spoke with us about his spiritual condition and told us that he has been thinking a lot about his wretched condition since Christmas. We told him he did not need to consider so many things, but just one: did he want to be the Savior's, to surrender to him and belong to him completely? He said this had been his intention from the beginning, when he came here from *Assünnünk*. If he had been seeking anything else he would have moved somewhere else rather than to our place, and he has the same intention now that he had then. His daughter who is 10 or 11 years old has been crying for a long time already that she wants to be baptized, and she is inconsolable. *Isaac*, who had gone to *White Eye's Town* on business,[899] visited him and talked with him a lot. He told us he had spoken very favorably of the Brothers. He did not want to hinder the Brothers or put any obstacles in their way, and he did not oppose them at all, although he might do something out of ignorance or misunderstanding or in matters he could not understand or comprehend. We were glad to hear his explanation and we have good hope that he will remain our friend.

THE 12TH   There are only 3 older boys here, so all the children had a service together. We read them the story about when Jesus was 12 years old[900] and discussed it. For some time now they have been emotional and sensitive. Their parents are often concerned and do not know how to comfort their children adequately when they cry bitter tears for baptism.

THE 14TH   Our visitors from *Schönbrunn* returned home. We began

---

Continental Congress, 6:1013). See Mohr, *Federal Indian Relations, 1774–1788*, 49–50. On the rather difficult military situation of the young United States and on the difficulties in securing provisions, see Middlekauff, *Glorious Cause*, passim; on the Moravians' attitude toward the American Revolution, see note 1063.

898. See Zeisberger to John Anderson, 8 Jan. 1777, excerpted in George Morgan Letterbook, vol. 1, fol. 30, CLP.

899. That is, White Eyes.

900. Luke 2:41–52.

school with the children, and they were very happy about this. However, we have not yet solved the problem of having no books for them.[901]

THE 15TH   Things are relatively calm now, so some Brothers went out to hunt for a number of days. Our dear Mother's[902] work of bringing them to the obedience of belief continues and does not allow them any peace until they resolve to belong to the Savior completely.

THE 19TH   *Welapachtschiechen* spoke with us about his children and told us it really touched him when he saw his children with tears on their faces day or night and he could really not help them. He had to cry with them then. He thought he was probably the reason his children had to endure so much and to remain so unhappy. Therefore he wanted to commend his children to us and ask us not to hold them back on his account. He would be very happy if his children preceded him and were baptized before him, and he would then follow them. We told him it was true that we were hesitant to baptize children if we did not know for sure if the parents completely appreciate the Savior and would stay with the congregation, because there had been cases when parents or friends took children away from the congregation after their baptism, which was sad. We spoke sincerely and directly with him and told him very plainly that being saved depended only on faith in the merits of Jesus; he should not try to do anything about this or earn this, but should go to the Savior as a sinner and seek forgiveness through his blood. As soon as he believed and felt that he was a sinner, then he had a right to the Savior, who came into the world to save sinners. He then said, I am a great sinner, it is true, and he began to repent for his youth and he confessed his sins. Then we told him he should go as a sinner, as he had told us, to the Savior who accepts sinners and so gladly forgives their sins. He would do this for him as well and make him a blessed human.

THE 20TH   The old widow *Justine* went to the Savior in blessing.

THE 21ST   Her earthly dwelling was buried and our God's Acre was thus dedicated. She was baptized in *Gnadenhütten* on the *Mahony* on *August* 16, 1749 by Brother *Martin Mack*, and she became a communicant on *September* 12, 1750. She became a widow in *January* 1760 when her husband *Nicodemus* died. In *June* 1772 she came here to *Gnadenhütten* and in *April* 1776 went to *Lichtenau*. We do not know anything about her life during this time, so we can only report what we saw in her and knew about her while she was here. She was a blessed widow. Her heart was firmly attached to the Savior and the Unity and she was eager for her blessed release. When we spoke with her she often said she was looking forward to going to the Savior soon.

We received news from elsewhere that the *Minque*, the riff-raff who murder and rob, had suffered a defeat and that their headman *Pluggy* was killed.[903]

901. See entry for 4 Dec. 1775.
902. See note 30 above.
903. Pluggy had been killed at McClelland's Station on 29 December 1776 (*RUO*, 206n47).

THE 22ND   The head people in *Goschgosching* would like to follow and fulfill *Netawatwe's* last will and testament, so they gathered their people by *Tribes* and admonished them to follow their former *Chief's* advice to accept God's word, as he had so often encouraged them, and not to abandon it. *Welapachtschiechen* did the same, because he is the eldest *Chief* in his *Tribe*. It is clear that the *Delaware* generally fear something terrible from the 6 *Nations*, who said the *Delaware* are becoming quite proud, and they would punish and humiliate them. This is because *White Eyes* spoke pretty severely in an address to the *Minque* at the last *Treaty*, and this annoyed them.[904]

THE 26TH   Various visitors, including *White Eye*, were here for the sermon. He was visiting his brother[905] here and told him he was happy that he lived with the congregation. He also hoped he would not stay here in vain but might find and enjoy something for his heart. He was very friendly to us. He went on to *Goschgosching* then, because he had come directly here from his *Town*.

THE 28TH   Yesterday and today the Brothers and Sisters went out looking for places to boil sugar and making preparations for this, because we have had such beautiful spring weather.

THE 30TH   We heard that the *Chiefs* in *Goschgosching* are determined to encourage and admonish the Indians to lead a better life. Therefore they decided in their *Councel* to do away with dancing at night and gaming during the day, and they have already begun this. However, such good intentions usually do not last very long. *Gelelemind's* wife is still unable to accept that she cannot be with the congregation, and she reminds her husband about this quite often. News arrived from the *Cherokee* that they have concluded peace with the White people. However, people say they want to take revenge on the 6 *Nations* because they are the cause of their unhappiness and incited them to go to war.[906]

[February]

FEBRUARY 8TH   We had a blessed Holy Communion, during which one Brother and one Sister participated for the first time.

THE 9TH   Early in the day we marked the beginning of Lent by having the *Liturgy* for *Communion* and then the sermon about the Savior's entry into Jerusalem[907] and his passion. Then there was a service for those who have been baptized.

904. See entry for 16 Nov. 1776 and note 858. On the reasons for the tensions between the Delaware and the Six Indian Nations, see Introduction, pp. 24–25.

905. White Eyes' brother was married to a sister of Isaac. He had visited Lichtenau on 13 August 1776.

906. In early November 1776 the majority of the Cherokee had capitulated to the advancing Virginian army and posted hostages until the conclusion of a peace treaty. That treaty was signed in April 1777. O'Donnell, *Southern Indians in the American Revolution*, 48–49, 55–58.

907. Matt. 21:1–11.

THE 10TH   Brothers *Johannes, Thomas, Gideon,* and *Isaac* went with *Welapachtschiechen* to *Goschgosching* to speak with their friendship.[908] They had been invited to go. The friendship of the latter, which is very widespread, had been talking about him and saying that he when he had gone to us he had left them very secretively and had not told them anything about his plans, so he found it necessary to explain himself. He did this after they had gathered. He told them the reason he had gone to the Brothers was this: a year ago he had visited in *Schönbrunn* and had heard the Brothers. At that time he had been certain in his heart that they were preaching the truth and the pure word of God was the only way to salvation. Before this he had lived his whole life as a pagan, and he had also listened to the Indian preachers and believed what they preached because he had not known any better.

As soon as he heard the Brothers, he had immediately realized that everything else was lies and empty straw. Therefore he had gone to the Brothers to be saved and to spend the rest of his days there. He could witness to them that he had become more certain every day that it was the truth since he had been with us. He admonished them to consider this, and they would then soon realize he had told them the truth. The Brothers confirmed his witness and *Thomas* and *Johannes* stayed with them after the rest of the Brothers had left. They told them about what the Savior had done for them through their own spiritual experiences, and what they had felt in their hearts. They testified strongly against pagan ways. *Johannes* finally stood at the post in the middle of the house, where there was a face carved out which is their house idol[909] and said to them, See, I am standing here beside your idol. It is nothing but a piece of wood, made by hand. I can chop it up and throw it in the fire and it will not say anything about this or complain. You worship this piece of wood as if it were a god and yet it has no life in it; it is dead. But you do not want to worship or know anything about the God and Creator of heaven and earth, who came into the world, became human like we are, and purchased and redeemed us from the power of Satan with his blood. We can all be saved through him alone. They could not argue with what he said, but had to admit it was the truth.

THE 12TH   We had a blessed conversation with *Welapachtschiechen* who visited us and told us about his spiritual condition. He is 61 years old and he

---

908. On Zeisberger's meaning of the term "friendship," see Introduction, pp. 16–19 and note 42.

909. Goddard, "Delaware," 219, cites seventeenth-century sources that mention "faces and images" in chiefs' houses. Kraft speaks of "Masked Beings" and "Mesingw" as one of the most important manitou of the Delaware (Kraft, *Lenape,* 169–76); see also Zeisberger, "History of the Northern American Indians," 141, where he mentions "images cut in wood" and life-sized sculptured images in "houses of sacrifice." We are not convinced that such "idols" were kept only in the houses of chiefs; in the entry here, for example, it is not stated that this was the house of a chief like Gelelemind or John Killbuck Sr.; instead Zeisberger insinuates that this was a house that was used as a meeting place for the "friendship"; see note 273 to entry for 22 Sept. 1773.

told us now that he was born at *Nazareth*, on the site where *Gnadenthal* stands. He lived there and moved here to the *Ohio* 42 years ago.

THE 13TH　*Gelelemind* visited here yesterday and asked us to take his 2 children into the school here. They themselves had requested this really wanted to be part of the congregation.

THE 16TH　Many Indians from the neighborhood had come for the sermon. Among them was a man and his wife who had come here form *Assün-nünk* in the fall.[910] They separated themselves like some others and settled between here and *Goschgosching*. The man told the Brothers about how he was caught between the unbelievers and us and could not decide where he wanted to turn. However, his heart always told him he should go to the congregation. The Brothers told him that he had to work this out himself. We did not tell anyone they should come to us, but we welcomed anyone who felt this in his heart and was concerned and worried about being saved and therefore wanted to come to the congregation.

THE 17TH　We received news that the *Wyandot* had arrived in the *Shawnee Town*s some time ago for a council being held there.[911] May God allow this to work for the best.

Joseph Peepi came here from *Gnadenhütten* for a visit and he talked with us about moving here. The *Conference* granted him permission to do this.[912]

THE 19TH　Early in the day Brother *David* and some Indian Brothers were called to *Goschgosching*. He received a packet of letters there from Brother *Mattheus* and informed the *Councel* about message from *Mr. Morgan*. Among other things it announced that the *Americans* had defeated the British troops.[913] Some of the *Counsellors* came here in the afternoon and Brother *David* wrote a reply to the *Fort* for them.[914]

THE 21ST　News arrived that the *Shawnee* are also starting to go to war again. They had already brought in 4 prisoners and some *Scalps,* and the warriors are no longer listening to the *Chief*s who want peace; they want to have war. *Detroit* would provide them with *Ammunition*.[915] Therefore some Indian Brothers were called to the *Councel* in *Goschgosching*. There the decision was made to prepare messengers immediately to send to the *Shawnee* and *Wyandot* to find out more about these matters and to give explanations.

Isaac had returned from *Schönbrunn* and was at *White Eye*'s overnight. He

---

910. See entries for 20 and 27 Oct. and 24 Nov. 1776.

911. The rumor proved to be wrong.

912. Helpers' Conference.

913. Five words crossed out, unreadable. The victory to which Zeisberger alludes could be either the military success at Trenton, New Jersey, on 26 Dec. 1776, or that at Princeton, New Jersey, on 3 Jan. 1777. We could not locate Morgan's letter.

914. We could not find Zeisberger's response.

915. This message agrees with other reports. See Colonel David Shepherd to Patrick Henry, 24 March 1777, *RUO*, 242–43 and 253–56. On the importance of Detroit, see entry for 23 Dec. 1776 and note 884.

had a long conversation with him and told *Isaac* about the *Situation* in which he currently finds himself. He sees himself standing completely alone and abandoned by both the Indian Believers and the Indians who do not believe. He thought he must have made some mistake to become so estranged from us; either he must not understand us correctly or we do not understand him. When he returned from *Philadelphia* a year ago and told the *Councel* in *Goschgosching* his *Intention* of bringing a *Minister* and schoolmaster here, this was immediately rejected. He had turned to us thinking that although the other Indians did not understand what he wanted, the Brothers would understand him, approve of his plan, and support him in this.[916] However, he realized he was wrong about this and saw that we did not treat him better than the Indians in *Goschgosching*. He had given up, because he thought we did not understand him any better than the Indians in *Goschgosching*. He was sad and distressed about this. *Isaac* replied that we understood very well what he wanted. The mistake was his, because he did not understand us. He wanted to go his own way, and this was not acceptable to us. That was why we could not join with him. We would continue on our path and not let anything deter us. Anyone who did not want to go with us would be left behind.

THE 22ND   *Welapachtschiechen's* son returned from the *Shawnee Towns*. He confirmed the news we had received from there yesterday.

THE 24TH   An Indian who came from *Kinhanschican*,[917] the *Minque Town*, reported that the *Nations* had held a council there about the White people. They wanted to destroy them, and when they had finished with them they would they remove those Indians who had not helped them from the face of the earth. They would come here and throw the *Delaware's Ministers* out of the houses and beat them to death. If the Indians intervened and opposed them, they would not treat them any better.[918]

THE 26TH   Most of the Brothers and Sisters went to the sugar huts and some of them went out hunting, so our *Town* was pretty empty.

March

MARCH 1ST   *Joseph Peepi* arrived here, and on THE 2ND Brothers *Marcus* and *Samuel* from *Gnadenhütten* and *Cornelius* and *Nathanael* from *Schönbrunn* also went. They had been called to a council that is supposed to be held in

---

916. See entries for 29 Oct. 1775 and 3, 11, 15, and 16 May 1776.

917. See entry for 23 July 1776 and note 804 on "Minque Town."

918. The GD provides additional information: the Wyandot, Chippewa, Tawa, Mingo, and Shawnee had accepted a red and white war belt on which a tomahawk had been inscribed. At the next full moon (23 March) they were resolved to attack the Virginians, and on their return journey they would fall on those Indians who were not their allies (GD, entry for 27 Feb., F 9, I 1a). The letter of the Delaware Council to George Morgan dated 26 Feb. 1777 reports the same story with more details (George Morgan Letterbook, vol. 1, fols. 47–49, CLP).

Goschgosching. The *Chiefs'* main purpose is to hold the Indians together, so that hostile Indians do not draw any of their people into the war. They should all remain quiet so that the *Delaware Nation* remains at peace. The *Chiefs* realize that the *Munsees* who are not standing firmly are wavering now, so they called the Brothers there to assist them and to speak in favor of peace. They know for sure they have their support.[919]

THE 4TH   Some *Shawnee* came here and through them we heard the unpleasant news that 64 of their warriors had gone to the *Settlements* of the White people to cause harm.[920] Our Indian Brothers were called from *Goschgosching* today to a hold a preparatory *Councel* with them and to consider what should be addressed in the *Councel*, because they have not yet all arrived.

THE 5TH   In the early service the poor and needy, the hungry and thirsty were invited to the fount of salvation, to the 5 little springs from which all our salvation flows.[921]

THE 7TH   The widow *Petty* returned from *Schönbrunn.* We received news from there that the *Minque* have decided to kill the White Brothers and Sisters, and since it is now time for sugar, they want to take advantage of the opportunity to steal away with some of us to the sugar huts and get the rest of us in our *Towns,* when most of the Brothers and Sisters are not at home. This sounds like it could be a true story, because some days ago a *Minque* was discovered here in *Munsee Town*[922] on the *Walhanding.* He had gone there and already recruited 3 *Munsees* there to go with him. However, the *Chiefs* stopped

919. For an identical argument, see entry for 12 June 1774.

920. See note 915 to entry for 21 Feb. 1777.

921. The "five little springs" representing the wounds at Jesus' side (John 19:34) and the nail marks on his hands and feet occupy a central place in Moravian theology.

922. I.e., Memehusing, "the Munsee settlement one day's journey from here," as Zeisberger phrased it in entry for 29 April 1778; see too entry for 1 Sept. 1776. The following entry in the diary for Schönbrunn for 3 March 1777 belongs to this context (MAB, B 141, F 9, unpaginated): "Nicolaus, the son of the Mingo Thomas, who the day before yesterday in the evening came accompanied by his father to fetch some corn, told first some brethren and finally me the following: Some days ago a Mingo entered his house at Wahlhanding and told him that it had been determined that as soon as it got warmer and people would boil sugar, a party of Mingo would come and fetch myself and brother Shebosch in the sugar huts, either to kill us or to make us prisoners, whichever would be the easiest. And the leader of the band had added that he knew well how we went about boiling sugar because he had staid overnight last spring in my house. After he had confided this to Nicolaus, he strictly forbade him to betray this to others but to keep the story to himself until it had been done. Yet he, Nicolaus, said, I will reveal this immediately. . . . Now, he continued: I have revealed to you all this, in order to induce you to be careful and not to leave town because many other evil things have been decided with relation to you. Seven days ago a group of one Mingo and some Munsee had been at the very place, yet I had them come back by bringing them myself a Belt of the Munsee chief. One Munsee, whom you know well, and who last year more than once came to you in your sugar hut, had offered to point the place out and then leave the rest to them. Further, he said that people say that as soon as everyone was out boiling sugar, it would be easy to bring the sisters Schmücks and Jungmanns out of the town, because it would then be empty. And that the brothers in Lichtenau intended to boil sugar across the river he had heard, too, and evil-minded people were already waiting for it. Therefore, Nicolaus continued: Write speedily to Brothers Schmück and David so that they can hear this; otherwise I will have no peace of mind. After he had confided all this to me I thanked him in our name."

them and it came out that they were planning to kill the White Brothers after they got more reinforcements, and indeed those in *Schönbrunn* first. The Indian Brothers therefore decided to stay home and that it would be better to leave the Sisters alone in the sugar huts.

THE 8TH   Our Indian Brothers were called to the *Councel* in *Goschgosching* and soon afterwards Brother *David* was also picked up and taken there to read something out loud to them from the *Treaty* held last fall.[923] It was uplifting to see how the Brothers all sat together directly across from the *Counsellors*, with *Welapachtschiechen* in their midst. *White Eye* was present and introduced matters, and everything proceeded very orderly and *venerably*.[924]

THE 9TH   The Brothers and Sisters had all returned from their sugar huts for the sermon. We could see and sense that they were hungry and eager for God's word. In the afternoon the Brothers were called to the *Councel* for a short while. They knew it was Sunday, so *White Eye* delivered the following *Speech* to our Brothers in a public council and nothing else was undertaken. He first addressed the *Mohican* Brothers in *Gnadenhütten* and said, Grandchildren living in *Gnadenhütten*, when you came here from the *Susquehanna* you planned to bring along your teachers, whom you had left behind. At the same time you were concerned that there might be bad times or war, and at that time you told your grandfather that he should watch your teachers to see that they suffered no harm. Therefore I am announcing that I will do all that is within my power, and if I see I no longer have power to protect them, I will inform you of this so that we can consider the matter further.

Then he gave them a *String of Wampum* and continued, My friends, Indian Believers in *Schönbrunn*, *Gnadenhütten*, and *Lichtenau*, 3 months ago you reminded me of what our old *Chief* left behind in his last *Testament* and you said we should see that this was not broken. Let us work together, therefore, so that we might be strong enough to bring this about and carry out the good work the *Chief* began. Then a *String of Wampum* followed and he continued,

My friends, Indian Believers, our *Chief* left behind a good relationship between you and us, yet we are still two kinds of people. Therefore, consider how we can become one people. Let us help each other to bring about the good work the *Chief* left behind for us. We are not yet as we should be, so it is our desire that you instruct us if we do not do something correctly and you should tell us how we should do it. Our people here in *Goschgosching* are ready and

923. On the congress, see note 884 to entry for 3 Oct. 1776.

924. The report that White Eyes chaired the Council meeting is remarkable in light of the fact that Gelelemind was the "designated" chief (see entry for 21 April 1776). This proves that the final decision about the successor of Netawatwees had still not been made and that in this interregnum the closest and most influential advisor of the former chief chaired the sessions of the Council—both qualifications fitted White Eyes. Another reason why White Eyes would have chaired the meeting is that the Council discussed matters that fell under the purview of the captain. Such a matter could have been related to the question of which course the Delaware should pursue in the conflict between England and the colonies.

determined to keep the *Chief*'s last will and *Testament*,[925] and none of us should break it. If it is ever broken, then it will be someone else or you yourself who do this; we will not break it. Then a white *Belt* was given.[926]

After a short pause he took a Bible and some schoolbooks in his hand and addressed the entire council as follows:

My friends, all who are present here, you have heard what our *Chief* accepted and followed, and he often said it was a good thing. See and hear now that I hold firmly to this. You Brothers also accepted the word. You also know that it is good and true. Some of us present here believe it is a good thing. There are others, however, who think there is nothing good in it. Therefore I am gathering my young people and children together, bowing down before Him from whom they proceeded, and asking Him to proclaim his word to us and to let us know his will. We also ask our dear Lord to reveal it to our children and children's children, because we cannot make those who are not yet born understand. Then he turned to the Brothers and said, My friends, you have heard my words now. Let us be strong and think about our children's welfare. Let us show them in a friendly way that we want what is best for them. We hope that our children's children will comprehend and understand better that we have sought their best interests. Brothers, take compassion on me and let us seek together the well-being of our children. Tears ran down his cheeks while he was speaking these words, so that he could not speak several times for crying.

THE 10TH   After the council had gathered the Indian Brothers offered the following reply, Friends who are gathered here, hear the words of the Indian Believers in *Schönbrunn*, *Gnadenhütten*, and *Lichtenau*. We have listened to you for five years now since you called us into this area, first to *Schönbrunn*, then to *Gnadenhütten*, and finally here to *Lichtenau*, and we are happy and grateful for this. Yesterday you informed us that those of you who live in *Goschgosching* want to remain faithful to and follow what the *Chief* left behind in his last *Testament*, to accept God's word and be concerned about the best interests of your youth. We were very pleased and happy to hear this. We Indian Believers assure you that we remain firmly committed to this and will not stray from it, but will seek to fulfill the *Chief*'s last will.

You also informed us that the *Chief* often told you he has found something good and precious and admonished you to accept it, and that now you have accepted the good word which was brought to you. You are gathering your young people and children and calling upon Him who made us to let us recognize and understand his word. We joyfully join you in this, and present our dear Lord not only to the young people and children but also to the elderly.

---

925. The formula "last will and Testament" is first used in the entry for 3 Dec. 1776, then again in the entry for 22 Jan. 1777. In both cases Zeisberger alludes to the decision of the Council, whose decision Netawatwees had communicated to the mission congregations on 28 Feb. 1775.

926. In the original the following paragraph is indented.

We will kneel before Him and ask Him to have mercy on everyone, to open our hearts and minds, and to reveal his sacred word to us.

THE 11TH   The council in *Goschgosching*, attended by Indians from all over,[927] ended. The *Delaware* agreed among themselves to keep quiet and not to help either party in the current war, but to live in peace with everyone. Especially since the *Congress* has not asked them to help the White people, but has always advised them to remain quiet and not get involved in the war.[928] Even if all the surrounding *Nations* wanted to wage war against the White people, they would stand firm and not allow themselves to be moved. In this way they hope to manage as well as possible during these times that seem so dangerous, because it looks now like trouble could break out again towards spring.

They want to inform the *Nations* about what the *Delaware Nation* plans to do and what they have decided among themselves, and to advise them to follow their example and accept the peace offered to them, in case they might listen to them.

There are only a small number of *Munsee* in this area, and they did not show themselves very strongly at this council. People are afraid they will still join in the war if they have a good opportunity, especially since they are planning to leave here and move closer to the *Minque*. *Newollike* left *Schönbrunn* this winter and has chosen pagan ways again.[929] Now he is saying he tried to become a Believer but was not able to and therefore there is nothing to the whole matter and it is not for the Indians, although it might be fine for the White people. He has now joined the side against the Brothers, who are also opponents of the *Chiefs* in *Goschgosching*. They are trying to gather a following from the bad people among the *Munsee* and to establish a separate *Town*. They hung their heads when they heard *White Eye*'s address to the Brothers. He said to *Newollike*, You went to the Brothers because you have not been able to find anything that can bless your heart anywhere in the world, and you believed you had found it with the Brothers. I heard these words from you personally. Yet you had hardly tried it when you gave up and returned to the old ways. You did not behave valiantly.

THE 12TH   The Brothers from *Schönbrunn* and *Gnadenhütten* returned home. They had attended the council and also enjoyed a 10-day visit here.

THE 14TH   We heard that the *Minque* in *Kinhanschican*[930] have supposedly decided to imprison or kill the White Brothers and Sisters in our 3 *Towns* within 3 days, and if the *Delaware* Indians resisted they would also kill them. This is exactly what *Chiefs White Eye* and *Gelelemind* have always feared, and

---

927. Zeisberger's precise remarks indicate that this was a Great Council.

928. See reports on the negotiations at Fort Pitt in the years 1775 and 1776 in entries for 29 Oct. 1775 and 20 Nov. 1776.

929. Newollike left Schönbrunn on 13 Feb. 1777; see note 936 to entry for 21 March 1777.

930. On this settlement (also called Kinhanschican), see entry for 23 July 1776 and note 804 on the term "Minque Town." This place is mentioned for the first time in the entry for 24 Feb. 1777.

if something like this happened, the Indians—the unbelievers as well as the Believers—would take up arms. They said that if the young people in *Goschgosching* received definite news that the *Minque* were coming here with evil intentions, they would not wait until they got here but would go all the way to their *Towns* to meet them. Therefore if trouble should happen, there would be war.

THE 16TH   *White Eye, Gelelemind*, and others came here for the sermon. Soon a messenger came after them with news that had just arrived; 3 Indians had been attacked while they were out hunting yesterday and one of them was wounded. People feared it might have been the *Minque*. We heard later that White people had done this[931] and therefore little more was made of it.

We also heard more from an Indian about the previously reported news that the lives of the White Brothers and Sisters were in danger. He asked us not to divulge who had told us this. *Pelewiechünk*[932] publicly said he would not rest until the White Brothers were out of the way. Our Indian Brothers think that he and his followers including *Newollike*, our archenemies, are behind this and that they are trying to accomplish their goal of using the *Minque* to get rid of the Brothers. There is indeed reason to think this. Because our *Town* is very weak, our Brothers met and decided to stop making sugar and stay at home, and to keep a good watch day and night. If something should happen they would immediately send word to *Goschgosching* to come to our assistance. At *White Eye*'s advice, we immediately sent *Johannes* to *Gnadenhütten* with this news to send on to *Schönbrunn*, so that the Brothers and Sisters would stay at home and be on their guard. We have many enemies, not only the *Minque* who say that the Brothers are the reason the *Delaware* do not join them in the war against the White people, but also our neighbors the *Munsee*. We are in greater danger from them than from the *Minque,* and they would be happy if the Brothers were cleared out of the way on this occasion. Both of them were silent at the council in *Goschgosching* and did not want to speak, which is not a good sign. Therefore it is easy to understand that the residents of *Goschgosching* have become closer to the Brothers, both to keep peace in general and also so they can outweigh the opposing side. The Savior will protect us and not allow the enemy to carry out his tricks on us, but will destroy his deceitful attacks.

THE 17TH   A messenger came from *Goschgosching* to inform us that a large party of warriors had been seen on the *Walhanding*. They had tracked them down and found out they were making their way through the bush directly to *Schönbrunn*. *White Eye* also sent word that the Indian Brothers here should be on their guard, because the time had come. We have already heard so much recently that we could only suppose they were heading for our Broth-

---

931. See *RUO*, 243.
932. Not identified.

ers and Sisters in *Schönbrunn*. We therefore thought more about them than about ourselves and pleaded with the Savior to cover them with his wings. We were somewhat comforted when we heard that an Indian had gone there this morning to report this to the Brothers. The Indians in *Goschgosching* sent us word that if the *Minque* actually came here, our Indian Brothers should just try to hold them off long enough to send a messenger to inform them of this, and they would come immediately to help us. May the Savior prevent this from happening, and mercifully keep all harm away.

THE 18TH   We had a conversation with our *Helpers*, who are worried about us White Brothers in these difficult times. We encouraged them not to lose heart and we comforted them that our entire work among the Indians was not the work of humans but of the Savior. He would not allow His Indian congregations, whom He had purchased with his blood, to be destroyed or ruined as long as we demonstrate our faithfulness, stand firmly, and do not give up. We told them we could not do much in this matter but put our trust in the Savior and look to him when we were in danger. At the same time, when we saw that something was being done to oppose the Savior's work or to harm it, for example if the *Chiefs* decided to send us White Brothers away, then it was really up to them to speak out against this and tell them, if they are torn from us, then no peace can be maintained and we also cannot make it. If we White Brothers told them this, the *Chiefs* might think that perhaps our Indian Brothers did not think this way. Nothing was as dangerous for them as taking the White Brothers away, unless we took the Sisters away in case of emergency. However, they should try to guide the *Chiefs* as much as possible to leave it up to us to choosewho would stay or go. We had this talk with the Brothers because *White Eye* and *Gelelemind* were coming here in the afternoon to discuss the dangerous circumstances and what should be done about our other sites. Our Indian Brothers would thus know in advance what our opinion was. Both Brother *David* and they told them our thoughts, which they were glad to hear. They explained to us that we should expect times to get even worse, because they thought the war would not really get going until this spring. They said that they would like to see us move closer together so that *Communication* would not be so difficult, because *Schönbrunn* is so far away. They are also afraid of the 6 *Nations,* who have threatened to punish the *Delaware Nation*.[933] Therefore, they asked us if our Indians in *Schönbrunn* would be willing to move here to *Lichtenau* and to stay until the war was over and there was peace again. Then their teachers, whose lives had been threatened, would not be in such danger because people would not dare to harm them so close to *Goschgosching*, much less to stain their *Councel-fire* with blood, which would be an obvious breach of

---

933. On similar concerns, see entry for 22 Jan. 1777; on the background, see Introduction, pp. 8–9, 24–25.

peace.[934] Brother *David* objected that stopping the work of our Indian Brothers and Sisters in *Schönbrunn* and moving them here would be very difficult and almost *impracticable*, because there was so little time. It was already spring and our people could not be moved from one *Town* to another very easily. However, they replied that if they stayed there they might have to flee in haste and leave behind everything they have. Then they would lose everything. It was not so dangerous yet and they could still bring everything here. Finally, they said they would consider this more and tell us their *Resolution* in two days.

THE 21ST   We were called to the *Councel* in *Goschgosching*, where a message had arrived from the *Fort* and Brother *David* had to read it out loud to them.[935] The *Delaware* were advised to consider their safety, because they had news in the *Fort* that the *Minque* were planning bad things against them. They also promised to help them, and said they should make suggestions about how this could be done. *Mr. Morgan, Superintendant of Indian Affairs,* had once again sent those *Nations* a message offering peace for the last time, and at the same time letting them know that they were preparing for war against the hostile Indians. Some of our Indian Brothers stayed behind after the *Councel* had broken up and Brother *David* had returned home. Some of the *Counsellors* gathered, called our Brothers, and informed them that they had decided our Indians from *Schönbrunn* and *Gnadenhütten* should all come here to *Lichtenau* so that they would be together. This should be done as soon as possible while there is still time and it would not be as dangerous now. It might be too late if we waited any longer. We should remain together until the war was over and then we could move back to our sites. If the Sisters or some of our White Brothers wanted to go home until times were better, they would leave this up to our choice and judgment. Finally, they said if one town, for example *Gnadenhütten*, did not want to move here, then they could not help them; they would have to leave them to fend for themselves. They were all being summoned, however. Brother *David* thus found it necessary after 5 months to travel back to *Gnadenhütten* escorted by Brothers *Isaac* and *Abraham*, where he

---

934. According to Native American perceptions of right and wrong, an attack on individuals in a settlement represented an infringement of custom that was to be dealt with, to use Zeisberger's terminology, by the "friendship." The "Council-Fire," by contrast, represented the whole nation; to attack the place of the "Council Fire" thus implied an attack on the whole nation and required a response by the whole nation. See the responses to the questions of Cass in Weslager, *Delaware Indian Westward Migration,* 94–100.

935. George Morgan sent messages dated 6 and 7 March 1777 to the Council of the Delaware (George Morgan Letterbook, vol. 1, fols. 49–52, CLP). In his first letter he asked for further information about a conference in one of the Shawnee settlements, in which Mingo, Shawnee, Wyandot, and supposedly also some Delaware had participated. He further requested that the Delaware Council again send messages to the Wyandot and Mingo and ask them to keep the peace. Morgan announced that he would soon be able to communicate "strange News about your old Father the French." His second letter criticized some Delaware for joining the British side and indicated that in case the mediation failed, a large army would move against the hostile tribes. At the same time he repeated his promise to do everything for the protection of those Delaware who remained friendly to the American cause.

first conferred with Brother *Schmick* about this. Then they arrived in *Schönbrunn* on the 23RD. After he had proposed the matter to them there, he found the *National Helpers* not only willing but indeed quite happy about being called to move to *Lichtenau*. Most of them said they had been waiting a long time for this and hoped they would be told to do so. After this had been announced to the whole congregation, we decided to make preparations for this right after the Easter holidays. They would begin as soon as they have some *Canow*s ready and could bring up the ones from *Lichtenau*. We were pleased that everything went so well and the Brothers and Sisters were so willing. We realized that under these circumstances a change needed to be made in *Schönbrunn*, not only because of the dangerous external situation, but also because of the spiritual life. For some time already there had been all sorts of *Confusion*. It was sad and painful for us that tempters had found their way in a while ago. They finally developed into a whole group including *Newollike, Jacob Gendaskind* and *Joseph*, who were head people and had already caused much harm. They were now making great efforts, working day and night to misguide people and get them away from the congregation if they could.[936] We could not do much about this matter except to commend them to the Savior and ask him to keep all tempters far away from his people, to bring back all who were confused and misguided, and to help them make things right. The worst thing was that *Jacob Gendaskund* had declared that they, the *Munsee*, had never accepted any teachers and they declared themselves free of the Brothers and the Unity. Therefore there is nothing more to be done. Even if we wanted to consider letting the *Munsee* settle alone somewhere, things have gone too far now.[937] Brother *David* did what he could, and he returned to *Lichtenau* with *Isaac* on THE 26TH, but left Brother *Abraham* there. In the meantime Brother *Edward* had taken care of the services there.

THE 27TH   The *communicants* enjoyed the *Holy Sacrament* of his Body and Blood on the night in which he was betrayed.[938] During this *Johannes* had the grace of observing for the first time.

936. Newollike, an influential Munsee chief who had been baptized Augustinus, had left Schönbrunn on 13 Feb. 1777; see entries for 13, 18, and 20 Feb. 1777 in Diary of Schönbrunn, MAB, B 141, F 9. How deep the rift between the Munsee and the mission congregations had become is evidenced by the Munsee's reaction to the resolve of the Delaware Council to concentrate all mission congregations in Lichtenau. According to the Diary of Schönbrunn, they declared on March 24 that White Eyes' speech did not apply to them because "they had given up believing" (ibid.). Jakob Gendaskund, like Newollike a Munsee, had been a war captain before his admission to the mission congregation at Goschgoschünk; on Christmas day 1770 he had been baptized at Friedensstadt ([Sensemann and Zeisberger], "Continuation of the Diary of the Brethren in Goschgoschuenk," 75). Joseph refers to Joseph Peepi, who around this time had moved from Gnadenhütten to Goschachgünk in order to "preach" there; see entry for 9 June 1777. Peepi, who on other occasions also acted rather independently, had assumed that he would retain his status as a member of the congregation in Lichtenau and had expected to be accepted into the community receiving Holy Communion, which, however, Zeisberger refused.

937. These remarks indicate that these withdrawals too were motivated by conflicts between the Munsee and other tribes.

938. Luke 22:47–48.

THE 28TH   Many tears were shed while we read the story of our Lord's passion[939] and people listened with great *Attention* and melted hearts. *Gelelemind* and his wife were among those present from *Goschgosching*. On Great Sabbath[940] we had a Lovefeast and on Easter morning, THE 30TH, we prayed the Easter *Litany* on our God's Acre and asked that those of us who belong to this place would enjoy eternal fellowship with Sister *Justina*, who died here.

Afterward we read today's story about our Lord's resurrection,[941] and Brother *Edward* then preached the sermon. Towards evening during the Congregational Service, *Gideon*'s 2nd son was baptized into Jesus' death with the name *Moses*. This was a blessed proceeding.

THE 31ST   Early in the day Wilhelm went to *Goschgosching* to speak with the head people. They had offered to help us bring our Brothers and Sisters here from *Schönbrunn*.[942] It is becoming clearer where the *Rum*ors about our lives being threatened are starting. The *Munsees* had sent a secret message to the *Wyandot* declaring they did not want to side with the White people but with them, and they wanted to distance themselves from the *Delaware*. We can conclude from the answer they received that they declared this because of the White Brothers here, and they gave the *Wyandot* the opportunity to say, among other things, that they would come here and get the *Ministers*, that is the White Brothers, and take them away. They heard our statement, although Brother *David* only spoke for himself, and then as a result of this matter the *Chiefs* resolved to live or die with them, no matter what happened. We were staking our lives on this, so they would also do what is within their power to save our lives. Secondly, since they are now sending messengers to the *Wyandot*, they will inform them at the same time that they have accepted God's word and have teachers among them, and anyone who harmed them harmed the entire *Delaware Nation*.

Threats once again arrived from the 6 *Nations*, saying they would attack the *Delaware*[943] as soon as it got warm, and we heard that 70 of the *Shawnee* warriors have returned. They did not have much *Success*, however, and they had lost a number of men.[944] We put our trust in the Lord. He alone knows ways

939. Probably they read the relevant sections from Samuel Lieberkühn's *Evangelien-harmonie*.
940. Holy Saturday.
941. See Introduction, pp. 53–54.
942. Two days earlier and in accordance with the requests of George Morgan, the Council had agreed on the texts of two letters to George Morgan and of messages to the Wyandot and Shawnee. In the first letter the Council complained about a group of white settlers who had robbed a hut in which furs had been stored and had shot at a Delaware. The second letter explained the messages to the Wyandot and Shawnee; the Council refused to send a similar message to the Munsee because of their hostility. The letter further discussed questions of security in case of threatened attacks and the concentration of all mission congregations in Lichtenau close to Goschachgünk, and included a list of goods most urgently needed. George Morgan Letterbook, vol. 1, fols. 83–88, CLP.
943. See entries for 22 Jan. and 18 March 1777.
944. In early March Shawnee had attacked the settlements Harrodsburgh and Boonesborough in Kentucky (*RUO*, 242n85).

and means to help us through. As our Watchword for today, which is the last for now, says, Behold, the LORD's hand is not shortened, that it cannot save; neither his ear heavy, that it cannot hear.[945]

[April]

APRIL 1ST   We sent all the *Canows* we had to *Schönbrunn* to help our Brothers and Sisters travel there and some people from *Goschgosching* helped bring them up.

THE 2ND   Brother *David* was called to *Goschgosching* with some Indian Brothers. A White man had arrived there from the *Fort* and claimed *Mr. Morgan* had sent him to *Detroit*. However, because he had nothing in writing to show them, the *Chiefs* detained him until further news comes. It turned out he was a *Deserteur*. The message to the *Wyandot* was prepared[946] in the *Council* and the *Chiefs* wanted to send a message along at the same time about us White Brothers here. They asked us to prepare an outline for this. We were very willing to do this and Brother *David* gave them information for this in a private conversation with *White Eye* and *Gelelemind*. After we had returned home, a messenger came from *Goschgosching* in the afternoon and brought us word that an Indian had just arrived from *Gnadenhütten* with the news that 18 *Minque* were in *Tuscarawi*. They had already gone to *Schönbrunn* yesterday evening and wanted to kill the White Brothers and Sisters. Brother Heckwelder had fled to *Gnadenhütten* during the night. We heard that the 18 *Minque* had been with *Newollike* some days ago and had crossed the *Ohio*. Our worries about the situation were calmed when we joyfully watched Brothers and Sisters *Jungmann* and *Conners*[947] arrive at our place in the evening. When they had received the news about the *Minque*, the Indian Brothers and Sisters advised them to go off to the side and at 10 o'clock Brothers *Abraham* and *Michael* had gone to *Gnadenhütten* by water and brought them here. We rejoiced sincerely with them and thanked the Savior in a childlike manner for protecting them.

White Eye and *Gelelemind*, who heard about their arrival while traveling past *Goschgosching*, also expressed their joy. During the night they sent another messenger here to learn what was going on and sent word that it would be better for us White Brothers and Sisters to go to *Goschgosching*, because only a few Indian Brothers are at home here. The rest had all gone to *Schönbrunn* with the *Canows*. They would clear out a house for us there until more Indian Brothers and Sisters returned here from *Schönbrunn*. We thanked them for this offer

---

945. Isa. 59:1; we cannot determine which collection of Watchwords Zeisberger was using; the Watchword he cites corresponds neither to the collection for 1769 nor to that for 1777.

946. See note 942.

947. I.e., the missionary couple Johann Georg and Anna Margaretha Jungmann, as well as Richard and Peggy Conner.

and again sent them word that we wanted to watch a little longer and wait until we had more news about the whole situation.

THE 5TH   Brothers *Isaac* and *Thomas* began their journey to the *Wyandot* with the messengers from *Goschgosching*. Our hearts and blessings accompanied them on their *expedition*, because our welfare and that of the entire country here depends upon this. The *Chiefs* were sending along a message about the White Brothers and Sisters, and they did not want to entrust this to any Indian because they feared it might not be delivered properly. Therefore they asked one or two of the Brothers from here go along to take it and to present it to the *Nations* in the name of the Indian Believers. We had no objections to this and indeed considered it necessary and proper. Such a message should have been sent a long time ago and Brother *David* had reminded the *Chiefs* of this in the winter. However, this could not be done before now because they were not yet in agreement with their people.[948] It is now easy to understand what *White Eye* and *Gelelemind* were working on in their *Councels* some time ago, trying to see that the matter of accepting the Gospel does not just remain with the *Chiefs*, but becomes more general and might be accepted by the people. After *White Eye* had first agreed with the people about this he then publicized it in a large council, as can be seen from his talk above.[949] Now it can also be made known to the *Nations*. Previously they could not have done this truthfully.

What does it mean, however, that the *Delaware* Nation has declared to the *Nations* that is has accepted God's word? Could it mean that all the Indians will become Believers? Although I hardly believe this will happen soon, I do not believe this is just an accident. The *Delaware Nation* is taking the concerns of the Indian Believers in its hands. It not only wants to maintain them and defend them as a people, but also to make this something lasting and eternal. The Savior alone knows what more will come of this.

The message says the following:

Uncles, some years ago we called our friends from the *Susquehanna* here to the *Allegheney*. They first came to *Goschgosching*, then to *Kaskaskunk*, where those who had remained behind all followed, and finally they came here to us.[950] These friends of ours accepted God's word more than 30 years ago, first the *Mohican*, then the *Munsee*, and now after they have joined us here also the

948. This means that the Council, unlike the people at large, was unanimous in acknowledging the Christian mission. Unanimity in the Council evidently came at a double cost: first, Captain Pipe and his supporters did not attend this meeting—at least his presence is not mentioned—and, second, the Munsee renegades, led by Newollike (see note 936 to entry for 21 March 1777), had seceded from the mission congregation and founded their own religious and nativistic party, which was busy recruiting members.

949. See entry for 9 March 1777.

950. On the beginning of the mission among the Delaware and the Munsee, see Introduction, pp. 47–51.

Unami Nation.[951] Our former *Chief* confessed this and left us this in his *Testament*. Until his end he admonished us to accept the Gospel and told us it would be precious for our children and for us. We followed our *Chief's* advice and are in agreement with our young people to remain with this and hold firmly to it. Therefore we desire to have peace with everyone and do not want to become involved in any war.

Having done this, however, we find that we are hated and persecuted by other *Nations* as a result, as if we had done something bad, although we know of nothing we have done. You, our uncles, did precisely the same thing many years ago and accepted *Ministers*[952] who are still with you today. Perhaps you know better than we do if this is good or bad. People call us *Virginians*[953] and say they sent us *Ministers* who misguided us. However, this is absolutely not true, because our friends who came to us already had teachers among them before people had heard much if anything among the Indians about *Virginians*. Therefore this is nothing new, but something more than 30 years old. Therefore, how can people call us *Virginians* and why are they trying to kill us? (That is to say, people are trying to kill our teachers, and thus the entire *Delaware* Nation).

THE 6TH   In the morning we had the sermon and in the afternoon a service for the baptized Brothers and Sisters, and we especially remembered the 6 who were baptized during the last year. We commended them to the Savior and to the care of our dear Mother,[954] to give them refuge in his wounds, away from all the trouble and noise on earth.

THE 7TH   Brother *Abraham* will go to *Munsee Town* a few miles from here.[955] He is very concerned about his *Nation*[956] and would like to advise them for their own good. He will talk with them because we heard they are preparing to move to the *Wyandot* or into that same area. This is a sign that they want to join in the war.

THE 8TH   8 *Canows* with some Brothers and Sisters arrived here from *Schönbrunn*. We learned from them that the 18 warriors had not gone there but to *Pittsburgh*, and that Brother *Heckewelder* is there again and will remain until the final departure.

THE 10TH   Brother *David* left with the *Canows* for *Schönbrunn*. He

951. On the usage and meaning of the term "Nation," see note 28 to entry for 5 June 1772.
952. On the Christian mission of the Jesuits among the Wyandot, see note 855 to entry for 12 Nov. 1776.
953. The term "Virginians" was shorthand for the brutal, land-greedy, unscrupulous whites, who during Lord Dunmore's war had enforced their unjust claims with brutal force. On the genesis of this abusive term, see entry for 1 Nov. 1774. Indians allied with England used the term "Virginians" for "anti-British" whites as well.
954. See note 30 above.
955. He was a Munsee. Abraham had been baptized on 25 Dec. 1765.
956. I.e., Memehusing; see entry for 7 March 1777 and note 922.

wanted to go some days ago, but he could not but because the *Minque* are roaming all around and making the road unsafe, as we have heard constantly in recent days. On the way he received a letter from Brothers *Schmick* and *Heckewelder*, who report that the savages are coming to *Schönbrunn* from all over, bothering our Brothers and Sisters there and being bossy. Brother *David* sent this news to Brother *Jungmann*, to inform *White Eye* about it and ask him for assistance. This was all done.

THE 13TH   A party of warriors came here from the *Settlements*, but we soon took them to *Goschgosching*. The White people set out after them because they had stolen horses, and therefore they could track them easily. They caught up with them not very far from here, killed one of them, and wounded one fatally. They had to leave him behind and turn over the horses and everything they had to the White people.[957]

THE 14TH   Another party of warriors passed through here with 5 prisoners, a woman and 4 children. The Brothers did not allow them to come into our *Town*, but took them to *Goschgosching*, where the *Chiefs* made great efforts to ransom the prisoners. Unfortunately they could not persuade the warriors to do this.

THE 26TH   Brother *David* returned from *Schönbrunn*. After he had arrived there and seen how rowdy the wild *Munsee* people were and that they were doing whatever they wanted, he immediately made preparations for the Brothers and Sisters to go *Gnadenhütten* in peace. This took place in a couple of days, with the help of the Brothers and Sisters in *Gnadenhütten*. On the 19th of this month we closed this little *Town* where we had enjoyed so many blessings and so much kindness from our dear Lord, where he so often blessed us inexpressibly with his dear presence. Hearts melted into tears. We thanked Him for all of this and asked Him to remain with us wherever He leads us in the future, to take us under His protection as a people who belong to Him, and to hide us in His wounds, away from all of Satan's temptations and seductions. The Savior revealed himself to us and granted us his peace. A contrite, blessed feeling could be sensed among the Brothers and Sisters, and many tears were shed. After the service the Brothers got busy tearing down the Meeting House, and the final departure took place on the 21st. Brothers *David* and *Heckewelder* left there with them for *Lichtenau* after they had made some more reed *Canows* in *Gnadenhütten*. Because we did not have enough *Canows*, 4 families had to remain in *Gnadenhütten* until they could be picked up, and 6 families are going to live there. One reed *Canow* wrecked on the way; 2 others sank at the *Falls*[958] and they lost many things. We all arrived in *Lichtenau* on the 26th. This week *Sam Evans*[959] and his family also moved here from *Gnadenhütten*.

957. See *RUO*, 250–55.

958. See entry for 14 April 1772.

959. Sam Evans was first mentioned in 1754; after further visits at Gnadenhütten he was baptized on 6 Jan. 1774. On 17 July 1780 he was appointed to the office of a helper; MAB, B 144, F2 and F 10.

THE 27TH   Yesterday we housed all the Brothers and Sisters as well as possible. This went better and smoother than anyone imagined it would, as did the whole move. Then today we had the sermon, which *White Eye, Gelelemind,* and many visitors from *Goschgosching* attended. Our *Meeting Hall* could hardly hold one third of them, and they had to stay outside.

THE 28TH   Brother *Heckewelder* and some Indian Brothers returned to *Gnadenhütten,* where he will remain for now.[960]

THE 29TH   The Brothers and Sisters were allotted land to clear and plant. In the afternoon Brother *David* and some Indian Brothers were picked up and taken to *Goschgosching.*

Messengers had returned there from the *Fort* with a *Speech* from *Mr. Morgan*[961] to *communicate* to the *Councel.* On *Mr. Morgan*'s orders, however, *Gelelemind* was first informed that only Brother *David* should read his letters out loud to the *Councel* and if they had anything to report to him he should write it for them, because *Traders* had done this several times.[962] This is really not the work we should be doing because it wastes a lot of time. However, we could not very well refuse since it is also for our own good. It will also stop when peace is fully restored. Among other things, a *Proclamation* and *Order* by *Gouverneur Patrick Henry* from *Virginia* to all the *Officiers* in the *Frontier Counties* was read. It said that because the *Delaware Nation* is in danger of being attacked by hostile *Nations,* and because they live in peace and friendship with the United States and do not side with hostile parties, he orders all *Officiers* on the *Frontiers* to defend the *Delaware Nation* with all their power, to protect them, preserve them, assist them in every way possible, and to defend their land. Further, if it becomes necessary and the *Delaware* Indians request it, they should build *Forts* in their country and occupy them with people to keep them safe. If they, or some of them, had to flee to the *Settlements* to seek protection among the White people, they would be well received and given *Provisions,* clothing, and *Ammunition.*[963] The most pleasant and delightful thing for us on this occasion

960. Six families had moved from Schönbrunn to Gnadenhütten; on 3 May 1777 they arrived at Lichtenau. The original inhabitants of Gnadenhütten still lived there and were looked after by Heckewelder until 27 May and thereafter, until 10 August 1777, by the couple Schmick. See entry for 6 May 1777.

961. Morgan's letter is dated 10 April 1777; enclosed with it was the report of a speech by Captain Pipe dated 5 April 1777, with news about attempts by the commanding officer of Fort Niagara to entice the Six Indian Nations and other tribes to war against the Americans. In this speech Pipe also announced that he and his people would retreat to Mahoning, "where I shall cultivate your Friendship & think of nothing but Peace." In his letter Morgan confirmed that he would procure and pay for the smith desired by the Council of the Delaware and send sufficient ammunition and guns for their defense, but he warned the Delaware that deserters were on their way from Fort Pitt. George Morgan Letterbook, vol. 1, fols. 78–80, 89–90, CLP.

962. An example of such a letter is in GD, F 9, I 1a; see entry for 2 April 1777. Through the trader James O'Hara, the chiefs wrote Morgan that they intended to send away all whites except Zeisberger. Morgan answered that they should retain and protect all missionaries. Schmick does not reveal the source of this information but adds that Zeisberger did not know anything about this.

963. From "he first made known to Gelelemind . . ." bracketed in a different hand, except in version H2. The governor's circular was related to the threats against the Delaware, especially by the

was that we received a packet of letters from Brother *Matthao*, dispatched through *Mr. Morgan's* messenger and delivered to Brother *David* during the *Councel*. From these we learned of the oppressive and difficult circumstances our Brothers and Sisters in Bethlehem* and other places are facing, and we felt much sympathy and compassion for them. Even so, it was sweet and pleasant to receive news from them. We thought we were enduring difficult and worrisome times, but we found many reasons to thank the dear Savior for dealing so mercifully and patiently with us. We do not yet have reason to complain.

May

THE 1ST   Brothers *Isaac* and *Thomas* sent news from *Sandusky* of their arrival and business there, and we learned that the *Wyandot* have received them well, were willing to listen to them, and are inclined to accept peace. However, because this matter concerns all the *Nations* and the *Chief* could not resolve it, he sent them across the *Lake* to the head seat of the *Wyandot*. All the *Nations* will gather[965] there, and people had already left for there 12 days ago. We can therefore hope that things will remain calm and peaceful among the *Nations* this summer. The *Minque* gang[966] alone is causing them all this trouble. They always incite the *Shawnee* and others to join them in going to war.

THE 3RD   All our Brothers and Sisters from *Schönbrunn* who had remained in *Gnadenhütten* finally arrived here by both water and by land. They brought all the rest of the cattle with them. We were happy about this and thanked the Savior for helping us this far again and bringing our Brothers and Sisters to rest.

THE 4TH   In addition to the usual Sunday services, we announced to the *communicants* that there will be Holy Communion next Saturday. This was happy news for them. It was sweet to hear the Savior and his death being proclaimed here and there in the houses and huts of our Brothers and Sisters, especially to the unbaptized.

Mingo. The expedition against the Mingo of Pluggy's Town had been shelved by the Continental Congress as a result of Morgan's conviction that this would have negative repercussions for relations with the Delaware, for the army would have to march through their territory. Other means had to be found, therefore, to protect the Delaware from the Mingo and keep them in the American camp. The governor's circular to the commanding officers of the militia in the frontier counties suggested the solution. Text of the circular in *RUO*, 244–45. On the expedition against Pluggy's Town, see McIlwaine, *Official Letters of the Governors of Virginia*, 1:118–22, 138; McIlwaine, *Journals of the Council of Virginia*, 1:365–66; Savelle, *George Morgan*, 168–69.

964. In the winter of 1776–77 a hospital for the army of the Continental Congress had been opened at Bethlehem; coupled with the many soldiers coming through the town, this caused serious unrest. Gilbert, "Bethlehem and the American Revolution."

965. See entry for 19 May 1777.

966. See entry for 9 May 1774, where Zeisberger speaks about "a gang of White people" who had "committed murders."

THE 6TH   The early service was about the comfort Believers enjoy in the merits and sufferings of our Lord, and from which they draw strength every day.

White Eye and Gelelemind came here for a visit, and Brother *David* spoke with them about our Brothers and Sisters in *Gnadenhütten*.[967] They had declared that they still wanted to wait until the messengers returned from the *Wyandot* before they move away, so they can first learn what news they would bring from there. We told them they would surely stay for now. We were happy that our Indian Brothers and Sisters from *Schönbrunn* were now here in peace. We would also be happy if our Brothers and Sisters in *Gnadenhütten* could remain at peace, which we hope. It would be too difficult for us if both places had to move here at one time. They should not think badly of them because of this, much less interpret it as disobedience, but let them enjoy friendship and love. *White Eye* replied that when they called us, they had no other purpose than bringing our Indians and their teachers to safety, because times were evil and dangerous and there was no indication of things improving. Therefore they had thought the best thing now would be to bring everyone here, where our Indians could be together and receive their teachers among them, since few people would dare harm them, especially if we were so close to them. They were happy that we were there. They had called the residents of *Gnadenhütten* once and that was enough. They would not say anything else to them about it.

THE 8TH   We worshipped our dear, still invisible Lord, and prayed for his invisible but even more obvious presence through all our days and hours.

THE 10TH   Both yesterday and today everyone was busy making fences. *White Eye* and *Gelelemind* came from *Goschgosching* with 100 men to help us his. They organized their people themselves and kept them orderly. This was a great help and we expressed our gratitude for this. We had Speakings with the Brothers and Sisters for Holy Communion. The Savior provided grace during this so that most of them rediscovered their hearts and the way to his wounds, and we were sincerely joyful and grateful. Then this evening we partook of the inexpressibly blessed enjoyment of his Body and Blood in the *Holy Sacrament*.

THE 11TH   In the morning we had the *Liturgy* for Holy Communion first, and then the sermon. *White Eye* and *Gelelemind* came here with a whole party of their people and Brother *David* used this opportunity to speak with them about the address to the Brothers in the *Councel* in *Goschgosching*[968] and what their hope and desire is. He told *White Eye* he had been wanting to ask him what he actually meant for a long time, because we had concluded from his talk that they would like to see the Brothers help them teach their children. They replied that we were absolutely correct. They would consider it a great

967. See entry for 28 April 1777 and note 960.
968. See entry for 9 March 1777.

favor and service if we could help them in this. Brother *David* told them that not much could be done about this now during such warlike times, until peace was restored. However, he would write our Brothers in Bethlehem about this. They were glad to hear this and said, Since we see now that our hope and desire has been considered this far, we have some degree of comfort and hope. Brother *David* discussed a number of other things with them about our congregational way of life and rules and how we must follow these and not be lax in them. He provided them an example of why, so they could understand it, and they received this well.

THE 12TH   A White man passed through here from the *Shawnee Towns* with the *Chief*'s son.[969] They were on their way to the *Fort*. We learned from them that most of the *Shawnee* were for peace. Many of them, however, were going to war with the *Minque*. Recently another 50 men had gone to the *Settlements* to commit murder, and they had already stolen about 300 horses.

THE 16TH   *Welapachtschiechen* spoke with *Gideon*'s mother, who had been *Netawatwe's* wife, and told her it his intention to live for the Savior and he wanted to live and die with the Brothers and the congregation. He wanted to tell her this because she was his close friend, and he hoped she would think about this since she was quite old after all, and did not know how soon she might die. She replied that this was precisely her intention. She really wanted to be saved as well, and this was why she had come to the congregation.

THE 18TH   The sermon was about the work of the Holy Spirit, who punishes humans for their unbelief and convicts them for not believing in the one God sent into the world so we would have eternal life through Him. We worshipped God the worthy Holy Spirit, our dear Mother,[970] prayed for forgiveness for all our mistakes and shortcomings, and for times we have not been faithful and attentive to her* reminders. We surrendered ourselves anew to her care and efforts to form us according to Jesus' heart, so that He might experience joy and honor from his Indian people, and we promised her new faithfulness and obedience. Brother *Edwards* led the Congregational Service. We were very happy to sense new life and feeling among our Brothers and Sisters; new life and emotion prevailed among them and our hearts were moved to praise the Savior for this and to thank Him.

THE 19TH   Brothers *Isaac* and *Thomas* returned safe and sound from the *Wyandot* across *Lake Erie* from *Detroit*.[971] As soon as they had arrived there,

969. The "White man" is the trader Robert George, see GD, F 9, Ia, entry for 15 May 1777. The "Chief's son" is probably the son of Cornstalk, El-i-nip-si-co.

970. See note 30 above.

971. On the background and reasons for this trip, see entries for 21 Feb., 11 and 31 March, 2 and 5 April, and 1 May 1777. On English political relations with western tribes and the importance of Lord Germain's instruction of 26 March 1766 to the commanding officer of Detroit, see note 1003 below.

rumors immediately circulated that two *Moravian Indians* were coming with an company of 10 men. One of them, that is *Isaac*, was the head man who was in charge of this *expedition*. Right away some of the *Wyandot* said, Now we will get to hear the truth, because the Indian Believers do not lie. The *Gouverneur*[972] himself received them cordially. After he had welcomed them he told *John Montour*,[973] who was part of the *Compagnie*, that he would really like to show the *Moravian Captain* kindness and provide him with the best hospitality possible. He wanted to know what he could offer him, because he knew well that he did him no service by offering him strong drink. However, he wanted to supply his *Compagnie* and him generously with *Provisions*, not only while they were there but also for their return journey. *Isaac* thanked him and answered that the greatest service and favor he could do was to give them enough to eat and spare them of strong drink. Then they stayed in *Wyandot Town*[974] for 10 days and *Isaac* also went along to their church and observed their worship. However, he said he was not pleased with this but saddened, because he just saw painted Indians with plumes and all sorts of figures in the church, and their lifestyle is not a hair better than other Indians who live a pagan life. After the *Nations* had gathered, *Isaac* delivered them the message in the *Fort* in the presence of the *Gouverneur*. Everything was written down there and very well received. They had heard repeatedly that an army would come into Indian country and to *Detroit* this summer,[975] and neither the *Governeur* nor the *Wyandot* expected otherwise. They were primarily trying to find out about this and *Isaac*, who was well informed about everything, gave them news about this to their complete *Satisfaction*. He told them that the *Virginians* (because all White people are now called this here) were not planning to come across the *Ohio* into Indian country unless they were forced to. They wanted to offer the *Nations* peace once more, but this would be the last time. If they accepted their message now and inclined their ears to suggestions of peace, they could be assured that they had nothing to fear from the *Virginians*, who would like to shake hands with them* and live in peace with the *Nations*. Therefore the *Wyandot* disciplined their people in the presence of the messengers and ordered them to stop carrying out further hostilities against the White people. They promised to

---

972. Henry Hamilton.

973. On John Montour, see entry for 17 Dec. 1774, note 563.

974. According to a Spanish report from the same year it was "located one-quarter league from the district of Detroit." *WHC*, 18:367.

975. Since the spring of 1776 Fort Detroit had awaited an attack from an American army (*RUO*, 145, 147–51). Thus the resolution of the Six Indian Nations to deny an American army right of passage through the confederation's territory can be viewed as a protective measure for Detroit and those tribes allied with England (*RUO*, 171–72); Morgan's concerns about the expedition against Pluggy's Town were based on this resolution, since it had been supported by the Shawnee as well as the Delaware. See note 961 to entry for 29 April 1777, and Williams, *Fort Pitt and the Revolution*, 70–71.

come to *Goschgosching* and restore peace with the *Colonies*. May God allow this to happen. However, they offered little response to the message they had sent along about us White Brothers. They said only that people call them *Virginians* because they listened to them, believed what they said, and had *Minister*s living with them. They knew of no other reason for this and it could not be helped.

THE 21ST   Brother *David* went with some Indian Brothers to the *Council* in *Goschgosching*. Messengers had returned there from the *Fort* with a written message to the Indians. He *communicated* this to them along with the main points of the *Treaty* held with the 6 *Nations* in *Easton* in *January* of this year.[976]

THE 22ND   After the early service some Indian Brothers were called to the *Councel* in *Goschgosching* once again, where they conferred about the *Treaty* to be held with the *Wyandot*.[977] They have concerns about having it in *Goschgosching* since there are so many hostile Indians around this area, and they fear it might not be carried out peacefully. The *Chief*s are therefore trying to decline and to arrange for the *Wyandot* to go to the *Fort*. This would also be calmer and better for us.

THE 24TH   Some time ago *Mr. Morgan* had promised the *Delaware Ammunition*[978] to use to defend themselves if they are attacked by other *Nations,* and if they did not need it for this they could use it for hunting. *Gelelemind* talked with us about this because they wanted to send some Indians to the *Fort* to pick it up and they wanted some of our people from here and *Gnadenhütten* to go along. However, we refused and told him that we would like to be left out of such matters. We did not want to have any part in this or in the *Presents*[979] at the *Treaties*, but would rather be spared of this. This did not really suit him, but he accepted it.

THE 26TH   Some *Counsellors* came here from *Goschgosching* and Brother

---

976. We have not found the letters. The negotiations with representatives of the Six Indian Nations took place on 30–31 January 1777. Pennsylvania was represented during these negotiations by members from the Pennsylvania Council of Safety, Colonel Joseph Dean, and Colonel John Bull, the Continental Congress by Robert Morris (*PCR,* 11:96, 108–9; *PA, 1st ser.,* 5:201, 203, 208). John Bull reported on 31 January that the negotiations thus far had been satisfactory: "the Indians seem to be Inclind to act the wise Part, with Respect to the present Dispute if they are to be relied on they mean to be Neuter, we have already Learnt their good Intentions & Great Expectations in Receiving Present" (*PA, 1st ser.,* 208). Neither Savelle, *George Morgan,* nor Mohr, *Federal Indian Relations, 1774–1788,* mentions these negotiations.

977. According to Zeisberger the Wyandot had declared that they would come to Goschachgünk for such negotiations; see entry for 19 May 1777. From the Wyandot's perspective, Goschachgünk was neutral ground, while negotiations in Fort Pitt had a different and more partial character; see entry for 5 July 1777. Zeisberger and the Christian Indians, especially, viewed such negotiations with apprehension because they threatened considerable unrest. See Zeisberger to General Edward Hand, *FDO,* 18–19.

978. See note 961 to entry for 29 April 1777.

979. On the importance of presents as part of these negotiations, see Jacobs, *Wilderness Politics and Indian Gifts.*

David had to write down a message for them from the *Gouverneur* in *Detroit* to the *Delaware*. They had received it yesterday and they immediately sent it to the *Fort* along with the *Wyandot'* reply. The *Gouverneur* seeks the friendship of the *Delaware*, encourages them to do what they can so peace will soon be restored among the *Nations*. He also recommends that they encourage and insist that the *Minque* stop causing further harm.[980]

THE 27TH   We had a *Conference* with the Helpers and spoke with *Joseph Peepi's* son *Petrus*, who moved from *Gnadenhütten* to *Goschgosching* with his father some time ago.[981] Now he wants to return to the Unity with his wife. He received permission to do this.

Once again we heard that a party of *Minque* and *Wyandot* had gone out to the *Settlements* of the White people to commit murders. The *Chiefs* in *Goschgosching* had sent messengers to the *Minque*, including *John Montour,* who can read and write. Brother *David* had to give him a *Copie* of the *Treaty* held in *Easton* with the 6 *Nations*[982] so that he could convince the *Minque* that the 6 *Nations* do not want war and therefore their claim that they had orders from them to go to war is not true.

THE 29TH   Brother *Jungmann* held the early service about how we know the Savior as our redeemer and must experience him in our hearts as the mighty Savior who freed us through his blood from the bondage of sin. We discussed some matters concerning the *Chiefs* in *Goschgosching* with the *National* Helpers, since it almost seems as if they wanted to involve us gradually in the *Chiefs Affairs* and in the worldly government. To some extent we can excuse them for this because they believe our Indians possess more understanding than the rest of them together, as they have often indicated. We reminded them about what we had agreed with them from the beginning and again just a year ago, so that they will not expect too much of us and will not leave all the work up to us in the end. We will always be faithful to this. We wanted to leave the worldly government completely up to them and it was also their responsibility to keep their people in order so that the Indian Believers could live calmly and peacefully among them. They should spare us of *Chief Affairs*, especially external ones, because that was their work and not ours. However, when they wanted our help and advice in their Councils, we would gladly help them in this way and would contribute what we could to support their *Chiefs*, for example *Wampum*, because nothing can be done without this. Now it is true we have

980. It is likely that the following remark in Henry Hamilton's letter to Governor Guy Carleton, dated Detroit, 11 May 1777, is related to the message Zeisberger mentioned: "As some of the Delawares appear wavering I have given one of their Chiefs a belt, with a present to induce them to come to the Council, when I make no doubt they will be influenced as I would wish." HP, 272.

981. Joseph Peepi had moved to Goschachgünk in order to preach there; see entries for 9 June and 21 March 1777 and note 936.

982. See entry for 21 May 1777.

gone further in these times of war and have done some things we would not have done at other times, but we did all this to achieve peace among the Indians wherever possible and to do what we could to keep an open Indian war from breaking out. After all, this is in our own interests. Therefore we sent some Indian Brothers from the *Conference* to *Goschgosching* to speak with the *Chiefs* and to remind them in a friendly way of our agreement with them, so that they do not forget it and would not think things would continue like this. However, *Gelelemind* soon yielded and asked us to have a little more patience and to support them and help them until they concluded the peace they were working on now among the *Nations*. Then they would gladly spare us and not ask us to do things that were difficult for us. We really could not raise any objections to this, because it is still up in the air whether we will have peace or an Indian war.

We discussed another matter with the *Chiefs*; we wanted to find out what they thought about the Indians' *Ceremonies* and customs about reconciliation. For example, when someone dies, is killed, dies drinking or in another way, then the friends of the one who died must be reconciled after a set amount of time has passed. This is generally done with *Wampum*. Now because it is too difficult for the perpetrator to come up with so much *Wampum*, since it sometimes adds up to between 1 to 200 *Klafter* of *Wampum*, his friends help him even if the whole *Tribe* cannot raise such a large amount. Then this will be given to a *Chief* of the injured *Tribe* to atone for it.[983] This happens often here and until now we have not been completely clear about this, so we are have now agreed with our Helpers to put aside this matter and stay out of it, which

---

983. Zeisberger, "History of the Northern American Indians," 90–91. In 1823, on the basis of interviews with Richard Conner's son, William, and Captain Pipe, among others, Charles C. Trowbridge defined the custom thus: "If a man in drunkenness or in the heat of passion commit any violence or injure another in his person or property, he goes to one of the Council Chiefs, delivers him a string of wampum, describes the circumstances of his transgression, confesses his sorrow for the event and solicits him to heal the breach between him and his friend. With a proper message the chief transmits the wampum to the injured party advising him to overlook the offence, and the matter is thus generally settled. But in case of refusal on the part of the latter it is returned to the aggressor, who prepares himself for any attempt of the other to avenge the wrong in his own way." This report also explains why it was so difficult for Welapachtschiechen to implement Zeisberger's proposed solution: Trowbridge's report clearly shows the central role of the chief. (Trowbridge's report is printed in full as appendix 3 in Weslager, *Delaware Indian Westward Migration;* quotation above is at 477–78). In both reports, however, the function of the "friendships" for the healing ceremonies remains unclear. Goddard mentions the custom as "Wergild of Wampum" ("Delaware," 216); a similar but probably more formal custom of the Six Indian Nations is described in Tooker, "League of the Iroquois," 418–41, esp. 438. Trowbridge says the Delaware knew only offenses against individual persons but not against a nation itself (see also Trowbridge's analysis of the Delaware's answers to a questionnaire by Lewis Cass in Weslager, *Delaware Indian Westward Migration,* 174: "No acts are considered offences gainst [sic] the body of the Nation—all are accounted personal injuries & and these may be commuted by presents"). The Delaware themselves, however, answered the question: "Are any acts considered as offences against the body of the nation?" with the words: "Nothing is considered as an offence against the Nation except murder and that done indicating war or an insult." See Weslager, *Delaware Indian Westward Migration,* 92, and entry for 18 March 1777.

we reported to the *Chiefs*. They answered us that some of their *Tribes* knew well enough that we did not like to participate in such matters, so they would also leave us out of it. However, because many were still not aware of this it would be good if we made a public statement about it. They thought there would be problems if *Welapachtschiechen* tried to renounce it completely though, because he is a *Chief*.

June

THE 1ST   Early in the day was the Helpers' *Conference* and then the sermon about those who are poor and wretched, but rich in faith. God has chosen them as heirs to the kingdom. Many visitors had come for this. Brother *Edwards* led the Children's Service and Brother *Jungmann* the Congregational Service.

THE 2ND   We received word from *Goschgosching* that a message from both the *Governeur* and the *Wyandot* in *Detroit* had arrived for the *Delaware Chiefs* in answer to the message sent to them about us White Brothers and Sisters here, which had been given to our *Isaac*. They did not answer it completely, however, but said they would hear more about it.[984] In brief, the message said they should treat their *Ministers* or teachers as a precious treasure, because they do much good among the Indians and seek their welfare and best interests in physical and spiritual matters. They should consider themselves lucky that they were with them, should protect them, and not let them out of their hands.

THE 6TH   Our Brothers and Sisters finished clearing and planting. They did this communally, planting the fields one after the other, because we saw that it was difficult and was going slowly, and also for the sake of the old and weak. In this way they all received assistance.

THE 8TH   We heard that another party of warriors including some *Munsee* had gone out to murder. It is feared that if peace cannot be negotiated with the *Nations* now, there could be a real Indian war. May the Savior prevent this.[985]

THE 9TH   After the early service, which Brother *Edwards* held, there

984. See entry for 19 May 1777.

985. Reacting to increasing Indian attacks, the commanding officers of the militias of the frontier counties had sent a petition to the Continental Congress in which they requested that the army take over the forts and that an experienced general be appointed for the region. This petition resulted on 10 April 1777 in the appointment of Brigadier General Edward Hand (1744–1802), an Irishman and a physician by profession, as commander of Fort Pitt. Between 1768 and 1772 Hand had been stationed at Fort Pitt as an officer of the 8th Royal Irish Regiment. On 1 June 1777 he arrived at Fort Pitt and initiated preparations for the improvement of the military protection of the settlements.

was a Helpers' Conference. An Indian from *Goschgosching* had asked to live here a long time ago and he received permission to do so, along with his wife. We informed them of our congregational rules. *Joseph Peepi* is now preaching in *Goschgosching* on Sundays. Even so, the Indians from there do attend our services as much as ever. When he got there he asked to attend our Holy Communion, but we could not allow him to do this.[986]

THE 11TH OF JUNE   A couple of Sisters from *Gnadenhütten* came here on business. They had almost been caught by a party of warriors yesterday evening. They ran quickly, because they heard their death screams, and they reached *Goschgosching*. The warriors passed by there this morning; it was *Wyandot* and they had a *Scalp*.[987] Some of our Sisters had also seen another party like this close by yesterday, marching toward the *Settlements*. They are trying to keep the peace negotiations from taking place and therefore are starting to commit more murders than ever before.

THE 13TH   We received a packet of news reports from *Europe* and *Bethlehem,* along with letters from our dear Brother *Matthao.* This brought us much joy and was very interesting.

THE 14TH   Brother *David* went to the *Council* in *Goschgosching. White Eye* had returned there from the *Fort* yesterday with a *Speech* from Mr. *Morgan.* He *communicated* this to them along with an *Invitation* to a *Treaty* in *Pittsburgh* that is supposed to take place at the end of this month. This will also be sent to the rest of the *Nations.*[988] Our Meeting House, which was begun 4 days ago, was finished today. It is built in the Indian style but is still spacious enough, and we held the first sermon in it on THE 15TH. *White Eye, Gelelemind,* and many others from *Goschgosching* came for this and the *Meeting Hall* was completely filled with attentive listeners. *White Eye* told Sister *Gertraud,* his close friend,[989] I have not yet forgotten what you once told me in *Schönbrunn.* I am glad to hear this, answered the Sister and she said, I am still concerned that you will let your eternal salvation slip away, because you always go to the *Fort* and *Philadelphia* on other business and forget to think about your spiritual salvation. You do not hear anything about the Savior and receive no nourishment for your heart, and a person can die at any time. *White Eye* answered, I think about that often, and sometimes I feel very badly because of this. However, my external *Affairs* prevent me, and I cannot free myself of these yet,

986. See note 981 to entry for 27 May 1777.

987. On 7 June Thomas McClearly was surprised and killed while fishing in the Wheeling Creek in Wheeling. *FDO,* 5–6; *PA,* 1st ser., 5:445.

988. *FDO,* 6. The message concerned those negotiations with the Wyandot that had been planned for a couple of months. See note 977 to entry for 22 May 1777 and also entry for 16 June 1777 and note 990.

989. Gertraud had come from Gekelemukpechünk; on 20 January 1771 she had been baptized in Langundoutenünk (MAB, B 137, F 2). At that time she had been a widow and was accompanied by grandchildren.

because if I withdrew from them now, great unhappiness and danger could come upon us and many people. When there is peace again, which I am now using all my powers to bring about, then I will rest and become a Believer.

THE 16TH   Some of the Helpers went to *Goschgosching* and took the *Chiefs* there a good amount of *Wampum* they had gathered here as a contribution to the upcoming peace negotiations with the *Nations*. They gratefully acknowledged and accepted this.[990]

We have had to cancel the evening devotions for some time because we did not have a place. Since we now have a Meeting House, we began our Singing Service here in the evening again. The Savior laid a special blessing on these and they are sweet and satisfying for the Brothers and Sisters.

THE 18TH   We received a letter from Brother *William Henry* in *Lancaster*, dispatched by *General Hand*.[991] We were comforted to learn from this that the Brothers have commended our Mission on the *Muskingum* to him and to his *Protection*. The *Shawnee Chief*[992] came here with quite a large number of his people on their journey to the *Fort* and they spent the night. He asked how things looked here and what we have heard from the *Fort*, and he was very happy to hear that things were peaceful and quiet here. He said that they heard and saw nothing but war at their place. 2 days ago, before they had left home, a party of *Minque*, *Wyandot*, and *Shawnee* warriors, along with others, had marched through their place with 8 white prisoners and 20 horses they had stolen, and were going to *Detroit*.

They had asked about *Isaac* and he welcomed them, provided them with hospitality, and told them that we usually had services in the evening and the morning. Any of them who wanted to go would be welcome. When they went to *Goschgosching* in the morning, they would find things different, because there was dancing there but not here. They were very quiet and orderly, and many attended the services. Their *Chief* told his good friend *Welapachtschiechen* that the *Minque* were really planning to begin a war against the *Delaware* in the spring,[993] and that they had come to them about this and had asked them for help because the *Delaware* were on the side of the White people and would not

990. The Wyandot had announced in their message (see entry for 19 May 1777) their imminent arrival at Goschachgünk, where they intended to conclude a peace treaty with the "Colonies." In conjunction with the missionaries and some Christian Indians, the chiefs had tried to have these negotiations transferred to Fort Pitt (see note 977 to entry for 22 May 1777). This was the reason for White Eyes' journey to Fort Pitt, where he had gotten Morgan's consent for the transfer of the negotiation. On 14 June 1777 he had returned with an official invitation to the Delaware to participate in such a congress at the end of June 1777 at Fort Pitt. On July 7 the Wyandot's message arrived, stating their refusal to participate in negotiations at Fort Pitt. In the final analysis, the plans for these negotiations failed as a consequence of the congress at Fort Detroit. See entry for 5 July 1777 and note 1003.

991. See note 158 to entry for 13 Feb. 1773.

992. Cornstalk, see GD, F 9, I 1b, entry for 24 June 1777.

993. See entries for 14, 16, and 21 March 1777.

fight against them. The *Shawnee*, however, had answered them that they could not and would not fight against their grandfather. Then the *Minque* had gone to the *Wyandot* and proposed the same thing to them. However, they told them that if they did that and began a war with the *Delaware Nation*, they should expect that the 6 *Nations* would all be destroyed because the *Delaware* Nation was not only strong itself, but also had alliances with so many *Nations*.

As a result they abandoned their plans, but they considered with each other and decided that they wanted to incite the *Delaware* and *Shawnee* to fight anyway. They wanted to reach this goal by going to war against the White people until they had lured them into Indian country among the *Delaware* and *Shawnee,* then they would stop and return to their *Nation*.

THE 21ST   After we had Speakings with the Brothers and Sisters yesterday, 56 in number had an unspeakably blessed enjoyment of his Body and Blood in the Holy Communion. One was readmitted. One Brother and one Sister participated for the first time. One watched for the 2nd and one, namely Sister *Conners*,[994] for the first time. Her husband *Richard Conner* had become a participant in the holy Sacrament already in *Schönbrunn*.

With this we conclude our diary, greet all congregations with all our people very cordially and commend ourselves to their faithful remembrance before our dear Savior.

Diary of the Indian Congregation in Lichtenau on the Muskingum from June 22nd until August 5th 1777.[995]

JUNE 22ND   Early in the day we had the Liturgy for Holy Communion and then the sermon about the text, There is therefore now no condemnation to them who are in Christ Jesus etc.[996] The *Shawnee* are staying in *Goschachgünk* for a few days on their way to the *Fort,* and their *Chief* visited us with some of his people and was very friendly. He also visited the Indian Brothers and Sisters in their huts.

THE 23RD   During the Singing Service in the evening we read our congregational rules and reviewed them for all the residents here.

THE 26TH   Several of our people traveled to *Gnadenhütten* to pick up the corn they had left there in the spring. We are hearing all kinds of bad news about the Indians on the *Walhanding* again, and particularly about something similar to a rebellion among the *Munsee.* People fear they might still join the warring party, so *Isaac* went to *Goschachgünk* with *White Eye* and *Gelelemind* to discuss this and make suggestions about how this can be avoided so the *Dela-*

994. Peggy Conner.
995. MAB, B 147, F 3, I 1, fol. 254.
996. Rom. 8:1.

ware Nation would not become involved in the war. As a result a *Councel* was called and everything was discussed peacefully and put aside.

THE 27TH   Two *Shawnee* came here on their return trip from the *Fort*. They had waited for 2 nights in *Goschachgünk* hoping the *Chiefs* might give them a message to take to their *Nation,* but they told us this did not happen. Therefore we arranged for *White Eye* and some people from his *Councel* to come here the next morning to do this.[997]

THE 29TH   In the morning was the sermon and in the afternoon the Children's Service. *Abraham* and a couple of other Brothers went to *Goschach-günk* for a visit. They proclaimed the Savior to some people there who were sick and lame and could not come here for the services, and they found attentive listeners.

July

THE 1ST   Most of the Brothers went a long day's journey from here to boil salt. They must have done without this for a long time because they had not gotten any since last fall.

THE 2ND   There were many things to consider in *Goschachgünk,* so our Indian Brothers were called there. It seems like all the things that have been accomplished and had provided hope that peace could be achieved will come to nothing [page 255a][998] because an incident near *Pittsburgh* has dashed almost all hopes. A party of *Senecas* had gone to the *Fort* and had a conversation or *Councel* there. When they were traveling back home, White people who thought they were hostile Indians shot at them. When that happened, a party of warriors who were lying in wait nearby attacked the White people and killed 3 of them.[999] An *express* messenger brought this news from the *Fort* yesterday, and today 10 more messengers were prepared to go to the *Mingo* and *Wyandot.* Brother *David* wrote to the *Fort*[1000] in the name of the *Chief,* and they immediately sent an *express* messenger there with this. We also used this opportunity to send letters and our diary to Bethlehem.

997. After Cornstalk had spent a number of days at Goschachgünk in negotiations with the chiefs, the Council at Goschachgünk may have seen no reason to send the Shawnee a message; the entry demonstrates, too, how far members of the mission congregations were involved in Council matters.

998. In fols. 251 to 255a of the manuscript are Zeisberger's letters to Matthäus Hehl dated 25 July 1777 and from Schmick to Hehl dated 30 July 1777.

999. Contemporaries kept silent about this incident; it was referred to, if at all, only indirectly (FDO, 85–86, with note, yet obviously dated wrongly by the editors; Heckewelder, *Narrative of the Mission,* 159, also dates the incident incorrectly). See the summary for 21 June 1777, where the warriors are identified as members of the "Pluggy's Gang" (FDO, 15).

1000. Letter not found.

THE 3RD   About 20 warriors, *Mingo* and *Wyandot*, came here and camped across the river from our *Town*. Brothers *David* and *Edward* were out working in the field just then and did not know anything about this. The latter suddenly had a feeling they should go home, and they went right away. Before they got home, 4 warriors came through the fields right where the Brothers had been and approached a couple of Sisters who were not far from there and then came into our *Town*. They were asked where they were going, and they said they were coming to visit us. However, they went to their *Compagnie* across the river soon. Later we heard that a woman who lives outside of *Goschachgünk* had directed these 4 warriors to our fields, gone with them part of the way, and told them that we worked there every day. The warriors themselves had told our Indians this. If we had stayed there just a few minutes longer, we would have seen the outcome of this and found out what they had planned for us. We kept a good watch during the night and they were also up the whole night, but they did not cause any trouble. We soon reported this to *Goschachgünk*. The *Chiefs* invited them to go there the following morning, spoke with them, and tried to stop them. They could not convince them to give up their plan though, and they continued their march to the *Settlements*.

THE 5TH   The messengers who had been sent to the *Mingo* and *Wyandot*, one of whom was our *Isaac*, returned. Not only had they met the previously mentioned warriors and relayed their message to them, but then they met a messenger who was coming from *Detroit*.[1001] From him they got a reliable account of what things are like there now, and therefore they did not need to go on. According to the news they brought, things look very bad and something bad and dangerous is in the works. People say that once again the *Governour* in *Detroit*[1002] presented the *Nations* the *War Belt* with the *Tomhawk* [*sic*] and the *Nations* had accepted it.[1003] The *Wyandot* want to keep their promise to come to *Goschachgünk* soon, but they absolutely refuse to go to *Pittsburgh*.[1004] Supposedly a general Indian war has been in the works secretly for many years among the *Nations* and they are trying hard now to get all the *Nations* to agree to this.[1005] The Savior seated on the throne above will destroy their plan, though.

1001. This refers to John Montour; see following entry.

1002. Henry Hamilton.

1003. On the causes for this congress from 17 to 24 June 1777, see Stevens, "'Placing Proper Persons at their Head.'" On 26 March 1777 Lord Germain had instructed Governor Guy Carleton "that the most vigorous Efforts should be made, and every means employed . . . for crushing the Rebellion & restoring the Constitution." Carleton was to order Hamilton "to assemble as many of the Indians of his District as he conveniently can, and placing proper persons at their Head, . . . employ them in making a Diversion and exciting an alarm upon the frontiers of Virginia and Pennsylvania" (Davies, *Documents of the American Revolution*, 14:51–53). However, this letter reached Hamilton only toward the end of the congress; see Henry Hamilton to Guy Carleton, 15 June 1777, in *WHC*, 12:45–46. A short report on the congress is in *FDO*, 7–13.

1004. See note 990 to entry for 16 June 1777.

1005. On the longevity of these efforts, see note 29 to entry for 6 June 1772.

THE 7TH   In *White Eye's* name, Brother *David* wrote to the *Fort* about this situation and sent this with an *express* messenger.[1006] *John Montour* had returned from *Detroit* and he also came here and told us that it was true that a full-scale Indian war might break out. Now it just depends on how things turn out when the *Wyandot* come here and what the *Delaware Nation* arranges with them. He also told us that he had talked with the *Governour* in *Detroit* about the Brothers here and asked him what would happen to them if there should be a war, because their lives were in danger. He said that he knew them and knew about them, but he could not help them. If they were closer to him he would do what he could to protect them.[1007] He had ordered all the Indians to spare everyone who was innocent and defenseless and only to fight those who are armed.[1008] The Indians do not do this, however, but attack the defenseless first.

THE 8TH   Most of the Indian Brothers were out boiling salt and things were beginning to get tense, so we sent messengers out to call them home.

THE 10TH   A *Councel* was held in *Goschachgünk* about the news from *Detroit,* and Indians from all over had gathered for this in recent days, including many who have joined with the *Mingo* and have worked diligently in recent days trying to incite the people. They have tried to persuade them to move closer to the *Wyandot,* where they would be safe. *White Eye* asked our Indian Brothers to support him and to speak confidently for *Neutrality,* which they did. They decided to remain quiet and wait until the *Wyandot* came, when they would hear more.

THE 12TH   All our Brothers came home from boiling salt. Many had made half a bushel in the eleven days they were gone from home, in addition to their hunting.[1009]

THE 13TH   The sermon in the morning was about what we are like by nature and what we can become through the grace of Jesus Christ. *White Eye, Gelelemind,* and many Indians, including 3 *Cherokees,* had gathered for this. *White Eye* later spoke with the latter about the preaching of the Gospel. He said it was God's will that all Indians should hear and accept God's word and he hoped all the Indians would be willing to do this. *Abraham,* who also came, spoke more with them about this and *White Eye* was his interpreter. They

1006. More details are given in a letter from Zeisberger to George Morgan, *PA,* 1st ser., 5:446–47.

1007. This is the first mention of transferring the missionaries and their Indian congregations closer to Fort Detroit, where they would be under better British protection and supervision.

1008. The protocol of the Detroit congress for 21 June 1777 read: "we desired to make war against men, and not against women or Children, and to forbear to dip their hands in the blood of the two latter." *FDO,* 12.

1009. It is not possible to offer a simple eighteenth-century definition of "bushel." A "bushel" was 35 liters, which probably was the equivalent of 30 to 35 kilograms. A "half bushel may have weighed between 30 and 35 pounds." See Zupko, *Dictionary of English Weights and Measures.*

listened very attentively during this. They came to this area here from their country a year ago and will return there any day now.

THE 15TH   News arrived once again that all the *Nations* on both sides of the *Lake*, all the way down to the *Mississippi*, had joined together to wage war against the *Colonies*. If this were true, then the entire *Delaware Nation* and we would be in danger of being attacked by other *Nations* and we would certainly all be destroyed. The following *Nations* are supposed to have united in this: the *Wyandot, Tawas*,[1010] Chippewa,[1011] Potawatomi,[1012] Twichtwees,[1013] Weas, Kickapoo,[1014] Kaskaskias,[1015] Chicasaw,[1016] and those who share the border with the latter.[1017] A messenger brought this news to the *Chiefs* in *Goschach-günk* yesterday. They were extremely upset about this and hardly know what they should do and how they should proceed to get control of the situation. Our heavenly Father will have to look at this situation and do what is best.

THE 17TH   An Indian who came from *Wabash*[1018] for a visit several days ago came here and asked the Brothers to tell him about the Savior. He himself said he had never heard anything about this in his whole life. He asked lots of questions, because he had heard many bad things about the Brothers

1010. See entry for 17 Sept. 1773 for the report on the visit of the Shawnee, and accompanying note 284.

1011. See entry for 5 June 1772 and note 29.

1012. Synonym for Potawatomi. See Clifton, "Potawatomi."

1013. See entry for 6 Aug. 1774 and note 488.

1014. On the Wewischtano (synonym for Wea) and Kigapa (synonym for Kickapoo), see entry for 22 May 1773 and note 198.

1015. On the Kaskaski (synonym for "Kaskaskia"), a tribe in the Illinois region, see Callender, "Illinois."

1016. On the Chicasaws (synonym for "Chickasaw"), see Gibson, *The Chickasaws.*

1017. In early July 1777, in preparation for Colonel Barry St. Leger's expedition against Fort Stanwix, Colonel John Butler invited the Six Indian Nations and the other northern tribes to a conference in Fort Oswego (*FDO*, 20); see the long report from Colonel Daniel Claus to William Knox, 16 Oct. 1777, *NYCD*, 8:718–23; and for similar negotiations with the southern tribes, see John Stuart to Augustine Prevost, 24 July 1777, Davies, *Documents of the American Revolution*, 14:147–50. From the British perspective, the following picture emerged: among the Six Indian Nations only the Mohawk (thanks to the pro-British activities of chief Joseph Brant; see Kelsay, *Joseph Brant*, 185–213) and parts of the Seneca (Wallace, *Death and Rebirth of the Seneca*, 138–46) were reliable British allies. Out west Hamilton had concluded alliances with all tribes in the Great Lakes and in the Mississippi region, but only with parts of the Shawnee (see Edward Hand to Yasper Yeates, 12 July 1777, *FDO*, 20) and the Delaware (according to Hamilton's own assessment in his letter dated 15 June 1777, cited in note 1003, only a few Shawnee and Delaware had come to Detroit). John Stuart and his agents had successfully concluded alliances with the Creek, Chickasaw, and Choctaw, but not with the Cherokee. This summary shows that the construction of a more or less solid western front with tribes allied with England depended to a large extent on the attitude of the Cherokee, Delaware, and Shawnee. After their heavy defeat in autumn 1776, the Cherokee were firmly tied to the Americans (see entry for 31 Jan. 1777). The Shawnee's relations to the Americans were still bad as a result of Lord Dunmore's war; thus the construction of a solid western front from a British perspective depended almost completely on the Delaware's attitude.

1018. "Wobash," more often "Wabash," was the settlement region of the Kickapoo and Wea; see entry for 22 May 1773 and note 198.

from other Indians. He therefore came to our place to see and hear if it were true. The Indian Brothers gave him a full explanation of everything and told him that the Savior had won our salvation here on earth and for all eternity through his incarnation, sufferings, and death. He could also share in this if he believed in Him. He returned here the following day and had them tell him more. He attended our services and said he saw now that everything he had been told about the Indian Believers was a lie. When he returned to *Wabash* he would tell them differently, because now he had seen and heard it himself.

THE 18TH   Brother *David* was picked up and taken to *Goschachgünk,* where he received a letter from *General Hand* along with a written message to the *Councel,* and he read these aloud to them.[1019] On this occasion we were also extremely happy to receive a packet of congregational news reports from *Europe* and letters from Bethlehem from the month of *September* through the end of last year.

THE 19TH   The 23 warriors mentioned on the 3rd of this month returned from the *Settlements.* When they approached our *Town,* they announced themselves as usual through death cries and then marched very quietly through our *Town* to *Goschachgünk.* They had 3 *Scalps* and 2 girls and one boy as prisoners and 8 horses they had stolen at the same time.[1020] The last time they were in *Goschachgünk* they were told not to come into the *Delaware Towns* here, but to take another road. They continue to come, however.

THE 20TH   *White Eye* and the entire *Councel* came for the sermon, and a crowd of Indians, men and women, came with them. They were also here for the Children's Service in the afternoon. The Savior blessed the services and He revealed himself to us, as the tears on people's cheeks attested. In the afternoon a messenger came and brought *White Eye* the news that the *Wyandot,* whom they had been expecting here for a long time now, were not far away. Then today 20 of them arrived in *Goschachgünk.*[1021] We immediately sent a messenger to *Gnadenhütten* to inform them of this and to tell them that some Brothers should come here for the *Councel.*

THE 21ST   Another party of warriors traveled past here by water, singing their war song.[1022] Some Indian Brothers went into the *Town* to greet the *Wyandot.* They had informed the *Chiefs* immediately upon their arrival there yesterday that they were in a hurry and would like to return home soon. How-

1019. Hand's letter dated 9 July 1777 has not been preserved; Zeisberger's answer dated 29 July 1777 is in *FDO,* 27–29.

1020. On 14 July 1777 Captain John Minor reported to George Morgan that two men and a boy had been killed and that a young woman and two children were missing. The dead were Jacob Farmer and Nathan Wirley; the missing children belonged to Jacob Jones and a daughter of Farmer. The incident occurred close to Fort Stradler. *PA,* 1st ser., 5:444.

1021. See entries for 16 June and 5 July 1777.

1022. In these months reports on Indian attacks multiplied. See *FDO,* 21–24, 33–42; Jefferds, *Captain Matthew Arbuckle,* 83–85.

ever, they offered them the peace pipe to smoke, for 2 days, when the council gathered and they could deliver their message. It seemed that they did not have much good to say. Brothers *Johann Martin* and *Andreas* came from *Gnaden-hütten* to attend the *Councel* in *Goschachgünk*.

When the Brothers had gathered, *Welapachtschiechen* said, Dear Brothers and friends, we are now hearing nothing but horrifying news from everywhere. Therefore let us pray all the more fervently to the Savior to help us through these dangerous times, because we need this now more than ever. I cannot actually count myself among the Believers yet, but I can tell you with my whole heart that I want to live and die with God's people. Where the Brothers remain, there I will also remain. Whatever happens to them will also happen to me. I will consider it a great grace to conclude my life with them. And if I do not attain the grace of being baptized, then at least people will be able to say this about me one day, *Welapachtschiechen* lies buried there. Although he could not be baptized, he still remained with the congregation until his end. After this confession, his wife *Rachel* felt at peace about him, because she still had doubts about whether he would remain with the congregation. She had often said, If my husband leaves the congregation, I cannot possibly go with him. I would not be able to endure it.

THE 22ND   The *Wyandot* presented what they had been sent to say in the council. In brief, the message was this: All the *Nations* on both the far side and this side of the *Lake*[1023] had accepted the *War Belt* from the *Governour* in *Detroit* and had united as one man to wage war against the *Colonies*. Therefore they wanted to know what their *Cousins* the *Delaware* would do. Then the *Chief* from *Sandusky*[1024] pulled out the *War Belt* and handed it to them. He suggested that they should move closer to them since there was war and it would be dangerous for the *Delaware*. They would prepare a place for them. The *Chiefs* promised to give them an answer the following day. Then they separated and considered what the best thing to do was. We laid this situation before the Savior and asked Him to guide the matter and the hearts of the *Chiefs* so that everything would go as He wanted it to. We drew a Watchword for this occasion which said, For my salvation is near to come, and my righteousness to be revealed.[1025] May the Savior soon fulfill this in us.

THE 23RD   Today was the day when the *Delaware Nation* was to make a decision about its *Resolution*. For our part, we had done as much as we could to prevent danger. The *Chiefs* and *Captains* (because the latter have precedence in *Affairs* of war) were all in agreement not to accept the *War Belt*. Therefore

---

1023. Zeisberger means "of the Great Lakes," i.e., Lakes Erie and Michigan.

1024. In his report on the arrival of the Wyandot and the negotiations with them and the resolves of the Council on 29 July 1777 to General Edward Hand, David Zeisberger names Half King as the chief who accompanied the Wyandot. *FDO*, 27–29.

1025. Isa. 56:1.

they returned this answer today and told the *Wyandot* they could not grant their request because at the peace agreement after the last war they had promised not to fight against the White people ever again as long as the sun shone and the water flowed.[1026] However, the *Wyandot* were not satisfied with this answer. They tried to force the *Belt* on them and to force the *Delaware* into going to war.[1027] Therefore we can only expect that this area will be swarming with warriors soon after the *Wyandot* have returned home. The following day in *Goschachgünk* they gathered all their people after the *Wyandot* were gone and ordered them not to allow themselves to be misguided; they would take no part in the war. Everyone promised this. It is good that they are in agreement and the people support the *Chiefs.* We hope it might continue like this.

THE 25TH   Brothers *Johann Martin* and *Andreas* returned to *Gnadenhütten* and some of our Brothers and Sisters also went there on business. Toward evening there was the burial of the blessed Sister *Verona,* a widow who died yesterday, and many Indians from *Goschachgünk* came for this. She came to the congregation in the beginning of *July* 1774. The occasion for this was that the White people had attacked a *Mingo Town* on the *Ohio* where she and her husband and children had just arrived, and they killed many of them. They saved themselves by fleeing, however, and came to *Gekelemukpechünk.* From there she and her husband, who was a great enemy of the Gospel, visited in *Schönbrunn.* Both were soon convinced in their hearts that the word of Jesus' death and sufferings is truth and life, because it had proved itself in their hearts. They returned home, but could find no more peace. In a few days they came back and asked for permission to come to the congregation, which they received. That same month her husband was baptized with the name *Seth,* and in *September* of last year, 1776, he died in blessing in *Schönbrunn.* She was baptized by Brother *Jungmann* on *December* 25th, 1774 and attained the enjoyment of Holy Communion on *September* 30, 1775. After her baptism she lived a blessed life and her heart was firmly attached to the Savior and the congregation. Last winter she was so weak that we expected her homegoing. She longed for this and said that nothing else stood in her way. However, this spring she came here with the Brothers and Sisters from *Schönbrunn,* and was very happy and grateful for this. She then lived in blessed anticipation of her release, which took place on the previously reported day. She leaves behind a married daughter in the congregation, as well as her mother.

THE 26TH   *Welapachtschiechen* came to *Goschachgünk* and was taken in by his friends. They spoke very seriously with him about going to the congregation and leaving all his friends. They even went so far as to threaten him with death. *Newollike,* who has been staying in *Goschachgünk* for a number of days

---

1026. This refers to the peace treaty after Pontiac's Rebellion of May 1765; see note 538 to entry for 5 Nov. 1774.

1027. In almost identical words Zeisberger reports this resolve in his letter to General Edward Hand, dated 29 July 1777; see note 1024 to entry for 22 July 1777.

now and prejudiced his friends against the Brothers, caused this. It annoys him that *Welapachtschiechen,* who is a *Chief,* is with the congregation while it did not work out with *him,* since he also wants to be a *Chief.*[1028] Until now they have tried to get him away from here through compliments and nice talk. Since this has not worked, they are trying to use threats to scare him into leaving. Neither has had any effect on him, however, except that he is all the more firmly committed to his intention of remaining with the congregation. Then on THE 27TH *Isaac* went with him to see his friends in the *Town.* They had just gathered when they found them and an Indian named *Gulpikamen.*[1029] He is a real enemy of the Gospel and was preaching to them that he had heard the *Quakers, Presbyterians* and also the Brothers, and had lived with the latter for a time. He thus knew that there was nothing to the whole matter and it was not at all for the Indians. Therefore he had turned back to what he had always heard from his ancestors. *Isaac,* who could hardly wait until he had finished talking, replied, I am glad I have come at just the right time, as if I had been called. Let me hear what you know and what your ancestors taught you. I would also like to know this and perhaps I have not heard it yet. When I know something good and especially something through which people can be saved, I am happy to let everyone know about it. I am not satisfied to know it myself, but I also want others to know it. You do the same and let me hear. I will observe it and examine it. He stood up right away and went into the house and told *Isaac* he did not want to say anything to him. *Isaac* then preached to those who were gathered about the Savior, his merits and sufferings, which alone could save them. He told them that nothing else could be found anywhere that saved people, except for Jesus Christ's blood, which was shed for their sins and the sins of the whole world.

THE 29TH Some *Shawnee,* friends of *Peggy Conner,* came here for a visit. We were somewhat concerned about this at first, because they live among the *Mingo* and are not very well disposed toward the White people. We could only presume they came to pick her up. Her Brother, who is a *Shawnee Captain* and was along in the company, had come through here just recently with a party of warriors and had prisoners with him.[1030]

THE 30TH About 20–30 warriors, including some French and English, went from *Detroit* to *Goschachgünk,* where they spent the night. They did not come here but marched to the *Fort* in the *Settlements*[1031] the next day.

THE 31ST During the early service we considered the beautiful Watchword, The Lord is round about his people from henceforth even for

1028. On Newollike, see entries for 11, 16, and 21 March 1777.

1029. On Gulpikamen, baptized Ludwig, see entries for 31 May and 25 June 1773.

1030. On Peggy Conner, see entry for 4 May 1775. Peggy Conner, a white prisoner, had been adopted into the family of the Shawnee chief; she was not his blood sister. The chief's visit demonstrates that adoption created very close bonds; see entry for 31 July 1777.

1031. See John Gibson to General Edward Hand, 1 Aug. 1777, FDO, 35–36.

ever.[1032] This comforting promise was very relevant to our circumstances. May He surround us so that no enemy can come in and protect us with his wings. We presume the *Shawnee Captain* did not come here without reason, but is planning to get his sister *Peggy Conner,* so the Brothers spoke with him and forestalled him before he made a demand. This worked well and he replied that he had indeed come with the *Intention* of picking her up because times were so dangerous now and he feared he would someday see his sister taken away as a prisoner, which he would not like. He had also heard much about us, and so he came here to see for himself. However, since he had been here all of his concerns had left him. He was very happy that she was here and he did not want to take her away. He had also seen that we were his friends, and when he went home he would tell the *Mingo* and warriors he saw not to harm us, because his friends lived here. He also wanted to turn away the warriors if possible so that they did not come here to our place as much.

[August]

AUGUST 1ST   Brother *Jungmann* led the early service. The *Shawnee Captain, Peggy Connor's* brother, and his company returned home today. They had faithfully attended our services during the days they were here and our Brothers had also spoken a great deal with them. They were very satisfied and promised to visit us again. They hoped that when peace was restored the Brothers would establish a *Settlement* in *Assünnünk* so that the Gospel would also reach the *Shawnee.* When they left, they told *Peggy* that there would be more bad times. They could not yet say when or what it would be, but when it happened we would realize and remember what he had told us. Therefore *Welapachtschiechen* went to *Goschachgünk* early on THE 2ND, where he spent the night and asked him more about what he meant by this and what he had wanted to say. He replied that they were in danger from the other *Nations* because of the great *War Belt*[1033] which had come from the 6 *Nations* and which all the *Nations* except the *Delaware* had accepted. He promised he would let us know quickly if he heard anything about evil plans against us.

After we had Speakings with the Brothers and Sisters, we had a blessed Holy Communion today, during which the Savior revealed himself to us especially closely and blessed us inexpressibly. A Brother named *Ephraim,* who is blind, participated in this high grace for the first time. Sister *Conner* watched for the 2nd time and *Susanna Minque* for the first time. The latter was so ill that she could not stand up. However, when Sister *Jungmann* brought to her

---

1032. Ps. 125:2, from the Collection of Watchwords for the year 1771. On 7 August 1777 Zeisberger noted in the diary that they would now use the Watchwords for the year 1771; see entry for 1 Jan. 1777.

1033. See entries for 22 and 23 July 1777.

the news that she could watch during Holy Communion for the first time and then told her that she would not be able to go to the Meeting Hall because she was so weak, she answered, Yes, that it is what I really long for. She stood up, came to the Meeting Hall, and was healthy from then on.

THE 3RD   The Liturgy for Holy Communion was read early in the day and then we had the sermon. In the afternoon the baptized Brothers and Sisters had a blessed service.

THE 4TH   A party of *Wyandot* returned from the war. They had lost their *Captain,* who was killed. Another party of 17 men went to the *Settlements.* Their *Captain* and some men came into our house here on THE 5TH, greeted us cordially, and shook all of our hands. We learned from them that many more would follow in a couple of days.[1034]

The *Councellors* in *Goschachgünk* sent word that things are beginning to get dangerous, so we should consider what would be best for the White Brothers and Sisters and their safety. We went there with the Helper Brothers and talked with them first about this and learned what they thought, and we then sent a couple of Brothers to discuss this further with the *Counsellors.* We White Brothers and Sisters considered what we should do about Brother and Sister *Jungmann,* who have surrendered themselves completely to the Savior's pleasure, either to hold out here or to go to the congregation according to His will. We looked to our dear Lord to advise us according to his heart, and He instructed us[1035] to take Brother and Sister *Jungmann* away from here and to safety in these dangerous circumstances. We were very sorry about losing this Brother and Sister. We do not want to lose them, but we also surrendered ourselves to the Savior's will and were happy to allow them their happiness of going to rest in the congregation once again after 7 years.[1036] We soon reported this to our Helpers' *Conference.* In their hearts they also agreed with this, because they realize it is the best and safest thing for them. We made preparations for them to depart as soon as possible.

Diary of Lichtenau *from* August 6 *until* September 23, 1777[1037]

AUGUST 6TH   After Brother and Sister *Jungmann* had prepared for their departure, the congregation gathered and blessed them for their journey. We prayed that the Savior and the dear angels might accompany them and bring them safely to their destination. They left from *Gnadenhütten* this eve-

---

1034. For reports on the attacks in the first half of August, see *FDO,* 33–42
1035. The formula means that the lot was drawn.
1036. This is the second missionary couple, after the Roth family, who left the congregations because of the dangers of the times. The Roths had returned to Bethlehem on 27 May 1775.
1037. MAB, B 147, F 4, I 1, fol. 393.

ning, accompanied by 5 Indian Brothers. The departure was emotional and touching and our tears accompanied them.

THE 7TH   Brother *Edward* led the early service about the Watchword, Put thou my tears into thy bottle: are they not in thy book?[1038] [Note: because we are not receiving Watchwords from Bethlehem, we are using the ones from the year 1771].[1039] In this situation we can do nothing but pray, cry, wonder what else will happen, and look faithfully to him to see how He will glorify His people among the heathen and miraculously preserve them and save them. Soon afterward we received news from *Goschachgünk* that about 100 warriors will come here today or tomorrow and another party of 100 men, who have taken another road, would presumably go through *Gnadenhütten*. All of them and those who are ahead will meet and go to the *Fort* in *Wilünk*.[1040] We immediately sent a messenger to *Gnadenhütten* with the news, so our Indian Brothers and Sisters gathered and considered how they could get food together for so many warriors and how they might assist those in *Goschachgünk*. There is nothing better to do here than to choke the ignorance of foolish people with good deeds. You could see the willingness of the Brothers and Sisters to give everything joyfully if it would help rescue and keep their teachers. They immediately got 5 oxen and 10 pigs together, which will be slaughtered for the warriors if this is needed. They can expect nothing in return for these.

THE 8TH   We had just gathered with the Helper Brothers in the morning when news came from *Goschachgünk* that a large party of warriors had arrived there, so the Brothers took the food they had prepared there. Brother *Schmick* sent a messenger from *Gnadenhütten* and we learned that Brother and Sister *Jungmann* had arrived there safely. We were even happier about this because we were worried about them since the bush is really swarming with warriors, and a party had come along the road at just the time they were going to *Gnadenhütten*. They had 4 *Scalps* and a prisoner, and from the news we had received, we did not think they could have avoided meeting them.

We had already talked with our Helper Brothers in recent days about the best and safest thing to do for the security of the White Brothers and Sisters under these circumstances, if we were flooded with so many warriors. We decided to deliver a *Speech* to the *Wyandot Captains* about this. Our Brothers had also talked with the leaders in *Goschachgünk* about this yesterday and informed them of our intention. However, they replied that they had no orders to do this. *White Eye* and *Gelelemind* were not at home and they were just stationed as watchmen to keep the young people from getting involved in the war. They

1038. Ps. 56:8.
1039. *Die täglichen Loosungen der Brüder-Gemeine für das Jahr 1771.*
1040. Their aim was Fort Henry in Wheeling. According to a note from Joseph Doddridge, Zeisberger informed General Edward Hand of the intentions of the Wyandot; Hand immediately ordered that Colonel David Shepherd strengthen Fort Henry. FDO, 46–48, 50–51, 54–58.

were not given the authority to negotiate *Affairs* with anyone. However, we told them that our Brothers would deliver the *Speech* themselves, and that we had informed them about it before and received their full approval and *Isaac* would be the speaker. They were very happy then and we were very glad about this.

Our Brothers asked and found out that the *Half King* and one of the most important *Wyandot Captains* were there, and our Brothers presented the following talk to the *Capitains* when they had gathered. The leaders from *Goschachgünk* were also present during this, Uncles, we your *Cousins,* the Indian Believers here in *Lichtenau* and *Gnadenhütten,* are happy that we have the chance to see you and speak with you. We want to cleanse your eyes of all the dust and whatever the wind may have blown into them, so that you can look at your *Cousins* with clear eyes and a cheerful face. We want to cleanse your ears and your heart of all evil and bad rumours that an evil wind may have blown into your ears, indeed even into your heart, during your journey here so that our words may enter into your ears and find a place in your hearts. Then a *String of Wampum* was offered and *Isaac* continued and said, Uncles, hear the words of the Indian Believers, your *Cousins* here in *Lichtenau* and *Gnadenhütten*. We herewith inform you that we accepted God's word more than 30 years ago, and therefore hold our meetings in the morning and evening every day. Know also that our teachers are here with us. They instruct our children and us in the word and in lessons. From God's word, which our teachers proclaim, we learn to live in peace with all people and to live with everyone in friendship, because God has commanded us to do so. Therefore we are a peace-loving people. Our teachers are not only our friends; we consider them our own flesh and blood and love them as such. Since we are your *Cousins,* our request and desire of you, *Uncles,* is that you also consider our teachers part of your own body and as your *Cousins,* because we are one body with them and cannot be separated from them. What you do to them, you do to us, whether it is good or harmful.[1041] Then a white *String* with a number of Klafters of *Wampum* was presented. Because we were saying this to warriors, who came with the hatchet in their hands, we thought it best to speak as briefly as possible. Everything is implied in the sentence that we are a peace-loving people. They can see and interpret this adequately if they want to, because their character has already been taken by the spirit of war and murder.

As soon as *Isaac* had finished talking, the *Half King* and highest *Captain* replied: My *Cousins,* Indian Believers. I am very happy to hear these words from you. They have reached my ears and entered into my heart. Just have a little patience until I have reported this to my *Warriors* and have spoken with them.

1041. In Native American terminology, Isaac told the Wyandot that the converted Indians had adopted their teachers and that they were therefore no longer whites but Native Americans. The far-reaching consequences of adoption are demonstrated by the Shawnee chief's attitude toward Peggy Conner; see entry for 29 July 1777.

Then I will give you my answer. He immediately called his warriors together, informed them of this, and addressed them. They responded to every sentence with a loud expression of satisfaction. During this the Brothers and everyone else was also allowed to listen. After they had considered together for a while, he gave the following answer, My *Cousins,* I am very glad and I am very happy that you have cleansed my eyes, ears, and my heart of all the evil the wind had blown in during this journey, because the journey I am on is not a common one. I am a man of war and am going to war. Therefore many things come over me and many bad thoughts go through my head and probably also into my heart. I am happy that my eyes are now bright and I can look at my *Cousins* with clear eyes. I am happy that I can listen to my *Cousins* with open ears and can take their words to heart. Then he offered a *String of Wampum* and continued, *Cousins,* you have informed me that you accepted God's word and have daily meetings and teachers at your place who instruct you and your children about God and his word, and that therefore you want to live in peace and friendship with all people. We are very glad to hear this. Stick with this. Do not allow yourselves to be disturbed in this; obey your teachers; they will only tell you good things about God, and do not worry at all that any harm will come to them. No one should hurt them. Hold your worship services and do not get involved in other affairs. You see that we are going to war now, but you should remain completely quiet and calm and do not think much about it. *Cousins,* we also have our teacher across the *Lake.* We call him our father and also hold our meetings where we hear about God. I hereby inform you that from now on I will view your teachers just as I view my father across the *Lake,* indeed as my own body.[1042] I will inform all the warriors I meet of this, and when I return home all the *Nations* will hear what we have agreed and decided together. I will come to you tomorrow, see my father, greet him and shake his hand.

He gave a *String of Wampum* after this talk.

While the Brothers were in *Goschachgünk,* we sent many sighs to the Savior, Oh, help us Lord! Let everything work out well. The Brothers had agreed that they would send one Brother ahead before the *Wyandot* had completely finished talking, to bring us the news quickly of whether things looked good or bad, and they did this. If things had turned out badly, we expected they might come soon and capture us or that we would have to flee.

The Lord did this and brought all of our Brothers and Sisters and us great joy, so that our hearts were moved to praise and honor Him for this according to our Watchword for today which says: Sing aloud unto God our strength: make a joyful noise unto the God of Jacob. Praise, honor and glory be brought to our Lamb of God, through whom we were elected.[1043]

1042. See note 855 to entry for 12 Nov. 1776.
1043. Ps. 81:1, "Preiss, Ehr und Macht, sey unserm Gottes Lamm gebracht, in der wir sind erwehlet," *Das kleine Brüder-Gesang-Buch* (1772), hymn no. 2000.

THE 9TH   Brother *Edward* led the early service about the Watchword, Thou shalt call me, My father.[1044] At noon the *Half King* and captain of the warriors came here with 82 men. First the handshaking ceremony was conducted. This took place in the schoolhouse, where Brothers *David* and *Edward* went for this purpose. *Half King* began, then the *Captains* followed, and then the whole *Compagnie* according to their rank. They shook hands with Brothers *David* and *Edward* and greeted them very cordially. This lasted a good while. When this was over, the *Capitains* and some others, 17 in all, remained in the school house with us and *Half King* told the Indian Brothers who were present and us that they were happy to see their father, with whom they had now shaken hands. From this day on they would acknowledge us and consider us their father, and we should also consider them our children and not allow anything to disturb us in this or be worried. This should last into eternity. He would also inform all the *Nations* of what had taken place here today. Without a doubt they would be happy about this too. Brother *David* replied that we were also glad to see our children, to greet them, and to shake hands with them. From this day on we would consider them our children. There would be no change in this on our part. We would not let ourselves become unsure about this; it would remain so. Then the *Captains* ate with some Brothers and us under a canopy of branches where food was served. The other warriors settled down in the shade at the other end of the *Town,* because there was not room for so many where they were being served. They all had plenty to eat because the Brothers had slaughtered a fat ox for them. Each person took food with him when they returned to *Goschachgünk* toward evening, and they were very satisfied. Before they left we told them that tomorrow was Sunday, when we had our services, and no one worked on that day.

THE 10TH   We gratefully held our Sunday services in undisturbed peace. In the afternoon a messenger brought us a letter from Brother *Schmick* in *Gnadenhütten.* We learned from this and also heard in person that Brother and Sister *Schmick* had already left for the *Fort* yesterday. We cannot describe how this made us feel. We had already spent many sleepless nights over it. There is no danger from elsewhere as there was several days ago and we can stop worrying about this now. However, it was still painful to think about these circumstances. We held all the more closely to the Savior, who is and will remain our comfort, guide, and assurance. Otherwise we have none.[1045]

THE 12TH   Warriors attended the early service both yesterday and today. Among others there was a White man who was born in *Philadelphia* and is now going to the war.[1046] Brother *David* had to bleed some of those who

1044. Jer. 3:19.

1045. After the return of the missionary couple Schmick to Bethlehem, only Zeisberger and Edwards were left to live with the converted Indians.

1046. This was probably a prisoner who had been adopted into the tribe while still a child and who had thus totally assimilated the traditions, language, and style of Native American life. On the problems related to the "white Savage," see note 633 to entry for 4 May 1775.

were ill, as they had requested. Another 50 men arrived in *Goschachgünk* today, and a party including 5 Frenchmen returned from the war with 2 *Scalps*. That was all they had stolen on the long, life-threatening journey, and they were half starved. There are already about 170 warriors here, and our house is full of them every day. They are all very orderly and polite, however, and treat us as friends.

THE 13TH   After the early service *Half King* arrived here with a party and informed our Brothers that they will set out from *Goschachgünk* tomorrow, march through here and then continue on. He thanked the Brothers warmly for all the kindness they had shown them and all the goodness they had enjoyed from us, and said they would not forget this. The Brothers reminded him of his promise to take another road when they returned and not come here, and explained to him that if the White people followed them, they would come into our *Town,* putting our women, children, and us into danger. He said they would not come back this way if they could help it. However, hunger would force them to come into our *Towns* no matter where we lived. If they were being followed by White people, they would hastily send a messenger in advance to warn us so that we could retreat for a short time. Quite a large party of *Mingo* from *Kinhanshican*[1047] who had arrived yesterday came here as well. Many of them knew Brother *David* very well and our house was full of them. They were all very polite and were very friendly toward us.

THE 14TH   Before the early service, *Half King* came here with his interpreter and first informed the Indian Brothers that they would not march away today because messengers had brought news yesterday evening that more warriors were joining them and they would wait for them. Then he came to us and said that he had written home and across the *Lake* both to the *Gouverneur* in *Detroit* and to the *Wyandot Chiefs* through a Frenchman and had reported to them what things were like here and how well we had received them, and that they had not lacked anything. He also reported what he had agreed and concluded with us, that they had accepted us White Brothers as their father and from now on would acknowledge us as such; they should inform all *Warriors* and all the *Nations* of this as soon as possible so that no harm comes to the Brothers here. He then said he had talked with the *Mingo* as soon as they had arrived in *Goschachgünk* and informed them of what they had agreed among themselves about us. They were very satisfied with this, accepted this, and rejoiced over it. Therefore we should be very peaceful and hold our meetings without disturbance. If warriors came here they would greet us cordially and consider us their friends. We should just give them something to eat if they were hungry, because this is why they came here. Finally he told us that he did not come here out of enmity against us White people, that they were now going to war. It was not their intention to do much harm, but they were

1047. See entry for 14 March 1777 and note 930.

required to do this and they were only doing it as a favor to the *Gouverneur* in *Detroit.* They hoped it would not last long and would soon be over.[1048]

THE 15TH   *Michael* returned from *Gnadenhütten.* Our *Conference* had sent him yesterday as a messenger to ask the Brothers and Sisters there for help supplying *Provisions* to the many people who are here, because our Brothers and Sisters are already quite exhausted. They were willing to do this and a couple of *Canows* loaded with Indian corn and meat were sent down that same night. They delivered this to *Half King,* who did not know how to express his gratitude adequately for this. He informed members of his *Council* that *White Eye* and *Gelelemind* were expected from the *Fort* any day now, so they had decided to wait here until they heard news from the *Fort.* Overall it seemed like they had not yet decided for sure what they would do.

Many different *Nations* and languages are gathering here now, *Tawas, Chippewa, Wyandot, Mingo* of all kinds, *Shawnee, Abenakis,* French, and *Potawatomi.*[1049] The latter come from far across the *Lakes* and we can consider it a *Direction* from the Savior that *Half King* is there. He orders all of them not to commit any *Excesses,* and if he were not here things would be chaotic and there would be no control. He asked the Brothers if his people behaved in an orderly fashion when they came into our *Town.* They told him that we had no complaints and were very satisfied with them. He said he was glad to hear this; they preferred to come to us and they did not visit anyone in *Goschachgünk.* Some *Mingo* had gone into the fields and taken some things from there and had also killed a pig. *Half King* got news of this and immediately ordered the *Mingo Captain* to keep his people in line better and not to rob or steal anything at all here. They had no reason to do this because they had been provided with plenty to eat. The *Wyandot* themselves told us that it was the *Tawas'* custom not to leave a single head of cattle, not even a dog, alive wherever they went, because they eat them.[1050] They take small children from the streets and the

1048. Half King's message illustrates the dilemma of Zeisberger and the mission congregation. For Half King believed that the mission congregations maintained strict neutrality; from this perspective the congregations were nothing but provisioning stations. From the point of view of the Americans, such a function designated the congregations pro-British support bases. The complete honesty with which Half King shared his plans with Zeisberger suggests that he did not suspect that Zeisberger would communicate the Wyandot's intentions to the American side. Zeisberger, on the other hand, believed he had no choice if he wanted to avoid sharing responsibility for the death of the settlers. It probably did not occur to him that his actions made him responsible, too, for the death of Wyandot warriors.

1049. For Zeisberger the "Woaponos" were Abenakis, who in the course of the eighteenth century had migrated from Maine to the region of Quebec (Snow, "Eastern Abenaki," 143–44). "Putawatamen" is a synonym for "Potawatomi." For these and the other tribes, see entry for 15 July 1777.

1050. Next to deer, dogs were an important meat source for the Huron (Heidenreich, "Huron," 382). The Huron probably introduced the Tawa (i.e., Ottawa) to the custom of eating dog meat; in any case, after the collapse of the tribe considerable numbers of Huron joined the Tawa, with whom they had maintained close contacts. See Cleland, *Rites of Conquest,* chap. 4. In 1830 Ottawa not only owned dogs but ate dog meat, too. Feest and Feest, "Ottawa," 781.

Indians then have to ransom them and buy them back. They said they were not allowed to do things like this now, however, since they were in their *Compagnie.*

THE 16TH   In the early service we read the Watchword and reminded the Brothers and Sisters not to forget to thank the Savior for the many acts of kindness and obvious protection, which exceeded all of our expectations, and to praise and honor Him for this.[1051]

THE 17TH   In the morning was the sermon and in the afternoon the Children's Service. The latter was about the text for today, Out of the mouth of babes and sucklings thou hast perfected praise.[1052] During this we admonished them to praise the Savior with heart and voice and to sing Him songs of praise and thanksgiving for all the goodness He shows us every day. Yesterday and today, warriors from various *Nations* visited us and attended our services. Many of them who had not seen us before came to visit us and to greet their father. Currently there are 250 warriors in *Goschachgünk.* If they stay much longer they will eat us out of house and home. They do not seem to be in much of a hurry to go to the *Settlements,* much less to have a battle with the White people. If they turned back it would be worth the trouble of entertaining them for so long. During this time the *Mingo* have been very impatient about staying here longer. They wanted to go on, but *Half King* did not let them go and told them, You just want to go kill innocent women and children. This is no honor; it will bring shame to you. And because I know this about you, you will not go alone.

An Indian who had brought *Rum* to *Goschachgünk* from the *Fort* several days ago worried us because we could foresee the danger if so many warriors got drunk. The trouble would be complete and the result would be murder and death among many *Nations.* Because the *Chiefs* were not at home, we did our best to prevent this, and the Savior helped us to succeed.[1053]

THE 18TH   Some Shawnee came here who told us that they were still quiet and peaceful and that none of them had gone to war yet.[1054] However, 80 warriors from various *Nations* were going to the *Canhawa.* We had always heard in recent days that there were 800 of them, which shows that most of the warriors come here to this area.

THE 19TH   *Half King* and a party of his people came here very early in the day to stop the 2 *Shawnee* who had spent the night here and wanted to go to the *Fort.* They did this because he did not want White people to get news of their plan.

1051. This was the Watchword from the Collection of Watchwords for 1771 (see entry for 7 Aug. 1777); the text of the day was Ps. 70:5

1052. Matt. 21:16.

1053. On the missionaries' attitude toward rum, see entry for 5 June 1776.

1054. Zeisberger knew that this message referred only to those settlements from which the person who brought the information came—in this case the settlements on the Scioto River that adhered to the neutralist policies of Cornstalk. On the attitude and policies of the Shawnee during the American Revolution, see in general Calloway, "'We have always been the frontier.'"

402   THE MORAVIAN MISSION DIARIES OF DAVID ZEISBERGER

In the evening our Brothers who had accompanied Brother and Sister *Jung-mann* to the *Fort* returned from there. We were happy to hear that they and Brother and Sister *Schmick* arrived there safely. In addition to receiving a letter from *Mr. Morgan*,[1055] we were very delighted to receive letters from Brother *Matthao* in *Litiz* and the Watchword Register through the end of *September*,[1056] as well as a letter from Brother *Sydrich*[1057] in *Philadelphia*.

THE 20TH   We had a very anxious day. More than 200 warriors came here from *Goschachgünk* to beg for tobacco and *provisions*. They danced through the whole *Town* going from house to house for this, as is their custom, and each person had to give them something. The Brothers went to meet them and informed them that we do not like to see such *Ceremonies* in our *Town*. We would give them enough to eat without doing this, and we would also collect some tobacco for them. They would not be deterred, however, because there were too many of them, and they danced circles around the *Town*. In the meantime we White Brothers had the house full of *Wyandot* and *Mingo*. Otherwise, everything went well and after they had completed their business they returned very quietly. They did not want to take anything by force or to steal it. Our house is full every day because they do not like to go anywhere else as well as here, but they have not stolen from us at all or taken anything secretly. If they wanted something, they asked for it. During the night we were scared by a blind commotion, when news came that everyone in *Goschachgünk* was drunk because a lot of *Rum* had been brought there from the *Fort* today. We sent messengers there to see if this was true, and we were reassured when we heard that *Half King* had sharply forbidden all the warriors from drinking anything, which they obeyed.

THE 21ST   *Whyte Eye* [sic] arrived yesterday and had already told the latest news from the *Fort* yesterday evening, most importantly that they were expecting a large army in Indian country soon.[1058] After the early service this morning they passed through here and camped in the bush at the end of our *Town,* where they finally spent the night because they were waiting for a party of *Wyandot,* who were returning from the war, so they could hear what was new. As a result, this was another very anxious day for us, since the *Town* was full of warriors. They did not harm us at all or cause any particular distur-

1055. We were unable to trace this letter.

1056. In the register of the Watchwords, only the place in the Bible, not the specific verse for each day, is given.

1057. Daniel Sydrich was born in 1727 in Frankfurt am Main; he came to North America in 1750, where he was assigned parishes at various places but most often in Philadelphia. He died in Lititz on 22 May 1790. Hamilton, "Ettwein," 133n7.

1058. At the end of July or in early August 1777, White Eyes went to Fort Pitt to inform the commanding officer and George Morgan about Half King's visit and the negotiations between them (see entries for 22 and 23 July 1777); White Eyes probably took with him Zeisberger's letter to Edward Hand dated 29 July 1777 (see note 1024 to entry for 22 July 1777). In response to the increasing attacks Hand decided around 10 August to organize an expedition "into the Indian Country," to quote his letter to Colonel William Fleming dated 12 Aug. 1777 (FDO, 42–43).

bances, except that they were swarming around us. Our greatest concern and fear was just that they might start drinking here. Brothers *Nathanael* and *Marcus* came from *Gnadenhütten* and the following day more from there came in *Canows* with provisions for the warriors.

THE 22ND   When we woke up very early in the morning we thanked the Savior with happy hearts and mouths for the peaceful and completely undisturbed night He had mercifully granted us. Even though we had more than 200 warriors camping here, it was as quiet the whole night as if we were completely alone, and you did not realize they were there. We even held our early service as usual, and a crowd of the warriors attended this and listened attentively. This morning a party returned from the *Settlements*. They had not done anything, though. The White people had attacked them and they did not stand against them so they were all chased away from each other and one of them was very badly wounded. Therefore 250 warriors left here this afternoon and marched to the river. We spoke with our Helpers from here and *Gnadenhütten,* some of whom were here, and encouraged them to be faithful servants of the Gospel and to join us in keeping the word of Jesus' death and sufferings. Above all, however, to let love, *harmony,* and unity of spirit prevail between the two places. The Savior added His blessing to this and graciously revealed Himself to us. The Brothers all expressed themselves so contritely and emotionally that we were able to rejoice over them sincerely and to take new courage and comfort. At the same time we also informed them that Brother *Edward* would go to *Gnadenhütten* with the Brothers now and stay with them, and they were very glad to hear this.[1059]

Until now we had not been waiting as much for the departure of all the warriors as for the return of the Brothers from the *Fort.* We had not heard anything from there in a long time.

THE 23RD   Brother *Edward* held the early service, and then he traveled to *Gnadenhütten* escorted by Brothers *Nathanael* and *Marcus.* We had said farewell yesterday evening and promised together in the Cup of Covenant[1060] to continue the Savior's work in one spirit and mind, despite all danger and future difficulties, until we see Him face to face. Today many warriors went after those who had marched off yesterday and we had another anxious and difficult day because of the drunken *Mingo.* So much *Rum* has arrived from the *Fort* that all the Indians in the whole area around us are drunk. Satan is loose and is raging more than a little. However, the Savior mercifully helped us escape this turmoil and granted us a peaceful day on THE 24TH, so that we were able to hold our Sunday services without being disturbed and the Brothers and Sisters were able to recover physically and spiritually. We cannot adequately thank the Savior

1059. After the return of the couple Schmick to Bethlehem, Gnadenhütten was without missionaries; Edwards was meant to fill this void.

1060. The formula means that Zeisberger and Edwards celebrated Holy Communion together; see Heb. 9:15 and 12:24.

for this. A false rumor was spread that the *Virginians* were marching and had already been seen at the little *Beaver Creek*.[1061] All the *Mingo* and many others, more than 100 warriors, returned here. They went home to take their women and children to safety because they feared an attack.[1062] Therefore only 140 of them went to the river and there is hope that not much will become of their *expedition.*

THE 25TH   Our Brothers were called to *Goschachgünk* for a *Councel,* where *White Eye* once again seriously admonished the people and warned the Indians tribe by tribe to remain quiet and not to go to war against the White people. He told them to prepare themselves now and keep their weapons ready so that they could defend themselves if they were attacked, because they still feared an attack by other *Nations.* He would give the signal first, however, and would place himself at their head. We hope it will not come to this, but believe *White Eye* is doing this out of politeness to keep the young people from going to war. We have clear enough indications that the *Mingo* have agreed to attack the *Delaware* and our *Towns.* At the same time, however, it is apparent that all of their suggestions are accompanied by much fear. We have heard that they are afraid to do anything against 4 Brothers here in *Lichtenau.* One *Mingo* Indian advised *Agnes, Isaac's* wife who is a *Mingo,* to leave with her husband and children because she was not safe here. We have heard the same thing from many people, and some even say that we will be attacked when the warriors return from the *Settlements.*

THE 26TH   We had a Helpers' *Conference* about the walk and spiritual lives of our Brothers and Sisters, as well as the situation mentioned above. There is constantly talk about the *Delaware Nation* being attacked, and some Brothers think the *Chiefs* might require us to take up arms then. Brother *David* replied that we are not going to war against anyone. We would leave everything and go away before anyone could get us to do this.[1063] If we feared an attack, we would keep a good watch. Generally it was useless to think about this too much in advance and to deliberate about it. The best and safest thing was to put our hope and trust in the Lord, to fix our eyes on Him, and to trust in Him as children that he would protect us from this and not let things get that far. The Brothers agreed with this absolutely and their hearts were in complete agreement.

1061. From the Little Beaver Creek Lichtenau was a two-and-a-half-day journey.

1062. This rumor is probably connected with the preparations for an expedition (see note 1058 to entry for 21 Aug 1777) against Pluggy's Town and the Wyandot settlements. Edward Hand had named these settlements in a letter to Jasper Yeates dated 25 Aug. 1777 (*FDO*, 48–49), in which he confessed: "the situation of the Delawares embarraces me much. I wish to preserve their friendship, how to do this & keep small parties in the Indian Country, (A measure I wish to Adopt) & steer Clear of the Delawares I cant tell." The difficulty stemmed from the Delaware's decision to follow the example of the Six Indian Nations and refuse the American army permission to cross their territory.

1063. On the pacifism of the Moravians, see circular dated 6 May 1775, Ettwain's comments in Hamilton, "Ettwein," 150–52, and Weinlick, "Moravians and the American Revolution," 3.

THE 28TH   *Gelelemind* sent word here from *Goschachgünk* asking Brother *David* if he thought it would be good to write a letter to the *Gouverneur* in *Detroit* and to inform him about the expenditures and costs the warriors had caused here, and also to ask if he would compensate them for this since he had sent them. However, Brother *David* declined this and suggested it would be better to do this in person through Indians. He was satisfied with this.

THE 29TH   In heart and mind, I was with my choir-relatives in the Unity. I let the Prince of our choir absolve, bless, and anoint me, and I gave myself to Him anew to serve Him and to belong to Him.

THE 31ST   *White Eye* and a party of Indians from *Goschachgünk* attended the sermon. In the afternoon the widows and widowers had a service for their festival day today, and the Savior mercifully revealed himself during this.

September

THE 2ND   Some of our Brothers had to come to *Goschachgünk* for the *Councel,* where they arranged to send a message to the *Wyandot* across the *Lake* once again so that this could be resolved and they could then await their fate.

The *Tawas* sent a message asking if it were true that the *Delaware* had accepted the *War-Belt.* When they heard the opposite, they promised to follow the example of their grandfather and not to go to war.[1064] I received a letter from Brother *Edward* in *Gnadenhütten* in which he reported that some Brothers and Sisters there are very sick, but that things there are peaceful for now, as they are here. We acknowledge this with much gratitude to the Savior and accept it from His hand.

THE 3RD   The early service was about the Watchword, Is there a God beside me? I know not any.[1065] Nor do we want to know of any other Savior besides the crucified Jesus, who is our only comfort, help, and assurance in all our troubles.

THE 5TH   A party of warriors returned and we heard that the 140 warriors had met the White people, and one of the *Wyandot* was killed. They transported by water some who were badly wounded.[1066] Finally Indians

---

1064. This message proved to be wrong; see entry for 17 Oct. 1778.

1065. Isa. 44:8. We could not locate this Watchword in any of the collections for the years 1772–77. Although Zeisberger noted in his entry for 19 Aug. 1777 that the Watchword registers for the time up to September 1777 had arrived, since early September he nevertheless used Watchwords not found in the Collection of Watchwords for 1777. Since we were unable to locate his Watchwords in any of the other collections, it is unclear to which Watchwords and texts Zeisberger is referring.

1066. This engagement was part of the effort to conquer Fort Henry; see next entry and note 1069 to entry for 7 Sept. 1777.

brought some goods here from *Sandusky*[1067] so that our Brothers and Sisters were able to get some clothing again.

THE 7TH   The married Brothers and Sisters had a blessed service for their festival today. *White Eye* had asked to attend this as well, and we permitted this.

A party of about 100 warriors returned with 11 *Scalps*. They had attacked the *Fort* in *Wilünk*[1068] and as far as they knew they had killed 14 men and collected a lot of loot from the houses they had plundered around the *Fort*. However, they could not do anything more at the *Fort*.[1069]

THE 8TH   Another party of warriors arrived with 6 *Scalps*. In the evening the *Communicants* were told that Holy Communion would be held next Saturday in a separate service.

THE 10TH   In the early service we considered the Watchword, Ho, every one that thirsteth, come ye to the waters etc., about the saving fountain of Jesus' 5 wounds, the source of all of our salvation.[1070] Soon afterward another party of warriors passed through here with 2 *Scalps* and a boy they had captured. We must watch all of this with sorrowful eyes, and yet we cannot change it. Our sincere hope and prayer to the Savior is that He would look upon this and put an end to the trouble soon. The *Wyandot Half King*, who came up with the wounded by water, came with the *Captains* to visit me and was happy to see me again.

THE 12TH   The past few days and today have been very anxious because of the warriors who fill the *Town* every day. During the Speakings with the Brothers and Sisters for Holy Communion, I was humbled to find them in a contrite, blessed relationship with the Savior. The difficult and desperate external circumstances affecting us now cause them to hold even more closely to the Savior, to take their refuge in him and seek comfort and help from Him. Late in the night I was called to *Goschachgünk*. Messengers from the *Fort* had arrived at the *Councel* there with a written message from *Mr. Morgan* and *General Hand*, which I *communicated* to them. It sounded good and was consistent with all the previous *Speeches* delivered to the Indians.[1071] What the messengers

1067. Since it was too dangerous for white Indian traders to travel and trade in this region, Indians had taken over this function.

1068. Wheeling, Fort Henry is meant; see next note.

1069. About two hundred Wyandot commanded by Half King had attacked Fort Henry on 1 September. Although forewarned by General Hand, who had heard of the intention to attack the fort from either Zeisberger or White Eyes during the latter's visit to Fort Pitt in early August, the officers of the fort had remained unconcerned. After the Wyandot had laid siege to the fort for two days and killed all the cattle in the vicinity, they gave up and retreated. The number of whites killed fluctuates between fourteen (FDO, 84) and twenty-one (Sosin, *Revolutionary Frontier*, 111). For reports of the siege, see FDO, 54–68, 72–73.

1070. Isa. 55:1. On the importance of Christ's wounds in Moravian theology, see Introduction, pp. 54–55.

1071. On 6 September 1777 both Morgan and Hand wrote to the Delaware that they should remain peaceful and not listen to bad people who wanted to lure them into the war (National Archives Microfilm 247, reel 180, I 163, fol. 293–94).

told us in person, however, was really horrifying. Another General had arrived in *Pittsburg*. He would not *Pardon* any Indian, friend or foe, but wanted to eradicate all of them. *Morgan* had told them secretly that they should defend themselves now and fight as well as they could and do their best, because they would die whether they fought or not. I encouraged *White Eye* and the *Councel* not to believe all of this right away, but first to try to get to the bottom of the matter, and I reminded them of all the previous *Speeches* from *Morgan* and showed them how this message was in harmony with those. I received no reply, however, but was astonished the next morning to hear that *White Eye* had burned the *Speech* publicly soon after I left, and he had summoned the young people to war that very evening. He had also told the *Wyandot* who were all still there that they should stay now and help them fight, because they had started the war. The messengers had also brought along word that the *Virginians* would be in *Goschachgünk* in a few days. This led to new confusion, fear, and horror.[1072] During the night *White Eye* sent messengers to *Gnadenhütten*, *Kaskaskunk*, *Cayahaga* etc. to inform the Indians about all of this and to call them all to gather here.

THE 13TH   We considered what we should do if the *Delaware* go to war, as it now seems likely. We thought we needed to hear something from our Brothers and Sisters in *Gnadenhütten* first, and we were expecting someone from there today. Therefore we did not decide anything further until we received news from there. This happened, and we heard that they were already leaving to come down here. In the meantime, we informed our Brothers and Sisters that we would stay together as much as possible if we had to leave in a hurry. We strictly forbade anyone who lives with us, whether baptized or not, from getting involved in fighting if it should come to that. Anyone who did this should immediately take his family and children away and not stay here anymore. We informed all the Brothers and Sisters and residents about this. In the evening 53 of us had a contrite and blessed Holy Communion in undisturbed peace, and during this inexpressibly blessed enjoyment we forgot all the wretchedness of life and all external dangers from outside. The Brothers and Sisters received new strength through this, and gathered new courage and trust in the Savior. We could see this in them the following days, and many could not adequately describe how mercifully the Savior had revealed himself in their hearts.

THE 14TH   Early in the day we prayed the *Liturgy* for *Communion* followed by the sermon. In the afternoon was the Children's Service, and in the evening the Congregational Service, all held in the peace of Jesus Christ. In the evening after all the services, we met with the Brothers and considered *White Eye's* actions and behavior, since he attached more importance to what the messengers said in person than to what *Morgan* and *General Hand* had sent to

1072. It is likely that these messages were planted by people in sympathy with England. There were at the time at least three men—Alexander McKee, Simon Girty, and Matthew Elliott—staying at Fort Pitt who were especially experienced in dealing with Native Americans. The messages proved wrong.

them in writing. We decided that a couple of wise Brothers should go to *Goschachgünk* with *Welapachtschiechen* to present our thoughts and see if they could not change *White Eye's* mind. Brothers *Wilhelm* and *Isaac* went to *Goschachgünk* with *Welapachtschiechen* during the night, and returned after midnight. We were comforted to learn that their statements had been well received. *White Eye* promised to consider our suggestion, and we thanked the Savior for this.

THE 15TH   *White Eye* himself came here, spoke with some Brothers, approved our *Proposition,* and resolved to send a message to the *Fort. Josua* came from *Gnadenhütten* to stay here for now. We learned from him that Brother *Edwards* [sic] would leave there with the Brothers and Sisters today and travel down here.

THE 16TH   In the early service we read the Watchword and text,[1073] and noted that we always want to try to do the Savior's will and to fulfill it, and not to go our own way and make room for our own spirit, which gets us into dangerous and unhappy situations. Many *Wyandot* and *Mingo* visitors came once again today.

THE 17TH   During the early service the Brothers and Sisters were admonished to endure and remain steadfast through all the danger and distress we are going to experience from elsewhere now, and to follow the example of the Savior, who remained steadfast in His sufferings in order to bring about our eternal redemption. He kept his courage until He had carried out and completed everything. In the morning we received news that the *Virginians* were marching toward *Goschachgünk.*[1074] In recent days we had posted a night watchman a distance from the *Town.* Trouble was starting again now and everyone was anxious and afraid. Many of the Indians in *Goschachgünk* were fleeing and many of the *Wyandot* had left. Parties were sent out everywhere people thought they might come, as far as the river,[1075] to get definite news about the situation. *Welapachtschiechen* insisted that Brother *David* write a letter that they would try to get to the *Virginians* in *Wilünk,*[1076] informing them that the *Delaware* had not yet taken up the hatchet and did not want to have a war. We heard that a party of White people was coming here to the *Delaware Towns,* so we asked them to take another road. If they would do this, we would always remain their friends. We agreed among ourselves where we would all meet if we had to take refuge, and the Brothers designated a site up the *Walhanding.*[1077] In the meantime, our Brothers and Sisters got ready to leave. I did this as well, and I burned most of my papers and kept only what was really indispensable.

1073. We do not know which Watchwords and texts Zeisberger referred to.
1074. See entry for 17 Sept. 1777; the message was wrong.
1075. Read: Ohio River.
1076. Wheeling.
1077. During Lord Dunmore's war, the region around Walhanding Creek had been designated an area to retreat to in case of danger; see entries for 3 and 11 July 1774.

My heart sank when I looked at everything in our household, since I had almost no time to get these things to safety. The best thing now was to have nothing except what was on our backs. I have enough to do with the Brothers and Sisters and should not bother with physical things. May the Savior have mercy on us and look upon our need and our distress. May he not abandon us, but help us and save us for the sake of His mercy, not because of our worthiness. Amen.

Late this evening, about midnight, some of the watchmen we had sent a couple of miles from the *Town* came running home with news that the *Virginians* were marching here and were not far away. All the Brothers and Sisters went to the river[1078] immediately and put their things, as many as they could grab in a hurry, into the *Canows*.[1079] With the help of the Brothers and Sisters, I carried my most important things to the *Canow*. However, most of the household items and all of the equipment remained behind. I did little to care for my physical needs, because I did not take along anything at all to eat. We traveled in the *Canow* to *Walhanding,* and some went by land. We got there a while before daybreak and stayed until morning, because everyone thought the fighting would begin at daybreak. The residents of *Goschachgünk* were all armed with the *Wyandot* and were just waiting for the attack. However, before it was really light, *White Eye* sent an express messenger with the happy news that it was all just rumors. During the night he himself had gone to the place where the *Virginians* were supposed to be, and lo and behold, it had just been a herd of wild horses at the *Like*.[1080] People from *Goschachgünk* had taken all their women and children across the river and only the men had stayed in the *Town*. We camped a little while up on the *Walhanding* and I went and visited the Brothers and Sisters from *Gnadenhütten,* who were camping very close to us. Our Brothers and Sisters visited them and they visited us. In the afternoon *White Eye, Winginund,* and some of the other *Counsellors* came to visit us. They were very pleased to see such a camp of Brothers and Sisters. As soon as we had arrived there during the night *White Eye* dutifully sent us word that we should only worry about the safety of our women and children and ourselves, and just take care of that. They would fight, and not once did it occur to them that we should help them. We would like to have returned home this morning, but we spent today, THE 18TH, there to make things more pleasant for the Brothers and Sisters and so they could visit each other. We all returned to *Lichtenau* in the morning on THE 19TH, after Brother *David* had once again visited those from *Gnadenhütten* and spoken with the Brothers of the *Conference.*

1078. Meaning Muskingum.

1079. In H3: "At once I threw the diary for Schönbrunn into the fire and brought with assistance from brothers and sisters."

1080. Zeisberger is referring to the Salt Licks "not far" from Schönbrunn, already mentioned in his entry for 7 July 1774, where on that date deer had triggered a similar alarm in the middle of the night.

A few Brothers had stayed in *Town* to keep watch. This turned out to be a small change of scenery and more of a pleasure trip than an escape. However, a whole crowd of Indians, mostly women and children, had immediately moved to where we were. The Watchword yesterday said, For I will contend with him that contendeth with thee, and I will save thy children. and the one for today said, I have seen his ways, and will heal him and restore comforts unto him and to his mourners.[1081]

THE 20TH   Brothers *Johann Martin* and *Marcus* came here with *White Eye* to discuss what we could do. The latter would like to have seen us all stay together in one place, but those from *Gnadenhütten* had no desire to do this. They preferred to live separately until we saw more clearly what times would be like. Brother *Edward* came here for a visit and spent the night.

White Eye spoke with Brother *David*, because *Communication* with *Pittsburgh* has now been completely blocked[1082] and they considered how we could manage[1083] to get a letter to the *Fort*. We also wanted to get news of what things were like there so that we did not have to be in constant fear of the White people. I wanted to get a letter to Bethlehem on this occasion as well, so our Brothers and Sisters would have some news from us. Unfortunately, no Indian can get there safely anymore. Therefore we wondered if Brother *Conner* could perhaps go there, escorted by one or several Indians. There were problems with this as well, though.

THE 21ST   We had our Sunday services as usual and thanked the Savior for the calm we are enjoying. Many of our Brothers and Sisters from *Gnadenhütten* came here for a visit. We had a *Conference* with the Helper-Brothers and discussed our escape further. We have already had a trial run, and we wanted to consider what needed to be done differently if we had to flee again.

THE 22ND   Very early in the day *White Eye* came here to talk to me again about sending a message to the *Fort*. I put this in writing and addressed it, along with a letter to *General Hand* in the *Fort*. The messengers were supposed to leave with these right away,[1084] but they were delayed until almost

1081. Isa 49:25 and 57:18.

1082. On 17 September 1777 Edward Hand confirmed in writing his earlier oral message to the Delaware that in these very dangerous circumstances the Delaware should refrain from sending Indian messengers to the fort. Both sides knew what was meant: the general and his officers, faced with enraged white settlers, could not guarantee the security of Native Americans friendly to the American side. *FDO*, 86–88.

1083. See Introduction, p. 23.

1084. Zeisberger to General Edward Hand, 22 Sept. 1777, *FDO*, 93–95. The text in the diary paraphrases the letter closely. Zeisberger omits, however, that he added to the letter the last information he had received about the movements and intentions of the English at Fort Detroit. The same day White Eyes wrote to the Continental Congress and reminded them about the agreements, demanded the continuation of the correspondence with George Morgan (because he trusted him), and added: "We made out with one another, that if any Army should march in the Indian Country it should take its march above & below our Towns that our Women & Children might remain quiet & not be too much frightened, which I hope you will remember and order it to be done according to our agreement" (*FDO*, 95–97).

evening because 2 White people arrived from the *Fort* as *express* messengers.[1085] Their news released us immediately from all our fear and worries, because we heard now that we have absolutely nothing to fear from the White people. This was also adequately expressed in the written message, and we were delighted and comforted. During the night Brother *David* was called to *Goschach-günk* to communicate this message from *Mr. Morgan* to them, as well as one from *General Hand,* who informed the Indians how *Affairs* were in the country down below.[1086] *Mr. Morgan* commended the White Brothers who are still here to the special care and protection of the Indians so that they would not be harmed, because they had been sent by God. When Brother *David* returned home around midnight with the Brothers who had escorted him to *Goschach-günk,* he found most of the Brothers and Sisters already prepared to leave again. They had heard that White people had arrived and concluded from this that an army would not be far away. Therefore we immediately called all the Brothers and Sisters together and delighted them with the good news, and then they all went happily to bed. We heard nothing among the Brothers and Sisters but praise and thanks to the Savior, who so miraculously helps us out of all of our troubles.

THE 23RD   After the early service Brother *David* had to go back to *Goschachgünk,* where *White Eye* and the *Counsellors* talked to him about what they should write and report to the *Fort.*[1087]

Dear Brothers and Sisters, the Lord has helped us thus far and we trust in Him as children to continue to guide us, protect us, and bring us in blessing through all difficulties and dangers. We are comforted by your prayers and remembrance before the Savior and join our Indian people in greeting all the congregations most sincerely.

Diary *of* Lichtenau *on the* Muskingum *From* September 24th 1777 *until* March 10, 1778[1088]

SEPTEMBER 24TH   I sent letters to Bethlehem with the two White people who had come here from the *Fort* as *express* messengers, and also to *Mr. Morgan* and *General Hand* in *Pittsburgh.* I had already written to the latter the

1085. The name of one of the two messengers is given as James Elliott in Edward Hand's letter dated 17 Sept. 1777, mentioned in note 1082 to entry for 20 Sept. 1777.

1086. In his letter dated 18 Sept. 1777, Morgan assured the Delaware that he would support their cause in the Continental Congress. The Delaware should convince their young people to remain peaceful and care for Zeisberger. In addition to Morgan's letter the messenger brought the letter from General Edward Hand mentioned in note 1082 and a letter from the governor of Virginia; they are printed in *FDO,* 88–92.

1087. H3: "In the early hour Brother David went to Goschachgünk." On the same day White Eyes confirmed that he had received the letter dated 18 Sept. (see note 1086) and reported that they were suffering from the Wyandot's ridicule yet hoped that friendship could be continued. The same day Zeisberger wrote General Edward Hand essentially the same good news about the attitudes of the western tribes that had arrived in Goschachgünk and added information about the state of defense of Fort Detroit. *FDO,* 100–103.

1088. MAB, B 147, F 5, I 1, fol. 278b.

day before yesterday, before the messengers had arrived, and explained why Brother *Edwards* and I are staying here; we had heard that 400 *Virginians* were coming to the *Delaware Towns* and would destroy them and we could not leave our Indians, much less watch the work of the Brothers among them be destroyed. The work has continued and been blessed for so many years despite numerous dangers and difficulties, and this would be destroyed if we left them alone. Therefore we were determined to endure everything with them and commended ourselves and our Indians to his *Protection*. We would stay with them as long as the *Delaware Nation* remained peaceful, as they had done unwaveringly until now. However, if we saw that they were going to war we would separate from them, as we had already agreed. The messengers also told us that on Sundays people in the churches in the country, primarily those not far from *Pittsburgh*, were praying for the Christian Indians on the *Ohio*. They personally had heard this numerous times and they said they believed this was now common in the entire country down there.[1089]

A White man from *Detroit*[1090] who came here several days ago spoke with me. He said that the White Brothers had nothing to fear from the warriors now. The discussion and agreement between *Half King* and the *Wyandot* and the Indian Believers was known far and wide among the *Nations* and they knew that they had accepted the Brothers as their father. The *Governour* in *Detroit* also knew it and this man assured me that if we got into trouble with our Indians or if we no longer felt safe here, the *Governor* would protect us if we put ourselves under his *Protection*. We would find enough food if we fled and had to leave all our food behind, because there was an abundance of *Provisions* in *Detroit*.[1091] Parties of warriors continue passing through here going to the *Settlements,* and in recent days more than 50 have passed through here.

THE 25TH   Very early, even before daybreak, the messengers returned to the *Fort* escorted by two Indian Brothers and two men from *Goschachgünk;* others accompanied them as far as *Gnadenhütten. White Eye* was going along to *Gnadenhütten* and I asked him to entrust the packet of letters to an Indian for protection if they met warriors along the way, so that it would not fall into their hands. Last night *White Eye* had a serious argument with some *Tawas* in *Goschachgünk* who wanted to get the 2 White people and take them to *De-*

1089. From "The messengers also" not in H3.

1090. It was Edward Hazle (or Hazel); see Henry Hamilton to Sir Guy Carleton, 25 April 1778, *FDO,* 284. Hamilton describes Hazle in another letter as "a very spirited young fellow, . . . trusty & I hope by good behavior will deserve to be put on a good footing," *FDO,* 274; see also the short biographical note at 275n31. In his letter to General Edward Hand dated 23 Sept. 1777, Zeisberger states distinctly that the white man "doth not choose to have his Name mentioned" (*FDO,* 103).

1091. In his letter dated 22 Sept. 1777, mentioned in note 1084 above, Zeisberger does not mention these assurances of Detroit's governor. Yet the letter contains detailed information about Fort Pitt as well as the news that in anticipation of the American army the British fort had received considerable reinforcements and was preparing for a siege.

troit.[1092] Brother *David* visited the Brothers and Sisters from *Gnadenhütten* on the other side of *Goschachgünk* and talked with them. They decided to return to *Gnadenhütten* but to leave some people who were weak and sickly here in *Lichtenau*. *Gelelemind* sent word to the Indian Brothers in both places that they should watch their teachers well, because the *Tawas* were angry that they had not gotten the 2 messengers from the *Fort*. People are afraid they might make the Brothers pay for this.

THE 26TH   *Isaac* returned from escorting the messengers to *Gnadenhütten*. *White Eye* had sent him back and while he was returning yesterday he met a party of warriors who had set out after the messengers from the *Fort*. It was evening and he saw that they were setting up their night camp, so he continued on his way. After he had considered the matter thoroughly, he returned during the night, reached the warriors at day break, and delivered a message in the name of *Welapachtschiechen* that they should abandon their plan to pursue the messengers. He told them he would not leave them until they had promised to obey, which they then did. They told him very directly that they were on their way to catch the 2 people, but after hearing the message from *Welapachtschiechen* they would do what he had told them. They sent him word that he could trust them not to pursue them further. I was worried not only about the messengers, but also about the letters, and I hope they reach the *Fort* safely.

THE 27TH   Brother *David* had to go to *Goschachgünk*, where he had to *communicate* the most recently received news to some *Shawnee* and Indians who had come from *Beaver Creek*.[1093] They had come to find out how things looked. At the same time we learned that the *Delaware* in *Cayahaga* are also starting to go to war.[1094] This is increasing and is also spreading among the *Delaware*. Some men from *Goschachgünk* have gone to war already.[1095] *White Eye* and the *Chiefs* are being worn down and do not have any real power anymore. Still, *Welapachtschiechen* makes great efforts to keep a hold on the residents of *Goschachgünk*.

THE 28TH   We had very blessed and happy Sunday services and we were so happy and grateful to the Savior for the peace He has given us for a while now.

THE 29TH   *White Eye* and *Gelelemind* came here with the above-mentioned *Shawnee* and joined the Brothers in preparing a message to the *Shawnee*, admonishing them to stand firm, and not to be persuaded to join in the war.

1092. This message contradicts what Zeisberger wrote in his letter to General Edward Hand on 22 Sept. 1777 (see note 1084): that Half King had informed White Eyes that the Twightees had refused acceptance of the war belt sent by the governor of Detroit. Zeisberger described this message as reliable, which underlines that these could be read as first indications that the alliances among tribes on the British side were showing signs of strain.

1093. Today called Beaver River.

1094. The Delaware of this settlement resolved shortly thereafter to move closer to the main settlement of Goschachgünk; see entry for 18 Feb. 1778.

1095. From "This is increasing" bracketed in another hand, not in H2 or H3.

THE 30TH   The Brothers and Sisters from *Gnadenhütten* returned there, but some families decided to stay here in *Lichtenau*. Others left their things stored here and want to wait and see what will happen. In the early service we comforted each other with our dear Savior's promise, according to today's text. He has promised to remain with us every day until the end of the world.[1096] We encouraged the Brothers and Sisters to ask the Savior for this every day. We thus concluded this month with praise and thanksgiving to the Lord for all the protection, kindness, and faithfulness He has shown us during this month as well, when He guided us so well and covered us with his wings. We want to continue allowing Him to do as He pleases, because He arranges everything so beautifully, beyond all our expectations, merits, and worthiness. We have also finished our Watchwords and texts and we ask our dear Lord to provide more for us soon.

October

THE 2ND   Some *Wyandot* from *Half King's Compagnie* came here as heralds to announce their arrival. We heard then that they had another battle with White people near *Wilünk*.[1097]

THE 4TH   He personally came with the entire *Compagnie,* which consisted of about 100 men, and he and his *Captains* visited me. My children are doing very badly, because they have killed another 27 White men. One *Wyandot* was killed and some were wounded and had to be carried the whole way. We gave them food to eat because they were very hungry. Then they went to *Goschachgünk,* but *Half King* camped with the wounded above the river. There was also a White man from *Detroit* with them. When Brother *David* asked him why he had gone to war in this manner, which brought him no honor, he replied that he had been forced to do so.[1098]

THE 5TH   *Half King* and a party of his men visited me and requested fresh food for his sick and wounded men. We provided this and he was very grateful. He also bought a couple of oxen for his people and promised to pay for them with goods. Since I had the opportunity, I informed him that the *Mingo* had stolen my horse in the spring and I told him where it was, because I had gotten news about this along with 2 others from our *Town.* He promised that not only would I get my horse back, but the others as well. They would not be lost because he would not allow the children to steal from their father.

1096. Matt. 28:20.

1097. Wheeling. On 26 September 1777 the companies of Captain William Foreman and Captain Joseph Ogle were ambushed in the vicinity of Fort Henry. They suffered heavy losses. *FDO,* 106–12.

1098. From "when Brother" bracketed in another hand, not in H2 or H3.

We held our Sunday services as usual, although a crowd of warriors was there. They did not cause us any further disturbances, and many of them attended the services and were attentive.

THE 6TH   *Half King* and all of his men marched out of this area to return home. We were very happy about this and grateful to the Savior, because there has not been a day free of warriors since he arrived here on the 8th of *August.* We hope it will never be like that again. From *Gnadenhütten* Brother *Edward* informed me that they had returned there safely, that the Brothers and Sisters were busy harvesting their fields, and that their houses had not been as badly plundered as they had imagined.

THE 7TH   We are now free from warriors again and we give the Savior many thousands of thanks for this. Since we can return to our usual routine, we began clearing things here out again. First we sent away a crowd of bad rabble who always like to come during such times. Some of them have left the congregation, and they were chased away like chaff in the wind. Recently some of our Brothers went a few miles from here to where the pigeons sleep. There are extraordinary numbers of them there, and they brought home many horse loads of them. They beat them to death in the night, and the pigeon droppings in that area are deeper than your shoes.[1099]

THE 8TH   A messenger returned from *Detroit.* The *Chiefs* had sent a message to the *Governor* there some time ago and asked him why he had sent the hatchet to the *Delaware*[1100] to use against the Americans. The messengers returned with the reply that he had no knowledge of the hatchet being sent to the *Delaware.* It must have come from somewhere else. He had indeed given it to the *Wyandot* because they had already asked him for this a number of times. However, he had told them not to cross the *Ohio,* but to keep watch on this side. If the *Virginians* came across, they should let him know immediately.

THE 9TH   The two Brothers returned from the *Fort* where they had escorted the 2 White people. All the news we received from *Mr. Morgan* and *General*[1101] was very good and positive for the *Delaware Nation* and for us. *Morgan* again proposed building them a *Fort* in their country for their safety if they wanted it, and putting a *Garrison* in it so they would not need to fear the other *Nations.*[1102] The *General* also sent us news of how *Affairs* down in the

1099. *Ectopistes migratorius* L. Mahr, "Delaware Terms for Plants and Animals," 21.

1100. See entry for 23 July 1777. On 22 July the Wyandot officially notified the Delaware that they had received the war belt from the governor of Detroit; the following day the Delaware refused the belt. The decision to send a delegation to Detroit to ascertain whether the Wyandot were bringing the war belt to the Delaware in the name of the governor of Detroit must have been made during that session.

1101. The words "and General" bracketed in another hand, missing in H3. For "General," read General Edward Hand.

1102. George Morgan to the Delaware, 1 Oct. 1777 (*FDO,* 117–18). On the same day Morgan dispatched another message to the chiefs, in which he sketched a speech he wanted the Delaware to deliver in front of the governor and the tribes assembled (*FDO,* 115–16).

country were going and about the victory the *Americans* had won, and he reassured the Indians that peace would soon be restored.[1103]

I have sensed something very ominous in Indian *Affairs* since the recent commotion here about an attack on the White people, and I have reason to believe there was something to the matter. Time will tell. We have all the more reason to thank our heavenly Father for keeping great misfortune from us when he allowed us to convince *White Eye* and the *Councellors* in *Goschachgünk* to abandon their plans. And although some people from *Goschachgünk* had gone to war, we were able to do enough that this was stopped and *White Eye* recognizes his mistake. Even on the night when he gave his people freedom to go to war and told them they could go that very night if they wanted to, he remembered us White Brothers and said that if they went to war against the White people they had to emphasize to all the Indians, no matter who they were, not to touch them or do them any harm because they should be considered their own flesh and blood and be protected.[1104]

THE 12TH   A number of people from *Goschachgünk* had come for the sermon, which was about the wedding garment of Christ's blood and righteousness, without which no one can stand before God.[1105] 2 messengers returned from *Pittsburgh*. They had had a letter for me from *General Hand,* but they did not stay on the road because they feared the White people and they had lost it in the bush. This was easier to bear, however, than if it had happened to letters from the Unity.[1106]

THE 13TH   We learned that large numbers of *Delaware* Indians in *Cayahaga* and further up the *Walhanding* are beginning to go to the war. We sent a *String* of *Wampum* and a *Speech* to the *Council* in *Goschachgünk* and explained to them the danger that would result if they did not control this evil and ward it off, and we offered suggestions so that this does not continue to spread and bring misfortune upon the *Delaware Nation.* We also reminded them that they had promised the states of *America* that they would keep peace from one time to the next, as long as the sun and moon shone.[1107] In the meantime, however, their people were going out to murder. We explained to them that they would be humiliated if this were ever investigated, which they could certainly expect.[1108] Then we told them that we looked only to them and were watching

---

1103. From "The General also" bracketed in another hand, not in H2 or H3. In his letter to the Delaware, dated 1 Oct. 1777, Hand described the battle at Brandywine Creek as an American victory in which the Americans had lost but six hundred while the British had lost some eighteen hundred soldiers (*FDO,* 112–14). In reality the Americans lost about a thousand and the British only 576 men.

1104. From "And although some people" bracketed in another hand, not in H2 or H3. See entry for 12 Sept. 1777.

1105. Matt. 22:11–14.

1106. From "They had had a letter" bracketed in another hand in H3. We were unable to locate the letter.

1107. See entry for 23 July 1777.

1108. From "We also reminded them" bracketed in another hand in H3.

their behavior. If we saw that they were staining their hands with blood, we knew what we had to do. However, we wanted to admonish them as friends not to be sleepy or negligent in the matter, but to warn their people and order them to sit quietly. This talk was really quite sharp, but they could not argue with it because they were convinced of the truth of the matter. It made an impact and led them reflect, so that they immediately resolved to call the Indian heads from all over to a *Councel.*

Marcus came here from *Gnadenhütten* for a visit, and we heard that *Tawas* and *Potawatomi* Indians who are going to the war were visiting them there.

THE 16TH   In the early service we read the Watchword, The angel of the Lord encampeth round about them that fear him[1109] and talked about the service the Savior provides us through the dear angels. Especially during these times, this keeps much misfortune and danger away from us, and we cannot adequately thank him for this.

THE 17TH   We received news that 2 *Shawnee* had been captured on the *Canhawa.* The *Chief* wanted to set them free because they had been sent there as messengers, but this was refused. We also learned that they are making great *Preparations* there for the army that is supposed to march into Indian country.[1110]

THE 18TH   We received news from the *Cayahaga,* from where we had not heard anything good for some time; 50 Frenchmen had come across the *Lake* and persuaded 40 men from the *Munsee* and *Delaware* to go with them to war in *Ligonier,* which was very unpleasant news.[1111] The evil continues to spread among the *Delaware.* We will do what we can to keep the residents of *Goschachgünk* and the Indians on the *Walhanding* from going to war, because what would become of us and where could we hide if the *Delaware Nation* should break out in war.[1112] May the Savior mercifully protect us from misfortune!

THE 19TH   We had blessed Sunday services. All of our Brothers came home yesterday. It was relatively peaceful now, so many of them had gone out

1109. Ps. 34:7. This Watchword is taken from the collection for 1771.

1110. On 19 September two messengers from the Shawnee arrived at Fort Randolph with "a speech with strong protestations of friendship." At the same time the Shawnee inquired about the reasons for George Morgan's message to the Delaware, informing them of the appointment of a new general and commander of Fort Pitt who planned to kill all Indians (see entry for 12 Sept. 1777). Both messengers were detained in the fort. Captain Matthew Arbuckle to General Edward Hand, 6 Oct. 1777, *FDO,* 125–28. Fort Randolph was the collection point for the expedition against Pluggy's Town and the settlements of the Wyandots on the Sandusky; see note 1058 to entry for 21 Aug. 1777.

1111. The attack was really intended to fall on Fort Wallace. On 8 November 1777 Colonel John Proctor reported to General Edward Hand: "Wallases fort was Attacted one tuesday last [4 Nov.] with a body of about forty or fifty White Men and indeans the people in the fort kild one of the white men and obliged the rest to retrate but they are Seen Evory Day in the Neibohud" (*FDO,* 151–52). On 16 November David Zeisberger repeated in his letter to Edward Hand the information about the plans for an attack of Fort Ligonier (*FDO,* 164–67).

1112. From "which was very unpleasant" bracketed in another hand, not in H2 or H3.

hunting for 14 days. The Brothers and Sisters encouraged each other, and it was sweet and uplifting to listen to the occasional singing and preaching in their houses.

THE 22ND   White Eye, Gelelemind, and 2 Shawnee came here. Brother David had to communicate the news received recently from Pittsburgh to them.[1113] The latter brought news here that their Chief named Corn Stock[1114] had also been arrested in the Fort on the Canhawa,[1115] and these 2 Shawnee had come here to get advice. They agreed with the Chiefs that all the peacefully inclined Shawnee would move here with the Delaware. With the help of our Indian Brothers, White Eye and Gelelemind therefore prepared a message to the Shawnee, and the messengers immediately went back with it.

THE 24TH   Yesterday and today we had Speakings with the Brothers and Sisters for Holy Communion, which we enjoyed most blissfully on THE 25TH. One Sister, Susanna Minque, participated for the first time.

Three Delaware warriors who had run away from the Mingo Town returned from the Settlements. 2 of them used to be Indian preachers. The latter of these two was killed and the other one came here wounded. They wanted to stay here for a few days. We sent them to Goschachgünk, however, and told them that we did not take in any warriors here. Every time Delaware have allowed themselves to be misguided, they have suffered misfortune. The leaders and Captains among them, who were always for the war, have now been gotten out of the way pretty well.

THE 26TH   After the Liturgy for Holy Communion was the sermon about the Gospel for today, which told how the Savior atoned and paid for all of our sins on the cross. In the afternoon was the Children's Service and in the evening a Congregational Service and after everything else the Helpers' Conference.

THE 29TH   In the devotions for married couples, the widower Adam was married to the single Sister Sabina. A party of warriors came from the Settlements with a Scalp and another party passed through here on their way there. The latter were Woaponos from the Wyandot Towns.[1116]

THE 31ST   A large council was held in Goschachgünk as a result of our

1113. This probably refers to the message from Edward Hand (?) dated 18 Oct. 1777, in which Hand had promised that the army would not march through Delaware settlements and that his men would build a fort for the protection of the Delaware settlements. Edward Hand Papers, Peter Force Transcripts, LOC.

1114. Cornstalk.

1115. Cornstalk had traveled to Fort Randolph because he wanted to find out why the Shawnee messengers were being detained (see note 1110) and to inform Colonel Matthew Arbuckle, commander of the fort, that the Shawnee had entered the war on the British side. He and his family were against entering the war, but the decision of the whole tribe made it impossible for him to ignore its implications. Arbuckle, on the other hand, in his letter to Edward Hand dated 8 Nov. 1777, confessed himself convinced that "the Shawnese are all our enemies" (FDO, 150); he imprisoned Cornstalk.

1116. See entry for 15 Aug. 1777 and note 1049.

recent address to the *Councel* there.[1117] The head people from *Cayahaga* and other places gathered there and some of our Indian Brothers were summoned. They agreed to keep their people in all the *Towns* close and well supervised so that the parties of warriors marching through would not misguide them. We thus had hope that it would not happen again as easily.

[November]

NOVEMBER 2ND   *Welapachtschiechen* had a thorough talk with me about his spiritual condition. Among other things he said, I have been in the congregation for almost one year now and I have not become better, but worse. In the beginning I did not believe I was as sinful a person as I now see in myself and realize. Therefore I am often afraid and worried about my condition. I directed him, exactly as he feels, to the Savior, who accepts sinners and saves them from their sins. *White Eye* came here to discuss various things with the Brothers, because they have much work ahead of them again sending messages to *Detroit*, to the *Shawnee*, and to the *Fort*. *Gelelemind* asked us to baptize his child who was born a couple of days ago. However, I told him we do not baptize any Indian children outside of the congregation because they are raised only in pagan ways and not for the Savior, and they could not be kept in the grace of baptism as long as they lived among the savages.

THE 4TH   We read the Watchword, And the Lord spake unto Moses face to face, as a man speaketh unto his friend.[1118] We extolled a daily relationship with the Savior to the Brothers and Sisters as the only necessary thing. The Brothers began finishing our schoolhouse so that the children can have school this winter at least sometimes. *Isaac* visited *Augustinus,* who is lying ill in *Goschachgünk,* in great pain and miserable circumstances.[1119] He actually admitted that he alone was responsible for his miserable and unhappy condition, but said his heart was completely dead. Even when he thought about turning to the Savior again, he thought about how greatly he had sinned against the congregation, because he had said many evil things against the congregation. For this reason he lacked the heart and courage to turn to the Savior. *Isaac* told him that the Savior offers forgiveness even for deserters and enemies, because on the cross he had prayed for his enemies.

THE 5TH   A couple of women from *Goschachgünk* came here especially for the early service. One of them was a widow who was baptized as a girl in *Gnadenhütten* on the *Mahony.* Afterward she told a Sister that the talk about

1117. See entry for 13 Oct. 1777.

1118. 2 Moses 33:11 (i.e., Exod. 33:11), Collection of Watchwords for 1771.

1119. His Indian name was Newollike; see entry for 11 March 1776. In the entries for 21 March and 26 July 1777 Zeisberger characterized Newollike as the center of opposition against the mission congregations.

the text, But many that are first shall be last; and the last shall be first,[1120] had been just for her and everything that was said was spoken to her. She had been baptized, and in baptism she had promised to give her heart to the Savior and to live for Him, but she had not kept her promise. As a result she had become one of the last, and many others who had become Believers had exceeded her. She could still remember very well how blessed she had been after her baptism. She had lost this, however, and she often thought about returning to the congregation. It is clear that those who have once been baptized have ears to hear, which is not the case among the raw savages.

THE 6TH   The highest-ranking *Captain* of the *Wyandot*[1121] came to *Goschachgünk* with 16 men. All of them had come across the *Lake* from *Detroit* to make another *Tour* of the *Settlements*. In their *Compagnie* were also two White people, an Englishman and a Frenchman, who visited me. The former told me that a *Wyandot* from *Half King's Compagnie* had wanted to kill me the last time they were here, because I had not given him something that he wanted. I did not know about this, though, and perhaps I had not understood him. When *Half King* and the *Captains* heard this, they had sharply warned the Indians and forbidden him from doing anything like this here. At the same time we heard that the 6 *Nations* had reprimanded the *Wyandot* for sending the hatchet to the *Delaware*. We can hope this will not happen again any time soon.

THE 9TH   During the sermon, the *Wyandot* marched through our *Town* to the river in absolute silence, and we were not aware of them at all until we heard about this later. During the Children's Service, the baby boy born to Brother *Lucas* and Sister *Paulina* on the 3rd of this month was baptized as *Daniel*. *White Eye* and many Indians from *Goschachgünk* attended this and the sermon in the morning.

THE 12TH   *Isaac* traveled to the *Shawnee* on *Chiefs Affairs*.[1122] They did not have anyone in *Goschachgünk* capable of this since most of the Indians have either gone out as messengers or are out hunting.

THE 13TH   We worshipped our *Chief* Elder and High Priest in the dust, asked for merciful *Absolution* for all of our mistakes and shortcomings and for times we have not acted according to His mind and heart.[1123] We also prayed he would continue to live among us and to guide his government, and we promised Him new faithfulness and obedience. *Joseph Peepi* visited me from *Goschachgünk* and asked me if I still remembered what he had told me when he came here in the beginning. I replied that I still remembered everything as if he had told me just today.[1124] Then he said he was already tired of living in

1120. Matt. 19:30.
1121. Not identified, probably Half King.
1122. See entry for 22 Oct. 1777.
1123. On the meaning of commemorating Christ's acceptance of the office of Elder on 13 Nov. 1741, see Introduction, p. 62–63.
1124. See entry for 9 June 1777.

Goschachgünk. He realized now that his presence there had no purpose and what he had imagined was not happening. Therefore he wanted to discuss this with me more in the future.

THE 14TH   Most of the Brothers went out to hunt for a while. We agreed that they should stay close by as much as possible, so that if anything happened they could be informed of this immediately and could come home if necessary. They were all very willing to do this.

THE 16TH   A whole crowd of women from *Goschachgünk* came for the sermon, because most of the men are out hunting now.

Nehemia and his wife *Johanna Maria,* who had left the congregation in the spring and came here yesterday, very humbly asked to be accepted again to live with the congregation. They have come into great poverty and misery. The woman was primarily responsible for them leaving the congregation, and she is now lame. She came from the river up to the congregation crawling on her knees. We had mercy on them and took them in, and they did not know how to express their gratitude adequately for this. One of her baptized children died on the *Walhanding* some days ago.

White Eye is going to the *Fort* tomorrow, and I wrote letters to send with him for *General Hand* and *Mr. Morgan* in *Pittsburgh.*[1125] I was hesitant to send letters to Bethlehem, although I did not know why, and did not do so.

THE 17TH   *Nicodemus* and *Matthew* and their families came from *Gnadenhütten* to live here. The widow *Naemi* also came here to stay.

THE 18TH   A party of warriors returned from the *Settlements.* One of them was wounded.

THE 20TH   16 *Wyandot*[1126] who had brought a *Scalp* and a prisoner came. We heard from them that the English had taken *Possession* of *Philadelphia.*[1127] Many of the *Wyandot* visited me the following day, and they were very orderly and friendly.

THE 23RD   There was the burial of *Adolph* and *Susanna's* baby boy *David,* who had died the day before yesterday.

Isaac returned from the *Shawnee* with the news that they had left and were on their way here.[1128] They ask the *Chiefs* to send them help transporting the elderly and infirm. Contrary to all our expectations, the famous *Gischenatsi* is also coming here.[1129]

THE 30TH   On the first of *Advent,* many listeners from other places attended both the sermon and the Children's Service in the afternoon. The

1125. Zeisberger's letter to General Edward Hand dated 16 Nov. 1777 is printed in *FDO,* 164–67. We could not locate Zeisberger's letter to Morgan.

1126. See entry for 6 Nov. 1777.

1127. On 26 September 1777 the English army had entered Philadelphia; in the battle at Germantown on 4 October 1777 they secured their new conquest.

1128. See entry for 12 Nov. 1777.

1129. For Gischenatsi (Hard Man), see Zeisberger's report about his journey to the Shawnee from 17 to 21 September 1773.

strangers really enjoy attending the Children's Services. A blessed feeling prevailed in all of our services, which dealt with our Savior's incarnation. *Rachel* said, During the services, when I hear that the Savior came into the world to bless sinners I think to myself, I am also a sinner. Therefore he came into the world for my sake as well and to save me. Then when I hear that we are saved through faith in Him alone, I hear in my heart, I believe with my whole heart that the Savior became human for me, was nailed to the cross for my sins, suffered bitter death, and shed his blood. I believe with my whole heart that I can and must be saved through his blood alone. However, she said that she was always worried about whether she had been baptized. She was born in *Philadelphia* and her father had gone to the *Presbyterian* Church, but he had led a bad life. Later they had moved to *Canegotschik,*[1130] where she was captured by the Indians in 1757. When she was 19 she had been taken away by *White Eye* and our *Isaac.* I told her that she should not question her baptism; she had surely been baptized. She should seek forgiveness for her sins from the Savior and through his blood; this was the most important thing.

[December]

THE 1ST   Most of the Brothers came home from the bush the day before yesterday to see if things were still calm and peaceful and today they went out to hunt again. Some *Mingo* came from the *Settlements* but did not do anything except steal some horses.

THE 3RD   News came that the *Shawnee Chief* and 3 others who were captured on the *Canhawa* had been killed,[1131] and 4 *Delaware* Indians from *Cayahaga* who had joined in the war with the French were killed. Old *Thamar* went home in *Goschachgünk*. In the spring she had moved there from *Gnadenhütten* with *Joseph Peepi*. She had visited here often and some Sisters from here visited her just yesterday, but they did not think her end was so near. She was sorry she had left the congregation and called out constantly, Dear Savior, have mercy on me! and then she died.

THE 6TH   *Joseph* arrived with his family from *Gnadenhütten* to stay here.

THE 8TH   *Lucas's* wife *Paulina* died in blessing. Her earthly dwelling was buried on THE 9TH. When the Brothers came to *Goschgosching* in 1768 she came to them with her husband, now a widower, and joyfully accepted the word of Jesus' redemption. Although there was much opposition to the Brothers at that time, she did not worry about this. She and her husband were the

---

1130. We were unable to identify the settlement. Rachel was the wife of Welapachtschiechen; see entries for 21 Oct. 1776 and 21 July 1777.

1131. Cornstalk, his son, and a companion were murdered at Fort Randolph on 10 November 1777 (reports about this event in *FDO,* 168–71, 175–77). On the official reaction of Virginia, see McIlwaine, *Official Letters of the Governors of Virginia,* 1:242–43.

first to be baptized on the *Ohio*, in *Lawunnakhannek*, on *December* 3, 1769, and she attained the enjoyment of Holy Communion on *January* 6, 1771, in *Langundouteniink*, where she was also one of the first. Since her baptism she continued in her blessed walk, was a *National* Helper, loved and was loved in return. Her last delivery, in which she gave birth to a baby boy on *November* 3rd, led to her death. When she was not feeling well she immediately said that she was going to the Savior this time. We always hoped she would recover and it appeared she would, but she still insisted on this, spoke of nothing but dying, and said she was finished. Nothing else was keeping her here in this world. She certainly had concerns at times about her children, and she leaves 8 behind in the congregation, but she had given them to Savior. On *December* 3rd Brother *David* reminded her of her baptismal day and told her that she would go to the Savior soon now. He had washed her with his blood and she had enjoyed his flesh and blood in the Holy *Sacrament* so often. Soon now she would see him face to face and remain with him always. She indicated her joy about this through gestures, because she could not talk any more. She died gently and blessedly on the said day with the Watchword we read, I will bless the Lord at all times; his praise shall continually be in my mouth. Until we sing with God's army, holy, holy is the Lord God, and see Him face to face in eternal joy and blessed light.[1132]

THE 11TH   Brother *David* went to *Gnadenhütten*, accompanied by *Samuel Nantikoks*. He had Speakings with the Brothers and Sisters there and then held Holy Communion on THE 13TH.[1133] We were also joyful and delighted to receive letters and news reports from Bethlehem at that time through *White Eye*, who arrived there from the *Fort* on the 12th. We spent the night together reading them. We felt sincere sympathy for the sufferings and the trouble our Brothers and Sisters and the entire congregation there are experiencing.[1134] Brother *David* returned home by water on THE 14TH and found everyone here well. In the early service on THE 15TH he extended greetings from Bethlehem to the Brothers and Sisters and shared with them some of the news we had received. They were very interested in this.

THE 16TH   All of the Helpers' *Conference* spoke with *Joseph Peepi* and his wife, who had reported to Brother *David* again yesterday and asked for reacceptance. He expressed his remorse not only for having left the congregation himself, but also for having hurt others by leading them away. He asked the Brothers and Sisters for forgiveness and for permission to move here before

---

1132. Ps. 34:1; *Des kleinen Brüder-Gesangbuchs Dritter Theil*, hymn no. 141. The German text: "Bis wir singen mit Gottes Heer, heilig, heilig ist Gott der Herr, und schauen Ihn von Angesicht in ewger Freud und selgem Licht."

1133. Since Edwards had not been ordained, he could not administer the holy supper.

1134. In September 1777, as a result of a concentration of British prisoners, numerous wounded soldiers, and heavy armaments of the Continental army, circumstances in Bethlehem were very difficult indeed; the army had requisitioned many buildings, of which many had been seriously damaged. Hamilton, "Ettwein," 256–59.

the holidays. We agreed to this and they were very joyful and grateful. At the same time, however, we informed them that this did not extend to the rest of his people, who are grown, and who left *Gnadenhütten* with him. They would have to speak for themselves and make their own requests. Then on THE 18TH he came to us with his wife. Brothers *Isaac* and *Michael* returned from the *Shawnee* with some others from *Gnadenhütten* who had gone with them, and they brought 10 horse loads of their belongings here.[1135] They left the *Shawnee* in their *Camp,* though, and they are waiting for men from *Goschachgünk* to pick them up. They do not dare come here alone because the *Mingo* have threatened to attack them on their march if they go any further. We also received definite news that the *Shawnee Chief* and 3 others were killed in the *Fort* on the *Canhawa.*[1136]

THE 19TH   *White Eye* came here and discussed various issues with the Brothers. The *Counsellors* in *Goschachgünk* look pretty weak because they are very divided among themselves. Therefore *White Eye* is thwarted and is taking refuge with the Brothers and asking them for advice and help. *Joseph Peepi* spoke with him before he moved here and informed him that he was moving back to the congregation. *White Eye* replied that he was very glad to hear this. He had thought about him on his trip to *Pittsburgh* and had hoped he would do this because he realized now that the Indians in *Goschachgünk* would not accept the Gospel and there would never be a congregation there as he had intended. That was their *Project,* that all of *Goschachgünk* should convert at once. It is very unlikely that a whole *Town* or *Nation* will ever convert at once, though. You must give them credit for doing their best though, and what they have done is certainly worthy of gratitude and praise.

THE 20TH   67 Brothers and Sisters celebrated Holy Communion, and *Johannes* watched for the second time during this.

THE 21ST   After the *Liturgy* for Communion there was the sermon about the text, Rejoice in the Lord always etc.[1137] There was such a large crowd of strangers present that our Meeting House, which at first seemed large enough, was completely full even though some of our people are not home. During the Children's Service the baby boy *William,* born to Brother and Sister *Conners* on the 10th of this month, was baptized.

THE 22ND   *Anna Johanna* from *Gnadenhütten,* who has been here for some time, returned there and took along young *Daniel,* the baby boy left by her Sister *Pauline,* so she could take care of him. *Isaac* had gone to *Goschachgünk* on business, and the residents sent a request through him for permission to come for Christmas Eve. We therefore sent word that anyone who appeared in an orderly manner had permission to come. However, those who came deco-

---

1135. See entries for 12 and 23 Nov. 1777.
1136. See note 1131 to entry for 3 Dec. 1777.
1137. Phil. 4:4.

rated and painted like warriors would be turned away. We made exceptions for those strangers who came from far away and were still ignorant, but we no longer considered them to be like this. They themselves had even told us that if they were not doing something correctly we should remind them, and we would do this now.

THE 23RD   Many Indians from the *Walhanding* had come for the holidays already so they would not miss them, because they have been planning on this for a long time. We could not turn them away although we really did not have enough room, and after all, we are here for their sakes. There has been a completely new spirit among our Brothers and Sisters and residents for some time now, and a real fire among young and old. It is like when people are first in love, and we are not at all aware that there is war in the country.

THE 24TH   We had a very happy and blessed Christmas Eve service, for which a crowd of people from *Goschachgünk* and other places had gathered here. Countless tears flowed down the cheeks of both children and adults.

THE 25TH   In the morning the sermon was about the text, For unto us a child is born, unto us a son is given etc.[1138] The strangers asked if they could attend the Children's Service, and the children sang songs very sweetly praising baby Jesus' birth in the manger. Their cheeks were covered with tears and many of the guests sat there and cried as well. In the Congregational Service 5 people were added to the congregation through Holy Baptism and one was received into it. *Welapachtschiechen* was baptized with the name *Israel,* along with 4 older girls, whose names are *Maria Cathrina, Johanna Salome, Friderica,* and *Marianne. Rachel, Israel's* wife, was received into the congregation. This blessed proceeding was still really touching the strangers this evening and some of them asked the Brothers to tell them more about the Savior, which they were very glad to do. They gathered in the schoolhouse and preached to them until late in the night, and the guests shed many tears during this.

Israel has been overrun with *Chief Affairs* in recent days because *Gelelemind* is not home. He did not want to have anything to do with this, though, and he asked the Brothers to help him, saying he had something else to think about now. We spared him as much as possible and the Brothers made arrangements with *White Eye,* who left for the *Shawnee* today and just used his name.

THE 28TH   A family from *Assünnünk,* from *Israel's* friendship, asked to live here and they received permission. They are some promising people.

THE 31ST   During the New Year's Eve Watchnight service we thanked our dear Lord with melted hearts for all the kindness He has shown us this year. We certainly cannot describe this sufficiently or praise Him adequately for this. We prayed for forgiveness for all of our mistakes and for the times we have not followed his heart with our actions. We commended ourselves to His

1138. Isa. 9:6.

grace and prayed for his constant walk among us, for the Father's continued protection, and our dear Mother's further care. Then we entered the New Year with comforted hearts.

At the conclusion of the year we also consider what the Savior has so miraculously arranged and guided during such dangerous external circumstances, and how he has brought us safely through so many troubles and dangers. We are amazed at this and we fall before his feet and worship him saying, The Lord did this. May His name continue to be glorified and praised among the heathen and by many who still walk in blindness and darkness, upon whom the glory of the wounds and the sun of grace will still rise.

At the very beginning of the year the *Prospects* for future peace were dim since the warriors were passing close by us going to the *Settlements*. Although they were not coming into the *Town* yet at that time, we could only presume they would come here eventually. In addition, the *Delaware Nation* feared attack by the *Mingo* or 6 *Nations*.

In *March* we received one report after another that the *Mingo* were coming and would either capture or kill all of us White Brothers and Sisters and that they threatened all who opposed them. This often caused our Indian Brothers and Sisters to worry. They did not know what they should do to keep their teachers safe from the warriors, if they came in great numbers. In *Schönbrunn* they had arranged to take all the White Brothers and Sisters to the *Fort* along with the Brothers in *Lichtenau*. Brother *David Zeisberger,* who went there at that time, discussed this with the Brothers and Sisters. The *Chiefs* in *Goschachgünk* had provided an opportunity to do this and they decided that they would all leave *Schönbrunn* together and move to *Lichtenau* as soon as possible.

Brother and Sister *Jungmann* were brought here on *April* 2nd when some *Mingo* went to *Tuscarawi,* not far from *Schönbrunn,* and Brother *David* went to assist Brother *Heckewelder,* who was there. Then all but a few of them came here on the 26th of that month.

In *July* things became very unsafe because of the warriors who were passing through here more and more, and we White Brothers and Sisters could not leave the *Town* safely. On the 22nd of the month the *War Belt* was forced upon the *Delaware Nation* in *Goschachgünk.* Here, we also experienced the kind of *confusion,* fear, and horror that a *War Belt* causes and saw how the spirit of murder and the power of darkness reveal themselves during this. However, we also saw how the Savior destroys all evil attacks and mercifully remembered us.

At the beginning of *August* news arrived that a large number from the *Wyandot* and other *Nations* were coming here on their way to fight in the *Settlements.* The *Chiefs* therefore sent us word that we should consider what to do now about the safety of the White Brothers and Sisters. They could neither help nor advise us further, and they were at their wits' end. We considered this together and Brother and Sister *Jungmann* then traveled to Bethlehem. Indian Brothers escorted them as far as *Pittsburgh.* This was very painful for those of us who remained behind, but the Savior comforted us richly in this as well. Two days later, on *August* 8, the *Wyandot Half King* came to *Goschachgünk* with his warriors. The Savior did something remarkable on that day. We submitted a *Speech* to *Half King* and his *Captains* about the safety of the White Brothers and Sisters. In his reply on behalf of his *Nation,* he accepted the Brothers as their father. This was then solemnly celebrated here in *Lichtenau* on *August* 9th. He immediately sent word of this event home and across the *Lake* and informed all the *Nations* that no warriors should harm the Brothers, no matter what *Nation* they belonged to. From that day on we felt completely safe among them and had nothing to fear. Our Indian Brothers were thus released and freed from their worry and concerns, because the safety of their teachers had always been the biggest problem they could not solve. However, the Savior had suddenly solved this now and settled the matter.

When Brother and Sister *Schmick* left *Gnadenhütten,* Brother *Edwards* went there to serve that congregation.

After the Savior had rescued us from one great trouble, there was another in *September* that was no smaller. The White people wanted to destroy the *Delaware Towns.* It was unclear to us to what extent this was actually true or not. In the meantime, the *Delaware Nation* came very close to breaking away and going to war. We did our best to prevent this and the Savior allowed us to succeed in this, and they were calmed down again. Our Brothers and Sisters in *Gnadenhütten* fled down the *Walhanding,* though. After camping there for 3 weeks they returned; we were also away from home for 2 nights once.

From *August* 8th until *October* 6th there was not one day free of warriors, and in the beginning 300 stayed there for more than 14 days. This cost our Brothers and Sisters several hundred bushels of corn, not including the loss of cattle they suffered. They gave gladly and willingly, however, and did not complain about it once. Although they were here in our *Town* every day, it was still a great relief to us that they camped in *Goschachgünk* rather than here.

Since that time, that is *October* 6th, the Savior has granted us external peace again and our dear Mother has doubled her work in the hearts of the Brothers and Sisters and plentifully restored everything for them, so that at the end of the year we could only sing praises and tell of grace and favor. We cannot praise and glorify Him sufficiently for this. However, he will accept our good intentions until the day we can do this perfectly in eternity.

It was also a great relief for us that *Communication* with *Pittsburgh* was not completely stopped, and all letters and news arrived as they should. We acknowledge this with gratitude and pray that the Savior allows this to continue.

This year 8 adults and 3 children were baptized here and one in *Schönbrunn.* One Sister, Rachel, was accepted into the congregation. We had Holy Communion 8 times, and 6 Brothers and Sisters here and 3 in *Schönbrunn* became communicants. One couple was married.

3 Sisters and 1 child here went to the congregation on high, as did one Sister in *Schönbrunn*.

Currently 232 people live here together.

January 1778

THE IST   In the morning a large crowd of listeners attended the sermon about the text, For ye are all the children of God by faith in Christ Jesus. For as many of you as have been baptized into Christ have put on Christ.[1139] Then the baptized Brothers and Sisters had a blessed service and time of adoration. A woman who was sick had urgently asked to be baptized, and this took place on her sick bed in the presence of a number of Brothers and Sisters. She received the name *Anna Justina*. During the Congregational Service 2 older girls, whose names are *Anna Sophia* and *Regina,* were baptized and many Indians from *Goschachgünk* were present for this. The grace which has prevailed among our Brothers and Sisters for some time is extending to the Indians elsewhere and many are being touched by it.

THE 2ND   A White man came here from *Sandusky* with goods. We heard from him and also from the Indians who came with him that *Gelelemind,* who returned from *Detroit* some days ago, once again accepted the *War Belt* from the *Governour* there and had brought it back. He is keeping this a secret, however, and has not said a word about it to anyone yet.[1140] People say the *Wyandot* and the other *Nations* are already preparing to continue the war in the spring, so we cannot expect much good. However, we want to do as our text for today teaches, Casting all your care upon him; for he careth for you. He who has chosen us for Him knows what we need.[1141]

THE 5TH   A widow and 4 children from *Goschachgünk* received permission to live here. She had requested this repeatedly and she shed many tears of joy.

THE 6TH   During the morning devotions today[1142] we prayed for blessings for all of our other congregations among the heathen and for ourselves, and asked Him to let his loving face shine upon us. He granted us this and laid his peace upon us, and hearts melted in tears. In a service of baptized Brothers

---

1139. Gal. 3:26–27.

1140. From "and also from the Indians" bracketed in another hand, not in H2 or H3. See entries for 10, 19, and 22 Jan. and 18 Feb. 1778, and White Eyes and Gelelemind to Morgan, dated March 1778, in which they briefly report the visit to Detroit without mentioning the war belt (George Morgan Letterbook, vol. 3, fols. 21–23, CLP). Gelelemind's visit to Fort Detroit is not mentioned in Lieutenant Governor Hamilton's letter to General Guy Carleton, 15 Jan. 1778 (HP, 430–33).

1141. 1 Pet. 5:7. *Das kleine Brüder-Gesang-Buch,* hymn no. 893. German text: "Er, der uns Ihm hat auserwehlt, der weiß auch gar wol was uns fehlt."

1142. On the importance of 6 January, see Introduction, pp. 62–63.

and Sisters, the great sinner *Joseph*[1143] was absolved. He and the others present shed many tears. A large number of strangers came for the sermon, which was about Isaiah 60, 1–4. There was such crying at the beginning that hardly anyone could hear what was being said. When Brother *David* wanted to stop because of this, a gentle hush suddenly arose, although countless tears flowed down people's cheeks. He then continued to preach and the service was accompanied by a powerful feeling of grace and the Savior of the heathen revealed himself mightily. In the afternoon there was a Lovefeast, and during the Congregational Service 4 were buried into His death in baptism and added to the congregation: *Israel's* 2 adult sons, one with the name *Anton* and the other *Jacob*, a single person named *Philippina,* and a 13 year-old girl *Anna Johanna* were baptized. The latter is from *Netawatwees'* family. May He receive thousands of expressions of thanks, praise, honor, and glory for this day.

THE 8TH   Indians from the *Walhanding* came here for a visit. They said they had heard that miraculous things were taking place here and they wanted to see and hear this. The Brothers replied, There are indeed miraculous things that you have perhaps never heard in your life, and they began to tell them that God the Creator of all things came into the world, became human, gave his life on the cross, and shed his blood for the sins of the whole world. Through this he redeemed us from the power of Satan and won our salvation. They preached to them about the Savior from his birth in the manger until his rest in the grave and they listened very attentively. It was already after midnight and *Isaac,* who was also there, wanted to go home and go to bed. One of the Indians, his former comrade, said to him, We used to spend many nights together celebrating or drinking, and we never got sleepy. Let us then also spend one night on this great matter now and discuss it thoroughly together. *Isaac* did this and stayed with them through the night. They passed the night asking questions and giving answers and returned home in the morning.

THE 10TH   *Gelelemind* visited me from *Goschachgünk.* He asked me what I would think about it if they made friends with the *Governour* in *Detroit,* who had invited them to a *Treaty* there in the spring, and whether this might be at all dangerous for them. I replied that it would be good for them to maintain a friendship with him, but above all they must be careful not to get mixed up in the war. If they agreed to go to war they would be in the gravest danger. They would be chased from their land and not know where they could flee and they would have no more hope of friendship with the *Americans.*[1144] He said he also believed this, but they wanted to make friends with the *Governour* because they were in constant fear of the other *Nations* who always threatened them because they would not go to war. Finally he told me his desires still lay

---

1143. This refers to Joseph Peepi, who on 19 December 1777 had received permission to move back to Lichtenau.

1144. From "They would be chased" bracketed in another hand, not in H2 or H3. See entry for 2 Jan. 1778.

with the congregation and he could not forget it. Therefore he wanted to have a house here at our place so that he would have a place to stay sometimes when things got too busy in *Goschachgünk,* or when he came here on Sunday. He wanted more information about this, and I told him he should consider it himself a little more first. Then I would give him an answer to this if he wanted one.

In *Goschachgünk* they told *Isaac* that many Indians there were well disposed toward *Lichtenau.* Therefore they all wanted to discuss whether they should stop making sacrifices or should continue to do this.[1145] He told them they could do as they wished. We did not forbid them to make sacrifices, but did not tell them to either.

THE 11TH   First everyone had blessed services together and then the baptized boys had their choir festival. The Savior graciously revealed himself during this.[1146]

THE 12TH   We resumed holding school for the children and Singing Services in the evenings. Both were pleasant for the children and adults.

THE 16TH   The old widow *Hanna* died in blessing and her earthly dwelling was buried on THE 18TH. She was baptized by Brother *Grube* in Bethlehem on *January* 9th, 1757, and then attained the enjoyment of Holy Communion, which was very important and precious to her. We do not know anything about her life during this time except what we saw in her since she came here to the *Muskingum,* but we can testify that she was a blessed widow whose heart was firmly attached to the Savior and the congregation. Since coming here to *Lichtenau* last spring, every time we spoke with her she said she hoped to go to the Savior soon. She also repeated this constantly during her illness, which lasted 10 days. This then took place on the date stated, and she died peacefully with the blessing of the congregation.

THE 19TH   *White Eye* and his men returned from picking up the *Shawnee* who want peace, whom they had left in *Woaketammeki.* 2 Frenchmen from *Detroit* arrived to see them at the same time *White Eye* did. They brought the *Shawnee* the *War Belt* from the *Governour*[1147] there and challenged them to go to the *Canhawa* with him. *White Eye* has this *War Belt* now, so there are now 2 *War Belts* in *Goschachgünk.* Time will tell what will happen with all this.

THE 20TH   *White Eye* came here with his *Counsellors.* The *Shawnee* had given him some *Copies* of a *Proclamation* which had been sent to them from the *Governour* in *Detroit.* They were supposed to leave them among the dead in the *Settlements* where they murdered, so that they would reach the residents of this country in this way. In the *Proclamation,* which he delivers in the name of

1145. On the importance of sacrifice, see entry for 23 Jan. 1774.
1146. The choir of the boys celebrated its festival on this day; see entry for 9 Jan. 1774.
1147. Henry Hamilton.

Governour Carleton,[1148] he promises many advantages to those who would serve the King, and when the war is over each will receive 200 acres of land.[1149] The *Shawnee* did not know what this said, however, so they did not do anything further with them.[1150]

THE 22ND   Some of our Brothers were called to the *Councel* in *Go-schachgünk,* where the news *Gelelemind* brought from the *Governour* in *Detroit* was *communicated* to the Indians. They only reported the best of this. No mention was made of the *War Belt* he had brought along, so only *White Eye* and a few others know about this matter.[1151] Then they decided once again to remain quiet and ordered their people not to let themselves be tempted to go to war if warriors come here in the spring, which they presume will happen.[1152]

In the afternoon was the burial of Sister *Anna Justina,* who died in blessing the day before yesterday. She was from *Salomon's* family and had lived with the Brothers in *Goschgosching* and *Lawunakhannek* as a young girl. She then moved with them to *Langundouteünk* and from there to *Schönbrunn,* so that she spent part of her youth with the congregation. As she advanced in years, people observed that the Savior often came upon her heart and she was sometimes very touched by grace. In *Schönbrunn* we once had her among the *candidates* for baptism. Unfortunately, our hopes for her were disappointed when her mother, who was worldly-minded and who had not become as good as she, led her away from the congregation. She was married, and then her mother died 2 years ago. Last fall when her husband wanted to go out hunting and she had been sickly for a long time already, he asked some of the Indian Brothers to let his wife stay here with her friends for that long, because she did not have anyone in *Goschachgünk* to take care of her. We gave him no hopes of this because it is not our custom. When Brother *David* heard this, however, he sent word to the man that he could leave his wife here until he came home from hunting, if she wanted to do this. She came here that very day and was extremely happy that she could be with the congregation. She attended services regularly as long as she could still walk. When her husband returned home from hunting and saw that she was worse instead of better, he asked if we would keep her here longer and gave her everything he had gotten on his fall hunt. At first she was very shy after coming here, and when Brother *David*

1148. Guy Carleton, 1st Baron of Dorchester (1724–1808), "Captain General and Governor in Chief" for Canada from 12 April 1768 until 27 June 1778. His successor was Frederick Haldimand (1718–91).

1149. Zeisberger's summary makes it clear that the reference is to Hamilton's proclamation dated 24 June 1777, printed in *FDO*, 14.

1150. From "THE 20TH" bracketed in another hand, not in H2 or H3.

1151. From "No mention was made" bracketed in another hand, not in H2 or H3. See entry for 2 Jan. 1778.

1152. On 14 March 1778 Zeisberger reported the results of the consultations to George Morgan. George Morgan Letterbook, vol. 3, fols. 25–26, CLP.

happened to go into her hut by accident, she was shocked even though he did not say anything to her. However, she became more confident after the Sisters had visited her often. When she could no longer get up or walk, Brother *David* visited her one time, had a sincere talk with her, and encouraged her to approach the Savior. Tears immediately flowed down her cheeks so that she could not speak. The following day, *December* 30th, she sent for him and told him that she wanted to give herself to the Savior, and the only thing she cared about in this world was that He would wash her of her sins with his blood before her end. Then she would gladly die. She joyfully received baptism on *January* 1st amid many tears, and she hardly slept at all that night for joy. She was inexpressibly blessed and said she wanted to go to the Savior as soon as possible now, and she no longer wanted to get well. She revived completely, and there was hope she would recover. However, after 14 days we saw that her end was approaching. The day before she went home, she asked a Sister who was visiting her, What could be keeping the Savior away, and what kind of hesitations does he still have about me that keep him from coming and taking me? The Sister replied, He will come soon. He is preparing a place for you. A couple of hours before her end this same Sister returned to her and she told her, He is coming now. She was conscious and maintained her ability to speak until her breathing stopped, and she died with the blessing of the congregation.

Her husband, who had gone to the *Shawnee* with *White Eye* and returned the previous evening, was very happy to see her still. He was especially glad that she had been baptized. It made a deep impression on him to hear from her personally how happily she was leaving this world, since she had been really afraid of death before, when she was still in *Goschachgünk*. He said he could see that something had happened to her because she seemed completely different than he had seen her before.

THE 24TH   *White Eye* and *Gelelemind* and the whole *Councel* came here, and the former addressed our Indian Brothers in the name of the rest. He confirmed this with 10 Klafter of *Wampum* and offered a reply to the talk and statement we had addressed to the *Councel* in *Goschachgünk* on *October* 13th last year, when we admonished them to watch over their people better so they would not bring unhappiness upon the *Delaware Nation*. They informed us that they had followed our advice and had done what we asked of them. The *Counsellors* all agreed to this and they had found it even more necessary since the *Shawnee* were coming here now. They do not want any of their people to go to war and they would hold more firmly to peace now than ever before. They also asked us to continue advising them, and if we observed that something harmful was going on among them, we should remind them. They would accept this gratefully. We were even happier to hear this because we had learned some time ago that there was opposition among the *Counsellors* and that they could not resolve anything.

THE 25TH   *White Eye* and *Gelelemind* and a number of Indians from

Goschachgünk came for the sermon. In the evening there was a blessed baptism. A widow who came here on the 5th of the month was baptized with the name *Anna Benigna,* a single person from *Israel's* family with the name *Martha Elisabeth,* and an older boy *Boas.*

THE 27TH   The Brothers and Sisters collected Indian corn for the *Shawnee,* as they are doing in all the *Delaware Towns,* to support them. We had learned that they are planning to settle between *Goschachgünk* and us, so we discussed this with the *Chiefs* early so they could prevent this. They promised to do this.

THE 28TH   Some Sisters who had been visiting here for a number of days returned to *Gnadenhütten.* In *Goschachgünk* they had collected *Wampum* to pacify the *Shawnee.* They also sent word to the *Walhanding* that they should do the same thing there, and a frivolous Indian from *Goschachgünk* had burst out that they were doing this because they wanted to make Brother *David* a *Chief.* Not only the common people but also some who sit in the *Councel* believed this and said they had been expecting this for a long time.

February

THE 1ST   Some *Shawnee* were among those present for the sermon. They arrived in *Goschachgünk* a couple of days ago. There are about 20 families of them and they are expecting more. *White Eye* came here with their *Chief* named *Nimho*[1153] and some people from the *Councel.* In the Children's Service the six-month-old baby daughter born to *Anna Benigna* was baptized with the name *Christina,* and during the Congregational Service 3 adults with the name *Daniel, Johann Jacob* and *Dorothea.* Both of the latter came to the congregation from *Israel's* friendship in *Assünnünk* on *December* 28th. The Savior is showing special grace to those from *Assünnünk.* An election of grace is resting upon them and even more of them want to move to our place.

THE 2ND   Some of the Helper Brothers went to *Goschachgünk* where they had something to discuss with *White Eye* and at the same time they welcomed the *Shawnee.*

THE 3RD   Brothers *Marcus* and *Josua* returned to *Gnadenhütten.* They were summoned by the *Councel* in *Goschachgünk* and had come here the day before yesterday.

THE 7TH   Many of the *Shawnee* came here for a visit. The Brothers used the opportunity to proclaim the Savior and what he has done for us. However, they do not yet have ears to hear the word of life.

THE 8TH   Our services were well attended by listeners from elsewhere and the Savior's presence accompanied and blessed them.

1153. Nimho, brother of Cornstalk and chief of the Mequochoke-Shawnee, who had joined the Delaware. Nimho died in 1780. *RUO,* 41n67, *FRO,* 73.

Israel spoke with some friends from *Goschachgünk* who were visiting him and told them, When we moved here together from *Assünnünk,* we had agreed to go to the congregation where we could hear about the Savior every day, and you were very willing to do this. However, when you came here you settled in *Goschachgünk* and despised the congregation. This bothered me, but I was determined to remain with the congregation even if you all left me. If you knew what I know and what I have felt and experienced in my heart, you would not stay in *Goschachgünk* another night. Out of love for you, I advise you to consider it yet and think about your eternal salvation, because there is still time. Do it soon though, because I am worried that you will be lost. *Johann Jacob* told his mother and friends, who are also from there, You probably think there is nothing to the whole matter or that there is just a lot of preaching here. I used to think like this too and just laughed about it. However, now I can tell you from personal experience that there is something great and amazing, a power of God that comes upon a person and crushes his heart when he hears what the Savior did and suffered for us and how much it cost him to redeem us poor, lost humans from Satan's power.

THE 10TH   An Indian woman came from *Detroit* some time ago. She had thought she would be baptized there, but she did not like it there so she did not do it. She told a Sister that the *Wyandot* talk about us a lot and praise us. Among other things, a *Wyandot* woman told her that she had been baptized 20 years ago and had attended church regularly and heard many things. However, she did not know that she had ever received anything in her heart or felt anything. All of it was empty, and she had not gained anything from it. She had heard many good things about the Indians here, however. Therefore she wanted to come here in the spring and hear the Brothers.

THE 11TH   We received written news via *Cayahaga* from *Mr. Morgan*[1154] in *Yorktown* and *General Hand*[1155] in *Pittsburgh* from *October* and *November* reporting what things are like in the country below. *Gelelemind* and the whole *Councel* came here to hear it. We were even happier about this for the sake of the Indians, because we had not heard anything from the *Fort* the whole winter.

THE 14TH   After having Speakings with the Brothers and Sisters in recent days, we had Holy Communion today, and one Brother joined as a participant for the first time. One Brother and 4 Sisters were readmitted after receiving *Absolution,* and 3 Brothers and Sisters, *Gideon,* young *Nathanael,* and *Rachel,* watched for the first time.

1154. On 16 October 1777 George Morgan informed the Delaware of the supposed successes of the American army in the east (*FDO,* 136–38). In his report he described the bloody defeat of the Americans at Germantown as a glorious American victory; of the capitulation of the British army under General Burgoyne on 7 October, he wrote, "our Army . . . routed the British Army commanded by their greatest Generals" (137). Morgan hoped that he would soon see Henry Hamilton as prisoner (Edward Hand Papers, Peter Force Transcripts, LOC).

1155. Hand's letter dated 3 Nov. 1777 is mentioned in *FDO,* 147.

THE 15TH   After the *Liturgy* for Holy Communion, the sermon was about 2 Peter: 16–19. *White Eye* and *Gelelemind* were here with a relatively large number of their people. We spoke with them a lot afterward and had heart to heart talks with them.

THE 18TH   The *Chiefs* had recently sent a message to *Cayahaga*, and we heard that the Indians there have finally decided to move here to *Goschachgünk* as well, and indeed before spring.[1156] Thus everyone is gathering here. Perhaps they shall hear the Gospel.

A White man came from *Detroit*.[1157] He had been here with the *Wyandot* a number of times last summer as well. He told me about the business that brought him here. He was to bring another *Proclamation* by the *Governour* in *Detroit*[1158] into the *Settlements* among the residents of the country. He is encouraging them either to go to *Detroit* or to another royal post where they would be well received and would enjoy protection and many advantages.[1159] He knows the *Delaware* have accepted the *War Belt,* so he is counting on *Assistenz* from them to carry this out.[1160] He asked me about this and I advised him to talk to *White Eye* about it. The *Wyandot* are planning to come here soon in order to go to war again.[1161]

THE 21ST   *Gideon* and his 2 sons returned from *Walhanding,* where they had been on business. A couple of old men there had questioned *Nathanael*, a youth, and asked him what he had gained or how he had improved from being with the Brothers now. They asked him many questions like this, and he answered them in such a way that one of them was soon made silent and had no arguments. However, the other said he wanted to spend half the night with him and see if he would be able to justify himself to an old man, since he was

1156. See entry for 27 Sept. 1777. The report of the conversation between White Eyes, Teytapankosheh, and the converted Indians Wilhelm and Isaac in Fort Pitt on 25 April 1778 suggests that this is based on the Council's highly controversial decision to concentrate all Delaware settlements in the region of Goschachgünk (George Morgan Letterbook, vol. 3, fols. 53–54, CLP).

1157. According to Henry Hamilton's letter to Sir Guy Carleton, 25 April 1778, this refers to Edward Hazle (*FDO*, 284); see also entry for 24 Sept. 1777 and note 1090.

1158. Henry Hamilton.

1159. In his letter to General Guy Carleton of 15 Jan. 1778, Hamilton wrote: "Four days since, a young man set out from this place to the Delaware towns, where a Moravian minister resides, with the design of engaging him to disperse some papers signed by several of the Prisoners taken and brought in by the Indians—the purport of them to show, that persons well affected to Government may be assured of a safe conduct to this place if they will agree upon a place of rendezvous, and that an officer (of the Indian Department) with an Interpreter shall be sent to escort them thro' the Indian Villages—I am in hopes some advantage may be drawn from this" (HP, 432). The proclamation is dated 15 Jan. 1778 (Barnhart, *Henry Hamilton and George Rogers Clark,* 32 and n. 51). The text of the proclamation is quoted in part in *FDO*, 254n9.

1160. The letter cited in note 1159 to entry for 18 Feb. 1778 suggests the opposite: Hamilton supposed, probably because he knew of the pro-British attitude of the Moravians at Bethlehem and from the talks with Half King about his conversations with Zeisberger, that Zeisberger would support such a pro-British measure, which, after all, would at the same time support the rightful government.

1161. From "A White Man came from Detroit" bracketed in another hand, not in H3; in H2 this entry is for 19 Feb. 1778.

just a boy after all. It was not long, however, before the old man said he had had enough already and advised *Nathanael* to stay with the congregation as long as he lived. He said that he personally was already so old and callous that he could not become a Believer.

THE 22ND   Various Indians from *Goschachgünk* and *Walhanding* came for the Sunday services, including some who were eager to listen. 3 older girls were baptized during the Congregational Service. Their names are: *Johanna Sabina, Anna Rosina,* and *Lucia.* The first two are daughters of *Anna Benigna.*

THE 24TH   Because the weather was so beautiful, our Brothers and Sisters went to their sugar huts yesterday and today. In our Helpers' *Conference* we considered our internal concerns. Among other things we found it necessary to designate a Brother to care for the widows, so that they can get help when they need it. We appointed Brother *Samuel Nantikok* for this. We also recommended that the Brothers consider how and in what manner we can help those who have moved here recently and need fields to be planted. There are quite a few of these.

THE 26TH   30 *Wyandot* warriors came here on their march to *Redstone.* They are beginning to go to war again.[1162] They camped at the end of our *Town* and stayed there until THE 28TH, when they moved on. They were all from *Sandusky* and had come and gone here a year ago. The Brothers told them we had received news there that smallpox was at the *Frontiers* of the White people, so they should take another route on their return march and not come through here. Otherwise they were completely quiet and orderly and did not cause any trouble.

[March]

MARCH 1ST   We entered into the season of our dear Lord's *Passion* in blessing. In the afternoon the baby boy born to Brother *Gideon* and Sister *Sara* on the 24th of last month was baptized with the name *Johannes Renatus.* News came from the *Wyandot Towns* that the *Munsee's* head people had gone there and secretly told the *Wyandot* that the Indians in *Goschachgünk* were just waiting until the *Virginians* came out with an army. Then they would join them and help them destroy the *Wyandot.* The *Munsee* are still trying to incite the *Nations* against the *Delaware* and particularly against us, as they did a year ago. In recent days some *Munsee* came here with the intention of picking up their friends because they said we would all be killed. No one listened to them, however, so they went back.

1162. Zeisberger related this information in a personal letter and in another letter written in the name of the Council of Goschachgünk to George Morgan; these are mentioned in Morgan's answer to the Delaware and to Zeisberger dated 27 March 1778, as well as in Morgan's letter to the president of the Continental Congress dated 31 March 1778. *FDO,* 241–45, 254–56.

THE 3RD   Many of the *Shawnee* came here to visit, including one old, gray-headed woman who attended the early service. Afterward she told the Sisters that she just wished she could understand what was being said, because she really liked everything here. Her children and friends would mock her when she would tell them she wanted to attend the service here.

THE 4TH   *Johann Jacob* came to *Goschachgünk* and his natural brother asked him, Do you believe that there is any truth to this whole matter about which so much is made here, and do you believe what the White people are preaching to you? I could also tell you and the Indian Believers a lot of things, but I do not want to start with them because there are too many of them and I would have all of them on my back. I want to tell you, though, that before one year is over their work will be finished and the Indian Believers will no longer exist. You are a fool to let yourself be seduced by the White people. It is true that they can talk a lot and preach to the people. They have learned this, but there is no truth in it. *Johann Jacob* told him, I talked to you recently. Did you not understand what I said then? He said, Yes. *Johann Jacob* answered, From what you say and from your questions, I see that you did not understand anything at all. You heard with your ears, but you do not know what you heard. I see it is useless to tell you much, because you do not understand your own language. I do not believe the White people just because they told me how I can be saved. Even before I was baptized I was convicted in my heart so that I could believe that the Savior is my Redeemer and the one who will save me. After I was baptized, however, I felt like I was a completely different person than before. My heart burned and I was so happy that I could not express it. It is still like this for me, and this is because the Savior has forgiven my sins and washed me with his blood. I used to speak as you do, because I did not know better. Therefore I understand you very well, but you do not understand me. I certainly do not know how you can say that the preaching of God's word will cease. You would just like this to be true. However, I tell you that what you say will not happen, but that God's word will be preached as long as the world exists. Do not waste any more effort trying to convince me that there is nothing to the matter. I know better.

THE 10TH   Brothers *Samuel Nantikok* and *Gideon* returned from the *Walhanding,* where they had gone yesterday. There they had also visited a headman of the *Delaware*[1163] who is ill and they told him about the Savior. He was more eager than he had ever been to hear, because after the Brothers were already asleep he sent for them and had them woken up. They had to go to him and preach the Savior to him and his entire friendship that had gathered, and others came as well. *Samuel* did this until morning. When they wanted to leave (because they were getting Indian corn) he told the Brothers they probably had no more business there now and he might not get to see them any

---

1163. This refers to Winginund; see entry for 21 March 1778.

more. He was very happy that they had come, however, because his people had never heard anything about the Savior except what the Indians had occasionally told. When the Brothers offered him hope that they would visit him more, he said he would really like that. Otherwise, we received news that the White people in *Sikhewunk* on the big *Beaver Creek* apparently had killed 10 Indians.[1164] Another party of *Wyandot,* 20 men strong, had gone through the *Settlements* in *Woaketammeki.* That is all for our diary for now. We greet all the congregations, as does our gathering of those elected to grace from among the heathen, and we commend ourselves to their prayer and intercession.

Diary of Lichtenau *on the* Muskingum *from* March 15th *until* July 6th, 1778[1165]

THE 15TH   Most of the Brothers and Sisters gathered from the bush, where they had been boiling sugar, for the Sunday services as if it were a holiday, and we had blessed services accompanied by his dear presence. Some *Shawnee* also listened to the sermon. Sometimes they may even gain something as well,[1166] as the Gospel lesson for today about the woman from *Cana* suggests.[1167] Afterward two of them talked for a long time with an Indian Brother who understands their language about what is in their hearts. They wished they could understand everything that had been said in the services. One said when he had said what he thought about the Brothers among his people, they said he was already one of them. In the service for those who are baptized, *Nehemia* was absolved and readmitted to the congregation.[1168]

THE 18TH   Messengers from *Goschachgünk* were sent to the *Fort* with

1164. In the middle of February General Edward Hand had set out with about five hundred militia soldiers for Cayahaga, after receiving information that the enemy had stored "a Quantity of Stores" there. The expedition was forced to turn back because of severe thawing weather. "About 40 miles up Beaver Creek we discovered Indian Tracts & Sent out reconnoitring Parties. Some of them returnd & Informd they had Found a Camp Containing between 50 & 60 Indians, I conjectured they were Warriors coming into Our Settlements & proceeded to Attack them. But to my great Mortification found only one Man with some Women & Children." A little later another group of soldiers killed three women and one boy (Hand to Jasper Ewing, 7 March 1778, *FDO,* 215–16; see also 216–23). Among the dead were Captain Pipe's sister and mother.

1165. MAB, B 147, F 6, I 1, fol. 296. On 18 March the letters mentioned in note 1162 to entry for 26 Feb. 1778 were sent, along with the diary, to Fort Pitt, whence George Morgan sent the diary to Bethlehem. In his letter of 14 March 1778 to Matthäus Hehl Zeisberger asked whether his report of the events of the war was too detailed and added, "I will leave that to you to decide whether every thing will be read in publick" (MAB, Lititz Records: Indian Mission). The same messenger carried letters dated 14 March 1778 to Nathaniel Seidel (MAB, B 229, F 15, I 13), and to Morgan (George Morgan Letterbook, vol. 3, fols. 25–26, CLP).

1166. The words "something as well" bracketed; "a piece of bread" written above them in another hand.

1167. Matt. 15:21–28.

1168. See entry for 16 Nov. 1777.

news, and I sent a packet with them for *Mr. Morgan* to send on to Bethlehem. We also received news that the Indians above *Gnadenhütten* have all fled again and *Gnadenhütten* is now the *Frontier* against the White people. The murder on *Beaver Creek* is what caused this.[1169]

THE 19TH   Brothers *Samuel Nantikok* and *Thomas* left for *Sandusky*. The 30 warriors who were mentioned on the 28th of last month returned from the *Settlements* and passed through here with 4 prisoners and 4 *Scalps*.[1170]

THE 21ST   *Abraham* returned from the *Walhanding,* where he had visited *Winginund* who is sick. He is our good friend and is always happy when the Brothers visit him.

MARCH 22.   The baby girl born to Brother *Jonas* and Sister *Amalia* on the 17th of this month was baptized with the name *Anna Christina,* as were *Johann Jacob's* wife with the name *Elisabeth* and their daughter, an older girl, who was baptized *Rahel*. The Savior revealed himself very graciously during this proceeding.

THE 24TH   A family from *Goschachgünk* who came here 3 days ago requested permission to live here and they received this.[1171]

THE 27TH   Brother *David* was called to *Goschachgünk,* where a messenger from the *Fort* had arrived.[1172] The reason we had not heard anything for so long was because they could not get anyone to go out in these times, and *Mr. Morgan* had finally gotten a *Wyandot* Indian coincidentally and sent him here. On this occasion I was very happy to receive letters from Brother *Matthao* in *Litiz*. *White Eye* and the *Chiefs* had been called to the *Fort* and we learned in the letters from there that an *Expedition* against the Indians was supposed to be carried out in one month's time.[1173] Therefore Brother *David* advised *White Eye*

1169. See entry for 10 March 1778.

1170. See George Morgan to the president of the Continental Congress, dated 31 March 1778: "The Parties of Wiandots mention'd in the Letter from Capt. White Eyes have committed several Murders in Monongahela County" (*FDO*, 255). Fort Redstone, which Zeisberger originally named as the warriors' destination, was on the Monongahela River (see entry for 26 Feb. 1778).

1171. Whole entry in H2 for date 23 March.

1172. The messengers brought George Morgan's letter dated 20 March 1778 to White Eyes, as well as the undated letter of the Commissioners of the Continental Congress and letters that had been dispatched earlier by another messenger who had fallen ill and therefore never arrived at Goschachgünk. *FDO*, 228–29.

1173. See the Report of Commissioners, c. 25 March 1778, *FDO*, 238–40. Probably around this time or shortly thereafter General Edward Hand, in a letter to James Wilson, sketched a plan designed to end the war in the west and in the Ohio region. He suggested, first, that the Delaware should be relocated to the European settled area and put under special protection; second, that the Delaware warriors should fight on the American side; and third: "If we have a general Indian war, it is my humble Opinion four expeditions will be necessary: One to the Southward, one to the Northward, one down the Ohio to establish a Strength on the Ohio, so as to cut off any communication with the Western and Southern Nations, and one other expedition to De Troit or to some part of the Country to the Westward, to cut off the communication between the Northern and Western Indians." Each army would have three thousand soldiers and a train of artillery. The conditions for concluding peace treaties would be secured by "large numbers of hostages . . . none but their chiefs or ruling men . . . and they should not be exchanged till we had good proof of their tribe or nation becoming agreeable people. That all the lands of the unoffending tribes or nations should be preserved to them,

to go there immediately and to have the rest follow him, so that our *Towns* and the *Delaware Towns* might be safe. He agreed to do this.[1174] Brothers *Samuel* and *Thomas* returned from *Sandusky* with *Confirmation* of the news we had already heard earlier, that the *Governour* of *Detroit* had sent word to the *Nations* that they should stop waging war against the *Colonies*.[1175]

THE 29TH   Many strangers came for the sermon, and during the Children's Service the baby daughter of *Johann Jacob* and *Elisabeth* was baptized into Jesus' death with the name *Maria Salome*. 20 *Wyandot* passed through here from the *Settlements* with 4 *Scalps* and 2 prisoners.

THE 30TH AND 31ST   More than 100 passed through in 3 different parties on their way to the *Settlements*. There were some *Munsee* among them, and no one could stop them.

[April]

APRIL 1st   Early in the day we received news from *Goschachgünk* that the messengers mentioned on *March* 18 had returned from the *Fort* and 6 White people, *Deserteurs*, had caught up with them on the way and come with them. *Mr. McKee*, the King's *Agent of Indian Affairs*, was with them, and the *Wyandot* immediately captured and bound him. They released him when they heard what was going on.[1176]

White Eye, who met them on his journey to the *Fort* and heard much bad news from them, came back with them. This caused difficulties later because the *Chiefs* were very upset by the bad news from the *Deserteurs*.

THE 2ND   Brother *David* was called to the *Councel* in *Goschachgünk*, where he *communicated Mr. Morgan's*[1177] message to the Indians who had gathered from all surrounding area. It actually sounded very nice, but it was all too easy to see that *White Eye* and the *Chiefs* gave it very little consideration. They

---

and a generous trade well regulated. And that all the lands of the offending Tribes or Nations should be forfeited, and that they should be restricted to hunt or live on such parts of it as should be directed by the commanding Officer or Governor who might be appointed to rule them." With regard to the Delaware he added, "To the Delawares we made promise of protection, and they now put our friendship to the test, and if we do not fulfil our promise they will undoubtedly be obliged to look for protection elsewhere, and we must suffer in their opinion and also in the opinion of all the other nations." Darlington, *Fort Pitt and Letters from the Frontier*, 229–31.

1174. H3 reads: "Because White Eyes and the chiefs were called to the Fort, Brother David agreed with White Eyes that our and the Delaware towns should be provided with security, to which he consented." From "and" to "consented" bracketed in another hand.

1175. It quickly became evident that this message was wrong.

1176. On 28 March Alexander McKee, Simon Girty, Matthew Elliott, Robert Surphlitt, and John Higgins of Pittsburgh ran away to Fort Detroit. *FDO*, 249–56; Horsman, *Matthew Elliott*, 18–24.

1177. George Morgan to the Delaware chiefs, 27 March 1778 (*FDO*, 241–43); Morgan to Zeisberger on the same day (*FDO*, 244).

were more influenced by what the *Deserteurs* said, that the *Delaware* really had reason to be on their guard because the militia on the *Frontiers* had been commanded and was prepared to march from *Pittsburgh* on *May* 1st and come into Indian country.[1178] We later heard that this was indeed true and had been planned, although people had never heard that they would go to the *Delaware Towns*. In the meantime, the *Chiefs* concluded that the gentlemen in the *Fort* were offering us peace with one hand and were using the hatchets against us with the other, and the *Affairs* on the *Canhawa* and *Beaver Creek*[1179] offered sufficient proof of this. *White Eye* finally addressed the *Councel*, but primarily addressed the Brothers and asked them for help. He said he was completely alone and would be overpowered by the many people around him, because he often weakened. Therefore we should advise them what the best thing for them to do was. They would gather again tomorrow for this purpose. Then they separated.

The *Wyandot* warriors captured and bound the *Wyandot* Indian who had been sent here as a messenger from the *Fort*. They marched home this morning and took him with them. This is against all the rules, because the *Chiefs* should have protected the messenger against violence and they did not do this. We commended ourselves to the Savior and the protection of the heavenly Father for grace and asked Him to advise us and guide us according to his heart so that his will might be carried out in us and through us.[1180]

APRIL 4TH   Yesterday and today were 2 difficult days. We were preparing to deliver a *Speech* to the *Councel*. They were supposed to give us a definite statement about it and reply to it. Most of the Brothers from the *Conference* went to *Goschachgünk* for this. However, the *Chiefs* were not well disposed to this and they had no ears to hear it. They were all very muddled and confused and not even in agreement among themselves. The situation was pretty extreme since this would determine whether they decided for peace or war, and it was a scary and anxious time for us. They would have broken away long ago if they did not fear we would separate from them, which we had indicated clearly enough to them.[1181] We asked the Savior in his mercy to help us out of this trouble and to show us how we could work for the best in this situation. In the meantime, we were happy that the *Deserteurs* had left; some went to *Detroit* and some to the *Shawnee* on the *Unami River*.[1182]

1178. See entry for 27 March 1778.

1179. The formula "Affairs on the Canhawa" refers to the murder of Cornstalk (see entry for 3 Dec. 1777), and the reference to Beaver Creek recalls the expedition of General Hand in February (see entry for 10 March 1778).

1180. Whole entry for 2 April missing in H3.

1181. Horsman's suggestion that the Delaware were at this time still firmly committed to neutrality, which worked in favor of the Americans, and that therefore the Elliotts' and the others' speeches were treated with disdain, is incorrect (*Matthew Elliott*, 23). The split among the Delaware is correctly described in Schaaf, *Wampum Belts and Peace Trees*, 197–98.

1182. This river is not mentioned in Heckewelder, "Names of Rivers, Streams, Places," or in Mahr, "Indian River and Place Names in Ohio," or in Kelton, *Indian Names of Places*, or in Russell, "Indian Geographical Names."

THE 5TH   In the morning was the sermon, for which many strangers had come, and in the afternoon was the Children's Service. Toward evening *Israel* went to *Goschachgünk* with a number of Brothers. We had appointed him to address *Gelelemind* alone. He encouraged him and admonished him not to give up but to do all he could to maintain peace. We also promised that if he accepted his advice, we would support him loyally and not abandon him. We were glad to hear that this talk, which *Israel* confirmed with a *Belt of Wampum*, was well received. *Johann Martin* had come here to visit and wanted to wait and see what happened in the *Affair* with the *Chiefs* and what they had decided. I sent letters with him to the Brothers and Sisters in *Gnadenhütten* inviting them all to come here to *Lichtenau* until the difficult times were over, as the Savior had advised and instructed. The reason for this was not only the situation in general, as far as I could see at that time, but also because I had been told in confidence that if the military should march, as had been decided, *Gnadenhütten* would be most in danger, and I was also told the reason for this.

THE 6TH   In the morning a messenger came from *Gnadenhütten* with unexpected news that delighted all of us; Brothers *Heckewelder* and *Schebosch* had arrived there safely yesterday evening.[1183] I was extremely happy to receive many letters and much news from Bethlehem and *Litiz* at the same time. I also received a letter then from the *Congress* gentlemen who were in the *Fort*, which I soon took to *Goschachgünk*, read it to the *Councel*, and addressed them. This provided an opportunity for *White Eye* to speak out and express his concerns and difficulties, so we could hope that everything will be worked out and set straight.[1184] In the evening Brother *Heckewelder* himself arrived here with *Anton*, which delighted all the Brothers and Sisters, and we received news that the Brothers and Sisters in *Gnadenhütten* have all decided to come here.

THE 7TH   Brother *Heckewelder* led the early service about the text, your sorrow shall be turned into joy etc.[1185] He extended greetings to the Brothers and Sisters from the congregations and returned to *Gnadenhütten* at noon. Some *Canows* from there loaded with corn arrived here. *White Eye* came here with the *Counsellors* and Brother *David* wrote a message to the *Fort* for them.[1186] Our Brothers who were going there to pick up our things Brothers *Heckewelder* and *Schebosch* had left behind were supposed to take this along, because the *Counsellors* decided not to go there.[1187]

THE 8TH   We sent all of our *Canows* to *Gnadenhütten* to help the Broth-

1183. Both had left for Bethlehem on 27 May 1777. GD, F 9, I 1b.
1184. Neither this letter nor a second by George Morgan, which John Heckewelder brought with him, seems to have survived. The Council, probably through Zeisberger, wrote to the commissioners on the same day (George Morgan Letterbook, vol. 3, fols. 37–40, CLP); and, also on the same day, Zeisberger to Morgan (ibid., fols. 40–42); these letter report what the deserters said.
1185. John 16:20.
1186. See note 1184 to entry for 6 April 1778.
1187. The group of brethren that returned to Fort Pitt was led by Schebosch; see entry for 2 May 1778 below.

ers and Sisters so they could arrive here before the holidays if possible. In the meantime, the rest of the Brothers who stayed here enlarged our Meeting House so that we will have enough room for everyone.

We see that the *Chiefs* are still in the dark about us and they do not quite know where they stand with us. Today they asked *Isaac* and *Wilhelm* what we would probably do if the White people attacked the *Delaware Towns*. The Brothers replied that if it came to that, we would know quickly what we had to do and would not need to deliberate long. However, until we saw a need for this or imminent danger, we did not consider it necessary to think about it much. *Gelelemind* then told them they had a question to ask us. We should not be afraid, however, if they told us what had been on their minds since we had come here to the *Ohio*. However, it seems that they had never had the heart to tell us, because it was never revealed afterward. Some of them also suggested that if they were not at peace here and the war was too difficult for them, they should leave this area and move to *Wabash,* completely out of the way of the war in a different part of the country.

THE 10TH   Another party of *Shawnee* arrived in *Goschachgünk* to stay. They camped across the river and stayed there a number of days.[1188]

THE 12TH   Early in the day Brother *Heckewelder* arrived here from *Gnadenhütten* with 20 *Canows* loaded with Indian corn and household supplies. It was not possible for them to come here before the holidays, so they decided they would all stay together there until after the holidays and then all travel down here together.

THE 14TH   *White Eye* came here with some *Counsellors*. Brother *David* spoke with the former alone, advised him to peace, and explained the danger that lay ahead of them if the *Delaware* became involved in the war. He said that everything I told him was true. However, he could not do anything else, and he explained the reason why. Brother *David* now saw and heard where the actual problem lay and promised we would do what was in our power to remove the stumbling blocks. Until now we had not been able to figure out exactly what the problem was, and therefore we could not do anything about this issue.[1189]

THE 16TH   In the evening we read the story of the Passion and then 75 *Communicants* participated in the inexpressibly blessed enjoyment of the Body and Blood of our Lord in Holy Communion. One Sister, *Rachel,* participated for the first time and her husband *Israel* observed for the first time.

THE 17TH   Early in the day we read the *Liturgy* for Holy Communion and then the story of the sufferings and death of our Lord. During this our

1188. The influx of Shawnee, mentioned repeatedly (see entry for 1 Feb. 1778), indicates that within the Shawnee settlements the pressure on those who preferred neutrality had become too strong—hence their move to the Delaware settlements.

1189. Whole entry for 14 April is missing in H3

hearts were nourished through his passion. Our eyes shed tears of tribute, and we were moved anew to live for Him, to be His joy alone.

THE 18TH   For Great Sabbath we had a Lovefeast and when we were returning from the Meeting Hall 10 warriors carrying a *Scalp* passed through on their way to *Goschachgünk*.

THE 19TH   We prayed the Easter *Litany* on God's Acre and asked for eternal fellowship with the 5 Brothers and Sisters who have died this year. Then today's story of the resurrection was read and afterward was the sermon. During the Children's Service the baby girl born to *Christian* and *Cathrine* on the 15th of this month was baptized with the name *Anna Maria*. Brother *Heckewelder* led the Congregational Service.

ON THE 16TH,   Brother *Schebosch* and the Indian Brothers returned safely from the *Fort* to *Gnadenhütten*.[1190] He brought along a letter to the *Chiefs* from *Mr. Morgan* and the *Commissioners*,[1191] as well as one for Brother *David*. Because of this *White Eye* and *Gelelemind* came here today and talked with our Indian Brothers for an hour about the current situation. The *Chiefs* are supposed to appear in the *Fort* in a very few days and if they do not do so within this period of time they will be considered enemies.

THE 20TH   Once again we sent 20 *Canows* to *Gnadenhütten* to help move the Brothers and Sisters down here. As part of his duties as *Chief, Israel* consoled the *Chiefs* in *Goschachgünk* for the loss of their old *Chief*[1192] and also admonished them to follow the rules he had left behind. Most importantly, shortly before his end he had instructed them not to take any part in the current war. They should remain quiet and peaceful.[1193] The day before yesterday our young Brothers had also encouraged the young people in *Goschachgünk* to obey their *Chiefs*. They told them they should offer the *Chiefs* an address in which they encouraged them to keep the peace firmly and not become tired or feeble, and the young people should also promise to support them as much as they could, and so on. Our Brothers contributed some Klafter of *Wampum* for this. They approved of this suggestion and instruction and carried it out.[1194]

1190. Fort Pitt.

1191. In a letter dated 13 April 1778 the commissioners asked the Delaware to maintain peace, not listen to the deserters, and come to Fort Pitt as soon as possible for consultations (*FDO,* 269–70). The threats Zeisberger reported are expressed much less strongly in the official letter; we could not find Morgan's letter to Zeisberger.

1192. On the death of Netawatwees, see entry for 5 Nov. 1776; the entry makes clear how far the missionaries' opinion had changed on the question of whether baptized members of the congregation could still exercise the functions of a chief. Until 1777 Zeisberger had insisted that that they could only if it served the interests of the mission congregation; now he was convinced that a baptized Indian could still fulfill functions of a chief as long as it did not harm the interests of the congregation. Israel, formerly Welapachtschiechen, thus not only directed messages to the former inhabitants of Assünnünk (see entry for 8 Feb. 1778) and acted as chief on behalf of the mission congregation (see entry for 5 April 1778), but according to Zeisberger he also looked after general chief affairs (see entry for 28 Dec. 1777).

1193. On Netawatwees' last will, see entry for 9 March 1777 and note 925.

1194. This advice to the young people of Goschachgünk reflected White Eyes' confession of 14 April 1778 that "he could not do anything else, and he explained the reason why." Faced with clashes

We really do not want to leave any stone unturned, but to remove anything in the way and do whatever we can to help preserve the *Delaware Nation.* Several days ago they told us there was no one among them who was able to do anything, but if we wanted to do something else we could. We do not want to let them down, and the Savior will do what is best.

THE 21ST   It was now high time for one of the *Chiefs* to go to the *Fort,* because the *Commissioners* had set the 25th as the deadline. All efforts made thus far to get someone to go were in vain but according to the last *Resolution* in the *Fort* the militia will march out to the *Frontiers* and into Indian country if they do not do this. This would be extremely dangerous for us, because they do not obey any *Commandos* or *Orders,* as we saw in the example of the *Action* at *Beaver Creek.*[1195] Therefore we instructed our *Israel* to do his best to get *White Eye,* who is his subordinate,[1196] to go to the *Fort.* All night long messengers went back and forth between here and *Goschachgünk,* and this continued until after the early service this morning, which was about the Watchword, Save thy people, who have nothing than your grace and live solely from it. The text was, For he saith, I have heard thee in a time accepted, and in the day of salvation have I succoured thee: behold, now is the accepted time; behold, now is the day of salvation.[1197] Then *Isaac* brought the good news that *White Eye* had decided to go. He requested Brothers *Willhelm* and *Isaac* as his companions and they left with him already today. The *Deserteurs* from the *Fort* laid the foundation for all of this *Confusion* and caused us so much work and trouble that it will be a while before everything is in order again. Still, we are happy and grateful to the Savior that a beginning has been made.[1198] For the past 14 days it has not been easy for us to speak with the *Chiefs.* They were turning over bad things in their minds, and whenever they began thinking about it we were immediately the wall they ran into and could not get past, because we always

---

between American settlers and soldiers on the one hand and Delaware on the other, under pressures from the British, the Munsee, and the Wyandot, and, finally, in light of the openly pro-British attitude of Captain Pipe and his considerable number of followers, the Council and White Eyes seemed unable to ignore the demands of the young warriors for a complete change of policy. Only the massive intervention of the missionary congregation seemed able to prevent this. The congregation reacted in two ways: Israel sent his message to the Council and the young members of the congregation tried to influence the young warriors, who commanded considerable influence within the tribe.

1195. See entry for 10 March 1778.

1196. See entry for 16 May 1776. At the same time this remark suggests the general problem of how the succession of Netawatwees had been arranged. Formulas like "White Eyes came here with some councillors" (entry for 14 April 1778) or "White Eyes and Gelelemind came here today and talked with our Indian Brothers" (entry for 19 April 1778) probably indicate that the succession had not yet been settled.

1197. Watchword is Ps. 28:9; *Des kleinen Brüder-Gesangbuchs Dritter Theil,* hymn no. 296, verse 2, "Hilf deinem Volk, das nichts hat als deine Gnad und nur lebet davon allein"; Text is 2 Cor. 6:2. Watchword and Text are taken from the Collection for 1778, *Die täglichen Loosungen der Brüdergemeine für das Jahr 1778.* The Collection of Watchwords evidently arrived with the mail of either 27 March or 6 April 1778.

1198. Until "has been made," whole entry for 21 April not in H3. On the deserters, see entries starting with 1 April 1778.

stuck to our *Text* and reminded them of the first time we had addressed them right after we came into this country. We told them that as long they were for peace, we would help them and support them and not leave them. In the opposite situation, however, they could expect the opposite from us.[1199] This was the only thing that was still holding them back, and sometimes they got very angry about this. One time recently they even told our Brothers that they wanted to give us alone the office of *Chief,* by which they meant the government.[1200] They probably said this just out of frustration, because they see they cannot do whatever they want to do with us. They often talk about how we are supposed to become one people with them (see *White Eye's Speech* to the Brothers on *March* 9 of last year in *Goschachgünk*). However, if this is going to happen, then *they* must become one people with us. If we are to become one people, they must convert to our ways; we will never be converted to theirs.[1201]

THE 22ND   Some loaded *Canows* arrived here from *Gnadenhütten* and then returned there immediately. In the evening the Brothers gathered in the schoolhouse and received news of what had happened and had been negotiated in recent days between the *Chiefs* and us. They listened to this and it had the *Effect* that they started preaching about this, which lasted until late in the night.

THE 24TH   46 *Warriors* returned from the *Settlements* with 7 prisoners, 3 *Scalps,* and 30 horses.[1202] The warriors were mostly *Mingo.* They stopped a little while at the end of our *Town* and our Brothers and Sisters took the prisoners something to eat. Then they went to *Goschachgünk.*

THE 25TH   Brother *Edwards* arrived here with the Brothers and Sisters from *Gnadenhütten* and they camped on the river until they could build huts for themselves.

THE 26TH   On Sunday *Quasimodogeniti,* 20 Brothers and Sisters who have been baptized in the past year, including one who was received into the congregation, were seated in front of the congregation. In a prayer we commended them to the Savior for protection and to the dear Mother for further care.

THE 27TH   The Brothers and Sisters from *Gnadenhütten* are all here and we are all together, so we gathered the *Conference* Brothers and Sisters and began establishing order among ourselves. We spoke with each of the young people from *Gnadenhütten* individually and informed them of our rules, and this had the desired *Effect.*[1203]

1199. On the messages, see entries for 23 Feb. and 1 June 1773.

1200. See entries for 22 Jan. 1778, in which it is reported that an Indian was spreading the rumor that Zeisberger was to be appointed a chief.

1201. On the problem of acculturation, see Introduction, pp. 7, 22.

1202. Indian attacks on American settlements had reached such proportions that the reports of leading military officers caused panic throughout the settlements. See *FDO,* 265–68, 273–74, 278–79.

1203. In light of the essential likeness of the statutes for Lichtenau and Gnadenhütten in all points, this is a rather remarkable proceeding; the only explanation for it is that Zeisberger had concluded that unpleasant deviations from the statutes had surfaced in Gnadenhütten. See Zeisberger

THE 29TH   At the request of the *Chiefs* in *Goschachgünk, Abraham* and some Brothers went to *Memehusing*,[1204] the *Munsee Town* a one-day journey from here. They had received and accepted the *War Belt* from *Detroit,* and they were taking them a message admonishing them to return the *War Belt* and not to have any part in the war. If they got involved in this war, they would not only bring misfortune upon themselves but also upon the entire *Delaware Nation.*[1205]

THE 30TH   Both yesterday and today the Brothers helped the Brothers and Sisters who had come to us from *Gnadenhütten* build huts. They continued this the following day until they were finished. We laid out a new street and built a long hut with a number of sections for the widows. Many *Mingo* warriors, who were camping in *Goschachgünk* with their prisoners, visited us today and in recent days.

May

THE 2ND   Brothers *Isaac* and *Wilhelm* returned from the *Fort* with *White Eye* and his company and brought us good news. People there were very happy to see both *White Eye* and the Brothers there, and the *Commissioners* asked in great detail about the latter and all of the circumstances here before dealing with the *Chiefs.*[1206] We were happiest to learn that the militia that was supposed to march into Indian country, which would have been one of the most dangerous things for us, has now been completely called off because they had carried out evil deeds and had not spared friend or enemy. One *Colonel* from the militia announced in *Pittsburgh* that as soon as they crossed the *Ohio,* one party would march directly to *Gnadenhütten* without letting anyone in the *Fort* know about

---

to Matthäus Hehl, 10 June 1778, MAB, Lititz Records: Indian Mission, where he discusses in detail the internal problems of the Gnadenhütten congregation.

1204. On earlier references to Memehusing, see entries for 1 Sept. 1776 and 7 March 1777.

1205. There was a conference at Fort Detroit on 11 March 1778 in which, according to Henry Hamilton's report, "one hundred & twenty-five warriors, Mingoes, Shawnese & Delawares"—all of whom had accepted the war belt—participated. Hamilton to Carleton, 25 April 1778, HP, 434. No Delaware from Goschachgünk seems to have attended this conference.

1206. See report on the negotiations of 25–26 April 1778 in George Morgan Letterbook, vol. 3, fols. 53–57, CLP. Subjects discussed were, first, the reasons for the conflicts within the Council of the Delaware; second, the number of friendly and hostile Indians; and, third, protection of the Indians against white attacks during their hunting season. On the first point, see note 1194. On the second point White Eyes offered the following information: At present the Delaware had some "300 strong (Men carrying Arms) and are collecting all our People from every Quarter." In addition, seventeen Shawnee families had joined the tribe. The number of hostile warriors White Eyes gave as four hundred, adding: "At present your Enemies are the Banditti of the Mingoes, & the Wiandots of Sandusky & Detroit & a few of the Ottawas & Chipwas & some Shawnese & a few Delawares." Of the Munsee he said: "The Munsies except about thirty have gone to live in the Senneca Country. They are so distant from us & times have been so troublesome that we have had no intercourse with those People." On the third point the participants agreed on the region between the Little Beaver Creek and the Hocking River as hunting territory, with the stipulation that hunters should not come within fifteen or twenty miles of the Ohio River.

it.[1207] We also heard that Brother *Schebosch* and the Indian Brothers who had gone to the *Fort* with him to pick up our things[1208] had experienced a special act of protection. When they returned from the *Fort* they were in the middle of two dangers, although they had no idea of this. Ahead of them were warriors who had committed murders near the *Fort*. Just before they had gone to *Sakunk* they had passed through here and forgotten some of their spoils there in their haste. Behind them were White people from the militia who had secretly set out after them as far as *Sakunk*. Because they had not caught them by then they had turned around. They had later reported this in the *Fort*, but people did not believe them. Rather everyone suspected they might have killed the Brothers. Now as soon as the Brothers got to the *Fort*, the first question was whether Brother *Schebosch* and his party had arrived safely and they were happy to hear this answer.

THE 3RD   Early in the day Brother *Heckewelder* went to *Goschachgünk* where he *communicated* the news from the *Fort* to the *Councel*. Brother *David* received friendly letters from both *Mr. Morgan* and the *Commissioners*.[1209] They recognize the work of the Brothers among the Indians as an act of kindness for the entire country and they say they are not ignorant of this. In a service for the communicant Brothers and Sisters, we asked the Savior to ground the 7 who became participants in Holy Communion this year in his death, so that they might remain in Him, the vine,[1210] and might prosper for Him.

THE 4TH   After the early service led by Brother *Heckewelder*, there was a Helpers *Conference*. The Brothers and Sisters were encouraged to consider together their work and things that come up daily and to support each other. *Abraham* returned from *Memehusing*, where they had urged the *Munsee* Indians to remain quiet and peaceful.[1211] From the stories the Brothers tell, we understand that it is a very dark area and the spirit of deception is in control.

THE 5TH   *Half King* of the *Wyandot* arrived here by water with 100 men. They traveled past *Goschachgünk* and before they arrived they fired off all their weapons and camped on the river. *Half King* soon came and greeted us, *shook hands* with us and said they were happy to see us again after a year. The following day our house was full of them all day. The *Wyandot* and *Mingo* were all orderly and polite. However, some of the *Shawnee* who were along let their coarseness be seen and they stood out. *White Eye* and *Gelelemind* came here with some *Councellors*[1212] and told them the news from the *Fort*.

1207. Other sources do not confirm this report, but in light of the incidents at Beaver River and the murder of Cornstalk, both the missionaries and the Indians were unanimous in the opinion that it nevertheless reflected the attitude of many militia soldiers.

1208. See entries for 7 and 19 April 1778.

1209. We could not locate the letters.

1210. John 15:5.

1211. See entry for 29 April 1778.

1212. H3 has text: "*Counsellors*, who met Half King and the chiefs in Council and communicated the news."

THE 7TH   A large party of warriors was present in the early service, and they were attentive and orderly. Soon afterward they traveled on to the Fort on the *Canhawa*.[1213] They had made some more *Canows* here yesterday. *Half King* informed us that they would not come here on their return march but would take another way instead.

THE 8TH   A Frenchman came here from the *Lake* with goods. It was a great benefit for our Brothers and Sisters to be provided with adequate goods from that area, and indeed for a very good price,[1214] since we cannot get anything from *Pittsburgh* at this time.

THE 13TH   The Brothers finished fencing in a field for the Brothers and Sisters from *Gnadenhütten*. They had been busy with this for several days.

THE 15TH   In the devotional service for married couples[1215] *Anton, Israel's* eldest son, was married to the single Sister *Philippina,* a very nice and promising Brother and Sister.

THE 17TH   The *Shawnee Chief Gischenatsi*[1216] and some of his people attended the sermon. During the Children's Service, which *White Eye* also attended with others, the baby girl born to Brother *Jacob* and Sister *Johannette* on the 11th of this month was baptized with the name *Anna Sabina.*

THE 22ND   A woman who had come along from *Assünnünk*[1217] but had settled in *Goschachgünk* later, brought her sick 6-year-old daughter here a couple of days ago. She asked that she be baptized before her end. 8 days ago last Sunday the woman and girl had attended the services as they usually did on Sundays and when they were going home the child cried because she wanted to stay here. When she got home, she immediately became ill and kept asking the mother until she brought her here. The child was very happy about this and said, Now I only want one more thing in the world; I would like to be baptized with the Savior's blood and then I will gladly go to Him. Today she was baptized with the name *Salome* and was very joyful. 2 days later she died and was buried in our God's Acre.

MAY 23RD   We received news that the *Governour* in *Detroit*[1218] had sent a message to the *Nations* that they should stop waging war against the *Colonies*

1213. The Wyandot spread anxiety and terror; on the reaction, see Colonel William Preston to Colonel William Fleming, 17 May 1778, *FAO,* 51–53. Also see entry for 9 June 1778.

1214. The traders hailed from Sandusky, a pro-British Wyandot settlement that got goods from Detroit. On April 25 1778 Hamilton reported to Carleton: "January the 25th some Traders to Sandooské having given room for suspecting they were carrying on a correspondence with the Rebels, I ordered a search to be made for some papers of which I had had notice, but tho' I was well assured my suspicions were well grounded, they eluded the search, however upon examining the goods conveyed out & comparing them with the Invoices, a considerable quantity was found for which a pass had not been asked." HP, 433–34.

1215. I.e., married people's quarter-of-an-hour devotion; H3: "Early hour."

1216. See entry for 23 Nov. 1777 and note 1129.

1217. See entry for 24 Nov. 1776.

1218. Henry Hamilton.

immediately, and those who had gone to war should be called back.[1219] It was announced that this message was for the *Wyandot, Mingo, Shawnee*s etc. and did not concern the *Delaware*, because they were not engaged in war. We could not find out the reason for this. In the meantime, this was pleasant news for us because it gives us hope for better times.

THE 24TH In the Children's Service the baby girl born to Brother *Ludwig* and Sister *Maria Juliana* on the 14th was baptized with the name *Rosina,* and the baby boy born to *Renatus* and *Johanna Sophia* on the 19th with the name *Samuel.*

THE 28TH We had a day of special blessing. Since our dear Lord has gone to heaven and is no longer visibly with us, He let us sense his invisible presence all the more powerfully and revealed himself to us especially during the Service of Adoration for the baptized Brothers and Sisters. We prayed for his company with him for all our days and hours. During the Congregational Service the above-mentioned widow from *Assünnünk*, whose child was baptized on the 22nd of this month, was also baptized into Jesus' death with the name *Anna Margaretha.*

THE 29TH Brothers *Samuel Nantikok* and *Thomas* returned from the *Lake*. They brought along *Confirmation* of the news that was reported on the 23rd of this month.

THE 30TH We had Speakings with the Brothers and Sisters in recent days, and then 110 *Communicants* celebrated Holy Communion. Two Brothers were readmitted. One watched for the first time and one for the second time.

THE 31ST After the *Liturgy* for Holy Communion there was the sermon, for which many strangers had gathered again. The baptized boys and girls then had a sweet and blessed service.

June

THE 3RD An Indian from the *Council* who is one of *Newollike's*[1220] followers is supposedly in the middle of bringing a secret accusation concerning the history of the congregation against the Indian Believers, and he has already

---

1219. This message was wrong. See entry for 29 May 1778 below. The origin of this message is not clear. It may have originated in a region under British control and was probably connected with the resignation of Governor Carleton. This message reached Fort Detroit in May; in any case, in his letter of 9 June 1778 to Carleton, Hamilton regretted Carleton's decision "to go to Europe." The same letter discussed Hamilton's plans to use the allied tribes in the war against the "rebels" and expressed the hope of getting Carleton's instructions before the latter's departure (HP, 440). Since the conference mentioned above began on 14 June, and since Hamilton began his letter with the words "The savages will in a few days meet in council," the editors' dating of this letter as "9th of July 78" must be wrong.

1220. On Newollike, see entries for 11 and 21 March (with note 936), 2 April, and 26 Aug. 1777.

been working on this secretly for some time and has tried to tempt some of our people. Therefore, some Brothers from the *Conference* went to *Goschachgünk* and brought this matter before the *Councel,* where he was supposed to answer for himself. He was not able to do this, however, and he was publicly shamed.

THE 4TH   28 more *Munsee* warriors came to *Goschachgünk* on their march to the *Settlements,* and many of them also came here. Our *Israel* had already recommended to the *Chiefs* yesterday that they should stop them if possible, and they promised to do this. They are the dregs of all bad people and the *Mingo* and *Wyandot* are quite an orderly people compared to them.[1221] The following day one party of them came into our house with their spears, which no warriors had done before. It hurt us to see that there were 3 people who had left the congregation in this *Compagnie.* They were so rude that I could no longer remain silent. I asked these three where they were going. They replied, Hunting. I told them that when I saw warriors going to war it did not matter which *Nation* they came from; I was not surprised and did not even think much about it, because they did not know better and had never heard any better. However, I was rightfully surprised at them, because they had lived with us and heard the Gospel, and they still went out murdering and robbing. One of them answered quite reasonably and said it was true that they had heard God's word, but they had then lost it all again. I replied that they had still heard it and knew it. Therefore they could not excuse themselves this way. Another one, however, became bitterly angry and could not hide his anger. He openly said he was going to bash in the brains of the White people. It was useless to try to persuade him to give up his intention. He continued on his way with some others. However, the rest all turned around. Then I said, many, many warriors have been here with me and I never said anything to them about going to the war. However, if they came to me now, I could not let them go like this without reminding them of what they had formerly heard from us and I would do this as often as they came into my house.

THE 6TH   After the early service was the burial of Sister *Johanna Sophia,* who died in blessing the day before yesterday. She was from the *Munsee Nation* and came to the congregation in *Schönbrunn* in 1774 with her husband *Renatus,* now a widower. She was baptized there on the 28th of *May,* 1775 and attained the enjoyment of Holy Communion on *May* 25, 1776. After her baptism she led a blessed life, grew in the grace she received, and remained faithful. Her father left the congregation last year when we pulled out of *Schoenbrunn,* and he tried hard to get her to leave as well. He then tried again here, but she remained firm and immovable about remaining with the Savior and the congregation as long as she lived. She had been sick for a long time, but since she delivered on May 19th we saw that her blessed end was approaching. She often said this herself, and added that she was concerned about her children; she

1221. H3 reads: "pretty orderly and civilized people."

leaves 5 behind in the congregation. However, she had surrendered herself and her children to the Savior. He would take care of them. Thus she died quite happily with the blessing of the congregation on the stated day.

JUNE 7TH   It was Pentecost and we thanked the worthy Holy Spirit for all the efforts and care he has made on our behalf. We asked for the forgiveness of all our mistakes and for times when we have not listened to his voice and reminders and promised him new faithfulness and obedience. He revealed himself to us in all of our services and gave us new comfort.

THE 8TH   Early in the day 2 *express* messengers[1222] from the *Fort* arrived here. We were also sincerely delighted to receive letters from our dear Brothers *Mattheus, Ettwein,* and *Grube* in *Litiz.* Brothers *David* and *Heckewelder* went to *Goschachgünk* soon afterward and *communicated* to them the news that had been sent from *Mr. Morgan* and *General Hand* to the *Councel.*[1223]

THE 9TH   We received news that the *Wyandot Half King* and his men had attacked the *Fort* on the *Canhawa*[1224] but did not fare very well, and that many of his people were wounded. Half of them then turned back, but the rest of them went further on into the country.

THE 10TH   *White Eye* came here with the *Councellors.* Brother *David* wrote a reply to the *Fort* for them.[1225] On this occasion he also wrote to Brother *Mattheus* in *Litiz.* The messenger, accompanied by some Indians from here and *Goschachgünk,* then returned to the *Fort* on the 11th.[1226] Many of our Brothers and Sisters from here went a day's journey away from here to boil salt.

THE 12TH   Our *Israel* and some Brothers went to *Goschachgünk,* where they settled a matter with *Gelelemind* concerning *White Eye,* who was offended

1222. The messengers were John Jones and Thomas Nichols. Both had participated in Lord Dunmore's war as scouts. *FAO,* 74; *DHDW,* 13n26.

1223. On 5 June 1778 Hand wrote to the Delaware chiefs about the treaty of friendship and alliance between the United States and France (*FAO,* 74). Hand had asked to be relieved of his command at Fort Pitt; the Continental Congress had accepted his wish on 2 May 1778 and asked George Washington to name a successor (*FDO,* 293–94).

1224. The commanding officer of Fort Randolph was Captain Matthew Arbuckle; reports of the siege of 16 May 1778 and the fights are printed in *FAO,* 64–73. See also Rice, *Allegheny Frontier,* 102–4. Since the attack failed, the pro-British Indians moved up the Kanawha River and laid siege to Fort Donally, were they suffered many losses and were defeated. See entry for 16 June 1778 and the cited reports.

1225. Printed in *FAO,* 83–84. White Eyes informed Morgan that Chippewa had told him they intended to follow the Delaware's example and stay neutral; he added that he had, as Morgan requested, talked to the Wyandot and gained the impression that they were now more willing to conclude a treaty of amity with the United States. The Shawnee asked him to convey to Morgan their decision to participate in the planned conference at Fort Pitt. He himself would be traveling to Detroit in a few days in consequence of an invitation from the governor there; upon his return he would go to Fort Pitt and report the events at Detroit.

1226. Zeisberger does not mention that on the same day he, too, had written a personal letter to George Morgan, printed in *FAO,* 82–83. In this letter Zeisberger conveyed information about British activities that he had received from John Montour and others. At the end of January Montour, who had tried to free prisoners, had himself been thrown into prison, but at the urgent requests of the Wyandot he had been released. Upon his return to Goschachgünk, Montour, according to Zeisberger, used his time "[to speak] against the Governour [Hamilton]."

by both the *Governour* in *Detroit* in *September*, 1776,[1227] and the Indians in *Go-schachgünk*.[1228] *Israel* had recently promised *White Eye* he would do this and told him he should just hurry to the *Fort* now so that the *Delaware Nation* would be removed from danger, because they had been informed by the *Fort*, through *Morgan* and the *Commissioners* appointed by *Congress*, that they would be considered enemies if they did not come at the appointed time. When he promised that everything could be set straight again, *White Eye* accepted and went. This brought peace and security not only to us, but also to the entire *Nation*. Today the baby boy born to the blessed Sister *Johanna Sophia* on the 19th of last month followed her into the kingdom of health. His earthly dwelling was buried on the 13th.

THE 16TH   We received news that the *Compagnie* of *Wyandot* who had left the *Fort* on the *Canhawa* and gone further into the country had suffered a serious defeat, and that 10 *Wyandot*, including 3 *Captains*, were killed and others were wounded. Some warriors who had been there brought this news here.[1229]

THE 19TH   Early in the day the widow *Cornelia's* little daughter, who was 9 years old, died unexpectedly. Yesterday she was still energetic and healthy until evening, when she began to complain that she did not feel well. This morning no one thought that she might die, but suddenly her end was there and her breathing stopped. The child had requested and cried for baptism quite often in the past couple of years. She had sometimes expressed her concern that she would die without experiencing the grace of being washed of her sins with the Savior's blood. On THE 20TH her earthly dwelling was buried on our God's Acre.

THE 22ND   The messengers returned from the *Fort*, and we received good news about the *Delaware*[1230] in a letter from *General Hand*.

THE 26TH   A *Compagnie* of *Munsee* came from the war with 2 *Scalps* and one prisoner.

1227. See entry for 14 Sept. 1776.

1228. This probably refers to the rupture in the Delaware Council that played a role in the negotiations of 25–26 April 1778 at Fort Pitt. During the altercations in the Council White Eyes had offered his resignation. See note 1206 to entry for 2 May 1778.

1229. See note 1224 to entry for 9 June 1778.

1230. Dated 16 June 1778, printed in *FAO*, 91–92. General Hand requested that White Eyes and the Council inform the Wyandot of the United States' final offer to conclude a treaty of amity with them at the forthcoming conference at Fort Pitt, provided they would immediately pull back all their warriors. Hand predicted that before the next winter was over the British forts in Detroit and Niagara would be conquered. In this letter Hand for the first time went beyond the usual requests and asked that ten Delaware warriors, who would be paid, observe a group of Canadian Indians who were considered particularly dangerous. He would consider acceptance of the request "a mark of your friendship." Hand of course must have known that granting this request would mean overstepping the line between friendly neutrality and active participation in the war on the American side. In response to the British attacks on American settlements, as reported by White Eyes, the Continental Congress resolved on 11 June 1778 to release funds for an expedition of three thousand soldiers against Fort Detroit and Indians hostile to the United States settling in that region. The resolve is printed in *FAO*, 88–89.

THE 29TH *Joseph Peepe* left with some *Councellors* to go to the *Wyandot* in *Sandusky* on business.[1231]

July

THE 2ND Yesterday and today about 50 warriors passed through here on their way to the *Settlements*. They informed us that we should expect large *Compagnies* of warriors soon. A *Compagnie* of 15 *Munsee* detained the Brothers until the next morning and *Israel* spoke with the *Munsee* in the evening and admonished them to put aside their plan and to turn back. Then they gave them a *String* with some Klafter of *Wampum*. However, the Brothers received no answer from them until the next morning, when they fired their rifles and marched on. However, 5 of them turned around. We also learned that a *Compagnie* of *Wyandot* who were waiting in *Goschachgünk* had gone to the *Fort*. We were not happy about this because we were expecting messengers from the *Fort* very soon, as *Mr. Morgan* had promised, and they might be caught.

THE 6TH The earthly dwelling of old *Simon*, left behind when he died in blessing yesterday, was laid to rest. He was a headman of the *Delaware Nation* and *Chief* in *Shenenge*[1232] on *Beaver Creek*. He had visited the Brothers in *Langundoutenünk*, where he once sat up the whole night with *Isaac*, talked with him, and asked him questions. He expressed all the hesitations and doubts he had about our teaching. *Isaac* gave him a complete explanation of this and although he was not yet completely convinced, he could not raise any objections to it. Then in 1773 he came to *Schönbrunn*, bought a *Canow* for the purpose of traveling several hundred miles to *Wabash* and enjoying a very plentiful hunt. He stayed for several days and the Brothers, especially *Nathanael Davis*, preached the Savior to him fervently and he was very attentive during this. He left then, but lost his *Canow* before he got out of this area. Therefore nothing came of his trip and he returned to *Schönbrunn*, where he stayed a while longer again and heard more about the salvation that comes from the merits and sufferings of Jesus. He then became completely convinced, felt no more peace, and asked the Brothers for permission to move to *Schönbrunn*, which he received. He then went home, told his wife what had happened to him and that he could not stay away from the Brothers any longer and he wanted to move to the congregation now. His wife did not cause any difficulties and in the fall of the above-stated year they came to Schönbrunn. On *April* 3, 1774, he was baptized and he attained the enjoyment of Holy Communion on *June* 21, 1777, in *Lichtenau*. He always treasured this, continued in grace, and did not allow himself to be disturbed or to worry much more about the things of

1231. On the background, see preceding note.
1232. On this place see entry for 10 May 1773 and note 191.

the earth. He must have been over 100 years old, because he could tell stories about when the first house was built in *Philadelphia,* when he himself had lived there as a boy. Despite his old age, he amazed everyone with his memory and his strength. During his 12-day illness, he surrendered to the Savior's will and wanted to be home with him if it pleased him. He experienced this happiness on the stated day and he died with the blessing of the congregation.

Diary of Lichtenau *on the* Muskingum *from* July 10th *until* August 17th, 1778[1233]

JULY 10TH   Today and in recent days many *Shawnee* from the *Unami River*[1234] came here to buy corn because there is great famine everywhere among the Indians.

THE 11TH   We strengthened ourselves in the Body and Blood of our Lord in Holy Communion. One Brother participated in this for the first time and one Sister observed for the first time.

THE 12TH   Early in the day we had the *Liturgy* for Holy Communion and then the sermon about the text, Therefore being justified by faith, we have peace with God through our Lord Jesus Christ etc.[1235] In the evening during the Congregational Service, *Marcus's* wife was baptized into Jesus' death with the name *Sara.* On this occasion the Watchword was, I shall give thee the heathen for thine inheritance, and the uttermost parts of the earth for thy possession. The abundance of the heathen is his hard earned reward.[1236]

Joseph Peepe and some of the *Council* returned from *Sandusky.* Once again they had advised the *Wyandot* there to peace and invited them to a *Treaty* in the name of the *Commissioners* in *Pittsburgh.*[1237] They would not listen to them, however, and they are actually trying to start the war again. Since last fall the *Chiefs* in *Goschachgünk* have been trying to establish a friendly relationship with *Governor Hamilton*[1238] in *Detroit* and are considering going to a *Treaty* there this spring. However, both the Whites and the Indians in *Sandusky* advised them not to go there because it had been decided that none of them would return if they went.

THE 16TH   A *Companie* of 80 *Wyandot* arrived here. Most of them came across the *Lake* from *Detroit* and visited us frequently throughout the day. Some of them looked at Brother *Heckewelder* very strangely because they had never

---

1233. MAB, B 147, F 7, fol. 306b.
1234. See note 1182 to entry for 4 April 1778.
1235. Rom. 5:1.
1236. Ps. 2:8; "Es ist die Füll der Heiden sein saurer Lohn" (*Das kleine Brüder-Gesang-Buch,* hymn no. 326).
1237. See entry for 29 June 1778 and note 1232.
1238. Henry Hamilton; see entry for 10 Jan. 1778.

seen him, and they asked him where he came from. They were satisfied, however, when Brother *David* said he was his Brother. When one of them went past the Meeting House, he knelt down before the door and offered his prayer. There were also some White people, French and English, in their *Companie,* and one of them brought Brother *David* an oral message from the *Governor* in *Detroit,* saying that the Indians had complained that Brother *David* always reported to *Pittsburgh* when warriors passed through here and that they would be betrayed and would suffer harm through this. He asked that this not be done any more. This was because the last *Company* of *Wyandot* had lost 17 men and someone had to be held responsible for this. Therefore not only Brother *David* but also *White Eye* and the *Chiefs* in *Goschachgünk* were accused of betraying them, although none of the *Delaware* had gone to the *Fort* the entire time they were out.[1239] Brother *David* sent him a reply saying that we were not concerned in the war, because that was not our business. He thought that the warriors were reasonable enough not to come here if they thought we would betray them, and that they would take another route. The fact that they all liked coming here so much was a sign that they did not fear anything from us, as indeed they had nothing to fear from us. We were situated between two warring parties and just watched; we wanted to live in peace with all people. The entire *Compagnie* spent the night here, so we spoke with the *Captains* of the warriors and asked them to spare us their war dances, since it is their custom to hold their dance wherever they spend the night. They immediately promised to forego this and they kept their word and behaved very quietly and politely.

White Eye came and talked with us and shared his concerns so we could consider them, and he asked us to advise him. First, he informed us that he had received news that the *Nations* are preparing to speak very sharply with the *Delaware* and wanted to force them to join in the war. This message was already on the way and they could expect it any day.[1240] Some parties of *Munsee*

1239. As far as the expedition of the Wyandot led by Half King in May 1778 is concerned, Zeisberger's defense is correct. Yet the more general rebuke of the governor of Detroit is equally justified. As late as 9 June 1778 Zeisberger had carefully reported all movements of the enemy in a letter to George Morgan; see note 1225 to entry for 10 June 1778. With this letter he enclosed the following note: "There is a small army of French 150 or 200 men that is for the frontiers, commanded by one Mr. Lemot. I imagine he is for his old hunting ground on Red Stone" (*FAO,* 83n1). This communication prompted General Hand's request that a group of Delaware warriors observe these hostile soldiers, cited in note 1230 above. But information flowed in more than one direction. Zeisberger's entry for 5 May 1778 states that White Eyes informed the Wyandot about the late events at Fort Pitt.

1240. Between 14 and 20 June 1778 there was a conference at Fort Detroit with the Indian Nations allied with England. The conference resolved to send a joint message to the Delaware; it is this message and its vigorous threats to which White Eyes refers. The message is printed in *FAO,* 94–95; the protocol of the conference, with even stronger hostile remarks against the Delaware, is printed in HP, 442–52. Considering the considerable military successes of the pro-British forces in the Ohio region, the question arises, what motivated Hamilton to increase pressure on the Delaware? Two reasons suggest themselves: first, provisioning Fort Detroit with English goods, and thus increasing the possibility of maintaining alliances with the Indian tribes, which had deteriorated considerably

warriors were guarding the road to the *Fort* and since *Mr. Morgan* had promised to send messengers here now, he feared they have already been captured or might be captured. The *Delaware* are constantly accused of betraying the warriors who pass through here, so the *Chiefs* no longer dare to send messengers there openly since this is not a secret among the Indians. However, they really would like to get news from the *Fort* and to know where they stand and also to report how things are. Most importantly, the *Delaware Nation* will get trapped in a corner if they do not receive assistance in one way or another. He said he was submitting this to us for our speedy consideration, because he cannot rely upon his people nor entrust them with such things. He had good hope, however, that we would not lack good advice and would share this with him. Things look very gloomy all around again, as if a storm were gathering above us. May the Savior look on this and help us make it through these complicated times in complete safety. Then we will praise Him and thank Him for this eternally.

JULY 17TH   A party of *Wyandot* was also present in the early service. Some of them knelt as soon as they entered the Meeting Hall and prayed their rosary in silence. Toward noon they continued their march, but they had hardly gotten out of the *Town* when a party of *Mingo* arrived with a *Scalp* and a prisoner whom the *Wyandot* had beaten badly, one man after the other, outside of the *Town*.[1241]

THE 20TH   2 Brothers, *Anton* and *Samuel Nantikok,* left for the *Fort.* We used this opportunity to send a packet to Brother *Mattheus.* No one in *Goschachgünk* except *White Eye* knew about these messengers.[1242] Some *Shawnee*

(see note 1282 to entry for 16 Sept. 1778); and second, the position of Detroit had deteriorated as a result of the French-American treaty of amity and the rapprochement between the United States and Spain, which immediately affected the attitude of the tribes in the Mississippi Valley (see note 1260 to entry for 17 Aug. 1778). Both factors necessitated a drastic increase in military activities, although these were considerably hampered by the geographical position of the Delaware settlements between the pro-British and the American settlements. At the instigation of the British, the Six Indian Nations had offered the Delaware a new territory at the "head of the Scioto," as Henry Hamilton reported to the *pro tempore* governor of Canada, Hector Theophilus Cramahé (d. 1788), in a letter dated 17 Aug. 1778. After the harvest the Delaware would move to the new territory and thus open the direct route to the American settlements in the east. Hamilton added: "If they do remove the Frontiers will repent it severely" (HP, 463–64). See Zeisberger's analysis in his diary entry for 17 Oct. 1778.

1241. According to James Smith, who had to survive a similar ordeal after being taken prisoner, this was a kind of initiation rite for white prisoners. Having survived the ordeal, they were usually adopted by an Indian family. Smith recalled his conversation with the Delaware: "I asked him if I had done any thing that had offended the Indians, which caused them to treat me so unmercifully? He said no, it was only an old custom the Indians had, and it was like how do you do; after that he said I would be well used. I asked him if I should be admitted to remain with the French? He said no—and told me that as soon as I recovered, I must not only go with the Indians, but must be made an Indian myself." Darlington, *Scoouwa: James Smith's Indian Captivity Narrative*, 22–24.

1242. Both Zeisberger and White Eyes wrote to Morgan on 19 July 1778. Reminding him of the resolves at the conference in Detroit, White Eyes requested the protection of the Delaware against the Wyandot and other hostile Indians (see note 1240 above). In his accompanying letter Zeisberger explained what White Eyes meant by this "that he wishes an army might come out now—the sooner the better, for its high time." Zeisberger added the latest information about the intentions of the

came from the *Unami River*[1243] with a *String of Wampum* from the women there, who asked us to contribute some Indian corn for their children and them. We did this and sent them a number of bushels, which they took back on THE 22ND. One of them had spoken with some of our Indian Brothers and told them that they, the *Shawnee*, had received a message from the *Mahican* Believers a number of years ago saying they should open the road for them to come to them. They had heard nothing more about this since then and would like to get more information about this and hear some more about it. Because we did not know anything about this message they had received, and could only guess it must have come from blessed Brother *Josua*,[1244] we gave him the following reply for his *Nation* for now, along with a *String of Wampum*. We, the Indian Believers from the *Mahicans*, *Munsee* and *Delaware*, were one people and had accepted God's word, and we carried this with us wherever we went. The Indian Believers not only from the *Mahicans*, but also from various *Nations*, informed them that if we heard they had a desire to share with us in the great peace we have with God, wanted to accept his word and hear about their Creator and Redeemer, we would always be willing and prepared to serve them in this way and to tell them what He has done for us and for them and what we know about this and have experienced of it. Otherwise however, neither hunting, nor land, nor anything else would move us to go into a certain area.

THE 23RD   A party of *Munsee* warriors came here. They were very angry and wanted to know why we gave something to eat to the prisoners the warriors were leading through here and would not allow them to be beaten. They said that all *Nations* were now in agreement to continue the war with all their might, and the *Delaware* alone remained. However, they would soon be forced to do this as well, and *White Eye* would not live much longer. Early the next morning they went to the *Fort* to lie in wait for the messengers from there, whom we had been expecting for some time, and to kill them.

THE 26TH   *White Eye* and a number of Indians from *Goschachgünk* came for the sermon. Today the former visited our *Munsee* Brothers separately and talked with them. In the afternoon, the earthly dwelling of Sister *Johanna Maria*, *Nehemia's* wife who died yesterday, was buried. She was baptized by Brother *Jungmann* in *Schönbrunn* on *November* 12th, 1775, and after her baptism was blessed and happy for a while. We were able to rejoice greatly over what the Savior had done in her, because she had a very angry disposition by nature. She knew and admitted this and it sometimes made her walk difficult. When *Schönbrunn* was abandoned last year, she was the reason her husband left the

---

enemy and their activities. Both requested that their correspondence be kept strictly secret. *FAO*, 117–20. Zeisberger's letter to Matthäus Hehl is in MAB, B 229, F 5, I 15.

1243. See note 1182 to entry for 4 April 1778.

1244. Josua Sr., a former chief and leader of the Mahicans in Gnadenhütten, had been buried on 2 August 1775.

congregation with her. They wandered around a while until she became ill and very lame. They decided then to return to the congregation and she came here with her husband and children on *November* 16th last year and asked to be reaccepted. They obtained this and she soon improved. However, when she was completely well, she forgot again how miserable she had been when she had first come here, and she had not known how to *express* her gratitude adequately for being allowed to be part of the congregation again. Her evil heart tempted her to leave again and to abandon her husband and children, who stayed here. However, it was not long until she became ill again. She sent word here and asked to come back and for her husband to pick her up, which was done about 3 weeks ago. From that time on her illness continued to worsen and she herself believed she would die this time and she asked for *Absolution* of her sins against the Savior and the congregation. It was as if she had been waiting just for this, because no one thought her end was that near when she received *Absolution,* but she died hardly an hour later and the faithful Shepherd of her soul took her to her eternal rest and assurance.

THE 27TH   In the early service we reflected on the Watchword, Keep me as the apple of the eye.[1245] With all of our hearts we joined *David* in this prayer to the Savior under these circumstances which seem so dangerous, and He reassured our hearts that He will carry this out in us. Everything now seems to point to the total ruin of the Indian congregation. All the news we have is consistent with and confirms that all the *Nations* have joined together and are united in continuing the war with all earnestness, and the *Delaware Nation* has been abandoned, realizes it is left standing completely alone and in danger of being overpowered. Assuming the *Governor* in *Detroit*[1246] managed to get the *Delaware Nation* to join in the war, this would still not suffice and the matter would not have been adequately dealt with. Then things would really happen to us and the doors would be opened for Satan to turn his full might upon us. Our Indians would be forced to join in the war, and if they refused they would be told: then you will all be killed and destroyed by the other *Nations*. For this reason our efforts and our intention have always been to keep the *Delaware* neutral as far as we are able. We cannot remain apathetic in this and think that they can do whatever they want and we will do the same, because we see in advance that we are pretty well finished if they get involved in the war. Some *Munsee* came here to pick up their friends, and they said that the Indians would get all their friends, that any who remain here would be killed, and that if the *Delaware* in *Goschachgünk* did not accept the hatchet, then all the White Brothers would be killed.

THE 30TH   A *Compagnie* of *Munsee* who were returning from the *Settle-*

1245. Ps. 17:8.
1246. Henry Hamilton.

ments came yesterday and brought a *Scalp* and a prisoner. They continued on after they had first worked among our *Munsee* Brothers and Sisters and tried to frighten them. Their *Captain* told them he knew something they did not know about, and that a decision had been made concerning the Indians in *Goschach-günk* and us because we did not want to join in the war. The *Munsee* accepted the hatchet so that it would not fall upon their heads, because the *Nations* had decided unanimously at the *Treaty* in *Detroit*[1247] that it would fall upon the head of anyone who did not accept it.

[August]

AUGUST 1ST   We buried the earthly dwelling left behind by the widow *Tabea,* who went to her eternal rest yesterday. She was baptized by Brother *Schmick* on *April* 16, 1775 in *Gnadenhütten* and became a participant in Holy Communion on *March* 9th, 1776. She was a blessed widow, spent her time quietly and in communion with the Savior, and was little concerned about the things of this earth. She came here from *Gnadenhütten* last fall and was very happy and well. During her illness she enjoyed it when anyone visited her and sang her little verses. She was happy about going to the Savior soon and seeing Him face to face, and then she died with the blessing of the congregation.

AUGUST 2ND   Brothers *David* and *Heckewelder* went to *Goschachgünk* and *communicated* a written message to the *Council* from *Governor Henry Hamilton* in *Detroit.* For some time we had been hearing many unpleasant and horrible things from there, but it turned out they were not as dangerous as people had thought.[1248] The *Governor* and the *Nations* urged the *Delaware* once more, and indeed for the last time, to unite with them.[1249] That means they should accept the hatchet and if they did not do this now they would regret it. Brothers *Anton* and *Samuel* returned from *Pittsburgh*[1250] and brought news from the country and a packet of European newsletters and reports from Bethlehem from *February, March,* and *April,* along with a letter from Brother *Mattheo* dated *May* 17, which brought us great joy. On the way, the Brothers had observed and sensed that the road is being carefully watched as far as the *Fort.* Still, they did not see any warriors and their arrival seemed as if it had been carefully planned, because 2 messengers were prepared to set out for *Pittsburgh* that same night and without a doubt they would have fallen into the hands of the warriors.

THE 3RD   We buried a child who was baptized on the 31st of last month with the name *Christian* and then died yesterday in the 12th month of

---

1247. See note 1240 to entry for 16 July 1778.
1248. See entry for 16 July 1778 and note 1240 accompanying it.
1249. Single bracket from another hand, not closed.
1250. See entry for 22 July 1778.

his life. A party of *Munsee* arrived here with a *Scalp* and a prisoner they had taken close to the *Fort*.

THE 8TH   In the *Council* where they had been called in *Goschachgünk,* the Brothers heard a message from the *Cherokees* and *Choctaws*[1251] who are renewing their friendship with the *Delaware*.

Job Challowey's wife, our *Samuel Moor's* sister, came here from *Great Island* on the *West Branch* of the *Susquehanna*.[1252] She said she had fled to save her life because the White people had killed all the Indians there, including her husband and her children.[1253]

AUGUST 9TH   *White Eye* and *Gelelemind* and a number of Indians from *Goschachgünk* were here for the sermon. Among them were 2 *Cherokees* who watched everything closely, paid attention to everything, and really liked it here. They visited us every day while they were in *Goschachgünk*.

THE 13TH   Together we remembered this important day,[1254] and the Brothers and Sisters were told what the Savior did for his Unity and church 51 years ago today when He acknowledged them as his people, grounded in His blood and death, and also what He has done among Christians and heathen through their service since then. This was also true here, since it has pleased him to elect and gather a people from the Indians. We thanked Him that we also have been chosen through grace to be his own people, who should proclaim what He has done for us and for all the world. In the afternoon the *Wyandot Companie* that had marched through here on their way to the *Settlements* on the 17th of last month returned. They had done little, and in almost a month's time the 80 men had gotten only 2 *Scalps* despite enduring much danger, hunger, and trouble. They brought a sick French man whom they carried on a stretcher. They spent the night here and went to *Goschachgünk* on THE 14TH.

The *Cherokee* messengers who were leaving today, and 2 Indians from *Goschachgünk* who were also going with them, came here this morning with the *Counsellors*. On this occasion we gave them a message for their *Nation,* which said in brief, *Grand Children!* We were happy to learn through your messengers that you have accepted your grandfather's advice and warning and want to join him in holding firmly to the peace agreement. Your grandfather, the Indian Believers, informs you that we have accepted God's word; we hold to it firmly and seek with all of our strength to live accordingly. We can tell you from experience that it is a precious treasure we have found and through which we will be saved in this world and in eternity. We live in peace with God and in

1251. On the Cherokee, see note 61 to entry for 8 Sept. 1772, and on the Choctaw, see McKee and Schlenker, *Choctaws*.

1252. See entry for 13 July 1772 and note 38 accompanying it.

1253. In his letter dated 19 Aug 1778, in which he conveyed further information about hostile movements, Zeisberger requested confirmation of the report from Petty, the wife of Job Challowey. *FAO,* 131–32.

1254. On this day of commemoration, see Introduction, pp. 62–63.

peace with all humans. It will make us very happy if you want to join us and share in this. We sent a *String of Wampum* along to confirm these words. Because this is the first message to the *Cherokees*, we wanted to keep it brief for now. More can be done in the future.

THE 15TH   Brother *David* had to go to *Goschachgünk*, where the *Chiefs* were talking with the *Wyandot Captain* about the written message that had recently reached them from *Detroit*. He instructed them thoroughly about this.[1255] *Isaac* had talked with the *Wyandot Chief* a lot again this time, as he had done the last time. This had the good *Effect* that the latter asked Brother *David* to write a message to *Pittsburgh* for him, which he promised to do. However, because Brother *David* could not get away the next day, Brother *Heckewelder* went there and did this in a *private Conference* that the *Wyandot Chief* held with *White Eye, Isaac,* and *Willhelm.* He spoke confidentially with them, and in the *Speech* Brother *Heckewälder* wrote to *Mr. Morgan,* he offered to shake hands with him and make peace. As soon as he heard that *Mr. Morgan* was willing to do this, he would lay down the hatchet immediately and all the *Nations* would do the same.[1256]

THE 16TH   In the afternoon was the burial of Sister *Agnes,* who died in blessing yesterday. In *May* of 1770 she came to the congregation in *Langun-doutenünk* with her husband, now the widower *Isaac.* She was from the *Mingo Nation,* and therefore she could not express her spiritual condition as easily in the *Delaware* language as she had often wished. She was baptized by Brother *David Zeisberger* on *February* 9, 1771 and attained the enjoyment of Holy Communion on *December* 26, 1772. Her walk in the congregation was humble and contrite, and people had a hard time comforting her when she sometimes made a mistake, because she took everything very seriously. Her heart was firmly attached to the Savior and to the congregation and we can attest that she was with the congregation for no other reason than because she valued the eternal welfare of her soul and she wanted to be saved through grace and for the sake of Jesus' blood. She was the only one from her friendship who was with the congregation. During her illness she was primarily concerned that her friends, the *Mingo,* would take her children away from the congregation. Because of this she urged her uncle, who was here with the *Wyandot* these days, and other friends of hers to please leave her children with the congregation. She said she was prepared otherwise. When the Savior came and took her she would go to Him joyfully. This blessed lot became hers on the stated day. At that time she received the blessing of the congregation.

1255. See entry for 2 Aug. 1778.
1256. Wyandot chief Bawbee to George Morgan, 16 Aug. 1778, *FAO,* 128–29. In this letter the chief offered to negotiate a treaty of amity if the Americans gave assurances that they had no intentions of violating Wyandot land beyond the Great Lakes region and that if they attacked Detroit they would spare the Wyandot settlements. Since no one in his nation knew of his initiative, Bawbee requested strict secrecy.

In the Congregational Service we took to heart the Watchword drawn by the *Unity* Elders' *Conference* for the Indian congregation, *In the multitude of my thoughts within me thy comforts delight my soul. Oh, you who transforms my tears into oil of gladness.*[1257] The Savior did this faithfully and graciously comforted us in our frequent distress. Can his equal be found on earth or in heaven? We say no.

THE 17TH   Brother *Heckewelder* went to *Goschachgünk* and wrote an answer for the *Chiefs* to the *Governor* in *Detroit*. It said in brief that they were determined to live in peace with all White people; they had not become so inclined just recently but had agreed on this with *Sir William Johnson* many years ago and promised him this, and they would never stray from this. We received news through the *Shawnee Chief* who returned from the *Unami River*[1258] that an army of *Virginians* and Frenchmen were marching around behind us westward to *Detroit* and that the *Twichtwees*[1259] had opened their land for them to pass through unhindered.[1260]

We join all of our brown Brothers and Sisters in greeting all the congregations with tender love, and we commend ourselves to their prayer and remembrance before the Savior.

Diary of Lichtenau *on the* Muskingum *from* August *19th until the end of the year* 1778[1261]

AUGUST 19TH   In the name of the *Chiefs* in *Goschachgünk*, Brother *David* wrote the *Commissioners* whom *Congress* had authorized to hold a *Treaty* with the *Delaware* in *Pittsburgh*. *Gelelemind* and others took it there today. I also used this opportunity to send our diary to Brother *Matthaus.*[1262]

THE 22ND   111 Brothers and Sisters enjoyed Jesus' Body and Blood in the Holy *Sacrament*. One Brother was readmitted. A Brother and a Sister watched for the 2nd time and one for the first time.

1257. Ps. 94:19; "O Du in Freuden Oel Verwandler meiner Zährlein," *Das kleine Brüder-Gesang-Buch*, hymn no. 1898, verse 1.

1258. The reference is to Nimhno. See Zeisberger to George Morgan, 19 Aug. 1778, *FAO*, 131–32.

1259. See entry for 6 Aug. 1774 and accompanying note 488.

1260. The news referred to the expedition army of George Rogers Clark, who conquered Kaskaskia and the other French settlements on the Illinois and who had invited the Indian tribes of that region to a conference (*FAO*, 131n4; James, *Clark Papers*, 46–67). In response to the news of a treaty of amity between Spain and the United States, and being informed of a message of the governor of Louisiana to the tribes in the Illinois region, Henry Hamilton called the chiefs of these tribes together for a conference between 29 June and 3 July 1778 at Fort Detroit in an effort to win them to the British side. HP, 452–58.

1261. MAB, B 147, F 8, I 1, fol. 312b.

1262. The whole entry for 19 Aug. is not in H3, but the heading reads "from 19 August"; Zeisberger to George Morgan, 19 Aug. 1778, *FAO*, 131–32; Zeisberger to Matthäus Hehl, 19 Aug. 1778, MAB, B 229, F 5, l 17.

THE 23RD   In the morning there was Holy Communion for the sick, the *Liturgy,* and then the sermon about the text, Christ hath redeemed us from the curse of the law, being made a curse for us etc.[1263] During the Congregational Service in the evening a widow named *Rebecca* was baptized into Jesus' blood. 2 white people[1264] from *Pittsburgh* came as *express* messengers with letters, and Brother *David* went the next day to *Goschachgünk* with them and *communicated* them to the *Council.*[1265] These messengers returned to the *Fort*[1266] on THE 26TH accompanied by 2 Indian Brothers with letters. Some *Mingo* had been seen close to here, so some more Brothers escorted them a distance beyond *Gnadenhütten.*

THE 27TH   Some *Chippewa*[1267] came to *Goschachgünk* on horse to capture the messengers from the *Fort.* They had heard about them in the *Munsee Town* and had borrowed their horses. The *Chiefs* prevented them from going

1263. Gal. 3:13.

1264. Not identified, but possibly the same who had been sent as messengers to Fort Pitt on 8 June 1778; see note 1222.

1265. Entry from "and Brother David" until "the next day" and from "went" bracketed in another hand, whole passage not in H2 or H3. The messengers probably brought with them letters of George Morgan from York to Delaware and Shawnee dated 25 June 1778, from Philadelphia dated 12 July 1778, and possibly also from Philadelphia dated 12 Aug. 1778 (George Morgan Letterbook, vol. 3, fols. 68–70, 73, 82–83, 91–92, CLP). We could not find the letter of the Commissioners of the Continental Congress dated 22 Aug. 1778 (see next note).

1266. On 25 August Zeisberger wrote to the commissioners at the fort (*FAO*, 132–33). This letter demonstrates impressively the psychological tension to which Zeisberger was prey. His anxieties about the fate of the mission congregations and the Delaware now prepared him, as we see in this letter, to deviate from his pacifist principles. He had read, he wrote, very carefully the letters of the commissioners dated 22 August, but "I found not in them what I was most desirous to see & to hear vizt that an Army was to come out, which at first disheartened me a little while till I heard it privately of the Messengers that it would be done which I wish it might be true—For it is my opinion that there will be no Peace & the Nations will not be quiet until they are subdued & Detroit is taken, and I think this will be the opinion of all who are acquainted with the affairs. . . . The Munsies have always shewn themselves & are yet Enemies to the white people, they ought therefore to be broken & no Chief of their own left them, cast out of the Council & to be deliver'd to the Delawares to be ruled by them, because they are not fit to be ruled by themselves. . . . Capᵗ White Eyes & the Delaware Head men are sensible that this is the only assistance you can afford them in sending an Army to Detroit & if that should not be done they would be in a miserable and dangerous situation." In conclusion Zeisberger announced that White Eyes and Gelelemind would take a delegation to Fort Pitt to participate in the treaty negotiation; with luck they would arrive on 2 September 1778. In the meantime the Continental Congress had abandoned the idea of sending an army to Detroit but resolved, on 25 July, to raise an army of fifteen hundred soldiers whose task it was to be, "without delay, to destroy such towns of the hostile tribes of *Indians* as he [General Hand] in his discretion shall think will most effectually tend to chastise and terrify the savages, and to check their ravages on the frontiers of these states" (printed in *FAO*, 121). Shortly thereafter, on 6 August, the successor of General Edward Hand, General Lachlan McIntosh, arrived as the new commanding officer of Fort Pitt (*FAO*, 125). On McIntosh (1725–1806), a doctrinaire and inflexible officer for whom discipline and obedience were most important values and whom Washington valued highly, see Jackson, *Lachlan McIntosh,* 74–91; Hawes, *Lachlan McIntosh Papers,* 29–33; Williams, "Revolutionary Journal and Orderly Book."

1267. See entry for 5 June 1772 and note 29.

any further, and it was good that the messengers were already more than a day's journey ahead.

THE 29TH   We had services with the single Brothers and older boys, accompanied by the Savior's presence.[1268] We White Brothers read a choir talk by Brother *Joseph* held on this day in 1770, which was a blessing for our hearts. In conclusion we strengthened ourselves on the Body and Blood of our Lord in the Holy *Sacrament* and gave Him our hearts and hands so that we may be his faithful servants until the end.

THE 30TH   Early in the day Brother *Heckewälder* went to *Goschachgünk*. Messengers had returned from the *Fort* with letters from the *Commissioners,* and he read them to the *Councel*.[1269] The *Commissioners* tore up and rejected the *Wyandot Chief's* message, which was mentioned in the last diary entry for the 10th of this month,[1270] as soon as they had read it. He had asked for peace in this and sent it to the *Fort* in writing. No answer followed either.[1271] In the morning was the sermon here and in the Children's Service which followed *Rebecca's* baby boy, one year old, was baptized into Jesus' death with the name *Johannes Thomas.*

AUGUST 31ST   In the early service we asked the Savior for special blessings for our widowed Brothers and Sisters on their festival day today.[1272] Then they had a service and time of adoration. The Savior graciously revealed himself to them and gave them his peace. Yesterday and today we had visits from *Chippewa*[1273] who had come here to go to war. After the *Chiefs* in *Goschach-günk* had spoken with them and advised them against this, they returned home.[1274] All the Indians were very attractive, of large stature, and were very friendly and polite to us. If we had first had them for the blood of the wounds, there would have been more of them than us in one hour.

September

THE 1ST   Brothers *Willhelm* and *Anton* left with the *Chiefs* for the *Fort,* where they had been called to a *Treaty.* The widow *Patty* and her daughter, *Joseph Challoway's* wife, accompanied them. The daughter wanted to go to her husband. He had sent her news of his arrival there.[1275]

1268. This refers to the choir festival of the single brethren.
1269. We could not locate these letters.
1270. See entry for 15 Aug. 1778 and note 1256.
1271. Entry from beginning until "followed either" not in H2 or H3, bracketed in another hand. This symbolic gesture meant the rejection of the Wyandot chief's peace initiative.
1272. This was the day the widows and widowers celebrated their choir festival.
1273. See entry for 5 June 1772 and note 29.
1274. From "After the Chiefs" not in H2 or H3, bracketed in another hand.
1275. See entry for 8 Aug. 1778.

THE 5TH   Many of our Brothers and Sisters returned from *Sikhewünk*, a day's journey from here. They had been boiling salt for a number of days and had made a good quantity.

THE 6TH   Brothers *Samuel Nantikok* and *Mattheus* returned from the *Fort* and delighted us with letters and news from our loved ones in Bethlehem. *Mr. Morgan* had sent us these from *Philadelphia*. We read through them together with interest and gratitude. The enclosed letters from our dear Brother *Joseph* in *Barby*, dated *January* 15 and 19 of this year, were like a balsam for our hearts. Later we shared these with the whole congregation. They were very happy about this and they responded whole-heartedly with Yes and Amen. The 2 Indian Brothers had been very welcome in the *Fort* and the *Commissioners* put on airs for them. A *Compagnie* of militia from *Redstone* happened to be there. The *Commissioners* brought their *Officiers* to them first, and then the common soldiers, one after the other and told them they were Christian Indians from the *Muskingum*. They shook all of their hands and some said, It is really a pleasure to see such Indians; they look like sheep. If only all Indians were like that.[1276]

THE 7TH   The married Brothers and Sisters had services for their choir festival.[1277] The Savior mercifully revealed himself to them and blessed them.

THE 8TH   Things had been quiet for a while regarding the Indian war, because the *Nations* presumed that some action was being taken against the hostile Indians and this had made them somewhat careful. Now we received news that 250 *Shawnee, Wyandot,* and others had gone to war again. In the meantime, the rumor that an army would enter Indian country relieved us a little, although this is not definite, because we did not know what they knew. The *Munsee* have started causing havoc, beating our cattle to death, acting proud and saying we should just wait another 3 or 4 weeks; then we would see something we have never experienced before. Supposedly there would not be any Indian congregation before long. If everything had gone according to plan, this could actually have happened. We could see this possibility pretty clearly before us. However, The Lord bringeth the counsel of the heathen to nought: he maketh the devices of the people of none effect. When they attack in the cleverest manner, God takes another way, according to the Watchword for the 4th of this month.[1278]

SEPTEMBER 12TH   The Savior took Sister *Willhelmina* home to himself in blessing. Her earthly dwelling was laid to rest on THE 13TH. In *April* 1773 she came to the congregation in *Schönbrunn* from *Kaskaskunk* with her husband *Noah*, the First Fruit of the *Cherokees*, who preceded her on *December* 26, 1776. She was baptized there by Brother *Jungmann* on *July* 4th of that same

1276. From "The 2 Indian Brothers" not in H2 or H3, bracketed in another hand.
1277. The married sisters celebrated their choir festival on this day.
1278. Ps. 33:10; "Wenn sies aufs Klügste greifen an, so geht Gott eine andre Bahn," *Das kleine Brüder-Gesang-Buch*, hymn no. 1138, verse 2.

year and became a communicant on *May 27, 1775*. When *Schönbrunn* was deserted a year ago, she stayed in *Gnadenhütten* because she was weak and came with the Indian congregation from there this spring. Her heart was completely surrendered to the Savior, was firmly attached to the Unity, and nothing would move her to be separated from it. After her husband's death she was also a blessed widow who put her hope in the Lord. During her protracted illness, which lasted since spring, she often said, Oh, when will the Savior come and take me to himself? It seems as if I am not yet prepared to go to him. The last 2 days she said, I am in a hurry and can hardly wait any longer. I want to go to the Savior. With this fervent desire, she died with the blessing of the congregation.

THE 16TH   Some Indian Brothers returned from *Sandusky*, where they had bought themselves clothing,[1279] and we heard that the *Wyandot* were preparing to flee because they were expecting an army. Their *Chief* had sent a message from *Goschachgünk* to *Pittsburgh* recently asking for peace.[1280] When he got to *Detroit* he returned the *War Belt* to the *Governor* and told him he was not going to war anymore. After they had argued with each other for a while, however, and the *Governor* had given him gifts, the *Wyandot* accepted the *War Belt* again after all.[1281] It is said that the negotiations with the Indians on this side of the *Lake* are going to be completely broken off.[1282]

THE 20TH   Two people went to the Savior in blessing: between here and *Goschachgünk Mattheus*, and here *Martha*, who was baptized here on the 17th of this month. Both were buried in our God's Acre on THE 21ST. Brother *Schmick* baptized the former as a 16-year-old boy in *Nain* near Bethlehem on *February 18, 1761*. Later he was with the Indian congregation in the *Barracks* in *Philadelphia* and in *Fridenshütten* on the *Susquehanna*, and then he came with the Indian congregation to the *Ohio*, specifically to *Gnadenhütten* on the *Muskingum* in *August* 1772. Last fall he moved here to *Lichtenau*. His walk had always been very inconsistent, and this is how things were here. This spring he and his wife left the congregation once again, as he had done numerous

1279. See entry for 8 May 1778 and note 1214.

1280. See entry for 15 Aug. 1778.

1281. The correspondence of Governor Henry Hamilton contains a cryptic hint ("I had previous intelligence of some designs to traverse the good dispositions of the Indians who at these times have always been tampered with") respecting the Wyandot's vacillations. See Hamilton's letter dated 22 Sept. 1778, HP, 464–82, quotation at 479. The Wyandot did not attend the conference on 24 September 1778, which irritated the other tribes (HP, 482–83).

1282. In summer and early autumn Governor Henry Hamilton reported repeatedly to Quebec that the goods expected and needed for 1778 had not yet arrived and that this had begun to affect his ability to supply provisions to the allied Indian tribes (see his letter to Guy Carleton dated 8 Aug. 1778, HP, 459). These difficulties may have prompted Hamilton more than ever to cut off trade in Sandusky with the neutral and pro-American tribes. See Hamilton's reports to Carleton's successor, Governor Haldimand, from early September (HP, 464–73, esp. 468), and from 17 Sept. 1778 (HP, 475–77). Hamilton was aware that the Americans faced equal difficulties: "they [the Rebels] are in the utmost distress for cloathing and other necessaries & that they are wearied out & unable to support the war any longer" (HP, 465).

times before. During his illness he turned to the Savior in his distress and asked the Brothers to forgive all of his unfaithfulness, to have mercy on him, to accept him again, and to allow him to return to the congregation. He was already too weak for this, however. Therefore Brother *David* went to him on the 19th of this month with some Brothers and Sisters and *absolved* him amid many tears. Many Indian strangers were standing around the house and listening (because there were numerous huts there.) They were completely amazed and broken-hearted when they saw that something was going on. He died on the day noted above, comforted, happy, and grateful for what the Savior had done in him.

2) Sister *Martha, Israel's Cousin,* came here on *October* 20, 1776, with those moving from *Assünnünk.* [1283] She had had a White husband there for a number of years already. He had given himself to *Israel* as his son and he accepted this. However, shortly before she came here he had been captured by the *Mingo* during *Israel's* absence and was taken to the *Wyandot.* [1284] The word of redemption through Jesus' blood found room in her heart and she was powerfully touched. She often asked for baptism, but we comforted her and advised her to be patient until her circumstances cleared up because we had hesitations about her husband. A year ago her husband came here with the *Wyandot,* who had accepted him into their *Nation.* She went with him to *Sandusky* then and from there to *Detroit.* However, she promised to leave her grown daughter in the congregation even if she herself could not be here, and she was later baptized. Because her heart was restless, she planned to be baptized there in the hope of finding peace for her soul. When she got there, she gave this up completely and did not have the courage to do it, because she did not find at all what she was looking for there. She returned here and spent the winter and you could see that her desire for spiritual healing continued. When she went to *Sandusky* again this spring to visit her husband, she said, The Savior knows my heart, and He knows that I seek and desire nothing in the world except to be saved. Therefore I will return after all, because I cannot stay away from here. She became ill there and was sick for a pretty long time, turned to the Savior and asked him to make her healthy again just long enough to get back to the congregation. This happened and before she was completely well again, she set out and arrived here about 10 days ago, happy and grateful that the Savior had granted her request. However, in a few days she had to lie down again and her illness got worse every day. She sent for Brother *David,* to whom she poured out her heart and her desire to be washed with the Savior's blood, and asked that this might happen soon. On that same day she was baptized on her sick bed in the presence of a relatively large number of Brothers and Sisters, and a

---

1283. See entry for 24 Nov. 1776.

1284. See entries for 25 Sept. and 25 and 28 Dec. 1776. The entry for 2 Nov. 1778 identifies the man as McCormick. Since Zeisberger pointedly describes him as "well known McCormick," this can only be the fur trader Alexander McCormick. In 1785 McCormick married Elizabeth Turner, who had probably been made prisoner by the Wyandot.

blessed feeling of grace prevailed during this. After her baptism she extended both hands to the Brothers and Sisters who were standing around her, to be faithful to Jesus and she was exceptionally happy and content. Thus she went happily to Jesus' arms and bosom on the 3rd day after her baptism. All the Brothers and Sisters loved her the entire time she lived with us and always considered her one of us although she was not yet baptized.

THE 23RD   One Sister experienced special protection when she was going home from the fields carrying a basket full of Indian corn. She heard a tree, being blown around by the wind, crack close to her. She could not see where it was because of her heavy load, so she ran, finally let the basket fall, and the tree fell down very close to her. It smashed the basket of Indian corn into the ground but did not cause her any more harm.

Last night the *Mahican Bartholomaus* died in *Goschachgünk*. When the Indian congregation moved from *Gnadenhütten* to *Lichtenau* in the spring, he had separated and moved with his family to their friends the *Shawnee*, to whom their hearts were always attached. Brothers and Sisters not only visited him frequently throughout the summer, but even daily during his illness, which lasted only a few days. They also kept watch by him every night. Unfortunately no time was left for remorse and repentance, because he was robbed of his ability to think and speak before he considered his end. Thus he died and was buried there.

SEPTEMBER 26TH   Brothers *Willhelm* and *Anton* returned with the *Chiefs* from the *Fort*. We received definite news through them that an army is coming out into Indian country. The front troops of 900 men are already lying at *Beaver Creek*. The *Chiefs* and all the Indians who were there were presented to the entire army, as many as were together, and were informed that from now on the *Delaware Nation* should be considered an ally of the *Colonies* of North America. The event was celebrated very solemnly and ceremoniously. They decided at first that a part of the army should march through *Goschachgünk*. However, they changed this and decided they would march through *Tuscarawi*. Since such a trip is now being made on account of the *Delaware,* we have reason to hope that everything will go well and our efforts to keep the *Nation* peaceful are now being well rewarded.[1285]

1285. Whole entry not in H2 or H3, bracketed in another hand. Between 12 and 19 September the Commissioners of the Continental Congress met for the fourth time with representatives of the Indian tribes of the Ohio region. Of all the tribes, only representatives of the Delaware and those Shawnee allied with the Delaware participated. On 19 September the Delaware signed a treaty of amity that contained the following stipulations: (1) all past hostilities should be forgiven and buried in oblivion; (2) the treaty of amity should last forever, "and if either of the parties are engaged in a just and necessary war with any other nation or nations, that then each shall assist the other in due proportion to their abilities"; (3) an American army received the right of passage through Delaware territory and the Delaware agreed to provide the army with provisions, horses, and other support, for which they would receive payment in addition to warriors for the expedition against the hostile tribes; in return the American army would provide protection for the children, women, and old people of the Delaware by building a fort in their region; (4) misdeeds and crimes would be adjudged by jointly manned courts and tribunals and by unilateral actions; (5) Delaware needs for European goods were

THE 30TH   Brother *David* had to go to *Goschachgünk*, where he read the *Treaty* concluded in *Pittsburgh*[1286] aloud to the entire crowd of *Delaware* gathered there from the entire area. It was signed and sealed by the *Commissioners*[1287] and the *Delaware Chiefs*[1288] and also signed by General McIntosh and the *Officers*.[1289] The *Delaware* alone are named in the 6 articles.

We have been hearing various things about the army on the *Wobash*, that they were marching to *Detroit*, that they had burned one Indian *Town* to ashes and had taken possession of the entire French *Settlement* on that river, and that the *Shawnee* are supposed to have suffered a bad defeat.[1290]

---

to be met by establishing trade under the supervision of an agent to be salaried by the United States; (6) the United States "do engage to guarantee to the aforesaid nation of Delawares, and their heirs, all their territoreal rights in the fullest and most ample manner. . . . And it is further agreed on between the contracting parties should it be for the future be found conducive for the mutual interest of both parties to invite any other tribes who have been friends to the interest of the United States, to join the present confederation, and to form a state whereof the Delaware nation shall be the head, and have a representation in Congress," provided the Congress approved such an agreement. The complete treaty is printed in Peters, *Public Statutes at Large*, 7:13–15; latest reprint, with distorting omissions, in Williams, *Fort Pitt and the Revolution*, 105–7. According to the protocol of the conference the treaty was not signed on 17 September, as stated in the statutes at large, but on 19 September (FAO, 144–45). There is no consensus on the interpretation of the treaty. Downes, *Council Fires*, 216–17, White, *Middle Ground*, 382–83, Williams, *Fort Pitt and the Revolution*, 107–8, and Dowd, *Spirited Resistance*, 72–73, believe that the Delaware were cheated, that they never intended to conclude a treaty of amity with obligations to provide military assistance but had gone to Fort Pitt with the intention of maintaining neutrality. Given Zeisberger's reports, this position is dubious. It also conflicts with White Eyes' and the Delaware Council's earlier demands for the erection of a fort and with Zeisberger's earlier abandonment of his neutrality. In general, both White Eyes and Captain Pipe were too experienced at negotiation to be duped on such vital matters. Dowd says that "in January 1779, an apparently altered version of the treaty of 1778 was read to the Delawares, who immediately challenged one very important article"—that is, the stipulation to provide military assistance (*Spirited Resistance*, 72), and he cites as proof Downes, *Council Fires*, 217; but in fact Downes nowhere maintains that copies of the treaty were exchanged in January. See note 1370 to entry for 27 Jan. 1779.

1286. This refers to Zeisberger, who translated the treaty and read it to the Council.

1287. Andrew Lewis and Thomas Lewis signed the treaty as Commissioners of the Continental Congress. Based on a July 1778 authorization of the Congress, both had been named by the governor of Virginia (Ford, *Journals of the Continental Congress*, 11:568, and McIlwaine, *Official Letters of the Governors of Virginia*, 1:290, 294); Pennsylvania had not used the same authorization.

1288. White Eyes, Gelelemind, and Captain Pipe.

1289. The following officers had signed: Daniel Brodhead, W. Crawford, John Campbell, John Stephenson, John Gibson, A. Graham, Lachlan McIntosh Jr., Benjamin Mills, Joseph L. Finley, and John Finley. Of these, John Gibson had established a special friendly relationship with the Delaware, whose language he spoke. About him, see note 102 to entry for 16 Nov. 1772. We assume that he played a significant role in the informal negotiations, an assumption supported by White Eyes' demand, in his public speech of 16 September, that "Colonel John Gibson may be appointed to have the charge of all matters between you & us. We esteem him as one of ourselves, he has always acted an honest part by us, & we are convinced he will make our common good his chief study, & not think only how he may get rich. We desire also that he may have the charge & take care of the Warriors of our people who may join you on the present Expedition" (FAO, 144). George Morgan, still the official agent of the Continental Congress, had remained in Philadelphia and did not participate in the conference.

1290. Whole entry for 30 Sept. not in H2 or H3, bracketed in another hand. The entry refers to the expedition of George Rogers Clark.

[October]

OCTOBER 2ND   During the night a whole party of *Munsee* came here. The *Chiefs* informed them that the *General*[1291] in the *Fort* did not speak *favorably* of them and that he was planning to pay them a visit. They are upset about this and came here to find out more about this. Without a doubt we would have a great influx of bad people who would force their way in among us now because they do not feel safe anywhere else. However, the articles of the *Treaty* expressly forbid the *Delaware* to take in or provide protection for any Indians who are involved in the war.[1292]

THE 3RD   We celebrated Holy Communion in quiet calm and in the peace of Jesus Christ. One Brother, our *Israel,* and one Sister joined us for the first time as participants. One Sister watched for the 2nd time and a Brother and a Sister for the first time.

THE 5TH   *Gelelemind* sent some of his *Counsellors* here. They informed us that *General McIntosch* has called the *Chiefs* to come to *Tuscarawi* as soon as the army has arrived there and asked that some of our Indian Brothers also go along, because the *General* still has a number of things to discuss with the Indians and then he will arrange his march with the army accordingly. We considered this matter with our Helpers and decided that it is good and necessary for some Brothers to go along there for a number of reasons. We immediately designated some to do this.

THE 8TH   Very early in the day, *Gelelemind* came here with *Captain Pipe.* Yesterday they had received a message from the *Munsee* asking for *Pardon* and peace. Brother *David* sent this in writing to the *General,* and two Brothers, *Samuel Nantikok* and *Mattheus,* immediately left for there.[1293]

THE 10TH   A party of *Wyandot* was seen not far from here. *Gideon,* who was out hunting, had spoken to them. They told him they were going to observe the army in order to see how strong it was. However, they could not find them anywhere. We also heard that an army would come from across the *Lake* to meet this one.[1294]

THE 12TH   *Gelelemind* came here and talked with our Indian Brothers

1291. Lachlan McIntosh.

1292. Article 6 stated: "And it is also the intent and meaning of this article, that no protection or countenance shall be afforded to any who are at present our enemies, by which they might escape the punishment they deserve." Peters, *Public Statutes at Large,* 7:14–15.

1293. Entry for whole day (8 Oct.) not in H2 or H3, bracketed in another hand. We could not find Zeisberger's letter.

1294. On 22 September 1778 Henry Hamilton wrote Governor Haldimand that he hoped to depart for the Illinois region on 1 October 1778 with an army from Detroit in order to recover the formerly French settlements that had been lost to George Rogers Clark. The rumor Zeisberger reported must refer to this expedition, since neither Hamilton nor Haldimand planned another expedition into the Ohio region at that time. HP, 477.

about the current circumstances since we have received more news about the *Wyandot* and the *6 Nations*. They are trying to persuade the *Delaware* through tough talk and threats and to force them to join with them in the war. They are telling them there is still time to change; if they unite with the *Nations,* they could still preserve themselves and be saved from their destruction. A *Shawnee* and a *Mahican* came from the *Unami River*[1295] with a message for our *Mahicans.* They are already inviting them for the 2nd time because they said it was too dangerous for them here now. They will allow them to bring their teachers along, and they promise they would not be forced to go to war with them or to have their lifestyle disrupted. The message sounded good, but this is no time to think about such things, and their only purpose anyway is to get their friends away from here. We dismissed them with the answer that we could not consider their *Invitation* at this time. Even if we fled there we did not think we would be safer there than where we are. However, if peace is completely restored, we might possibly be able to consider this more easily.

THE 13TH   Some Brothers from our *Conference* had to go to the *Councel* in *Goschachgünk* and because things look dangerous for the *Delaware* again on account of the *Nations,* they quickly prepared messengers to go to the *Tawas*[1296] and *Chippewa*[1297] with the following message: *Grandchildren!* Some years ago you let me know that most of your wise old men and *Chiefs* had died, that you acknowledge your grandfather (the *Delaware*) as your *Chief* and want to follow him in all matters. I want to remind you of this again on this occasion. My uncle (the *Wyandot*) gave me the pipe at the beginning of this war with the words that I should keep quiet and smoke my pipe. I did this, but soon afterward I saw him get up with the hatchet in his hand to help his father (the *Governor* in *Detroit*) kill his own children (the Americans). Until now I have just watched and smoked my pipe, and now it is completely used up. I have not helped either party. Now things have reached the point that your father and his children will soon meet each other and fight each other bravely. Therefore I want to advise you, my *Grandchildren,* to stay out of the way. Let them fight it out with each other. You should watch quietly and not help any party. In this way you will preserve the lives of your people, young and old, women and children, and I will also do the same.

THE 16TH   We received favorable news about the western *Nations* on the *Wobash* through some *Shawnee*. Most of them have declared themselves for peace; at least they are not hostile and are leaving the army there alone, although it is very weak, so that no real progress can be made in the Indian war. This is always *profitable* for us.

THE 17TH   The Indian Brother *Daniel* had gone to *Sandusky* some time

1295. See note 1182 to entry for 4 April 1778.
1296. See entry for 17 Oct. 1773, where the visit to the Shawnee is reported, esp. note 284.
1297. See entry for 5 June 1772 and note 29.

ago to buy himself necessities, but because trade had stopped there he went on to *Detroit*. He returned from there today. We were often very concerned about him, and we had good reason to be, because the *Delaware* from this area cannot show themselves publicly there. He did not stay there long and he remained *incognito*, as good friends among the White people there had advised him.

As soon as he got there he heard people talking freely and openly about the *Governor* planning an *Expedition* against *Goschachgünk* and *Lichtenau* and that in a few days 2 *Captains* would march here with men and Indians and capture *White Eye* and *Gelelemind* in *Goschachgünk* and us White Brothers here. They would take them to *Detroit* dead or alive, because they were the reason the *Delaware* cannot be persuaded to go to war. He feels sure the rest would agree soon if they were out of the way. He also realizes that as long as he does not have the *Delaware* with him, nothing can come of the Indian war in this part of the country because most of the *Nations,* such as the *Chippewa, Tawas, Twichtwees,*[1298] *Shawnee* etc., depend on the *Delwares* to a certain extent. We heard more about this a few days later, and the reason this *Expedition* had not taken place was because both *Captains* had died suddenly. One of them was well known here because he came and went here with the *Wyandot* warriors a year ago and this spring. The *Governor* also received news that the army was marching to *Detroit*.[1299] This was another reason he had set aside his plan. If you take the *Munsee's* threats and this together, then you can believe that they were not ignorant of this, if not actually the perpetrators.[1300]

THE 18TH   Brother *Nicolai* died the day before yesterday and his earthly dwelling was buried. He was from the *Mingo* family and was baptized in *Schochari*,[1301] came to the congregation in *Schönbrunn* in the fall of 1774, and was received into the congregation on *January* 1st, 1775. However, the *confusion* that arose among this whole family caused him and most of them to leave the congregation in 1776. Despite this, we still always felt that he loved the Brothers and he often told his sister, who remained with the congregation, You are fortunate to be in the congregation. Stay here and do not let yourself be turned against them. You will not be better off anywhere else. About 3 months ago he got consumption. During his illness they always wanted to bring him Indian *Doctors* who were supposed to make him well. He did not accept any, however, but said they could not help him. If they wanted to help him they should bring him here to *Lichtenau,* then he would die. That was the only thing he wanted but no one wanted to assist him in this way. Instead they refused him until his brother finally took pity on him because of his continual requests, and he

1298. See entry for 6 Aug. 1774 and note 488.
1299. This refers to the expedition of George Rogers Clark.
1300. From "As soon as" not in H2 or H3, bracketed in another hand.
1301. Schochari, normally Schoharie, a settlement on the Schoharie Creek in the colony/state of New York. The Schoharie Creek flowed into the Mohawk River. See Cappon et al., *Atlas of Early American History,* map "The American Colonies c. 1775: The Middle Colonies and Quebec," 4, E7.

brought him a long way down the *Walhanding* in a *Canow* and arrived here on the 15th of this month. When the Brothers carried him out of the *Canow* he thanked them for the love they had shown him and said he was happy to be with the congregation again now. He had longed for this for so long, although he was not worthy of it. Then he asked his sister *Susanna* to call Brother *David* soon. When he came to him, he gave an honest and humble spiritual talk of his own accord and asked for *Absolution* for his sins against the Savior and the church and that this might be done soon, because his time was short. He had hardly finished talking when he fell unconscious, because talking was difficult for him. After he had come to himself again, he was *absolved* in the presence of some Brothers and Sisters. There was a moving and compassionate feeling during this and all the Brothers and Sisters were sincerely happy for him to receive this blessed happiness. He then said, I am happy to go to the Savior now, because I have received mercy. Then on the 16th he could no longer talk, and on the evening of that same day he died peacefully and happily with the blessing of the congregation.

THE 19TH   Early in the day *Gelelemind* came here. He brought Brother *David* a letter from *Colonel Gibson*[1302] in *Fort McIntosh*[1303] on *Beaver Creek*, which was just recently built. He reported that the army will march through here in just a few days and they were now preparing a plan to protect and defend the *Delaware Nation* and us as well as they could. At the same time he assured us that the welfare and progress of our mission was important to him and that he was happy to provide us any service he could. From his letter we could see that a *Fort* is supposed to be built close to us here. This was also reported in the recently held *Treaty* in *Pittsburgh*.[1304]

THE 20TH   *Samuel Nantikok* returned from *Fort McIntosh*. He had been sent to the *General*[1305] with the *Munsee's* message. In reply they had sent word that he was very upset about it and could not talk to them until he got further into Indian country and then he would see if and what he would answer them.

We also had the joy and the pleasure of receiving letters from Brother *Mattheo* and *Grube* from Litiz on this occasion.

OCTOBER 23RD   Some *Munsee* came here to pick up their friends because they said we would all be killed by the *Nations*. They realize they did not

1302. On John Gibson, see notes 102 and 1289.

1303. On 8 October a company began with the building of Fort McIntosh; shortly thereafter General Lachlan McIntosh transferred his headquarters to that fort. See Williams, "Revolutionary Journal and Orderly Book," 165–66 and n. 11. For the exact location of the fort, see Williams, *Fort Pitt and the Revolution*, 114–16, 118. The fort stood close to where the Beaver River entered the Ohio. The army followed the route Colonel Henry Bouquet had taken in 1764.

1304. Entry for the whole day of 19 Oct. not in H2 or H3, bracketed in another hand. This is the fort later named Fort Laurens. The stipulation Zeisberger mentions is in article 3 of the treaty: "and for the better security of the old men, women and children of the aforesaid nation, whilst their warriors are engaged against the common enemy, it is agreed . . . that a fort of sufficient strength and capacity be built at the expense of the said states." Peters, *Public Statutes at Large*, 7:13.

1305. Lachlan McIntosh.

receive the *favorable* answer from the *General* they had been expecting for some time, so now they all want to run away. They had asked the *Wyandot* for advice about what they should do, and they replied that they should go to them and not worry about all their corn and food, because they would find this at their place, though it is well known that the *Wyandot* themselves have little since they planted almost none. Despite the fact that the *Munsee* are so horrified and scared, they are still malicious. They had often before threatened us that after they defeated the army, they would all overrun us and destroy us. Now they are saying they would not wait until the army came, but would do this first. First we White Brothers would either be killed or captured and taken to *Detroit*.

THE 25TH   The *Munsee Chief* himself came here and announced that he had something to say to our *Munsee* Brothers. We replied that we did not distinguish between *Munsee* and others who lived here, because we were not two but one people. Therefore we called together the Brothers we thought appropriate. First he reported that since times were dangerous and they were no longer safe in their town, they were planning to flee to the *Wyandot,* from whom they had received an *Invitation* to go there. He then took out a *String of Wampum* and said he had come here now to learn what they (he meant our *Munsee* Brothers) were planning to do and where they would turn, because it would be very dangerous for them to stay here. They could see in advance that they would be caught between two fires and would be annihilated by one side or the other. The *Nations* would muster all their warriors and engage in a battle with the army and when it was over, things around us here would look very bad. The Brothers, especially *Abraham* who is a *Munsee,* reminded him that one year ago and again this year, we had advised him well and had asked him to put aside his thoughts of war and follow the council of the *Chiefs.* We had sent many Klafter of *Wampum* to him with *Speeches* but until this day he still owed us an answer. Now he came to us with *Speeches* and *Wampum.* He should know now that we would not accept anything from him because he was not concerned about the welfare of his *Nation,* but was promoting their destruction. Then they gave him back his *String of Wampum.* The *Munsee Chief* and another man who was with him exerted great efforts trying to get someone from here to go with them. However, when they realized this was all in vain they finally wanted to take along an older unbaptized girl. They claimed to have a right to her, but we did not allow this and they then moved on.

THE 27TH   Yesterday and today we heard so many unpleasant and terrible stories that all the Indians in the area went into a state of fear and horror. We have to listen to horrifying threats about beating us to death, and all of this comes from the *Munsee.* They are fleeing now, so they want to do as much damage as they can first. It would bring them great joy if they could make us all run away. From midnight last night until noon today, one piece of horrifying news after another arrived. In order to make it quite believable, they said they were forbidden to tell people here what was going on, but they really wanted to tell their good friends here in order to save them from danger. Some of our *Munsee* will be shaken up once again by this and tested, so that it is really hard for them. May the Savior help us and allow the hour of affliction and temptation to pass soon and end in blessing. We see very well that they could still do great harm if the Savior did not hold his hand above us and allowed them to do this. The *Munsee* are our greatest enemies and they know why they are hostile toward us. Other Indians and *Nations* know of no reason they should hate us; they do not have the knowledge of the *Munsee*, who have heard the Gospel.

OCTOBER 28TH   Times and circumstances were getting worse and more dangerous each day, because late this evening we received the unpleasant news that *Captain Pipe* and *Winginund*, two headmen of the *Delaware* on the *Walhanding*, had left there with most of the Indians and gone over to the enemies.[1306] People were saying that in 4 or 5 days a crowd of warriors will gather up on the *Walhanding* and engage the army in battle, and then they would come here. *Pipe* had called them and sent word that they should not be concerned about food, because those who fled there would have to leave everything behind; they would find plenty of this there. The danger for us seemed greater now than it had ever been and we could not let our Brothers and Sisters know this at all. Although we cannot believe everything, we cannot help but think there must be something to the matter and that we are in danger, and indeed mostly from *Detroit*. During the night Brothers *Isaac* and *Marcus* went to *Goschachgünk* to take the news to *Gelelemind*, who came here very early on THE 29TH and discussed it with us. 2 *express* messengers were immediately prepared to take the news to General *McIntosh*. He also sent him word that he should march here with the army without delay.[1307] The texts in recent days offered us strength and encouragement. The one for the day before yesterday said, Stand therefore, having your loins girt about with truth, and having on the breastplate of righteousness.[1308] Yesterday it was, Put on the whole armour of God, that ye may be able to stand against the wiles of the devil, and today, If

1306. Pipe and Winginund transferred their settlements to the region near Sandusky and Cuyahuga controlled by the Wyandot chief Half King; such a Delaware settlement is not in Cappon et al., *Atlas of Early American History*, 21, map "Indian Settlements. Indian Villages. Ohio, Pennsylvania, New York 1760–1794," but it is marked under the name of "Pipe 1" on the map "Frontier in Transition, 1772–81. The Ohio Country and Canada," in Tanner, *Atlas*, before p. 81. Zeisberger seems to have believed that Pipe and Winginund were motivated by their pro-British sympathies, but this seems unlikely. Pipe's energetic distancing of himself from the treaty, concluded in September 1778 (White, *Middle Ground*, 382–83; Dowd, *Spirited Resistance*, 72–73), suggests that his real motive was the abandonment of the neutral policy between the belligerents and the rejection of the acculturation policy agreed to in the treaty.

1307. Entry from "late this evening" not in H2 or H3, bracketed in another hand. Letter not found.

1308. Eph. 6:14; Eph. 6:11; Rom. 8:31; "Hab ich das Haupt zum Freunde und bin beliebt bey Gott, was kan mir thun der Feinde und Wiedersacher Rott" is the second part of the first verse of the choral "Ist Gott für mich, so trete," printed in *Das kleine Brüder-Gesang-Buch*, hymn no. 783.

God be for us, who can be against us? If the Head is my friend and I am loved by God, what can the enemy and ranks of adversaries do to me? May He preserve us and not allow our confidence in Him to fail. This evening a party of *Munsee* came here and spread their lies again and frightened those of weak character, mostly by saying that we would be attacked and killed in 3 days.

THE 30TH   We heard that the Indians in *Goschachgünk* are already beginning to flee. The *Confusion* among the Indians is indescribable. No one can say why they are running and yet they are going off and leaving behind the corn they have harvested without considering, what will we eat, what will we drink? This already has spread to our place because so many terrible and horrifying stories have been brought here, and the fear is contagious. Therefore we considered the circumstances with our Helpers and decided to stand firm and remain calm. We informed the Brothers and Sisters of this in a Congregational Council this evening and we encouraged them to remain confident and undaunted, and not to believe lies that lead them into distress and danger. All these lies come from the evil *Munsee,* who always send their apostles here and try to deceive people. We are a stumbling block to them and they are always trying to ruin the congregation. They even know when the time is right, so their work will not be in vain.

THE 31ST   An old widow and *Nehemia* ran away from here. This was the 2nd time the latter left the congregation.[1309]

[November]

NOVEMBER 1ST   Early in the day we had a Helpers' *Conference* and discussed the people who come here every day to pick up their friends. We decided to question them, send them away, and forbid them from doing this. We also did this immediately with some who had come here for this purpose tonight. This had a good *Effect,* because when we urged them to explain why they wanted to take their friends away they had no reply except that that they did not know. They said we should ask the *Munsee Chief,* however; he would know why. Then they left quickly.

After this was the sermon about the wedding garment, Christ's blood and righteousness, without which no one can stand before God.[1310] In the afternoon the congregation gathered and the Helpers, especially Brothers *Abraham, Isaac,* and *Willhelm,* spoke words of comfort and encouragement to the Brothers and Sisters. They admonished them not to listen to the lies brought here daily claiming that we will be destroyed by either the Indian *Nations* or the White

1309. See entry for 26 July 1778; the necrology for Johanna Maria, wife of Nehemia, states that "she had been the cause that her husband left with her the congregation."
1310. Matt. 22:11.

people. They should not give in to fear, but remain confident and unconcerned about this because we would let them know when we saw that danger was imminent. We would inform them then what the best thing for us to do was. In the evening during the Congregational Service, we remembered our fellowship with the Church triumphant and comforted ourselves with the blessed hope of praising Him in the great congregation throughout eternity.

NOVEMBER 2ND   Last night was the time when people said we were supposed to be attacked because we would not join the hostile Indians and flee with them, since it was now obvious enough that we were on the side of the *Virginians,* as the *Americans*[1311] are now being called. However, we slept peacefully enough. In the meantime *Jonas,* an old widower, his mother *Beata* who can hardly crawl, and *Priscilla,* also an old widow, left here during the night. The Brothers and Sisters tried as hard as they could to overcome their fear, but it was all in vain. Today *Israel* was in *Goschachgünk* the entire day and he helped *Gelelemind* with his business. He has no more helpers now except *Israel,* because they have all left him.[1312] This morning the latter talked to Brother *David* in the company of some Brothers and said he would remain with the Brothers, even if only a few of them stayed together. Others wanted to take up their weapons tonight, because they heard that Indian strangers who were talking carelessly had come here, and they knew the attack was supposed to happen tonight.[1313] Our acquaintance *McCormick,* husband of our recently deceased Sister *Martha,* came here from *Sandusky.*[1314] We heard from him that the *Wyandot* were quiet; he did not believe we had anything to fear from them or the other *Nations.* If there were to be any problem, it would be from the *Munsee.*

THE 3RD   Last night another party of *Munsee* came here to cause trouble as usual and to misguide people. They left at daybreak, however, because they like to do their evil work at night. We had recovered somewhat and were calm for the most part, so we had a *Conference* with the Helpers. We gave them the job of speaking with some of our young people and Brothers and Sisters today.

THE 5TH   Messengers had arrived yesterday evening from *Fort McIntosh* on *Beaver Creek,* and we heard from them that the *General*[1315] was already marching to *Tuscarawi* with the army. The *General* had kept our Brothers *Marcus* and *Nathanael,* who were the last messengers sent there, as well as *Daniel* who had been sent previously, because it had been agreed at the last *Treaty* that

---

1311. From "because we" not in H2 or H3, bracketed in another hand. On the origins of "Virginians" as an abusive term, see entry for 1 Nov. 1774 and note 533. On the identification of "Virginians" with "Americans," see Introduction, p. 23.

1312. White Eyes was with the army of General Lachlan McIntosh; see entry for 7 Nov. 1778.

1313. From "Others wanted" not in H2 or H3, bracketed in another hand.

1314. See entry for 20 Sept. 1778.

1315. Lachlan McIntosh.

there would always be at least 4 Indians with the army.[1316] Our *Israel* was in *Goschachgünk* with some Brothers again today. *Gelelemind* must now hold the *Councel* with our Brothers,[1317] because almost all of his *Counsellors* have left him.

THE 7TH   The *Wyondat Half King* from *Sandusky* visited us very early in the day. He had come to *Goschachgünk* the day before yesterday to get news of how things were there. He greeted us cordially and said he had wanted to see us once again, because he believed he would not see us again for a long time. *Isaac* spoke with him alone about all we had heard about the *Nations* making evil plans against us since we were not running away, which was a sign that we were on the side of the *Virginians*.[1318] He replied that he knew nothing about this and assured him that he was our friend. He also promised he would let us know if he heard such things. Yesterday *Gelelemind* had delivered a message for his *Nation* and the other *Nations* to him. He wanted to prepare the way once again through this for them to join in the peace concluded by the *Delaware Nation*. He did not accept this, however, but gave it back. Brothers *Marcus* and *Nathanael* returned from the army. They had marched with them from *Fort McIntosh* for 2 days and had enjoyed nothing but kindness and friendship and could not talk about this enough. *White Eye,* who has been made a *Colonel,* told them confidentially that the army was above *Walhanding,* and if we were in danger they would go through *Goschachgünk* and *Lichtenau.*[1319]

At the conclusion of this week, the congregation strengthened itself through the Body and Blood of the Lord in the Holy *Sacrament*. One Sister, *Anna Margretha,* participated for the first time during this and *Gideon* observed for the 2nd time.

THE 8TH   Early in the day we read the *Liturgy* for Holy Communion. The text for today was, For by one Spirit are we all baptized into one body; and have been all made to drink into one Spirit,[1320] and we discussed it and then had the sermon. In the afternoon we shared news of the current situation with the Brothers and Sisters and told them that we were in no imminent danger. *Marcus* told them about the approach of the army and how well the *Delaware* Indians are being treated and said, there is real peace.[1321]

THE 10TH   Brothers *Israel* and *Isaac* and some others set out from here,

1316. On the subject of the Delaware warriors, the written protocol contains only White Eyes' remarks in his speech of 16 Sept. 1778: "We desire also that he [Colonel John Gibson] may have the charge & take care of the Warriors of our people who may join you on the present Expedition" (*FAO,* 144). Zeisberger's more detailed information in this entry suggests the interpretation that the American military did not expect active participation in the war, which would have been pointless if only four warriors were involved, but only scouting and securing the flanks of the army.

1317. From "The General has kept" not in H2 or H3, bracketed in another hand.

1318. From "which was a sign" not in H2 or H3, bracketed in another hand.

1319. From "Yesterday Gelelemind" not in H2 or H3, bracketed in another hand.

1320. 1 Cor. 12:13.

1321. From "Marcus" not in H2 or H3, bracketed in another hand.

and *Gelelemind* left from *Goschachgünk*, to meet the army before they arrive at *Tuscarawi*, where *General McIntosh* will decide if he will come here or not.[1322] *Gelelemind* came here and informed us that he had left word with his people in *Goschachgünk*, that if they heard bad news from the *Nations* and things were looking dangerous, they would bring their women and children here to us for safety. We were not really very happy about this, but we did not think this would actually happen and it would not be necessary. This indeed turned out to be the case.

THE IITH   Until now we have always just guessed that something dangerous to us was going on, but we could not find out what kind of danger it was or where it was coming from. Today we received news about the source of the fear among the Indians for some time. Some of them may have known this, but did not want to say it directly. The *Governor* in *Detroit*,[1323] who wanted to incite the *Nations* against the *Delaware* because they would not join in the war against the *Colonies*, recently gave the *War Belt* to the *Wyandot* first and then to the other *Nations* to wage war against the *Delaware*.[1324] The former accepted it. The *Chippewa*, however, one of the strongest *Nations*, said that the *Delaware Nation* was not only its grandfather, but also its *Chief* and they were therefore one *Nation*. The *Governor* wanted them to kill each other, however, and destroy themselves. They did not want to be this foolish and threw the *War Belt* to the ground in front of him. When the *Tawas* and *Putewoatamen*, who are also the *Grand Children* of the *Delaware*, heard this they agreed with them. The *Chippewa* thus fended off and destroyed the plot designed against us. We have this news from a reliable source.[1325]

NOVEMBER 13TH   During the early service we mentioned the importance of today and then in a service for baptized Brothers and Sisters we told them what had happened in the Unity 31 years ago, when the Savior declared himself Chief Elder and Lord of his Unity. Through grace we also belong to this, since the Gospel came to us through them, and the Savior has gathered himself a congregation from the Indians, through which his name will be glorified and his death proclaimed among the *Nations*.[1326] In the dust we prayed to our Lord and Chief Elder, asked for *Absolution* for all our mistakes and shortcomings, and promised Him obedience and faithfulness anew.

From elsewhere we received the news that 11 *Mingo* had gone to spy on the army. They had met it on the small *Beaver Creek,* however, and gotten 2

1322. From "Brothers Israel and Isaac" not in H2 or H3. The lack of a closing bracket indicates that the whole entry, and that for 11 Nov., were to be left out.

1323. Henry Hamilton.

1324. See entry 16 July 1778 and note 1240.

1325. Entry for 11 Nov. not in H2 or H3; an additional end-quotation mark suggests that the whole entry for 10 Nov. was to be left out. The details reported in this entry are not supported by evidence in HP.

1326. See Introduction, pp. 62–63, on the importance of the commemorating Christ's acceptance of the office of Elder on 13 Nov. 1741.

Scalps from it. We reported this to *General McIntosh* immediately, so that he would not suspect the *Delaware.* In recent days and today, most of the Indians from *Goschachgünk* left to go to the army in *Tuscarawi,* although everyone had wanted to run away only a few days ago. Their fear left them completely, however, after they had heard such good news from people coming here from there.[1327] A family from *Goschachgünk* asked for permission to move here, and after receiving this they moved here today.

THE 15TH   We heard through *Shawnee* from the *Unami River* that the *Nations* were holding a *Councel* and trying to unite so that they could engage the army in *Tuscarawi* in a battle when they think they are strong enough. May the Savior mercifully prevent this, because we would have the warriors on our backs whether it turned out well or badly.

THE 16TH   *Stephan* returned from *Gokhossing*[1328] where he had gone to get his grandmother who had fled from here. He could not find her there any more. He said that the Indians who fled are in miserable circumstances, suffering from hunger and cold. They do not even know why they flee but are just following some evil Indians. They are evil and threatened to capture *Stephan* because he was a *Virginian.*

THE 20TH   We received news in a letter from *Colonel Gibson* that the first troops[1329] from the army had arrived at *Tuscarawi* yesterday evening, and also that *Colonel White Eye* had died not far from *Pittsburgh* 15 days ago today.[1330] He had an old illness and then got small pox in addition to that.[1331] Brothers *Isaac* and *Israel* informed us that they were all well and had been well received by the army and also by the *General,* and that they heard and enjoyed nothing but kindness there.[1332]

THE 22ND   In the devotion for married couples, the single Brother *Nathanael, Gideon's* son who is a communicant, was married to the single Sister *Martha Elisabeth.*

THE 23RD   The Helpers spoke with some young people and told two of them that they had to leave the congregation. We learned through an Indian who came from *Tuscarawi* that our Brother *Daniel* had gotten small pox there.

THE 24TH   *Israel* returned from *Tuscarawi* where *General McIntosh* had conferred with the *Chiefs* because things had taken such a turn with the *Delaware. Captain Pipe* had left there with so many Indians[1333] and now the hostile

1327. From "From elsewhere," whole paragraph not in H2 or H3, at the margin a sign in another hand.
1328. Probably identical with Goschahossink, mentioned in entry for 8 March 1773; see note 166.
1329. H2 and H3: "The 20th we heard that the advance troops."
1330. The words "15 days ago" not in H2 or H3.
1331. In reality White Eyes had been murdered by a white settler (White, *Middle Ground,* 385). Zeisberger and his contemporaries believed the story as here reported.
1332. From "Brothers Isaac and Israel" not in H2 or H3, bracketed in another hand.
1333. See entry for 28 Oct. 1778 and note 1306.

ones were all mixed up with those who had been well inclined until now. This is just what the hostile ones had been trying to achieve and they have reached their goal now.[1334] Therefore the *General* had to change his *Resolution* and for the sake of the *Delaware* who had run away, he and the *Chiefs* decided to send a message to all the *Nations* and invite them to *Tuscarawi,* where he will speak with them. All the *Nations* who want to accept peace will have it, except for the *Mingo.*[1335]

THE 27TH   In the Helpers' *Conference* we commended our Brother *Israel* and his affairs to the Brothers and asked that they help him so that the *Chief Affairs* of his tribe, which now fall completely upon him since *White Eye* has died, do not become a burden for him. In *Tuscarawi* in the presence of all the Indians and the *General, Gelelemind* declared him the *Chief* upon whom he could best rely now, and he asked him to help him.[1336]

THE 29TH   On the first of *Advent* our services were about the incarnation of our Lord, and we rejoiced over God our Savior, who is our Redeemer. *Johann Martin* returned from *Tuscarawi,* where he had gone to visit his sick Brother *Daniel.* When he got there, however, he had already been buried. He was baptized by Brother *Schmick* in *Fridenshütten* on *April* 3, 1768 and became a communicant on *September* 17, 1774. For the past year his heart had not felt right, and he had wavered when the Indian congregation came here from *Gnadenhütten* in the spring. Still, a hidden hand preserved him and an election to grace rested upon him. Some time ago he went with another Brother to *Fort McIntosh* as a messenger. Since then he had remained with the army and he also went to *Tuscarawi* with them. Not a single person in the army had had small pox, but he got them there.[1337] The *General* and the *Doctors* did their best to save him, but the small pox beat him and he died on the 25th of this month and was buried there.

General McIntosh had a long talk with *Johann Martin* and asked him all sorts of physical and spiritual questions. *Johann Martin* answered them to his complete *Satisfaction* so that the *General* was completely amazed to see and hear an

1334. From "This is just what the hostile" not in H2 or H3.

1335. From "and for the sake of the Delawares" not in H2 or H3. On 22 November General McIntosh declared in a speech to the Delaware that all Indians had to make peace with him within the next two weeks, otherwise he would attack them. At the same time he asked the Delaware for provisions, which made his threat less than convincing (*FAO*, 178–80). Close to the place where in 1764 Henry Bouquet had built a fort, McIntosh erected a new fort on the Tuscarawas, which was baptized Fort Laurens; see note 1303 to entry for 19 Oct. 1778. See also Pieper and Gidney, *Fort Laurens.*

1336. This note suggests that the succession of Netawatwees had finally been settled: Gelelemind was the new chief. After White Eyes' death Gelelemind, as chief, appointed Israel, alias Welapachtschiechen, whom the Americans called Captain Johnny, his most important counselor. With this decision this office remained within the Turkey clan.

1337. H3: "to Fort McIntosch, where he was infected with the small pox. The General . . ." Zeisberger's remark ("Not a single person in the army had had small pox, but he got them there") indicates that he had begun to wonder why small pox infected the Delaware but not others.

Indian who had such understanding and knowledge. *Johann Martin* told him among other things, I cannot actually read the Bible, but still I know it is written and we have been taught this by our teachers. The *General* can read the Bible and will know if what I say is the truth. He answered him, You are right; what you say is the truth and I am really happy to see such an Indian. Now I see indeed that you are no longer heathen, but Christian Indians, and I will help you and serve you as much as I am able.

[December]

DECEMBER 1ST   Brothers *Isaac* and *Tobias* went to *Tuscarawi* with some horses loaded with Indian corn.[1338] The army is very close now and this has provided us some peace because everything is quiet and the warriors who previously talked so grandly here have gone far away. Our Brothers therefore went out to hunt for a couple of weeks.

THE 2ND   A White man from the army[1339] came here to buy some fresh *Provisions* for the *Officiers*. We heard then that they will not move on this winter but will stay in this area until spring. If it were not for the sake of the *Delaware* Indians who were in danger, the army would have spent the winter in *Fort McIntosh*. People say they want to take possession of the Indian land and to occupy it as far as they go. The Indians, however, imagine that when peace is restored the army will return home, as happened before. It is currently 3,000 men strong.[1340]

THE 4TH   The *General* and *Colonels Gibson* and *Broadhead*[1341] really wanted to see one of us White Brothers, so Brother *Heckewelder* left for there today with *Johann Martin*.

THE 7TH   Brother *David* received a letter from the *General* in *Fort Lawrence*[1342] in *Tuscarawi*, which is now completed. In this he informs him that he would like to see and speak with him before he returns. Brother *David* set out to go there but he could not cross the river because of high waters, so he had to come back. We also heard that the Brothers House, schoolhouse, and one other building in *Gnadenhütten* were burned down. The Meeting House and

1338. On the miserable provision of the troops at Fort Laurens, see *FAO*, 172–76, 181–82; Pieper and Gidney, *Fort Laurens*, 37–38.

1339. Not identified.

1340. H3: "It is said that it numbers at the present 3000 men." Zeisberger mentions in passing a rumor that would be a decisive factor in destroying the good relations between the Delaware and the soldiers in Fort Laurens in the following weeks.

1341. Colonel Daniel Brodhead (1736–1809), since March 1777 commanding officer of the 8th Pennsylvania Regiment, was appointed general of the army after McIntosh's recall; he retained this office until 1781. At this time he was involved in very serious conflicts with Colonel John Gibson, who succeeded him in this office in 1781 (*FAO*, 58n2); for Brodhead, see Appel, "Colonel Daniel Brodhead."

1342. That is, Fort Laurens.

others were also set on fire, but apparently the fire either went out by itself or someone extinguished it.

THE 11TH   We had a *Conference* with the female Helpers and they received their assigned work for today of speaking with various members of their sex.

THE 14TH   Brother *Heckewelder* returned from *Fort Lawrence* early in the day. He had such a long and difficult journey there because of the high waters and he did not get there for several days. As a result he missed the *General*, who had returned to *Fort McIntosh* the previous day.[1343] In the meantime he was welcomed and the *Officiers* were happy to see someone from here. *Colonel Gibson*, the *Commandant* and *Agent of Indian Affairs*, told him that the *Commissioners* who had been in *Pittsburgh* for some time had written to *Congress* about our mission and had highly *recommended* the Brothers.[1344] *General McIntosh* would do the same now and soon we would hear something good for us which would please us. The *General* returned with the army and left an occupying force of 200 men there, so nothing else will happen there until spring. Now we also learned from there that a great danger had been hovering above us this past summer. The Savior had mercifully kept it away from us, and the eye and guardian of *Israel* had watched over us although we knew nothing about it, nor could we have guessed it. The residents of the *Frontiers* across the river from us had submitted a *Petition* to *Congress* asking for permission to set out after the warriors who continued attacking the *Settlements* and to pursue them. If they had received permission to do this, which they did not, they would have followed the warriors' path directly into our *Town,* which they had no intention of sparing. Once when they set out after a party of warriors, they were actually only about 20 miles from here when they turned back again. The residents on the *Frontiers* around *Pittsburgh* also submitted a similar *Petition* and actually received permission to go to the *Mingo-Towns* above *Goschgosching* and to destroy them.[1345]

1343. The retreat of McIntosh's army began on 9 December. One hundred seventy soldiers, mostly from the 13th Virginia Regiment, were stationed under the command of Colonel John Gibson at Fort Laurens. The 8th Pennsylvania Regiment under Brodhead manned Fort McIntosh, while the other soldiers returned to Fort Pitt, where they arrived on 25 December. Pieper and Gidney, *Fort Laurens,* 41–47.

1344. The report of the commissioners, together with the treaty of amity concluded on 19 September, was presented to Congress on 6 October 1778 (Ford, *Journals of the Continental Congress,* 12:986). The Congress asked a commission of three to report on the report; the Congress does not seem to have taken any further action.

1345. "Goschgosching" is a variant of Goschgoschünk. From "So nothing there will happen" not in H2 or H3, bracketed in another hand. On 18 May 1778 a letter from Thomas Smith of Bedford County to James Smith, a delegate for Pennsylvania, dated 11 May 1778, was presented to the Continental Congress. After reading the letter, the Congress resolved to forward it to the Board of War with the request "to take such measures of affording present relief to the western frontiers" (Ford, *Journals of the Continental Congress,* 11:507; see too Henry Laurens to David Espy and others, 17 May 1778, Smith et al., *Letters of Delegates to Congress,* 9:693–94). On 21 May 1778 a letter dated 19 May 1778 from the Assembly of Pennsylvania was presented to the Continental Congress together with a petition "from sundry inhabitants on the Western Frontier." That letter and petition were also for-

THE 16TH   *Gelelemind* came here with some *Shawnee* and *Counsellors* and we learned that the *Wyandot Half King* and many *Nations* had accepted the *Invitation* to go to *Tuscarawi*[1346] and they have promised to speak with the *General*. We received news that a party of *Mingo* had gone to *Fort Lawrence* to get *Scalps*. *Colonel Gibson* had asked us to let him know when we heard about things like this, so we sent an *express* messenger to him with the news.[1347]

THE 17TH   After a long illness, the single Brother *Stephan* went to the Savior in blessing and on **the 18th** his earthly dwelling was buried. Brother *Schmick* baptized him on *January* 6, 1775, and a year ago in the fall he came here with his parents to live. His heart was tender and sensitive to the Savior. The entire time he was here, he lived his blessed life quietly. During his illness, which was consumption, he was always happy when someone visited him and talked with him about the Savior and sang verses, and he expressed his gratitude whenever this happened.

THE 23RD   There was the burial of Brother *Jeremia,* who died yesterday in blessing. He was the natural brother of the blessed *Johannes Papunhanks*[1348] and first heard the Gospel in *Wyalusing*[1349] in 1762, two years before the Indian congregation moved there from the *Barracks* in *Philadelphia.*[1350] When an Indian war broke out soon thereafter, he moved to *Goschgoshing* on the *Ohio* with many other Indians. Then when the Brothers went there in 1768[1351] he was one of the first to join them and from then on he remained with them. He was baptized on *January* 21, 1770, in *Lawunakhannek* and on *January* 6, 1771, became a communicant. In the spring of 1770 he moved to *Langundoutenünk* with the Brothers, from there to *Schönbrunn* in 1772, and in 1776 to *Lichtenau.* Thus he was present at the beginning of each of the Brothers' *Settlements* on the *Ohio.* He was a faithful and willing congregational servant and *National*-Helper. Because he was weak and could not do much hunting, he let his service to the congregation be his primary concern. He was always ready and willing to do this and it was important to him and a great blessing for him. He did anything assigned to him with much faithfulness and care. If he saw disorder anywhere he diligently worked against this, so that he sometimes offended the Brothers and Sisters and had to be cautioned about this. This subsided in the last few years and he learned to treat the Brothers and Sisters with more love and

---

warded to the Board of War (Ford, *Journals of the Continental Congress,* 11:518). This was the "Petition from the Township of Peters, in the County of Cumberland, praying, in effect, Protection from the Indian Ravages," as the summary of its contents in the protocol of the Supreme Executive Council of Pennsylvania dated 18 May reports. A delegation from the assembly had presented the petition to the council. Both council and assembly resolved to present the petition to the Continental Congress (*PCR,* 11:491). We have found no other indications of further petitions from the western counties.

1346. Fort Laurens.
1347. From "We received news" not in H2 or H3, bracketed in another hand.
1348. See entry for 16 May 1775.
1349. On Wyalusing, variant of Wihilusing, see Introduction, xx–xx.
1350. See entry for 9 May 1774 and note 368.
1351. See entry Introduction, pp. 48–49.

patience. He loved and was loved in return, and he will really be missed in the congregation now. About 4 weeks ago he was overtaken by an illness but at first did not think it would be his end. He surrendered himself to the Savior's will, however, and when he saw that his illness would not break, he quickly reconciled himself, spoke of nothing but his death, and hoped the Savior would take him quickly. He said a sweet farewell to his wife, admonished her to remain with the Savior and the congregation, and then he died peacefully and happily with blessing of the congregation.

THE 24TH   We began the Christmas Eve service with a Lovefeast, celebrated the birth of our baby Jesus in song, praised Him with happy hearts and mouths, adored Him in his manger, and thanked Him for his holy incarnation. There were many strangers from *Goschachgünk* present, including some *Shawnee* who had asked permission to attend.

THE 25TH   In the morning was the sermon about the text, For unto us a child is born, unto us a son is given etc.[1352] During the Congregational Service *Israel's* sister, a widow, was buried into Jesus' death through baptism. She received the name *Eva* in Holy Baptism, and it was a blessed event full of grace. *Joseph Peepe* returned from *Fort Lawrence* with another unbaptized person from here. They had been kept there until other Indians from *Goschachgünk* took their place.

THE 26TH   At the conclusion of the blessed holidays, our dear Lord allowed us to eat and drink of his Body and Blood in Holy Communion. One Brother, *Gideon,* participated in this for the first time. One Sister watched for the 2nd time, and one for the first time.

THE 27TH   The baby girl born to Brother *Gottfried* and Sister *Justina* on the 20th of this month was baptized with the name *Charlotte.*

THE 28TH   *Mr. Samples,* the *Quarter Master*[1353] from *Fort Lawrence,* was here to trade goods for cattle and various items from our Indian Brothers and Sisters. Trade with *Detroit* has ceased here, but until now good friends have always provided us with goods so that our Brothers and Sisters have not had any shortages. Now trade is beginning on this side again and actually at the same price it was in peacetime. And so things are always taken care of for us in advance, and our dear heavenly Father is aware of our needs. *Mr. Samples* could not adequately express his amazement at the order and the quiet behavior in our *Town.* I can easily see, he said, that these Indians are completely different from the ones in *Goschachgünk.* They are an orderly and diligent people; I did not expect to see such Indians in the bush. It is worth helping them.

THE 29TH   An Indian from *Wobash*[1354] had asked the Brothers about the foundation of our teaching and what held us so strongly together, and he

1352. Isa. 9:5.
1353. Samuel Samples's civil occupation in Pittsburgh was running a guesthouse. *FAO,* 186n2.
1354. On the tribes of this region, see entry for 22 May 1773 and note 198.

believed this must be a secret. *Thomas,* his natural brother, spoke with him and preached the Savior to him. He had not been talking to him for long when the Indian said, That is enough now. Please stop, because my heart feels very strange when you are talking. I cannot put it into words, but I can already tell that if I thought about it much, I would not be able to continue carrying out my business (messenger to the *Nations*).

THE 31ST   During the Watchnight Service we contritely concluded this year, asked for all of our mistakes to be pardoned, and thanked the Savior for being with us and comforting and blessing us so richly with his sweet presence. Also for the mighty protection of our dear heavenly Father, which we have often experienced very directly, and for the work and care of our dear Mother, who has kept our hearts in relationship with Him and has clarified His wounds and suffering for us daily so that we have not strayed from Him. We prayed that He would continue this in the coming year. He let his loving face shine upon us and granted us his peace. In conclusion, the Lord's blessing was laid upon the congregation and we entered into the New Year with comforted and happy hearts.

The Brothers and Sisters have now seen in the Diary most of the noteworthy events in the year now ending. We are confident they will agree with us that praise, honor, and glory should be brought to the Savior for what He has done for his Indian congregation during this year and they will join us in thanking the Lord for this. Therefore we will keep this brief and just add the following:

The celebration days of the incarnation and birth, sufferings, death, resurrection and ascension of our Lord and Savior, Pentecost, and *November* 13th were blessed days for us, along with other days. They were accompanied by his dear presence and made a lasting impression in our hearts. Above all else was the very blessed enjoyment of His Body and Blood in Holy Communion, which we enjoyed 8 times during the year. We cannot adequately thank Him for continuing to preserve and grant us this great kindness. If we no longer had this, how much shorter this would have been, and where would we be now?

In *April* Brothers *Heckewelder* and *Schebosch* returned to us from Bethlehem safely and without any difficulties. It turned out that if they had made the trip a little bit later, they could have fallen into the hands of the warriors.

That same month, the Brothers and Sisters from *Gnadenhütten* moved here to *Lichtenau.* Now we hope they will be able to return there soon.

During the year 23 adults were baptized.

12 children were born and baptized; 8 girls and 4 boys and in *Gnadenhütten* 3 girls and 1 boy.

7 Brothers and Sisters became communicants

2 couples were married

In *Lichtenau* 14 adults died and 3 elsewhere

and 3 children died here and 2 in *Gnadenhütten*

6 young people were sent away by the congregation

7 left the congregation

Currently 108 married Brothers and Sisters live here

11 single Brothers

6 single Sisters

9 widowers

31 widows

15 older boys

21 older girls

30 baptized little boys

38 baptized little girls

30 unbaptized boys

29 unbaptized girls

Total: 328

Diary of Lichtenau *on the* Muskingum *from* January *until* April *and of the resettling of* Schönbrunn *and its continuation through* November 1779[1355]

JANUARY 1ST   A pretty large number of strangers came in the morning for the sermon. Afterward we had a service with the baptized Brothers and Sisters, and with humbled hearts we thanked the Savior for all the grace and acts of kindness we have enjoyed from Him. We gave ourselves to Him anew to be his own people, commended ourselves to Him, to the protection of our heavenly Father, and to the merciful care of our dear Mother in this year also. We had not received any Watchwords and texts for this year, so we used the ones from the beginning of last year.

THE 2ND   This morning the Savior quickly took *Marie,* sister of the blessed *Josua,*[1356] home to himself in blessing. Her earthly dwelling was buried on THE 3RD. She was baptized on *March* 26, 1747, in Bethlehem and later became a communicant. She lived in the single Sisters' house there for a number of years, later came with the Indian congregation to the *Barracks* in *Philadelphia,* and she went to *Fridenshütten* on the *Susquehanna* with them in 1765. She came to *Gnadenhütten* on the *Muskingum* in 1772 and then here in the spring of last year. We know nothing about her walk through this mortal life except what we saw in her while she was here, and we can testify that her heart was attached to the Savior and to the congregation. During all the external difficulties and troubles she had to endure, she remained calm and held tightly to the Savior. A few days ago she told one Sister that she felt like she would go to

1355. MAB, B 147, F 9, fol. 326b.
1356. Josua had been buried on 2 August 1775; see entry under this date.

the Savior soon, although she was fit and healthy and nothing was wrong with her. She even gave instructions about how she wanted things done after her homegoing. On *December* 30th she was busy all day getting in wood for the holidays, until almost evening when she came home and felt bad. Soon afterward, however, she was found in her house, lying there with seizures, and she was not aware of anything. She remained in this state until she died with the blessing of the congregation on the stated date.

THE 6TH   We celebrated our festival[1357] with grace and blessing. Our dear Lord revealed himself to us very graciously during all the services and laid his peace upon us.

THE 8TH   In our Helpers' *Conference* we decided that some Brothers should go to *Gnadenhütten* since the spring weather is so beautiful and the time for making sugar is approaching. They should also take care of the *Town* so that it is not completely ruined before the Brothers and Sisters are able to move back there. Brothers *Samuel Nantikok* and *Petrus* went to *Fort Laurence* to spend 14 days there, until others replace them.[1358]

THE 10TH   The baby boy born to *Adolph* and *Susanna* on the 5th of this month was baptized with the name *Johannes Petrus.*

THE 14TH   We heard that the *Nations* have been meeting in *Sandusky* for some time and are still holding council. We will hear the results of this soon, but we cannot expect it to be anything good.[1359] There is also a division

1357. On the importance of 6 January, see Introduction, pp. 62–63.

1358. From "Brothers Samuel" bracketed in another hand, not in H3. There is no copy of this part of the diary in MAB. The willingness of the Christian Indians to serve the soldiers of Fort Laurens, with the non-Christian Delaware as guides and scouts, prompted the British side, as the letter of Richard B. Lernoult to Henry Hamilton dated 9 Feb. 1779 proves, to adopt an interpretation that explains the following events: "Girty says . . . that about 70 Moravian Indians were in the Virginian Interest and were lying near Beaver Creek; that two of them were Constantly detained as hostages, for the rest Girtie thinks they will Join the Other Indians when occasion offers." James, *Clark Papers,* 108–9.

1359. Zeisberger's source for this information is unclear. He probably received it from the messenger who brought Captain Pipe's and Half King's speeches to the Council of Goschachgünk, whence Gelelemind carried the speech to Fort Laurens on 20–21 December. On 21 December Colonel Gibson wrote the speech down. In his message, Half King, chief of the Wyandot, informed the Delaware that he could accept the invitation for peace negotiations only if he were authorized by the Council of the Wyandot; at the same time he requested that the Delaware avoid his settlement on their trip to Detroit because he was unable to guarantee their safety (*FAO*, 187–88). According to a memorandum in the hand of Capt. Richard B. Lernoult, who acted as commanding officer of Fort Detroit during the absence of Lieutenant Governor Henry Hamilton, the hostile tone of Half King's message was supported by speeches of other Wyandot chiefs delivered on 2 January 1779 (*FAO*, 191–92). On the other hand, in a letter dated 9 Feb. 1779 to Henry Hamilton, Lernoult bemoaned the greatly wavering attitude of the Wyandot (James, *Clark Papers,* 108–9). Hamilton was more optimistic, reporting on 24 January to Governor Haldimand that together with the southern tribes he intended a large-scale campaign against the "rebells": "The various reports brought to me by the savages agree in the mean [main] as to the design of the Southern Indians, who were to make four several parties for the ensuing spring, one towards Kaskasquias to attack the rebels there, another to go up the Ohio to assist the Shawanese, a third to come to this place [Vincennes] to make peace with the Ouabash Indians and drive the Americans out of their country, and the fourth to remain in the mouth of the Cherokee River to intercept any boats coming up the Mississippi or going down the

among the Indians in *Goschachgünk* and most of them are working on moving to *Assünnünk* this spring.[1360]

THE 17TH   An *express* messenger from *Mr. Morgan* in *Pittsburgh* brought us a *Paquet* of Bethlehem reports from *July, August,* and *September* of last year, as well as weekly news reports from the *Unity* Elders' *Conference* and letters from Brothers *Matthao* and *Grube* in *Litiz,* from which we learned how things were going in the congregations.[1361]

THE 19TH   We heard that a party of warriors had gone to *Tuscarawi* and that the *Wyandot* and other *Nations* are meeting and planning to lay siege to the *Fort.*[1362] They want to cut off *Communication* with them and to come and get us White Brothers here. All the news we had indicated that things are not yet over and we can once again expect something to happen.

THE 20TH   A message with a *String of Wampum* came to *Israel* from his tribe and friends[1363] in *Goschachgünk.* They would like for him to leave the congregation, and it was easy to see what their plan is. They want him to be *Chief* in *Assünnünk,* because most of them are planning to move there.[1364] *Israel* told us what he thought about this and that his intentions were the same as they had been from the beginning when he came to the congregation. The Helper Brothers helped him prepare a reply, which he took to them. They could not argue with it.

THE 21ST   Two of our young people who were sent away some time ago have returned and asked to be reaccepted. They received permission to stay here on a provisional basis.

JANUARY 23RD   The older girl *Phoebe, Isaac's* stepdaughter, went home yesterday and her earthly dwelling was buried today. Brother *Jungmann* baptized her in *Schönbrunn* on *April* 16, 1775. She was a quiet and meek girl and loved the Savior. During her illness she often said she wanted to go to the

Ohio" (Davies, *Documents of the American Revolution,* 17:48). On the one hand Lernoult envisioned the complete collapse of the British position in the west in the face of American initiatives and the wavering attitude of the Great Lakes tribes, while on the other Hamilton predicted that 1779 would be the great turning point in favor of England as a result of the grand coalition between the southern, western, and northern tribes.

1360. This pessimistic interpretation contrasts sharply with the positive tone of Captain Pipe's message (*FAO,* 187–88); Pipe had assured the American general: "I never meant to quit the hold I have of the friendship subsisting Between us."

1361. On the weekly news reports from the Unity's Elders' Conference ("Wöchentlichen Nachrichten der Unitäts Aeltesten Conferenz"), see note 313 to entry for 17 Nov. 1773.

1362. The reference is to Fort Laurens. See Richard B. Lernoult to Henry Hamilton, 9 Feb. 1779: "Girty says . . . that the Six Nations, Delewares, Shanees and Wiandots, to the Number of 700 are assembled at the little Village of St. Dusky [Sandusky] that they Intend marching off the 14th to Attack the Virginians at Tuscarawas, if they Cannot decoy them out they will drive off and destroy their Cattle and if the main Army Advances they will Attack them in the Night." James, *Clark Papers,* 108–9.

1363. On the meaning of "friends" and "friendship" within Delaware society, see Introduction, pp. 16–19 and note 142.

1364. The settlement Assünnünk was close to the Shawnee settlement southwest of the Delaware settlement and thus at a considerable distance from where the major military actions were expected.

Savior and be with her mother, who preceded her in *August* of last year. The quartermaster *Mr. Samples*[1365] came here from *Fort Laurence.* He took 7 men from the *Garrison* with him to *Goschachgünk,* one of whom was killed by hostile Indians across the river shortly after they had arrived.[1366]

THE 24TH   The baby girl born to *David* and *Salome* on *December* 23rd was baptized *Anna Susanna.* News arrived that there were about 60 warriors on the *Walhanding* who wanted come to *Goschachgünk* tonight and kill the White people. We can also expect troubles because of this now, so 10 Brothers kept watch in the *Town* tonight.

THE 25TH   We received news through an *express* messenger from *Fort Laurence* that there had been a battle with the Indians there; 2 White people were killed and one was taken prisoner.[1367] A rumor reached us that there is a party of warriors across the river near *Goschachgünk.* They wanted to cross and kill the White people there,[1368] so they brought them to us late in the night. We were then scared that people here might be murdered also. We could not do anything about this though, so we remained hopeful and trusted in the Savior to keep all harm from us in His mercy. He did this, and we heard the next morning that it had just been a rumor.

Colonel Gibson wrote to *Gelelemind* and us that we should consider what was the best thing to do, and we should all come to *Fort Laurence* together if we thought it would be better.[1369] We could not agree to this, however, because the war will go wherever there is a *Fort,* and we are safest far away from there.

THE 27TH   During the night a couple of suspicious Indians were seen around our *Town* with rifles and spears. We immediately reported this to *Goschachgünk* and sent them word to keep good watch over the White people there. They saw them shortly thereafter and chased them away. The next morning they looked for them in the bush between here and *Goschachgünk,* found them, and questioned them. However, they let them go again after they had promised not to do any harm, and they stayed there until the next morning when two of the White people they had been waiting for came on their return journey here to our *Town.* They fired at them and wounded one. Our *Israel,* who was going down the road just then, was not far behind them. He yelled

1365. On Samples, see note 1353 above.

1366. From "The quartermaster" not in H3, bracketed in another hand. The soldier killed was John Nash. See Colonel John Gibson to General Lachlan McIntosh, 13 Feb. 1779, *FAO,* 224.

1367. The commanding officer of this expedition against Fort Laurens was Simon Girty; according to a report by Lachlan McIntosh (to Archibald Lochry, dated 29 Jan. 1779), the battle took place three miles from Fort Laurens. The "Mingoes . . . killed two of our Men, wounded four, and took one prisoner." On 19 January Zeisberger had warned Gibson and on 20 January Morgan of the imminent attack (*FAO,* 210, 202). The letter to Gibson (printed in "Letters from the Canadian Archives," *Collections of the Illinois State Historical Library* 1 [1903]: 381–82) was intercepted and carried to Fort Detroit. Zeisberger asserted in this letter that he had received the information from two hostile warriors. This letter and other intercepted communications by Zeisberger are further proof that the missionary was actively supporting the American cause in this war.

1368. That is the quartermaster Sample and his company.

1369. We could not locate the letter.

at the Indians, who immediately ran away, and the wounded one narrowly escaped.[1370]

THE 30TH   *Mr. Samples* had written to the *Commandant* in *Fort Laurence*[1371] to have a *Commando* of soldiers pick up his people and him, but he informed him that he could not send any men. Therefore it was decided a convoy of Indians should accompany them there, which was then done. We had to provide 10 of our Indian Brothers for this, and they took the wounded man there by water. They made many promises about how they would protect us, but we did not receive any protection from them. On the contrary, they bring the war into our *Town* and we then have to protect them. *Mr. Samples* spent most of the time here with us, because he did not believe he was safe in *Goschachgünk*. We can truthfully say, Give us help from trouble: for vain is the help of man.[1372] To conclude this week and after the unpleasant circumstances of recent days, the congregation had Holy Communion. One Sister participated in this for the first time and one watched for the 2nd time.

THE 31ST   Early in the day was the *Liturgy* for Holy Communion and then the sermon about the text, Even as the Son of man came not to be ministered unto, but to minister, and to give his life a ransom for many.[1373] Warriors were seen here again. They stayed hidden in the bush and were lying in wait for a chance to cause harm.

[February]

FEBRUARY 1ST   We have had the most beautiful spring weather for some time, so our Brothers and Sisters went out to make preparations for boiling sugar.

1370. Colonel John Gibson reports this incident in a letter to General Lachlan McIntosh, Fort Laurens, 13 Feb. 1779, *FAO*, 224–26; the wounded soldier was Peter Parchment. Gibson further reports how far the relations between himself and his soldiers and the Delaware had deteriorated. While Gibson assumes in his report that the Delaware had generally changed their pro-American attitude, Gelelemind in his written apology blamed the incident on supporters of Captain Pipe. On 30 January Pipe informed Gibson in a message sent via Gelelemind that he had strictly commanded his warriors "not to join any Body of Warriors, be they who they would that he also had no dealings or Concern with them & their undertakings & if any of his foolish young men should actually Go to war with the Enemy they were disobedient towards his orders and Might stand their Chance" (*FAO*, 214). At the same time both Gelelemind and the Council in Goschachgünk, in letters to George Morgan dated 20 January, complained that they had been betrayed during the negotiations in Fort Pitt in September 1778. They claimed that the Delaware had definitively not given up their neutrality in the September 1778 treaty but had resolved "to sit quite still & let you & the English make out the matter together." In short, Gelelemind wrote, "the Articles of the Treaty . . . are wrote down false, & as I did not understand the Interpreter what he spoke I could not contradict his Interpretation, but now I will speak the truth plain & tell you what I spoke" (*FAO*, 202–5). This is the first time that the charge of betrayal was made; see also Zeisberger's entries for 26 and 27 Sept. 1778 and the notes thereto.

1371. John Gibson.

1372. Ps. 60:13.

1373. Matt. 20:28.

THE 2ND   We heard that the *Shawnee* who lived in *Goschachgünk* for one year[1374] went to *Woakatammeki* recently. They want to move back to their former site of residence this spring and it looks the same with those from *Goschachgünk*. We hear there is a division among them though, because many of them want to move to *Assünnünk* and elsewhere.[1375]

THE 5TH   Once again we received nothing but bad news from the *Wyandot Towns*. We could not learn anything definite, because everything is being kept very secret and Indians are forbidden to go into that area. Therefore the people from *Goschachgünk* cannot learn what they are planning. Still, we could see that something that is not good is going on again and we cannot expect peace yet. We presumed that the *Nations* are planning an attack on *Fort Laurence*.[1376]

THE 6TH   *Gelelemind* came here and discussed the current circumstances, which appear serious. His messengers from the *Wyandot* have returned but did not bring him any answer except what they had heard incidentally. This was nothing but horrible news, because the *Nations* are threatening the *Delaware* once again.[1377] Therefore *Gelelemind* asked us what we would think about it if a *Fort* were built close to us, as they had been offered a number of times before. He said he would propose it as soon as he went to the *Fort* if the Indians agreed to it. He knows very well that few Indians in *Goschachgünk* will consent to this but he would still like to see it done. It seemed like he wanted to try to get our approval for this so that he could later blame us for wanting it if the Indians asked him to explain himself. We told him we would leave it up to him, because he was the *Chief* and was concerned for the welfare of his people. We did want to tell him our thoughts about having a *Fort* here, though. Then he could do and act as he saw fit. We thought we would constantly have

1374. For the arrival of the Shawnee in Goschachgünk, see entries for 1 to 3 March and 10 April 1778.

1375. Entire entry for this day bracketed in another hand. On the intention to move to Assünnünk, see entries for 14 and 20 Jan. 1779.

1376. Gelelemind had sent two messengers to Half King in Sandusky; both returned without much success on 5 February 1779; their reports form the basis for this entry. Heckewelder and Gelelemind reported to Colonel John Gibson and Colonel George Morgan on 10 February what the two messengers had learned. According to Gelelemind, after the letters intercepted by Girty (see entry for 25 Jan. 1779 and note 1367) had been read to Half King in Sandusky, Half King sent the following message to the Delaware: "Cousin at Cooschacking I have told you a Year ago leave of[f] sending letters to the Virginians, & quit them entirely, I have pealed bark & stop't the road between them & you, that you might not come together any more, but you still continue to go to them, now I tell you once more, leave entirely your Correspondence with the Virginians & send no more letters to them, Consider yourself Cousin, you alone are diverse from all other Nations, all the Nations are of one mind but you I am quite astonished at you & your works, & must needs think you are the Cause of the Virginians building a Fort at Tucarawas, I cannot think otherwise but you have sold them that land entirely. I now tell you again Cousin at Cooschaking do not go any more to the Virginians neither towards them, for if I see you there, I will Consider you as a Virginian, & kill you the same as I will kill the Virginians." Gelelemind reported that Captain Pipe "is looked on by the Wyondotts as a Virginian, on account of his not joining them" (*FAO*, 223).

1377. See preceding note.

the war before our doors if there were a *Fort* here, while it was still distant from us now.[1378] We also thought he would do what he had told us, and we would not seek safety from the warring parties with the *Nations* but would claim our own place and not leave this area for now. He finally said he was glad he had heard what we thought and he believed what we had told him was true. He said the latter because he is well aware that there is a division and separation among his people in *Goschachgünk* and most want to move away. However, nothing came of this later because they received news from the *Fort* that an army was supposed to march on the road where they had planned to move, that is, to *Assünnünk,* to learn what we were thinking and what we are planning to do.[1379]

Because of all of these circumstances and the news we had received, we met to discuss this together and most importantly to learn the Savior's counsel and desire. It is getting to be spring, so we must decide whether our Indian congregation will remain together like this for another year or if it is time to split up again now. He mercifully instructed us[1380] and we were comforted and joyful that he indicated we should not only occupy *Gnadenhütten* again but should also begin a site on up the river, which we could not determine at this time. After receiving the Savior's guidance, we were able to hope and believe that things related to the Indian war would not be as dangerous as they had seemed and this strengthened our faith.

THE 7TH   The twins born to Brother *Thomas* and Sister *Sabina* on *January* 29th were baptized into Jesus' death. They received the names *Isaac* and *Maria Salome* in Holy Baptism.

THE 9TH   Messengers returned from *Pittsburgh* with a *Speech* from *Colonel Morgan* to the *Councel* in *Goschachgünk.* We had not heard anything from him in a long time. I also received a friendly letter from him.[1381] The 10 Brothers who had taken the wounded man to *Fort Laurence* in a *Canow* returned from there. *Colonel Gibson* expressed his deep gratitude for the kindness his people had received from us here and for the help we had given them.[1382] When the Brothers said farewell to the wounded man, who soon recovered, he cried,

1378. This negative attitude is contradicted by what Colonel John Gibson wrote to General Lachlan McIntosh, 13 Feb. 1779: "The Moravians wish a Fort built near their town as they could then assist with provisions and men" (*FAO,* 225).

1379. From "However, nothing came" not in H3, bracketed in another hand. On 9 February messengers from Fort Pitt arrived at Goschachgünk with a message from George Morgan for the Council of the Delaware; no expedition is mentioned in this message or in the letter addressed to Zeisberger; see entry for 9 Feb. 1779. At the same time, however, George Washington exchanged letters with General Lachlan McIntosh about the possibility and necessity of sending an expedition from Fort Pitt against Fort Detroit. [Washington], *Writings of George Washington,* 14:59–62 (31 Jan. 1779), 114–18 (15 Feb. 1779). It is possible that the messengers had learned about this and carried it as a rumor to Lichtenau.

1380. The formula means that the lot had been drawn.

1381. George Morgan to the Council of the Delaware and Morgan to Zeisberger, both dated 30 Jan. 1779, in *FAO,* 215–16.

1382. We could not locate the letter.

expressed his gratitude to them for taking such good care of him, and said he was just sorry they could not stay with him any longer.[1383]

THE 10TH   In *Morgan's Speech* to the *Councel* in *Goschachgünk* he recommended that they look out for the White people and protect them so that they are not harmed.[1384] As a result of this, they held a counsel to consider what they should do about us. They did not believe they were in a position to protect us from the hostile Indians, so most of them thought the best and safest thing would be to take us to *Pittsburgh*. When they thought that it was already correct and agreed upon, however, old *Killbuck*[1385] threw this plan out and told them, You have decided to send the White Brothers away, which is easily and quickly said. However, you have not considered what the results of this will be and I can tell you this: If you send away the teachers of the Indian Believers, you can be sure that none of our friends who are with them will stay here. What will you say if this happens? Have the White Brothers not served and helped us a great deal? We cannot last without them, and when messages come from the *Fort* we cannot read them. Then some replied it would be enough if *one* were there; the others could go. It does not matter to us what they decide about us in the council, however. We are not concerned about this, but will do what we should and want to.

THE 13TH   In the morning an earthquake was felt here and also in all the places where our Brothers and Sisters were in their sugar huts in the bush. Later we heard from the *Shawnee, Mingo,* and *Wyandot* warriors that it had been felt at their distant sites at the same time as well.[1386]

THE 14TH   During a Congregational Council, it was recommended among other things that the Brothers make as many *Canows* as they can now while they are in their sugar huts, because we will need them this spring. Late in the evening a sign was seen in the air, a large fiery ball heading north. For a few minutes it made everything as bright as lightning. It had a long fiery tail behind it that shot fire and there was a powerful bang three times about 3 or 4 minutes after it had disappeared, and it made a great racket. Everyone who saw it agreed it was heading straight toward *Detroit*.[1387]

1383. On the background, see entry for 27 Jan. 1779 and note 1370.

1384. The letter dated 30 Jan. 1779 and addressed to the Council (see note 1381) does not contain such a remark. Possibly this is a misunderstanding; the security of the missionaries had acquired new urgency as a result of the threats contained in Half King's message (see note 1376 to entry for 5 Feb. 1779).

1385. I.e., the father of Gelelemind.

1386. According to Hobbs, "Earthquakes in Michigan," an earthquake was registered in 1779, but Hobbs does not give details or the precise date of this event. Stover and Loffman, *Seismicity of the United States,* 328, records only one earthquake in this region, close to the Muskingam, during the summer of 1776. We received this information from the U.S. Geological Survey Center, whose help is gratefully acknowledged. Bradley and Bennett, "Earthquake History of Ohio," do not record any earthquakes for this time.

1387. From "Everyone who" not in H3, bracketed in another hand. Evidently Zeisberger describes here the fall of a meteorite; for contemporary meaning and interpretation in general, see Burke, *Cosmic Debris.* The meteorite described here is not listed in Graham et al., *Catalogue of Meteorites.*

THE 17TH   Brothers *Johann Martin* and *Marcus* went to *Gnadenhütten* with some Brothers and Sisters to boil sugar there and also to take care of the *Town* so it does not fall into further ruin before the Brothers and Sisters can all move there. Brother *David* wrote a message to the *Wyandot Chief* across the *Lake* for *Gelelemind*.[1388]

THE 18TH   Late in the evening *Gelelemind* came and brought us the following news that 2 Indians from the *Wyandot Towns* had delivered this evening: the *Governor* from *Detroit* had recaptured a *Fort* on the *Wobash* that the *Americans* had taken in the summer,[1389] and the *Wyandot, Mingo, Shawnee,* and *Munsee* had been marching to *Fort Laurence* for a number of days already to occupy it. We also heard many stories that sounded terrible.[1390]

FEBRUARY 19TH   Two Indians who had come here from the *Wyandot Towns* brought many horrible rumors here. Most of them could be lies, especially that we White Brothers were in danger and that people were out to kill us. Therefore they held a council about us in *Goschachgünk*, and *Gelelemind* came here with some *Counsellors* and informed us that he and his *Councel* had something to tell us. We called the Brothers from the Helpers' *Conference* together to listen to them. The former told them that things looked very dangerous now; people were out to kill their teachers and they did not know how to protect us. Therefore they had decided to take us to *Pittsburgh* for a short time until the commotion was over and then we could return. The Brothers listened to them and replied that this was nothing new to us at all; since we had been in this area it had been repeated over and over that their teachers would be killed. Under these circumstances we commended ourselves to the grace of the eye and guardian of our souls and resolved not to worry about all the rumors, but to act as if we did not hear them.

THE 20TH   We heard that there were 7 warriors across the river who were after us and they were just the first members of a larger *Compagny*. In the evening, however, when it was already dark, *Gelelemind* sent a messenger here in great haste and informed our Indian Brothers that they should guard the safety of the White Brothers, because there were 30 warriors across the river and some of them were already on this side. They said they had come to get the White Brothers. For a while this caused a gloomy and confused night, because everyone believed there must be something to the matter since the message had been sent by *Gelelemind*. He finally came here personally, sent *Isaac* to Brother *David*, and informed him that he thought the safest thing for

---

1388. From "Brother David wrote" not in H3, bracketed in another hand. This was probably the answer to Half King's message; see entry for 5 Feb. 1779 and note 1376.

1389. This refers to Vincennes, which was occupied by Henry Hamilton on 17 December 1778. On 24 February 1779 Hamilton and his soldiers had to surrender to George Rogers Clark. James, *Clark Papers*, 87–113; HP, 492–505; Barnhart, *Henry Hamilton and George Rogers Clark*, 146–87.

1390. At Gelelemind's behest Zeisberger sent the information the same day in a letter to General Lachlan McIntosh and George Morgan (*FAO*, 231–32).

us would be to do what he had proposed and go to *Pittsburgh*. If we consented to this, he would have us taken away this very night yet. Brother *David* sent word that it was dark now; we would wait until morning and then consider the matter by the light of day. However, no warriors came into the *Town* and the next morning we heard that it had been just talk and that the 7 warriors who had been across the water came over here, but they were not planning to do us any harm.

THE 22ND   We sent an Indian with a message about us White Brothers to the *Wyandot Half King,* because the Indian who had been staying here a number of days offered to do this. Our Brothers were in favor of this, too, so we had this done because we thought it would not cause any harm even if it did not help. However, when the Indian got to *Goschachgünk* and let them know he had a message to the *Wyandot* from us, they took the *String of Wampum* away from him and kept it. From this it was clear enough that they do not want us to find out the truth of the matter and that the lies are all being made up in *Goschachgünk* to get rid of us in this way. Then when we are finally gone, the *Chiefs* will make themselves masters of our people and do what they want with our Indians. Therefore we sent Brothers *Isaac, Thomas,* and *Michael* to the *Wyandot Half King* in *Tuscarawi* on THE 24TH to speak with him and his *Captains* about the safety of the White Brothers and to get his reassurance about this. We had news that he was surrounding the *Fort* there with 200 warriors. We had also asked *Gelelemind* to send along one Indian from his people, but this did not happen and so they continued on their way. We had not expected these Brothers to do anything like this, because it is really not pleasant to travel with such a crowd of warriors. However, they were courageous, especially *Isaac,* and offered this themselves, so we could not oppose it. Although we did not believe we were in as much danger as people said and claimed, we still thought we had to do something for the sake of our Brothers and Sisters so that we could ease their anxiety and fear. When they are in constant fear for us they eventually begin thinking it would be better to take us away to safety for a while until things were calmer. Some Brothers had talked like this recently and in their fear actually asked us just to allow them to take us away. They said they would take care of everything else and get us safely to *Pittsburgh* because they could not see us killed. It did not satisfy them when we replied that we would just see if they killed us. They said they would have no more hope of getting us back then, but they knew they could have us back again if they took us away for a little while. However, we told them that we absolutely could not agree to this and leave them, because as surely as we left, our *Town* would be the savages' *Town* within a few days; they would immediately make themselves masters of it and carry out all kinds of mischief.

THE 24TH[1391]   During the night some warriors from the party camped

---

1391. In H₃ corrected as "25."

in *Tuscarawi* were seen and spoken to around our *Town*, but they left soon. 2 messengers came from *Fort Laurence*. From them we learned that the warriors were swarming around the *Fort* but had not yet attacked or done any harm.[1392] However, on THE 26TH the warriors personally brought news that 16 White people had been killed in a battle there and 2 had been taken prisoner.[1393] The warriors had accomplished this by tricking them and luring them out. None of them got back into the *Fort*.

THE 27TH   Many warriors who had been in *Tuscarawi* came here during the battle. During the night an *express* messenger from *Fort McIntosh* arrived with the news that 200 men were coming up the *Muskingum*[1394] with boats. We feared there might be a battle close to us here because there are so many warriors in this area, so that night we sent more messengers to meet them and to advise them to turn back, which they did. Already the next morning some warriors came and brought 2 *Scalps* from there.

THE 28TH   The baby girls born to Brother *Johannes* and Sister *Hanna* on the 22nd and to *Wilhelm* and *Martha* on the 23rd were baptized into Jesus' death, the former with the name *Agnes* and the latter *Regina*.

[March]

MARCH 1ST   *Isaac* returned from *Tuscarawi* with Brothers *Johannes* and *Michael*.[1395] They had not found *Half King* there because the warriors had already left. However, they had spoken with a party of *Mingo* from whom they learned that we had nothing to fear. We also learned that the *Shawnee* were on the way to lay siege to *Fort Laurence* with even more force and that they wanted to storm it.

THE 4TH   The Watchword was, He remembered us, when we were oppressed,[1396] and we adopted this promise for ourselves in the current critical circumstances, since we can expect something noteworthy to happen any day which might turn out to be for our good or might harm us. We reassured ourselves that our dear Lord remembers us well and nothing will happen to us without his will and permission. He will watch over us and will command the

---

1392. Between 22 February and 20 March 1779 Fort Laurens was besieged by Indian allies of the British. See report of General Lachlan McIntosh dated 12 March 1779, *FAO*, 240–42; Pieper and Gidney, *Fort Laurens*, 59.

1393. In the report cited in the preceding note, General Lachlan McIntosh assumed that "18 men . . . were fired upon, and all killed and scalped in sight of the Fort."

1394. The information was not entirely correct; the two hundred men were in reality a series of boats under the command of Major Richard Taylor that brought provisions for Fort Laurens. See the detailed instructions in General Lachlan McIntosh to Major Richard Taylor, 8 Feb. 1779, *FAO*, 221, and McIntosh's report dated 12 March 1779, cited in note 1392.

1395. See entry for 20 Feb. 1779.

1396. Ps. 136:23, from the Collection of Watchwords for 1778.

enemy not to harm us. Warriors continued going to *Fort Laurence* and we heard that the attack would happen either tonight or tomorrow.

THE 5TH　　A party of *Mingo* who had been at the battle in *Tuscarawi* came here. They said we would have to pay for it if Indians were lost during the current attack at *Fort Laurence,* and they would take revenge on us for this. We had already heard this many times.

THE 7TH　　We informed our Helpers that we would divide again this spring and occupy *Gnadenhütten* and another site. We had hesitated to inform them of this any sooner because times are so uncertain. We could not postpone it any longer, however, because the time is approaching. Therefore we sent *Isaac* to *Goschachgünk* to inform *Gelelemind* of this. On THE 8TH he then came here with his *Counsellors,* gave the Brothers a *String of Wampum,* and asked us to stay there one more year because he was planning to go to *Philadelphia* soon and discuss everything with *Congress.*[1397] We postponed our reply to this until a more suitable time. We received news from *Tuscarawi* that the *Shawnee* had given up the siege on *Fort Laurence.* The *Chiefs* in *Goschachgünk* had sent messengers to them and advised them to abandon their plan if they wanted to stay alive. After the messengers had talked to them twice, they agreed and promised to come to *Goschachgünk,* which was indeed the best thing. All our worries were thereby removed, because if they had captured the *Fort* they would have come here with very proud spirits, and if they had lost people they would have poured out their rage over this here. However, a letter from *General McIntosh* to the *Chiefs* brought us new trouble.[1398] He had given the *Delaware Chiefs* the *War Belt* at the *Treaty* last fall. If this had been executed, it might have meant that our Indians had to serve in the war. Although it was not publicly known among the Indians, there was still murmuring about this, and it was a primary cause for the split among the *Delaware.*[1399] Until now we had reassured our-

---

1397. In his letter dated 5 Jan. 1779, Colonel George Morgan had invited the Council of the Delaware to travel with him to Philadelphia and to negotiate there directly with representatives of the Continental Congress. *FAO,* 193–94; see also Morgan's letter dated 30 Jan. 1779, *FAO,* 215.

1398. *FAO,* 236–38. The letter is dated 25 Feb. 1779.

1399. This part of the treaty negotiations of September 1778 had in the meantime become the subject of a public controversy. In his letter to the Delaware Council dated 5 Jan. 1779, Colonel George Morgan was the first to voice criticism (*FAO,* 193–94). Gelelemind repeated this critique in his answer dated 20 Jan. 1779. In his letter, cited in 1370, he wrote Morgan that the text of the treaty had been incorrectly written down. Now he realized the error. He enclosed the relevant resolves and complaints of the Council of the Delaware. The complaints focused on two stipulations: first, that the request that Colonel John Gibson rather than George Morgan become agent of the Delaware originated with the Delaware representatives. This, he claimed, was wrong: during the negotiations he had demanded only that Gibson be appointed commanding officer of the fort to be built close to the Delaware settlements. Second, the critique focused on the conclusion of the military compact between the Delaware and the United States: "The Tomahawk was handed to me at Fort Pitt but not in a Warlike manner, we all standing & at no Council Fire, neither did I understand the meaning of it. I neither desired any Implements of War, all what I agreed to was to pilot the Army 'till beyond our bounds, & my great Capt White Eyes with several others to go before the Army & convey them to the Enemy in order to be of use to both Parties, in case they should desire to speak or treat with one another" (*FAO,* 202–5, quotation on p. 204). It is noteworthy that the complaint about falsifica-

selves that it would pass by quietly and have no further consequences. Now, however, the *General* is claiming it and insisting upon it. Therefore he asks for 2 *Captains* with 60 men for his use. The *Chiefs* are not in a position to gather such a strong force because there are very few of them, so it could even affect our Indians. However, the Savior who has released us from so many afflictions will also help us out of this problem.

THE 9TH   Some messengers from the warriors in *Tuscarawi* arrived here. They brought us news that about 200 were on the way here and they had nothing to eat, so we had to send them something. Some Indian Brothers came here from *Gnadenhütten* and we heard that things are very calm there and they had not seen any signs of warriors the entire time they were there.

THE 11TH AND 12TH   Our *Town* was full of warriors the entire day. Even though they were camping in *Goschachgünk*, they were still here most of the time. There were *Wyandot, Mingo,* and *Delaware,* but most were *Shawnee.* On the 13TH, however, they all came here to our place and set up their quarters, presumably because they did not get enough to eat in *Goschachgünk*. We spoke with the *Captains* and asked them to keep order among their people and to ensure that they did not dance or act wildly. They promised to do this and they kept their promise. A party came from the *Settlements* with a couple of children they had captured and 5 *Scalps*.[1400]

THE 14TH   A whole party of *Mingo* and *Shawnee* warriors attended the sermon. Oh, if only they had ears to hear! The *Captains* of the warriors told some of our Indian Brothers confidentially that the *Nations* are now quietly preparing to begin the war anew and when they are ready we would have the following sign that they had told us the truth: a party would come in advance. They would kill our cattle and take what they wanted. As soon as we saw that, we should believe that all the *Nations* were united and things would be very dangerous for us. Our Watchword said, For the oppression of the poor, for the sighing of the needy, now will I arise, saith the Lord.[1401] We sent letters to Bethlehem with *Samuel Moor,* who was going to *Pittsburgh* on business.[1402]

---

tion refers only to the remarks about the appointment of Gibson as agent of the Delaware and not to those stipulations that dealt with the military assistance the Delaware were to give. In the latter instance the critique concerned only an infringement of diplomatic forms: the tomahawk had not been handed over in such a way as to suggest the forging of a military alliance, according to the Delaware understanding. On 30 January Morgan answered: "I see by my absence some strange things have been spoken of last Summer & Fall; When we meet again we will set these matters right: I therefore desire that you may not be uneasy about what is past" (*FAO,* 215).

1400. Heckewelder explained on 12 March 1779: "They took 5 Children out of a house, somewhere about Redstone, then went to another house to murder, but their being some Men in the same, found it a difficult Matter, their Captn (Delaware Georges Uncle) being killed there and another one very much Stabbed, they however killed two men in that house." *FAO,* 244.

1401. Ps. 12:5, from the Collection of Watchwords for 1778. Zeisberger does not repeat the whole verse: "saith the Lord; I will set *him* in safety *from him,* that puffeth at him."

1402. Zeisberger to Matthäus Hehl, 13 March 1779, MAB, B 229, F 5, I 20. Moore also carried with him a letter from John Heckewelder to the commanding officer of Fort Pitt (*FAO,* 242–47). After a long, detailed, and very pessimistic analysis of the situation, Heckewelder counsels more energetic measures and suggests that preparations for the conquest of Fort Detroit be intensified.

THE 15TH   We learned several days ago that the *Shawnee* had something to tell us. This may actually have been the reason they camped with us, and now we learned that they had changed their way of thinking because they realized it was useless to propose anything to us alone. Therefore the *Captains* went to *Goschachgünk,* where our Indian Brothers were also called, gave a talk to the *Councel,* and demanded that the *Delaware* go to war. They also wanted to move the Indians and us to another place further west. However, the following day they received an answer that shamed and dejected them completely and they left the area quickly.[1403]

THE 16TH   The baby daughter of *Christian* and *Catharina,* who died yesterday at exactly 11 months old, was buried.

THE 19TH   The warriors had now moved on, so we thanked the Savior for bringing us peace again and hope that this will have been the worst problem for this year. They cost us a lot during these 8 days and more, however, because we had to keep them completely by ourselves, with no assistance from *Goschachgünk.* However, we were just happy they did not do us any other harm. On this occasion we witnessed what the *Shawnee* are like: the worst people of all the *Nations,* who are truly ruled by the power of darkness.[1404] They and the *Mingo* tried to persuade some of their friends who live with us to go with them, but they did not accomplish anything. They go around with an old story which they consider a secret, that the *Delaware* in *Goschachgünk* and we would be destroyed and annihilated by the *Nations* because we do not want to participate in the war. The 6 *Nations* supposedly decided this.[1405] There may be something to this, but it is the least of our worries.

THE 22ND   An *express* messenger from *Colonel Gibson* came here from *Fort Laurence.* He informed us in a letter that *General McIntosh* was on the way and was expected there tomorrow.[1406] He asked one of us to go there because

---

At the same time he names two sources from whom Zeisberger and he received information—a man from Virginia who had been a prisoner of the Shawnee since 1778 and who had participated in the siege of Fort Laurens, and the Indian trader Alexander McCormick, the most important source of information about the plans and behavior of the Wyandot in Sandusky and events beyond the lake. Parts of the information contained in Heckewelder's letter are repeated in Gelelemind's letter to General Lachlan McIntosh of the same day (*FAO,* 248–49).

1403. A different version of the negotiations is contained in Gelelemind's letter to General Lachlan McIntosh dated 15 March 1779, to which Gelelemind added the Shawnee's answer to the Delaware. *FAO,* 254–55.

1404. Zeisberger's formula means that among the Shawnee, native religious customs (usually called "nativistic") were of the greatest importance. See Dowd, *Spirited Resistance,* 42–49, who describes the Shawnee as one of the important forces in shaping a pan-Indian movement but ascribes to them nativistic motives only for the 1790s. See also Introduction, pp. 20, 37.

1405. For the last threat of this kind ascribed to the Six Indian Nations, see entry for 12 Oct. 1778.

1406. In his letter of 13 March 1779 to the president of the Continental Congress, Henry Laurens (after whom Fort Laurens was named), Lachlan McIntosh explained why he returned to Fort Laurens even though he had already been recalled: his only motive was to help the fort in a particularly precarious situation. *FAO,* 249–51.

he had been wanting to see and speak with one of us White Brothers since winter. Therefore on THE 24TH[1407] Brother *Heckewelder* left to go there in the company of some Indian Brothers. A party of *Wyandot* with 3 *Scalps* and a prisoner passed through here coming from the *Settlements*.

THE 25TH   We rejoiced in God our Savior and thanked Him for taking on our flesh and blood in the Virgin Mary, becoming a sacrifice for us, and redeeming us through this.[1408]

We received reliable news from *Sandusky* that a *Captain* with men and *Canons* had crossed the *Lake* to join the Indians in laying siege to *Fort Laurence*. We will just watch and see what comes of this and commend ourselves to the protection of the heavenly Father, because if this happens it almost cannot fail, or we will be harmed. His will be done!

THE 26TH   *Israel* went to *Pittsburgh* with the *Chiefs* who had been called to *Philadelphia*.[1409] It had not been his *Intention* to go on with them, as he ended up doing. It happened so quickly that we could hardly send along a letter to Bethlehem.[1410] A party of *Shawnee* came here with 3 prisoners, including an old man who was 80 years old. Our Brothers and Sisters took great pity on him because it was very difficult for him to leave with them. Therefore they collected about 14 Klafter of *Wampum* and other things to ransom him, in the hope that they might be glad to surrender him because he was so old and would just be trouble for them. However, the warriors would not give him up. Later the 2 young men who were prisoners with him were tortured and burned to death in the *Shawnee Towns* and he was supposed to meet the same fate. Therefore he fled and Brother *Isaac* found him in the bush not far from here, after he had lived on nothing but grass for 10 days. He brought him here while there was still a little life left in him. It is indescribable how very happy he was when he saw that he was in our *Town* again. Soon afterward he was taken to *Pittsburgh*.[1411]

THE 29TH   Brother *Heckewelder* returned from *Fort Laurence* but had not found *General McIntosh* there.[1412] On the return journey, he and the Indian Brothers who were with him looked at another site above the old *Town Gekelem-ukpechünk*, where we were planning to live if it was suitable and comfortable.

[April]

APRIL 1ST   During Holy Communion for Maundy Thursday, Sister *Hanna, Johannis's* wife, participated for the first time.

1407. In H3 written at first as "28," then corrected to "23."

1408. On 25 March the "incarnation of Christ" was commemorated.

1409. On George Morgan's invitation to Philadelphia, see note 1399 to entry for 7 March 1779. Because of the precarious situation of Fort Laurens, the departure had to be pushed back repeatedly.

1410. Zeisberger to Nathanael Seidel, 26 March 1779, MAB, B 229, F 5, I 21.

1411. Whole sentence later added.

1412. According to the report of the new commanding officers of Fort Laurens, Major Frederick Vernon, to Colonel Daniel Brodhead, dated 28 March 1779, Heckewelder had reported: "we may

THE 2ND   Our hearts were nourished by the passion of our God. During the reading of the story the blessed feeling stirred in us anew and the Savior granted us such an impression of this that eyes and hearts overflowed during the reflection on his sufferings for us.

THE 4TH   We prayed the Easter *Litany* on God's Acre and prayed for eternal fellowship with the 14 adult Brothers and Sisters and 5 children who have gone home this year. The sermon was about the Gospel lesson of the disciples at *Emmaus,* especially the words, Did not our heart burn within us, while he talked with us by the way etc.[1413] *Bartholomaus's* widow *Elisabeth* received permission to move to *Gnadenhütten* with the Brothers and Sisters again, after long, repeated requests, on a provisional basis. Her son, however, did not.

THE 5TH   We talked with the Helpers about both the Brothers and Sisters who are moving to *Gnadenhütten* and those who are moving to the new site, and we prepared for the journey. The residents of *Goschachgünk* were not really happy that we were moving away. However, we were not concerned about this.

ON THE 6TH   Brother *Edwards* then left for *Gnadenhütten* with about 20 families, and Brother *David* with about 20. Brother *Heckewelder* remained in *Lichtenau* with the rest. In the evening we came to *White Eyes Town* and on THE 7TH above the old *Town Gekelemukpechünk* to the site where we were planning to build. Then the *Canows* all arrived there on THE 8TH. The Brothers and Sisters from *Gnadenhütten* did not stay there long, but soon traveled on. We went together and looked over the area and the site, but we did not find it suitable and comfortable for various reasons. We had no choice now, so we quickly decided to move to *Schönbrunn* and traveled on further that same day. We passed *Gnadenhütten* on THE 9TH and the Brothers and Sisters there were very happy when they saw us and heard that we had decided to move to *Schönbrunn.* They had all arrived there yesterday and had already moved into their houses. We arrived there early on THE 10TH, and we saw the destruction but also remembered vividly how much blessing and goodness we had enjoyed there from our dear Lord. Just a few houses were still standing and the site was overgrown with grass, like a meadow. We camped on the bank of the *Muskingum* across from the *Town* to be newly settled, above it but within site of it. We were planning to camp there until we have planted and then we could think about building.[1414] Those who came by land and by water arrived here together this evening and brought some deer they had shot to the *Camp.*

THE 11TH   The sermon was preached under the open skies about the text, I am come to send fire on the earth etc.?[1415] We remembered the 5 adult

depend there will be a large party of Indians and some English, with several pieces of artillery, [who] will pay us a visit in a short time." *FAO,* 264–65. See entry for 25 March 1779.

1413. Luke 24:32.

1414. Zeisberger himself always called the settlement "Schönbrunn." Later the name "Neu Schönbrunn" was used. Although this entry makes it clear that the settlement was indeed built anew, we have followed Zeisberger's usage.

1415. Luke 12:49.

Brothers and Sisters who were baptized during this year, one of whom is already with the Savior, and we commended those who are still on their pilgrimage here below to His protection and to our dear Mother's care.

THE 12TH   After the early service about the Watchword, The consumption decreed shall overflow with righteousness,[1416] the Brothers and Sisters began building huts. Some Brothers traveled to *Lichtenau* to pick up a couple of families who had to stay behind because of a shortage of *Canows*.

THE 13TH   I wrote to *Commandant Vernon*[1417] in *Fort Laurence* and informed him of our arrival here in case any of his men should scout into this area. In a written reply, he expressed his satisfaction and pleasure that we are closer to them. *Tobias* passed through here going from *Lichtenau* to *Tuscarawi*. Through him Brother *Heckewelder* informed me in writing that the *Munsee* and *Mingo* were after the *Scalps* of the White Brothers because a certain sum of money has supposedly been set on each white *Scalp*.[1418]

THE 15TH   The Watchword, As one whom his mother comforteth, so will I comfort you[1419] was our blessed reflection. Indeed He does this richly, beyond all of our thoughts, requests, and understanding. Today we began dividing the fields. Many old trees have ruined them. Still, it is a great help for us that the fences are still pretty good and can be repaired with little effort.

Note. Because we had so many copies of the Watchwords and Daily Texts from 1775, we used these when we separated from each other in *Lichtenau* until we get the ones from this year.[1420]

THE 17TH   The 3 families who had stayed behind arrived here as well. It has been as warm as summer for a good while now and we have had the most beautiful weather, as if the Savior had provided us this especially for our move, and we accepted this with gratitude. Today and in the following days, however, it snowed and we were happy that we had a roof over our heads.

THE 28TH   Brother *Heckewelder* informed me once again from *Lichtenau* that someone was trying to kill me because I had forced our Indians to move here to *Schönbrunn*. Our Indian Brothers there thought we would have to return to *Lichtenau* because *Fort Laurence* would be occupied by the English any day.[1421] This is how we felt about this: it might be possible, but we were very calm and not worried and we believe the Savior will take care of us.

1416. Isa. 10:22. This Watchword is taken from the Collection of Watchwords for 1775. See entry for 15 Aug. 1779.

1417. Major Frederick Vernon (d. 1795 or 1796) did not follow the example of his father and brother, who joined the British side but enlisted in the Continental army. In September 1778 he participated with other officers in the negotiations with the Delaware. With Lachlan McIntosh he came to Fort Laurens, where he succeeded Colonel John Gibson, who had returned with McIntosh to Fort Pitt.

1418. Half a line crossed out and unreadable.

1419. Isa. 66:13.

1420. "Nota"—this paragraph in the original indented.

1421. See the report of Colonel Daniel Brodhead to George Washington about his talks with the Delaware delegation during their stay at Fort McIntosh on 3 April 1779. *FAO*, 272.

[May]

MAY 1ST   *Thomas* and *Samuel* went to *Fort Laurence* with a *Paquet* of letters that had come here from *Pittsburgh* via *Gnadenhütten.*

We finished making fences today. We have been busy with this for some days now. *Abel,* a single person who was sent away from the congregation about a year ago, returned and asked for reacceptance. He received this provisionally.

THE 3RD   The Brothers built a Meeting House, which they finished on THE 4TH.

THE 6TH   For the National Day of Prayer and Repentance,[1422] the sermon was about Isaiah 57: 15,16, For I will not contend for ever, neither will I be always wroth. We asked the Savior to have mercy on the country and to delight us with peace soon.

THE 9TH   The baby daughter born on the 4th of this month to *Zacharias* and *Anna Elisabeth* was baptized with the name *Marie.*

THE 13TH   We worshipped our dear Lord, who ascended to heaven for us, and asked that we might feel His precious presence, unseen though it is, every day and hour. In the sermon that followed, a child was baptized with the name *Elisabeth.* At the conclusion of this blessed day we strengthened ourselves on His Body and Blood in Holy Communion.

THE 15TH   The heavy rains in recent days caused the *Muskingum* to rise so that we were in danger of being flooded. We were already surrounded by water and if it had risen one more foot we would have had to leave. However, it cleared up and the water stopped rising. Therefore Brother *David* went to *Lichtenau* with some *Canows,* because there was no way to travel on land. He had Speakings with the Brothers and Sisters there and held Holy Communion for them, on the 21st had a Helpers' *Conference* and a Congregational Council in *Gnadenhütten,* and on the 22nd he returned to *Schönbrunn* where he found everyone well. The Brothers and Sisters had been very busy planting in the meantime.

THE 23RD   It was Pentecost and we asked our dear Mother to forgive all of our debts, commended ourselves anew to her care, prayed that she would clarify Jesus' wounds in our hearts every day and grant us more understanding and knowledge of the Gospel, and we promised her new faithfulness and obedience.

THE 24TH   The Brothers returned in 8 *Canows* loaded with Indian corn. The widow *Priscilla* also returned with them from her flight last winter and very humbly asked for reacceptance, which she was granted.[1423]

1422. See *By His Excellency the President and Council of the Commonwealth of Pennsylvania. A Proclamation* (Philadelphia: Hall & Sellers, 1779). In this proclamation the president and council of Pennsylvania declared the first Thursday in May a national day of prayer and repentance. The proclamation is dated 16 April 1779.

1423. See entry for 2 Nov. 1778.

THE 31ST   Brother *David* went to *Gnadenhütten*, where he married the single Brother *Abraham* and the single Sister *Anna Pauline* and he returned from there on JUNE 1ST. He had barely arrived when an Indian messenger from *Tuscarawi* passed through here with the news that the first warriors had arrived there. He had spoken with one who told him that the English were marching from *Detroit* to *Fort Laurence* with a large number of Indians and would be there in a few days to besiege it. We could not doubt the truth of the news because we had received reliable news about this a long time ago and our only hope was that the Savior would arrange things so that nothing came of it. Our hope was not disappointed, as we later saw.

[June]

THE 2ND   We received news that the White people had attacked the *Shawnee Towns* 4 days ago, and they had sent to the other *Nations* for help.[1424]

THE 6TH   Brother *Heckewelder* informed me in writing through a messenger that *Isaac* had returned from the *Wyandot Towns* yesterday.[1425] He had been sent to *Half King* with our concerns, and he had ordered him to hurry home and take good care of their teachers, the White Brothers, because he knew for sure now that people were trying to kill them and he no longer had any power to help us.[1426] We knew very well where this came from and what kind of danger it was. I could not be very worried or fearful, but commended us to the Savior. I wrote to Brothers *Edwards* and *Heckewelder*, and also sent word to the Indian Brothers in *Gnadenhütten* not to leave their *Town* empty until further notice. On THE 10TH we received news that the English, who were already on this side of the *Wyandot Towns* and marching to *Fort Laurence*, had turned back around.[1427] This led to the *American* attack on the *Shawnee Towns*, because all the Indians left there and hurried to the *Shawnee*.

1424. In the last days of May, about three hundred militia soldiers commanded by the county lieutenant colonel, John Bowman, attacked Chillicothe, one of the chief settlements of the Shawnee. Chief Blackfish died in the attack. The attackers got a rich booty, and indeed the prospect of booty had motivated soldiers to participate in the attack. When British troops commanded by Girty arrived, the American militia retreated. Talbert, "Kentucky Invades Ohio, 1779."

1425. On earlier attempts to establish direct contacts with Half King, chief of the Wyandot in Sandusky, see entries for 22 Feb. and 1 March 1779.

1426. The number of messages from Sandusky warning about imminent military actions against Fort Laurens and the Moravian settlements increased. At the same time, Colonel Daniel Brodhead, commanding officer of Fort Pitt, reported to George Washington the growing willingness of the Wyandot to distance themselves from the British and move closer to the American side. Brodhead probably based his assessment on Half King's friendly message to Goschachgünk, which arrived there on 4 May (*FAO*, 309–10), and on a further positive report dated 29 May (*FAO*, 347–48) on pro-American leanings among the Wyandot.

1427. On 13 June 1779 this news was sent from Goschachgünk to Colonel Daniel Brodhead. *FAO*, 361–62.

THE 11TH   *Jonas* and his mother *Beata*, who had fled from *Lichtenau* last winter,[1428] returned to our place. They were sick in body and soul and asked that we have mercy on them and take them in again. After talking with them we did so.

THE 13TH   Yesterday evening some *Munsee* warriors came here from *Fort Laurence,* where they had tried to catch a prisoner. They returned home this morning without accomplishing their task. The Brothers talked with them and admonished them to stop causing trouble, which they promised to do.

THE 16TH   An Indian messenger from *Pittsburgh* came here with a *Paquet* of letters for *Fort Laurence.* He knew there was something there for Brother *David,* so he asked Brother *David* to break it open. When Brother *David* refused, he wanted to do it himself. Brother *David* stopped him, however, and sent him on to *Fort Laurence.* He later received a letter from there from Mr. *Brainerd* of *Philadelphia,*[1429] with his best wishes for our *Mission,* about which he had heard many good things.

THE 23RD   In the evening 8 *Mingo* came here by way of *Tuscarawi* and spent the night. There was one White man with them. They said they were not planning to cause any harm, but just to see what things here looked like.

THE 24TH   The Brothers and Sisters in *Gnadenhütten* were expecting a large party of Indians, including a party of *Cherokees,* to march through on their way to *Pittsburgh.* Our Brothers and Sisters there are short of food supplies, so our Brothers and Sisters collected Indian corn for them and sent it there. We learned that the *Chiefs* had arrived in *Pittsburgh* from *Philadelphia.*[1430] We were happy to hear this, because we hoped to receive letters from the congregation.

1428. See entry for 2 Nov. 1778.

1429. The author was the missionary John Brainerd (1720–81), who in the 1750s had visited Bethlehem and read the reports of the missionaries Charles Beatty and Daniel McClure (see entries for 26 Sept. to 9 Oct. 1772), which had made him familiar with the Moravian missions in North America in general and the work of Zeisberger in particular. Brainerd, *Life of John Brainerd,* 197–98, 203–5, 364–69, 392–95. See entry for 25 Dec. 1772 and note 116.

1430. On the invitation of Colonel Morgan, see note 1399 to entry for 7 March 1779. On 31 May 1779 the chiefs had sent a petition to George Washington and the Continental Congress that summarized their services and their expectations (*FAO,* 317–21). Paragraph five mentioned that Moravian missionaries and their congregations lived among them, which had been helpful in maintaining "considerable order, Regularity and love of Peace" in their own settlements. Paragraph six was devoted to a complaint about how, in September 1778, the tomahawk had been handed to them; they added that they had "since return'd the said Tomahawk and Belt into the Hands of the Agent for the United States." In the seventh paragraph they requested the confirmation of a firm title to the land they lived on. George Washington's answer, dated 12 May 1779, did not go beyond pleasantries (*FAO,* 322–24); the Continental Congress's answer, dated 26 May 1779, blamed England for the difficulties the Delaware had experienced, promised help in promoting the Christianizing and civilizing efforts of David Zeisberger, who was expressly mentioned, denied the confirmation of a firm title to the land, and concluded with promises of better times (*FAO,* 340–42). Morgan, who had accompanied the chiefs to Philadelphia and had looked after them during their stay there, resigned his office as Indian agent of the Continental Congress on 28 May 1779 (*FAO,* 345). In these talks General Lachlan McIntosh accused Morgan of hampering military efforts; McIntosh saw Morgan as responsible for the Delaware's breaking the treaty of September 1778 and playing a key role in the siege of Fort Laurens (Savelle, *George Morgan,* 164–66). In resigning Morgan not only reacted to these essentially unprovable

The next day a letter from Brother *Mattheo* indeed arrived, and I learned from this that a *Paquet* for us was on the way. A *Munsee* Indian stranger came here and entered my hut with a spear in his hand. I was at home completely alone because the Brothers and Sisters were all working in the fields. I could not find out where he came from or what he wanted. He then went on and no one knew where.

THE 26TH   We had a blessed Holy Communion during which one Sister observed for the first time.

THE 30TH   Brother *David*, escorted by the Indian Brother *Michael*, went through *Gnadenhütten* and on to *Lichtenau* where he arrived the next day. On the way he met Mr. *McCormick*[1431] from *Sandusky*, the former husband of Sister *Martha*, who has gone home. He was very surprised that Brother *David* dared to go out so far with just one Indian and asked him not to do this unless he had 4 or 5 Indians with him. A certain White man[1432] had told him personally that he hoped to be fortunate enough yet to take one of us White Brothers or all of us to *Detroit*, and people expected him to return from the *Settlements* any day now with his *Companie*. In *Lichtenau* Brother *David* spoke with the Brothers and Sisters and held Holy Communion on the 3RD. On JULY 4TH he set out for *Gnadenhütten* again with the 2 Brothers *Michael* and *Isaac*. On the way, an Indian from *Goschachgünk* happened to join him, and before they got to *White Eyes Town* they met the above-mentioned *Simon Girtey*[1433] with 8 *Mingo*. They were coming from the *Settlements* and had a prisoner. We can only presume that something would have happened there if Brother *David* had been alone with *Michael* and *Isaac*. Everything had been very carefully planned in advance, because as the *Compagnie* of *Mingo* was meeting us, a party of *Delaware* came up behind them. They were just coming from *Pittsburgh* and watched until one of them tried to attack Brother *David*. When *Simon* saw him, he called to his *Compagnie*, Look, the person we have wanted to see for a long time is coming toward us there. Now do what you think you should! However, the *Mingo Captain* remained silent and shook his head. They asked some questions, which Brother *David* answered for them. Then they moved on and gave a *War Whoop*.

There is no doubt that the *Mingo* would try to do something if they had a good opportunity, especially since they are now encouraged to do so. *Captain Bird*[1434] from *Detroit*, who was marching to *Fort Laurence*, told the above-men-

---

and untenable attacks but also to the meaningless reactions of Washington and the Continental Congress to the petition of the Delaware chiefs. The chiefs returned empty-handed.

1431. See note 840 to entry for 25 Sept. 1776.

1432. Alexander McCormick probably had in mind Simon Girty, who played a leading role in imprisoning Zeisberger and orchestrating the evacuation of the mission congregations in 1781.

1433. H3: "Gisley."

1434. Since the Seven Years' War Captain Henry Bird (d. 1800) belonged to the British army; he was stationed at Fort Detroit from 1778. In the next years he played a leading role in military activities originating from Fort Detroit. *FAO*, 252n2.

tioned *McCormick* that one of the main reasons he wanted to go there was to get the *Ministers,* and he specifically named Brother *David,* whom he was determined to get. The latter said he could assure him the *Ministers* were not doing them any harm and were not getting involved in any war, but were doing much good among the Indians. He replied, I am well aware they are not concerned about the war. However, if we just got the *Ministers* out of the way, then we would get not only the *Delaware* to join with us in the war, but also all the *Nations.* It was not his intention to harm Brother *David;* he wanted to take him to *Detroit.* They needed *Ministers* there more than the *Savages* did. (He is well informed and has good intentions.)

[July]

THE 5TH   Brother *David* returned to *Schönbrunn* via *Gnadenhütten,* where he had held a *Conference* with the Helpers. We learned that a party of *Mingo* had left here this morning to go to *Gnadenhütten,* but we had not met them.

THE 12TH   Brother *Schebosch* came here for a visit and helped us lay out our new *Town.* The Interim Chief[1435] in the absence of those who have gone to *Philadelphia* came here from *Goschachgünk.* Warriors were seen around here again and we saw one in the *Town* during the night when there was thunder and lightning. He was out recruiting, but did not do well.[1436]

THE 14TH   Brother *David* wrote to *Commandant Colonel Campbell*[1437] in *Fort Laurence.* He had asked to see our sites here and in *Gnadenhütten* and he advised him to wait a little longer to do this, because things were very unsafe now due to the warriors. A couple of days later we heard that 2 of his people had been killed.

THE 18TH   The baby girl born to *Samuel* and *Sara Nantikok* yesterday was baptized into Jesus' death with the name *Augustina.*

THE 21ST   *Isaac* came here from *Lichtenau* to speak with Brother *David* personally about the Brothers and Sisters in *Lichtenau.* He also brought along a letter about this from Brother *Heckewelder.* This evening I was overjoyed to receive long expected letters, Bethlehem news reports, and weekly reports of the *Unity* Elders' *Conference,* as well as Watchwords and texts for this year via

1435. The interim chief was Big Cat, who in the absence of Gelelemind and leading counselors signed the letters to the commanding officer of Fort Pitt. His Indian name was Maghingua Keeshoch; see White, *Middle Ground,* 455–60.

1436. Annotation at the margin.

1437. On 14 June 1779 Colonel Richard Campbell of Frederick County, Virginia, since 1776 a member of the Continental army, had been ordered with a convoy and provisions to Fort Laurens, where he was to succeed Major Vernon as commanding officer of the Fort. *FAO,* 59n2, 364.

Gnadenhütten.[1438] We were most especially interested in and delighted by the arrival of dear Brother and Sister *Reichel* with their party from *Europe,*[1439] and the next day we extended greetings to the Brothers and Sisters from our congregations both here and in *Europe* and assured them of their remembrance and prayers before the Savior on our behalf.

THE 22ND   Brother *David* went to *Gnadenhütten.* He returned from there on THE 23RD.

THE 25TH   The Indian Brother *Thomas* brought letters and some things that had been sent here from *Pittsburgh.* Through him, the *Commandant* sent our Brothers and Sisters a barrel of salt as a *Present,* as he had sent them a quantity of flour when they were planting some time ago.

THE 31ST   *Tobias* came here from *Lichtenau* as a messenger. Brother *Heckewelder* informed us in a letter that the Indians in *Goschachgünk* have been called to *Pittsburgh* and asked to join the army against the *Mingo Towns* as soon as possible, along with other news.[1440] Once again we paid no attention to this,

---

1438. *Die täglichen Loosungen und Lehrtexte der Brüdergemeine für das Jahr* 1779. On the "Wöchentlichen Nachrichten" ("Weekly News") of the Bethlehem congregation and the "Wöchentlichen Nachrichten der Unitäts Aeltesten Conferenz" ("Weekly News of the Unity's Elders' Conference"), see note 313 to entry for 17 Nov. 1773. It is likely that this package also contained John Ettwein's letter to the missionaries, which Ettwein must have composed some time in the spring of 1779 (MAB, E.P., B 965, F 42, no. 1047). In this letter Ettwein criticized sharply the missionaries' attitudes: "we cannot but share with you our concerns that the news received from you have caused us. You seem to us to get too deeply involved with worldly affairs and thus lose the character as a friend to all mankind. You seem to trust too much in the favour and power of one party and this has destroyed your balance and led you into troubled territory. Above all our trust should rest in Him, our Lord and God. Doing all that you can to guard the peace and quietness of the congregations in your trust as children of peace is your duty and obligation; but we are not concerned with things outside. The best we can do is to ignore their doings and take no notice of them."

1439. Bishop Johann Friedrich Reichel had been charged by the Unity's Elders' Conference with the visitation of the congregations in Pennsylvania, New Jersey, and New York. Together with a sizeable group he arrived at Bethlehem on 17 April 1779; his visitation lasted until 1781. Hegner, *Fortsetzung,* 239–45.

1440. On 23 June 1779 George Washington had signed orders for an expedition against the Seneca in the region of the Allegheny River (*FAO,* 371–72). These orders prompted Colonel Daniel Brodhead's efforts to initiate new negotiations with the Wyandot as the most important tribe in the Great Lakes region and with the Cherokee as the largest tribe in the southern region. The success of these negotiations would have isolated the Seneca in the Ohio region, who contemporaries usually called Mingo, as well as the Shawnee and the British in Detroit, but would have strengthened the position of the Delaware in the region. Negotiations with the Cherokee took place in the second half of July and were concluded with the signing of a treaty of peace and amity on 22 July 1779 (*FAO,* 392–400, treaty at 397–400). This treaty continued and extended the concept of confederation first formulated in the treaty of amity concluded with the Delaware in September 1778. Similar efforts failed with the Wyandot; despite pointed warnings, Alexander McCormick and John Heckewelder sent messages from Goschachgünk to Fort Pitt on 29 and 30 June 1779 (*FAO,* 382–83, 385–86) that the Wyandot were insincere and treacherous. Colonel Daniel Brodhead began negotiations with Chiefs Bawbee and Half King, but these were soon terminated without tangible results (*FRO,* 46–47, 66–72). Simultaneously, on 12 July 1779, Gelelemind officially notified the commanding officer of Fort Pitt that the Council of the Delaware had resolved "[that] we have unanimously agreed that when any of your Young Men go to War, our Young Men shall accompany them, this is the agreement & consent of all the Chiefs of the Delaware Nation" (*FAO,* 387–88). Brodhead, on the other

and we will be happy and thank the Savior if we manage in this way. Otherwise we will take things as they come.

[August]

AUGUST 3RD   The Brothers began cutting down wood at the building site. I received a letter from the *Commandant* in *Fort Laurence* in which he informed me that the *Fort* had been evacuated and he had retreated with his men today.[1441]

THE 5TH   Brothers *Marcus* and *Johann Martin* came here from *Gnadenhütten* with a letter from Brother *Heckewelder*. In this he reported that a message had arrived from *Gelelemind* in *Pittsburgh* explicitly requesting that our Indians come there and go with the army.[1442] The *Counsellors* in *Goschachgünk* reported this to our Indian Brothers in *Lichtenau,* who gave them the appropriate answer. Brother *David* wrote to *Colonel Brodhead* in *Pittsburgh* about this and he especially urged the Brothers in *Gnadenhütten* to keep watch over our young people.

THE 7TH   During Holy Communion one Sister watched for the 2nd time.

THE 8TH   In the morning was the *Liturgy* in Preparation for Holy Communion and then the sermon. Then the children listened to a serious admonition that had a good *Effect.* The communicant Brothers all listened to *Zacharias,* a married man who had to be told to leave here some weeks ago; he had returned and publicly recounted his sins against the congregation. Then the Helpers *Conference* readmitted him the next day.

THE 10TH   The Brothers had cut down all the trees on the building site, which was extremely dense. Then yesterday and today they felled more than 600 additional trees for timber, not including what the Sisters had felled.

---

hand, informed the commanding officer of Fort Laurens that Washington had decided to evacuate Fort Laurens as soon as possible (389). As with Bowman's expedition (see entry for 2 June 1779 and note 1424, remuneration of the participating militia men depended on whatever could be plundered, as there were no official funds for the expedition (390).

1441. See preceding note.

1442. See note 1440 to entry for 31 July 1779, citing the resolve of the Council of the Delaware. This resolve was not based on a full meeting of the Council, as Gelelemind had maintained in his letter. Neither the chiefs who had remained in Goschachgünk nor Captains Pipe and Winginund had participated in the Council's meeting at Fort Pitt. Pipe and Winginund arrived with the Wyandot chief Bawbee in Goschachgünk in early August (FRO, 46–47). It is likely, however, that Israel (Welapachtschiechen, who as "Weylapachecon call'd Israel or Capt Johnny—2ᵈ Chief" had signed the petition to the Continental Congress dated 10 May 1779; FAO, 321) had participated in the Council meeting that passed the resolve. After the delegation returned from Philadelphia Israel did not return to the mission congregation. Because Gelelemind remained at Fort Pitt, Israel (under his original Delaware name) resumed his functions as a chief in Goschachgünk. Messages to Daniel Brodhead at this time and in the next years are usually signed by him; see for example the message dated 30 March, which informed Brodhead that "a few Men" were prepared to accompany Brodhead in his expedition against the enemy (FRO, 158). This development also meant that the split Zeisberger had feared between Christian Indians and unconverted Delaware had become a reality; see entry for 20 Aug. 1779.

AUGUST 11TH   Brother *David* went to *Gnadenhütten* and from there on to *Lichtenau* on the 12TH. He returned there on THE 17TH. In the meantime the Helper *Samuel Nantikok* held the services, which were a blessing for the Brothers and Sisters.[1443]

THE 20TH   A messenger came in great haste from *Gnadenhütten* with a sealed letter to the *Council* in *Goschachgünk* from *Colonel Brodhead*. Most of them were in *Gnadenhütten* on their way to *Pittsburgh* and they asked Brother *David* to go there. Because it also concerned our 3 *Towns*, he went there and read them the *Speeches*, which in brief said that the *Delaware* warriors should come to the army quickly. In his *Speech*, *Gelelemind* once again explicitly demanded that our Indians arise immediately and go with him; if they refused they would suffer the consequences with the rest of the *Nations*. However, *Brodhead's Speech* did not specifically name the Indian Brothers, but just the *Delaware* in general. We told the *Counsellors* we had already shared our thoughts about this with them once very clearly and we would stick to this; there was nothing to negotiate. The *Chiefs* were very angry at this because they saw that they could not get anywhere with us like this. However, nothing like this has ever been expected of us again since then.

THE 31ST   The widowers and widows celebrated their choir festival in grace. The Savior graciously revealed himself to them and blessed them with his precious presence.

[September]

SEPTEMBER 3RD   Some Brothers and Sisters from *Gnadenhütten* who had enjoyed a happy visit here returned home. This evening the Brothers and Sisters held Singing Services in almost all of the huts. Because the huts are so close together in a small area, it sounded as if they were together in the congregational Meeting Hall. It was sweet to hear.

THE 4TH   The Brothers cleared the road on the building site because there were layers of trees lying all over each other in every direction. Next winter the Brothers and Sisters will work themselves out of the wood a little.

THE 7TH   The married Brothers and Sisters had a blessed choir festival. All the services were accompanied by the Savior's presence. The reading of their text on this occasion had a very blessed effect on them, so that we were able to praise and worship Him for this with contrite, happy hearts.

THE 9TH   Brother *Heckewelder* came here from *Lichtenau* for a visit and Brother *Edwards* came along with him from *Gnadenhütten*. We discussed various matters together and they returned the next day.[1444]

1443. This is the first mention in the diary that an Indian Helper, rather than a missionary, officiated at a religious service.

1444. See the following note.

THE 13TH   *Johann Martin* came with some Brothers from *Gnadenhütten* to help our Brothers at the building site and we framed in some houses this week.

THE 17TH   Brother *David* went to *Gnadenhütten* and he returned there on THE 18TH.

THE 22ND   For a number of reasons, Brother *David* decided to travel to *Pittsburgh* and he began his trip today, accompanied by some Indian Brothers. He returned from there *October* 3rd after he had taken care of the necessary business.[1445] In the meantime, the Helper *Abraham* held the daily services and took care of other matters. Some Indians who came from the *Fort* offered the Brothers and Sisters cold comfort, when they brought news that the Indian Brothers would not return for a long time and Brother *David* not at all, because we would all be arrested together. While he was gone the widower *Jonas* went home and his earthly dwelling was buried here on the old God's Acre. He was from the *Munsee Nation* and among the first in *Goschgosching* who came to the Brothers in 1768. He moved with the Brothers to *Lawunakhanek, Langundoutenünk,* and *Schönbrunn,* where he was baptized on *January* 1, 1774. He was a poor, weak character and was easily confused and led astray by the lies of the savage Indians. Indeed the reason he fled from *Lichtenau* last winter was because he believed we would all be destroyed either by the *Nations* or by the White people. If one side did not do it, the other side surely would; at that time this was what the Indians generally said. After spending the winter in the bush, he saw that the congregation remained unharmed and everything had not turned out as had been prophesied. Last spring he returned to *Lichtenau* and then here, and he was reaccepted at his request.[1446] However, he was always somewhat shy and no longer as obliging toward the Brothers as previously. During his illness the Brothers visited him regularly and in all of his misery directed him to the Savior. He remained coherent until his end, and he called out, Dear Savior, have mercy on me and be gracious to me, a sinner.

[October]

THE 4TH   We had a Helpers *Conference.* Brother *David* reported what he had seen during his trip to the *Fort* and what needed to be noted.[1447] He

---

1445. The reasons for this trip were, first, that the security for the transport of these letters from Schönbrunn to Fort Pitt was not guaranteed; second, the purchase of wine for Holy Communion; third, talks with the commanding officer, Daniel Brodhead (see Zeisberger to the Brothers in Bethlehem, Pittsburgh, 28 Sept. 1779, MAB, B 229, F 5, I 22). Zeisberger reported the resolution to disband the settlement at Lichtenau and transfer its inhabitants to Schönbrunn and Gnadenhütten or alternatively to found a new settlement for them.

1446. See entries for 2 Nov. 1778 and 11 June 1779.

1447. After the essentially successful expeditions between 11 August and 14 September 1779 against the Seneca and Munsee, whose most important settlements in the Allegheny River region were

particularly informed them of the danger which is hovering over our people and young people. Many efforts are being made to seduce them. The Helpers then gathered our people and they decided among themselves that no one would allow himself to be persuaded through threats or compliments to join in the war. May the Savior, who earned and purchased his Indian congregation with his own precious blood, protect them and enclose them in his vest of wounds, so that none of them are stolen.

THE 6TH   Brother *David* went to *Gnadenhütten,* held a *Conference* there with the *National* Helpers and returned home on THE 7TH.

THE 9TH   One Sister joined the congregation in partaking of the Body and Blood of our Lord in the holy *Sacrament* for the first time.

THE 10TH   The Indian *Zacharias* was *absolved* on his sick bed.[1448] A party of *Wyandot* Indians came here, bought some supplies, and quickly continued on.

THE 16TH   I received a letter from Brother *Heckewelder* in *Lichtenau,* in which he reported that the Brothers and Sisters there are all healthy and well, but that there is much confusion among people in *Goschachgünk.*

THE 19TH   The Brothers were busy building and the Sisters busy in the fields harvesting. Praise be to God, we have a plentiful and blessed harvest. Everything produced well, beyond our expectations. It is common here for illnesses to rage in the fall, and we have not been completely free of them now. Still, there has not been a period of fever as there used to be here, although we are on the bank of the *Muskingum* and are waiting to move into our new town, which we always have before our eyes.

THE 24TH   The sermon was about the text, Be strong in the Lord, and in the power of his might.[1449] Then the Sisters had a service. A talk of admonition was held for them about various matters, which had a healing *Effect.* The Congregational Service was about the remarkable Watchword for today, And when ye shall hear of wars and rumours of wars, be ye not troubled.[1450] We

---

destroyed and plundered (*FRO,* 55–66), Brodhead began to intensify his efforts to reestablish diplomatic relations with the other Indian tribes of the region. After negotiations with those Shawnee who had joined the Delaware in Goschachgünk (*FRO,* 73–75), further negotiations with the Delaware took place at least on 24 September (75–76). Remarks by Zeisberger, who at this time stayed at Fort Pitt, indicate that these talks led to a confirmation of the treaty of amity of September 1778, including the paragraph that obliged the Delaware to participate actively on the American side in the war. Brodhead acquiesced in the Delaware's demand for a place on the Beaver River for a new "Council Fire"; his decision was motivated by the desire to move the Delaware settlements from the Muskingum Valley closer to Fort Pitt, where they could better be protected by the American army. In order to maintain the advantages that accrued from the closeness of Goschachgünk to the mission settlements, Gelelemind and the Council of the Delaware secured Brodhead's support in their endeavor to induce the mission congregations to move with them to the Beaver Creek. See entry for 12 March 1780 and note 1469.

1448. See entry for 8 Aug. 1779.
1449. Eph. 6:10.
1450. Mark 13:7.

have indeed heard enough about this in past years, and therefore we found all the more reason to thank the Savior who has so mercifully protected and assisted us until now, and also for the peace we are now enjoying.

THE 26TH   *Tobias* came here from *Lichtenau* and on THE 27TH Brother *Edwards* visited me. He soon returned home as well. The Brothers had noticed that the bears were getting into the chestnuts frequently, so most of them stopped building and went to look for them, and in recent days they shot over 20.

THE 31ST   Some Indians came here from the *Walhanding*. Visits by Indian strangers are currently something unusual at our place, and we have no objections to this. They have no ears to hear the Gospel now, because their minds are preoccupied with other things, so that they have no time.[1451]

[November]

NOVEMBER IST   We remembered our fellowship with the congregation on high in the blessed hope of also being perfected one day and becoming one with them.

THE 3RD   2 widows, *Eva* and her daughter *Anna Margretha,* came here from *Lichtenau* to stay. The former is *Israel's* natural sister.

THE 7TH   The widower *Lucas* was bound to the widow *Anna* Caritas in holy matrimony. *David* arrived here from *Gnadenhütten* with his wife *Salome* to stay.

NOVEMBER 13TH   This was a day of special blessing for us. The Savior revealed himself to us as our Chief Elder. We allowed ourselves to be absolved by him and promised Him faithfulness and obedience anew.[1452] Two Sisters were absolved and added anew to the congregation. In conclusion the communicant congregation enjoyed His Body and Blood in the Holy *Sacrament,* during which one Brother and one Sister were readmitted. On THE 14TH the baby boy born to *Nathanael* and *Martha Elisabeth* on the 11th of this month was baptized with the name *Johann Gottlieb.* We join the Indian congregation on the *Muskingum* in greeting all the congregations, and we commend ourselves to their continued remembrance and prayer.

1451. Another important reason for the decline of visitors to Schönbrunn was that the distance from Schönbrunn to the next non-Christian settlement was much greater than that from Lichtenau. The removal from Lichtenau also meant that Zeisberger escaped further entanglements in the diplomatic and political activities of Goschachgünk. John Heckewelder, who was responsible for the congregation at Lichtenau, also began to distance himself from the discourse between the Council at Goschachtünk and Fort Pitt after he was reproached for describing the situation in the Ohio region in too negative terms. *FRO,* 45–46.

1452. On the meaning of commemorating Christ's acceptance of the office of the Elder on 13 November 1741, see Introduction, pp. 62–63.

Diary of Schönbrunn *and* Gnadenhütten *on the* Muskingum *from* November *1779 until* August *1780.*[1453]

NOVEMBER 18TH   There was the burial of Brother *Jacob,* who went home in blessing the day before yesterday. He was baptized in *Friedenshütten* [*sic*] on *May* 19th, 1771, by Brother *Gregor,*[1454] then came to *Langundouteniünk* on the *Ohio* in the fall, where he was joined in holy matrimony on *June* 14th, 1772, to the single Sister *Johannette,* now a widow, and attained the enjoyment of Holy Communion on *March* 9th, 1776. His father who died blessedly in *Fridenshütten* was from the *Catawba Nation*[1455] and his mother died in *Schoenbrunn* in 1773. He had many trials and tests to endure through his friends, the nonbelievers, who really tried to take him away from the congregation, especially when external conditions were difficult. However, the faithful friend of souls did not take his hand away from him, and always brought him back to the right path quickly. Right in the beginning of his illness he said he would go to the Savior this time and did not want to become healthy again. In his last hours he testified that he believed in the one he was going to see.

THE 19TH   I sent letters and our diary to Bethlehem via *Pittsburgh.*[1456]

THE 21ST   The usual Sunday services were accompanied by our dear Savior's presence.

THE 26TH   2 Brothers had accidents during the construction of our houses, which the Brothers were very busy throughout this week trying to finish quickly. One split his foot and the other had a fall, and both had to be carried home.

THE 28TH   We had blessed *Advent* services. The Savior renewed the feeling in the hearts of the Brothers and Sisters that He had clothed himself in our poor flesh and blood, and we thanked Him with melted hearts for his holy incarnation. The children also celebrated this during their service with sweet singing.

THE 30TH   There was a Helpers *Conference.* They had Speakings with some Brothers and Sisters, as instructed. The female Helpers were especially encouraged to care for the Sisters faithfully and diligently.

1453. MAB, B 141, F 10, fol. 540.

1454. On 16 November 1770, members of the Unity's Elders' Conference Christian Gregor and Johannes Loretz, along with Hans Christian Alexander von Schweinitz, arrived at Bethlehem as visitors from the Unity. After their visits to congregations in different colonies, Loretz and Gregor, along with Bishop Nathanael Seidel, visited Friedenshütten, arriving there on 15 May 1771. On Whitsunday, 19 May, they jointly baptized five Indians. MAB, Diarium Friedenshütten, B 131, F 8, entries for 15 to 19 May 1771.

1455. I.e., Catawba; see note 425 to entry for 23 June 1774.

1456. Zeisberger to Nathanael Seidel, 17 Nov. 1779, MAB, B 229, F 5, I 24. In this letter Zeisberger defended himself against the rebuke for too much involvement in political affairs and political partiality (see note 1438 to entry for 31 Oct. 1779). Diary and letter were taken to Fort Pitt by a delegation of the Council of Goschachgünk; the delegation arrived at Fort Pitt on 22 Nov. 1779. FRO, 115–16.

[December]

DECEMBER 6TH   We moved together from our *Camp* into our recently constructed *Town* on the west side of the *Muskingum,* where the houses were now all ready to occupy.

THE 7TH   Brother *Heckewelder* came here from *Lichtenau* via *Gnadenhütten* and returned on THE 8TH.

THE 11TH   About half of our Brothers went out to hunt for a while. This year they have really been kept from doing this by all the work.

THE 17TH   The Savior took a child who was born on the 11th of last month, *Nathanael* and *Martha Elisabeth's* baby boy *Johann Gottlieb,* home to himself quickly. His earthly dwelling was buried on THE 19TH and thus our God's Acre on the West side of the *Muskingum* was dedicated.

THE 20TH   Brother *David* went to *Gnadenhütten,* where we were overjoyed to receive letters from Brothers *Matthao* and *Grube,* as well as reports from Bethlehem from the months *March, April, May,* and *June,* and weekly news reports of the *Unity* Elders' *Conference.*[1457] On THE 21ST the single Brother *Joseph Schebosch* was married to the single Sister *Helena in Gnadenhütten.* In the meantime the Brothers in *Schoenbrunn* finished building an *Interim* Meeting House, where we had the first service on THE 22ND. At the same time Brother *David* greeted the Brothers and Sisters and assured them of the congregation's remembrance and prayer before the Savior on our behalf. He hears these so graciously and until now has protected us so obviously.

THE 24TH   Christmas Eve began with a Lovefeast. We rejoiced over the birth of our Savior and knelt and thanked Him for becoming incarnate out of love for us poor and wretched people.

In the diary from *Gnadenhütten*[1458] it also says, We had a happy and blessed Christmas Eve Watch Service. During the Lovefeast and adoration we could sense the Savior's nearness and he granted us his peace.

THE 25TH   In the morning was a sermon and in the afternoon a Children's Service. In a song they worshipped baby Jesus in the manger sweetly and emotionally and brought him their childlike *Gratias.* During the Congregational Service a single man was baptized into Jesus' death with the name *Andreas,* during which a blessed feeling of his presence prevailed. This was the first baptism for a year.

THE 26TH   During the devotional service in preparation for Holy Communion the Brothers and Sisters were admonished to bury everything inconsistent with Jesus' intention at the Savior's feet and not to carry anything with them into the New Year.

1457. For the other news, see note 313 to entry for 17 Nov. 1773.

1458. As the title makes clear, Zeisberger reported events at Gnadenhütten in this section of the diary.

THE 31ST   Throughout this week the blessed work of the dear Mother[1459] could be felt among the Brothers and Sisters. They cleared things up among themselves in cases where one of them had something against someone else that had disturbed the love, and where something was hidden, the Savior revealed this. Thus through His grace we made a contrite, blessed conclusion to the year, thanked Him with shame and humility for all the grace, goodness, and faithfulness shown to us, for all his forgiveness and his acknowledgment of us poor ones, for the protection of our dear heavenly Father and the dear Mother's care, and we entered into the New Year with comforted hearts.

When we moved here in *April,* we could not expect that we would remain so peaceful and undisturbed the way things looked elsewhere. However, the Savior protected us and covered us with his wings so that no misfortune came close to us. And when we White Brothers were in more danger than ever before last summer, and did not see any way we could escape this, we looked to our dear Lord who never lacks good counsel, surrendered it up to Him and just watched to see how He would arrange things so wonderfully. Before we expected it, the evil attacks against us were destroyed and the danger which threatened us was turned away, because we heard that an attack on the *Shawnee Towns* had taken place. This is what led to our release.

We camped on the east side of the *Muskingum* until the beginning of *December* and took care of the planting. The Savior blessed us so that we not only did not lack anything, but we even had extra and could share with others who were in need during the great famine caused among the Indians by the war.

The Savior graciously revealed himself in our daily services. The Watchwords and texts are the daily food for the Brothers and Sisters. They serve to instruct and admonish them, to comfort them and enable them to flourish in the grace, knowledge and love of Jesus Christ, and we are happy to see that the Brothers and Sisters have ears to hear.

No one joined the congregation this year. Visits by strangers were also very rare.

The choir festival days which are always very great and important to the Brothers and Sisters were blessed and marked by the presence of the Savior, which could be felt. Above everything, however, is the inexpressible enjoyment of Holy Communion, which we had 7 times this year. One Sister joined us in this for the first time. Since spring one adult and 4 children have been baptized here. Two adults and one child went home.

At the conclusion of the year, the little gathering consists of 17 married couples, 1 widower, 9 widows, 9 single Brothers and older boys, 7 older girls, 15 little boys, and 25 little girls. Altogether 100 people.[1460]

1459. "Mother" underlined; the words "Holy Ghost" added above the word in similar hand.
1460. Added in another hand: "Among the Brothers and sisters some 40 participants at the Holy Communion (see date 9 July)."

The diary from *Gnadenhütten* notes on this day: At night we gathered and remembered all the grace, mercy, and good deeds the Lord has shown us this year. We also confessed to Him our poverty and shortcomings and prayed to Him for *Absolution* for all our mistakes, shortcomings, and misdeeds, and that He will reveal himself to us further as He has until now and will bless us with His comforting presence. At the beginning of this year we were in *Lichtenau*. On *April* 8th we returned here. At first we had much work to do on our houses and fields, repairing them, and the dear Savior blessed the work of our hands so that we have had a plentiful harvest and now he is letting us enjoy it in peace. He revealed himself graciously to us in our daily services and turned our hearts blissfully to His merits and sufferings. Since we have been back here we have had Holy Communion 5 times. 2 children have been born and baptized. 3 couples were married and 2 children went home. The little congregation in *Gnadenhütten* consists of 86 baptized adults and children, among whom 34 are communicants, 13 are not baptized, altogether 99 souls.

January 1780

THE 1ST   In the morning was a sermon about Galatians 3:22, For ye are all the children of God by faith in Christ Jesus.[1461] In the service for those who have been baptized, two young people were *absolved* and many tears were shed. They confessed the sins to which they had succumbed during times of temptation. We knelt and prayed, commending ourselves and especially these two to the Savior for protection, and we prayed for his sweet presence throughout this year. At the conclusion of this day, the communicant congregation enjoyed His Body and Blood in the Holy *Sacrament,* as a seal on all the kindness He has bestowed upon us in recent days. One Sister watched as a *Candidate* for the first time.

3 Brothers and 2 Sisters were readmitted during Holy Communion in *Gnadenhütten*. We have not yet received any Watchwords, so we used those from the beginning of last year.

THE 2ND   In the morning was the *Liturgy* for Holy Communion and a sermon and in the evening Congregational Service. Today and last night it snowed so much that the snow was generally 2 feet deep, which is something unusual here. Our Brothers and Sisters are in good shape because they have an overabundance of wood lying before their doors.

THE 6TH   We had a blessed choir festival with our little Brown gathering, accompanied by his sweet presence.[1462] During the morning devotion we

1461. Zeisberger's references are to Galatians 3:26. Evidently he cites from memory. The text reads: "For ye are all the children of God by faith in Jesus Christ."
1462. On the importance of 6 January, see Introduction, pp. 62–63.

commended ourselves and our congregations in *Gnadenhütten* and *Lichtenau* to the Savior for grace and prayed to Him to grant us the blessing of his blood today and thanked Him for choosing us through grace to be His own people. One person was *absolved* during the service for those who are baptized, and in the Congregational Service one person was buried into Jesus' death through baptism with the name *Jonathan.* He revealed Himself to us and let us feel his peace during all the services as well as during the Lovefeast and Service of Adoration.

The Brothers and Sisters in *Gnadenhütten* also celebrated a blessed choir festival through the Savior's grace. He let them feel his comforting presence during all their services. Two of the Sisters were *absolved.*

THE 9TH   During the Children's Service we commended our youth, and especially the older boys, to the Savior's grace. We knelt and prayed that he would let them prosper completely for Him and would grow up in His knowledge and love.

THE 10TH   Despite the deep snow, the 2 Brothers *Samuel Nantikok* and *Stephanus* set out on the road through *Gnadenhütten* to *Lichtenau*, whence we have not heard anything for a long time now.

THE 11TH   Brother *Edwards* came from *Gnadenhütten* and also returned there that same day.

THE 16TH   The usual Sunday services were held in blessing. During the Congregational Service a single man was baptized into Jesus' death with the name *Paulus.* Brothers *Samuel* and *Stephanus* returned from *Lichtenau* after all the services in the evening and delighted us with letters from Brother *Heckewelder.* We learned from these that our Brothers and Sisters there are doing well and how the Savior has revealed himself to them.

THE 17TH   The Watchword was, Then had the churches rest and were edified,[1463] and the Lord indeed fulfilled this in us at all 3 sites and we thanked Him with childlike hearts for the peace He has allowed us to enjoy internally and externally and for the comfort He has poured out on us through his Holy Spirit.

THE 20TH   A couple of Sisters came here from *Gnadenhütten* for a visit. They returned there the next day. The Brothers and Sisters encouraged and uplifted each other and told each other what the Savior and the dear Mother[1464] are doing in their hearts. Every evening they hold their own Singing Service in their houses, and instead of hearing nothing except for noise and heathen entertainment as in the savages' *Towns,* here you hear the Lord being praised and the crucified Savior being preached. An Indian stranger came here a number of days ago and we proclaimed the Savior to him. He said, I have attended

1463. Acts 9:31. The text reads: "Then had the churches rest throughout all Judaea and Galilee and Samaria, and were edified; and walking in the fear of the Lord, and in the comfort of the Holy Ghost, were multiplied."

1464. The words "the dear Mother" crossed out and "his Ghost" written above in another hand.

the services in *Lichtenau* a number of times, but I heard nothing. Now for the first time I have heard something.

THE 22ND   *Augustus* and his wife *Lydia* arrived in *Gnadenhütten* from *Lichtenau* to stay there.

THE 24TH   Some Brothers went to *Lichtenau* and on THE 27TH Brothers *Schebosch* and *Johann Martin* came here from *Gnadenhütten* for a visit.

THE 30TH   The sermon about today's Gospel, about the sower,[1465] and the rest of the services were held as usual. There was much talk among the Brothers and Sisters about what they had heard in the sermon and they examined themselves about which group they could count themselves among. One said he felt like he was among those meant when the seed of God's words falls onto the road and is trod upon and the birds eat it. Another when the seed fell among the thorns and was smothered. This one found that good and evil was mixed up together in him and he had not yet surrendered everything to the Savior. A third counted himself among the rocky hearts, where the word has not yet taken root.

THE 31ST   We concluded this first month with praise and thanksgiving to our dear Lord for revealing Himself among us so graciously at the beginning of this year, revealing himself to us in a way we could feel, and revitalizing the hearts of the Brothers and Sisters through the power of His blood.

[February]

THE 5TH   Some Brothers returned from *Lichtenau* and they brought letters from Brother *Heckewelder* and on THE 10TH Brother *Edwards* came here and then returned home. Some Indian strangers have also come here to visit in recent days.

THE 12TH   After we had Speakings with the Brothers and Sisters, we had a blessed Holy Communion during which a Brother and Sister watched for the first time, and in *Gnadenhütten* one Sister joined the congregation in partaking for the first time.

THE 13TH   Early in the day was the Liturgy for Holy Communion. During the Children's Service the baby girl born to *Christian* and *Catharina* on the 8th was baptized into Jesus' death with the name *Sophia.*

THE 14TH   Brother *David* went to *Gnadenhütten* and on THE 16TH from there on to *Lichtenau* with Brother *Edwards,* accompanied by Brother *Lucas.* We 3 Brothers had a discussion there as well as with the Brothers and Sisters who are Helpers about their move away from there.[1466] We learned that most of the Indian Brothers and Sisters were planning to settle 6 miles below *Gnadenhütten,* except for a few who will move to *Schönbrunn* and a few who will

---

1465. Matt. 13:1–23.
1466. The removal started at the end of March; on 5 April the first arrived at Schönbrunn and on 24 April the arrival of the last from Lichtenau was registered in Schönbrunn.

move to *Gnadenhütten*. On THE 19TH Brother *David* arrived back in *Schönbrunn*, where he found everyone well. He had had a difficult return journey because the *Muskingum*, which had to be crossed several times, had already broken up in many places.

THE 22ND   *Josua* had to be sent away from *Lichtenau* a month ago and since then he has wandered from one place to another in despair. He has had no peace night or day and could not eat or sleep. He pleaded urgently for permission to live here, and he was inexpressible comforted and overjoyed that he received this.

THE 27TH   We were delighted by letters and congregational news reports from Bethlehem dated *November* 17th last year. We also received the Watchwords for this year[1467] through *May*. During the Congregational Service in the evening, the Brothers and Sisters were very interested when we shared with them some news from these and many greetings. This brought them much joy.

THE 28TH   There is now beautiful spring weather, so the Brothers and Sisters went out to look for place to boil sugar and to build huts for this purpose. This is very convenient and close for them here.

THE 29TH   A couple of confused sheep who had distanced themselves from the congregation a long time ago returned and urgently asked to be reaccepted. The Helpers spoke with them and learned of their request.[1468]

[March]

MARCH 1ST   The *Muskingum,* which had been frozen over here since before Christmas, broke up. We were concerned that all the low land would be flooded and much harm would be done to cattle and fields because of the deep snow. However, it did not rise as high as usual for this time of year.

THE 5TH   The Brothers and Sisters gathered for the usual Sunday services. They come home for the services every morning as well, because they are not very far away. However, we really like to take advantage of the nice weather for this work, so in the afternoons they were dismissed early to go to their sugar huts. While they were there, everyone gathered in their houses in between services and Brothers *Abraham* and *Samuel* preached without ceasing.

THE 12TH   I received a letter from Colonel *Brodhead Commandant* from *Pittsburgh*[1469] in which he requests that we settle our Indian congregation in

---

1467. The Watchwords for 1780 had been printed again in Philadelphia; as was the case before 1776, this happened in more than one installment. See *Die täglichen Loosungen der Brüdergemeine für das Jahr 1780.*

1468. See entry for 22 March 1780.

1469. Daniel Brodhead to Zeisberger, 10 Feb. 1780, *PA,* 1st ser., 12:203–4. Brodhead justified his request as follows: "having since had some conversation with Capts. Pipe & Killbuck relative to the Coochocking Indians coming to live on big Beaver Creek, they seem to think it will be of advantage to them to do so, but seem to wish your people would likewise form a town or more in their Neighborhood."

Kaskaskunk, closer to *Pittsburgh.* This has happened numerous times, but now he asked more insistently. He listed all sorts of reasons for this, for example, where we now lived we were too exposed to warriors whom we had to entertain for our own safety when they came into our *Towns.* Also we had to be distressed by seeing the *Scalps* of the *Americans* carried through our *Towns* and the prisoners led through here, which must be very unpleasant. Also, as long as we lived here they had to spare the Indians who are really their enemies for our sake, so he would prefer it if we were not in this area. Then they would know that they had no one but enemies before them. Brother *David* replied to him about this and explained the impossibility of this. He asked him to let us remain in possession of our *Settlements* if possible.[1470]

THE 14TH   Brothers *Conner* and *Willhelm* came here for a visit. They returned there on THE 17TH. Recently our Brothers here have been busy making *Canows.* They finished 6 of them to assist the Brothers and Sisters in *Lichtenau.*

THE 19TH   In the morning on Palm Sunday was the sermon about Philippians 2:5, He became obedient unto death, even the death of the cross,[1471] and asked Him through his Holy Spirit to paint the image of His suffering and death clearly before our hearts and eyes as we enter the passion week.

THE 22ND   The 2 people mentioned on the 29th of last month, *Joseph* and *Maria Catharina,* received permission to live here again at their repeated request.

THE 23RD   In the evening the story of our Savior's bitter spiritual suffering and bloody sweat for the sake of our sins was heard with emotional hearts. Afterward the communicant Brothers and Sisters gathered and received merciful *Absolution* for our many shortcomings and faults and we enjoyed His Body and Blood in Holy Communion. One Brother joined us in partaking for the first time. 2 Sisters were readmitted and one watched for the first time.

THE 24TH   We spent this day reading the passion story and reflecting on all the pain our Lord and God suffered for our sakes. His wounds and chastisement, his head crowned with thorns, and how they spit into His face, His crucifixion and how He bowed His head, and the piercing of His side, made a deep impression on our hearts and caused us to sigh, Oh, may we live in constant reflection on his sufferings and always nourish our hearts with this; then we would always be blessed and secure.

THE 25TH   For *Mary's* annunciation, the story[1472] was read in the general service and we considered and sang praises of His meritorious incarnation.

1470. This letter is dated not before 2 April, David Zeisberger to Daniel Brodhead, Tupaking, 2 April 1780, *PA,* 1st ser., 8:158–59.
1471. Phil. 2:5–11, verse 8.
1472. Luke 1:26–38.

In the service for those baptized, two received *Absolution*. The older girls had a separate service. They were committed to the remembrance of the Brothers and Sisters both this morning in the service and also during the Lovefeast in the afternoon.

THE 26TH   Early in the day we prayed the Easter Litany in the Meeting Hall, and asked for eternal communion with the 3 who have gone home from here. Then the story of the Lord's resurrection[1473] was read and then was the sermon. During the Congregational Service, two people once again received *Absolution,* so that now all of our young people who suffered harm in the evil times have been restored and accepted to grace. May the Savior be praised for this and allow them to prosper completely for Him.

Brother *Edwards* reports from *Gnadenhütten:* We had very happy holidays, which the Savior blessed. On Maundy Thursday He blessed us in an inexpressible manner during Holy Communion. The story of His bitter sufferings and death was heard with emotional hearts. He, our dear Lord, was close to us in all our services on Good Friday, while we reflected on his incarnation and many sufferings, on the Great Sabbath, when we considered both his holy incarnation and His body in the grave, during the Lovefeast on that day, and during the Easter *Litany* on God's Acre Easter morning. Our hearts were full of shame and gratitude that He suffered and endured so much for us.

THE 27TH   We sent all of our *Canows* to *Lichtenau* to assist the Brothers and Sisters there in their departure.

THE 29TH   We received a packet of news reports from Bethlehem and *Europe* from *Pittsburgh,* along with Watchwords[1474] for this year, and letters from Brothers *Matthao* and *Grube* from the month of *February.*

We received word from *Pittsburgh* about a great massacre carried out by the Indians, and that they suspected the *Delaware* in *Goschachgünk.* The latter, however, is not true.[1475]

[April]

APRIL 1ST   Once again news arrived that more than 20 people had been captured at the mouth of the *Muskingum* and some have been killed.[1476]

1473. E.g., Mark 16:1–7.
1474. See note 1467 to entry for 27 Feb. 1780.
1475. This refers to an incident on Raccoon Creek. Daniel Brodhead to David Zeisberger, 22 March 1780, *PA,* 1st ser., 12:214–15. In his letter dated 2 April 1780 (see note 1470 above), Zeisberger informed Brodhead that this attack had been the work of Wyandot warriors. See also *FRO,* 150–54, for eyewitness reports and for Council of Delaware to Daniel Brodhead, 30 March 1780 (157–59).
1476. See Council of Delaware to Daniel Brodhead, 30 March 1780 (*FRO,* 157–59): "I am at once surprised to see three Warriors at the head of a large party carrying Your Flesh and Blood by here. . . . These three Warriors were first the Mingo Hawtatscheek. Neeshawsh a Mohican. Washenaws a Monsy. These three carried 20 Children and 3 grown People Prissonners past here Yesterday" (157). In his letter of 2 April (see note 1470 above), Zeisberger confirmed this information. Other reports in *FRO,* 160, 163–64.

THE 2ND   We remembered our Brothers and Sisters who have been baptized during the last year, 3 from here and 9 in *Lichtenau,* and we asked the Savior to protect them from the evil and to allow them to prosper in the congregation.

THE 4TH   I sent letters to Bethlehem via *Gnadenhütten* and *Pittsburgh.*

THE 5TH   Brother and Sister *Conners* arrived here and some other families from *Lichtenau* came here on THE 6TH to live.[1477] Otherwise we heard that things are beginning to get very restless in the *Nations* again and there remains little hope of peace.

THE 8TH   We sent our *Canows* back to *Lichtenau* to assist the Brothers and Sisters there.

THE 9TH   During the service for the communicant Brothers and Sisters we remembered those who have become communicants during the last year. 2 of them are here and one is in *Gnadenhütten.* We asked the Savior to keep them in Him, the vine, and to let them bear fruit.[1478]

THE 10TH   Some more widows came here to live, as did *Rachel.*

THE 18TH   The Brothers began building huts together for the Brothers and Sisters who have arrived from *Lichtenau.* They continued with this the entire week. In the *Gnadenhüttenn* diary it says on this date: Most of the Brothers and Sisters in *Lichtenau,* have already arrived at their new site 6 miles from here. Today Brother *Edwards* visited it and returned home from there in the evening.

THE 20TH   I received a friendly letter from *Colonel Brodhead* in *Pittsburgh* which said in brief that he does not want to insist at all that we move away from here, nor expect anything of us that would be troublesome for us. However, he was glad we had left *Goschachgünk* and that our Indian congregations now lived closer together.[1479]

THE 24TH   *Ignatius* and his family arrived here from *Gnadenhütten* to live. In recent days we had many visits from Indians strangers.

THE 25TH   Our Brothers were hungry for meat during their work and went out hunting. Toward evening they brought 10 deer home.

Leonhard and his family arrived in *Gnadenhütten* from *Lichtenau* to live there.

[May]

MAY 1ST   Because the *Muskingum* was very high, Brother *David* traveled by water to *Gnadenhütten* and from there by land to our new *Settlement*[1480]

1477. See entry for 14 Feb. 1780.
1478. After John 15:5.
1479. Daniel Brodhead to Zeisberger, 15 April 1780, *PA,* 1st ser., 12:221.
1480. This refers to the new settlement called Salem, six miles from Gnadenhütten. The first mention of the name of this new settlement appears in the entry for 21 May 1780.

and visited the Brothers and Sisters there. He returned to *Gnadenhütten* in the evening on THE 2ND, where he held a *Conference* with the Helpers. On THE 3RD he returned home.

THE 4TH   For Ascension Day we read the story of the day[1481] and worshipped our dear Lord. We asked for His unseen presence and that our relationship with him would continue always.

In *Gnadenhütten* the story of our dear Lord's departure from his disciples and his ascension was also read and the Brothers and Sisters prostrated themselves before our unseen but close Lord. Brother *Edwards* preached the sermon there about the Savior's words, Lo, I am with you alway, even unto the end of the world.[1482]

Brother *David* had gotten a sore throat but still led the Congregational Service in the afternoon. Later this evening he lost his voice because his throat was swollen.

THE 5TH   Brother *Edwards* came here. He led the early service on THE 6TH and returned home.

THE 7TH   The Helper *Samuel* held the service in the morning and the Helper *Abraham* in the afternoon.

THE 8TH   Early before daybreak the Brothers sent a message to Brother *Heckewelder,* who then came here this morning. In the meantime the Indian Brothers and Sisters had all worked hard and filled the house with *Beson* (that is, roots and herbs).[1483] With the Savior's help however, the swelling in his throat subsided and Brother *David* got his voice back. The Brothers and Sisters were overjoyed and they thanked the Savior for this.

THE 9TH   Brothers *Edwards* and *Schebosch* also came here. They returned home, as did Brother *Heckewelder,* who led the early service this morning.

THE 11TH   Brother *David* held the early service again about the Watchword for the day, A bruised reed shall he not break, and smoking flax shall he not quench etc.[1484]

Some Brothers from both here and *Gnadenhütten* went to the new *Town* to help the Brothers and Sisters there with the construction of their Meeting House. In *Gnadenhütten* they finished fencing in a new piece of land today. On THE 13TH we also finished fencing in 30 acres[1485] on the West side of the *Muskingum.*

THE 14TH   It was Pentecost and we had a blessed day. God the worthy Holy Spirit revealed Himself powerfully among us and let us feel his presence in all the services. We joined with the baptized Brothers and Sisters in asking

---

1481. Acts 1:1–14.
1482. Matt. 28:20.
1483. See entry for 25 Dec. 1772 and note 117.
1484. Matt. 12:20.
1485. See entry for 15 May 1773 and note 193.

for forgiveness for all our mistakes and shortcomings and for times we have not listened to His voice and have caused Him sorrow. We surrendered ourselves anew to His blessed care and asked Him to remain with us and to make Jesus' wounds and suffering clearer in our hearts each day. And we received the comfort and assurance from Him that He will do this and even more for us.

It says this about today in *Gnadenhütten:* We asked for obedient hearts to hear the voice of the Holy Spirit and for forgiveness for everything we have done to cause him sorrow, and we promised anew to be His obedient children. Today the baby boy born to Brother *Thomas* and Sister *Polly* on the 3rd of this month was also baptized with the name *Christian.*

THE 16TH   Brother *David* went to *Gnadenhütten* accompanied by Brother *Lucas.* Indian strangers followed from *Schönbrunn* just a little while after him, and he learned from them that he had almost fallen into the hands of a party of warriors who had gone through the bush and crossed the road. He had Speakings with the Brothers and Sisters there in preparation for Holy Communion, which they celebrated on the 20th, and they returned home on THE 18TH. In the meantime Brothers *Abraham* and *Samuel* had taken care of the services.

THE 20TH   After we had had Speakings with the Brothers and Sisters, we had Holy Communion. One Brother watched as a *Candidate* for the first time during this.

THE 21ST   In the morning was the *Liturgy* for Holy Communion and the sermon. In the afternoon Brother *David* and some Indian Brothers went straight through the bush to the new *Town,* where he arrived in the evening. On THE 22ND they had the dedication of their Meeting House for which most of the Brothers and Sisters from *Gnadenhütten* had also come. On THE 23RD after Speakings had been held with the Brothers and Sisters, they had Holy Communion. We were also happy to receive letters from Brother *Matthao* and Brother *Grube* through a French *Major Lanetot*[1486] who was going to *Goschachgünk* on Indian *Affairs.* From these we can see hope that we get reinforcements of Brothers and Sisters this spring. Then on the 24TH Brother *David* returned home from *Salem*[1487] via *Gnadenhütten.*

THE 27TH   Indians from *Walhanding* came here dressed as warriors.[1488] However, they denied that they were going to war when they were asked. One *Munsee* Indian who came here from *Niagara,* where he had been staying for a long time, brought news here that when all the Indians had to flee there last

1486. Daniel-Maurice Godefroy de Linctot (1739–83), son of a French family from Montreal who had seen active duty in the Seven Years' War. He returned to France with his family in 1762, but two years later he came back to North America. In 1770 at the latest he lived as an Indian trader in the Mississippi Valley. After the arrival of George Rogers Clark he joined the American side; in the spring of 1779 he was appointed Indian agent of the Illinois region.

1487. On the new settlement, see note 1480.

1488. Zeisberger means dressed and painted as warriors.

year, 300 men, women, and children from various *Nations* died from an epidemic and 80 on the *Ohio* from smallpox.[1489]

THE 30TH   The office of *Servant for Visitors* was given to *Thomas,* and he accepted this willingly. We found this even more necessary because so many strangers are visiting us now.

THE 31ST   The French *Agent* returned from *Goschachgünk* on his way to *Pittsburgh.* He sent messages to the *Nations* because the *Chiefs* in *Goschachgünk* did not think it advisable for him to go see them personally as he had intended; now we will see how they take this.[1490]

It seems he is not ignorant of the Brothers' Mission among the Indians. He said he liked our *Towns* better than any *Towns* he had ever seen and really praised the behavior and the lifestyle of our Indians.

[June]

JUNE 1ST   Many of the *Chiefs* from *Goschachgünk* came here with the French *Major* to discuss a message they had received from *Pittsburgh.* A large sum of money has been set on Indian *Scalps* so word was sent from *Pittsburgh* that the road there will not be safe for Indians to travel because of the parties going out after *Scalps.* In *Pittsburgh* the *Delaware* were given *Commissions* to go after the hostile Indians and they are supposed to be rewarded for this.[1491] The *Chiefs* returned on THE 3RD.

THE 4TH   The French *Agent* attended the sermon. During the service for married Brothers and Sisters, the single Brother *Abel* was married to the widow *Johannette.*

THE 7TH   We received news from *Sandusky* that the English have marched from *Detroit* to *Kentucky*[1492] with several hundred Indians.[1493]

THE 9TH   Some Brothers and Sisters returned from *Mochweshünk* (formerly *Lichtenau*). They still have cattle there and had gone to fetch them. They said that it now was a much worse place than *Goschachgünk.* It did not look at all the same anymore and they had not felt well there at all.

THE 11TH   One *Delaware* Indian came here with a White man who

1489. Zeisberger to Daniel Brodhead, 1 June 1780. *FRO,* 189.

1490. With more details, John Heckewelder to Daniel Brodhead, 7 June 1780, and Gelelemind to Brodhead on the same day. *FRO,* 190–92.

1491. Daniel Brodhead to the Council of the Delaware, 27 May 1780 (*FRO,* 183–84). Some of the Council's resolves are reported in Gelelemind and Council to Daniel Brodhead, 7 June 1780 (*FRO,* 190–92).

1492. This refers to Kentucky County south of the Ohio River.

1493. In a letter dated 1 June 1780 (cited in note 1489 above), Gelelemind mentions three hundred English soldiers and five hundred Indian warriors marching toward Kentucky (*FRO,* 191). On 7 June Colonel Arthur Campbell mentions six hundred English soldiers and a thousand warriors en route to Kentucky (*FRO,* 192). Zeisberger communicated this information, which he probably received from Alexander McCormick, to Daniel Brodhead on 12 June (see note 1495).

was a prisoner of the *Wyandot.* They were on their way to the *Fort.* He is a well-to-do man from *Virginia,*[1494] where his family lives. He was amazed to see our 3 *Settlements* and so many Christian Indians and to see that we had maintained our position thus far in the war. He said this is not the work of men, but of God.

THE 12TH   *Gelelemind* came here from *Goschachgünk* with the rest of the *Chiefs.* On the 14th they continued their journey to the *Fort* with the French *Officier* and the *Virginian.* I had also written to *Colonel Brodhead* on this occasion about the Brothers and Sisters we are expecting and asked him to send a messenger to inform us as soon as they arrived at the *Fort,* so that we could pick them up.[1495] On THE 16TH, however, we were extremely happy to learn that he had arrived there with his traveling company. We learned this through a personal letter from Brother *Grube* in *Pittsburgh,* which was delivered to us by Indians who came from the *Fort.* Therefore, we immediately made arrangements to pick them up as soon as possible. Otherwise, many strangers visited us this week.

THE 17TH   One *Delaware* Indian who had been in *Lower Sandusky* came here with 6 White people from *Pittsburgh.* They had taken two *Wyandot* women prisoner there and are returning with them.[1496] People fear the *Nations* will still get tangled up in war among themselves, because the *Delaware* have become too involved in this.[1497]

THE 18TH   A good number of Indian Brothers from all 3 sites left on horse to go to the *Fort* and pick up our Brothers and Sisters who have arrived there. The waters there are very high because of the heavy rains and we were worried they would have a slow trip.

JUNE 20TH   A party of *Munsee* Indians who had bought corn here returned to *Sandusky.* We did not fail to proclaim the Savior to them while they were here.

THE 23RD   Brothers *Ignatius* and *Johannes* returned from *Sandusky,* where they had traded skins for clothing and goods. We had already gotten word that they might have trouble because of the event reported on the 17th of this month. We were therefore even happier to see that they returned without experiencing any hardships. They had been cordially received and well treated everywhere they went and they heard nothing but good things said about the Indian Believers. They say we alone are the luckiest people because we are not concerned about any war. All the *Nations* were our friends because we lived in

---

1494. Not identified.

1495. Dated 12 June 1780.

1496. This group had been commanded by Colonel Samuel Brady. See Daniel Brodhead to George Washington, 29 June 1780, *PA,* 1st ser., 12:243.

1497. This is the first indication in the diary that those Delaware who had thus far been neutral and who had since had joined the American camp were now actively engaged in the war. The composition of the warriors suggests that settlers had hired the Delaware as trackers.

peace with everyone. As a result we did not even suffer food shortages, while other Indians were suffering from hunger and distress. The *Wyandot* told them to inform people here that if our Indians needed anything, they should just come and buy it. They did not need to fear anyone and there were plenty of goods available there.

THE 27TH   Today and in recent days many strangers came here, mostly *Munsee* Indians. They stayed here for several days.

THE 30TH   We were very happy to welcome our dear Brother *Grube* and Brother and Sister *Sensemann* and Sister *Sara Ohneberg*. Their arrival was a beautiful and happy sight for us.[1498] All the Indian Brothers and Sisters were very happy to greet these dear Brothers and Sisters and welcome them among us. They were busy with them well into the night. We thanked the dear Savior who had protected them from all harm and misfortune on their journey and who had the dear angels guide them here so safely. On their trip here from *Pittsburgh,* after they were past *Fort McIntosh,* between the large and small *Beaver Creek,* White people who were out to get Indian *Scalps* fired on the Indians who were in front. They shot one of them, who does not actually live with us, through the sleeve of his shirt. However, they soon realized how large the company of Indians was and they ran away.

[July]

JULY 1ST   Brother *Grube* led the early service about the text, Put on therefore, as the elect of God, holy and beloved, bowels of mercies, kindness, humbleness of mind, meekness, longsuffering.[1499] In conclusion he extended greetings to the Brothers and Sisters from the congregations both here in this country and over in Europe.

THE 2ND   Brother *David* preached the sermon and Brother *Sensemann* led the Children's Service. In the afternoon Brothers *Edwards* and *Heckewelder* came here to see and welcome these dear Brothers and Sisters, and many Indian Brothers and Sisters from *Gnadenhütten* and *Salem* came with them. During a Lovefeast for the White Brothers and Sisters, we celebrated the engagement of

---

1498. Bernhard Adam Grube inspected the mission congregations on the Muskingum; in early August he returned to Bethlehem. His travel report, "Reise Diarium der Geschwister Grube, Sensemanns und Sara Ohnebergin nach Pittsburg und Muskingum," is preserved in MAB, B 211, F 15, I 3. The Rev. Gottlob Sensemann (1745–1800) had accompanied Zeisberger on his trip to Goschgoschink in 1768; until 20 August 1781 he assisted Zeisberger, as Heckewelder had done earlier, in his mission at Schönbrunn. On 11 May 1780, shortly before starting his trip, Sensemann had married Anna Brucker (1747–1815). Anna Brucker was born in Bethlehem; immediately after the marriage she was ordained an acolyte and prepared for work in the congregation. On 4 July 1780 Grube joined in marriage Sarah Ohneberg (1746–1815), daughter of a Moravian missionary couple living in the Danish–West Indian island of St. Croix, and John Heckewelder. MAB, Memoirs, B 7, 1811–20, F 1815.

1499. Col. 3:12.

Brother *Johann Heckewelder* to the single Sister *Sara Ohneberg*. During this, Brother *Grube* talked about complete devotion to the Savior and encouraged this Brother and Sister to be faithful servants in the Savior's work among the Indians here. In the evening he led the Congregational Service about the Watchword.[1500] The Savior knows and sees the longing and desire a poor, troubled heart has for Him; He gladly approaches them and comforts and delights them. In a fervent prayer on his knees, he laid His Indian congregation before the Savior on his faithful heart. During a *Conference* in the evening, we White Brothers and Sisters discussed the Holy Communion scheduled for next Saturday and how we can hold this at all three of our sites. Brother *Grube* also offered some practical comments and reminders.

THE 3RD   Brother *Grube* led the early service about the text, Be ready, always to give an answer to every man that asketh you a reason of the hope that is in you. We want to be eternal witnesses that grace and freedom from all sins can be found only in Jesus' sacrifice, for all the world.[1501] He said that anyone who has sought and attained grace and the forgiveness for his sins in Jesus' blood could testify later from personal experience what He has done for his soul. Finally, he informed the Brothers and Sisters of the upcoming marriage of Brother *Heckewelder* to Sister *Sara Ohneberg,* which will take place in *Salem.* Then he and the 2 Sisters traveled by water as far as *Gnadenhütten* today.[1502]

THE 4TH   Brothers *David* and *Sensemann* and some Indian Brothers also went to *Salem.* The former returned on THE 5TH and Brother and Sister *Sensemann* on THE 6TH.

THE 7TH   Brother *Sensemann* led the early service. We had Speakings with the Brothers and Sisters today and the following day in preparation for Holy Communion.

THE 9TH   The sermon was about the text, We have also a more sure word of prophecy etc.[1503] In the afternoon Brother *Grube* came from *Gnadenhütten,* and in the evening he led the Congregational Service about the Watchword, For he is thy Lord; and worship thou him.[1504] Then the 45 *Communicants* partook of His Body and Blood in Holy Communion. One Sister was readmitted after receiving *Absolution* and one Brother watched as a Candidate for confirmation for the 2nd time.

THE 10TH   After the early service Brother *Grube* held the *Liturgy* in Preparation for Holy Communion. He knelt and prayed that the Savior would

1500. Ps. 94:4.

1501. 1 Pet. 3:15; the choral beginning with "Wir wollen ewiglich Zeugen seyn, daß im Opfer Jesu allein zu finden Gnade und Freiheit von allen Sünden für alle Welt" is in *Gesangbuch zum Gebrauch der evangelischen Brüdergemeinen,* hymn no. 1390, verse 10.

1502. Anna Sensemann and Sarah Ohneberg. The wedding ceremony took place on 4 July (see note 1498). Grube, "Reise Diarium der Geschwister Grube," entry for 4 July 1780, MAB, B 211, F 15, I 3.

1503. 2 Pet., 1:19.

1504. Ps. 45:11; the Collection of Watchwords incorrectly has verse 2.

show the Brothers and Sisters what He had given them through the very blessed enjoyment of His Body and Blood in Holy Communion.

THE 11TH   He led the early service about the text, Examine yourselves, whether ye be in the faith; prove your own selves etc.[1505] It is important for each person to ask himself frequently if he is healthy in faith and in heart and walks in the knowledge of his wretchedness. This causes us to approach the Savior, where we always experience the comfort of his grace.

Yesterday and today he visited the Brothers and Sisters in their houses, which everyone enjoyed.

THE 14TH   Brother *Sensemann* led the early service. We used the past days to read reports from the Synod of 1776 in *Barby*. This was a great blessing for our hearts.[1506]

THE 15TH   Brother *Grube* held a blessed service for the Helpers, of which there are 6 Brothers and 5 Sisters, and reminded them what their duty was and what the Savior and the Brothers who are with them and whom they assist in the Savior's work expect from them, and he admonished them to live in love and harmony according to *John* 17,[1507] and to provide their Brothers and Sisters a good example in this particularly, as well as in their entire walk. He said a Brother or Sister who was leading an improper life or causing offence, or who lost the privilege of Holy Communion because of sins, could not remain one of the Helpers. They were also informed and instructed about how our baptized children are received into the congregation, which has not been introduced here yet.[1508] In conclusion, Brother *Grube* knelt and commended these Brothers and Sisters to the Savior for blessing and prayed they would receive the necessary grace for all they do for Him and His Indian congregation.

THE 16TH   In the sermon, Brother *Grube* read from Paul's letters and

---

1505. 2 Cor. 13:5.

1506. In 1776 there was no synod in Barby; Zeisberger is thinking of the synod of 1775. In the report of the resolutions entitled "Verlaß des im Jahr 1775 zu Barby gehaltenen Synodi der Evangelischen Brüder-Unität" (manuscript in MAB, without call number), section XII summarized the synod's resolves on mission. According to these resolves in 1775, about 160 persons were working in the different mission fields. Most resolves dealt with problems arising from the mission fields in the West Indian Islands. Resolutions no. 7 and 8, however, dealt with mission in North America. They read: "7. The query of one of the mission congregations receives the answer from the synod that accepting children born in the congregation should follow the rules laid down as introduced in the congregations in Greenland." The eighth resolve requested permission to train more Indian Helpers and included the admonition that in order to avoid becoming arrogant, Helpers should never be alone but always form a group.

1507. John 17:21–23.

1508. Until then baptized children were treated the same way as were adults baptized outside mission congregations. On 30 June 1775 Zeisberger had raised with the Provincial Helpers' Conference the status of these children with respect to their candidacy for participating in Holy Communion. The conference had replied that this problem had been dealt with by the synod of the Unity but that the conference harbored no doubts that the missionaries should deal with the problem according to the rules followed in the mission congregations in Greenland, whereby "the same are accepted into the congregations as regular members" (MAB, Protokoll der Provincial Helfer Conferenz, fol. 39). The resolve of the 1775 Synod of Barby is cited in note 1506 above.

clearly explained what the Savior achieved for us through his meritorious incarnation, life, sufferings, and death. Through this he brought about our eternal salvation, which we are now able to enjoy through faith in Him. Afterward he also held a service for the married Brothers and Sisters and the Savior laid his blessing upon this. Then he went to *Gnadenhütten* with Brother *David* and most of the Helper Brothers. The latter returned on THE 17TH, but Brother *Grube* stayed there for 8 days.

We received news that the English who marched to *Kentucky* have returned from there with 300 prisoners, mostly women and children.[1509]

THE 18TH   The French *Major Lanetot*[1510] returned here from *Pittsburgh* with another French *Officier*.[1511] They were on their way to *Goschachgünk* to try to move the *Nations* to peace once again.

THE 22ND   Brother *Sensemann* held the early service. In a letter from Brother *Heckewelder* we learned that many parties of warriors have gone to the *Settlements* again and the road to the *Fort* is therefore unsafe. Some messengers who had been sent there from *Goschachgünk* turned back because of this.

THE 24TH   An Indian family wants to come to the congregation. During the Helpers' *Conference* we discussed them and their circumstances and shared our advice with them, which they gladly accepted. Some of our Brothers who were out hunting tracked a large party of warriors who had marched to *Pittsburgh* after completely burning down the houses in *Fort Lawrence*.[1512]

1509. Between 24 and 26 June Captain Henry Bird used his two cannons effectively in forcing two fortified frontier houses to capitulate. His Indian allies plundered these houses as American vigilante militia units had done and took the inhabitants prisoners; for contemporary reports, see Young, *Westward into Kentucky*, 80–81. In a report in the hand of John Heckewelder addressed to Daniel Brodhead, Gelelemind speaks of 340 prisoners (*FRO*, 217–20). This letter also contains a detailed report on the conference at Fort Detroit with the Indian tribes of the region, at which both captains, Pipe and Wingenund, had participated. According to this report Half King uttered a serious warning against the Delaware at Goschachgünk because of their participation in the attack in which two Wyandot women were taken prisoner. See entry for 17 June 1780 and note 1496.

1510. H3: Lometot. On Daniel-Maurice Godefroy de Linctot, see note 1486. Daniel Brodhead's instructions for Godefroy, dated 7 July 1780, are printed in *PA*, 1st ser., 12:246.

1511. According to a report by Augustin Mottin de La Balme dated 27 June 1780 (printed in Alvord, *Kaskaskia Records*, 163–68), three French were at Fort Pitt at this time: he himself, Godefroy, and a third person whose name he did not give. He intended, he continued, to travel by river into the Mississippi Valley, while Godefroy would follow him on the overland route. The person whose name is not known must be the third person Zeisberger refers to. According to Brodhead's letter to George Washington dated 21 Aug. 1780 (*PA*, 1st ser., 12:258), shortly before 21 August a "Captain Duplantier" arrived from the "Delaware Towns" at Fort Pitt. And another letter from Brodhead to Godefroy in Goschachgünk dated 31 July 1780 (*FRO*, 234) states that he was accompanied by a "Captain." Since Godefroy spoke no English, one must assume that this captain too was French, and it seems reasonable to conclude that the "French Officer" Zeisberger mentions is Duplantier. This is probably Louis-Gabriel Du Plantier, whose petition for acknowledging his French officer's patent Washington had denied on 6 Feb. 1780. [Hamilton], *Papers of Alexander Hamilton*, 2:264.

1512. These warriors were ambushed close to Fort McIntosh; Captain Thomas McIntyre defeated them and killed many of them. See Brodhead to Washington on 21 July and to Heckewelder on 31 July (*FRO*, 223, 232–33), and Brodhead to Joseph Reed on 21 July 1780 (*PA*, 1st ser., 12:251–52). John Heckewelder supplements these reports with information from Sandusky in his letter dated 14 Aug. 1780 (*FRO*, 245–46).

THE 27TH   Some Indians from *Sandusky* who had bought corn here returned home. There is great famine among the Indians everywhere, which is forcing them to stay home still and take care of their families. If it were not for this, everyone would go to war.

THE 31ST   Brother *Heckewelder* had gotten sick and both he and Brother *Grube* could not come here as planned, so Brother *David* and Brother and Sister *Sensemann* went to *Salem* today. Brother *Edwards* also went there from *Gnadenhütten,* and we White Brothers and Sisters had a *Conference* this evening and the following day and discussed present and future concerns. Brother *Grube's* return journey was set for *August* 13th. On AUGUST 2ND the latter returned with Brother *David* to *Schönbrunn* via *Gnadenhütten,* where he had Speakings with some Brothers and Sisters. However, Brother *Sensemann* had gotten sick and he and his wife had to remain in *Salem* until he recovers.

[August]

AUGUST 3RD   Brother *Grube* led the early service about the Watchword, Put on the whole armour of God, that ye may be able to stand against the wiles of the devil[1513] and then began the Speakings with the Brothers and Sisters.

THE 4TH   After the early service he held sweet services first for the little boys and then for the little girls. They all promised him with voice and a handshake they would belong completely to the Savior.

THE 5TH   In the early service he spoke directly and openly with the Brothers and Sisters about the text, If we say that we have no sin, we deceive ourselves, and the truth is not in us. If we confess our sins, he is faithful and just to forgive us our sins, and to cleanse us from all unrighteousness.[1514] The Savior laid his blessing on this and many came and talked honestly with us about their hearts. Afterward he held separate services for the single men and older boys and then also for the single women and older girls and had Speakings with them. During most of these he found hearts made tender by Jesus' blood. The tears on their cheeks were proof of this. In the evening he held a talk for the communicant Brothers and Sisters about the Watchword, Rejoice evermore. Pray without ceasing. In every thing give thanks.[1515] Oh, if only each person lived for him his whole life with a happy spirit and praised and glorified him.[1516] He talked about the Brothers' and Sisters' prayer and intercession for the congregations and for all people, which is good and pleasing to the Savior. He instructed the Brothers and Sisters to designate a certain time daily, day or

---

1513. Eph. 6:11.
1514. 1 John 1:8–9.
1515. 1 Thess. 5:16–18.
1516. *Gesangbuch zum Gebrauch der evangelischen Brüdergemeinen* (1778), hymn no. 1639, verse 1.

night, for this important task of speaking personally with the Savior, laying on His heart the concerns about their own spiritual condition and those of the congregation and the word of God in this part of the country, so that many heathen might yet come to the knowledge of the truth.[1517] Then *Josua* was *absolved* when Brother *Grube* laid on hands and in a sincere prayer commended this company to the Savior.

Indians from *Goschachgünk* came to get Indian corn. The *Chiefs* had requested this because a *Council* is supposed to be held there with the *Wyandot* and they have a shortage of food.

THE 6TH   Brother *David* preached the sermon and Brother *Grube* held blessed services first for the married Sisters, then for the married Brothers, then both together, and then also for the widows. The *Communicants* were informed that Holy Communion would be held on the 13th of this month, and in conclusion there was a Congregational Service.

THE 7TH   Brother *Grube* had Speakings with some more Brothers and Sisters and finished with this today. We found much cause to thank the Savior and to praise Him that His grace is not in vain in the hearts of the Brothers and Sisters.

THE 9TH   Brother *Grube* held an impressive and anointed talk about the Watchword, I will never leave thee, nor forsake thee, and the text, Therefore if any man be in Christ, he is a new creature etc.[1518] He spoke sincerely and emotionally about this with the Brothers and Sisters and poured out his heart to them. He admonished them to hold to the Savior whenever they felt their misery and to remain with Him in all circumstances since He would always grant them the comfort of His grace and would not abandon them. He knelt and prayed, thanking the Savior for the grace He has poured out on this little Indian congregation until now, and he commended them to his further faithful care, to the dear heavenly Father's protection and guidance, and to the Holy Spirit's care. The service was concluded with the New Testament benediction. Afterward the Brothers and Sisters came and said farewell and sent many greetings to the congregations all the way across the big water.

1517. See Grube's report in his travel diary for 5 Aug. 1780: "In the evening assembly Grube communicated to them the idea of a horary prayer, as it is practiced in all our other congregations, even in Greenland, and what the purpose of it is. Therefore the community partaking of the Holy supper was, too, requested to form such a prayer community, that would daily present their dire difficulties and conditions of their souls and circumstances to Jesus Christ; this would bring them into a closer and childlike communication with Jesus Christ." "Reise-Diarium der Geschwister Grube," MAB, B 211, F 15, I 3. In Herrnhut since 1727 and in Bethlehem since its beginning, groups of inhabitants prayed each hour of the day for the concerns, problems, and needs of the congregations. The result was the establishment of uninterrupted chains of prayers. We do not know whether the mission congregations were able to establish such strict chains of prayers. Grube's remarks make it clear that the duties of these praying assemblies were not restricted to their meeting every second week but were to be performed on a daily basis. Grube introduced these praying assemblies in Lichtenau on 5 August, in Salem on 11 August, and in Gnadenhütten on 14 August. See entry for 27 Aug. 1780.

1518. Heb. 13:5. Text: 2 Cor. 5:17.

Diary of Schönbrunn *from* August *13th 1780 until* March *25th, 1781.*[1519]

AUGUST 13TH   During a Lovefeast, the Brothers and Sisters were reminded of the important event 53 years ago in the congregation in Herrnhut, of what the Savior did for his Unity on that day, and what he has done through them among Christians and heathen since then and how he has revealed himself in the glory of his wounds. We have also participated in this great grace through her service, and we cannot thank Him enough for this.[1520] We were assured of the grace of being members of His body during Holy Communion today. One Brother and one Sister were readmitted during this. One Brother participated for the first time and one Brother and one Sister were *confirmed.*[1521]

THE 14TH   After the early service and *Liturgy* for Holy Communion, Brother *David* and a number of Brothers and Sisters went to *Gnadenhütten,* where the congregation had another Lovefeast on the occasion of the farewell of Brother Grube. Brother and Sister *Heckewelder* also came from *Salem* for this and many Indian Brothers and Sisters accompanied them there. Brother *Grube* held his final farewell *Conference* with the White Brothers and Sisters and workers, and after he had said good-bye to the Brothers and Sisters in the early service on THE 15TH, and we White Brothers and Sisters had recommitted ourselves to be faithful in our service to the Lord in the Cup of Covenant, he left for *Pittsburgh* with Brother *Schebosch* and a number of Indian Brothers. Brother *David* returned to *Schönbrunn* with Brother and Sister *Sensemann,* who had come from *Salem* yesterday. He had had to stay there a while because he was ill, but he was somewhat better now.

THE 17TH   The Watchword was, This is the generation of them that seek him, that seek thy face etc.[1522] We commended our little girls to the Savior in a prayer and asked Him to let them grow in love and knowledge of Him and to prosper for Him. We received news that a party of warriors had passed through *Tuscarawi* on their way to *Fort Pitt,* so we were concerned about our dear Brother *Grube* who was on his way there. We commended him to the guardian of *Israel* and the guidance of the dear angels.

THE 18TH   We had already heard yesterday that the *Americans* had attacked the *Shawnee,* destroyed and burned down 2 *Towns* and cut down all their fields, and that they were advancing further against the rest of the *Towns.* Today Indians from *Sandusky* brought us definite news of this.[1523]

1519. MAB, B 141, F 11, fol. 556.

1520. On this day of commemoration, see Introduction, p. 62.

1521. According to Kortz, it was the Synod of Berthelsdorf in 1782 that declared confirmation the precondition for participation in Holy Communion (Kortz, "Liturgical Development of the American Moravian Church," 110–11). The term "Confirmation," meaning "Being admitted to the Holy Communion," was already used in Langundoutenünk (MAB, B 137, passim).

1522. Ps. 24:6.

1523. Together with about a thousand soldiers, most of them probably warriors, George Rogers Clark marched into the settlement area of the Shawnee in August, destroying on 6 August Chillicothe

THE 22ND   Brother *David* and many Indian Brothers and Sisters went to *Gnadenhütten.* There he held the burial of Sister *Esther,* who went home in blessing yesterday. For many years she was a faithful and blessed *National* Helper among her gender, and her memory will remain a blessing to them.

THE 26TH   The Brothers who had accompanied Brother *Grube* to the *Fort* returned today, and we were delighted that they brought us word and also personally written news of his safe arrival there.

THE 27TH   After the usual Sunday service there was a prayer meeting[1524] with the communicant Brothers and Sisters. The text, Praying always with all prayer and supplication in the Spirit etc.[1525] was discussed and they were instructed about which matters they should take to the Savior in prayer and should commend to His remembrance. This would be a blessing and benefit for their own hearts, and they would become closer to Him and more familiar with Him.

THE 29TH   Brother *Heckewelder,* who came here from *Salem* yesterday, led the early service about the text, For whether we live, we live unto the Lord etc.[1526] Brother *Edwards* also came from *Gnadenhütten* and the single Brothers celebrated their choir festival with a Lovefeast and rededicated themselves to serve the Prince of their choir with body and soul. Both Brothers *Heckewelder* and *Edwards* returned home today, as did *Christina Schebosch,* who came here yesterday with some Sisters from *Gnadenhütten* for a visit.[1527]

One of the Indians hired by *English Traders* came here from Sandusky with goods to trade for cattle.

THE 31ST   In the early service we prayed for the Savior's comfort and special blessings for our widows and widowers,[1528] from the bounty earned through his blood. Then they had a service about their text and a time of adoration. He let them sense his presence and filled their hearts with the comfort of the Holy Spirit.

[September]

SEPTEMBER 3RD   In the morning was the sermon and in the afternoon the baptized Brothers and Sisters had a blessed service about the text, Faithful is he that calleth you, who also will do it etc.[1529] Brother *Sensemann* led the Congregational Service.

---

and on 8 August the Shawnee settlements on the Miami River, after battles that cost Clark, according to his own statements, fourteen soldiers and the Shawnee forty warriors. G. R. Clark to Governor Thomas Jefferson, 17 Oct. 1780, James, *Clark Papers,* 451–53.

1524. See note 1517 to entry for 5 Aug. 1780.
1525. Eph. 6:18.
1526. Rom. 14:8.
1527. From "As did Christina" not in H3.
1528. Refers to choir festival.
1529. 1 Thess. 5:24.

Otherwise there are many illnesses now, as is usual at this time of year. During the summer there was seldom any wind at all and intense heat, and the weather now is variable and cool weather. This may contribute a lot to this.

THE 7TH   The married Brothers and Sisters celebrated their choir festival in grace and blessing. In the Morning Devotion we asked the Savior to pour out on them the abundance earned through his blood, and the entire congregation blessed them with heart and voice. Then they had a service about the Watchword for today, The Lord shall increase you more and more, you and your children, and the text, But speaking the truth in love, may grow up into him in all things, which is the head, even Christ etc.[1530] During the Lovefeast, which the entire congregation celebrated with them, we also talked with the children about becoming the Savior's own and thus bringing joy to Him and to their parents. They were especially delighted and enjoyed this great and important day of their parents. We concluded this blessed day with a time of adoration and the New Testament benediction. The Savior let them feel his presence in all the services and his loving face shone upon them.

THE 8TH   Pimoacan, the Half King of the Wyandot sent us word through an Indian who came here from Sandusky. He said, My Cousins, Indian Believers, you have spoken to the Chiefs in Goschachgünk often and repeatedly since you came into this area, and when you had a concern you took it before them. However, they have not paid much attention to this, nor have they let me or us know anything about this. Therefore your Speeches to them have all been lost. I am your friend and love the Indian Believers. If you have concerns about your 3 Towns just let me know, your requests will be granted. Presumably he heard that we submitted a Speech to the Council in Goschachgünk in the spring about establishing Salem, which had not yet been accepted,[1531] and this was probably the reason for this message. We sent him our Compliments and assured him of our love and friendship. We did not think it would be good to send him a reply now, however, because we have been instructed not to send any messages through Indian strangers.

THE 10TH   3 Delaware Indians came here from Pittsburgh. The Helper Brothers were suspicious of them, so they questioned them closely about their business in that area. They finally admitted that they had killed 2 White people a couple of miles from Pittsburgh but did not let their Scalps be seen, and they soon continued on.[1532]

1530. Ps. 115:14; text, Eph. 4:15.

1531. The diary does not mention such a speech to the Council at Goschagünk; it is possible that such a speech was resolved upon during Zeisberger's visit to Lichtenau on 16 February 1780 and sent from there to Goschachgünk; see entry for 14 Feb. 1780. During the Delaware Council's stay at Schönbrunn on 1 and again on 12 June 1780, these problems were not discussed, according to Zeisberger's entries in his diary. See entries for 1 and 12 June 1780.

1532. Both men were killed at "Robinson's Run" (a tributary of Chartier's Creek, a few miles from Pittsburgh) on 4 or 5 September 1780. See Daniel Brodhead to George Washington, 5 Sept. 1780, FRO, 271.

THE 11TH   In the morning we buried the earthly remains of our Sister *Charlotte,* who went to her eternal rest yesterday morning after a difficult and long-lasting illness. She came to *Langundoutenünk* with her husband and children, 4 daughters and 2 sons. They are all in the congregation and most of them are married. She was baptized there on *January 26, 1772,* and came to *Schönbrunn* on the *Muskingum* in the spring of 1773, where she became a communicant on *May 14, 1774.* After her baptism she remained faithful to the Savior. She treasured the grace she had experienced and her heart was firmly attached to the Savior and the congregation. She was a faithful servant of the congregation. It was great and important to her to be able to do something for the Savior. She also had a special gift for relating to the Sisters, encouraging them, and speaking sincerely with them. She said a moving farewell to her children and admonished them to remain faithful to the Savior. She longed to be released soon and to be at home with the Lord. Her desire was fulfilled yesterday and she fell asleep peacefully and in blessing. Sister *Sensemann* laid the blessing upon her while Brother *David* read the *Liturgy.*

In the evening the son of Brother *Johannes* and Sister *Hanna* was baptized into Jesus' death in his sickbed. He received the name *Samuel.*

THE 12TH   The Brothers began building a schoolhouse and a house for Brother *David.*

THE 15TH   *Samuel,* who was baptized on the 11th of this month and went home yesterday, was buried, two months before he would have turned 8. He was a dear child and loved the Savior and the Brothers. Shortly before he died, he told his father to call Brother *David.* When he came, he told him, I am going home now, but what should I wear? Brother *David* replied, You are already dressed and have been beautifully clothed with Christ's blood and righteousness in Holy Baptism; you do not need anything else. Good, he said, now I am happy, and then he died as Brother *David* was blessing him.

THE 18TH   Brother and Sister *Heckewelder* came here from *Salem* and Brother *Edwards* from *Gnadenhütten* for our usual *Conference,* and we considered our concerns before the Savior. On THE 19TH the latter led the early service and then they returned to their homes.

THE 23RD   After having Speakings with the Brothers and Sisters in the past few days, the *Communicants* partook of His Body and Blood in Holy Communion and one Brother and one Sister enjoyed this great good for the first time.

THE 24TH   After the *Liturgy* in Preparation for Holy Communion, the sermon was preached about the greatest commandment[1533] and in the evening the Congregational Service was about the text, Be not thou therefore ashamed of the testimony of our Lord.[1534]

1533. Matt. 22:37–38.
1534. 2 Tim. 1:8.

THE 28TH   Brother *David* went to *Gnadenhütten,* had Speakings with the Brothers and Sisters there, and held Holy Communion for them on THE 30TH. He returned from there on OCTOBER 1ST. Brother *Sensemann* was ill, so the Helpers *Abraham* and *Samuel* held the services in the meantime.

[October]

OCTOBER 2ND   After the early service there was a Helpers' *Conference.* *Gelelemind* came from *Goschachgünk* with *Captain Pipe* and a company of Indians on their way to the *Fort.*[1535] *Anna Benigna* and her daughter, and Brothers *Jonas, Marcus,* and *Christian,* also came from *Salem* to go out on the fall hunt.

THE 3RD   The single Brother *Nicolaus* was married to the single Sister *Johanna Sabina* from *Salem* in the devotional service for married couples.

OCTOBER 4TH   I sent letters to Brother *Mattheus* and *Grube* with the French *Major* and a *Captain*[1536] who were going to *Pittsburgh,* and on THE 5TH the *Chiefs* from *Goschachgünk* also left to go there. Their people did not behave well and killed our Indians' pigs.

THE 6TH   There was a Helpers' *Conference* and we also put a roof on our schoolhouse today.

THE 8TH   The baby boy born to Brother and Sister *Connors* last night was baptized into Jesus' death with the name *Henry.*

THE 10TH   Many people were going out to hunt, and one Brother said that he had been a great hunter before he came to the congregation. However, since he had come to know the Savior he did not enjoy doing this anymore. He went out sometimes just to get meat for his household; previously he had left most of this lying in the bush for the animals. He preferred to work at home and did not want to miss any services, which were important to him and served as his daily food. He had never heard about the Savior going out to hunt in the bush for many days while he was in the world; he had worked with his hands instead.

THE 14TH   Some Brothers took cattle to *Lower Sandusky* to trade them for goods and clothing for themselves for winter. They are highly valued there.

THE 15TH   The sermon was held at the usual time and in the afternoon we read to the married Brothers and Sisters about marriage from the *Idea fidei.*[1537] After the Congregational Service, which Brother *Sensemann* led, the communicant Brothers and Sisters, or Prayer Group had their service.

1535. Big Cat had announced this visit on 12 September 1780, in a letter to Daniel Brodhead in the handwriting of John Heckewelder. According to Brodhead's report to George Washington dated 17 Oct. 1780, the chiefs arrived "with upwards of thirty warriors" to assist him in the planned expedition against hostile tribes. *FRO,* 273, 284.

1536. Major Daniel-Maurice Godefroy de Linctot and probably Captain Louis-Gabriel Du Plantier.

1537. Spangenberg, *Idea fidei fratrum.*

THE 23RD   The Savior took *Agnes*, the one-and-a-half-year-old baby daughter of *Johannes* and *Hanna*, home to himself. She was buried on THE 24TH. On THE 27TH old *Debora*, a widow who had lived near *Philadelphia* when there were still just a few houses there, followed her. She came to the congregation in *Schönbrunn* from *Tuscarawi* in 1773 and had been with us for a very short time when her own son, who lived among the savages, accused her of having cursed his child.[1538] He said the child died because of this, and that this may have been one of the reasons she came to the congregation. Therefore we told her to appear before the *National* Helpers with her son, who had come for a visit. They spoke with both of them. She justified herself to his satisfaction and he stopped suspecting her, although others did not completely lose their suspicions as long as she lived. She was baptized by Brother *Jungmann* on *January* 1, 1774, and she became a communicant on *November* 11, 1775. She led a quiet and orderly life and we saw nothing improper in her behavior. When we talked with her we also noticed that she had feeling in her heart. Even so, we always had some concerns about her, which we excused because of her advanced age. After her death, however, a very small heathen idol,[1539] that is a *Beson* such as old women who live among the savages usually have, was found among her things. They believe that if they have this they will not suffer any lack in their old age. Now we will never really know if she put any hope in this or if she had forgotten that she still had something like this. Otherwise, she loved all the Brothers and Sisters. Her earthly dwelling was buried on THE 28TH.

Joseph Schebosch junior came here with some Brothers from *Gnadenhütten*. He was on his way to the *Fort* to pick up his father.[1540] Indians who came from there gave them the news that he had arrived there from Bethlehem with another Brother, so they left for there today.

THE 28TH   Our Brothers returned from *Sandusky*.[1541] They brought along news that the war is supposed to begin again next spring and the *Nations* were preparing for this. They had been told in confidence that if our Indians needed to buy anything, they should do so this winter, since it would not be advisable for them to go there in the spring because of all the warriors.

A sick girl who was 10 years old sent for Brother *David* and told him she might go home that night. She had not yet been baptized with the Savior's blood, and she really wanted this; if she experienced this grace, then she would gladly go to the Savior. After she had spoken these words, she had a seizure and lay unconscious for a while. After she came back to herself, Brother *David* baptized her into Jesus' death with the name *Sara* in the presence of a number of Brothers and Sisters. She was very grateful for this and it comforted her.

1538. On the function of magic and witchcraft among the Delaware, see note 264 to entry for 11 Sept. 1773.

1539. See for the importance of pagan gods or idols note 273 to entry for 22 Sept. 1773.

1540. See entry for 14 Aug. 1780.

1541. Bracketed in another hand, but in H3. See entry for 14 Oct. 1780.

THE 29TH   The baby boy born to *Josua* and *Sophia* on the 16th of this month was baptized with the name *Thomas*.

THE 30TH   Brother *David* went to *Gnadenhütten*, and Brother *Heckewelder* also went there from *Salem*. We workers held a *Conference* together there. However, Brother and Sister *Sensemann*, who are both still fighting a fever, had to stay home. In the meantime, Brother *Sensemann* had held the burial of a child named *Sophia*, the one-year-old baby daughter of *Christian* and *Catharina* who had died yesterday. Brother *David* returned home late in the evening.

[November]

NOVEMBER 2ND   We remembered our fellowship with the Church triumphant, in the blessed hope of being joined with them one day and remaining at home with the Lord throughout eternity.

THE 4TH   We had a blessed Holy Communion during which one Sister was confirmed and one watched for the first time as a *Candidate*.

THE 7TH   Brother *Schebosch* came here. He had arrived in *Gnadenhütten* yesterday from Bethlehem and Litiz, after accompanying our dear Brother *Grube*. We were delighted and interested to learn, through word of mouth and in writing, of his safe arrival there. The single Brother *Michael Jung*[1542] came with him from Bethlehem to serve the *Mission*. He is staying with Brother *Edwards* in *Gnadenhütten* for now.

Here old *Erdmuth* went to the Savior in blessing. Neither she nor anyone else knew if she was 90 or 100 years old. Her earthly dwelling was buried on THE 8TH. She was baptized in *Fridenshütten* on the *Susquehanna* by Brother *Schmick* on *December 26, 1766* and became a communicant there on *June 6, 1772*, just before the Indian congregation left for the *Ohio*. She moved here to *Gnadenhütten* with the Brothers and Sisters and then went with them to *Lichtenau* in 1778. Once when things looked dangerous, she let her friends talk her into leaving the congregation out of fear. When *Lichtenau* was abandoned in 1779, she came here to *Schönbrunn*, regretted that she had wasted her time like this, and asked to be reaccepted, which was granted to her.[1543] After a while she was also readmitted to Holy Communion, for which she asked urgently. Since this time she appreciated even more what she had in the grace of the congregation and often told how she had spent the brief time she was away from the congregation in pure fear and restlessness. She was happy and thankful that the Savior had shown her mercy again. For a couple of months she could not attend services because she was weak, and she could only crawl now,

---

1542. Franz Michael Jung (1743–1826) had emigrated to America in the year 1751 and had joined the Moravians in Bethlehem in 1767.

1543. Leaving and renewed admission are not specially noted in the diary.

although she did not feel ill. She was old and had lived long enough and often wished the Savior would take her. This took place on the stated day, when she was released from all trouble.

THE 9TH   The old widow *Naemi* then followed her. She was also baptized in *Gnadenhütten* on *August* 18, 1774, by Brother *Schmick* and *admitted* to Holy Communion there on *April* 4, 1776. Last spring she also moved here from *Lichtenau*. She was happy and content, held firmly to the Savior during all the circumstances of recent years that often looked so serious, indeed terrible, and she put her hope in Him. After she came here she was especially blessed and lived in a close relationship with the Savior. Soon after the beginning of her illness, which was brief, she said that she was going home. Whenever anyone visited her, she repeated her desire for this and said she was completely worn out. Nothing else was keeping her in this world; she wanted to go to the Savior. This took place with the blessing of the congregation. Her earthly remains were buried on THE 10TH.

THE 13TH   We brought our dear Lord and Chief Elder our debt of gratitude and honor for his blessed and merciful reign in the *Unitas Fratrum,* to which He elected and called us through grace, and for which he gathered some of the heathen to be His own people.[1544] We prayed for merciful *Absolution* for our many mistakes and shortcomings and also prayed that He would continue forming and shaping us according to his heart and mind until he has completely achieved his purpose for us, so that we might become his complete joy. We also surrendered ourselves to Him anew and promised Him faithfulness and obedience. We could feel Him close to us during all our services, and He allowed us to experience his peace quite joyfully.

THE 15TH   There was the burial of Brother *Timotheus,* who went home in blessing yesterday. When the Indian congregation left the *Barraks* in *Philadelphia*[1545] for *Fridenshütten* in 1765, he came to the congregation right at the start. Brother *David Zeisberger* baptized him there on *March* 30, 1766, and he became a communicant on *April* 16, 1767. In 1772 he went with the Indian congregation from *Fridenshütten* to *Langundouteniünk* and the next spring on to *Schönbrunn,* where he became one of the *National* Helpers. During all the distractions and changes the Indian congregation had to undergo during times of war, he remained steadfast and did not allow himself to become anxious or fearful; he trusted in the Savior to protect His people and to help them through this. He felt sorry for those who let their doubts and fear drive them to seek safety among the savages and thus threw themselves into misfortune, both externally and internally. He led an exemplary life and was loved by his people, and the welfare of the Indian congregation lay upon his heart. He lived in a

1544. On the meaning of commemorating Christ's acceptance of the office of the Elder on 13 November 1727, see Introduction, pp. 62–63.

1545. See entry for 9 May 1774 and note 368.

blessed relationship with the [page 562Aa]¹⁵⁴⁶ Savior. A little more than 2 months ago he starting getting sickly and emaciated, and he finally said he believed his time here below was over; the Savior was going to take him to him and he would be glad to go to him. A few days before his end he told Brother *David*, who was visiting him, that he was waiting eagerly for the Savior to come and take him. He also asked the Brothers to forgive him if he had offended anyone. Then Brother *David* assured him that we had no grudges against him, but loved him sincerely. This was also reported to the Brothers and Sisters in the Meeting Hall. He was especially glad to listen when the Brothers and Sisters sang verses for him, which Brother *David* did many times as well. He always folded his hands during this, as he did when he received the blessing even though he had already lost his ability to speak. Thus he died, and we were happy for him to experience the joy of being at home with the Lord.

THE 16TH   During the early service the baby daughter born to Brother *Ludwig* and Sister *Maria Juliana* on the 11th of this month was baptized into Jesus' death with the name *Elisabeth*. Both Brother *David* and the Helper Brothers spoke with *Israel*, who came here from the *Fort*. They admonished him to abandon his errant ways and turn to the Savior, while there was still time.¹⁵⁴⁷ He took this well and expressed his gratitude that we still honored him with good advice. He said he had not forgotten what he had heard in the congregation, but he also complained to us about his troubles. He had tried to free himself from the *Chiefs*, but they had bound him anew and did not want to let him [page 562Ab]¹⁵⁴⁸ go. We told him if he waited for them to let him go, nothing would ever happen. Otherwise he is friendly and shows love for the Brothers, but he would like to serve God and *mammon* at the same time as we explained to him very directly. On THE 19TH he went to *Goschachgünk* and promised to visit us again.

THE 18TH   All of our Brothers, except for a few who stayed home, went out for the fall hunt until around Christmas. Since they did not have time to hunt last year, we were glad to let them go and admonished them to remain close to the Savior while they are in the bush. We sang the verse that has been translated into the Indian language, As the woodsman might desire to hunt until that day, so I desire to be in the Savior's heart,¹⁵⁴⁹ and we gave them this to take along on their hunt.

THE 21ST   *Joseph* came here from *Goschachgünk*.¹⁵⁵⁰ When external conditions were bad he had acted so badly in *Lichtenau* that he did not receive permission to live in one of our congregations when that town was abandoned

---

1546. Pagination added later.

1547. See entry for 5 Aug. 1779 and note 1442.

1548. Pagination added later.

1549. "Wie sich Waldmann verwünschen mag, jagen zu woll'n bis an jenen Tag; so verwünsche ich mich ins Heilands Herze." We did not locate the source.

1550. For Joseph Peepi, see entries for 27 May, 9 June, and 16 Dec. 1777, and 6 Jan. 1778.

last spring. Now he is asking to be reaccepted. We refused, however, and did not become involved with him.

THE 23RD   Brother and Sister *Sensemann* returned from their visit in *Salem,* where they had gone on the 21st. This journey and change had the desired *Effect* of completely freeing them from their fever.

THE 26TH   The sermon, held at the usual time, dealt with the righteousness revealed to us through Jesus Christ: the forgiveness of sins through faith in him.

Brothers *Samuel* and *Stephanus* returned home from hunting, but the latter was sick.

[December]

DECEMBER 3RD   On the first Sunday of *Advent,* the sermon was about the text from John I, And the Word was made flesh, and dwelt among us etc.[1551] The Brothers and Sisters were moved to rejoice in God our Savior and to be sincerely grateful to Him for taking on flesh and blood for our sake, in order to become a sacrifice for our sins. The Brothers and Sisters were also reminded to be grateful to the Savior for the first baptism on the *Ohio* in *Lawunakhannek* 11 years ago today, when the first Sunday in Advent was also on *December* 3, and about what the Savior has done for the poor heathen since that time through the power of his blood.

Joseph returned here a number of days ago and since then he has asked us unceasingly and with many tears to allow him to live with us again. Out of compassion for him we finally gave him provisional permission to live here as long as he behaves in accordance with the rules proscribed for him.

THE 4TH   *Israel's* son *Anton* also came here. He had left the congregation in *Lichtenau* a year ago and has been wandering around on the *Wobash* among other *Nations.* His restless heart and conscience tortured him everywhere he went until he finally decided to return to the congregation, and now he also was asking to be taken in again.[1552]

THE 8TH   *Colonel Brodhead, Commandant* of *Pittsburgh* sent a letter asking our Indians to go hunting for buffalo and elk, then to salt the meat and take it to the first and nearest *Fort,* and they would then be paid for it.[1553]

DECEMBER 10TH   Brother and Sister *Schebosch* came here from *Gnadenhütten* for a visit. A family from *Salem* did the same yesterday.

Anton spoke with the *Conference* and received permission to live with the congregation again.

1551. John 1:14.
1552. Anton was last mentioned by name in entry for 26 Sept. 1779.
1553. Daniel Brodhead to Zeisberger, 2 Dec. 1780, *FRO,* 300.

THE 12TH   *Elisabeth,* the little daughter of Brother *Ludwig* and Sister *Maria Juliana,* who went home yesterday, was buried.

THE 18TH   Brother *David* and Brother and Sister *Sensemann* went to *Salem* with some Indian Brothers and Sisters. They cut through the bush because the river was too high to go the usual way. Brothers *Edwards* and *Michael Jung* also arrived there, and after we had discussed and agreed upon the necessary things in a *Conference,* we returned home again on THE 19TH.

THE 23RD   After having Speakings with the Brothers and Sisters in recent days, we partook of our Lord's Body and Blood in the Holy *Sacrament* with hungry and thirsty souls. One Sister joined the congregation in partaking for the first time and one Sister watched as a *Confirmande.*

THE 24TH   We began the Christmas Eve service with a Lovefeast, during which we read the story of our Lord's birth.[1554] We rejoiced over his holy incarnation and brought him our childlike *Gratias* for this, and after reflecting upon the Watchword and text for today,[1555] we worshipped Him in his little manger. In conclusion, wax candles were given to the children, who always look forward to Christmas Eve especially. Then they went happily home.

THE 25TH   Brother *Sensemann* preached the sermon in the morning, and in the afternoon there was a blessed service for the baptized Brothers and Sisters in which *Anton* was *absolved* and rejoined the congregation. The Congregational Service was about the text, The first human was of the earth and earthly. The other human is the Lord of heaven.[1556] We concluded with the New Testament benediction.

THE 31ST   During the Watchnight Service at the conclusion of the year, we remembered the grace and kindness the Savior has shown us, his poor and wretched people, during this year, how He revealed Himself to us despite all of our shortcomings, guided and carried us with motherly hands, showed us so much kindness, and blessed us with his priceless and comforting presence. We also confessed to Him our mistakes and failures, as we often did not please his heart and caused Him sorrow. We asked Him for merciful *Absolution* for this, and we then entered into the New Year with comforted hearts.

The following items should also be noted to the glory of the Savior:

This spring at the end of *March* and beginning of *April, Lichtenau* was completely abandoned and a new *Settlement* was begun 6 miles below *Gnadenhütten.* It was named *Salem.*

We cannot adequately thank the Savior for granting us more peace and quiet from elsewhere than in past years, so that our lives were not disturbed in the least.

He truly blessed our Indian Brothers and Sisters and us through the visit

1554. Luke 2:1–20.
1555. Watchword, 1 Pet. 4:14; text, 2 Tim. 1:9–10.
1556. 1 Cor. 15:47.

and *Visitation* of our dear Brother *Grube* from the Unity, and this remains fresh in our memories. Brother and Sister *Sensemann* and the single Sister *Sara Ohneberg* came here with him to be assistants at the *Mission*. On *July* 4th she and Brother *Heckewelder* were joined in holy matrimony by Brother *Grube* in *Salem*, and Brother and Sister *Sensemann* came here as assistants. On this occasion we were also delighted to receive news from the Unity again. The Synod Report provides us with true blessing, instruction, comfort, and encouragement. May the Savior grant us the grace to surrender more and more to the rules and customs of His house.

During Brother *Grube's* stay here we also made new arrangements in the congregation: a Prayer Meeting with the communicant congregation will be held every 14 days, and this is important and a blessing for the Brothers and Sisters.

There will also be congregational days, held every 6 weeks, when news will be shared with the Brothers and Sisters.

The *conferences* of the workers from the 3 sites were also *regulated* and brought into order.

The Savior has maintained us through the Word of his redemption. Our hearts have received nourishment from this daily and He has illuminated it through his Holy Spirit and given us a greater understanding of the Gospel.

The festivals and holidays at Easter, Pentecost, *August* 13 and *November* 13, and Christmas were special days of blessing for us, accompanied by his presence.

With Brother *Schebosch,* who had escorted Brother *Grube* home, the single Brother *Michael Jung* came here from Bethlehem. He will serve the Indian congregation in *Gnadenhütten* with Brother *Edwards.*

This year we had Holy Communion 8 times. In the spring 6 families came from *Lichtenau* to live here and 2 families came from *Gnadenhütten*. 3 families who had gone astray found their way back again.

3 adults were baptized and 5 children.

5 individuals, 3 Brothers and 2 Sisters attained Holy Communion.

2 couples were married.

5 adults went home, 1 Brother and 4 Sisters, and 4 children.

The Indian congregation in *Schönbrunn* currently consists of the following: 24 married couples, 2 widowers, 12 widows, 5 single men and 3 single women, and 6 older boys, 12 older girls, 21 little boys and 34 little girls. Total: 143

One adult and 26 children among them have not been baptized.

January 1781

THE 1ST   Brother *Sensemann* preached the sermon about the Gospel for today. We presented ourselves and the baptized Brothers and Sisters before our dear Lord, commended ourselves anew to Him for grace, and prayed that he would pour out his blessings upon us throughout this year and complete all the plans of peace He has for us in his heart.

We have not received Watchwords and texts yet, so we used the ones from the beginning of last year, and the Congregational Service was about the text, Grace and peace, from God our Father, and from the Lord Jesus Christ, be unto you and all those who pray to the name of our Lord Jesus Christ etc.[1557] During this an older girl was baptized into Jesus' death with the name *Lucia*.

THE 3RD   The Brothers spoke with some strangers who had come here for a visit and explained the way to salvation. *Abraham* closed with the words, Now we have told you how you can be saved. If you accept this, you will experience that what we have told you is the truth. Even if you do not accept it, we have fulfilled our responsibility. You will not be able to say someday that you went to the Believers and they did not tell you what you should do to be saved. We tell this to all Indians who come to our place and show them the way to eternal life so that in the future they cannot accuse us of having neglected to do this.

THE 4TH   Some Brothers and Sisters from *Gnadenhütten* and *Salem* who were here visiting returned home.

THE 6TH   Brother *Sensemann* led the Morning Devotion and asked the dear Savior to give the congregation on this day the blessing earned through his blood, from his abundance.[1558] In the service for those who have been baptized, one Brother and one Sister were *absolved*. During the Lovefeast in the afternoon, the Brothers and Sisters were reminded that the Savior especially entrusted the *Unitas Fratrum* with proclaiming the Gospel among the heathen, who had never heard anything about it. So that we could see that this is good and pleasing to Him, he lets them see the fruits of their efforts and work. He lays his blessing upon this so that thousands who used to be blind heathens and part of Satan's poor regiments have already come to know and believe in the Savior through the preaching of the word of redemption. During the Congregational Service in the evening, 3 people were buried into His death through baptism, an older boy with the name *Levi* and 2 older girls, one with the name *Lea*, the other *Benigna*.

THE 7TH   In a service for the older boys, they were encouraged to follow Jesus when he was a boy, who presented himself to them as a model and example, and to try to be like Him in this world. We knelt and prayed to the Savior to grant them this.

THE 8TH   Brothers *Edwards* and *Schebosch* came from *Gnadenhütten* and Brother *Heckewelder* came from *Salem* with some of his Helpers. We discussed *Gelelemind* with them and the Helpers from here. He has asked once again to come to the congregation. We considered the talk he delivered to the Indian

---

1557. 1 Cor. 1:2–3, Collection of Watchwords for 1780.
1558. On the meaning of 6 January, see Introduction, pp. 62–63.

Brothers in *Salem* and looked at his walk since he has wanted to come to the congregation. He has entangled himself more and more with the world, both with the White people and the Indians, and also with the war, to the point that he himself does not know how to escape this. He wants an answer now, so we agreed to give him the following reply: The affairs of a *Chief* and the word of God were two different kinds of things and did not belong together. We had accepted God's word and were committed to that; we would leave *Chief's Affairs* up to those appropriate and preferred to have nothing to do with them. Therefore if someone wanted to come and live with us, he cannot bring worries and troubles to us in the congregation. Before he could consider coming to us, he must first free himself from everything else. He could not ask us how he could become free of these things either, because if we helped him we would first have to become quite involved in *Chief Affairs,* which would not be fitting for us.[1559]

THE 9TH   Brother *Edwards* led the early service. Afterward we had a *Conference* with the Helpers. Then the Brothers returned to *Gnadenhütten* and *Salem.*[1560]

THE 10TH   Brothers *Connor* and *Willhelm* and some others left for the *Fort.* I used this opportunity to write *Colonel Brodhead* about the *Proposition* he made us in *December* to go hunting for his troops. We told him we could not take on such work and then explained the reasons for this.[1561]

THE 14TH   Brother *David* preached the sermon and then led the devotion in preparation for Holy Communion, and Brother *Sensemann* led the Congregational Service.[1562]

THE 15TH   The early service was about how we must become obedient to God's word. So that we would not have doubts about it being God's pure word, the text for today told us that God's men and the prophets had not spoken of their own accord, but through God's inspiration. After the Savior came into the world, we received this from his own mouth, and He will preserve this for us until the end.[1563]

THE 18TH   The baby son born yesterday to *Zacharias* and *Anna Elisabeth* was baptized into Jesus' death with the name *Jonas.* Unfortunately he went home on the 22nd.

THE 21ST   *Tobias* and some Brothers from *Salem* who had been here visiting for a number of days returned there.[1564]

1559. See the earlier result concerning "Chief-affairs" in entry for 29 May 1777. As a result of this conversation, Gelelemind informed Daniel Brodhead, on 15 Jan. 1781 from Salem, that he had resigned his office as chief and asked Brodhead to assist in electing a new chief from the "Turtle Tribe." *FRO,* 316–17.

1560. From "Afterward" not in H3.

1561. On 21 Jan. 1781, in response to this letter, Daniel Brodhead accepted Zeisberger's arguments. *FRO,* 320–21.

1562. Entire entry for 14 Jan. not in H3.

1563. 1 Cor. 2, 14.

1564. Entire entry for 21 Jan. not in H3.

THE 27TH   Throughout this entire week we had snow and rainy weather, although this winter until now had been beautiful spring weather.

The Brothers gather in their houses almost every evening and hold a Singing Service. They share their hearts, what is happening with them, and what the Savior and the Holy Spirit are doing for them. The Helpers spoke with some of them and made peace where there was discord. This sometimes happens in household matters and in relationships with one another. For the most part, the Helpers are successful in these efforts. However, this takes a lot of time because there is much preaching on such occasions and they can sometimes mediate matters of public concern better than we workers can. They just need to be instructed not to let the reputation of the person influence them.

[February]

FEBRUARY 1.   Our Brothers returned from the *Fort*. They brought us letters from *Litiz* and news from Bethlehem and *Europe*, along with several months of Watchwords for this year.[1565] A White man[1566] from the *Fort* came with them too. We also learned that the *Chiefs* in *Goschachgünk* tried to cast suspicion on our 3 *Towns* by spreading lies in the *Fort* that we were on the side of the hostile Indians.[1567] We heard much about a *Campaign* in Indian country this summer and that we also should expect a visit, although a friendly one.

THE 3RD   During Holy Communion one Sister partook for the first time and two people were readmitted.

THE 4TH   Early in the day was the Liturgy in Preparation for Holy *Communion*. We had to cancel the sermon because of stormy weather and heavy rains, since it had leaked into the Meeting House everywhere. The Brothers repaired this on THE 5TH.

THE 7TH AND 8TH   We received unpleasant news from the Indians in *Goschachgünk* that they were making intense preparations to go to war. It therefore seems like things might turn out badly for the *Delaware*, who have stayed relatively neutral until now.[1568]

THE 9TH   Brother *Samuel* went to *Sandusky* with 3 others. The White

1565. *Die täglichen Loosungen der Brüdergemeine für das Jahr 1781.* As in earlier years these Watchwords were printed in installments and bound after all parts had been finished.

1566. Not identified.

1567. The letter of the Delaware Council to Daniel Brodhead is not preserved; Brodhead mentions the Council's reproaches in a letter to Zeisberger dated 21 Jan. 1781: "As to the mockery of the savages, it is common with them against persons living in a religious way." *FRO*, 320–21.

1568. See "William Penn and the Councellors of Cooshockung" to Daniel Brodhead on 13 Jan. 1781: "I assure You, that I am not afraid of any body, and I tell You now, that I am resolved to get up and Fight. I have considered this matter from my Heart. I am able to Fight any one of my Colour. I am no coward that You know Yourself, and You will find it so for the future." Brodhead responded to the Council of the Delaware on 4 Feb. 1781 that he was glad about their willingness to enter the war. *FRO*, 315–16, 328–29.

man who came here from *Pittsburgh,* and who had been recommended by *Colonel Brodhead,* went with them too. During the war we frequently had to cancel our Singing Services because we did not have enough candles, but we began holding them again. They are very important services to the Brothers and Sisters.

THE 13TH   *Winginund,* a headman of the *Delaware* who was here visiting for many days and heard much about the Savior, returned to *Kinhanschican*[1569] where he lives.

Brother and Sister *Schebosch* brought their daughter *Christiana* here. She was engaged to *Jacob, Rachel's* son, and they were married in the devotional service for married couples on THE 14TH.

THE 16TH   The Brothers and Sisters went out to get ready to boil sugar, and on THE 19TH several families of strangers who wanted to buy cattle came here. From them we heard once again that the *Delaware* everywhere are arming themselves and preparing for war. Others also confirmed this in the following days. We heard that the *Wyandot* talked a lot about the Indian Believers and what a good life they led, and people saw nothing reproachful in them. They said, We have also been baptized, but we cannot see that we are better than other heathens; we are the same as we were before our baptism. This is not the case among the Indian Believers, however. They have become different people through baptism and they no longer live in sin and vice like other heathens. Why is this? They must really know something and have been taught something about which we know nothing; there must be something else that we have not heard. If only we had them closer to us so that we could understand the secret. If they would move closer to us, we would clear an area of land where they could live alone and in peace. *We* are sure that the *Wyandot* are our friends, because they have demonstrated this adequately during this war and their *Half King* has assisted our mission in many ways. However, we must act very reserved toward them because of the war.

THE 25TH   For the beginning of Lent we prayed to the dear Mother to clarify Jesus' sufferings and death and the reason for this in our hearts, and to guide us to reflect constantly on what our redemption cost Him.

[March]

MARCH 1ST   The Brothers returned from *Lower Sandusky,* next to the *Lake,* where they had traded skins with the English *Traders* for clothing and necessities. There they met some of our baptized *Munsee* who were lost. They

1569. See entries for 23 July 1776, with note 804, and for 14 March 1777, with note 930.

spoke with them and admonished them to turn back to their doctor and re-deemer, and some of them promised to visit us soon. They had gone there from *Niagara,* where they stayed with the *Mingo* since their *Towns* had been destroyed,[1570] and they said that all the *Munsee* and other Indians from the *Susquehanna* who had fled there had left and were moving further this way.

THE 5TH   Brother *David* and Brother and Sister *Sensemann* went to *Gnadenhütten,* where we had a *Conference* with the Helpers from the three sites. Together we discussed the Indians in *Goschachgünk;* we learned that they have decided that some of them who were not joining in the war against the White people (because they just cannot) will settle close to *Salem* and they want to force themselves in here at our place, because they do not think they are safe from the White people where they are. They hope if the White people attacked them they would be spared for our sakes. We *resolved* to tell them we do not want to have anything to do with them, and they should leave us in peace and stay where they are, because we do not desire their company. Some of the people from *Goschachgünk* went to *Salem* and some Helpers from the 3 settlements informed them of this. We have to wait to see what the result will be.

We workers considered the circumstances and concerns of our 3 towns and sought the Savior's instruction where it was necessary. Most of us were concerned that Brother *David* would be absent in the current situation, because the external circumstances look so serious and tense. Therefore we found it necessary to learn the Savior's intention in this matter. He instructed us that Brother *David* should begin his trip to the Congregation before Easter in accordance with his call.[1571]

Brother *David* returned home on THE 6TH. Brother and Sister *Sensemann* went down to *Salem* for a visit, and they returned from there on THE 8TH.

THE 10TH   We had Holy Communion, and one Brother watched during this for the first time.

THE 11TH   Brother *Sensemann* held the *Liturgy* in Preparation for Holy Communion and Brother *David* preached the sermon. Then we dismissed the Brothers and Sisters because they had a lot of work in their sugar huts, since the weather was so nice.

THE 13TH   Some Indian strangers came here to buy cattle. They had goods the English *Traders* in *Sandusky* had sent.

THE 14TH   Brother *Edwards* came here on business with Brother *Schebosch* and both returned home on THE 15TH. They brought the news that the residents of *Goschachgünk* are planning to move here after all, against our wishes, and to settle a short distance below *Salem*. If this happens it will cause all sorts of bad consequences.

THE 17TH   2 families moved from here to *Salem: Rachel* and *Johannes,* and *Hanna* and her children.

1570. See entry for 4 Oct. 1779 and note 1447.
1571. Zeisberger had three reasons for traveling to Bethlehem: (1) participation in the synod, (2) clarification of questions relating to the mission, and (3) concern about the security of the mission congregations.

THE 18TH   During the service for those who have been baptized, the Brothers and Sisters were informed after the sermon of Brother *David's* trip. They were also reassured that he would return from there soon. We had a *Conference* with the Helpers, who were admonished to be very vigilant during Brother *David's* absence, not to allow any disorder to slip in, and to report everything promptly to Brother and Sister *Sensemann* so that any problems could be prevented. Because there were not enough servants for the Meeting Hall, Brother *Thomas* and Sister *Sabina* were appointed to this. They accepted this humbly. *Augustine,* a single woman who had left the congregation more than a year ago but was now fervently asking to be taken in again, received provisional permission to live here.

THE 23RD   Brothers *Heckewelder, Edwards,* and *Michael Jung* came here. We held a *Conference* once again and discussed how things should be done in Brother *David's* absence. They returned home on the 24th.

THE 25TH   We thanked the Savior for his holy incarnation, sufferings, and death, through which he achieved so much good that is now ours to enjoy. In the sermon and in the service for those who have been baptized, we could feel his presence as we adored him and he blessed us. The older girls had a separate service for their choir festival today. In closing, we commended them to the Savior for grace in a prayer, asked that He would form them to be his heart's delight and would allow them to grow and prosper completely for Him. Brother *Sensemann* led the Congregational Service about the Watchword, Lo, this is our God; we have waited for him, and He will help us.[1572] He will indeed do this now, though things once again do not look very *favorable* in Indian country.

Some warriors came here. We learned from them that many parties of warriors have gone into the White people's *Settlements.* They were on their way to the *Fort* and said that there are already many of them there, and the road to *Pittsburgh* is thus not very safe. Despite this, Brother *David* decided to go on with his journey there.[1573]

1572. Isa. 25:9.

1573. On 19 April 1781 Zeisberger arrived at Bethlehem; on 21 April the problems relating to the mission congregations were discussed at length in the Provincial Helpers' Conference in Zeisberger's presence. Zeisberger voiced his anxiety and concern on this occasion that the American army would increase its pressure on the mission congregations and that this would make it necessary that he travel to Philadelphia to secure the assurance of Washington and the president of the Continental Congress that the young confederation would be protected; this request was granted by the conference. The protocol clearly indicates that Zeisberger did not expect serious problems from Fort Detroit or the British side in general. The other consultations in May 1781 focused on the question whether it would be possible to increase the number of missionaries in the three mission congregations. The suggestion was approved, and it was resolved to dispatch once more the Jungmanns and that Zeisberger should be married. Zeisberger was married to Susanne Lecron of Lititz on 4 June 1781 (MAB, Protocoll der Provincial Helfer Conferenz, 1774–82, fols. 267–90). After the synod adjourned, Zeisberger traveled to Philadelphia, where he discussed the issue of the security of the mission congregations with Joseph Reed, president of the Supreme Executive Council of Pennsylvania, among others. Schweinitz, *Zeisberger,* 480–82.

APPENDIX

DOCUMENT NO. I

PROTOCOL OF THE CONFERENCE AT LANGUNDO-UTENÜNK ON 12 AUGUST 1772[1]

Present: Johannes Ettwein, David Zeisberger, Brother and Sister Jungmann, and Brother and Sister Roth

1st Since Brother David Zeisberger has come to us from the Muskingum in order to discuss with us when the Indian congregation would continue its journey and related issues, and because the Brethren who have arrived want to know soon where they will be staying in the winter, it is necessary that we agree about the Holy Communion, the journey to Gekelemukpechünk, the affairs at this place, and other issues.

2nd Although not yet all members of the Holy Communion congregation have arrived, it is impossible to put off the next Holy Communion beyond next Saturday. We will therefore begin talking to the sisters and brothers tomorrow. Brother Ettwein and Sister and Brother Jungmann will do this.

3rd Brother Ettwein, David, and John Heckewelder will journey next week from here to the new place with as many of the Indian brethren as want to accompany them. From there they will continue to Gekelemukpechünk with five or six Brethren in order to salute the Chief there and have talks with him. The Brethren Johannes, Nathanael, Wilhelm, Josua, Cornelius, Joseph, and Anton have been proposed to accompany them.

4th Because of the many drunk people in the neighborhood, the Indian Brethren are tired and want to leave this place; therefore the Brethren assumed that this place would be totally given up. Yet because some people from these regions still come to us in order to listen to the sermons, and because it would

1. MAB B 315, F 2, I 4

complicate matters if we all move together to the new site, in particular because all the land there has yet to be cleared, it would probably be better that some stay here a little bit longer. We would have to accept it if none of the Indian Brethren want to stay here. Yet we want to be told by our dear Lord what we will have to consider in relation to this issue. We therefore prepared three * [the asterisk is the Moravian symbol for "lot"].

    a. The Savior approves that we intend to leave this place next spring.

    b. The Savior does not approve.

    c. *————[empty lot]

The lot drawn showed that the Savior does not approve that we totally give up this place next spring.

5th By sending messages and belts to the Chiefs in the name of the Mahicans, Old Josua has started separate negotiations; on our journey we have noted, too, that the old differences between the Mahicans and the Delaware still exist. For the Mahicans at least, Josua confirms this. At Bethlehem we already were of the opinion that an opportunity might arise to settle the two [tribes] in two different towns. We therefore decided to ask the Savior whether we should pursue this thought any further:

    a. The Savior approves that we now plan to settle the Mahicans and the Delaware in separate places.

    b. The Savior does not approve.

    c. *————

The latter was pulled.

We will have to see how things develop.

6th Concerning the name of the new town, we thought of Bethel, Enon, Gosen, and Welik Tuppeek or good lovely spring. We prepared lots for all, including one empty one. We pulled the lot for Welik Tuppeek.

7th Because we have to care for two different places, circumstances demand that Brother and Sister Jungmann and Heckewelder go with David to Welik Tuppeek, while Brother and Sister Roth will stay here in Langunto-Utenünk; the latter would have preferred that we draw the lot about this, yet we were unable to do so.

AUGUST 15 ABOUT THE HOLY COMMUNION

Brother Ettwein, Brother and Sister Jungmann talked to the married couples, David, Ettwein, and Jungmann talked to the single Brethren and the Sisters Jungmann and Roth to the single Sisters.

All desire the Holy Communion.

Salomo's daughter Maria Elisabeth, a widow, will participate for the first time.

Whether Anna Salome, the wife of Nathanael, will become a candidate? Denied by the *
Whether the blind Pommachgute is to be baptized tomorrow? Denied by the *!
Whether his Brother can be baptized? Empty *
Whether Michael's son? Empty *
Whether the Jannetgen be accepted into the congregation? Approved by the *!

AUGUST 17TH

Present: the above mentioned

1st Brother David Zeisberger is the Helper or Oeconomus[2] of the Indian affairs in this area and as such must also often visit Landunto-Utenünk from Welik Tuppeek. Sister and Brother Jungmann are his closest assistants, wherever they are; next are Sister and Brother Roth. These five sisters and brothers constitute for the time being the conference.

2nd Brother Heckewelder is here in order to learn the language; he is to assist wherever needed. Yet one has to be mindful that he does not become stupid and tired; occasionally he should therefore be asked to direct a religious meeting. He can, however, not sing. In Welik Tuppeek he will be responsible for the boys' school.

3rd The following is expected from the brothers: Always to send two copies of their diaries to Bethlehem, of which one is to be written on sturdy paper to be sent to Europe. The brothers objected. They pointed out that they would be unable to produce such copies and that frequently sending large packages would be dangerous.

4th The congregation news that is to be copied for this place is to be read first by those where it arrives, then handed on to the others, and after that Brother David is to collect it and put it into the archive, for which he will be responsible as well as for

5th the congregation's registers and that all baptisms, admissions into the congregation, etc., are tidily noted in the registers; that these things are only noted in the diary or jotted down on little octavo pieces of paper is not good. Brother Ettwein will get a book and will note in it what has thitherto been done by the Brethren in the Ohio region. Brother David will then continue it.

6th Since we do not know what Josua intends to do with his Mahicans, we are unable to resolve anything concerning them. On the one hand we hear

2. Responsible for the worldly affairs.

that they want to go directly from Sakunk to Gekelemukpechünk; then we hear again that they intend to come to this place. If Josua comes and inquires after Ettwein and David are gone, one will tell him that one would have liked to see him because we heard much from him; the Brothers do not object, indeed would like it if his Mahicans and some Delawares would start a separate settlement. In such a case they would be served with the gospel as frequently as possible until Sister and Brother Schmick or another missionary couple arrive.

7th Brothers Jungmann and Roth will draw up a new inventory of all things that belong to the mission deaconry. When the things were sold at Friedenshütten much was left behind; therefore it is necessary to compose a new inventory. Whatever Brother Roth needs here he will keep; all the other things will be brought to the Muskingum.

8th It is not good that the one or other keeps horses or cattle on his own account; everything that a Brother acquires is joint property of the mission deaconry, yet when something is sold, his will be returned to him; everything else that is acquired by raising cattle will be the property of the Mission to be used for the purchase of, for example, salt, flour, coffee, tea, etc.

9th To send supplies from Bethlehem will now be even more costly; the Mission Deaconry has large expenses that exceed its income; frugality is therefore recommended to all Mission congregations. However, that does not mean that anyone should neglect his health or his bodily needs, for that would profit neither the Savior nor the brethren. Brother David's way of living during the summer is not to be approved; he should be more concerned about his bodily needs.

In spring the sisters and brothers will jointly inform Bethlehem of their needs and what is to be sent to them from hence; they should then have it by autumn. Once the Indian brethren and sisters are settled again, one will have to find out whether they cannot jointly procure and meet the expenses for the wine for the Holy Communion.

10th In Welik Tuppeek the two Brothers Johannes and Nathanael will be appointed to the office of the warden; wardens here are Anton and Abraham. These four brothers together with Salomon, Josua, Cornelius, and Shebosch will form the Board of Overseers for both places. Together with Joachim, Jo Pepi, Samuel Moor, Wilhelm, Jacob, Petrus, Jeremias, Nicodemus, John Martin, Isaac, Lucas, and the Sisters Christiana, Anna Johanna, Johanna, Esther, Lucia and Anna Caritas, they will be the Helpers' Conference for both places.

11th We want to use more words in the Indian language such as "amen, hallelujah, lamb, agape," and we want to define rules for writing these words in order to avoid using too many K's and write them in a more uniform style. [Baptism, baptism, Lord Supper inserted later by Zeisberger]

No verse is to be introduced without being first reviewed and revised by those Brethren responsible for this, that is, David, Roth, Anton, Nathanael, Jo Pepi, Samuel, Wilhelm, Shebosh, Abraham, Johannes, and the other white Brethren present.

DOCUMENT NO. 2

CONFERENCE HELD AT SCHÖNBRUNN ON 19 AUGUST 1773.[3]

Present: David, Sisters and Brothers Schmick, Jungmann, and Roth.

First a letter from the Provincial Helpers' Conference at Bethlehem addressed to the conference was read, which instructs us that Sister and Brother Schmick are to be sent to serve the little congregation at Gnadenhütten and Sister and Brother Roth are to work here at Schönbrunn. The former we will as far as possible gladly provide with all things necessary.

Brother Jungmann Jr., who arrived with the others and who is destined to live with the Schmicks at Gnadenhütten, will stay here until a living place has been found for him, which will not take long.

Since we are now to work at two distinct towns in the Indian country, it is good and necessary that we follow certain rules and serve the Lord among the Indians with one mind. This requires that we agree what course we will pursue in certain matters.

1st With respect to the chiefs we have to be very circumspect not to give them any occasion to become prejudiced or suspicious against us.

Whenever people behave so badly that we have to banish them from the towns—which happens often to those whom we accept on trial for a time and who cause trouble after they have lived with us for a while—it is best to have the Board of Overseers or, if they are too few, members of the Helpers' Conference talk to them and send them away. If they have friends in the congregation it will be best to involve them, too, because they can contribute much good if they are with us and agree with us. Thus it will be possible to shield us from suspicion or be viewed by the Indians as if we wanted to rule over the people. In the same way we will deal with Indians who desire to live with us; they too will be talked to by the Conference sisters and brothers who will read to them the Statutes[4] or who will inform them orally what kind of behavior is expected of them.

---

3. MAB B 229, F 4, I 9.
4. See Document No. 3 below.

2nd   These conference brothers and sisters will do nothing on their own, they will receive their instructions from us, they will receive the information and materials from us, and we will even suggest the words they are to use and how they are to treat a particular problem.

3rd   As yet we have no example where we had to send away a baptized member of the congregation and we hope that it may never happen. Yet should it be necessary we have to be especially careful with married couples, whom we want to treat with more leniency and for many reasons apply the rules less strictly than to unmarried members.

4th   We have to be careful not to lose our independence by yielding to them out of kindness and thus become servants of them with respect to who directs the congregational affairs and determines the cause of our Lord. If we once start to yield in a particular point they will not stop until they have subjugated us and thus do to us what they want. We want to deal with them honestly and openly and stick to what we initially declared to the chiefs that we are willing to contribute to the success of good things, but as far as war or heathenish things are concerned we want to have nothing to do with those. We have done so, for example, in the affair with the Cherokee who had come to negotiate a peace to which we contributed wampum, or, for example, the affair of the poison, with which we refused to have anything to do and hope that in future we will not have anything else to do with it.

5th   It is possible that our Indian brothers and sisters out of good intentions will want to please the chiefs. This happened at Gnadenhütten, where they live closer to them. They had the idea of cutting firewood for the chief in Gekelemukpechünk. The first time they would do this for the chief as a favor without being asked; another time it would be asked of them and gradually this would be considered a service due from them. This would grow; they soon would be expected to plant for him or build houses, which indeed has already been asked of them, and if it would suit in one but not in another place it would cause bad feelings. Therefore it is better that we refrain from doing such favors, for which in the end our Indian brothers and sisters would only suffer. It is written: Do not become other men's servants.

6th   If we have anything to say to the Chiefs or to negotiate with them, it has to be done with the consent of both towns. No town should act only for itself. Similarly, messages from the Chiefs should be dealt with jointly by both towns.

7th   With respect to the religious meetings and affairs and related customs, we want to stick as much as possible to the same rules in both places. Normally during the week there will be an early morning religious meeting where we will speak about the text of the day, and in the evening we will have the singing hour. If the text requires it, it will occasionally be possible to continue the discussion in the evening. As far as time and circumstances permit, but especially during the winter, lectures from the Bible should be read once or twice per week so that our Indian sisters and brothers will become acquainted with the Bible and thus grow in knowledge.

On Sunday morning there will be a sermon, in the afternoon the children's hour, devotions for the baptized and the married couples alternatively, and in the evenings congregational hours. Before the sermon we will pray the Lord's Prayer in the Delaware language—but sometimes this can be dropped in order to avoid boredom. We have not yet introduced the liturgy because its revision is not yet completed.

8th Whoever has sinned in public and regains his grace will be absolved publicly before the whole congregation. Yet we will not make it a rule that everyone has to apologize publicly. Yet if any brother or sister desires it, we will allow it.

9th We will not introduce anything new but will follow as much as possible the customs and usages of the congregation {i.e., at Bethlehem}.

10th For the baptism of children, thus far godparents have not yet been introduced; in this instance, too, we will not introduce alterations but continue the current practice.

11th We will continue to celebrate the choir festivals; they are always blessed days for the brothers and sisters with their morning blessings, their lovefeasts, their choir devotions, and their prayers.

12th Owing to a shortage of wine we celebrated the Holy Communion for a while only every eight weeks; yet this is too long a time span and we noted that the sisters and brothers missed it. Therefore, since we have received wine from Bethlehem, we will celebrate the Holy Communion, as formerly, every six weeks, for we congregational brothers and sisters suffer too.

13th It is not possible to keep our people from going out to hunt. For this is their only chance to acquire the means for purchasing clothing and what else they need. On the other hand it is not good for them to be out too long on a hunt. Their heart suffers. We cannot really lament this; indeed it would be better if some would be more diligent hunters and thus avoid becoming so poor. In this case too we have to keep the best for our people in mind. If someone has been baptized only recently it certainly is not good for him to go out on extended hunting trips.

14th Why is it that once couples are married, the wives start to criticize their husbands and demand things from them they before would never have dreamed of, as for example that they demand that they work on their plantations and elsewhere, work that originally was the wives' concerns. And if the men do not live up to their wives' expectations, quarrel and disunity between the partners result. This is continued right down to the Holy Communion, by which they want to turn their husbands into servants. Of course this is not generally the case, but it happens often enough and it is then our duty constantly to arbitrate between them. This is not a problem nature has given them. Among savages these are not causes for altercation and fighting. The women know what their duties are and what it behooves them to do; it never comes to their mind to expect these things from their husbands. It is good and we like to see husbands helping their wives; indeed, if necessary we admonish them to do so. The sisters, however, should not push things too far and we therefore will have to let them know that they have no right to demand it from their husbands.

15th We have to take care that our young people, both baptized as well as unbaptized, get married as soon as they are ready for marriage and as soon as we note that it is necessary for them to marry. We must then talk to their parents and tell them that getting their young ones married is part of their duty, which indeed we have done so repeatedly in public. This has to be done in order to shield the parents from confusion and prevent children from having to go into the world or get involved in bad things, which would result in their getting sent out of the congregation.

16th We will not concern ourselves with marriages of unbaptized people; neither will we marry them. But if this problem arises to relation to children of baptized parents, we are willing to assist as far as we can, yet let friends and the sisters and brothers concerned settle the affair to ensure that the two come together in an orderly fashion. Our sisters and brothers are, however, to do nothing in these affairs without our prior knowledge and consent.

17th We will pay strict regard that baptized and unbaptized will not marry each other; yet we cannot be too strict in this, but if we can avoid it we will do so.

18th We cannot tolerate that our sisters' and brothers' daughters and friends, who befriend men outside the congregation, come back to the congregation when pregnant or after having given birth to children, and live here until they decide to leave their children in the congregation. And if they do not leave soon, they start making mischief.

19th If Indian men who have two wives come to us and ask whether they can live with us, they must leave one of their two wives first. For there is none among us who has two wives. Others could think that if he has two women, why not me?

20th When a woman leaves her husband and goes out into the world, the reason most commonly is that she wants to be a whore and becomes a whore. In such a case the man is not bound to remain single if he does not want to. There is no reason why he should be ruined because of her doings. Such a thing happened this summer at Gnadenhütten, when Anna Johanna left her husband and has now taken a savage.

21st As far as the poison story and similar things are concerned, we must be on our guard and prevent anything from coming into our congregations in order to ensure that this whole affair becomes totally extinct. As we have hitherto done, we will continue to try to ridicule these things as fables and demonstrate on all occasions that there is nothing to the whole affair.

DOCUMENT NO. 3

"STATUTES & RULES AGREED UPON BY THE CHRISTIAN INDIANS AT LANGUNDO UTENÜNK AND WELHIK TUPPEK, AUGUST 1772"[5]

1st We will know of no other God and pray to no other but him who has made us and all creatures and who came into this World to Save us poor Sinners.

2nd We will rest from all Labour on Sunday and attend the usual meetings.

3rd We will honor father and mother and do for them what we can, if they grow old and needy.

4th Nobody shall get leave to dwell with us, without the Consent of our Teachers, when they have been examined by the Helpers.

5th With Thiefs, murderers, whoremongers & adulterers and Drunkards, we will have nothing to do[6] till they repent of their bad ways.

---

5. MAB, Ettwein MSS, Item 1634; the text, except the additions marked as such, is in Ettwein's handwriting. These statutes were agreed upon at the conference on 17 August 1772; cf. Document No. 1 above and diary entry for 9 Aug. 1772.
6. From here to end of sentence added later.

6th We will not go to any Dances, offerings or heathenish festivals, or sinful plays.

7th We will use no tshapiet, or witchcraft, in hunting.

8th We will renounce and abhor all Jugles, cheats, lies, and deceits of Satan.

9th We will be obedient to our Teachers and the helpers who are appointed to keep good order in our meetings, the Town and in the fields.

10th We will not be idle & lazy; we will not scold or beat anybody. We will not tell lies.

11th Whosoever does hurt anybody's goods shall make the Damage good.

12th A man shall have only one Wife, and shall love her & care for her and his children.
A Woman shall have only one husband, and be obedient unto him, she shall take good care of the Children, and shall be cleanly in all things.

13th We will not admit any rum or strong liquor into our Towns; If Strangers or Traders bring any, the helpers shall get it from them, and not deliver it until they get from the place.

14th None of the Inhabitants shall run into debt to Traders. None shall receive any goods to sell for Traders without the consent of the helpers.

15th If any one will go a hunting or on a journey they shall inform the minister or the Stewards of it.

16th Young people shall not marry without the consent of their parents and the ministers.

17th If the Stewards or Helpers appoint a time to make fences or some other work, we will all assist and do as we are bid.

18th We will freely contribute when Corn or sugar is gathered for Lovefeasts or to entertain Strangers.
[7]Not to go to War, nor to buy any thing being of Warriors supposed to have been taken at War.

---

7. Later addition in another hand.

DOCUMENT NO. 4

CALENDAR OF FESTIVALS OF THE MORAVIAN BRETHREN[8]

Festivals

1 January	The New Year; festival of circumcision and of name of Jesus.
6 January	Day commemorating the appearance of the three heathen kings {who were the first heathens to adore Christ} Epiphanias.
2 February	Presentation of Jesus in the Temple [If appropriate] Beginning of Passiontide

25 March	Festival of the incarnation of Christ
	[If appropriate] Beginning of Passion Week
	      Maundy Thursday
	      Good Friday
	      Easter Sabbath
	      Easter
	      Ascension of Christ
	      Whitsunday
	      Festival of the Holy Trinity

24 June	Day commemorating John the Baptist
2 July	Visitation of Mary
29 Sept.	Festival of Angels
End November	Advent
24 December	Night Christ was born
25 December	Christmas

Days of Commemoration

19 January 1733	Beginning of Mission among the Heathen in Greenland
1 March 1456	Beginning of Church of Moravian Brethren
3 May 1728	Beginning of Watchwords at Herrnhut
12 May 1724	Foundation of first prayer hall of Herrnhut congregation
1727	Consent to the first statutes of the Herrnhut congregation
1749	British Parliament passes act that officially recognizes the Moravian Church and grants dispensation from military service and the right of affirmation
17 June 1722	Beginning of Herrnhut Congregation

8. Based on the appendices to the Collections of Watchwords for the years 1772 to 1781.

25 June 1530	Confession of Augsburg officially handed to the emperor
6 July 1415	"Johann Hus sealed the testimony of the Holy Gospel to his martyr's death"
13 August 1727	In receiving Holy Communion in the church at Berthelsdorf the congregation at Herrnhut experienced a special dispensation of grace
21 August 1732	First mission among the heathen among the Negroes on the Island of St. Thomas [Day of departure of first missionary to St. Thomas]
27 August 1727	Beginning of Horary Prayer
16 Sept. 1741	Disciples' Day [The synod of the Moravian Church at London decided by lot that Jesus Christ himself as Elder accepted the direction of the church; day to commemorate the servants of the church]
31 Oct. 1517	Beginning of Luther's Reformation
13 November 1741	Blessed experience of Jesus as the Elder of the Church of the Brethren [The decision by lot of 16 Sept. 1741 was communicated to the congregation on this day]

Choir Festivals

25 March	Festival for all choirs together
24 June	Festival for choir of small boys
17 August	Festival for choir of girls
10 Sept. 1772	Festival for choir of all children
28 Sept. 1775	Festival for choir of all children
28 Sept. 1776	Festival for choir of all children
12 January 1772	Festival for choir of big boys
10 January 1773	Festival for choir of big boys
8 January 1775	Festival for choir of big boys
7 January 1776	Festival for choir of big boys
12 January 1777	Festival for choir of big boys
11 January 1778	Festival for choir of big boys
10 January 1779	Festival for choir of big boys
9 January 1780	Festival for choir of big boys
7 January 1781	Festival for choir of big boys
25 March	Festival for choir of big girls
24 August	Festival for choir of big girls
29 August	Festival for choir of single brethren
24 May	Festival for choir of single brethren
4 May	Festival for choir of single sisters
11 Sept.	Festival for choir of single sisters

7, 8, 9 Sept.	Festival for choir of married couples
8 May	Festival for choir of married couples
2 February	Festival for choir of widows and widowers
31 August	Festival for choir of widows and widowers
12 Sept.	Festival for choir of widows
26 April 1772	Festival of the choir of baptized adults who had been admitted into the congregation
18 April 1773	Festival of the choir of baptized adults who had been admitted into the congregation
23 April 1775	Festival of the choir of baptized adults who had been admitted into the congregation
14 April 1776	Festival of the choir of baptized adults who had been admitted into the congregation
6 April 1777	Festival of the choir of baptized adults who had been admitted into the congregation
26 April 1778	Festival of the choir of baptized adults who had been admitted into the congregation
11 April 1779	Festival of the choir of baptized adults who had been admitted into the congregation
2 April 1780	Festival of the choir of baptized adults who had been admitted into the congregation
22 April 1781	Festival of the choir of baptized adults who had been admitted into the congregation
3 May 1772	Festival of the choir of those allowed to participate in Holy Communion for the first time
25 April 1773	Festival of the choir of those allowed to participate in Holy Communion for the first time
30 April 1775	Festival of the choir of those allowed to participate in Holy Communion for the first time
21 April 1776	Festival of the choir of those allowed to participate in Holy Communion for the first time
13 April 1777	Festival of the choir of those allowed to participate in Holy Communion for the first time
3 May 1778	Festival of the choir of those allowed to participate in Holy Communion for the first time
18 April 1779	Festival of the choir of those allowed to participate in Holy Communion for the first time
9 April 1780	Festival of the choir of those allowed to participate in Holy Communion for the first time
29 April 1781	Festival of the choir of those allowed to participate in Holy Communion for the first time

DOCUMENT NO. 5

PROTOCOL OF THE CONFERENCE AT DETROIT, 1781[9]

INDIAN COUNCIL

In Council at Detroit Nov. 9, 1781

Present

Major At. S. De Peyster, Commandant

Messrs. D. Baby and P. Druillard, Interpreters

Capt'n Pipe & Winginam, Delaware chiefs to a number of warriors from the Shawanese Country.

Capt'n Pipe speaks

Father! As soon as Mr. [Matthew] Elliot had returned to the Shawanese Touns having executed your orders, in bringing away the Moravians the same was immediately communicated to you through Capt'n McKee, since which you have directed that they should be brought to you. In obedience thereto we have taken them by the hand and are come here to hear what you have to say. for my part I am happy that they are here with us and as they are our friends I hope you will speak nothing but what is good to them.—

He then speaks on 14 scalps.

Father! You may recollect that eighteen years are now elaps'd since Sir William Johnson call'd a council of us Delawares. He then assured us that the English would never deceive us, but I find that they do.

On presenting the scalps he says—

Father! These were all your friends as well as mine, but as they used us ill we put our hands on their throats and chocked them. You recommended to us brown skins to do your will we have done so, and we now expect that you will take care of all our people by providing for our men, women and children to cloathing and other necessaries for the winter. do not say you have not any because we know your store abounds to plenty and we hope you will give us in profusion.

Father! When your vessel came to the Miamis River I sent you some fresh meat (Prisoners), as I apprehended you would have said it was your flesh and would ask them from me. I therefore would not subject myself to that and sent them before me—

. . . .

Major De Peyster then said to Capt'n Pipe,

After having listened to what you had to say, I must now desire you and your people will pay attention to what I shall say—ever since I have presided amongst you it has been the universal Complaint of the Warriors who came into me "that the Moravian Teachers had always apprized the Enemy of our

Manouvers" by which means they were always frustrated, after repeated Informations of this nature I sent strings of Wampum to the Moravian Indians inviting them to come in to me, as I was desirous to speak to them, but they never came—I then sent Indian officers to Indians to desire them to come in, but no sooner had my Indian Children rec'd my orders, than they executed them, in bringing them and their Teachers in by force, before they had yet my Speeches, now as we are together and the Moravian Teachers before us, I request of you to inform me whether or not the report I have received respecting them be true and when I have your reply to this, I shall then speak further—

Capt'n Pipe then said—

Father! Tis very true what you have said, and as the Moravian Teachers are here present to us, we must take care that they send no more intelligence to the Enemy—You say, true, these people did write letters for the Kooshacking Delawares who were once my people but not at Fort Pitt—

Major De Peyster then put the following Interrogatories to the Moravian Teachers who replyed as under.

Q. How many are there of your mission?

A. Six.

Q. Where are you from?

A. Bethleheme in Pennsylvania and two sent to each Town—

Q. By what authority do you act?

A. By that of our Bishops at Bethleheme.

Q. How long have you been in the Indian Country?

A. I have been on the Muskingum River since 1768 and many followed me.

Q. By what did you pass?

A. By permission of Congress.

Q. I suppose you must have rec'd instructions from the Congress.

A. Not any of us—

Q. What correspondence could you have carried on with the Enemy, which I have been informed by my Interpreters that you have practised from time to time.

A. Being obliged to draw near to the Kooshaking Indians we were often importuned by them to write to Fort Pitt and after two years residence with them we found they were rather troublesome which obliged us to quit their Towns and retreat to our former villages as we had long declined writing for them, we drew their resentment upon us, since when we have never wrote any.

Q. How many Indians are there who belong to your Mission?

A. Including Men, Women and Children 350.

Q. Have they ever joined in the War?

A. Not any.

Q. Where are the Kooshacking Indians?

A. Dispersed every where, as they have deserted their villages.

Major De Peyster then spoke to Capt'n Pipe.

I wish to be informed whether the Christian Indians are desirous that their teachers remain amongst them?

Capt'n Pipe replies.

Father! I can say nothing in answer to your question where the Christian Indians mean to place them, but I imagine it will rest intirely with you and if you have no objection we shall be glad to have them with us to instruct our people—

Major De Peyster then said—

Children the Delawares

Since it is your desire that the teachers remain with you, I agree to it, until the General in Chief's pleasure be known—My design in having them brought in was to learn whether or not they had been meddling to Public Matters, for if they had I should have withheld them, but since I find they were compel'd to do what they did I admit of their going back with your people, provided they behave themselves as good Subjects—

[The Moravian Teachers say they never rec'd any speeches from the Commandant of Detroit, or else would have made an answer.]

Indian Council.

In Council, Detroit 8th December 1781

Present
Major At. S. De Peyster, Commandant
D. Baby
J. Chesne   Sworn Interpreters
W. Tucker

Buckagihitas with his band of 240 Delaware warriors, 70 women, and 90 children.

Buckagihitas Speaks on 16 scalps
[Reports on his deeds against the enemy and requests provisions for his band]

Major De Peyster then said
[Thanks Buckagihitas for his deeds and promises goods]

In Council Detroit 11th December, 81

Maj'r A. S. De Peyster Commandant, and the Gentlemen who composed the Council on the 10th.

Buckagihitas Delaware Chief speaks on a War belt and sings the war song—

Brethren! I salute you all and pray you will listen to what I am going to say to our father, I could wish that our uncles the Hurons were present, that they might see this War Belt which they introduced amongst us Delawares and we were the first of our Nation who readily accepted it from their hands, after the Kooshacking Indians had refused it. It's sufficiently notorious that we have made use of our father's ax ag'st the Enemy for these five years past as may appear by the blood we have made fly throughout the Frontiers and we now find that it has made in part this as dull which has obliged us to come in to our father who alone is able to sharpen it for us, by supplying us all with Rifles and other Implements of War to enable us to continue the war.

Father! This War Belt is not only for war but serves amongst us brown skins as a token of alliance and amity—

Major De Peyster then said
[Thanks the Delaware for speech and for efforts against common Enemy]
Buckagihitas Speaks, after each Warrior had sung the war song.

Father! You see with how much alacrity we have hastened to sharpen your ax and its my duty to recommend to you to provide for my people good Rifles which may kill at a distance, otherwise the Enemy would have the advantage over us, as they are well armed—we want good Kettles, Tomhawks, and other necessaries for warriors—the Tomhawks we received formerly were of no use as they would brake to pieces not only on the heads of the Enemy but on the Smallest branch in the woods, I therefore pray you will order us good strong Tomhawks.

Major de Peyster then said.
[Promises goods; regrets bad quality of tomahawks but does not have others, announces restrictions on alcohol "because you drink to excess"]

Buckagihitas says
Father! I have one thing more to mention to you which is the surprize that my people and myself are in at your allowing the Moravians to return after having them brought in to you, for we know them to be our Enemies who try to do us all the injury they can. I therefore most earnestly request of you in behalf of myself and people that you send for them and keep them close—

Major De Peyster then said
Children! As soon as I had heard that the Moravian Teachers and their adherents had arrived at Saindooskey and that the Hurons had given them a spot of land in order to have them under their Eye, I immediately sent a belt to Captain McKee desiring him to send them in as I wanted to examine them. He informed me that Captain Pipe and Buckagihitas were bringing them in but sometime after Captain Pipe arrived with them. He told me that Buckagihitas could not come in with him. I examined the Moravians in his presence and

could find no harm ag't them. He told me as they were with us they could do no injury to the cause. he desired I would allow them to go back to take care of their families who were starving in the woods, on which I consented to their returning to Saindooskey on their behaving as good subjects until I heard the General's pleasure. If any one had appeared to accuse them, they should have been secured—Since I find you are against their being at liberty as you know them for Enemies I shall order them in here early in the Spring and send them to the General to be dealt with as he may please to direct."

REGISTER OF PERSONS

Explanation of symbols

b.	born
bap.	baptized
m.	married
d.	died
bur.	buried
(B)	in the diary the date of death is accompanied by a short biographical note
F#	number under which the person can be identified in the so-called Fliegel Index. Where the Fliegel Index does not list a number, we have written F# —.

Note: If the date of marriage is known it is given. If no date is given, then the partners lived together before their baptism.

The entry "no children" means that we could not find any children in the register of baptism or in the other registers of the congregation.

The place of baptism is given only if the baptism occurred during the period covered by Zeisberger's diary. Dates of baptisms and marriages occasionally differ between the diary and the registers. In such cases we usually opted for the date given in the diary. Dates given without additions are from the Fliegel Index.

Children born after 1781 or otherwise mentioned in the Fliegel Index do not receive a separate entry in this register. For the period after 1782, all other persons are identified only by their date of death.

MEMBERS OF THE MISSION CONGREGATION

Aaron, alias Tachenos, bap. 4 Oct. 1772 in Langundoutenünk; m. Henriette (bap. 25 Dec. 1772); child: Anna Maria (b. 29 Aug. 1772, bur. 8 Sept. 1772, F# 717); d. before 1798 (F# 721).

Abel, bap. 7 April 1776 in Schönbrunn, son of Magdalene; readmitted 1 May 1779; m.4 June 1780 to Johanette (bap. 12 April 1772); child: Jonas (b. 4 Sept. 1781); d. 8 March 1782 (F# 838).

Abigail, bap. 31 Aug. 1766, daughter of Abraham, alias Sakima (bap. 25 Dec. 1765) and Salome (bap. 20 Oct. 1765); m. Petrus, alias Sapan (bap. 25 Dec. 1766); children: Beata (bap.

1766), Abraham (bap. 1769), Anna Salome (b. 6 Nov. 1771): family refused admission to Gnadenhütten on 7 Sept. 1774 and expelled from the congregation of Schönbrunn on 4 Oct. 1774; readmitted 13 Nov. 1796; d. 1804 outside the congregation; Munsee (F# 556).

Abigail, bap. 7 Feb. 1772, daughter of Willhelm, alias Bill Chelloway (bap. 6 Jan. 1771) and Martha (bap. 19 May 1771); d. 27 June 1773 (F# 705).

Abraham, bap. 21 Aug. 1749 in Gnadenhütten I, son of Jonathan and Anna; m. 1 June 1779 to Anna Paulina (bap. 7 June 1772); d. 8 March 1782; Mahican (F# 212).

Abraham, alias Sakima, bap. 25 Dec. 1765 in Wyalusing; m. Salome (bap. 20 Oct. 1765); child of this marriage: Abigail (bap. 31 Aug. 1766); m. 16 Jan. 1774 to Anna (bap. 6 Jan. 1771); widowed; m. 15 Feb. 1784 to Martha (bap. 10 Aug. 1766); d. 3 Nov. 1791; Munsee (F# 543); National Helper, preacher, and frequent messenger.

Adam, bap. 1 Jan. 1776 as son of Charlotte (bap. 1 Jan. 1776) in Gnadenhütten II (F# 814).

Adam, alias Scheechganìm, bap. 1 Jan. 1776 as son of Jephta, alias Queelpacheno (bap. 6 Jan. 1774) and Zipora (bap. 12 April 1772) in Schönbrunn; m. Dorothea (bap. 1 Jan. 1776); m. 29 Oct. 1777 to Sabina (bap. 26 May 1776); children: Elisabeth (b. 5 May 1779), Augustus (1786), Wilhelmina (bap. 9 Aug. 1791, F# 1512), Adolph (1794), Charles (bap. 5 Dec. 1798, bur. 8 Dec. 1798, F# 1571), Gottfried (1802), d. before 11 Jan. 1814 (F# 808).

Adam, alias Wulalowechen, bap. 2 Jan. 1780 in Lichtenau; m. 28 March 1780 to Cornelia (bap. 28 May 1775); child: Anna Elisabeth (b. 22 April 1781); d. 8 March 1782 (F# 879).

Adolph, bap. 29 Oct. 1772 as son of Tanguk or Tankug (mother) in Langundoutenünk; d. 2 Nov. 1772 (F# 722); see Nathanael (bap. 21 Sept. 1772, twin brother).

Adolph, alias Tschálok, bap. 13 Feb. 1774 in Schönbrunn; m. 29 June 1774 to Susanna (bap. 20 July 1766); children: David (b. 8 June 1776), Johannes Petrus (b. 5 Jan. 1779), Philippina (1786); d. 24 June 1789 (F# 754).

Agnes, b. 22 Feb. 1779, daughter of Johannes, alias Netanewund (bap. 28 July 1776) and Hanna (bap. 7 Jan. 1758), bap. 28 Feb. 1779 in Lichtenau, d. 23 Oct. 1780 (F# 1405).

Agnes, bap. 9 Feb. 1771 in Langundoutenünk; child from earlier marriage: Phoebe (bap. 16 April 1775), m. Isaac, alias Glikhican (bap. 24 Dec. 1770); children: Jonathan (bap. 30 June 1773), Benigna (bap. 8 Feb. 1772); d. 15 Aug. 1778; Mingo (F# 667).

Amalia, bap. 23 Feb. 1766; m. Cornelius (admitted 6 Jan. 1766); children: Esther (bap. 22 March 1767), Matthäus (bap. 7 Jan. 1770), Anton (bap. 21 Sept. 1770), Petrus (bap. 6 Jan. 1771), Paulina (bap. 20 Oct. 1771), Lea (bap. 25 Sept. 1775), Anna (b. 13 July 1776), d. after 1810; Munsee (F# 562).

Amalia, bap. 20 June 1771 in Langundoutenünk, m. Nicolaus (admitted 20 June 1771); children: Tobias (b. 5 Oct. 1771), Lea and twin sister Amalia (b. 24 Sept. 1775) (F# 688). *Not mentioned in diary after Sept. 1775.*

Amalia, bap. 6 Jan. 1775 in Gnadenhütten, m. Jonas (bap. 6 Jan. 1775); children: Lea (b. 12 Oct. 1775), Anna Christina (b. 17 March 1778), Elisabeth (bap. 6 Jan. 1780); d. 8 March 1782 (F# 777). See Tabea (mother, bap. 16 April 1775), Helper.

Amalia, b. 24 Sept. 1775, daughter of Nicolaus (admitted 20 June 1771) and Amalia (bap. 20 June 1771); bap. 25 Sept. 1775 in Schönbrunn (F# 1352). See Lea (twin sister).

Andreas, bap. 7 Aug. 1743 in Checomeco; m. Lea (bap. 26 March 1744, d. 23 March 1749, F# 67); child: Elias (b. 27 Aug. 1749, d. after 18 July 1764, F# 214); m. 5 Dec. 1750 to Anna Justina (bap. 17 Dec. 1749); no children; d. after 28 Dec. 1780; Wampanoag (F# 53). See Philippus Sr. (brother, bap. 12 Dec. 1742).

Andreas, alias Tschemipachgennesch, bap. 7 Jan. 1776 in Schönbrunn; m. Maria Theresia, alias Gochgachganemau (bap. 4 Feb. 1776); children: Samuel (bap. 23 Oct. 1773), Philippus (bap. 8 Feb. 1776); d. before 18 July 1806 (F# 817).

Andreas, bap. 25 Dec. 1779 in Schönbrunn; m. 1784 to Anna Sophia (bap. 1 Jan. 1778); no children; d. 5 Jan. 1814 (F# 877).

Andreas, b. 18 Sept. 1780 as son of Gabriel (bap. before 1755) and Lydia (bap. 22 Sept. 1771); bap. 24 Sept. 1780 in Gnadenhütten (F# 1423).

Anna, bap. 4 Aug. 1765, daughter of Josua Jr. (bap. 23 Jan. 1749) and Sophia (bap. 11 June 1765); d. 8 March 1782 (F# 541).

Anna, bap. 6 Jan. 1771 as widow in Langundoutenünk; m. 16 Jan. 1774 to Abraham, alias Sakima (bap. 25 Dec. 1765); d. 6 Sept. 1783 (F# 661), National Helper.

Anna [Paulina], b. 30 July 1772, daughter of Lucas, alias Gatshenis (bap. 3 Dec. 1769) and Paulina (bap. 3 Dec. 1769); bap. 2 Aug. 1772 in Schönbrunn; bur. 23 March 1790 (F# 1310).

Anna, bap. 10 Aug. 1773, daughter of Ludwig, alias Gokschewéhemen (bap. 16 April 1775) and Marie Juliane, alias Mattamis (bap. 7 Jan. 1776); d. 10 Aug. 1773, great-granddaughter of Salomo, alias Allemewi (bap. 25 Dec. 1769) (F# 1318).

Anna, b. 13 July 1776, daughter of Cornelius (admitted 6 Jan. 1766) and Amalia (bap. 23 Feb. 1766); bap. 14 July 1776 in Schönbrunn; bur. 24 March 1813 (F# 1370).

Anna, bap. 25 March 1780 in Lichtenau; m. Petrus of Goschachgünk (bap. 2 Jan. 1780); bur. 27 March 1780 (F# 889).

Anna, alias Nansy, bap. 22 July 1780 in Gnadenhütten; d. 25 July 1780 (F# 890).

Anna Benigna, bap. 25 Jan. 1778 in Lichtenau as widow; children from earlier marriage: Christina (bap. 1 Feb. 1778), Johanna Sabina (bap. 22 Feb. 1778), Anna Rosina (bap. 22 Feb. 1778), Petrus (bap. 2 Jan. 1780); m. 20 May 1779 to Isaac, alias Glikhican (bap. 24 Dec. 1770); child: Martinus (b. and bap. 26 March 1780); d. 8 March 1782 (F# 862).

Anna Caritas, bap. 21 Jan. 1770 in Lawunnakhannek, m. Jeremias, alias Tschechquoapesek (bap. 21 Jan. 1770); m. 7 Oct. 1779 to Lucas, alias Gatshenis, widower (bap. 3 Dec. 1769); bur. 15 March 1789; Munsee (F# 645), niece of a Munsee chief, National Helper.

Anna Catharina, bap. 4 Feb. 1776 as grandson of Silas (bap. 1 Jan. 1774) in Schönbrunn (F# 834).

Anna Christina, b. 17 March 1778, daughter of Jonas (bap. 6 Jan. 1775) and Amalia (bap. 6 Jan. l775); bap. 22 March 1778 in Lichtenau; d. 8 March 1782 (F# 1390).

Anna Elisabeth, bap. 14 May 1769; m. 6 May 1770 to Marcus (bap. 8 Sept. 1749); child: Ludwig (bap. 10 March 1771); d. before 11 April 1773; Unami (F# 617).

Anna Elisabeth, alias Tiangan, bap. 16 April 1775, daughter of Anna (bap. 6 Jan. 1771) in Schönbrunn; m. 8 Aug. 1776 to Zacharias (bap. 7 Jan. 1776); children: Maria (b. 4 May 1779), Jonas (b. 17 Jan. 1781), Johannes (bap. 17 Oct. 1784), Jonathan (bap. 17 May 1787), Esra (bap. 29 Sept. 1799); d. after 1810 (F# 785).

Anna Elisabeth, bap. 17 Oct. 1776 as eight-year-old daughter of Fridrich (bap. 7 April 1776) and Bathseba (bap. 7 April 1776); "before her demise" in Schönbrunn; d. after 17 Oct. 1776 (F# —).

Anna Elisabeth, b. 22 April 1781, daughter of Adam (bap. 2 Jan. 1780) and Cornelia (bap. 28 May 1775); bap. 23 April 1781 in Salem; d. 8 March 1782 (F# 1432).

Anna Helena, b. 29 March 1775, daughter of Samuel Nantikok (bap. 10 Aug. 1766) and Sarah Nantikok (bap. 27 Jan. 1772); bap. 30 March 1775 in Schönbrunn; d. 4 May 1775; bur. 5 May 1775 (F# 1343).

Anna Helena, bap. 7 April 1776, daughter of Nathanael, alias James Davis (bap. 18 June 1769) and Anna Salome (bap. 6 Oct. 1770) in Schönbrunn; m. 11 Januar 1780 to Daniel, alias Tschitquiechen (bap. 1 Feb. 1778) in Lichtenau; no children (F# 840), probably identical to Anna Helena, d. 1 March 1805 (F# 986).

Anna Johanna, b. 8 June 1756, daughter of Daniel (bap. 17 Sept. 1749) and Elsje or Elsie (of Westenhuck, F# 360b); bap. 10 June 1756, raised by her grandmother Judith (bap. 30 Oct. 1743) in Checomeco; m. 12 Aug. 1771 to Nathanael (b. before 1749); children: Jonathan (b. 26 May 1775), Rebecca (b. 2 March 1778); expelled from the congregation in 1781 (F# 404).

Anna Johanna, bap. 10 Aug. 1766, m. Johannes Papunhank (bap. 26 June 1763); children: Sophia (bap. 11 June 1765), Anna Paulina (bap. 7 June 1772); d. 1 July 1814; Munsee (F# 552). See Paulina (sister, bap. 3 Dec. 1769).

Anna Johanna, bap. 6 Jan. 1778 in Lichtenau as a thirteen-year-old relative of Netawatwees (F# 860).

Anna Justina, bap. 17 Dec. 1749 in Gnadenhütten I; m. 5 Dec. 1750 to Andreas (bap. 7 Aug. 1743); no children; d. before 27 Aug. 1785; Unami (F# 242).

Anna Justina, b. 19 Oct. 1771, daughter of Philippus Jr. (bap. 1749) and Eleanore (bap. 7 Sept. 1767); bap. 20 Oct. 1771 in Friedenshütten; d. 8 Oct. 1773; bur. 11 Oct. 1773; Mahican (F# 695).

Anna Justina, bap. 13 Nov. 1775, daughter of Anna Maria (bap. 12 Nov. 1775) at age eighteenth months in Gnadenhütten, bur. 6 Dec. 1803 (F# 1355).

Anna Justina, alias Matschikis, bap. 1 Jan. 1778 as relative of Salomo, alias Allemewi (bap. 25 Dec. 1769) in Lichtenau; d. 20 Jan. 1778; bur. 22 Jan. 1778; (B) (F# 854).

Anna Justina, b. 23 Jan. 1778, daughter of Philippus Jr. (bap. 1749) and Eleanore (bap. 7 Sept. 1767); bap. 8 Feb. 1778 in Gnadenhütten (F# —). See Sara (twin sister).

Anna Margaretha, admitted as widow on 20 Jan. 1771; children: Nicolaus (admitted 20 June 1771), Jannetje (admitted 20 Jan. 1771), Susanna (admitted 25 Dec. 1774); grandchild: Ludwig (b. 20 Nov. 1773) (F# 719).

Anna Margaretha, widow, bap. 28 May 1778, daughter of Eva (bap. 25 Dec. 1778) in Lichtenau; d. 27 Aug. 1790 (F# 872). See Martha (sister, bap. 17 Sept. 1778).

Anna Maria, bap. 12 Nov. 1775 as widow in Gnadenhütten; child from first marriage: Anna Justina (bap. 13 Nov. 1775); m. 18 Sept. 1779 to Joachim (bap. 14 June 1760); children: Martin (b. 8 Oct. 1780), Henriette (bap. 19 Sept. 1789), Johann Jakob (bap. 4 March 1790); d. 6 June 1809 (F# 799), Helper, sister of Martha (bap. 19 May 1771).

Anna Maria, b. 15 April 1778, daughter of Christian Gottlieb (bap. before 1768) and Catharina, alias Mamtscha (bap. 25 Dec. 1775); bap. 19 April 1778 in Lichtenau; d. 15 March 1779 (F# 1393).

Anna Paulina, bap. 7 June 1772, daughter of Johannes Papunhank (bap. 26 June 1763) and Anna Johanna (bap. 10 Aug. 1766) in Friedenshütten; m. 31 May 1779 to Abraham (bap. 21 Aug. 1749); d. after 1809 (F# 713).

Anna Regina, alias Quewus, bap. 2 Sept. 1774 "as a sick woman" and widow in Schönbrunn (F# 765).

Anna Regina, bap. 3 June 1781 in Schönbrunn, single, "daughter of Amelia's sister," m. 22 Feb. 1784 to Renatus (bap. 12 Nov. 1775) (F# 904).

Anna Rosina, alias Rosina, bap. 11 May 1755; m. Matthäus (bap. 18 Feb. 1761); d. after 1791; Wampanoag (F# 381).

Anna Rosina, bap. 22 Feb. 1778 as big girl and daughter of Anna Benigna (bap. 25 Jan. 1778) in Lichtenau; d. 8 March 1782 (F# 868).

Anna Sabina b. 11 May 1778, daughter of Jacob (bap. 19 May 1771) and Johanette (bap. 12 April 1772); bap. 17 May 1778 in Lichtenau (F# 1394).

Anna Salome, bap. 6 Oct. 1770; m. Nathanael, alias James Davis (bap. 18 June 1769); children: Gottlieb (bap. 8 Oct. 1770), Catharina (bap. 6 Jan. 1773), Eleonora (b. 21 Aug. 1774), Leonhard (bap. 6 Jan. 1775), Anna Helena (bap. 7 April 1776); left congregation in 1789 and moved to Maumee River; returned to congregation in 1801; left again in 1803; Unami (F# 653), Helper.

Anna Salome, b. 6 Nov. 1771, daughter of Petrus, alias Sapan (bap. 25 Dec. 1766) and Abigail (bap. 31 Aug. 1766); bap. 10 Nov. 1771 in Langundoutenünk; m. 9 Aug. 1798 to Simon (bap. 8 March 1789); d. before end of 1803 (F# 697).

Anna Salome, bap. 26 March 1775 as big girl and daughter of Johann Martin (bap. 22 Jan. 1750) and Regine (bap. 19 April 1767) in Gnadenhütten (F# 783).

Anna Sophia, bap. 1 Jan. 1778 as big girl and daughter of Samuel Nantikok (bap. 10 Aug. 1766) in Lichtenau; m. 25 Jan. 1784 to Andreas (bap. 25 Dec. 1779); d. and bur. 5 Dec. 1784 (F# 855).

Anna Susanne, bap. 24 Jan. 1779, daughter of David Jr., alias Kutschias (bap. 6 Feb. 1774) and Salome (bap. 6 Jan. 1772); m. 26 Dec. 1796 to Christian Gottlieb (bap. 4 April 1790); children: Jeremias Henry (bap. 22 Oct. 1799), Francis (bap. 30 Dec. 1802), Benjamin Henry (bap. 31 March 1805), Jane (bap. 2 March 1806), Joseph (bap. 16 June 1806), Nanzy (bap. 18 July 1813), William (bap. 7 July 1816), Salome (bap. 15 Nov. 1818), John (bap. 18 Jan. 1821); d. after 23 Sept. 1821 (F# 1402).

Anna Sybilla, bap. 1 Jan. 1776 in Schönbrunn; m. Christoph, alias Wuligawan (bap. 20 Aug. 1775); no children (F# 810).

Anton, bap. 8 Feb. 1750 in Bethlehem, husband of Johanna (bap. 8 Feb. 1750, d. after 16 May 1770, F# 250); no children; d. 5 Sept. 1773 (B), bur. 6 Sept. 1773; Unami (F# 249). See Augustinus, alias Newollike (brother, bap. 12 May 1774), National Helper, preacher, translator.

Anton, bap. 21 Sept. 1770, son of Cornelius (admitted 6 Jan. 1766) and Amalia (bap. 23 Feb. 1766) in Friedenshütten; d. 12 Sept. 1770; Munsee (F# 652).

Anton, alias Welochalent, bap. 19 May 1771, son of Joseph Peepi (bap. before 1748 by Presbyterians) and Hanna (bap. 30 July 1769) in Friedenshütten; m. to Juliana (bap. 30 May 1771); children: Elisabeth (bap. 1 July 1771), Joseph (b. 15 Oct. 1772), Marcus (b. 25 Feb. 1775), Gertraud (b. 28 Jan. 1778), Christian Gottlieb (b. 20 May 1781); d. after 1804; Unami (F# 682).

Anton, bap. 6 Jan. 1774 as adult son of John Martin (bap. 22 Jan. 1750) and Anna (admitted 26 March 1752); d. 8 March 1782 (F# 748). See Joseph Peepi (grandfather, bap. before 1748 by Presbyterians).

Anton, bap. 6 Jan. 1778, son of Israel, alias Welapachtschiechen (bap. 25 Dec. 1777) and Rahel (admitted 25 Dec. 1777) in Lichtenau; m. 15 May 1778 to Philippina (bap. 6 Jan. 1778); expelled from congregation before 4 Dec. 1780; readmitted 25 Dec. 1780; d. after 1812 (F# 943).

Augustine, bap. 6 Jan. 1767, daughter of Job Chelloway (frequent visitor of congregation) in Friedenshütten; m. 1 Feb. 1767 to Christian (bap. 4 March 1750); children: Martha (bap. 1 Jan. 1768), Christian (bap. 22 Oct. 1769), Christiana (bap. 10 Sept. 1775); d. 8 March 1782; Unami (F# 569).

Augustine, b. 17 July 1779, daughter of Samuel Nantikok (bap. 10 Aug. 1766) and Sarah Nantikok (bap. 27 Jan. 1772) in Schönbrunn; Nantikok (F# 1412).

Augustinus, alias Newollike, bap. 12 May 1774 in Schönbrunn; m. Regina (bap. 3 April 1774); no children; left congregation 13 Feb. 1777; Munsee (F# 760); influential Munsee chief. See Anton (brother, bap. 8 Feb. 1750).

Augustus, bap. 19 Aug. 1766; m. 1 Feb. 1767 to Lydia (bap. 26 Dec. 1766); no children; d. after 1780; Canai (F# 554).

Balthasar, bap. 7 Jan. 1776 as adult son of Jonas (bap. 6 Jan. 1775) (F# 827).

Bartholomäus, bap. 26 March 1744 in Checomeco; m. Elisabeth (bap. before 1753); children: Jeremias (bap. before 1771), Elisabeth (b. 28 July 1764, F# 534), Christina (bap. 5 March 1767, d. 3 July 1768, F# 573), Anna (bap. 28 April 1771, F# 677); d. in Goschachgünk 22 Sept. 1778 (B); Wampanoag? (F# 66).

Bathseba, bap. 7 Aug. 1743 in Checomeco; m. before 1755 to Josua Sr. (bap. 4 Sept. 1742); no children; d. 11 March 1799; Mahican (F# 58), Helper.

Bathseba, bap. 13 May 1767, daughter of Josua Jr. (bap. before 1747) and Sophia (bap. 11 June 1765); d. 8 March 1782 (F# —).

Bathseba, bap. 7 April 1776 in Schönbrunn; m. Fridrich, alias Weschnasch (bap. 7 April 1776); child: Anna Elisabeth (bap. 17 Oct. 1776) (F# 839).

Bathseba, bap. 5 Aug. 1780 "in her sickness" as two-year-old daughter of Joseph (bap. 2 March 1751) (F# —).

Beata, bap. 25 Jan. 1770 in Lawunnakhannek, mother of Lucas, alias Gatshenis (bap. 3 Dec. 1769) and Jonas, alias Pilawetsch (bap. 1 Jan. 1774); d. 7 Feb. 1790; Munsee (F# 646).

Beata, b. 28 Aug. 1771, daughter of Samuel Nantikok (bap. 10 Aug. 1766) and Sarah Nantikok (bap. 27 Jan. 1772); bap. 27 Jan. 1772 in Friedenshütten; d. 25 Aug. 1773; Nantikok (F# 704).

Beata, b. 19 March 1775, daughter of Ignatius, alias Tschimachtschis (bap. 6 Jan. 1773) and Christina (bap. 6 Jan. 1774); bap. 20 March 1775 in Schönbrunn; m. 28 Jan. 1792 to Joseph (bap. 25 Dec. 1789); left congregation 1821 (F# 1342).

Beata, b. 20 April 1775, daughter of Daniel (bap. 3 April 1768) and Johanna (bap. 11 Sept. 1768); bap. 23 April 1775 in Gnadenhütten; m. 12 Feb. 1797 to Jephta (bap. 6 Jan. 1797); bur. 19 June 1806 (F# 1344).

Benigna, bap. 13 Jan. 1754 in Gnadenhütten I; m. 26 Oct. 1755 to Joachim (bap. before 1747); children: Maria, alias Ahtschem (bap. 6 Jan. 1763, d. 11 July 1764, F# 517), Heinrich (bap. 8 Jan. 1758, F# 427), Joachim (bap. 14 June 1760); d. 10 June 1785; Unami (F# 353).

Benigna, bap. 8 Feb. 1772 in Langundoutenünk as little daughter of Agnes (bap. 9 Feb. 1771) and Isaac, alias Glikhican (bap. 24 Dec. 1770) (F# 707).

Benigna, b. 19 April 1776, daughter of Sem, alias Tschuwisch (bap. 25 Dec. 1775) and Lucia (bap. 4 Feb. 1776); bap. 7 July 1776 in Schönbrunn; d. 8 March 1782 (F# 1368).

Benigna, bap. 7 Jan. 1781 as adult daughter of Samuel Nantikok (bap. 10 Aug. 1766) in Schönbrunn; d. 1814 (F# 902).

Benjamin, b. 22 April 1773, son of Daniel (bap. 3 April 1768) and Johanna (bap. 11 Sept. 1768); bap. 29 April 1773 in Gnadenhütten; d. 8 March 1782 (F# 1315).

Benjamin, bap. 2 July 1773, son of Rebecca (b. c. 1713) in Schönbrunn; d. 9 July 1773 (F# 731).

Benjamin, alias Kaschoos, bap. 6 Jan. 1774 in Gnadenhütten (F# 747).

Benjamin, bap. 7 Jan. 1776, son of Nathanael, alias James Davis (bap. 18 June 1769) in Schönbrunn (F# 818).

Bibiane, bap. 25 Dec. 1775 as thirteen-year-old daughter of Esra, alias Apallochgacan (bap. 20 May 1773) (F# 802).

Boas, alias Lelawoapaneuche, bap. 23 May 1771, son of Maria (bap. 7 June 1772); m. Theodora (bap. 20 Jan. 1771); child: Susanna (bap. 20 Jan. 1771); d. after 1798; Munsee (F# 679).

Boas, bap. 25 Jan. 1778 as twelve-year-old son of Gideon, alias Saktelaeuche (bap. 25 Dec. 1776) (F# 861).

Boas, alias Apallauwis (Allais), bap. 14 Jan. 1781 in Salem; Unami (F# 903).

Catharina, bap. 17 Dec. 1772 as three-year-old daughter of Samuel Moor (bap. 6 Jan. 1771); d. 28 Dec. 1772 (F# —).

Catharina, bap. 6 Jan. 1773 as adult daughter of Nathanael Davis (bap. 18 June 1769) and Anna Salome (bap. 6 Oct. 1770); m. 14 Aug. 1774 to Jeremias (bap. before 1771) in Gnadenhütten; children: Johanan (b. 14 Nov. 1775), Martin (b. 19 Dec. 1777); d. 8 March 1782 (F# 727).

Catharina, alias Mamtscha, bap. 25 Dec. 1775 as "big girl" and daughter of Jacob, alias Menatschis (bap. 29 Dec. 1765) and Rebecca (bap. 7 June 1772) in Schönbrunn; probably m. to Christian Gottlieb (bap. 22 Feb. 1752); children: Anna Maria (b. 15 April 1778), Sophia (b. 8 Feb. 1780); d. after 1816 (F# 803). Possible brothers and sister—see Levi (bap. 3 April 1768), Jacob (bap. 19 May 1771), Benjamin (bap. 2 July 1773), Christina (bap. 6 Jan. 1774).

Charlotte, bap. 6 Jan. 1772 in Langundoutenünk; m. Michael, alias Paatschpatsch (bap. 6 Jan. 1772); children: Sabina (bap. 2 Feb. 1772), Johanette (bap. 12 April 1772), Gottfried (bap. 25 Dec. 1774), Ruth (bap. 4 Feb. 1776), Sabina (bap. 26 May 1776), Mariane (bap. 25 Dec. 1777), Lea (bap. 6 Jan. 1781); bur. 11 Sept. 1780 (F# 702).

Charlotte, bap. 1 Jan. 1776 in Gnadenhütten, sister of Johanna (bap. 11 Sept. 1768), mother of Adam (bap. 1 Jan 1776) (F# 813).

Charlotte, bap. 27 Dec. 1778, daughter of Gottfried (bap. 25 Dec. 1774) and Justina (bap. 25 Dec. 1774) in Gnadenhütten (F# 1400).

Christian, bap. 4 March 1750, son of Nicodemus (d. 1760) and Justine (bap. 16 Aug. 1749) in Gnadenhütten I; m. 7 Oct. 1762 to Martha (bap. 6 Jan. 1762, d. 16 July 1764, F# 506); m. 1 Feb. 1767 to Augustine (bap. 6 Jan. 1767); children: Martha (bap. 1 Jan. 1768), Christian (bap. 22 Oct. 1769), Christiana (bap. 10 Sept. 1775); d. 8 March 1782; Unami (F# 256), Helper.

Christian, bap. 23 Aug. 1767, son of Elias (bap. 6 Jan. 1768) and Louisa (bap. 6 Jan. 1768); m. 22 Oct. 1790 to Johannette (bap. 1 Jan. 1787, d. after 2 June 1810, F# 935), no children; d. after 2 Sept. 1802; Unami (F# 584). See Jacob (brother, bap. 11 Dec. 1768).

Christian, bap. 22 Oct. 1769, son of Christian (bap. 4 March 1750) and Augustine (bap. 6 Jan. 1767); Unami (F# 637).

Christian, bap. 2 Feb. 1776, son of Ludwig, alias Gokschewéhemen (bap. 16 April 1775) and Marie Juliane, alias Mattamis (bap. 7 Jan. 1776) in Schönbrunn, great-grandson of Salomo, alias Allemewi (bap. 25 Dec. 1769) (F# 1359).

Christian, bap. 31 July 1778, son of Christina (bap. 6 Jan. 1774) and grandson of Jacob, alias Menatschis (bap. 29 Dec. 1765); d. 3 Aug. 1778 in Lichtenau (F# 1398).

Christian, b. 3 May 1780, son of Thomas (admitted 19 May 1771) and Polly (bap. in the Jerseys); bap. 14 May 1780 in Gnadenhütten (F# 1419).

Christian David, bap. 24 Sept. 1780 in Salem; d. after 1781; Shawnee (F# 895).

Christian Gottlieb, bap. 12 May 1758, son of Gottlieb (bap. 25 April 1756) and Amalia (bap. 8 May 1749); probably m. to Catharina, alias Mamtscha (bap. 25 Dec. 1775); children: Anna Maria (b. 15 April 1778), Sophia (b. 8 Feb. 1780); d. after 1785; Unami (F# 438).

Christian Gottlieb, b. 20 May 1781, son of Anton, alias Welochalent (bap. 19 May 1771) and Juliana (bap. 30 May 1771); bap. 27 May 1781 in Salem; d. 8 March 1782 (F# 1433).

Christian Gottlieb, bap. 4 April 1790; m. 26 Dec. 1796 to Anna Susanne (bap. 24 Jan. 1779); children: Jeremias Henry (bap. 22 Oct. 1799), Francis (bap. 30 Dec. 1802), Benjamin Henry (bap. 31 March 1805), Jane (bap. 2 March 1806), Joseph (bap. 16 June 1806), Nanzy (bap. 18 July 1813), William (bap. 7 July 1816), Salome (bap. 15 Nov. 1818), John (bap. 18 Jan. 1821); d. after 10 Oct. 1821 (F# 970).

Christiana, bap. 12 July 1746; m. 12 Jan. 1747 to John Joseph Bull, alias Schebosch (b. 22May 1721); children: Johann Martin (bap. 17 Aug. 1750), Joseph (bap. 25 Dec. 1758), Christina (bap. 9 May 1764); d. 7 Sept. 1787; Mahican (F# 82).

Christiana, bap. 2 July 1749; m. Ludwig (bap. 27 April 1749); separated from husband and moved to Goschachgünk 28 April 1777; Unami (F# 184).

Christiana, bap. 10 Sept. 1775, daughter of Christian (bap. 4 March 1750) and Augustine (bap. 6 Jan. 1767) in Gnadenhütten; d. 8 March 1782 (F# 1350).

Christina, bap. 9 May 1764, daughter of John Joseph Bull, alias Schebosch (b. 22 May 1721) and Christiana (bap. 12 July 1764); m. 12 Feb. 1781 to Jacob (bap. 6 Jan. 1778); children: Elisabeth (1786), Martin (1790), Mary (1792), Rahel (1800), Josephus (1801), Ketura (1803), Christian Jacob (1807); d. after 1813 (F# 527).

Christina, bap. 6 Jan. 1774, daughter of Jacob, alias Menatschis (bap. 29 Dec. 1765) and Rebecca (bap. 7 June 1772) in Schönbrunn; m. to Ignatius, alias Tschimachtschis (bap. 6 Jan. 1773); children: Beata (b. 19 March 1775), Christian (bap. 3 Aug. 1778), Elisabeth (b. 2

Nov. 1779), Heinrich (bap. 29 Feb. 1784), Philippus (b. 9 Dec. 1787), Anna Benigna (bap. 9 Nov. 1791, d. 22 May 1812), Agnes (bap. 13 May 1795, bur. 26 Sept. 1801), Anna Maria (b. before 1803); d. 23 Oct. 1821 (F# 744). See Levi (brother, bap. 3 April 1768), Jacob (brother, bap. 19 May 1771), Catharina, alias Mamtscha (sister, bap. 19 May 1771), Benjamin (brother, bap. 2 July 1773).

Christina, admitted 19 Aug. 1775, daughter of Thomas (admitted 1 Jan. 1775) and Maria (admitted 12 Feb. 1775); m. 24 April 1776 to Petrus (bap. 6 Jan. 1771) (F# 915).

Christina, bap. 4 Oct. 1776 at six years "in her illness," probably daughter of Helena, alias Quelpinawos (bap. 13 April 1755) (F# —).

Christina, bap. 1 Feb. 1778 at six months, daughter of Anna Benigna (bap. 25 Jan. 1778) in Lichtenau (F# 1385).

Christina, b. 15 Sept. 1780, daughter of Gideon, alias Saktelaeuche (bap. 25 Dec. 1776) and Sara (bap. 6 Jan. 1777); bap. 24 Sept. 1780 in Salem; d. 8 March 1782 (F# 1422).

Christine, admitted 19 Aug. 1775, daughter of Thomas Onondaga (admitted 1 Jan. 1775) and Marie (admitted 12 Feb. 1775) (F# 915).

Christoph, alias Wuligawan, bap. 20 Aug. 1775 in Schönbrunn; m. Anna Sybilla (bap. 1 Jan. 1776); no children (F# 793).

Cornelia, bap. 6 Jan. 1771 in Langundoutenünk; d. 20 Aug. 1773 in Schönbrunn (B); Munsee (F# 660). See Isaac, alias Glikhican (son, bap. 24 Dec. 1770).

Cornelia, bap. 28 May 1775; children from first marriage: Maria Susanna (bap. 4 Feb. 1776), Johanna Salome (bap. 25 Dec. 1777); m. 28 March 1780 to Adam, alias Wulalowechen (bap. 2 Jan. 1780); child: Anna Elisabeth (b. 22 April 1781) (F# 791).

Cornelia, b. 9 Sept. 1777, daughter of Leonhard (bap. 6 Jan. 1775) and Rahel (bap. 6 Jan. 1776); bap. 14 Dec. 1777 in Gnadenhütten (F# —).

Cornelius, bap. 6 Jan. 1766; admitted; m. Amalia (bap. 23 Feb. 1766); children: Esther (bap. 22 March 1767), Matthäus (bap. 7 Jan. 1770), Anton (bap. 21 Sept. 1770), Petrus (bap. 6 Jan. 1771), Paulina (bap. 20 Jan. 1771), Lea (bap. 25 Sept. 1775), Anna (b. 13 July 1776); d. 26 Feb. 1793 "almost one hundred years old and blind"; Munsee (F# 545).

Daniel, bap. 3 April 1768, son of Paulus (bap. 10 June 1764); m. Johanna (bap. 11 Sept. 1768); children: Samuel (bap. 12 Sept. 1768), Gottlieb (bap. 6 Jan. 1771), Benjamin (b. 22 April 1773), Rahel (bap. 1 Jan. 1775), Beata (b. 20 April 1775), Johannes (b. 27 May 1779); d. 25 Nov. 1778; Munsee (F# 595). See Johann Martin (brother, bap. 22 Jan. 1750), Paulina (sister, bap. 6 Jan. 1774), Theodora (mother, F# 232).

Daniel, b. 3 Nov. 1777, son of Lucas, alias Gatshenis (bap. 3 Dec. 1769) and Paulina (bap. 3 Dec. 1769); bap. 9 Nov. 1777 in Lichtenau (F# 1381).

Daniel, alias Tschitquiechen, bap. 1 Feb. 1778, son of Helena (bap. 6 Jan. 1777) in Lichtenau; m. 11 Jan. 1780 to Anna Helena (bap. 7 April 1776); m. to Dorothea (bap. 1 Feb. 1778); children: Anna Marie (1803), Anna Johanna (1803), Eva (1809), Joel (1810); d. after 1811 (F# 865). *Note: Fliegel's entries for Dorothea and Daniel are contradictory.*

David Jr., alias Kutschias or Kutschiaheft of Gekelemukpechünk, bap. 6 Feb. 1774 in Gnadenhütten; m. 27 March 1774 to Salome (bap. 6 Jan. 1772); children: Timotheus (bap. 26 April 1775), David (bap. 16 March 1776), Anna Susanne (bap. 24 Jan. 1779), Anna Margaretha (bap. 15 March 1790), Benjamin (bap. 24 Jan. 1792), Augustina (bap. 2 Oct. 1803), Silas (bap. 30 Dec. 1802); d. after 18 April 1813 (F# 753), Helper.

David, bap. 16 March 1776, son of David Jr., alias Kutschias (bap. 6 Feb. 1774) and Salome (bap. 6 Jan. 1772) in Gnadenhütten; d. 23 March 1776; bur. 25 March 1776 (F# 1364).

David, b. 8 June 1776, son of Adolph, alias Tschàlok (bap. 13 Feb. 1774) and Susanna (bap. 20 July 1766); bap. 9 June 1776 in Schönbrunn; bur. 23 Nov. 1777 (F# 1367).

David, bap. 6 Jan. 1780, son of Israel, alias Welapachtschiechen (bap. 25 Dec. 1777) and Rahel (admitted 25 Dec. 1777); d. 8 March 1782 (F# 885).

Debora "von Tuscarawi," bap. 1 Jan. 1774 in Schönbrunn as widow, mother of Michael (bap. 6 Jan. 1772); d. 27 Oct. 1780; bur. 28 Oct. 1780 in Schönbrunn (F# 738).

Debora, bap. 16 April 1775 in Schönbrunn, sister of Gertraud (bap. 20 Jan. 1771) (F# 787).

Dorothea, bap. 1 Jan. 1776; m. Adam, alias Scheechganìm (bap. 1 Jan. 1776); d. probably before 29 Oct. 1777 (F# 811).

Dorothea, bap. 1 Feb. 1778 as big girl and granddaughter of Israel, alias Welapachtschiechen (bap. 25 Dec. 1777); m. probably to Daniel, alias Tschitquiechen (bap. 1 Feb. 1778); children: Anna Marie (1800) Anna Johanna (1803), Eva (b. 10 Feb. 1809), Joel (1810) (F# 866). *Note: Fliegel's entries for Dorothea and Daniel are obviously contradictory.*

Eleanora (frequently referred to as Lorel), bap. 7 Sept. 1767, daughter of Petrus (?); m. Philippus Jr. (bap. 23 Jan. 1749); children: Thomas (b. 26 June 1769), Anna Justina (b. 19 Oct. 1771), Jonas (b. 11 Nov. 1774), Levi (bap. 14 Jan. 1776), Anna Justina and twin sister Sara (b. 23 Jan. 1778); d. 8 March 1782; Munsee (F# 587). See Salome (sister, bap. 17 Oct. 1773) and Martha (sister).

Eleonora, b. 21 Aug. 1774, daughter of Nathanael (bap. 18 June 1769) and Anna Salome (bap. 6 Oct. 1770); bap. 28 Aug. 1774 in Schönbrunn (F# 1333).

Elias, bap. 6 Jan. 1768; m. Louisa (bap. 6 Jan. 1768); children: Christian (bap. 23 Aug. 1767), Jacob (bap. 11 Dec. 1768), Matthaeus (bap. 8 May 1774); d. after 19 March 1777; Unami (F# 592).

Elias, bap. 30 July 1780 as adult in Salem; m. Rosina (not identified) (F# 891).

Elisabeth, admitted 10 March 1754 (bap. in Westenhuk); m. Bartholomäus (bap. 26 March 1744); children: Elisabeth (b. 28 July 1764, F# 534), Christina (bap. 5 March 1767, d. 3 July 1768, F# 573), Anna (bap. 28 April 1771, F# 677), Jeremias (bap. 19 May 1771); d. after 1779; Shawnee (F# 356).

Elisabeth, bap. 1 July 1771, daughter of Anton, alias Welochalent (bap. 19 May 1771) and Juliana (bap. 30 May 1771); d. before 11 April 1773; Unami (F# 691).

Elisabeth, b. and bap. 20 Oct. 1774, daughter of Willhelm, alias Bill Chelloway (bap. 6 Jan. 1771) and Martha (bap. 19 May 1771) in Schönbrunn; m. before 1798 to Tobias (bap. 25 Oct. 1769); d. after 1810 (F# 1335).

Elisabeth, bap. 22 March 1778 in Lichtenau; m. Johann Jacob, alias Trenchtees (bap. 1 Feb. 1778); children: Maria Salome (bap. 29 March 1778), Rahel (bap. 22 March 1778) (F# 870).

Elisabeth, b. 5 May 1779, daughter of Adam (bap. 1 Jan. 1776) and Sabina (bap. 26 May 1776); bap. 13 May 1779 in Schönbrunn (F# —).

Elisabeth, b. 2 Nov. 1779, daughter of Ignatius, alias Tschimachtschis (bap. 6 Jan. 1773) and Christina (bap. 6 Jan. 1773); bap. 13 Nov. 1779 in Gnadenhütten (F# —).

Elisabeth, bap. 6 Jan. 1780, daughter of Jonas (bap. 6 Jan. 1775) and Amalia (bap. 6 Jan. 1775) in Lichtenau; d. 8 March 1782 (F# 886).

Elisabeth, b. 11 Nov. 1780, daughter of Ludwig, alias Gokschewéhemen (bap. 16 April 1775) and Marie Juliane, alias Mattamis (bap. 7 Jan. 1776), great-grandson of Salomo, alias Allemewi (bap. 25 Dec. 1769); bap. 16 Nov. 1780 in Schönbrunn; bur. 12 Dec. 1780 (F# 1427).

Ephraim, alias Pomachgutte, bap. 25 Dec. 1772 in Schönbrunn, blind; d. before 1796 (F# 724).

Ephraim, bap. 7 Jan. 1776 in Gnadenhütten, cousin of Petrus Echpalawehund (bap. 4 Feb. 1774) (F# 826).

Erdmuth, bap. 12 June 1770 in Langundoutenünk; m. to Salomo, alias Allemewi (bap. 25 Dec. 1769); children: Theodora (bap. 20 Jan. 1771), Maria Elisabeth (bap. 31 March 1771); left congregation with her husband on 4 July 1774; Munsee (F# 649). See Levi (grandson, bap. 6 Jan. 1781), Marie Juliane (granddaughter, bap. 7 Jan. 1776, Anna (great-granddaughter, bap. 10 Aug. 1773), Anna Justina (relative, bap. 1 Jan. 1778).

Esra, alias Apallochgacan, bap. 20 May 1773; child from earlier marriage: Bibiane (bap. 25 Dec. 1775); m. Lazara (bap. 30 June 1771); children: Jonathan (b. 29 May 1772), Thomas (b. 31 July 1774); d. after 1776 (F# 730), Helper. See Jephta, alias Queelpachena (brother, bap. 4 Jan. 1774), Nicodemus (brother, bap. 7 Dec. 1775), Sem, alias Tschuwisch (brother, bap. 25 Dec. 1775).

Esther, bap. 22 Aug. 1742; d. 21 Aug. 1780; bur. 22 Aug. 1780.

Esther, bap. 22 March 1767, daughter of Cornelius (admitted 6 Jan. 1766) and Amalia (bap. 23 Feb. 1766); bur. 22 Aug. 1780. *Note: Fliegel's entry is contradictory (F# 574).*

Esther, bap. 2 Jan. 1780, daughter of Israel, alias Welapachtschiechen (bap. 25 Dec. 1777) and Rahel (admitted 25 Dec. 1777); m. 16 Jan. 1787 to Ludwig (bap. 1 Jan. 1787); children: Nathanael (1788), Caleb (1790), Johannes (1796), widowed 1799; m. 10 April 1803 to Israel; children: Jesse (1804), Philippina (1806); d. after 1808 (F# 882).

Eva, bap. 25 Dec. 1778 as widow and sister of Israel, alias Welachpatschiechen (bap. 25 Dec. 1777), mother of Anna Margaretha (bap. 28 May 1778); d. 7 Aug. 1789 (F# 876).

Friderica, bap. 25 Dec. 1777 as granddaughter of Gertraud (bap. 20 Jan. 1771) at age thirteen in Lichtenau; d. after 1790 (F# 852).

Fridrich, bap. 1 Jan. 1776 in Gnadenhütten as cousin of Isaac, alias Eschecanahunt (bap. 25 Dec. 1775) (F# 815).

Fridrich, alias Weschnasch, bap. 7 April 1776 in Schönbrunn; m. to Bathseba (bap. 7 April 1776); child: Anna Elisabeth (bap. 17 Oct. 1776); d. after 1787 (F# 837).

Gabriel, bap. 15 March 1749, son of Abel and Caritas, brother of Batseba; m. 10 Jan. 1773 to Lydia (bap. 22 Sept. 1771); children: Judith (b. 11 April 1774), Regina (bap. 31 March 1777), Andreas (b. 18 Sept. 1780); bur. 24 Aug. 1791 (F# 160).

Georg, bap. 22 Jan. 1775 as "big boy" and son of Magdalena (not identified) (F# 780).

Gertraud, bap. 20 Jan. 1771 in Langundoutenünk, from Gekelemukpechünk; bur. 18 Dec. 1791 (F# 666B). See Friderica (granddaughter, bap. 25 Dec. 1777), Levi (grandson, bap. 6 Jan. 1781), Debora (sister, bap. 16 April 1775) and Zeno (brother).

Gertraud, b. 11 March 1775, daughter of Maria Magdalena (bap. 13 March 1775); bap. 18 March 1775 in Schönbrunn (F# 1340); d. and bur. 19 March 1775.

Gertraud, b. 28 Jan. 1778, daughter of Anton, alias Welochalent (bap. 19 May 1771) and Juliana (bap. 30 May 1771); bap. 8 Feb. 1778 in Gnadenhütten; d. 8 March 1782 (F# 1388).

Gideon, alias Saktelaeuche, bap. 25 Dec. 1776 in Lichtenau, son of Netawatwees; children from earlier marriage: Moses (bap. 30 March 1777), Boas (bap. 25 Jan. 1778); m. Sara (Sarah) (bap. 6 Jan. 1777); children: Johannes (bap. 8 Jan. 1777), Johannes Renatus (b. 2 Feb. 1778), Christina (b. 15 Sept. 1780); d. before 15 Nov. 1787 (F# 843).

Gottfried, bap. 25 Dec. 1774, son of Michael, alias Paatschpatsch (bap. 6 Jan. 1772) and Charlotte (bap. 6 Jan. 1772) in Schönbrunn; m. to Justina (bap. 25 Dec. 1774); children: Lydia (bap. 16 Jan. 1775), Martin (bap. 22 Oct. 1775), Charlotte (bap. 27 Dec. 1778); d. after 27 Dec. 1778 (F# 768).

Gottlieb, bap. 8 Oct. 1770, son of Nathanael, alias James Davis (bap. 18 June 1769) and Anna Salome (bap. 6 Oct. 1770) (F# 654).

Gottlieb, bap. 6 Jan. 1771, son of Daniel (bap. 3 April 1768) and Johanna (bap. 11 Sept. 1768); d. 8 March 1782 (F# 662).

Gottlob, bap. 22 Feb. 1776, son of Johannes, alias [Captain] Douty (bap. 7 Jan. 1776) and Rebecca (bap. 1 Jan. 1776), (F# —).

Hanna, bap. 9 Jan. 1757 by Grube in Bethlehem; child: Anna Elisabeth (bap. 14 May 1769); d. 16 Jan. 1778 (B) (F# 413).

Hanna, bap. 7 Jan. 1758 at age thirteen, daughter of Paulus (bap. 9 Jan. 1757) and Magdalena (bap. 9 Jan. 1757); m. Johannes, alias Netanewund (bap. 28 July 1776); children: Joseph (b. 12 Nov. 1776), Agnes (b. 22 Feb. 1779), Samuel (bap. 11 Sept. 1780), Sarah (bap. 28 Oct. 1780) (F# 426).

Hanna, bap. 30 July 1769 in Friedenshütten; children from first marriage: Lydia (bap. 22 Sept. 1771), Ludwig (bap. 1 Jan. 1774), Michael (bap. 15 Jan. 1776); m. Joseph Peepi (bap. before 1748 by Presbyterians); children: Anton, alias Welochalent (bap. 19 May 1771), Jonas (bap. 6 Jan. 1775), Polly (bap. in the Jerseys); d. 8 March 1782 (F# 635).

Hanna, b. 2 March 1776, daughter of Petrus, alias Mose (bap. 14 April 1775) and Mary (bap. in Stockbridge), bap. 3 March 1776 in Gnadenhütten; d. 8 March 1782 (F# 1363).

Hanna, b. 9 April 1776, daughter of Leonhard (bap. 6 Jan. 1775) and Rahel (bap. 6 Jan. 1776); bap. 10 April 1776 in Schönbrunn (F# 1365).

Heinrich, b. and bap. 22 Aug. 1773, son of Samuel Nantikok (bap. 10 Aug. 1766) and Sarah Nantikok (bap. 27 Jan. 1772) in Schönbrunn; d. 9 Nov. 1773; bur. 10 Nov. 1773 (F# 1320).

Heinrich, bap. 9 Jan. 1774 at age fourteen, son of Noah (bap. 2 July 1773) and Willhelmine (bap. 4 July 1773) in Schönbrunn; d. 8 March 1782 (F# 751).

Heinrich, alias Tschananges, bap. 7 Jan. 1776 in Gnadenhütten; m. 31 Aug. 1780 to Johanna Salome (bap. 25 Dec. 1777); d. 8 March 1782 (F# 824).

Heinrich, bap. 25 Dec. 1778 in Lichtenau; d. after 1780 (F# 878), from Wabash.

Helena, alias Quelpinawos, bap. 13 April 1755 at age fourteen, readmitted 4 Feb. 1776; children: Sybilla (bap. 22 Jan. 1775), Sigmund (bap. 18 Feb. 1776), Christina (bap. 4 Oct. 1776), Martha (bap. 2 Jan. 1780); bur. 22 Jan. 1777; Unami (F# 377).

Helena bap. 13 April 1768 as widow; m. 13 June 1773 to widower Samuel Moor (bap. 6 Jan. 1771); child: Louisa (b. 26 July 1774); left congregation in 1791; Unami (F# 583). See Nathanael, alias James Davis (brother, bap. 18 June 1769).

Helena, bap. 1 Jan. 1775, daughter of Magdalena (bap. 20 July 1766) and Nathanael, alias Gochgachgaholen (bap. 9 Feb. 1767, d. 26 May 1767, F# 555) in Gnadenhütten; m. 21 Dec. 1779 to Joseph Schebosch (bap. 25 Dec. 1758); no children (F# 772).

Helena, bap. 6 Jan. 1777 in Lichtenau, sister of Isaac, alias Glikhican (bap. 24 Dec. 1770); children: Martha (bap. 2 Jan. 1780), Daniel (bap. 25 Jan. 1778); d. 10 June 1785 (F# 846).

Helena, bap. 8 Dec. 1780, daughter of Killbuck Sr. in Gnadenhütten; d. after 1781 (F# 897).

Henriette, bap. 25 Dec. 1772 in Schönbrunn; m. Aaron, alias Tachenos (bap. 4 Oct. 1772); child: Anna Maria (b. 29 Aug. 1772, bur. 8 Sept. 1772, F# 717); readmitted 1789; bur. 14 Dec. 1798 (F# 725).

Henry Conner, European, b. 7 Oct. 1780, son of Richard and Peggy Conner (both admitted 7 April 1776); bap. 8 Oct. 1780 in Schönbrunn (F# —).

Ignatius, alias Tschimachtschis, bap. 6 Jan. 1773 in Schönbrunn; m. Christina (bap. 6 Jan. 1774); children: Beata (b. 19 March 1775), Elisabeth (b. 2 Nov. 1779), Heinrich (bap. 29 Feb. 1784), Philippus (b. 9 Dec. 1787), Anna Benigna (bap. 9 Nov. 1791, d. 22 May 1812), Agnes (bap. 13 May 1795, bur. 26 Sept. 1801), Anna Maria (b. before 1803); d. 11 Sept. 1806 (F# 726), Helper.

Isaac, alias Glikhican, bap. 24 Dec. 1770 in Langundoutenünk, son of Cornelia (bap. 6 Jan. 1771); child probably from earlier marriage: Ludwig, alias Gulpikamen (bap. before 1749); m. Agnes (bap. 9 Feb. 1771); children: Jonathan (bap. 30 June 1773), Benigna (bap. 8 Feb. 1772); m. 20 May 1779 to Anna Benigna (bap. 25 Jan. 1778); child: Martinus (b. and bap. 26 March 1780); d. 8 March 1782; Munsee (F# 659). Isaac was war captain of Wolf clan before baptism, influential counselor, messenger, brother of Indian preacher Wangomen, friend of White Eyes. See Simon, alias Panipachgihillen (brother, bap. 1 Jan. 1771), Helena (sister, bap. 6 Jan. 1777), Martha (niece, bap. 2 Jan. 1780), Maria Magdalena (niece, bap. 13 March 1775), Gertraud (grandniece, bap. 11 March 1755).

Isaac, alias Eschecanahunt, bap. 25 Dec. 1775, son of chief Packanke; m. 10 May 1781 to the widow Sophia (bap. 14 May 1749); no children; d. after 6 Jan. 1801 (F# 805). Before his baptism member of the council at Kuskuski, spoke Mohawk, Shawnee, and Delaware; Helper.

Isaac, b. 29 Jan. 1779, son of Thomas, alias Gutkigamen (bap. 11 Sept. 1774) and Sabina (bap. 11 Sept. 1774); bap. 7 Feb. 1779 in Lichtenau; d. after 1821 (F# 1403). See Maria Salome (twin sister).

Israel, bap. 3 Dec. 1769, son of Lucas, alias Gatshenis (bap. 3 Dec. 1769) and Paulina (bap. 3 Dec. 1769) in Lawunnakhannek; m. 21 Feb. 1789 to Salome (bap. 29 March 1771); d. after 1810; Munsee (F# 641).

Israel, alias Welapachtschiechen, Captain Johnny, bap. 25 Dec. 1777 in Schönbrunn; m. Rahel (admitted 25 Dec. 1777); children: Jacob (bap. 6 Jan. 1778), Anton (bap. 6 Jan. 1778), David (bap. 6 Jan. 1780), Esther (bap. 2 Jan. 1780); d. 8 March 1782 (F# 849). Before baptism chief of Turtle clan, See Eva (sister, bap. 25 Dec. 1778), Martha Elisabeth (grand-daughter, bap. 25 Jan. 1778), Dorothea (granddaughter, bap. 1 Feb. 1778), Polly (grand-daughter, bap. before 1792), Johann Jacob, alias Trenchtees (cousin, bap. 1 Feb. 1778), Martha (cousin, bap. 17 Sept. 1778).

Jacob, alias Menatschis, bap. 29 Dec. 1765 in Wyalusing; m. Rebecca [marriage c. 1735] (bap. 7 June 1767); children: Jacob (bap. 19 May 1771), Levi (bap. 3 April 1768), Catharina, alias Mamtscha (bap. 25 Dec. 1775), Christina (bap. 6 Jan. 1774), Benjamin (bap. 2 July 1773); d. 1 Oct. 1770; Catawba (F# 544).

Jacob, bap. 11 Dec. 1768, son of Elias (bap. 6 Jan. 1768) and Louisa (bap. 6 Jan. 1768); d. 9 July 1801 (murdered by his brother Christian, bap. 23 Aug. 1767); Unami (F# 611).

Jacob (Jakob) Gendaskund, bap. 24 Dec. 1770 in Langundoutenünk, m. Rosina (bap. 21 March 1771), children: Philippina (b. 1 March 1774), Sophia (bap. 6 Jan. 1774), Rosina (bap. 16 April 1772), Wangegias (d. 26 Jan. 1773, not baptized); left congregation 23 March 1777; d. after 3 May 1799; Munsee (F# 658). Before baptism chief of Munsee. See Simon, alias Panipachgihillen (father-in-law, bap. 1 Jan. 1772).

Jacob, bap. 19 May 1771, adult son of Jacob, alias Menatschis (bap. 29 Dec. 1765) and Rebecca (bap. 7 June 1767); m. 14 June 1772 to Johanette (bap. 12 April 1772); children: Maria Magdalena (b. 2 Nov. 1773), Michael (b. 3 Jan. 1776), Anna Sabina (b. 11 May 1778); bur. 16 Nov. 1779 (B); Munsee (F# 683). See Levi (brother, bap. 3 April 1768), Catharina, alias Mamtscha (sister, bap. 25 Dec. 1775), Christina (sister, bap. 6 Jan. 1774), Benjamin (bap. 2 July 1773).

Jacob, alias Tschimapehellus or Schimapehellus, bap. 26 Dec. 1773 in Gnadenhütten; m. Marie (bap. 26 April 1745); children: Theodora (bap. 6 Jan. 1774), Nathanael (b. 9 Aug. 1774), Christina (1777); expelled with family from congregation 26 Dec. 1781 (F# 736).

Jacob, b. and bap. 19 Oct. 1776, son of Willhelm, alias Bill Chelloway (bap. 6 Jan. 1771) and Martha (bap. 19 May 1771) in Lichtenau (F# 1374).

Jacob, bap. 6 Jan. 1778, son of Israel, alias Welapachtschiechen (bap. 25 Dec. 1777) and Rahel (admitted 25 Dec. 1777); m. 12 Feb. 1781 to Christina (bap. 9 May 1764); children: Elisa-beth (1786), Martin (1790), Rahel (1800), Josephus (1801), Ketura (1803), Christian Jacob (1807); d. after 1814 (F# 857).

Jacobina, bap. 4 Feb. 1776, adult daughter of Lucas, alias Gatshenis (bap. 3 Dec. 1769) and Paulina (bap. 3 Dec. 1769) in Schönbrunn; m. Matthaeus before 1784; d. 27 June 1797 (F# 835).

Jael, bap. 25 Dec. 1775 as big girl and daughter of Samuel Nantikok (bap. 10 Aug. 1766) and Sarah Nantikok (bap. 27 Jan. 1772) in Schönbrunn; d. 19 Jan. 1808; Nantikok (F# 804).

Jannetje, admitted 16 Aug. 1772, daughter of Anna Margaretha (admitted 20 Jan. 1771); child from earlier marriage: Johanan (bap. 3 Dec. 1773); m. 11 May 1774 to Petrus, alias Echpalawehund (bap. 6 Feb. 1774); no children (F# 907).

Jephta, alias Queelpacheno, bap. 6 Jan. 1774 in Schönbrunn; m. to Zipora (bap. 12 April 1772); children: Joseph (bap. 12 Jan. 1773), Adam, alias Scheechganìm (bap. 1 Jan. 1776); d. 3 Feb. 1776; bur. 5 Feb. 1776 in Schönbrunn (B) (F# 743), "in early times a great medical doctor amongst the Indians." See Esra, alias Apallochgacan (brother, bap. 20 May 1773), Sem, alias Tschuwisch (brother, bap. 25 Dec. 1775).

Jeremias bap. before 1771; admitted 19 May 1771; son of Bartholomäus (bap. 26 March 1744) and Elisabeth (bap. before 1753); m. 14 Aug. 1774 to Catharina (bap. 6 Jan. 1773); children: Johanan (b. 14 Nov. 1775), Martin (b. 19 Dec. 1777); d. after 1777; Mahican (F# 681).

Jeremias, alias Tschechquoapesek, bap. 21 Jan. 1770 in Lawunnakhannek; m. Anna Caritas (bap. 21 Jan. 1770); d. 23 Dec. 1778 (B); Munsee (F# 644), National Helper. See Johannes Papunhank (brother, bap. 26 June 1763), Johanna (sister, bap. 10 Aug. 1766).

Joachim, bap. 5 Sept. 1745; m. 26 Oct. 1755 to Benigna (bap. 13 Jan. 1754); children: Maria, alias Ahtschem (bap. 6 Jan. 1763), Heinrich (bap. 8 Jan. 1758, F# 427), Joachim (bap. 14 June 1760); d. 13 Dec. 1798; Unami (F# 75), translator, Helper.

Joachim, bap. 14 June 1760, son of Joachim (bap. 5 Sept. 1745) and Benigna (bap. 13 Jan. 1754); m. 18 Sept. 1779 to Anna Maria (bap. 12 Nov. 1775); children: Martin (b. 8 Oct. 1780), Henriette (bap. 19 Sept. 1789), Johann Jakob (bap. 4 March 1790); d. 26 Jan. 1814; Unami (F# 482), Helper.

Joachim, alias Moochwe, bap. 1 Jan. 1776 in Schönbrunn as "adult son of Jacob" (F# 806). *We were unable to identify his father.*

Job Chelloway, father of Augustine (bap. 6 Jan. 1767), frequent visitor of congregation, "common law husband" of Petty; d. before 1780 (F# —). See Willhelm, alias Bill Chelloway (brother, bap. 6 Jan. 1771).

Joel, bap. 1 Jan. 1776 in Schönbrunn (F# 807).

Johanan, b. 15 Nov. 1775, son of Jeremias (bap. before 1771) and Catharina (bap. 6 Jan. 1773); bap. 16 Nov. 1775 in Schönbrunn; d. 21 Jan. 1776 (F# 1356).

Johanan, bap. 3 Dec. 1773, son of Jannetje (admitted 20 Jan. 1771) in Schönbrunn (F# 1324).

Johanette, bap. 12 April 1772, daughter of Michael, alias Paatschpatsch (bap. 6 Jan. 1772) and Charlotte (bap. 6 Jan. 1772) in Langundoutenünk; m. 14 June 1772 to Jacob (bap. 19 May 1771); children: Maria Magdalena (b. 2 Nov. 1773), Michael (b. 3 Jan. 1776), Anna Sabina (b. 11 May 1778); m. 4 June 1780 to Abel (bap. 7 April 1776); child: Jonas (b. 4 Sept. 1781) (F# 709).

Johann Gottlieb, b. 11 Nov. 1779, son of Nathanael (bap. 25 Dec. 1776) and Martha Elisabeth (bap. 25 Jan. 1778); bap. 14 Nov. 1779 in Schönbrunn; bur. 19 Dec. 1779 (F# 1416).

Johann Jacob, alias Trenchtees, bap. 1 Feb. 1778 in Lichtenau; m. Elisabeth (bap. 22 March 1778); children: Maria Salome (bap. 29 March 1778), Rahel (bap. 22 March 1778) (F# 864). See Israel, alias Welapachtschiechen (cousin, bap. 25 Dec. 1777).

Johann Martin, bap. 22 Jan. 1750, son of Theodora (F# 232); m. 27 March 1752 to Anna (admitted 26 March 1752, bur. 5 July 1753, F# 329); child: Anton (bap. 6 Jan. 1774); m. before 1767 to Regine (bap. 19 April 1767); child: Anna Salome (bap. 26 March 1775); d. 8 March 1782; Unami (F# 248). See Daniel (brother, bap. 3 April 1768).

Johann Thomas, bap. 30 Aug. 1778 as one-year-old son of widow Rebecca (bap. 23 Aug. 1778) in Lichtenau; d. 8 March 1782 (F# 1399).

Johanna, bap. 11 Sept. 1768; m. Daniel (bap. 3 April 1768); children: Samuel (bap. 12 Sept. 1768), Gottlieb (bap. 6 Jan. 1771), Benjamin (b. 22 April 1773), Rahel (bap. 1 Jan. 1775), Beata (b. 20 April 1775), Johannes (b. 27 May 1779); d. 20 May 1795; Unami (F# 608). See Charlotte (sister, bap. 1 Jan. 1775).

Johanna, b. 7 May 1776, daughter of Thomas, alias Gutkigamen (bap. 11 Sept. 1774) and Sabina (bap. 11 Sept. 1774); bap. 12 May 1776 in Lichtenau; children: Benjamin (bap. 1 Jan. 1802), Caty (bap. 15 Sept. 1803), Amos (1804), Betheia (1804); d. 16 Jan. 1804; bur. 17 Jan. 1804 (F# 1366).

Johanna, bap. 30 March 1777, daughter of Josua Jr. (bap. 23 Jan. 1749) and Sophia (bap. 11 June 1765) in Gnadenhütten; bur. 31 March 1777 (F# 1376).

Johanna Christiana, bap. 7 Jan. 1776 as adult daughter of Salome (unclear status) in Schönbrunn (F# 820).

Johanna Maria, bap. 12 Nov. 1775 in Schönbrunn; child from earlier marriage: Regina (bap. 1 Jan. 1778); m. Nehemia, alias Wisawoapamend (bap. 12 Nov. 1775); child: Silpa (bap. 24 Dec. 1775); bur. 26 July 1778 (F# 798).

Johanna Sabina, bap. 22 Feb. 1778 as big daughter of Anna Benigna (bap. 25 Jan. 1778); m. 3 Oct. 1780 to Nicolaus (bap. 6 Jan. 1775); no children; d. 8 March 1782 (F# 867).

Johanna Salome, bap. 25 Dec. 1777 at age thirteen, daughter of Cornelia (bap. 28 May 1775) in Lichtenau; m. 31 Aug. 1780 to Heinrich (bap. 7 Jan. 1776); d. 8 March 1782 (F# 851).

Johanna Sophia, bap. 28 May 1775 in Schönbrunn; m. Renatus, alias Wunak (bap. 12 Nov. 1775); children: Sulamith (bap. 6 Aug. 1775), Samuel (b. 19 May 1778); d. 6 June 1778 (F# 790).

Johannes, b. 23 April 1774, son of Thomas, alias Gutkigamen (bap. 11 Sept. 1774) and Sabina (bap. 11 Sept. 1774); bap. 18 Sept. 1774 in Schönbrunn; d. 25 Aug. 1775; bur. 26 Aug. 1775 (F# 1334).

Johannes, alias [Captain] Douty, bap. 7 Jan. 1776 in Gnadenhütten; m. Rebecca (bap. 1 Jan. 1776); child: Gottlob (bap. 22 Feb. 1776); d. after 1777 (F# 823). See Justina (niece, bap. 6 Jan. 1777, F# 847).

Johannes, bap. 4 Feb. 1776 as adult son of Lucas, alias Gatshenis (bap. 3 Dec. 1769) and Paulina (bap. 3 Dec. 1769) in Schönbrunn; m. Anna before 1800; d. 11 May 1813 (F# 836).

Johannes, alias Netanewand, bap. 28 July 1776, grandson of Netawatwees in Lichtenau; m. Hanna (bap. 9 Jan. 1757); children: Joseph (b. 12 Nov. 1776), Agnes (b. 22 Feb. 1779), Samuel (bap. 10 Sept. 1780), Sarah (bap. 28 Oct. 1780); d. 8 March 1782 (F# 842).

Johannes, bap. 8 Jan. 1777, son of Gideon, alias Saktelaeuche (bap. 25 Dec. 1776) and Sara (bap. 6 Jan. 1777) in Lichtenau (F# 1377).

Johannes, b. 27 May 1779, son of Daniel (bap. 3 April 1768) and Johanna (bap. 11 Sept. 1768); bap. 30 May 1779 in Gnadenhütten (F# —).

Johannes Papunhank, bap. 26 June 1762 in Wyalusing; m. Anna Johanna (bap. 10 Aug. 1766); children: Sophia (bap. 11 June 1765), Anna Paulina (bap. 7 June 1772); d. 15 May 1775 (B); Munsee (F# 520). Before baptism Indian prophet, elder of congregation. See Samuel Moor (grandson, bap. 6 Jan 1771).

Johannes Petrus, b. 5 Jan. 1779, son of Adolph, alias Tschálok (bap. 13 Feb. 1774) and Susanne (bap. 20 July 1766); bap. 10 Jan. 1779 in Lichtenau; d. after 1811 (F# 1401).

Johannes Renatus, b. 2 Feb. 1778, son of Gideon, alias Saktelaeuche (bap. 25 Dec. 1776) and Sara (bap. 6 Jan. 1777); bap. 1 March 1778 in Lichtenau (F# 1389).

John Conner, European, b. 19 Aug. 1775, son of Richard and Peggy Conner (both admitted on 7 April 1776), bap. 27 Aug. 1775 in Schönbrunn (F# —).

Jonas, alias Pilawetsch, bap. 1 Jan. 1774, son of Beata (bap. 25 Jan. 1770) in Schönbrunn; d. 3 Oct. 1779 (B); Munsee (F# 739). See Lucas (brother, bap. 3 Dec. 1769).

Jonas, b. 11 Nov. 1774, son of Philippus Jr. (bap. 1749) and Eleanore (bap. 7 Sept. 1767); bap. 14 Nov. 1774 in Gnadenhütten (F# 1336).

Jonas, bap. 6 Jan. 1775, son of Joseph Peepi (bap. before 1748 by Presbyterians) and Hanna (bap. 30 July 1769); child from earlier marriage: Balthasar (bap. 7 Jan. 1776); m. Amalia (bap. 6 Jan. 1766); children: Lea (b. 12 Oct. 1775), Anna Christina (b. 17 March 1778), Elisabeth (bap. 6 Jan. 1780); d. 8 March 1782 (F# 776), Helper.

Jonas, b. 17 Jan. 1781, son of Zacharias (bap. 7 Jan. 1776) and Anna Elisabeth, alias Tiangan (bap. 16 April 1775); bap. 18 Jan. 1781 in Schönbrunn; d. 22 Jan. 1781 (F# 1429).

Jonas, b. 4 Sept. 1781, son of Abel (bap. 7 April 1776) and Johanette (bap. 12 April 1772) in Schönbrunn; bap. 9 Sept. 1781 in Salem; d. 8 March 1782 (F# 1436).

Jonathan, bap. 18 April 1749 in Bethlehem, formerly of Meniolagomeka; m. Verona (bap. 27 April 1749, d. 17 March 1764, F# 177); according to diary entry for 11 Jan. 1776 married to a "black woman"; Unami (F# 173).

Jonathan, b. 29 May 1772, son of Esra, alias Apallochgacan (bap. 20 May 1773) and Lazara (bap. 30 June 1771); bap. 31 May 1772 in Schönbrunn (F# 711).

Jonathan, bap. 30 June 1773, ill, son of Isaac, alias Glikhican (bap. 24 Dec. 1770) and Agnes (bap. 9 Feb. 1771) (F# —).

Jonathan, b. 26 May 1775, son of Nathanael (bap. 19 Dec. 1748) and Anna Johanna (b. 8 June 1756); bap. 28 May 1775 in Gnadenhütten; d. 8 March 1782 (F# 1346).

Jonathan, bap. 6 Jan. 1780, son of Susanna Minque (bap. before 2 Aug. 1777) in Schönbrunn (F# 884).

Joseph, bap. 2 March 1751, son of Gottlieb (bap. 26 April 1745, F# 73) and Marie (bap. 26 April 1745, F# 74); readmitted 30 July 1780; child from earlier marriage: Bathseba (bap. 5 Aug. 1780); m. 30 Aug. 1780 to Petty (admitted 31 March 1771); d. after 1782; Unami (F# 296 and 925).

Joseph, b. 15 Oct. 1772, son of Anton, alias Welochalent (bap. 19 May 1771) and Juliana (bap. 30 May 1771); bap. 25 Oct. 1772 in Schönbrunn (F# 1311).

Joseph, bap. 12 Jan. 1773 "shortly before his death," son of Jephta, alias Queelpacheno (bap. 4 Jan. 1774) and Zipora (bap. 12 April 1772) (F# —).

Joseph, bap. 1 Jan. 1774, son of Gideon, alias Teedyuskung (bap. 8 March 1750) in Gnadenhütten I; probably m. Maria Catharina (bap. 25 Dec. 1777); moved from Gekelemukpechünk to Lichtenau; d. after 19 Sept. 1787 (F# 741).

Joseph, bap. 15 April 1774 at age four, son of Joseph, alias Gutkigamen (bap. 1 Sept. 1774) "in his illness" in Schönbrunn; d. and bur. 16 April 1774 (F# 1326).

Joseph, admitted 25 May 1775 as son of Thomas Onondaga (admitted 1 Jan. 1775) and Marie (admitted 12 Feb. 1775) (F# 913).

Joseph, b. 6 July 1776, son of Thomas (admitted 19 May 1771) and Polly (bap. in the Jerseys); bap. 7 July 1776 in Gnadenhütten (F# 1369).

Joseph, b. 12 Nov. 1776, son of Johannes, alias Netanewand (bap. 28 July 1776) and Hanna (bap. 7 Jan. 1758); bap. 17 Nov. 1776 in Lichtenau; d. 8 March 1782 (F# 1375).

Joseph, bap. 5 Aug. 1779, grandson of Helena (bap. 6 Jan. 1777) in Lichtenau; d. 23 Aug. 1779 (F# 1413).

Joseph Peepi (Piipi, Peepe), bap. before 1748 by Presbyterians; admitted 30 July 1769 in Friedenshütten; child from earlier marriage: Petrus, alias Mose (bap. 14 April 1775); m. Hanna (bap. 30 July 1769); children: Anton, alias Welochalent (bap. 19 May 1771), Jonas (bap. 6 Jan. 1775), Polly (bap. in the Jerseys) (F# 634). See Maria (mother, d. 2 Sept. 1770).

Joseph Schebosch, bap. 25 Dec. 1758, son of John Joseph Bull, alias Schebosch (bap. 27 May 1721) and Christiana (bap. 12 July 1764); m. 21 Dec. 1779 to Helena (bap. 1 Jan. 1775); no children; d. 28 March 1782 (F# 457).

Josua Sr., Mahican, bap. 4 Sept. 1742 in Bethlehem; m. to Salome (bap. 12 Dec. 1742, d. 16 Sept. 1746, F# 28); children: Gabriel (bap. 20 May 1744, F# 70), Josua Jr. (bap. 23 Jan. 1749); m. before 1755 to Bathseba (bap. 7 Aug. 1743); no children; bur. 2 Aug. 1775 (F# 12); Helper, translator, founder of Gnadenhütten II.

Josua Jr., bap. 23 Jan. 1749, son of Josua Sr. (bap. 4 Sept. 1742) and Salome (bap. 12 Dec. 1742, d. 3 Sept. 1747); m. 26 June 1764 to Sophia (bap. 11 June 1765); children: Anna (bap. 4 Aug. 1765), Bathseba (bap. 13 May 1767), Salome (bap. 29 March 1771), Nathanael (bap. 17 Aug. 1773), Sophia (b. 5 July 1774), Johanna (bap. 30 March 1777), Josua (b. 9 April 1779), Thomas (b. 16 Oct. 1780); d. before 1806; Mahican (F# 130); played the harpsichord, National Helper.

Josua, b. 9 April 1779, son of Josua Jr. (bap. 23 Jan. 1749) and Sophia (bap. 11 June 1765) in Lichtenau; bap. 18 April 1779; d. 29 April 1779 (F# 1408).

Judith, b. 11 April 1774, daughter of Gabriel (bap. 15 March 1749) and Lydia (bap. 22 Sept. 1771); bap. 20 April 1774 in Gnadenhütten (F# 1327).

Judith, bap. 12 May 1774 in Schönbrunn; m. Simon, alias Laweloochwalend (bap. 3 April 1774); d. 8 March 1782 (F# 761).

Juliana, bap. 7 May 1769 in Friedenshütten; m. Moses (bap. 17 Sept. 1749); children: Beata (bap. 8 May 1769), Anna Maria (bap. 20 Oct. 1772); d. after 4 Jan. 1773; Unami (F# 615).

Juliana, bap. 30 May 1771; m. Anton, alias Welochalent (bap. 19 May 1771); children: Elisabeth (bap. 1 July 1771), Joseph (b. 15 Oct. 1772), Marcus (b. 25 Feb. 1775), Gertraud (b. 28 Jan. 1778), Christian Gottlieb (b. 20 May 1781); bur. 21 Aug. 1781; Unami (F# 690).

Juliana, bap. 1 Jan. 1775, daughter of Phoebe (bap. 22 May 1774) in Gnadenhütten; d. 8 March 1782 (F# 773).

Justina, bap. 25 Dec. 1774, daughter of Seth, alias Netawastond (bap. 16 July 1774) and Verona (bap. 25 Dec. 1774); m. Gottfried (bap. 25 Dec. 1774); children: Lydia (bap. 16 Jan. 1775), Charlotte (bap. 27 Dec. 1778), Martin (bap. 22 Oct. 1775) (F# 769).

Justina, bap. 6 Jan. 1777 at age sixteen in Gnadenhütten, niece of Johannes alias [Captain] Douty (bap. 7 Jan. 1776); m. Jephta (bap. 27 June 1790, d. after 1804, F# 974); children: Elisabeth (bap. 22 Nov. 1801), Lisette, alias Quetit (bap. 6 Jan. 1803); d. after 1810 (F# 847).

Laban, alias Woachihillen, bap. 7 Jan. 1776 in Schönbrunn (F# 816).

Lazara, bap. 30 June 1771, daughter of Jephta (bap. 6 Jan. 1774) in Langundoutenünk; m. Esra, alias Apallochgacan (bap. 20 May 1773); children: Jonathan (b. 29 May 1772), Thomas (b. 31 July 1774); d. after 1776 (F# 687).

Lea, bap. 6 Jan. 1772; m. Simon, alias Panipachgihillen (bap. 1 Jan. 1771) (F# 700).

Lea, b. 12 Oct. 1775, daughter of Jonas (bap. 6 Jan. 1775) and Amalia (bap. 6 Jan. 1766); bap. 17 Oct. 1775 in Gnadenhütten; d. 8 March 1782 (F# 1353).

Lea, b. 24 Sept. 1775, daughter of Nicolaus (admitted 20 June 1771) and Amalia (bap. 20 June 1771); bap. 25 Sept. 1775 in Schönbrunn (F# 1351). See Amalia (twin sister).

Lea, bap. 6 Jan. 1781, daughter of Michael, alias Paatschpatsch (bap. 6 Jan. 1772) and Charlotte (bap. 6 Jan. 1772) in Schönbrunn (F# 900). See Johanette (sister, bap. 12 April 1772).

Leonhard, bap. 8 Sept. 1749 in Meniolagomeka; m. Lucia (bap. 2 Jan. 1751, d. after 9 Aug. 1771, F# 288); d. after 9 Sept. 1773; Unami (F# 213).

Leonhard, bap. 6 Jan. 1775 as adult son of Nathanael Davis (bap. 18 June 1769) and Anna Salome (bap. 6 Oct. 1770) in Schönbrunn; m. to Rahel (bap. 6 Jan. 1775); children: Lucia (bap. 16 Jan. 1775), Hanna (b. 9 April 1776), Cornelia (b. 9 Sept. 1777), Samuel (b. 19 Aug. 1781); left congregation before 1788 (F# 774).

Levi, bap. 3 April 1768, son of Jacob, alias Menatschi (bap. 29 Dec. 1765) and Rebecca (bap. 7 June 1772) and grandson of Salomo, alias Allemewi (bap. 25 Dec. 1769); m. Salome (bap. 11 Sept. 1768); children: David (bap. 16 April 1769, bur. 22 Oct. 1769), Anna (bap. 19 Aug. 1770, d. 1771), Sophia (bap. 5 April 1772, d. 24 April 1772), Rebecca (b. 18 March 1773, d. 17 July 1773); expelled from Schönbrunn 19 Sept. 1774; d. after 18 Aug. 1804 (F# 596). See Jacob (brother, bap. 19 May 1771), Christiana (sister, bap. 6 Jan. 1774), Catarina, alias Mamtscha (sister, bap. 19 May 1777).

Levi, bap. 14 Jan. 1776 as adult son of Philippus Jr. (bap. 23 Jan. 1749) and Eleanore (bap. 7 Sept. 1767); in 1774 lived in Gekelemukpechünk, in 1804 on White River; d. after 18 Aug. 1804 (F# 828).

Levi, bap. 6 Jan. 1781, grandson of Gertraud (bap. 20 Jan. 1771) in Schönbrunn; d. after 6 Feb. 1809 (F# 899).

Loida, bap. 1 Jan. 1776 in Schönbrunn; m. Moses (bap. 12 Nov. 1775); child: Phoebe (b. 16 July 1776); d. after 1808 (F# 809).

Louisa, bap. 6 Jan. 1768 in Friedenshütten; m. Elias (bap. 6 Jan. 1768); children: Christian (bap. 23 Aug. 1767), Jacob (bap. 11 Dec. 1768), Matthaeus (bap. 8 May 1774); d. after 1803; Unami (F# 593).

Louisa, b. 26 July 1774, daughter of Samuel Moor (bap. 6 Jan. 1771) and Helena (bap. 13 April 1768); bap. 27 July 1774 in Schönbrunn (F# 1330).

Lucas, alias Gatshenis, bap. 3 Dec. 1769 in Lawunnakhannek, son of Beata (bap. 25 Jan. 1770); m. Paulina (bap. 3 Dec. 1769); children: Israel (bap. 3 Dec. 1769), Anna [Paulina] (b. 30 July 1772), Paulus (b. and bap. 19 March 1775), Jacobina (bap. 4 Feb. 1776), Johannes (bap. 4 Feb. 1776), Daniel (b. 3 Nov. 1777); m. 7 Oct. 1779 to Anna Caritas (bap. 21 Jan. 1770); no children; m. 10 Feb. 1793 to Cornelia; d. 31 Jan. 1808; Munsee (F# 639), National Helper. See Jonas alias Pilawetsch (brother, bap. 1 Jan. 1774).

Lucas, alias Netoochghallent, bap. 24 April 1774 in Gnadenhütten; m. Lucia (bap. 24 April 1774); d. 8 March 1782 (F# 758).

Lucas, bap. 6 Jan. 1775, son of Sam Evans (bap. 6 Jan. 1774) and Ruth (bap. before 1749) in Philadelphia, was epileptic; d. 12 Feb. 1775 (F# 538).

Lucia, bap. 10 April 1757, widow; d. 31 Aug. 1773 (B), bur. 1 Sept. 1773 (F# 416).

Lucia, bap. 24 April 1774 in Gnadenhütten; m. Lucas, alias Gatshenis (bap. 24 April 1774); d. 8 March 1782 (F# 759). See Phoebe (sister, bap. 22 May 1774), Anna Begina (sister, bap. 25 June 1778), Rebecca (bap. 23 Aug. 1778).

Lucia, bap. 16 Jan. 1775, daughter of Leonard (bap. 6 Jan. 1775) and Rahel (bap. 6 Jan. 1775) age one year (F# 1338).

Lucia bap. 4 Feb. 1776 in Schönbrunn; m. Sem, alias Tschuwisch (bap. 25 Dec. 1775); child: Benigna (b. 19 April 1776); d. after 1798 (F# 831).

Lucia, bap. 22 Feb. 1778 as adult daughter probably of Phoebe (bap. 22 May 1774) and Nicodemus, alias Acootschees (Acheutschis) (bap. 7 Jan. 1776) in Lichtenau (F# 869).

Lucia, bap. 1 Jan. 1781 in Schönbrunn, granddaughter of Maria Elisabeth (bap. 31 March 1771); d. after 2 June 1810 (F# 898).

Ludwig, alias Gulpikamen, bap. 27 April 1749, son of Isaac, alias Glikhican (bap. 24 Dec. 1770); Unami (F# 176).

Ludwig, bap. 10 March 1771, son of Marcus (bap. 8 Sept. 1749) and Anna Elisabeth (bap. 14 May 1769); d. 6 Sept. 1772 (F# 669).

Ludwig, b. 20 Nov. 1773, grandson of Anna Margaretha (admitted 20 Jan. 1771); bap. 2 Dec. 1773 in Schönbrunn; bur. 2 March 1774 (F# 1323).

Ludwig, bap. 1 Jan. 1774, son of Hanna (bap. 30 July 1769) and Joseph Peepi (bap. before 1748 by Presbyterians); m. Ruth (bap. 4 Feb. 1776); child: Samuel (b. 9 Oct. 1779); d. 8 March 1782 (F# 742).

Ludwig, alias Gokschewéhemen, bap. 16 April 1775 in Schönbrunn; m. Marie Juliane, alias Mattamis (bap. 7 Jan. 1776); children: Christian (bap. 2 Feb. 1776), Rosina (bap. 24 May 1778), Elisabeth (b. 11 Nov. 1780) (F# 784).

Ludwig, bap. 1 Jan. 1787 in Cuyahoga; m. 16 Jan. 1787 to Esther (bap. 2 Jan. 1780); children: Nathanael (1788), Caleb (1790), Johannes (1796), Salome (1800); bur. 30 Dec. 1799 (F# 932).

Lydia, bap. 26 Dec. 1766 in Friedenshütten; m. 1 Feb. 1767 to Augustus (bap. 19 Aug. 1766); no children; d. after 1780; Munsee (F# 566).

Lydia, bap. 22 Sept. 1771, daughter of Hanna (bap. 30 June 1769) from her first marriage; m. 10 Jan. 1773 to Gabriel (bap. before 1755); children: Judith (b. 11 April 1774), Regina

(bap. 31 March 1777), Andreas (b. 18 Sept. 1780); bur. 24 Aug. 1791; Unami (F# 693).
Note: In her biography the date of baptism is given as 26 Dec. 1766. We believe that Zeisberger erred and confused Lydia, wife of Gabriel, with Lydia, wife of Augustus.

Lydia, bap. 16 Jan. 1775, daughter of Gottfried (bap. 25 Dec. 1774) and Justina (bap. 25 Dec. 1774) in Schönbrunn (F# 1337).

Magdalena, bap. 9 Jan. 1757; m. Paulus (bap. 9 Jan. 1757, d. 12 July 1758, F# 411); child: Hanna (bap. 7 Jan. 1758); d. before 1776 in Gekelemukpechünk; Unami (F# 412).

Magdalena, bap. 20 July 1766 in Friedenshütten; m. Nathanael, alias Gochgachgaholen (bap. 9 Feb. 1767, d. 26 May 1767, F# 555); children: Anna (bap. 12 Jan. 1768, d. 21 Jan. 1768, F# 594), Rosina (bap. 12 June 1768, d. 20 June 1768, F# 603), Helena (bap. 1 Jan. 1775); d. after 29 Aug. 1776; Munsee (F# 549).

Magdalena, bap. 3 April 1774 at age thirty-three; m. Petrus (not identified) in Schönbrunn; d. before 1 Nov. 1804 (F# 757). See Willhelmine (sister, bap. 4 July 1773).

Marcus, bap. 8 Sept. 1749; m. before 1764 to Anna (bap. 31 July 1743, d. 21 June 1769, F# 51); children: Nathanael, Abraham, Christian and Marie Elisabeth (all admitted in 1769); m. 6 May 1770 to Anna Elisabeth (bap. 14 May 1769); child: Ludwig (bap. 10 March 1771); m. before 12 July 1778 to Sarah (bap. 12 July 1778); no children; d. before 10 Nov. 1783; Mahican (F# 217), National Helper, played the violin.

Marcus, b. 25 Feb. 1775, son of Anton, alias Welochalent (bap. 19 May 1771) and Juliana (bap. 30 May 1771); bap. 26 Feb. 1775 in Schönbrunn; d. 8 March 1782 (F# 1339).

Marcus, bap. 30 July 1780 as adult in Salem; m. 18 Feb. 1781 to Susanna (bap. 2 Jan. 1780); d. 8 March 1782 (F# 892), from Wabash.

Maria, bap. 7 June 1772 by Jungmann in Langundoutenünk, mother of Boas (bap. 23 May 1771) (F# 712).

Maria, b. 4 May 1779, daughter of Zacharias (bap. 7 Jan. 1776) and Anna Elisabeth, alias Tiangan (bap. 16 April 1775); bap. 9 May 1779 in Schönbrunn (F# —).

Maria Catharina, bap. 25 Dec. 1777 at age fifteen, daughter of Magdalene in Lichtenau; m. Joseph (bap. 1 Jan. 1774) (F# 850).

Maria (Marie) Elisabeth, bap. 31 March 1771, daughter of Salomo, alias Allemewi (bap. 25 Dec. 1769) and Erdmuth (bap. 12 June 1770) in Langundoutenünk, widow; bur. 12 May 1802 (F# 676). See Lucia (grandson, bap. 1 Jan. 1781).

Maria Magdalena, b. 2 Nov. 1773, daughter of Jacob (bap. 19 May 1771) and Johanette (bap. 12 April 1772); bap. 3 Nov. 1773 in Schönbrunn (F# 1322).

Maria Magdalena, bap. 13 March 1775 in Schönbrunn; d. 14 March 1775, mother of Gertraud (b. 11 March 1775, d. 19 March 1775) (F# 782). See Isaac, alias Glikhican (relative, probably uncle, bap. 24 Dec. 1770).

Maria Salome, bap. 29 May 1778 at age one, daughter of Johann Jacob (bap. 1 Feb. 1778) and Elisabeth (bap. 22 March 1778) in Lichtenau (F# 1392).

Maria Salome, b. 29 Jan. 1779, daughter of Thomas, alias Gutkigamen (bap. 11 Sept. 1774) and Sabina (bap. 11 Sept. 1774); bap. 7 Feb. 1779 in Lichtenau; m. before 28 Dec. 1803 to Wichtsch; child: Cornelius (bap. 28 Dec. 1803); bur. 11 Oct. 1804 (F# 1404).

Maria Susanna, bap. 4 Feb. 1776, oldest daughter of Cornelia (bap. 28 May 1775) in Schönbrunn; d. 8 March 1782 (F# 832).

Maria Theresia, alias Gochgachganemau, bap. 4 Feb. 1776 as adult daughter of Theodore (probably identical to Theodora, bap. 20 Jan. 1771) in Schönbrunn; m. Andreas, alias Tschemipachgennesch (bap. 7 Jan. 1776); children: Samuel (bap. 23 Oct. 1773), Philippus (bap. 8 Feb. 1776); d. before 18 July 1806 (F# 830).

Mariane bap. 25 Dec. 1777 at age twelve, daughter of Michael, alias Paatschpatsch (bap. 6 Jan. 1772) and Charlotte (bap. 6 Jan. 1772) in Lichtenau (F# 853).

Marie, bap. 26 April 1745; m. Gottlieb (bap. 26 April 1745, d. 31 July 1753, F# 73); children: Samuel (bap. 3 April 1749, d. 28 March 1750, F# 172), Sophia (bap. 14 May 1749), Joseph (bap. 2 March 1751, d. after 26 April 1754, F# 296), Gottlieb (b. 4 Sept. 1753, d. after 26 April 1754); m. Jacob, alias Tschimapehellus or Schimapehellus (bap. 26 Dec. 1773); children: Nathanael (b. 10 Aug. 1774), Theodora (bap. 6 Jan. 1774), Christiana (1777), Sophia (bap. 14 April 1779); d. after 14 April 1779; Unami (F# 74).

Marie, admitted 12 Feb. 1775 to Schönbrunn congregation; m. Thomas Onondaga (admitted 1 Jan. 1775); children: Joseph (admitted 25 May 1775), Nicolaus (admitted 1 Jan. 1775), Christine (admitted 19 Aug. 1775), Polly (admitted 25 May 1775) (F# 912).

Marie Elisabeth, bap. 15 May 1767 in Friedenshütten, daughter of Marcus (bap. 8 Sept. 1749) and Anna (bap. 31 July 1743); d. 8 March 1782; Mahican (F# 579).

Marie Juliane, alias Mattamis, bap. 7 Jan. 1776, as granddaughter of Salomo, alias Allemewi (bap. 25 Dec. 1769) and Erdmuth (bap. 12 June 1770); m. Ludwig (bap. 7 Jan. 1776); children: Christian (bap. 2 Feb. 1776), Rosina (bap. 24 May 1778), Elisabeth (b. 11 Nov. 1780) (F# 819).

Martha, bap. 10 Aug. 1766; m. Timotheus, alias Tuteleu (bap. 30 March 1766); child: Salome (bap. 6 Jan. 1772); separated from her husband 26 May 1776; m. 15 Feb. 1784 to Abraham, alias Sakima (bap. 25 Dec. 1765); bur. 16 Nov. 1807 (F# 553).

Martha, bap. 1 Jan. 1768, daughter of Christian (bap. 4 March 1750) and Augustine (bap. 6 Jan. 1767) in Friedenshütten; d. 1803; Unami (F# 591).

Martha, bap. 19 May 1771; m. Willhelm, alias Bill Chelloway (bap. 6 Jan. 1771); children: Abigail (bap. 7 Feb. 1772), Elisabeth (bap. 20 Oct. 1774), Jacob (bap. 19 Oct. 1776), Regina (b. 23 Feb. 1779), Anton (bap. 4 April 1784, d. after 1808, F# 1458), Mattheus (bap. 17 Sept. 1786, bur. 8 July 1789, F# 1469), Gertraud (bap. 3 Sept. 1789, bur. 17 Sept. 1791, F# 1487); bur. 14 Dec. 1810; Unami (F# 685). See Anna Maria (sister, bap. 12 Nov. 1775).

Martha, bap. 17 Sept. 1778 in Lichtenau; m. white Indian trader Alexander McCormick; child: Martha Elisabeth (bap. 25 Jan. 1778); d. 20 Sept. 1778 (B) (F# 875). See Israel, alias Welapachtschiechen (cousin, bap. 25 Dec. 1777), Anna Margretha (sister? bap. 28 May 1778). *Note: The biography mentions a baptized daughter from the clan of Israel. Only Martha Elisabeth fits the description.*

Martha, bap. 2 Jan. 1780 at age twelve, probably daughter of Helena, alias Quelpinawos (bap. 13 April 1755) in Lichtenau; d. 8 March 1782 (F# 883).

Martha, sister of Salome (bap. 17 Oct. 1773) and Eleanore (bap. 7 Sept. 1767) according to death notice for Salome (F# —).

Martha Elisabeth, bap. 25 Jan. 1778 in Lichtenau, grandson of Israel, alias Welapachtschiechen (bap. 25 Dec. 1777); m. 22 Nov. 1778 to Nathanael (bap. 25 Dec. 1776); child: Johann Gottlieb (b. 11 Nov. 1779) (F# 863).

Martin, b. 19 Oct. 1775, son of Gottfried (bap. 25 Dec. 1774) and Justina (bap. 25 Dec. 1774); bap. 22 Oct. 1775 in Schönbrunn (F# 1354).

Martin, b. 19 Dec. 1777, son of Jeremias (bap. 19 May 1771) and Catharina (bap. 6 Jan. 1773); bap. 25 Dec. 1777 in Gnadenhütten (F# —).

Martin, b. 8 Oct. 1780, son of Joachim (bap. before 1762) and Anna Maria (bap. 12 Nov. 1775); bap. 15 Oct. 1780 in Gnadenhütten (F# 1425).

Martinus, b. and bap. 26 March 1780, son of Isaac, alias Glikhican (bap. 24 Dec. 1770) and Anna Benigna (bap. 25 Jan. 1778) in Lichtenau; d. 19 May 1780 (F# 1418).

Mary, bap. in Stockbridge; admitted 25 Dec. 1772; m. Petrus, alias Mose (bap. 14 April 1775); child: Hanna (b. 2 March 1776) (F# 908).

Mary, bap. in the Jerseys, admitted 25 Dec. 1772, sister of Samuel Nantikok (bap. 10 Aug. 1766) (F# —).

Matthaeus, b. and bap. 8 May 1774, son of Elias (bap. 6 Jan. 1768) and Louisa (bap. 6 Jan. 1768) in Gnadenhütten; d. after 26 Sept. 1790 (F# 1328).

Matthäus, bap. 18 Feb. 1761 at age sixteen; m. Anna Rosina (bap. 11 May 1755); d. 20 Sept. 1778 (B) (F# 495).

Matthäus, bap. 7 Jan. 1770, son of Cornelius (admitted 6 Jan. 1766) and Amalia (bap. 23 Feb. 1766) in Friedenshütten; d. before 1791 (F# 643).

Matthäus, alias Tom, bap. 6 Jan. 1781, son of Elisabeth (not identified) in Gnadenhütten; half Shawnee (F# 901).

Michael, alias Paatschpatsch, bap. 6 Jan. 1772, son of Debora (bap. 1 Jan. 1774) in Langundoutenünk; m. Charlotte (bap. 26 Jan. 1772); children: Johanette (bap. 12 April 1772), Sabina (bap. 2 Feb. 1772), Gottfried (bap. 25 Dec. 1774), Ruth (bap. 4 Feb. 1776), Sabina (bap. 26 May 1776), Mariane (bap. 25 Dec. 1777), Lea (bap. 6 Jan. 1781); d. before 15 May 1780; Munsee (F# 699).

Michael, b. 3 Jan. 1776, son of Jacob (bap. 19 May 1771) and Johanette (bap. 12 April 1772); bap. 5 Jan. 1776 in Schönbrunn; d. 5 July 1814 (F# 1358).

Michael, bap. 15 Jan. 1776 as adult son of Hanna (bap. 30 July 1769) in Gnadenhütten; d. 8 March 1782 (F# 829).

Michael, b. 25 Nov. 1777, son of Petrus (bap. before 25 Nov. 1777) and Pauline (bap. before 25 Nov. 1777); bap. 26 Nov. 1777 in Gnadenhütten (F# —).

Moses, bap. 17 Sept. 1749, son of Moses (bap. 12 Dec. 1742) and Miriam (bap. 12 Dec. 1742); m. 9 Feb. 1750 to Rosina (d. 30 Aug. 1750); m. Juliana (bap. 7 May 1769); children: Beata (bap. 8 May 1769), Anna Maria (bap. 20 Oct. 1772); d. after 1773; Mahican (F# 221).

Moses, alias Nono, bap. 12 Nov. 1775, son of Priscilla (bap. 20 Aug. 1775) in Schönbrunn; m. Loida (bap. 1 Jan. 1776); child: Phoebe (b. 16 July 1776); d. after 1804 (F# 796).

Moses, bap. 30 March 1777, son of Gideon, alias Saktelaeuche (bap. 25 Dec. 1776); m. 16 Nov. 1779 to Sybilla (bap. 22 Jan. 1775); deported by hostile warriors in 1781 (F# 848).

Naemi, bap. 14 Aug. 1774 in Gnadenhütten; d. 9 Nov. 1780 (F# 764). See Petrus, alias Echpalawehund (son, bap. 6 Feb. 1774), Nicolaus (grandson, bap. 6 Jan. 1775).

Nathan, b. and bap. 7 Sept. 1775, son of Timotheus, alias Kabaasch (bap. 19 May 1771) and Sarah (bap. before 19 Aug. 1775) in Schönbrunn (F# 1349).

Nathanael, bap. 19 Dec. 1748, son of Jonathan (bap. 10 Oct. 1742) and Anna (bap. 31 July 1743); m. 12 Aug. 1771 to Anna Johanna (b. 8 June 1756); children: Jonathan (b. 26 May 1775), Rebecca (b. 2 March 1778); d. 22 Sept. 1780; Mahican (F# 119).

Nathanael, alias James Davis, known as Nathanael Davis, bap. 18 June 1769; child from earlier marriage: Benjamin (bap. 7 Jan. 1776); m. Anna Salome (bap. 6 Oct. 1770); children: Gottlieb (bap. 8 Oct. 1770), Catharina (bap. 6 Jan. 1773), Eleonora (b. 21 Aug. 1774), Leonhard (bap. 6 Jan. 1775), Anna Helena (bap. 7 April 1776); left congregation in 1789 and moved to Maumee River; Unami (F# 621), Helper.

Nathanael, bap. 21 Sept. 1772, son of Tanguk or Tankug (mother) in Langundoutenünk; d. 24 Sept. 1772 (F# 723). See Adolph (twin brother, bap. 29 Oct. 1772).

Nathanael, bap. 17 Aug. 1773, son of Josua Jr. (bap. 23 Jan. 1749) and Sophia (bap. 11 June 1765) in Gnadenhütten; d. 9 Sept. 1773 (F# 1319).

Nathanael, b. 9 Aug. 1774, son of Jacob, alias Tschimapehellus or Schimapehellus (bap. 26 Dec. 1773) and Marie (bap. before 6 Jan. 1747); bap. 10 Aug. 1774 in Gnadenhütten (F# 1332).

Nathanael, bap. 25 Dec. 1776, stepson of Gideon, alias Saktelauche (bap. 25 Dec. 1776); m. 22 Nov. 1778 to Martha Elisabeth (bap. 25 Jan. 1778) in Lichtenau; child: Johann Gottlieb (b. 11 Nov. 1779) (F# 844).

Nehemia, alias Wisawoapamend, bap. 12 Nov. 1775 in Schönbrunn; m. Johanna Maria (bap. 12 Nov. 1775); child: Silpa (bap. 24 Dec. 1775); left congregation on 31 Oct. 1778 (F# 797).

Nicodemus, bap. 10 June 1764 in Philadelphia, widower; d. 26 June 1774; Munsee (F# 528).

Nicodemus, alias Zelotschis, bap. 7 Dec. 1775 in Schönbrunn; d. 10 Dec. 1775 (F# 800). See Esra, alias Apallochgacan (brother, bap. 20 May 1773), Jephta, alias Queelpacheno (brother, bap. 4 Jan. 1774), Sem, alias Tschuwisch (brother, bap. 25 Dec. 1775).

Nicodemus, alias Achgutschisch or Acootschees orAcheutschis, bap. 7 Jan. 1776 in Gnadenhütten; m. Phoebe (bap. 22 May 1774); children: Stephanus (bap. 6 Jan. 1775), Juliana (bap. 1 Jan. 1775), and unbaptized son; deported by hostile Indians with his children on 7 May 1781 (F# 822).

Nicolaus, admitted 20 June 1771 to Langundoutenünk, son of Anna Margaretha (admitted 20 Jan. 1771); m. Amalia (bap. 20 June 1771); children: Tobias (b. 5 Oct. 1771), Lea and twin sister Amalia (b. 24 Sept. 1775); d. 16 Oct. 1778; bur. 18 Oct. 1778 (B) (F# 720, 906).

Nicolaus, admitted 1 Jan. 1775 to Schönbrunn as son of Thomas Onondaga (admitted 1 Jan. 1775) and Marie (admitted 12 Feb. 1775); m. 17 April 1776 to Sophia (bap. 6 Jan. 1774); no children; d. 18 Oct. 1778 (F# 911).

Nicolaus, bap. 6 Jan. 1775 in Gnadenhütten as adult son (stepson?) of Petrus, alias Echpalawehund (bap. 6 Feb. 1774) and grandson of Naemi (bap. 14 Aug. 1774); m. 3 Oct. 1780 to Johanna Sabina (bap. 22 Feb. 1778); no children; d. 8 March 1782 (F# 779).

Noah, alias Tassewochwe, bap. 2 July 1773 in Schönbrunn; m. Willhelmine (bap. 4 July 1773); child: Heinrich (bap. 9 Jan. 1774); d. 26 Dec. 1776; "First Fruit" of the Cherokee (F# 732).

Paulina, bap. 3 Dec. 1769 in Lawunnakhannek; m. Lucas, alias Gatshenis (bap. 3 Dec. 1769); children: Israel (b. March 1769), Anna {Paulina} (bap. 30 July 1772), Paulus (b. and bap. 19 March 1775), Jacobina (bap. 4 Feb. 1776), Johannes (bap. 4 Feb. 1776), Daniel (b. 3 Nov. 1777); d. 8 Dec. 1777 (F# 640), National Helper. See Anna Johanna (sister, bap. 10 Aug. 1766).

Paulina, bap. 20 Oct. 1771, daughter of Cornelius (admitted 6 Jan. 1766) and Amalia (bap. 23 Feb. 1766) in Friedenshütten; d. after 1804 (F# 694).

Paulina, bap. 6 Jan. 1774 as widow and daughter of Paulus (bap. 10 June 1764) in Gnadenhütten; d. after 1 Jan. 1804 (F# 749).

Pauline, bap. before 25 Nov. 1777; m. to Petrus (bap. before 25 Nov. 1777); child: Michael (b. 25 Nov. 1777) (F# —).

Paulus, alias Sesapsit, bap. 16 Jan. 1780 in Schönbrunn; d. 8 March 1782 (F# 888).

Paulus, b. and bap. 19 March 1775, son of Lucas, alias Gatshenis (bap. 3 Dec. 1769) and Paulina (bap. 3 Dec. 1769) in Schönbrunn; d. after 1801 (F# 1341).

Paulus, bap. 10 June 1764 in Philadelphia; children: Daniel (bap. 3 April 1768), Paulina (bap. 6 Jan. 1774); d. before 27 Aug. 1785; Munsee (F# 529).

Peggy Conner, European, during Seven Years' War taken prisoner by Shawnee and adopted into Shawnee family; m. Richard Conner; freed after Lord Dunmore's war; admitted 7 April 1776 with her husband; children: James (b. 1772), John (b. 19 Aug. 1775), William (b. 10 Dec. 1777), Henry (b. 7 Oct. 1780) (F# —).

Petrus, alias Sapan, bap. 25 Dec. 1766 in Friedenshütten; m. Abigail (bap. 31 Aug. 1776); children: Beata (bap. 1766), Abraham (bap. 1769), Anna Salome (bap. 1771); family refused admission to Gnadenhütten 7 Sept. 1774; d. after 1777 (F# 564).

Petrus, bap. 6 Jan. 1771, son of Cornelius (admitted 6 Jan. 1766) and Amalia (bap. 23 Feb. 1766) in Friedenshütten; m. 24 April 1776 to Christina (admitted 19 Aug. 1775); d. after 1777; Munsee (F# 665).

Petrus, alias Echpalawehund, bap. 6 Feb. 1774, son of Naemi (bap. 14 Aug. 1774) in Gnadenhütten; child from earlier marriage: Nicolaus (bap. 6 Jan. 1775); m. 11 May 1774 to Jannetje (daughter of Anna Margaretha); no children; d. 19 March 1775 (F# 752); before his baptism was chief.

Petrus, alias Mose, bap. 14 April 1775, son of Joseph Peepi (bap. before 1748 by Presbyterians) in Gnadenhütten; m. Mary (bap. in Stockbridge); children: Hanna (b. 2 March 1776); left congregation before 1780 (F# 788).

Petrus, bap. before 25 Nov. 1777; m. Pauline (bap. before 25 Nov. 1777); child: Michael (b. 25 Nov. 1777) (F# —).

Petrus, bap. 2 Jan. 1780 at age nineteen, son of Anna Benigna (bap. 25 Jan. 1778) in Lichtenau; m. Anna (bap. 25 March 1780) (F# 880a; *contrary to Fliegel we assume that the son of Anna Benigna was not married to Magdalena*), from Goschachgünk.

Petty, "common law wife" of Job Chelloway 1772, widow; m. 30 Aug. 1780 to Joseph (bap. 2 March 1751); d. 10 Jan. 1791 (F# 923).

Philippina, b. 1 March 1774, daughter of Jacob (Jakob) Gendaskund (bap. 24 Dec. 1770) and Rosina (bap. 31 March 1771); bap. 6 March 1774 in Schönbrunn (F# 1325).

Philippina, bap. 6 Jan. 1778 as single person and sister of Hanna (not identified)]; m. 15 May 1778 to Anton (bap. 6 Jan. 1778); no children (F# 859).

Philippus Sr., bap. 12 Dec. 1742 in Checomeco; m. to Lydia (bap. 12 Dec. 1742, F# 27); children: Philippus Jr. (bap. 23 Jan. 1749), Maria Salome (bap. 3 Jan. 1751, bur. 18 March 1754, F# 293), Petrus (bap. 12 Jan. 1758, bur. 28 Aug. 1765, F# 414); d. 15 Feb. 1776; bur. 16 Feb. 1776 in Gnadenhütten; Wampanoag (F# 20). See Thamar (sister, d. after 1763, F# 50), Andreas (brother, bap. 7 Aug. 1743).

Philippus Jr. bap. 23 Jan. 1749, son of Philippus Sr. (bap. 12 Dec. 1742) and Lydia (bap. 12 Dec. 1742, F# 27); m. 18 May 1760 to Judith (d. 8 Nov. 1764, F# 448); child: Joseph (d. 16 Nov. 1762); m. before 27 Feb. 1766 to Eleanore (frequently Lorel, bap. 7 Sept. 1767); children: Thomas (b. 26 June 1769), Anna Justina (b. 19 Oct. 1771), Jonas (b. 11 Nov. 1774), Levi (bap. 14 Jan. 1776), Sara and twin sister Anna Justina (b. 23 Jan. 1778); Wampanoag (F# 128).

Philippus, bap. 8 Feb. 1776, one-year-old son of Andreas, alias Tschemipachgennesch (bap. 7 Jan. 1776) and Maria Theresia, alias Gochgachganemau (bap. 4 Feb. 1776); d. 31 May 1806 (F# 1360).

Phoebe, bap. 6 Jan. 1767 as widow in Friedenshütten, mother of unbaptized children, sister of chief of Shommunk (Schammungk); d. 17 Jan. 1774; bur. 18 Jan. 1774 (F# 568).

Phoebe, bap. 22 May 1774 in Gnadenhütten; m. Nicodemus, alias Achgutschisch orAcootschees orAcheutschis (bap. 7 Jan. 1776); children: Juliana (bap. 1 Jan. 1775), unbaptized son, probably Lucia (bap. 22 Feb. 1778); d. in Lichtenau on 31 Dec. 1779; bur. 1 Jan. 1780 (B) (F# 762). See Lucia (sister, bap. 24 April 1774), Rebecca (sister, bap. 23 Aug. 1778), Anna Begina (sister, bap. 25 June 1778).

Phoebe, bap. 16 April 1775, daughter of Agnes (bap. 9 Feb. 1771) and (according to Fliegel) stepdaughter of Isaac, alias Glikhican (bap. 24 Dec. 1770) in Schönbrunn; d. 23 Jan. 1779 in Lichtenau (F# 786).

Phoebe, b. 16 July 1776, daughter of Moses, alias Nono (bap. 12 Nov. 1775) and Loida (bap. 1 Jan. 1776); bap. 21 July 1776 in Schönbrunn (F# —).

Polly, bap. in the Jerseys, daughter of Joseph Peepi (bap. before 1748 by Presbyterians) and Hanna (bap. 30 July 1769); admitted 19 May 1771; m. 28 May 1771 as widow to Thomas (admitted 19 May 1771); children: Joseph (b. 6 July 1776), Christian (b. 3 May 1780); left congregation in 1789; Unami (F# 680).

Polly, admitted 25 May 1775 to Schönbrunn, daughter of Thomas Onondaga (admitted 1 Jan. 1775) and Marie (admitted 12 Feb. 1775) (F# 914).

Priscilla, bap. 20 Aug. 1775 in Schönbrunn, mother of Renatus (bap. 12 Nov. 1775) and Moses (bap. 12 Nov. 1775); d. after 1779 (F# 792).

Rahel, bap. 1 Jan. 1775 as adult daughter of Daniel (bap. 3 April 1768) and Johanna (bap. 11 Sept. 1768) in Gnadenhütten; d. 8 March 1782 (F# 771).

Rahel, bap. 6 Jan. 1775 in Schönbrunn; m. Leonhard (bap. 6 Jan. 1775); children: Lucia (bap. 16 Jan. 1775), Hanna (b. 9 April 1776), Cornelia (b. 9 Sept. 1777), Samuel (b. 19 Aug. 1781); probably left with her husband before 1788 (F# 775).

Rahel, European, 1757 captured by Indians; admitted 25 Dec. 1777; m. Israel, alias Welapacht-schiechen (bap. 25 Dec. 1777); children: Jacob (bap. 6 Jan. 1778), Anton (bap. 6 Jan. 1778), David (bap. 6 Jan. 1780), Esther (bap. 2 Jan. 1780); d. 16 March 1783 (F# 922).

Rahel, bap. 22 March 1778 as big girl and daughter of Johann Jacob (bap. 1 Feb. 1778) and Elisabeth (bap. 22 March 1778) in Lichtenau (F# 871).

Rebecca, b. c. 1713, bap. 7 June 1767, oldest daughter of Salomo, alias Allemewi (bap. 25 Dec. 1769); m. c. 1735 to Jacob, alias Menatschis (bap. 29 Dec. 1765); children: Jacob (bap. 19 May 1771), Levi (bap. 3 April 1768), Benjamin (bap. 2 July 1773), Christina (bap. 6 Jan. 1774), Catharina, alias Mamtscha (bap. 25 Dec. 1775); d. 18 Sept. 1773 (B); Munsee (F# 581).

Rebecca, b. 18 March 1773, daughter of Levi (bap. 3 April 1768) and Salome (bap. 11 Sept. 1768); bap. 21 March 1773 in Schönbrunn; d. 17 July 1773 (F# 1313).

Rebecca Nantikok, alias Sara, widow, bap. 25 Dec. 1773 in Schönbrunn; m. 11 May 1774 to Tobias, alias Melimius (bap. 11 April 1773); no children (F# 735).

Rebecca, bap. 1 Jan. 1776 in Gnadenhütten; m. Johannes, alias [Captain] Douty (bap. 7 Jan. 1776); child: Gottlob (bap. 22 Feb. 1776); d. 11 May 1777 (F# 812).

Rebecca, b. 26 Feb. 1777, daughter of Samuel Nantikok (bap. 10 Aug. 1766) and Sarah Nanti-kok (bap. 27 Jan. 1772), bap. 2 March 1777 in Schönbrunn; d. 10 Nov. 1783; Nantikok (F# 1379).

Rebecca, b. 2 March 1778, daughter of Nathanael (bap. 19 Dec. 1748) and Anna Johanna (b. 8 June 1756); bap. 8 March 1778 in Gnadenhütten (F# 1391).

Rebecca, bap. 23 Aug. 1778 in Lichtenau, widow; child: Johann Thomas (bap. 30 Aug. 1778); d. 8 March 1782 (F# 874). *According to the Baptism Register she was sister of Phoebe (bap. 22 May 1774), Anna Benigna (bap. 25 Jan. 1778) and Lucia (bap. 24 April 1774).*

Regina, b. 23 Feb. 1779, daughter of Willhelm, alias Bill Chelloway (bap. 6 Jan. 1771) and Martha (bap. 19 May 1771); bap. 28 Feb. 1779 in Lichtenau (F# 1406).

Regina, b. and bap. 31 March 1777, daughter of Gabriel (bap. before 1755) and Lydia (bap. 22 Sept. 1771) in Gnadenhütten (F# 1373).

Regina, bap. 1 Jan. 1778 as big girl and daughter of Johanna Maria (bap. 12 Nov. 1775) in Lichtenau (F# 856).

Regine, bap. 19 April 1767; m. Johann Martin (bap. 22 Jan. 1750); child: Anna Salome (bap. 26 March 1775); d. after 1775; Unami (F# 575).

Regine, bap. 3 April 1774 in Schönbrunn; m. Augustinus, alias Newollike (bap. 12 May 1774); no children (F# 756).

Renatus, alias Wunank, bap. 12 Nov. 1775, son of Priscilla (bap. 20 Aug. 1775) in Schönbrunn; m. Johanna Sophia (bap. 28 May 1775); children: Sulamith (bap. 6 Aug. 1775), Samuel (b. 19 May 1778); d. 2 March 1814 (F# 795). See Moses, alias Nono (brother, bap. 12 Nov. 1775).

Richard Conner, European, Indian trader, admitted 7 April 1776, originally from Fredericks-town, Maryland; m. to Peggy (admitted 7 April 1776); children: James (b. 1772), John (b. 19 Aug. 1775), William (b. 10 Dec. 1777), Henry (b. 7 Oct. 1780) (F# —).

Rosina, bap. 31 March 1771 in Langundoutenünk, possibly daughter of Simon, alias Panipach-gihillen (bap. 1 Jan. 1772); m. Jacob (Jakob) Gendaskund (bap. 24 Dec. 1770); children: Philippina (b. 1 March 1774), Sophia (bap. 6 Jan. 1774), Rosina (bap. 16 April 1772, d. 16 April 1772, F# —); Wangegias (d. 26 Jan. 1773 unbaptized); Munsee (F# 675).

Rosina, bap. 24 May 1778, daughter of Ludwig, alias Gokschewéhemen (bap. 16 April 1775) and Marie Juliane, alias Mattamis (bap. 7 Jan. 1776) in Lichtenau, great-granddaughter of Salomo, alias Allemewi (bap. 25 Dec. 1769) (F# 1396).

Rosina; see Anna Rosina (bap. 11 May 1755).

Ruth, bap. 4 Feb. 1776, daughter of Michael, alias Paatschpatsch (bap. 6 Jan. 1772) and Charlotte (bap. 6 Jan. 1772) in Schönbrunn; m. Ludwig (bap. 1 Jan. 1774); child: Samuel (b. 9 Oct. 1779); d. 8 March 1782 (F# 833).

Ruth, bap. 11 March 1749, widowed 1754; m. Sam Evans (bap. 6 Jan. 1774); children: Lucas (bap. 6 Jan. 1765), Tobias (bap. 25 Oct. 1769), Sabina (bap. 1 Oct. 1775); d. 31 May 1804; bur. 1 June 1804; Unami (F# 147).

Sabina, bap. 2 Feb. 1772, daughter of Michael, alias Paatschpatsch (bap. 6 Jan. 1772) and Charlotte (bap. 6 Jan. 1772); d. 15 July 1773 (F# 706).

Sabina, bap. 11 Sept. 1774 in Schönbrunn; m. Thomas, alias Gutkigamen (bap. 11 Sept. 1774); children: Johannes (b. 23 April 1774), Johanna (b. 7 May 1776), Isaac and twin sister Maria Salome (b. 29 Jan. 1779), Judith (bap. 25 Dec. 1784, d. after 14 May 1804, F# 1463), Abel (bap. 23 Aug. 1789, bur. 24 April 1805, F# 959), Ruth (bap. 10 Sept. 1789, d. after 14 Oct. 1810, F# 1488), Lea (bap. 6 Jan. 1793, F# 1525); d. after 28 March 1809 (F# 767), National Helper.

Sabina, bap. 1 Oct. 1775, daughter of Sam Evans (bap. 6 Jan. 1774) and Ruth (bap. 11 March 1749) in Gnadenhütten (F# 794).

Sabina, bap. 26 May 1776, daughter of Michael, alias Paatschpatsch (bap. 6 Jan. 1772) and Charlotte (bap. 6 Jan. 1772) in Lichtenau; m. 29 Oct. 1777 to Adam, alias Scheechganím (bap. 1 Jan 1776); children: Elisabeth (b. 5 May 1779), Augustus (1786), Wilhelmina (bap. 9 Aug. 1791, F# 1512), Adolph (1794), Charles (bap. 5 Dec. 1798, bur. 8 Dec. 1798, F# 1571), Gottfried (1802); d. 16 May 1806 (F# 841).

Salome, bap. 20 Oct. 1765; m. Abraham, alias Sakima (bap. 25 Dec. 1765); child: Abigail (b. 31 Aug. 1766); d. 21 Sept. 1772; Munsee (F# 542).

Salome, bap. 11 Sept. 1768 in Friedenshütten; m. Levi (bap. 3 April 1768); children: David (bap. 16 April 1769, bur. 22 Oct. 1769), Anna (bap. 19 Aug. 1770, d. 1771), Sophia (b. 30 March 1772), Rebecca (b. 18 March 1773, d. 17 July 1773); probably followed her husband, who had to leave the congregation; Munsee (F# 609).

Salome, bap. 29 March 1771, daughter of Josua Jr. (bap. before 1747) and Sophia (bap. 11 June 1765) in Friedenshütten, m. 21 Feb. 1789 to Israel (bap. 3 Dec. 1769), d. 4 March 1802 (F# 673).

Salome, bap. 6 Jan. 1772, daughter of Timotheus, alias Tuteleu (bap. 30 March 1766) and Martha (bap. 10 Aug. 1766) in Friedenshütten, m. 27 March 1774 to David Jr. (bap. 6 Feb. 1774), children: Timotheus (bap. 26 April 1775), David (b. 16 March 1776), Anna Susanne (bap. 24 Jan. 1779), Anna Margaretha (bap. 15 March 1790), Benjamin (bap. 24 Jan. 1792), Augustina (bap. 2 Oct. 1803), Silas (bap. 30 Dec. 1802), d. 24 March 1813 (no F#), Helper.

Salome, b. 9 April 1773, daughter of unbaptized parents and granddaughter of Isaac, alias Glikhican (bap. 24 Dec. 1770); bap. 19 April 1773 in Schönbrunn; d. 20 April 1773 (F# 1314).

Salome, bap. 17 Oct. 1773, daughter of Petrus (?) and sister of Eleanore (bap. 7 Sept. 1767) in Gnadenhütten, widow; settled at Gnadenhütten 22 April 1774; m. 27 April 1774 to Stephanus, alias Weskhattees (bap. 1 Jan. 1774); no children; d. 21 Aug. 1813 (F# 734), Helper.

Salome, bap. 22 May 1778 as a sick six-year-old girl in Lichtenau, relative of Israel, alias Welapachtschiechen (bap. 25 Dec. 1777) (F# —).

Salome, bap. 23 March 1779 as sick four-year-old girl and granddaughter of Jacob, alias Tschimapehellus or Schimapehellus (bap. 26 Dec. 1773) and Marie (bap. 6 Jan. 1747) in Lichtenau (F# —).

Salome, bap. 6 Jan. 1780 as twelve-year-old daughter of Tobias, alias Melimius (bap. 11 April 1773) in Lichtenau; d. 8 March 1782 (F# 887).

Salomo, alias Allemewi, bap. 25 Dec. 1769 in Lawunnakhannek; m. Erdmuth (bap. 12 June 1770); children: Rebecca (bap. 7 June 1767), Theodora (bap. 20 Jan. 1771), Maria Elisabeth (bap. 31 March 1771); left congregation 4 July 1774; returned shortly before his death; bur. 28 Sept. 1775 (B); Munsee (F# 642), chief of Munsee. See Levi (grandson, bap. 3 April 1768), Marie Juliane, alias Mattamis (granddaughter, bap. 7 Jan. 1776), Anna (great-grand-daughter, bap. 10 Aug. 1773), Christian (great-grandson, bap. 2 Feb. 1776), Rosina (great-granddaughter, bap. 31 March 1771), Elisabeth (great-granddaughter, bap. 11 Nov. 1780), Anna Justina (relative, bap. 1 Jan. 1778).

Sam Evans, bap. 6 Jan. 1774 in Gnadenhütten, lived at Gnadenhütten I from 1754; m. Ruth (bap. 11 March 1749); children: Lucas (bap. 6 Jan. 1765), Tobias (bap. 25 Oct. 1769), Sabina (bap. 1 Oct. 1775); d. after 1 Oct. 1779 (F# 746).

Samuel, bap. 12 Sept. 1768, son of Daniel (bap. 3 April 1768) and Johanna (bap. 11 Sept. 1768) in Friedenshütten; m. before 1794 to Polly (bap. before 1792); d. after 1810; Munsee (F# 612).

Samuel, bap. 23 Oct. 1773 at three months, son of Andreas, alias Tschemipachgennesch (bap. 7 Jan. 1776) and Maria Theresia, alias Gochgachganemau (bap. 4 Feb. 1776) in Schönbrunn; d. same day (F# 1321).

Samuel, b. 19 May 1778, son of Renatus (bap. 12 Nov. 1775) and Johanna Sophia (bap. 28 May 1775); bap. 24 May 1778 in Lichtenau; d. 12 June 1778 (F# 1397).

Samuel, b. 9 Oct. 1779, son of Ludwig (bap. 1 Jan. 1774) and Ruth (bap. 4 Feb. 1776); bap. 10 Oct. 1779 in Lichtenau; d. 25 Oct. 1779 (F# 1414).

Samuel, bap. 11 Sept. 1780, son of Johannes, alias Netanewund (bap. 28 July 1776) and Hanna (bap. 7 Jan. 1758) in Schönbrunn, age over seven years; bur. 15 Sept. 1780 (F# 1421).

Samuel, b. 19 Aug. 1781, son of Leonhard (bap. 6 Jan. 1775) and Rahel (bap. 6 Jan. 1776); bap. 24 Aug. 1781 in Gnadenhütten (F# 1434).

Samuel Moor, bap. 6 Jan. 1771 in Friedenshütten, grandson of Johannes Papunhank (bap. 26 June 1763); child from earlier marriage: Catharina (bap. 17 Dec. 1772); m. 13 June 1773 as widower to the widow Helena (bap. 13 April 1768); child: Louisa (b. 26 July 1774); d. 8 March 1782; Unami (F# 664), National Helper.

Samuel Nantikok, bap. 10 Aug. 1766 in Friedenshütten; m. Sarah Nantikok (bap. 27 Jan. 1772); children: Beata (b. 28 Aug. 1771), Heinrich (b. 22 Aug. 1773), Anna Helena (b. 29 March 1775), Jael (bap. 25 Dec. 1775), Rebecca (b. 26 Feb. 1777), Augustine (b. 17 July 1779), Anna Sophia (bap. 1 Jan. 1778), Benigna (bap. 7 Jan. 1781), Anna Maria (b. 19 Aug. 1785), Amalia (b. 27 Oct. 1786), Mercy (1790); d. 1805 (F# 551), National Helper, lay preacher.

Sarah, admitted 19 Aug. 1775; m. Timotheus, alias Kabaasch (bap. 19 May 1771) (F# 916).

Sara (Sarah), bap. 6 Jan. 1777 in Lichtenau; child from earlier marriage: Nathanael (bap. 25 Dec. 1776); m. Gideon, alias Saktelaeuche (bap. 25 Dec. 1776); children: Johannes (bap. 8 Jan. 1777), Johannes Renatus (b. 2 Feb. 1778), Christina (b. 15 Sept. 1780) (F# 845).

Sara, b. 23 Jan. 1778, daughter of Philippus Jr. (bap. 1749) and Eleanore (bap. 7 Sept. 1767); bap. 8 Feb. 1778 in Gnadenhütten; d. 8 March 1782 (F# 1386). See Anna Justina (twin sister).

Sarah, bap. 12 July 1778 in Lichtenau; m. Marcus (bap. 8 Sept. 1749); no children (F# 873).

Sarah, bap. 28 Oct. 1780 in Schönbrunn at age eleven, daughter of Johannes, alias Netanewand (bap. 28 July 1776) and Hanna (bap. 7 Jan. 1758); d. and bur. 1 May 1781 (F# 896).

Sarah Nantikok, bap. 27 Jan. 1772 in Friedenshütten; m. Samuel Nantikok (bap. 10 Aug. 1766); children: Beata (b. 28 Aug. 1771), Heinrich (b. 22 Aug. 1773), Anna Helena (b. 29 March 1775), Jael (bap. 25 Dec. 1775), Rebecca (b. 26 Feb. 1777), Augustine (b. 17 July 1779), Anna Sophia (bap. 1 Jan. 1778), Benigna (bap. 7 Jan. 1781), Anna Maria (b. 19 Aug. 1785), Amalia (b. 27 Oct. 1786), Mercy (1790); d. 8 April 1798; Nantikok (F# 703).

Sem, alias Tschuwisch, bap. 25 Dec. 1775 in Schönbrunn; m. Lucia (bap. 4 Feb. 1776); child: Benigna (b. 19 April 1776); d. after 1777 (F# 801). See Esra, alias Apallochgacan (brother, bap. 20 May 1773), Jephta, alias Queelpacheno (brother, bap. 4 Jan. 1774), Nicodemus (brother, bap. 7 Dec. 1778).

Seth, alias Netawastond, bap. 16 July 1774 in Schönbrunn; m. Verona (bap. 25 Dec. 1774); child: Justina (bap. 25 Dec. 1774); d. 17 Sept. 1776 (F# 763). See Simon, alias Lawalooch-walend (brother, bap. 2 April 1774).

Sigmund, bap. 18 Feb. 1776 at age six months, probably son of Helena, alias Quelpinawos (bap. 13 April 1755) in Schönbrunn (F# 1361).

Silas, alias Quequeslpa, bap. 1 Jan. 1774 in Schönbrunn, grandfather of Anna Catharina (bap. 4 Feb. 1776) (F# 737), from Tuscarawi.

Silpa, bap. 24 Dec. 1775 at age ten months, daughter of Nehemia, alias Wisawoapamend (bap. 12 Nov. 1778) and Johanna Maria (bap. 12 Nov. 1775) in Schönbrunn; d. summer 1777 "at the Walhanding" (F# —).

Simon, alias Panipachgihillen, bap. 1 Jan. 1772 in Langundoutenünk; m. Lea (bap. 6 Jan. 1772); d. 31 Oct. 1773; Munsee (F# 698). See Isaac, alias Glikhican (brother, bap. 11 Sept. 1768).

Simon, alias Laweloochwalend, b. c. 1680; bap. 2 April 1774 in Schönbrunn; m. Judith (bap. 12 May 1774); bur. 6 July 1778 (B) (F# 755), before his baptism chief at Shenenge. See Seth, alias Netawastond (brother, bap. 17 July 1774).

Sophia, bap. 14 May 1749 in Gnadenhütten I, daughter of Gottlieb (bap. 26 April 1745, F# 73) and Marie (bap. 26 April 1775, F# 74), admitted to Lichtenau 25 July 1779; m. 10 May 1781, as widow, to Isaac, alias Eschecanahunt (bap. 25 Dec. 1775); no children; Unami (F# 189, 924). See Joseph (brother, bap. 2 March 1751).

Sophia, bap. 11 June 1765, daughter of Johannes Papunhank (bap. 26 June 1763) and Anna Johanna (bap. 10 Aug. 1766) in Philadelphia; m. 26 June 1764 to Josua Jr. (bap. 23 Jan. 1749); children: Anna (bap. 4 Aug. 1765), Bathseba (bap. 13 May 1767), Salome (bap. 29 March 1771, d. 4 March 1802, F# 673), Nathanael (bap. 17 Aug. 1773), Sophia (b. 5 July 1774), Johanna (bap. 30 March 1777), Josua (b. 9 April 1779), Thomas (b. 16 Oct. 1780); d. 2 Feb. 1801; Munsee (F# 530).

Sophia b. 30 March 1772, daughter of Levi (bap. 3 April 1768) and Salome (bap. 11 Sept. 1768); bap. 5 April 1772 in Langundoutenünk; d. 24 April 1772 on the journey to Schönbrunn; Munsee (F# 708).

Sophia, bap. 6 Jan. 1774, daughter of Jacob Gendaskund (bap. 24 Dec. 1770) and Rosina (bap. 21 March 1771) in Schönbrunn; m. 17 April 1776 to Nicolaus (bap. 1 Jan. 1775); no children; d. after 16 Feb. 1805 (F# 745).

Sophia, bap. 5 July 1774, daughter of Josua Jr. (bap. 23 Jan. 1749) and Sophia (bap. 11 June 1765) in Gnadenhütten; m. before 1798 to James (bap. 6 Jan. 1790, d. 21 June 1813, F# 968); bur. 15 Aug. 1801 (F# 1329).

Sophia, bap. 14 April 1779, daughter of Jacob, alias Tschimapehellus or Schimapehellus. (bap. 26 Dec. 1773) and Marie (bap. 6 Jan. 1747) (F# —).

Sophia, b. 8 Feb. 1780, daughter of Christian Gottlieb (bap. before 1768) and Catharina, alias Mamtscha (bap. 25 Dec. 1775); bap. 13 Feb. 1780 in Schönbrunn; d. 29 Oct. 1780 (F# 1417).

Sophia, mother of Susanna (bap. 2 Jan. 1780), no further identification possible (F# —).

Stephanus, alias Weskhattees, bap. 1 Jan. 1774; m. 26 April 1774 to Salome (bap. 17 Oct. 1773); no children; d. after 5 Oct. 1813 (F# 740), from Tuscarawi, Helper, messenger.

Stephanus, bap. 6 Jan. 1775 as adult son of Nicodemus, alias Achgutschisch orAcootschees or Acheutschis (bap. 7 Jan. 1776) in Gnadenhütten; d. 17 Dec. 1778 (B); bur. 18 Dec. 1778 (F# 778).

Sulamith, bap. 9 Feb. 1771 as widow in Langundoutenünk; lived in Schönbrunn in 1774; Munsee (F# 668).

Sulamith, bap. 6 Aug. 1775 at age six months, daughter of Renatus (bap. 12 Nov. 1775) and Johanna Sophia (bap. 28 May 1775) in Schönbrunn; m. before 1800 to Abel (bap. 23 Aug. 1789 as son of Thomas [bap. 11 Sept. 1774] and Sabine [bap. 11 Sept. 1774]); d. 25 June 1803 (F# 1347).

Susanna, bap. 20 July 1766, daughter of Agnes (bap. 25 Aug. 1751) in Friedenshütten; m. 29 May 1774 to Adolph, alias Tschàlok (bap. 13 Feb. 1774); children: David (bur. 23 Nov. 1777), Johannes Petrus (b. 5 Jan. 1779), Philippina (1786); m. Zachäus before 1803; Unami (F# 550).

Susanna, bap. 20 Jan. 1771 as little daughter of Theodora (bap. 20 Jan. 1771) and Boas, alias Lelawoapaneuche (bap. 23 May 1771) in Langundoutenünk (F# 671).

Susanna, admitted to Schönbrunn 25 Dec. 1774, daughter of Anna Margaretha (admitted 20 Jan. 1771) (F# 909).

Susanna, bap. 2 Jan. 1780 at age sixteen, daughter of Sophia (?) in Lichtenau; m. 18 Feb. 1781 to Marcus (bap. 20 July 1780) (F# 881).

Susanna Minque, bap. before 2 Aug. 1777, mother of Jonathan (bap. 6 Jan. 1780); d. after 18 Nov. 1789 (F# 920). See Nicodemus, alias Zelotschis (brother, bap. 7 Dec. 1775).

Sybilla, bap. 22 Jan. 1775 as big girl and daughter of Helena, alias Quelpinawos (bap. 13 April 1755) in Schönbrunn; m. 16 Nov. 1779 to Moses (bap. 30 March 1777) (F# 781).

Tabea, bap. 16 April 1775 in Gnadenhütten as widow and mother of Amalia (bap. 6 Jan. 1775); bur. 1 Aug. 1778 (B) (F# 789).

Tanguk or Tankug, mother of Nathanael (bap. 21 Sept. 1772) and Adolph (bap. 29 Oct. 1772) in Langundoutenünk (F# —).

Thamar, bap. 7 Jan. 1776, maternal aunt of Hanna (not further identified) in Gnadenhütten; d. in Goschachgünk 3 Dec. 1777 (F# 821).

Theodora, bap. 20 Jan. 1771, daughter of Salomo, alias Allemewi (bap. 25 Dec. 1769) and Erdmuth (bap. 12 June 1770); m. Boas, alias Lelawoapaneuche (bap. 23 May 1771); children: Susanna (bap. 20 Jan. 1771), probably also Maria Theresia, alias Gochgachganemau (bap. 4 Feb. 1776); Munsee (F# 666).

Theodora, bap. 6 Jan. 1774, daughter of Jacob, alias Tschimapehellus or Schimapehellus (bap. 26 Dec. 1773) and Marie (bap. 6 Jan. 1747) (F# —).

Thomas, bap. 8 Feb. 1760; admitted 19 May 1771; m. 28 May 1771 to Polly (bap. in the Jerseys); children: Joseph (b. 6 July 1776), Christian (b. 3 May 1780); d. before 1789; Unami (F# 496).

Thomas, b. 26 June 1769, son of Philippus Jr. (bap. 23 Jan. 1749) and Eleanore (bap. 7 Sept. 1767); bap. 2 July 1769 in Friedenshütten; d. 30 June 1786 on Cuyahoga River; Mahican (F# 622).

Thomas, b. 31 July 1774, son of Esra, alias Apallochgacan (bap. 20 May 1773) and Lazara (bap. 30 June 1771); bap. 1 Aug. 1774 in Schönbrunn (F# 1331).

Thomas, alias Gutkigamen, bap. 11 Sept. 1774 in Schönbrunn; m. Sabina (bap. 11 Sept. 1774); children: Johannes (b. 23 April 1774), Johanna (b. 7 May 1776), Isaac and Maria Salome (b. 29 Jan. 1779), Judith (bap. 25 Dec. 1784, d. after 14 May 1804, F# 1463), Abel (bap. 23 Aug. 1789, bur. 24 April 1805, F# 959), Ruth (bap. 10 Sept. 1789, d. after 14 Oct. 1810, F# 1488); d. 8 May 1792 (F# 766), grandson of Netawatwees, National Helper, sexton, lay preacher.

Thomas, b. 16 Oct. 1780, son of Josua Jr. (bap. 23 Jan. 1749) and Sophia (bap. 11 June 1765); bap. 29 Oct. 1780 in Schönbrunn (F# 1426).

Thomas Onondaga, admitted 1 Jan. 1775 to Schönbrunn; m. Marie (admitted 12 Feb. 1775); children: Joseph (admitted 25 May 1775), Nicolaus (admitted 1 Jan. 1775), Christine (admitted 19 Aug. 1775), Polly (admitted 25 May 1775); d. after 6 April 1777 (F# 910).

Timotheus, alias Tuteleu, bap. 30 March 1766 in Wyalusing; m. Martha (bap. 10 Aug. 1766); child: Salome (bap. 6 Jan. 1772); d. and bur. 15 Nov. 1780 (F# 546).

Timotheus, alias Kabaasch, bap. 19 May 1771 in Friedenshütten, son of a Shawnee from Woaketameki; m. Sarah (admitted 19 Aug. 1775); child: Nathan (b. and bap. 7 Sept. 1775) (F# 684).

Timotheus, b. 25 April 1775, son of David Jr., alias Kutschias (bap. 6 Feb. 1774) and Salome (bap. 6 Jan. 1772); bap. 26 April 1775; bur. 27 April 1775 (F# —).

Tobias, bap. 25 Oct. 1769 in Friedenshütten, son of Sam Evans (bap. 6 Jan. 1774) and Ruth (bap. before 1749); survived massacre at Gnadenhütten II; m. before 1798 to Elisabeth (bap. 20 Oct. 1774); d. after 1814; Unami (F# 638), Helper, translator.

Tobias, b. 5 Oct. 1771, son of Nicolaus (admitted 20 June 1771) and Amalia (bap. 20 June 1771); bap. 6 Oct. 1771 in Langundoutenünk; d. 9 July 1773; Munsee (F# 718).

Tobias, alias Melimius, bap. 11 April 1773 in Langundoutenünk; child from earlier marriage: Salome (bap. 6 Jan. 1780); m. Rebecca Nantikok (bap. 25 Dec. 1773); d. 8 March 1782 (F# 729), Helper.

Tobias, bap. 10 May 1781 in Gnadenhütten II, grandson of Eva (bap. 25 Dec. 1778) (F# —).

Verona, bap. 6 Jan. 1772 in Langundoutenünk as widow; d. after 5 Feb. 1774; Munsee (F# 701).

Verona, bap. 25 Dec. 1774 in Schönbrunn, m. Seth, alias Netawastond (bap. 16 July 1774); child: Justine (bap. 25 Dec. 1774); bur. 25 July 1777 (B) as widow (F# 770).

William Conner, European, b. 10 Dec. 1777, son of Richard and Peggy Conner (both admitted to congregation 7 April 1776); bap. 21 Dec. 1777 in Schönbrunn (F# —).

Willhelm, alias Bill Chelloway, bap. 6 Jan. 1771 in Friedenshütten; m. Martha (bap. 19 May 1771); children: Abigail (bap. 7 Feb. 1772), Elisabeth (bap. 20 Oct. 1774), Jacob (bap. 19 Oct. 1776), Regina (b. 23 Feb. 1779), Anton (bap. 4 April 1784, d. after 1808, F# 1458), Mattheus (bap. 17 Sept. 1786, bur. 8 July 1789, F# 1469), Gertraud (bap. 3 Sept. 1789, bur. 17 Sept. 1791, F# 1487); d. 22 Sept. 1791; Unami (F# 663), Helper.

Willhelmine, bap. 4 July 1773 in Schönbrunn, m. Noah (bap. 2 July 1773); child: Heinrich (bap. 9 Jan. 1774); d. 12 Sept. 1778 (B), bur. 13 Sept. 1778; Unami (F# 733), von Kuskuski. See Magdalena (sister, bap. 3 April 1774).

Zacharias, bap. 7 Jan. 1776 in Gnadenhütten; m. 8 Aug. 1776 to Anna Elisabeth, alias Tiangan (bap. 16 April 1775); children: Maria (b. 4 May 1779), Jonas (b. 17 Jan. 1781), Johannes (bap. 17 Oct. 1784), Jonathan (bap. 17 May 1787), Esra (bap. 29 Sept. 1799); d. after 1811 (F# 825).

Zeno, brother of Gertraud (bap. 20 Jan. 1771) and Debora (bap. 16 April 1775), participated in assault on Gnadenhütten I on 24 Nov. 1755 (F# —).

Zipora, bap. 12 April 1772 in Langundoutenünk; m. Jephta, alias Queelpacheno (bap. 4 Jan. 1774); children: Joseph (bap. 12 Jan. 1773), Adam, alias Scheechganìm (bap. 1 Jan. 1776); d. 22 April 1784; Munsee (F# 710).

EURO-AMERICANS

Anderson, John. According to Heckewelder the Indians called him "the honest Quaker trader." Cooperated in 1774 in efforts to prevent Lord Dunmore's war; after 1775–76 the Continental Congress frequently entrusted him with Indian affairs.

Beatty, Charles Clinton (c. 1715–72). Irish, arrived in North America in 1729, read theology at William Tennent's Log College in Neshaminy, preached in Pennsylvania, Virginia, and North Carolina. In 1766 visited Indian tribes in the Ohio region.

Bird, Henry (d. 1800). Captain in the British army since the Seven Years' War, stationed at Fort Detroit from 1778, played important role in military activities organized from Detroit.

Bouquet, Henry (1719–65). Swiss, first enlisted in Dutch army, after 1755 in English army, came with army to North America in 1756, played prominent role in conquest of Fort Duquesne in 1758. As commander of Fort Pitt he was responsible for crushing Pontiac's Rebellion and for establishing satisfactory conditions in the Ohio region.

Brainerd, David (1718–47). Congregational missionary, at first among Indians living in neighborhood of Stockbridge, Massachusetts, then in the region of Easton in Pennsylvania and New Jersey. Shortly before his death he moved his mission congregation to Crossweeksung in New Jersey.

Brainerd, John (1720–81). Missionary, continued mission work of his brother, David; became familiar with Moravian mission activities in the 1750s through visits to Bethlehem and through reports of Charles Beatty and Daniel McClure.

Brodhead, Daniel (1736–1809). Colonel, commanding officer of 8th Pennsylvania Regiment beginning in March 1777; McIntosh's successor as commanding officer of Fort Pitt until 1781, relieved after serious conflicts with Col. John Gibson, who succeeded him.

Brother Joseph. See Spangenberg, August Gottlieb.

Brother Matteus. See Hehl, Matthäus.

Bull, John Joseph (1721–88). Son of Quakers in Skippack, Pennsylvania, joined the Moravian Church in 1742, married Christiana, a Mahican, served as Zeisberger's adjunct and assistant until his death. In the diary usually referred to by his Indian name Schebosh ("running water").

Butler, John (1728–96). Indian agent, commander of Fort Niagara and commanding officer of warriors of Six Indian Nations as English allies.

Butler, Richard (1743–91). Irish, Indian agent of Continental Congress 1775–76, officer of the Continental army, became brigadier general in 1783.

Cammerhoff, Johann Christoff Friedrich (1721–51). Studied theology at the University of Jena, Germany, became bishop in the Moravian Church in 1746, from 1747 Spangenberg's assistant in North America, prominent representative of "sifting period."

Campbell, Richard (d. 1781). Colonel from Frederick County, Virginia, joined Continental army in 1776. On 14 June 1779 entrusted to command of a convoy of provisions for Fort Laurens, where he was to relieve Major Frederick Vernon as commanding officer.

Carleton, Guy, 1st Baron of Dorchester (1724–1808). Captain general and governor-in-chief of Canada from 12 April 1768 until 27 June 1778. Succeeded by Frederick Haldimand.

Clark, George Rogers (1752–1818). Surveyor and soldier, commanded militia units in Lord Dunmore's war and in Revolutionary War; in 1778 conquered French settlements in the Mississippi Valley.

Conner, Richard and Peggy. Admitted on 8 May 1775 as first Europeans to Schönbrunn congregation. Peggy Conner, a prisoner, was adopted after the Seven Years' War by a chief of the Shawnee, freed after Lord Dunmore's war. Richard Conner, an Indian trader until 1775, and his wife operated a guesthouse in a Shawnee village, from which they supplied information about Shawnee military plans and activities.

Connolly, John (c. 1743–1813). Medical doctor, captain of militia of Augusta County, Virginia. In 1773 he usurped command of Fort Pitt for Virginia, loyalist, prisoner of Continental Congress until 1780.

Cresap, Michael (1742–75). Son of Thomas Cresap, settler and land speculator in western Virginia. At the beginning of Lord Dunmore's war he was involved in an assault on Mingo chief John Logan; commanded a militia unit from Virginia in Lord Dunmore's war.

Croghan, George (d. 1782). Indian trader, land speculator, and from 1756 to 1771 representative of Sir William Johnson as superintendent for Indian Affairs in the Ohio region. Very knowledgeable about Indian affairs in the Ohio region; supported Virginia's position in conflict with Pennsylvania over ownership of Fort Pitt region.

Dartmouth, William Legge, 2nd Earl of (1731–1801). Influential English politician, from 1772 to 1775 secretary of state responsible for British colonies.

De Peyster, Arent Schuyler (1736–1832). Member of a prominent New York family of Dutch descent. Joined British army at the beginning of Seven Years' War, served in the region of Fort Detroit, appointed commander of that fort in 1779. After 1783 he retired with his family to Dumfries, Scotland.

Dodge, John (1749–94). Indian trader, lived in Wyandot settlement Sandusky, accompanied Wyandot to congress at Fort Pitt in 1775, imprisoned in Jan. 1776 for his pro-American activities, escaped to Boston in 1778.

Duffield, George (1732–90). Born in Pequea, Lancaster County, Pennsylvania, Presbyterian preacher, especially in Cumberland County, Pennsylvania. In 1766 he visited the Indian tribes in the Ohio region with Charles Beatty; after the American Revolution he became an active supporter of the new United States.

Dunmore. See Murray, John.

Edwards, Jonathan (1703–58). Perhaps the leading congregational divine of eighteenth-century America; his activities and writings between 1735 and the 1740s were important forces in shaping the First Great Awakening. Between 1751 and 1758 he served a mission congregation of the Housatonic tribe in Stockbridge, Massachusetts, as pastor.

Edwards, William (1724–1801). Born in England, joined Moravians in 1749, deacon, replaced Zeisberger at Schönbrunn in Nov. 1776.

Elliott, Matthew (c. 1739–1814). Migrated in 1761 from Ireland to Pennsylvania, Indian trader with close ties to the Shawnee. In 1778, with Alexander McKee and Simon Girty, escaped to Fort Detroit where they joined the British army as Indian agents.

Ettwein, Johann (1721–1802). Succeeded Nathanael Seidel as chairman of the Provincial Helpers' Conference in Bethlehem; responsible for mission among Native Americans, most important correspondent of Zeisberger, consecrated bishop in 1784.

Frisbie, Levi (1748–1806). Presbyterian preacher, visited Indian settlements in the Ohio region with David McClure in 1772; unable to proceed beyond Fort Pitt because of illness.

Gambold, Hector Ernest (1719–88). One of five Moravian pastors born in England who toured the middle Atlantic colonies, first as itinerant preachers, then as circuit preachers. From 1764 to 1784 pastor of a Moravian congregation on Staten Island, New York.

Germain, George Sackville, 1st Viscount Sackville (1716–85). British army general during Seven Years' War; from 1775 to 1782 secretary of state for the American colonies. Usually called "Lord Germain."

Gibson, John (1740–1822). Indian trader with close ties to Shawnee and Delaware, later commander of Fort Laurens, married to a Shawnee who lived in Gekelemukpechünk and who was murdered in late April 1774.

Girty, Simon (c. 1745–1818). Learned the Seneca language while prisoner between 1756 and 1759; interpreter at conferences in Fort Pitt and Indian agent until his flight, with Alexander McKee and Matthew Elliott, to Fort Detroit in 1778. At Detroit he coordinated Native American military expeditions against American settlements in the Ohio region.

Grube, Bernhard Adam (1715–1808). Lutheran pastor at Erfurt before he joined the Moravian Church; stationed as missionary at Wechquetank. Between 1763 and 1765 accompanied and assisted the Christian Indians quartered in Philadelphia; in 1780 conducted a formal visitation of the mission settlements in the Muskingum valley.

Hagen, Johann (d. 1747). Probably from Brandenburg, Germany, arrived in Georgia in 1740, worked as missionary among the Cherokee. Went to Bethlehem in 1742, where he married Margaret Dismann from Providence Township near Philadelphia. Continued to work as missionary in Checomeco and Shamokin, where he died.

Haldimand, Sir Frederick (1718–91). Swiss, British army officer, arrived in North America in 1756. In the 1760s superintendent for Indian Affairs in Florida, between 1777 and 1786 successor of Carleton and governor general of Canada.

Hamilton, Henry (c. 1734–96). Irish, joined British army in North America at the beginning of Seven Years' War. Appointed civil governor for the Detroit region in 1775. Tried unsuccessfully to stop George Rogers Clark's conquest of French settlements in the Mississippi Valley. On 25 Feb. 1779 capitulated at Vincennes and was prisoner of the Continental army for eighteen months. Between 1781 and 1785 lieutenant governor of Quebec and thereafter governor of a variety of British colonies in the West Indies.

Hand, Edward (1744–1802). Irish, medical doctor, brigadier general in the Continental army. Appointed commander of Fort Pitt in 1777; improved military protection of European and Delaware settlements.

Heckewelder, Johann (John) Gottlieb Ernestus (1743–1823) (occasionally Heckewalder). Born in Bedford, England, came to Pennsylvania in 1754, Zeisberger's assistant beginning in 1771; consecrated deacon in 1778.

Heckewelder, Johanna Maria. Born 16 April 1781, daughter of Johann and Sarah Heckewelder, baptized 17 April 1781 in Salem.

Heckewelder, Sarah, born Ohneberg (1746–1815). Daughter of a Moravian missionary couple, married 4 July 1780 by Grube to John Heckewelder.

Hehl, Matthäus (1704–87). From Württemberg, Germany, studied at Tübingen University, came to Bethlehem, Pennsylvania, as assistant to A. G. Spangenberg, later pastor of Moravian congregation at Lititz.

Henry, William (1729–86). Merchant and member of Moravian congregation at Lancaster, Pennsylvania; important link between Bethlehem and Fort Pitt.

Heston, Zebulon. Quaker, traveling friend who between July and Sept. 1773, with his friend John Parrish, visited Delaware settlements and Schönbrunn in the Ohio region.

Johnson, Guy (1740–88). Relative of Sir William Johnson and from 1774 onward his successor as superintendent for Indian Affairs. Between 1776 and 1779 delegated most of his duties to John Butler (Fort Niagara) and Daniel Claus (Montreal); between 1779 and 1783 planned and directed massive Iroquois attacks against American settlements.

Johnson, Sir William (1715–74). Irish, came in 1738 to New York, merchant, fur trader, owned large tracts of land in the Mohawk River valley, established close relations with the Mohawk and Six Indian Nations. At beginning of Seven Years' War appointed superintendent of Indian Affairs.

Jones, David (1736–1820). Baptist preacher, between May 1772 and April 1773 visited Shawnee and Delaware settlements in the Ohio region as a missionary. Served as American army chaplain during Revolutionary War and supported the American cause in his sermons.

Joseph, Brother. See Spangenberg.

Jung, Franz Michael (1743–1826). Emigrated to America in 1751, joined the Moravians at Bethlehem in 1767, from 6 Nov. 1780 assistant to William Edwards at Gnadenhütten II.

Jungmann, Anna Margaretha, born Bechtel (1722–93). First marriage to the Moravian missionary Gottlieb Büttner (d. 1745), remarried the Moravian missionary Johann Georg Jungmann. Spoke Mahican and Delaware, was stationed at Checomeco, Gnadenhütten I, Pachgatgoch, Langundoutenünk, and from 1772 until 1777 and again from 1781 in the mission settlements on the Muskingum. Deaconess in the Moravian Church.

Jungmann, Johann (John) (1749–1843). Son of the missionary couple Jungmann who lived at Schönbrunn. Until 1775 he lived at Gnadenhütten in order to learn the Mahican language.

Jungmann, Johann Georg (1720–1808). Moravian missionary at Gnadenhütten I, Pachgatgoch, Langundoutenünk, and from Sept. 1772 collaborator of Zeisberger in Schönbrunn; married to Anna Margaretha Jungmann (1722–93). Deacon in the Moravian Church.

Krogstrup, Otto Christian (1714–85). After studying theology emigrated in 1753 to America, where he served as pastor of the Moravian congregations at Lititz, Graceham, York, and Lancaster; died on 10 Oct. 1785 in Bethlehem.

Lernoult, Richard B. Since 1774 and until the arrival of Henry Hamilton commander of Fort Detroit, served as substitute for Hamilton during his absence in spring 1779 as civil governor and commander of Fort Detroit.

Lewis, Andrew (1720–81). Irish, wealthy planter and influential politician in western Virginia. In autumn 1774 commander of second Virginia army against Shawnee; his command culminated in the battle of Point Pleasant.

Linctot, Daniel-Maurice Godefroy de (1739–83). From Montreal, participated in Seven Years' War; in 1762 returned for two years to France; from 1770 Indian trader in the Mississippi Valley region. Joined the American side after arrival of George Rogers Clark, who appointed him Indian agent for the Illinois region in the spring of 1779.

Logan, James (1674–1751). Merchant, representative of the Penn family in Pennsylvania and provincial secretary of the colony, shaped and enforced new political concept that defined Shawnee and Delaware as dependent tribes of the Six Indian Nations.

Mack, Johann Martin (1715–84). From Laichingen, Württemberg, Germany, arrived in Georgia in 1736, co-founder of Bethlehem, from 1742 assistant to missionary Christian Heinrich Rauch at Moravian mission settlement at Checomeco. Married Jeanette Rauch on 14 Sept. 1742, ordained on 13 Nov. 1742 by Zinzendorf and David Nietschmann. After the closure of Checomeco transferred to Pachgatgoch. In 1745 he was entrusted with the overall direction of the mission work in North America; he initiated the foundation of Gnadenhütten I. From 1762 to 1784 he served as missionary in the West Indies.

Matthao, Brother. See Hehl, Matthäus

McClure, David (1748–1820). Presbyterian preacher and missionary who visited Indian settlements in the Ohio region and especially in the Muskingum valley in 1772.

McCormick, Alexander (d. 1803). Before 1776 Indian trader in Pittsburgh, taken prisoner by Wyandot before Nov. 1776, adopted into the family of Wyandot chief Half King at the request of Delaware and then set free. Thereafter Indian trader at Sandusky, the settlement of Half King.

McDonald, Angus (1727–79). Colonel in the Virginia militia, commanded the expedition army against the Shawnee settlement Woaketammeki in 1774.

McIntosh, Lachlan (1725–1806). Scot, successor to General Edward Hand, appointed commander of Fort Pitt on 6 Aug. 1778. Inflexible and little experienced in Indian warfare, he alienated the Delaware and aggravated the military situation of the Delaware settlements.

McKee, Alexander (c. 1735–99). Indian trader and agent, assistant of George Croghan; in 1771 appointed Croghan's successor as representative of Sir William Johnson in the Ohio region. Married to a Shawnee woman; in 1778, with Simon Girty, Matthew Elliott, Robert Surphlitt, and John Higgins, fled to the British Fort Detroit.

Montour, John (1744–after 1789). Son of Andrew Montour and the daughter of a Delaware chief. From 1756 attended the English school in Philadelphia; after school lived in Fort Pitt until 1775; friend of White Eyes; served as commanding officer of a band of Delaware warriors in 1780–81.

Morgan, George (1742–1810). Indian trader and land speculator. On 10 April 1776 appointed Indian agent of the Middle Department by Continental Congress; he resigned in May 1779.

Murray, John (1732–1809). Fourth Earl and Lord Dunmore, governor of Virginia 1771–76, defended British policies against critique of the Virginia House of Burgesses; mobilized Virginia militia against Shawnee in 1774; invaded Shawnee territory with two armies during Lord Dunmore's war in order to crush Shawnee resistance against white settlers occupying Shawnee hunting ground.

Occom, Samson (1723–92). Mohegan from New London, Connecticut. Received his education in theology in school of congregational pastor Eleazar Wheelock between 1743 and 1747–48; ordained preacher in 1759; preached to Indian congregations in the Housatonic valley and to Montauk on Long Island until his removal during the American Revolution to Brotherton, a Christian Indian settlement in the territory of the Oneida.

Parrish, John (1729–1807). Quaker, traveling friend, who from July until Sept. 1773, with Zebulon Heston and the young John Lacey, visited Delaware settlements in the Ohio region as well as Schönbrunn.

Post, Christian Friedrich (1710–85). From Conitz in Prussia, Germany, arrived at Bethlehem in 1742. Beginning in 1743 served as missionary in Checomeco and then in Pachgatgoch, and after his return from a visit to Europe served as missionary in Wyoming from 1754 on. During the Seven Years' War he brought government messages to Shawnee and Delaware settlements in the Ohio region and acted as mediator between these tribes and the colonial government. In 1761–62 independent missionary in the Delaware settlements on the Tuscarawas, and between 1762 and 1784 missionary on the Mosquito Coast, Nicaragua. Died 1785 in Germantown, Pennsylvania.

Powell, Joseph (1710–74). From Shropshire, England, originally follower of George Whitefield, joined Moravians in Bethlehem in 1742; missionary in Shamokin 1747–48; thereafter preacher in various Moravian congregations; later missionary at Wechquanach, Connecticut, where he died in 1774.

Pyrlaeus, Johann Christian (1713–85). From Saxony, Germany, studied at University of Leipzig, joined the Moravian Church in 1739, came to Bethlehem in 1741, learned Mohawk. Between 1744 and 1746 ran a school that prepared young men for work as missionaries; then teacher in Frederickstown close to Philadelphia; returned to England in 1751 with his wife Susanna, a daughter of the Quaker Anthony Benezet. From 1769 he worked in a German Moravian congregation.

Reichel, Johann Friedrich (1731–1809). Bishop of the Moravian Church, sent as member of the Unity's Elders' Conference to conduct a visitation of the Moravian congregations in the middle Atlantic states. He arrived in Bethlehem on 17 April 1779; his visitation was completed in 1781.

Roth, Johann (1726–91). Deacon, from Saarmund, Mark Brandenburg, Germany, by trade a locksmith, joined Moravian Church in 1748, arrived at Bethlehem in 1756, in 1770 married Anna Maria (1735–1805); served as missionary in Schechschiquanünk, Langundoutenünk and from April until Aug. 1773 in Gnadenhütten II, and until May 1774 in Schönbrunn.

Roth, Johann Ludwig. Born 4 Aug. 1773 to Johann and Anna Maria Roth, baptized 5 Aug. 1773 in Gnadenhütten.

Roth, Maria Agnes, born Pfingstag (1735–1805). From Wirsche, Württemberg, Germany, arrived in North America in 1737, joined Moravian Church in 1748, married Johann Roth in 1770 and worked with him as missionary in the mission congregations of the Muskingum valley.

Schebosch. See Bull, John Joseph.

Schmick, Johann Jacob (1714–78). From Königsberg, Germany, Lutheran pastor, joined the Moravian Church in 1748, arrived in North America in 1751 and married Johanna, born Heid (1721–95) the same year. Between 1757 and 1777 they both worked as missionaries; the last four years they served the congregation in Gnadenhütten II.

Schmick, Johanna, born Heid (1721–95). Born in Larwick, Norway, joined the Moravian Church before 1745 in Norway, came to North America via Herrnhut, Germany. In 1751 married Johann Jacob Schmick and worked with him in mission congregations.

Seidel, Nathanael (1718–82). Became bishop of the Unitas Fratrum in 1758; guided the Moravian Church in North America beginning in 1762.

Sensemann, Anna Maria, born Brucker (1747–1815). Born in Bethlehem, married Gottlob Sensemann in 1780; between 1781 and 1785 and between 1790 and 1800 both worked as missionaries; she was an ordained acolyte.

Sensemann, Christian David. Baptized 30 Aug. 1781 in Schönbrunn, son of Gottlob and Anna Maria Sensemann.

Sensemann, Gottlob (1745–1800). Son of missionary Heinrich Joachim Sensemann and his wife Anna Katharina, accompanied Zeisberger on his trip to Goschgoschink in 1768; in 1780 married Anna Maria Brucker (1747–1815); assisted Zeisberger in his work as a missionary between 1780 and 1785 and between 1790 and 1800. He was ordained a deacon.

Sensemann, Heinrich Joachim (d. 1774). A baker by occupation, came from Hessen Kassel, Germany, arrived in Bethlehem in 1742 with his wife, Anna Maria. Served as missionary in Checomeko and Gnadenhütten I, where his wife was killed in the 1755 massacre. In 1766 he went with his second wife, Christina, as a missionary to Jamaica, where he died in 1774.

Sergeant, John (1710–49). Took care of the Housatonic Indian congregation at Stockbridge between 1735 and 1749. Having learned the language of the Housatonic, he translated the catechism, parts of the Bible, and songs into Housatonic.

Spangenberg, August Gottlieb (1704–92). Born in the Harz mountains (Lower Saxony, Germany), studied law and theology at Jena, served for a short time as teacher in the orphanage of August Hermann Francke at Halle, joined Moravians and from 1733 on was closely associated with Zinzendorf in Herrnhut. From 1735 to 1739, 1744 to 1749, and 1751 to 1762 he was in charge of the Moravian Church in North America. Ordained bishop in 1744; after 1762 most influential member of the directorate and Unity's Elders' Conference; he was responsible for the church's finances and for the mission work. Author of the first biography of Zinzendorf, wrote the first systematic treatise of Moravian theology, *Idea Fidei Fratrum* (1779).

St. Clair, Arthur (1736–1818). Justice of the peace in Westmoreland County, Pennsylvania, in the 1770s; prominently represented Pennsylvania's interest in the contest with Virginia about rival claims to the Pittsburgh region; first governor of the Northwest Territory.

Stuart, John (c. 1700–1779). Scot, superintendent of Indian Affairs from 1762, generous and efficient administrator of Indian-English relations in the southern colonies; less successful in organizing and coordinating Indian attacks against American frontier settlements.

Sydrich, Daniel (1727–90). From Frankfurt am Main, Germany, emigrated to North America in 1750, where he served as pastor of numerous Moravian congregations, most often in Philadelphia; he died at Lititz.

Thrane, Amadaeus Paul (1718–76). Born in Jütland, Germany, studied theology, arrived at Bethlehem in 1761, in the same year was appointed pastor of the Bethlehem congregation; he fulfilled that office until his death on 19 April 1776.

Vernon, Frederick (d. 1795 or 1796). Did not follow the example of his father and brother but joined the Continental army at the beginning of the American Revolution; in Sept. 1778 he took part in the negotiations at Fort Pitt that led to the conclusion of a treaty with the Delaware; with Lachlan McIntosh he transferred to Fort Lawrence, where he succeeded Colonel John Gibson.

Weiser, Conrad (1696–1760). Palatinate immigrant, learned Mohawk as a youth; from the early 1740s Indian agent of Pennsylvania and influential link between that colony and the Head Council of the Six Indian Nations. In the early 1740s he entertained friendly relations with Moravians; later his daughter married Heinrich Melchior Mühlenberg, then the most influential Lutheran pastor in Pennsylvania.

Zeisberger, David (1721–1808). See Introduction, pp. 72–74.

Zeisberger, Susanna, born Lecron (1744–1824). Born in Lancaster, daughter of German immigrants and joined the Moravian Church with them in 1764; on 4 June 1781 married David Zeisberger. She was an ordained deaconess.

Zinzendorf and Pottendorf, Nicolaus Ludwig Graf and Herr von (1700–1760). Educated in the Francke'schen Anstalten in Halle, where he was strongly influenced by August Hermann Francke's pietism. Studied law at the University at Wittenberg, became a civil servant of Saxonia, married Erdmuthe Dorothea, Countess of Reuss and Ebersdorf, in 1722; granted Bohemian brethren asylum on his estates and founded the town of Herrnhut, which became the center of the Moravian Church. Moravian theology encompassed Reformed, Lutheran, and pietistic concepts that he blended into a remarkably pronounced Christology that defined Moravian theology as a separate movement within pietism. His travels to North America and the West Indies prove his far-flung interests in the mission work of the Moravian Church, or Unitas Fratrum.

UNCONVERTED INDIANS

Allemewi. See Salomon (bap. 25 Dec. 1768).

Alomosbey. Chief of the Delaware, resided in Shamokin. Described as "old and deaf" In 1747.

Baby. See Bawbee.

Baubee. See Bawbee.

Bawbee. Also Baubee, Baby, Odingquanooron. Wyandot chief who on 16 August 1778 offered George Morgan secret negotiations aimed at ending Wyandot attacks on American settlements in exchange for a guarantee that the Americans would respect the integrity of Wyandot territory in case of an American attack of Fort Detroit. The negotiations did not materialize.

Beaver King (d. 1771). Also Tamaqua, head chief of the Delaware. After his death the settlement where he had lived was given up; in autumn 1772 Gnadenhütten II was founded at this location.

Bemineo. See Killbuck Sr.

Bemino. See Killbuck Sr.

Big Cat (d. after 1792). Also Chotachpaschies, Maghingua Keeshoch, Machíngwe Púshees. Delaware chief. In the absence of Gelelemind signed letters of Delaware Council to commander of Fort Pitt; deserted American side in 1780 and retreated to the Miami River region, where he died.

Buckagihitas. See Pachgantschihilas.

Buckongahelas. See Pachgantschihilas.

Canasatego (d. 1750). Chief of Onondaga, speaker of the Council of the Six Indian Nations in negotiations with Pennsylvania at Easton (1742) and Lancaster (1744).

Captain Johnny. See Welapachtschiechen.

Chotachpaschies. See Big Cat.

Coquethagechton. See White Eyes.

Corn Stock. See Cornstalk.

Cornstalk (c. 1720–77). Also Corn Stock, Semachquaan, Simaquan, Coleschqua. Influential chief of Shawnee, leader of pro-American faction; imprisoned at Fort Randolph with his son and murdered on 10 Nov. 1777.

Custaloga. See Packanke.

Dunquat. See Half King.

Echpalawehund. See Petrus (bap. 14 Aug. 1774).

Gaiachoton. See Kayahsota.

Gajachschuta. See Kayahsota.

Gelélemend. See Gelelemind.

Gelelemind (1737–1811). Also Gelélemend, John Killbuck, Killbuck Jr. Eldest son of Killbuck Sr. and grandson of Netawatwees, member of Turtle clan. After Netawatwees' death chief of Turtle clan and leader of neutral, then of pro-American, faction within the Delaware tribe. Beginning in 1776 maintained close relationship with David Zeisberger; after a period of estrangement enjoyed increasingly close relations with Moravian congregation. Baptized on 12 April 1789 as William Henry.

Geyesutha. See Kayahsota.

Gischenatsi. Also Kishanathathe, Kissonaucththa, Kishanosity, Kishshinottisthee, Keesnateta (English: Hard Man). Influential Shawnee chief.

Glikhican. See Isaac (bap. 24 Dec. 1770).

Guyasuta. See Kayahsota.

Half King (d. after 1817). Also Pimoagan, Pomoacan, Dunquat. Wyandot chief, lived in Upper Sandusky, directed and organized Wyandot warriors' attacks on American settlements.

Hard Man. See Gischenatsi.

Hopocan. See Pipe.

John Killbuck. See Gelelemind.

John Logan (c. 1725–80). Also Logan, Tahgahjuta, Oneida, son of Shikellemi. As chief exercised considerable influence over Mingo in the Ohio region; his seat was Logan's Town, near Pittsburgh.

Kayahsota (c. 1725–c. 1794). Also Kayashota, Gaiachoton, Geyesutha, Guyasuta, Kayashoton, Kiyasuta, Kiashuta, Quiasutha, Gajachschuta. Influential Seneca chief, represented interests of Six Indian Nations in the region and in negotiations at Fort Pitt.

Kayahsota. See Kayahsota.

Kayashoton. See Kayahsota.

Keesnateta. See Gischenatsi.

Kiashuta. See Kayahsota.

Killbuck Jr. See Gelelemind.

Killbuck Sr. (d. after Feb. 1779). Also Bemino, Bemineo. Blind son of Netawatwees, member of Head Council at Gekelemukpechünk, chief of Wolf clan, one of the determined opponents of the Moravian mission congregation until Sept. 1775; attended a Moravian religious service for the first time on 19 May 1775. Children of Killbuck belonged to the mission congregation at Schönbrunn.

Kishanathathe. See Gischenatsi.

Kishanosity. See Gischenatsi.

Kishshinottisthee. See Gischenatsi.

Kissonaucththa. See Gischenatsi.

Kiyasuta. See Kayahsota.

Kogeshquanohel. See Pipe.

Kogieschquanoheel. See Pipe.

Koquethagachton. See White Eyes.

Kuckquetacton. See White Eyes.

Laweloochwalend. Before 1774 chief of Shenenge (c. 1680–1778). See Simon (bap. 2 April 1774).

Logan. See John Logan.

Machíngwe Púshees. See Big Cat.

Maghingua Keeshoch. See Big Cat.

Neatotwhealomen. See Netawatwees.

Neolin. Delaware prophet in the 1760s.

Netawatees. See Netawatwees.

Netawatwees (c. 1677–31 Oct. 1776). Also Netawatwes, Netawatees, Netawatwelemend, Neatotwhealomen (English: Newcomer). Chief of the Turtle clan and head chief of the Delaware with seat at Gekelemukpechünk; a number of relatives were members of the mission congregation: his grandsons were Johannes, alias Netanewand (bap. 28 July 1776), Gideon, alias Saktelaeuche (bap. 25 Dec. 1776), Thomas, alias Gutgikamen (bap. 11 Sept. 1774); Helena was the daughter of Killbuck (bap. 8 Dec. 1780), his son.

Netawatwelemend. See Netawatwees.

Netawatwes. See Netawatwees.

Newcomer. See Netawatwees.

Newollike. See Augustinus (bap. 12 May 1774).

Nimho (d. Jan. 1780). Also Nimwho, Nimwha, Nymwha. Brother of Cornstalk and chief of the Mequochoke-Shawnee; joined the Delaware in Feb. 1778.

Nimwha. See Nimho.

Nimwho. See Nimho.

Nymwha. See Nimho.

Odingquanooron. See Bawbee.

Onkiswathetmi. See Shikellemi.

Pachanke. See Packanke.

Pachgantschihilas (d. c. 1805). Also Buckagihitas, Buckongahelas. Delaware captain, pro-British from 1776; according to the protocol of David Zeisberger's Nov. 1781 hearing, 240 warriors, 70 women, and 90 children belonged to his group.

Packanke (d. after 1775). Also Pachanke, Pankanke, Custaloga. Chief of Wolf clan, Munsee, lived at Kaskaskunk; his war captain was Pipe. His most influential counselor was Glikhican (baptised Isaac) before his conversion. A number of members of "Packanke's friendship" joined the mission congregation; his son Isaac (alias Eschenanáhunt) was baptized on 25 Dec. 1775.

Pankanke. See Packanke.

Papunhank. See Johannes (bap. 26 June 1763).

Paxenoos (before 1680–after 1757). Also Paxinos, Paxinoso. Shawnee chief; in Sept. 1772 Zeisberger stayed overnight in the house of one of his sons during his first journey to the Shawnee.

Paxinos. See Paxenoos.

Paxinoso. See Paxenoos.

Pimoagan. See Half King.

Pipe, Captain (c. 1725–1823). Also Hopocan, Kogeshquanohel, Kogieschquanoheel. War captain of the Wolf clan and successor of Packanke; according to Heckewelder "sensible, Ambitious & bold, which led him to seek popularity." Opponent of the pro-Moravian faction in Delaware Head Council and defender of a neutralist cause in the struggle between England and the colonies. Left the Head Council and in 1779 transferred his settlement from the Muskingum valley to the Wyandot settlements. Most authors believe that Pipe died in 1794; Weslager (*Delaware Indian Westward Migration*, 474) affirms that in 1823 Pipe was interviewed by Lewis Cass.

Pluggy (d. 1776). Chief of Mingo, lived at Pluggy's Town, one of the most active allies of the Shawnee in Lord Dunmore's war, joined pro-British side in late 1775, was killed on 29 Dec. 1776 close to McClelland's Station.

Pomoacan. See Half King.

Quequedegatha. See White Eyes.

Quiasutha. See Kayahsota.

Scarouady (d. 1756). Oneida and successor of Tanaghrisson, "Half King" of the Mingo in the Ohio region.

Scattameck. Indian prophet, Wolf clan, focused his preaching activities on the Delaware settlements in the region of the Allegheny River.

Semachquaan. See Cornstalk.

Shikellamy. See Shikellemi.

Shikellemi (d. 1748). Also Shikellamy, Shikellemy, Onkiswathetmi. Originally French, taken prisoner and adopted by the Oneida, became chief of Oneida, representative of the Six Indian Nations in Pennsylvania and Ohio region with residence at Shamokin; died in Shamokin.

Shikellemy. See Shikellemi.

Simaquan, Coleschqua. See Cornstalk.

Tadeuskung. See Teedyuskung.

Tahgahjuta. See John Logan.

Tamaqua. See Beaver King.

Tanaghrisson (c. 1700–1754). Catawba adopted by the Seneca, chief of Seneca and from the 1740s "Half King" of Mingo in Ohio region.

Teedyuskung (1700–1763). Also Tadeuskung. Delaware chief, member of Moravian mission congregation at Gnadenhütten I, baptized Gideon on 8 March 1750; accused Pennsylvania of land fraud in so-called Walking Purchase (1737); in the 1750s chief negotiator of Delaware in negotiations at Easton.

Wangomen (d. after 1782). Also Wangomend. Influential Munsee preacher from the 1750s, resided in Kaskaskunk and Goschgoschünk; determined opponent of the Moravian missionaries in Goschgoschünk and cause for transfer of mission congregation to the Delaware settlements in the Muskingum valley.

Wangomend. See Wangomen.

Welapachtschiechen. Also Captain Johnny. See Israel (bap. 25 Dec. 1777).

White Eyes (d. 1778). Also Koquethagachton, Kuckquetacton, Coquethagechton, Quequedegatha. Captain of the Turkey clan, member of Head Council at Gekelemukpechünk and Go-schachgünk, one of the closest counselors of Netawatwees and speaker of Head Council, lived in his own settlement (White Eyes Town); after death of Netawatwees and until his murder in Oct. 1778 most influential Delaware chief. White Eyes was a close friend of Glikhican.

Winginund (d. 1791). Captain of Wolf clan, resided from 1778 at Kinhanschican on Scioto River close to Shawnee settlements. Friendlier in his attitude toward the Moravian mission congregations, he nevertheless stuck to the policy advocated by Captain Pipe.

INDEX OF PLACE AND RIVER NAMES AND
OTHER GEOGRAPHICAL TERMS

This index lists the names of villages, settlements, rivers, creeks, and regions mentioned in the Introduction and in the diaries of David Zeisberger. Variations in the spelling are mentioned in the main entry; the individual variation of a name is listed with reference to the main entry. Most settlements are listed in the map at the back of the volume.

Albanien. See Albany.

Albany. Also "Albanien." Colony in New York, center of fur trade to the Six Indian Nations and most imporant conference town for negotiations betweeen the colonies and Native American tribes in the middle Atlantic and northern regions

Allegene. Synonym for Allegheny River region.

Assinink. See Assünnünk.

Assünink. See Assünnünk.

Assünnünk. Also Assinink, Assününk, Assünink, Standing Stone. Delaware settlement, renamed Shawnee Town in 1777, settlement of King Beaver (sometimes also called Beaver's Town), afterward, until 1776, settlement of Welapachtschiechen, "a tough 3 day journey from here [i.e., Schönbrunn] on the Hokhokung Creek [Hocking River] a day's journey from the Shawnee towns" (Zeisberger entry for 30 Jan. 1776) (E 4).

Assününk. See Assünnünk.

Attike. Indian name Kittanning, former settlement of the Delaware, at the mouth of the Cowanshannock creek into the Allegheny River, fifty miles north of Pittsburgh (D 7).

Beaver Creek. See Beaver River.

Beaver River. Also Great Beaver Creek, Great Beaver River, Big Beaver Creek, Big Beaver River, Bieber-Creek. Tributary of the Ohio. The Delaware settlements around Kaskaskunk were situated at Beaver River. The distance from Pittsburgh to the entrance of the Beaver River into the Ohio was twenty-nine miles (C-D 6).

Bedford. Originally Ray's Town, settlement in western Pennsylvania on the Juniata River (D 8).

Bethlehem. On the Lehigh River, Pennsylvania, main settlement of the Moravians in North America.

Bieber-Creek. See Beaver River.

Big Beaver Creek. See Beaver River.

Canacoshick. See Canegotschik.

Canegotschik. Also Canacoshick, Conococheague. Creek that enters the Potomac River south of Franklin County, Pennsylvania.

Canhawa. See Kanawha River.

1776 Pennsylvania and Virginia disputed possession of the fort; beginning in 1777 it was the seat of the commanding general of the Continental army for the Ohio region (D 6–7).

Fort Randolph. Also "Fort at the Canhawa." Located where the Kanawha River enters the Ohio, built in the summer of 1776 on the site of Fort Blair, burned down in 1775 by the Shawnee (F 4).

Fridenshütten. See Friedenshütten.

Friedenshütten. Also Fridenshütten. Moravian mission settlement founded in 1764, located on the east side of the east branch of the Susquehanna River opposite the mouth of Sugar Creek and two miles below Wyalusing. The settlement was abandoned in 1772 (C 10).

Friedensstadt. See Langundoutenünk.

Gekelemukpechünk. Also Kighalampegha, Kekalemahpehoong, Newcomer's Town. Situated on the Muskingum, until 1775–76 head settlement of the Delaware on the Muskingum and seat of the chief and the Great Council of the Delaware Nation (D 5).

Gnadenhütten I. Moravian mission settlement for the Mahican from Checomeco, situated where the Mahony Creek enters the Lehigh River, destroyed on 24 Nov. 1755.

Gnadenhütten II. Mission settlement of the Moravians located on the Tuscarawas, founded in autumn 1772 at the place where King Beaver (d. 1771) and members of the Turkey tribe had lived formerly. The place was settled mostly by Christian Mahican (D 5).

Goschachgünk. Also Coshocton, Cooschacking, Newcomerstown II. Head settlement of the Delaware founded in the spring of 1775, located at the confluence of the Walhanding and Tuscarawas (D 5).

Goschahossink. See Cushaughking.

Goschgosching. See Goschgoschünk.

Goschgoschünk. Also Goschgosching. Munsee settlement on the western bank of the Allegheny River at the mouth of Tionesta Creek (C 7).

Great Beaver Creek. See Beaver River.

Great Island. See Gros-Eiland.

Great Miami River. Tributary of the Ohio.

Greenville, Ohio. Settlement close to the Great Miami River, where in 1795 the treaty was signed under which the tribes of the Ohio region relinquished their lands to the United States.

Gros Eyland. See Gros-Eiland.

Gros-Eiland. Also Gros Eyland, Great Island. Settlement located at the site of present-day town Lock Haven on the right bank of the west branch of the Susquehanna River in Clinton County, Pennsylvania (C 9).

Harris's Ferry. Located on the Susquehanna River, Lancaster County, Pennsylvania; ferry place for the road from Philadelphia to Pittsburgh via Lancaster (D 10). Zeisberger mistakenly called it Harrisons Ferry.

Harrisons Ferry. See Harris's Ferry.

Hell I. A Delaware and Munsee settlement on the tributary of the Mohican, a river that enters the Walhanding River (D 4).

Hockhocking. See Hockhocküng.

Hockhocküng. Also Hockhocking. Settlement on the Hocking River (a.k.a. Hokhokung Creek) close to Assünnünk (E 4).

Hocking River. Also Hokhokung Creek. Enters the Ohio River from the northwest; the Delaware settlement Assünnünk was on the Hocking River (E 4–5).

Hokhokung Creek. See Hocking River.

Jerseys. Colony of New Jersey, which was divided into East Jersey and West Jersey.

Juniata River. Tributary of the Susquehanna River.

Kanawha River. Also Canhawa, Kenhawa. Tributary of the Ohio; the distance from the mouth of the Muskingum into the Ohio to the mouth of the Kanawha into the Ohio was 100 miles (F 4–5).

Kaskaskia. Originally a French settlement at the mouth of the Kaskasia River where it enters the Mississippi.

Kaskaskunk. Also Kuskuskies, Kuskuski. Main settlement of the Delaware on the Beaver River between Friedensstadt and Shenango; home of Chief Packanke (C-D 6).

Kenhawa. See Kanawha River.

Kekalemahpehoong. See Gekelemukpechünk.

Kekionga. Mingo settlement on the Maumee River in present-day Indiana (C 1).

Kighalampegha. See Gekelemukpechünk.

Kinhanschican. See Minque Town.

Kittanning. See Attike.

Kleinen Bieber-Creek. See Little Beaver Creek; from which it took two and a half days to reach Lichtenau.

Kuskuski. See Kaskaskunk.

Kuskuskies. See Kaskaskunk.

Lancaster. Town on the Susquehanna in Pennsylvania.

Langundo-Utenünk. See Langundoutenünk.

Langundoutenünk. Also Langundo-Utenünk, Languntennenk, German name Friedensstadt. A Moravian mission settlement founded in 1770 close to Kaskaskunk on the Beaver River (D 6).

Languntennenk. See Langundoutenünk.

Lawunachannek. See Lawunnakhannek.

Lawomakhannek. Also Lawunakhannek. Moravian mission settlement on the Allegheny River above Goschgoschünk, founded in 1770 (C 7).

Lichtenau. Founded in 1776, third Moravian mission settlement on the east bank of the Wal-handing River immediately south of Goschachgünk (D 5).

Ligonier. An American fort on the Loyalhanna Creek, Pennsylvania (D 7).

Lititz. Town ten miles north of Lancaster, Pennsylvania, named after the Bohemian barony Litiz (the spelling Zeisberger uses); Matthäus Hehl (1704–87) was the pastor of the Moravian congregation at Lititz.

Little Beaver Creek. Tributary of the Ohio, smaller than the the Beaver River (which on older maps was sometimes referred to as a creek). The route from Pittsburgh to the Delware settlements on the Muskingum crossed the Little Beaver Creek not far from its headwaters; the distance from that point to Lichtenau took about two and a half days to cover (D 6).

Little Shawnee Womans. See Mochwesüng.

Little Turtles. Mingo settlement on the Maumee near Lake Erie (C 2).

Logan's Town. Located at the mouth of the Beaver River where it joins the Ohio, on the main road from Pittsburgh to the Delaware settlements on the Muskingum (D 6).

Loggs Town. See Logstown.

Logstown. Also Loggs Town. Settlement of the Six Indian Nations between Fort Pitt and the mouth of the Beaver River where it joins the Ohio, a center of trade (D 6).

Lower Sandusky. Trading center, Wyandot settlement on the Sandusky River about ten miles from Sandusky Bay (C 3).

Loyalhanna Creek. Tributary of the Allegheny River.

Machiwihilusing. Munsee settlement near present-day Wyalusing in Bradford County, Pennsyl-vania, located on the Susquehanna River; home of the Munsee prophet Papunhank; for a short time Moravian settlement called Friedenshütten (C 10).

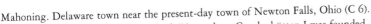

Mahoning. Delaware town near the present-day town of Newton Falls, Ohio (C 6).

Mahony Creek. Tributary of the Lehigh River where Gnadenhütten I was founded.

Maumee River. Originates in the northeastern part of Indiana, crosses the state of Ohio, and enters into Lake Erie (C 1–3).

Mechedachpisink. Not identified.

Memehusing. "A Munsee Town a one-day journey from here [Lichtenau]," according to Zeisberger's entry for 29 April 1778.

Meniolagomeka. Outpost settlement of Gnadenhütten I from 1749 to 1754; located on the Aquanshicola River in eastern Pennsylvania, five miles from Wechquetank.

Middle Town. Settlement near Harris's Ferry on the Susquehanna River in Lancaster County, Pennsylvania, on the route from Philadelphia via Lancaster to Pittsburgh.

Mighchetaghpiestagh. Also Mighchetaghpustagh. Settlement with salt springs about ten miles from Sikhewünk, today part of Salt Creek Township.

Mingo Town. Situated between Logstown and Wheeling on the Ohio River, possibly synonym for Logan's Town.

Minque Town. Mingo settlement and home of Winginund, probably identical to Kinhanschican and Hell I, located on the Mohican River, a headwater of the Walhanding River (D 4).

Mochwesüng. Also Mochwesünk, Moghwheston, Moughwersssing, Moschwasünk, Moquesin, Mow-hey-sink, Mouhweissing, Little Shawnee Womans. Munsee settlement between Woaketameki and White Eyes Town, a few miles from Woaketameki (D 5).

Mochwesünk. See Mochwesüng.

Moghwheston. See Mochwesüng

Mohok River. Also Mohawk River. River in the colony of New York.

Monongahela River. Headwater of the Ohio, at Pittsburgh joins the Allegheny River to become the Ohio River.

Moquesin. See Mochwesüng.

Moschwasünk. See Mochwesüng.

Moughwersssing. See Mochwesüng.

Mouhweissing. See Mochwesüng.

Mow-hey-sink. See Mochwesüng.

Muschkingum. See Muskingum.

Mushkingum. See Muskingum.

Muskingum. Tributary of the Ohio where most of the Delaware settlements were located; its headwaters were the Walhanding and the Tuscarawasee. Zeisberger did not differentiate between the Tuscarawas and the Muskingum (D–E 4–5).

Nain I. Coastal settlement and Moravian mission settlement in northern Labrador (see Scobel, *Andrees Allgemeiner Handatlas,* 158–59) (L 3).

Nain II. Christian Mahican settlement from 1757 to 1763, located two miles north of Bethlehem on the west bank of the Monocacy Creek.

Newcomer's Town. See Gekelemukpechünk.

Newcomerstown II. See Goschachgünk.

Niagara. See Fort Niagara.

Oberer Town. First Mahican settlement, established autumn 1772 before the Mahican moved to and founded Gnadenhütten II.

Oghkitawmikaw. See Woaketameki.

Ohio River. Tributary of the Mississippi.

Onenge. Also Onengo. Seneca settlement at the mouth of the French Creek and the Allegheny River.

Onengo. See Onenge.

Onondaga. Seat of the Head Council of the Six Indian Nations, south of Lake Ontario (B 10).

Pachgatgoch. Moravian Mission settlement two miles southwest of the present-day town of Kent, Connecticut, today called Scaticook.

Pennsylvania. Also Pennsylvanien. Colony between New Jersey and Maryland founded in 1682 by William Penn.

Pipe l. Delaware settlement in the region of the headwaters of the Cuyahoga River north of the Tuscarawas in Wyandot territory in the region controlled by the British; probably a synonym for the place to which the captains Pipe and Winginund transferred their settlements in 1777 (C 5).

Pittsburgh. Merchant settlement around Fort Pitt (D 6–7).

Pluggy's Town. Mingo settlement on the Olentangy, a tributary of the Scioto River (D 3).

Point Pleasant. Located at the confluence of the Ohio and the Kanawha where Fort Randolph was built; this was the place where the only battle during Lord Dunmore's war between an army from Virginia and the Shawnee was fought (10 Oct. 1774) (F 4).

Ray's Town. See Bedford.

Redstone. Town south of Pittsburgh where Redstone Creek and Dunlap's Creek enter the Monongahela River.

Robinson's Run. Tributary of Chartier's Creek a few miles from Pittsburgh.

Sakunk. Located at the mouth of the Beaver River and the Ohio close to Fort McIntosh (D 6).

Salem. Moravian mission settlement founded in 1780 on the Tuscarawas below Gnadenhütten II (D 5).

Salt Licks I. Mingo settlement on the Scioto River (E 3).

Salt Licks II. Delaware settlement close to present-day Niles, Ohio.

Salt Licks III. See Sikhewünk.

Salt Licks. Places where salt veins reach the surface and attract deer; American Natives procured their salt from these places. There was a salt lick not far from Schönbrunn.

Sandusky River. Flows into Lake Erie; the region around this river represented the main settlement area of the Wyandot (C 3).

Sarepta. Town in the governmental district of Saratow, Russia, and home to a Moravian congregation (see Scobel, *Andrees Allgemeiner Handatlas,* 115) (I/J 4).

Schechschiquanünk. Also Sheshequon, Sheshequin. Settlement founded in 1769 on the west bank of Susquehanna River, north of Wyalusing and Friedenshütten, six miles below Tioga Point, today seat of the town of Ulster, Bradford County, Pennsylvania (C 10).

Schochari. See Schoharie.

Schoharie. Also Schochari. Settlement on the Schoharie Creek in the colony of New York; the Schoharie Creek was a tributary of the Mohawk River.

Schönbrunn. Delaware name Welhik Thuppeck, also Tuppeek. Moravian mission settlement on the Tuscarawas (which Zeisberger called the Muskingum) founded in 1772, located south of what is today New Philadelphia, Ohio (D 5).

Scioto River. Also Sioto. Tributary of the Ohio and settlement region of the Shawnee (E–F 3–4).

Se-key-unck. See Sikhewünk.

Shamokin. Also Shomoko, Shomoco. Seat of the Pennsylvania representative of the Six Indian Nations and for some time Moravian mission settlement. Located at the confluence of the west and east branches of the Susquehanna River (D 10).

Shawnee Lower Towns. Until 1777–78 main settlement region of the Shawnee; its capital was Chillicothe (E 3–4).

Shawnee Womans. Shawnee settlement south of Woaketameki (D 4).

Shenango. See Shenenge.

Shenenge. Also Shenango, Zenenge. Delaware settlement on the Shenango, a headwater of the Beaver River situated above Kaskaskunk. Until 1773–74 the seat of Chief Laweloochwalend (C 6).

Sheshequin. See Schechschiquanünk.

Sheshequon. See Schechschiquanünk.

Sikhewünk. Also Se-key-unck, Will's Town, Sughchaung, Sukahunig, Salt Licks. Delaware town at the mouth of Salt Creek and Muskingum, a day's journey from Lichtenau.

Sioto. See Scioto River.

Snakes. Shawnee settlement near Woaketameki (D 4).

Snipes I. Wyandot settlement at one of the headwaters of the Sandusky River (D 3).

Stockbridge. Western Massachusetts town on the Houssatonic River, home of the Muhhakaneok or Stockbridge Indians, mission settlement of Jonathan Edwards.

Sugar Creek. Also Zucker Creek. River that enters the Tuscarawas River two miles northwest of Schönbrunn.

Sughchaung. See Sikhewünk.

Sukahunig. See Sikhewünk.

Susquehanna River. Pennsylvania river that enters the Chesapeake Bay in Maryland; Friedenshütten was located at its east branch.

Tennessee River. In colonial and revolutionary times usually called Cherokee River, a tributary of the Ohio; the Cherokee's main settlement area lay on the upper part of this river, primarily in North Carolina and extending into Georgia.

Tionesta Creek. Joined the Allegheny River near Goschgoschünk.

Tuscarawas. See Gnadenhütten II.

Tuscarawas River. One of the two headwaters of the Muskingum. The lake where the Tuscarawas originates is noted on Thomas Hutchins's map, "Map of Col. Bouquet's Indian Campaigns" (1764) (D 5).

Tuscarawi. Settlement north of the Tuscarawas River and according to Zeisberger forty miles north of Gekelemukpechünk, where Delaware lived by the winter of 1772–73 (D 5).

Unami River. Not identified.

Upper Sandusky. Wyandot town on the Sandusky River where Half King (Indian name Pomoacan) lived (D 3).

Venango. First a Delaware and later a Seneca settlement on the upper Allegheny River, where Fort Venango was built in 1760 (C 7).

Vincennes. Originally a French settlement on the Wabash River.

Virginia. Also Virginien. The oldest English colony in North America, bordering Pennsylvania to the west. In 1773 Virginia claimed the region around Pittsburgh, including Fort Pitt.

Wabash. Also Wobash. Region of the Wabash River, a tributary of the Ohio, and settlement territory of the Kickapoo and Wea tribes.

Wakataumika. See Woaketameki.

Wakatomica. See Woaketameki.

Waketameki. See Woaketameki.

Walhanding Creek. Also Walhonding. One of the two headwaters of the Muskingum. Zeisberger considered the Walhanding a tributary of the Muskingum; consequently he called the Tuscarawas River the Muskingum. By today's geography Schönbrunn and Gnadenhütten II were on the Tuscarawas River, but according to Zeisberger's understanding they were on the Muskingum River (D 4–5).

Walhanding. Also Walhonding, Walhandünk. Town on the river of the same name, about seventeen miles upstream from Goschachgünk (D 4).

Walhandünk. See Walhanding.

Walhonding. See Walhanding.

Wayomik. See Wyoming.

Wechquetank. Also Wequetank, Wequitank. Moravian mission settlement founded in 1760 and abandoned in 1763, located on Hoeth's Creek, a tributary of the Lehigh River, six miles north of the Blue Mountains in Pennsylvania.

Welhik Thuppeck. Also Tuppeek. See Schönbrunn.

Wequetank. See Wechquetank.

Wequitank. See Wechquetank.

Wheeling. Town near Fort Henry at the mouth of Wheeling Creek and the Ohio River (D 6).

White Eyes Town. Located on the Tuscarawas, the closest of the three settlements between Woaketameki and Gekelemukpechünk to Gekelemukpechünk; seat of White Eyes (D 5).

Wihilasing. See Wyalusing.

Wihilusing. See Wyalusing.

Will's Town. See Sikhewünk.

Wilünk. See Wheeling.

Wisancksican. Not identified.

Woaketameki. Also Woaketammeki, Oghkitawmikaw, Wakataumika, Wakatomica, Waketameki. Located on the Muskingum, chief settlement of the Shawnee in this region, abandoned after Lord Dunmore's war (D 5).

Wobash. See Wabash.

Wyalusing. Also Wihilusing, Wihilasing. Settlement of Papunhank, baptized Johannes, situated at the north branch of the Susquehanna at the mouth of Wyalusing Creek near the Moravian mission settlement of Friedenshütten; founded in 1765 (C 10).

Wyoming. Also Wayomik. Shawnee and Delaware settlement, situated on the east branch of the Susquehanna River (C 11).

Wyondat Town. According to a Spanish report, "located one-quarter league from the district of Detroit."

Yellow Creek. Enters the Ohio River about forty miles north of the town of Wheeling.

Zane's. Also Zanes. Mingo settlement in the headwater region of the Miami River (D 3).

Zeninge. See Chenango.

Zucker Creek. See Sugar Creek.

BIBLIOGRAPHY

MANUSCRIPT COLLECTIONS

Moravian Archives, Bethlehem, Pa.
  Bethlehem Diary
    Box 112
    Box 121
    Box 131
    Box 137
    Box 141
    Box 144
    Box 147
    Box 148
    Box 211
    Box 217
    Box 229
    Box 311
    Box 315
    Diaconate of Bethlehem, Ledger A
    Ettwein Papers [E.P.], Box 965
    Letters received by the Provincial Helpers' Conference in general, from the Unity's Elders' Conference, 1770–93
    Memoirs Box 6, 1805
    Memoirs Gemeinnachrichten 1793
    Memoirs Diary Bethlehem, vols. 37–38
    Memoirs Box 7, 1811–20
    Memoirs Box 8, 1824
    Protokoll der Provincial-Helfer-Conferenz, 1774–82 (uncatalogued)
    Verlaß der General Synode in Philadelphia vom 25.–27. 3. 1746 (uncatalogued)
    Verlaß der Pennsylvanischen Religions Conferenz gehalten zu Philadelphia, Juli 31 seq. 1746 (without call numbers)
    Verlaß des im Jahr 1775 zu Barby gehaltenen Synodi der Evangelischen Brüder-Unität (without call number)
    "Wöchentliche Nachrichten der Unitäts Aeltesten Conferenz" (volumes for 1764–73, 1774–80, and 1781–85)

Archives of the Moravian Church at Herrnhut, Germany
  R 15 H 1 b 14–17.
  R 3 A 8 2a

Carnegie Library of Pittsburgh
Morgan Letterbook, vols. 1–3

National Archives, Washington, D.C.
Edward Hand Papers, National Archives Microfilm 247, reel 180

Library of Congress, Manuscript Division
Edward Hand Papers, Peter Force Transcripts

Historical Society of Pennsylvania, Philadelphia
"Bishop Cammerhoff's Letters to Zinzendorf, 1747–1749," transcripts by J. W. Jordan
Richard Peters Manuscripts

John Rylands Library, Manchester, England
Minutes, etc., of Provincial Conferences and Synods of the Moravian Brethren in England,
1743–55. Copied from the records in the Provincial Archives of the Moravian Church at
22 Fetter Lane, London, vol. 1, MSS R 92072, Ryl. Eng. MS 1054. We have used:
Minutes of the Provincial Conference at Northampton House, Bloomsbury Square, London,
16–20 Jan. 1749
Minutes of the Provincial Conference at Ingatestone Hai, 17–19 May 1752, No. 9
Minutes of the Provincial Synod at Lindsey House, London, 13–20 May 1754
Minutes, etc., of Provincial Conferences and Synods of the Moravian Brethren in England,
1743–55. Copied from the records in the Provincial Archives of the Moravian Church at
22 Fetter Lane, London, vol. 3, R 92072, Ryl. Eng. Ms. 1056. We have used:
Minutes of the Provincial Synod at Lindsey House, 12–22 May 1765
Result of the Provincial Synod, 3–14 Aug. 1766

Ohio Historical Society, Columbus, Ohio
MSS 215, August C. Mahr Papers

PRINTED SOURCES

"Letters from the Canadian Archives." *Collections of the Illinois State Historical Library* 1 (1903):
290–457.
"The Haldimand Papers." *Michigan Pioneer and Historical Collections* 9 (1886): 343–658.
Alvord, Clarence Walworth, ed. *Kaskaskia Records, 1778–1790*. Collections of the Illinois State
Historical Library 5, Virginia Series 2. Springfield, Ill., 1909.
Barnhart, John D., ed. *Henry Hamilton and George Rogers Clark in the American Revolution, with the
Unpublished Journal of Lieut. Gov. Henry Hamilton*. Crawfordsville, Ind., 1951.
[Beatty, Charles]. *Journals of Charles Beatty, 1762–1769*, ed. Guy Soulliard Klett. University
Park, Pa., 1962.
Beyreuther, Erich, and Gerhard Meyer, eds. *Ergänzungsbände zu den Hauptschriften*, vols. 1–14.
Hildesheim, 1966–85.
Bray, William. "'*Observations on the Indian Method of Picture-Writing*.' In a Letter to the Secretary,"
American Philosophical Society Proceedings (1781): 159–62.
Brüdergemeine. *Altes und Neues Brüdergesangbuch*, Theil 1. London, 1753.
———. *Das kleine Brüder-Gesang-Buch in einer Harmonischen Samlung von kurzen Liedern, Versen,
Gebeten und Seufzern bestehend*. Barby, 1763.
———. *Des Evangelischen Lieder-Buches unter dem Titel Brüder-Gesang von den Tagen Henochs bisher
Zweyter Band*. London 1754.

————. *Des kleinen Brüder-Gesangbuchs Dritter Theil, enthaltend eine abermalige Samlung alter und neuer Verse.* Barby, 1772.

————. *Gesangbuch zum Gebrauch der evangelischen Brüdergemeinen.* Barby, 1778.

————. *Die Lehr-Texte der Brüder-Gemeine für das Jahr 1772.* Philadelphia: Gedrukt bey Henrich Miller, 1771.

————. *Die Lehr-Texte der Brüder-Gemeine für das Jahr 1773.* Philadelphia: Gedrukt bey Henrich Miller, 1772.

————. *Die Lehrtexte der Brüder-Gemeine für das Jahr 1774.* Philadelphia: Gedruckt bey Henrich Miller, im Jahr 1773.

————. *Die Lehrtexte der Brüder-Gemeine für das Jahr 1775.* Philadelphia: Gedruckt bey Henrich Miller, 1774.

————. *Die Lehrtexte der Brüder-Gemeine für das Jahr 1776. Enthaltend lauter Worte unsers lieben Herrn und Heilandes.* Philadelphia: Gedruckt bey Henrich Miller, 1775.

————. *Die täglichen Loosungen der Brüder-Gemeine für das Jahr 1771.* Philadelphia: Gedrukt bey Henrich Miller, 1770.

————. *Die täglichen Loosungen der Brüder-Gemeine für das Jahr 1772.* Philadelphia: Gedrukt bey Henrich Miller, 1771.

————. *Die täglichen Loosungen der Brüder-Gemeine für das Jahr 1773.* Philadelphia: Gedrukt bey Henrich Miller, 1772.

————. *Die täglichen Loosungen der Brüder-Gemeine für das Jahr 1774.* Philadelphia: Gedruckt bey Henrich Miller, 1773.

————. *Die täglichen Loosungen der Brüder-Gemeine für das Jahr 1775.* Philadelphia: Gedruckt bey Henrich Miller, 1774.

————. *Die täglichen Loosungen der Brüder-Gemeine für das Jahr 1776.* Philadelphia: Gedruckt bey Henrich Miller, 1775.

————. *Die täglichen Loosungen der Brüdergemeine für das Jahr 1778. Zu finden in den Brüdergemeinen.* 1777 [N.p., preface dated "Barby 21 April 1777"].

————. *Die täglichen Loosungen und Lehrtexte der Brudergemeine für das Jahr 1779* [N.p., preface dated "Barby den 1ten Merz 1778"].

————. *Die täglichen Loosungen der Brüdergemeine für das Jahr 1780.* Philadelphia: Gedruckt bey Steiner und Cist, n.d..

————. *Die täglichen Loosungen der Brüdergemeine für das Jahr 1781.* Philadelphia: Gedruckt bey Steiner und Cist, n.d.

Butterfield, Consul Willshire, ed. *The Washington-Crawford Letters, Being the Correspondence Between George Washington and William Crawford, from 1767 to 1781, Concerning Western Lands.* Cincinnati, 1877.

By His Excellency the President and Council of the Commonwealth of Pennsylvania. A Proclamation. Philadelphia, 1779.

[Connolly, John]. "A Narrative of the Transactions, Imprisonment, and Sufferings of John Connolly, an American Loyalist and Lieut. Col. in His Majesty's Service." *Pennsylvania Magazine of History and Biography* 12 (1888): 310–24, 407–20; 13 (1889): 61–79, 153–67, 281–91.

Cranz, David. *Historie von Grönland, enthaltend die Beschreibung des Landes . . . insbes. die Geschichte der dortigen Mission der Evangelischen Brüder zu Neu-Herrnhut und Lichtenfels.* Barby, 1765.

————. *Alte und Neue Brüder-Historie oder kurzgefaßte Geschichte der Ev. Brüder-Unität.* Barby, 1771.

Crèvecoeur, Hector St. John de. *Letters from an American Farmer.* London, 1782.

Darlington, William M., ed. *Scoouwa: James Smith's Indian Captivity Narrative*, annotated by John J. Barsotti. Columbus, Ohio, 1992.

Darlington, Mary C., ed. *Fort Pitt and Letters from the Frontier.* Pittsburgh, 1892.

Davies, K. G., ed. *Documents of the American Revolution.* 21 vols. Shannon, Dublin, 1970–83.

Dexter, Franklin B., ed. *Diary of David McClure, Doctor of Divinity, 1748–1820*. New York, 1899.

[Dodge, John]. "A Narrative of the Capture and Treatment of John Dodge by the English at Detroit." *The Remembrancer, or, Impartial Repository of Public Events for the Year 1779* (London, 1779): 73–81.

Edwards, Jonathan. *The Life of David Brainerd*, ed. Norman Pettit. In *The Works of Jonathan Edwards*, ed. Perry Miller et al., vol. 7. New Haven, 1985.

[Ettwein, John]. "Brother Ettwein's Account of His Visit in Langundo-Utenünk on the Beaver Creek, and Welhik Tupeck, on the Muskingum River." In Kenneth G. Hamilton, *John Ettwein and the American Revolution*, 341–57. Bethlehem, Pa., 1940.

———. "John Ettwein's Notes of Travel from the North Branch of the Susquehanna to the Beaver River, Pennsylvania, 1772," ed. John W. Jordan. *Pennsylvania Magazine of History and Biography* 25 (1901): 208–19.

[Ettwein, John, Gottlob Sensemann, and David Zeisberger]. "Report of the Journey of John Ettwein, David Zeisberger and Gottlob Senseman to Friedenshuetten and Their Stay There," ed. Archer B. Hulbert and Nathaniel Schwarze. *The Moravian Records 2, Ohio Archaeological and Historical Quarterly* 21 (1912): 32–42.

Force, Peter, ed. *American Archives*, 4th ser., 6 vols. Washington, D.C., 1837–44.

———. *American Archives*, 5th ser., 3 vols. Washington, D.C., 1848–53.

Ford, Worthington C., ed. *Journals of the Continental Congress, 1774–1789*. 34 vols. Washington, D.C., 1904–37.

[Franklin, Benjamin]. *The Interest of Great Britain Considered, With Regard to her Colonies, and the Acquisitions of Canada and Guadaloupe. To which are added, Observations concerning the Increase of Mankind, Peopling of Countries, etc.* London, 1760. Reprinted in Leonard W. Labaree, et al., eds., *The Papers of Benjamin Franklin*, 9:59–100. New Haven, 1966.

Freylinghausen, Johann Athanasius. *Grundlegung der Theologie darin die Glaubenslehren aus göttlichem Wort deutlich vorgetragen und zum tätigen Christentum wie auch evangelischen Trost angewendet werden*, 4th ed. Halle, 1712.

Grube, Bernhard Adam. *Dellawaerisches Gesang-Büchlein. Wenn ich des Morgens frühaufsteh etc. Translat. 1. Enda wopanachinaane*. Friedensthal bei Bethlehem, Pa., [1763?].

Hale, Duane K., ed. *Turtle Tales: Oral Traditions of the Delaware Tribe of Western Oklahoma*. Anadarko, Okla., 1984.

[Hamilton, Alexander]. *The Papers of Alexander Hamilton*. 27 vols. Ed. Harold C. Syrett and Jacob E. Cooke. New York, 1961–87.

Harcourt, Edward W., ed. *The Harcourt Papers*. 12 vols. Oxford, 1880–1905.

Hastings, Hugh, ed. *Ecclesiastical Records, State of New York*. 7 vols. Albany, N.Y., 1901–16.

Hawes, Lilla Mills, ed. *Lachlan McIntosh Papers in the University of Georgia Libraries*. University of Georgia Libraries Miscellanea Publications, no. 7. Athens, 1968.

Hawkins, Ernest, ed. *Historical Notices of the Missions of the Church of England in the North American Colonies, Previous to the Independence of the United States: Chiefly from the MSS Documents of the Society for the Propagation of the Gospel in Foreign Parts*. London, 1845.

Hazard, Samuel, ed. *Colonial Records*. 16 vols. Harrisburg, Pa., 1852–56.

Hazard, Samuel, et al., eds. *Pennsylvania Archives, Selected and Arranged from Original Documents in the Office of the Secretary of the Commonwealth*. 138 vols. in 9 series. Philadelphia and Harrisburg, 1852–1935.

Heckewelder, John. *History, Manners, and Customs of the Indian Nations who Once Inhabited Pennsylvania and the Neighbouring States*, ed. William C. Reichel. Memoirs of the Historical Society of Pennsylvania 12 (Philadelphia, 1881).

———. "Names which the Lenni Lenape or Delaware Indians, who once inhabited this country, had given to Rivers, Streams, Places," ed. Peter S. Du Ponceau. *Transactions of the American Philosophical Society*, n.s. 4 (1834): 351–96.

———. *A Narrative of the Mission of the United Brethren Among the Delaware and Mohegan Indians, from Its Commencement, in the Year 1740, to the Close of the Year 1808*. Philadelphia, 1820. Reprint, New York, 1971.

[Heckewelder, John]. "A Canoe Journey from the Big Beaver to the Tuscarawas in 1773: A Travel Diary of John Heckewelder," ed. and trans. August C. Mahr. *Ohio Archaeological and Historical Quarterly* 61 (1952): 283–98.

Hegner, J. K., ed. *Fortsetzung von David Cranzens Brüder-Historie*. Barby: Gnadau, 1791–1816.

Heston, Zebulon, and John Parrish. "Journal of a Mission to the Indians in Ohio, by Friends from Pennsylvania, July–September 1773." *Historical Magazine and Notes and Queries, Concerning the Antiquities, History, and Biography of America*, 2d ser., 7 (1870): 103–7.

Horn, William F., ed. *The Horn Papers. Early Westward Movement on the Monongahela and Upper Ohio, 1765–1795*. 3 vols. Scottsdale, Pa., 1945.

Hulbert, Archer B., and Nathaniel Schwarze, eds. "The Diaries of Zeisberger Relating to the First Missions in the Ohio Basin." *Ohio Historical Quarterly* 21 (1912): 1–125.

———. *The Moravian Records* 2, *Ohio Archaeological and Historical Quarterly* 21 (1912): 1–115.

James, Alton James, ed. *George Rogers Clark Papers, 1771–1781*. Collections of the Illinois State Historical Library 8, Virginia Series 3. Springfield, Ill., 1912.

Jones, David. *A Journal of Two Visits Made to some Nations of the Indians on the West Side of the River Ohio, in the Years 1772 and 1773*. Philadelphia, 1774. Reprinted for Joseph Sabin with a biographical notice of the author, by Horatio Gates Jones. New York, 1865.

Kappler, Charles J., ed. *Indian Affairs, Laws, and Treaties*. Washington, D.C., 1903.

Kellogg, Louise P., ed. *The British Régime in Wisconsin and the Northwest*. Publications of the State Historical Society of Wisconsin, Collections 2. Madison, Wis., 1935.

———. *Frontier Advance on the Upper Ohio, 1778–1779*. Publications of the State Historical Society of Wisconsin, Collections 23, Draper Series 4. Madison, Wis., 1916.

———. *Frontier Retreat on the Upper Ohio, 1779–1781*. Publications of the State Historical Society of Wisconsin, Collections 24, Draper Series 5. Madison, Wis., 1917.

Kinietz, Vernon, and Erminie W. Voegelin, eds. *Shawnee Traditions. C. C. Trowbridge's Account. Occasional Contributions from the Museum of Anthropology of the University of Michigan*, no. 9. Ann Arbor, Mich. 1939.

[Kirkland, Samuel]. *Journals of Samuel Kirkland, 18th-century Missionary to the Iroquois, Government Agent, Father of Hamilton College*, ed. Walter Pilkington. Clinton, N.Y., 1980.

[Lacey, John]. "Memoirs of Brigadier-General John Lacey, of Pennsylvania." *Pennsylvania Magazine of History and Biography* 25 (1901): 1–13.

"Letters from the Canadian Archives." *Collections of the Illinois State Historical Library* 1 (1903): 290–457.

Lindeström, Peter. *Geographica Americae, with an Account of the Delaware Indians Based on Surveys and Notes Made in 1654–1656*, ed. Amandus Johnson. Philadelphia, 1925.

Loskiel, Georg Heinrich. *Geschichte der Mission der evangelischen Brüder unter den Indianern in Nordamerika*. Barby, 1789.

McIlwaine, Henry R., ed. *Journals of the Council of the State of Virginia*. 6 vols. Richmond, 1925–66.

———. *Official Letters of the Governors of the State of Virginia*. 3 vols. Richmond, 1926–29.

McIlwaine, Henry R., Henry Read, and John Pendleton Kennedy, eds. *Journals of the House of Burgesses of Virginia*. 13 vols. Richmond, 1905–15.

McIlwaine, Henry R., Henry Read, Wilmer L. Hall, and Benjamin I. Hillman, eds. *Executive Journals of the Council of Colonial Virginia {1680–1775}*. 6 vols. Richmond, 1925–66.

Mulkearn, Lois, ed. *George Mercer Papers Relating to the Ohio Company of Virginia*. Pittsburg, Ohio, 1954.

Neisser, Georg. *A History of the Beginnings of Moravian Work in America,* ed. William N. Schwarze and Samuel H. Gapp. Archives of the Moravian Church, Publications, no. 1. Bethlehem, Pa., 1955.

O'Callaghan, Edmund B., et al., eds. *Documents Relative to the Colonial History of the State of New-York.* 15 vols. Albany, N.Y., 1853–87.

Oldendorp, Christian Georg Andreas. *Geschichte der Mission der evangelischen Brüder auf den caraibischen Inseln: S. Thomas, S. Croix und S. Jan.* Barby, 1777.

[Parrish, John]. "Extract from the Journal of John Parrish, 1773." *Pennsylvania Magazine of History and Biography* 16 (1892): 443–48.

[Penn, William]. *William Penn's Own Account of the Lenni Lenape or Delaware Indians,* ed. Albert Cook Myers. Wilmington, 1970.

Peters, Richard, ed. *The Public Statutes at Large of the United States of America.* 8 vols. Boston, 1860–67.

Robinson, W. Stitt, ed. *Virginia Treaties, 1723–1775.* Vol. 5 of *Early American Indian Documents: Treaties & Laws, 1607–1789.* Frederick, Md., 1983.

[Schmick, Johann Jacob]. *Schmick's Mahican Dictionary,* ed. Carl Masthay. In Memoirs of the American Philosophical Society 197. Philadelphia, 1991.

Scribner, Robert L., et al., eds. *Revolutionary Virginia: The Road to Independence.* 7 vols. Charlottesville, 1973–83.

[Sensemann, Gottlob, and David Zeisberger]. "Diary of David Zeisberger and Gottlob Zenseman. Journey to Goschgoschink on the Ohio and their Arrival There, 1768," ed. Archer B. Hulbert and Nathaniel Schwarze. *The Moravian Records* 2, *Ohio Archaeological and Historical Quarterly* 21 (1912): 42–69.

———. "Continuation of the Diary of the Brethren in Goschgoschuenk on the Ohio, August 1768," ed. Archer B. Hulbert and Nathaniel Schwarze. *The Moravian Records* 2, *Ohio Archaeological and Historical Quarterly* 21 (1912): 69–104.

Smith, Paul H. et al., eds. *Letters of Delegates to Congress.* 26 vols. Washington, D.C., 1976–2000.

[Smith, William]. *An Historical Account of the Expedition Against the Ohio Indians, in the Year 1764. Under the Command of Henry Bouquet, Esq; . . . Including His Transactions with the Indians, relative to the delivery of their prisoners and the preliminaries of Peace.* Philadelphia: William Bradford, 1765.

Smith, William H., ed. *The St. Clair Papers. The Life and Public Services of Arthur St. Clair.* 2 vols. Cincinnati, 1882.

Spangenberg, August G. *Idea fidei fratrum, oder kurzer Begriff der Christlichen Lehre in den evangelischen Brüdergemeinen.* Barby, 1779.

———. *Leben des Herrn Nicolaus Ludwig Grafen und Herrn von Zinzendorf und Pottendorf,* 8 parts. Barby, 1772–75.

Stevens, Sylvester K., and Donald H. Kent, eds. *The Papers of Henry Bouquet.* 19 vols. Harrisburg, Pa., 1940–43.

Stevens, Sylvester K., Donald H. Kent, and Louis M. Waddell, eds. *The Papers of Henry Bouquet.* 5 vols. Harrisburg, Pa., 1951–84.

Stock, Leo Francis et al., eds. *Proceedings and Debates of the British Parliaments Respecting North America, 1542–1754.* 5 vols. Washington, D.C., 1924–41.

Sullivan, James et al., eds. *The Papers of Sir William Johnson.* 14 vols. Albany, N.Y., 1921–65.

Thornely, Samuel, ed. *The Journal of Nicholas Cresswell, 1774–1777.* New York, 1924.

Thwaites, Reuben G., ed. *The British Regime in Wisconsin 1760–1800. Collections of the State Historical Society of Wisconsin* 18 (1908).

———. *Early Western Travels, 1748–1846.* 32 vols. Cleveland, Ohio, 1904–7.

Thwaites, Reuben G., and Louise P. Kellogg, eds. *Documentary History of Dunmore's War, 1774.* Draper Series 1. Madison, Wis., 1905.

————. *Frontier Defense on the Upper Ohio, 1777–1778.* Draper Series 3. Madison, Wis., 1912.

————. *Revolution on the Upper Ohio, 1775–1777.* Draper Series 2. Madison, Wis., 1908.

Wainwright, Nicholas B., ed. "Turmoil at Pittsburgh. Diary of Augustine Prevost, 1774." *Pennsylvania Magazine of History and Biography* 85 (1961): 111–62.

Wallace, Paul A. W., ed. *Travels of John Heckewelder in Frontier America.* Pittsburgh, 1958.

[Washington, George]. *The Diaries of George Washington.* 6 vols. Ed. Donald Jackson and Dorothy Twohig. Charlottesville, 1976–79.

————. *The Writings of George Washington.* 39 vols. Ed. John C. Fitzpatrick. Washington, D.C., 1931–44.

Williams, Samuel Cole, ed. *Adair's History of the American Indians.* Johnson City, Tenn., 1930.

————. "Presbyterian Mission to the Cherokees, 1757–1759." *Tennessee Historical Magazine,* 2d ser., 1 (1930–31): 125–38.

Williams, Edward W., ed. "The Journal of Richard Butler, 1775. Continental Congress' Envoy to the Western Indians." *Western Pennsylvania Historical Magazine* 46 (1963): 381–95, and 47 (1964): 31–46, 141–56.

————. "A Revolutionary Journal and Orderly Book of General Lachlan McIntosh's Expedition, 1778." *Western Pennsylvania Historical Magazine* 43 (1960): 1–17, 157–77, 267–88.

Young, Chester R., ed. *Westward into Kentucky: The Narrative of Daniel Trabue.* Lexington, Ky., 1981.

Zeisberger, David. *A Collection of Hymns for the Use of the Christian Indians, of the Missions of the United Brethren in North America.* Philadelphia, 1803; Bethlehem, Pa., 1847.

————. *Essay of a Delaware Indian and English Spelling Book for the Use of the Schools of the Christian Indians on Muskingum River.* Philadelphia, 1776. Republished as *Delaware Indian and English Spelling Book, for the Schools of the Mission of the United Brethren.* Philadelphia, 1806.

————. "History of the Northern American Indians," ed. Archer B. Hulbert and William Nathaniel Schwarze. *Ohio State Archaeological and Historical Quarterly* 19 (1910): 1–189. Reprint, New York, 1991, and Lewisburg, Pa., 1999.

————. *A Lenapé–English Dictionary,* ed. Daniel G. Brinton and Albert Seqaqkind Anthony. Pennsylvania Student Series 1. Philadelphia, 1889.

Zeisberger's Indian Dictionary, English, German, Iroquois—the Onondaga and Algonquin—the Delaware. Cambridge, Mass., 1887.

[Zeisberger, David]. "Diary of David Zeisberger's Journey to the Ohio, Called in Delaware the Allegene, from Sept. 20th to Nov. 16, 1767," ed. Archer B. Hulbert and Nathaniel Schwarze. *The Moravian Records* 2, *Ohio Archaeological and Historical Quarterly* 21 (1912): 8–32.

Zinzendorf, Nikolaus Ludwig von. *Hauptschriften in sechs Bänden,* ed. Erich Beyreuther and Gerhard Meyer. Hildesheim, 1962–63.

[Zinzendorf, Nikolaus Ludwig von]. *Texte zur Mission. Mit einer Einführung in die Missionstheologie Zinzendorfs,* ed. Helmut Bintz. Hamburg, 1979.

————. *Die wichtigsten Missionsinstruktionen Zinzendorfs,* ed. Otto Uttendörfer. Herrnhut, 1913.

SECONDARY SOURCES

Abel, Annie H. "Proposals for an Indian State, 1778–1878." *American Historical Association Annual Report* 1 (1907): 87–104.

Abler, Thomas S., and Elizabeth Tooker. "Seneca." In *Northeast,* ed. Bruce G. Trigger, 505–17. Vol. 15 of *Handbook of North American Indians,* ed. William C. Sturtevant. Washington, D.C., 1978.

Alden, John Richard. *John Stuart and the Southern Colonial Frontier: A Study of Indian Relations, War, Trade, and Land Problems in the Southern Wilderness, 1754–1775.* Ann Arbor, 1944.

Alvord, Clarence Walworth. *The Mississippi Valley in British Politics: A Study of the Trade, Land*

Speculation, and Experiments in Imperialism Culminating in the American Revolution. 2 vols. Cleveland, Ohio, 1917. Reprint, New York, 1959.

Appel, John C. "Colonel Daniel Brodhead and the Lure of Detroit." *Pennsylvania History* 38 (1971): 265–82.

Arndt, Karl John Richard, and Reimer C. Eck, eds. *The First Century of German Language Printing in the United States of America: A Bibliography Based on the Studies of Oswald Seidensticker and Wilbur H. Oda*. 2 vols. Göttingen, 1989.

Axtell, James. *The Invasion Within: The Contest of Cultures in Colonial North America*. Vol. 1 of *The Cultural Origins of North America*. New York, 1985.

———. "The White Indians of Colonial America" *William & Mary Quarterly*, 3d ser., 32 (1975): 55–88.

Barclay, Wade Crawford. *History of Methodist Missions*. Part 1: *Early American Methodism, 1769–1844*, vol. 1: *Missionary Motivation and Expansion*. New York, 1949.

Bechler, Theodor. *August Gottlieb Spangenberg und die Mission*. Hefte zur Missionskunde (Herrnhuter Missionsstudien), nos. 28–29. Herrnhut, 1933.

Beck, Hartmut. *Brüder in vielen Völkern: 250 Jahre Mission der Brüdergemeine*. Erlangen, 1981.

Becker, Marshall J. "The Boundary Between the Lenape and Munsee: The Forks of Delaware as a Buffer Zone." *Man in the Northeast* 26 (fall 1983): 1–20.

Bettermann, Wilhelm. *Theologie und Sprache bei Zinzendorf*. Gotha, 1935.

Beyreuther, Erich. "Christozentrismus und Trinitätsauffassung" and "Lostheorie und Lospraxis." In Erich Beyreuther, *Studien zur Theologie Zinzendorfs: Gesammelte Aufsätze*, 9–34 and 109–39. Neukirchen, 1962.

Bonomi, Patricia U. *Under the Cope of Heaven: Religion, Society, and Politics in Colonial America*. New York, 1986.

Bonvillain, Nancy. *The Mohawk*. New York, 1992.

Boyd, Jesse L. *A History of Baptists in America Prior to 1845*. New York, 1957.

Bradley, E. A., and T. J. Bennett. "Earthquake History of Ohio." *Seismological Society of America Bulletin* 55 (1965): 745–52.

Brainerd, Thomas. *The Life of John Brainerd: The Brother of David Brainerd, and His Successor as Missionary to the Indians of New Jersey*. Philadelphia, 1865.

Brasser, Ted J. "Mahican." In *Northeast*, ed. Bruce G. Trigger, 198–212. Vol. 15 of *Handbook of North American Indians*, ed. William C. Sturtevant. Washington, D.C., 1978.

Brecht, Martin et al., eds. *Geschichte des Pietismus*, vols. 1–4. Göttingen, 1993–2004.

Brown, Parker B. "The Battle of Sandusky: June 4–6, 1782." *Western Pennsylvania Historical Magazine* 65 (1982): 115–51.

———. "The Fate of Crawford Volunteers Captured by Indians Following the Battle of Sandusky in 1782." *Western Pennsylvania Historical Magazine* 65 (1982): 323–40.

Brunner, Daniel L. *Halle Pietists in England: Anthony William Boehm and the Society for Promoting Christian Knowledge*. Göttingen, 1993.

Burke, John G. *Cosmic Debris: Meteorites in History*. Berkeley, 1986.

Bushnell, David I., Jr. "The Virginia Frontier in History—1778." *Virginia Magazine of History* 23 (1915): 113–23, 256–68, 337–57, and 24 (1916): 168–79.

Callender, Charles. "Illinois," "Miami," and "Shawnee." In *Northeast*, ed. Bruce G. Trigger, 673–80, 681–89, 622–35. Vol. 15 of *Handbook of North American Indians*, ed. William C. Sturtevant. Washington, D.C., 1978.

Callender, Charles, Richard K. Pope, and Susan M. Pope. "Kickapoo." In *Northeast*, ed. Bruice G. Trigger, 656–67. Vol. 15 of *Handbook of North American Indians*, ed. William C. Sturtevant. Washington, D.C., 1978.

Calloway, Colin G. "'We have always been the frontier': The American Revolution in Shawnee Country." *American Indian Quarterly* 16 (1992): 39–52.

Cappon, Lester J. et al., eds. *Atlas of Early American History: The Revolutionary Era, 1760–1790.* Princeton, 1976.

Cleland, Charles E. *Rites of Conquest: The History and Culture of Michigan's Native Americans.* Ann Arbor, 1992.

Clifton, James A. "Potawatomi." In *Northeast,* ed. Bruce G. Trigger, 725–42. Vol. 15 of *Handbook of North American Indians,* ed. William C. Sturtevant. Washington, D.C., 1978.

Cogley, Richard W. "John Eliot and the Origins of the American Indians." *Early American Literature* 21 (1986–87): 210–25.

Conrad, A. Mark. "The Cherokee Mission of Virginia Presbyterians." *Journal of Presbyterian History* 58 (1980): 35–48.

[Cornstalk]. "Sketch of Cornstalk, 1759–1777." *Ohio Archaeological and Historical Society Publications* 21 (1912): 245–62.

Cutcliffe, Stephen H. "Colonial Indian Policy as a Measure of Rising Imperialism: New York and Pennsylvania, 1700–1755." *Western Pennsylvania Historical Magazine* 64 (1981): 237–68.

Daiutolo, Robert, Jr. "The Early Quaker Perception of the Indian." *Quaker History* 72 (1983): 103–19.

Dean, Nora Thompson. "A Reply to 'A Further Note on Delaware Clan Names.'" *Man in the Northeast* 9 (spring 1975): 63–65.

Doddridge, Joseph. *Notes on the Settlements and Indian Wars of the Western Parts of Virginia and Pennsylvania from 1763–1783.* Pittsburgh, 1912.

Dowd, Gregory Evans. *A Spirited Resistance: The North American Indian Struggle for Unity, 1745–1815.* Baltimore, 1992.

Downes, Randolph C. *Council Fires on the Upper Ohio: A Narrative of Indian Affairs in the Upper Ohio Valley Until 1795.* Pittsburgh, 1940.

Dubbs, J. H. "The Jones Family of Bethlehem Township." *Pennsylvania Magazine of History and Biography* 4 (1880): 209–17.

Duffy, John. *Epidemics in Colonial America.* Baton Rouge, 1953.

Duke, Mary A. "Iroquois Treaties: Common Forms, Varying Interpretations." In *The History and Culture of Iroquois Diplomacy: An Interdisciplinary Guide to the Treaties of the Six Nations and Their League,* ed. Francis Jennings and William N. Fenton, et al., 85–98. Syracuse, N.Y., 1985.

Dunn, Jacob Piatt. *True Indian Stories, with Glossary of Indiana Indian Names.* Indianapolis, 1908.

Edmunds, R. David. *The Shawnee Prophet.* Lincoln, Neb., 1983.

Erbe, Hellmuth. *Bethlehem, Pa.: Eine kommunistische Herrnhuter Kolonie des 18. Jahrhunderts.* Stuttgart, 1929.

Fausz, J. Frederick. "Middlemen in Peace and War" *Virginia Magazine of History and Biography* 95 (1987): 41–64.

Feest, Christian F. "Nanticoke and Neighboring Tribes." In *Northeast,* ed. Bruce G. Trigger, 240–52. Vol. 15 of *Handbook of North American Indians,* ed. William C. Sturtevant. Washington, D.C., 1978.

Feest, Johanna E., and Christian F. Feest. "Ottawa." In *Northeast,* ed. Bruce G. Trigger, 772–86. Vol. 15 of *Handbook of North American Indians,* ed. William C. Sturtevant. Washington, D.C., 1978.

Fenton, William N. *The Great Law and the Longhouse: A Political History of the Iroquois Confederacy.* Norman, 1998.

Fenton, William N., and Elisabeth Tooker. "Mohawk." In *Northeast,* ed. Bruce G. Trigger, 466–80. Vol. 15 of *Handbook of North American Indians,* ed. William C. Sturtevant. Washington, D.C., 1978.

Fenton, William N., and Gertrude P. Kurath. "The Feast of the Dead, or Ghost Dance, at Six Nations Reserve, Canada." In *Half a Century of Dance Research: Essays,* ed. Gertrude Prokosch Kurath, 95–117. Flagstaff, 1986.

Fliegel, Carl John. *Index to the Records of the Moravian Mission Among the Indians of North America.* New Haven, 1970.

Forell, George Wolfgang. "The Moravian Mission Among the Delawares in Ohio During the Revolutionary War." *Transactions of the Moravian Historical Society* 23 (1977): 41–60.

Foster, Michael K. "Another Look at the Function of Wampum in Iroquois-White Councils." In *The History and Culture of Iroquois Diplomacy: An Interdisciplinary Guide to the Treaties of the Six Nations and Their League,* ed. Francis Jennings and William N. Fenton, et al., 99–114. Syracuse, N.Y., 1985.

Frank, Armin Paul et al., eds. *Übersetzen, verstehen, Brückenbauen: Geisteswissenschaftliches und literarisches Übersetzen im internationalen Kulturaustausch.* Berlin, 1993.

Franz, Georg W. *Paxton: A Study of Community Structure and Mobility in the Colonial Pennsylvania Backcountry.* New York, 1989.

Frazier, Patrick. *The Mohicans of Stockbridge.* Lincoln, Neb., 1992.

Galloway, Patricia Kay. "Talking with Indians: Interpreters and Diplomacy in French Louisiana." In *Race and Family in the Colonial South,* ed. Winthrop D. Jordan and Sheila L. Skemp, 109–29. Jackson, Miss., 1986

Gibson, Arrell Morgan. *The Chickasaws.* Norman, 1971.

Gibson, John B. "General John Gibson." *Western Pennsylvania Historical Magazine* 5 (1922): 298–310.

Gilbert, Bill. *God Gave Us This Country: Tekamthi and the First American Civil War.* New York, 1989.

Gilbert, Daniel R. "Bethlehem and the American Revolution." *Transactions of the Moravian Historical Society* 23 (1977): 17–40.

Glatfelter, Charles H. *Pastors and People: German Lutheran and Reformed Churches in the Pennsylvania Field, 1717–1793.* Vol. 2, *The History.* Publications of the Pennsylvania German Society 13. Breinigsville, Pa., 1980.

Goddard, Ives. "Delaware." In *Northeast,* ed. Bruce G. Trigger, 213–40. Vol. 15 of *Handbook of North American Indians,* ed. William C. Sturtevant. Washington, D.C., 1978.

———. "A Further Note on Delaware Clan Names," *Man in the Northeast* 7 (spring 1974): 106–8.

Gollin, Gillian Lindt. *Moravians in Two Worlds, a Study of Changing Communities.* New York, 1967.

Goodwin, Gary C. *Cherokees in Transition: A Study of Changing Culture and Environment Prior to 1775.* Chicago, 1977.

Goodwin, Gerald J. "Christianity, Civilization, and the Savage: The Anglican Mission to the American Indians." *Historical Magazine of the Protestant Episcopal Church* 42 (1973): 93–110.

Graham, Andrew A., et al. *Catalogue of Meteorites.* Tucson, 1985.

Gramly, Richard Michael. *Fort Laurens, 1778–79: The Archaeological Record.* N.p., 1978.

Gray, Elma E., with Leslie Rob Gray. *Wilderness Christians: The Moravian Mission to the Delaware Indians.* Ithaca, 1956.

Graymont, Barbara. *The Iroquois in the American Revolution.* Syracuse, N.Y., 1972.

Greiert, Steven G. "The Board of Trade and Defense of the Ohio Valley, 1748–1753." *Western Pennsylvania Historical Magazine* 64 (1981): 1–32.

[Grube, Bernhard Adam]. "Biographical Sketch of . . . Grube." *Pennsylvania Magazine of History and Biography* 25 (1901): 14–19.

Hagedorn, Nancy L. " 'A Friend to Go Between Them': The Interpreter as Cultural Broker During Anglo-Iroquois Councils, 1740–1770." *Ethnohistory* 5 (1988–89): 60–80.

Halpenny, Francess G., George W. Brown, and David M. Hayne, eds. *Dictionary of Canadian Biography.* 10 vols. Toronto, 1966–90.

Hamilton, Kenneth Gardiner. "John Ettwein and the Moravian Church During the Revolutionary Period." *Transactions of the Moravian Historical Society* 12, parts 3–4, Bethlehem, Pa., 1940.

Hanna, Charles A. *The Wilderness Trail, or The Ventures and Adventures of the Pennsylvania Traders on the Allegheny Path*. 2 vols. New York, 1911.

Hedican, Edward J. "Algonquian Kinship Terminology: Some Problems of Interpretation." *Man in the Northeast* 40 (spring 1990): 1–15.

Heidenreich, Conrad E. "Huron." In *Northeast*, ed. Bruce G. Trigger, 368–88. Vol. 15 of *Handbook of North American Indians*, ed. William C. Sturtevant. Washington, D.C., 1978.

Herrick, James William. "Iroquois Medical Botany." Ph.D. diss., State University of New York, Albany, 1977.

Hertrampf, Stefan. *"Unsere Indianer-Geschwister waren lichte und vergnügt": Die Herrnhuter Missionare bei den Indianern Pennsylvanias, 1745–1765*. Frankfurt am Main, 1997.

Hinderaker, Eric. *Elusive Empires: Constructing Colonialism in the Ohio Valley, 1673–1800*. New York, 1997.

Hindle, Brooke. "The March of the Paxton Boys." *William & Mary Quarterly*, 3d ser., 3 (1946): 461–86.

Hobbs, William Herbert. "Earthquakes in Michigan." *Michigan Geological and Biological Survey* 5, Geological Series 3, 69–87. Lansing, 1911.

Hoberg, Walter R. "A Tory in the Northeast." *Pennsylvania Magazine of History and Biography* 59 (1939): 32–41.

Hodge, Frederick W., ed. *Handbook of American Indians North of Mexico*. Washington, D.C., 1912.

Horsman, Reginald. *Matthew Elliott, British Indian Agent*. Detroit, 1964.

Howard, James H. *Shawnee! The Ceremonialism of a Native Indian Tribe and Its Cultural Background*. Athens, Ohio, 1981.

Hoyt, Anne Kelley. *Bibliography of the Chickasaw*. Metuchen, N.J., 1987.

Hudson, Charles M. *The Catawba Nation*. Athens, Ga., 1970.

Hutton, Joseph Edmund. *A History of Moravian Missions*. London, 1923.

Jackson, Harvey H. *Lachlan McIntosh and the Politics of Revolutionary Georgia*. Athens, Ga., 1979.

Jacobs, Wilbur R. *Wilderness Politics and Indian Gifts: The Northern Colonial Frontier, 1748–1763*. Lincoln, Neb., 1966.

Jakle, John A. *Images of the Ohio Valley: A Historical Geography of Travel, 1740–1860*. New York, 1977.

Jefferds, Joseph C. *Captain Matthew Arbuckle: A Documentary Biography*. Charleston, W.V., 1981.

Jennings, Francis. *The Ambiguous Iroquois Empire: The Covenant Chain Confederation of Indian Tribes with English Colonies from its Beginnings to the Lancaster Treaty of 1744*. New York, 1984.

———. *Empire of Fortune: Crowns, Colonies, and Tribes in the Seven Years' War in America*. New York, 1988.

Jennings, Francis, and William N. Fenton, eds. *The History and Culture of Iroquois Diplomacy: An Interdisciplinary Guide to the Treaties of the Six Nations and Their League*. Syracuse, N.Y., 1985.

Jeyaraj, Daniel. *Inkulturation in Tranquebar. Der Beitrag der frühen dänisch-halleschen Mission zum Werden einer indisch-einheimischen Kirche (1706–1730)*. Erlangen, 1996.

Jordan, Francis, Jr. *The Life of William Henry of Lancaster, Pennsylvania, 1729–1786, Patriot, Military Officer, Inventor of the Steamboat: A Contribution to Revolutionary History*. Lancaster, Pa., 1910.

Kaiser, Siegrun. "Die Delaware und die Herrnhuter Brüdergemeine: Konflikte einer Missionierung, 1741–1806." Master's thesis, University of Frankfurt am Main, 1992.

Kellaway, William. *The New England Company, 1649–1776: Missionary Society to the American Indians*. London, 1961.

Keller, Robert H. "America's Native Sweet: Chippewa Treaties and the Right to Harvest Maple Sugar." *American Indian Quarterly* 13 (1989): 117–35.

Kelsay, Isabel Thompson. *Joseph Brant, 1743–1807, Man of Two Worlds*. Syracuse, N.Y., 1984.

Kelton, Dwight H. *Indian Names of Places Near the Great Lakes*. Detroit, 1888.

Kittel, Harald, and Armin Paul Frank, eds. *Interculturality and the Historical Study of Literary Translations*. Berlin, 1991.

Kortz, Edwin W. "The Liturgical Development of the American Moravian Church." Ph.D. diss., Temple University, 1955.

Kraft, Herbert C. *The Lenape: Archaeology, History, and Ethnography*. Newark, N.J., 1986.

Krusche, Rolf. "The Origin of the Mask Concept in the Eastern Woodlands of North America." *Man in the Northeast* 31 (spring 1986): 1–47.

Kurath, Gertrude Prokosch. "Native Choreographic Areas of North America." In *Half a Century of Dance Research: Essays*, ed. Gertrude Prokosch Kurath, 230–43. Flagstaff, 1986.

Leibert, Eugene. "Sketch of the History of the Congregation on Staten Island, New York." *Transactions of the Moravian Historical Society* 1 (1876): 57–63.

———. "Wechquetank." *Transactions of the Moravian Historical Society* 7, part 2 (1903): 57–82.

Levering, Joseph Mortimer. *A History of Bethlehem, Pennsylvania, 1741–1892, with some Account of Its Founders and Their Early Activity in America*. Bethlehem, Pa., 1903.

Lewin, Howard. "A Frontier Diplomat: Andrew Montour." *Pennsylvania History* 33 (1966): 153–86.

Loges, Ilse. "Irokesen und Delawaren im Spiegel der Herrnhuter Mission: Versuch einer vergleichenden Stammesmonographie nach den Herrnhuter Quellen des 18. Jahrhunderts." Ph.D. diss., University of Göttingen, 1956.

Mahr, August C. "A Chapter of Early Ohio Natural History." *Ohio Journal of Science* 49 (1949): 45–69.

———. "Delaware Terms for Plants and Animals in the Eastern Ohio Country: A Study in Semantics." *Anthropological Linguistics* 4, no. 5 (1962): 1–48.

———. "Health Conditions in the Moravian Indian Missions of Schoenbrunn in the 1770s." *Ohio Journal of Science* 50 (1950): 121–31.

———. "How to Locate Indian Place Names on Modern Maps." *Ohio Journal of Science* 53 (1953): 129–37.

———. "Indian River and Place Names in Ohio." *Ohio Historical Quarterly* 66 (1957): 137–58.

———. "Moravian Influence on Indian Life in the Tuscarawas Missions, 1772–1777." *Ohio Journal of Science* 48 (1948): 178–84.

Mancall, Peter C. *Deadly Medicine: Indians and Alcohol in Early America*. Ithaca, 1995.

Mark, Conrad A. "The Cherokee Mission of Virginia Presbyterians." *Journal of Presbyterian History* 58 (1980): 35–48.

Marsh, Thelma R. *Moccasin Trails to the Cross: A History of the Mission to the Wyandot Indians on the Sandusky Plains*. Sandusky, Ohio, 1974.

Mayer, Brantz. *Tah-Gah-Jute; or, Logan and Cresap, an Historical Essay*. Albany, N.Y., 1867.

McConnell, Michael N. *A Country Between: The Upper Ohio Valley and Its Peoples, 1724–1774*. Lincoln, Neb., 1992.

———. "Kuskusky Towns and Early Western Pennsylvania Indian History, 1748–1778." *Pennsylvania Magazine of History and Biography* 116 (1992): 33–58.

———. "Pisquetomen and Tamaqua: Mediating Peace in the Ohio Country." In *Northeastern Indian Lives*, ed. Robert S. Grumet, 273–94. Amherst, Mass., 1996.

McKee, Jesse O., and Jon A. Schlenker. *The Choctaws: Cultural Evolution of a Native American Tribe*. Jackson, Miss., 1980.

Merrell, James H. *Into the American Woods: Negotiators on the Pennsylvania Frontier*. New York, 1999.

Merrell, James H., and Shikellemi. "A Person of Consequence." In *Northeastern Indian Lives*, ed. Robert S. Grumet, 227–57. Amherst, Mass., 1996.

Merritt, Jane T. *At the Crossroads: Indians and Empire on a Mid-Atlantic Frontier, 1700–1763*. Chapel Hill, 2003.

Meyer, Dieter. *Der Christozentrismus des späten Zinzendorf: Eine Studie zu dem Begriff 'täglicher Umgang mit dem Heiland.* Bern, Frankfurt am Main, 1973.

Meyer, Dietrich. "Zinzendorf und Herrnhut." In *Geschichte des Pietismus,* ed. Martin Brecht, et al., 2:5–106. Göttingen, 1995.

Middlekauff, Robert. *The Glorious Cause: The American Revolution, 1763 to 1789.* Oxford, 1982.

Miller, Jay. "Delaware Clan Names." *Man in the Northeast* 6 (fall 1973): 57–60.

———. "A Cultural View of Delaware Clan Names as Contrasted with a Linguistic View." *Man in the Northeast* 9 (spring 1975): 60–63.

———. "Delaware Masking." *Man in the Northeast* 41 (spring 1991): 105–10.

———. "Delaware Personhood." *Man in the Northeast* 42 (fall 1991): 17–27.

Mohr, Walter H. *Federal Indian Relations, 1774–1788.* Philadelphia, 1933.

Müller, Karl. *200 Jahre Brüdermission.* Herrnhut, 1931.

Nebenzahl, Kenneth. *Atlas of the American Revolution.* Text by Don Higginbotham. Chicago, 1974.

Newcomb, William W. *The Culture and Acculturation of the Delaware Indians.* Ann Arbor, 1956.

O'Donnell, James H. *Southern Indians in the American Revolution.* Knoxville, 1973.

Olmstead, Earl P. *Blackcoats Among the Delaware: David Zeisberger on the Ohio Frontier.* Kent, Ohio, 1991.

———. *David Zeisberger: A Life Among the Indians.* Kent, Ohio, 1997.

Orrill, Lawrence A. "General Edward Hand." *Western Pennsylvania Historical Magazine* 25 (1942): 99–112.

Palm, Mary Borgias. *The Jesuit Missions of the Illinois Country, 1673–1763.* Cleveland, Ohio, 1933.

Pieper, Thomas J., and James B. Gidney. *Fort Laurens, 1778–1779: The Revolutionary War in Ohio.* Kent, Ohio, 1976.

Ramsay, Jack C., Jr. "Francis Borland: Presbyterian Missionary to the Americas." *Journal of Presbyterian History* 62 (1984): 1–17.

Reichel, Jörn. *Dichtungstheorie und Sprache bei Zinzendorf.* Bad Homburg, 1969.

Rice, Otis K. *The Allegheny Frontier: West Virginia Beginnings, 1730–1830.* Lexington, Ky., 1970.

Richter, Daniel K. "Cultural Brokers and Intercultural Politics." *Journal of American History* 75 (1988–89): 40–67.

Roeber, A. Gregg. "Der Pietismus in Nordamerika im 18. Jahrhundert." In *Geschichte des Pietismus,* ed. Martin Brecht, et al., 2:668–99. Göttingen, 1995.

Rogers, E. S. "Southeastern Ojibwa." In *Northeast,* ed. Bruce G. Trigger, 760–71. Vol. 15 of *Handbook of North American Indians,* ed. William C. Sturtevant. Washington, D.C., 1978.

Russell, Errett. "Indian Geographical Names." *Magazine of Western History* 2 (1885): 51–59, 238–46.

Sacks, Francis W. *The Philadelphia Baptist Tradition of Church and Church Authority, 1707–1814.* Lewiston, N.Y., 1989.

Salone, Emile. "Les Sauvages du Canada et les Malades Importées de France au xviii siècle: La Pictoe de l'alcoholism." *Journal de la Société des Américanistes* 4 (1904): 1–17.

Sandgren, Ulla. *The Tamil New Testament and Bartholomäus Ziegenbalg.* Uppsala, 1991.

Savelle, Max. *George Morgan, Colony Builder.* New York, 1932.

———. *The Origins of American Diplomacy: The International History of Angloamerica, 1492–1763.* New York, 1967.

Schaaf, Gregory. *Wampum Belts and Peace Trees: George Morgan, Native Americans, and Revolutionary Diplomacy.* Golden, Colo., 1990.

Scharf, John Thomas. *History of Western Maryland. Being a History of Frederick, Montgomery, Carroll, Washington, Allegeny, and Garrett Counties from the Earliest Period to the Present Day; Including Biographical Sketches of their Representative Men.* 2 vols. Philadelphia, 1882.

Schwartz, Sally. *"A Mixed Multitude": The Struggle for Toleration in Colonial Pennsylvania.* New York, 1987.

Schweinitz, Edmund A., de. *The Life and Times of David Zeisberger.* Philadelphia, 1870.

Schweitzer, Christoph E. "The Significance of a Newly Discovered Volume of Verse by Matthaeus Gottfried Hehl." *Yearbook of German-American Studies* 16 (1981): 67–71.

Scobel, Albert, ed. *Andrees Allgemeiner Handatlas.* 4th ed. Bielefeld and Leipzig, 1899.

Sheehan, Bernard W. *Seeds of Extinction: Jeffersonian Philanthropy and the American Indian.* Chapel Hill, 1973.

Simmons, William S. "Conversion from Indian to Puritan." *New England Quarterly* 52 (1979): 197–218.

Smaby, Beverly Prior. *The Transformation of Moravian Bethlehem: From Communal Mission to Family Economy.* Philadelphia, 1988.

Smylie, James H., ed. "The United Presbyterian Church in Mission: An Historical Overview." *Journal of Presbyterian History* 57 (1979): 183–423.

Snow, Dean R. "Eastern Abenaki." In *Northeast,* ed. Bruce G. Trigger, 137–47. Vol. 15 of *Handbook of North American Indians,* ed. William C. Sturtevant. Washington, D.C., 1978.

Sosin, Jack M. *The Revolutionary Frontier, 1763–1783.* New York, 1967.

———. "The Use of Indians in the War of the American Revolution: A Re-Assessment of Responsibility." *Canadian Historical Review* 46 (1965): 101–21.

Stevens, Paul L. "The Indian Diplomacy of Capt. Richard B. Lernoult, British Military Commandant of Detroit, 1774–1775." *Michigan Historical Review* 13 (1987): 47–82.

———. " 'Placing Proper Persons at Their Head': Henry Hamilton and the Establishment of the British Revolutionary-Era Indian Department at Detroit, 1777." *The Old Northwest* 12 (1986): 279–317.

Stover, Carl W., and Jerry L. Loffman. *Seismicity of the United States, 1568–1989.* Washington, D.C., 1993.

Sturtevant, William C., ed. *Handbook of North American Indians.* Vols. 4–13, 15, 17. Washington D.C., 1978–2001.

Szasz, Margaret Connell, ed. *Between Indian and White Worlds: The Cultural Broker.* Norman, 1994.

Talbert, Charles G. "Kentucky Invades Ohio, 1779." *Kentucky Historical Society Register* 51 (1953): 228–35.

Tanner, Helen Hornbeck. *Indians of Ohio and Indiana Prior to 1795.* New York, 1974.

———, ed. *Atlas of Great Lakes Indian History.* Norman, 1986.

Tantaquidgeon, Gladys. *Folk Medicine of the Delaware and Related Algonkian Indians.* Harrisburg, Pa., 1972.

Thayer, Theodore. "The Friendly Association." *Pennsylvania Magazine of History and Biography* 67 (1943): 356–76.

Tolles, Frederick B. "Nonviolent Contact: The Quakers and the Indians." *Proceedings of the American Philosophical Society* 107 (1963): 93–101.

Tooker, Elisabeth. "The League of the Iroquois: Its History, Politics, and Ritual," and "Wyandot." In *Northeast,* ed. Bruce G. Trigger, 418–41 and 398–406. Vol. 15 of *Handbook of North American Indians,* ed. William C. Sturtevant. Washington, D.C., 1978.

Trigger, Bruce G. *The Huron: Farmers of the North.* New York, 1969.

———, ed. *Northeast.* Vol. 15 of *Handbook of North American Indians,* ed. William C. Sturtevant. Washington, D.C., 1978.

Vachon, François. "History of Brandy in Canada." *Mid-America* 33 (1951): 42–63.

Vaughan, Alden T. "Frontier Banditti and the Indians: The Paxton Boys' Legacy, 1763–1775." *Pennsylvania History* 51 (1984): 1–29.

Victor, I. Henry. "Tamil Translation of the Bible by the Danish-Halle Mission During the Eighteenth Century." *Indian Church History Review* 16 (1982): 72–85.

Voegelin, Charles F. *The Shawnee Female Deity.* New Haven, 1936.

Vogel, Virgil J. *American Indian Medicine*. Norman, 1970.

"Volk, Nation, Nationalismus, Masse." In *Geschichtliche Grundbegriffe*, ed. Otto Brunner, Werner Conze, and Reinhart Koselleck, 7:141–431. Stuttgart, 1992.

Wainwright, Nicholas B. *George Croghan, Wilderness Diplomat*. Chapel Hill, 1959.

Wallace, Anthony F. C. *The Death and Rebirth of the Seneca*. New York, 1970.

———. *King of the Delawares: Teedyuscung, 1700–1763*. Philadelphia, 1949.

Wallace, Paul A. W. *Conrad Weiser, 1696–1760, Friend of Colonist and Mohawk*. Philadelphia, 1945.

———. *Indians in Pennsylvania*. Harrisburg, Pa., 1961.

———. "They Knew the Indian: The Men Who Wrote the Moravian Records." *American Philosophical Society Proceedings* 95 (1951): 290–95.

Washburn, Wilcomb E., ed. *History of Indian-White Relations*. Vol. 4 of *Handbook of North American Indians*, ed. William C. Sturtevant. Washington, D.C., 1988.

Weinlick, John R. "The Moravians and the American Revolution." *Transactions of the Moravian Historical Society* 23 (1977): 1–17.

Wellenreuther, Hermann. "Bekehrung und Bekehrte: Herrnhuter Mission unter den Delaware, 1772–1781." In *Pietismus und Neuzeit: Ein Jahrbuch zur Geschichte des neueren Protestantismus* 23 (1997): 152–74.

———. "Deux modèles de mission piétiste: Halle et Herrnhut." In *Les piétismes à l'âge classique: Crise, Conversion, Institutions*, ed. Anne Lagny, 145–66. Villeneuce-d'Ascq (Nord), 2001.

———. "England und Europa: Überlegungen zum Problem des englischen Sonderwegs in der europäischen Geschichte." In *Liberalitas: Festschrift für Erich Angermann zum 65. Geburtstag*, ed. Norbert Finzsch and Hermann Wellenreuther, 89–123. Stuttgart 1992.

———. *Glaube und Politik in Pennsylvania, 1681–1776. Die Wandlungen der Obrigkeitsdoktrin und des Peace Testimony der Quaker*. Cologne and Vienna, 1972.

———. "Land, Herrschaft, Alltag: Die Indianer und die englischen Kolonien vor der Amerikanischen Revolution." In *Amerika, eine Hoffnung, zwei Visionen*, ed. Hans Thomas, 213–43. Herford, 1991.

———. "Der Vertrag zu Paris (1763)." *Niedersächsisches Jahrbuch für Landesgeschichte* 71 (1999): 83–110.

Weslager, Clinton A. *The Delaware Indians: A History*. New Brunswick, N.J., 1972.

———. *The Delaware Indian Westward Migration, with Texts of Two Manuscripts, 1821–22, Responding to General Lewis Cass's Inquiries About Lenape Culture and Language*. Wallingford, Pa., 1978.

Wessel, Carola. "Connecting Congregations: The Net of Communications Among the Moravians as Exemplified by the Interaction Between Pennsylvania, the Upper Ohio Valley, and Germany (1772–1774)." In *The Distinctiveness of Moravian Culture: Essays and Documents in Moravian History in Honor of Vernon H. Nelson on his Seventieth Birthday*, ed. Craig D. Atwood and Peter Vogt, 153–72. Nazareth, Pa., 2003.

———. "Die Delawares in der Amerikanischen Revolution." Ph.D. diss., University of Göttingen, 1995.

———. *Delaware-Indianer und Herrnhuter Missionare im Upper Ohio Valley*. Tübingen, 1999.

———. "Missionary Diaries as a Source for Native American Studies: David Zeisberger and the Delaware." *European Review of Native American Studies* 10:2 (1996) 31–37.

———. "Missionsvorstellung und Missionswirklichkeit der Herrnhuter Brüdergemeine in Nordamerika im 18. Jahrhundert." Master's thesis, University of Göttingen, 1989.

———. "'We do not want to introduce anything new . . .': Transplanting the Communal Life from Herrnhut to the Upper Ohio Valley." In *In Search of Peace and Posterity*, ed. Hartmut Lehmann, Hermann Wellenreuther, and Renate Wilson, 246–62. University Park, Pa., 2000.

Wheeler-Voegelin, Erminie. "Ethnohistory of Indian Use and Occupancy in Ohio and Indiana Prior to 1795." In *Indians of Ohio and Indiana Prior to 1795*, 1:59–319, 2:320–656. New York, 1974.

White, Richard. *The Middle Ground: Indians, Empires, and Republics in the Great Lakes Region, 1650–1815.* Cambridge, 1991.

Williams, Edward G. *Fort Pitt and the Revolution on the Western Frontier.* Pittsburgh, 1978.

———. "A Note on Fort Pitt and the Revolution on the Western Frontier." *Western Pennsylvania Historical Magazine* 60 (1977): 265–76.

Williams, Thomas J. C. *History of Frederick County, Maryland, from the Earliest Settlements to the Beginning of the War Between the States, Continued from the Beginning of the Year 1861 down to the Present Time, by Folger McKinsey.* 2 vols. Frederick, Md., 1910.

Witthöft, Harald. *Umrisse einer historischen Metrologie zum Nutzen der wirtschafts- und sozialgeschicht-lichen Forschung.* 2 vols. Göttingen, 1979.

Woodward, Grace Steele. *The Cherokees.* Norman, 1963.

Zupko, Ronald Edward. *A Dictionary of English Weights and Measures, from Anglo-Saxon Times to the Nineteenth Century.* Madison, Wis., 1968.

MAPS OF OHIO REGION

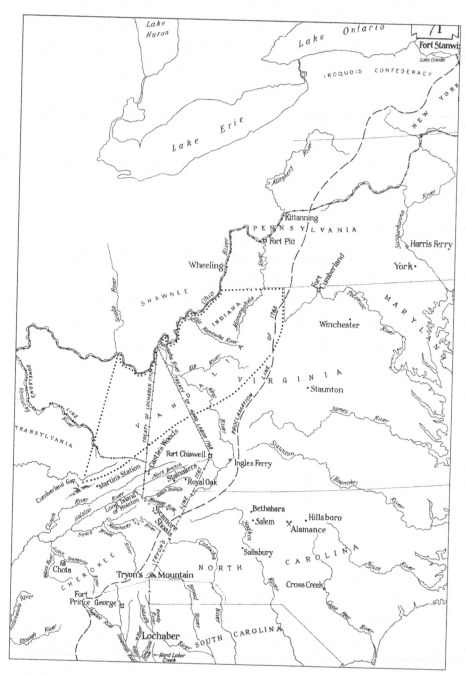

1. Border between English and Native American settlements according to the royal proclamation of 1763. Source: Kenneth T. Jackson, ed., *Atlas of American History* (New York, 1978), 70–71.

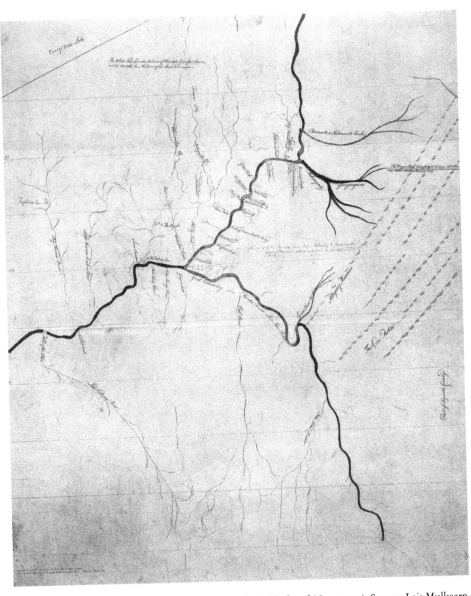

2. John Mercer's map of the Ohio Land Company (drafted before 6 Nov. 1752). Source: Lois Mulkearn, ed. *George Mercer Papers Relating to the Ohio Company of Virginia* (Pittsburg, Ohio, 1954), 72–73.

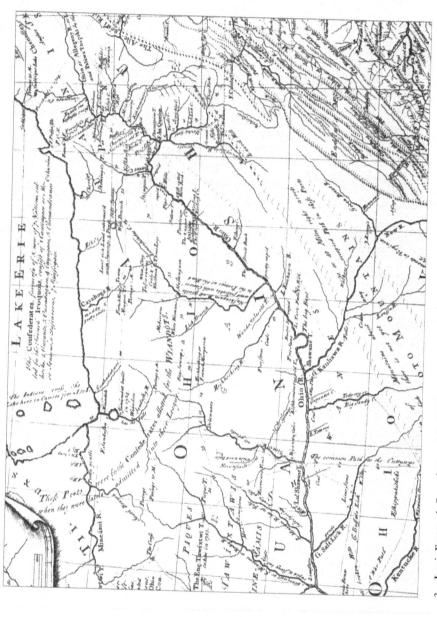

3. Lewis Evans, *A General Map of the Middle British Colonies*, 1755 (section). Source: Lawrence Henry Gipson, *Lewis Evans* (Philadelphia, 1939), map 6 in the appendix.

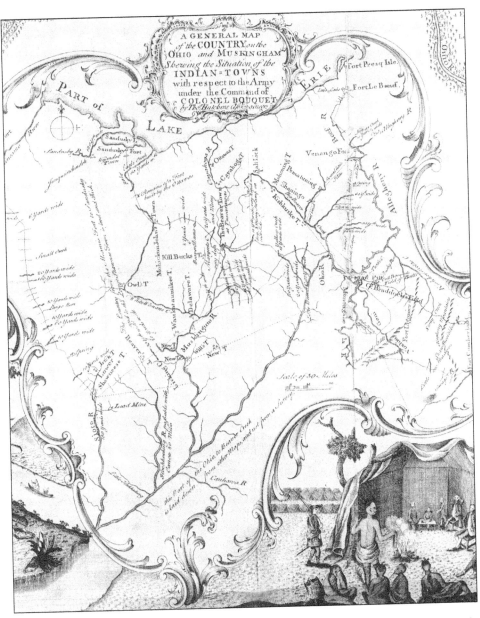

4. Thomas Hutchins, *A Topographical Plan of That Part of the Indian Country Through Which the Army Under the Command of Colonel Bouquet Marched in the Year 1764.* Source: William Smith, ed. *An Historical Account of the Expedition Against the Ohio Indians, in the Year 1764. Under the Command of Henry Bouquet* (Philadelphia, 1765), illustration 1 in appendix, after page 71.

Remarks.

Captain White Eyes Says, at the Head of Big Beaver Creek there is a Pond, out of the Northwest end of Which the Water of this pond runs to Lake Erié as the Country between the Head of Beaver C. and Lake Erié is very level. Much over grown with Beech and full of Small Ponds, it is possible it may be So; especially when the Waters are high, as the may, then Drain off that way & empty into Cherâge Elk Creek of capahogo R.; thence in to lake Erié. I am of Opinion that John Anderson (of whom I had the Sketch of Big Beaver Creek (No 1) is not so well acquainted with this part of the Country as White-Eyes is Who assures me that Anderson was Mistaken in this particular as well as in his Opinion of the Heading of the Westernmost Branches of this Creek against Captenin & c. as Mentioned in page 2.

As lieut.ant Hutchins has an actual Survey of the Road on which the Army under the Command of Colonel Bouquette Marches from fort pitt to Tuscaraway's on Muskingum, I need only observe, that by attending to the Remarks on the Sketch of Scioto Rx. he will be enabled effectually to adjust all these Sketches on our Map and I am of opinion he will find Scioto laid too much to the Westward.

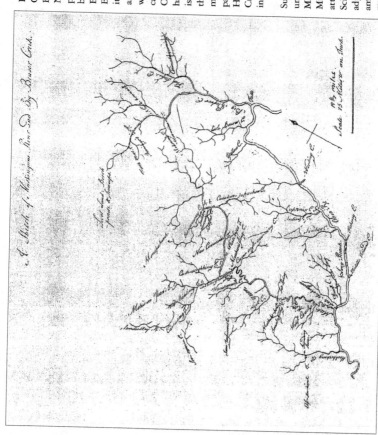

5. *A Sketch of Muskingum River and Big Beaver Creek, ca. 1775* (section). Source: Bibliothèque de la Service Hydrographique, c. 4044, no. 92, reproduced from copy in Library of Congress, Map Division, Washington, D.C.

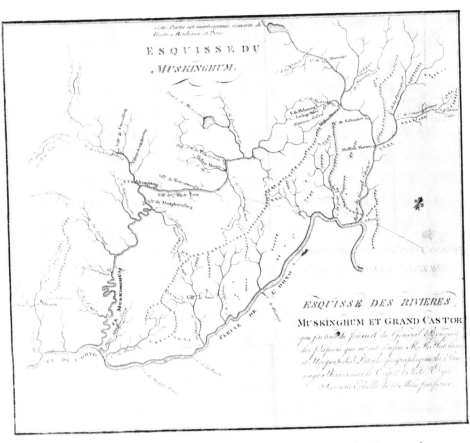

6. *Esquissé des Rivières Muskingum et grand Castor.* Source: J. Hector St. John de Crèvecoeur, *Lettres d'cultivateur Americain,* vol. 3 (Paris, 1787), between pages 412 and 413.

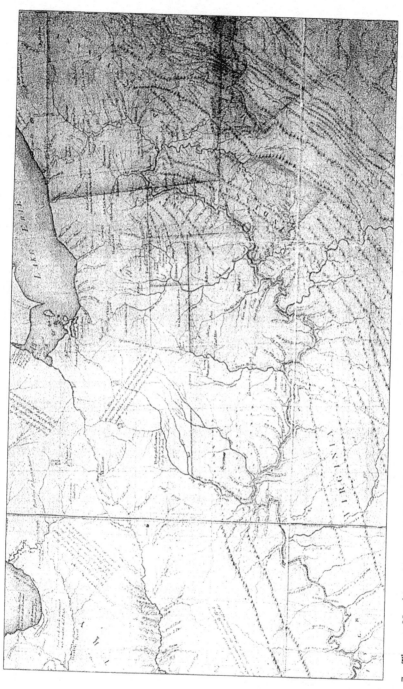

7. Thomas Hutchins, *A Map of the Western Parts of Virginia, Pennsylvania, Maryland, and North Carolina* (London, 1778). Source: Library of Congress, Map Division, GT 3700. 1778. H 8 Vault.

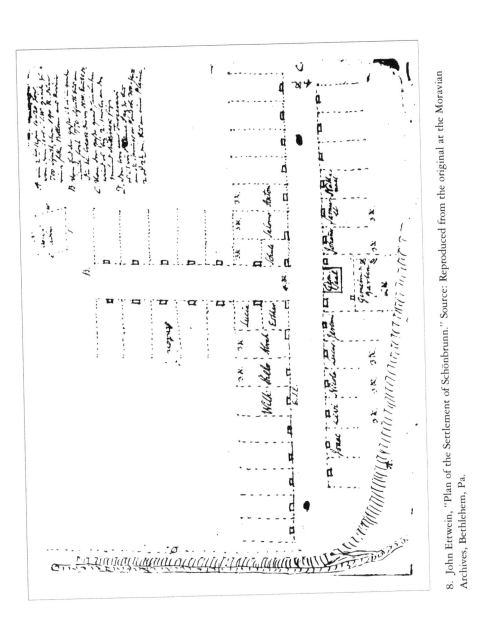

8. John Ettwein, "Plan of the Settlement of Schönbrunn." Source: Reproduced from the original at the Moravian Archives, Bethlehem, Pa.

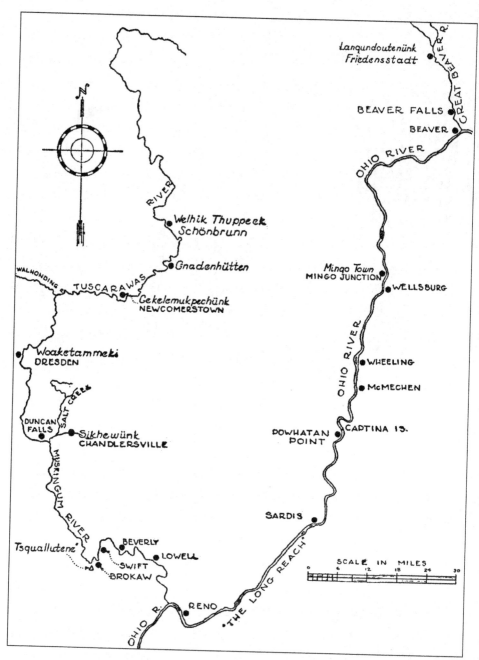

9. "Map of River Route of John Heckewelder's Party from Friedensstadt on the Great Beaver River to Schönbrunn on the Tuscarawas, 13 April–5 May, 1773." Source: August C. Mahr, ed. and trans. "A Canoe Journey from the Big Beaver to the Tuscarawas in 1773: A Travel Diary of John Heckewelder," *Ohio Archaeological and Historical Quarterly* 61 (1952): 291.

INDEX

French settlers: Fort Pitt negotiations and, 533 n.
1511; in Lichtenau, 400; negotiations with,
430; warriors' incited by, 417
Freylinghausen, J. A., 52 n. 175
Fridenshütten, Christian Indians in, 99, 116, 121,
125
Friderica (bap. 1777), 425
Fridrich (bap. 1776) (Eschecanahunt), 308
Fridrich (bap. in old Gnadenhütten), 317
"Friendly Association," 39, 317 n. 771
friendship: Moravian concept of, 126 n. 142, 160;
tribal concept of, 201, 356, 366, 381 n. 983,
490
Frisbie, Levi, 39, 104 n. 64, 105 n. 69
funeral rites of Native Americans, Zeisberger's description of, 164

Gabriel (bap. 1749), 125–26
Gachnawage tribe, 204
Gage, Thomas, 97 n. 29, 202 n. 414
Gambold, Hector Ernest, 130
Gatshenis (also Lucas), 91, 99–100. See also Lucas
(bap. 1769)
Gekelemukpechünk: Baptist missionaries in, 130;
Christian Indians in, 130–32, 144, 146; Conference of 19 August 1772 in, 102; ethnography
of Native American tribes and, 17–21; expansion of settlements around, 502–3; expulsion of
Native Americans from, 184; Five Families of
Indian Brothers and Sisters in, 91–103; geographical history of, 11–13; illness in, 149; migration of tribal converts from, 128–34,
259–60, 264–65, 327; Moravian settlement in
area of, 91–103; Native American preachers at,
186; Native Americans in, 92–93; peace negotiations in, 183, 203–5; Quakers in, 150–51,
156; traders in, 115 n. 102; tribal unrest in,
135–44, 149–50, 164–73, 186, 193–213; Virginia war and, 217–28, 230–69; Zeisberger's
visits to, 92 n. 6, 108–9
"Gelegenheiten" (devotional services), 53
Gelelemind (John Killbuck), 31, 34–36, 81, 83;
British-warrior expeditions discussed by, 528 n.
1493, 533 n. 1509; Brodhead's negotiations
with, 513 n. 1446; death of White Eye and,
482; Delaware alliances in Revolution and, 443,
470 n. 1285; 470 n. 1288, 473, 475–76, 492
n. 1370; Fort Detroit negotiations and, 400,
405, 428–30; fortifications at Goschachgünk
and, 347, 493–94; Fort Laurens negotiations
and, 489 n. 1359, 491, 493 n. 1376; Fort Pitt
negotiations and, 303, 338, 444, 448, 463, 471,
499 n. 1399, 510 n. 1440, 511–12; Goschachgünk tribal councils and, 314–15, 317, 320,
380–85, 431–14, 432–33, 478–79; involvement in mission activities, 329 n. 807, 353,

419, 435, 461, 464 n. 1266, 548–49; letter to
McIntosh, 501 nn. 1402–3; at Lichtenau, 311–
13, 319, 322–26, 343–45, 349–52, 358, 368,
373, 375–76, 387; meeting with army, 480;
migration from Goschachgünk, 529; Mingo
hostilities and, 364–66, 369–70; Morgan and,
347 n. 874, 379, 499 n. 1399; Netawatwees'
succession dispute and, 312 n. 765, 344–47,
356, 361 n. 924; return to Gnaddenhütten and,
499; in Schönbrunn, 540; Shawnee negotiations
and, 418, 432, 485; Welapachtschiechen and,
442, 452–53; Wyandot negotiations and,
496–98; Zeisberger's references to, 106
Gendaskund, Jacob, 146–47, 182, 367; death of
daughter, 188–89; negotiations with Shawnee
and, 230, 233–34, 242
Gendowe (Sunday) Indians, Zeisberger's references
to, 169
General Synod, of Moravian Unity Church, 43, 296
George, Robert, 376 n. 969
George (bap. 1775), 256
George III (King of England), 24, 280 n. 665; Cher-
okee treaty with, 331
Georgia, colony of, Moravian missionary expansion
and, 43, 72
Germain, George Sackville (Lord), 329 nn. 9–6,
342 n. 854, 386 n. 1003
Germantown, Battle of, 421, 434 n. 1154
Gertraud (bap. 1775), 262
Gertraut (bap. 1771), 99, 134, 382
Gibson, John, 10, 32, 116 n. 101, 197 n. 398, 291;
British-tribal alliances in Revolution, 327 n.
798; at Fort Laurens, 483–84, 489 n. 1359,
491, 493 n. 1376, 494–95; Fort Pitt negotiations and, 274, 285 n. 682, 290, 479 n. 1316;
Lichtenau fort proposal and, 494 n. 1378; relations with Delaware, 336, 470 n. 1289, 474,
481, 492 n. 1370, 499 n. 1399, 501–2; Virginia war and, 220–21, 222 n. 486, 223, 231,
257; white prisoners of Shawnee and, 306–7
Gideon (bap. 1776) (Saktelaeuche), 350, 354, 357,
368, 376, 435–38, 471, 486
Girty, Simon, 23, 33, 407 n. 1072, 440 n. 1176,
489 n. 1358, 490 n. 1362, 491 n. 1367; attack
on Fort Laurens, 506 n. 1424; imprisonment of
Zeisberger and, 508
Gischenatsi ("Hard Man"), 161 n. 275; in Lichtenau, 421, 449; role in tribal conflicts of, 204,
205 n. 425, 222, 306 n. 743; Zeisberger's meeting with, 165–73
Gist, Christopher, 10, 230 n. 516
Glikhican (Indian Captain), 49, 91, 98, 104, 108–9,
111–12, 114, 116. See also Isaac (bap. 1770);
baptism as Isaac, 138 n. 186
Gnadenhütten: attacks on, 212; Christian Indian

Zeisberger, David (*continued*)
and tribal concepts discussed by, 71–72; Native American council meetings attended by, 17–18, 35–37; Native Americans in diaries of, 8, 16, 30, 34–35; negotiations with Shawnee, 164–73; Six Indian Nations and, 48–49; translations of religious works into Delaware by, 96 n. 24

Zeno, Gnadenhütten massacre and, 99

Zinzendorf, Nikolaus Ludwig (Count), 42–45, 226 n. 499; mission method and theory and, 51–58, 68, 70–71

CPSIA information can be obtained
at www.ICGtesting.com
Printed in the USA
BVOW08s0324010317
477402BV00001B/12/P